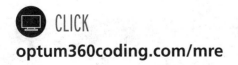

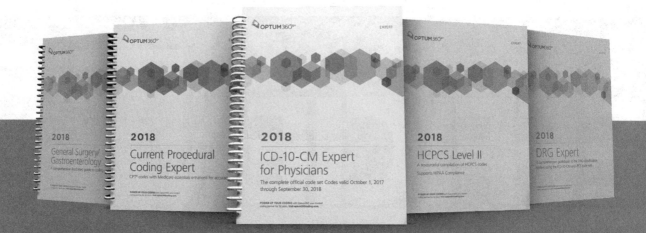

Keep your go-to coding resources up to date.

Stay current and compliant with our 2018 edition code books.
With more than 30 years in the coding industry, Optum360® is proud to
be your trusted resource for coding, billing and reimbursement resources.
Our 2018 editions include tools for ICD-10-CM/PCS, CPT®, HCPCS, DRG,
specialty-specific coding and much more.

SAVE UP TO 25% ON ADDITIONAL CODING RESOURCES

Visit us at optum360coding.com
and enter promo code **FOBA18ED**
to save 25%.

Call 1-800-464-3649, option 1,
and be sure to mention promo
code **FOBA18ED** to save 20%.

A modern approach to CDI matches the pace of change in health care.

The move to value-based care increases the need for accuracy in clinical documentation—across every patient and payer.

A modern CDI approach makes the work of CDI specialists more efficient by automatically reviewing every patient record and prioritizing those that require intervention.

Using case-finding logic and state-of-the-art natural language processing, Optum CDI 3D connects clinical indicators to identify records with gaps or deficiencies and enables timely documentation improvement, cleaner claims, faster reimbursement and accurate reporting.

Optum CDI 3D, together with Optum's market-leading Enterprise CAC, provides unmatched capabilities in a single, fully integrated CDI and coding solution.

OPTUM CDI 3D

- Automates 100-percent record review and identifies clinical documentation improvement opportunities

- Identifies co-morbidities, HACs and patient safety indicators

- Streamlines the query loop between CDIS and physicians

- Enhances code assignment efficiency, compliance and quality reporting

Modernizing your CDI program starts here.
Visit optum360.com/CDI3D to learn more.

Visit: optum360.com/CDI3D
Email: optum360@optum.com

Let Optum360 help you find
the best product for your needs

Together with you, Optum360® can help drive financial results across your organization with industry-leading resources that cut through the complexity of medical coding challenges.

Let us help you find the best coding solution, at the best price.

Contact your Medallion representative directly or call Customer Service at 1-800-464-3649, option 1.

OPTUM360°®

Optum360 **Learning**

Earn your CEUs with US

You've worked hard for your coding credentials, and now you need an easy way to maintain your certification.

Optum360® offers the most complete training in the marketplace, designed to address exactly what you and your organization need. We offer eLearning courses you can take online at your desk; you can invite a specialist to your office for on-the-job preparation; or ask our consulting professionals to create a tailor-made program specific for your organization.

Our strategy is simple — education must be concise, relevant and accurate. Choose the delivery method that works best for you:

- **eLearning:** Web-based courses offered at the most convenient times for your learners. eLearning courses are interactive, task-focused and developed around practical scenarios. These self-paced courses include "try-it" functionality, knowledge checks and downloadable resources.

- **Instructor-led training (ILT):** On-site or remote courses, built specifically for your organization.

- **Webinars:** Online courses, geared toward a broad market of learners, delivered in a live or recorded setting.

- **Podcasts and videos:** Physician-focused online courses available when and where convenient.

NO MATTER HOW YOU CHOOSE TO EARN YOUR CEUs, OPTUM360 IS HERE TO HELP YOU.

 VISIT

optum360coding.com/learning

 CALL

1-800-464-3649, option 1

RE NEW

It's time to renew your Optum360 coding tools.

SAVE UP TO 25%*

when you renew your 2018 coding essentials.

ITEM #	TITLE INDICATE THE ITEMS YOU WISH TO PURCHASE	QUANTITY	PRICE PER PRODUCT	TOTAL
			Subtotal	
	(AK, DE, HI, MT, NH & OR are exempt)		Sales Tax	
	1 item $10.95 • 2–4 items $12.95 • 5+ CALL		Shipping & Handling	
			TOTAL AMOUNT ENCLOSED	

Save up to 25% when you renew.

PROMO CODE: RENEW18B

 Visit **optum360coding.com** and enter the promo code above.

 Call **1-800-464-3649, option 1,** and mention the promo code above.

 Fax this order form with purchase order to **1-801-982-4033.** *Optum360 no longer accepts credit cards by fax.*

 Mail this order form with payment and/or purchase order to: **Optum360, PO Box 88050, Chicago, IL 60680-9920.** *Optum360 no longer accepts credit cards by mail.*

Name _____

Address _____

Customer Number _____ Contact Number _____

○ CHECK ENCLOSED (PAYABLE TO OPTUM360)

○ BILL ME ○ P.O.# _____

(____) _____
Telephone

(____) _____
Fax

_____@_____
E-mail

Optum360 respects your right to privacy. We will not sell or rent your email address or fax number to anyone outside Optum360 and its business partners. If you would like to remove your name from Optum360 promotions, please call 1-800-464-3649, option 1.

Contents

Introduction

The purpose of the *Complete Guide for Interventional Radiology* is to provide a reference for hospitals and physicians for reporting interventional radiology and cardiology procedures in the context of today's complex requirements for coding, billing, and reimbursement. Coding for these types of procedures is widely recognized as one of the most complex and challenging under Medicare's reimbursement programs, especially the ambulatory payment classification (APC) program.

This guide is intended to help both technical, professional, and coding staff select the appropriate codes to accurately report the services performed in the interventional radiology and cardiology settings.

CPT and Medicare have continued to revise reporting requirements for interventional radiology services to keep up with technological changes, techniques, and methods for performing procedures. Certain components of an interventional procedure, such as contrast media, supplies and devices, or additional imaging procedures, have increased both the complexity and cost. In order for Medicare to keep up with these changes in terms of billing and payment, specific HCPCS codes and other unique coding requirements such as surgical component codes may be required.

Specificity in reporting interventional radiology procedures requires a good basic understanding of CPT® coding. Providers are expected to report each procedure component by revenue code, CPT/HCPCS code related description, modifiers if applicable, and the number of units used or performed.

The most common components of an interventional radiology procedure are the surgical intervention, imaging, supplies, contrast media, and pharmacy. Complexity of a procedure may require reporting several CPT codes. Where appropriate, this book includes CPT codes that are not cardiovascular or radiology-related.

Case examples of procedures are provided in this publication as a guide to learning and understanding the various aspects of the service. The case examples in this publication follow basic Medicare guidance for reporting; however, many payers accept these guidelines. Standardized reporting should be the goal of all providers with specific exceptions from individual payers on a case-by-case basis. When possible, coding for the professional components should closely match the coding submitted for the technical components.

Documentation for each procedure must be in the medical record and must include detailed descriptions of each component of the procedure, such as advancement and exact placement of catheters, surgical component descriptors, and the type and amount of low osmolar contrast media and the special devices used. These documentation requirements hold true for both radiology and cardiology interventions.

Providers should review their process for reporting interventional services at least semi-annually and in conjunction with newly released Medicare transmittals to ensure proper claims processing.

Coding described throughout this publication is for normal anatomy and transfemoral percutaneous approach unless otherwise specified.

CPT Codes and Descriptions

Physicians' Current Procedural Terminology (CPT) was developed by the American Medical Association and is used to report medical services and procedures performed by physicians and some allied health providers. The codes are updated every year.

Indented Procedures

CPT descriptions are developed to stand alone, but sometimes they appear to be incomplete. The format is employed to conserve space on the printed page. Some CPT codes that share a common procedure are grouped together and the common procedure is listed fully only with the first code. The codes that follow are indented to indicate that a portion of their description is found in a previous code.

CPT Code descriptions appear in bold text followed by the lay description of the service provided.

For example:

70120   **Radiologic examination, mastoids; less than 3 views per side**

70130   **complete, minimum of 3 views per side**

The common portion of these codes precedes the semicolon (;) in the full description of 70120. The complete description of 70130 is:

70130   **Radiologic examination, mastoids; complete, minimum of 3 views per side**

When the information for an indented code is the same as the information for the code with the full description, these codes will be grouped together in a range. When the information varies greatly, they will be listed separately.

Unlisted CPT Codes

Coding guidelines instruct providers to report unlisted CPT codes when there is no existing code that exactly describes the procedure performed. Unlisted CPT codes provide a method for reporting procedures that have not been assigned codes. This usually occurs because the procedures are new or uncommon. Following are the unlisted procedure codes for procedures specific to radiology and cardiology:

17999	Unlisted procedure, skin, mucous membrane and subcutaneous tissue
19499	Unlisted procedure, breast
20999	Unlisted procedure, musculoskeletal system, general
21499	Unlisted musculoskeletal procedure, head
22899	Unlisted procedure, spine
22999	Unlisted procedure, abdomen, musculoskeletal system
23929	Unlisted procedure, shoulder
24999	Unlisted procedure, humerus or elbow
25999	Unlisted procedure, forearm or wrist
26989	Unlisted procedure, hands or fingers
27299	Unlisted procedure, pelvis or hip joint
27599	Unlisted procedure, femur or knee
27899	Unlisted procedure, leg or ankle
28899	Unlisted procedure, foot or toes
33999	Unlisted procedure, cardiac surgery
36299	Unlisted procedure, vascular injection
37999	Unlisted procedure, vascular surgery
38999	Unlisted procedure, hemic/lymphatic system
43499	Unlisted procedure, esophagus
43999	Unlisted procedure, stomach
44799	Unlisted procedure, small intestine
47999	Unlisted procedure, biliary tract
49999	Unlisted procedure, abdomen, peritoneum and omentum
53899	Unlisted procedure, urinary system
76496	Unlisted fluoroscopic procedure (eg, diagnostic, interventional)
76497	Unlisted computed tomography procedure (eg, diagnostic, interventional)
76498	Unlisted magnetic resonance procedure (eg, diagnostic, interventional)
76499	Unlisted diagnostic radiographic procedure
76999	Unlisted ultrasound procedure (eg, diagnostic, interventional)
93799	Unlisted cardiovascular service or procedure

Procedure Codes

Following the specific CPT code and its narrative, you will find a combination of the following features:

Illustrations

The illustrations accompanying the *Complete Guide for Interventional Radiology* provide readers a better understanding of the medical procedures referenced by the codes and data. The graphics offer coders a visual link between the technical language of the operative report and the cryptic descriptions accompanying the codes. The depictions usually include a labeled view of the affected body area, and occasionally tools and devices pertinent to the referenced procedure. Since many codes within a given set are similar in nature, graphics have been developed to highlight differences for clearer code selection.

The illustrations are almost always simplified schematic representations, oftentimes of complex and delicate medical procedures. In many instances, proper anatomical detail is minimized to present a clearer picture of coding the procedure. As such, only a lay knowledge of a given procedure can be obtained from any depiction. All graphic material was computer generated by Optum360 staff. Valuable reference was drawn from a broad spectrum of surgical, clinical, and anatomic publications.

Explanation

Every CPT code or series of similar codes is presented with its official CPT code description. However, sometimes these descriptions do not provide the reader with sufficient information to make a proper code selection. In the *Complete Guide for Interventional Radiology*, you will find a step-by-step clinical description of the procedure, in simple terms. Technical language potentially used by the physician is included and defined.

The *Complete Guide for Interventional Radiology* describes the most common method or methods for performing each procedure, using key words often found in operative reports. If our description varies too greatly from the operative report, another code might be more appropriate. If a satisfactory code description cannot be matched to the patient's record, consult the physician.

Coding Tips

Coding tips provide information on how the code should be used, modifier assignment, HCPCS codes reported instead of or in addition to the procedure, offer other codes frequently reported with the procedures, and information regarding when not to use the code. A chart is also provided as a quick glance at the component codes typically reported for the procedure. This information comes from consultants and technical editors at Optum360 and from the coding guidelines provided in the CPT book.

The coding tips have been expanded to include physician-specific indications, such as when to append modifier 26 to radiology procedures and CPT codes reported by physicians when a code is specific to facilities.

HCPCS Level II Codes

HCPCS is an acronym (pronounced "hick-picks") for the Healthcare Common Procedural Coding System. This field presents Level II (national) codes that provide a uniform method for reporting medical supplies and equipment, as well as select services provided on an outpatient basis. Level II codes were developed and are maintained by the Centers for Medicare and Medicaid Services (CMS) for Medicare reporting, but they are rapidly gaining recognition in the commercial payer industry. CPT codes are considered Level I codes of HCPCS.

CMS mandates the use of HCPCS codes on outpatient Medicare claims and many states also require them on Medicaid forms.

ICD-10-CM Diagnosis Codes

ICD-10-CM diagnosis codes listed are common diagnoses or reasons the procedure may be necessary. This list in most cases is inclusive to radiology or cardiology.

Several conventions specific to the *Complete Guide for Interventional Radiology* must be understood for effective use of this feature.

"Code First" and "Code Also" Instructions

Notes and rules in ICD-10-CM sometimes instruct the coder to use a second code when reporting specific diagnoses. For instance:

J95.02   **Infection of tracheostomy stoma**
          Use additional code to identify type of infection, such as:
              cellulitis of neck (L03.8)
              sepsis (A40, A41.-)

In our list of clinical indications, a note would be attached to J95.02 to include this information:

J95.02   **Infection of tracheostomy stoma – (Use additional code to identify type of infection: A40, A41.-, L03.8)**

Unspecified and Not Otherwise Specified Codes
Because specific diagnoses are sometimes linked in the ICD-10-CM index to nonspecific codes, and because the patient record may sometimes leave no other option for the coder, unspecified and not otherwise specified codes have been included in our crosswalk. Typically, nonspecific codes will have a final digit of 0, 8, or 9, but are most easily identified by their descriptions. These codes should be used only when a more specific code cannot be located in the *Complete Guide for Interventional Radiology* and in ICD-10-CM. Remember, some payers may reject claims based on nonspecific diagnoses.

Correct Coding Initiative
The "CCI Edits" section includes a list of codes from the official Centers for Medicare and Medicaid Services' National Correct Coding Policy Manual for Part B Medicare carriers considered to be an integral part of the comprehensive code or mutually exclusive of it and should not be reported separately. CMS has also implemented the requirement that state Medicaid programs must incorporate NCCI methodologies into their Medicaid Management Information Systems (MMIS) and began to edit claims using NCCI effective for claims filed on or after October 1, 2010.

Unbundling is the practice of reporting components of a surgical service in addition to the major service. Medicare and private payers consider unbundling as fraudulent billing.

Medicare divides its unbundles into two categories: component codes and mutually exclusive codes. Component codes are considered part of the main surgical service, while mutually exclusive codes are considered codes that for other reasons should not be billed.

Beginning with the MUE release updated on July 2, 2014, an additional component of the MUE became effective. This edit is the MUE Adjudication Indicator, or MAI. This edit is the result of an audit by the Office of Inspector General (OIG) that identified inappropriate billing practices that bypassed the MUE edits. These included inappropriate reporting of bilateral services and split billing.

There are three MAIs:

MAI 1 will continue to be adjudicated as the line edit on the claim. These will be auto-adjudicated by the contractor.

MAI 2 is identified as the "absolute date-of-service edit" and is based on policy. The total unit of services (UOS) for that CPT code and that date of service (DOS) are combined for this edit. They are considered to be firm limits that are based upon subregulatory guidance or directly on a regulation or statute. The Medicare contractor is required to look at all claims for the same patient, same date of service, and same provider as identified by the national provider identifier (NPI), rendering provider, or supplier number.

This review considers the current submitted claim and/or a previously submitted claim. If the total MUE is exceeded, the current claim is denied; however, previously paid claims are not adjusted.

MAI 3 is also a date-of-service edit but is based upon clinical benchmarks. The review considers current and previously submitted claims, looking at the same patient, same date of service, and same provider. Claims in excess of the MUE are denied on the current claim. However, "if there is adequate documentation of medical necessity," the claim may bypass the edit or be resubmitted. Instructions indicate that the MUE/MAI edit is a coding denial and not a medical necessity denial. It would be inappropriate to have a beneficiary sign an advance beneficiary notice (ABN), and signing one does not shift the liability for the claim to the beneficiary. For those claims with an MAI value of 3, the contractor can consider whether the "services were medically reasonable and necessary" if provided and documented.

The *Complete Guide for Interventional Radiology* includes the most up-to-date ICD-10-CM, CPT, and HCPCS codes. The codes in the CCI are from version 23.3, the most current version available at press time. CCI version 23.3 does not address the 2018 CPT and HCPCS new code changes. So that current information is available before the next edition, Optum360 posts updated CCI edits on a website specific to this publication. The website address is https://www.optumcoding.com/Products/Updates/FIR/ and the password is FIR18.

For instance:

75710   Angiography, extremity, unilateral, radiologic supervision and interpretation

has the following component code unbundles:

> 01916, 01924-01926, 35201-35206, 35226, 35261-35266, 35286, 36000, 36005, 36410, 36500, 36591-36592, 75630, 75820, 75822, 75893, 76000-76001, 76942, 76998, 77001-77002, 96372, 96376-96377, 99446-99449

To conserve space, we have listed codes in ranges whenever possible. The two codes listed and any codes that fall into the numeric sequence between the two codes listed, are considered part of the Correct Coding Initiative unbundle edit.

Unbundles listed directly under the "CCI Edits" heading apply to all codes in the code range addressed on that page.

Case Examples

Authentic case examples are provided to give the reader a realistic application of the code(s) discussed in the section. Key terms appear in red text to help the reader understand how the terms lead to proper code selection. These cases are coded using Medicare and AMA guidelines. Individual MACs and third party payers should be consulted for specific coding guidelines.

Medicare Information

Medicare edits are provided for most codes. These Medicare edits were current as of November 2017.

Chapter 1: The Basics

APC Basics–Why are they important?

Why are APCs (ambulatory payment classification) important to interventional radiology and cardiology? The simple answer is: correct coding and charge capture equals correct APC assignment equals correct payment to the hospital for the services provided. Additionally, capturing and reporting all applicable and appropriate codes helps set future APC payment rates.

APCs apply only to hospitals. Physicians are paid according to the current fee schedule. The majority of hospitals today are paid for Medicare outpatient services via the ambulatory payment classification system (APC). Procedures are grouped into similar categories and assigned a fixed payment rate.

Under APCs, Medicare pays hospitals at "a rate per service basis" for outpatient services performed in a hospital-based setting. On August 1, 2000, Medicare initiated the outpatient prospective payment system (OPPS) as an attempt to cap payments for services in outpatient departments rather than paying 80 percent of total charges. Rural and critical access hospitals (CAH) are exempt from APCs but have been coming under various versions of capped reimbursement in recent years.

Medicare uses a formula to group like types of service by cost and type into APC categories with an assigned payment rate. Healthcare Common Procedural Coding System (HCPCS), which includes Level I CPT® codes, is used to report services. Codes are linked to each APC grouping.

The imaging, surgical, and certain supply components of an interventional service have specific HCPCS or HCPCS II codes required to be reported by line item on a UB-04 claim. Medicare reviews each line item and groups the codes using the Outpatient Code Editor (OCE). The OCE is a system of edits all claims must pass through. This system ensures all required fields on the claim are completed properly. If they are not, the claim is flagged as incorrect. Adjunct costs such as routine pharmacy and supplies routinely reported are recognized as cost, but are bundled into the actual APC (procedure) payment and not separately paid. Pre- and post-procedure costs such as patient preparation and post-procedure monitoring are included in the APC rate as well.

Each interventional service should have at least one related diagnosis or symptom linking it to the necessity of the procedure. The diagnosis is incorporated into the OCE claims editing process to identify medical necessity.

Medicare has established unique APC groups for new technology services based on cost. These are considered temporary until enough data are collected to assign a permanent APC category. Virtually all interventional procedures, however, are grouped into established APC categories with associated payment rates.

Status Indicators

What are status indicators and why are they important to interventional radiology and invasive cardiology services?

Table 1. Excerpt from Addendum B, 2018 Final Rule (OPPS Facility Payment)

HCPCS Code	Short Descriptor	CI	SI	APC	Relative Weight	Payment Rate	National Unadjusted Copayment	Minimum Unadjusted Copayment
27096	Inject sacroiliac joint		B					
33967	Insert i-aort percut device		C					
36200	Place catheter in aorta		N					
36224	Place cath carotd art	CH	Q2	5184	54.2330	$4,264.67		$852.94
36225	Place cath subclavian art	CH	Q2	5183	31.6976	$2,492.57		$498.52
49465	Fluoro exam of g/colon tube	CH	Q1	5522	1.5100	$118.74		$23.75
75710	Artery x-rays arm/leg	CH	Q2	5183	31.6976	$2,492.57		$498.52
92928	Prq card stent w/angio 1 vsl		J1	5193	133.6503	$10,509.72		$2,101.95
93458	L hrt artery/ventricle angio		J1	5191	35.7776	$2,813.41	$865.56	$562.69
93613	Electrophys map 3d add-on		N					
93620	Electrophysiology evaluation		J1	5212	67.5765	$5,313.95		$1,062.79
93653	Ep & ablate supravent arrhyt		J1	5213	235.4500	$18,514.85		$3,702.97
93654	Ep & ablate ventric tachy		J1	5213	235.4500	$18,514.85		$3,702.97
93655	Ablate arrhythmia add on		N					
93656	Tx atrial fib pulm vein isol		J1	5213	235.4500	$18,514.85		$3,702.97
93657	Tx l/r atrial fib addl		N					

Table 2. Status Indicators Affecting Interventional Procedures

Status Indicator	Description	OPPS Payment Status
B	Codes that are not recognized by OPPS when submitted on an outpatient hospital Part B bill type (12x and 13x).	Not paid under OPPS. • May be paid by MACs when submitted on a different bill type—for example, 75x (CORF)—but not paid under OPPS. • An alternate code that is recognized by OPPS when submitted on an outpatient hospital Part B bill type (12x and 13x) may be available.
C	Inpatient Procedures	Not paid under OPPS. Admit patient. Bill as inpatient.
D	Discontinued Codes	Not paid under OPPS or any other Medicare payment system.
E1	Items and services: • Not covered by any Medicare outpatient benefit category • Statutorily excluded by Medicare • Not reasonable and necessary	Not paid by Medicare when submitted on outpatient claims (any outpatient bill type).
E2	Items and services for which pricing information and claims data are not available	Not paid by Medicare when submitted on outpatient claims (any outpatient bill type).
G	Pass-through drugs and biologicals	Paid under OPPS; separate APC payment.
H	Pass-through device categories	Separate cost-based pass-through payment; not subject to copayment.
J1	Hospital Part B services paid through a comprehensive APC	Paid under OPPS; all covered Part B services on the claim are packaged with the primary "J1" service for the claim, except services with OPPS SI=F,G, H, L and U; ambulance services; diagnostic and screening mammography; all preventive services; and certain Part B inpatient services.
J2	Hospital Part B services that may be paid through a comprehensive APC	Paid under OPPS; addendum B displays APC assignments when services are separately payable. (1) Comprehensive APC payment based on OPPS comprehensive-specific payment criteria. Payment for all covered Part B services on the claim is packaged into a single payment for specific combinations of services, except services with OPPS SI=F,G, H, L and U; ambulance services; diagnostic and screening mammography; all preventive services; and certain Part B inpatient services. (2) Packaged APC payment if billed on the same claim as a HCPCS code assigned status indicator "J1." (3) In other circumstances, payment is made through a separate APC payment or packaged into payment for other services.
K	Non-pass-through drugs and nonimplantable biologicals, including therapeutic radiopharmaceuticals	Paid under OPPS; separate APC payment.
N	Items and services packaged into APC rates	Paid under OPPS; payment is packaged into payment for other services. Therefore, there is no separate APC payment.
Q1	STV-packaged codes	Paid under OPPS; addendum B displays APC assignments when services are separately payable. (1) Packaged APC payment if billed on the same claim as a HCPCS code assigned status indicator "S," "T," or "V." (2) Composite APC payment if billed with specific combinations of services based on OPPS composite-specific payment criteria. Payment is packaged into a single payment for specific combinations of services. (3) In other circumstances, payment is made through a separate APC payment.
Q2	T-packaged codes	Paid under OPPS; addendum B displays APC assignments when services are separately payable. (1) Packaged APC payment if billed on the same claim as a HCPCS code assigned status indicator "T." (2) In other circumstances, payment is made through a separate APC payment.

Status Indicator	Description	OPPS Payment Status
Q3	Codes that may be paid through a composite APC	Paid under OPPS; addendum B displays APC assignments when services are separately payable. Addendum M displays composite APC assignments when codes are paid through a composite APC. (1) Composite APC payment based on OPPS composite-specific payment criteria. Payment is packaged into a single payment for specific combinations of services. (2) In other circumstances, payment is made through a separate APC payment or packaged into payment for other services.
S	Procedure or service, not discounted when multiple	Paid under OPPS; separate APC payment.
T	Procedure or service, multiple procedure reduction applies	Paid under OPPS; separate APC payment.
U	Brachytherapy sources	Paid under OPPS; separate APC payment.
	* Note—Payments "under a fee schedule or payment system other than OPPS" may be contractor priced.	

Status indicators are categories in which APCs are assigned based upon Medicare's coverage of the service and the method of how they are paid. Status indicators provide guidance in properly reporting items and services on outpatient claims. Each HCPCS and CPT code is assigned a status indicator. These indicators can be found in addendum B of the Changes to the Hospital Outpatient Prospective Payment System Final Rule released each November. The list is updated by the Centers for Medicare and Medicaid Services (CMS) on a quarterly basis. Table 1 is an excerpt from addendum B of the 2018 Outpatient Prospective Payment System Final Rule.

There are several status indicators affecting interventional radiology and cardiology services. See Table 2. For a complete listing of the OPPS status indicators, please refer to appendix E.

Status Indicator B—For interventional radiology and cardiology, items and services assigned status indicator B are typically items for which a new code exists or for services billed only by physicians and paid under the physician fee schedule. An example is code 27096 Injection procedure for sacroiliac joint. Codes G0259 and G0260 report this service to Medicare.

Status Indicator C—Procedures assigned status indicator C have been determined to be complex enough to be deemed medically unsafe to perform on an outpatient basis and have thus been classified as not eligible for payment on an OP claim. They are paid only on an IP claim under the DRG reimbursement system. If an outpatient is scheduled to have a procedure on the inpatient-only list, the appropriate hospital financial personnel should be alerted so they can handle the encounter in a way that facilitates payment for the services. Refer to appendix D for a list of interventional radiology and cardiology procedures with status indicator C for 2018.

Status Indicator D—Procedure codes deleted from the OPPS list are assigned status indicator D. Some may be assigned a different code while others are eliminated altogether from the APC system. Usually a program transmittal is issued detailing the new or changed reporting guidelines. Items assigned status indicator D should not be reported on claims to Medicare. CPT code 36140 is deleted for 2018 and is therefore assigned status indicator D.

Status Indicator E1 and E2—Most items and services assigned status indicators E1 and E2 are simply not covered by Medicare and are therefore not paid. There may be an alternate code required to report the service. Some examples of non-covered services are CPT codes 61640–61642 Balloon dilatation of intracranial vasospasm. These services are not covered by Medicare. It is important to inform the patient when noncovered procedures are requested, as the patient becomes responsible for the charges. An advance beneficiary notice (ABN) should be completed before service is provided to document notification to Medicare. Items assigned status indicators E1 and E2 should not be reported on claims to Medicare.

Status Indicator H—A few device items still qualify for OPPS payment. There are currently no items assigned status indicator H.

Items assigned status indicator H should be separately reported and appear on Medicare claims with the HCPCS code.

Status Indicator J1—When a code is assigned this status indicator, all other reported services are packaged into this code. In other words, this code is the only payable code for the claim. An example is 37221 Iliac endovascular revascularization with stent placement.

Status Indicator K—Items assigned status indicator K consist primarily of drugs, biologicals, and some radiopharmaceutical agents. Several of the drugs used during interventional vascular procedures are assigned to status indicator K. Items with this status indicator are paid under OPPS and carry a separate APC payment. Items assigned status indicator K should be separately reported and appear on Medicare claims with the HCPCS code and revenue code 0636.

Status Indicator N—Items and services assigned status indicator N are covered by Medicare and paid under the OPPS system; however, payment is packaged into the payment for other services. In the case of interventional radiology and cardiology, payment for these items is included in the APC payment for the procedure itself. Most of the CPT codes reporting catheter placement (36215, 36216, etc.) are assigned status indicator N. Many of the supplies used in interventional procedures such as guide wires (C1769) and catheters are assigned status indicator N. Even though these items do not carry separate payment, they should still be reported separately on Medicare claims. Claims will be rejected if the required coding is not present. Claims will also be rejected if a status indicator N item appears alone. These items must always be reported with another code and service.

Status Indicator Q—Status indicator Q has been split into four separate categories—Q1, Q2, Q3, and Q4. Payment for Q1 codes is packaged when the service is performed with certain procedures but paid separately when performed alone. Payment for Q2 codes is packaged when the service is performed with procedures assigned status indicator T but paid separately when performed alone. Q3 codes may be paid under the new composite payment criteria. The composite payment criteria applies to interventional radiology codes and electrophysiology procedures. Q4 applies only to laboratory.

Status Indicator S—Services assigned status indicator S are considered to be significant procedures involving a wide variety of hospital resources. The APC payment is not discounted when performed with other procedures. Many angiography, interventional radiology, and cardiac catheterization procedures have been assigned to the composite status indicators. Code 76000 has S status.

Status Indicator T—Procedures assigned status indicator T are surgical procedures also considered significant procedures involving significant hospital resources. However, they are considered to carry some duplicate components when performed with other procedures and are discounted when reported with other procedures. For example, the procedure described by CPT code 93505 Endomyocardial biopsy, is usually performed with cardiac catheterization procedures. Both procedures would contain duplicate services such as room preparation. Payment is reduced under the OPPS system in order to not pay twice for such components.

Status Indicator U—This status indicator is used to report brachytherapy sources. These items are paid by separate APC payment. Assign the applicable HCPCS Level II code.

Physician Payment Methodology

Payment for physician services is determined by the Resource-Based Relative Value Scale (RBRVS), implemented in 1992 to provide consistent payment policies by Medicare Part B.

There are three factors in determining payment within the RBRVS system:

- Relative value units (RVU)
- Conversion factor (CF)
- Geographic practice cost indices (GPCI)

In addition to these three major indicators, other instances affect reimbursement such as the use of modifiers, location where service is provided, global surgical parameters, and supplies.

RVUs are established for a procedure or service based on three components:

- Work RVU: The physician work RVU (RVUw) includes the skill, time, and effort needed to provide the service.
- Practice expense RVU: The practice expense RVU (PE-RVU) includes the cost of providing space, equipment, and associated staff to provide the service.
- Malpractice RVU: The malpractice RVU (RVUm) includes the cost of the physician's liability insurance based on a percentage of revenue.

There are two types of PE-RVUs: facility, which includes a hospital, skilled nursing facility, or ambulatory surgery center, and nonfacility, which includes a physician's office or patient's home. For services performed in only one setting, there is only one PE-RVU.

The conversion factor is a standard dollar amount equating relative values with payment amounts. In 2017, the current physician CF is $35.8887. Any 2018 update to the conversion factor is not included in this update since it was not available at press time. Please check www.cms.gov for the most current CF. Geographical practice cost indexes (GPCI) take into consideration the cost per unit based on the geographic location where the service is performed compared to the national average of the cost per unit.

The general payment formula is:

Payment = [(RVUw x GPCI work) + (PE-RVU x GPCI practice expense) + (RVUm x GPCI malpractice)] x CF

The payment amount is rounded to the nearest cent and the amount reimbursed by Medicare is 80 percent of the actual charge or 80 percent of the fee schedule amount, whichever is lower. The exceptions to this payment methodology are:

- National codes without established national values
- Services required by report payment or carrier priced
- Services outside the standard physician service definition

Services with established national codes, but no assigned relative value, will be paid based on local carrier relative values or a flat rate payment. However, the carrier cannot determine relative values for services deemed noncovered, bundled, or paid by report.

CCI Edits–Why are they important?

Why are the CCI edits important to interventional radiology and cardiology? Reporting services assigned with codes affected by the many CCI edits could cause the claim or bill to be either delayed or denied altogether. CCI edits apply to all providers reporting services to CMS for reimbursement. An awareness of these edits at the point of charge capture can alleviate delays in receiving payment and help hospital and practice financial performance.

The Correct Coding Initiative (CCI) was developed as a result of a report issued to Congress in May 1995 by the General Accounting Office (GAO), which outlined billing code abuses in the health care system. The Correct Coding Initiative (CCI) was developed by AdminaStar Federal, Inc., Indianapolis, Indiana, as a result of their contracted work in subsequent years. Phase I of the CCI issued approximately 87,000 code edits in an attempt to develop a national, standardized coding policy. Phase II added 16,000 more edits in 1996. Since that time, updated versions of the CCI are released for payers and providers to use in editing claims data. The ultimate goal is to reduce inappropriate reimbursement to providers by monitoring details of claims submitted for payment.

All Medicare carriers and intermediaries are required to use the CCI edits, which can also detect fraud and abuse patterns. Virtually all edits are incorporated into the OCE, which is used primarily by fiscal intermediaries. CMS has also implemented the requirement that state Medicaid programs must incorporate NCCI methodologies into their Medicaid Management Information Systems (MMISs) and begin to edit claims using NCCI effective for claims filed on or after October 1, 2011.

Providers should maintain correct coding policies within their organizations to be shared with coding and billing staff in addition to point-of-service staff who assign codes at the time of service. Policies should incorporate information about CCI edits that can be used as a reference when verifying code assignments.

Interventional radiology and cardiology claims are subject to CCI edits through the OCE. Incorrect codes, mutually exclusive code sets, and over-coding can be detected by the editor. Code errors should be returned to the department submitting the codes for correction prior to submitting the claim to Medicare or other payers. Departmental staff should understand the intention of these edits. When queried by billing or coding staff, the clinician frequently responds that the service was provided but does not necessarily understand that the service in question may be included in another service performed. Good communication between the billing, coding, and department clinical staff is essential to correctly applying the CCI edits.

The CCI edits address two major types of coding situations. First, those formerly known as comprehensive and component codes are now simply known as Column 1/Column 2 edits. These edits apply to code combinations where one code is considered to be a component of the more comprehensive code. The codes in Column 1 are considered to be the major procedure when reported on the same claim as the code in Column 2. The Column 2 code is considered to be included in the Column 1 code when performed at the same time. The edit allows payment for the comprehensive (Column 1) code only. Many of these edits will allow reporting of the Column 2 code with a modifier when appropriate. Examples of Column 1/Column 2 edits are CPT codes 75625 (Column 1) and 76000 (Column 2) and CPT codes 93530 (Column 1) and 93561 (Column 2). In the first example, fluoroscopy is included in angiography and would not be reported at the same time. In the second example, indicator dilution studies are considered to be part of the right heart catheterization procedure and would not be separately reported at the same time.

The second type of CCI edit is known as the mutually exclusive codes. CPT codes mutually exclusive of one another based either on the CPT definition or the medical impossibility/improbability the procedures could be performed at the same session can be identified as code pairs. These edits represent code pairs that should not be reported together. Examples are CPT code pairs 93619 (Column 1) and 93620 (Column 2) and 33226 (Column 1) and 33221 (Column 2). In the first code pair, the CPT definitions lead us to choose either with attempted arrhythmia induction or without attempted arrhythmia induction. In the second code pair, the code definition leads to a code for either a repositioning of an existing pacemaker electrode, including removal, insertion or replacement of a pulse generator, or the placement of a pacemaker pulse generator with existing electrodes. These two codes are mutually exclusive of one another.

There are also medically unlikely edits (MUEs). These edits provide the maximum number of units a provider reports for a single patient on one date of service. All HCPCS/CPT codes do not have an MUE.

It is important to remember CCI edits are updated quarterly and facilities should be aware of changes to the CCI edits to ensure appropriate reporting of services.

Recovery Audit Contractors (RAC)

The RAC program was mandated by the Medicare Prescription Drug, Improvement, and Modernization Act of 2003 to find and correct inappropriate Medicare Part A and Part B payments. Four regional RACs utilize data mining techniques to identify claims with potential overpayment (and in some cases underpayment). The RACs are paid on a contingency fee basis; the three-year demonstration project was considered a resounding success, with collection of more than $1.03 billion in inappropriate payments. The nationwide program was implemented in early 2010, with both automated and complex reviews.

In response to RACs, providers, and their associations, CMS has modified the additional documentation request limits for the RAC program in FY 2010 for institutional providers. The limits will be set by each RAC on an annual basis to establish a cap per campus on the maximum number of medical records that may be requested per 45-day period. A campus unit may consist of one or more separate facilities/practices under a single organizational umbrella; each limit will be based on that unit's prior calendar year Medicare claims volume.

In 2013, providers appealed 30.7 percent (500,629) of the RAC determinations. Overall, the data indicated that of all the RAC overpayment determinations (151,645), only 9.3 percent were overturned on appeal. It is recommended that providers track denials carefully and appeal when appropriate.

Coding Basics

Coding is the basis by which health care providers are paid for services they provide to patients. Codes tell the story of why and what occurred during a patient encounter. There are different sets of codes. They are:

- Diagnosis codes—The ICD-10-CM code set is currently used to report diagnoses.
- Level I HCPCS codes—CPT procedure codes and modifiers
- Level II HCPCS codes—HCPCS codes and modifiers for procedures, supplies and drugs
- Revenue codes

These sets of codes communicate the story of the patient encounter to the payer via the UB-04 form for hospitals and the CMS-1500 form for physicians. The claim form is defined by the National Uniform Billing Committee (NUBC). Refer to appendix C for sample claim forms.

Diagnosis coding is the responsibility of the health information or medical records department in most hospitals. This information is reported in the form of ICD-10-CM codes. ICD-10-CM is the acronym for International Classification of Diseases, 10th Revision, Clinical Modification. Beginning October 1, 2015, providers began using the 10th revision of this code set, ICD-10-CM. Clinical departments play an important role in obtaining clinical data and documentation to support the procedures being billed to the payer. Coders translate the clinical data into ICD-10-CM codes applied to the claim. These codes support the medical necessity of the procedures and affect whether or not payment is justified. If the ICD-10-CM codes do not match approved clinical indications to support the procedure paid, reimbursement will be affected.

Interventional radiology and cardiology procedures are reported using CPT and HCPCS codes. CPT (Current Procedural Terminology) codes are created and managed by the American Medical Association (AMA). It is important for hospital staff to understand this set of codes was created by physicians for physician use. They do not always easily translate to what happens in the hospital department. CMS, rather than creating its own coding system, contracts with the AMA to use the CPT system. CMS determines which CPT codes are covered by the Medicare system and how they will be paid.

Since CPT codes describe only physician services, CMS created HCPCS (Healthcare Common Procedure Coding System) for hospitals to report items and services unique to the facility setting. HCPCS codes are national codes consisting of one alphanumeric character followed by four digits.

General Coding Guidelines

General coding guidelines apply to all areas of service and all providers.

The CPT code submitted to describe a procedure or service must exactly match the service provided. If there is not a CPT code matching what was done, then the unlisted code for the applicable section should be reported. This holds true for both the surgical and radiology code sections of the CPT manual. It also applies to the medicine section of CPT where the interventional cardiology codes are located.

The fact that a code exists does not mean it is appropriate to report it to the payer. Check the status indicator section of this manual for guidance. Refer to addendum B of the *Federal Register* to determine the status indicator of each code.

An excerpt from addendum B can be found in appendix A of this book. The codes listed are those typically used in the interventional radiology and cardiology settings.

It is important to again point out the CPT manual's intended use is to report physician services. Facilities should remember to disregard reference to physician use in the CPT manual language. Much of the language does not pertain to hospitals.

HCPCS codes take precedence over CPT codes when reporting to Medicare. If both a CPT code and a HCPCS code describe the procedure provided, hospitals must report the HCPCS code to Medicare. The status indicator assignment helps identify whether a specific code is appropriate to report to Medicare.

Report the most comprehensive procedure describing the service provided. If one code describes all components of the procedure, then multiple different codes for each component should not be reported separately.

CPT codes are updated annually. CMS may make changes to HCPCS codes at any time during the year. It is important for facilities to stay informed of coding updates released by CMS.

Modifiers for Outpatient Hospital Radiology and Cardiology Procedures

Modifiers are used to provide additional information about the procedure performed. They inform payers the service or procedure has been altered or "modified" in some way, although the definition of the service has not changed. For example, there are modifiers to report the procedure performed was bilateral, only part of the procedure was performed, the procedure was performed more than once, or unusual events occurred during the procedure. Modifiers provide more specific or complete information about the procedure performed. Appropriate use of modifiers enhances correct coding and impacts reimbursement. APC payment for procedures appended with modifier 52 is reduced to 50 percent. These modifiers apply to Medicare claims. Verify modifier use with other payers.

This book lists CPT and HCPCS Level II modifiers used most often with cardiology and radiology-related procedures in a hospital outpatient department. CPT modifiers appropriate for radiology and cardiology hospital outpatient claims are as follows:

50	Bilateral procedure
52	Reduced services
59	Distinct procedural service
73	Discontinued outpatient procedure prior to anesthesia administration
74	Discontinued outpatient procedure after anesthesia administration

HCPCS Level II modifiers that may be appropriate are:

RT	Right side (used to identify procedures performed on the right side of the body)
LT	Left side (used to identify procedures performed on the left side of the body)
LC	Left circumflex, coronary artery
LD	Left anterior descending, coronary artery
LM	Left main coronary artery
RC	Right coronary artery
RI	Ramus intermedius, coronary artery
XE	Separate encounter
XP	Separate practitioner
XS	Separate structure
XU	Unusual non-overlapping service

50—Bilateral procedure

Assign modifier 50 for bilateral or procedures performed on both sides when the code is not inherently bilateral. CMS now prefers using modifier 50 rather than modifiers RT and LT. However, modifier 50 does not work well for catheter placement codes. Modifier 59 is best used when multiple catheter placement codes are reported or when a diagnostic procedure is performed before a therapeutic service. Please note that to separately report the diagnostic service, the documentation must clearly state it was needed and then used to make a clinical decision to proceed with intervention. Otherwise, diagnostic procedures are considered part of the therapeutic procedure.

Example: Angiography is performed on both vertebral arteries. Report CPT code 36226 with modifier 50.

52—Reduced services

Assign modifier 52 for discontinued or partially reduced radiologic procedures and other services not requiring anesthesia. Modifier 52 should not be assigned to procedures requiring another existing procedure code to be reported. Modifier 52 is rarely used in interventional radiology. Refer to modifiers 73 and 74.

Example: Only an AP view of the femur is taken. Report CPT code 73550 Radiologic examination, femur, 2 views, and assign modifier 52 to indicate a reduced service was performed.

59—Distinct procedural service

Assign modifier 59 to a distinct service that is not a component of another reported procedure HCPCS/CPT code. This modifier should not be utilized to unbundle procedure codes.

Example: Assign modifier 59 when more than one artery is catheterized during an angiogram procedure. When both the right internal and external carotid arteries are selected during a cerebral angiogram case, assign modifier 59 to tell the payer this is not a duplicate code.

73—Discontinued outpatient procedure prior to anesthesia administration

Assign modifier 73 to report a discontinued surgical or diagnostic procedure prior to anesthesia.

Example: The patient is prepped (including pre-medication), placed on the procedure room table and before the incision, intubation, insertion of scope, local anesthesia, regional block, or conscious sedation/anesthesia, is administered, the procedure is terminated due to extenuating or life-threatening circumstances.

74—Discontinued outpatient procedure after anesthesia administration

Assign modifier 74 to indicate a discontinued surgical or diagnostic procedure after conscious sedation/anesthesia has been induced. This modifier will be the most often used modifier to report reduced services in the interventional radiology and cardiology settings. Append this modifier for unsuccessful interventional attempts. Procedures appended with modifier 74 are paid at 100 percent of the assigned APC rate.

Example: The patient is prepped and draped. After local anesthesia, conscious sedation, scope, or regional block has been administered and/or the incision has been made, the procedure is terminated due to extenuating or life-threatening circumstances.

Do not report modifiers 73 and 74 for elective cancellation.

Note: For Medicare billing purposes, anesthesia is defined as any type of anesthesia including local and conscious sedation.

RT (right side) and LT (left side)

Assign right and left modifiers to radiology procedures for extremity and organ pairs when only one side is imaged or has an intervention performed. Verify the use of RT and LT modifiers versus reporting modifier 50 for bilateral procedures with individual payers and fiscal intermediaries. Policies will differ among payers.

LC—Left circumflex, coronary artery

Modifier LC is used to designate the left circumflex coronary artery and its branches. It is appended to coronary interventional procedure codes to depict the vessel treated.

LD—Left anterior descending coronary artery

Modifier LD is used to designate the left anterior descending coronary artery and its branches. It is appended to coronary interventional procedure codes to depict the vessel treated.

RC—Right coronary artery

Modifier RC is used to designate the right coronary artery and its branches. It is appended to coronary interventional procedure codes to depict the vessel treated.

RI—Ramus intermedius, coronary artery

Modifier RI is used to designate interventional procedure performed in the ramus intermedius artery. It is appended to coronary interventional procedure codes to depict the vessel treated.

XE—Separate encounter, a service that is distinct because it occurred during a separate encounter

A subset of modifier 59, assign modifier XE when a normally included service is performed during a separate encounter from the main service.

XP—Separate practitioner, a service that is distinct because it was performed by a different practitioner

A subset of modifier 59, assign modifier XP when a normally included service is performed by a different practitioner.

XS—Separate structure, a service that is distinct because it was performed on a separate organ/structure

A subset of modifier 59, assign modifier XS when a normally included service is performed on a separate organ or structure from the main service.

XU—Unusual non-overlapping service, the use of a service that is distinct because it does not overlap usual components of the main service

A subset of modifier 59, assign modifier XU to report a non-overlapping service as the main service.

It is important to point out here the importance of following CMS guidelines for appropriate modifier assignment. Failure to do so could result in compliance violations leading to fines and penalties to the provider.

Modifiers for Physician Services

Modifiers are designed to give Medicare and commercial payers additional information needed to process a claim. The examples included in this text are the modifiers most commonly utilized within interventional radiology and cardiology. These include HCPCS Level I (Physicians' Current Procedural Terminology [CPT]) and HCPCS Level II modifiers. Appendix A of *CPT 2016* includes a list of 32 HCPCS Level I (CPT) modifiers applicable to CPT 2016 codes and 13 HCPCS Level I (CPT) modifiers approved for use in outpatient facilities.

There are two levels of modifiers within the HCPCS coding system. Level I (CPT) modifiers are developed by the American Medical Association (AMA) while HCPCS Level II modifiers are developed by the Centers for Medicare and Medicaid Services (CMS). HCPCS modifiers can be found in a current version of the HCPCS Level II code book.

Level I Modifiers

26	Professional component
50	Bilateral procedure
51	Multiple procedures
52	Reduced services
53	Discontinued procedure
59	Distinct procedural service
76	Repeat procedure or service by same physician or other qualified health care professional
77	Repeat procedure or service by another physician or other qualified health care professional
78	Unplanned return to the operating/procedure room by the same physician or other qualified health care professional following initial procedure for a related procedure during the postoperative period
79	Unrelated procedure or service by the same physician or other qualified health care professional during the postoperative period

Level II Modifiers

GD	Units of service exceeds medically unlikely edit value and represents reasonable and necessary services
LC	Left circumflex, coronary artery
LD	Left anterior descending, coronary artery
LT	Left side
RC	Right coronary artery
RI	Ramus intermedius
RT	Right side
TC	Technical component
XE	Separate encounter
XP	Separate practitioner
XS	Separate structure
XU	Unusual non-overlapping service

26—Professional component

Certain procedures are a combination of a physician component and a technical component. When the physician component is reported separately, the service is identified by adding modifier 26 to the usual procedure number.

Example: A unilateral adrenal angiogram radiological supervision and interpretation is performed in an outpatient hospital setting. Report code 75731 with modifier 26.

50—Bilateral procedure

Assign modifier 50 to indicate a bilateral service or for procedures performed on both the right and left sides when the code is not inherently bilateral. CMS now prefers the use of modifier 50 rather than modifiers RT and LT. However, modifier 50 does not work well for catheter placement codes and modifier 59 is a more appropriate choice when multiple catheter placement codes are reported.

Example: Angiography is performed on both vertebral arteries. Report code 36226 with modifier 50.

51—Multiple procedures

When multiple procedures, other than E/M services, physical medicine and rehabilitation services, or provision of supplies (e.g., vaccines), are performed at the same session by the same provider, the primary procedure or service may be reported as listed. The additional procedures or services are identified by appending modifier 51 to the additional procedure or service codes.

Note: This modifier should not be appended to designated add-on codes.

Example: The physician initially inserts a gastrostomy tube via a percutaneous approach for feeding due to gastrointestinal obstruction. Upon completion, the physician determines there is a need to convert the gastrostomy tube to a gastrojejunostomy tube. Report 49440 and 49446 with modifier 51.

52—Reduced services

Under certain circumstances a service or procedure is partially reduced or eliminated at the physician's discretion. Under these circumstances, the service provided is identified by its usual procedure number and the addition of modifier 52, signifying the service was reduced. This modifier provides a means of reporting reduced services without disturbing the identification of the basic service.

Example: A patient is scheduled for a percutaneous thrombectomy of the right femoral vein. The pre-procedural angiogram indicated more extensive thrombus requiring re-evaluation of treatment. The physician expressed the need to repeat a portion of the prior angiogram in order to review further images of the vein and evaluate the size of the thrombus in order to proceed with stent placement. Report code 75820 with modifier 52 on the second angiogram since a complete study is not required.

53—Discontinued procedure

Under certain circumstances, the physician may elect to terminate a surgical or diagnostic procedure. Due to extenuating circumstances or those threatening the well-being of the patient, it may be necessary to indicate a surgical or diagnostic procedure was started but discontinued. This circumstance is reported by adding modifier 53 to the code reported by the physician for the discontinued procedure.

Example: A patient presents for cardiac catheterization. However, the procedure was discontinued when the catheter could not be advanced into the heart and was withdrawn without obtaining any diagnostic data. Continuing with the procedure would have put the patient at risk. Report 93451 with modifier 53 since the procedure was not completed.

59—Distinct procedural service

Assign modifier 59 to a distinct service not considered a component of another reported procedure. This modifier should not be utilized to unbundle procedure codes.

Example: Assign modifier 59 when more than one artery is catheterized during an angiogram. When both the right internal and external carotid arteries are selected during a cerebral angiogram case, assign modifier 59 to tell the payer this is not a duplicate code.

76—Repeat procedure or service by same physician or other qualified health care professional

It may be necessary to indicate a procedure or service was repeated subsequent to the original procedure or service. This circumstance is reported by adding modifier 76 to the repeated procedure/service.

Example: A patient underwent revision of a pacemaker lead due to malfunction in the morning. Later in the evening, symptoms recurred indicating a return to the OR with the same physician. The previous pacemaker incision was reopened and the pacemaker wires exposed; the right atrial lead was repositioned at the atrial appendage. Proper pacing thresholds were obtained and the leads were reattached to the pacemaker generator. Report code 33208 with modifier 76 to indicate the same procedure was performed by the same physician at a different encounter in order to indicate the service was not a duplicate reporting issue.

77—Repeat procedure or service by another physician or other qualified health care professional

The physician may need to indicate a basic procedure or service performed by another physician, or other qualified health care professional, had to be repeated. This situation may be reported by adding modifier 77 to the repeated procedure/service.

Example: A patient may have a single view chest x-ray to evaluate the placement of a catheter or line and, in some cases, if their condition does not improve, a repeat chest x-ray may be done by another physician to evaluate current positioning of the catheter. Report code 71045 with modifier 77 for the second chest x-ray.

78—Unplanned return to the operating/procedure room by the same physician or other qualified health care professional following initial procedure for a related procedure during the postoperative period

It may be necessary to indicate another procedure was performed during the postoperative period of the initial procedure. When this subsequent procedure is related to the first and requires the use of the operating room, it is reported by adding modifier 78 to the related procedure.

Example: A single vessel coronary graft is performed. In the patient's room that evening it is noted his vital signs are unstable, and it is observed that hemorrhagic complications following the surgery have occurred. The patient is returned to the operating room on the same date to locate and control the source of hemorrhage. Report 33510 and 35820 with modifier 78.

79—Unrelated procedure or service by the same physician or other qualified health care professional during the postoperative period

The physician may need to indicate the performance of a procedure or service during the postoperative period was unrelated to the original procedure. This circumstance may be reported by using modifier 79.

Example: A patient, having had a femoral-popliteal graft performed one week previously, presents to his physician with symptoms of acute renal failure. He is admitted for care but does not respond to the prescribed treatment. His physician discusses the possibility of hemodialysis with the patient and his family. They agree that it is a viable option. The same surgeon inserts a cannula for hemodialysis. Report code 36810 with modifier 79 since the insertion of the cannula for hemodialysis was not related to the femoral-popliteal graft that was performed earlier.

GD—Units of service exceeds MUE value

Modifier GD is reported to indicate the units of service reported exceed the medically unlikely edit value yet still represent reasonable and necessary services. Currently, only CMS is using medically unlikely edits (MUE) and the provider documentation must support the medical necessity of exceeding the MUE.

LC—Left circumflex, coronary artery

Modifier LC is used to designate the left circumflex coronary artery and its branches. It is appended to coronary interventional procedure codes to depict the vessel treated.

LD—Left anterior descending coronary artery

Modifier LD is used to designate the left anterior descending coronary artery. It is appended to coronary interventional procedure codes to depict the vessel treated.

LT—Left side (used to identify procedures performed on the left side of the body)

Assign modifier LT to radiology procedures for extremity and organ pairs when only one side is imaged or has an intervention performed. Verify the use of LT vs. modifier 50 for bilateral procedures with individual payers and fiscal intermediaries. Policies will differ among payers.

RC—Right coronary

Modifier RC is used to designate the right coronary artery and its branches. It is appended to coronary interventional procedure codes to depict the vessel treated.

RI—Ramus intermedius, coronary artery

Modifier RI is used to designate interventional procedure performed in the ramus intermedius artery. It is appended to coronary interventional procedure codes to depict the vessel treated.

RT—Right side (used to identify procedures performed on the right side of the body)

Assign modifier RT to radiology procedures for extremity and organ pairs when only one side is imaged or has an intervention performed. Verify the use of RT vs. modifier 50 for bilateral procedures with individual payers and fiscal intermediaries. Policies will differ among payers.

TC—Technical component

Under certain circumstances, a charge may be submitted for the technical component alone. Under those circumstances, the technical component charge is identified by adding modifier TC to the usual procedure number. Technical component charges are institutional charges and not billed separately by physicians. However, portable x-ray suppliers bill only for the technical component and should use modifier TC. The charge data from portable x-ray suppliers are then used to build customary and prevailing profiles. There are stand-alone procedure codes describing the technical component only (e.g., staff and equipment costs) of diagnostic tests. They also identify procedures covered only as diagnostic tests and, therefore, do not have a related professional component. Do not use modifier TC on these codes.

XE—Separate encounter, a service that is distinct because it occurred during a separate encounter

A subset of modifier 59, assign modifier XE when a normally included service is performed during a separate encounter from the main service.

XP—Separate practitioner, a service that is distinct because it was performed by a different practitioner

A subset of modifier 59, assign modifier XP when a normally included service is performed by a different practitioner.

XS—Separate structure, a service that is distinct because it was performed on a separate organ/structure

A subset of modifier 59, assign modifier XS when a normally included service is performed on a separate organ or structure from the main service.

XU—Unusual non-overlapping service, the use of a service that is distinct because it does not overlap usual components of the main service

A subset of modifier 59, assign modifier XU to report a non-overlapping service as the main service.

Radiology Services

Radiology services may be reported with both the technical and professional components or by separate entities on separate claims. The technical component, indicated by modifier TC, includes the cost associated with a service as it relates to equipment and technical staff utilized to provide the service. The professional component, indicated by modifier 26, includes physician service, supervision, and interpretation.

Hospitals bill the technical component and physicians bill the professional component. Hospital billing utilizes the UB-04 form while physician billing utilizes the CMS-1500 form (or electronic version 837i). Refer to appendix C for examples of these forms. If the physician is employed by the hospital, the professional billing would be done on the UB-04 (or electronic version 837p). When services are provided within the physician facility or freestanding center, the technical component would be reported on the CMS-1500 form. If both the technical and professional components are provided by the same entity, no modifier is necessary.

Revenue Codes

Revenue codes are four-digit codes used by hospitals to classify facility charges by the type of service provided. The use of these codes is defined by the National Uniform Billing Committee (NUBC). Revenue codes affect reimbursement, particularly for outpatient claims. These codes do not determine where an individual hospital posts revenue in its internal accounting system. Revenue codes are not used for physician services reported on the CMS-1500 form.

After APCs were implemented, CMS eased many of the previous restrictions on hospitals for revenue code assignment. Some restrictions still exist for supplies and drugs. As a general rule, hospitals should assign the revenue code matching the department where the service was provided. Fourth-digit specificity is recommended. For example, report 0481 rather than 0480 for cardiac cath procedures. Some FIs and other third-party payers may have additional revenue code restrictions. Be sure to consult with the individual payer for guidance. Revenue codes should be reported consistently for all payers. The hospital billing office is a good internal resource to help with assigning revenue codes for various payer restrictions. Revenue code assignment is often handled by someone in patient financial services. Revenue codes most commonly used in interventional radiology and cardiology are listed in Table 3.

Table 3. Revenue Codes for Interventional Imaging Services

Revenue Code	Description	Guidelines
0250	General pharmacy	Used for drugs other than contrast media and other drugs not eligible for pass-through payment
0255	Drugs incident to radiology	Use for drugs not eligible for pass-through payment and high osmolar contrast media.
0271	Med/surg supplies, nonsterile	Use to report non-sterile supplies.
0272	Med/surg supplies, sterile	Use for sterile supplies and devices with pass-through status.
0275	Med/surg supplies, pacemaker	Use for pacemaker generators and leads, AICD. Report the appropriate HCPCS code(s).
0278	Med/surg supplies, other implants	Use to report stents and other implants. Report the appropriate HCPCS code if available.
0320	Radiology-diagnostic, general	Use for general radiology procedures including fluoroscopy guidance.
0323	Radiology-arteriography	Recommended for all arteriography procedures.
0333	Radiation therapy	Use to report brachytherapy procedures.
0343	Diagnostic radiopharmaceuticals	Use for agents used in diagnostic procedures.
0344	Therapeutic radiopharmaceuticals	Use for agents used in therapeutic procedures.
0350	CT Scan, general	Use for CT guidance.
0360	Operating room services, general	May be used for interventional radiology surgical component codes Use for pacemaker procedures.
0361	Operating room services, minor surgery	Recommended for use with interventional radiology surgical component codes.
0371	Anesthesia incident to radiology	If separately billed, use this code for anesthesia during radiology procedures.
0372	Anesthesia incident to other diagnostic services	If separately billed, use this code for anesthesia during cardiology procedures.
0402	Ultrasound	Use for ultrasound guidance.
0480	Cardiology, general	Use for electrophysiology procedures.
0481	Cardiac cath lab	Recommended for procedures performed in the cath lab.
0610	MRI, general	Use for MRI guidance.
0621	Supplies incident to radiology	May be used to report radiology supplies. Do not use with pass-through status devices.
0622	Supplies incident to other diagnostic services	May be used to report cath lab supplies. Do not use with pass-through status devices.
0624	FDA investigational devices	Use to report investigational devices and procedures for FDA approved clinical trials.
0636	Drugs requiring detailed coding	Use to report drugs and biologicals requiring specific HCPCS code including LOCM.
0972	Professional fees, radiology, diagnostic	Use to report the professional component for diagnostic imaging procedures when billed by hospitals.
0973	Professional fees, radiology, therapeutic	Use to report the professional component for therapeutic procedures when billed by hospitals.

General Interventional Radiology Coding Guidelines for Selective and Nonselective Catheter Placements

Interventional radiology procedures are coded using a mixture of comprehensive procedure codes and the component coding methodology. There are several *components* to an interventional radiology procedure. There is the procedure of placing the catheter into the vascular system known as catheter placement. There is often a *surgical* component to the procedure, and there is the *imaging* or radiologic supervision and interpretation portion of the procedure. Most interventional radiology procedures have two of these components, and many include all three. More recently, interventional radiology coding is returning to comprehensive codes. These codes include all components of the procedure, namely the catheter placement, imaging, and surgical procedure. It is important to note there is often not a one-to-one coding correlation with the surgical and the radiology supervision and interpretation components. It is also important to note this component coding methodology is not applied consistently. Comprehensive codes have replaced component coding for some diagnostic procedures. Please review the appropriate sections in chapters 2–12 carefully.

Nonselective catheter placement is defined as the final placement of the catheter either in the aorta or vena cava from the point of origin, or placement of the catheter so that it is not advanced beyond the vessel of original access.

Selective catheter placement means the catheter is advanced from the vessel of origin into the aorta or vena cava and then *beyond* into another vessel.

There are specific and special rules guiding coding of interventional radiology procedures.

Nonselective Coding

- Regardless of the access site (femoral, axillary, or brachial) or the number of injections made in the aorta, if the catheter does not advance beyond the aorta it is nonselective catheter placement, catheter in aorta, report CPT code 36200.
- Regardless of the access site, if the catheter is not advanced beyond the access vessel, the access is considered nonselective.
- Code a nonselective and selective catheter placement CPT code only if there are two puncture sites or there are two separate patient encounters on the same date of service.

Selective Coding

The intent of the catheterization determines the degree of selectivity of the code assigned for the procedure performed. If the catheter is unintentionally placed into a vessel, this placement is not coded. Catheterizations to assist with forming loops in the catheter in order to assist in placement are also not coded.

- Know each puncture site.
- Know each final catheter placement.
- Place precedence on selective CPT codes over nonselective CPT codes.
- Code each vascular family separately.
- Code each vascular family to the highest degree of selectivity within that vascular family.
- Code only one second- or third-order selective catheter placement code within each vascular family.
- Code each additional second- or third-order catheter placement within a vascular family with the appropriate CPT code.
- Code each diagnostic and therapeutic procedure when performed together.
- Do not assume one exam is included in another; code each exam separately as appropriate.
- Understand the intention of the procedure such as the degree of selectivity or number of separately coded PTAs that may be coded in an upper extremity.
- Ensure documentation supports coding for all procedure codes assigned to claims.

The specific catheter placement code reported will depend upon the number of vessel branches the catheter passes to reach its final position and on the site of access. For example, from the femoral artery approach, the left common carotid artery is a first-order selective artery. If the approach is achieved by direct arterial stick, the catheterization becomes nonselective as no movement of the catheter is necessary from the point of origin.

The number of catheter placement codes reported depends upon the individual patient's anatomy and, of course, how many vascular families are selectively catheterized. The dictated procedure report should state the presence of anatomic variations and clearly describe the variation.

Comprehensive codes continue to replace previously reported component codes. Revised guidelines now apply. Please refer to the applicable sections in subsequent chapters for details.

Vascular Families

A vascular family is defined as a primary branch off of the aorta or vena cava and all of that vessel's subsequent branch vessels. Below are the most common arterial vascular families:

- Head and Neck—2, 3, and sometimes 4 families

  Most common families based upon normal anatomy are:
  - right carotid (brachiocephalic)
  - left carotid
  - right vertebral
  - left vertebral or subclavian
- Pulmonary—2 (typically exams are sub-selective-upper, middle, and lower lobes of the lung)
  - RT pulmonary
  - LT pulmonary
- Aortography—high and low (arch, thoracic, proximal/distal abdominal)
- Renals—1–4 families
  - right renal—if two right renal arteries are present, each is a separate family.
  - left renal—if two left renal arteries are present, each is a separate family.
- Visceral—many families
  - Each vessel arising directly from the aorta such as intercostal or spinal arteries
  - Inferior mesenteric artery (IMA)
  - Superior mesenteric artery (SMA)
  - Celiac artery
- Extremities—upper and lower, 1–4 families (branches)

Catheter Placement Codes for Interventional Radiology

Nonselective Catheter Placements—Arterial

36140   Introduction of needle or intracatheter; upper or lower extremity artery
Report this code when access is made into any extremity artery when the catheter is not advanced any further.

36160   Introduction of needle or intracatheter, aortic, translumbar
Report this code for translumbar access directly into the aorta when the catheter is not advanced beyond the aorta.

36200   Introduction of catheter, aorta
Report this code for peripheral access when the catheter is advanced to the aorta but not beyond.

Selective CPT Codes—Arterial, Above the Diaphragm

Note: Catheter placement becomes "selective" when the catheter goes from the point of initial access and is then advanced beyond the aorta and into another vessel.

36215   Selective catheter placement, arterial system; each first order thoracic or brachiocephalic branch, within a vascular family

36216   Selective catheter placement, arterial system; initial second order thoracic or brachiocephalic branch, within a vascular family

36217   Selective catheter placement, arterial system; initial third order or more selective thoracic or brachiocephalic branch, within a vascular family

36218   Selective catheter placement, arterial system; additional second order, third order, and beyond, thoracic or brachiocephalic branch, within a vascular family (List in addition to code for initial second or third order vessel as appropriate)

Note: For catheter placement of carotid and vertebral arteries, refer to chapter 2.

Selective CPT Codes—Arterial, Below the Diaphragm

36245   Selective catheter placement, arterial system; each first order abdominal, pelvic, or lower extremity artery branch, within a vascular family

36246   Selective catheter placement, arterial system; initial second order abdominal, pelvic, or lower extremity artery branch, within a vascular family

36247   Selective catheter placement, arterial system; initial third order or more selective abdominal, pelvic, or lower extremity artery branch, within a vascular family

36248   Selective catheter placement, arterial system; additional second order, third order, and beyond, abdominal, pelvic, or lower extremity artery branch, within a vascular family (List in addition to code for initial second or third order vessel as appropriate)

Selective CPT Codes—Renal Arteries

36251   Selective catheter placement (first-order), main renal artery and any accessory renal artery(s) for renal angiography....; unilateral

36252   Selective catheter placement (first-order), main renal artery and any accessory renal artery(s) for renal angiography....; bilateral

36253   Superselective catheter placement (one or more second order or higher renal artery branches) renal artery and any accessory renal artery(s) for renal angiography....; unilateral

36254   Superselective catheter placement (one or more second order or higher renal artery branches) renal artery and any accessory renal artery(s) for renal angiography....;bilateral

Nonselective CPT Codes—Venous

36005   Injection procedure for extremity venography (including introduction of needle or intracatheter)

36010   Introduction of catheter, superior or inferior vena cava

Selective CPT Codes—Venous

36011   Selective catheter placement, venous system; first order branch (eg, renal vein, jugular vein)

36012   Selective catheter placement, venous system; second order, or more selective, branch (eg, left adrenal vein, petrosal sinus)

Pulmonary, Arterial

36013   Introduction of catheter, right heart or main pulmonary artery

36014   Selective catheter placement, left or right pulmonary artery

36015   Selective catheter placement, segmental or subsegmental pulmonary artery (upper, middle, or lower lobe)

Portal

36481   Percutaneous portal vein catheterization by any method
Use venous selective codes to report catheterization of portal system branches in addition to portal access (36481).

Anatomical Variants

In cases where anatomical variants exist such as hepatic artery origin from the superior mesenteric artery, code assignments are based upon the anatomical variant. These cases require very detailed documentation of the anatomy in the dictated report to provide support for code assignment.

General Cardiac Procedure Coding Guidelines

Coding Guidelines for Diagnostic Cardiac Catheterization Procedures

- Code changes in 2011 incorporated the most common injection codes with the catheterization codes. However, there are still some injection codes available to report in addition to the catheterization codes. For example, report CPT code 93567 for aortic root injection performed during cardiac catheterization.

- Imaging supervision is included in the codes reported for cardiac catheterization and is not reported separately.

- During the left cardiac catheterization procedure, if the catheter does not pass through the aortic valve and into the left ventricle report CPT code 93454 or 93455.

- Fluoroscopy is included in the cardiac catheterization procedure codes and is not reported separately.

- Dilution studies and cardiac output measurements are included in cardiac catheterization procedures. Do not separately report CPT codes 93561 or 93562.

- Pulse oximetry is not reported separately. It is considered to be a part of the patient monitoring needed to accomplish the procedure.

Coding Guidelines for Coronary Interventions

Coding guidelines for interventional coronary procedures were revised in 2013. Refer to chapter 11 and chapter 12 for details.

Documentation

Diagnostic Radiology Report

The dictated operative report is the best and most appropriate document to support procedure charges as images are usually destroyed after five or seven years.

In October 1995 the American College of Radiology (ACR) revised the standards of communication for diagnostic radiology's written interpretations. The following is a summary of a policy statement by the ACR in an attempt to promote optimal patient care and enhance effective documentation supporting appropriate coding methods of all diagnostic and therapeutic interventional radiology procedures performed by physicians.

For example, a dictated operative report should be organized as follows:

- Date of the procedure (and time if relevant)
- Preoperative diagnosis
- Postoperative diagnosis (conclusion or impression)
- Precise name or title of procedures performed (specific selective catheter placement). For example:
    1. Arch aortogram
    2. Bilateral selective common (or cervical) carotid angiogram
    3. Bilateral selective cerebral (or internal) carotid angiogram
    4. Unilateral selective left vertebral angiogram

In the example above we can assume an arch study was performed with the catheter in the aorta. The catheter was likely advanced into the right and left common and/or internal carotid arteries and injected. Images were obtained of both bilateral common and internal carotid arteries. The left vertebral artery was also injected and imaged. In order to conclusively assign catheter placement CPT codes, coders need to know each catheter puncture site and final catheter placement within each vascular family.

Without precise titles of procedures and complete narrative description of selective and nonselective catheter placements, coders and other department staff will not be able to accurately represent procedures performed on claims.

Body of procedure report should contain descriptions of:

- Actual process and events of how procedures were approached and performed
- Utilized materials, drugs, contrast, guide wires and catheters
- Precise anatomic terminology and names of vessels observed or studied
- Identifiable limiting factors
- Other pertinent clinical issues, such as patient condition, complications, etc.
- Comparisons with previous studies where applicable

Summary of findings (conclusion, impression or diagnosis) should contain:

- A precise diagnosis if possible
- Recommendations for follow-up or additional diagnostic or therapeutic procedures

Patient demographic and other pertinent information should be contained in the procedure report format such as patient name, facility name, patient account number, patient date of birth, referring physician name, date and time procedure dictated, date and time report was transcribed, as well as name of physician performing procedure.

Transcribed report revisions or edits should be performed per individual facility health information and medical staff guidelines.

Supply Device Codes

Prior to the issuance of *Changes to the Hospital Outpatient Prospective Payment System and Calendar Year 2005 Rates*; Final Rule, Medicare (CMS) encouraged hospitals to report the appropriate Healthcare Common Procedural Coding System (HCPCS) codes only for supply devices. Additionally, CMS requested that hospitals include the charges for the devices used during procedures when they billed for all of the related services in the device-dependent ambulatory payment classifications (APCs). As a result, hospitals were not providing sufficient data to CMS.

In 2005, to improve the quality of claims data, CMS began requiring hospitals to report device category HCPCS codes on the claim when such devices are used in conjunction with procedures billed and paid for under the OPPS system. For example, if APC 5192 Level II Endovascular Procedures, is reported on a Medicare claim, a device HCPCS code is required to appear on the same claim. CMS updates the device dependent codes quarterly. Refer to appendix B for a current listing of supply HCPCS codes.

Beginning January 1, 2005, Medicare required all hospitals include device category codes on claims with those APCs impacted by this regulatory update. Medicare has developed a crosswalk of procedures to devices to assist providers listed in Table 19 in the November 15, 2004 (final rule). If more than one potential device code maps to a particular APC, the provider will be required to report at least one of the device HCPCS codes for the claim to be accepted by Medicare. If this coding information is not present, the claim will be returned to the provider for correction and delay reimbursement (lengthen the revenue cycle).

While CMS required the use of the device category codes, edits did not apply to Medicare claims until April 1, 2005. The Outpatient Code Editor (OCE) ensured certain procedure codes were accompanied by an appropriate device category code. Effective January 2017, CMS implemented Device Dependent Procedure edits. Any claim containing a device-intensive procedure code is required to contain at least one device HCPCS code. If the device code is absent, the claim is returned to the provider without payment. The claim also fails the edits if it contains a device code but does not also contain the applicable procedure code. These edits do not apply for claims with modifier 52, 73, or 74.

Providing CMS with accurate data will aid in establishing future rates for device dependent APC payments.

Refer to appendix B for a listing of supply codes, category descriptions and other helpful information on supply reporting.

Stark/Anti-Kickback Legislation

Anti-kickback legislation applies to nearly all health care providers—everyone from physicians to suppliers of medical equipment. In general, it prohibits them from giving or receiving (offering or soliciting) cash or other incentives for:

*   Referrals of Medicare or Medicaid beneficiaries (or arranging such referrals)
*   The buying, leasing, or ordering of goods or services payable by Medicare or Medicaid (or arranging for such purchases or leases). Office space, pharmaceuticals, and clerical help are examples of such goods

The waiver of copayments/deductibles also may apply to providers. Under Medicare Part B, providers may waive copayments and deductibles for patients undergoing genuine financial hardship. However, providers who do so must adjust their bills to Medicare downward accordingly or risk a charge of fraud.

Providers who do not comply with this policy can be charged with making false statements and submitting false claims to the federal government.

Stark Self-Referral Regulations

In 1989, Congress enacted the Stark I law because of concern about potential kickbacks to physicians. The law, named after sponsor Rep. Fortney "Pete" Stark (D, Calif.), is designed to prevent physicians from referring Medicare patients for certain "designated health services" to clinical laboratories or other entities in which the physician holds a financial stake, unless a particular exception applies.

The bill's passage came in the wake of increased business activities in the health care industry. Studies showed physicians who had ownership in labs ordered tests more frequently than physicians who referred to independent laboratories.

By 1993, the law was expanded to include Medicaid services and 10 additional designated health services, such as physical and occupational therapy, radiology services (including MRI, CT, and ultrasound), durable medical equipment and supplies, home health services, and outpatient prescription drugs. The expanded law is known as Stark II.

Because of the complexities of the law, Congress did not release rules to enforce Stark I until 1995. Also due to the complexities of regulating and monitoring physician referrals, CMS did not publish rules on Stark II until the final rule on January 4, 2001. These rules generated nearly 13,000 comments from doctors and other providers. The changes became effective January 4, 2002. In future years, the intent is to use a January 1 effective date to coincide with the effective date for new HCPCS or CPT codes. The full text of each of the versions of the Stark regulations can be found at the *Federal Register* section of the Government Printing Office website at www.gpoaccess.gov/fr/.

The majority of regulations were contained in phase I of the Stark legislation, including ownership and compensation arrangement, definitions, employment agreements, and personal service contracts, and regulatory exceptions. Phase II, implemented July 26, 2004, focused on new regulatory definitions and exceptions, as well as public comments pertaining to phase I.

The Stark III final rule, published in the *Federal Register* on November 15, 2007, became effective immediately and delayed until December 4, 2008, the "stand in the shoes" provisions made final in the rule with respect to certain compensation arrangements.

"Stand in the Shoes Provision"
CMS defines the "stand-in-the shoes" provision as one that provides a physician owner of (or investor in) a physician organization stands in the shoes of the physician organization for the purpose of analyzing the financial relationships between DHS entities and referring physicians if the physician has the ability or right to receive financial benefits of the ownership or investment. However, a merely titular owner (one who does not have the ability or right to receive the financial benefits of ownership or investment) is not required to stand in the shoes of his or her physician organization. (However, we are

permitting nonowner physicians and titular owners to stand in the shoes of their physician organization if they choose to do so.) CMS is not finalizing its proposal to consider a DHS entity with a 100 percent ownership interest in an organization to be standing in the shoes of the organization. Finally, CMS is finalizing its proposed revisions to the definitions of "physician" and "physician organization."

What's Prohibited

In general, the Stark II regulation is an attempt to clarify prohibited activities and to allow "particular and reasonable" exceptions to the regulations. It is important to remember the prohibitions surrounding self-referrals apply specifically to Medicare and Medicaid patients. However, medical practices still must abide with the specific state statutes applied to all patients, regardless of the insurer.

Under Stark II, a physician cannot refer Medicare or Medicaid patients to a health care entity in which a financial interest is held for the following services:

- Physical therapy services
- Occupational therapy services
- Radiology services and supplies
- Radiation therapy services and supplies
- Durable medical equipment and supplies
- Parenteral and enteral nutrients, equipment, and supplies
- Prosthetics, orthotics, and prosthetic devices, and supplies
- Home health services
- Outpatient prescription drugs
- Inpatient and outpatient hospital services
- Clinical lab tests

Exclusions for Medical Groups

Stark II does allow certain referrals within a medical group practice. These exceptions include ancillary services performed in office and referrals to physicians practicing within the same medical group.

Ancillary services (such as physical therapy, interpreting x-rays, or echocardiograms) must be personally performed by the referring physician, another member of the physician group, or an in-office employee supervised by the physician.

Physicians may refer patients to other doctors within their medical group. In order to qualify for these exceptions, medical group practices must meet the following guidelines: Under the rule, a medical group must demonstrate:

- Billing, auditing, accounting, and financial statements originate from a centralized entity with overall responsibility for the group.
- Decision making is handled by a centralized unit exercising responsibility and control over budget, salaries, compensation, assets, and liabilities.
- At least 75 percent of patient care is provided by group members. This includes owners and employees of the group, not independent contractors. In addition, at least 75 percent of group members' income must derive from practice within the group.

Rural Provider Exception

The rural provider exception in section 1877(d)(2) of the Act states "... in the case of DHS furnished in a rural area (as defined in section 1886(d)(2)(D)) by an entity, if substantially all of the DHS furnished by such entity are furnished to individuals residing in such a rural area."

An ownership or investment interest in the Diagnostic Center must pass a two-part test in order to qualify for the rural provider exception. The first requirement of the rural provider exception is the DHS must be furnished in a rural area. The second requirement of the rural provider exception is substantially all of the DHS furnished by an entity (at least 75 percent) must be furnished to individuals residing in a rural area.

Chapter 2: Diagnostic Angiography

Cervicocerebral Angiography—Carotid and Vertebral Arteries

Cerebral angiography involves imaging of one or both carotid arteries and/or one or both vertebral arteries. These codes report selective and nonselective imaging of the arch, carotid (internal and external), and vertebral arteries. All imaging procedures are included in these catheter placement codes. Refer to the Coding Tips section for additional information.

36221   **Non-selective catheter placement, thoracic aorta, with angiography of the extracranial carotid, vertebral, and/or intracranial vessels, unilateral or bilateral, and all associated radiological supervision and interpretation, includes angiography of the cervicocerebral arch, when performed**
A local anesthetic is applied over the access artery. The artery is percutaneously punctured with a needle. A guidewire is inserted through the needle and into the arterial system. A catheter is threaded over the guidewire. The physician directs the catheter to the aortic arch or upper thoracic aorta. The guidewire is removed. Contrast medium is injected through the catheter and into the aortic arch. Radiographic images are taken of the extracranial and/or intracranial circulation. Imaging of the arch is included when performed.

36222   **Selective catheter placement, common carotid or innominate artery, unilateral, any approach, with angiography of the ipsilateral extracranial carotid circulation and all associated radiological supervision and interpretation, includes angiography of the cervicocerebral arch, when performed**
A local anesthetic is applied over the access artery. The artery is percutaneously punctured with a needle. A guidewire is inserted through the needle and into the arterial system. A catheter is threaded over the guidewire. The physician directs the catheter to the innominate or common carotid artery. The guidewire is removed. Contrast medium is injected through the catheter into the carotid arterial system. Radiographic images are obtained to visualize the extracranial carotid circulation.

36223   **Selective catheter placement, common carotid or innominate artery, unilateral, any approach, with angiography of the ipsilateral intracranial carotid circulation and all associated radiological supervision and interpretation, includes angiography of the extracranial carotid and cervicocerebral arch, when performed**
A local anesthetic is applied over the access artery. The artery is percutaneously punctured with a needle. A guidewire is inserted through the needle and into the arterial system. A catheter is threaded over the guidewire. The physician directs the catheter to the innominate or common carotid artery. The guidewire is removed. Contrast medium is injected through the catheter into the carotid arterial system. Radiographic images are obtained to visualize the intracranial carotid circulation.

36224   **Selective catheter placement, internal carotid artery, unilateral, with angiography of the ipsilateral intracranial carotid circulation and all associated radiological supervision and interpretation, includes angiography of the extracranial carotid and cervicocerebral arch, when performed**
A local anesthetic is applied over the access artery. The artery is percutaneously punctured with a needle. A guidewire is inserted through the needle and into the arterial system. A catheter is threaded over the guidewire. The physician directs the catheter to the internal carotid artery. The guidewire is removed. Contrast medium is injected through the catheter into the carotid arterial system. Radiographic images are obtained to visualize the intracranial carotid circulation.

36225   **Selective catheter placement, subclavian or innominate artery, unilateral, with angiography of the ipsilateral vertebral circulation and all associated radiological supervision and interpretation, includes angiography of the cervicocerebral arch, when performed**
A local anesthetic is applied over the access artery. The artery is percutaneously punctured with a needle. A guidewire is inserted through the needle and into the arterial system. A catheter is threaded over the guidewire. The physician directs the catheter to the subclavian or the innominate artery. The guidewire is removed. Contrast medium is injected through the catheter into the vertebral arterial system. Radiographic images are obtained to visualize the vertebral circulation.

36226   **Selective catheter placement, vertebral artery, unilateral, with angiography of the ipsilateral vertebral circulation and all associated radiological supervision and interpretation, includes angiography of the cervicocerebral arch, when performed**
A local anesthetic is applied over the access artery. The artery is percutaneously punctured with a needle. A guidewire is inserted through the needle and into the arterial system. A catheter is threaded over the guidewire. The physician directs the catheter to the vertebral artery. The guidewire is removed. Contrast medium is injected through the catheter into the vertebral arterial system. Radiographic images are obtained to visualize the vertebral circulation.

36227   **Selective catheter placement, external carotid artery, unilateral, with angiography of the ipsilateral external carotid circulation and all associated radiological supervision and interpretation (List**

separately in addition to code for primary procedure)
The physician directs the catheter to the vertebral artery. The guidewire is removed. Contrast medium is injected through the catheter into the external carotid arterial system. Radiographic images are obtained to visualize the external carotid circulation.

36228 **Selective catheter placement, each intracranial branch of the internal carotid or vertebral arteries, unilateral, with angiography of the selected vessel circulation and all associated radiological supervision and interpretation (eg, middle cerebral artery, posterior inferior cerebellar artery) (List separately in addition to code for primary procedure)**
During selective angiography of the internal carotid or vertebral artery, the physician further manipulates the catheter into additional intracranial branches of the artery, such as the middle cerebral or posterior inferior cerebellar arteries. Contrast medium is injected into the catheter for arteriography, including the selected vessels circulation.

CPT® Coding for Cervicocerebral Artery Angiography

Imaging Service Performed	Catheter Location	CPT Code(s) Reported
Aortic arch and great vessel origins	Aorta or aortic arch	36221
Carotid artery cervical portion, with or without arch	Innominate artery or common carotid artery	36222
Carotid artery cervical portion, when performed, with or without arch	Innominate artery or common carotid artery	36223
Carotid artery cervical portion, when performed, with or without arch	Internal carotid artery	36224
Vertebral artery, with or without arch	Innominate artery or subclavian artery	36225
Vertebral artery, with or without arch	Vertebral artery	36226

Coding Tips

1. All codes discussed in this section include fluoroscopy. Do not separately report 76000, 76001, or 77002.
2. All codes discussed in this section include radiologic imaging, supervision, and interpretation. Imaging includes all vascular phases: arterial through venous.
3. All codes include catheter placement. Do not separately report codes 36215–36218.
4. For physician reporting, vascular closure is included and not separately reported.
5. For facility reporting of vascular closure, refer to payer guidelines and policies. For Medicare, refer to HCPCS Level II code G0269.
6. Selective catheter placement codes 36222–36228 are unilateral procedures. To report a bilateral catheter placement procedure, use modifier 50. Exceptions apply; see next coding tip.
7. Modifier 59 may be required if imaging of a different vascular territory is performed on the opposite side. For example, diagnostic study of the right intracranial carotid circulation and left vertebral circulation would need modifier 59 to specify that different arteries were studied.
8. Modifiers RT and LT are not recommended for use with these codes.
9. These codes are based on the level of catheter placement selectivity. Report the code for the highest selectivity performed. For example, if the catheter is placed in the right internal carotid artery for intracranial imaging, report 36224 rather than 36223.
10. Codes 36222–36226 include arch angiography. Do not separately report 36221.
11. For external carotid angiography, report 36227 in addition to the base catheterization procedure performed. For example, if external carotid angiography is the only imaging performed, first report 36222 and then add 36227.
12. A maximum of two additional codes (36227 or 36228) may be reported. Code 75774 should not be reported for angiography of the carotid or vertebral vessels. Code 75774 may be reported if diagnostic studies of the upper extremity or other noncerebral vessels, such as the internal mammary, are imaged during the diagnostic session.
13. Separately report 76376 or 76377 for three dimensional imaging performed with these diagnostic procedures.
14. Refer to 76937 if ultrasound guidance is used for vascular access. Criteria must be met before reporting 76937.
15. Report interventional procedures separately according to interventional coding guidelines. Refer to chapter 4 for additional information.
16. Diagnostic angiography may be reported during the same session as an interventional procedure provided the guidelines are met. Refer to chapter 4 for details.

17. The dictated report should discuss the intracranial vessels as appropriate verification for imaging the cerebral carotid circulation. The vessels mentioned could include, but are not limited to, the distal portion of the internal carotid artery; the anterior, middle, or posterior cerebral arteries; the Circle of Willis; and/or the anterior/posterior communicating arteries.

18. Report all applicable HCPCS Level II codes. Refer to the HCPCS section for possible codes.

19. Hospitals should continue to separately report LOCM contrast media with HCPCS Level II codes Q9965-Q9967. Report contrast media by milliliter rather than by bottle or other unit.

20. Physician Reporting: These codes have both a technical and professional component. To report only the professional component, append modifier 26. To report only the technical component, append modifier TC. To report the complete procedure (i.e., both the professional and technical components), submit without a modifier.

Internal Carotid and Vertebral Arterial Anatomy—Femoral Approach

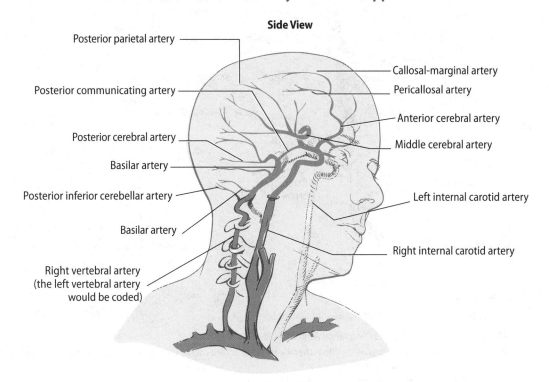

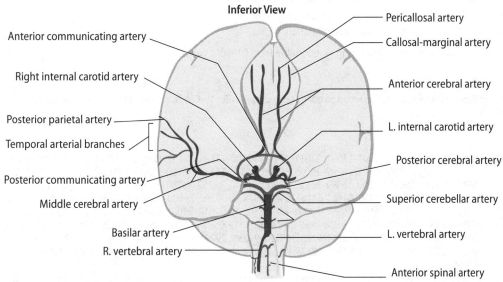

External Carotid Arterial Anatomy—Femoral Approach

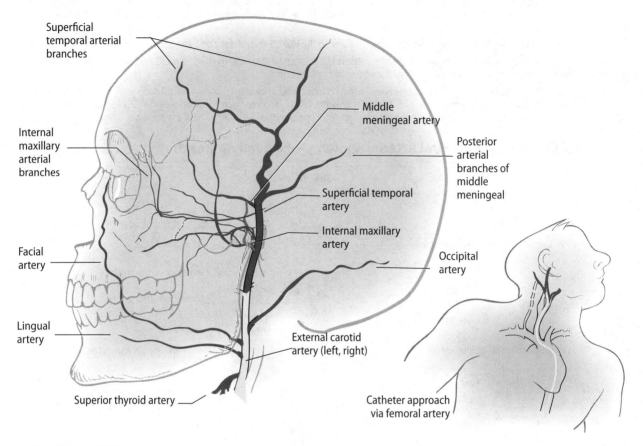

Superficial temporal arterial branches

Middle meningeal artery

Internal maxillary arterial branches

Posterior arterial branches of middle meningeal

Superficial temporal artery

Internal maxillary artery

Facial artery

Occipital artery

Lingual artery

External carotid artery (left, right)

Superior thyroid artery

Catheter approach via femoral artery

Facility HCPCS Coding

Some applicable codes may include but are not limited to:

C1760	Closure device, vascular (implantable/insertable)
G0269	Placement of occlusive device into either a venous or arterial access site, post surgical or interventional procedure (e.g., AngioSeal plug, vascular plug)
Q9965	LOCM, 100-199 mg/ml iodine concentration, per ml
Q9966	LOCM, 200-299 mg/ml iodine concentration, per ml
Q9967	LOCM, 300-399 mg/ml iodine concentration, per ml

Note: See appendix B for a complete listing of reportable HCPCS Level II codes.

ICD-10-CM Coding

The application of these codes is too broad to adequately present ICD-10-CM diagnosis code links here. Refer to the current ICD-10-CM book.

CCI Edits

36221 01916, 01924-01926, 12001-12007, 12011-12057, 13100-13133, 13151-13153, 35201-35206, 35226-35236, 35256-35266, 35286, 36000, 36002-36005, 36100, 36120-36140, 36160-36200, 36215-36218, 36400-36410, 36420-36430, 36440, 36500, 36591-36592, 36600, 36640, 43752, 51701-51703, 62320-62327, 64400-64410, 64413-64435, 64445-64450, 64461-64463, 64479-64530, 69990, 75600, 75605, 75774, 75860, 75870, 75872, 75893, 76000-76001, 76942, 76970, 76998, 77001-77002, 92012-92014, 93000-93010, 93040-93042, 93050, 93318, 93355, 93567, 94002, 94200, 94250, 94680-94690, 94770, 95812-95816, 95819, 95822, 95829, 95955, 96360-96368, 96372, 96374-96377, 99155-99157, 99211-99223, 99231-99255, 99291-99292, 99304-99310, 99315-99316, 99334-99337, 99347-99350, 99374-99375, 99377-99378, 99446-99449, 99495-99496, G0269, G0463, G0471, J0670, J1642-J1644, J2001

36222 01916, 01924-01926, 12001-12007, 12011-12057, 13100-13133, 13151-13153, 35201-35206, 35226-35236, 35256-35266, 35286, 36000, 36002-36005, 36100, 36120-36140, 36160-36200, 36215-36218, 36221, 36400-36410, 36420-36430, 36440, 36500, 36591-36592, 36600, 36640, 43752, 51701-51703, 62320-62327, 64400-64410,

64413-64435, 64445-64450, 64461-64463, 64479-64530, 69990, 75600, 75605, 75774, 75860, 75870, 75872, 75893, 76000-76001, 76942, 76970, 76998, 77001-77002, 92012-92014, 93000-93010, 93040-93042, 93050, 93318, 93355, 94002, 94200, 94250, 94680-94690, 94770, 95812-95816, 95819, 95822, 95829, 95955, 96360-96368, 96372, 96374-96377, 99155-99157, 99211-99223, 99231-99255, 99291-99292, 99304-99310, 99315-99316, 99334-99337, 99347-99350, 99374-99375, 99377-99378, 99446-99449, 99495-99496, G0269, G0463, G0471, J0670, J1642-J1644, J2001

36223 01916, 01924-01926, 12001-12007, 12011-12057, 13100-13133, 13151-13153, 35201-35206, 35226-35236, 35256-35266, 35286, 36000, 36002-36005, 36100, 36120-36140, 36160-36200, 36215-36218, 36221-36222, 36400-36410, 36420-36430, 36440, 36500, 36591-36592, 36600, 36640, 43752, 51701-51703, 62320-62327, 64400-64410, 64413-64435, 64445-64450, 64461-64463, 64479-64530, 69990, 75600, 75605, 75774, 75860, 75870, 75872, 75893, 76000-76001, 76942, 76970, 76998, 77001-77002, 92012-92014, 93000-93010, 93040-93042, 93050, 93318, 93355, 94002, 94200, 94250, 94680-94690, 94770, 95812-95816, 95819, 95822, 95829, 95955, 96360-96368, 96372, 96374-96377, 99155-99157, 99211-99223, 99231-99255, 99291-99292, 99304-99310, 99315-99316, 99334-99337, 99347-99350, 99374-99375, 99377-99378, 99446-99449, 99495-99496, G0269, G0463, G0471, J0670, J1642-J1644, J2001

36224 01916, 01924-01926, 12001-12007, 12011-12057, 13100-13133, 13151-13153, 35201-35206, 35226-35236, 35256-35266, 35286, 36000, 36002-36005, 36100, 36120-36140, 36160-36200, 36215-36218, 36221-36223, 36400-36410, 36420-36430, 36440, 36500, 36591-36592, 36600, 36640, 43752, 51701-51703, 62320-62327, 64400-64410, 64413-64435, 64445-64450, 64461-64463, 64479-64530, 69990, 75600, 75605, 75774, 75860, 75870, 75872, 75893, 76000-76001, 76942, 76970, 76998, 77001-77002, 92012-92014, 93000-93010, 93040-93042, 93050, 93318, 93355, 94002, 94200, 94250, 94680-94690, 94770, 95812-95816, 95819, 95822, 95829, 95955, 96360-96368, 96372, 96374-96377, 99155-99157, 99211-99223, 99231-99255, 99291-99292, 99304-99310, 99315-99316, 99334-99337, 99347-99350, 99374-99375, 99377-99378, 99446-99449, 99495-99496, G0269, G0463, G0471, J0670, J1642-J1644, J2001

36225 01916, 01924-01926, 12001-12007, 12011-12057, 13100-13133, 13151-13153, 35201-35206, 35226-35236, 35256-35266, 35286, 36000, 36002-36005, 36100, 36120-36140, 36160-36200, 36215-36217, 36221, 36400-36410, 36420-36430, 36440, 36500, 36591-36592, 36600, 36640, 43752, 51701-51703, 62320-62327, 64400-64410, 64413-64435, 64445-64450, 64461-64463, 64479-64530, 69990, 75600, 75605, 75774, 75860, 75870, 75872, 75893, 76000-76001, 76942, 76970, 76998, 77001-77002, 92012-92014, 93000-93010, 93040-93042, 93050, 93318, 93355, 94002, 94200, 94250, 94680-94690, 94770, 95812-95816, 95819, 95822, 95829, 95955, 96360-96368, 96372, 96374-96377, 99155-99157, 99211-99223, 99231-99255, 99291-99292, 99304-99310, 99315-99316, 99334-99337, 99347-99350, 99374-99375, 99377-99378, 99446-99449, 99495-99496, G0269, G0463, G0471, J0670, J1642-J1644, J2001

36226 01916, 01924-01926, 12001-12007, 12011-12057, 13100-13133, 13151-13153, 35201-35206, 35226-35236, 35256-35266, 35286, 36000, 36002-36005, 36100, 36120-36140, 36160-36200, 36215-36217, 36221, 36225, 36400-36410, 36420-36430, 36440, 36500, 36591-36592, 36600, 36640, 43752, 51701-51703, 62320-62327, 64400-64410, 64413-64435, 64445-64450, 64461-64463, 64479-64530, 69990, 75600, 75605, 75774, 75860, 75870, 75872, 75893, 76000-76001, 76942, 76970, 76998, 77001-77002, 92012-92014, 93000-93010, 93040-93042, 93050, 93318, 93355, 94002, 94200, 94250, 94680-94690, 94770, 95812-95816, 95819, 95822, 95829, 95955, 96360-96368, 96372, 96374-96377, 99155-99157, 99211-99223, 99231-99255, 99291-99292, 99304-99310, 99315-99316, 99334-99337, 99347-99350, 99374-99375, 99377-99378, 99446-99449, 99495-99496, G0269, G0463, G0471, J0670, J1642-J1644, J2001

36227 35201-35206, 35226-35236, 35256-35266, 35286, 36160-36200, 36215-36218, 36221, 36591-36592, 51702, 75774, 76000-76001, 93050, G0269, G0471

36228 35201-35206, 35226-35236, 35256-35266, 35286, 36160-36200, 36215-36218, 36221, 36591-36592, 51702, 75774, 76000-76001, 93050, G0269, G0471

Case Example

Via right femoral approach, a guidewire and catheter were advanced into the abdominal aorta. The **catheter** was selectively **advanced into** the **right common carotid artery**. Injection of contrast and imaging of **the carotid bifurcation and intracranial arteries were performed**. The **catheter** was then withdrawn from the right carotid artery and advanced into the left common carotid artery where injection of contrast and **imaging of the carotid bifurcation and intracranial arteries were performed**. The catheter was then **placed** into the **right vertebral artery** where injection of contrast and **imaging of the vertebral basilar system** were performed. The catheter was withdrawn to the femoral artery where hand injection of contrast revealed the vessel to be patent. **A vascular closure** device was successfully **deployed** and the patient was transported to recovery. A total **of 80 cc of Isovue 300** was used during the procedure.

CPT/HCPCS Codes Reported:
36223-50, 36226, G0269 (per payer policy)

Other HCPCS Codes Reported:
Q9967 x 80, C1769, C1760

Aorta Angiography—Thoracic and Abdominal

Thoracic aorta angiography is a nonselective procedure involving catheter placement in the superior portion of the descending aorta and imaging of the aorta to the level of the diaphragm.

Abdominal aorta angiography is a nonselective procedure involving catheter placement in the distal aspect of the thoracic aorta usually just above the renal artery origins. This procedure is rarely performed as a stand-alone procedure. Imaging usually includes the iliac arteries.

In the event renal angiography is interpreted, for example, during the course of an abdominal aortography without having selected the renal arteries, CPT code 36251 or 36252 should not be reported and this nonselective renal angiography would be included in the abdominal aortography. Refer to the renal angiography section of this manual for details.

75600   **Aortography, thoracic, without serialography, radiological supervision and interpretation**

75605   **Aortography, thoracic, by serialography, radiological supervision and interpretation**
A local anesthetic is applied over the common femoral artery. The artery is percutaneously punctured with a needle and a guidewire is inserted and fed through the artery into the thoracic aorta. A catheter is threaded over the guidewire to the point of study and the guidewire is removed. Contrast medium is injected and films are taken by serialography, producing a series of individual x-ray films. This code reports the radiological supervision and interpretation. Use a separately reportable code for the catheterization.

75625   **Aortography, abdominal, by serialography, radiological supervision and interpretation**
A local anesthetic is applied over the common femoral artery. The artery is percutaneously punctured with a needle and a guidewire is inserted and fed through the artery into the abdominal aorta. A catheter is threaded over the guidewire to the point of study and the guidewire is removed. Contrast medium is injected and films are taken by serialography, producing a series of individual x-ray films. This code reports the radiological supervision and interpretation. Use a separately reportable code for the catheterization.

CPT Coding for Aorta Angiography

Imaging Service Performed	CPT Code(s) Reported
Thoracic aorta imaging	75605, 36200
Abdominal aorta imaging	75625, 36200
Arch or cervicocerebral aorta imaging	36221

Coding Tips

1. Report both components of the procedure: the surgical component or catheter placement codes and the radiology S&I codes.
2. These codes are not intended for use with cardiac catheterization procedures. Refer to the Cardiac Catheterization section of this manual for more information.
3. Thoracic aortography is frequently reported in error when arch aortography is actually the procedure performed. CPT code 36221 is used to report imaging of the aortic arch.
4. If an arch study is performed in addition to a thoracic study, report CPT code 36221 separately. If the abdominal aorta is imaged, also report CPT code 75625. Do not separately report 36200.
5. If all three portions of the aorta are studied in the same operative session, only one nonselective catheter placement (CPT code 36221) is reported.
6. Abdominal aorta CPT code 75625 is included in the codes reported for renal and visceral artery imaging. Do not report this code in addition to CPT code 36251, 36252, 36253, 36254, or 75726. Refer to the appropriate following sections for additional information.
7. Conscious sedation is not included in these codes. Separately report 99151–99157 per payer policy and coding guidelines. Hospitals may choose to include the costs associated with the service as part of the procedure rather than reporting them separately.
8. Report all applicable HCPCS Level II codes. Refer to the HCPCS section for possible codes.
9. Hospitals are requested to continue reporting LOCM separately with HCPCS codes Q9965–Q9967. Report contrast media by milliliter.
10. Physician Reporting: These radiology S&I codes have both a technical and professional component. To report only the professional component, append modifier 26. To report only the technical component, append modifier TC. To report the complete procedure (i.e., both the professional and technical components), submit without a modifier.

Facility HCPCS Coding

Some applicable codes may include but are not limited to:

C1760   Closure device, vascular (implantable/insertable)

G0269   Placement of occlusive device into either a venous or arterial access site, post surgical or interventional procedure (e.g., AngioSeal plug, vascular plug)

Q9965   LOCM, 100-199 mg/ml iodine concentration, per ml

Q9966   LOCM, 200-299 mg/ml iodine concentration, per ml

Q9967   LOCM, 300-399 mg/ml iodine concentration, per ml

Note: See appendix B for a complete listing of reportable HCPCS Level II codes.

ICD-10-CM Coding

A52.Ø1	Syphilitic aneurysm of aorta
I25.3	Aneurysm of heart
I25.41	Coronary artery aneurysm
I25.42	Coronary artery dissection
I25.5	Ischemic cardiomyopathy
I25.6	Silent myocardial ischemia
I25.83	Coronary atherosclerosis due to lipid rich plaque
I25.84	Coronary atherosclerosis due to calcified coronary lesion
I25.89	Other forms of chronic ischemic heart disease
I25.9	Chronic ischemic heart disease, unspecified
I67.Ø	Dissection of cerebral arteries, nonruptured
I7Ø.Ø	Atherosclerosis of aorta
I71.ØØ	Dissection of unspecified site of aorta
I71.Ø1	Dissection of thoracic aorta
I71.Ø3	Dissection of thoracoabdominal aorta
I71.1	Thoracic aortic aneurysm, ruptured
I71.2	Thoracic aortic aneurysm, without rupture
I71.3	Abdominal aortic aneurysm, ruptured
I71.4	Abdominal aortic aneurysm, without rupture
I71.5	Thoracoabdominal aortic aneurysm, ruptured
I71.6	Thoracoabdominal aortic aneurysm, without rupture
I71.8	Aortic aneurysm of unspecified site, ruptured
I71.9	Aortic aneurysm of unspecified site, without rupture
I74.Ø1	Saddle embolus of abdominal aorta
I74.Ø9	Other arterial embolism and thrombosis of abdominal aorta
I74.1Ø	Embolism and thrombosis of unspecified parts of aorta
I74.11	Embolism and thrombosis of thoracic aorta
I74.19	Embolism and thrombosis of other parts of aorta
I77.81Ø	Thoracic aortic ectasia
I77.812	Thoracoabdominal aortic ectasia
I77.819	Aortic ectasia, unspecified site
I79.Ø	Aneurysm of aorta in diseases classified elsewhere
Q25.21	Interruption of aortic arch
Q25.29	Other atresia of aorta
Q25.3	Supravalvular aortic stenosis
Q25.4Ø	Congenital malformation of aorta unspecified
Q25.41	Absence and aplasia of aorta
Q25.42	Hypoplasia of aorta
Q25.43	Congenital aneurysm of aorta
Q25.44	Congenital dilation of aorta
Q25.45	Double aortic arch
Q25.46	Tortuous aortic arch
Q25.47	Right aortic arch
Q25.48	Anomalous origin of subclavian artery

Q25.49	Other congenital malformations of aorta
Q25.9	Congenital malformation of great arteries, unspecified
S25.00XA	Unspecified injury of thoracic aorta, initial encounter
S25.01XA	Minor laceration of thoracic aorta, initial encounter
S25.02XA	Major laceration of thoracic aorta, initial encounter
S25.09XA	Other specified injury of thoracic aorta, initial encounter
S35.00XA	Unspecified injury of abdominal aorta, initial encounter
S35.01XA	Minor laceration of abdominal aorta, initial encounter
S35.02XA	Major laceration of abdominal aorta, initial encounter
S35.09XA	Other injury of abdominal aorta, initial encounter
T82.310A	Breakdown (mechanical) of aortic (bifurcation) graft (replacement), initial encounter
T82.320A	Displacement of aortic (bifurcation) graft (replacement), initial encounter
T82.330A	Leakage of aortic (bifurcation) graft (replacement), initial encounter
T82.390A	Other mechanical complication of aortic (bifurcation) graft (replacement), initial encounter
T82.595A	Other mechanical complication of umbrella device, initial encounter
T82.598A	Other mechanical complication of other cardiac and vascular devices and implants, initial encounter
T82.818A	Embolism of vascular prosthetic devices, implants and grafts, initial encounter
T82.838A	Hemorrhage of vascular prosthetic devices, implants and grafts, initial encounter
T82.858A	Stenosis of vascular prosthetic devices, implants and grafts, initial encounter

Abdominal Aorta and Major Branch Anatomy

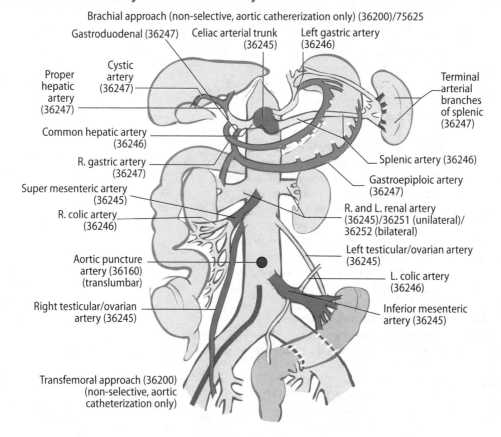

Brachial approach (non-selective, aortic cathererization only) (36200)/75625

Gastroduodenal (36247)

Celiac arterial trunk (36245)

Left gastric artery (36246)

Cystic artery (36247)

Proper hepatic artery (36247)

Terminal arterial branches of splenic (36247)

Common hepatic artery (36246)

R. gastric artery (36247)

Splenic artery (36246)

Gastroepiploic artery (36247)

Super mesenteric artery (36245)

R. colic artery (36246)

R. and L. renal artery (36245)/36251 (unilateral)/ 36252 (bilateral)

Aortic puncture artery (36160) (translumbar)

Left testicular/ovarian artery (36245)

L. colic artery (36246)

Right testicular/ovarian artery (36245)

Inferior mesenteric artery (36245)

Transfemoral approach (36200) (non-selective, aortic catheterization only)

CCI Edits

75600 01916, 01924-01926, 35201-35206, 35226, 35261-35266, 35286, 36000, 36005, 36410, 36500, 36591-36592, 75827, 75893, 76000-76001, 76942, 76970, 76998, 77001-77002, 93567, 96372, 96376-96377, 99446-99449, J1642-J1644

75605 01916, 01924-01926, 35201-35206, 35226, 35261-35266, 35286, 36000, 36005, 36410, 36500, 36591-36592, 75600, 75827, 75893, 76000-76001, 76942, 76970, 76998, 77001-77002, 93567, 96372, 96376-96377, 99446-99449

75625 01916, 01924-01926, 35201-35206, 35226, 35261-35266, 35286, 36000, 36005, 36410, 36500, 36591-36592, 75825, 75893, 76000-76001, 76942, 76970, 76998, 77001-77002, 93567, 96372, 96376-96377, 99446-99449

Case Example

Via left **femoral artery approach**, the pigtail **catheter was advanced to the distal thoracic aorta.** 40 cc of Omnipaque 300 were injected and **images were obtained over the abdomen and pelvis area.** The catheter and guidewire were removed and manual pressure was held until hemostasis was achieved.

CPT/HCPCS Codes Reported:
75625, 36200

Other HCPCS Codes Reported:
Q9967 x 40, C1769

Internal Mammary and Spinal Angiography

Angiography of the internal mammary artery involves catheterizing the subclavian or internal mammary arteries and imaging the internal mammary artery. CPT code 75756 is unilateral. This code is reported with modifier 50 appended if the procedure is bilateral. The code includes as many injections and projections as necessary to image the vessel. Imaging may be obtained via traditional film methods and/or utilizing digital techniques.

Spinal artery angiography involves selectively catheterizing one of the intercostals or lumbar spinal arteries. CPT code 75705 is unilateral and may be reported twice with the appropriate modifiers appended to the second code. This code is commonly reported multiple times.

75705   **Angiography, spinal, selective, radiological supervision and interpretation**
A local anesthetic is applied over the artery of access, usually the common femoral artery. The artery is percutaneously punctured with a needle and a guidewire is inserted and fed through the artery into the aorta. Under fluoroscopic guidance, a catheter is threaded over the guidewire to the aorta and advanced directly into a spinal artery suitable for viewing the study area. The guidewire is removed. Contrast medium is then injected in the lowest level first and then just above that in sequence and films are taken until the study has covered the entire area of interest. This code reports the radiological supervision and interpretation only. Use a separately reportable code for the catheterization.

75756   **Angiography, internal mammary, radiological supervision and interpretation**
A local anesthetic is applied over the site where the catheter is to be introduced; this is most often either the common femoral or brachial artery. The artery is percutaneously punctured with a needle and a guidewire is inserted and fed through the artery to the internal mammary. A catheter is threaded over the guidewire to the point of study and the guidewire is removed. Contrast medium is injected and a series of x-rays performed to visualize the vessels and evaluate any abnormalities, such as blockages, narrowing, or aneurysms. This code reports the radiological supervision and interpretation only. Use a separately reportable code for the catheterization.

Internal Mammary and Spinal Angiography

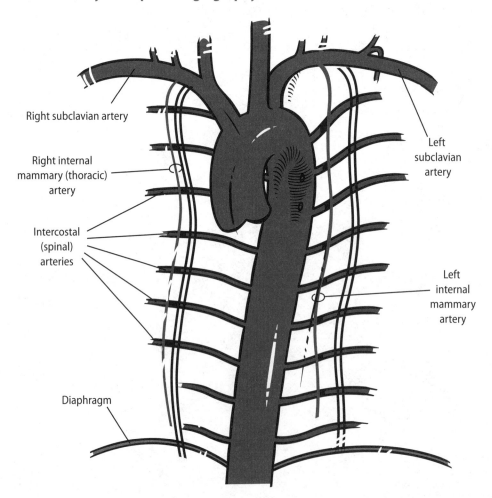

Right subclavian artery

Right internal mammary (thoracic) artery

Intercostal (spinal) arteries

Diaphragm

Left subclavian artery

Left internal mammary artery

CPT Coding for Internal Mammary and Spinal Angiography

Service Performed	Surgical Component	Radiology S&I Component
Internal mammary angiography	36216	75756
Spinal artery angiography	varies	75705
Catheter placement in a first order above the diaphragm artery	36215	
Catheter placement in a second order above the diaphragm artery	36216	
Catheter placement in a first order below the diaphragm artery	36245	
Catheter placement in a second order below the diaphragm artery	36246	

Coding Tips

1. Report both components of the procedure: the surgical component or catheter placement codes and the radiology S&I codes.

2. Catheter placement codes will change depending upon the approach taken. Refer to the Basic Interventional Radiology Coding section of this manual for guidance.

3. Report the catheter placement code for each artery catheterized. Append modifier 59 or XS as appropriate.

4. Report CPT code 75705 for each spinal artery catheterized. This code is unilateral. Append modifier 50, 59, XS, RT, or LT as appropriate.

5. CPT code 75756 is intended for radiology use. When injecting the internal mammary artery as part of a cardiac catheterization to study bypass grafts, report CPT code 93457.

6. Conscious sedation is not included in these codes. Separately report 99151–99157 per payer policy and coding guidelines. Hospitals may choose to include the costs associated with the service as part of the procedure rather than reporting them separately.

7. Report all applicable HCPCS Level II codes. Refer to the HCPCS section for possible codes.

8. Hospitals are requested to continue reporting LOCM separately with HCPCS codes Q9965–Q9967. Report contrast media by milliliter.

9. Diagnostic angiography performed during the same surgical encounter as an interventional procedure may be reported separately if no previous catheter-based angiogram has been performed. A complete diagnostic exam must also be performed and the decision to perform an interventional procedure should be based on diagnostic exam results. When a previous diagnostic exam was performed, documentation must indicate the condition of the patient changed since that exam, anatomy was not optimally identified in the previous exam, or a change during the surgical encounter required another evaluation beyond the area being treated during the intervention. Under these circumstances, append modifier 59 to the diagnostic evaluation.

10. Physician Reporting: These radiology S&I codes have both a technical and professional component. To report only the professional component, append modifier 26. To report only the technical component, append modifier TC. To report the complete procedure (i.e., both the professional and technical components), submit without a modifier.

11. Angiograms performed after angioplasty, stent, and atherectomy procedures are included in the interventional codes and are not reported separately.

Facility HCPCS Coding

Some applicable codes may include but are not limited to:

C1760 Closure device, vascular (implantable/insertable)

G0269 Placement of occlusive device into either a venous or arterial access site, post surgical or interventional procedure (e.g., AngioSeal plug, vascular plug)

Q9965 LOCM, 100-199 mg/ml iodine concentration, per ml

Q9966 LOCM, 200-299 mg/ml iodine concentration, per ml

Q9967 LOCM, 300-399 mg/ml iodine concentration, per ml

Note: See appendix B for a complete listing of reportable HCPCS Level II codes.

ICD-10-CM Coding

G95.11 Acute infarction of spinal cord (embolic) (nonembolic)

G95.19 Other vascular myelopathies

I63.00 Cerebral infarction due to thrombosis of unspecified precerebral artery

I63.09 Cerebral infarction due to thrombosis of other precerebral artery

I63.10 Cerebral infarction due to embolism of unspecified precerebral artery

I63.19 Cerebral infarction due to embolism of other precerebral artery

I63.29	Cerebral infarction due to unspecified occlusion or stenosis of other precerebral arteries
I65.8	Occlusion and stenosis of other precerebral arteries
I65.9	Occlusion and stenosis of unspecified precerebral artery
I70.8	Atherosclerosis of other arteries
I70.90	Unspecified atherosclerosis
I70.91	Generalized atherosclerosis
I72.5	Aneurysm of other precerebral arteries
I72.6	Aneurysm of vertebral artery
I72.8	Aneurysm of other specified arteries
I74.8	Embolism and thrombosis of other arteries
I74.9	Embolism and thrombosis of unspecified artery
I75.89	Atheroembolism of other site
I77.0	Arteriovenous fistula, acquired
I77.1	Stricture of artery
I77.2	Rupture of artery
I77.3	Arterial fibromuscular dysplasia
I77.5	Necrosis of artery
I77.6	Arteritis, unspecified
I77.79	Dissection of other artery
I77.89	Other specified disorders of arteries and arterioles
I77.9	Disorder of arteries and arterioles, unspecified
I79.1	Aortitis in diseases classified elsewhere
I79.8	Other disorders of arteries, arterioles and capillaries in diseases classified elsewhere
I87.9	Disorder of vein, unspecified
I99.9	Unspecified disorder of circulatory system
M31.8	Other specified necrotizing vasculopathies
M31.9	Necrotizing vasculopathy, unspecified
Q27.30	Arteriovenous malformation, site unspecified
Q27.39	Arteriovenous malformation, other site
Q27.4	Congenital phlebectasia
Q28.8	Other specified congenital malformations of circulatory system
Q28.9	Congenital malformation of circulatory system, unspecified

CCI Edits

75705 01916, 01924-01926, 01935-01936, 35201-35206, 35226, 35261-35266, 35286, 36000, 36005, 36410, 36500, 36591-36592, 75893, 76000-76001, 76942, 76970, 76998, 77001-77002, 96372, 96376-96377, 99446-99449

75756 01916, 01924-01926, 35201-35206, 35226, 35261-35266, 35286, 36000, 36005, 36410, 36500, 36591-36592, 75893, 76000-76001, 76942, 76970, 76998, 77001-77002, 96372, 96376-96377, 99446-99449

Case Example #1

Through a **transfemoral approach**, the posterior **intercostal arteries at levels T8-T12 and the 1st through 4th lumbar arteries were selectively catheterized bilaterally** with subsequent angiography performed.

CPT/HCPCS Codes Reported:
36215-50 x 5, 36245-50 x 4, 75705, 75705-XS x17

Note: Add modifier 59 to each 75705 coded after the first. Some payers may require modifier 59 instead of modifier 50, which would require changing the number of units. In any event, 10 separate intercostals vessels and 8 separate lumbar vessels were selectively catheterized with 18 spinal angiograms performed.

Case Example #2

Spinal Angiogram

Lower extremity weakness, numbness, neurogenic bladder and impotency. Spinal AVM cannot be excluded on MRI and CT angiography.

After providing informed consent, the patient was prepped and draped in typical sterile fashion. Lidocaine was infiltrated in the right groin. A small incision was made and single wall puncture technique was used to obtain **access in the right CFA**. Over a J wire, a 5F sheath was placed. Through the sheath, a 5F pigtail catheter was advanced over a Glidewire and the **ascending aorta** was cannulated. Biplane **DSA was done**. Biplane **DSA of the abdominal aorta** was also performed. At the end of the spinal angiogram, repeat abdominal **angiography was done** to focus on the **L3 portion** of the aorta as the L3 lumbar arteries could not be cannulated directly. The cervical evaluation was performed with a Simmons 1 Glide catheter in which the hook was formed of the aortic valve. The spinal angiogram was performed using the Simmons catheter as well as a 5F Mikal catheter. The **bilateral T5 through T12 intercostal as well as the bilateral L1, L2, and L4 lumbar arteries were evaluated**. The intercostals **above T5 could not be cannulated** and were therefore evaluated by the thoracic aortogram. The L2 and L4 arteries each have a common pedicle that in turn gives rise to their right and left branches. **The median sacral artery injection was obtained** with the **catheter at the vessel ostium**. **Both internal iliac arteries** were also cannulated and injected during DSA. The supreme and superior intercostal arteries could not be cannulated as described above. **The bilateral vertebral, external carotid, internal carotid, common carotid, thyrocervical, and costocervical arteries were selectively evaluated**. The left thyrocervical and costocervical arteries arose from a common trunk. The left vertebral artery arose directly from the arch. The patient tolerated the procedure well, and the results were discussed with the patient. 262 ml nonionic 300 contrast was given during the procedure.

Findings:

- Arch aortogram: The brachiocephalic, left CCA, left vertebral, and left subclavian arteries arise from the arch and have a normal appearance. The subclavian arteries and both internal thoracic arteries are patent. The upper thoracic intercostal arteries are visualized and are unremarkable in appearance without evidence of early draining vein over the spinal canal.
- Abdominal aortogram: There is no evidence of early draining vein over the spinal canal.
- Right vertebral artery: This vessel is dominant and fills the basilar and right PICA. There is no significant plaque and no early draining vein over the neck or posterior fossa.
- Right common carotid artery: The carotid bifurcation is fully patent at the C3 level. There is no early draining vein over the cervical canal.
- Right ICA: The right ICA is patent to the terminus where there is normal filling of the anterior and middle cerebral arteries as well as of the ophthalmic, PCOM, and anterior choroidal artery. There is a PCOM infundibulum incidentally noted. There is no early draining vein.
- Right external carotid artery: There is no early draining vein over the cervical canal.
- Right costocervical: There is no early draining vein over the canal.
- Right thyrocervical: There is no early draining vein.
- Left subclavian artery: The thyrocervical and costocervical arteries have a normal appearance with a common origin. The dorsal scapula artery also shares this origin. The internal thoracic artery is unremarkable.
- Left thyrocervical/costocervical: There is no evidence of early draining vein over the cervical and upper thoracic canal.
- Left vertebral artery: The left vertebral artery is patent to the basilar. These vessels are unremarkable in appearance and there is no early draining vein over the posterior fossa or cervical canal. The left PICA is patent. Both posterior cerebral arteries are unremarkable.
- Left common carotid artery: The carotid bifurcation is free of stenosis and is located at the C4 level. There is no early draining vein.
- Left ICA: The left ICA is patent to the terminus where there is normal filling of the left anterior, middle cerebral, and ophthalmic arteries. A sizable left PCOM artery is seen arising from an infundibulum. Flash filling of the ACOM is noted. There is no early draining vein.
- Left external carotid artery: There is no early draining vein over the cervical canal.
- Bilateral T5 through T12 intercostal arteries: All negative.
- Bilateral L1 intercostal arteries: Negative.
- Left and right L2: Negative.
- Left and right L4: Negative.
- Median sacral: Negative.
- Right hypogastric: Negative.
- Left hypogastric: Negative.
- Impression: No angiographic evidence of intracranial or spinal vascular malformation. The artery of Adamkiewicz is not localized/visualized by spinal angiography.

Case Example #2 (Continued)

CPT/HCPCS Codes Reported:

75625, 75710, 75774 x 4, 75705, 75705-XS x 18, 75736, 75736-XS, 36226-50, 36227-50, 36224, 36223-50, 36222-XS, 36215-XS, 36218 x 4, 36215-50 x 8

Note: Add modifier 59 or XS to each 75705 after the first. Add modifier 59 or XS to the second 75736 code.

Other HCPCS Codes Reported:

Q9967 x 262, C1769, C1894

Visceral Angiography—Celiac, Hepatic, Splenic, Inferior Phrenic, Superior and Inferior Mesenteric Arteries, and Bronchial Arteries

Visceral angiography includes selective catheterization of one of the arteries supplying blood to the viscera and encompasses arteries within the thoracic and abdominal viscera. CPT code 75726 is selective or superselective. Arteries covered by this code include the celiac, hepatic, splenic, gastric, inferior phrenic, superior and inferior mesenteric arteries, and bronchial arteries, as well as other branches. The code includes the performance of an aortogram and as many injections and projections as necessary to image each vessel.

75726   **Angiography, visceral, selective or supraselective, (with or without flush aortogram), radiological supervision and interpretation**
An artery supplying the organ of concern is examined radiologically by injecting contrast material. A local anesthetic is applied over the area of access, usually the common femoral artery. The artery is percutaneously punctured with a needle and a guidewire inserted and fed through the artery to the point of study. A catheter is threaded over the guidewire until it, too, reaches the point of study and the guidewire is removed. Contrast medium is injected through the catheter and a series of x-rays or fluoroscopic images taken to visualize the vessels and evaluate any abnormalities such as blockages, narrowing, or aneurysms. The catheter is removed and pressure applied to the site. This code reports the radiological supervision and interpretation. Use separately reportable code for the catheterization.

Superior and Inferior Mesenteric Arteries and Branches

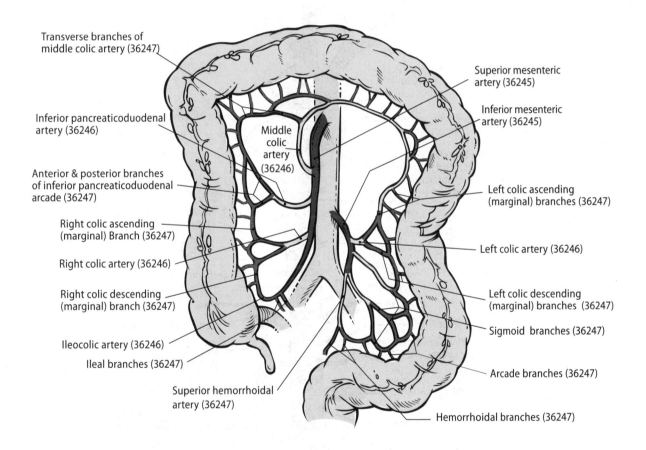

© 2017 Optum360, LLC

CPT Coding for Visceral Angiography

Service Performed	Surgical Component	Radiology S&I Component
Celiac artery	36245	75726
Left gastric artery	36246	See coding tip #2 and #5
Splenic artery	36246	See coding tips #2 and #5
Common hepatic artery	36246	See coding tip #2 and #5
Right gastric artery	36247	See coding tip #2 and #5
Inferior phrenic	36245	See coding tip #2 and #5
Superior mesenteric	36245	75726 See coding tip #2
Inferior mesenteric	36245	75726 See coding tip #2
Bronchial artery	36215 or 36245 depending upon location	75726 See coding tip #2
Each additional vessel after the basic exam	See coding tip #2	75774

Thoracic and Abdominal Arteries

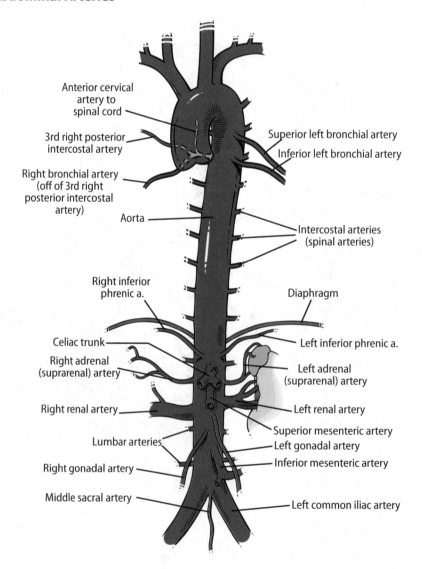

Anterior cervical artery to spinal cord

3rd right posterior intercostal artery

Right bronchial artery (off of 3rd right posterior intercostal artery)

Aorta

Right inferior phrenic a.

Celiac trunk

Right adrenal (suprarenal) artery

Right renal artery

Lumbar arteries

Right gonadal artery

Middle sacral artery

Superior left bronchial artery

Inferior left bronchial artery

Intercostal arteries (spinal arteries)

Diaphragm

Left inferior phrenic a.

Left adrenal (suprarenal) artery

Left renal artery

Superior mesenteric artery

Left gonadal artery

Inferior mesenteric artery

Left common iliac artery

Celiac Artery and Branches

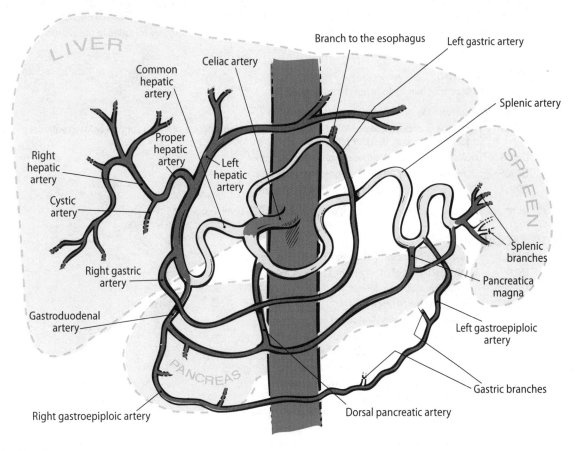

Coding Tips

1. Report both components of the procedure: the surgical component or catheter placement codes and the radiology S&I codes.

2. If multiple vessels are studied during the same session, CPT code 75774 is reported for each vessel after the initial vessel. Catheter placement is coded for each vascular family. Any of the arteries in the group listed can be studied by themselves. CPT code 75726 and one catheter placement code would be reported in this situation. It is more common to study multiple vessels during the same session.

3. Do not report CPT code 75625 in addition to 75726 if the aorta is injected during the exam. The aorta is included as part of this procedure.

4. These vessels can have many congenital variations in their location and take off from the aorta. This affects catheter placement coding. Anatomy should be detailed in the dictated report.

5. When multiple branches of the celiac are catheterized be sure to report 36248 instead of 36246 or 36247 as appropriate. The celiac and its branches are one vascular family.

6. Conscious sedation is not included in these codes. Separately report 99151–99157 per payer policy and coding guidelines. Hospitals may choose to include the costs associated with the service as part of the procedure rather than reporting them separately.

7. Report all applicable HCPCS Level II codes. Refer to the HCPCS section for possible codes.

8. Hospitals are requested to continue reporting LOCM separately with HCPCS codes Q9965–Q9967. Report contrast media by milliliter.

9. Diagnostic angiography performed during the same surgical encounter as an interventional procedure may be reported separately if no previous catheter-based angiogram has been performed. A complete diagnostic exam must also be performed and the decision to perform an interventional procedure should be based on diagnostic exam results. When a previous diagnostic exam was performed, documentation must indicate the condition of the patient changed since that exam, anatomy was not optimally identified in the previous exam, or a change during the surgical encounter required another evaluation beyond the area being treated during the intervention. Under these circumstances, append modifier 59 to the diagnostic evaluation.

10. Physician Reporting: These radiology S&I codes have both a technical and professional component. To report only the professional component, append modifier 26. To report only the technical component, append modifier TC. To report the complete procedure (i.e., both the professional and technical components), submit without a modifier.

11. Angiograms performed after angioplasty, stent, and atherectomy procedures are included in the interventional codes and are not reported separately.

Facility HCPCS Coding

Some applicable codes may include but are not limited to:

C1760   Closure device, vascular (implantable/insertable)
G0269   Placement of occlusive device into either a venous or arterial access site, post surgical or interventional procedure (e.g., AngioSeal plug, vascular plug)
Q9965   LOCM, 100-199 mg/ml iodine concentration, per ml
Q9966   LOCM, 200-299 mg/ml iodine concentration, per ml
Q9967   LOCM, 300-399 mg/ml iodine concentration, per ml

Note: See appendix B for a complete listing of reportable HCPCS Level II codes.

ICD-10-CM Coding

D18.03   Hemangioma of intra-abdominal structures
I70.8   Atherosclerosis of other arteries
I70.90   Unspecified atherosclerosis
I70.91   Generalized atherosclerosis
I71.00   Dissection of unspecified site of aorta
I71.02   Dissection of abdominal aorta
I71.03   Dissection of thoracoabdominal aorta
I71.3   Abdominal aortic aneurysm, ruptured
I71.4   Abdominal aortic aneurysm, without rupture
I71.5   Thoracoabdominal aortic aneurysm, ruptured
I71.6   Thoracoabdominal aortic aneurysm, without rupture
I71.8   Aortic aneurysm of unspecified site, ruptured
I71.9   Aortic aneurysm of unspecified site, without rupture
I74.01   Saddle embolus of abdominal aorta
I74.09   Other arterial embolism and thrombosis of abdominal aorta
I74.10   Embolism and thrombosis of unspecified parts of aorta
I74.19   Embolism and thrombosis of other parts of aorta
K31.811   Angiodysplasia of stomach and duodenum with bleeding
K31.819   Angiodysplasia of stomach and duodenum without bleeding
K31.82   Dieulafoy lesion (hemorrhagic) of stomach and duodenum
K55.011   Focal (segmental) acute (reversible) ischemia of small intestine
K55.012   Diffuse acute (reversible) ischemia of small intestine
K55.019   Acute (reversible) ischemia of small intestine, extent unspecified
K55.021   Focal (segmental) acute infarction of small intestine
K55.022   Diffuse acute infarction of small intestine
K55.029   Acute infarction of small intestine, extent unspecified
K55.031   Focal (segmental) acute (reversible) ischemia of large intestine
K55.032   Diffuse acute (reversible) ischemia of large intestine
K55.039   Acute (reversible) ischemia of large intestine, extent unspecified
K55.041   Focal (segmental) acute infarction of large intestine
K55.042   Diffuse acute infarction of large intestine
K55.049   Acute infarction of large intestine, extent unspecified
K55.051   Focal (segmental) acute (reversible) ischemia of intestine, part unspecified
K55.052   Diffuse acute (reversible) ischemia of intestine, part unspecified
K55.059   Acute (reversible) ischemia of intestine, part and extent unspecified
K55.061   Focal (segmental) acute infarction of intestine, part unspecified
K55.062   Diffuse acute infarction of intestine, part unspecified
K55.069   Acute infarction of intestine, part and extent unspecified

K55.1	Chronic vascular disorders of intestine
K55.8	Other vascular disorders of intestine
K55.9	Vascular disorder of intestine, unspecified
K76.6	Portal hypertension
S35.00XA	Unspecified injury of abdominal aorta, initial encounter
S35.01XA	Minor laceration of abdominal aorta, initial encounter
S35.02XA	Major laceration of abdominal aorta, initial encounter
S35.09XA	Other injury of abdominal aorta, initial encounter
S35.211A	Minor laceration of celiac artery, initial encounter
S35.212A	Major laceration of celiac artery, initial encounter
S35.218A	Other injury of celiac artery, initial encounter
S35.219A	Unspecified injury of celiac artery, initial encounter
S35.221A	Minor laceration of superior mesenteric artery, initial encounter
S35.222A	Major laceration of superior mesenteric artery, initial encounter
S35.228A	Other injury of superior mesenteric artery, initial encounter
S35.229A	Unspecified injury of superior mesenteric artery, initial encounter
S35.231A	Minor laceration of inferior mesenteric artery, initial encounter
S35.232A	Major laceration of inferior mesenteric artery, initial encounter
S35.238A	Other injury of inferior mesenteric artery, initial encounter
S35.239A	Unspecified injury of inferior mesenteric artery, initial encounter
S35.291A	Minor laceration of branches of celiac and mesenteric artery, initial encounter
S35.292A	Major laceration of branches of celiac and mesenteric artery, initial encounter
S35.298A	Other injury of branches of celiac and mesenteric artery, initial encounter
S35.299A	Unspecified injury of branches of celiac and mesenteric artery, initial encounter
S35.8X1A	Laceration of other blood vessels at abdomen, lower back and pelvis level, initial encounter
S35.8X8A	Other specified injury of other blood vessels at abdomen, lower back and pelvis level, initial encounter
S35.8X9A	Unspecified injury of other blood vessels at abdomen, lower back and pelvis level, initial encounter
T82.310A	Breakdown (mechanical) of aortic (bifurcation) graft (replacement), initial encounter
T82.332A	Leakage of femoral arterial graft (bypass), initial encounter
T82.390A	Other mechanical complication of aortic (bifurcation) graft (replacement), initial encounter
T82.392A	Other mechanical complication of femoral arterial graft (bypass), initial encounter
T82.524A	Displacement of infusion catheter, initial encounter
T82.530A	Leakage of surgically created arteriovenous fistula, initial encounter
T82.531A	Leakage of surgically created arteriovenous shunt, initial encounter
T82.534A	Leakage of infusion catheter, initial encounter
T82.590A	Other mechanical complication of surgically created arteriovenous fistula, initial encounter
T82.591A	Other mechanical complication of surgically created arteriovenous shunt, initial encounter
T82.594A	Other mechanical complication of infusion catheter, initial encounter

CCI Edits

75726 01916, 01924-01926, 35201-35206, 35226, 35261-35266, 35286, 36000, 36005, 36410, 36500, 36591-36592, 75810, 75889, 75891, 75893, 76000-76001, 76942, 76970, 76998, 77001-77002, 96372, 96376-96377, 99446-99449

Case Example #1

Via **right common femoral artery approach**, a 5-French Simmons-2 catheter was advanced through a sheath to the descending thoracic aorta. The catheter was reformed in the thoracic aorta. The **celiac artery was selectively cannulated** and Visipaque 270 was injected while digital subtraction **radiographs of the abdomen were obtained** in the AP projection. The catheter was then **selectively placed** into the **common hepatic artery** and, during contrast injection, digital subtraction **radiographs of the liver were obtained** in the anterior-posterior (AP), right anterior oblique (RAO), and left anterior oblique (LAO) projections. The catheter was then placed into the **superior mesenteric artery** and digital subtraction **radiographs of the abdomen** were obtained. The catheter and sheath were removed and pressure maintained until hemostasis was achieved. A total of 85 cc of contrast was used.

CPT/HCPCS Codes Reported:
36245-XS, 36246, 75726-XS, 75726, 75774

Note: Verify modifier assignment with payer requirements.

Other HCPCS Codes Reported:
Q9966 x 85, C1894

Case Example #2

Procedure:
Using the usual sterile technique and local anesthesia, a 5-French sheath was inserted into **right common femoral artery** via the Seldinger technique. A 5-French Simmons-2 catheter then was advanced through the sheath to the descending thoracic aorta. The Simmons-2 catheter was reformed in the descending thoracic aorta. The **celiac artery then was selectively cannulated** and a 35 ml bolus of Visipaque 270 was injected at a rate of 7 ml/sec while digital subtraction **radiographs of the abdomen** were obtained in the AP projection. The catheter was then **selectively placed** into the **common hepatic artery** and 30 ml boluses of Visipaque 270 were injected at rates of 6 ml/sec while digital subtraction **radiographs of the liver** were obtained in the AP, RAO and LAO projections. The catheter then was **replaced into the superior mesenteric artery** and 35 ml bolus of Visipaque 270 was injected at a rate of 7 ml/sec while digital subtraction radiographs of the abdomen were obtained.

Following the procedure, the catheter and sheath were removed and pressure was maintained at the percutaneous puncture site until hemostasis was achieved. The patient tolerated the procedure well and left the department in no distress.

Celiac Arteriogram:
The celiac artery gives rise to the left gastric, common hepatic, and splenic arteries. The common hepatic artery gives rise to the gastroduodenal and to the proper hepatic artery. The arterial, capillary, and venous phases of the celiac arteriogram were normal. The hepatic arteriogram demonstrated a normal hepatic arterial anatomy. The capillary and venous phases appeared normal. The venous phase demonstrates a widely patent portal vein with hepatopetal flow demonstrated.

Superior Mesenteric Arteriogram:
No displaced hepatic arteries are demonstrated off of the superior mesenteric artery. Superior mesenteric arteriogram appeared normal. The venous drainage demonstrates a widely patent portal vein with hepatopetal flow demonstrated.

Impression:
1. Normal appearing hepatic arterial and venous anatomy with no evidence of abnormal vasculature nor evidence of a tumor blush.

2. There is a widely patent portal vein with hepatopetal flow demonstrated.

CPT/HCPCS Codes Reported:
75726, 75726-XS, 75774, 36246, 36245-XS

Other HCPCS Codes Reported:
Q9966 x 150 units

Note: Verify modifier assignment with payer requirements. Add modifier 59 to each 75726 coded after the first.

Case Example #3

Bronchial Arteriogram

Indication: Patient presents with bleeding hemoptysis from a large mass in the right lobe, which is cavitating. The patient is a nonsurgical candidate.

Procedure:

A **right femoral approach** was utilized. Using micropuncture technique, a needle, guidewire and originally a 5-French pigtail catheter was placed in the **arch for arteriography**. This was then retracted to the thoracic aorta for **thoracic arteriography**. The previous CTA had noted **two arteries off the right side of the medial aspect of the aorta. Each of these was catheterized selectively** using Michelson catheters and Simmons-1 and Simmons-2 catheters. **Imaging** was **obtained** of **each artery** selected. Embolization was recommended.

CPT/HCPCS Codes Reported:

75605, 75726, 75726-XS x 2, 36215 x 3

Note: Contrast media should be documented to accurately report the type and amount administered and/or used. Add modifier 59 to each 75726 coded after the first.

Bronchial Artery Anatomy

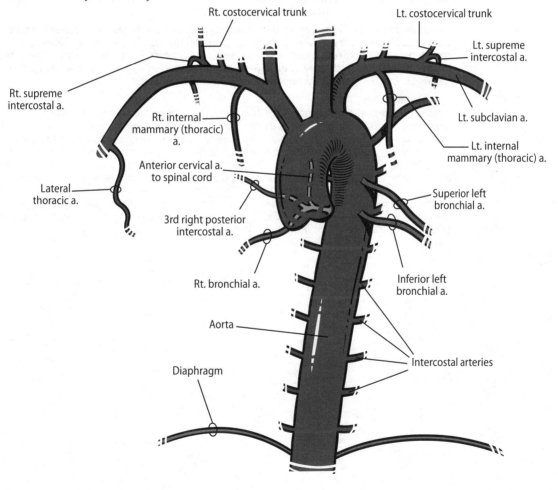

Renal Angiography

Angiography of the renal arteries involves selectively catheterizing one or both of the renal arteries and imaging the kidneys. Unilateral or bilateral imaging may be performed. The codes include as many injections and projections as necessary to image the vessels. These codes also include fluoroscopy, image postprocessing, and pressure gradient measurements when performed. Codes are available for selection of the main renal artery and super selection of renal artery branches. Codes are also separated for unilateral and bilateral procedures.

36251   **Selective catheter placement (first-order), main renal artery and any accessory renal artery(s) for renal angiography, including arterial puncture and catheter placement(s), fluoroscopy, contrast injection(s), image postprocessing, permanent recording of images, and radiological supervision and interpretation, including pressure gradient measurements when performed, and flush aortogram when performed; unilateral**

36252   **bilateral**

Patients with a renal complication are first well hydrated with a drip and given medications to protect the kidney from further damage by the contrast agent. A local anesthetic is applied over the access artery, usually the common femoral artery, which is percutaneously punctured with a needle. A guidewire is inserted and fed through until it reaches the renal artery. A catheter is threaded over the guidewire and the guidewire is removed. Contrast medium is injected and a series of x-rays or fluoroscopic images are taken to visualize the vessels and evaluate any abnormalities. If a flush aortogram is performed, the catheter is directed to the aorta and dye is injected as x-rays are taken to look for plaque build-up. The catheter is removed and pressure applied to the site. These codes report the complete procedure

36253   **Superselective catheter placement (one or more second order or higher renal artery branches) renal artery and any accessory renal artery(s) for renal angiography, including arterial puncture, catheterization, fluoroscopy, contrast injection(s), image postprocessing, permanent recording of images, and radiological supervision and interpretation, including pressure gradient measurements when performed, and flush aortogram when performed; unilateral**

36254   **bilateral**

A superselective catheterization is performed on one or more of the second order (branch) or higher of the renal artery branches. Superselective catheterization is needed for extremely small vessels or vessels that have sharp angles when branching to another order. The physician inserts a needle through the skin and into an underlying artery, usually a lower extremity artery, and threads a guidewire through the needle and into the artery. The needle is removed. The wire is threaded into the targeted artery and any accessory renal arteries of the second order or higher. A super fine and small catheter follows the wire into the arteries. The wire is removed. Contrast material for arteriography is injected into the catheter. Images are taken, the catheter is removed, and pressure is applied to stop bleeding at the injection site. These codes include image postprocessing, permanent recording of images, and radiological supervision and interpretation (e.g., pressure gradient measurements and flush aortogram).

Renal Artery Anatomy—Femoral Approach

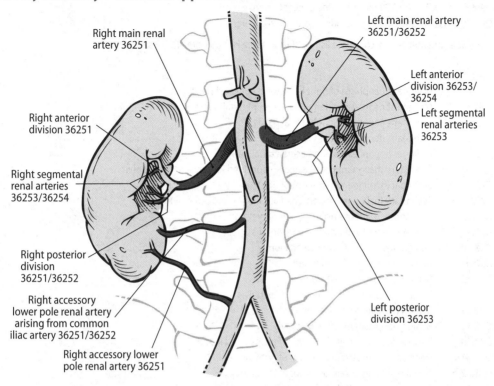

CPT Coding for Renal Angiography

Service Performed	Main Renal Artery	Second or Higher Order Artery(s)
Unilateral angiogram	36251	36253
Bilateral angiogram	36252	36254

Coding Tips

1. Use of these codes requires *selective* catheterization of the renal arteries. Report aortography if nonselective imaging is performed.

2. Unilateral and bilateral codes exist for renal arteriography. Do not use modifier 50 and do not report 36251 or 36253 twice.

3. The kidneys could have more than one artery providing blood supply to one or both kidneys. These accessory arteries arise directly off the aorta.

4. Catheterization and imaging of any accessory renal arteries is included in 36251–36254. Do not report 75774 for additional arteries imaged.

5. For unilateral renal angiography, assign the appropriate side modifier, LT or RT, to codes 36251 and 36253. Refer to payer guidelines.

6. Aortography is included in CPT codes 36251–36254. Do not report 75625 in addition to these codes.

7. Report all applicable HCPCS Level II codes. Refer to the HCPCS section for possible codes.

8. Hospitals are requested to continue reporting LOCM separately with HCPCS codes Q9965–Q9967. Report contrast media by milliliter.

9. Conscious sedation is not included in these codes. Separately report 99151–99157 per payer policy and coding guidelines. Hospitals may choose to include the costs associated with the service as part of the procedure rather than reporting them separately.

Facility HCPCS Coding

Some applicable codes may include but are not limited to:

C1760   Closure device, vascular (implantable/insertable)

G0269   Placement of occlusive device into either a venous or arterial access site, post surgical or interventional procedure (e.g., AngioSeal plug, vascular plug)

Q9965	LOCM, 100-199 mg/ml iodine concentration, per ml
Q9966	LOCM, 200-299 mg/ml iodine concentration, per ml
Q9967	LOCM, 300-399 mg/ml iodine concentration, per ml

Note: See appendix B for a complete listing of reportable HCPCS Level II codes.

ICD-10-CM Coding

C64.1	Malignant neoplasm of right kidney, except renal pelvis
C64.2	Malignant neoplasm of left kidney, except renal pelvis
C65.1	Malignant neoplasm of right renal pelvis
C65.2	Malignant neoplasm of left renal pelvis
C65.9	Malignant neoplasm of unspecified renal pelvis
C79.00	Secondary malignant neoplasm of unspecified kidney and renal pelvis
C79.01	Secondary malignant neoplasm of right kidney and renal pelvis
C79.02	Secondary malignant neoplasm of left kidney and renal pelvis
D09.10	Carcinoma in situ of unspecified urinary organ
D09.19	Carcinoma in situ of other urinary organs
D30.00	Benign neoplasm of unspecified kidney
D30.01	Benign neoplasm of right kidney
D30.02	Benign neoplasm of left kidney
D30.10	Benign neoplasm of unspecified renal pelvis
D30.11	Benign neoplasm of right renal pelvis
D30.12	Benign neoplasm of left renal pelvis
D41.00	Neoplasm of uncertain behavior of unspecified kidney
D41.01	Neoplasm of uncertain behavior of right kidney
D41.02	Neoplasm of uncertain behavior of left kidney
D41.10	Neoplasm of uncertain behavior of unspecified renal pelvis
D41.11	Neoplasm of uncertain behavior of right renal pelvis
D41.12	Neoplasm of uncertain behavior of left renal pelvis
D41.20	Neoplasm of uncertain behavior of unspecified ureter
D41.21	Neoplasm of uncertain behavior of right ureter
D41.22	Neoplasm of uncertain behavior of left ureter
D49.511	Neoplasm of unspecified behavior of right kidney
D49.512	Neoplasm of unspecified behavior of left kidney
D49.519	Neoplasm of unspecified behavior of unspecified kidney
D49.59	Neoplasm of unspecified behavior of other genitourinary organ
I15.0	Renovascular hypertension
I15.1	Hypertension secondary to other renal disorders
I15.8	Other secondary hypertension
I16.0	Hypertensive urgency
I16.1	Hypertensive emergency
I16.9	Hypertensive crisis, unspecified
I70.1	Atherosclerosis of renal artery
I72.2	Aneurysm of renal artery
I75.81	Atheroembolism of kidney
I77.73	Dissection of renal artery
N17.0	Acute kidney failure with tubular necrosis
N17.1	Acute kidney failure with acute cortical necrosis
N17.2	Acute kidney failure with medullary necrosis
N17.8	Other acute kidney failure
N17.9	Acute kidney failure, unspecified
N26.1	Atrophy of kidney (terminal)
N26.2	Page kidney
N26.9	Renal sclerosis, unspecified
N27.0	Small kidney, unilateral
N27.1	Small kidney, bilateral

N27.9	Small kidney, unspecified
N28.0	Ischemia and infarction of kidney
N28.82	Megaloureter
N28.89	Other specified disorders of kidney and ureter
Q27.1	Congenital renal artery stenosis
Q27.2	Other congenital malformations of renal artery
S35.401A	Unspecified injury of right renal artery, initial encounter
S35.402A	Unspecified injury of left renal artery, initial encounter
S35.403A	Unspecified injury of unspecified renal artery, initial encounter
S35.411A	Laceration of right renal artery, initial encounter
S35.412A	Laceration of left renal artery, initial encounter
S35.413A	Laceration of unspecified renal artery, initial encounter
S35.491A	Other specified injury of right renal artery, initial encounter
S35.492A	Other specified injury of left renal artery, initial encounter
S35.493A	Other specified injury of unspecified renal artery, initial encounter
S37.001A	Unspecified injury of right kidney, initial encounter
S37.002A	Unspecified injury of left kidney, initial encounter
S37.009A	Unspecified injury of unspecified kidney, initial encounter
S37.011A	Minor contusion of right kidney, initial encounter
S37.012A	Minor contusion of left kidney, initial encounter
S37.019A	Minor contusion of unspecified kidney, initial encounter
S37.021A	Major contusion of right kidney, initial encounter
S37.022A	Major contusion of left kidney, initial encounter
S37.029A	Major contusion of unspecified kidney, initial encounter
S37.061A	Major laceration of right kidney, initial encounter
S37.062A	Major laceration of left kidney, initial encounter
S37.069A	Major laceration of unspecified kidney, initial encounter
S37.091A	Other injury of right kidney, initial encounter
S37.092A	Other injury of left kidney, initial encounter
S37.099A	Other injury of unspecified kidney, initial encounter

CCI Edits

36251 01916, 01924-01926, 0213T, 0216T, 0228T, 0230T, 12001-12007, 12011-12057, 13100-13133, 13151-13153, 35201-35206, 35226-35236, 35256-35266, 35286, 36000, 36005, 36120-36140, 36160-36200, 36245-36247, 36400-36410, 36420-36430, 36440, 36500, 36591-36592, 36600, 36640, 43752, 51701-51703, 62320-62327, 64400-64410, 64413-64435, 64445-64450, 64461-64463, 64479-64530, 69990, 75625, 75831, 75833, 75893, 76000-76001, 76942, 76970, 76998, 77001-77002, 92012-92014, 93000-93010, 93040-93042, 93050, 93318, 93355, 94002, 94200, 94250, 94680-94690, 94770, 95812-95816, 95819, 95822, 95829, 95955, 96360-96368, 96372, 96374-96377, 99155-99157, 99211-99223, 99231-99255, 99291-99292, 99304-99310, 99315-99316, 99334-99337, 99347-99350, 99374-99375, 99377-99378, 99446-99449, 99495-99496, G0269, G0463, G0471, J0670, J1642-J1644, J2001

36252 01916, 01924-01926, 0213T, 0216T, 0228T, 0230T, 12001-12007, 12011-12057, 13100-13133, 13151-13153, 35201-35206, 35226-35236, 35256-35266, 35286, 36000, 36005, 36120-36140, 36160-36200, 36245-36247, 36251, 36400-36410, 36420-36430, 36440, 36500, 36591-36592, 36600, 36640, 43752, 51701-51703, 62320-62327, 64400-64410, 64413-64435, 64445-64450, 64461-64463, 64479-64530, 69990, 75625, 75831, 75833, 75893, 76000-76001, 76942, 76970, 76998, 77001-77002, 92012-92014, 93000-93010, 93040-93042, 93050, 93318, 93355, 94002, 94200, 94250, 94680-94690, 94770, 95812-95816, 95819, 95822, 95829, 95955, 96360-96368, 96372, 96374-96377, 99155-99157, 99211-99223, 99231-99255, 99291-99292, 99304-99310, 99315-99316, 99334-99337, 99347-99350, 99374-99375, 99377-99378, 99446-99449, 99495-99496, G0269, G0463, G0471, J0670, J1642-J1644, J2001

36253 01916, 01924-01926, 0213T, 0216T, 0228T, 0230T, 12001-12007, 12011-12057, 13100-13133, 13151-13153, 35201-35206, 35226-35236, 35256-35266, 35286, 36000, 36005, 36120-36140, 36160-36200, 36245-36247, 36251, 36252, 36400-36410, 36420-36430, 36440, 36500, 36591-36592, 36600, 36640, 43752, 51701-51703, 62320-62327, 64400-64410, 64413-64435, 64445-64450, 64461-64463, 64479-64530, 69990, 75625, 75831, 75833, 75893, 76000-76001, 76942, 76970, 76998, 77001-77002, 92012-92014, 93000-93010, 93040-93042, 93050, 93318, 93355, 94002, 94200, 94250, 94680-94690, 94770, 95812-95816, 95819, 95822, 95829, 95955, 96360-96368, 96372, 96374-96377, 99155-99157, 99211-99223, 99231-99255, 99291-99292, 99304-99310, 99315-99316, 99334-99337, 99347-99350, 99374-99375, 99377-99378, 99446-99449, 99495-99496, G0269, G0463, G0471, J0670, J1642-J1644, J2001

36254 01916, 01924-01926, 0213T, 0216T, 0228T, 0230T, 12001-12007, 12011-12057, 13100-13133, 13151-13153, 35201-35206, 35226-35236, 35256-35266, 35286, 36000, 36005, 36120-36140, 36160-36200, 36245-36247, 36251-36253, 36400-36410, 36420-36430, 36440, 36500, 36591-36592, 36600, 36640, 43752, 51701-51703, 62320-62327, 64400-64410, 64413-64435, 64445-64450, 64461-64463, 64479-64530, 69990, 75625, 75831, 75833, 75893, 76000-76001, 76942, 76970, 76998, 77001-77002, 92012-92014, 93000-93010, 93040-93042, 93050, 93318, 93355, 94002, 94200, 94250, 94680-94690, 94770, 95812-95816, 95819, 95822, 95829, 95955, 96360-96368, 96372, 96374-96377, 99155-99157, 99211-99223, 99231-99255, 99291-99292, 99304-99310, 99315-99316, 99334-99337, 99347-99350, 99374-99375, 99377-99378, 99446-99449, 99495-99496, G0269, G0463, G0471, J0670, J1642-J1644, J2001

Case Example #1

Access was made via the **right femoral artery**. A sheath was placed and a guidewire advanced into the aorta. A flush catheter was then positioned in the proximal aorta. The aortogram was taken in the AP, LAO, and RAO views. The flush catheter was exchanged for an SOS #2 catheter and **positioned into the orifice of the left renal** artery. **Selective renal arteriogram** was performed. The catheter was then **positioned into the right renal artery orifice and selective angiograms** were obtained. The guidewire, catheter, and sheath were then removed from the artery and pressure maintained until hemostasis was achieved. A total of 100 cc of Omnipaque 300 was used for the procedure.

CPT/HCPCS Codes Reported:
36252

Other HCPCS Codes Reported:
Q9967 x 100, C1769

Case Example #2

Access was made via the **right femoral artery**. A sheath was placed and a guide wire and flush catheter was advanced into the aorta. An aortogram was obtained in the AP projection. The injection revealed **two renal arteries on the right**. The flush catheter was exchanged for a Cobra catheter and **positioned into the left renal artery and each right renal artery consecutively**. Selective angiograms were taken of each artery. The catheter and sheath were then removed and pressure maintained until hemostasis was achieved.

CPT/HCPCS Codes Reported:
36252

Adrenal Angiography

Angiography of the adrenal arteries involves selectively catheterizing one or both of the adrenal arteries and imaging the adrenal glands. Unilateral and bilateral codes exist for adrenal angiography.

75731   **Angiography, adrenal, unilateral, selective, radiological supervision and interpretation**
The left or right adrenal gland, located on top of the upper end of each kidney is examined radiologically by injecting contrast material. A local anesthetic is applied over the common femoral artery. The artery is percutaneously punctured with a needle and a guidewire inserted and fed through the artery, the aorta, and then further into the renal artery. A catheter is threaded over the guidewire until it, too, reaches the point of study and the guidewire is removed. Contrast medium is injected through the catheter and a series of x-rays or fluoroscopic images taken to visualize the vessels and evaluate any abnormalities such as blockages, narrowing, or aneurysms. The catheter is removed and pressure applied to the site. This code reports the radiological supervision and interpretation. Use separately reportable code for the catheterization.

75733   **Angiography, adrenal, bilateral, selective, radiological supervision and interpretation**
The adrenal glands located on top of the upper end of each kidney are examined radiologically by injecting contrast material. A local anesthetic is applied over the common femoral artery. The artery is percutaneously punctured with a needle and a guidewire inserted and fed through the artery, the aorta, and then further into the renal arteries. A catheter is threaded over the guidewire until it, too, reaches the point of study and the guidewire is removed. Contrast medium is injected through the catheter and a series of x-rays or fluoroscopic images taken to visualize the vessels and evaluate any abnormalities such as blockages, narrowing, or aneurysms. The catheter is removed and pressure applied to the site. This code reports the radiological supervision and interpretation. Use separately reportable code for the catheterization.

Other Visceral Arterial Anatomy—Adrenal Arteries

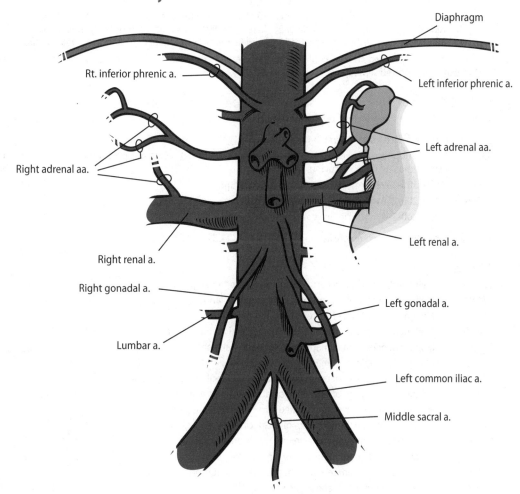

CPT Coding for Adrenal Angiography

Service Performed	Surgical Component	Radiology S&I Component
Unilateral adrenal angiogram	Varies	75731
Bilateral adrenal angiogram	Varies	75733
Each additional artery		75774

Coding Tips

1. Report both components of the procedure: the surgical component or catheter placement codes and the technical radiology S&I codes.

2. Unilateral and bilateral codes exist for adrenal arteriography. Do not use modifier 50 and do not report 75731 twice.

3. The adrenal glands could have more than one artery providing blood supply. There are many congenital variations of artery origin; therefore catheter placement coding will vary. A catheter placement code is reported for each artery selected. Use modifier 59 to denote the separate catheterization. Report CPT code 75774 for each additional artery imaged.

4. Do not report CPT codes 75731 or 75733 unless selective catheterization and imaging is performed and documented.

5. Conscious sedation is not included in these codes. Separately report 99151–99157 per payer policy and coding guidelines. Hospitals may choose to include the costs associated with the service as part of the procedure rather than reporting them separately.

6. Report all applicable HCPCS Level II codes. Refer to the HCPCS section for possible codes.

7. Hospitals are requested to continue reporting LOCM separately with HCPCS codes Q9965–Q9967. Report contrast media by milliliter.

8. Physician Reporting: Procedures 75731 and 75733 have both a technical and professional component. To report only the professional component, append modifier 26. To report only the technical component, append modifier TC. To report the complete procedure (i.e., both the professional and technical components), submit without a modifier.

9. Angiograms performed after angioplasty, stent, and atherectomy procedures are included in the interventional codes and are not reported separately.

Facility HCPCS Coding

Some applicable codes may include but are not limited to:

C1760   Closure device, vascular (implantable/insertable)

G0269   Placement of occlusive device into either a venous or arterial access site, post surgical or interventional procedure (e.g., AngioSeal plug, vascular plug)

Q9965   LOCM, 100-199 mg/ml iodine concentration, per ml

Q9966   LOCM, 200-299 mg/ml iodine concentration, per ml

Q9967   LOCM, 300-399 mg/ml iodine concentration, per ml

Note: See appendix B for a complete listing of reportable HCPCS Level II codes.

ICD-10-CM Coding

C74.00   Malignant neoplasm of cortex of unspecified adrenal gland
C74.01   Malignant neoplasm of cortex of right adrenal gland
C74.02   Malignant neoplasm of cortex of left adrenal gland
C74.10   Malignant neoplasm of medulla of unspecified adrenal gland
C74.11   Malignant neoplasm of medulla of right adrenal gland
C74.12   Malignant neoplasm of medulla of left adrenal gland
C74.90   Malignant neoplasm of unspecified part of unspecified adrenal gland
C74.91   Malignant neoplasm of unspecified part of right adrenal gland
C74.92   Malignant neoplasm of unspecified part of left adrenal gland
C79.70   Secondary malignant neoplasm of unspecified adrenal gland
C79.71   Secondary malignant neoplasm of right adrenal gland
C79.72   Secondary malignant neoplasm of left adrenal gland
C7A.1   Malignant poorly differentiated neuroendocrine tumors
C7A.8   Other malignant neuroendocrine tumors
C7B.00   Secondary carcinoid tumors, unspecified site
C7B.09   Secondary carcinoid tumors of other sites
C7B.8   Other secondary neuroendocrine tumors

D09.3	Carcinoma in situ of thyroid and other endocrine glands
D09.8	Carcinoma in situ of other specified sites
D18.00	Hemangioma unspecified site
D18.03	Hemangioma of intra-abdominal structures
D35.00	Benign neoplasm of unspecified adrenal gland
D35.01	Benign neoplasm of right adrenal gland
D35.02	Benign neoplasm of left adrenal gland
D44.10	Neoplasm of uncertain behavior of unspecified adrenal gland
D44.11	Neoplasm of uncertain behavior of right adrenal gland
D44.12	Neoplasm of uncertain behavior of left adrenal gland
D49.7	Neoplasm of unspecified behavior of endocrine glands and other parts of nervous system
E24.0	Pituitary-dependent Cushing's disease
E24.2	Drug-induced Cushing's syndrome
E24.3	Ectopic ACTH syndrome
E24.4	Alcohol-induced pseudo-Cushing's syndrome
E24.8	Other Cushing's syndrome
E24.9	Cushing's syndrome, unspecified
E25.0	Congenital adrenogenital disorders associated with enzyme deficiency
E25.8	Other adrenogenital disorders
E25.9	Adrenogenital disorder, unspecified
E26.01	Conn's syndrome
E26.02	Glucocorticoid-remediable aldosteronism
E26.09	Other primary hyperaldosteronism
E26.1	Secondary hyperaldosteronism
E26.81	Bartter's syndrome
E26.89	Other hyperaldosteronism
E26.9	Hyperaldosteronism, unspecified
E27.0	Other adrenocortical overactivity
E27.1	Primary adrenocortical insufficiency
E27.2	Addisonian crisis
E27.3	Drug-induced adrenocortical insufficiency
E27.40	Unspecified adrenocortical insufficiency
E27.49	Other adrenocortical insufficiency
E27.5	Adrenomedullary hyperfunction
E27.8	Other specified disorders of adrenal gland
E27.9	Disorder of adrenal gland, unspecified

CCI Edits

75731   01916, 01924-01926, 35201-35206, 35226, 35261-35266, 35286, 36000, 36005, 36410, 36500, 36591-36592, 75840, 75842, 75893, 76000-76001, 76942, 76970, 76998, 77001-77002, 96372, 96376-96377, 99446-99449

75733   01916, 01924-01926, 35201-35206, 35226, 35261-35266, 35286, 36000, 36005, 36410, 36500, 36591-36592, 75731, 75840, 75842, 75893, 76000-76001, 76942, 76970, 76998, 77001-77002, 96372, 96376-96377, 99446-99449

Case Example

Clinical History:
The patient was a 69-year-old male who presented with possible bleeding in the right suprarenal region. He presented for evaluation of the adrenal artery.

Technique:
The right groin was prepped and draped in usual fashion. Using a 5-French micropuncture set, the **right common femoral artery was accessed**. A 5-French sheath was placed in the right common femoral artery. Through the sheath a 5-French C2 catheter was advanced into the abdominal aorta. **Selective catheterization of the right inferior adrenal artery** was then performed. **This artery was a branch off the renal artery**. Angiography demonstrated two branch vessels of the adrenal artery that had extravasation of contrast material on the run. Embolization was recommended.

CPT/HCPCS Codes Reported:
36246, 75731

Note: Contrast media should be documented to accurately report the type and amount administered and/or used.

Extremity Angiography

Upper extremity angiography typically involves selective catheterization of the subclavian or axillary artery and imaging the vessels of the upper extremity. Retrograde brachial angiography involves placing the catheter in the brachial artery and injecting contrast media in the retrograde direction toward the chest in order to obtain images of the arm.

Lower extremity angiography involves selective catheterization of the iliac or femoral artery and imaging the lower extremity. Unilateral and bilateral codes exist to report extremity angiography. Codes are available to report bilateral iliofemoral arteriography in conjunction with an aortogram.

75630   **Aortography, abdominal plus bilateral iliofemoral lower extremity, catheter, by serialography, radiological supervision and interpretation**
A local anesthetic is applied over the common femoral artery. The artery is percutaneously punctured with a needle and a guidewire is inserted and fed through the artery into the abdominal aorta. A catheter is threaded over the guidewire to the point of study and the guidewire is removed. Contrast medium is injected into the abdominal aorta and a series of continuous films are taken of the contrast flow through the aorta and its runoff into the arteries of both legs. This code reports the radiological supervision and interpretation. Use a separately reportable code for the catheterization.

75710   **Angiography, extremity, unilateral, radiological supervision and interpretation**
The arteries of one arm, leg, hand, or foot not normally seen in an x-ray, are examined radiologically by injecting contrast material. A local anesthetic is applied over the area of access which could be femoral, brachial, subclavian, or axillary artery. The artery is percutaneously punctured with a needle and a guidewire inserted and fed through the artery to the point of study. A catheter is threaded over the guidewire until it, too, reaches the point of study and the guidewire is removed. Contrast medium is injected through the catheter and a series of x-rays or fluoroscopic images taken to visualize the vessels and evaluate any abnormalities such as blockages, narrowing, or aneurysms. The catheter is removed and pressure applied to the site. This code reports the radiological supervision and interpretation. Use a separately reportable code for the catheterization.

75716   **Angiography, extremity, bilateral, radiological supervision and interpretation**
The arteries of both arms or legs not normally seen in an x-ray, are examined radiologically by injecting contrast material. A local anesthetic is applied over the area of access which could be femoral, brachial, subclavian, or axillary artery. The artery is percutaneously punctured with a needle and a guidewire inserted and fed through the artery to the point of study. A catheter is threaded over the guidewire until it, too, reaches the point of study and the guidewire is removed. Contrast medium is injected through the catheter and a series of x-rays or fluoroscopic images taken to visualize the vessels and evaluate any abnormalities such as blockages, narrowing, or aneurysms. The catheter is removed and pressure applied to the site. This code reports the radiological supervision and interpretation. Use a separately reportable code for the catheterization.

CPT Coding for Extremity Angiography

Service Performed	Surgical Component	Radiology S&I Component
Unilateral extremity angiography	Varies	75710
Bilateral extremity angiography	Varies	75716
Aortography plus bilateral iliofemoral run-off	36200	75630
Each additional artery		75774
Catheter placement in the right subclavian using a femoral approach	36216	
Catheter placement in the left subclavian using a femoral approach	36215	

Coding Tips

1. Report both components of the procedure: the surgical component or catheter placement codes and the technical radiology S&I codes.

2. Unilateral and bilateral codes exist for extremity angiography. Do not use modifier 50 and do not report 75710 twice, unless a unilateral upper extremity and unilateral lower extremity are studied, as the bilateral extremity code would not be accurate in this case.

3. It is appropriate to report 75710 if only the subclavian artery is imaged.

4. Code 75658 Retrograde brachial angiography, is deleted. Use 75710 for all unilateral angiography regardless of the approach.

5. CPT code 75774 is reported if additional selective arteries are catheterized after the initial complete exam is performed. Do not report 75774 to obtain images to "complete" the lower extremity run-off procedure or for additional views.

6. Documentation of catheter placement in the dictated report is critical in extremity angiography. If catheter placement or repositioning of the catheter is not clearly described, lesser codes should be reported. Discuss the importance of this with the physician performing the procedure.

7.   CPT code 75736 is not appropriate to report for imaging the iliac arteries. Please refer to the Pelvic Angiography section in this chapter for more details.

8.   Catheter placement codes will change depending upon the approach taken. Refer to the Basic Interventional Radiology Coding section of this manual for guidance.

9.   Conscious sedation is not included in these codes. Separately report 99151–99157 per payer policy and coding guidelines. Hospitals may choose to include the costs associated with the service as part of the procedure rather than reporting them separately.

10. Report all applicable HCPCS Level II codes. Refer to the HCPCS section for possible codes.

11. Hospitals are requested to continue reporting LOCM separately with HCPCS codes Q9965–Q9967. Report contrast media by milliliter.

12. Physician Reporting: These radiology S&I codes have both a technical and professional component. To report only the professional component, append modifier 26. To report only the technical component, append modifier TC. To report the complete procedure (i.e., both the professional and technical components), submit without a modifier.

Upper Extremity Arterial Anatomy

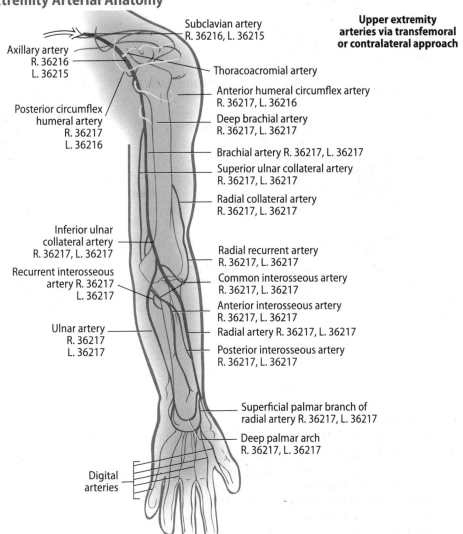

Subclavian artery R. 36216, L. 36215

Upper extremity arteries via transfemoral or contralateral approach

Axillary artery R. 36216 L. 36215

Thoracoacromial artery

Anterior humeral circumflex artery R. 36217, L. 36216

Posterior circumflex humeral artery R. 36217 L. 36216

Deep brachial artery R. 36217, L. 36217

Brachial artery R. 36217, L. 36217

Superior ulnar collateral artery R. 36217, L. 36217

Radial collateral artery R. 36217, L. 36217

Inferior ulnar collateral artery R. 36217, L. 36217

Radial recurrent artery R. 36217, L. 36217

Recurrent interosseous artery R. 36217 L. 36217

Common interosseous artery R. 36217, L. 36217

Anterior interosseous artery R. 36217, L. 36217

Ulnar artery R. 36217 L. 36217

Radial artery R. 36217, L. 36217

Posterior interosseous artery R. 36217, L. 36217

Superficial palmar branch of radial artery R. 36217, L. 36217

Deep palmar arch R. 36217, L. 36217

Digital arteries

Extremity Arterial Anatomy—Contralateral, Axillary or Brachial Approach Lower

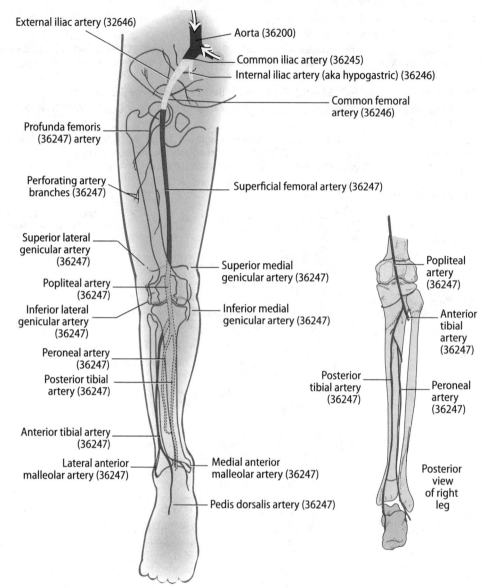

External iliac artery (32646)

Aorta (36200)

Common iliac artery (36245)

Internal iliac artery (aka hypogastric) (36246)

Common femoral artery (36246)

Profunda femoris (36247) artery

Perforating artery branches (36247)

Superficial femoral artery (36247)

Superior lateral genicular artery (36247)

Superior medial genicular artery (36247)

Popliteal artery (36247)

Inferior lateral genicular artery (36247)

Inferior medial genicular artery (36247)

Peroneal artery (36247)

Posterior tibial artery (36247)

Anterior tibial artery (36247)

Lateral anterior malleolar artery (36247)

Medial anterior malleolar artery (36247)

Pedis dorsalis artery (36247)

Popliteal artery (36247)

Anterior tibial artery (36247)

Posterior tibial artery (36247)

Peroneal artery (36247)

Posterior view of right leg

Facility HCPCS Coding

Some applicable codes may include but are not limited to:

C1760   Closure device, vascular (implantable/insertable)

G0269   Placement of occlusive device into either a venous or arterial access site, post surgical or interventional procedure (e.g., AngioSeal plug, vascular plug)

Q9965   LOCM, 100-199 mg/ml iodine concentration, per ml

Q9966   LOCM, 200-299 mg/ml iodine concentration, per ml

Q9967   LOCM, 300-399 mg/ml iodine concentration, per ml

Note: See appendix B for a complete listing of reportable HCPCS Level II codes.

ICD-10-CM Coding

The application of these codes is too broad to adequately present ICD-10-CM diagnosis code links here. Refer to the current ICD-10-CM book.

CCI Edits

75630   01916, 01924-01926, 35201-35206, 35226, 35261-35266, 35286, 36000, 36005, 36410, 36500, 36591-36592, 75625, 75716, 75820, 75822, 75825, 75893, 76000-76001, 76942, 76970, 76998, 77001-77002, 93567, 96372, 96376-96377, 99446-99449

75710   01916, 01924-01926, 35201-35206, 35226, 35261-35266, 35286, 36000, 36005, 36410, 36500, 36591-36592, 75630, 75820, 75822, 75893, 76000-76001, 76942, 76970, 76998, 77001-77002, 96372, 96376-96377, 99446-99449

75716   01916, 01924-01926, 35201-35206, 35226, 35261-35266, 35286, 36000, 36005, 36410, 36500, 36591-36592, 75710, 75820, 75822, 75893, 76000-76001, 76942, 76970, 76998, 77001-77002, 96372, 96376-96377, 99446-99449

Case Example #1

Via **right femoral approach**, a guidewire and catheter were advanced through a sheath into the abdominal aorta. The catheter was positioned in the aorta. An aortogram was performed using 40 cc of Omnipaque 300. The **catheter was then pulled into the distal aorta. Bilateral femoral run-off images to** the ankles were obtained. The catheter and vascular sheath were removed and pressure was applied to the puncture site to achieve hemostasis. A total of 125 cc of contrast was used.

CPT/HCPCS Codes Reported:
75625, 75716, 36200

Other HCPCS Codes Reported:
Q9967 x 125, C1769

Case Example #2

Via **right femoral approach**, a guidewire and catheter were advanced through a sheath into the abdominal aorta. A 5-French vertebral **catheter** was then **advanced** over a guidewire **into the right axillary artery**. A right **upper extremity run-off** was performed with magnification views of the right hand. The catheter was then removed and hemostasis obtained.

CPT/HCPCS Codes Reported:
36217, 75710-RT

Other HCPCS Codes Reported:
Q9967, C1769, C1894

Case Example #3

Brachial Arteriogram
Patient was placed supine on the fluoroscopy table. The skin overlying the left arm was prepped and draped in the usual sterile fashion. Local anesthesia was achieved. Using a micropuncture system, the **left brachial** artery was **accessed**. A .035 Glidewire was advanced through the dilator, which was removed and a 5-French sheath was advanced over the Glidewire. Contrast was injected for **left brachial arteriogram**, revealing normal flow within the brachial artery and visualized portions of the radial, interosseous, and ulnar arteries. The sheath was removed and hemostasis obtained using direct pressure.

CPT/HCPCS Codes Reported:
36140, 75710-LT

Note: In all cases, examples of contrast media should be documented to accurately report the type and amount administered and/or used.

Pelvic Artery Angiography

Pelvic angiography involves selective catheterization of the internal iliac artery, also known as the hypogastric artery, or its branches and imaging the arteries that supply the pelvis. Some of the arteries may include the hypogastric, uterine, ovarian, iliolumbar, umbilical, inferior gluteal, and the internal pudendal. CPT code 75736 is unilateral. This code is repeated with a modifier if the procedure is bilateral.

75736   **Angiography, pelvic, selective or supraselective, radiological supervision and interpretation**

An angiogram is done on operative candidates for pelvic fixation to rule out retroperitoneal arterial bleeding. A local anesthetic is applied over the common femoral artery. The artery is percutaneously punctured with a needle and a guidewire inserted and fed through the artery into the study area in the pelvic region. A catheter is threaded over the guidewire until it, too, reaches the point of study and the guidewire is removed. Contrast medium is injected through the catheter and a series of x-rays or fluoroscopic images taken to visualize the vessels and evaluate for any transected or bleeding arteries. Embolization may be dictated by angiography results to hemorrhaging for definitive stabilization treatment. The catheter is removed and pressure applied to the site. This code reports the radiological supervision and interpretation. Use separately reportable code for the catheterization.

CPT Coding for Pelvic Angiography

Service Performed	Surgical Component	Radiology S&I Component
Unilateral pelvic angiography	**Varies**	75736
Bilateral pelvic angiography	**Varies**	75736-50. Note: Some third-party payers may require modifier 59 appended to the second code in order to secure appropriate reimbursement.
Each additional artery		75774

Coding Tips

1. Report both components of the procedure: the surgical component or catheter placement codes and the radiology S&I codes.

2. CPT code 75736 is unilateral. It would be appropriate to report this code with modifier 50 if the procedure is bilaterally performed with only injection of the internal iliac arteries. Some third-party payers may require modifier 59 appended to the second code in order to secure appropriate reimbursement.

3. CPT code 75774 is reported if additional selective branches of the internal iliac are catheterized and imaged after the initial procedure has been completed.

4. Do not report CPT code 75736 for imaging of the common iliac arteries. This code is selective and may only be reported when catheterization occurs of the internal iliac artery, one of its branches, or in a branch of the aorta or iliac artery that supplies the pelvis.

5. Catheter placement codes will change depending upon the approach taken. However, regardless of approach, the uterine arteries are considered 3rd order selective. Refer to the Basic Interventional Radiology Coding section of this manual for guidance.

6. Conscious sedation is not included in these codes. Separately report 99151–99157 per payer policy and coding guidelines. Hospitals may choose to include the costs associated with the service as part of the procedure rather than reporting them separately.

7. Report all applicable HCPCS Level II codes. Refer to the HCPCS section for possible codes.

8. Hospitals are requested to continue reporting LOCM separately with HCPCS codes Q9965–Q9967. Report contrast media by milliliter.

9. Physician Reporting: These radiology S&I codes have both a technical and professional component. To report only the professional component, append modifier 26. To report only the technical component, append modifier TC. To report the complete procedure (i.e., both the professional and technical components), submit without a modifier.

10. Angiograms performed after angioplasty, stent, and atherectomy procedures are included in the interventional codes and are not reported separately.

Pelvic Arterial Anatomy

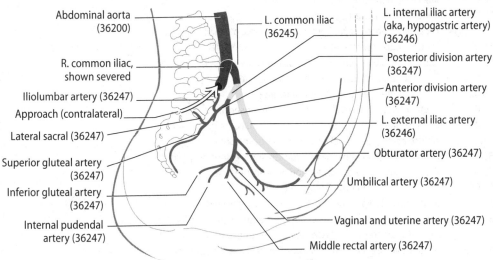

Contralateral approach (R. groin)

Abdominal aorta (36200)
L. common iliac (36245)
L. internal iliac artery (aka, hypogastric artery) (36246)
R. common iliac, shown severed
Posterior division artery (36247)
Iliolumbar artery (36247)
Anterior division artery (36247)
Approach (contralateral)
L. external iliac artery (36246)
Lateral sacral (36247)
Obturator artery (36247)
Superior gluteal artery (36247)
Umbilical artery (36247)
Inferior gluteal artery (36247)
Vaginal and uterine artery (36247)
Internal pudendal artery (36247)
Middle rectal artery (36247)

Facility HCPCS Coding

Some applicable codes may include but are not limited to:

C1760	Closure device, vascular (implantable/insertable)
G0269	Placement of occlusive device into either a venous or arterial access site, post surgical or interventional procedure (e.g., AngioSeal plug, vascular plug)
Q9965	LOCM, 100-199 mg/ml iodine concentration, per ml
Q9966	LOCM, 200-299 mg/ml iodine concentration, per ml
Q9967	LOCM, 300-399 mg/ml iodine concentration, per ml

Note: See appendix B for a complete listing of reportable HCPCS Level II codes.

Pelvic Arterial Anatomy—Anterior

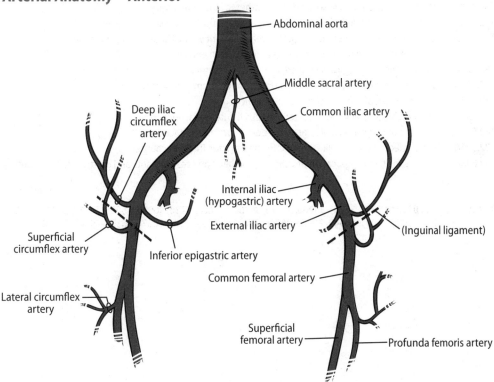

Abdominal aorta
Middle sacral artery
Deep iliac circumflex artery
Common iliac artery
Internal iliac (hypogastric) artery
Superficial circumflex artery
External iliac artery
(Inguinal ligament)
Inferior epigastric artery
Common femoral artery
Lateral circumflex artery
Superficial femoral artery
Profunda femoris artery

ICD-10-CM Coding

I72.3	Aneurysm of iliac artery
I74.5	Embolism and thrombosis of iliac artery
I77.72	Dissection of iliac artery
K55.011	Focal (segmental) acute (reversible) ischemia of small intestine
K55.012	Diffuse acute (reversible) ischemia of small intestine
K55.019	Acute (reversible) ischemia of small intestine, extent unspecified
K55.021	Focal (segmental) acute infarction of small intestine
K55.022	Diffuse acute infarction of small intestine
K55.029	Acute infarction of small intestine, extent unspecified
K55.031	Focal (segmental) acute (reversible) ischemia of large intestine
K55.032	Diffuse acute (reversible) ischemia of large intestine
K55.039	Acute (reversible) ischemia of large intestine, extent unspecified
K55.041	Focal (segmental) acute infarction of large intestine
K55.042	Diffuse acute infarction of large intestine
K55.049	Acute infarction of large intestine, extent unspecified
K55.051	Focal (segmental) acute (reversible) ischemia of intestine, part unspecified
K55.052	Diffuse acute (reversible) ischemia of intestine, part unspecified
K55.059	Acute (reversible) ischemia of intestine, part and extent unspecified
K55.061	Focal (segmental) acute infarction of intestine, part unspecified
K55.062	Diffuse acute infarction of intestine, part unspecified
K55.069	Acute infarction of intestine, part and extent unspecified
K55.1	Chronic vascular disorders of intestine
K55.8	Other vascular disorders of intestine
S35.511A	Injury of right iliac artery, initial encounter
S35.512A	Injury of left iliac artery, initial encounter
S35.513A	Injury of unspecified iliac artery, initial encounter
T82.398A	Other mechanical complication of other vascular grafts, initial encounter
T82.41XA	Breakdown (mechanical) of vascular dialysis catheter, initial encounter
T82.42XA	Displacement of vascular dialysis catheter, initial encounter
T82.43XA	Leakage of vascular dialysis catheter, initial encounter
T82.49XA	Other complication of vascular dialysis catheter, initial encounter
T82.510A	Breakdown (mechanical) of surgically created arteriovenous fistula, initial encounter
T82.511A	Breakdown (mechanical) of surgically created arteriovenous shunt, initial encounter
T82.514A	Breakdown (mechanical) of infusion catheter, initial encounter
T82.520A	Displacement of surgically created arteriovenous fistula, initial encounter
T82.521A	Displacement of surgically created arteriovenous shunt, initial encounter
T82.524A	Displacement of infusion catheter, initial encounter
T82.530A	Leakage of surgically created arteriovenous fistula, initial encounter
T82.531A	Leakage of surgically created arteriovenous shunt, initial encounter
T82.594A	Other mechanical complication of infusion catheter, initial encounter
T82.898A	Other specified complication of vascular prosthetic devices, implants and grafts, initial encounter

CCI Edits

75736 01916, 01924-01926, 35201-35206, 35226, 35261-35266, 35286, 36000, 36005, 36410, 36500, 36591-36592, 75825, 75893, 76000-76001, 76942, 76970, 76998, 77001-77002, 96372, 96376-96377, 99446-99449

Case Example

Via a **right common femoral arterial approach,** a 5-French vascular sheath was placed. A 5-French pigtail catheter was then placed in the distal descending abdominal aorta and an AP pelvic angiogram was obtained. The pigtail catheter was then exchanged for a 5-French Cobra II catheter, which was **positioned in the left internal iliac artery.** AP and bilateral oblique pelvic **angiograms were obtained.** Using road-map technique, the Cobra catheter was used to **select the left uterine artery** and an AP digital subtraction **angiogram was obtained.** The catheter was **placed in the right internal iliac artery.** AP and oblique pelvic **angiograms were obtained.** The Cobra catheter was then used to **select the right uterine artery.** AP digital subtraction **images were obtained.** Sixty (60) cc of Visipaque 270 were used. The catheter and sheath were removed and hemostasis was achieved.

CPT/HCPCS Codes Reported:
75736, 75736-XS, 75774 x 2, 36247, 36247-XS

Other HCPCS Codes Reported:
Q9966 x 60, C1894

Pulmonary Artery Angiography

The pulmonary arterial system is considered to be a separate vascular system. It is the only arterial system that carries venous blood. There are separate catheter placement codes for this system. There are selective and nonselective radiological S&I codes for pulmonary angiography. Angiography of the pulmonary system involves catheterizing the peripheral venous system, passing the catheter through the heart and into the pulmonary artery.

75741   **Angiography, pulmonary, unilateral, selective, radiological supervision and interpretation**
A local anesthetic is applied over the site where the catheter is to be introduced; this is most often either the common femoral or internal jugular vein. The vein is percutaneously punctured and the catheter selectively manipulated through the vena cava, right atrium, and right ventricle into the left or right pulmonary artery. Contrast medium is injected and films are taken to visualize the vessels and evaluate any abnormalities, such as blockages, narrowing, or aneurysms. This code reports the radiological supervision and interpretation only. Use a separately reportable code for the catheterization.

75743   **Angiography, pulmonary, bilateral, selective, radiological supervision and interpretation**
A local anesthetic is applied over the site where the catheter is to be introduced; this is most often either the common femoral or internal jugular vein. The vein is percutaneously punctured and the catheter selectively manipulated through the vena cava, right atrium, and right ventricle into the pulmonary arteries. Contrast medium is injected and films taken bilaterally to visualize the vessels and evaluate any abnormalities, such as blockages, narrowing, or aneurysms. This code reports the radiological supervision and interpretation only. Use a separately reportable code for the catheterization.

75746   **Angiography, pulmonary, by nonselective catheter or venous injection, radiological supervision and interpretation**
Local anesthetic is applied over the site of catheter introduction; this is most often either the common femoral or internal jugular vein. The vein is percutaneously punctured, and the catheter is manipulated to the main pulmonary artery or the right atrium. Contrast medium is injected, and images are taken of the pulmonary arteries to evaluate for abnormalities such as blockages, narrowing, or aneurysms. This code reports the radiologic supervision and interpretation only. Report the catheterization separately.

Pulmonary Arterial Anatomy

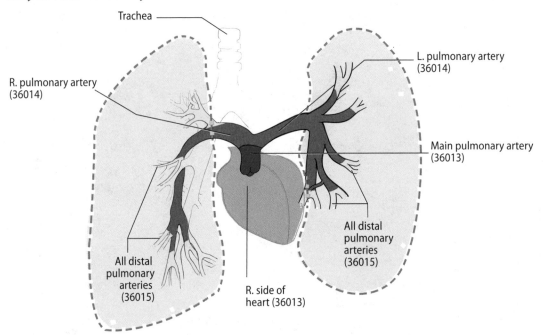

CPT Coding for Pulmonary Angiography

Service Performed	Surgical Component	Radiology S&I Component
Unilateral selective pulmonary angiography	36014	75741
Bilateral selective pulmonary angiography	36014-50	75743
Nonselective pulmonary angiography	36013	75746
Catheter placement in the right heart or main pulmonary artery	36013	
Catheter placement in the right or left pulmonary artery	36014	
Catheter placement in a segmental or subsegmental pulmonary artery	36015	

Coding Tips

1. Report both components of the procedure: the surgical component or catheter placement codes and the radiology S&I codes.

2. Unilateral and bilateral codes exist for pulmonary angiography. Do not use modifier 50 and do not report 75741 twice.

3. CPT code 75774 is reported if additional selective catheterizations are performed after an initial pulmonary angiogram is done.

4. Inferior venacavagram (CPT code 75825) may be reported provided the procedure is appropriately indicated and documented. CPT code 36010 would be reported for the catheter placement code. Refer to the venous chapter for additional information.

5. Non-selective pulmonary angiography is reported with CPT codes 36013 and 75746 when the injection is made from the right atrium, right ventricle, or the main pulmonary artery.

6. For pulmonary angiography during cardiac catheterization, report CPT code 93568. Do not report 75741, 75743, or 75746 for pulmonary artery injections during cardiac catheterization procedures.

7. Conscious sedation is not included in these codes. Separately report 99151–99157 per payer policy and coding guidelines. Hospitals may choose to include the costs associated with the service as part of the procedure rather than reporting them separately.

8. Report all applicable HCPCS Level II codes. Refer to the HCPCS section for possible codes.

9. Hospitals are requested to continue reporting LOCM separately with HCPCS codes Q9965–Q9967. Report contrast media by milliliter.

10. Physician Reporting: These radiology S&I codes have both a technical and professional component. To report only the professional component, append modifier 26. To report only the technical component, append modifier TC. To report the complete procedure (i.e., both the professional and technical components), submit without a modifier.

11. Angiograms performed after angioplasty, stent, and atherectomy procedures are included in the interventional codes and are not reported separately.

Facility HCPCS Coding

Some applicable codes may include but are not limited to:

Q9965   LOCM, 100-199 mg/ml iodine concentration, per ml
Q9966   LOCM, 200-299 mg/ml iodine concentration, per ml
Q9967   LOCM, 300-399 mg/ml iodine concentration, per ml

Note: See appendix B for a complete listing of reportable HCPCS Level II codes.

ICD-10-CM Coding

D18.00   Hemangioma unspecified site
I26.02   Saddle embolus of pulmonary artery with acute cor pulmonale
I26.09   Other pulmonary embolism with acute cor pulmonale
I26.90   Septic pulmonary embolism without acute cor pulmonale
I26.92   Saddle embolus of pulmonary artery without acute cor pulmonale
I26.99   Other pulmonary embolism without acute cor pulmonale
I27.0   Primary pulmonary hypertension
I27.1   Kyphoscoliotic heart disease
I27.20   Pulmonary hypertension, unspecified
I27.21   Secondary pulmonary arterial hypertension
I27.22   Pulmonary hypertension due to left heart disease
I27.23   Pulmonary hypertension due to lung diseases and hypoxia

I27.24	Chronic thromboembolic pulmonary hypertension
I27.29	Other secondary pulmonary hypertension
I27.81	Cor pulmonale (chronic)
I27.82	Chronic pulmonary embolism
I27.83	Eisenmenger's syndrome
I27.89	Other specified pulmonary heart diseases
I27.9	Pulmonary heart disease, unspecified
I28.0	Arteriovenous fistula of pulmonary vessels
I28.1	Aneurysm of pulmonary artery
I28.8	Other diseases of pulmonary vessels
I28.9	Disease of pulmonary vessels, unspecified
I36.0	Nonrheumatic tricuspid (valve) stenosis
I36.1	Nonrheumatic tricuspid (valve) insufficiency
I36.2	Nonrheumatic tricuspid (valve) stenosis with insufficiency
I36.8	Other nonrheumatic tricuspid valve disorders
I36.9	Nonrheumatic tricuspid valve disorder, unspecified
I37.0	Nonrheumatic pulmonary valve stenosis
I37.1	Nonrheumatic pulmonary valve insufficiency
I37.2	Nonrheumatic pulmonary valve stenosis with insufficiency
I37.8	Other nonrheumatic pulmonary valve disorders
I37.9	Nonrheumatic pulmonary valve disorder, unspecified
I42.0	Dilated cardiomyopathy
I42.5	Other restrictive cardiomyopathy
I42.8	Other cardiomyopathies
I42.9	Cardiomyopathy, unspecified
I50.1	Left ventricular failure
I50.21	Acute systolic (congestive) heart failure
I50.22	Chronic systolic (congestive) heart failure
I50.23	Acute on chronic systolic (congestive) heart failure
I50.31	Acute diastolic (congestive) heart failure
I50.32	Chronic diastolic (congestive) heart failure
I50.33	Acute on chronic diastolic (congestive) heart failure
I50.41	Acute combined systolic (congestive) and diastolic (congestive) heart failure
I50.42	Chronic combined systolic (congestive) and diastolic (congestive) heart failure
I50.43	Acute on chronic combined systolic (congestive) and diastolic (congestive) heart failure
I50.810	Right heart failure, unspecified
I50.811	Acute right heart failure
I50.812	Chronic right heart failure
I50.813	Acute on chronic right heart failure
I50.814	Right heart failure due to left heart failure
I50.82	Biventricular heart failure
I50.83	High output heart failure
I50.84	End stage heart failure
I50.89	Other heart failure
I72.9	Aneurysm of unspecified site
I77.1	Stricture of artery
I82.91	Chronic embolism and thrombosis of unspecified vein
O88.011	Air embolism in pregnancy, first trimester
O88.012	Air embolism in pregnancy, second trimester
O88.013	Air embolism in pregnancy, third trimester
O88.019	Air embolism in pregnancy, unspecified trimester
O88.02	Air embolism in childbirth
O88.03	Air embolism in the puerperium
O88.211	Thromboembolism in pregnancy, first trimester
O88.212	Thromboembolism in pregnancy, second trimester
O88.213	Thromboembolism in pregnancy, third trimester

O88.219	Thromboembolism in pregnancy, unspecified trimester
O88.22	Thromboembolism in childbirth
O88.23	Thromboembolism in the puerperium
O88.311	Pyemic and septic embolism in pregnancy, first trimester
O88.312	Pyemic and septic embolism in pregnancy, second trimester
O88.313	Pyemic and septic embolism in pregnancy, third trimester
O88.319	Pyemic and septic embolism in pregnancy, unspecified trimester
O88.32	Pyemic and septic embolism in childbirth
O88.33	Pyemic and septic embolism in the puerperium
O88.811	Other embolism in pregnancy, first trimester
O88.812	Other embolism in pregnancy, second trimester
O88.813	Other embolism in pregnancy, third trimester
O88.819	Other embolism in pregnancy, unspecified trimester
O88.82	Other embolism in childbirth
O88.83	Other embolism in the puerperium
Q20.0	Common arterial trunk
Q20.1	Double outlet right ventricle
Q20.2	Double outlet left ventricle
Q20.3	Discordant ventriculoarterial connection
Q20.4	Double inlet ventricle
Q20.5	Discordant atrioventricular connection
Q20.8	Other congenital malformations of cardiac chambers and connections
Q21.0	Ventricular septal defect
Q21.1	Atrial septal defect
Q21.3	Tetralogy of Fallot
Q22.0	Pulmonary valve atresia
Q22.1	Congenital pulmonary valve stenosis
Q22.2	Congenital pulmonary valve insufficiency
Q22.3	Other congenital malformations of pulmonary valve
Q23.8	Other congenital malformations of aortic and mitral valves
Q23.9	Congenital malformation of aortic and mitral valves, unspecified
Q24.8	Other specified congenital malformations of heart
Q25.5	Atresia of pulmonary artery
Q25.6	Stenosis of pulmonary artery
Q25.71	Coarctation of pulmonary artery
Q25.72	Congenital pulmonary arteriovenous malformation
Q25.79	Other congenital malformations of pulmonary artery
Q33.9	Congenital malformation of lung, unspecified
S25.401A	Unspecified injury of right pulmonary blood vessels, initial encounter
S25.402A	Unspecified injury of left pulmonary blood vessels, initial encounter
S25.409A	Unspecified injury of unspecified pulmonary blood vessels, initial encounter
S25.411A	Minor laceration of right pulmonary blood vessels, initial encounter
S25.412A	Minor laceration of left pulmonary blood vessels, initial encounter
S25.419A	Minor laceration of unspecified pulmonary blood vessels, initial encounter
S25.421A	Major laceration of right pulmonary blood vessels, initial encounter
S25.422A	Major laceration of left pulmonary blood vessels, initial encounter
S25.429A	Major laceration of unspecified pulmonary blood vessels, initial encounter
S25.491A	Other specified injury of right pulmonary blood vessels, initial encounter
S25.492A	Other specified injury of left pulmonary blood vessels, initial encounter
S25.499A	Other specified injury of unspecified pulmonary blood vessels, initial encounter
S27.321A	Contusion of lung, unilateral, initial encounter
S27.322A	Contusion of lung, bilateral, initial encounter
S27.329A	Contusion of lung, unspecified, initial encounter
T80.0XXA	Air embolism following infusion, transfusion and therapeutic injection, initial encounter
T81.718A	Complication of other artery following a procedure, not elsewhere classified, initial encounter
T81.72XA	Complication of vein following a procedure, not elsewhere classified, initial encounter

T82.817A	Embolism of cardiac prosthetic devices, implants and grafts, initial encounter
T82.818A	Embolism of vascular prosthetic devices, implants and grafts, initial encounter
T82.828A	Fibrosis of vascular prosthetic devices, implants and grafts, initial encounter
T82.838A	Hemorrhage of vascular prosthetic devices, implants and grafts, initial encounter
T82.848A	Pain from vascular prosthetic devices, implants and grafts, initial encounter
T82.858A	Stenosis of vascular prosthetic devices, implants and grafts, initial encounter
T82.868A	Thrombosis of vascular prosthetic devices, implants and grafts, initial encounter
T82.898A	Other specified complication of vascular prosthetic devices, implants and grafts, initial encounter
T82.9XXA	Unspecified complication of cardiac and vascular prosthetic device, implant and graft, initial encounter

CCI Edits

75741 01916, 01924-01926, 35201-35206, 35226, 35261-35266, 35286, 36000, 36005, 36410, 36500, 36591-36592, 75746, 75893, 76000-76001, 76942, 76970, 76998, 77001-77002, 93568, 96372, 96376-96377, 99446-99449

75743 01916, 01924-01926, 35201-35206, 35226, 35261-35266, 35286, 36000, 36005, 36410, 36500, 36591-36592, 75741, 75746, 75893, 76000-76001, 76942, 76970, 76998, 77001-77002, 93568, 96372, 96376-96377, 99446-99449

75746 01916, 01924-01926, 35201-35206, 35226, 35261-35266, 35286, 36000, 36005, 36410, 36500, 36591-36592, 75893, 76000-76001, 76942, 76970, 76998, 77001-77002, 93568, 96372, 96376-96377, 99446-99449

Case Example #1

Via **right femoral vein** approach, a guidewire and catheter were advanced through a sheath up the inferior vena cava, across the tricuspid valve, and initially **positioned within the main pulmonary** artery where pressures were obtained. The catheter was **advanced selectively into the right pulmonary artery** where injections of Isovue 300 contrast were given as images were obtained over the right hemithorax in the AP and LAO projections. The catheter was then **advanced selectively into the left pulmonary artery** where similar injections of contrast were given and images obtained over the left hemithorax in the AP and RAO projections. The catheter and vascular sheath were removed and pressure applied to the puncture site to achieve hemostasis. A total of 100 cc contrast was used.

CPT/HCPCS Codes Reported:
75743, 36014-50

Other HCPCS Codes Reported:
Q9967 x 100, C1894

Case Example #2

Pulmonary Arteriogram
Patient has a history of multiple arterial venous anomalies. The patient had previous embolizations performed on multiple settings.

After informed consent was obtained, a **right common femoral venous puncture** was made. Using an H1 catheter, a Glidewire access into the pulmonary artery was achieved. This was exchanged for a 6-French 90 cm long sheath placed in the **main pulmonary artery.** Contrast injections were performed through a 100 cm pigtail catheter **placed within the left pulmonary artery**. This revealed no obvious significant arteriovenous fistulas. Using a Glidewire access into the **right pulmonary artery**, contrast was injected and **angiography** was **performed** of the **right pulmonary artery system**. This revealed an arterial venous anomaly within the right middle lobe region. This arteriovenous fistula represents the finding on CT exam. The rest of the right lung showed one arterial-to-arterial anastomotic vascular lesion, but there was no venous flow accompanying this lesion. The other areas previously embolized remain closed. Embolization was recommended. 80 cc of Isovue 300 was used.

CPT/HCPCS Codes Reported:
75743, 36014-50

Other HCPCS Codes Reported:
Q9967 x 80, C1769, C1894

Chapter 3: Diagnostic Venography

Cerebral Veins

Cerebral venography is typically performed with an interventional procedure such as embolization. Cerebral venography involves selective catheterization of the internal jugular vein by direct stick or via a peripheral approach. Jugular venography may be performed non-selectively by direct stick or via peripheral approach.

Orbital venography involves selective catheterization of the internal jugular vein or beyond in order to image the orbital veins and the cavernous sinus.

Epidural venography involves selective catheterization of the epidural veins via the common iliac vein. This procedure is now obsolete and is no longer or rarely performed. Less invasive CT and MRI procedures are now used for disc herniation diagnosis.

75860   **Venography, venous sinus (eg, petrosal and inferior sagittal) or jugular, catheter, radiological supervision and interpretation**
A local anesthetic is applied over the site where the catheter is to be introduced and the access vein is percutaneously punctured with a needle. A guidewire is inserted and advanced through the vein until it reaches the desired location in the venous system for imaging the sinus (petrosal, inferior sagittal) or jugular vein. A catheter is threaded over the guidewire to the selected point and the wire is removed. Non-ionic diluted contrast medium is injected over approximately 30 seconds through the catheter that has traveled to an area upstream of the site under investigation. Images are acquired. This code reports the radiological supervision and interpretation only. Use a separately reportable code for the catheterization.

75870   **Venography, superior sagittal sinus, radiological supervision and interpretation**
A local anesthetic is applied over the site where the catheter is to be introduced and the access vein is percutaneously punctured with a needle. A guidewire is inserted and advanced through the dominant jugular vein until it reaches the desired location for studying the superior sagittal sinus, which is the primary venous drainage for the cranial vasculature. A catheter is threaded over the guidewire into the selected point in the vein and the wire is removed. Non-ionic diluted contrast medium is injected through the catheter that has traveled to an area upstream of the site under investigation. Images are acquired. This code reports the radiological supervision and interpretation only. Use a separately reportable code for the catheterization.

Cerebral Venous Anatomy

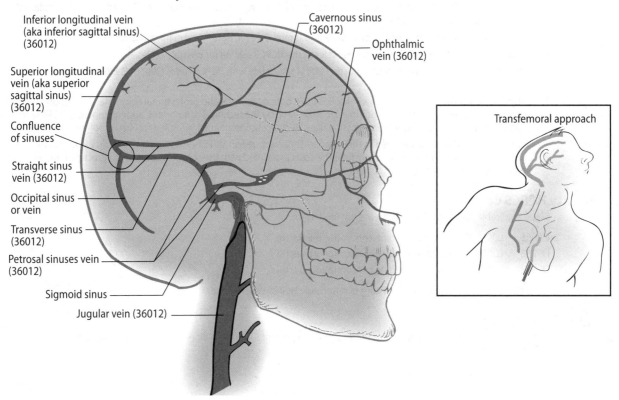

Inferior longitudinal vein (aka inferior sagittal sinus) (36012)

Cavernous sinus (36012)

Ophthalmic vein (36012)

Superior longitudinal vein (aka superior sagittal sinus) (36012)

Confluence of sinuses

Straight sinus vein (36012)

Occipital sinus or vein

Transverse sinus (36012)

Petrosal sinuses vein (36012)

Sigmoid sinus

Jugular vein (36012)

Transfemoral approach

75872   **Venography, epidural, radiological supervision and interpretation**
A local anesthetic is applied over the site where the catheter is to be introduced and the access vein is percutaneously punctured with a needle. A guidewire is inserted and advanced into the common iliac vein for imaging the epidural veins. Contrast media is injected through the catheter and images are acquired. This code reports the radiological supervision and interpretation only. Use a separately reportable code for the catheterization.

75880   **Venography, orbital, radiological supervision and interpretation**
The physician introduces a needle or catheter through a puncture site in the skin into a peripheral vein. A guidewire is inserted and selectively fed through the vein until it reaches the desired location in the venous system for imaging the orbital veins. A catheter is threaded over the guidewire into the selected point in the vein and the wire is removed. Radiopaque dye is administered into the facial or frontal veins, and x-rays are taken to visualize the orbital veins and cavernous sinuses. This code reports the radiological supervision and interpretation only. Use a separately reportable code for the catheterization.

CPT® Coding for Cerebral Venography

Service Performed	Surgical Component	Radiology S&I Component
Venous sinus or jugular venography		75860
Superior sagittal sinus venography		75870
Epidural venography		75872
Orbital venography		75880
Catheter introduction into the superior or inferior vena cava	36010	
Selective catheter placement in a first order branch of the venous system	36011	
Selective catheter placement in a second order branch of the venous system	36012	

Coding Tips

1. Report both components of the procedure: the surgical component or catheter placement codes and the radiology S&I codes.
2. CPT® code 75860 is unilateral. It is appropriate to report this code with modifier 50 if the procedure is performed bilaterally.
3. Do not report 36012 (Second order selective venous catheterization) when direct access is made into the jugular vein. Rather report the unlisted code 36299.
4. Epidural venography is an obsolete procedure and is rarely, if ever, performed in hospitals today.
5. Report all applicable HCPCS Level II codes. Refer to the HCPCS section for possible codes.
6. Hospitals are requested to continue reporting LOCM separately with HCPCS codes Q9965–Q9967. Report contrast media by milliliter.
7. Physician Reporting: These radiology S&I codes have both a technical and professional component. To report only the professional component, append modifier 26. To report only the technical component, append modifier TC. To report the complete procedure (i.e., both the professional and technical components), submit without a modifier.
8. Conscious sedation is not included in these codes. Separately report 99151–99157 per payer policy and coding guidelines. Hospitals may choose to include the costs associated with the service as part of the procedure rather than reporting them separately.

Facility HCPCS Coding

Some applicable codes may include but are not limited to:

Q9965   LOCM, 100-199 mg/ml iodine concentration, per ml
Q9966   LOCM, 200-299 mg/ml iodine concentration, per ml
Q9967   LOCM, 300-399 mg/ml iodine concentration, per ml

Note: See appendix B for a complete listing of reportable HCPCS Level II codes.

ICD-10-CM Coding

The application of these codes is too broad to adequately present ICD-10-CM diagnosis code links here. Refer to the current ICD-10-CM book.

CCI Edits

75860 01916, 01924-01926, 35201-35206, 35226, 35261-35266, 35286, 36000, 36005, 36410, 36500, 36591-36592, 76000-76001, 76942, 76970, 76998, 77001-77002, 96360, 96365, 96372, 96374-96377, 99446-99449

75870 01916, 01924-01926, 35201-35206, 35226, 35261-35266, 35286, 36000, 36005, 36410, 36500, 36591-36592, 75860, 76000-76001, 76942, 76970, 76998, 77001-77002, 96360, 96365, 96372, 96374-96377, 99446-99449

75872 01916, 01924-01926, 35201-35206, 35226, 35261-35266, 35286, 36000, 36005, 36410, 36500, 36591-36592, 76000-76001, 76942, 76970, 76998, 77001-77002, 96360, 96365, 96372, 96374-96377, 99446-99449

75880 01916, 01924-01926, 35201-35206, 35226, 35261-35266, 35286, 36000, 36005, 36410, 36500, 36591-36592, 76000-76001, 76942, 76970, 76998, 77001-77002, 78456-78458, 96360, 96365, 96372, 96374-96377, 99446-99449

Case Example

History:
Recent arteriogram showed a suspected dural sinus fistula, which was treated with coil embolization. Further evaluation was clinically indicated to determine the success of this prior therapy.

Procedure:
The **left femoral vein** was punctured in cephalad direction. A 9-French sheath was **advanced to the left jugular vein**. Through this a 5-French Kumpe catheter was **advanced into the abnormal dural sinus** involved in the fistula. Then using this as a coaxial introducer, a Renagade microcatheter was **advanced into the region of the fistula**. A **subselective venogram** was performed. This demonstrated significantly decreased flow into the fistula. The procedure was then discontinued.

CPT/HCPCS Codes Reported:
36012, 75860

Note: Contrast media should be documented to accurately report the type and amount administered and/or used.

Central Veins—Superior and Inferior Vena Cava

Central venography is performed on the superior and/or inferior vena cava. Vena cava angiography involves catheterization of the vena cava by subclavian or femoral approach. Central venography may also be performed from a peripheral injection rather than via a catheter.

75825   **Venography, caval, inferior, with serialography, radiological supervision and interpretation**

75827   **Venography, caval, superior, with serialography, radiological supervision and interpretation**

A local anesthetic is applied over a distal vein (typically antecubital, internal jugular, subclavian, or femoral) and the vein is percutaneously punctured with a needle. A guidewire is inserted and fed through the vein to the inferior vena cava in 75825 and the superior vena cava in 75827. The physician may slide an introducer sheath over the guidewire into the venous lumen before inserting a catheter. The catheter is inserted into the vein and threaded over the guidewire to the inferior (75825) or superior (75827) vena cava. The guidewire is removed. Contrast medium is injected and a series of x-rays performed to visualize and evaluate any abnormalities, such as blockages, narrowing, or aneurysms. In venography, contrast medium is injected into the catheter that has traveled to an area upstream of the site under investigation. These codes report the radiological supervision and interpretation only. Use a separately reportable code for the catheterization.

CPT Coding for Vena Cava

Service Performed	Surgical Component	Radiology S&I Component
Inferior vena cavogram	36010	75825
Superior vena cavogram	36010	75827
Catheter introduction into the superior or inferior vena cava	36010	

Coding Tips

1. Report both components of the procedure: the surgical component or catheter placement codes and the radiology S&I codes.

2. It is appropriate to report the vena cavogram CPT code when performed with pulmonary angiography.

3. It is appropriate to report inferior vena cavogram (CPT code 75825) in addition to selective renal venography. Refer to the Renal Venography section for additional information.

4. It is appropriate to report the vena cavogram CPT code when performed during the percutaneous placement of an inferior vena cava (IVC) filter. Refer to the Vascular Interventional Procedure section for additional information.

5. Vena cavogram is not reported separately when performed with a venous sampling study (CPT code 75893) or a dialysis fistulogram (CPT codes 36901–36909). Refer to the sections below for additional information.

6. Report all applicable HCPCS Level II codes. Refer to the HCPCS section for possible codes.

7. Hospitals are requested to continue reporting LOCM separately with HCPCS codes Q9965–Q9967. Report contrast media by milliliter.

8. Physician Reporting: These radiology S&I codes have both a technical and professional component. To report only the professional component, append modifier 26. To report only the technical component, append modifier TC. To report the complete procedure (i.e., both the professional and technical components), submit without a modifier.

9. Conscious sedation is not included in these codes. Separately report 99151-99157 per payer policy and coding guidelines. Hospitals may choose to include the costs associated with the service as part of the procedure rather than reporting them separately.

Facility HCPCS Coding

Some applicable codes may include but are not limited to:

Q9965   LOCM, 100-199 mg/ml iodine concentration, per ml
Q9966   LOCM, 200-299 mg/ml iodine concentration, per ml
Q9967   LOCM, 300-399 mg/ml iodine concentration, per ml

Note: See appendix B for a complete listing of reportable HCPCS Level II codes.

Central Venous Anatomy

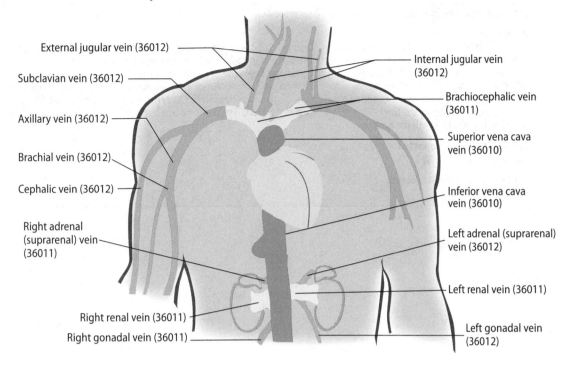

ICD-10-CM Coding

I82.21Ø	Acute embolism and thrombosis of superior vena cava
I82.211	Chronic embolism and thrombosis of superior vena cava
I82.22Ø	Acute embolism and thrombosis of inferior vena cava
I82.221	Chronic embolism and thrombosis of inferior vena cava
Q26.Ø	Congenital stenosis of vena cava
Q26.1	Persistent left superior vena cava
S25.2ØXA	Unspecified injury of superior vena cava, initial encounter
S25.21XA	Minor laceration of superior vena cava, initial encounter
S25.22XA	Major laceration of superior vena cava, initial encounter
S25.29XA	Other specified injury of superior vena cava, initial encounter
S35.11XA	Minor laceration of inferior vena cava, initial encounter
S35.12XA	Major laceration of inferior vena cava, initial encounter
S35.19XA	Other injury of inferior vena cava, initial encounter
T82.7XXA	Infection and inflammatory reaction due to other cardiac and vascular devices, implants and grafts, initial encounter
T82.818A	Embolism of vascular prosthetic devices, implants and grafts, initial encounter
T82.828A	Fibrosis of vascular prosthetic devices, implants and grafts, initial encounter
T82.838A	Hemorrhage of vascular prosthetic devices, implants and grafts, initial encounter
T82.848A	Pain from vascular prosthetic devices, implants and grafts, initial encounter
T82.858A	Stenosis of vascular prosthetic devices, implants and grafts, initial encounter
T82.868A	Thrombosis of vascular prosthetic devices, implants and grafts, initial encounter
T82.898A	Other specified complication of vascular prosthetic devices, implants and grafts, initial encounter
T82.9XXA	Unspecified complication of cardiac and vascular prosthetic device, implant and graft, initial encounter
T85.9XXA	Unspecified complication of internal prosthetic device, implant and graft, initial encounter

CCI Edits

75825	01916, 01924-01926, 35201-35206, 35226, 35261-35266, 35286, 36000, 36005, 36410, 36500, 36591-36592, 36598, 76000-76001, 76942, 76970, 76998, 77002, 96360, 96365, 96372, 96374-96377, 99446-99449
75827	01916, 01924-01926, 35201-35206, 35226, 35261-35266, 35286, 36000, 36005, 36410, 36500, 36591-36592, 36598, 76000-76001, 76942, 76970, 76998, 77002, 96360, 96365, 96372, 96374-96377, 99446-99449

Case Example

Patient returned for evaluation for possible IVC filter removal.

Procedure:
The **right internal jugular vein** was punctured. Over a 0.018 guidewire a 5-French catheter was introduced. Exchange was then made over a 0.035 guidewire and a 5-French sheath was introduced. Through this sheath a multi-side hole straight flush catheter was introduced and **advanced** over the guidewire down the superior vena cava and **subsequently into the inferior vena cava. Inferior venacavography** was then **performed.** A moderate amount of thrombus was identified within the IVC filter. This thrombus measured approximately 2 cm in superior-inferior dimension x 1 cm right-to-left dimension and appeared constrained by the filter. Given this volume clot the IVC filter removal was not performed at that time. I discussed the presence of a clot with the patient.

CPT/HCPCS Codes Reported:
36010, 75825

Other HCPCS Codes Reported:
C1769 x 2, C1894

Renal and Adrenal Veins

Renal and adrenal venography procedures are performed with selective catheter placement. Inferior vena cavagram is not included with these codes and is reported separately. Imaging may be obtained via traditional film methods and/or utilizing digital techniques.

75831   **Venography, renal, unilateral, selective, radiological supervision and interpretation**

75833   **Venography, renal, bilateral, selective, radiological supervision and interpretation**
A local anesthetic is applied over the site where the catheter is to be introduced; this is most often the common femoral vein. The vein is percutaneously punctured with a needle and a guidewire is inserted and selectively fed through the vein until it reaches the desired location in the venous system. A catheter is threaded over the guidewire into the selected point in the vein and the wire is removed. Contrast medium for venography is injected through the catheter that has traveled to an area upstream of the site under investigation. X-rays are taken. Code 75831 reports the radiological supervision and interpretation only for venography of either the left or right renal vein and 75833 is used for both renal veins. Use a separately reportable code for the catheterization.

75840   **Venography, adrenal, unilateral, selective, radiological supervision and interpretation**

75842   **Venography, adrenal, bilateral, selective, radiological supervision and interpretation**
A local anesthetic is applied over the site where the catheter is to be introduced; this is most often the common femoral vein. The vein is percutaneously punctured with a needle and a guidewire is inserted and selectively fed through the vein until it reaches the desired location in the venous system. A catheter is threaded over the guidewire into the selected point in the vein and the wire is removed. Contrast medium for venography is injected through the catheter that has traveled to an area upstream of the site under investigation. X-rays are taken. Code 75840 reports the radiological supervision and interpretation only for venography of either the left or right adrenal vein and 75842 is used for both adrenal veins. Use a separately reportable code for the catheterization.

Central Venous Anatomy

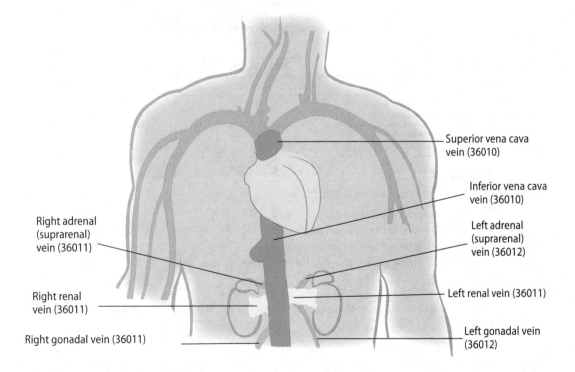

Superior vena cava vein (36010)

Inferior vena cava vein (36010)

Right adrenal (suprarenal) vein (36011)

Left adrenal (suprarenal) vein (36012)

Right renal vein (36011)

Left renal vein (36011)

Right gonadal vein (36011)

Left gonadal vein (36012)

Coding Tips

1. Report both components of the procedure: the surgical component or catheter placement codes and the radiology S&I codes.

2. Unilateral and bilateral codes exist for renal and adrenal venography. Do not use modifier 50 and do not report 75831 or 75840 twice.

3. Inferior vena cavography is not included with these codes. Report 75825 in addition to the CPT codes for renal and/or adrenal venography.

4. Do not report renal venography if the procedure is performed for venous sampling. Renal venography is included in CPT code 75893. Selective catheter placement is also included with CPT code 36500, the surgical component for venous sampling.

5. Ovarian venography is included in the renal venography codes.

6. Report all applicable HCPCS Level II codes. Refer to the HCPCS section for possible codes.

7. Hospitals are requested to continue reporting LOCM separately with HCPCS codes Q9965–Q9967. Report contrast media by milliliter.

8. Physician Reporting: These radiology S&I codes have both a technical and professional component. To report only the professional component, append modifier 26. To report only the technical component, append modifier TC. To report the complete procedure (i.e., both the professional and technical components), submit without a modifier.

9. Conscious sedation is not included in these codes. Separately report 99151-99157 per payer policy and coding guidelines. Hospitals may choose to include the costs associated with the service as part of the procedure rather than reporting them separately.

CPT Coding for Renal and Adrenal Venography

Service Performed	Surgical Component	Radiology S&I Component
Unilateral renal venography	36011	75831
Bilateral renal venography	36011-50 Note: Some third-party payers may require modifier -59 appended to the second code in order to secure appropriate reimbursement.	75833
Unilateral adrenal venography	36011-RT, 36012-LT	75840
Bilateral adrenal venography	36011-RT, 36012-LT	75842
Each additional vein		75774
Selective catheter placement into the first order branch of the venous system	36011	
Selective catheter placement into the second order branch of the venous system	36012	

Facility HCPCS Coding

Some applicable codes may include but are not limited to:

Q9965   LOCM, 100-199 mg/ml iodine concentration, per ml
Q9966   LOCM, 200-299 mg/ml iodine concentration, per ml
Q9967   LOCM, 300-399 mg/ml iodine concentration, per ml

Note: See appendix B for a complete listing of reportable HCPCS Level II codes.

ICD-10-CM Coding

The application of these codes is too broad to adequately present ICD-10-CM diagnosis code links here. Refer to the current ICD-10-CM book.

CCI Edits

75831   01916, 01924-01926, 35201-35206, 35226, 35261-35266, 35286, 36000, 36005, 36410, 36500, 36591-36592, 76000-76001, 76942, 76970, 76998, 77001-77002, 96360, 96365, 96372, 96374-96377, 99446-99449

75833   01916, 01924-01926, 35201-35206, 35226, 35261-35266, 35286, 36000, 36005, 36410, 36500, 36591-36592, 75831, 76000-76001, 76942, 76970, 76998, 77001-77002, 96360, 96365, 96372, 96374-96377, 99446-99449

75840   01916, 01924-01926, 35201-35206, 35226, 35261-35266, 35286, 36000, 36005, 36410, 36500, 36591-36592, 76000-76001, 76942, 76970, 76998, 77001-77002, 96360, 96365, 96372, 96374-96377, 99446-99449

75842   01916, 01924-01926, 35201-35206, 35226, 35261-35266, 35286, 36000, 36005, 36410, 36500, 36591-36592, 75840, 76000-76001, 76942, 76970, 76998, 77001-77002, 96360, 96365, 96372, 96374-96377, 99446-99449

Case Example

History:
This was a 36-year-old female with pelvic congestion syndrome.

Procedure:
After the right neck was prepped and draped the **right internal jugular vein was accessed**. Over a wire, an Ansel 3 catheter was advanced to the inferior aspect of the IVC. Using a 60 cm Kumpe catheter and over the wire the **left renal vein was accessed**. With a Valsalva maneuver a venogram was performed, which demonstrated significant reflux in a dilated left renal vein, which filled dilated pelvic varicosities and severely dilated ovarian vein. Embolization of the ovarian vein was recommended.

CPT/HCPCS Codes Reported:
36011, 75831

Note: Renal venography includes ovarian vein venography.

Extremity Veins

Upper extremity venography is typically performed by direct injection of contrast into a peripheral vein. It may also be performed via catheter placement. Lower extremity venography is also usually performed by direct injection of contrast into a peripheral vein. Catheter placement is also possible, but extremely rare. Imaging may be obtained via traditional film methods and/or utilizing digital techniques.

75820   **Venography, extremity, unilateral, radiological supervision and interpretation**

75822   **Venography, extremity, bilateral, radiological supervision and interpretation**

The physician performs a radiographic study on the veins of either the left or right lower extremity in 75820 and of both lower extremities in 75822. A local anesthetic is applied over the site where the catheter is to be introduced; this is most often the common femoral vein. The vein is percutaneously punctured with a needle and a guidewire is inserted and fed through the vein to the point where dye will be injected. A catheter is threaded over the guidewire and the guidewire is removed. Contrast medium is injected and a series of x-rays performed to visualize the vessels and evaluate any abnormalities, such as blockages, narrowing, or aneurysms. In venography, contrast medium is injected into the catheter that has traveled to an area upstream of the site under investigation. These codes report the radiological supervision and interpretation only. Use a separately reportable code for the catheterization.

Lower Extremity Venous Anatomy

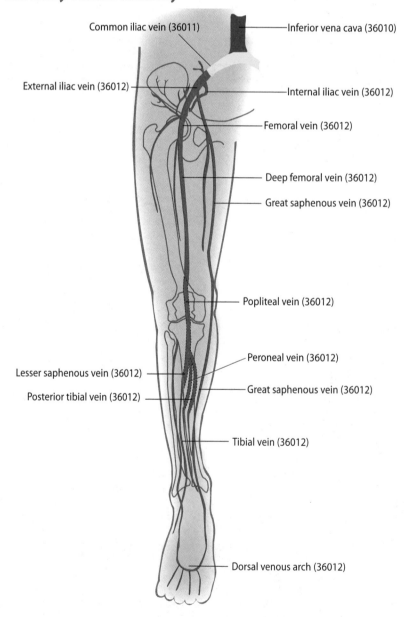

Common iliac vein (36011)

Inferior vena cava (36010)

External iliac vein (36012)

Internal iliac vein (36012)

Femoral vein (36012)

Deep femoral vein (36012)

Great saphenous vein (36012)

Popliteal vein (36012)

Peroneal vein (36012)

Lesser saphenous vein (36012)

Great saphenous vein (36012)

Posterior tibial vein (36012)

Tibial vein (36012)

Dorsal venous arch (36012)

CPT Coding for Extremity Venography

Service Performed	Surgical Component	Radiology S&I Component
Unilateral non-selective extremity venography	36005	75820
Bilateral non-selective extremity venography	36005-50 Note: Some third-party payers may require modifier -59 appended to the second code in order to secure appropriate reimbursement.	75822
Selective catheter placement into a first order branch of the venous system	36011	
Selective catheter placement into a second order branch of the venous system	36012	

Coding Tips

1. Report both components of the procedure: the surgical component or catheter placement codes and the radiology S&I codes.

2. Unilateral and bilateral codes exist for extremity venography. Do not use modifier 50 and do not report 75820 twice.

3. Extremity venography is not reported separately when performed as part of an A-V dialysis shunt procedure. It is included in CPT codes 36901–36909.

4. Report all applicable HCPCS Level II codes. Refer to the HCPCS section for possible codes.

5. Hospitals are requested to continue reporting LOCM separately with HCPCS codes Q9965–Q9967. Report contrast media by milliliter.

6. Physician Reporting: These radiology S&I codes have both a technical and professional component. To report only the professional component, append modifier 26. To report only the technical component, append modifier TC. To report the complete procedure (i.e., both the professional and technical components), submit without a modifier.

Facility HCPCS Coding

Some applicable codes may include but are not limited to:

Q9965   LOCM, 100-199 mg/ml iodine concentration, per ml
Q9966   LOCM, 200-299 mg/ml iodine concentration, per ml
Q9967   LOCM, 300-399 mg/ml iodine concentration, per ml

Note: See appendix B for a complete listing of reportable supply pass-through codes and HCPCS Level II codes.

ICD-10-CM Coding

The application of these codes is too broad to adequately present ICD-10-CM diagnosis code links here. Refer to the current ICD-10-CM book.

CCI Edits

75820   01916, 01924-01926, 35201-35206, 35226, 35261-35266, 35286, 36000, 36410, 36500, 36591-36592, 76000-76001, 76942, 76970, 76998, 77002, 78456-78458, 96360, 96365, 96372, 96374-96377, 99446-99449

75822   01916, 01924-01926, 35201-35206, 35226, 35261-35266, 35286, 36000, 36410, 36500, 36591-36592, 75820, 76000-76001, 76942, 76970, 76998, 77002, 96360, 96365, 96372, 96374-96377, 99446-99449

Case Example

With the patient in a 30-degree upright position on the fluoroscopy table, a tourniquet was applied to the right ankle and a 19-gauge **needle** was advanced **into the vein** over the dorsum of the foot. Additional tourniquets were applied above the ankle and also above the knee. One hundred (100) cc of Visipaque 270 was injected with fluoroscopic monitoring. Spot films were obtained of **the right leg** with eventual removal of the tourniquets and supine positioning of the patient. The veins were flushed with normal saline and the needle withdrawn.

CPT/HCPCS Codes Reported:
36005, 75820-RT

Other HCPCS Codes Reported:
Q9966 x 100

Portal and Hepatic Veins and TIPS

Hepatic venography is typically performed via femoral approach by catheter through the inferior vena cava and selectively catheterizing the hepatic vein.

Portal venography is performed by percutaneous approach through the abdomen directly into the portal vein.

Splenoportography involves a percutaneous entry via an incision directly into the splenic vein for imaging the splenic vein.

37182 **Insertion of transvenous intrahepatic portosystemic shunt(s) (TIPS) (includes venous access, hepatic and portal vein catheterization, portography with hemodynamic evaluation, intrahepatic tract formation/dilatation, stent placement and all associated imaging guidance and documentation)**

37183 **Revision of transvenous intrahepatic portosystemic shunt(s) (TIPS) (includes venous access, hepatic and portal vein catheterization, portography with hemodynamic evaluation, intrahepatic tract recanulization/dilatation, stent placement and all associated imaging guidance and documentation)**
A transvenous intrahepatic portosystemic shunt is inserted in 37182 and replaced in 37183. Shunts are placed to manage the complications of portal hypertension and control variceal bleeding and ascites. Access is made into the jugular vein, and a catheter is advanced into the hepatic vein. Images and pressures are obtained. A long needle is then placed through a long sheath to create a tract from the hepatic vein to the portal vein. This tract is then dilated with a balloon catheter, and a stent is placed to maintain the tract. Blockages can occur along the shunt so later revisions may be necessary. Revisions are reported with 37183.

75810 **Splenoportography, radiological supervision and interpretation**
The physician makes an incision in the lower left axilla. An 18 or 20-gauge sheath catheter is inserted into the middle of the soft, sponge-like tissue of the spleen. The splenic vein is visualized and the catheter is placed. 2.0-3.0 cc of radiopaque dye is injected per second, totaling about 15.0-20.0 cc of dye. X-rays are taken every second for about 12 seconds. The catheter is removed and the incision covered with a dressing. This code reports the radiological supervision and interpretation only. Use a separately reportable code for the splenoportography injection procedure.

75885 **Percutaneous transhepatic portography with hemodynamic evaluation, radiological supervision and interpretation**
A radiographic exam of the portal vein of the liver is done by inserting a needle through the abdomen. The patient's right side is cleansed and a local anesthetic given at the puncture site. A needle is inserted into the skin just under the ribs and diaphragm and advanced to the liver under fluoroscopic guidance. The needle is aimed at the portal vein and when blood returns from the needle, a small amount of contrast is injected to help confirm placement into the portal vein. When in place, a guidewire is inserted and a catheter follows. More contrast is injected, radiographs taken and intravenous, hemodynamic pressures in the portal vein are recorded. This code reports the radiological supervision and interpretation only. Use a separately reportable code for the catheterization.

75887 **Percutaneous transhepatic portography without hemodynamic evaluation, radiological supervision and interpretation**
A radiographic exam of the portal vein of the liver is done by inserting a needle through the abdomen. The patient's right side is cleansed and a local anesthetic given at the puncture site. A needle is inserted into the skin just under the ribs and diaphragm and advanced to the liver under fluoroscopic guidance. The needle is aimed at the portal vein and when blood returns from the needle, a small amount of contrast is injected to help confirm placement into the portal vein. When in place, a guidewire is inserted and a catheter follows. More contrast is injected and radiographs are taken. This code reports the radiological supervision and interpretation only. Use a separately reportable code for the catheterization.

75889 **Hepatic venography, wedged or free, with hemodynamic evaluation, radiological supervision and interpretation**

75891 **Hepatic venography, wedged or free, without hemodynamic evaluation, radiological supervision and interpretation**
A local anesthetic is applied over the common femoral vein and a guidewire is then inserted and fed through until it reaches the hepatic vein. A catheter is threaded over the guidewire and the guidewire is removed. For wedged hepatic venography, the catheter is wedged into a small hepatic vein branch to approximate the portal pressure occurring in liver disease. For free hepatic venography, the catheter tip lies free in the hepatic vein. Correct positioning of the catheter is monitored by fluoroscopy. Contrast medium is injected into the vein and x-rays are taken. Report 75889 if this is done together with hemodynamic evaluation in which blood movement through the liver is monitored by indwelling catheters connected to transducers. The pressure forces within the arteries and veins are then converted to electrical signals and displayed on screen. Report 75891 if hepatic venography is performed without the hemodynamic evaluation. These codes report the radiological supervision and interpretation only.

Portal System

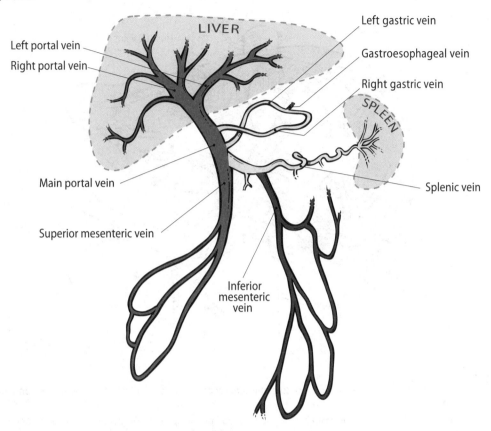

CPT Coding for Portal System

Service Performed	Surgical Component	Radiology S&I Component
Splenoportography	38200	75810
Percutaneous transhepatic portography, with hemodynamic evaluation	36481	75885
Percutaneous transhepatic portography, without hemodynamic evaluation	36481	75887
Hepatic venography with hemodynamic evaluation	varies	75889
Hepatic venography without hemodynamic evaluation	varies	75891
Selective catheter placement into a first order branch of the venous system	36011	
Selective catheter placement into a second order branch of the venous system	36012	
Insertion of a transvenous intrahepatic portosystemic shunt	37182	
Revision of a transvenous intrahepatic portosystemic shunt	37183	

T.I.P.S. Placement

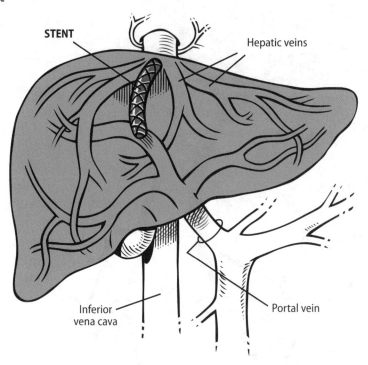

Coding Tips

1. Report both components of the procedure: the surgical component or catheter placement codes and the radiology S&I codes.

2. Report inferior vena cavagram (CPT code 75825) in addition to splenoportography, portography, or hepatic venography when performed.

3. CPT code 36481 includes only nonselective portal vein catheter placement. Report additional veins imaged with CPT code 75774 after initial complete exam. Report additional catheterization codes as well.

4. If a transvenous intrahepatic portosystemic shunt (TIPS) procedure is performed, do not report CPT code 36481. The catheterization is included in the CPT codes for TIPS. CPT codes 37182 and 37183 are inclusive of all imaging services used in performing TIPS procedures. Radiology S&I codes—75885 and 75887—are not reported in addition to the TIPS codes.

5. Separately report any other interventions such as embolization or thrombolysis when performed in addition to the TIPS procedure.

6. CPT code 37182 is on the "inpatient-only" procedure list for Medicare patients. Medicare will not cover this service for outpatients.

7. Report all applicable HCPCS Level II codes. Refer to the HCPCS section for possible codes.

8. Hospitals are requested to continue reporting LOCM separately with HCPCS codes Q9965–Q9967. Report contrast media by milliliter.

9. Physician Reporting: These radiology S&I codes have both a technical and professional component. To report only the professional component, append modifier 26. To report only the technical component, append modifier TC. To report the complete procedure (i.e., both the professional and technical components), submit without a modifier.

10. Conscious sedation is not included in CPT code 37182. Depending upon payer policy, hospitals may choose to separately report codes 99151–99157.

Facility HCPCS Coding

Some applicable codes may include but are not limited to:

Q9965   LOCM, 100-199 mg/ml iodine concentration, per ml

Q9966   LOCM, 200-299 mg/ml iodine concentration, per ml

Q9967   LOCM, 300-399 mg/ml iodine concentration, per ml

Note: See appendix B for a complete listing of reportable HCPCS Level II codes.

ICD-10-CM Coding

75810

C26.0	Malignant neoplasm of intestinal tract, part unspecified
C26.1	Malignant neoplasm of spleen
C26.9	Malignant neoplasm of ill-defined sites within the digestive system
C78.7	Secondary malignant neoplasm of liver and intrahepatic bile duct
C78.80	Secondary malignant neoplasm of unspecified digestive organ
C78.89	Secondary malignant neoplasm of other digestive organs
C82.07	Follicular lymphoma grade I, spleen
C82.17	Follicular lymphoma grade II, spleen
C82.27	Follicular lymphoma grade III, unspecified, spleen
C82.37	Follicular lymphoma grade IIIa, spleen
C82.47	Follicular lymphoma grade IIIb, spleen
C82.67	Cutaneous follicle center lymphoma, spleen
C82.87	Other types of follicular lymphoma, spleen
C82.97	Follicular lymphoma, unspecified, spleen
D01.7	Carcinoma in situ of other specified digestive organs
D01.9	Carcinoma in situ of digestive organ, unspecified
D57.02	Hb-SS disease with splenic sequestration
D57.212	Sickle-cell/Hb-C disease with splenic sequestration
D57.412	Sickle-cell thalassemia with splenic sequestration
D57.812	Other sickle-cell disorders with splenic sequestration
D73.0	Hyposplenism
D73.1	Hypersplenism
D73.2	Chronic congestive splenomegaly
D73.3	Abscess of spleen
D73.4	Cyst of spleen
D73.5	Infarction of spleen
D73.89	Other diseases of spleen
D73.9	Disease of spleen, unspecified
S36.00XA	Unspecified injury of spleen, initial encounter
S36.020A	Minor contusion of spleen, initial encounter
S36.021A	Major contusion of spleen, initial encounter
S36.029A	Unspecified contusion of spleen, initial encounter
S36.039A	Unspecified laceration of spleen, initial encounter
S36.09XA	Other injury of spleen, initial encounter

75885–75887

I81	Portal vein thrombosis
K70.0	Alcoholic fatty liver
K70.30	Alcoholic cirrhosis of liver without ascites
K70.31	Alcoholic cirrhosis of liver with ascites
K75.1	Phlebitis of portal vein
K76.6	Portal hypertension

75889-75891

D18.00	Hemangioma unspecified site
K70.0	Alcoholic fatty liver
K70.2	Alcoholic fibrosis and sclerosis of liver
K70.30	Alcoholic cirrhosis of liver without ascites
K70.31	Alcoholic cirrhosis of liver with ascites
K70.9	Alcoholic liver disease, unspecified
K76.4	Peliosis hepatis
K76.5	Hepatic veno-occlusive disease
K76.6	Portal hypertension

CCI Edits

37182 0075T, 0213T, 0216T, 0228T, 0230T, 11000-11006, 11042-11047, 12001-12007, 12011-12057, 13100-13133, 13151-13153, 35201-35206, 35226-35236, 35256-35266, 35286, 36000, 36010-36012, 36400-36410, 36420-36430, 36440, 36481, 36500, 36591-36592, 36600, 36640, 37140, 37183, 37217-37218, 37236, 37238, 43752, 47010, 49405, 51701-51703, 62320-62327, 64400-64410, 64413-64435, 64445-64450, 64461-64463, 64479-64530, 69990, 75885, 75887, 76000-76001, 76380, 76942, 76970, 76998, 77001-77002, 77012, 77021, 92012-92014, 93000-93010, 93040-93042, 93318, 93355, 94002, 94200, 94250, 94680-94690, 94770, 95812-95816, 95819, 95822, 95829, 95955, 96360-96368, 96372, 96374-96377, 97597-97598, 97602, 99155-99157, 99211-99223, 99231-99255, 99291-99292, 99304-99310, 99315-99316, 99334-99337, 99347-99350, 99374-99375, 99377-99378, 99446-99449, 99495-99496, G0463, G0471

37183 0075T, 0213T, 0216T, 0228T, 0230T, 11000-11006, 11042-11047, 12001-12007, 12011-12057, 13100-13133, 13151-13153, 35201-35206, 35226-35236, 35256-35266, 35286, 36000, 36010-36012, 36400-36410, 36420-36430, 36440, 36481, 36500, 36591-36592, 36600, 36640, 37140, 37217-37218, 37236, 37238, 43752, 47010, 49405, 51701-51703, 62320-62327, 64400-64410, 64413-64435, 64445-64450, 64461-64463, 64479-64530, 69990, 75885, 75887, 76000-76001, 76380, 76942, 76970, 76998, 77001-77002, 77012, 77021, 92012-92014, 93000-93010, 93040-93042, 93318, 93355, 94002, 94200, 94250, 94680-94690, 94770, 95812-95816, 95819, 95822, 95829, 95955, 96360-96368, 96372, 96374-96377, 97597-97598, 97602, 99155-99157, 99211-99223, 99231-99255, 99291-99292, 99304-99310, 99315-99316, 99334-99337, 99347-99350, 99374-99375, 99377-99378, 99446-99449, 99495-99496, G0463, G0471, J0670, J1642-J1644, J2001

75810 01916, 01924-01926, 35201-35206, 35226, 35261-35266, 35286, 36000, 36005, 36410, 36500, 36591-36592, 76000-76001, 76942, 76970, 76998, 77001-77002, 96360, 96365, 96372, 96374-96377, 99446-99449

75885 01916, 01924-01926, 35201-35206, 35226, 35261-35266, 35286, 36000, 36005, 36410, 36500, 36591-36592, 75887, 76000-76001, 76942, 76970, 76998, 77001-77002, 96360, 96365, 96372, 96374-96377, 99446-99449

75887 01916, 01924-01926, 35201-35206, 35226, 35261-35266, 35286, 36000, 36005, 36410, 36500, 36591-36592, 76000-76001, 76942, 76970, 76998, 77001-77002, 96360, 96365, 96372, 96374-96377, 99446-99449

75889 01916, 01924-01926, 35201-35206, 35226, 35261-35266, 35286, 36000, 36005, 36410, 36500, 36591-36592, 75891, 76000-76001, 76942, 76970, 76998, 77001-77002, 96360, 96365, 96372, 96374-96377, 99446-99449

75891 01916, 01924-01926, 35201-35206, 35226, 35261-35266, 35286, 36000, 36005, 36410, 36500, 36591-36592, 76000-76001, 76942, 76970, 76998, 77001-77002, 96360, 96365, 96372, 96374-96377, 99446-99449

Case Example #1

Ultrasound was used to visualize the right internal jugular vein and subsequently used to gain **access into the right internal jugular vein**. A guidewire was passed into the region of the right atrium without difficulty. Over the guidewire, a 5-French catheter was advanced and successfully negotiated across the right atrium into the inferior vena cava (IVC). With some difficulty, the right hepatic vein was successfully catheterized and a guidewire and catheter were then **advanced from the right hepatic vein** across the TIPS and successfully advanced **to the level of the extra-hepatic portal vein**. **Portal venogram** was obtained with digital subtraction imaging and Isovue 300 contrast. The study was terminated and the catheter removed from the right internal jugular site. Standard compression was applied and adequate hemostasis achieved.

CPT/HCPCS Codes Reported:
36012, 75885

Note: Ultrasound guidance CPT code 76937 can be reported only if permanent images are recorded and obtained in the medical record.

Case Example #2

The **right internal jugular vein was accessed** and a sheath placed. A 5-French Cobra **catheter** was **placed** into the **portal vein and a main portal venogram performed**. Intravenous portal-systemic pressures were obtained from the main portal vein to the right atrium. A 12 mm **balloon angioplasty** was performed **across the stenosis** at the **hepatic venous end of the shunt**. Angioplasty was repeated after venogram showed no significant decrease in stenosis. Subsequent final venogram was performed and pullback pressures were obtained across the shunt. The catheter and sheath were removed and hemostasis achieved.

CPT/HCPCS Codes Reported:
37183

No supply codes are reported for this inpatient-only procedure. However, supplies should be billed separately in the sterile medical supplies revenue code, 0272. Also report contrast media separately with the appropriate pharmacy revenue code (0255 is preferred for inpatient-performed procedures).

Venous Sampling

Blood samples from organ outflow are sometimes required to assist in evaluation of chemical or hormone levels in the blood. This is done by catheter placement into the veins of the organ.

36500   **Venous catheterization for selective organ blood sampling**
The physician inserts a needle through the skin and into a peripheral vein. A guidewire is threaded through the needle into the vessel. The needle is removed. The wire is manipulated into the vein draining from the organ to be sampled. The catheter follows the guidewire into the vein. Once the catheter has been placed, the guidewire is removed and the blood sample obtained. The catheter is removed and pressure is applied to the puncture site to stop the flow of blood.

75893   **Venous sampling through catheter, with or without angiography (eg, for parathyroid hormone, renin), radiological supervision and interpretation**
Venous sampling involves withdrawing blood from a patient's vein into a vacuum tube. For parathyroid hormone or renin testing, a catheter is used for sampling. The catheter must be advanced through the abdominal aorta and into the renal arteries from an outside access point, usually the common femoral vein. When the catheter is correctly placed, several samples are withdrawn. This code reports the radiological supervision and interpretation only.

Coding Tips

1. Catheter placement is included in CPT code 36500 and is not reported separately.

2. Angiography is included in CPT code 75893 and is not reported separately.

3. All blood sampling is included in CPT code 36500 regardless of where in the venous system the sample is obtained.

4. These codes are unilateral. Report the codes with modifier 50 if performed bilaterally.

5. CPT code 75893 has been assigned payment status by CMS for 2015. Be sure to report all codes and supplies associated with the procedure.

6. Renal venography is included and is not reported separately.

7. Physician Reporting: These radiology S&I codes have both a technical and professional component. To report only the professional component, append modifier 26. To report only the technical component, append modifier TC. To report the complete procedure (i.e., both the professional and technical components), submit without a modifier.

Facility HCPCS Coding

Report any applicable codes for supplies. Refer to appendix B for a complete listing.

ICD-10-CM Coding

The application of these codes is too broad to adequately present ICD-10-CM diagnosis code links here. Refer to the current ICD-10-CM book.

CCI Edits

36500   0213T, 0216T, 0228T, 0230T, 12001-12007, 12011-12057, 13100-13133, 13151-13153, 35201-35206, 35226-35236, 35256-35266, 35286, 36000, 36002-36015, 36400-36410, 36420-36430, 36440, 36591-36592, 36600, 36640, 43752, 51701-51703, 62320-62327, 64400-64410, 64413-64435, 64445-64450, 64461-64463, 64479-64530, 69990, 76000-76001, 77001-77002, 92012-92014, 93000-93010, 93040-93042, 93318, 93355, 94002, 94200, 94250, 94680-94690, 94770, 95812-95816, 95819, 95822, 95829, 95955, 96360-96368, 96372, 96374-96377, 99155-99157, 99211-99223, 99231-99255, 99291-99292, 99304-99310, 99315-99316, 99334-99337, 99347-99350, 99374-99375, 99377-99378, 99446-99449, 99495-99496, G0463, G0471

75893   01916, 01924-01926, 35201-35206, 35226, 35261-35266, 35286, 36000, 36410, 36591-36592, 75810, 75820, 75822, 75825, 75827, 75831, 75833, 75840, 75842, 75860, 75870, 75872, 75880, 75885, 75887, 75889, 75891, 76000-76001, 76942, 76970, 76998, 77001-77002, 96360, 96365, 96372, 96374-96377, 99446-99449

Case Example

Via **right femoral vein** approach, a **catheter** was advanced into the vena cava and then selectively **placed into the right renal vein**. **Blood samples** were obtained. The catheter was then placed into the **left renal vein** where additional **blood samples** were obtained. Final blood samples were **obtained from the vena cava**. The catheter was withdrawn and manual pressure maintained until hemostasis was achieved.

CPT/HCPCS Codes Reported:
36500-50, 75893-50

Note: Verify modifier assignment with payer requirements.

Chapter 4: Dialysis Circuit Interventions

Patients on dialysis require a way to access the vascular system for repeated hemodialysis, which could be needed for years. There are several methods used to create an arteriovenous circuit, the most common of which in interventional radiology is arteriovenous fistula.

Commonly located in the arm, the arteriovenous fistula comprises two segments, the peripheral and the central. The peripheral segment begins at the arterial anastomosis and ends at the central segment. The central segment for the upper extremity begins with the subclavian vein; for the lower extremity, the central portion begins at the external iliac vein. The central segment begins with these veins and includes the veins leading to either the superior or inferior vena cava. The arterial anastomosis is where the graft is patched into the artery (refer to the illustration "Arteriovenous Fistula Anatomy" in this chapter). The arterial inflow into the circuit is considered to be a separate vessel. Refer to the guidelines detailed in this chapter for reporting separate vessels.

Arteriovenous Fistula (Dialysis Circuit) Diagnostic Angiography

36901   **Introduction of needle(s) and/or catheter(s), dialysis circuit, with diagnostic angiography of the dialysis circuit, including all direct puncture(s) and catheter placement(s), injection(s) of contrast, all necessary imaging from the arterial anastomosis and adjacent artery through entire venous outflow including the inferior or superior vena cava, fluoroscopic guidance, radiological supervision and interpretation and image documentation and report**
The physician inserts a needle or catheter into a dialysis circuit via a puncture in the skin overlying the circuit of a dialysis patient. The catheter is guided into the circuit and vessel to an area upstream of the site under investigation, and contrast material is injected into it.

Arteriovenous Fistula Anatomy

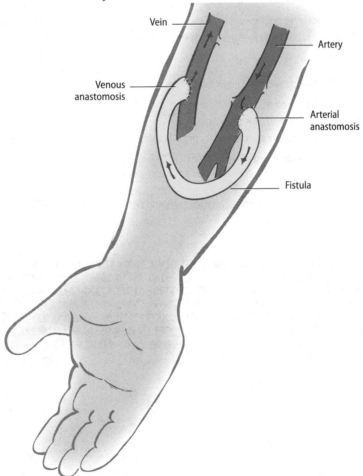

Coding Tips

1. Codes 36147 and 36148 (access into the fistula) have been deleted and replaced with the new code 36901.

2. Report 36901 for diagnostic study of the dialysis circuit. This procedure is commonly known as the AV fistulogram.

3. Code 36901 is reported only once and covers imaging of the entire circuit—both peripheral and central segments.

4. All catheterizations needed to complete the diagnostic study are included in 36901. Advancing the catheter to the vena cava is included and is not separately reported.

5. Catheterizations of accessory veins to the circuit are included in 36901.

6. Crossing the arterial anastomosis to study the peri-anastomotic region is also included.

7. Code 36901 includes the imaging portions of the procedure—fluoroscopy, image guidance, angiography, and radiological supervision and interpretation.

8. Selective catheterization *beyond* the peri-anastomotic inflow region is *not* included, and an additional catheterization may be reported. Refer to 36215 or 36245.

9. Angiography of the artery beyond the peri-anastomotic inflow region may be additionally reported with imaging code 75710.

10. Closure of the puncture access into the circuit is included in this code.

11. This code is reported when only the diagnostic study is performed. If an intervention is also done, see codes 36902–36909.

12. If a diagnostic study is performed via an existing access or via catheter based arterial access, then modifier 52 is appended to 36901 to depict the reduced service.

13. Although not typically used to access a dialysis circuit, ultrasound guidance may be separately reported with 76937. Refer to the coding guidelines for the required elements before reporting this code.

14. As with any imaging or interventional study, complete and detailed documentation of the procedure should be provided in the physician's procedure note.

15. Conscious sedation is not included in this code. Separately report 99151–99157 per payer policy and coding guidelines. Hospitals may choose to include the costs associated with the service as part of the procedure rather than reporting them separately.

16. Hospitals should separately report contrast media with HCPCS codes Q9965–Q9967. Report these codes per milliliter.

17. Report all applicable supply HCPCS Level II codes. Refer to the HCPCS section for possible codes.

Facility HCPCS Coding

Some applicable codes may include but are not limited to:

Q9965   LOCM, 100-199 mg/ml iodine concentration, per ml
Q9966   LOCM, 200-299 mg/ml iodine concentration, per ml
Q9967   LOCM, 300-399 mg/ml iodine concentration, per ml

Note: See appendix B for a complete listing of reportable HCPCS Level II codes.

ICD-10-CM Coding

The application of these codes is too broad to adequately present ICD-10-CM diagnosis code links here. Refer to the current ICD-10-CM book.

CCI Edits

36901   01916, 01924-01926, 01930, 0213T, 0216T, 0228T, 0230T, 12001-12007, 12011-12057, 13100-13133, 13151-13153, 35201-35207, 35211-35286, 36000, 36002-36012, 36140, 36200, 36261, 36400-36410, 36420-36430, 36440, 36500, 36591-36592, 36600, 36640, 36832-36833, 43752, 51701-51703, 62320-62327, 64400-64410, 64413-64435, 64445-64450, 64461-64463, 64479-64530, 69990, 75658, 75820, 75822, 75825, 75827, 75893, 76000-76001, 76942, 76998, 77001-77002, 77012, 77021, 92012-92014, 93000-93010, 93040-93042, 93318, 94002, 94200, 94250, 94680-94690, 94770, 95812-95816, 95819, 95822, 95829, 95955, 96360-96368, 96372, 96374-96377, 96523, 99155-99157, 99211-99223, 99231-99255, 99291-99292, 99304-99310, 99315-99316, 99334-99337, 99347-99350, 99374-99375, 99377-99378, J0670, J1644, J2001

Case Example

Procedure:

Using the standard sterile technique and local anesthesia, a 4 French catheter was initially inserted into the **right upper extremity arterial venous dialysis fistula** via the Seldinger technique. Pressure was initially applied to the venous outflow as **contrast material was injected** to reflux to the arterial anastomosis as digital **radiographs were obtained** over the upper arm in the AP and oblique projections. Additional injections were then made as serial digital radiographs were obtained over the upper arm, axilla, upper chest, and mediastinum.

Findings:

Comparison was made to previous arterial venous dialysis shunt study. The arterial anastomosis of the fistula appears normal. Dilatation of the venous limb in the upper arm is without change when compared with the prior study. Minimal recurrent narrowing is seen within the right innominate vein in the region of a previously placed stent, yet this does not appear hemodynamically significant and excellent antegrade flow is seen into the superior vena cava through this area.

CPT/HCPCS Codes Reported:

36901

Arteriovenous Fistula (Dialysis Circuit) Angioplasty and Stenting

Arteriovenous dialysis circuits are prone to failure and complications over time. Interventions such as transcatheter angioplasty and stent placements are required to repair the circuits so they may continue to be used for the patient's dialysis.

For the purposes of coding dialysis circuit interventions, the circuit is divided into the central and peripheral segments (defined at the beginning of this chapter). These interventions are built upon a progressive hierarchy from less intensive to the most intensive service. This section will discuss the less intensive services of angioplasty and stent interventions.

36902			**Introduction of needle(s) and/or catheter(s), dialysis circuit, with diagnostic angiography of the dialysis circuit, including all direct puncture(s) and catheter placement(s), injection(s) of contrast, all necessary imaging from the arterial anastomosis and adjacent artery through entire venous outflow including the inferior or superior vena cava, fluoroscopic guidance, radiological supervision and interpretation and image documentation and report; with transluminal balloon angioplasty, peripheral dialysis segment, including all imaging and radiological supervision and interpretation necessary to perform the angioplasty**

A catheter with a balloon attached is inserted into the peripheral dialysis segment and fed into the narrowed portion, where its balloon may be inflated several times in order to stretch the diameter to allow a more normal flow of blood through the area.

36903			**with transcatheter placement of intravascular stent(s), peripheral dialysis segment, including all imaging and radiological supervision and interpretation necessary to perform the stenting, and all angioplasty within the peripheral dialysis segment**

A catheter with a stent-transporting tip is threaded over the guidewire into the peripheral dialysis segment, and the wire is extracted. The catheter travels to the point where the vessel needs additional support. The compressed stent is passed from the catheter into the vessel, where it deploys, expanding to support the vessel walls. Once the procedure is complete, the catheter is removed and pressure is applied over the puncture site.

36907			**Transluminal balloon angioplasty, central dialysis segment, performed through dialysis circuit, including all imaging and radiological supervision and interpretation required to perform the angioplasty (List separately in addition to code for primary procedure)**

A catheter with a balloon attached is inserted into the central dialysis segment and fed into the narrowed portion, where its balloon may be inflated several times in order to stretch the diameter to allow a more normal blood flow through the area.

36908			**Transcatheter placement of intravascular stent(s), central dialysis segment, performed through dialysis circuit, including all imaging and radiological supervision and interpretation required to perform the stenting, and all angioplasty in the central dialysis segment (List separately in addition to code for primary procedure)**

A catheter with a stent-transporting tip is threaded over the guidewire into the central dialysis segment, and the wire is extracted. The catheter travels to the point where the vessel needs additional support. The compressed stent is passed from the catheter out into the vessel, where it deploys, expanding to support the vessel walls. Once the procedure is complete, the catheter is removed and pressure is applied over the puncture site. All imaging and radiological supervision and interpretation is included.

Coding Tips

1. These codes are used when the intervention is performed via puncture of the dialysis circuit. For angioplasty and stent placement performed through an access other than the dialysis circuit, please refer to codes 37238, 37239, 37248, and 37249, described in the next chapter of this publication.

2. Use code 36902 to report angioplasty of the peripheral dialysis circuit segment.

3. Use code 36907 to report additional angioplasty of the central dialysis circuit segment. Code 36907 is an add-on code reported in addition to 36901–36906. This code may also be reported in addition to codes 36818–36833, surgical codes describing the creation of the dialysis circuit.

4. Codes 36902 and 36907 include the diagnostic services described by code 36901. Do not report 36901 in addition to 36902 or 36907.

5. Code 36902 is reported only once regardless of how many separate angioplasties are performed in the peripheral segment.

6. Code 36907 is reported only once regardless of how many separate angioplasties are performed in the central segment.

7. Angioplasty of the peri-anastomotic region is included and is not separately reported.

8. Use code 36903 to report transcatheter stent placement within the peripheral dialysis circuit segment.

9. Use code 36908 to report additional stent placement in the central dialysis circuit segment. Code 36908 is an add-on code reported in addition to 36901–36906. This code may also be reported in addition to codes 36818–36833, surgery codes describing the creation of the dialysis circuit.

10. Code 36903 includes any angioplasty described in 36902. Do not report these codes together.

11. Code 36903 is reported only once. Any number of stents placed and all lesions treated within the peripheral segment are included and are not separately reported.

12. Code 36908 is reported only once regardless of how many stents are placed or how many separate lesions in the central segment are treated.

13. If angioplasty is performed in one area and a stent is placed in another area, report only 36903 and only once.

14. Codes 36903 and 36908 include the diagnostic services described by code 36901. Do not report 36901 in addition to 36903 or 36908.

15. Although not typically used to access a dialysis circuit, ultrasound guidance may be separately reported with 76937. Refer to the coding guidelines for the required elements before reporting this code.

16. As with any imaging or interventional study, complete and detailed documentation of the procedure should be provided in the physician's procedure note.

17. Conscious sedation is not included in this code. Separately report 99151–99157 per payer policy and coding guidelines. Hospitals may choose to include the costs associated with the service as part of the procedure rather than reporting them separately.

18. Hospitals should separately report contrast media with HCPCS codes Q9965–Q9967. Report these codes per milliliter.

19. Report all applicable supply HCPCS Level II codes. Refer to the HCPCS section for possible codes.

Facility HCPCS Coding

Some applicable codes may include but are not limited to:

C1725	Catheter, transluminal angioplasty, non-laser
C1769	Guidewire
C1874	Stent, coated/covered, with delivery system
C1875	Stent, coated/covered, without delivery system
C1876	Stent, non-coated/non-covered, with delivery system
C1877	Stent, non-coated/non-covered, without delivery system
C1885	Catheter, transluminal angioplasty, laser
C2623	Catheter, transluminal angioplasty, drug-coated, non-laser
Q9965	LOCM, 100-199 mg/ml iodine concentration, per ml
Q9966	LOCM, 200-299 mg/ml iodine concentration, per ml
Q9967	LOCM, 300-399 mg/ml iodine concentration, per ml

Note: See appendix B for a complete listing of reportable HCPCS Level II codes.

ICD-10-CM Coding

The application of these codes is too broad to adequately present ICD-10-CM diagnosis code links here. Refer to the current ICD-10-CM book.

CCI Edits

36902   01916, 01924-01926, 01930, 0213T, 0216T, 0228T, 0230T, 12001-12007, 12011-12057, 13100-13133, 13151-13153, 35201-35207, 35211-35286, 36000, 36002-36012, 36140, 36200, 36261, 36400-36410, 36420-36430, 36440, 36500, 36591-36592, 36600, 36640, 36832-36833, 36901, 43752, 51701-51703, 62320-62327, 64400-64410, 64413-64435, 64445-64450, 64461-64463, 64479-64530, 69990, 75658, 75820, 75822, 75825, 75827, 75893, 76000-76001, 76942, 76998, 77001-77002, 77012, 77021, 92012-92014, 93000-93010, 93040-93042, 93318, 94002, 94200, 94250, 94680-94690, 94770, 95812-95816, 95819, 95822, 95829, 95955, 96360-96368, 96372, 96374-96377, 96523, 99155-99157, 99211-99223, 99231-99255, 99291-99292, 99304-99310, 99315-99316, 99334-99337, 99347-99350, 99374-99375, 99377-99378, J0670, J1642-J1644, J2001

36903   01916, 01924-01926, 01930, 0213T, 0216T, 0228T, 0230T, 12001-12007, 12011-12057, 13100-13133, 13151-13153, 35201-35207, 35211-35286, 36000, 36002-36012, 36140, 36200, 36261, 36400-36410, 36420-36430, 36440, 36500, 36591-36592, 36600, 36640, 36832-36833, 36901-36902, 37237, 37239, 43752, 51701-51703, 62320-62327, 64400-64410, 64413-64435, 64445-64450, 64461-64463, 64479-64530, 69990, 75658, 75820, 75822, 75825, 75827, 75893, 76000-76001, 76942, 76998, 77001-77002, 77012, 77021, 92012-92014, 93000-93010, 93040-93042, 93318, 94002, 94200, 94250, 94680-94690, 94770, 95812-95816, 95819, 95822, 95829, 95955, 96360-96368, 96372, 96374-96377, 96523, 99155-99157, 99211-99223, 99231-99255, 99291-99292, 99304-99310, 99315-99316, 99334-99337, 99347-99350, 99374-99375, 99377-99378, J0670, J1642-J1644, J2001

36907   01916, 01924-01926, 01930, 0213T, 0216T, 0228T, 0230T, 12001-12007, 12011-12057, 13100-13133, 13151-13153, 35201-35207, 35211-35286, 36000, 36002-36012, 36140, 36200, 36261, 36400-36410, 36420-36430, 36440, 36500, 36591-36592, 36600, 36640, 43752, 51701-51703, 62320-62327, 64400-64410, 64413-64435, 64445-64450, 64461-64463, 64479-64530, 69990, 75658, 75820, 75822, 75825, 75827, 75893, 76000-76001, 76942, 76998, 77001-77002, 77012, 77021, 92012-92014, 93000-93010, 93040-93042, 93318, 94002, 94200, 94250, 94680-94690, 94770, 95812-95816, 95819, 95822, 95829, 95955, 96360-96368, 96372, 96374-96377, 96523, 99155-99157, 99211-99223, 99231-99255, 99291-99292, 99304-99310, 99315-99316, 99334-99337, 99347-99350, 99374-99375, 99377-99378, J0670, J1642-J1644, J2001

36908   01916, 01924-01926, 01930, 0213T, 0216T, 0228T, 0230T, 12001-12007, 12011-12057, 13100-13133, 13151-13153, 35201-35207, 35211-35286, 36000, 36002-36012, 36140, 36200, 36261, 36400-36410, 36420-36430, 36440, 36500, 36591-36592, 36600, 36640, 36907, 37239, 43752, 51701-51703, 62320-62327, 64400-64410, 64413-64435, 64445-64450, 64461-64463, 64479-64530, 69990, 75658, 75820, 75822, 75825, 75827, 75893, 76000-76001, 76942, 76998, 77001-77002, 77012, 77021, 92012-92014, 93000-93010, 93040-93042, 93318, 94002, 94200, 94250, 94680-94690, 94770, 95812-95816, 95819, 95822, 95829, 95955, 96360-96368, 96372, 96374-96377, 96523, 99155-99157, 99211-99223, 99231-99255, 99291-99292, 99304-99310, 99315-99316, 99334-99337, 99347-99350, 99374-99375, 99377-99378, J0670, J1642-J1644, J2001

Case Example

The patient had formation of **cephalic vein to brachial artery arteriovenous fistula in the right upper extremity**. The patient developed problems with access of the fistula and poor dialysis. The skin overlying the fistula was prepped and draped in sterile fashion. A stab wound was made and a needle was introduced into the fistula. A guidewire was advanced and a sheath placed directly toward the arterial anastomotic area. A **fistulogram was performed** with hand injections of Omnipaque 300. A stenosis was present very **near the arterial anastomosis**. A Bentson guidewire was advanced into the brachial artery and a 4x20 mm ultrathin **balloon** was placed across the stenosis. The balloon was inflated to 10 atmospheres. No waist was seen. A completion angiogram was performed demonstrating improvement in the stenosis. The catheter and sheath were withdrawn and the wound repaired with 3-0 silk. The patient maintained a pulse and a thrill within the fistula at the completion of the procedure.

CPT/HCPCS Codes Reported:
36902

Other HCPCS Codes Reported:
C1725, C1729, C1894, Q9967, C1769

Note: Assign the appropriate device code for the angioplasty catheter used.

Arteriovenous Fistula (Dialysis Circuit) Thrombectomy

Arteriovenous dialysis fistulas and grafts periodically form blood clots within the circuit, resulting in the occlusion or blockage of the circuit. When this happens, dialysis cannot be done. Interventions are required to remove the clot or occlusion so dialysis may be performed. The codes in this section are reported for this type of intervention.

36904   **Percutaneous transluminal mechanical thrombectomy and/or infusion for thrombolysis, dialysis circuit, and method, including all imaging and radiological supervision and interpretation, diagnostic angiography, fluoroscopic guidance, catheter placement(s), and intraprocedural pharmacological thrombolytic injection(s);**

The physician treats the dialysis circuit occlusion with mechanical thrombectomy and/or thrombolysis infusion. The devices used for mechanical thrombectomy include those that fragment the thrombus with or without removal of the clot, as well as those that come into contact with the vessel wall. The dialysis circuit is cannulated to gain access, and 5,000 units of heparin are administered. Angiography is performed to confirm the occluded segment. A hydrophilic wire is passed across the occlusion, followed by passing of the Trellis device over a stiff exchange length wire. The distal and proximal balloons are inflated in the segment on either side of a treatment zone containing infusion to isolate the treatment zone and to sustain the fluid concentration that is infused. One milligram of tissue plasminogen activator (TPA) is infused into the treatment zone. The Turbo Trellis is run at 4,000 rpm for five minutes. After the proximal balloon is deflated, small clots are removed via the integral aspiration port to prevent embolization. Thrombolysis infusion may be performed with a catheter threaded over the wire for pharmaceutical administration directly within the thrombosis. When the procedure is complete, the instruments are removed and pressure is applied over the puncture site to stop the bleeding.

36905   **with transluminal balloon angioplasty, peripheral dialysis segment, including all imaging and radiological supervision and interpretation necessary to perform the angioplasty**

The peripheral dialysis segment is treated with balloon angioplasty. A catheter with a balloon attached is inserted into the segment and fed into the narrowed portion, where its balloon may be inflated several times in order to stretch the diameter to allow a more normal flow of blood through the area.

36906   **with transcatheter placement of intravascular stent(s), peripheral dialysis segment, including all imaging and radiological supervision and interpretation necessary to perform the stenting, and all angioplasty within the peripheral dialysis circuit**

The peripheral dialysis segment is treated with an intravascular stent. A catheter with a stent-transporting tip is threaded over the guidewire into the vessel, and the wire is extracted. The catheter travels to the point where the vessel needs additional support. The compressed stent is passed from the catheter into the vessel, where it deploys, expanding to support the vessel walls. Once the procedure is complete, the catheter is removed and pressure is applied over the puncture site.

Coding Tips

1. For code 36904, the entire dialysis circuit is considered to be one vessel.

2. Code 36904 is reported when either percutaneous mechanical thrombectomy or infusion thrombolysis is used to remove the clot.

3. Removal of an arterial plug is included in code 36904. Do not add 36905 for this element.

4. These codes include access into the circuit and any imaging required. Do not also report 36901.

5. Code 36904 includes all diagnostic imaging, fluoro guidance, catheter placement(s), and any maneuvers and techniques required to remove the thrombus.

6. Code 36905 is not reported in addition to 36904 when angioplasty is performed in the peripheral segment of the circuit. If angioplasty is also performed in the central segment during the encounter, use 36907.

7. Code 36906 is not reported in addition to 36904 when stent placement is performed in the peripheral segment of the circuit. If stent(s) are also placed in the central segment during the encounter, use 36908.

8. Code 36906 includes angioplasty. Do not also report 36905.

9. For open thrombectomy of the dialysis circuit, see codes 36831 and 36833.

10. Although not typically used to access a dialysis circuit, ultrasound guidance may be separately reported with 76937. Refer to the coding guidelines for the required elements before reporting this code.

11. As with any imaging or interventional study, complete and detailed documentation of the procedure should be provided in the physician's procedure note.

12. Conscious sedation is not included in this code. Separately report 99151–99157 per payer policy and coding guidelines. Hospitals may choose to include the costs associated with the service as part of the procedure rather than reporting them separately.

13. Hospitals should separately report contrast media with HCPCS codes Q9965–Q9967. Report these codes per milliliter.

14. Report all applicable supply HCPCS Level II codes. Refer to the HCPCS section for possible codes.

Facility HCPCS Coding

Some applicable codes may include but are not limited to:

C1725	Catheter, transluminal angioplasty, non-laser
C1757	Catheter, thrombectomy/embolectomy
C1769	Guidewire
C1874	Stent, coated/covered, with delivery system
C1875	Stent, coated/covered, without delivery system
C1876	Stent, non-coated/non-covered, with delivery system
C1877	Stent, non-coated/non-covered, without delivery system
C1885	Catheter, transluminal angioplasty, laser
C2623	Catheter, transluminal angioplasty, drug-coated, non-laser
Q9965	LOCM, 100-199 mg/ml iodine concentration, per ml
Q9966	LOCM, 200-299 mg/ml iodine concentration, per ml
Q9967	LOCM, 300-399 mg/ml iodine concentration, per ml

Note: See appendix B for a complete listing of reportable HCPCS Level II codes.

ICD-10-CM Coding

The application of these codes is too broad to adequately present ICD-10-CM diagnosis code links here. Refer to the current ICD-10-CM book.

CCI Edits

36904 01844, 01916, 01924-01926, 01930, 0213T, 0216T, 0228T, 0230T, 11000-11001, 11004-11006, 11042-11047, 12001-12002, 12004-12007, 12011, 12013-12018, 12020-12021, 12031-12032, 12034-12037, 12041-12042, 12044-12047, 12051-12057, 13100-13102, 13120-13122, 13131-13133, 13151-13153, 35201, 35206-35207, 35211, 35216, 35221, 35226, 35231, 35236, 35241, 35246, 35251, 35256, 35261, 35266, 35271, 35276, 35281, 35286, 35800, 35860, 36000, 36002, 36005, 36010, 36011-36012, 36140, 36200, 36261, 36400, 36405-36406, 36410, 36420, 36425, 36430, 36440, 36500, 36591-36593, 36600, 36640, 36800, 36810, 36815, 36821, 36825, 36830, 36832-36833, 36835, 36860-36861, 36901-36903, 37186, 37188, 37211-37214, 43752, 51701-51703, 62320-62327, 64400, 64402, 64405, 64408, 64410, 64413, 64415-64418, 64420-64421, 64425, 64430, 64435, 64445-64450, 64461-64463, 64479-64480, 64483, 64484, 64486-64495, 64505, 64508, 64510, 64517, 64520, 64530, 69990, 75658, 75820, 75822, 75825, 75827, 75893, 76000-76001, 76942, 76998, 77001-77002, 77012, 77021, 92012, 92014, 93000, 93005, 93010, 93040-93042, 93050, 93318, 93355, 94002, 94200, 94250, 94680-94681, 94690, 94770, 95812-95813, 95816, 95819, 95822, 95829, 95955, 96360-96361, 96365-96368, 96372, 96374-96377, 96523, 97597-97598, 97602, 99155-99157, 99211-99215,99217-99223, 99231-99236, 99238-99239, 99241-99245, 99251-99255, 99291-99292, 99304-99310, 99315-99316, 99334-99337, 99347-99350, 99374-99375, 99377-99378, 99446-99449, 99495-99496, G0463, G0471, J0670, J1642, J1644, J2001

36905 01844, 01916, 01924-01926, 01930, 0213T, 0216T, 0228T, 0230T, 11000-11001, 11004-11006, 11042-11047, 12001-12002, 12004-12007, 12011, 12013-12018, 12020-12021, 12031-12032, 12034-12037, 12041-12042, 12044-12047, 12051-12057, 13100-13102, 13120-13122, 13131-13133, 13151-13153, 35201, 35206-35207, 35211, 35216, 35221, 35226, 35231, 35236, 35241, 35246, 35251, 35256, 35261, 35266, 35271, 35276, 35281, 35286, 35800, 35860, 36000, 36002, 36005, 36010-36012, 36140, 36200, 36261, 36400, 36405-36406, 36410, 36420, 36425, 36430, 36440, 36500, 36591-36593, 36600, 36640, 36800, 36810, 36815, 36821, 36825, 36830, 36832, 36833, 36835, 36860-36861, 36901-36904, 37186-37188, 37211-37214, 37246-37247,37248-37249, 43752, 51701-51703, 62320-62327, 64400, 64402, 64405, 64408, 64410, 64413, 64415-64418, 64420-64421, 64425, 64430, 64435, 64445-64450, 64461-64463, 64479-64480, 64483-64484, 64486-64495, 64505, 64508, 64510, 64517, 64520, 64530, 69990, 75658, 75820, 75822, 75825, 75827, 75893, 76000-76001, 76942, 76998, 77001-77002, 77012, 77021, 92012, 92014, 93000, 93005, 93010, 93040, 93041-93042, 93050, 93318, 93355, 94002, 94200, 94250, 94680-94681, 94690, 94770, 95812-95813, 95816, 95819, 95822, 95829, 95955, 96360-96361, 96365-96368, 96372, 96374-96377, 96523, 97597-97598, 97602, 99155-99157, 99211-99215, 99217-99223, 99231-99236, 99238-99239, 99241-99245, 99251-99255, 99291-99292, 99304-99316, 99334-99337, 99347-99350, 99374-99375, 99377-99378, 99446-99449, 99495-99496, G0463, G0471, J0670, J1642, J1644, J2001

36906   01844, 01916, 01924-01926, 01930, 0213T, 0216T, 0228T, 0230T, 11000-11006, 11042-11047, 12001-12007,
12011-12057, 13100-13133, 13151-13153, 33951-33954, 35201-35207, 35211-35286, 35800, 35860, 36000,
36002-36012, 36140, 36200, 36261, 36400-36410, 36420-36430, 36440, 36500, 36591-36593, 36600, 36640,
36800-36815, 36821, 36825-36830, 36832-36833, 36835, 36860-36861, 36901-36905, 37184, 37186-37188,
37211-37214, 37236-37239, 37246-37249, 43752, 51701-51703, 62320-62327, 64400-64410, 64413-64435,
64445-64450, 64461-64463, 64479-64530, 69990, 75658, 75820, 75822, 75825, 75827, 75893, 76000-76001, 76942,
76998, 77001-77002, 77012, 77021, 92012-92014, 93000-93010, 93040-93042, 93050, 93318, 93355, 94002, 94200,
94250, 94680-94690, 94770, 95812-95816, 95819, 95822, 95829, 95955, 96360-96368, 96372, 96374-96377, 96523,
97597-97598, 97602, 99155-99157, 99211-99223, 99231-99255, 99291-99292, 99304-99310, 99315-99316,
99334-99337, 99347-99350, 99374-99375, 99377-99378, 99446-99449, 99495-99496, G0463, G0471, J0670,
J1642-J1644, J2001

Case Example

Procedure:
Dialysis graft thrombolysis with venous angioplasty

Clinical History:
An 81-year-old male with renal failure and a thrombosed dialysis graft. We were requested to declot the graft.

Technique:
The patient was placed on the angiography table with the left upper arm prepped and draped in the usual sterile fashion. 1% lidocaine was used for local anesthesia. A 21 gauge needle was used to **puncture** the **arterial portion of the graft** in an antegrade fashion and a 0.18 wire was then placed. A 4-French dilator was then placed. A 0.035 glidewire was inserted and the dilator was exchanged for a 6-French vascular sheath. A **second** 21-gauge needle was then used to **puncture** the **venous portion** of the dialysis graft near the venous anastomosis in a retrograde fashion. A 0.018 wire was placed followed by a 4-French dilator. A 0.035 glidewire was inserted and the dilator was exchanged for a 5-French **Fogarty balloon catheter.** Holding pressure over the venous and arterial anastomosis, approximately **2 mg of t-PA was slowly infused**. This was allowed to flow for approximately five minutes. A 6 mm **angioplasty balloon** was then introduced via the antegrade directed vascular sheath and the entire length of the **dialysis graft was dilated**. The **venous anastomosis** was then **dilated using** a combination of **the Fogarty** catheter and a 0.35 glidewire. The Fogarty catheter was manipulated across the arterial anastomosis and arterial blood was withdrawn into the graft. A fistulogram was then obtained. The **graft and venous anastomosis** was then **again dilated** to 6 mm. A 7 mm x 4 cm angioplasty balloon was introduced into the graft and the venous anastomosis was dilated a total of two times to 20 atmospheres. A final fistulogram to the level of the right atrium was obtained. The catheter and sheath were removed. The graft puncture sites were closed with 3.0 Vicryl suture. There were no immediate complications.

Medications:
2 mg t-PA and 3,000 units heparin were administered during the procedure for prophylaxis.

Findings:
Initially the patient's left upper arm dialysis graft was completely thrombosed. There is diffuse moderate stenosis to the upper half of the dialysis graft that was dilated initially to 6 mm and then to 7 mm. Additionally, there was a high grade stenosis of the venous anastomosis that was treated initially with a 6 mm balloon with moderate residual stenosis. Following dilatation to 7 mm there was minimal residual stenosis. No other significant stenosis was identified.

Impression:
Successful thrombolysis of left upper arm dialysis graft described above.

CPT/HCPCS Codes Reported:
36905

Other HCPCS Codes Reported:
C1769 x 2, C1757, C1725

Arteriovenous Fistula (Dialysis Circuit) Embolization

Arteriovenous dialysis circuits sometimes develop veins that "steal" the circulation from the circuit. These veins need to be cut off from the circuit for dialysis to be conducted successfully. This is where the interventionalist could use embolization or vessel occlusion.

36909   **Dialysis circuit permanent vascular embolization or occlusion (including main circuit or any accessory veins), endovascular, including all imaging and radiological supervision and interpretation necessary to complete the intervention (List separately in addition to code for primary procedure)**

The physician performs embolization or occlusion of a dialysis circuit (main circuit or any accessory vein) due to complications or to assist in circuit maturity and/or patency. A needle is inserted through the skin and into a blood vessel. A guidewire is threaded through the needle into the vessel. The needle is removed. A catheter is threaded into the vessel, and the wire is extracted. The catheter travels to the appropriate blood vessel, and beads, coils, or another vessel-blocking device is released. The beads or other devices block the vessel. The catheter is removed, and pressure is applied over the puncture site to stop bleeding.

Coding Tips

1. Code 36909 is reported only once per encounter per day.
2. This code is an add-on code. Report it in addition to 36901–36906.
3. Do not use code 37241 to report these services.
4. Use this code to report embolization of the main circuit and/or any accessory vessels.
5. If angioplasty or stent placement of the central segment is also performed, add code 36907 or 36908 as appropriate.
6. When an open procedure is done, refer to 37607.
7. Although not typically used to access a dialysis circuit, ultrasound guidance may be separately reported with 76937. Refer to the coding guidelines for the required elements before reporting this code.
8. As with any imaging or interventional study, complete and detailed documentation of the procedure should be provided in the physician's procedure note.
9. Conscious sedation is not included in this code. Separately report 99151–99157 per payer policy and coding guidelines. Hospitals may choose to include the costs associated with the service as part of the procedure rather than reporting them separately.
10. Hospitals should separately report contrast media with HCPCS codes Q9965–Q9967. Report these codes per milliliter.
11. Report all applicable supply HCPCS Level II codes. Refer to the HCPCS section for possible codes.

Facility HCPCS Coding

Some applicable codes may include but are not limited to:

C1769   Guidewire
C2628   Catheter, occlusion
Q9965   LOCM, 100-199 mg/ml iodine concentration, per ml
Q9966   LOCM, 200-299 mg/ml iodine concentration, per ml
Q9967   LOCM, 300-399 mg/ml iodine concentration, per ml

Note: See appendix B for a complete listing of reportable HCPCS Level II codes.

ICD-10-CM Coding

This is an add-on code. Refer to the corresponding primary procedure code for ICD-10-CM diagnosis code links.

CCI Edits

36909   01916, 01924-01926, 01930, 0213T, 0216T, 0228T, 0230T, 12001-12007, 12011-12057, 13100-13133, 13151-13153, 35201-35207, 35211-35286, 36000, 36002-36012, 36140, 36200, 36261, 36400-36410, 36420-36430, 36440, 36470-36471, 36500, 36591-36592, 36600, 36640, 43752, 51701-51703, 62320-62327, 64400-64410, 64413-64435, 64445-64450, 64461-64463, 64479-64530, 69990, 75658, 75820, 75822, 75825, 75827, 75893, 76000-76001, 76942, 76998, 77001-77002, 77012, 77021, 92012-92014, 93000-93010, 93040-93042, 93318, 94002, 94200, 94250, 94680-94690, 94770, 95812-95816, 95819, 95822, 95829, 95955, 96360-96368, 96372, 96374-96377, 96523, 99155-99157, 99211-99223, 99231-99255, 99291-99292, 99304-99310, 99315-99316, 99334-99337, 99347-99350, 99374-99375, 99377-99378, J0670, J1644, J2001

Case Example

Patient with end-stage renal disease and slowly maturing fistula in the left forearm. Angiogram with possible intervention is requested.

The left upper extremity was prepped and draped. Local anesthesia was applied, and a 21-gauge needle was used to **puncture** the **venous outflow** and directed toward the arterial inflow. A wire was advanced and the needle exchanged for a sheath. A Kumpe catheter was used to select the arterial inflow. **Contrast was injected**, which caused the fistula to occlude due to severe stenosis in the arterial **anastomosis**. Subsequently, a Newton wire was advanced and a 3x40mm balloon dilation catheter inserted to perform **angioplasty of** this area. Repeat angiogram shows still occluded arterial anastomosis. Next a 5x20mm balloon catheter was inserted and **repeat angioplasty** performed. Slight flow improvement was noted with residual stenosis remaining. **Angioplasty** was again **repeated** using a 5x40mm catheter.

Next, the Kumpe catheter was utilized to **select the two larger collaterals arising from the mid fistula**. These were **embolized** using a combination of Nestor and Tornado coils. Repeat angiogram shows improvement of flow through the fistula.

Next, **another small branch was selected** and **embolization** performed. Residual flow through at least three collaterals were noted. At this point, the decision was made to end the procedure due to patient discomfort. The sheaths were removed. Hemostasis was achieved with 2-0 silk purse-string stitches.

Impression:
Small left upper extremity arteriovenous fistula with severe arterial anastomotic stenosis and multiple collaterals. The anastomosis was angioplastied up to 3mm. Residual stenosis noted. Three collaterals were embolized. However, there were at least 3 large collaterals remaining. If this does not work, patient may need repeat fistulogram and further intervention.

CPT/HCPCS Codes Reported:
36902, 36909

Other HCPCS Codes Reported:
C1725, C1769

Chapter 5: Vascular Interventions

Percutaneous Embolization—Other than Cerebral, Head and Neck

Transcatheter embolization is performed with the intent to occlude the blood vessels supplying a previously determined abnormality such as a tumor or aneurysm. Once the blood supply to the abnormality is determined, selective or super-selective catheterization of the feeder vessels is performed and embolic material is injected or placed in each vessel. The most common embolic materials available are gelfoam, coils, glue, balloons, microspheres, and polyvinyl alcohol. Chemo drugs are also used for certain embolization situations. Follow-up angiography performed to determine the success of the therapy is included.

37241   **Vascular embolization or occlusion, inclusive of all radiological supervision and interpretation, intraprocedural roadmapping, and imaging guidance necessary to complete the intervention; venous, other than hemorrhage (eg, congenital or acquired venous malformations, venous and capillary hemangiomas, varices, varicoceles)**

37242   **arterial, other than hemorrhage or tumor (eg, congenital or acquired arterial malformations, arteriovenous malformations, arteriovenous fistulas, aneurysms, pseudoaneurysms)**
Embolization or occlusion of a blood vessel is performed. A needle is inserted through the skin and into a blood vessel. A guidewire is threaded through the needle into the vessel. The needle is removed. A catheter is threaded into the vessel, and the wire is extracted. The catheter travels to the appropriate blood vessel, and beads, coils, or another vessel-blocking device is released. The beads or other devices block the vessel. The catheter is removed, and pressure is applied over the puncture site to stop bleeding.

37243   **for tumors, organ ischemia, or infarction**
Embolization or occlusion of an artery is performed to treat tumors or organ infarction/ischemia. A needle is inserted through the skin and into the artery. A guidewire is threaded through the needle and the needle is removed. A catheter is threaded into the vessel over the guidewire and the wire is extracted. The catheter travels to the appropriate site and beads, coils, or another vessel-blocking device is released. The beads or other device block the artery that supplies the tumor or that portion of the organ with blood. The catheter is removed and pressure is applied over the puncture site to stop bleeding.

37244   **for arterial or venous hemorrhage or lymphatic extravasation**
Embolization or occlusion of a blood vessel is performed to treat hemorrhage. A needle is inserted through the skin and into a blood vessel. A guidewire is threaded through the needle, and the needle is removed. A catheter is threaded into the vessel over the guidewire, and the wire is extracted. The catheter travels to the appropriate site and beads, coils, or another vessel-blocking device is released. The beads or other devices block the vessel. The catheter is removed, and pressure is applied over the puncture site to stop the bleeding.

Coding Tips

1. Transcatheter vascular embolization is reported with comprehensive codes 37241–37244. These codes include radiological guidance and imaging directly related to the intervention procedure.
2. Do not additionally report CPT® code 75894 or 75898.
3. Separately report catheter placement code(s).
4. Separately report diagnostic angiography per guidelines detailed in chapter 2.
5. A stent or stents placed to facilitate deployment of embolization codes are included in the embolization codes and not separately reported.
6. Stent placement for treatment of aneurysm, extravasation, etc., is reported with stent placement codes rather than with embolization codes.
7. Embolization codes are reported only once per each surgical field. If multiple different surgical fields are treated, additional codes may be reported. Append modifier 59, or appropriate X modifier, per payer guidelines.
8. Use code 37241 for embolization procedures performed within the venous system. Exception: hemorrhage (see 37244).
9. Use code 37241 for embolization of arteriovenous fistula outflow vein branches. See chapter 3 for details.
10. Use code 37242 for embolization procedures performed within the arterial system. Exception: hemorrhage (see 37244). AV (arterio-venous) malformation treatment would be reported with this code.
11. Use 37243 for uterine fibroid embolization. For embolization for hemorrhage of uterine arteries, see 37244.
12. Use 37243 for organ embolization such as the kidney for tumor embolization, etc.
13. Use 37244 for embolization treatment of a hemorrhage, gastrointestinal (GI) bleed and bronchial hemoptysis.
14. For embolization of a dialysis circuit, see code 36909.
15. If chemoembolization is performed, report CPT code 96420 in addition to the embolization procedure codes.

Percutaneous Embolization

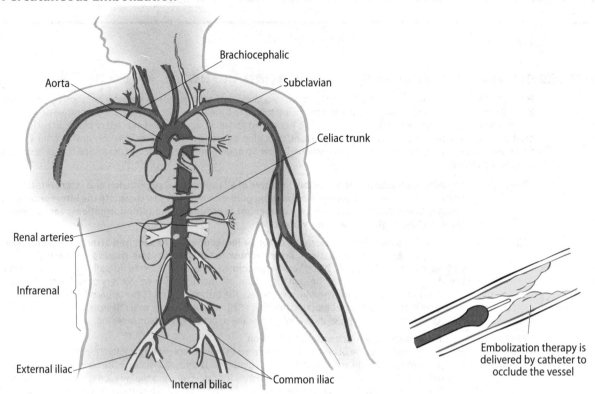

Labels on diagram: Aorta, Brachiocephalic, Subclavian, Celiac trunk, Renal arteries, Infrarenal, External iliac, Internal biliac, Common iliac

Embolization therapy is delivered by catheter to occlude the vessel

16. Conscious sedation is not included in these codes. Separately report 99151–99157 per payer policy and coding guidelines. Hospitals may choose to include the costs associated with the service as part of the procedure rather than reporting them separately.

17. Report all applicable pass-through HCPCS codes. Refer to the HCPCS section for possible codes.

18. Hospitals are requested to continue reporting LOCM separately with HCPCS codes Q9965–Q9967. Report contrast media by milliliter.

19. Physician Reporting: These radiology S&I codes have both a technical and professional component. To report only the professional component, append modifier 26. To report only the technical component, append modifier TC. To report the complete procedure (i.e., both the professional and technical components), submit without a modifier.

Facility HCPCS Coding

Some applicable codes may include but are not limited to:

C1760	Closure device, vascular (implantable/insertable), if used
C1769	Guidewire
C2628	Catheter, occlusion
G0269	Placement of occlusive device into either a venous or arterial access site, post surgical or interventional procedure (e.g., AngioSeal plug, vascular plug), if performed
Q9965	LOCM, 100-199 mg/ml iodine concentration, per ml
Q9966	LOCM, 200-299 mg/ml iodine concentration, per ml
Q9967	LOCM, 300-399 mg/ml iodine concentration, per ml

Note: See appendix B for a complete listing of reportable HCPCS Level II codes.

ICD-10-CM Coding

The application of these codes is too broad to adequately present ICD-10-CM diagnostic code links here. Refer to the current ICD-10-CM book.

CCI Edits

37241   0075T, 01916, 01924-01926, 0213T, 0216T, 0228T, 0230T, 0395T, 12001-12007, 12011-12057, 13100-13133, 13151-13153, 34812-34813, 35201-35206, 35226-35236, 35256-35266, 35286, 36000, 36002, 36005-36010, 36013, 36400-36410, 36420-36430, 36440, 36468, 36470-36479, 36500, 36591-36592, 36600-36640, 36909, 37211-37218, 37221, 37223, 37226-37227, 37230-37231, 37236-37239, 43752, 49185, 51701-51703, 61623, 61635, 61645, 62320-62327, 64400-64410, 64413-64435, 64445-64450, 64461-64463, 64479-64530, 69990, 75600, 75605, 75625, 75630, 75635, 75658, 75705, 75710, 75716, 75726, 75731, 75733, 75736, 75741, 75743, 75746, 75756, 75810, 75820, 75822, 75825, 75827, 75831, 75833, 75840, 75842, 75860, 75870, 75872, 75880, 75885, 75887, 75889, 75891, 75893-75894, 75898, 76000-76001, 76380, 76942, 76970, 76998, 77001-77002, 77012, 77021, 77750, 77778, 92012-92014, 93000-93010, 93040-93042, 93318, 93355, 94002, 94200, 94250, 94680-94690, 94770, 95812-95816, 95819, 95822, 95829, 95955, 96360-96368, 96372, 96374-96377, 99155-99157, 99211-99223, 99231-99255, 99291-99292, 99304-99310, 99315-99316, 99334-99337, 99347-99350, 99374-99375, 99377-99378, 99446-99449, G0463, G0471, J0670, J1642-J1644, J2001

37242   0075T, 01916, 01924-01926, 0213T, 0216T, 0228T, 0230T, 0395T, 12001-12007, 12011-12057, 13100-13133, 13151-13153, 34812-34813, 35201-35206, 35226-35236, 35256-35266, 35286, 36000, 36100, 36120-36140, 36200, 36221-36226, 36251-36254, 36400-36410, 36420-36430, 36440, 36473, 36475-36478, 36500, 36591-36592, 36600-36640, 36909, 37211-37218, 37221, 37223, 37226-37227, 37230-37231, 37236-37241, 43752, 49185, 51701-51703, 61623, 61635, 61645, 62320-62327, 64400-64410, 64413-64435, 64445-64450, 64461-64463, 64479-64530, 69990, 75600, 75605, 75625, 75630, 75635, 75658, 75705, 75710, 75716, 75726, 75731, 75733, 75736, 75741, 75743, 75746, 75756, 75774, 75893-75894, 75898, 76000-76001, 76380, 76942, 76970, 76998, 77001-77002, 77012, 77021, 77750, 77778, 92012-92014, 93000-93010, 93040-93042, 93050, 93318, 93355, 94002, 94200, 94250, 94680-94690, 94770, 95812-95816, 95819, 95822, 95829, 95955, 96360-96368, 96372, 96374-96377, 99155-99157, 99211-99223, 99231-99255, 99291-99292, 99304-99310, 99315-99316, 99334-99337, 99347-99350, 99374-99375, 99377-99378, 99446-99449, G0463, G0471, J0670, J1642-J1644, J2001

37243   0075T, 00840, 00860, 01916, 01924-01926, 0213T, 0216T, 0228T, 0230T, 0395T, 12001-12007, 12011-12057, 13100-13133, 13151-13153, 34812-34813, 35201-35206, 35226-35236, 35256-35266, 35286, 36000, 36100, 36120-36140, 36200, 36221-36226, 36251-36254, 36400-36410, 36420-36430, 36440, 36468, 36470-36473, 36475-36479, 36500, 36591-36592, 36600-36640, 37211-37218, 37221, 37223, 37226-37227, 37230-37231, 37236-37242, 43752, 49185, 51701-51703, 61623, 61635, 61645, 62320-62327, 64400-64410, 64413-64435, 64445-64450, 64461-64463, 64479-64530, 69990, 75600, 75605, 75625, 75630, 75635, 75658, 75705, 75710, 75716, 75726, 75731, 75733, 75736, 75741, 75743, 75746, 75756, 75774, 75893-75894, 75898, 76000-76001, 76380, 76942, 76970, 76998, 77001-77002, 77012, 77021, 77750, 77778, 92012-92014, 93000-93010, 93040-93042, 93050, 93318, 93355, 94002, 94200, 94250, 94680-94690, 94770, 95812-95816, 95819, 95822, 95829, 95955, 96360-96368, 96372, 96374-96377, 99155-99157, 99211-99223, 99231-99255, 99291-99292, 99304-99310, 99315-99316, 99334-99337, 99347-99350, 99374-99375, 99377-99378, 99446-99449, G0463, G0471, J0670, J1642-J1644, J2001

37244   0075T, 01916, 01924-01926, 0213T, 0216T, 0228T, 0230T, 0395T, 12001-12007, 12011-12057, 13100-13133, 13151-13153, 34812-34813, 35201-35206, 35226-35236, 35256-35266, 35286, 36000, 36005-36010, 36013, 36100, 36120-36140, 36200, 36221-36226, 36251-36254, 36400-36410, 36420-36430, 36440, 36468, 36470-36473, 36475-36479, 36500, 36591-36592, 36600-36640, 37211-37218, 37221, 37223, 37226-37227, 37230-37231, 37236-37243, 43752, 49185, 51701-51703, 61623, 61635, 61645, 62320-62327, 64400-64410, 64413-64435, 64445-64450, 64461-64463, 64479-64530, 69990, 75600, 75605, 75625, 75630, 75635, 75658, 75705, 75710, 75716, 75726, 75731, 75733, 75736, 75741, 75743, 75746, 75756, 75774, 75810, 75820, 75822, 75825, 75827, 75831, 75833, 75840, 75842, 75860, 75870, 75872, 75880, 75885, 75887, 75889, 75891, 75893-75894, 75898, 76000-76001, 76380, 76942, 76970, 76998, 77001-77002, 77012, 77021, 77750, 77778, 92012-92014, 93000-93010, 93040-93042, 93050, 93318, 93355, 94002, 94200, 94250, 94680-94690, 94770, 95812-95816, 95819, 95822, 95829, 95955, 96360-96368, 96372, 96374-96377, 99155-99157, 99211-99223, 99231-99255, 99291-99292, 99304-99310, 99315-99316, 99334-99337, 99347-99350, 99374-99375, 99377-99378, 99446-99449, G0463, G0471, J0670, J1642-J1644, J2001

Case Example #1

Pulmonary Arteriogram and Embolization

Patient has a history of multiple arterial venous anomalies. The patient had previous embolizations performed on multiple settings. The patient **returns for embolization of the right middle lobe lesion** seen on CT exam.

After informed consent was obtained, a **right common femoral venous puncture** was made. Using an H1 catheter, a Glidewire access into the pulmonary artery was achieved. This was exchanged for a 6-French 90 cm long **sheath placed in the main pulmonary artery**. Contrast **injections** were performed through a 100 cm pigtail catheter **placed within the left pulmonary artery**. This revealed no obvious significant arteriovenous fistulas. Using a Glidewire, **access into the right pulmonary artery contrast was injected** and **angiography** was performed of the **right pulmonary artery system**. This revealed an arterial venous anomaly within the right middle lobe region. This arteriovenous fistula represents the finding on CT exam. The rest of the right lung showed one arterial-to-arterial anastomotic vascular lesion, but there was no venous flow accompanying this lesion. The other areas previously embolized remain closed. **We proceeded with embolization.**

The H1 catheter was **placed into the feeding vessel of the right mid-lung arteriovenous fistula**. Demonstration of the fistula was easily performed with contrast injection visualizing the anastomosis and draining vein across the pulmonary parenchyma to the left atrium. Four 7 mm x 4 cm **tornado coils were deployed** through the H1 catheter into the **feeding pulmonary artery to the AV fistula**. **Post-embolization imaging** demonstrates complete occlusion of the AV fistula within the right middle lobe region. Coil deployment was performed utilizing an LLT wire in the H1 catheter with no side holes.

Impression:

Successful coil embolization of the right middle lobe arteriovenous fistula within the right lung.

CPT/HCPCS Codes Reported:

75743, 36014, 36015-XS, 37241

Case Example #2

Bronchial Arteriogram with Embolization

Indication: Patient presents with **bleeding hemoptysis** from a large mass in the **right lobe**, which is cavitating. The patient is a nonsurgical candidate.

Procedure:

A **right femoral approach** was utilized. Using micropuncture technique, a needle, guidewire, and originally a 5-French pigtail catheter was **placed in the arch for arteriography**. This was then **retracted** to the thoracic aorta for **thoracic arteriography**. The previous CTA had noted **two arteries off the right side of the medial aspect of the aorta. Each of these was catheterized selectively** using Michelson catheters and Simmons-1 and Simmons-2 catheters and **imaging obtained**. The **decision** was **made to proceed** with **embolization**. A 5-French long sheath was placed into the descending thoracic aorta. The **right bronchial arteries were entered with microcatheter technique. Embolization was performed** with 3mm X 2mm microcoils. **Multiple branches were embolized**. The spinal artery was not seen, and no particle embolizations were performed. Final imaging revealed there was significant decrease of blood flow to the area of the right upper lobe mass with no significant residual blood flow. Finally, a **Headhunter catheter was placed selectively into the right subclavian artery** where **injection** revealed no evidence of bleeding from the internal mammary artery, the subclavian artery, or the axillary artery. The catheter and sheath were removed and hemostasis achieved.

Impression:

Successful embolization of bronchial arteries on the right for hemoptysis in a patient with a large cavitating lung carcinoma.

CPT/HCPCS Codes Reported:

36221, 75726, 75726-XS, 36215x3, 75774, 37244

Note: Add modifier XS to each 75726 coded after the first.

Case Example #3

Uterine Fibroid Embolization (UFE)

Indication: Uterine fibroids

Via **right femoral approach**, a guidewire was advanced into the abdominal aorta and a sheath was placed. A 5-French pigtail **catheter** was **advanced** and **placed in the distal abdominal aorta** and **AP pelvic angiogram** obtained. The pigtail was exchanged for a Cobra II **catheter** and **positioned into the left internal iliac artery**. AP and bilateral oblique **pelvic angiograms** were obtained. Using road-map technique, the Cobra catheter was used to **select the left uterine artery**, and an AP digitally subtracted **angiogram** was **obtained**. A tracker **catheter** was **positioned** in the **descending portion of the left uterine artery**. The left uterine artery was then **embolized** with approximately one-half of one vial of 500–700 micron embole spheres. A **final angiogram** was **obtained**. A Waltman's loop was then formed, and the Cobra catheter was used to **select the right uterine artery**, and an AP angiogram was obtained. A tracker catheter was positioned in the distal portion of the right uterine artery, and the **right uterine artery was embolized** with approximately 1.5 vials of 500–700 micron embole spheres. A **final angiogram was obtained**. The catheter and sheath were removed, and hemostasis was achieved with manual compression. A total of 165 cc of Isovue 300 was used during the procedure.

CPT/HCPCS Codes Reported:

37243, 36247-50

Other HCPCS Codes Reported:

Q9967 x 165, C1769

Transcatheter Thrombolysis Other Than Intracranial

Transcatheter thrombolysis involves placing the catheter into an occluded vessel and slowly injecting a de-clotting agent. Do not confuse thrombolytic agents (e.g., tPA-tissue plasminogen activator, alteplase, streptokinase, reteplase, abbokinase, anistreplase) with anti-coagulants (e.g., heparin, coumadin). Thrombolysis requires a thrombolytic agent. Anti-coagulants do not meet this requirement. Follow-up angiography is frequently performed during the course of the therapy.

37211   **Transcatheter therapy, arterial infusion for thrombolysis other than coronary or intracranial, any method, including radiological supervision and interpretation, initial treatment day**

37212   **Transcatheter therapy, venous infusion for thrombolysis, any method, including radiological supervision and interpretation, initial treatment day**

37213   **Transcatheter therapy, arterial or venous infusion for thrombolysis other than coronary, any method, including radiological supervision and interpretation, continued treatment on subsequent day during course of thrombolytic therapy, including follow-up catheter contrast injection, position change or exchange, when performed**

37214   **cessation of thrombolysis including removal of catheter and vessel closure by any method**

Transcatheter thrombolysis infusion is most commonly used to treat symptomatic inferior vena cava thrombosis that is responding poorly to the routine anticoagulation regimen or symptomatic iliofemoral or femoropopliteal deep vein thrombosis (DVT) in patients with a low risk of bleeding. A diagnostic arteriography or venography is performed to pinpoint the extent of the thrombosis. The physician places a needle into the blood vessel. A guidewire is threaded through the needle to the site of the clot using fluoroscopic guidance, and the needle is removed. An infusion catheter is threaded to the site, and the wire is extracted. A thrombolytic pharmaceutical is administered directly to the thrombosis. During the infusion, the patient is on bed rest with frequent monitoring. Once the thrombosis has dissipated satisfactorily, the infusion is stopped and the catheter removed. Pressure is applied over the puncture site to stop the bleeding. Report 37211 for the first day of arterial transcatheter therapy; 37212 for the first day of venous transcatheter therapy; 37213 for each subsequent day of arterial or venous therapy, including follow-up catheter contrast injection, position change, or exchange, if applicable; and 37214 for the last day the thrombolysis is administered, including removal of the catheter and closure of the access site. These codes are not for use when thrombolysis is performed on coronary or intracranial arteries.

CPT Coding for Thrombolysis Procedures

Service Performed	Code(s) Reported
Thrombolysis, transcatheter, arterial, initial day	37211
Thrombolysis, transcatheter, venous, initial day	37212
Thrombolysis, transcatheter, subsequent day, arterial or venous	37213
Catheter exchange	Included in 37213
Catheter removal at treatment end	37214

Coding Tips

1. Transcatheter thrombolysis is reported with comprehensive codes 37211–37214. Codes are reported per treatment day. Report 37211 or 37212 for the initial day of therapy. Use 37213 per subsequent day of therapy. Use 37214 for the final day of therapy. If therapy is completed in a single day, report only 37211 or 37212.
2. Code separately for each selective catheter placement.
3. Diagnostic angiography is separately reported.
4. Other interventions, such as angioplasty, performed during or after thrombolysis are reported separately.
5. These codes are not intended for bolus injections of a thrombolytic drug. They are intended for therapy performed over time.
6. For intracranial infusion for thrombolysis, see code 61645.
7. For a bilateral procedure performed from two separate accesses, add modifier 50.
8. Conscious sedation is not included in these codes. Separately report 99151–99157 per payer policy and coding guidelines. Hospitals may choose to include the costs associated with the service as part of the procedure rather than reporting them separately.
9. Report all applicable pass-through HCPCS codes. Refer to the HCPCS section for possible codes. Device edits apply to some of the codes in this section. Refer to appendixes E and F for the applicable edits.
10. Hospitals are requested to continue reporting LOCM separately with HCPCS codes Q9965–Q9967. Report contrast media by milliliter.

11. Physician Reporting: These codes have both a technical and professional component. To report only the professional component, append modifier 26. To report only the technical component, append modifier TC. To report the complete procedure (i.e., both the professional and technical components), submit without a modifier.

Facility HCPCS Coding

Some applicable codes may include but are not limited to:

C1751 Catheter, infusion, inserted peripherally, centrally or midline (other than hemodialysis)

C1757 Catheter, thrombectomy; embolectomy

C1769 Guidewire

C1760 Closure device, vascular (implantable/insertable), if used

G0269 Placement of occlusive device into either a venous or arterial access site, post surgical or interventional procedure (e.g., AngioSeal plug, vascular plug), if performed

Q9965 LOCM, 100-199 mg/ml iodine concentration, per ml

Q9966 LOCM, 200-299 mg/ml iodine concentration, per ml

Q9967 LOCM, 300-399 mg/ml iodine concentration, per ml

Note: See appendix B for a complete listing of reportable HCPCS Level II codes.

ICD-10-CM Coding

The application of these codes is too broad to adequately present ICD-10-CM diagnosis code links here. Refer to the current ICD-10-CM book.

CCI Edits

37211 0075T, 01916, 01924-01926, 01930-01933, 0213T, 0216T, 0228T, 0230T, 12001-12007, 12011-12057, 13100-13133, 13151-13153, 34812-34813, 35201-35206, 35226-35236, 35256-35266, 35286, 36000, 36005, 36221-36227, 36400-36410, 36420-36430, 36440, 36500, 36591-36593, 36600-36640, 37213-37214, 37217-37218, 43752, 51701-51703, 62320-62327, 64400-64410, 64413-64435, 64445-64450, 64461-64463, 64479-64530, 69990, 75600, 75605, 75625, 75630, 75635, 75658, 75705, 75710, 75716, 75726, 75731, 75733, 75736, 75741, 75743, 75746, 75756, 75774, 75809-75810, 75820, 75822, 75825, 75827, 75831, 75833, 75840, 75842, 75860, 75870, 75872, 75880, 75885, 75887, 75889, 75891, 75893, 75894, 75898, 76000-76001, 76380, 76942, 76970, 76998, 77001-77002, 77012, 77021, 92012-92014, 92977, 93000-93010, 93040-93042, 93050, 93318, 93355, 94002, 94200, 94250, 94680-94690, 94770, 95812-95816, 95819, 95822, 95829, 95955, 96360-96368, 96372, 96374-96377, 99155-99157, 99201-99255, 99291-99292, 99304-99310, 99315-99318, 99324-99328, 99334-99350, 99354-99360, 99374-99375, 99377-99378, 99415-99416, 99446-99449, 99460-99463, 99495-99497, G0463, G0471, G0505

37212 0075T, 01916, 01924-01926, 01930-01933, 0213T, 0216T, 0228T, 0230T, 12001-12007, 12011-12057, 13100-13133, 13151-13153, 34812-34813, 35201-35206, 35226-35236, 35256-35266, 35286, 36000, 36005, 36221-36227, 36400-36410, 36420-36430, 36440, 36500, 36591-36593, 36600-36640, 37213-37214, 37217-37218, 43752, 51701-51703, 62320-62327, 64400-64410, 64413-64435, 64445-64450, 64461-64463, 64479-64530, 69990, 75600, 75605, 75625, 75630, 75635, 75658, 75705, 75710, 75716, 75726, 75731, 75733, 75736, 75741, 75743, 75746, 75756, 75774, 75809-75810, 75820, 75822, 75825, 75827, 75831, 75833, 75840, 75842, 75860, 75870, 75872, 75880, 75885, 75887, 75889, 75891, 75893, 75894, 75898, 76000-76001, 76380, 76942, 76970, 76998, 77001-77002, 77012, 77021, 92012-92014, 92977, 93000-93010, 93040-93042, 93318, 93355, 94002, 94200, 94250, 94680-94690, 94770, 95812-95816, 95819, 95822, 95829, 95955, 96360-96368, 96372, 96374-96377, 99155-99157, 99201-99255, 99291-99292, 99304-99310, 99315-99318, 99324-99328, 99334-99350, 99354-99360, 99374-99375, 99377-99378, 99415-99416, 99446-99449, 99460-99463, 99495-99497, G0463, G0471, G0505

37213 0075T, 01916, 01924-01926, 01930-01933, 0213T, 0216T, 0228T, 0230T, 12001-12007, 12011-12057, 13100-13133, 13151-13153, 34812-34813, 35201-35206, 35226-35236, 35256-35266, 35286, 36000, 36005, 36221-36227, 36400-36410, 36420-36430, 36440, 36500, 36591-36593, 36600-36640, 37214, 37217-37218, 43752, 51701-51703, 62320-62327, 64400-64410, 64413-64435, 64445-64450, 64461-64463, 64479-64530, 69990, 75600, 75605, 75625, 75630, 75635, 75658, 75705, 75710, 75716, 75726, 75731, 75733, 75736, 75741, 75743, 75746, 75756, 75774, 75809-75810, 75820, 75822, 75825, 75827, 75831, 75833, 75840, 75842, 75860, 75870, 75872, 75880, 75885, 75887, 75889, 75891, 75893, 75894, 75898, 76000-76001, 76380, 76942, 76970, 76998, 77001-77002, 77012, 77021, 92012-92014, 92977, 93000-93010, 93040-93042, 93050, 93318, 93355, 94002, 94200, 94250, 94680-94690, 94770, 95812-95816, 95819, 95822, 95829, 95955, 96360-96368, 96372, 96374-96377, 99155-99157, 99201-99255, 99291-99292, 99304-99310, 99315-99318, 99324-99328, 99334-99350, 99354-99360, 99374-99375, 99377-99378, 99415-99416, 99446-99449, 99460-99463, 99495-99497, G0463, G0471, G0505

37214   0075T, 01916, 01924-01926, 01930-01933, 0213T, 0216T, 0228T, 0230T, 11000-11006, 11042-11047, 12001-12007, 12011-12057, 13100-13133, 13151-13153, 34812-34813, 35201-35206, 35226-35236, 35256-35266, 35286, 36000, 36005, 36221-36227, 36400-36410, 36420-36430, 36440, 36500, 36591-36593, 36600-36640, 37217-37218, 43752, 51701-51703, 62320-62327, 64400-64410, 64413-64435, 64445-64450, 64461-64463, 64479-64530, 69990, 75600, 75605, 75625, 75630, 75635, 75658, 75705, 75710, 75716, 75726, 75731, 75733, 75736, 75741, 75743, 75746, 75756, 75774, 75809-75810, 75820, 75822, 75825, 75827, 75831, 75833, 75840, 75842, 75860, 75870, 75872, 75880, 75885, 75887, 75889, 75891, 75893, 75894, 75898, 76000-76001, 76380, 76942, 76970, 76998, 77001-77002, 77012, 77021, 92012-92014, 92977, 93000-93010, 93040-93042, 93050, 93318, 93355, 94002, 94200, 94250, 94680-94690, 94770, 95812-95816, 95819, 95822, 95829, 95955, 96360-96368, 96372, 96374-96377, 97597-97598, 97602, 99155-99157, 99201-99255, 99291-99292, 99304-99310, 99315-99318, 99324-99328, 99334-99350, 99354-99360, 99374-99375, 99377-99378, 99415-99416, 99446-99449, 99460-99463, 99495-99497, G0463, G0471, G0505

Case Example

The patient was brought into the angiography suite and the skin site over the right femoral vessels was prepared with Betadine scrub. The skin and deeper tissues were anesthetized with 8 mL 1 percent aqueous lidocaine and the **right common femoral artery punctured** with a 21-gauge needle. Utilizing Seldinger technique, a 0.018 guidewire and 5-French catheter were introduced. Exchange was then made over a 0.035 Glidewire and a 5-French Omniflush **catheter** was introduced and **positioned at the level of the hemidiaphragms**. The **abdominal aortogram was performed** in the AP projection. The **catheter** was then **withdrawn to the aortic bifurcation** and bolus chase **arteriography** was obtained **of both lower extremities** to the feet. **Multiple emboli were identified within both lower extremity vessels**.

Thrombolysis therapy was discussed with the patient's vascular surgeon and **thrombolysis was elected**. Exchange was then made over a 0.035 Glidewire and an 8-French hemostatic sheath was introduced into the right common femoral artery. Through this sheath, a 5.5-French Balkan sheath was introduced and advanced over the aortic bifurcation and down to the left common femoral artery. Through this Balkan sheath, a 5-French Fountain catheter was introduced over the Glidewire and advanced down the left superficial femoral artery to the left popliteal artery with the catheter tip extending into the left posterior tibial artery. **Tissue plasminogen activator thrombolysis infusion was initiated with** direct infusion into the clotted arterial segment at the left popliteal artery and at the left distal common femoral artery. Indirect infusion at the right common femoral artery was performed with the right common femoral artery sheath. Low-dose intravenous heparin infusion was also initiated at this time.

A total of 100 mL Isovue-300 contrast material was injected intravascularly for this procedure. 1 mg Versed and 100 mcg Fentanyl were injected intravenously for sedation.

Findings:
The **abdominal aortogram** was normal. Both renal arteries are well visualized and appear normal. The superior mesenteric artery appears normal as visualized. The common and external iliac arteries are normal bilaterally. The **right common femoral artery and right** profundus femoris **artery appear normal**. Right superficial femoral artery is entirely normal. The popliteal artery demonstrates a distal intraluminal filling defect beginning below the knee joint line and extending into the proximal anterior tibial artery and into the tibioperoneal trunk. This filling defect is noted to be mobile during the time of the examination and is typical for emboli lodged within the distal popliteal artery and proximal trifurcation vessels. A segmental occlusion is present at the mid and distal right posterior tibial artery, probably peripheral emboli, as well as a short-segment occlusion of the distal anterior tibial artery, likely related to the distal emboli.

Left lower extremity arteriogram demonstrates an embolus with a saddle configuration extending from the profundus femoris artery into the proximal left superficial femoral artery. This embolus is nearly occlusive in this position. The left superficial femoral artery is entirely patent. The left popliteal artery demonstrates an occlusive embolus beginning at the position 3 cm above the joint line. There is distal reconstitution of the anterior tibial artery and posterior tibial artery from collateral vessels. This distal reconstitution occurs at a position approximately 14 cm below the knee joint line.

Impression:
Evidence of embolic disease involving both lower extremities with occlusive embolus in the right popliteal artery, as well as near occlusive embolus in the left distal common femoral artery, with occlusive embolus noted in the left distal popliteal artery. **Thrombolysis infusion was initiated** after identification of these multiple emboli.

CPT/HCPCS Codes Reported:
36247, 75716, 75625, 37211

Other HCPCS Codes Reported:
Q9967 x 100, C1769 x 2, C1894, C1751

Percutaneous Thrombectomy

These CPT codes describe the procedure of removing a thrombus from within a vessel. Mechanical thrombectomy is performed using special transcatheter devices which mechanically break up or remove a thrombus or clot from the inside of a vessel. Mechanical thrombectomy may be performed in addition to pharmacological thrombolysis described in another section. here are codes available to report mechanical thrombectomy when it is the planned primary procedure performed and there are codes to report mechanical thrombectomy when performed as an unplanned adjunctive procedure to another intervention such as angioplasty. Separate codes are available for arterial versus venous vessel intervention.

37184   **Primary percutaneous transluminal mechanical thrombectomy, noncoronary, non-intracranial, arterial or arterial bypass graft, including fluoroscopic guidance and intraprocedural pharmacological thrombolytic injection(s); initial vessel**

37185   **second and all subsequent vessel(s) within the same vascular family (List separately in addition to code for primary mechanical thrombectomy procedure)**

The physician treats an acute noncoronary arterial occlusion with a combination of thrombolytic drugs and percutaneous mechanical thrombectomy. The devices used for mechanical thrombectomy include those that fragment the thrombus with or without removal of the clot, as well as those that come into contact with the wall of the vessel. For the procedure using the Trellis device, the artery is cannulated to gain access and 5,000 units of heparin are administered. Angiography is performed to confirm the occluded arteries. A hydrophilic wire is passed across the occlusion, followed by passing of the Trellis device over a stiff exchange length wire. The distal and proximal balloons are inflated in the artery on either side of a treatment zone containing infusion to isolate the treatment zone and to sustain the fluid concentration that is infused. One milligram of tissue plasminogen activator (TPA) is infused into the treatment zone. The Turbo Trellis is then run at 4,000 rpm for five minutes. After the proximal balloon is deflated, small clots are removed via the integral aspiration port to prevent embolization. Fluoroscopic guidance services and injections administered during the course of the procedure are included in the service. Separately reportable procedures include other percutaneous interventions such as stent placement and diagnostic studies. Report 37184 for the first vessel and 37185 for the second and subsequent vessels in the same vascular family.

37186   **Secondary percutaneous transluminal thrombectomy (eg, nonprimary mechanical, snare basket, suction technique), noncoronary, non-intracranial, arterial or arterial bypass graft, including fluoroscopic guidance and intraprocedural pharmacological thrombolytic injections, provided in conjunction with another percutaneous intervention other than primary mechanical thrombectomy (List separately in addition to code for primary procedure)**

The physician performs a secondary thrombectomy of a noncoronary arterial occlusion. Prior to or after a percutaneous intervention is performed, such as by balloon angioplasty or placement of a stent, the transcatheter removal of small sections of the thrombus or embolism is performed using suction, a snare basket, or a mechanical thrombectomy device under fluoroscopic guidance. Thrombolytic injections may also be used during the procedure.

37187   **Percutaneous transluminal mechanical thrombectomy, vein(s), including intraprocedural pharmacological thrombolytic injections and fluoroscopic guidance**

37188   **repeat treatment on subsequent day during course of thrombolytic therapy**

The physician performs a percutaneous transluminal mechanical venous thrombectomy. A catheter sheath is inserted through a small incision in the vein, most commonly a groin incision in the femoral vein or an incision below the knee in the popliteal vein. Contrast is injected through the sheath and a separately reportable venography is performed to visualize the area of the vein being treated. Fluoroscopic guidance may be used. A guidewire is inserted through the sheath and advanced past the clot. A catheter is passed over the wire to the blocked area. A device at the tip of the catheter, a mechanical tool or a high-velocity liquid jet, is used to break up the clot. A thrombolytic agent may be injected. When the procedure is completed, all instruments are removed and a compression bandage is applied. Report 37187 for the initial treatment. Report 37188 for repeat treatment on a subsequent day during the course of thrombolytic therapy.

CPT Coding for Percutaneous Thrombectomy Procedures

Service Performed	Surgical Component	Radiology S&I Component
Arterial mechanical thrombectomy of an initial vessel	**37184**	none
Arterial mechanical thrombectomy of an subsequent vessel	**37185**	none
Arterial mechanical thrombectomy of an secondary vessel	**37186**	none
Venous mechanical thrombectomy	**37187**	none
Subsequent venous mechanical thrombectomy	**37188**	none

Coding Tips

1. There are no corresponding radiologic supervision and interpretation codes for these thrombectomy procedures. Radiologic supervision and interpretation is included in codes 37184–37188. All other imaging is not included and should be reported separately.

2. Report CPT 37184 for each vascular family treated. Report 37185 for each subsequent vessel within the same vascular family. Report these codes when mechanical thrombectomy is the primary planned procedure.

3. Report 37186 when thrombectomy is performed as a result of complication from another intervention. CPT code 37186 is not reported in addition to 37184 and 37185.

4. CPT codes 37184–37188 include fluoroscopy. Do not separately report 76000 or 76001.

5. Report catheter placement codes in addition to the thrombectomy codes.

6. Separately report diagnostic angiography or diagnostic venography.

7. Separately report other transcatheter interventions performed on the same vessel such as angioplasty or stent placement.

8. Thrombolytics injected during mechanical thrombectomy are not separately reported. However, if thrombolytic infusion is required subsequently to mechanical thrombectomy to further treatment success, it is separately reported.

9. For mechanical thrombectomy of a dialysis circuit, see codes 36904–36906. Refer to the AV intervention section of chapter 3 for more information.

10. For coronary mechanical thrombectomy, CPT code 92973 is reported. Refer to the Cardiac Interventional section of chapter 10 for more information.

11. Report CPT code 37187 for venous mechanical thrombectomy. This code is used to report venous thrombectomy performed either as a stand alone procedure or in addition to another percutaneous venous interventional procedure.

12. Report CPT code 37188 for repeat venous mechanical thrombectomy during the course of therapy.

13. Report all applicable HCPCS Level II codes. Refer to the HCPCS section for possible codes. Device edits apply to some of the codes in this section. Refer to appendixes E and F for the applicable edits.

14. Conscious sedation is not included in these codes. Separately report 99151–99157 per payer policy and coding guidelines. Hospitals may choose to include the costs associated with the service as part of the procedure rather than reporting them separately.

15. Hospitals are requested to continue reporting LOCM separately with HCPCS codes Q9965–Q9967. Report contrast media by milliliter.

16. Physician Reporting: These codes have both a technical and a professional component. To report only the professional component, append modifier 26. To report only the technical component, append modifier TC. To report the complete procedure (i.e., both the professional and technical components), submit without a modifier.

Facility HCPCS Coding

C1757	Catheter thrombectomy/embolectomy
Q9965	LOCM, 100-199 mg/ml iodine concentration, per ml
Q9966	LOCM, 200-299 mg/ml iodine concentration, per ml
Q9967	LOCM, 300-399 mg/ml iodine concentration, per ml

Note: See appendix B for a complete listing of reportable HCPCS Level II supply codes.

ICD-10-CM Coding

The application of these codes is too broad to adequately present ICD-10-CM diagnosis code links here. Refer to the current ICD-10-CM book.

CCI Edits

37184 01924-01926, 0213T, 0216T, 0228T, 0230T, 11000-11006, 11042-11047, 12001-12007, 12011-12057, 13100-13133, 13151-13153, 35201-35206, 35226-35236, 35256-35266, 35286, 36000, 36400-36410, 36420-36430, 36440, 36591-36592, 36600, 36640, 36860-36861, 36904-36905, 37186, 37211-37214, 43752, 51701-51703, 61645, 61651, 62320-62327, 64400-64410, 64413-64435, 64445-64450, 64461-64463, 64479-64530, 69990, 75600, 75605, 75625, 75630, 75635, 75658, 75705, 75710, 75716, 75726, 75731, 75733, 75736, 75741, 75743, 75746, 75756, 75774, 76000-76001, 77001-77002, 92012-92014, 93000-93010, 93040-93042, 93050, 93318, 93355, 94002, 94200, 94250, 94680-94690, 94770, 95812-95816, 95819, 95822, 95829, 95955, 96360-96368, 96372, 96374-96377, 97597-97598, 97602, 99155-99157, 99211-99223, 99231-99255, 99291-99292, 99304-99310, 99315-99316, 99334-99337, 99347-99350, 99374-99375, 99377-99378, 99446-99449, 99495-99496, G0463, G0471

37185 0213T, 0216T, 11000-11006, 11042-11047, 36000, 36410, 36591-36592, 43752, 61645-61650, 62324-62327, 64415-64417, 64450, 64486-64490, 64493, 69990, 76000, 77001-77002, 93000-93010, 93040-93042, 93050, 94770, 96360, 96365, 96372, 96374-96377, 97597-97598, 97602, 99155-99157

37186 01924-01926, 0213T, 0216T, 11000-11006, 11042-11047, 35201-35206, 35226-35236, 35256-35266, 35286, 36000, 36410, 36591-36592, 37211-37214, 43752, 61645-61651, 62324-62327, 64415-64417, 64450, 64486-64490, 64493, 69990, 76000-76001, 77001-77002, 93000-93010, 93040-93042, 93050, 94770, 96360, 96365, 96372, 96374-96377, 97597-97598, 97602, 99155-99157

37187 01930-01933, 0213T, 0216T, 0228T, 0230T, 11000-11006, 11042-11047, 12001-12007, 12011-12057, 13100-13133, 13151-13153, 35201-35206, 35226-35236, 35256-35266, 35286, 36000, 36400-36410, 36420-36430, 36440, 36591-36592, 36600, 36640, 36860-36861, 36904, 37211-37214, 43752, 51701-51703, 61645, 62320-62327, 64400-64410, 64413-64435, 64445-64450, 64461-64463, 64479-64530, 69990, 75810, 75820, 75822, 75825, 75827, 75831, 75833, 75840, 75842, 75860, 75870, 75872, 75880, 75885, 75887, 75889, 75891, 76000-76001, 77001-77002, 92012-92014, 93000-93010, 93040-93042, 93318, 93355, 94002, 94200, 94250, 94680-94690, 94770, 95812-95816, 95819, 95822, 95829, 95955, 96360-96368, 96372, 96374-96377, 97597-97598, 97602, 99155-99157, 99211-99223, 99231-99255, 99291-99292, 99304-99310, 99315-99316, 99334-99337, 99347-99350, 99374-99375, 99377-99378, 99446-99449, 99495-99496, G0463, G0471

37188 01930-01933, 0213T, 0216T, 0228T, 0230T, 11000-11006, 11042-11047, 12001-12007, 12011-12057, 13100-13133, 13151-13153, 35201-35206, 35226-35236, 35256-35266, 35286, 36000, 36400-36410, 36420-36430, 36440, 36591-36592, 36600, 36640, 36860-36861, 37211-37214, 43752, 51701-51703, 61645, 62320-62327, 64400-64410, 64413-64435, 64445-64450, 64461-64463, 64479-64530, 69990, 75810, 75820, 75822, 75825, 75827, 75831, 75833, 75840, 75842, 75860, 75870, 75872, 75880, 75885, 75887, 75889, 75891, 76000-76001, 77001-77002, 92012-92014, 93000-93010, 93040-93042, 93318, 93355, 94002, 94200, 94250, 94680-94690, 94770, 95812-95816, 95819, 95822, 95829, 95955, 96360-96368, 96372, 96374-96377, 97597-97598, 97602, 99155-99157, 99211-99223, 99231-99255, 99291-99292, 99304-99310, 99315-99316, 99334-99337, 99347-99350, 99374-99375, 99377-99378, 99446-99449, 99495-99496, G0463, G0471

Case Example

Procedure:
Selective right iliac angiography with right superficial femoral angiography; Angiojet thrombectomy of right popliteal, right tibioperoneal trunk and right posterior tibial arteries

Reason for exam:
Ischemic disease

History:
The patient is an 86-year-old female with known peripheral vascular disease with previous laser atherectomy and stenting for dissection of the right popliteal artery. She has recently presented with an acutely painful ischemic right lower extremity. She has improved with heparin but still has absent palpable pulses distally.

Procedure:
The patient was pre-medicated and brought to the IR lab where both groins were prepped and draped in typical sterile fashion. A 6-French **sheath** was **placed** in the **left femoral artery.** A pigtail catheter was used to **selectively engage the right external iliac. Unilateral extremity angiogram** was obtained with runoff to the foot. Images revealed **total occlusion of the right popliteal artery** at the level of the knee well above the previously placed stent. After a 0.035 wire was used to exchange the pigtail for a 45 cm Pinnacle destination sheath, ACT was checked and found to be sub-therapeutic and an additional 3000 units of heparin was administered. The area of total occlusion was easily crossed with an Ironman wire and **Angiojet** catheter was then placed at the area of total occlusion and **thrombectomy performed distally into the peroneal.** Repeat angiograms revealed an excellent result with total resolution of the thrombus of the popliteal artery. The stent was widely patent with a very smooth 50% in-stent stenosis. There was still considerable thrombus in the tibioperoneal trunk and into the posterior tibial artery on the right. The Ironman wire was then **redirected into the posterior tibial artery** and another Angiojet catheter run made with **thrombectomy performed** in both antegrade and retrograde fashion. Follow-up angiograms revealed much improved flow in the tibioperoneal trunk. There was some dissection of distal disease in the posterior tibial artery, but two vessel flow was present to the foot. The long Pinnacle Destination sheath was exchanged over a 0.035 wire for a short 6-French sheath and she was sent to the nursing unit to be maintained on full dose heparin treating her distal disease. No complications occurred.

Impression:
Peripheral vascular disease with total occlusion of the right popliteal artery.

Successful Angiojet thrombectomy with removal of extensive thrombus in the **popliteal artery** well **into the tibioperoneal trunk and posterior tibial artery.** Distal disease is present just above the foot, but patent three-vessel flow is present into the foot.

CPT/HCPCS Codes Reported:
36247, 75710, 37184, 37185

Other HCPCS Codes Reported:
C1757, C1769, C1894

Percutaneous Vascular Filter Placement, Repositioning, and Removal

Vascular filters are placed in the inferior vena cava (IVC) in patients at risk of pulmonary embolism from known deep vein thrombosis. In the interventional radiology area, these filters are placed via percutaneous transcatheter approach. Special catheters containing a pre-loaded filter are inserted into the IVC via femoral vein or internal jugular approach and the filter is deployed. The filter grips the walls of the vena cava and is designed to "catch" clots migrating from the lower extremities. Filters may be temporary or permanent.

37191   **Insertion of intravascular vena cava filter, endovascular approach including vascular access, vessel selection, and radiological supervision and interpretation, intraprocedural roadmapping, and imaging guidance (ultrasound and fluoroscopy), when performed**

37192   **Repositioning of intravascular vena cava filter, endovascular approach including vascular access, vessel selection, and radiological supervision and interpretation, intraprocedural roadmapping, and imaging guidance (ultrasound and fluoroscopy), when performed**

37193   **Retrieval of intravascular vena cava filter, endovascular approach including vascular access, vessel selection, and radiological supervision and interpretation, intraprocedural roadmapping, and imaging guidance (ultrasound and fluoroscopy), when performed**

A filter is placed into the inferior vena cava percutaneously, usually through the right internal jugular vein. Fluoroscopy is used to monitor and guide the process. An incision is made just above the clavicle and then another small incision is made into the vein once it is identified. A catheter loaded with the filter is inserted into the vein and threaded through until it reaches the inferior vena cava. The filter is released from the catheter and opens to fill the diameter and grip the walls of the vena cava. The filter-loaded catheter may also be advanced over a guidewire to the vena cava after needle puncture of the internal jugular vein.

Central Venous Anatomy—Femoral Approach

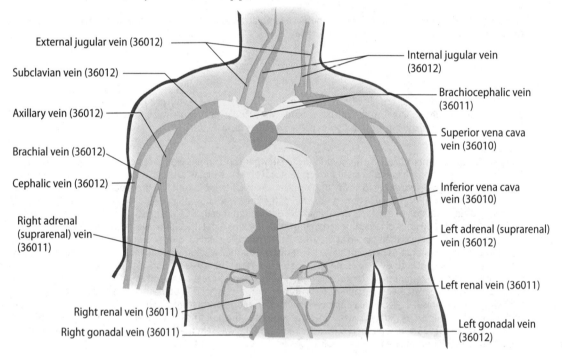

External jugular vein (36012)

Subclavian vein (36012)

Axillary vein (36012)

Brachial vein (36012)

Cephalic vein (36012)

Right adrenal (suprarenal) vein (36011)

Right renal vein (36011)

Right gonadal vein (36011)

Internal jugular vein (36012)

Brachiocephalic vein (36011)

Superior vena cava vein (36010)

Inferior vena cava vein (36010)

Left adrenal (suprarenal) vein (36012)

Left renal vein (36011)

Left gonadal vein (36012)

IVC Filter Placement

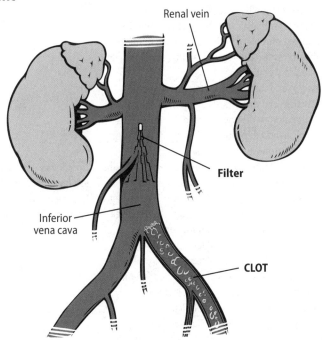

CPT Coding for IVC Filter Procedures

Service Performed	Code Reported
IVC filter placement	**37191**
IVC filter repositioning	**37192**
IVC filter removal	**37193**

Coding Tips

1. These codes are comprehensive codes. Component coding no longer applies.

2. Catheter placement is included in codes 37191–37193 and is not separately reported.

3. Intravascular ultrasound is included in these procedures. Do not separately report 37252 or 37253.

4. Report diagnostic inferior vena cavagram with CPT code 75825 only when performed for diagnostic purposes and results are used to make the clinical decision to proceed with filter placement. Append modifier 59 or appropriate X modifier.

5. Temporary and permanent filter placement is coded in the same manner.

6. Report the procedure to reposition a previously placed filter with CPT code 37192. This repositioning must be a separately documented procedure.

7. Report the procedure to remove a previously placed filter with CPT code 37193.

8. Conscious sedation is not included in these codes. Separately report 99151–99157 per payer policy and coding guidelines. Hospitals may choose to include the costs associated with the service as part of the procedure rather than reporting them separately.

9. Report the applicable device codes (HCPCS codes) in addition to the procedure code. Refer to the HCPCS section below for possible codes.

10. Hospitals are requested to continue reporting low osmolar contrast media separately with HCPCS Level II codes Q9965-Q9967. Report contrast media by milliliter.

Facility HCPCS Coding

Some applicable codes may include but are not limited to:

C1773   Retrieval device, insertable
C1880   Vena cava filter
Q9965   LOCM, 100-199 mg/ml iodine concentration, per ml
Q9966   LOCM, 200-299 mg/ml iodine concentration, per ml
Q9967   LOCM, 300-399 mg/ml iodine concentration, per ml

Note: See appendix B for a complete listing of reportable HCPCS Level II codes.

© 2017 Optum360, LLC   **111**

ICD-10-CM Coding

I26.Ø1	Septic pulmonary embolism with acute cor pulmonale
I26.Ø9	Other pulmonary embolism with acute cor pulmonale
I26.9Ø	Septic pulmonary embolism without acute cor pulmonale
I26.99	Other pulmonary embolism without acute cor pulmonale
I27.82	Chronic pulmonary embolism
I82.22Ø	Acute embolism and thrombosis of inferior vena cava
I82.221	Chronic embolism and thrombosis of inferior vena cava
I82.29Ø	Acute embolism and thrombosis of other thoracic veins
I82.291	Chronic embolism and thrombosis of other thoracic veins
I82.3	Embolism and thrombosis of renal vein
I82.4Ø1	Acute embolism and thrombosis of unspecified deep veins of right lower extremity
I82.4Ø2	Acute embolism and thrombosis of unspecified deep veins of left lower extremity
I82.4Ø3	Acute embolism and thrombosis of unspecified deep veins of lower extremity, bilateral
I82.4Ø9	Acute embolism and thrombosis of unspecified deep veins of unspecified lower extremity
I82.411	Acute embolism and thrombosis of right femoral vein
I82.412	Acute embolism and thrombosis of left femoral vein
I82.413	Acute embolism and thrombosis of femoral vein, bilateral
I82.419	Acute embolism and thrombosis of unspecified femoral vein
I82.421	Acute embolism and thrombosis of right iliac vein
I82.422	Acute embolism and thrombosis of left iliac vein
I82.423	Acute embolism and thrombosis of iliac vein, bilateral
I82.429	Acute embolism and thrombosis of unspecified iliac vein
I82.431	Acute embolism and thrombosis of right popliteal vein
I82.432	Acute embolism and thrombosis of left popliteal vein
I82.433	Acute embolism and thrombosis of popliteal vein, bilateral
I82.439	Acute embolism and thrombosis of unspecified popliteal vein
I82.441	Acute embolism and thrombosis of right tibial vein
I82.442	Acute embolism and thrombosis of left tibial vein
I82.443	Acute embolism and thrombosis of tibial vein, bilateral
I82.449	Acute embolism and thrombosis of unspecified tibial vein
I82.491	Acute embolism and thrombosis of other specified deep vein of right lower extremity
I82.492	Acute embolism and thrombosis of other specified deep vein of left lower extremity
I82.493	Acute embolism and thrombosis of other specified deep vein of lower extremity, bilateral
I82.499	Acute embolism and thrombosis of other specified deep vein of unspecified lower extremity
I82.4Y1	Acute embolism and thrombosis of unspecified deep veins of right proximal lower extremity
I82.4Y2	Acute embolism and thrombosis of unspecified deep veins of left proximal lower extremity
I82.4Y3	Acute embolism and thrombosis of unspecified deep veins of proximal lower extremity, bilateral
I82.4Y9	Acute embolism and thrombosis of unspecified deep veins of unspecified proximal lower extremity
I82.4Z1	Acute embolism and thrombosis of unspecified deep veins of right distal lower extremity
I82.4Z2	Acute embolism and thrombosis of unspecified deep veins of left distal lower extremity
I82.4Z3	Acute embolism and thrombosis of unspecified deep veins of distal lower extremity, bilateral
I82.4Z9	Acute embolism and thrombosis of unspecified deep veins of unspecified distal lower extremity
I82.5Ø1	Chronic embolism and thrombosis of unspecified deep veins of right lower extremity
I82.5Ø2	Chronic embolism and thrombosis of unspecified deep veins of left lower extremity
I82.5Ø3	Chronic embolism and thrombosis of unspecified deep veins of lower extremity, bilateral
I82.5Ø9	Chronic embolism and thrombosis of unspecified deep veins of unspecified lower extremity
I82.511	Chronic embolism and thrombosis of right femoral vein
I82.512	Chronic embolism and thrombosis of left femoral vein
I82.513	Chronic embolism and thrombosis of femoral vein, bilateral
I82.519	Chronic embolism and thrombosis of unspecified femoral vein
I82.521	Chronic embolism and thrombosis of right iliac vein
I82.522	Chronic embolism and thrombosis of left iliac vein
I82.523	Chronic embolism and thrombosis of iliac vein, bilateral
I82.529	Chronic embolism and thrombosis of unspecified iliac vein

I82.531	Chronic embolism and thrombosis of right popliteal vein
I82.532	Chronic embolism and thrombosis of left popliteal vein
I82.533	Chronic embolism and thrombosis of popliteal vein, bilateral
I82.539	Chronic embolism and thrombosis of unspecified popliteal vein
I82.541	Chronic embolism and thrombosis of right tibial vein
I82.542	Chronic embolism and thrombosis of left tibial vein
I82.543	Chronic embolism and thrombosis of tibial vein, bilateral
I82.549	Chronic embolism and thrombosis of unspecified tibial vein
I82.591	Chronic embolism and thrombosis of other specified deep vein of right lower extremity
I82.592	Chronic embolism and thrombosis of other specified deep vein of left lower extremity
I82.593	Chronic embolism and thrombosis of other specified deep vein of lower extremity, bilateral
I82.599	Chronic embolism and thrombosis of other specified deep vein of unspecified lower extremity
I82.5Y1	Chronic embolism and thrombosis of unspecified deep veins of right proximal lower extremity
I82.5Y2	Chronic embolism and thrombosis of unspecified deep veins of left proximal lower extremity
I82.5Y3	Chronic embolism and thrombosis of unspecified deep veins of proximal lower extremity, bilateral
I82.5Y9	Chronic embolism and thrombosis of unspecified deep veins of unspecified proximal lower extremity
I82.5Z1	Chronic embolism and thrombosis of unspecified deep veins of right distal lower extremity
I82.5Z2	Chronic embolism and thrombosis of unspecified deep veins of left distal lower extremity
I82.5Z3	Chronic embolism and thrombosis of unspecified deep veins of distal lower extremity, bilateral
I82.5Z9	Chronic embolism and thrombosis of unspecified deep veins of unspecified distal lower extremity
I82.811	Embolism and thrombosis of superficial veins of right lower extremities
I82.812	Embolism and thrombosis of superficial veins of left lower extremities
I82.813	Embolism and thrombosis of superficial veins of lower extremities, bilateral
I82.819	Embolism and thrombosis of superficial veins of unspecified lower extremity
T82.515A	Breakdown (mechanical) of umbrella device, initial encounter
T82.518A	Breakdown (mechanical) of other cardiac and vascular devices and implants, initial encounter
T82.525A	Displacement of umbrella device, initial encounter
T82.528A	Displacement of other cardiac and vascular devices and implants, initial encounter
T82.535A	Leakage of umbrella device, initial encounter
T82.538A	Leakage of other cardiac and vascular devices and implants, initial encounter
T82.595A	Other mechanical complication of umbrella device, initial encounter
T82.598A	Other mechanical complication of other cardiac and vascular devices and implants, initial encounter
T82.7XXA	Infection and inflammatory reaction due to other cardiac and vascular devices, implants and grafts, initial encounter
T82.818A	Embolism of vascular prosthetic devices, implants and grafts, initial encounter
T82.828A	Fibrosis of vascular prosthetic devices, implants and grafts, initial encounter
T82.848A	Pain from vascular prosthetic devices, implants and grafts, initial encounter
T82.856A	Stenosis of peripheral vascular stent, initial encounter
T82.858A	Stenosis of vascular prosthetic devices, implants and grafts, initial encounter
T82.868A	Thrombosis of vascular prosthetic devices, implants and grafts, initial encounter
T82.898A	Other specified complication of vascular prosthetic devices, implants and grafts, initial encounter
T82.9XXA	Unspecified complication of cardiac and vascular prosthetic device, implant and graft, initial encounter

CCI Edits

37191   01916, 01924-01926, 01930, 01932, 0213T, 0216T, 0228T, 0230T, 11000-11006, 11042-11047, 12001-12007, 12011-12057, 13100-13133, 13151-13153, 35201-35206, 35226-35236, 35256-35266, 35286, 36000, 36005-36010, 36400-36410, 36420-36430, 36440, 36500, 36591-36592, 36600, 36640, 37192, 37252-37253, 43752, 51701-51703, 62320-62327, 64400-64410, 64413-64435, 64445-64450, 64461-64463, 64479-64530, 69990, 75825, 75827, 75893, 76000-76001, 76937, 76942, 76970, 76998, 77001-77002, 92012-92014, 93000-93010, 93040-93042, 93318, 93355, 93975-93979, 94002, 94200, 94250, 94680-94690, 94770, 95812-95816, 95819, 95822, 95829, 95955, 96360-96368, 96372, 96374-96377, 97597-97598, 97602, 99155-99157, 99211-99223, 99231-99255, 99291-99292, 99304-99310, 99315-99316, 99334-99337, 99347-99350, 99374-99375, 99377-99378, 99446-99449, 99495-99496, G0269, G0463, G0471, J0670, J2001

37192 01916, 01924-01926, 01930, 01932, 0213T, 0216T, 0228T, 0230T, 12001-12007, 12011-12057, 13100-13133, 13151-13153, 35201-35206, 35226-35236, 35256-35266, 35286, 36000, 36005-36010, 36400-36410, 36420-36430, 36440, 36500, 36591-36592, 36600, 36640, 37252-37253, 43752, 51701-51703, 62320-62327, 64400-64410, 64413-64435, 64445-64450, 64461-64463, 64479-64530, 69990, 75825, 75827, 75893, 76000-76001, 76937, 76942, 76970, 76998, 77001-77002, 92012-92014, 93000-93010, 93040-93042, 93318, 93355, 93975-93979, 94002, 94200, 94250, 94680-94690, 94770, 95812-95816, 95819, 95822, 95829, 95955, 96360-96368, 96372, 96374-96377, 99155-99157, 99211-99223, 99231-99255, 99291-99292, 99304-99310, 99315-99316, 99334-99337, 99347-99350, 99374-99375, 99377-99378, 99446-99449, 99495-99496, G0269, G0463, G0471, J0670, J2001

37193 01916, 01924-01926, 01930-01933, 0213T, 0216T, 0228T, 0230T, 11000-11006, 11042-11047, 12001-12007, 12011-12057, 13100-13133, 13151-13153, 35201-35206, 35226-35236, 35256-35266, 35286, 36000, 36005-36010, 36251, 36253, 36400-36410, 36420-36430, 36440, 36500, 36591-36592, 36600, 36640, 37191, 37197, 37252-37253, 43752, 51701-51703, 62320-62327, 64400-64410, 64413-64435, 64445-64450, 64461-64463, 64479-64530, 69990, 75600, 75605, 75625, 75630, 75635, 75658, 75705, 75710, 75716, 75726, 75731, 75733, 75736, 75741, 75743, 75746, 75756, 75774, 75810, 75820, 75822, 75825, 75827, 75831, 75833, 75840, 75842, 75860, 75870, 75872, 75880, 75885, 75887, 75889, 75891, 75893, 76000-76001, 76937, 76942, 76970, 76998, 77001-77002, 92012-92014, 93000-93010, 93040-93042, 93318, 93355, 94002, 94200, 94250, 94680-94690, 94770, 95812-95816, 95819, 95822, 95829, 95955, 96360-96368, 96372, 96374-96377, 97597-97598, 97602, 99155-99157, 99211-99223, 99231-99255, 99291-99292, 99304-99310, 99315-99316, 99334-99337, 99347-99350, 99374-99375, 99377-99378, 99446-99449, 99495-99496, G0269, G0463, G0471, J0670, J2001

Case Example

Via right femoral access, a vascular sheath was placed into the femoral vein. A Greenfield vena cava filter system was advanced through the sheath into the inferior vena cava. The filter was deployed below the level of the renal veins. Follow up venography showed good positioning of the filter. The catheter and sheath were removed and manual pressure maintained until hemostasis was achieved.

CPT/HCPCS Codes Reported:
37191

Other HCPCS Codes Reported:
C1880

Percutaneous Transcatheter Retrieval of Foreign Body

When devices break off inside the body, percutaneous retrieval of the fractured device is performed via catheter when the device can be reached using this method.

37197   **Transcatheter retrieval, percutaneous, of intravascular foreign body (eg, fractured venous or arterial catheter), includes radiological supervision and interpretation, and imaging guidance (ultrasound or fluoroscopy), when performed**
The vascular system is accessed based on the location of the foreign body and a guidewire is advanced. A retrieval device is placed over the guidewire and advanced to the foreign body. The retrieval device is used to grasp the fractured device and remove it via the catheter.

Coding Tips

1. Transcatheter retrieval of a foreign body is reported with comprehensive code 37197.

2. Code separately for each selective catheter placement.

3. Do not report this code for retrieval of vena cava filters; see 37191–37193.

4. Removal of a permanent leadless pacemaker is reported with CPT category III code, 0388T.

5. Report diagnostic angiography separately.

6. Separately report other interventions, such as stent placement, if performed.

7. Conscious sedation is not included in these codes. Separately report 99151–99157 per payer policy and coding guidelines. Hospitals may choose to include the costs associated with the service as part of the procedure rather than reporting them separately.

8. Report all applicable pass-through device HCPCS codes. Refer to the HCPCS section for possible codes.

9. Although CMS has not issued device edits for this code, hospitals are strongly encouraged to separately report C1773 Retrieval device, when used.

Facility HCPCS Coding

Some applicable codes may include but are not limited to:

C1773   Retrieval device, insertable

C1769   Guidewire

C1887   Catheter, guiding (may include infusion/perfusion capability)

C1894   Introducer/sheath, other than guiding, intracardiac, electrophysiological, non-laser

C1760   Closure device, vascular (implantable/insertable), if used

G0269   Placement of occlusive device into either a venous or arterial access site, post surgical or interventional procedure (e.g., AngioSeal plug, vascular plug), if performed

Q9965   LOCM, 100-199 mg/ml iodine concentration, per ml

Q9966   LOCM, 200-299 mg/ml iodine concentration, per ml

Q9967   LOCM, 300-399 mg/ml iodine concentration, per ml

Note: See appendix B for a complete listing of reportable HCPCS Level II codes.

ICD-10-CM Coding

T81.500A	Unspecified complication of foreign body accidentally left in body following surgical operation, initial encounter
T81.501A	Unspecified complication of foreign body accidentally left in body following infusion or transfusion, initial encounter
T81.502A	Unspecified complication of foreign body accidentally left in body following kidney dialysis, initial encounter
T81.503A	Unspecified complication of foreign body accidentally left in body following injection or immunization, initial encounter
T81.505A	Unspecified complication of foreign body accidentally left in body following heart catheterization, initial encounter
T81.507A	Unspecified complication of foreign body accidentally left in body following removal of catheter or packing, initial encounter
T81.508A	Unspecified complication of foreign body accidentally left in body following other procedure, initial encounter
T81.509A	Unspecified complication of foreign body accidentally left in body following unspecified procedure, initial encounter
T81.510A	Adhesions due to foreign body accidentally left in body following surgical operation, initial encounter
T81.511A	Adhesions due to foreign body accidentally left in body following infusion or transfusion, initial encounter
T81.512A	Adhesions due to foreign body accidentally left in body following kidney dialysis, initial encounter
T81.513A	Adhesions due to foreign body accidentally left in body following injection or immunization, initial encounter

T81.515A	Adhesions due to foreign body accidentally left in body following heart catheterization, initial encounter
T81.517A	Adhesions due to foreign body accidentally left in body following removal of catheter or packing, initial encounter
T81.518A	Adhesions due to foreign body accidentally left in body following other procedure, initial encounter
T81.519A	Adhesions due to foreign body accidentally left in body following unspecified procedure, initial encounter
T81.520A	Obstruction due to foreign body accidentally left in body following surgical operation, initial encounter
T81.521A	Obstruction due to foreign body accidentally left in body following infusion or transfusion, initial encounter
T81.522A	Obstruction due to foreign body accidentally left in body following kidney dialysis, initial encounter
T81.523A	Obstruction due to foreign body accidentally left in body following injection or immunization, initial encounter
T81.525A	Obstruction due to foreign body accidentally left in body following heart catheterization, initial encounter
T81.527A	Obstruction due to foreign body accidentally left in body following removal of catheter or packing, initial encounter
T81.528A	Obstruction due to foreign body accidentally left in body following other procedure, initial encounter
T81.529A	Obstruction due to foreign body accidentally left in body following unspecified procedure, initial encounter
T81.530A	Perforation due to foreign body accidentally left in body following surgical operation, initial encounter
T81.531A	Perforation due to foreign body accidentally left in body following infusion or transfusion, initial encounter
T81.532A	Perforation due to foreign body accidentally left in body following kidney dialysis, initial encounter
T81.533A	Perforation due to foreign body accidentally left in body following injection or immunization, initial encounter
T81.535A	Perforation due to foreign body accidentally left in body following heart catheterization, initial encounter
T81.537A	Perforation due to foreign body accidentally left in body following removal of catheter or packing, initial encounter
T81.538A	Perforation due to foreign body accidentally left in body following other procedure, initial encounter
T81.539A	Perforation due to foreign body accidentally left in body following unspecified procedure, initial encounter
T81.590A	Other complications of foreign body accidentally left in body following surgical operation, initial encounter
T81.591A	Other complications of foreign body accidentally left in body following infusion or transfusion, initial encounter
T81.592A	Other complications of foreign body accidentally left in body following kidney dialysis, initial encounter
T81.593A	Other complications of foreign body accidentally left in body following injection or immunization, initial encounter
T81.595A	Other complications of foreign body accidentally left in body following heart catheterization, initial encounter
T81.597A	Other complications of foreign body accidentally left in body following removal of catheter or packing, initial encounter
T81.598A	Other complications of foreign body accidentally left in body following other procedure, initial encounter
T81.599A	Other complications of foreign body accidentally left in body following unspecified procedure, initial encounter
T82.310A	Breakdown (mechanical) of aortic (bifurcation) graft (replacement), initial encounter
T82.311A	Breakdown (mechanical) of carotid arterial graft (bypass), initial encounter
T82.312A	Breakdown (mechanical) of femoral arterial graft (bypass), initial encounter
T82.318A	Breakdown (mechanical) of other vascular grafts, initial encounter
T82.319A	Breakdown (mechanical) of unspecified vascular grafts, initial encounter
T82.390A	Other mechanical complication of aortic (bifurcation) graft (replacement), initial encounter
T82.391A	Other mechanical complication of carotid arterial graft (bypass), initial encounter
T82.392A	Other mechanical complication of femoral arterial graft (bypass), initial encounter
T82.398A	Other mechanical complication of other vascular grafts, initial encounter
T82.399A	Other mechanical complication of unspecified vascular grafts, initial encounter
T82.41XA	Breakdown (mechanical) of vascular dialysis catheter, initial encounter
T82.49XA	Other complication of vascular dialysis catheter, initial encounter
T82.513A	Breakdown (mechanical) of balloon (counterpulsation) device, initial encounter
T82.514A	Breakdown (mechanical) of infusion catheter, initial encounter
T82.515A	Breakdown (mechanical) of umbrella device, initial encounter
T82.518A	Breakdown (mechanical) of other cardiac and vascular devices and implants, initial encounter
T82.593A	Other mechanical complication of balloon (counterpulsation) device, initial encounter
T82.594A	Other mechanical complication of infusion catheter, initial encounter
T82.595A	Other mechanical complication of umbrella device, initial encounter
T82.598A	Other mechanical complication of other cardiac and vascular devices and implants, initial encounter
T82.599A	Other mechanical complication of unspecified cardiac and vascular devices and implants, initial encounter
T82.898A	Other specified complication of vascular prosthetic devices, implants and grafts, initial encounter
T82.9XXA	Unspecified complication of cardiac and vascular prosthetic device, implant and graft, initial encounter

CCI Edits

37197 01916, 01924-01926, 01930-01933, 0213T, 0216T, 0228T, 0230T, 0388T, 12001-12007, 12011-12057, 13100-13133, 13151-13153, 34812-34813, 35201-35206, 35226-35236, 35256-35266, 35286, 36000, 36005, 36400-36410, 36420-36430, 36440, 36500, 36591-36592, 36600-36640, 37211-37214, 37252-37253, 43752, 51701-51703, 61645, 62320-62327, 64400-64410, 64413-64435, 64445-64450, 64461-64463, 64479-64530, 69990, 75600, 75605, 75625, 75630, 75635, 75658, 75705, 75710, 75716, 75726, 75731, 75733, 75736, 75741, 75743, 75746, 75756, 75774, 75810, 75820, 75822, 75825, 75827, 75831, 75833, 75840, 75842, 75860, 75870, 75872, 75880, 75885, 75887, 75889, 75891, 75893, 76000-76001, 76380, 76942, 76970, 76998, 77001-77002, 77012, 77021, 92012-92014, 93000-93010, 93040-93042, 93050, 93318, 93355, 94002, 94200, 94250, 94680-94690, 94770, 95812-95816, 95819, 95822, 95829, 95955, 96360-96368, 96372, 96374-96377, 99155-99157, 99211-99223, 99231-99255, 99291-99292, 99304-99310, 99315-99316, 99334-99337, 99347-99350, 99374-99375, 99377-99378, 99446-99449, 99495-99496, G0463, G0471, J0670, J2001

Case Example

The patient is brought to the IR suite and placed on the imaging table. The skin overlying the **right jugular vein** is prepped and draped in typical sterile fashion. The skin is anesthetized and the **access needle is placed into the jugular vein**. Using fluoro guidance, a guidewire is advanced, the needle removed, and an 8 French sheath placed. A loop snare is advanced through the sheath and into the SVC where the catheter fragment is located. The **fragment is successfully snared and retracted** into the sheath. The entire assembly is removed from the patient and pressure held over the access site until hemostasis is achieved. The patient left the IR suite in satisfactory condition.

CPT/HCPCS Codes Reported:
C1773

Other HCPCS Codes Reported:
37197

Intravascular Ultrasound, Non-coronary

Intravascular ultrasound, or IVUS, is a transcatheter procedure performed percutaneously with a special catheter with ultrasound capability. The catheter contains a tiny ultrasound probe allowing imaging of the inside of the vessel. It requires the use of ultrasound imaging equipment in addition to the fluoroscopy equipment usually found in the interventional radiology imaging suite. There are separate CPT codes available to report IVUS performed of coronary arteries. Refer to the Diagnostic Cardiac Catheterization section of this book for further details.

37252	**Intravascular ultrasound (noncoronary vessel) during diagnostic evaluation and/or therapeutic intervention, including radiologic supervision and interpretation; initial vessel (List separately in addition to code for primary procedure)**
37253	**each additional noncoronary vessel (List separately in addition to code for primary procedure)**

An ultrasound is performed on the inside of a blood vessel previously treated for an obstruction or stricture. The ultrasound may be done during or after a therapeutic procedure such as dilation, stent deployment, or atherectomy. A special intravascular ultrasound catheter is threaded over an already placed guidewire to the study area and its external end is connected to the display monitor. Ultrasonic images of the vessel are displayed on the monitor and if satisfactory, the catheter is removed and the therapeutic procedure completed.

Coding Tips

1. These codes are comprehensive. Do not separately report radiologic guidance.
2. Code each vessel separately. Follow the same guidelines as for angioplasty discussed earlier in this chapter.
3. Code separately for each selective catheter placement.
4. Report diagnostic angiography separately.
5. Report other interventions such as angioplasty separately as well.
6. Do not report these codes for intravascular ultrasound of the coronary arteries. Separate codes are available. Refer to the cardiac catheterization chapter for information.
7. These codes are included in the inferior vena cava filter procedures. Do not separately report them with procedure code 37191, 37192, 37193 or 37197.
8. Many fiscal intermediaries have individual coverage policies for IVUS procedures. Verify reporting requirements with your payer.
9. Report all applicable device HCPCS codes. Refer to the HCPCS section for possible codes.
10. Hospitals are strongly encouraged to separately report the device code for the ultrasound catheter, C1753.
11. Physician Reporting: Report only the technical component, append modifier TC. To report the complete procedure (i.e., both the professional and technical components), submit without a modifier.

Facility HCPCS Coding

Some applicable codes may include but are not limited to:

C1753   Catheter, intravascular ultrasound

Note: See appendix B for a complete listing of reportable HCPCS Level II codes.

ICD-10-CM Coding

These codes are add-on codes. Refer to the corresponding primary procedure code for ICD-10-CM diagnosis code links.

CCI Edits

37252	01916, 01924-01926, 01930-01933, 0213T, 0216T, 0228T, 0230T, 12001-12007, 12011-12057, 13100-13133, 13151-13153, 35201-35206, 35226, 35261-35266, 35286, 36000, 36005, 36400-36410, 36420-36430, 36440, 36500, 36591-36592, 36600, 36640, 43752, 51701-51703, 62320-62327, 64400-64410, 64413-64435, 64445-64450, 64461, 64463, 64479, 64483, 64486-64490, 64493, 64505-64530, 69990, 75893, 76000-76001, 76376-76377, 76942, 76970, 76998, 77001-77002, 92012-92014, 93000-93010, 93040-93042, 93050, 93318, 93978-93979, 94002, 94200, 94250, 94680-94690, 94770, 95812-95816, 95819, 95822, 95829, 95955, 96360, 96365, 96372, 96374-96377, 99155-99157, 99211-99223, 99231-99255, 99291-99292, 99304-99310, 99315-99316, 99334-99337, 99347-99350, 99374-99375, 99377-99378, 99446-99449
37253	0213T, 0216T, 0228T, 0230T, 12001-12007, 12011-12057, 13100-13133, 13151-13153, 36000, 36400-36410, 36420-36430, 36440, 36600, 36640, 43752, 51701-51703, 62320-62327, 64400-64410, 64413-64435, 64445-64450, 64461, 64463, 64479, 64483, 64486-64490, 64493, 64505-64530, 69990, 92012-92014, 93000-93010, 93040-93042, 93050, 93318, 94002, 94200, 94250, 94680-94690, 94770, 95812-95816, 95819, 95822, 95829, 95955, 96360, 96365, 96372, 96374-96377, 99155-99157, 99211-99223, 99231-99255, 99291-99292, 99304-99310, 99315-99316, 99334-99337, 99347-99350, 99374-99375, 99377-99378

Case Example

Indications for study:
Abdominal aortic aneurysm, pre-reconstructive arteriographic and intravascular ultrasound evaluation for implantation of endovascular graft.

Studies performed:
#1 Abdominal aortogram and pelvic arteriogram

2 Intravascular abdominal aortic and unilateral left iliac ultrasound

Technique:
The **left common femoral artery** was entered with a thin wall needle, and a J-tipped 0.035 inch guidewire was passed centrally under fluoroscopic guidance. A pigtail **catheter** was then placed in a **suprarenal position**, and **abdominal aortography** was **performed**. The abdominal aorta was imaged in anterior posterior plane, with slight cranio-caudal angulation of the image intensifier. The **common iliac arteries** were **imaged** in opposite oblique projection, with **retrograde injections** from the femoral sheaths.

A **left transfemoral intravascular ultrasound** was then performed. Measurements were obtained for the diameter of the perirenal and infrarenal aortic neck, the length of the infrarenal aortic neck, the length of the **infrarenal aorta**, the length of the **left common iliac** artery, and the diameter of the left distal common iliac findings and for the endo graft.

Findings:
The perirenal aorta had no significant stenotic disease. Mild ectasia of the infrarenal aortic neck was present. There was a fusiform aneurysm of the distal infrarenal aortic segment. Ectasia of the common iliac arteries was noted bilaterally, left worse than right. Single main renal arteries were present bilaterally, without significant stenosis.

The infrarenal aortic neck was approximately 5 cm in length, with visible flaring of the diameter in the lower 3 cm of that segment. There was no significant stenotic disease in the common iliac arteries. Moderate luminal irregularity was present. The length of the common iliac arteries was documented, using the marker pigtail catheter.

Intravascular ultrasound documented a 19.4-19.9 mm diameter of the immediate infrarenal aortic segment, confirming the appropriateness of the chosen 26-88 mm main body and the graft device. There was no significant change in diameter within 2 cm of the most inferior left main renal artery. The distal left common iliac artery diameter was 19.2 X. 19.9 mm, indicating the appropriateness of the 22-54 mm ipsilateral iliac leg.

Conclusions:
#1 Large infrarenal abdominal aortic aneurysm

#2 Bilateral common iliac artery ectasia, left greater than right

#3 Single, bilateral main renal arteries, without significant stenosis

#4 Satisfactory aorto-iliac anatomy for implantation of the Zenith modular endoprosthesis

CPT/HCPCS Codes Reported:
36200, 75625, 37252, 37253

Other HCPCS Codes Reported:
C1753

Transcatheter Biopsy

Transcatheter biopsies are performed via vascular access rather than direct needle puncture. Special biopsy needles are required to obtain the specimen. These procedures are most commonly performed on the liver to evaluate for possible transplant status.

37200	**Transcatheter biopsy**
75970	**Transcatheter biopsy, radiological supervision and interpretation**

A biopsy specimen is obtained through a catheter. The biopsy catheter may be inserted through an already existing drainage tube or catheter, through a tract or pathway, such as the urethra during cystourethroscopy, or through the skin and into the access artery. Fluoroscopy is used to help guide the catheter through its course from whatever entry to the point of study to be biopsied. A biopsy brush, a fine biopsy needle, or biting forceps may be used through the catheter to obtain the cells or tissue for examination. This code reports the radiological supervision and interpretation only.

Coding Tips

1. Report both components of the procedure—the surgical component and/or catheter placement codes and the technical radiology S&I codes.
2. Separately report diagnostic angiography.
3. Separately code for catheter placements.
4. Report the surgical biopsy code for the applicable location of the biopsy, i.e., liver.
5. Do not report imaging guidance. It is included in CPT code 75970.
6. Report all applicable pass-through HCPCS codes. Refer to the HCPCS section for possible codes.
7. Physician Reporting: These radiology S&I codes have both a technical and professional component. To report only the professional component, append modifier 26. To report only the technical component, append modifier TC. To report the complete procedure (i.e., both the professional and technical components), submit without a modifier.

Facility HCPCS Coding

Some applicable codes may include but are not limited to:

C1769   Guidewire

Note: See appendix B for a complete listing of reportable HCPCS Level II codes.

ICD-10-CM Coding

The application of these codes is too broad to adequately present ICD-10-CM diagnosis code links here. Refer to the current ICD-10-CM book.

CCI Edits

37200   01924-01926, 0213T, 0216T, 0228T, 0230T, 12001-12007, 12011-12057, 13100-13133, 13151-13153, 34812-34820, 34833-34834, 35201-35206, 35226-35236, 35256-35266, 35286, 36000, 36400-36410, 36420-36430, 36440, 36500, 36591-36592, 36600, 36625-36640, 43752, 51701-51703, 62320-62327, 64400-64410, 64413-64435, 64445-64450, 64461-64463, 64479-64530, 69990, 75600, 75605, 75625, 75630, 75635, 75658, 75705, 75710, 75716, 75726, 75731, 75733, 75736, 75741, 75743, 75746, 75756, 75774, 75810, 75820, 75822, 75825, 75827, 75831, 75833, 75840, 75842, 75860, 75870, 75872, 75880, 75885, 75887, 75889, 75891, 75893, 76000-76001, 76380, 76942, 76970, 76998, 77001-77002, 77012, 77021, 92012-92014, 93000-93010, 93040-93042, 93050, 93318, 93355, 94002, 94200, 94250, 94680-94690, 94770, 95812-95816, 95819, 95822, 95829, 95955, 96360-96368, 96372, 96374-96377, 99155-99157, 99211-99223, 99231-99255, 99291-99292, 99304-99310, 99315-99316, 99334-99337, 99347-99350, 99374-99375, 99377-99378, 99446-99449, 99495-99496, G0463, G0471

75970   01916, 01924-01926, 01930-01933, 35201-35206, 35226, 35261-35266, 35286, 36000, 36005, 36410, 36500, 36591-36592, 75600, 75605, 75625, 75630, 75635, 75658, 75705, 75710, 75716, 75726, 75731, 75733, 75736, 75741, 75743, 75746, 75756, 75774, 75810, 75820, 75822, 75825, 75827, 75831, 75833, 75840, 75842, 75860, 75870, 75872, 75880, 75885, 75887, 75889, 75891, 75893, 76000-76001, 76942, 76970, 76998, 77001-77002, 96360, 96365, 96372, 96375-96377, 99446-99449

Case Example

Transjugular Liver Biopsy

Access was obtained via the right internal jugular and an 8-French sheath was placed. Through the sheath, a 5-French hockey stick type catheter was used to attempt catheterization of a hepatic vein. Only a tiny caudate hepatic vein could be catheterized. Subsequently, a pigtail catheter was advanced into the inferior vena cava and an inferior vena cavagram was performed to evaluate for inflow from the larger hepatic veins. Subsequently, the 5-French hockey stick catheter was used to catheterize the right hepatic vein. Over an Amplatz super stiff guidewire, an 18-gauge transjugular liver biopsy needle was advanced and four specimens were obtained. The needle and sheath were removed and hemostasis obtained.

CPT/HCPCS Codes Reported:
75825-XS, 36012, 75970, 37200

Transcatheter Endovascular Revascularization—Overview

Endovascular revascularization is performed to improve blood flow in arteries occluded or partially occluded due to atherosclerotic disease. These procedures may require one type or multiple types of treatment to achieve satisfactory results. Treatment types include angioplasty, atherectomy, and/or stent insertion. Angioplasty involves using a catheter-mounted balloon which is expanded inside the narrowing within the vessel to open the flow. Atherectomy involves special cutting type catheters designed to "cut" and remove the plaque from the artery. Catheter-mounted stents are inserted inside the artery to hold open the artery at the point of narrowing.

Significant coding changes occurred January 1, 2011. Providers should pay particularly close attention to these rules and guidelines. These codes describe therapies provided in three separate vascular territories: iliac, femoral/popliteal, and tibial/peroneal. The codes in this section do not apply to other vascular territories such as visceral and brachiocephalic. Please refer to separate sections in this publication addressing these territories.

Coding Tips—CPT Codes 37220–37235, Iliac, Femoral-Popliteal, and Tibial/Peroneal Territories

1. Report the code inclusive of all therapies provided for each specified vessel.
2. Codes 37220–37235 are used to report procedures when performed specifically for vascular occlusive disease.
3. These codes include selective vascular catheterization. Do not report 36245–36248 with these codes.
4. These codes include radiologic supervision and interpretation.
5. Angioplasty, if performed, is included in all codes 37220–37235.
6. Angiography performed for diagnostic purposes is reported separately. Do not report angiography performed to size the vessel, confirm catheter placement, or to confirm the presence of a known lesion.
7. Mechanical thrombectomy and thrombolysis are not included and should be reported separately when performed.
8. Multiple stent placement within the same vessel is reported only once.
9. When therapies are performed in multiple territories in the same leg, one primary revascularization code is reported for each territory.
10. Apply modifier 59, or appropriate X modifier, when therapies are performed on the same territory in both legs during the same session.
11. Conscious sedation is not included in these codes. Separately report 99151–99157 per payer policy and coding guidelines. Hospitals may choose to include the costs associated with the service as part of the procedure rather than reporting them separately.
12. Device codes are required for the codes in this section. Hospitals should report all applicable device codes used. Refer to the HCPCS section for possible codes.
13. Hospitals are requested to continue reporting low osmolar contrast media with HCPCS codes Q9965–Q9967. Report all contrast media by milliliter rather than by vial.

Revascularization Device

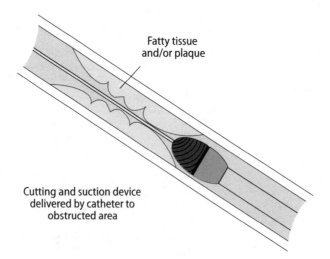

Fatty tissue and/or plaque

Cutting and suction device delivered by catheter to obstructed area

CPT Coding for Transcatheter Endovascular Revascularization

Service	Iliac Territory	Femoral/Popliteal Territory	Tibial/Peroneal Territory
Angioplasty only	**37220 – initial vessel** **37222 – additional vessel**	**37224**	**37228 – initial vessel** **37232 – additional vessel**
Stent, with or without angioplasty	**37221 – initial vessel** **37223 – additional vessel**	**37226**	**37230 – initial vessel** **37234 – additional vessel**
Atherectomy only	**0238T**	n/a	n/a
Atherectomy with or without angioplasty	**0238T and** **37220 – initial vessel** **37222 – additional vessel**	**37225**	**37229 – initial vessel** **37233 – additional vessel**
Stent with Atherectomy, with or without angioplasty	**0238T and** **37221 – initial vessel** **37223 – additional vessel**	**37227**	**37231 – initial vessel** **37235 – additional vessel**

Transcatheter Endovascular Revascularization—Iliac Vascular Territory

The iliac territory includes the following vessels:

- Common iliac artery
- Internal iliac artery
- External iliac artery

Angioplasty, only:

37220   **Revascularization, endovascular, open or percutaneous, iliac artery, unilateral, initial vessel; with transluminal angioplasty**

37222   **Revascularization, endovascular, open or percutaneous, iliac artery, unilateral, each additional ipsilateral iliac vessel; with transluminal angioplasty (List separately in addition to code for primary procedure)**

Stent placement:

37221   **Revascularization, endovascular, open or percutaneous, iliac artery, unilateral, initial vessel; with transluminal stent placement(s), includes angioplasty within the same vessel, when performed**

37223   **Revascularization, endovascular, open or percutaneous, iliac artery, unilateral, each additional ipsilateral iliac vessel; with transluminal stent placement(s), includes angioplasty within the same vessel, when performed (List separately in addition to code for primary procedure)**

Atherectomy:

0238T   **Transluminal peripheral atherectomy, open or percutaneous, including radiological supervision and interpretation; iliac artery, each vessel**

Coding Tips—Iliac Territory

1. CPT codes 37220–37223 report unilateral service.
2. Report only one primary code for the initial iliac artery treated in each leg.
3. Report additional iliac vessel treatment with the add-on codes, 37222 or 37223. Up to two additional vessel codes may be reported for each leg.
4. Do not report multiple codes for different lesions within the same vessel. Treatment of multiple lesions in one vessel is covered by a single vessel code.
5. For atherectomy of an iliac vessel, use category III CPT code 0238T.
6. Code 0238T does not include angioplasty. Separately report with code 37220 or 37222.
7. Code 0238T does not include catheter placement, embolic protection, other interventions of the same or other vessels, or arteriotomy closure. Report these services separately.

Facility HCPCS Coding

Some applicable codes may include but are not limited to:

C1714   Catheter, transluminal atherectomy, directional
C1724   Catheter, transluminal atherectomy, rotational
C1725   Catheter, transluminal angioplasty, non-laser
C1760   Closure device vascular (implantable/insertable), if used
C1769   Guidewire
C1874   Stent, coated/covered, with delivery system
C1875   Stent, coated/covered, without delivery system
C1876   Stent, non-coated/non-covered, with delivery system
C1877   Stent, non-coated/non-covered, without delivery system
C1885   Catheter transluminal angioplasty, laser
G0269   Placement of occlusive device into either a venous or arterial access site, post surgical or interventional procedure (e.g., angioSeal plug, vascular plug), if performed
Q9965   LOCM, 100-199 mg/ml iodine concentration, per ml
Q9966   LOCM, 200-299 mg/ml iodine concentration, per ml
Q9967   LOCM, 300-399 mg/ml iodine concentration, per ml

Note: See appendix B for a complete listing of reportable HCPCS Level II codes.

Pelvic Arterial Anatomy—Anterior

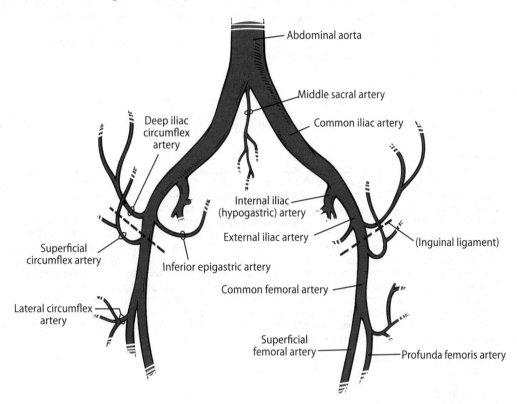

ICD-10 CM-Coding

The application of these codes is too broad to adequately present ICD-10-CM diagnosis code links here. Refer to the current ICD-10-CM book.

CCI Edits

37220 01924, 11000-11006, 11042-11047, 12001-12007, 12011-12057, 13100-13133, 13151-13153, 35201-35206, 35226-35236, 35256-35266, 35286, 36000, 36002-36005, 36120-36140, 36160-36200, 36245-36247, 36400-36410, 36420-36430, 36440, 36500, 36591-36592, 36600-36640, 37246-37247, 43752, 51701-51703, 62320-62327, 64400-64410, 64413-64435, 64445-64450, 64461-64463, 64479-64530, 69990, 75630, 75710, 75716, 75736, 75774, 75893, 76000-76001, 76942, 76970, 76998, 77002, 92012-92014, 93000-93010, 93040-93042, 93050, 93318, 93355, 94002, 94200, 94250, 94680-94690, 94770, 95812-95816, 95819, 95822, 95829, 95955, 96360-96368, 96372, 96374-96377, 97597-97598, 97602, 99155-99157, 99211-99223, 99231-99255, 99291-99292, 99304-99310, 99315-99316, 99334-99337, 99347-99350, 99374-99375, 99377-99378, 99446-99449, 99495-99496, G0269, G0463, G0471, J0670, J1642-J1644, J2001

37221 01924, 11000-11006, 11042-11047, 12001-12007, 12011-12057, 13100-13133, 13151-13153, 34812-34820, 34833-34834, 35201-35206, 35226-35236, 35256-35266, 35286, 36000, 36002-36005, 36120-36140, 36160-36200, 36245-36247, 36400-36410, 36420-36430, 36440, 36500, 36591-36592, 36600-36640, 37220, 37236, 37238, 37246-37247, 43752, 51701-51703, 62320-62327, 64400-64410, 64413-64435, 64445-64450, 64461-64463, 64479-64530, 69990, 75630, 75710, 75716, 75736, 75774, 75893, 76000-76001, 76942, 76970, 76998, 77002, 92012-92014, 93000-93010, 93040-93042, 93050, 93318, 93355, 94002, 94200, 94250, 94680-94690, 94770, 95812-95816, 95819, 95822, 95829, 95955, 96360-96368, 96372, 96374-96377, 97597-97598, 97602, 99155-99157, 99211-99223, 99231-99255, 99291-99292, 99304-99310, 99315-99316, 99334-99337, 99347-99350, 99374-99375, 99377-99378, 99446-99449, 99495-99496, G0269, G0463, G0471, J0670, J1642-J1644, J2001

37222 11000-11006, 11042-11047, 35201-35206, 35226-35236, 35256-35266, 35286, 36591-36592, 93050, 97597-97598, 97602, G0269, J1642-J1644

37223 11000-11006, 11042-11047, 34812-34820, 34833-34834, 35201-35206, 35226-35236, 35256-35266, 35286, 36591-36592, 37236, 37238, 93050, 97597-97598, 97602, G0269, J1642-J1644

0238T	01924, 11000-11006, 11042-11047, 35201-35206, 35226-35236, 35256-35266, 35286, 36000, 36002-36005, 36400-36410, 36420-36430, 36440, 36500, 36591-36592, 36600-36640, 43752, 51701-51703, 61650, 62320-62327, 64400-64410, 64413-64435, 64445-64450, 64461, 64463, 64479, 64483, 64486-64490, 64493, 64505-64530, 69990, 75630, 75635, 75710, 75716, 75736, 75774, 75893, 76000-76001, 76942, 76970, 76998, 77002, 93000-93010, 93040-93042, 93050, 93318, 93355, 94002, 94200, 94250, 94680-94690, 94770, 95812-95816, 95819, 95822, 95829, 95955, 96360, 96365, 96372, 96374-96377, 97597-97598, 97602, 99155-99157, 99446-99449, G0471

Case Example #1

History:
The patient was a 66-year-old diabetic male with a non-healing right toe ulcer. A stent was previously placed in the right mid iliac system.

Procedure:
Access was achieved via the right common femoral artery and a 6-French long sheath was placed. A diagnostic angiography of the right iliac system was performed through the sheath. The angiogram revealed a relatively short stent present in the mid right iliac system. The right internal iliac artery was not visualized and presumably occluded. There was also some mild irregular narrowing in the more proximal right common iliac artery region. Angioplasty of these lesions was pursued. Through the sheath, a 6mm x 2cm balloon catheter was advanced and positioned in the proximal vessel of the common iliac region. The balloon was inflated twice to 10 atmospheres for 30 seconds each. The balloon was then deflated and withdrawn down to the stented site in the mid iliac. This area was also inflated twice to 10 atmospheres for 30 seconds each. The balloon catheter was then removed, leaving a safety guide wire in place. A repeat angiography demonstrated marked improvement at both sites, though some residual stenosis persisted at the stented region. Therefore, a 7mm x 2cm balloon catheter was advanced through the sheath and a repeat angioplasty was performed at both areas of stenosis. The balloon catheter was removed and a repeat angiography was performed. The repeat angiography demonstrated complete resolution of any stenosis or abnormality of the right iliac system. Therefore, the procedure was discontinued. All catheters were removed and manual compression was applied to the groin with adequate hemostasis obtained. A total of 60cc Omnipaque 240 was used during the procedure.

CPT/HCPCS Codes Reported:
75710-XS, 37220

Other Codes Reported:
C1769, C1894, C1725, Q9966 x 60

Case Example #2

Indication:
Limiting claudication of both lower extremities

Procedure:
The patient was brought to the procedure room and after adequate IV sedation was obtained, both groins were prepped and draped in the usual sterile fashion. Then 1% Xylocaine was infiltrated into the skin overlying the left common femoral arterial pulsation and an 11 blade used to make a small stab incision. Retrograde access through the left common femoral artery was then obtained using a micropuncture needle technique. The micropuncture catheter was exchanged over a guidewire for a 5 French sheath and a diagnostic omni flush catheter advanced into the pararenal aorta under fluoroscopic guidance using guidewire technique. An abdominal aortogram was performed. The diagnostic catheter was withdrawn to the level of the bifurcation and bilateral lower extremity angiograms were obtained. The decision was made to proceed with intervention and the diagnostic catheter was then exchanged for a 7 French Raabe sheath, which was advanced into the right common femoral artery. Using a glidewire and glide catheter, the chronic total occlusion of the distal superficial femoral artery on the right was crossed in the subintimal plane using an Outback re-entry catheter. The true lumen of the proximal popliteal artery was re-accessed and an angiogram performed, demonstrating true lumen location of the distal catheter in the popliteal artery. A 5mm x 10cm Powerflex balloon was then chosen and angioplasty performed of the distal superficial femoral artery at the adductor canal. The completion angiogram demonstrated good results. Attention was then directed to the proximal superficial femoral artery at the level of the origin, where there was a severe stenosis present. A 5mm x 2cm balloon was advanced and angioplasty performed under fluoroscopic guidance with excellent angiographic results. A 6mm x 2cm balloon was next advanced to the level of the right external iliac artery and angioplasty performed with excellent results. The sheath was then withdrawn to the level of the left external iliac artery and a 7mm x 4cm balloon was chosen, advanced to a severe stenosis involving the left proximal external iliac artery and angioplasty performed. The completion angiogram demonstrated acceptable results. No further intervention was performed and all guidewires and catheters were withdrawn. The sheath was withdrawn and hemostasis obtained via manual pressure. The patient was transferred to recovery in satisfactory condition.

Case Example #2 (Continued)

Findings:
There is evidence of renal artery occlusive disease involving the proximal third of the right renal artery, causing a 50% stenosis. There is also atherosclerotic occlusive disease involving the distal renal arteries. The infrarenal aorta is patent with mild diffuse atherosclerotic changes. There is diffuse moderate to severe atherosclerosis involving the common internal and external iliac arteries bilaterally. There is a plaque in the distal aspect of the right common iliac artery causing a 50% narrowing. There is severe focal stenosis involving the distal external iliac artery on the right. There is diffuse disease involving the common deep and superficial femoral artery. There is a 4cm chronic total occlusion of the distal superficial femoral artery at the level of the adductor canal. The popliteal artery is patent with diffuse moderate atherosclerotic changes. There is severe tibial arterial occlusive disease with single vessel runoff to the level of the ankle via peroneal artery. Peroneal artery does reconstitute a posterior tibial artery at the level of the ankle which crosses the ankle to form a plantar arch. The left superficial femoral artery occludes at its origin and reconstitutes at the adductor canal via collaterals. The popliteal is patent. There is single vessel runoff to the level of the ankle via the peroneal artery, which reconstitutes a posterior tibial artery at the level of the ankle and crosses the ankle to form a plantar arch.

CPT/HCPCS Codes Reported:
75625-XS, 75716-XS, 37220, 37222, 37224

Other Codes Reported:
C1769, C1894, C1725

Case Example # 3

Under satisfactory anesthesia, the patient was prepped and draped. A percutaneous stick was made into the **right common femoral artery**, and a sheath was inserted. Through the sheath, a guidewire and pigtail **catheter** were inserted and **advanced to the distal abdominal aorta. Contrast was injected,** and **images of both legs** were **taken from the bifurcation to and including the tibial peroneal trunk**. A high-grade **stenosis** was identified **in the left external iliac.** We decided to proceed with intervention, and **angioplasty was selected as the therapy to use**. We selected the appropriate angioplasty catheter and advanced through a guiding catheter to the **left common iliac. Angioplasty was performed**. A follow-up angiogram demonstrated only partial resolution of the stenosis. We then **decided to proceed with atherectomy** to remove the remaining plaque. We selected the **Diamondback system** and prepped it for the procedure. The 2.5 Diamondback bur was then **passed to the left external iliac**. Several high-speed passes were made through the vessel. A subsequent angiogram then demonstrated 0% stenosis in the left external iliac. The walls of the vessel appeared smooth. All devices and catheters were removed. **Vascular closure was achieved using an angio-seal**.

CPT/HCPCS Codes Reported:
75716-XS, 37220, 0238T, G0269 (per payer policy)

Other HCPCS Codes Reported:
C1769, C1724, C1725, C1887

Transcatheter Endovascular Revascularization—Femoral/Popliteal Vascular Territory

The femoral/popliteal territory consists of the following segments:

- Common femoral artery
- Deep femoral artery
- Superficial femoral artery
- Popliteal artery

Angioplasty, only:

37224   **Revascularization, endovascular, open or percutaneous, femoral, popliteal artery(s), unilateral; with transluminal angioplasty**

Atherectomy, with or without angioplasty:

37225   **Revascularization, endovascular, open or percutaneous, femoral, popliteal artery(s), unilateral; with atherectomy, includes angioplasty within the same vessel, when performed**

Stent placement, with or without angioplasty:

37226   **Revascularization, endovascular, open or percutaneous, femoral, popliteal artery(s), unilateral; with transluminal stent placement(s), includes angioplasty within the same vessel, when performed**

Stent placement and atherectomy, with or without angioplasty:

37227   **Revascularization, endovascular, open or percutaneous, femoral, popliteal artery(s), unilateral; with transluminal stent placement(s) and atherectomy, includes angioplasty within the same vessel, when performed**

Coding Tips—Femoral/Popliteal Territory

1. For endovascular revascularization CPT coding the entire femoral/popliteal territory is considered to be a single vessel.
2. The number of separate lesions treated within this defined territory does not impact coding. Report only one code describing the complexity of the therapy performed. For example, if a stent is placed in one lesion in the common femoral and atherectomy is performed on a lesion in the superficial femoral, only 37227 is reported.

Facility HCPCS Coding

Some applicable codes may include but are not limited to:

C1714   Catheter, transluminal atherectomy, directional

C1724   Catheter, transluminal atherectomy, rotational

C1725   Catheter, transluminal angioplasty, non-laser

C1760   Closure device vascular (implantable/insertable), if used

C1769   Guidewire

C1874   Stent, coated/covered, with delivery system

C1875   Stent, coated/covered, without delivery system

C1876   Stent, non-coated/non-covered, with delivery system

C1877   Stent, non-coated/non-covered, without delivery system

C1885   Catheter transluminal angioplasty, laser

G0269   Placement of occlusive device into either a venous or arterial access site, post surgical or interventional procedure (e.g., angioSeal plug, vascular plug), if performed

Q9965   LOCM, 100-199 mg/ml iodine concentration, per ml

Q9966   LOCM, 200-299 mg/ml iodine concentration, per ml

Q9967   LOCM, 300-399 mg/ml iodine concentration, per ml

Note: See appendix B for a complete listing of reportable HCPCS Level II codes.

Extremity Arterial Anatomy—Contralateral, Axillary or Brachial Approach Lower

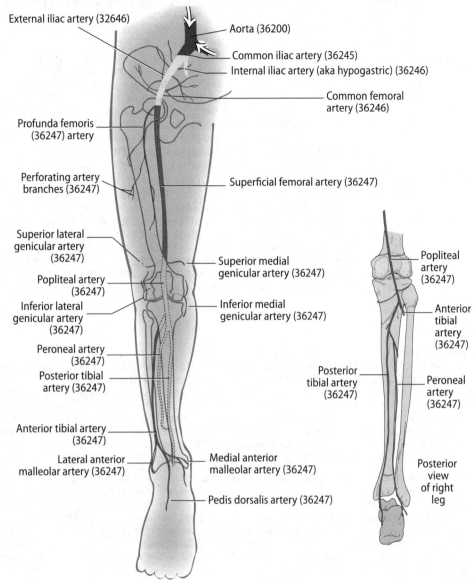

External iliac artery (32646)

Aorta (36200)

Common iliac artery (36245)

Internal iliac artery (aka hypogastric) (36246)

Common femoral artery (36246)

Profunda femoris (36247) artery

Perforating artery branches (36247)

Superficial femoral artery (36247)

Superior lateral genicular artery (36247)

Superior medial genicular artery (36247)

Popliteal artery (36247)

Inferior lateral genicular artery (36247)

Inferior medial genicular artery (36247)

Peroneal artery (36247)

Posterior tibial artery (36247)

Anterior tibial artery (36247)

Lateral anterior malleolar artery (36247)

Medial anterior malleolar artery (36247)

Pedis dorsalis artery (36247)

Popliteal artery (36247)

Anterior tibial artery (36247)

Posterior tibial artery (36247)

Peroneal artery (36247)

Posterior view of right leg

ICD-10 CM-Coding

The application of these codes is too broad to adequately present ICD-10-CM diagnosis code links here. Refer to the current ICD-10-CM book.

CCI Edits

37224   01924, 11000-11006, 11042-11047, 12001-12007, 12011-12057, 13100-13133, 13151-13153, 35201-35206, 35226-35236, 35256-35266, 35286, 36000, 36002-36005, 36120-36140, 36160-36200, 36245-36247, 36400-36410, 36420-36430, 36440, 36500, 36591-36592, 36600-36640, 37246-37247, 43752, 51701-51703, 62320-62327, 64400-64410, 64413-64435, 64445-64450, 64461-64463, 64479-64530, 69990, 75630, 75710, 75716, 75736, 75774, 75893, 76000-76001, 76942, 76970, 76998, 77002, 92012-92014, 93000-93010, 93040-93042, 93050, 93318, 93355, 94002, 94200, 94250, 94680-94690, 94770, 95812-95816, 95819, 95822, 95829, 95955, 96360-96368, 96372, 96374-96377, 97597-97598, 97602, 99155-99157, 99211-99223, 99231-99255, 99291-99292, 99304-99310, 99315-99316, 99334-99337, 99347-99350, 99374-99375, 99377-99378, 99446-99449, 99495-99496, G0269, G0463, G0471, J0670, J1642-J1644, J2001

37225   01924, 11000-11006, 11042-11047, 12001-12007, 12011-12057, 13100-13133, 13151-13153, 35201-35206, 35226-35236, 35256-35266, 35286, 35302-35303, 36000, 36002-36005, 36120-36140, 36160-36200, 36245-36247, 36400-36410, 36420-36430, 36440, 36500, 36591-36592, 36600-36640, 37186, 37224, 37226, 37246-37247, 43752, 51701-51703, 62320-62327, 64400-64410, 64413-64435, 64445-64450, 64461-64463, 64479-64530, 69990, 75630,

75710, 75716, 75736, 75774, 75893, 76000-76001, 76942, 76970, 76998, 77002, 92012-92014, 93000-93010, 93040-93042, 93050, 93318, 93355, 94002, 94200, 94250, 94680-94690, 94770, 95812-95816, 95819, 95822, 95829, 95955, 96360-96368, 96372, 96374-96377, 97597-97598, 97602, 99155-99157, 99211-99223, 99231-99255, 99291-99292, 99304-99310, 99315-99316, 99334-99337, 99347-99350, 99374-99375, 99377-99378, 99446-99449, 99495-99496, G0269, G0463, G0471, J0670, J1642-J1644, J2001

37226 01924, 11000-11006, 11042-11047, 12001-12007, 12011-12057, 13100-13133, 13151-13153, 34812-34820, 34833-34834, 35201-35206, 35226-35236, 35256-35266, 35286, 36000, 36002-36005, 36120-36140, 36160-36200, 36245-36247, 36400-36410, 36420-36430, 36440, 36500, 36591-36592, 36600-36640, 37224, 37236, 37238, 37246-37247, 43752, 51701-51703, 62320-62327, 64400-64410, 64413-64435, 64445-64450, 64461-64463, 64479-64530, 69990, 75630, 75710, 75716, 75736, 75774, 75893, 76000-76001, 76942, 76970, 76998, 77002, 92012-92014, 93000-93010, 93040-93042, 93050, 93318, 93355, 94002, 94200, 94250, 94680-94690, 94770, 95812-95816, 95819, 95822, 95829, 95955, 96360-96368, 96372, 96374-96377, 97597-97598, 97602, 99155-99157, 99211-99223, 99231-99255, 99291-99292, 99304-99310, 99315-99316, 99334-99337, 99347-99350, 99374-99375, 99377-99378, 99446-99449, 99495-99496, G0269, G0463, G0471, J0670, J1642-J1644, J2001

37227 01924, 11000-11006, 11042-11047, 12001-12007, 12011-12057, 13100-13133, 13151-13153, 34812-34820, 34833-34834, 35201-35206, 35226-35236, 35256-35266, 35286, 35302-35303, 36000, 36002-36005, 36120-36140, 36160-36200, 36245-36247, 36400-36410, 36420-36430, 36440, 36500, 36591-36592, 36600-36640, 37186, 37224-37226, 37236, 37238, 37246-37247, 43752, 51701-51703, 62320-62327, 64400-64410, 64413-64435, 64445-64450, 64461-64463, 64479-64530, 69990, 75630, 75710, 75716, 75736, 75774, 75893, 76000-76001, 76942, 76970, 76998, 77002, 92012-92014, 93000-93010, 93040-93042, 93050, 93318, 93355, 94002, 94200, 94250, 94680-94690, 94770, 95812-95816, 95819, 95822, 95829, 95955, 96360-96368, 96372, 96374-96377, 97597-97598, 97602, 99155-99157, 99211-99223, 99231-99255, 99291-99292, 99304-99310, 99315-99316, 99334-99337, 99347-99350, 99374-99375, 99377-99378, 99446-99449, 99495-99496, G0269, G0463, G0471, J0670, J1642-J1644, J2001

Case Example

Procedure:
After adequate preoperative evaluation, the patient was taken to the operating room and placed in the supine position where adequate general endotracheal anesthesia was administered without complication. The right groin was prepped and draped in the standard sterile fashion. A longitudinal incision was created in the right groin and carried down through the skin and subcutaneous tissue with electrocautery. The proximal end of the right femoral-popliteal bypass graft and the anastomosis were then dissected and the patient heparinized. Vessel loops were placed proximally and distally around the graft and a **transverse incision made in the graft**. A #6 Fogarty **embolectomy** catheter was passed first distally and then proximally and a large amount of grumous material removed. The material appeared to be chronic rather than acute. There was no acute clot. Good inflow was obtained proximally.

An 11-French sheath was then **passed distally and a 0.035 glidewire was passed distally into the popliteal artery** and on into the peroneal artery. A glide catheter was then passed over the wire and the wire exchanged for a 0.014 run-through wire. The **Silver Hawk MSM** device was then used to **perform plaque excision** to the **proximal popliteal artery including** the **distal anastomosis of the femoral-popliteal bypass graft**. Two runs were made with a total of eight passes each with the SilverHawk. A large amount of plaque material was obtained. Repeat angiography showed much better flow through the graft into the popliteal artery; however, there remained a significant amount of residual stenosis. Therefore, a 4x40 mm Agiltrac balloon was passed into the **distal popliteal artery** and **proximal popliteal artery**, and **balloon angioplasty** was **performed** to 8 atm for two minutes each.

There was also residual disease in the anterior tibial, peroneal, tibioperoneal trunk, and posterior tibial arteries. A 2x120 mm **balloon** was passed over the run-through wire and through the **anterior tibial artery** distally on **into the dorsalis pedis artery**. The balloon was dilated to 8 atm distally. A 3x120 mm balloon was then passed over the wire **into the proximal anterior tibial artery** and this vessel was dilated to 8 atm. The wire was then directed into the **peroneal artery**.

The 3x100 mm balloon was then **directed into the peroneal artery and dilated** to 8 atm for one minute. The wire was then placed in the **posterior tibial artery** and 3x100 mm was passed over the wire into the artery and **balloon angioplasty performed** at 8 atm for one minute. Balloons, catheter, and wires were then removed. **Nitroglycerin was infused** and repeat angiography showed good flow through the graft into the popliteal artery and into the tibial and peroneal vessels with no evidence of residual stenosis or flow-limiting dissection. The arteriotomy was then closed using a running continuous suture of 5-0 Prolene. Good Doppler signals were obtained after the artery was back-flushed and air was vented. Clamps were released and after adequate hemostasis was assured the patient was given protamine and the wound closed in layers using Vicryl sutures. Sterile dressings were applied and the patient moved to recovery in stable condition having tolerated the procedure well without complications.

CPT/HCPCS Codes Reported:
35875, 37225, 37228, 37232 x 2

Other Codes Reported:
C1769, C1894, C1725, C1757, C1724

Transcatheter Endovascular Revascularization—Tibial/Peroneal Vascular Territory

The tibial/peroneal territory includes these vessels:

- Anterior tibial artery
- Posterior tibial artery
- Peroneal artery

Angioplasty, only:

37228   **Revascularization, endovascular, open or percutaneous, tibial, peroneal artery, unilateral, initial vessel; with transluminal angioplasty**

37232   **Revascularization, endovascular, open or percutaneous, tibial, peroneal artery, unilateral, each additional vessel; with transluminal angioplasty (List separately in addition to code for primary procedure)**

Atherectomy, with or without angioplasty:

37229   **Revascularization, endovascular, open or percutaneous, tibial, peroneal artery, unilateral, initial vessel; with atherectomy, includes angioplasty within the same vessel, when performed**

37233   **Revascularization, endovascular, open or percutaneous, tibial, peroneal artery, unilateral, each additional vessel; with atherectomy, includes angioplasty within the same vessel, when performed (List separately in addition to code for primary procedure)**

Stent placement, with or without angioplasty:

37230   **Revascularization, endovascular, open or percutaneous, tibial, peroneal artery, unilateral, initial vessel; with transluminal stent placement(s), includes angioplasty within the same vessel, when performed**

37234   **Revascularization, endovascular, open or percutaneous, tibial, peroneal artery, unilateral, each additional vessel; with transluminal stent placement(s), includes angioplasty within the same vessel, when performed (List separately in addition to code for primary procedure)**

Stent placement and atherectomy, with or without angioplasty:

37231   **Revascularization, endovascular, open or percutaneous, tibial/peroneal artery, unilateral, initial vessel; with transluminal stent placement(s) and atherectomy, includes angioplasty within the same vessel, when performed**

37235   **Revascularization, endovascular, open or percutaneous, tibial/peroneal artery, unilateral, each additional vessel; with transluminal stent placement(s) and atherectomy, includes angioplasty within the same vessel,when performed (List separately in addition to code for primary procedure)**

Coding Tips—Tibial/Peroneal Territory

1. CPT codes 37228–37235 report unilateral service.
2. Report only one primary code for the initial tibial/peroneal artery treated in each leg.
3. Report additional vessel treatments with the appropriate add-on codes, 37232–37235. Up to two additional vessel codes may be reported for each leg since there are three arteries.
4. Do not report multiple codes for different lesions within the same vessel. Treatment of multiple lesions in one vessel is covered by a single vessel code.
5. The common tibio-peroneal trunk is part of the tibial/peroneal territory but is not considered to be a separate vessel.

Facility HCPCS Coding

Some applicable codes may include but are not limited to:

C1714   Catheter, transluminal atherectomy, directional
C1724   Catheter, transluminal atherectomy, rotational
C1725   Catheter, transluminal angioplasty, non-laser
C1760   Closure device, vascular (implantable/insertable), if used
C1769   Guidewire
C1874   Stent, coated/covered, with delivery system
C1875   Stent, coated/covered, without delivery system
C1876   Stent, non-coated/noncovered, with delivery system
C1877   Stent, non-coated/noncovered, without delivery system

C1885   Catheter, transluminal angioplasty, laser

G0269   Placement of occlusive device into either a venous or arterial access site, post surgical or interventional procedure (e.g., angioSeal plug, vascular plug), if performed

Q9965   LOCM, 100-199 mg/ml iodine concentration, per ml

Q9966   LOCM, 200-299 mg/ml iodine concentration, per ml

Q9967   LOCM, 300-399 mg/ml iodine concentration, per ml

Note: See appendix B for a complete listing of reportable HCPCS Level II codes.

ICD-10-CM Coding

The application of these codes is too broad to adequately present ICD-10-CM diagnosis code links here. Refer to the current ICD-10-CM book.

CCI Edits

37228   01924, 11000-11006, 11042-11047, 12001-12007, 12011-12057, 13100-13133, 13151-13153, 35201-35206, 35226-35236, 35256-35266, 35286, 36000, 36002-36005, 36120-36140, 36160-36200, 36245-36247, 36400-36410, 36420-36430, 36440, 36500, 36591-36592, 36600-36640, 37246-37247, 43752, 51701-51703, 62320-62327, 64400-64410, 64413-64435, 64445-64450, 64461-64463, 64479-64530, 69990, 75630, 75710, 75716, 75736, 75774, 75893, 76000-76001, 76942, 76970, 76998, 77002, 92012-92014, 93000-93010, 93040-93042, 93050, 93318, 93355, 94002, 94200, 94250, 94680-94690, 94770, 95812-95816, 95819, 95822, 95829, 95955, 96360-96368, 96372, 96374-96377, 97597-97598, 97602, 99155-99157, 99211-99223, 99231-99255, 99291-99292, 99304-99310, 99315-99316, 99334-99337, 99347-99350, 99374-99375, 99377-99378, 99446-99449, 99495-99496, G0269, G0463, G0471, J0670, J1642-J1644, J2001

37229   01924, 11000-11006, 11042-11047, 12001-12007, 12011-12057, 13100-13133, 13151-13153, 35201-35206, 35226-35236, 35256-35266, 35286, 35304-35306, 36000, 36002-36005, 36120-36140, 36160-36200, 36245-36247, 36400-36410, 36420-36430, 36440, 36500, 36591-36592, 36600-36640, 37186, 37228, 37230, 37246-37247, 43752, 51701-51703, 62320-62327, 64400-64410, 64413-64435, 64445-64450, 64461-64463, 64479-64530, 69990, 75630, 75710, 75716, 75736, 75774, 75893, 76000-76001, 76942, 76970, 76998, 77002, 92012-92014, 93000-93010, 93040-93042, 93050, 93318, 93355, 94002, 94200, 94250, 94680-94690, 94770, 95812-95816, 95819, 95822, 95829, 95955, 96360-96368, 96372, 96374-96377, 97597-97598, 97602, 99155-99157, 99211-99223, 99231-99255, 99291-99292, 99304-99310, 99315-99316, 99334-99337, 99347-99350, 99374-99375, 99377-99378, 99446-99449, 99495-99496, G0269, G0463, G0471, J0670, J1642-J1644, J2001

37230   01924, 11000-11006, 11042-11047, 12001-12007, 12011-12057, 13100-13133, 13151-13153, 34812-34820, 34833-34834, 35201-35206, 35226-35236, 35256-35266, 35286, 36000, 36002-36005, 36120-36140, 36160-36200, 36245-36247, 36400-36410, 36420-36430, 36440, 36500, 36591-36592, 36600-36640, 37228, 37236, 37238, 37246-37247, 43752, 51701-51703, 62320-62327, 64400-64410, 64413-64435, 64445-64450, 64461-64463, 64479-64530, 69990, 75630, 75710, 75716, 75736, 75774, 75893, 76000-76001, 76942, 76970, 76998, 77002, 92012-92014, 93000-93010, 93040-93042, 93050, 93318, 93355, 94002, 94200, 94250, 94680-94690, 94770, 95812-95816, 95819, 95822, 95829, 95955, 96360-96368, 96372, 96374-96377, 97597-97598, 97602, 99155-99157, 99211-99223, 99231-99255, 99291-99292, 99304-99310, 99315-99316, 99334-99337, 99347-99350, 99374-99375, 99377-99378, 99446-99449, 99495-99496, G0269, G0463, G0471, J0670, J1642-J1644, J2001

37231   01924, 11000-11006, 11042-11047, 12001-12007, 12011-12057, 13100-13133, 13151-13153, 34812-34820, 34833-34834, 35201-35206, 35226-35236, 35256-35266, 35286, 35304-35306, 36000, 36002-36005, 36120-36140, 36160-36200, 36245-36247, 36400-36410, 36420-36430, 36440, 36500, 36591-36592, 36600-36640, 37186, 37228-37230, 37236, 37238, 37246-37247, 43752, 51701-51703, 62320-62327, 64400-64410, 64413-64435, 64445-64450, 64461-64463, 64479-64530, 69990, 75630, 75710, 75716, 75736, 75774, 75893, 76000-76001, 76942, 76970, 76998, 77002, 92012-92014, 93000-93010, 93040-93042, 93050, 93318, 93355, 94002, 94200, 94250, 94680-94690, 94770, 95812-95816, 95819, 95822, 95829, 95955, 96360-96368, 96372, 96374-96377, 97597-97598, 97602, 99155-99157, 99211-99223, 99231-99255, 99291-99292, 99304-99310, 99315-99316, 99334-99337, 99347-99350, 99374-99375, 99377-99378, 99446-99449, 99495-99496, G0269, G0463, G0471, J0670, J1642-J1644, J2001

37232   11000-11006, 11042-11047, 35201-35206, 35226-35236, 35256-35266, 35286, 36591-36592, 93050, 97597-97598, 97602, G0269, J1642-J1644

37233   11000-11006, 11042-11047, 35201-35206, 35226-35236, 35256-35266, 35286, 35304-35306, 36591-36592, 37186, 93050, 97597-97598, 97602, G0269, J1642-J1644

37234   11000-11006, 11042-11047, 34812-34820, 34833-34834, 35201-35206, 35226-35236, 35256-35266, 35286, 36591-36592, 37236, 37238, 93050, 97597-97598, 97602, G0269, J1642-J1644

37235   11000-11006, 11042-11047, 34812-34820, 34833-34834, 35201-35206, 35226-35236, 35256-35266, 35286, 35304-35306, 36591-36592, 37186, 37236, 37238, 37246-37247, 93050, 97597-97598, 97602, G0269, J1642-J1644

Case Example

Preoperative diagnoses:
Chronic arterial insufficiency, threatened left lower extremity

The patient is brought to the operating room for angiography followed by revascularization for limb salvage as indicated.

Procedure Description:
After adequate preoperative evaluation, the patient was taken to the operating room and placed in supine position where adequate intravenous sedation was administered without complication. Both groins were prepped and draped in the usual sterile fashion. The **right common femoral artery** was cannulated retrograde with a 5-French sheath over a J wire. The wire was then advanced to the **suprarenal aorta**. The pigtail **catheter was advanced** over the wire and the wire was removed. Then, 30 ml of contrast media was injected at 10 ml per second and the contrast bolus used to **visualize** the **abdominal aorta** and its branches using digital subtraction angiography. There were single renal arteries bilaterally.

There was no evidence of renal artery stenosis. The infrarenal aorta was normal. There was a 70 percent right common iliac artery stenosis and the left common iliac artery was normal. Both internal iliac arteries were patent. There was diffuse disease involving the left external iliac artery ranging from 70 to 90 percent. The **catheter was** then **withdrawn into the right external iliac artery** and 25 ml of contrast media was injected at 5 ml per second and the bolus was followed **distally** using high level fluoroscopy on pulse mode **down the right lower extremity**. The right external iliac, right common femoral, and right profunda femoris were normal. The right superficial femoral artery was occluded just beyond its origin. The right popliteal artery reconstituted at the adductor hiatus. The trifurcation vessels below the knee were all normal on the right. The catheter was then directed over the aortic bifurcation to the left external iliac artery.

Again, 25 ml of contrast media was injected at 5 ml per second and the bolus **followed down the left lower extremity**. There was diffuse disease involving the left external iliac artery ranging from 70 to 90 percent. The left common femoral artery also had an 80 percent stenosis. The left profunda femoris was normal. The left superficial femoral artery was occluded at its origin. The popliteal artery did not reconstitute above the knee. A short segment of popliteal artery reconstituted below the knee just proximal to the takeoff of the anterior tibial which had a 90 percent stenosis at its ostium. The tibioperoneal trunk, posterior tibial, and peroneal arteries were patent. A stiff angled glide catheter was then passed through the catheter into the profunda femoris and the catheter and sheath exchanged for a 7-French Pinnacle Destination **sheath** which was passed over the aortic bifurcation through the left external iliac disease **into the left common femoral artery**. The patient was then heparinized. The stiff angled glidewire was then used to successfully pass through the long occluded segment of the left superficial femoral and popliteal artery into the tibioperoneal trunk and peroneal artery. The **angled glide catheter** was then passed over the wire and the wire exchanged for a 0.014 Miracle Brothers wire which **was placed in the peroneal artery**. A **SilverHawk LXN device** was then used to **perform plaque excision to the long occluded segment of the left superficial femoral artery**. A large amount of bulky plaque was removed. However, there remained a significant amount of disease with the residual luminal narrowing which could not be removed with the SilverHawk device. Therefore, **three separate stents** were **placed from the popliteal artery proximally into the proximal portion of the superficial femoral artery**. A 6x150 mm **stent was placed in the left popliteal artery**. A 6x150 mm Viabond **stent was placed in the left superficial femoral artery** and a 6x100 mm Viabond **stent was placed in the proximal left superficial femoral artery**. Just above this, a 75mm LifeStent noncovered self-expanding **stent** was **placed up to the ostium of the left superficial femoral artery**. A 3x200mm NanoCross balloon was then used to **perform balloon angioplasty to the tibioperoneal trunk and peroneal artery**. The wire was then directed into the left anterior tibial artery using the glide catheter, and the ostial stenosis in the **anterior tibial artery was then dilated** using the 3x200mm NanoCross balloon. The wire was then placed into the posterior tibial and again **balloon angioplasty** was **performed to the posterior tibial** using 3x200 mm NanoCross balloon. Attention was then turned to the **left external iliac artery**. A 7x120 mm Flex Star self-expanding **stent** was then **placed into the left external iliac artery**. This was then post-dilated using a 7x80 mm balloon. The sheath was withdrawn to the right external iliac artery. The wire was placed in the suprarenal aorta and the **right common iliac artery stenosis was stented** using a 10x37mm Visipro balloon expandable stent to 12 atm. The flush catheter was replaced and repeat aortography was performed demonstrating good flow through both iliac arteries and to the left superficial femoral artery, popliteal, and trifurcation vessels below the knee without evidence of residual luminal stenosis and no flow-limiting lesions. The sheath was replaced with a short 7-French sheath. The right common femoral arteriotomy was closed using the boomerang closure device. Sterile dressings were applied. The patient was returned to the recovery room in stable condition, having tolerated the procedure well without complications.

CPT/HCPCS Codes Reported:
75625, 75716, 37227, 37228, 37232x2, 37221, 37221-XS

Other HCPCS Codes Reported:
C1724, C1769, C1725, C1876x5

Transluminal Atherectomy for Supra-Inguinal Arteries

Atherectomy involves special cutting type catheters designed to "cut" and remove the plaque from the artery. This set of codes reports atherectomy procedures for arteries located above the inguinal ligament.

0234T   **Transluminal peripheral atherectomy, open or percutaneous, including radiological supervision and interpretation; renal artery**

A stenosed renal artery is treated intraluminally to relieve blockage. A needle is used to access the arterial system and is followed by a guidewire and an introducer sheath to protect and enclose the opening. Various catheters and guidewires are inserted to transverse the stenosed area. A special atherectomy catheter is used to cut or drill a channel through the plaque lesion and reopen the artery. This code reports both the surgical procedure and the radiological supervision and interpretation for atherectomy of the renal artery.

0235T   **Transluminal peripheral atherectomy, open or percutaneous, including radiological supervision and interpretation; visceral artery (except renal), each vessel**

A stenosed visceral (abdominal) artery is treated intraluminally to relieve blockage. A needle is used to access the arterial system and is followed by a guidewire and an introducer sheath to protect and enclose the opening. Various catheters and guidewires are inserted to transverse the stenosed area. A special atherectomy catheter is used to cut or drill a channel through the plaque lesion and reopen the artery. This code reports both the surgical procedure and the radiological supervision and interpretation for atherectomy of a visceral artery.

0236T   **Transluminal peripheral atherectomy, open or percutaneous, including radiological supervision and interpretation; abdominal aorta**

The abdominal aorta is treated intraluminally to relieve blockage. A needle is used to access the arterial system and is followed by a guidewire and an introducer sheath to protect and enclose the opening. Various catheters and guidewires are inserted to transverse the stenosed area. A special atherectomy catheter is used to cut or drill a channel through the plaque lesion and reopen the artery. This code reports both the surgical procedure and the radiological supervision and interpretation for atherectomy of the abdominal aorta.

0237T   **Transluminal peripheral atherectomy, open or percutaneous, including radiological supervision and interpretation; brachiocephalic artery, each vessel**

A stenosed brachiocephalic artery is treated intraluminally to relieve blockage. A needle is used to access the arterial system and is followed by a guidewire and an introducer sheath to protect and enclose the opening. Various catheters and guidewires are inserted to transverse the stenosed area. A special atherectomy catheter is used to cut or drill a channel through the plaque lesion and reopen the artery. This code reports both the surgical procedure and the radiological supervision and interpretation for atherectomy of a brachiocephalic artery.

0238T   **Transluminal peripheral atherectomy, open or percutaneous, including radiological supervision and interpretation; iliac artery, each vessel**

A stenosed iliac artery is treated intraluminally to relieve blockage. A needle is used to access the arterial system and is followed by a guidewire and an introducer sheath to protect and enclose the opening. Various catheters and guidewires are inserted to transverse the stenosed area. A special atherectomy catheter is used to cut or drill a channel through the plaque lesion and reopen the artery. This code reports both the surgical procedure and the radiological supervision and interpretation for atherectomy of an iliac artery.

Coding Tips

1. These codes include radiologic supervision and interpretation.
2. Catheter placement is not included and is reported separately.
3. Report closure of arteriotomy separately, if performed.
4. This code set does not include embolic protection, if used.
5. Other interventions are not included and are reported separately if performed. Report separately other interventions (stent placement and angioplasty) following coding guidelines for multiple interventions.
6. Angiography performed for diagnostic purposes is reported separately. Do not report angiography performed to size the vessel, confirm catheter placement or to confirm the presence of a known lesion.
7. Atherectomy is coded per vessel treated. Do not report separately each lesion treated within the same vessel.
8. Report all applicable pass-through device HCPCS codes. Refer to the HCPCS section for possible codes.
9. Hospitals are strongly encouraged to separately report all devices used and associated codes.
10. Hospitals are requested to continue reporting low osmolar contrast media (LOCM) separately with HCPCS codes Q9965–Q9967. Report all contrast media by milliliter.
11. Code 0235T is covered by Medicare as an inpatient procedure only.

Pelvic Arterial Anatomy—Anterior

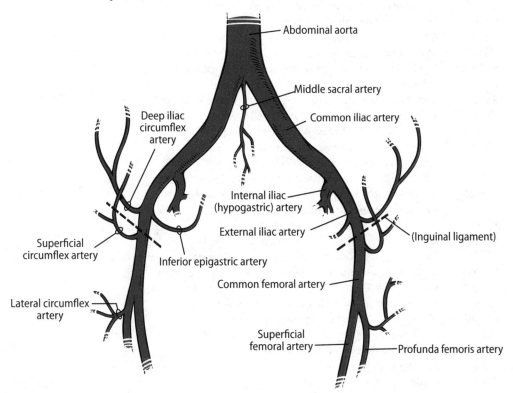

Facility HCPCS Codes

Some applicable codes may include but are not limited to:

C1714	Catheter, transluminal atherectomy, directional
C1724	Catheter, transluminal atherectomy, rotational
C1725	Catheter, transluminal angioplasty, non-laser
C1760	Closure device, vascular (implantable/insertable), if used
C1769	Guidewire
C1885	Catheter, transluminal angioplasty, laser
G0269	Placement of occlusive device into either a venous or arterial access site, post surgical or interventional procedure (e.g., angioSeal plug, vascular plug), if performed
Q9965	LOCM, 100-199 mg/ml iodine concentration, per ml
Q9966	LOCM, 200-299 mg/ml iodine concentration, per ml
Q9967	LOCM, 300-399 mg/ml iodine concentration, per ml

Note: See appendix B for a complete listing of reportable HCPCS Level II codes.

ICD-10-CM Coding

G45.1	Carotid artery syndrome (hemispheric)
G45.2	Multiple and bilateral precerebral artery syndromes
I65.21	Occlusion and stenosis of right carotid artery
I65.22	Occlusion and stenosis of left carotid artery
I65.23	Occlusion and stenosis of bilateral carotid arteries
I65.29	Occlusion and stenosis of unspecified carotid artery
I70.0	Atherosclerosis of aorta
I70.1	Atherosclerosis of renal artery
I70.8	Atherosclerosis of other arteries
I74.01	Saddle embolus of abdominal aorta
I74.09	Other arterial embolism and thrombosis of abdominal aorta

I74.5	Embolism and thrombosis of iliac artery
I74.8	Embolism and thrombosis of other arteries
I74.9	Embolism and thrombosis of unspecified artery
I75.81	Atheroembolism of kidney
I75.89	Atheroembolism of other site
K55.Ø11	Focal (segmental) acute (reversible) ischemia of small intestine
K55.Ø12	Diffuse acute (reversible) ischemia of small intestine
K55.Ø19	Acute (reversible) ischemia of small intestine, extent unspecified
K55.Ø21	Focal (segmental) acute infarction of small intestine
K55.Ø22	Diffuse acute infarction of small intestine
K55.Ø29	Acute infarction of small intestine, extent unspecified
K55.Ø31	Focal (segmental) acute (reversible) ischemia of large intestine
K55.Ø32	Diffuse acute (reversible) ischemia of large intestine
K55.Ø39	Acute (reversible) ischemia of large intestine, extent unspecified
K55.Ø41	Focal (segmental) acute infarction of large intestine
K55.Ø42	Diffuse acute infarction of large intestine
K55.Ø49	Acute infarction of large intestine, extent unspecified
K55.Ø51	Focal (segmental) acute (reversible) ischemia of intestine, part unspecified
K55.Ø52	Diffuse acute (reversible) ischemia of intestine, part unspecified
K55.Ø59	Acute (reversible) ischemia of intestine, part and extent unspecified
K55.Ø61	Focal (segmental) acute infarction of intestine, part unspecified
K55.Ø62	Diffuse acute infarction of intestine, part unspecified
K55.Ø69	Acute infarction of intestine, part and extent unspecified
K55.9	Vascular disorder of intestine, unspecified
N28.Ø	Ischemia and infarction of kidney
Q27.1	Congenital renal artery stenosis

CCI Edits

0234T 01924-01926, 0213T, 0216T, 11000-11006, 11042-11047, 34812, 34820, 34833-34834, 35201-35206, 35226-35236, 35256-35266, 35286, 36000, 36002-36005, 36400-36410, 36420-36430, 36440, 36500, 36591-36592, 36600-36640, 37184, 43752, 49000-49002, 51701-51703, 61645-61650, 62320-62327, 64400-64410, 64413-64435, 64445-64450, 64461, 64463, 64479, 64483, 64486-64490, 64493, 64505-64530, 69990, 75893, 76000-76001, 76942, 76970, 76998, 77002, 93000-93010, 93040-93042, 93050, 93318, 93355, 94002, 94200, 94250, 94680-94690, 94770, 95812-95816, 95819, 95822, 95829, 95955, 96360, 96365, 96372, 96374-96377, 97597-97598, 97602, 99155-99157, 99446-99449, G0471

0235T 01924-01926, 0213T, 0216T, 11000-11006, 11042-11047, 34812, 34820, 34833-34834, 35201-35206, 35226-35236, 35256-35266, 35286, 36000, 36002-36005, 36400-36410, 36420-36430, 36440, 36500, 36591-36592, 36600-36640, 37184, 43752, 49000-49002, 51701-51703, 61645-61650, 62320-62327, 64400-64410, 64413-64435, 64445-64450, 64461, 64463, 64479, 64483, 64486-64490, 64493, 64505-64530, 69990, 75726, 75736, 75774, 75893, 76000-76001, 76942, 76970, 76998, 77002, 93000-93010, 93040-93042, 93050, 93318, 93355, 94002, 94200, 94250, 94680-94690, 94770, 95812-95816, 95819, 95822, 95829, 95955, 96360, 96365, 96372, 96374-96377, 97597-97598, 97602, 99155-99157, 99446-99449, G0471

0236T 01924-01926, 0213T, 0216T, 11000-11006, 11042-11047, 32551, 32556-32557, 34812, 34820, 34833-34834, 35201-35206, 35226-35236, 35256-35266, 35286, 36000, 36002-36005, 36400-36410, 36420-36430, 36440, 36500, 36591-36592, 36600-36640, 37184, 43752, 49000-49002, 51701-51703, 61645-61650, 62320-62327, 64400-64410, 64413-64435, 64445-64450, 64461, 64463, 64479, 64483, 64486-64490, 64493, 64505-64530, 69990, 75600, 75605, 75625, 75630, 75635, 75893, 76000-76001, 76942, 76970, 76998, 77002, 93000-93010, 93040-93042, 93050, 93318, 93355, 94002, 94200, 94250, 94680-94690, 94770, 95812-95816, 95819, 95822, 95829, 95955, 96360, 96365, 96372, 96374-96377, 97597-97598, 97602, 99155-99157, 99446-99449, G0471

0237T 01924-01926, 0213T, 0216T, 11000-11006, 11042-11047, 34834, 35201-35206, 35226-35236, 35256-35266, 35286, 36000, 36002-36005, 36400-36410, 36420-36430, 36440, 36500, 36591-36592, 36600-36640, 37184, 43752, 51701-51703, 61645-61650, 62320-62327, 64400-64410, 64413-64435, 64445-64450, 64461, 64463, 64479, 64483, 64486-64490, 64493, 64505-64530, 69990, 75605, 75658, 75710, 75716, 75893, 76000-76001, 76942, 76970, 76998, 77002, 93000-93010, 93040-93042, 93050, 93318, 93355, 94002, 94200, 94250, 94680-94690, 94770, 95812-95816, 95819, 95822, 95829, 95955, 96360, 96365, 96372, 96374-96377, 97597-97598, 97602, 99155-99157, 99446-99449, G0471

0238T   01924, 11000-11006, 11042-11047, 35201-35206, 35226-35236, 35256-35266, 35286, 36000, 36002-36005,
36400-36410, 36420-36430, 36440, 36500, 36591-36592, 36600-36640, 43752, 51701-51703, 61650, 62320-62327,
64400-64410, 64413-64435, 64445-64450, 64461, 64463, 64479, 64483, 64486-64490, 64493, 64505-64530, 69990,
75630, 75635, 75710, 75716, 75736, 75774, 75893, 76000-76001, 76942, 76970, 76998, 77002, 93000-93010,
93040-93042, 93050, 93318, 93355, 94002, 94200, 94250, 94680-94690, 94770, 95812-95816, 95819, 95822, 95829,
95955, 96360, 96365, 96372, 96374-96377, 97597-97598, 97602, 99155-99157, 99446-99449, G0471

Case Example

Clinical History:
The patient has known atherosclerotic disease of the left common iliac artery.

Procedure:
Access was made into the left common femoral artery by percutaneous needle placement. A guidewire was successfully
passed through the area of stenosis and into the abdominal aorta. A 7 French sheath was placed. A bolus of 3000 units of
heparin was given. Mechanical atherectomy was then performed using the Fox hollow device. The atherectomy device
was withdrawn and follow-up angiography performed of the left leg. Most of the focal stenosis was reduced to
approximately 80 percent and good distal flow was maintained. All catheters and wires were removed and hemostasis
achieved with a Perclose device.

Impression:
Successful mechanical atherectomy of the left common iliac artery as described with residual stenosis of approximately
20 percent without complication.

0 pressure gradient across the area of atheromatous disease in the left common iliac artery.

Three vessel run-off with normal caliber anterior and posterior arteries.

CPT/HCPCS Codes Reported:
0238T, G0269

Other HCPCS Codes Reported:
C1714, C1769

Endovascular Transluminal Angioplasty— Visceral and Brachiocephalic Arteries, Aorta

Angioplasty is a common procedure performed to improve blood flow in arteries or veins that have become narrowed or blocked. In the interventional radiology area, these procedures are performed by percutaneous technique using specially designed balloon catheters.

37246   **Transluminal balloon angioplasty (except lower extremity artery(ies) for occlusive disease, intracranial, coronary, pulmonary, or dialysis circuit), open or percutaneous, including all imaging and radiological supervision and interpretation necessary to perform the angioplasty within the same artery; initial artery**

37247   **each additional artery (List separately in addition to code for primary procedure)**

A narrowing or stricture of a peripheral artery is stretched to allow a normal flow of blood. A local anesthetic is applied over the access site, usually the femoral artery, and the skin is percutaneously punctured with a needle. A guidewire is inserted and fed through the blood vessel and the needle is removed. A catheter with a deflated balloon is then advanced over the guidewire to the narrowed portion of the vessel. The balloon is inflated to stretch the vessel to a larger diameter allowing a more normal flow of blood. Several inflations may be performed along the narrowed area. Transluminal angioplasty may be done through an incision in the skin overlying the artery of access. Vessel clamps are applied and then the artery is nicked to create an opening for the balloon catheter.

Angioplasty

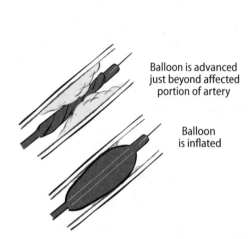

Balloon is advanced just beyond affected portion of artery

Balloon is inflated

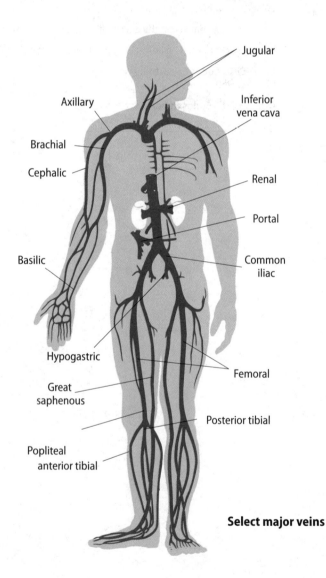

Jugular

Axillary

Inferior vena cava

Brachial

Cephalic

Renal

Portal

Basilic

Common iliac

Hypogastric

Femoral

Great saphenous

Posterior tibial

Popliteal anterior tibial

Select major veins

Coding Tips

1. These codes apply to angioplasty procedures performed on the renal and other visceral arteries, the brachiocephalic arteries and the aorta. Also use this code set to report angioplasty of the extremities when performed for reasons other than occlusive disease.

2. These codes are used for open or percutaneous approaches and cover all types of angioplasty devices.

3. Code separately for each selective catheter placement in addition to the angioplasty procedure code.

4. Angiography performed for diagnostic purposes is reported separately. Do not report angiography performed to size the vessel, confirm catheter placement, or to confirm the presence of a known lesion.

5. Angioplasty is coded per vessel treated. Do not report separately each lesion treated within the same vessel. Report one code for lesions extending across two vessels treated with single intervention.

6. Report 37247 when angioplasty is performed in a separate and distinct vessel, either ipsilateral or contralateral.

7. When performed, intravascular ultrasound (IVUS) is separately reported. See codes 37252 and 37253.

8. When performed, thrombectomy is separately reported. See codes 37184–37188 and 37211–37214.

9. Do not use these codes with 37215–37237 when intervention is in the same artery and during the same encounter.

10. Do not use these codes with the visceral endograft codes, 36841–36848.

11. Device codes are required for the codes in this section. Hospitals should report all applicable device codes used. Refer to the HCPCS section for possible codes.

12. Conscious sedation is not included in these codes. Separately report 99151–99157 per payer policy and coding guidelines. Hospitals may choose to include the costs associated with the service as part of the procedure rather than reporting them separately.

13. The angioplasty procedure includes roadmapping, guiding angiography or other contrast injections, and follow-up angiography to determine the success of the dilation.

14. Angioplasty is not reported in the following cases:

    a. When performed to pre-dilate a lesion for stent placement

    b. When performed to deploy a stent

    c. If the intent of the procedure was to place a stent

    d. To further dilate a newly deployed stent

15. Do not report vascular angioplasty codes for balloon dilatation of nonvascular structures.

16. Angiography may be reported in addition to angioplasty if there is a clinical change in the patient symptoms post angioplasty intervention. These changes must be documented.

17. Report all applicable pass-through device HCPCS codes. Refer to the HCPCS section for possible codes.

18. Hospitals are requested to continue reporting low osmolar contrast media (LOCM) separately with HCPCS codes Q9965–Q9967. Report all contrast media by milliliter.

19. Physician Reporting: These radiology S&I codes have both a technical and professional component. To report only the professional component, append modifier 26. To report only the technical component, append modifier TC. To report the complete procedure (i.e., both the professional and technical components), submit without a modifier.

Facility HCPCS Coding

Some applicable codes may include but are not limited to:

C1725	Catheter, transluminal angioplasty, non-laser
C1760	Closure device, vascular (implantable/insertable), if used
C1885	Catheter, transluminal angioplasty, laser
C2623	Catheter, transluminal angioplasty, drug-coated
G0269	Placement of occlusive device into either a venous or arterial access site, post surgical or interventional procedure (e.g., AngioSeal plug, vascular plug), if performed
Q9965	LOCM, 100-199 mg/ml iodine concentration, per ml
Q9966	LOCM, 200-299 mg/ml iodine concentration, per ml
Q9967	LOCM, 300-399 mg/ml iodine concentration, per ml

Note: See appendix B for a complete listing of reportable HCPCS Level II codes.

Upper Extremity Arterial Anatomy

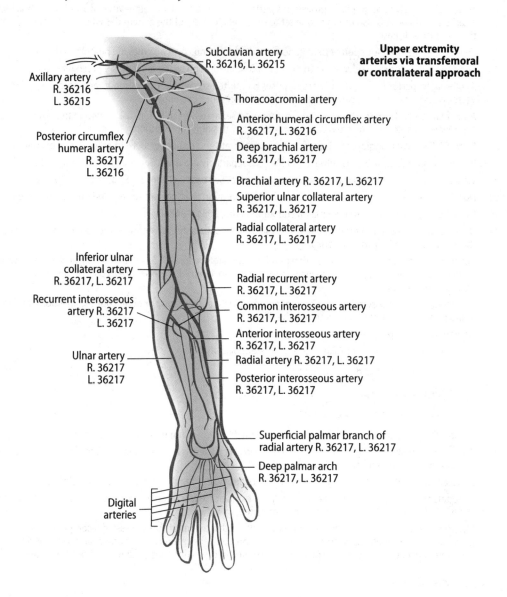

Upper extremity arteries via transfemoral or contralateral approach

Subclavian artery
R. 36216, L. 36215

Axillary artery
R. 36216
L. 36215

Thoracoacromial artery

Anterior humeral circumflex artery
R. 36217, L. 36216

Posterior circumflex
humeral artery
R. 36217
L. 36216

Deep brachial artery
R. 36217, L. 36217

Brachial artery R. 36217, L. 36217

Superior ulnar collateral artery
R. 36217, L. 36217

Radial collateral artery
R. 36217, L. 36217

Inferior ulnar
collateral artery
R. 36217, L. 36217

Radial recurrent artery
R. 36217, L. 36217

Recurrent interosseous
artery R. 36217
L. 36217

Common interosseous artery
R. 36217, L. 36217

Anterior interosseous artery
R. 36217, L. 36217

Ulnar artery
R. 36217
L. 36217

Radial artery R. 36217, L. 36217

Posterior interosseous artery
R. 36217, L. 36217

Superficial palmar branch of
radial artery R. 36217, L. 36217

Deep palmar arch
R. 36217, L. 36217

Digital
arteries

Thoracic Abdominal Arteries

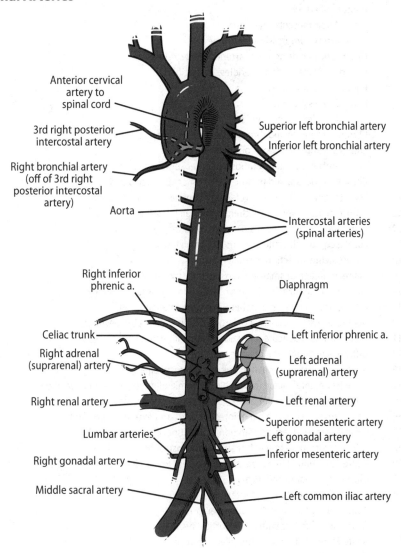

ICD-10-CM Coding

G45.3	Amaurosis fugax
I10	Essential (primary) hypertension
I12.Ø	Hypertensive chronic kidney disease with stage 5 chronic kidney disease or end stage renal disease
I12.9	Hypertensive chronic kidney disease with stage 1 through stage 4 chronic kidney disease, or unspecified chronic kidney disease
I13.Ø	Hypertensive heart and chronic kidney disease with heart failure and stage 1 through stage 4 chronic kidney disease, or unspecified chronic kidney disease
I13.1Ø	Hypertensive heart and chronic kidney disease without heart failure, with stage 1 through stage 4 chronic kidney disease, or unspecified chronic kidney disease
I13.11	Hypertensive heart and chronic kidney disease without heart failure, with stage 5 chronic kidney disease, or end stage renal disease
I13.2	Hypertensive heart and chronic kidney disease with heart failure and with stage 5 chronic kidney disease, or end stage renal disease
I15.Ø	Renovascular hypertension
I15.1	Hypertension secondary to other renal disorders
I16.Ø	Hypertensive urgency
I16.1	Hypertensive emergency
I16.9	Hypertensive crisis, unspecified
I7Ø.1	Atherosclerosis of renal artery

I77.1	Stricture of artery
I77.2	Rupture of artery
I77.3	Arterial fibromuscular dysplasia
I77.4	Celiac artery compression syndrome
I77.89	Other specified disorders of arteries and arterioles
I77.9	Disorder of arteries and arterioles, unspecified
I81	Portal vein thrombosis
I82.0	Budd-Chiari syndrome
I82.1	Thrombophlebitis migrans
I82.291	Chronic embolism and thrombosis of other thoracic veins
I82.3	Embolism and thrombosis of renal vein
I82.890	Acute embolism and thrombosis of other specified veins
I82.891	Chronic embolism and thrombosis of other specified veins
K55.011	Focal (segmental) acute (reversible) ischemia of small intestine
K55.012	Diffuse acute (reversible) ischemia of small intestine
K55.019	Acute (reversible) ischemia of small instestine, extent unspecified
K55.021	Focal (segmental) acute infarction of small intestine
K55.022	Diffuse acute infarction of small intestine
K55.029	Acute infarction of small intestine, extent unspecified
K55.031	Focal (segmental) acute (reversible) ischemia of large intestine
K55.032	Diffuse acute (reversible) ischemia of large intestine
K55.039	Acute (reversible) ischemia of large intestine, extent unspecified
K55.041	Focal (segmental) acute infarction of large intestine
K55.042	Diffuse acute infarction of large intestine
K55.049	Acute infarction of large intestine, extent unspecified
K55.051	Focal (segmental) acute (reversible) ischemia of intestine, part unspecified
K55.052	Diffuse acute (reversible) ischemia of intestine, part unspecified
K55.059	Acute (reversible) ischemia of intestine, part and extent unspecified
K55.061	Focal (segmental) acute infarction of intestine, part unspecified
K55.062	Diffuse acute infarction of intestine, part unspecified
K55.069	Acute infarction of intestine, part and extent unspecified
K55.1	Chronic vascular disorders of intestine
K55.8	Other vascular disorders of intestine
N17.0	Acute kidney failure with tubular necrosis
N17.1	Acute kidney failure with acute cortical necrosis
N17.2	Acute kidney failure with medullary necrosis
N17.8	Other acute kidney failure
N17.9	Acute kidney failure, unspecified
N26.2	Page kidney
N28.0	Ischemia and infarction of kidney
Q27.1	Congenital renal artery stenosis
Q27.2	Other congenital malformations of renal artery

CCI Edits

37246 01924-01926, 0213T, 0216T, 0228T, 0230T, 11000-11001, 11004-11006, 11042-11047, 12001-12002, 12004-12007, 12011, 12013-12018, 12020-12021, 12031-12032, 12034-12037, 12041-12042, 12044-12047, 12051-12057, 13100-13102, 13120-13122, 13131-13133, 13151-13153, 34812-34813, 34833- 34834, 35201, 35206-35207, 35211, 35216, 35221, 35226, 35231, 35236, 35241, 35246, 35251, 35256, 35261, 35266, 35271, 35276, 35281, 35286, 36000, 36002, 36400, 36405-36406, 36410, 36420, 36425, 36430, 36440, 36591-36592, 36600, 36640, 36902-36904, 37184, 37216, 37222-37223, 37232-37234, 37237, 43752, 51701-51703, 61645, 62320-62327, 64400, 64402, 64405, 64408, 64410, 64413, 64415-64418, 64420-64421, 64425, 64430, 64435, 64445-64450, 64461-64463, 64479-64480, 64483-64484, 64486-64495, 64505, 64508, 64510, 64517, 64520, 64530, 69990, 75600, 75605, 75625, 75630, 75658, 75705, 75710, 75716, 75726, 75731, 75733, 75736, 75741, 75743, 75746, 75756, 75774, 76000-76001, 76942, 77001-77002, 77012, 77021, 92012, 92014, 93000, 93005, 93010, 93040-93042, 93050, 93318, 93355, 94002, 94200, 94250, 94680-94681, 94690, 94770, 95812-95813, 95816, 95819, 95822, 95829, 95955, 96360-96361, 96365-96368, 96372, 96374-96377, 96523, 97597-97598, 97602, 99155-99157, 99211-99215, 99217-99223, 99231-99236, 99238-99239, 99241-99245, 99251-99255, 99291-99292, 99304-99310, 99315-99316, 99334-99337, 99347-99350, 99374-99375, 99377-99378, 99446-99449, 99495-99496, G0463, G0471, J0670, J1642, J1644, J2001

37247   01924-01926, 0213T, 0216T, 0228T, 0230T, 11000-11006, 11042-11047, 12001-12007, 12011-12057, 13100-13133, 13151-13153, 34812-34813, 34833-34834, 35201-35207, 35211-35286, 36000, 36002, 36400-36410, 36420-36430, 36440, 36591-36592, 36600, 36640, 36902-36904*, 37184, 37216, 37222-37223, 37232-37234, 37237, 43752, 51701-51703, 61645, 62320-62327, 64400-64410, 64413-64435, 64445-64450, 64461-64463, 64479-64530, 69990, 75600, 75605, 75625, 75630, 75658, 75705, 75710, 75716, 75726, 75731, 75733, 75736, 75741, 75743, 75746, 75756, 75774, 76000-76001, 76942, 77001-77002, 77012, 77021, 92012-92014, 93000-93010, 93040-93042, 93050, 93318, 93355, 94002, 94200, 94250, 94680-94690, 94770, 95812-95816, 95819, 95822, 95829, 95955, 96360-96368, 96372, 96374-96377, 96523, 97597-97598, 97602, 99155-99157, 99211-99223, 99231-99255, 99291-99292, 99304-99310, 99315-99316, 99334-99337, 99347-99350, 99374-99375, 99377-99378, 99446-99449, 99495-99496, G0463, G0471

Case Example

History:
Renovascular hypertension

Procedure:
Access was made via the right common femoral artery and a 6-French sheath was placed. The right renal artery was selectively catheterized and images were taken of the right renal arterial system. The catheter was then placed into the origin of the left renal artery and images were taken of the left renal arterial system. The images revealed an 80 percent stenosis in the right renal artery. The decision was made to proceed with angioplasty. A balloon catheter was advanced and positioned into the right renal artery. A glide wire was used to cross the stenosis and the balloon catheter was advanced. The balloon was inflated twice then removed. Repeat angiography demonstrated marked improvement in the area of stenosis. The procedure was discontinued. All catheters were removed and manual pressure was applied until hemostasis was achieved. A total of 50 cc of Omnipaque 240 was used during the procedure.

CPT/HCPCS Codes Reported:
36252, 37246

Other HCPCS Codes Reported:
Q9966x50, C1725, C1769

Endovascular Transluminal Angioplasty—Venous System

Angioplasty is a common procedure performed to improve blood flow in vessels that have become narrowed or blocked. In the interventional radiology area, these procedures are most commonly performed by percutaneous technique using specially designed balloon catheters. This section pertains to angioplasty performed in venous vessels.

37248 **Transluminal balloon angioplasty (except dialysis circuit), open or percutaneous, including all imaging and radiological supervision and interpretation necessary to perform the angioplasty within the same vein, initial vein**

37249 **each additional vein (List separately in addition to code for primary procedure)**

Coding Tips

1. Codes 37248 and 37249 apply to angioplasty procedures performed in any vein, including the portal venous structures. They do not apply to interventions performed in the dialysis circuit. See previous chapter for coding of dialysis circuit procedures.

2. These codes are used for open or percutaneous approaches and cover all types of angioplasty devices.

3. Code separately for each selective catheter placement in addition to the angioplasty procedure code.

4. Angiography performed for diagnostic purposes is reported separately. Do not report angiography used to size the vessel, confirm catheter placement, or to confirm the presence of a known lesion.

5. Angioplasty is coded per vessel treated. Do not report separately each lesion treated within the same vessel. Report one code for lesions extending across two vessels treated with a single intervention.

6. Report 37248 when angioplasty is performed in a separate and distinct vessel, either ipsilateral or contralateral.

7. When performed, intravascular ultrasound (IVUS) is separately reported. See codes 37252 and 37253.

8. When performed, thrombectomy is separately reported. See codes 37184–37188 and 37211–37214.

9. Device codes are required for the codes in this section. Hospitals should report all applicable device codes used. Refer to the HCPCS section for possible codes.

10. Conscious sedation is not included in these codes. Separately report 99151–99157 per payer policy and coding guidelines. Hospitals may choose to include the costs associated with the service as part of the procedure rather than reporting them separately.

Facility HCPCS Coding

Some applicable codes may include but are not limited to:

C1769	Guidewire
C1725	Catheter, angioplasty
C1885	Catheter, transluminal angioplasty, laser
C2623	Catheter, transluminal angioplasty, drug-coated
Q9965	LOCM, 100-199 mg/ml iodine concentration, per ml
Q9966	LOCM, 200-299 mg/ml iodine concentration, per ml
Q9967	LOCM, 300-399 mg/ml iodine concentration, per ml

Note: See appendix B for a complete listing of reportable HCPCS Level II codes.

ICD-10-CM Coding

The application of these codes is too broad to adequately present ICD-10-CM diagnosis code links here. Refer to the current ICD-10-CM book.

CCI Edits

37248 01916, 01924-01926, 01930-01933, 0213T, 0216T, 0228T, 0230T, 11000-11006, 11042-11047, 12001-12007, 12011-12057, 13100-13133, 13151-13153, 35201-35207, 35211-35286, 36000, 36002-36005, 36400-36410, 36420-36430, 36440, 36591-36592, 36600, 36640, 36860-36861, 36902-36903, 36907-36908, 37239, 43752, 51701-51703, 62320-62327, 64400-64410, 64413-64435, 64445-64450, 64461-64463, 64479-64530, 69990, 75810, 75820, 75822, 75825, 75827, 75831, 75833, 75840, 75842, 75860, 75870, 75872, 75880, 75885, 75887, 75889, 75891, 76000-76001, 76942, 76998, 77001-77002, 77012, 77021, 92012-92014, 93000-93010, 93040-93042, 93318, 93355, 94002, 94200, 94250, 94680-94690, 94770, 95812-95816, 95819, 95822, 95829, 95955, 96360-96368, 96372, 96374-96377, 96523, 97597-97598, 97602, 99155-99157, 99211-99223, 99231-99255, 99291-99292, 99304-99310, 99315-99316, 99334-99337, 99347-99350, 99374-99375, 99377-99378, 99446-99449, 99495-99496, G0463, G0471, J0670, J1642-J1644, J2001

37249   01916, 01924-01926, 01930-01933, 0213T, 0216T, 0228T, 0230T, 11000-11006, 11042-11047, 12001-12007, 12011-12057, 13100-13133, 13151-13153, 35201-35207, 35211-35286, 36000, 36002-36005, 36400-36410, 36420-36430, 36440, 36591-36592, 36600, 36640, 36860-36861, 36902-36903, 36907-36908, 37239, 43752, 51701-51703, 62320-62327, 64400-64410, 64413-64435, 64445-64450, 64461-64463, 64479-64530, 69990, 75810, 75820, 75822, 75825, 75827, 75831, 75833, 75840, 75842, 75860, 75870, 75872, 75880, 75885, 75887, 75889, 75891, 76000-76001, 76942, 76998, 77001-77002, 77012, 77021, 92012-92014, 93000-93010, 93040-93042, 93318, 93355, 94002, 94200, 94250, 94680-94690, 94770, 95812-95816, 95819, 95822, 95829, 95955, 96360-96368, 96372, 96374-96377, 96523, 97597-97598, 97602, 99155-99157, 99211-99223, 99231-99255, 99291-99292, 99304-99310, 99315-99316, 99334-99337, 99347-99350, 99374-99375, 99377-99378, 99446-99449, 99495-99496, G0463, G0471

Case Example

Patient with pain and swelling of the right leg.

The patient is prepped and draped in the typical sterile fashion. The **right external iliac vein** was percutaneously punctured. A guidewire was inserted and directed down into the femoral vein. The wire was then exchanged for a straight flush catheter. Contrast was injected demonstrating a 2cm segment of narrowing in the distal portion of the deep femoral vein. The flush catheter was exchanged for the balloon angioplasty catheter. The angioplasty catheter was directed to the stenosis. A wire was carefully directed through the area of the stenosis and the angioplasty catheter was then guided through the stenosis. The wire was removed and the **balloon catheter was used to perform angioplasty** of the stenosed area. The balloon was deflated and the catheter was retracted back to the femoral vein. Contrast injection was then performed. **Venography** demonstrated near complete resolution of the stenosed area. The catheter was removed and pressure over the entry site held until hemostasis was achieved.

CPT/HCPCS Codes Reported:
75820-RT, 36012, 37248

Other HCPCS Codes Reported:
C1769, C1725

Transcatheter Stent Placement—Visceral and Brachiocephalic Arteries; Venous System

In the interventional radiology setting, vascular stents are performed via percutaneous technique. Vascular surgeons perform stent placement via percutaneous or open technique. Special catheters are routed to the area of stenosis. Stents can be self-expanding or require balloon expansion for deployment. Stents may be placed as the primary or intended procedure or they may be deployed after failed angioplasty or atherectomy. Multiple stents may be required to fully treat the area of stenosis. There are separate CPT codes available to report stent placement performed on the peripheral, carotid, cerebral, and vertebral arteries. Refer to other sections in this chapter for details. There are separate CPT codes available to report stent placement performed on coronary arteries. Refer to the Interventional Cardiology chapter of this book for further details.

37236	**Transcatheter placement of an intravascular stent(s) (except lower extremity artery(s) for occlusive disease, cervical carotid, extracranial vertebral or intrathoracic carotid, intracranial, or coronary), open or percutaneous, including radiological supervision and interpretation and including all angioplasty within the same vessel, when performed, initial artery**
37237	**each additional artery (List separately in addition to code for primary procedure)**
37238	**Transcatheter placement of an intravascular stent(s) open or percutaneous, including radiological supervision and interpretation and including angioplasty within the same vessel, when performed; initial vein**
37239	**each additional vein (List separately in addition to code for primary procedure)**

The physician places one or more intravascular stents through a catheter into an artery other than a coronary, cervical, or intrathoracic carotid, extracranial vertebral, iliac, intracranial, or lower extremity artery, or into a vein. The procedure may be performed via a percutaneous or an open approach. In the percutaneous approach, a guidewire is threaded through the needle into the blood vessel, and the needle is removed. In the open approach, the physician makes an incision in the skin overlying the vessel to be catheterized. The vessel is dissected and nicked with a small blade. After the approach, a catheter with a stent-transporting tip is threaded over the guidewire into the vessel and the wire is extracted. The catheter travels to the point where the vessel needs additional support. The compressed stent is passed from the catheter out into the vessel, where it deploys, expanding to support the vessel walls. The catheter is removed, and pressure is applied over the puncture site or layered closure is performed. Report 37236 for stents placed in the initial artery and 37237 for each additional artery where a stent is placed. Report 37238 for stents placed in the initial vein and 37239 for each additional vein where a stent is placed.

Coding Tips

1. These codes apply to stent procedures performed on the renal and other visceral arteries, the brachiocephalic arteries, the aorta, and any vein. Also use this code set to report stent placement of the extremities when performed for reasons other than occlusive disease.

2. Code separately for each selective catheter placement in addition to the stent surgical procedure code and radiology S&I codes.

3. Angiography performed for diagnostic purposes is reported separately. Do not report angiography performed to size the vessel, confirm catheter placement, or to confirm the presence of a known lesion.

4. Stent placement is coded per vessel treated. Do not report separately each lesion treated within the same vessel. Do not report multiple stents placed in the same vessel as a separate procedure.

5. Do not report angiography performed to measure vessel for stent sizing.

6. Do not report angiography performed as follow-up to stent deployment.

7. Do not code angioplasty performed on the treated vessel.

8. For lesions extending across two vessels and treated as a single lesion, report the stent code only once.

9. Separately report angioplasty of a different vessel.

10. These codes include all imaging related to stent placement.

11. Separately report extensive artery repair or replacement.

12. Ultrasound guidance for vascular access may be separately reported provided all criteria for reporting code 76937 are met.

13. Separately report mechanical thrombectomy or thrombolytic treatment.

14. Do not report these codes for stents placed for deployment of embolization coils.

15. Conscious sedation is not included in these codes. Separately report 99151–99157 per payer policy and coding guidelines. Hospitals may choose to include the costs associated with the service as part of the procedure rather than reporting them separately.

16. Report all applicable pass-through device HCPCS codes. Refer to the HCPCS section for possible codes.

17. Hospitals are requested to continue reporting low osmolar contrast media (LOCM) separately with HCPCS codes Q9965–Q9967. Report all contrast media by milliliter.

Facility HCPCS Coding

Some applicable codes may include but are not limited to:

C1760	Closure device, vascular (implantable/insertable), if used
C1769	Guidewire
C1874	Stent, coated/covered, with delivery system
C1875	Stent, coated/covered, without delivery system
C1876	Stent, non-coated/noncovered, with delivery system
C1877	Stent, non-coated/noncovered without delivery system
G0269	Placement of occlusive device into either a venous or arterial access site, post surgical or interventional procedure (e.g., AngioSeal plug, vascular plug), if performed
Q9965	LOCM, 100-199 mg/ml iodine concentration, per ml
Q9966	LOCM, 200-299 mg/ml iodine concentration, per ml
Q9967	LOCM, 300-399 mg/ml iodine concentration, per ml

Note: See appendix B for a complete listing of reportable HCPCS Level II codes.

Upper Extremity Arterial Anatomy

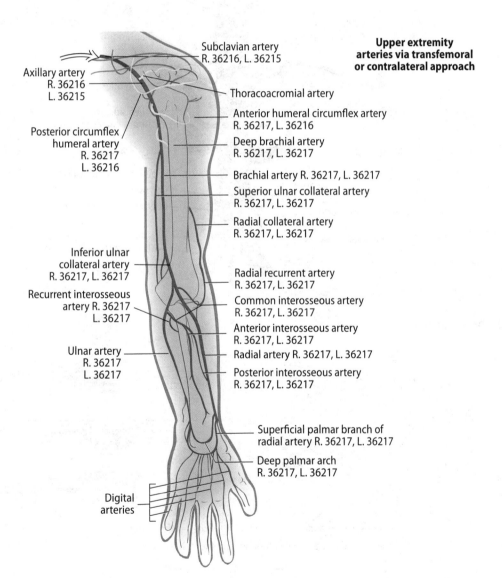

Subclavian artery
R. 36216, L. 36215

Upper extremity arteries via transfemoral or contralateral approach

Axillary artery
R. 36216
L. 36215

Thoracoacromial artery

Anterior humeral circumflex artery
R. 36217, L. 36216

Posterior circumflex
humeral artery
R. 36217
L. 36216

Deep brachial artery
R. 36217, L. 36217

Brachial artery R. 36217, L. 36217

Superior ulnar collateral artery
R. 36217, L. 36217

Radial collateral artery
R. 36217, L. 36217

Inferior ulnar
collateral artery
R. 36217, L. 36217

Radial recurrent artery
R. 36217, L. 36217

Recurrent interosseous
artery R. 36217
L. 36217

Common interosseous artery
R. 36217, L. 36217

Anterior interosseous artery
R. 36217, L. 36217

Ulnar artery
R. 36217
L. 36217

Radial artery R. 36217, L. 36217

Posterior interosseous artery
R. 36217, L. 36217

Superficial palmar branch of
radial artery R. 36217, L. 36217

Deep palmar arch
R. 36217, L. 36217

Digital
arteries

Thoracic and Abdominal Arteries

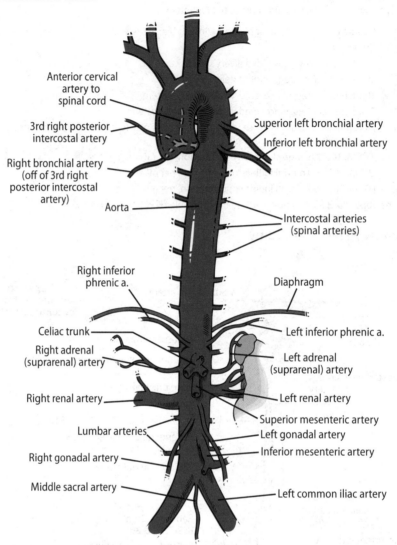

Anterior cervical artery to spinal cord

3rd right posterior intercostal artery

Right bronchial artery (off of 3rd right posterior intercostal artery)

Aorta

Right inferior phrenic a.

Celiac trunk

Right adrenal (suprarenal) artery

Right renal artery

Lumbar arteries

Right gonadal artery

Middle sacral artery

Superior left bronchial artery

Inferior left bronchial artery

Intercostal arteries (spinal arteries)

Diaphragm

Left inferior phrenic a.

Left adrenal (suprarenal) artery

Left renal artery

Superior mesenteric artery

Left gonadal artery

Inferior mesenteric artery

Left common iliac artery

Transcatheter Stent

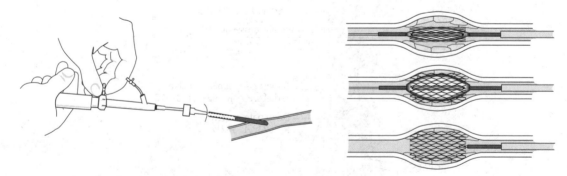

A balloon is expanded inside the stent to support the vessel

The balloon and catheter are withdrawnand the stent is left in place

ICD-10-CM Coding

The application of these codes is too broad to adequately present ICD-10-CM diagnosis code links here. Refer to the current ICD-10-CM book.

CCI Edits

37236 01924-01926, 0213T, 0216T, 0228T, 0230T, 0254T, 11000-11006, 11042-11047, 12001-12007, 12011-12057, 13100-13133, 13151-13153, 34812-34820, 34833-34834, 35201-35206, 35226-35236, 35256-35266, 35286, 36000, 36400-36410, 36420-36430, 36440, 36500, 36591-36592, 36600-36640, 36831-36833, 36860-36861, 36903, 37184, 37239, 37246-37247, 43752, 51701-51703, 61645, 62320-62327, 64400-64410, 64413-64435, 64445-64450, 64461-64463, 64479-64530, 69990, 75600, 75605, 75625, 75630, 75635, 75658, 75705, 75710, 75716, 75726, 75731, 75733, 75736, 75741, 75743, 75746, 75756, 75774, 75810, 75820, 75822, 75825, 75827, 75831, 75833, 75840, 75842, 75860, 75870, 75872, 75880, 75885, 75887, 75889, 75891, 75893, 76000-76001, 76380, 76942, 76970, 76998, 77001-77002, 77012, 77021, 92012-92014, 93000-93010, 93040-93042, 93050, 93318, 93355, 94002, 94200, 94250, 94680-94690, 94770, 95812-95816, 95819, 95822, 95829, 95955, 96360-96368, 96372, 96374-96377, 97597-97598, 97602, 99155-99157, 99211-99223, 99231-99255, 99291-99292, 99304-99310, 99315-99316, 99334-99337, 99347-99350, 99374-99375, 99377-99378, 99446-99449, G0269, G0463, G0471, J0670, J1642-J1644, J2001

37237 0075T, 01924-01926, 0213T, 0216T, 0228T, 0230T, 0254T, 11000-11006, 11042-11047, 12001-12007, 12011-12057, 13100-13133, 13151-13153, 34812-34820, 34833-34834, 35201-35206, 35226-35236, 35256-35266, 35286, 36000, 36400-36410, 36420-36430, 36440, 36500, 36591-36592, 36600-36640, 36831-36833, 36860-36861, 37184, 37215, 37217-37218, 43752, 51701-51703, 61645-61650, 62320-62327, 64400-64410, 64413-64435, 64445-64450, 64461, 64463, 64479, 64483, 64486-64490, 64493, 64505-64530, 69990, 75600, 75605, 75625, 75630, 75635, 75658, 75705, 75710, 75716, 75726, 75731, 75733, 75736, 75741, 75743, 75746, 75756, 75774, 75810, 75820, 75822, 75825, 75827, 75831, 75833, 75840, 75842, 75860, 75870, 75872, 75880, 75885, 75887, 75889, 75891, 75893, 76000-76001, 76380, 76942, 76970, 76998, 77001-77002, 77012, 77021, 93000-93010, 93040-93042, 93050, 93318, 93355, 94002, 94200, 94250, 94680-94690, 94770, 95812-95816, 95819, 95822, 95829, 95955, 96360, 96365, 96372, 96374-96377, 97597-97598, 97602, 99155-99157, 99211-99223, 99231-99255, 99291-99292, 99304-99310, 99315-99316, 99334-99337, 99347-99350, 99374-99375, 99377-99378, 99446-99449, G0463, G0471, J1644

37238 0075T, 01924-01926, 0213T, 0216T, 0228T, 0230T, 0254T, 11000-11006, 11042-11047, 12001-12007, 12011-12057, 13100-13133, 13151-13153, 34812-34820, 34833-34834, 35201-35206, 35226-35236, 35256-35266, 35286, 36000, 36005, 36400-36410, 36420-36430, 36440, 36500, 36591-36592, 36600-36640, 36831-36833, 36860-36861, 36903, 36908, 37184, 37215, 37217-37218, 37237, 37248-37249, 43752, 51701-51703, 61645, 62320-62327, 64400-64410, 64413-64435, 64445-64450, 64461-64463, 64479-64530, 69990, 75600, 75605, 75625, 75630, 75635, 75658, 75705, 75710, 75716, 75726, 75731, 75733, 75736, 75741, 75743, 75746, 75756, 75774, 75810, 75820, 75822, 75825, 75827, 75831, 75833, 75840, 75842, 75860, 75870, 75872, 75880, 75885, 75887, 75889, 75891, 75893, 76000-76001, 76380, 76942, 76970, 76998, 77001-77002, 77012, 77021, 92012-92014, 93000-93010, 93040-93042, 93318, 93355, 94002, 94200, 94250, 94680-94690, 94770, 95812-95816, 95819, 95822, 95829, 95955, 96360-96368, 96372, 96374-96377, 97597-97598, 97602, 99155-99157, 99211-99223, 99231-99255, 99291-99292, 99304-99310, 99315-99316, 99334-99337, 99347-99350, 99374-99375, 99377-99378, 99446-99449, G0269, G0463, G0471, J0670, J1642-J1644, J2001

37239 0075T, 01924-01926, 0213T, 0216T, 0228T, 0230T, 0254T, 11000-11006, 11042-11047, 12001-12007, 12011-12057, 13100-13133, 13151-13153, 34812-34820, 34833-34834, 35201-35206, 35226-35236, 35256-35266, 35286, 36000, 36005, 36400-36410, 36420-36430, 36440, 36500, 36591-36592, 36600-36640, 36831-36833, 36860-36861, 37184, 37215, 37217-37218, 43752, 51701-51703, 61645-61650, 62320-62327, 64400-64410, 64413-64435, 64445-64450, 64461, 64463, 64479, 64483, 64486-64490, 64493, 64505-64530, 69990, 75600, 75605, 75625, 75630, 75635, 75658, 75705, 75710, 75716, 75726, 75731, 75733, 75736, 75741, 75743, 75746, 75756, 75774, 75810, 75820, 75822, 75825, 75827, 75831, 75833, 75840, 75842, 75860, 75870, 75872, 75880, 75885, 75887, 75889, 75891, 75893, 76000-76001, 76380, 76942, 76970, 76998, 77001-77002, 77012, 77021, 93000-93010, 93040-93042, 93318, 93355, 94002, 94200, 94250, 94680-94690, 94770, 95812-95816, 95819, 95822, 95829, 95955, 96360, 96365, 96372, 96374-96377, 97597-97598, 97602, 99155-99157, 99211-99223, 99231-99255, 99291-99292, 99304-99310, 99315-99316, 99334-99337, 99347-99350, 99374-99375, 99377-99378, 99446-99449, G0463, G0471, J1644

Case Example #1

Indication:
A previous aortogram was performed. The patient was found to have severe bilateral renal artery stenosis associated with peripheral vascular disease. At that time, bilateral renal stent placement was recommended as a revascularization procedure.

Procedure:
Vascular **access** was achieved **via the right groin** using a 6-French sheath. A 6-French catheter was advanced into the abdominal aorta. The abdominal aortogram demonstrated patent aorta with runoff to the renals, demonstrating bilateral renal artery stenosis at the ostium. **A selective left renal angiogram was performed**. There was an eccentric ostial renal stenosis of approximately 80 percent with an inferior takeoff. A flexible guidewire was advanced through the lesion without difficulty. Subsequently, the **left renal artery was stented** using a 4.5 x 18 Herculink stent. Inadequate results were seen with 30 percent residual stenosis; therefore, a 5.0 ViaTrac balloon was used for **balloon angioplasty**. The final result was 10 percent residual stenosis with excellent patency. Attention was then turned to the right renal artery. A selective **right renal angiogram** was performed. The right renal artery was small in caliber at 3.0mm in diameter; therefore, a 3.0 x 15 **coronary balloon** Crossail was used to pre-dilate the lesion. The 95 percent renal stenosis did not improve significantly with the balloon angioplasty; therefore, a 3.0 x 13 Penta **stent was deployed**. A residual 10 percent stenosis was seen with excellent angiographic results. The patient received IV heparin and was transferred to recovery.

CPT/HCPCS Codes Reported:
37236, 37237, 36252

Other HCPCS Codes Reported:
C187x, C1725

Case Example #2

Indication:
Renovascular hypertension

Procedure:
Access was made into the **right femoral artery**. A catheter was advanced and placed in the left renal artery. Renal **angiogram revealed** a 20% lesion of the proximal left renal artery. The remainder of the artery is unremarkable. The catheter was then placed in the **origin of the right renal** artery. **Renal angiogram** revealed an 85% stenosis of the proximal right renal artery. The **decision** was made to **proceed** with intervention.

Angioplasty was performed of the right renal artery resulting in partial relief of the stenosis from 85% to 80%. A 6x18 Herculink **stent was deployed** at 14 atmospheres, resulting in a reduction of the stenosis to 10%. No evidence of distal dissection is noted. There is now normal flow into the distal right renal artery.

Conclusions:
- Severe renal artery stenosis involving the right renal artery (85%).
- **Unsuccessful angioplasty** of the right renal artery (80% residual stenosis).
- **Successful stenting** of the right renal artery (10% residual stenosis).
- Mild left renal artery stenosis (20%).

CPT/HCPCS Codes Reported:
36252, 37236

Other HCPCS Codes Reported:
C1725, C1876

Chapter 6: Neurovascular Interventions

Cerebral Endovascular Therapeutic Interventions

Cerebral Vascular Territories

Just as vascular territories have been defined for lower extremity interventions, territories have been defined for cerebral vascular interventions. The intracranial arteries fall into the following defined vascular territories:

- Right carotid circulation
  - right external carotid and branches
  - right internal carotid and branches
- Left carotid circulation
  - left external carotid and branches
  - left internal carotid and branches
- Vertebro-basilar circulation
  - left vertebral and branches
  - right vertebral and branches

Coding rules differ depending on the procedure performed. Please note these guidelines for each of the codes in this section.

61645 **Percutaneous arterial transluminal mechanical thrombectomy, and/or infusion for thrombolysis, intracranial, any method, including diagnostic angiography, fluoroscopic guidance, catheter placement, and intraprocedural pharmacological thrombolytic injections**
This code describes cerebral thrombolysis.

61650 **Endovascular intracranial prolonged administration of pharmacologic agent(s) other than for thrombolysis, arterial, including catheter placement, diagnostic angiography, and imaging guidance; initial vascular territory**

61651 **each additional vascular territory (List separately in addition to code for primary procedure)**

These codes describe prolonged administration of drugs such as chemotherapy or antispasmotic drugs. They are intended for infusions longer than 10 minutes.

A catheter is directed into the affected cerebral artery and positioned at the location of the occlusion. For infusion of a thrombolytic drug, an infusion line is attached to the catheter and the drug is infused until desired results are achieved. For mechanical thrombectomy, a device is used to extract the occlusion. Upon completion of the intervention, all the devices are removed and the patient is monitored.

Coding Tips

1. These codes include selective catheterization within the treated vascular territory. Do not separately report 36215–36218 unless a noncerebral artery is selected.
2. These codes include diagnostic angiography and all post-intervention angiography. Do not separately report 36222–36228 unless a nontreated cerebral artery is studied.
3. Radiologic supervision is included when pertaining to the treated vascular territory.
4. These codes also include fluoro guidance, patient monitoring (e.g., hemodynamic or neurologic), and arteriotomy closure.
5. Code 61645 is reported once for each treated territory.
6. Code 61645 includes revascularization by any method including mechanical retrieval device or aspiration catheter. It also includes the use of thrombolytic drugs.
7. Codes 61650 and 61651 are not used to report administration of nonthrombolytic agents such as nitroglycerin or heparin, which are typically given during interventions.
8. Do not report 61645 with 61650 or 61651 for the same vascular territory.
9. Diagnostic angiography of a nontreated territory may be separately reported.
10. Do not report 61650 or 61651 with 96420–96425 (intra-arterial chemotherapy) for the same vascular territory.
11. Conscious sedation is not included in these codes and may be separately reported.
12. Report all applicable HCPCS codes. Refer to the HCPCS coding section for possible codes.

13. Facilities should separately report low osmolar contrast media (LOCM) with HCPCS codes Q9965–Q9967. Report contrast media per milliliter.

Facility HCPCS Coding

Some applicable codes may include but are not limited to:

C1757	Catheter, thrombectomy; embolectomy
C1760	Closure device, vascular (implantable/insertable)
C1769	Guidewire
C1887	Catheter, guiding
C1894	Introducer/sheath, other than guiding, intracardiac electrophysiological, non-laser
Q9965	LOCM, 100-199 mg/ml iodine concentration, per ml
Q9966	LOCM, 200-299 mg/ml iodine concentration, per ml
Q9967	LOCM, 300-399 mg/ml iodine concentration, per ml

ICD-10-CM Coding

The application of these codes is too broad to adequately present ICD-10-CM diagnosis code links here. Refer to the current ICD-10-CM book.

CCI Edits

61645   0075T, 01916, 01924-01926, 01930-01933, 0213T, 0216T, 0228T, 0230T, 11000-11006, 11042-11047, 12001-12007, 12011-12057, 13100-13133, 13151-13153, 34101-34111, 34812-34813, 35201-35206, 35226-35236, 35256-35266, 35286, 36000, 36005, 36221-36228, 36400-36410, 36420-36430, 36440, 36500, 36591-36593, 36600-36640, 36860-36861, 36904-36906, 37195, 37211-37214, 37217-37218, 43752, 51701-51703, 61650-61651, 62320-62327, 64400-64410, 64413-64435, 64445-64450, 64461-64463, 64479-64530, 69990, 75600, 75605, 75625, 75630, 75635, 75658, 75705, 75710, 75716, 75726, 75731, 75733, 75736, 75741, 75743, 75746, 75756, 75774, 75809-75810, 75820, 75822, 75825, 75827, 75831, 75833, 75840, 75842, 75860, 75870, 75872, 75880, 75885, 75887, 75889, 75891, 75893, 75894, 75898, 76000-76001, 76380, 76942, 76970, 76998, 77001-77002, 77012, 77021, 92012-92014, 92585, 92977, 93000-93010, 93040-93042, 93318, 93355, 94002, 94200, 94250, 94680-94690, 94770, 95812-95816, 95819, 95822, 95829, 95860-95870, 95907-95913, 95925-95933, 95937-95941, 95955, 96360-96368, 96372, 96374-96377, 97597-97598, 97602, 99155-99157, 99201-99255, 99291-99292, 99304-99310, 99315-99318, 99324-99328, 99334-99350, 99354-99360, 99374-99375, 99377-99378, 99415-99416, 99446-99449, 99460-99463, 99495-99497, G0453, G0463, G0471, G0505

61650   0213T, 0216T, 0228T, 0230T, 12001-12007, 12011-12057, 13100-13133, 13151-13153, 34812, 36000, 36005-36100, 36120-36140, 36160-36200, 36215-36216, 36221-36226, 36228, 36245-36246, 36400-36410, 36420-36430, 36440, 36591-36592, 36600-36640, 36800-36815, 36821, 36825-36833, 36835, 36860-36861, 37200, 37211-37214, 43752, 51701-51703, 61641-61642, 62320-62327, 64400-64410, 64413-64435, 64445-64450, 64479-64530, 69990, 75600, 75605, 75625, 75630, 75635, 75658, 75705, 75710, 75716, 75726, 75731, 75733, 75736, 75741, 75743, 75746, 75756, 75774, 75810, 75820, 75822, 75825, 75827, 75831, 75833, 75840, 75842, 75860, 75870, 75872, 75880, 75885, 75887, 75889, 75891, 75893, 75898, 76000-76001, 76380, 76942, 76970, 76998, 77001-77002, 77012, 77021, 92012-92014, 92585, 93000-93010, 93040-93042, 93318, 93355, 94002, 94200, 94250, 94680-94690, 94770, 95812-95816, 95819, 95822, 95829, 95860-95870, 95907-95913, 95925-95933, 95937-95941, 95955, 96360, 96365, 96372-96377, 96420, 96422-96425, 99155-99157, 99211-99223, 99231-99255, 99291-99292, 99304-99310, 99315-99316, 99334-99337, 99347-99350, 99374-99375, 99377-99378, 99446-99449, 99495-99496, G0453, G0463, G0471

61651   0213T, 0216T, 0228T, 0230T, 12001-12007, 12011-12057, 13100-13133, 13151-13153, 34812, 36000, 36005-36100, 36120-36140, 36160-36200, 36215-36216, 36221-36226, 36228, 36245-36246, 36400-36410, 36420-36430, 36440, 36591-36592, 36600-36640, 36800-36815, 36821, 36825-36833, 36835, 36860-36861, 37200, 37214, 43752, 51701-51703, 62320-62327, 64400-64410, 64413-64435, 64445-64450, 64479, 64483, 64486-64490, 64493, 64505-64530, 69990, 75600, 75605, 75625, 75630, 75635, 75658, 75705, 75710, 75716, 75726, 75731, 75733, 75736, 75741, 75743, 75746, 75756, 75774, 75810, 75820, 75822, 75825, 75827, 75831, 75833, 75840, 75842, 75860, 75870, 75872, 75880, 75885, 75887, 75889, 75891, 75893, 75898, 76000-76001, 76380, 76942, 76970, 76998, 77001-77002, 77012, 77021, 92012-92014, 92585, 93000-93010, 93040-93042, 93318, 93355, 94002, 94200, 94250, 94680-94690, 94770, 95812-95816, 95819, 95822, 95829, 95860-95870, 95907-95913, 95925-95933, 95937-95941, 95955, 96360, 96365, 96372-96377, 96420-96425, 99155-99157, 99211-99223, 99231-99255, 99291-99292, 99304-99310, 99315-99316, 99334-99337, 99347-99350, 99374-99375, 99377-99378, 99446-99449, 99495-99496, G0453, G0463, G0471

Case Example

Indication:
Cerebral infarct per CT scan

Procedure:
Angiogram performed revealed **complete occlusion of the left middle cerebral artery.** We selected a Tracker-18 microcatheter for the purpose of **thrombolysis.** The Tracker was advanced and placed in the proximal left MCA. **Urokinase was infused** for 20 minutes. Angiogram revealed no change in the occlusion. Urokinase was infused for an additional 20 minutes. Angiogram was again performed demonstrating significant lysis of the thrombus. The infusion was continued with the catheter slowly advanced during the next 20 minutes. Final angiogram revealed good flow with no residual thrombus.

CPT/HCPCS Codes Reported:
61650

Other HCPCS Codes Reported:
C1887, C1769

Percutaneous Embolization—Cerebral (Extracranial and Intracranial)

Transcatheter embolization is performed of the carotid or vertebral arteries with the intent to occlude the blood vessels supplying a previously identified abnormality such as a tumor, arteriovenous malformation, or aneurysm. Once the blood supply of the abnormality is identified, selective or super-selective catheterization of the feeder vessels is performed, and embolic material is injected into each vessel. The most common embolic materials available are gel foam, coils, glue, balloons, microspheres, and polyvinyl alcohol. Follow-up angiography is performed to determine the success of the therapy and is coded separately.

61624 **Transcatheter permanent occlusion or embolization (eg, for tumor destruction, to achieve hemostasis, to occlude a vascular malformation), percutaneous, any method; central nervous system (intracranial, spinal cord)**
The physician accesses an artery of the central nervous system (internal carotid or vertebral) percutaneously to permanently occlude or embolize a vascular malformation, destroy a tumor, or achieve hemostasis for a bleeding aneurysm. The access artery is percutaneously punctured with a needle, and a guidewire is inserted and fed through the artery into the target vessel. A catheter is threaded over the guidewire to the point of intended occlusion, and the guidewire is removed. When the catheter is in position, the defect is occluded or embolized with materials injected through the catheter to achieve occlusion. Radiographic methods are used to position the catheter and test for successful occlusion.

61626 **Transcatheter permanent occlusion or embolization (eg, for tumor destruction, to achieve hemostasis, to occlude a vascular malformation), percutaneous, any method; non-central nervous system, head or neck (extracranial, brachiocephalic branch)**
The physician uses a percutaneous catheter to access an arterial venous malformation, tumor, or bleeding aneurysm. The defect lies outside the central nervous system, in the head or neck regions (common carotid, external carotid, vertebral and their branches). The physician places a catheter in a peripheral artery (eg, femoral artery). Using fluoroscopic guidance, the physician locates the lesion with the catheter. The defect is occluded or embolized with materials placed through the catheter to accomplish occlusion.

75894 **Transcatheter therapy, embolization, any method, radiological supervision and interpretation**
This code reports the radiologic supervision and interpretation of the previously described transcatheter occlusion or embolization procedures.

75898 **Angiography through existing catheter for follow-up study for transcatheter therapy, embolization or infusion, other than for thrombolysis**
Angiography is performed during or following transcatheter infusion or embolization through an existing catheter to reassess the therapy's effectiveness. A radiopaque contrast medium is injected through the catheter and by fluoroscopic images recorded of the vessel, the radiologist interprets the status of the blood vessel and the effectiveness of the treatment rendered.

Coding Tips

1. Report both components of the procedure—the surgical component and/or catheter placement codes and the radiology S&I codes.

2. Angiography performed for diagnostic purposes is separately reported.

3. Road mapping and imaging performed to confirm catheter placement are not reported separately.

4. CPT codes 61624 and 61626 are reported once per surgical field. Do not report these codes for each vessel treated.

5. CPT code 61624 is assigned status indicator C for Medicare to indicate inpatient-only status. It is not paid if the procedure is performed in the outpatient setting.

6. Separately report a catheter placement code for each vessel selectively catheterized to achieve embolization/occlusion.

7. CPT code 75898 reports angiography following transcatheter embolization. Report this code once for each angiogram performed.

8. If chemoembolization is performed, report CPT code 96420 in addition to the embolization procedure codes. Consult individual payer policies for restrictions.

9. Report all applicable HCPCS codes. Refer to the HCPCS section for possible codes. Device edits apply to some of the codes in this section. Refer to the Device Edits section below for the applicable edits.

10. Facilities should continue to separately report low osmolar contrast media (LOCM) with HCPCS codes Q9965–Q9967. Report contrast media per milliliter.

11. Physician Reporting: These radiology S&I codes have both a technical and professional component. To report only the professional component, append modifier 26. To report only the technical component, append modifier TC. To report the complete procedure (i.e., both the professional and technical components), submit without a modifier.

Facility HCPCS Coding

Some applicable codes may include but are not limited to:

C1760 Closure device, vascular (implantable/insertable), if used
C1769 Guidewire
C2628 Catheter, occlusion
G0269 Placement of occlusive device into either a venous or arterial access site, post surgical or interventional procedure (eg, AngioSeal plug, vascular plug), if performed
Q9965 LOCM, 100-199 mg/ml iodine concentration, per ml
Q9966 LOCM, 200-299 mg/ml iodine concentration, per ml
Q9967 LOCM, 300-399 mg/ml iodine concentration, per ml

Note: See appendix B for a complete listing of reportable HCPCS Level II device codes.

Internal Carotid and Vertebral Arterial Anatomy

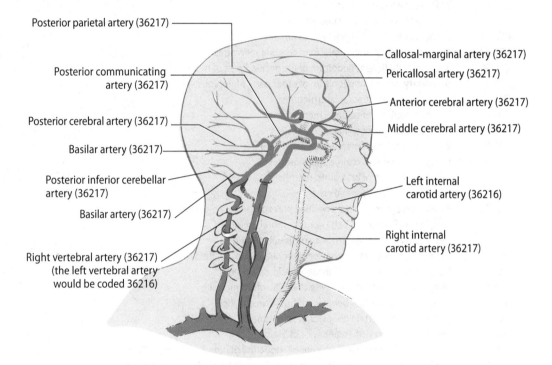

Posterior parietal artery (36217)
Callosal-marginal artery (36217)
Posterior communicating artery (36217)
Pericallosal artery (36217)
Anterior cerebral artery (36217)
Posterior cerebral artery (36217)
Middle cerebral artery (36217)
Basilar artery (36217)
Posterior inferior cerebellar artery (36217)
Left internal carotid artery (36216)
Basilar artery (36217)
Right internal carotid artery (36217)
Right vertebral artery (36217) (the left vertebral artery would be coded 36216)

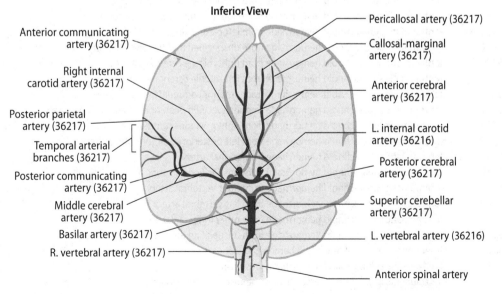

Inferior View

Pericallosal artery (36217)
Anterior communicating artery (36217)
Callosal-marginal artery (36217)
Right internal carotid artery (36217)
Anterior cerebral artery (36217)
Posterior parietal artery (36217)
L. internal carotid artery (36216)
Temporal arterial branches (36217)
Posterior cerebral artery (36217)
Posterior communicating artery (36217)
Superior cerebellar artery (36217)
Middle cerebral artery (36217)
Basilar artery (36217)
L. vertebral artery (36216)
R. vertebral artery (36217)
Anterior spinal artery

ICD-10-CM Coding

61624

C70.0	Malignant neoplasm of cerebral meninges
C70.9	Malignant neoplasm of meninges, unspecified
C71.0	Malignant neoplasm of cerebrum, except lobes and ventricles
C71.1	Malignant neoplasm of frontal lobe
C71.2	Malignant neoplasm of temporal lobe
C71.3	Malignant neoplasm of parietal lobe
C71.4	Malignant neoplasm of occipital lobe
C71.5	Malignant neoplasm of cerebral ventricle
C71.6	Malignant neoplasm of cerebellum
C71.8	Malignant neoplasm of overlapping sites of brain
C71.9	Malignant neoplasm of brain, unspecified
C72.0	Malignant neoplasm of spinal cord
C72.1	Malignant neoplasm of cauda equina
C79.31	Secondary malignant neoplasm of brain
C79.32	Secondary malignant neoplasm of cerebral meninges
C79.40	Secondary malignant neoplasm of unspecified part of nervous system
C79.49	Secondary malignant neoplasm of other parts of nervous system
D18.02	Hemangioma of intracranial structures
D32.0	Benign neoplasm of cerebral meninges
D32.1	Benign neoplasm of spinal meninges
D32.9	Benign neoplasm of meninges, unspecified
D33.0	Benign neoplasm of brain, supratentorial
D33.1	Benign neoplasm of brain, infratentorial
D33.4	Benign neoplasm of spinal cord
D33.7	Benign neoplasm of other specified parts of central nervous system
D42.0	Neoplasm of uncertain behavior of cerebral meninges
D42.1	Neoplasm of uncertain behavior of spinal meninges
D42.9	Neoplasm of uncertain behavior of meninges, unspecified
D43.0	Neoplasm of uncertain behavior of brain, supratentorial
D43.1	Neoplasm of uncertain behavior of brain, infratentorial
D43.2	Neoplasm of uncertain behavior of brain, unspecified
D43.4	Neoplasm of uncertain behavior of spinal cord
D49.6	Neoplasm of unspecified behavior of brain
D49.7	Neoplasm of unspecified behavior of endocrine glands and other parts of nervous system
I60.00	Nontraumatic subarachnoid hemorrhage from unspecified carotid siphon and bifurcation
I60.01	Nontraumatic subarachnoid hemorrhage from right carotid siphon and bifurcation
I60.02	Nontraumatic subarachnoid hemorrhage from left carotid siphon and bifurcation
I60.10	Nontraumatic subarachnoid hemorrhage from unspecified middle cerebral artery
I60.11	Nontraumatic subarachnoid hemorrhage from right middle cerebral artery
I60.12	Nontraumatic subarachnoid hemorrhage from left middle cerebral artery
I60.2	Nontraumatic subarachnoid hemorrhage from anterior communicating artery
I60.30	Nontraumatic subarachnoid hemorrhage from unspecified posterior communicating artery
I60.31	Nontraumatic subarachnoid hemorrhage from right posterior communicating artery
I60.32	Nontraumatic subarachnoid hemorrhage from left posterior communicating artery
I60.4	Nontraumatic subarachnoid hemorrhage from basilar artery
I60.50	Nontraumatic subarachnoid hemorrhage from unspecified vertebral artery
I60.51	Nontraumatic subarachnoid hemorrhage from right vertebral artery
I60.52	Nontraumatic subarachnoid hemorrhage from left vertebral artery
I60.6	Nontraumatic subarachnoid hemorrhage from other intracranial arteries
I60.7	Nontraumatic subarachnoid hemorrhage from unspecified intracranial artery
I60.8	Other nontraumatic subarachnoid hemorrhage
I60.9	Nontraumatic subarachnoid hemorrhage, unspecified
I61.0	Nontraumatic intracerebral hemorrhage in hemisphere, subcortical

I61.1	Nontraumatic intracerebral hemorrhage in hemisphere, cortical
I61.2	Nontraumatic intracerebral hemorrhage in hemisphere, unspecified
I61.3	Nontraumatic intracerebral hemorrhage in brain stem
I61.4	Nontraumatic intracerebral hemorrhage in cerebellum
I61.5	Nontraumatic intracerebral hemorrhage, intraventricular
I61.6	Nontraumatic intracerebral hemorrhage, multiple localized
I61.8	Other nontraumatic intracerebral hemorrhage
I61.9	Nontraumatic intracerebral hemorrhage, unspecified
I67.1	Cerebral aneurysm, nonruptured
Q27.9	Congenital malformation of peripheral vascular system, unspecified
Q28.2	Arteriovenous malformation of cerebral vessels
Q28.3	Other malformations of cerebral vessels

61626

C47.0	Malignant neoplasm of peripheral nerves of head, face and neck
C49.0	Malignant neoplasm of connective and soft tissue of head, face and neck
C79.89	Secondary malignant neoplasm of other specified sites
C79.9	Secondary malignant neoplasm of unspecified site
D18.00	Hemangioma unspecified site
D18.09	Hemangioma of other sites
D21.0	Benign neoplasm of connective and other soft tissue of head, face and neck
D48.1	Neoplasm of uncertain behavior of connective and other soft tissue
D48.2	Neoplasm of uncertain behavior of peripheral nerves and autonomic nervous system
D49.2	Neoplasm of unspecified behavior of bone, soft tissue, and skin
I72.0	Aneurysm of carotid artery
I77.0	Arteriovenous fistula, acquired
Q27.39	Arteriovenous malformation, other site
Q27.8	Other specified congenital malformations of peripheral vascular system
Q27.9	Congenital malformation of peripheral vascular system, unspecified
S15.001A	Unspecified injury of right carotid artery, initial encounter
S15.002A	Unspecified injury of left carotid artery, initial encounter
S15.009A	Unspecified injury of unspecified carotid artery, initial encounter
S15.011A	Minor laceration of right carotid artery, initial encounter
S15.012A	Minor laceration of left carotid artery, initial encounter
S15.019A	Minor laceration of unspecified carotid artery, initial encounter
S15.021A	Major laceration of right carotid artery, initial encounter
S15.022A	Major laceration of left carotid artery, initial encounter
S15.029A	Major laceration of unspecified carotid artery, initial encounter
S15.091A	Other specified injury of right carotid artery, initial encounter
S15.092A	Other specified injury of left carotid artery, initial encounter
S15.099A	Other specified injury of unspecified carotid artery, initial encounter

CCI Edits

61624 01924, 01926, 0213T, 0216T, 0228T, 0230T, 0333T, 0464T, 12001-12007, 12011-12057, 13100-13133, 13151-13153, 36000, 36400-36410, 36420-36430, 36440, 36591-36592, 36600, 36640, 37236, 37238, 37241-37244, 37600-37609, 43752, 51701-51703, 62320-62327, 64400-64410, 64413-64435, 64445-64450, 64461-64463, 64479-64530, 92012-92014, 92585, 93000-93010, 93040-93042, 93318, 93355, 94002, 94200, 94250, 94680-94690, 94770, 95812-95816, 95819, 95822, 95829, 95860-95870, 95907-95913, 95925-95933, 95937-95940, 95955, 96360-96368, 96372, 96374-96377, 99155-99157, 99211-99223, 99231-99255, 99291-99292, 99304-99310, 99315-99316, 99334-99337, 99347-99350, 99374-99375, 99377-99378, 99446-99449, 99495-99496, G0453, G0463, G0471

61626 01924, 0213T, 0216T, 0228T, 0230T, 0333T, 0464T, 12001-12007, 12011-12057, 13100-13133, 13151-13153, 36000, 36400-36410, 36420-36430, 36440, 36591-36592, 36600, 36640, 37236, 37238, 37241-37244, 37600-37609, 43752, 51701-51703, 62320-62327, 64400-64410, 64413-64435, 64445-64450, 64461-64463, 64479-64530, 92012-92014, 92585, 93000-93010, 93040-93042, 93318, 93355, 94002, 94200, 94250, 94680-94690, 94770, 95812-95816, 95819, 95822, 95829, 95860-95870, 95907-95913, 95925-95933, 95937-95940, 95955, 96360-96368, 96372, 96374-96377, 99155-99157, 99211-99223, 99231-99255, 99291-99292, 99304-99310, 99315-99316, 99334-99337, 99347-99350, 99374-99375, 99377-99378, 99446-99449, 99495-99496, G0453, G0463, G0471

75894   01916, 01924-01926, 01930-01933, 35201-35206, 35226, 35261-35266, 35286, 36000, 36005, 36410, 36500, 36591-36592, 36600-36640, 75600, 75605, 75625, 75630, 75635, 75658, 75705, 75710, 75716, 75726, 75731, 75733, 75736, 75741, 75743, 75746, 75756, 75774, 75810, 75820, 75822, 75825, 75827, 75831, 75833, 75840, 75842, 75860, 75870, 75872, 75880, 75885, 75887, 75889, 75891, 75893, 76000-76001, 76942, 76970, 76998, 77001-77002, 96360, 96365, 96372, 96374-96377, 99446-99449

75898   01916, 35201-35206, 35226, 35261-35266, 35286, 36000, 36005, 36410, 36500, 36591-36592, 75600, 75605, 75625, 75630, 75635, 75658, 75705, 75710, 75716, 75726, 75731, 75733, 75736, 75741, 75743, 75746, 75756, 75774, 75810, 75820, 75822, 75825, 75827, 75831, 75833, 75840, 75842, 75860, 75870, 75872, 75880, 75885, 75887, 75889, 75891, 75893, 76000-76001, 76942, 76970, 76998, 77001-77002, 96360, 96365, 96372, 96374-96377, 99446-99449

Case Example

Procedure:
Cerebral angiogram and left superselective internal maxillary artery embolization

History:
A 34-year-old male with 1-2 days of **severe left-sided epistaxis**. Diagnostic angiography and embolization of the left internal maxillary artery are requested as further treatment.

Following consent and local anesthesia, single wall puncture technique of the **right common femoral artery** was performed without difficulty. A 6-French sheath was placed. A 6-French Guider introducing **catheter** was advanced in conjunction with a .035 glide wire and used to select the following vessels: the **right common carotid, the left internal carotid and left external carotid**. Following this, the tip of the Guider was advanced into the origin of the LECA and set to a continuous heparinized saline flush. Through the Guider in a coaxial fashion, a Cordis Rapid transit **microcatheter** was advanced and using roadmap guidance used to **select the distal most aspect of the left internal maxillary artery**. **Superselective diagnostic angiography** was then **performed**. This failed to demonstrate any vascular malformations or other definite abnormality. No active bleeding was identified. I then proceeded to **perform empiric embolization of this vessel**. A small amount of Embospheres particles measuring 300-500 microns in diameter was prepared. Under live digital subtraction, these particles were infused through the microcatheter until complete stasis in the terminal internal maxillary artery was obtained. I then deposited a solitary Vortex fibered **platinum coil** measuring 2 x 3 mm **in the terminal internal maxillary artery**. **Repeat angiography** of this vessel demonstrated near complete stasis of flow with marked devascularization of this vessel. The procedure was discontinued at this point. All catheters were removed and the right groin arteriotomy site sutured with a Perclose device with adequate hemostasis obtained. He was neurologically intact without complication. He was returned to his hospital room uneventfully. A total of 120 cc of Omnipaque 240 were injected as contrast.

Sedation was achieved with a combination of IV Versed and fentanyl.

Findings:
Selective RCCA angiography failed to demonstrate any significant abnormalities. Intracranially, no abnormalities are found. The right external carotid artery distribution appears normal.

Selective LICA angiography is also unremarkable without any aneurysm, vascular malformation or other abnormality. The left ophthalmic artery is noted to arise normally off the LICA.

Selective LECA angiography is also unremarkable though some nonspecific hyper vascularity in the nasal region is identified. Following **coil and particle embolization** as described above, there is complete devascularization of the terminal internal maxillary artery distribution.

Impression:
1.   Unremarkable RCCA, LICA, and LECA angiography. Specifically, no aneurysms or vascular malformations identified.

2.   Technically successful empiric particulate and coil embolization of the terminal left internal maxillary artery as treatment for this patient's epistaxis.

CPT/HCPCS Codes Reported:
36223, 36224, 36227, 36228, 75894, 75898, 61626

Other HCPCS Codes Reported:
Q9966 x 120, C1769, C1894

Temporary Balloon Occlusion

61623   **Endovascular temporary balloon arterial occlusion, head or neck (extracranial/intracranial) including selective catheterization of vessel to be occluded, positioning and inflation of occlusion balloon, concomitant neurological monitoring, and radiologic supervision and interpretation of all angiography required for balloon occlusion and to exclude vascular injury post occlusion**

Temporary balloon occlusion (TBO) is done on arteries of the head or neck to control blood flow during procedures such as intracranial or extracranial aneurysm surgery. The balloon catheter, such as a double lumen Swan-Ganz, is placed in the artery and positioned at the point where occlusion is to occur. Selective catheterization is done first. The access artery is percutaneously punctured with a needle, and a guidewire is inserted and fed through the artery into the target vessel, such as the cerebral carotid. A catheter is threaded over the guidewire to the point where the occlusion is to be performed, and the guidewire is removed. The balloon is then inflated under fluoroscopy to the minimal size necessary for occlusion, which is confirmed with small amounts of contrast material injected through the catheter and checked for stasis in the contrast column. The patient is monitored for change in neurologic status. The TBO is maintained only for about 20 to 30 minutes, and angiographic studies may be done after occlusion to rule out post-procedure vascular injury.

Coding Tips

1. Component coding rules do not apply to this code. The code is all-inclusive and includes all imaging before, during, and after occlusion.
2. Do not separately report catheter placement codes.
3. Do not separately report neurological monitoring.
4. Do report all applicable HCPCS codes. Refer to the HCPCS coding section for possible codes.
5. Facilities should continue to separately report low osmolar contrast media (LOCM) with HCPCS codes Q9965–Q9967. Report contrast media per milliliter.

Facility HCPCS Coding

Some applicable codes may include but are not limited to:

C1760	Closure device, vascular (implantable/insertable), if used
C1769	Guidewire
C2628	Catheter, occlusion
G0269	Placement of occlusive device into either a venous or arterial access site, post surgical or interventional procedure (eg, AngioSeal plug, vascular plug), if performed
Q9965	LOCM, 100-199 mg/ml iodine concentration, per ml
Q9966	LOCM, 200-299 mg/ml iodine concentration, per ml
Q9967	LOCM, 300-399 mg/ml iodine concentration, per ml

Note: See appendix B for a complete listing of reportable HCPCS Level II device codes.

ICD-10-CM Coding

C47.0	Malignant neoplasm of peripheral nerves of head, face and neck
C49.0	Malignant neoplasm of connective and soft tissue of head, face and neck
C79.89	Secondary malignant neoplasm of other specified sites
C79.9	Secondary malignant neoplasm of unspecified site
D18.00	Hemangioma unspecified site
D18.09	Hemangioma of other sites
D21.0	Benign neoplasm of connective and other soft tissue of head, face and neck
D48.1	Neoplasm of uncertain behavior of connective and other soft tissue
D48.2	Neoplasm of uncertain behavior of peripheral nerves and autonomic nervous system
D49.2	Neoplasm of unspecified behavior of bone, soft tissue, and skin
I72.0	Aneurysm of carotid artery
I77.0	Arteriovenous fistula, acquired
Q27.39	Arteriovenous malformation, other site
Q27.8	Other specified congenital malformations of peripheral vascular system
Q27.9	Congenital malformation of peripheral vascular system, unspecified
S15.001A	Unspecified injury of right carotid artery, initial encounter
S15.002A	Unspecified injury of left carotid artery, initial encounter
S15.009A	Unspecified injury of unspecified carotid artery, initial encounter

S15.Ø11A   Minor laceration of right carotid artery, initial encounter
S15.Ø12A   Minor laceration of left carotid artery, initial encounter
S15.Ø19A   Minor laceration of unspecified carotid artery, initial encounter
S15.Ø21A   Major laceration of right carotid artery, initial encounter
S15.Ø22A   Major laceration of left carotid artery, initial encounter
S15.Ø29A   Major laceration of unspecified carotid artery, initial encounter
S15.Ø91A   Other specified injury of right carotid artery, initial encounter
S15.Ø92A   Other specified injury of left carotid artery, initial encounter
S15.Ø99A   Other specified injury of unspecified carotid artery, initial encounter

CCI Edits

61623   01924-01926, 0213T, 0216T, 0228T, 0230T, 0333T, 0464T, 12001-12007, 12011-12057, 13100-13133, 13151-13153, 36000, 36100, 36120-36140, 36215-36217, 36400-36410, 36420-36430, 36440, 36591-36592, 36600, 36640, 37606-37609, 43752, 51701-51703, 62320-62327, 64400-64410, 64413-64435, 64445-64450, 64461-64463, 64479-64530, 92012-92014, 92585, 93000-93010, 93040-93042, 93318, 93355, 94002, 94200, 94250, 94680-94690, 94770, 95812-95816, 95819, 95822, 95829, 95860-95870, 95907-95913, 95925-95933, 95937-95940, 95955, 96360-96368, 96372, 96374-96377, 99155-99157, 99211-99223, 99231-99255, 99291-99292, 99304-99310, 99315-99316, 99334-99337, 99347-99350, 99374-99375, 99377-99378, 99446-99449, 99495-99496, G0453, G0463, G0471

Case Example

Procedure:
Balloon occlusion test

Indication:
Cerebral aneurysm

Technique:
Following informed consent, the patient was placed on the angiography table and the right groin was prepped and draped in usual sterile fashion. Local anesthesia was achieved and the right common femoral artery was percutaneously accessed by micro puncture needle. A guide wire was placed and then exchanged for a 4-French transition sheath. A JB1 catheter was advanced over a glide wire into the proximal left internal carotid artery. Digital angiography was performed in the AP and lateral projections. The angiogram demonstrated aneurysm arising from the left posterior communicating artery. No critical stenosis or filling defects were noted within the internal carotid artery or its branches. The AC and NC arterial branches appear within normal limits. The **catheter was exchanged for a 5-French balloon occlusion catheter**. The catheter was positioned in the petrous portion of the left internal carotid artery and the balloon was inflated for 30 minutes. 5,000 units of heparin were administered via occlusion catheter. An additional 2,000 units of heparin were administered 10 minutes after balloon occlusion. **During the balloon occlusion**, EEG and other neurophysiological tests were conducted by the department of neurology. The **balloon was deflated after 30 minutes** and repeat digital subtraction angiography was performed. This demonstrated no evidence of development of filling defects within the left internal carotid artery or its branches to suggest thrombosis. No spasm or dissection was identified. The catheter was removed and hemostasis achieved with manual compression.

Impression:
Successful balloon occlusion of the petrus portion of the left internal carotid artery for future neurosurgical intervention.

CPT/HCPCS Codes Reported:
61623

(Note: the applicable EEG codes are also reported, and for this example we assume the hospital EEG department reports these codes.)

Percutaneous Intracranial Angioplasty

61630	**Balloon angioplasty, intracranial (eg, atherosclerotic stenosis), percutaneous**

The physician performs a percutaneous balloon angioplasty of an intracranial vessel, most often as an alternative to surgical carotid endarterectomy for carotid stenosis in high-risk patients. The patient undergoes an appropriate neurological and vascular work up preoperatively. A standard percutaneous transfemoral approach is most frequently used. Light intravenous sedation is administered. Standard diagnostic carotid and cerebral angiography is performed to confirm the suspected lesion and evaluate the cerebral circulation. The patient is anticoagulated and an antiplatelet agent is given. Using the femoral approach, the balloon is introduced on the tip of an angiographic catheter passed through the circulatory tree until it reaches the stenotic lesion. Once in place, the balloon is inflated, dilating the vessel and improving blood flow to the brain.

61640	**Balloon dilatation of intracranial vasospasm, percutaneous; initial vessel**
61641	**each additional vessel in same vascular family (List separately in addition to code for primary procedure)**
61642	**each additional vessel in different vascular family (List separately in addition to code for primary procedure)**

The physician treats intracranial vasospasm via an endovascular approach most often performed under general anesthesia. Angioplasty is performed using a percutaneous transfemoral approach, usually with a six or seven French sheath. Heparin is administered to minimize the risk of thromboembolic events. Prior to the procedure, diagnostic angiography is performed to confirm the clinical suspicion of vasospasm and to correlate the findings with the clinical symptoms, since treatment is directed only at the areas of vasospasm correlating with symptoms. The custom-designed silicone microballoon, which conforms to the shape of the vessel, is guided through the intracranial vessels, and inflated to dilate the spastic vessel. Among other etiologies, vasospasm is a documented complication of a ruptured cerebral aneurysm and subarachnoid hemorrhage, and may lead to reduced cerebral blood flow with subsequent ischemia. This procedure is useful in improving blood flow to ischemic cerebral tissue by treating focal, as well as diffuse, areas of spasm involving more than one vascular territory. Report 61640 for balloon dilation of the first vessel; 61641 for each additional vessel in the same vascular family; and 61642 for vessels in different vascular families.

Coding Tips

1. Refer to the CMS national coverage determination (NCD) for angioplasty of intracranial arteries for coverage details. Coverage involves IDE clinical trial protocols. All other indications remain noncovered by Medicare. Verify coverage policy with other payers.

2. CPT code 61630 is assigned inpatient only status. CMS will not cover this procedure when performed as an outpatient.

3. Code 61630 includes all diagnostic angiography and selective catheterization performed when the intent of the procedure is to perform the intervention or the need for the intervention is discovered during the study. This differs from conventional interventional radiology coding rules.

4. Diagnostic angiography of a separate vessel family from the one treated can be separately reported.

5. Codes 61640–61642 include selective catheterization, contrast injection, and post-intervention angiography. Diagnostic angiography is not included in these codes and should be separately reported.

6. Fluoroscopy is included and is not separately reported.

7. Since these are noncovered procedures, HCPCS coding is not necessary; however, all devices and contrast used should be billed as with any other interventional procedure.

ICD-10-CM Coding

G45.Ø	Vertebro-basilar artery syndrome
G45.1	Carotid artery syndrome (hemispheric)
G45.2	Multiple and bilateral precerebral artery syndromes
G45.8	Other transient cerebral ischemic attacks and related syndromes
G45.9	Transient cerebral ischemic attack, unspecified
G46.Ø	Middle cerebral artery syndrome
G46.1	Anterior cerebral artery syndrome
G46.2	Posterior cerebral artery syndrome
G46.3	Brain stem stroke syndrome
G46.4	Cerebellar stroke syndrome
G46.5	Pure motor lacunar syndrome
G46.6	Pure sensory lacunar syndrome
G46.7	Other lacunar syndromes
G46.8	Other vascular syndromes of brain in cerebrovascular diseases

G97.31	Intraoperative hemorrhage and hematoma of a nervous system organ or structure complicating a nervous system procedure
G97.32	Intraoperative hemorrhage and hematoma of a nervous system organ or structure complicating other procedure
I63.3Ø	Cerebral infarction due to thrombosis of unspecified cerebral artery
I63.311	Cerebral infarction due to thrombosis of right middle cerebral artery
I63.312	Cerebral infarction due to thrombosis of left middle cerebral artery
I63.319	Cerebral infarction due to thrombosis of unspecified middle cerebral artery
I63.321	Cerebral infarction due to thrombosis of right anterior cerebral artery
I63.322	Cerebral infarction due to thrombosis of left anterior cerebral artery
I63.329	Cerebral infarction due to thrombosis of unspecified anterior cerebral artery
I63.331	Cerebral infarction due to thrombosis of right posterior cerebral artery
I63.332	Cerebral infarction due to thrombosis of left posterior cerebral artery
I63.339	Cerebral infarction due to thrombosis of unspecified posterior cerebral artery
I63.341	Cerebral infarction due to thrombosis of right cerebellar artery
I63.342	Cerebral infarction due to thrombosis of left cerebellar artery
I63.349	Cerebral infarction due to thrombosis of unspecified cerebellar artery
I63.39	Cerebral infarction due to thrombosis of other cerebral artery
I63.4Ø	Cerebral infarction due to embolism of unspecified cerebral artery
I63.411	Cerebral infarction due to embolism of right middle cerebral artery
I63.412	Cerebral infarction due to embolism of left middle cerebral artery
I63.419	Cerebral infarction due to embolism of unspecified middle cerebral artery
I63.421	Cerebral infarction due to embolism of right anterior cerebral artery
I63.422	Cerebral infarction due to embolism of left anterior cerebral artery
I63.429	Cerebral infarction due to embolism of unspecified anterior cerebral artery
I63.431	Cerebral infarction due to embolism of right posterior cerebral artery
I63.432	Cerebral infarction due to embolism of left posterior cerebral artery
I63.439	Cerebral infarction due to embolism of unspecified posterior cerebral artery
I63.441	Cerebral infarction due to embolism of right cerebellar artery
I63.442	Cerebral infarction due to embolism of left cerebellar artery
I63.449	Cerebral infarction due to embolism of unspecified cerebellar artery
I63.49	Cerebral infarction due to embolism of other cerebral artery
I63.5Ø	Cerebral infarction due to unspecified occlusion or stenosis of unspecified cerebral artery
I63.511	Cerebral infarction due to unspecified occlusion or stenosis of right middle cerebral artery
I63.512	Cerebral infarction due to unspecified occlusion or stenosis of left middle cerebral artery
I63.519	Cerebral infarction due to unspecified occlusion or stenosis of unspecified middle cerebral artery
I63.521	Cerebral infarction due to unspecified occlusion or stenosis of right anterior cerebral artery
I63.522	Cerebral infarction due to unspecified occlusion or stenosis of left anterior cerebral artery
I63.529	Cerebral infarction due to unspecified occlusion or stenosis of unspecified anterior cerebral artery
I63.531	Cerebral infarction due to unspecified occlusion or stenosis of right posterior cerebral artery
I63.532	Cerebral infarction due to unspecified occlusion or stenosis of left posterior cerebral artery
I63.539	Cerebral infarction due to unspecified occlusion or stenosis of unspecified posterior cerebral artery
I63.541	Cerebral infarction due to unspecified occlusion or stenosis of right cerebellar artery
I63.542	Cerebral infarction due to unspecified occlusion or stenosis of left cerebellar artery
I63.549	Cerebral infarction due to unspecified occlusion or stenosis of unspecified cerebellar artery
I63.59	Cerebral infarction due to unspecified occlusion or stenosis of other cerebral artery
I63.6	Cerebral infarction due to cerebral venous thrombosis, nonpyogenic
I63.8	Other cerebral infarction
I63.9	Cerebral infarction, unspecified
I66.Ø1	Occlusion and stenosis of right middle cerebral artery
I66.Ø2	Occlusion and stenosis of left middle cerebral artery
I66.Ø3	Occlusion and stenosis of bilateral middle cerebral arteries
I66.Ø9	Occlusion and stenosis of unspecified middle cerebral artery
I66.11	Occlusion and stenosis of right anterior cerebral artery
I66.12	Occlusion and stenosis of left anterior cerebral artery
I66.13	Occlusion and stenosis of bilateral anterior cerebral arteries
I66.19	Occlusion and stenosis of unspecified anterior cerebral artery

I66.21	Occlusion and stenosis of right posterior cerebral artery
I66.22	Occlusion and stenosis of left posterior cerebral artery
I66.23	Occlusion and stenosis of bilateral posterior cerebral arteries
I66.29	Occlusion and stenosis of unspecified posterior cerebral artery
I66.3	Occlusion and stenosis of cerebellar arteries
I66.8	Occlusion and stenosis of other cerebral arteries
I66.9	Occlusion and stenosis of unspecified cerebral artery
I67.2	Cerebral atherosclerosis
I67.81	Acute cerebrovascular insufficiency
I67.82	Cerebral ischemia
I67.841	Reversible cerebrovascular vasoconstriction syndrome
I67.848	Other cerebrovascular vasospasm and vasoconstriction
I67.89	Other cerebrovascular disease
I67.9	Cerebrovascular disease, unspecified
I68.0	Cerebral amyloid angiopathy
I68.8	Other cerebrovascular disorders in diseases classified elsewhere
I97.810	Intraoperative cerebrovascular infarction during cardiac surgery
I97.811	Intraoperative cerebrovascular infarction during other surgery
I97.820	Postprocedural cerebrovascular infarction during cardiac surgery
I97.821	Postprocedural cerebrovascular infarction during other surgery
O99.411	Diseases of the circulatory system complicating pregnancy, first trimester
O99.412	Diseases of the circulatory system complicating pregnancy, second trimester
O99.413	Diseases of the circulatory system complicating pregnancy, third trimester
O99.419	Diseases of the circulatory system complicating pregnancy, unspecified trimester
O99.42	Diseases of the circulatory system complicating childbirth
O99.43	Diseases of the circulatory system complicating the puerperium
Q27.30	Arteriovenous malformation, site unspecified
Q27.4	Congenital phlebectasia
Q28.0	Arteriovenous malformation of precerebral vessels
Q28.1	Other malformations of precerebral vessels
Q28.8	Other specified congenital malformations of circulatory system

CCI Edits

61630 01924, 01926, 01930, 01933, 0213T, 0216T, 0333T, 0464T, 11000-11006, 11042-11047, 35201-35206, 35226-35236, 35256-35266, 35286, 36000, 36100, 36120-36140, 36200, 36215-36217, 36410, 36591-36592, 36620-36625, 37215, 37217-37218, 37236, 37238, 37246-37247, 51701-51703, 61645-61650, 62324-62327, 64415-64417, 64450, 64486-64490, 64493, 76000-76001, 76380, 76942, 76970, 76998, 77001-77002, 77012, 77021, 92585, 95822, 95860-95870, 95907-95913, 95925-95933, 95937-95940, 96360, 96365, 96372, 96374-96377, 97597-97598, 97602, G0453, G0471

61640 12001-12007, 12011-12057, 13100-13133, 13151-13153, 36000, 36400-36410, 36420-36430, 36440, 36591-36592, 36600, 36640, 43752, 61650-61651, 62320-62327, 64400-64410, 64413-64435, 64445-64450, 64461-64463, 64479-64530, 92012-92014, 93000-93010, 93040-93042, 93318, 93355, 94002, 94200, 94250, 94680-94690, 94770, 95812-95816, 95819, 95822, 95829, 95955, 96360-96368, 96372, 96374-96377, 99155-99157, 99211-99223, 99231-99255, 99291-99292, 99304-99310, 99315-99316, 99334-99337, 99347-99350, 99374-99375, 99377-99378, 99446-99449, 99495-99496, G0463

61641 36591-36592, 61651

61642 36591-36592, 61651

Case Example

Intracranial Angioplasty

The patient was placed on the angiography table in supine position and prepped and draped in normal sterile fashion. The **right groin** was **selected for puncture**, and 1% lidocaine was used for local anesthesia. Modified Seldinger technique was used with micropuncture needle to access the right common femoral artery. A 7 French sheath was placed. A glide wire was inserted into the aorta, and a UCSF catheter was inserted over the wire. **Selective catheterization of the right common carotid artery** was performed. Injection was performed and **imaging** carried out **over the cervical and cranial circulation**. The catheter was **advanced into the right internal carotid artery**, and **imaging** over the **cranial circulation** was performed. There is a significant stenosis present in the M1 segment. The **decision was made to angioplasty** this segment. A Viatrac 6mm x 20mm balloon **catheter was guided into the M1 segment** and the stenosis was traversed. The **balloon was inflated** and then retracted. Post-angioplasty imaging revealed satisfactory results, and the procedure was concluded.

CPT/HCPCS Codes Reported:
61630

Other HCPCS Codes Reported:
C1725, C1769, C1894

Transcatheter Vascular Stent Placement—Cervical Carotid

37215   **Transcatheter placement of intravascular stent(s), cervical carotid artery, open or percutaneous, including angioplasty, when performed, and radiological supervision and interpretation; with distal embolic protection**

37216   **without distal embolic protection**

The physician places an intravascular stent most often as an alternative to surgical carotid endarterectomy for carotid stenosis in patients at high surgical risk. Angioplasty may also be performed. Using the femoral approach, a guiding catheter is placed from the groin into the common carotid artery. A microwire is passed through the guiding catheter and crosses the stenotic lesion in the artery. The distal embolic protection device (if used) is placed distal to the lesion to catch any clot that may break away during angioplasty or stent placement. In the event the stenosis is too tight to pass the stent, an angioplasty balloon is used to predilate the stenosis prior to the stent placement. The wire is left across the dilated segment, the balloon catheter is removed, and the stent delivery device is placed. Once positioned, the stent is deployed across the region of the stenosis. If necessary, a balloon may be placed inside the stent to assist with proper stent deployment.

37217   **Transcatheter placement of intravascular stent(s), intrathoracic common carotid artery or innominate artery by retrograde treatment, open ipsilateral cervical carotid artery exposure, including angioplasty, when performed, and radiological supervision and interpretation**

Placing stents into the intrathoracic common carotid artery or innominate artery via a catheter is a less invasive alternative to open endarterectomy. The procedure is carried out by making an incision exposing the cervical carotid artery and creating an arteriotomy. A catheter is inserted through the artery and threaded to the target. A stent delivery system, which may also include an embolic capturing device, is loaded into a delivery pod and advanced to the blocked or narrowed artery through the catheter. The embolic protection device is deployed first, distal to the lesion so that any emboli are collected as the blood passes through the device. The stent is advanced out of the pod until it expands to open the narrowing. The instruments are removed. The artery and overlying tissues are closed. The procedure includes radiologic supervision and interpretation, as well as angioplasty, when performed.

37218   **Transcatheter placement of intravascular stent(s), intrathoracic common carotid artery or innominate artery, open or percutaneous antegrade approach, including angioplasty, when performed, and radiological supervision and interpretation**

The physician places an intravascular stent via open or percutaneous antegrade approach through a catheter into the intrathoracic common carotid artery or innominate artery. A catheter is inserted through the artery and threaded to the target. A stent delivery system, which may also include an embolic capturing device, is loaded into a delivery pod and advanced to the blocked or narrowed artery through the catheter. The embolic protection device is deployed first, distal to the lesion, so that any emboli are collected as the blood passes through the device. The stent is advanced out of the pod until it expands to open the narrowing. The instruments are removed. The artery and overlying tissues are closed. The procedure includes radiologic supervision and interpretation, as well as angioplasty, when performed.

Coding Tips

1. Component coding rules do not apply to these codes. They are all-inclusive and include imaging supervision and interpretation.

2. Angiography of the stented vessel is included in these codes and is not separately reported.

3. Selective catheterization of the target vessel is included and is not separately reported.

4. All angioplasty is included and is not separately reported.

5. CPT codes 37215, 37217 and 37218 are assigned status indicator C and are covered by Medicare only when done as inpatient procedures.

6. CPT code 37216 is assigned status indicator E and is not covered by Medicare.

7. If not previously studied, the carotid vessel not being stented may be imaged during the same session and may be reported separately as a unilateral study. Refer to the cerebral angiography section for guidelines.

8. If diagnostic angiography was previously performed and there is no documented clinical change in the patient's condition, separate angiography may not be reported at the same time as these codes.

9. If bilateral carotid stenting is performed, report CPT code 37215 or 37216 with modifier 50 or 59 depending upon payer policy.

10. Code 37217 includes open vessel exposure and vascular access closure, all access, traversing the lesion and standard closure of arteriotomy by suture.

11. Report 37218 when stent placement in the intrathoracic common carotid artery or innominate artery is inserted from an antegrade approach, i.e., from the aortic arch via peripheral access.

12. Carotid artery revascularization services (33891, 35301, 35509, 35510, 35601, 35606) may be reported separately.

13. Medicare has strict coverage rules for carotid stent procedures. Refer to the most recent national coverage determination for details.

14. Conscious sedation is not included in these codes. Separately report 99151–99157 per payer policy and coding guidelines. Hospitals may choose to include the costs associated with the service as part of the procedure rather than reporting them separately.

15. Do report all applicable HCPCS codes. Refer to the HCPCS coding section for possible codes.

16. Facilities should continue to separately report low osmolar contrast media (LOCM) with HCPCS codes Q9965–Q9967. Report contrast media per milliliter.

Facility HCPCS Coding

Some applicable codes may include but are not limited to:

C1760	Closure device, vascular (implantable/insertable), if used
C1769	Guidewire
C1887	Catheter, guiding
C1885	Catheter, transluminal angioplasty, laser
C1725	Catheter, transluminal angioplasty, non-laser
C1884	Embolization protective system
C1894	Introducer/sheath, other than guiding, other than intracardiac electrophysiological, non-laser
C1874	Stent, coated/covered with delivery system
C1875	Stent, coated/covered, without delivery system
C1876	Stent, non-coated/non-covered, with delivery system
C1877	Stent, non-coated/non-covered, without delivery system
G0269	Placement of occlusive device into either a venous or arterial access site, post surgical or interventional procedure (eg, AngioSeal plug, vascular plug), if performed
Q9965	LOCM, 100-199 mg/ml iodine concentration, per ml
Q9966	LOCM, 200-299 mg/ml iodine concentration, per ml
Q9967	LOCM, 300-399 mg/ml iodine concentration, per ml

Note: See appendix B for a complete listing of reportable HCPCS Level II device codes.

ICD-10-CM Coding

G45.1	Carotid artery syndrome (hemispheric)
G45.8	Other transient cerebral ischemic attacks and related syndromes
G45.9	Transient cerebral ischemic attack, unspecified
I63.031	Cerebral infarction due to thrombosis of right carotid artery
I63.032	Cerebral infarction due to thrombosis of left carotid artery
I63.039	Cerebral infarction due to thrombosis of unspecified carotid artery
I63.131	Cerebral infarction due to embolism of right carotid artery
I63.132	Cerebral infarction due to embolism of left carotid artery
I63.139	Cerebral infarction due to embolism of unspecified carotid artery
I63.231	Cerebral infarction due to unspecified occlusion or stenosis of right carotid arteries
I63.232	Cerebral infarction due to unspecified occlusion or stenosis of left carotid arteries
I63.239	Cerebral infarction due to unspecified occlusion or stenosis of unspecified carotid arteries
I63.8	Other cerebral infarction
I63.9	Cerebral infarction, unspecified
I65.21	Occlusion and stenosis of right carotid artery
I65.22	Occlusion and stenosis of left carotid artery
I65.23	Occlusion and stenosis of bilateral carotid arteries
I65.29	Occlusion and stenosis of unspecified carotid artery
I67.81	Acute cerebrovascular insufficiency
I67.82	Cerebral ischemia
I67.848	Other cerebrovascular vasospasm and vasoconstriction
I67.89	Other cerebrovascular disease
I72.0	Aneurysm of carotid artery
I76	Septic arterial embolism
I77.1	Stricture of artery
I77.3	Arterial fibromuscular dysplasia
I77.70	Dissection of unspecified artery
I77.71	Dissection of carotid artery

I77.75	Dissection of other precerebral arteries
I77.76	Dissection of artery of upper extremity
I77.77	Dissection of artery of lower extremity
I77.89	Other specified disorders of arteries and arterioles
I77.9	Disorder of arteries and arterioles, unspecified

CCI Edits

37215 0075T, 01924-01926, 0213T, 0216T, 0228T, 0230T, 11000-11006, 11042-11047, 12001-12007, 12011-12057, 13100-13133, 13151-13153, 34812, 34820, 34834, 35201-35206, 35226-35236, 35256-35266, 35286, 36000, 36100, 36120-36140, 36200, 36215-36217, 36222-36224, 36245, 36400-36410, 36420-36430, 36440, 36500, 36591-36592, 36600-36640, 37184, 37217-37218, 37236, 37246-37247, 43752, 51701-51703, 61645, 62320-62327, 64400-64410, 64413-64435, 64445-64450, 64461-64463, 64479-64530, 69990, 75605, 75893, 76000-76001, 76380, 76942, 76970, 76998, 77001-77002, 77012, 77021, 92012-92014, 93000-93010, 93040-93042, 93050, 93318, 93355, 94002, 94200, 94250, 94680-94690, 94770, 95812-95816, 95819, 95822, 95829, 95955, 96360-96368, 96372, 96374-96377, 97597-97598, 97602, 99155-99157, 99211-99223, 99231-99255, 99291-99292, 99304-99310, 99315-99316, 99334-99337, 99347-99350, 99374-99375, 99377-99378, 99446-99449, 99495-99496, G0463, G0471

37216 11000-11006, 11042-11047, 12001-12007, 12011-12057, 13100-13133, 13151-13153, 36222-36224, 36400-36406, 36420-36430, 36440, 36591-36592, 36600, 36640, 37236, 43752, 62320-62323, 64400-64410, 64413, 64418-64435, 64445-64449, 64461-64463, 64479-64530, 92012-92014, 93000-93010, 93040-93042, 93050, 93318, 93355, 94002, 94200, 94250, 94680-94690, 94770, 95812-95816, 95819, 95822, 95829, 95955, 96360-96368, 96372, 96374-96377, 97597-97598, 97602, 99155-99157, 99211-99223, 99231-99255, 99291-99292, 99304-99310, 99315-99316, 99334-99337, 99347-99350, 99374-99375, 99377-99378, 99446-99449, 99495-99496, G0463

37217 0075T-0076T, 01924-01926, 0213T, 0216T, 0228T, 0230T, 11000-11006, 11042-11047, 12001-12007, 12011-12057, 13100-13133, 13151-13153, 34812-34820, 34833-34834, 35201-35206, 35226-35236, 35256-35266, 35286, 36000, 36100, 36120-36140, 36200, 36215-36217, 36221-36227, 36245, 36400-36410, 36420-36430, 36440, 36500, 36591-36592, 36600-36640, 36831-36833, 36860-36861, 37184, 37218, 37236, 37246-37247, 43752, 51701-51703, 62320-62327, 64400-64410, 64413-64435, 64445-64450, 64461-64463, 64479-64530, 69990, 75600, 75605, 75893, 76000-76001, 76380, 76942, 76970, 76998, 77001-77002, 77012, 77021, 92012-92014, 93000-93010, 93040-93042, 93050, 93318, 93355, 94002, 94200, 94250, 94680-94690, 94770, 95812-95816, 95819, 95822, 95829, 95955, 96360-96368, 96372, 96374-96377, 97597-97598, 97602, 99155-99157, 99211-99223, 99231-99255, 99291-99292, 99304-99310, 99315-99316, 99334-99337, 99347-99350, 99374-99375, 99377-99378, 99446-99449, G0463, G0471

37218 0075T-0076T, 01924-01926, 0213T, 0216T, 0228T, 0230T, 11000-11006, 11042-11047, 12001-12007, 12011-12057, 13100-13133, 13151-13153, 34812-34820, 34833-34834, 35201-35206, 35226-35236, 35256-35266, 35286, 36000, 36100, 36120-36140, 36200, 36215-36217, 36221-36227, 36245, 36400-36410, 36420-36430, 36440, 36500, 36591-36592, 36600-36640, 36831-36833, 36860-36861, 37184, 37236, 37246-37247, 43752, 51701-51703, 62320-62327, 64400-64410, 64413-64435, 64445-64450, 64461-64463, 64479-64530, 69990, 75600, 75605, 75893, 76000-76001, 76380, 76942, 76970, 76998, 77001-77002, 77012, 77021, 92012-92014, 93000-93010, 93040-93042, 93050, 93318, 93355, 94002, 94200, 94250, 94680-94690, 94770, 95812-95816, 95819, 95822, 95829, 95955, 96360-96368, 96372, 96374-96377, 97597-97598, 97602, 99155-99157, 99211-99223, 99231-99255, 99291-99292, 99304-99310, 99315-99316, 99334-99337, 99347-99350, 99374-99375, 99377-99378, 99446-99449, G0463, G0471

Case Example #1

Indication:
The patient has a history of prior left carotid endarterectomy. She presents with a high-grade recurrent stenosis and ipsilateral hemispheric symptoms.

Technique:
The right groin was prepped and draped in the usual fashion. The **right common femoral artery** was **accessed** using a 5 French micropuncture system. A 5 French pigtail catheter was advanced over a glide wire into the ascending thoracic aorta. **Arch aortography** was **performed** in the LAO projection. Pigtail catheter was exchanged for a Davis catheter. This catheter was used to **select** the **left common carotid artery**, and a **cervical carotid arteriogram** was **performed. Intracranial angiography** was then **performed.** The catheter was then used to **select** the **right common carotid artery. Cervical carotid angiography** was performed in multiple projections. **Intracranial angiography was performed.** The Davis catheter was withdrawn.

A focal high-grade stenosis of the left internal carotid artery was confirmed. Diameter and length measurements were obtained in preparation for placement of carotid stent. The patient was given additional boluses of IV heparin. The ACT was monitored and maintained between 250 and 300 throughout the procedure.

A Zilver 6 x 40 self-expanding stent was prepared in the usual fashion. A filter wire EZ 300cm long cerebral anti-embolization device was brought on the field and prepared in the usual fashion. The right femoral sheath was removed over an exchange length stiff glide wire. A 6 French shuttle select sheath was loaded with a 6.5 French JB1 catheter. The sheath and catheter were then advanced over the glide wire through the right femoral artery and into the aortic arch under fluoroscopic guidance. The JB1 catheter and stiff glide wire were used to select the left common carotid artery. The shuttle select sheath was advanced over the JB1 catheter into the common carotid artery. Once appropriate positioning of the sheath was obtained, the JB1 catheter and stiff glide wire were removed. The sheath was connected to a pressurized heparinized saline flush bag. Angiogram of the left carotid artery was performed with hand injection of contrast through the sheath. The **filter wire** was then advanced through the sheath and used to **cross the left internal carotid stenosis.** The **filter wire** was positioned and **deployed** by withdrawing the filter delivery sheath. A **left** carotid angiogram was performed with hand injection of contrast through the sheath to confirm patency of the filter. The **internal carotid stenosis** was **pre-dilated** using a 3 x 2 Gazelle balloon, which was advanced over the filter wire. Following pre-dilation, a left carotid arteriogram was performed with hand injection of contrast through the sheath. The balloon was removed. The Zilver 6 x 40 self-expanding stent was advanced over the filter wire and positioned across the left internal carotid stenosis using roadmap guidance. Once the **stent** was in the appropriate position, it **was deployed** in the usual fashion.

Following stent deployment, the stent delivery catheter was removed and a left carotid arteriogram was performed with hand injection of contrast through the sheath. A residual stenosis was noted in the mid portion of the stent. This was post-dilated using a 5 x 2 Gazelle angioplasty balloon. Cervical carotid angiography was performed with hand injection of contrast through the sheath. Intracranial angiography was then performed with injection of contrast through the sheath. The sheath was removed over a wire. The sheath was then exchanged over a guide wire for a short 6 French sheath. This sheath was connected to a pressure infusion system and sutured in place. At the end of the procedure the patient was at her baseline neurologic status.

Findings:
Arch aortogram: The aortic arch shows mild to moderate diffuse calcification. There is standard great vessel anatomy. Extremely slow flow is noted in the right common carotid artery. The left common carotid artery shows mild luminal irregularity at its origin. The left vertebral artery is large and appears free of stenosis. The right vertebral artery is not visualized. The innominate artery is patent. The right subclavian is patent. The left subclavian is patent throughout its course.

Left carotid arteriogram: The distal left common carotid artery shows mild luminal irregularity with a long, mild, tapered stenosis. There is a focal high-grade stenosis at the origin of the left internal carotid artery. This produces an 80% stenosis. The remainder of the cervical internal carotid artery is normal in appearance. There is a focal high grade stenosis at the origin of the external carotid artery. The remainder of the artery is patent. The intracranial arteriogram shows no significant intracranial arterial disease. There is brisk left to right cross-filling with the left carotid circulation supplying the right anterior cerebral and middle cerebral arteries. The capillary and venous phases are unremarkable.

Right carotid arteriogram: Selective injection of the right common carotid artery shows occlusion at the level of the carotid bifurcation with distal reconstitution of the internal carotid artery via a network of tortuous small vessels consistent with vasovasorum. The reconstituted internal carotid artery demonstrates slow flow and shows diffuse luminal irregularity. Multiple surgical clips are superimposed over the level of the carotid bifurcation. Reflux of contrast into the subclavian artery during injection of the common carotid artery demonstrates antegrade flow in the right vertebral artery. There is a focal stenosis at the origin of the vertebral artery. The remainder of the cervical segment of the vertebral artery shows no significant luminal irregularities. The intracranial arteriogram demonstrates flow within the intracranial portion of the internal carotid artery and faint visualization of the middle cerebral artery and its branches. The anterior cerebral artery is not well visualized. In addition, the intracranial arteriogram demonstrates continued flow through the right vertebral system into the basilar artery. The right posterior cerebral artery is well visualized. The left posterior cerebral artery is faintly visualized.

Case Example #1 (Continued)

Left carotid stent placement: A 6 x 40 self-expanding stent was placed across the left carotid stenosis. A filter wire is present and appears well opposed to the wall of the internal carotid artery. Flow is present through the filter wire. Following initial stent placement, there is a moderate residual stenosis within the mid portion of the stent. The external carotid artery remains patent. However, a high grade stenosis persists at its origin. The stent extends into the common carotid artery. Following post stent angioplasty, the previously noted residual stenosis is no longer present. Completion intracranial angiography was performed with injection of contrast in the left common carotid artery. This demonstrates normal pattern of flow through the left middle cerebral and left anterior cerebral artery with brisk left to right cross-filing supplying the right anterior cerebral and right middle cerebral arteries. No focal abnormalities are identified and there is no significant change when compared with the pre-intervention angiogram.

Impression:
Focal high-grade stenosis at the left carotid bifurcation producing an 80 percent stenosis of the proximal internal carotid artery.

The left carotid stenosis was successfully treated with stent placement and post-stent angioplasty with complete resolution of the stenosis.

Chronic occlusion of the right internal carotid artery at the level of the carotid bifurcation. There is reconstitution of the internal carotid artery via a network of vasovasorum.

The right internal carotid artery provides minimal flow to the right hemisphere. The majority of the right hemispheric flow is via well developed left to right cross-filling.

The left vertebral artery is dominant. The right vertebral artery shows a focal stenosis at its origin.

CPT/HCPCS Codes Reported:
36223, 36216, 37215

Other HCPCS Codes Reported:
C1725, C1769, C1876, C1884, C1894

Case Example #2:

Indication:
Brain attack

Procedure:
Clinical emergency consent was obtained. Sedation was performed. The patient was placed on the angiography table in supine position and prepped and draped in normal sterile fashion. The right groin was selected for puncture and 2% lidocaine was used for local anesthesia. A modified Seldinger technique was used with micropuncture needle to **access the right common femoral artery**. A 7 French sheath was placed.

Using a glide wire and UCSF catheter, the left common carotid artery was selected. Digital subtraction angiography was performed through the common carotid artery. Angiography demonstrated **occlusion of the left internal carotid artery at its origin**. A high-grade stenosis was present at the origin of the left internal carotid artery. The glide wire was removed. An exchange length wire was placed. The proximal left internal carotid artery was traversed. A guide catheter was placed in the left internal carotid artery. Digital subtraction angiography was performed. There was occlusion at the carotid terminus without opacification of the ACA or MCA.

Subsequently, a microcatheter and micro wire were advanced into the **left middle cerebral artery**. A **Merci device** was loaded and advanced beyond the filling defect. The Merci device was deployed. This was withdrawn through the clot and withdrawn under suction into the guiding catheter. Post **thrombectomy** angiography was performed. Digital subtraction angiography of the carotid terminus was performed. There was interval increase in flow. Filling defect and clot was demonstrated at the M2 M3 bifurcation.

Subsequently, a Merci microcatheter was inserted into the MCA. A Merci clot removal device was used to **perform thrombectomy within the MCA**. Device was deployed beyond the clot and withdrawn under suction. Two passes were performed. The post angiography demonstrated interval improvement in flow. 5.0 mg of **t-PA was administered intra-arterially**. Post t-PA angiography demonstrated interval incremental improvement in flow. Distal filling defects and emboli were present. **Mechanical thrombectomy of M3 M4 branches was performed**. **Superselective administration** of additional 2.5 mg of **t-PA into the distal M3 branches was performed**. There was interval improvement in flow. Selected parietal branches MCA remain occluded.

Subsequently, microcatheters and wires were removed. **Angiography** of the **left common carotid bifurcation** was performed. There is a moderate to high-grade stenosis at the origin of the left internal carotid. Crescentic filling defect was present within the proximal left internal carotid artery. This was most consistent with **a dissection**. After **discussion** with the clinical service, **stent placement was planned**.

Long guiding catheter was withdrawn over a wire. **Two** overlapping Zilver **self expanding stents** 9 x 30 and 8 x 30 **were deployed across the stenosis and a dissection**. The stenosis and dissection flap was further angioplastied using a balloon catheter. Post angioplasty and stent angiography demonstrated interval increase in internal carotid flow.

Whole brain angiography was performed through the left internal carotid artery. There is interval increase in flow through the MCA territory. Some distal branches within the posterior parietal lobe remain occluded.

All catheters and wires were removed. Angioseal closure device was used to obtain hemostasis. Dressing was applied. The patient tolerated the procedure well and was transferred out in stable condition.

Findings/Impression:
1.   Technically moderately successful administration of **t-PA and thrombectomy using Merci device**. Interval improvement
      in flow within the left internal carotid artery, MCA and distal branches. Persistent parietal branch occlusions.

2.   Successful **angioplasty and stent of the left internal carotid** artery stenosis and dissection.

3.   Insertion of angioseal in common femoral artery.

CPT/HCPCS Codes Reported:
37184, 37185, 37216, G0269 (per payer guidelines)

Other HCPCS Codes Reported:
C1757, C1760, C1769, C1876, C1894

Transcatheter Vascular Stent Placement—Intracranial

61635   **Transcatheter placement of intravascular stent(s), intracranial, (eg, atherosclerotic stenosis), including balloon angioplasty, if performed**

The physician places an intravascular stent in an intracranial vessel. Angioplasty may also be performed. Using the femoral approach, a guiding catheter is placed from the groin into the common carotid artery. A microwire is passed through the guiding catheter and crosses the stenotic lesion in the artery. Angioplasty may be performed to predilate the stenosis prior to the stent placement. The wire is left across the dilated segment, the balloon catheter is removed, and the stent delivery device is placed. Once positioned, the stent is deployed across the region of the stenosis. If necessary, a balloon may be placed inside the stent to assist with proper stent deployment.

Internal Carotid and Vertebral Arterial Anatomy

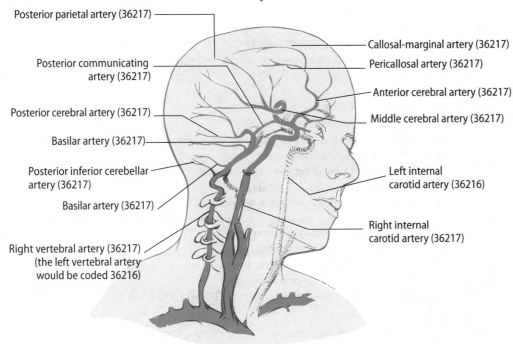

Inferior View

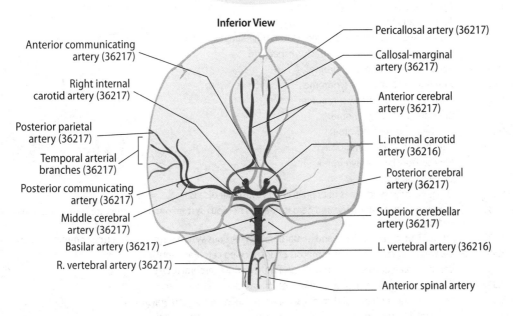

Coding Tips

1. The typical component coding rules do not apply to this code. The code includes imaging supervision and interpretation.
2. Angiography of the stented vessel family is included and is not separately reported.
3. Selective catheterization of the target vessel is included and is not separately reported.
4. All angioplasty is included and is not separately reported.
5. Diagnostic angiography of a separate vessel family from the one treated can be separately reported.
6. Do not report with 61645 when performed in the same vascular territory.
7. CPT code 61635 is assigned status indicator C and is not covered by Medicare when performed as an outpatient.
8. Do report all applicable HCPCS codes. Refer to the HCPCS coding section for possible codes.
9. Facilities should continue to separately report low osmolar contrast media (LOCM) with HCPCS codes Q9965–Q9967. Report contrast media per milliliter.

Facility HCPCS Coding

Some applicable codes may include but are not limited to:

C1760	Closure device, vascular (implantable/insertable), if used
C1769	Guidewire
C1887	Catheter, guiding
C1885	Catheter, transluminal angioplasty, laser
C1725	Catheter, transluminal angioplasty, non-laser
C1894	Introducer/sheath, other than guiding, other than intracardiac electrophysiological, non-laser
C1874	Stent, coated/covered with delivery system
C1875	Stent, coated/covered, without delivery system
C1876	Stent, non-coated/non-covered, with delivery system
C1877	Stent, non-coated/non-covered, without delivery system
G0269	Placement of occlusive device into either a venous or arterial access site, post surgical or interventional procedure (eg, AngioSeal plug, vascular plug), if performed
Q9965	LOCM, 100-199 mg/ml iodine concentration, per ml
Q9966	LOCM, 200-299 mg/ml iodine concentration, per ml
Q9967	LOCM, 300-399 mg/ml iodine concentration, per ml

Note: See appendix B for a complete listing of reportable HCPCS Level II device codes.

ICD-10-CM Coding

G45.0	Vertebro-basilar artery syndrome
G45.1	Carotid artery syndrome (hemispheric)
G45.2	Multiple and bilateral precerebral artery syndromes
G45.8	Other transient cerebral ischemic attacks and related syndromes
G45.9	Transient cerebral ischemic attack, unspecified
G46.0	Middle cerebral artery syndrome
G46.1	Anterior cerebral artery syndrome
G46.2	Posterior cerebral artery syndrome
G46.3	Brain stem stroke syndrome
G46.4	Cerebellar stroke syndrome
G46.5	Pure motor lacunar syndrome
G46.6	Pure sensory lacunar syndrome
G46.7	Other lacunar syndromes
G46.8	Other vascular syndromes of brain in cerebrovascular diseases
G97.31	Intraoperative hemorrhage and hematoma of a nervous system organ or structure complicating a nervous system procedure
G97.32	Intraoperative hemorrhage and hematoma of a nervous system organ or structure complicating other procedure
I63.30	Cerebral infarction due to thrombosis of unspecified cerebral artery
I63.311	Cerebral infarction due to thrombosis of right middle cerebral artery
I63.312	Cerebral infarction due to thrombosis of left middle cerebral artery
I63.319	Cerebral infarction due to thrombosis of unspecified middle cerebral artery
I63.321	Cerebral infarction due to thrombosis of right anterior cerebral artery
I63.322	Cerebral infarction due to thrombosis of left anterior cerebral artery
I63.329	Cerebral infarction due to thrombosis of unspecified anterior cerebral artery

I63.331	Cerebral infarction due to thrombosis of right posterior cerebral artery
I63.332	Cerebral infarction due to thrombosis of left posterior cerebral artery
I63.339	Cerebral infarction due to thrombosis of unspecified posterior cerebral artery
I63.341	Cerebral infarction due to thrombosis of right cerebellar artery
I63.342	Cerebral infarction due to thrombosis of left cerebellar artery
I63.349	Cerebral infarction due to thrombosis of unspecified cerebellar artery
I63.39	Cerebral infarction due to thrombosis of other cerebral artery
I63.40	Cerebral infarction due to embolism of unspecified cerebral artery
I63.411	Cerebral infarction due to embolism of right middle cerebral artery
I63.412	Cerebral infarction due to embolism of left middle cerebral artery
I63.419	Cerebral infarction due to embolism of unspecified middle cerebral artery
I63.421	Cerebral infarction due to embolism of right anterior cerebral artery
I63.422	Cerebral infarction due to embolism of left anterior cerebral artery
I63.429	Cerebral infarction due to embolism of unspecified anterior cerebral artery
I63.431	Cerebral infarction due to embolism of right posterior cerebral artery
I63.432	Cerebral infarction due to embolism of left posterior cerebral artery
I63.439	Cerebral infarction due to embolism of unspecified posterior cerebral artery
I63.441	Cerebral infarction due to embolism of right cerebellar artery
I63.442	Cerebral infarction due to embolism of left cerebellar artery
I63.449	Cerebral infarction due to embolism of unspecified cerebellar artery
I63.49	Cerebral infarction due to embolism of other cerebral artery
I63.50	Cerebral infarction due to unspecified occlusion or stenosis of unspecified cerebral artery
I63.511	Cerebral infarction due to unspecified occlusion or stenosis of right middle cerebral artery
I63.512	Cerebral infarction due to unspecified occlusion or stenosis of left middle cerebral artery
I63.519	Cerebral infarction due to unspecified occlusion or stenosis of unspecified middle cerebral artery
I63.521	Cerebral infarction due to unspecified occlusion or stenosis of right anterior cerebral artery
I63.522	Cerebral infarction due to unspecified occlusion or stenosis of left anterior cerebral artery
I63.529	Cerebral infarction due to unspecified occlusion or stenosis of unspecified anterior cerebral artery
I63.531	Cerebral infarction due to unspecified occlusion or stenosis of right posterior cerebral artery
I63.532	Cerebral infarction due to unspecified occlusion or stenosis of left posterior cerebral artery
I63.539	Cerebral infarction due to unspecified occlusion or stenosis of unspecified posterior cerebral artery
I63.541	Cerebral infarction due to unspecified occlusion or stenosis of right cerebellar artery
I63.542	Cerebral infarction due to unspecified occlusion or stenosis of left cerebellar artery
I63.549	Cerebral infarction due to unspecified occlusion or stenosis of unspecified cerebellar artery
I63.59	Cerebral infarction due to unspecified occlusion or stenosis of other cerebral artery
I63.6	Cerebral infarction due to cerebral venous thrombosis, nonpyogenic
I63.8	Other cerebral infarction
I63.9	Cerebral infarction, unspecified
I66.01	Occlusion and stenosis of right middle cerebral artery
I66.02	Occlusion and stenosis of left middle cerebral artery
I66.03	Occlusion and stenosis of bilateral middle cerebral arteries
I66.09	Occlusion and stenosis of unspecified middle cerebral artery
I66.11	Occlusion and stenosis of right anterior cerebral artery
I66.12	Occlusion and stenosis of left anterior cerebral artery
I66.13	Occlusion and stenosis of bilateral anterior cerebral arteries
I66.19	Occlusion and stenosis of unspecified anterior cerebral artery
I66.21	Occlusion and stenosis of right posterior cerebral artery
I66.22	Occlusion and stenosis of left posterior cerebral artery
I66.23	Occlusion and stenosis of bilateral posterior cerebral arteries
I66.29	Occlusion and stenosis of unspecified posterior cerebral artery
I66.3	Occlusion and stenosis of cerebellar arteries
I66.8	Occlusion and stenosis of other cerebral arteries
I66.9	Occlusion and stenosis of unspecified cerebral artery
I67.2	Cerebral atherosclerosis
I67.81	Acute cerebrovascular insufficiency
I67.82	Cerebral ischemia

I67.841	Reversible cerebrovascular vasoconstriction syndrome
I67.848	Other cerebrovascular vasospasm and vasoconstriction
I67.89	Other cerebrovascular disease
I67.9	Cerebrovascular disease, unspecified
I68.0	Cerebral amyloid angiopathy
I68.8	Other cerebrovascular disorders in diseases classified elsewhere
I97.810	Intraoperative cerebrovascular infarction during cardiac surgery
I97.811	Intraoperative cerebrovascular infarction during other surgery
I97.820	Postprocedural cerebrovascular infarction during cardiac surgery
I97.821	Postprocedural cerebrovascular infarction during other surgery
Q27.30	Arteriovenous malformation, site unspecified
Q28.0	Arteriovenous malformation of precerebral vessels
Q28.1	Other malformations of precerebral vessels

CCI Edits

61635 01924, 01926, 01930, 01933, 0213T, 0216T, 0333T, 0464T, 11000-11006, 11042-11047, 35201-35206, 35226-35236, 35256-35266, 35286, 36000, 36100, 36120-36140, 36200, 36215-36217, 36410, 36591-36592, 36620-36625, 37215, 37217-37218, 37236, 37238, 37246-37247, 51701-51703, 61630, 61645-61650, 62324-62327, 64415-64417, 64450, 64486-64490, 64493, 76000-76001, 76380, 76942, 76970, 76998, 77001-77002, 77012, 77021, 92585, 95822, 95860-95870, 95907-95913, 95925-95933, 95937-95940, 96360, 96365, 96372, 96374-96377, 97597-97598, 97602, G0453, G0471

Case Example

Indication:
Cerebral angiography and stenting of left internal carotid artery for acute stroke; status post neurosurgery.

Technique:
The patient was brought to the interventional neuroangiography suite and placed supine on the angiography table. The patient was prepped and draped in the usual sterile fashion. Using a modified Seldinger technique, a 5 French vascular sheath was placed in the **right common femoral artery**. Using a Davis diagnostic catheter to select the **left internal carotid artery, angiography** was **performed** and **imaging obtained of the head and neck**. An exchange length Bentson guidewire was placed in the left internal carotid artery and the diagnostic catheter removed. A 7 French guiding catheter was placed with its tip in the left internal carotid artery at C2 and the guidewire removed. A power 14 microcatheter was **advanced** into the **left M1 segment** over a Transcend EX Platinum guidewire. The guidewire was removed. **Angiography** was **performed** by injecting 0.5 cc of nonionic contrast and obtaining AP and lateral projections.

An exchange length Transcend guidewire was **advanced** into the **angular branch of the left middle cerebral artery M3 segment**. The Prowler microcatheter was removed. An IV bolus of 2000 units porcine heparin was administered. A 3.5 mm x 20 mm **neuroform stent was advanced into the intracranial segment of the internal carotid artery**. The **stent** was **deployed** with its distal most aspect in the **proximal left M1 segment** and its proximal markers in the cavernous internal carotid artery.

Angiography was performed by injecting 8 cc of nonionic contrast through the guiding catheter. The guidewire and catheter was removed.

Interpretations and Findings:
Left internal carotid artery: Initial angiography demonstrates occlusion of the left internal carotid artery just beyond the ophthalmic artery origin. Subselective angiography of the left middle cerebral artery performed reveals no major branch occlusions. After delivery of the neuroform stent, there is excellent restoration of luminal diameter with mild tapering of the supraclinoid internal carotid artery.

Impression:
1. Left supraclinoid internal carotid artery occlusion presumed secondary to dissection from recent surgery.

2. Reopening of the left supraclinoid internal carotid artery dissection using a neuroform stent with good result.

CPT/HCPCS Codes Reported:
61635

Other HCPCS Codes Reported:
C1769, C1876, C1887, C1894

Transcatheter Vascular Stent Placement—Extracranial Vertebral or Intrathoracic Carotid Artery

0075T   **Transcatheter placement of extracranial vertebral artery stent(s), including radiologic supervision and interpretation, open or percutaneous; initial vessel**

0076T   **each additional vessel (List separately in addition to code for primary procedure)**

The physician places an intravascular stent most often as an alternative to surgical carotid endarterectomy for stenosis in patients at high surgical risk. Angioplasty may also be performed. Using the femoral approach, a guiding catheter is placed from the groin into the artery to be treated. A microwire is passed through the guiding catheter and crosses the stenotic lesion in the artery. The distal embolic protection device (if used) is placed distal to the lesion to catch any clot that may break away during angioplasty or stent placement. In the event the stenosis is too tight to pass the stent, an angioplasty balloon is used to predilate the stenosis prior to the stent placement. The wire is left across the dilated segment, the balloon catheter is removed, and the stent delivery device is placed. Once positioned, the stent is deployed across the region of the stenosis. If necessary, a balloon may be placed inside the stent to assist with proper stent deployment.

Coding Tips

1. The typical component coding rules do not apply to these codes. They are all-inclusive and include imaging supervision and interpretation.
2. Angiography of the stented vessel is included in these codes and is not separately reported.
3. Selective catheterization of the target vessel is included and is not separately reported.
4. All angioplasty is included and is not separately reported.
5. The codes are used to report stent procedures performed on lesions of precranial vertebral lesions.
6. If not previously studied, the carotid vessel not being stented may be imaged during the same session and may be reported separately as a unilateral study. Refer to the cerebral angiography section for guidelines.
7. If diagnostic angiography was previously performed and there is no documented clinical change in the patient's condition, separate angiography may not be reported at the same time as these codes.
8. Do report all applicable HCPCS codes. Refer to the HCPCS coding section for possible codes.
9. Facilities should continue to separately report low osmolar contrast media (LOCM) with HCPCS codes Q9965–Q9967. Report contrast media per milliliter.
10. 0075T and 0076T are assigned inpatient only status. These codes will not be paid if reported on an outpatient claim.

Facility HCPCS Coding

Some applicable codes may include but are not limited to:

C1760	Closure device, vascular (implantable/insertable), if used
C1769	Guidewire
C1887	Catheter, guiding
C1885	Catheter, transluminal angioplasty, laser
C1725	Catheter, transluminal angioplasty, non-laser
C1884	Embolization protective system
C1894	Introducer/sheath, other than guiding, other than intracardiac electrophysiological, non-laser
C1874	Stent, coated/covered with delivery system
C1875	Stent, coated/covered, without delivery system
C1876	Stent, non-coated/noncovered, with delivery system
C1877	Stent, non-coated/noncovered, without delivery system
G0269	Placement of occlusive device into either a venous or arterial access site, post surgical or interventional procedure (eg, AngioSeal plug, vascular plug), if performed
Q9965	LOCM, 100-199 mg/ml iodine concentration, per ml
Q9966	LOCM, 200-299 mg/ml iodine concentration, per ml
Q9967	LOCM, 300-399 mg/ml iodine concentration, per ml

Note: See appendix B for a complete listing of reportable HCPCS Level II device codes.

ICD-10-CM Coding

G45.0	Vertebro-basilar artery syndrome
I63.011	Cerebral infarction due to thrombosis of right vertebral artery
I63.012	Cerebral infarction due to thrombosis of left vertebral artery
I63.013	Cerebral infarction due to thrombosis of bilateral vertebral arteries
I63.019	Cerebral infarction due to thrombosis of unspecified vertebral artery
I63.033	Cerebral infarction due to thrombosis of bilateral carotid arteries
I63.111	Cerebral infarction due to embolism of right vertebral artery
I63.112	Cerebral infarction due to embolism of left vertebral artery
I63.113	Cerebral infarction due to embolism of bilateral vertebral arteries
I63.119	Cerebral infarction due to embolism of unspecified vertebral artery
I63.133	Cerebral infarction due to embolism of bilateral carotid arteries
I63.211	Cerebral infarction due to unspecified occlusion or stenosis of right vertebral arteries
I63.212	Cerebral infarction due to unspecified occlusion or stenosis of left vertebral arteries
I63.213	Cerebral infarction due to unspecified occlusion or stenosis of bilateral vertebral arteries
I63.219	Cerebral infarction due to unspecified occlusion or stenosis of unspecified vertebral arteries
I63.233	Cerebral infarction due to unspecified occlusion or stenosis of bilateral carotid arteries
I63.313	Cerebral infarction due to thrombosis of bilateral middle cerebral arteries
I63.323	Cerebral infarction due to thrombosis of bilateral anterior arteries
I63.333	Cerebral infarction to thrombosis of bilateral posterior arteries
I63.343	Cerebral infarction to thrombosis of bilateral cerebellar arteries
I63.413	Cerebral infarction due to embolism of bilateral middle cerebral arteries
I63.423	Cerebral infarction due to embolism of bilateral anterior cerebral arteries
I63.433	Cerebral infarction due to embolism of bilateral posterior cerebral arteries
I63.443	Cerebral infarction due to embolism of bilateral cerebellar arteries
I63.513	Cerebral infarction due to unspecified occlusion or stenosis of bilateral middle arteries
I63.523	Cerebral infarction due to unspecified occlusion or stenosis of bilateral anterior arteries
I63.533	Cerebral infarction due to unspecified occlusion or stenosis of bilateral posterior arteries
I63.543	Cerebral infarction due to unspecified occlusion or stenosis of bilateral cerebellar arteries
I65.01	Occlusion and stenosis of right vertebral artery
I65.02	Occlusion and stenosis of left vertebral artery
I65.03	Occlusion and stenosis of bilateral vertebral arteries
I65.09	Occlusion and stenosis of unspecified vertebral artery
I67.848	Other cerebrovascular vasospasm and vasoconstriction
I67.89	Other cerebrovascular disease
I76	Septic arterial embolism
I77.1	Stricture of artery
I77.74	Dissection of vertebral artery
I77.89	Other specified disorders of arteries and arterioles
I77.9	Disorder of arteries and arterioles, unspecified

CCI Edits

0075T	01924-01926, 0213T, 0216T, 34812-34820, 34833-34834, 35201-35206, 35226, 35261-35266, 35286, 36000, 36100, 36120-36140, 36200, 36215-36217, 36410, 36591-36592, 36620-36625, 36831-36833, 36860-36861, 37236, 37246-37247, 61650, 62324-62327, 64415-64417, 64450, 64486-64490, 64493, 69990, 75600, 75605, 76000-76001, 76380, 76942, 76970, 76998, 77001-77002, 77012, 77021, 93050, 96360, 96365, 96372, 96374-96377, 99446-99449
0076T	36591-36592, 37236, 37246-37247, 93050, 99446-99449

Case Example

Indication:
Stroke, distal left common carotid artery stenosis

Procedure:
The patient was placed on the angiography table and prepped and draped in the usual sterile fashion. The right groin was selected for puncture and 2% lidocaine was used for local anesthesia. A modified Seldinger technique was used with micropuncture needle to **access the right common femoral artery**. A 7 French sheath was placed.

Using a pigtail catheter and glide wire, the ascending aorta was selected. **Arch aortography was performed**. Using a guidewire and Davis catheter, the left common carotid artery was selected. Glidewire was exchanged for an exchange length Amplatz wire. Davis catheter was removed over the wire. An Arrow long 7 French guiding catheter was inserted into the descending aorta. Using a 4 mm by 40 mm Agilitrac balloon angioplasty catheter, the high grade stenosis of **the distal left common carotid artery was angioplastied**. Digital subtraction angiogram demonstrated interval improvement. The balloon catheter was removed and a 9 mm x 28 mm Omnilink **stent was deployed across the origin of the left common carotid artery**. Balloon expansion was performed. Post stent angiography demonstrated optimal positioning. The vessel is widely patent. Stent geometry is optimal. All catheters and wires were removed. Hemostasis was obtained.

Findings:
1.   Arch aortogram

2.   Left common carotid artery angiogram

3.   Left common carotid artery angioplasty and stent placement

Impression:
Successful angioplasty and stent of the left distal common carotid artery origin with near complete resolution of high-grade origin stenosis.

CPT/HCPCS Codes Reported:
0075T

Other HCPCS Codes Reported:
C1725, C1769, C1876, C1887, C1894

Chapter 7: Vascular Access Device Placement and Therapy

Vascular access devices are placed into a central or venous structure to facilitate fluid delivery. The devices are used to facilitate delivery of chemotherapy, dialysis, antibiotics, parenteral nutrition and other fluids necessary in the care of the patient. Codes for these devices are classified into "tunneled," or implanted under the skin, or those placed via direct puncture or "non-tunneled," for temporary purposes. It is common for long-term devices to require intervention to maintain patency. There are separate codes defining these services. Placement and manipulation of many of these devices require imaging guidance. Imaging guidance can be provided by fluoroscopy, ultrasound, or CT.

General Coding Tips for Vascular Access Devices

1. CPT® code 77001 specifically describes fluoroscopy guidance for central venous access device placement procedures. This code covers guidance for access, device placement, replacement, removal, manipulation, and confirmation of catheter tip location. Do not report CPT code 76000, 76001, or 77002 for this service.

2. CPT code 76937 specifically describes ultrasound guidance for central venous access device placement procedures. This code is reported for documentation of vessel patency, evaluation of potential access sites and real-time imaging for needle placement into the vessel. As with other ultrasound guidance codes, reporting this code requires permanent image recording and report interpretation as part of the patient's medical record. Do not report CPT code 76942 for this service.

3. If both fluoroscopy and ultrasound guidance are used in the placement of a vascular access device, both codes may be reported provided the above guidelines are met.

4. Do not separately report venography performed through a central venous access catheter. It is included in the services covered under CPT code 77001. Venography performed through a separate access site may be reported provided medical necessity supports the study. Separate interpretation of the venography is required.

5. In order to accurately code central venous access procedures, the entry site, age of patient, type of device, and method of placement (tunneled, non-tunneled) must be provided.

6. CPT code 36598 is used to report contrast injection or "catheter check" of an existing central venous access device. This code includes fluoroscopy. Do not separately report CPT code 76000, 76001, or 77001.

7. To report extremity venogram or superior vena cavogram, documentation must describe the vessel injected and discuss findings. Location of the catheter tip will not justify separate reporting of 75820 or 75827.

8. Conscious sedation is not included in these codes. Separately report 99151–99157 per payer policy and coding guidelines. Hospitals may choose to include the costs associated with the service as part of the procedure rather than reporting them separately.

Non-Tunneled Vascular Access Device Placement

36555   **Insertion of non-tunneled centrally inserted central venous catheter; under 5 years of age**

36556   **age 5 years or older**

A central venous access device (CVAD) or catheter is one in which the tip terminates in the subclavian, brachiocephalic, or iliac vein; the superior or inferior vena cava; or the right atrium. A centrally inserted CVAD has an entry site in the inferior vena cava or the jugular, subclavian, or femoral vein. For insertion of a non-tunneled, centrally inserted CVAD, standard sterile preparations are made and the site over the access vein (e.g., subclavian, jugular) is injected with local anesthesia and punctured with a needle. A guidewire is inserted. The central venous catheter is then placed over the guidewire. Ultrasound guidance may be used to gain venous access and/or fluoroscopy to check the positioning of the catheter tip. The catheter is secured into position and dressed. Non-tunneled catheters are percutaneously inserted for short term (five to seven days) use; to infuse medications, fluids, blood products, and parenteral nutrition; and to take blood draws. Report 36555 for insertion for children younger than 5 years of age and 36556 for a patient 5 years of age or older.

36568   **Insertion of peripherally inserted central venous catheter (PICC), without subcutaneous port or pump; under 5 years of age**

36569   **age 5 years or older**

A central venous access device or catheter is one in which the tip terminates in the subclavian, brachiocephalic, or iliac vein; the superior or inferior vena cava; or the right atrium. A peripherally inserted central venous catheter (PICC) has an entry site in the basilic or cephalic vein in the arm and is threaded into the superior vena cava above the right atrium. PICC lines are used for antibiotic therapy, chemotherapy, total parenteral nutrition, lab work, pain medications, blood transfusions, and hydration the same as a central line. For insertion of a (non-tunneled), peripherally inserted central venous catheter, without subcutaneous port or pump, standard sterile preparations are made and the site over the access vein (basilic or cephalic) is injected with local anesthesia and punctured with a needle. A guidewire is inserted. The central venous catheter is then placed over the guidewire. Ultrasound guidance may be used to gain venous access and/or fluoroscopy to check the positioning of the catheter tip. The catheter is secured into position, and dressed. Report 36568 for insertion for children younger than 5 years of age and 36569 for a patient 5 years of age or older.

36570   **Insertion of peripherally inserted central venous access device, with subcutaneous port; under 5 years of age**

36571   **age 5 years or older**

A central venous access device or catheter is one in which the tip terminates in the subclavian, brachiocephalic, or iliac vein; the superior or inferior vena cava; or the right atrium. A peripherally inserted central venous catheter (PICC) has an entry site in the basilic or cephalic vein in the arm and is threaded into the superior vena cava above the right atrium. PICC lines are used for antibiotic therapy, chemotherapy, total parenteral nutrition, lab work, pain medications, blood transfusions, and hydration the same as a central line. For insertion of a peripherally inserted central venous catheter with a subcutaneous port, standard sterile preparations are made and the site over the access vein (basilic or cephalic) is injected with local anesthesia and punctured with a needle. A guidewire is inserted. The central venous catheter is then placed over the guidewire and fed through the vein in the arm into the superior vena cava.

The port may be placed in the chest in a subcutaneous pocket created through an incision in the chest wall, or placed in the arm through a small incision just above or halfway between the elbow crease and the shoulder on the inside of the arm. The port is attached to the catheter and checked. Ultrasound guidance may be used to gain venous access and/or fluoroscopy to check the positioning of the catheter tip. The catheter and port are secured into position and incisions are closed and dressed. Report 36570 for insertion for children younger than 5 years of age and 36571 for a patient 5 years of age or older.

Coding Tips

1. Imaging guidance may or may not be used for these services. If imaging is used, it should be documented in the procedure note.

2. Non-tunneled devices may be inserted either peripherally or centrally. Peripheral access sites include the basilic and cephalic veins. Central access sites include the jugular, subclavian, and femoral veins.

3. Report all applicable pass-through HCPCS codes. Refer to the HCPCS section for possible codes.

4. Hospitals are requested to continue reporting LOCM separately with HCPCS codes Q9965–Q9967. Report contrast media by milliliter.

PICC Placement

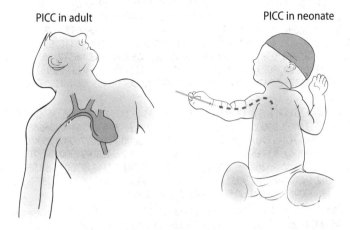

PICC in adult   PICC in neonate

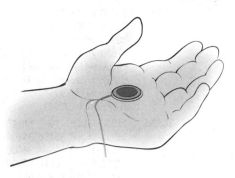

Subcutaneous ports for children and babies can be very small

CPT Coding for Non-Tunneled Devices

Service Performed	Surgical Component	Radiology S&I Component
Insertion of a non-tunneled central venous catheter in a patient under 5 years old	36555	Fluoroscopy guidance-77001 Ultrasound guidance-76937
Insertion of a non-tunneled central venous catheter in a patient 5 years or older	36556	Fluoroscopy guidance-77001 Ultrasound guidance-76937
Insertion of a peripheral central venous catheter without a subcutaneous port or pump in a patient under 5 years old	36568	Fluoroscopy guidance-77001 Ultrasound guidance-76937
Insertion of a peripheral central venous catheter without a subcutaneous port or pump, 5 years or older	36569	Fluoroscopy guidance-77001 Ultrasound guidance-76937
Insertion of a peripheral central venous catheter with subcutaneous port in a patient under 5 years old	36570	Fluoroscopy guidance-77001 Ultrasound guidance-76937
Insertion of a peripheral central venous catheter with a subcutaneous port in a patient 5 years or older	36571	Fluoroscopy guidance-77001 Ultrasound guidance-76937

Facility HCPCS Coding

Some applicable codes may include but are not limited to:

C1750   Catheter, hemodialysis, long-term

C1751   Catheter, infusion, inserted peripherally, centrally or midline (other than hemodialysis)

C1752   Catheter, hemodialysis, short-term

C1769   Guidewire

C1788   Port, indwelling (implantable)

Q9965   LOCM, 100-199 mg/ml iodine concentration, per ml

Q9966   LOCM, 200-299 mg/ml iodine concentration, per ml

Q9967   LOCM, 300-399 mg/ml iodine concentration, per ml

Note: See appendix B for a complete listing of reportable HCPCS Level II codes.

ICD-10-CM Coding

The application of these codes is too broad to adequately present ICD-10-CM diagnosis code links here. Refer to the current ICD-10-CM book.

CCI Edits

36555 11000-11006, 11042-11047, 12001-12007, 12011-12057, 13100-13133, 13151-13153, 35201-35206, 35226-35236, 35256-35266, 35286, 35800-35860, 36000, 36002-36005, 36010, 36013, 36400-36410, 36420-36430, 36440, 36556, 36568-36569, 36591-36592, 36597, 36600, 36640, 43752, 51701-51703, 64461-64463, 64486-64495, 69990, 71010, 71020, 76000-76001, 76942, 76970, 76998, 77002, 92012-92014, 93000-93010, 93040-93042, 93318, 93355, 94002, 94200, 94250, 94680-94690, 94770, 95812-95816, 95819, 95822, 95829, 95955, 96360-96368, 96372, 96374-96377, 97597-97598, 97602, 99155-99157, 99211-99223, 99231-99255, 99291-99292, 99304-99310, 99315-99316, 99334-99337, 99347-99350, 99374-99375, 99377-99378, 99446-99449, 99495-99496, G0463, G0471, J0670, J1642-J1644, J2001

36556 11000-11006, 11042-11047, 12001-12007, 12011-12057, 13100-13133, 13151-13153, 35201-35206, 35226-35236, 35256-35266, 35286, 35800-35860, 36000, 36002-36005, 36010, 36400-36410, 36420-36430, 36440, 36568-36569, 36591-36592, 36597, 36600, 36640, 43752, 51701-51703, 69990, 71010, 71020, 76000-76001, 76942, 76970, 76998, 77002, 92012-92014, 93000-93010, 93040-93042, 93318, 93355, 94002, 94200, 94250, 94680-94690, 94770, 95812-95816, 95819, 95822, 95829, 95955, 96360-96368, 96372, 96374-96377, 97597-97598, 97602, 99155-99157, 99211-99223, 99231-99255, 99291-99292, 99304-99310, 99315-99316, 99334-99337, 99347-99350, 99374-99375, 99377-99378, 99446-99449, 99495-99496, G0463, G0471, J0670, J1642-J1644, J2001

36568 11000-11006, 11042-11047, 12001-12007, 12011-12057, 13100-13133, 13151-13153, 35201-35206, 35226-35236, 35256-35266, 35286, 35800-35860, 36000, 36002-36005, 36400-36410, 36420-36430, 36440, 36569, 36591-36592, 36597, 36600, 36640, 43752, 51701-51703, 64461-64463, 64486-64495, 69990, 71010, 71020, 76000-76001, 76942, 76970, 76998, 77002, 92012-92014, 93000-93010, 93040-93042, 93318, 93355, 94002, 94200, 94250, 94680-94690, 94770, 95812-95816, 95819, 95822, 95829, 95955, 96360-96368, 96372, 96374-96377, 97597-97598, 97602, 99155-99157, 99211-99223, 99231-99255, 99291-99292, 99304-99310, 99315-99316, 99334-99337, 99347-99350, 99374-99375, 99377-99378, 99446-99449, 99495-99496, G0463, G0471, J0670, J1642-J1644, J2001

36569 11000-11006, 11042-11047, 12001-12007, 12011-12057, 13100-13133, 13151-13153, 35201-35206, 35226-35236, 35256-35266, 35286, 35800-35860, 36000, 36002-36005, 36400-36410, 36420-36430, 36440, 36591-36592, 36597, 36600, 36640, 43752, 51701-51703, 64461-64463, 64486-64495, 69990, 71010, 71020, 76000-76001, 76942, 76970, 76998, 77002, 92012-92014, 93000-93010, 93040-93042, 93318, 93355, 94002, 94200, 94250, 94680-94690, 94770, 95812-95816, 95819, 95822, 95829, 95955, 96360-96368, 96372, 96374-96377, 97597-97598, 97602, 99155-99157, 99211-99223, 99231-99255, 99291-99292, 99304-99310, 99315-99316, 99334-99337, 99347-99350, 99374-99375, 99377-99378, 99446-99449, 99495-99496, G0463, G0471, J0670, J1642-J1644, J2001

36570 0213T, 0216T, 0228T, 0230T, 11000-11006, 11042-11047, 12001-12007, 12011-12057, 13100-13133, 13151-13153, 35201-35206, 35226-35236, 35256-35266, 35286, 35800-35860, 36000, 36005-36013, 36400-36410, 36420-36430, 36440, 36555-36558, 36568-36569, 36571, 36591-36592, 36600, 36640, 43752, 51701-51703, 62320-62327, 64400-64410, 64413-64435, 64445-64450, 64461-64463, 64479-64530, 69990, 71010, 71020, 76000-76001, 76942, 76970, 76998, 77002, 92012-92014, 93000-93010, 93040-93042, 93318, 93355, 94002, 94200, 94250, 94680-94690, 94770, 95812-95816, 95819, 95822, 95829, 95955, 96360-96368, 96372, 96374-96377, 96522, 97597-97598, 97602, 99155-99157, 99211-99223, 99231-99255, 99291-99292, 99304-99310, 99315-99316, 99334-99337, 99347-99350, 99374-99375, 99377-99378, 99446-99449, 99495-99496, G0463, G0471, J0670, J1642-J1644, J2001

36571 0213T, 0216T, 0228T, 0230T, 11000-11006, 11042-11047, 12001-12007, 12011-12057, 13100-13133, 13151-13153, 35201-35206, 35226-35236, 35256-35266, 35286, 35800-35860, 36000, 36005-36013, 36400-36410, 36420-36430, 36440, 36555-36558, 36568-36569, 36591-36592, 36600, 36640, 43752, 51701-51703, 62320-62327, 64400-64410, 64413-64435, 64445-64450, 64461-64463, 64479-64530, 69990, 71010, 71020, 76000-76001, 76942, 76970, 76998, 77002, 92012-92014, 93000-93010, 93040-93042, 93318, 93355, 94002, 94200, 94250, 94680-94690, 94770, 95812-95816, 95819, 95822, 95829, 95955, 96360-96368, 96372, 96374-96377, 96522, 97597-97598, 97602, 99155-99157, 99211-99223, 99231-99255, 99291-99292, 99304-99310, 99315-99316, 99334-99337, 99347-99350, 99374-99375, 99377-99378, 99446-99449, 99495-99496, G0463, G0471, J0670, J1642-J1644, J2001

Case Example

Indication:
A 79-year-old female was referred for PICC line placement.

Procedure:
Following site preparation and local anesthesia, access to the right basilic vein was achieved under ultrasound guidance. A 5-French Bard double lumen catheter was inserted under fluoroscopic guidance. Final position in the superior vena cava was confirmed with fluoroscopy.

Impression:
It was a successful PICC line placement. The device was ready to use.

CPT/HCPCS Codes Reported:
36569, 77001

Note: There was no documentation provided of permanent ultrasound images recorded. Code 76937 should not be reported in this example.

Tunneled Vascular Access Device Placement

36557   **Insertion of tunneled centrally inserted central venous catheter, without subcutaneous port or pump; under 5 years of age**

36558   **age 5 years or older**

A central venous access device (CVAD) or catheter is one in which the tip terminates in the subclavian, brachiocephalic, or iliac vein; the superior or inferior vena cava; or the right atrium. A centrally inserted CVAD has an entry site in the inferior vena cava or the jugular, subclavian, or femoral vein. A tunneled catheter has an entrance site at a distance from its entrance into the vascular system; they are "tunneled" through the skin and subcutaneous tissue to a great vein. For insertion of a tunneled, centrally inserted CVAD, without subcutaneous port or pump, standard sterile preparations are made and the site over the access vein (e.g., subclavian, jugular) is injected with local anesthesia and punctured with a needle or accessed by cutdown approach. A guidewire is inserted. A subcutaneous tunnel is then created using a blunt pair of forceps or sharp tunneling tools, over the clavicle from the anterior chest wall to the venotomy site, which is dilated to the right size. The catheter is passed through this tunnel over the guidewire and into the target vein. Ultrasound guidance may be used to gain venous access and/or fluoroscopy to check the positioning of the catheter tip. The catheter is secured into position and any incisions are sutured. Report 36557 for insertion for children younger than 5 years of age and 36558 for a patient 5 years of age or older.

36560   **Insertion of tunneled centrally inserted central venous access device, with subcutaneous port; under 5 years of age**

36561   **Insertion of tunneled centrally inserted central venous access device, with subcutaneous port; age 5 years or older**

36563   **Insertion of tunneled centrally inserted central venous access device with subcutaneous pump**

For insertion of a tunneled, centrally inserted CVAD, with subcutaneous port/pump, standard sterile preparations are made and the site over the access vein (e.g., subclavian, jugular) is injected with local anesthesia and punctured with a needle or accessed by cutdown approach. A guidewire is inserted. A subcutaneous tunnel is created using a blunt pair of forceps or sharp tunneling tools, over the clavicle, from the anterior chest wall to the venotomy site, which is dilated to the right size. The catheter is then passed through this tunnel over the guidewire and into the target vein. The subcutaneous pocket for the port/pump is created with an incision through the skin overlying the second rib, a few centimeters from the midline. Blunt dissection and cautery are used to create the pocket in the chest wall and the port/pump is placed. The catheter is connected to the port/pump and checked by injection. Ultrasound guidance may be used to gain venous access and/or fluoroscopy to check the positioning of the catheter tip. The catheter and port/pump are secured into position and any incisions are sutured. Report 36560 for insertion with a port for children younger than 5 years of age and 36561 for a patient 5 years of age or older. Report 36563 for insertion with a pump.

36565   **Insertion of tunneled centrally inserted central venous access device, requiring two catheters via two separate venous access sites; without subcutaneous port or pump (eg, Tesio type catheter)**

For insertion of a tunneled, centrally inserted CVAD, requiring two catheters via two separate venous access sites, without subcutaneous port/pump, standard sterile preparations are made and the sites of access (e.g., subclavian, jugular vein) for each catheter are injected with local anesthesia and two punctures are made with a needle or cutdown approach. Guidewires are inserted. Two subcutaneous tunnels are then created using a blunt pair of forceps or sharp tunneling tools, over the clavicle, from the anterior chest wall to the venotomy sites, which are dilated to the right size. The catheters are each passed through their tunnel, over the guidewires, and into their venotomy sites. Ultrasound guidance may be used to gain venous access and/or fluoroscopy to check the positioning of the catheter tip. The catheters are secured into position and any incisions are sutured.

36566   **with subcutaneous port(s)**

For insertion of a tunneled, centrally inserted CVAD, requiring two catheters via two separate venous access sites, with subcutaneous ports, standard sterile preparations are made and the sites of access (e.g., subclavian, jugular vein) for each catheter are injected with local anesthesia and two punctures are made with a needle or cutdown approach. Guidewires are inserted. Two subcutaneous tunnels are then created using a blunt pair of forceps or sharp tunneling tools, over the clavicle, from the anterior chest wall to the venotomy sites, which are dilated to the right size. The catheters are each passed through their tunnel over the guidewires and into their venotomy sites. Two subcutaneous pockets for the ports are created with incisions through the skin in the chest wall, a few centimeters from the midline. Blunt dissection and cautery are used to create the pockets in the chest wall and the ports are placed. The catheters are connected to their respective ports and checked by injection. Ultrasound guidance may be used to gain venous access and/or fluoroscopy to check the positioning of the catheter tip. The catheters and ports are secured into position and any incisions are sutured.

Tunneled Device Placement

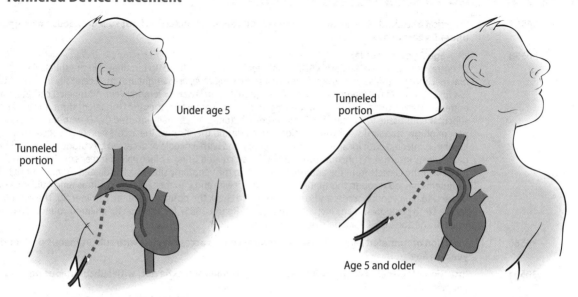

Under age 5

Tunneled portion

Tunneled portion

Age 5 and older

CPT Coding for Tunneled Devices

Service Performed	Surgical Component	Radiology S&I Component
Insertion of a tunneled centrally inserted central venous catheter without a port or pump in a patient under 5 years old	**36557**	Fluoroscopy-77001 Ultrasound-76937
Insertion of a tunneled centrally inserted central venous catheter without a port or pump in a patient 5 years or older	**36558**	Fluoroscopy-77001 Ultrasound-76937
Insertion of a tunneled centrally inserted central venous catheter with a Port in a patient under 5 years old	**36560**	Fluoroscopy-77001 Ultrasound-76937
Insertion of a tunneled centrally inserted central venous catheter with a port in a patient 5 years or older	**36561**	Fluoroscopy-77001 Ultrasound-76937
Insertion of a tunneled centrally inserted central venous catheter with a pump	**36563**	Fluoroscopy-77001 Ultrasound-76937
Insertion of a tunneled centrally inserted central venous catheter requiring two catheters via two separate access sites without a port or pump	**36565**	Fluoroscopy-77001 Ultrasound-76937
Insertion of a tunneled centrally inserted central venous catheter requiring two catheters via two separate access sites with port(s)	**36566**	Fluoroscopy-77001 Ultrasound-76937

Coding Tips

1. Imaging guidance may or may not be used for these services. If imaging is used, it should be documented in the procedure note.
2. Tunneling is performed by placing the catheter directly into the vein and then making a second counter-incision and pulling the catheter through the "tunnel" and securing it into place. A subcutaneous pocket may be formed for placement of the port.
3. Report all applicable pass-through HCPCS codes. Refer to the HCPCS section for possible codes.
4. Hospitals are requested to continue reporting LOCM separately with HCPCS codes Q9965–Q9967. Report contrast media by milliliter.

Facility HCPCS Coding

Some applicable codes may include but are not limited to:

C1750   Catheter, hemodialysis, long-term

C1751   Catheter, infusion, inserted peripherally, centrally or midline (other than hemodialysis)

C1752   Catheter, hemodialysis, short-term

C1769   Guidewire

C1788   Port, indwelling (implantable)

Q9965   LOCM, 100-199 mg/ml iodine concentration, per ml

Q9966   LOCM, 200-299 mg/ml iodine concentration, per ml

Q9967   LOCM, 300-399 mg/ml iodine concentration, per ml

Note: See appendix B for a complete listing of reportable HCPCS Level II codes.

ICD-10-CM Coding

The application of these codes is too broad to adequately present ICD-10-CM diagnosis code links here. Refer to the current ICD-10-CM book.

CCI Edits

36557   0213T, 0216T, 0228T, 0230T, 11000-11006, 11042-11047, 12001-12007, 12011-12057, 13100-13133, 13151-13153, 35201-35206, 35226-35236, 35256-35266, 35286, 35800-35860, 36000, 36002-36005, 36010-36013, 36400-36410, 36420-36430, 36440, 36555-36556, 36558, 36568-36569, 36591-36592, 36597, 36600, 36640, 43752, 51701-51703, 62320-62327, 64400-64410, 64413-64435, 64445-64450, 64461-64463, 64479-64530, 69990, 71010, 71020, 76000-76001, 76942, 76970, 76998, 77002, 92012-92014, 93000-93010, 93040-93042, 93318, 93355, 94002, 94200, 94250, 94680-94690, 94770, 95812-95816, 95819, 95822, 95829, 95955, 96360-96368, 96372, 96374-96377, 97597-97598, 97602, 99155-99157, 99211-99223, 99231-99255, 99291-99292, 99304-99310, 99315-99316, 99334-99337, 99347-99350, 99374-99375, 99377-99378, 99446-99449, 99495-99496, G0463, G0471, J0670, J1642-J1644, J2001

36558   0213T, 0216T, 0228T, 0230T, 11000-11006, 11042-11047, 12001-12007, 12011-12057, 13100-13133, 13151-13153, 35201-35206, 35226-35236, 35256-35266, 35286, 35800-35860, 36000, 36002-36005, 36010-36013, 36400-36410, 36420-36430, 36440, 36555-36556, 36568-36569, 36591-36592, 36597, 36600, 36640, 43752, 51701-51703, 62320-62327, 64400-64410, 64413-64435, 64445-64450, 64461-64463, 64479-64530, 69990, 71010, 71020, 76000-76001, 76942, 76970, 76998, 77002, 92012-92014, 93000-93010, 93040-93042, 93318, 93355, 94002, 94200, 94250, 94680-94690, 94770, 95812-95816, 95819, 95822, 95829, 95955, 96360-96368, 96372, 96374-96377, 97597-97598, 97602, 99155-99157, 99211-99223, 99231-99255, 99291-99292, 99304-99310, 99315-99316, 99334-99337, 99347-99350, 99374-99375, 99377-99378, 99446-99449, 99495-99496, G0463, G0471, J0670, J1642-J1644, J2001

36560   0213T, 0216T, 0228T, 0230T, 11000-11006, 11042-11047, 12001-12007, 12011-12057, 13100-13133, 13151-13153, 35201-35206, 35226-35236, 35256-35266, 35286, 35800-35860, 36000, 36005-36013, 36400-36410, 36420-36430, 36440, 36555-36558, 36561-36565, 36568-36571, 36591-36592, 36600, 36640, 43752, 51701-51703, 62320-62327, 64400-64410, 64413-64435, 64445-64450, 64461-64463, 64479-64530, 69990, 71010, 71020, 76000-76001, 76942, 76970, 76998, 77002, 92012-92014, 93000-93010, 93040-93042, 93318, 93355, 94002, 94200, 94250, 94680-94690, 94770, 95812-95816, 95819, 95822, 95829, 95955, 96360-96368, 96372, 96374-96377, 96522, 97597-97598, 97602, 99155-99157, 99211-99223, 99231-99255, 99291-99292, 99304-99310, 99315-99316, 99334-99337, 99347-99350, 99374-99375, 99377-99378, 99446-99449, 99495-99496, G0463, G0471, J0670, J1642-J1644, J2001

36561   0213T, 0216T, 0228T, 0230T, 11000-11006, 11042-11047, 12001-12007, 12011-12057, 13100-13133, 13151-13153, 35201-35206, 35226-35236, 35256-35266, 35286, 35800-35860, 36000, 36005-36013, 36400-36410, 36420-36430, 36440, 36555-36558, 36565, 36568-36571, 36591-36592, 36600, 36640, 43752, 51701-51703, 62320-62327, 64400-64410, 64413-64435, 64445-64450, 64461-64463, 64479-64530, 69990, 71010, 71020, 76000-76001, 76942, 76970, 76998, 77002, 92012-92014, 93000-93010, 93040-93042, 93318, 93355, 94002, 94200, 94250, 94680-94690, 94770, 95812-95816, 95819, 95822, 95829, 95955, 96360-96368, 96372, 96374-96377, 96522, 97597-97598, 97602, 99155-99157, 99211-99223, 99231-99255, 99291-99292, 99304-99310, 99315-99316, 99334-99337, 99347-99350, 99374-99375, 99377-99378, 99446-99449, 99495-99496, G0463, G0471, J0670, J1642-J1644, J2001

36563   0213T, 0216T, 0228T, 0230T, 11000-11006, 11042-11047, 12001-12007, 12011-12057, 13100-13133, 13151-13153, 35201-35206, 35226-35236, 35256-35266, 35286, 35800-35860, 36000, 36005-36013, 36400-36410, 36420-36430, 36440, 36555-36558, 36561, 36565, 36568-36571, 36591-36592, 36600, 36640, 43752, 51701-51703, 62320-62327, 64400-64410, 64413-64435, 64445-64450, 64461-64463, 64479-64530, 69990, 71010, 71020, 76000-76001, 76942, 76970, 76998, 77002, 92012-92014, 93000-93010, 93040-93042, 93318, 93355, 94002, 94200, 94250, 94680-94690, 94770, 95812-95816, 95819, 95822, 95829, 95955, 96360-96368, 96372, 96374-96377, 96522, 97597-97598, 97602, 99155-99157, 99211-99223, 99231-99255, 99291-99292, 99304-99310, 99315-99316, 99334-99337, 99347-99350, 99374-99375, 99377-99378, 99446-99449, 99495-99496, G0463, G0471, J0670, J1642-J1644, J2001

36565   0213T, 0216T, 0228T, 0230T, 11000-11006, 11042-11047, 12001-12007, 12011-12057, 13100-13133, 13151-13153, 35201-35206, 35226-35236, 35256-35266, 35286, 35820, 36000, 36005, 36011-36013, 36400-36410, 36420-36430, 36440, 36555-36556, 36557-36558, 36568-36569, 36570-36571, 36591-36592, 36600, 36640, 43752, 51701-51703, 62320-62327, 64400-64410, 64413-64435, 64445-64450, 64461-64463, 64479-64530, 69990, 71010, 71020, 76000-76001, 76942, 76970, 76998, 77002, 92012-92014, 93000-93010, 93040-93042, 93318, 93355, 94002, 94200, 94250, 94680-94690, 94770, 95812-95816, 95819, 95822, 95829, 95955, 96360-96368, 96372, 96374-96377, 97597-97598, 97602, 99155-99157, 99211-99223, 99231-99255, 99291-99292, 99304-99310, 99315-99316, 99334-99337, 99347-99350, 99374-99375, 99377-99378, 99446-99449, 99495-99496, G0463, G0471, J0670, J1642-J1644, J2001

36566   0213T, 0216T, 0228T, 0230T, 11000-11006, 11042-11047, 12001-12007, 12011-12057, 13100-13133, 13151-13153, 35201-35206, 35226-35236, 35256-35266, 35286, 35800-35860, 36000, 36005-36013, 36400-36410, 36420-36430, 36440, 36555-36556, 36557-36558, 36560-36565, 36568-36569, 36570-36571, 36591-36592, 36600, 36640, 43752, 51701-51703, 62320-62327, 64400-64410, 64413-64435, 64445-64450, 64461-64463, 64479-64530, 69990, 71010, 71020, 76000-76001, 76942, 76970, 76998, 77002, 92012-92014, 93000-93010, 93040-93042, 93318, 93355, 94002, 94200, 94250, 94680-94690, 94770, 95812-95816, 95819, 95822, 95829, 95955, 96360-96368, 96372, 96374-96377, 96522, 97597-97598, 97602, 99155-99157, 99211-99223, 99231-99255, 99291-99292, 99304-99310, 99315-99316, 99334-99337, 99347-99350, 99374-99375, 99377-99378, 99446-99449, 99495-99496, G0463, G0471, J0670, J1642-J1644, J2001

Case Example

Indication:
The patient was a 77-year-old male with chronic renal failure.

Procedure:
Ultrasound was used to reveal a patent right subclavian vein. Images were recorded. The region was anesthetized following standard preparation and draping. **Access to the right subclavian** vein was gained under direct ultrasound guidance with a 19-gauge needle. A guidewire was advanced into the venous system. The **subcutaneous tunnel** was then anesthetized with lidocaine with epinephrine. Incisions were made at the venotomy and the chest wall exit site. A 24 cm 14-French **Ashsplit catheter** was **advanced from the chest wall exit site to the venotomy site** with the supplied tunneling device.

Serial fascial dilation was then performed over the previously placed guidewire with final placement of a 15-French peel-away sheath into the subclavian vein. The dilator and wire were removed followed by placement of the Ashsplit catheter into the venous system. The **catheter was positioned at the cavoatrial junction** under fluoroscopy. The peel-away sheath was removed. The venotomy was closed with a single 3-0 Vicryl suture followed by Dermabond tissue.

CPT/HCPCS Codes Reported:
36558, 77001, 76937

Other HCPCS Codes Reported:
C1769, C1750, C1894

Repair/Replacement/Removal of Vascular Access Device

36575   **Repair of tunneled or non-tunneled central venous access catheter, without subcutaneous port or pump, central or peripheral insertion site**

This code reports repair of a central venous access device (CVAD) that has external catheters with the access ports outside the body, and no subcutaneous ports or pumps, whether centrally or peripherally inserted, tunneled or non-tunneled. The repair is done on the catheter that is placed without any replacement of components. A Hickman catheter is an example of a tunneled CVAD with an external port.

36578   **Replacement, catheter only, of central venous access device, with subcutaneous port or pump, central or peripheral insertion site**

The catheter only of a central venous access device with a subcutaneous port or pump is replaced, whether centrally or peripherally inserted. Local anesthesia is given and the subcutaneous pocket over the port is incised. The catheter is disconnected. A guidewire is placed through the existing catheter, which is then removed over the guidewire. A new central venous catheter of correct length is then placed into position and connected to the port/pump device that has not been removed or replaced. The connection with the new catheter is checked, as well as the catheter and port secured, and the wound is dressed.

36580   **Replacement, complete, of a non-tunneled centrally inserted central venous catheter, without subcutaneous port or pump, through same venous access**

A non-tunneled, centrally inserted central venous catheter, without subcutaneous port or pump, is replaced through the same venous access site. Local anesthesia is given. A guidewire is first passed through the existing central line catheter and then the catheter is removed. A new central venous catheter is then placed back into position over the guidewire, secured into position, and dressed.

36581   **Replacement, complete, of a tunneled centrally inserted central venous catheter, without subcutaneous port or pump, through same venous access**

A tunneled, centrally inserted central venous catheter, without subcutaneous port or pump is replaced. Local anesthesia is given and the sutures securing the cuff of the indwelling catheter are freed from the skin. A guidewire is next placed through the existing catheter, which is then removed, and a new central venous catheter is inserted into the tunneled position over the guidewire. The new catheter is secured into position and the wound is dressed.

36582   **Replacement, complete, of a tunneled centrally inserted central venous access device, with subcutaneous port, through same venous access**

36583   **Replacement, complete, of a tunneled centrally inserted central venous access device, with subcutaneous pump, through same venous access**

A tunneled, centrally inserted central venous catheter, along with a subcutaneous port (36582) or pump (36583) device is replaced. Local anesthesia is given and the subcutaneous pocket over the port/pump device is incised. The pump/port is dissected free and tested. The catheter is disconnected and the pump/port device is removed from its pocket. A guidewire is placed over the existing catheter, which is removed, and a new central venous catheter is threaded into position over the guidewire. A new pump/port device is inserted into the subcutaneous pocket and the catheter is connected. The connection is checked with an injection. The new pump/port is secured into the pocket, incisions are closed, and the wound is dressed.

36584   **Replacement, complete, of a peripherally inserted central venous catheter (PICC), without subcutaneous port or pump, through same venous access**

A peripherally inserted central venous catheter (PICC), without subcutaneous port or pump, is

replaced through the same venous access site. Local anesthesia is given and the sutures securing the cuff of the catheter with external port are freed from the skin and it is partially withdrawn. A sheath is then placed over the nonfunctioning catheter and it is completely withdrawn. A guidewire is inserted into the access site through the sheath and advanced. A new catheter of correct length is placed over the guidewire and the sheath and guidewire are removed. The catheter is fastened in position and the wound is dressed.

36585   **Replacement, complete, of a peripherally inserted central venous access device, with subcutaneous port, through same venous access**

A peripherally inserted central venous catheter (PICC), along with a subcutaneous port, is replaced through the same venous access site. Local anesthesia is given, the skin over the subcutaneous pocket is incised, and the port is dissected free. A sheath is then placed over the nonfunctioning catheter and it is completely withdrawn. A guidewire is inserted into the access site through the sheath and advanced. A new catheter of correct length is placed over the guidewire and the sheath and guidewire are removed. The catheter is fastened in position and the wound is dressed.

36589   **Removal of tunneled central venous catheter, without subcutaneous port or pump**

A tunneled central venous catheter without subcutaneous port or pump is removed. Local anesthesia is given and the sutures securing the cuff of the tunneled catheter's external port are freed from the skin. A guidewire is next placed through the catheter, which is withdrawn over the guidewire. After the guidewire is removed, the wound is dressed.

36590   **Removal of tunneled central venous access device, with subcutaneous port or pump, central or peripheral insertion**

A tunneled central venous access device, both catheter and subcutaneous port or pump, is removed. Local anesthesia is given and the subcutaneous pocket over the port/pump device is incised and the pump/port is dissected free. The catheter is disconnected and the pump/port device is removed from its pocket. A guidewire is placed over the existing catheter, which is withdrawn over the guidewire, and the guidewire is removed. The incisions are closed and the wound is dressed.

36597   **Repositioning of previously placed central venous catheter under fluoroscopic guidance**

A previously placed central venous catheter needs to be repositioned. It is possible for catheter position to change significantly after the procedure is completed. Catheter position change and tip migration occur most often with subclavian venous access, in women and obese patients, owing to the fact that the soft tissues of the chest wall move inferiorly with standing and often cause the catheter to get pulled back. When a catheter tip is incorrectly placed, it can increase the risks of thrombosis, fibrin sheath formation, perforation of the vein, and even arrhythmias. Fluoroscopy is used to check the positioning of the catheter tip and guide it to its correct position. Local anesthesia is given and the sutures securing the cuff of the catheter may be freed from the skin. The catheter is partially withdrawn and a sheath may be placed over the catheter at the existing venous access site. A guidewire is then inserted through the catheter and advanced. The central venous catheter is maneuvered back into correct position and monitored with fluoroscopy to view correct placement of the tip.

36598   **Contrast injection(s) for radiologic evaluation of existing central venous access device, including fluoroscopy, image documentation and report**

A previously placed central venous access device is evaluated for complications that may be interfering with its proper functioning or the ability to draw blood from the catheter. Complications may include the presence of a fibrin sheath around the end of the catheter, migration of the catheter tip, patency of the tubing, kinking, fracture, or leaks. A small amount of contrast agent is injected into the catheter, and the central venous access device is examined under fluoroscopy as the flow is evaluated. Images are documented, and a radiological report is prepared.

Coding Tips

1. Imaging guidance may or may not be used for these services. If imaging is used, it should be documented in the procedure note.

2. Replacement codes include the removal of the old catheter. Do not separately report removal in this situation.

3. Replacement of an old catheter with a new catheter through the same access site includes placement of the new catheter. Report only the replacement code. If the new catheter is placed through a different access site, report the new catheter placement. If the catheter is tunneled, report the removal code in addition to new site placement.

4. There is no code to report removal of non-tunneled devices. This removal is included in the evaluation and management service. Hospital departments may report low level evaluation and management codes based upon their facility guidelines.

5. CPT code 36598 reports contrast injection or "catheter check" of central venous access devices. This code includes fluoroscopy. Do not separately report 77001, 76000, or 76001.

6. Report all applicable pass-through HCPCS codes. Refer to the HCPCS section for possible codes.

7. Hospitals are requested to continue reporting LOCM separately with HCPCS codes Q9965–Q9967. Report contrast media by milliliter.

Tunneled Device

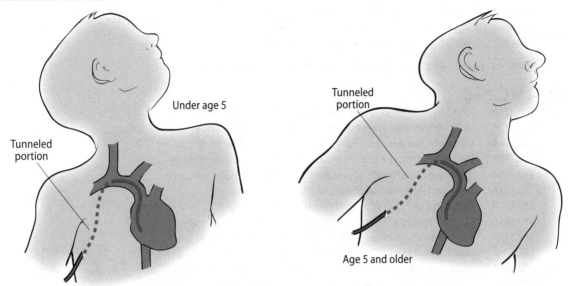

Under age 5

Tunneled portion

Tunneled portion

Age 5 and older

CPT Coding for CVAD Repair/Replacement/Removal

Service Performed	Surgical Component	Radiology S&I Component
Repair of a tunneled or non-tunneled central venous access catheter without a port or pump that is central or peripherally inserted	36575	77001-Fluoroscopy 76937-Ultrasound
Repair of a central venous access device with a port or pump that is central or peripherally inserted	36576	77001-Fluoroscopy 76937-Ultrasound
Replacement of a catheter only of a central venous access device with a port or pump that is central or peripherally inserted	36578	77001-Fluoroscopy 76937-Ultrasound
Complete replacement of a non-tunneled, centrally inserted, central venous catheter without a port or pump at the same access site	36580	77001-Fluoroscopy 76937-Ultrasound
Complete replacement of a tunneled, centrally inserted, central venous catheter without a port or pump at the same access site	36581	77001-Fluoroscopy 76937-Ultrasound
Complete replacement of a tunneled, centrally inserted, central venous catheter with a port at the same access site	36582	77001-Fluoroscopy 76937-Ultrasound
Complete replacement of a tunneled, centrally inserted, central venous catheter with a pump at the same access site	36583	77001-Fluoroscopy 76937-Ultrasound
Complete replacement of a peripherally inserted, central venous catheter without a port or pump at the same access site	36584	77001-Fluoroscopy 76937-Ultrasound
Complete replacement of a peripheral inserted, central venous catheter with a port at the same access site	36585	77001-Fluoroscopy 76937-Ultrasound
Removal of tunneled central venous catheter without a port or pump	36589	77001-Fluoroscopy
Removal of a tunneled central venous catheter, with port or pump, central or peripherally inserted	36590	77001-Fluoroscopy
Repositioning of a previously placed central venous catheter	36597	76000-Fluoroscopy
Contrast injection for evaluation of an existing central venous catheter	36598	none

Facility HCPCS Coding

Some applicable codes may include but are not limited to:

C1750   Catheter, hemodialysis, long-term

C1751   Catheter, infusion, inserted peripherally, centrally or midline (other than hemodialysis)

C1752   Catheter, hemodialysis, short-term

C1769   Guidewire

C1788	Port, indwelling (implantable)
Q9965	LOCM, 100-199 mg/ml iodine concentration, per ml
Q9966	LOCM, 200-299 mg/ml iodine concentration, per ml
Q9967	LOCM, 300-399 mg/ml iodine concentration, per ml

Note: See appendix B for a complete listing of reportable HCPCS Level II codes.

ICD-10-CM Coding

T80.211A	Bloodstream infection due to central venous catheter, initial encounter
T80.212A	Local infection due to central venous catheter, initial encounter
T80.218A	Other infection due to central venous catheter, initial encounter
T80.219A	Unspecified infection due to central venous catheter, initial encounter
T82.41XA	Breakdown (mechanical) of vascular dialysis catheter, initial encounter
T82.42XA	Displacement of vascular dialysis catheter, initial encounter
T82.43XA	Leakage of vascular dialysis catheter, initial encounter
T82.49XA	Other complication of vascular dialysis catheter, initial encounter
T82.514A	Breakdown (mechanical) of infusion catheter, initial encounter
T82.524A	Displacement of infusion catheter, initial encounter
T82.534A	Leakage of infusion catheter, initial encounter
T82.594A	Other mechanical complication of infusion catheter, initial encounter
T82.598A	Other mechanical complication of other cardiac and vascular devices and implants, initial encounter
T82.7XXA	Infection and inflammatory reaction due to other cardiac and vascular devices, implants and grafts, initial encounter
T82.818A	Embolism of vascular prosthetic devices, implants and grafts, initial encounter
T82.828A	Fibrosis of vascular prosthetic devices, implants and grafts, initial encounter
T82.838A	Hemorrhage of vascular prosthetic devices, implants and grafts, initial encounter
T82.848A	Pain from vascular prosthetic devices, implants and grafts, initial encounter
T82.856A	Stenosis of peripheral vascular stent, initial encounter
T82.858A	Stenosis of vascular prosthetic devices, implants and grafts, initial encounter
T82.868A	Thrombosis of vascular prosthetic devices, implants and grafts, initial encounter
T82.898A	Other specified complication of vascular prosthetic devices, implants and grafts, initial encounter
T82.9XXA	Unspecified complication of cardiac and vascular prosthetic device, implant and graft, initial encounter
Z45.2	Encounter for adjustment and management of vascular access device
Z45.89	Encounter for adjustment and management of other implanted devices
Z46.89	Encounter for fitting and adjustment of other specified devices

CCI Edits

36575   0213T, 0216T, 0228T, 0230T, 11000-11006, 11042-11047, 12001-12007, 12011-12057, 13100-13133, 13151-13153, 35201-35206, 35226-35236, 35256-35266, 35286, 36000, 36005, 36400-36410, 36420-36430, 36440, 36591-36592, 36597, 36600, 36640, 43752, 51701-51703, 62320-62327, 64400-64410, 64413-64435, 64445-64450, 64461-64463, 64479-64530, 69990, 71010, 71020, 76000-76001, 76942, 76970, 76998, 77002, 92012-92014, 93000-93010, 93040-93042, 93318, 93355, 94002, 94200, 94250, 94680-94690, 94770, 95812-95816, 95819, 95822, 95829, 95955, 96360-96368, 96372, 96374-96377, 97597-97598, 97602, 99155-99157, 99211-99223, 99231-99255, 99291-99292, 99304-99310, 99315-99316, 99334-99337, 99347-99350, 99374-99375, 99377-99378, 99446-99449, 99495-99496, G0463, G0471, J0670, J1642-J1644, J2001

36578   0213T, 0216T, 0228T, 0230T, 11000-11006, 11042-11047, 12001-12007, 12011-12057, 13100-13133, 13151-13153, 35201-35206, 35226-35236, 35256-35266, 35286, 36000, 36005, 36400-36410, 36420-36430, 36440, 36575-36576, 36580-36581, 36584, 36591-36592, 36597, 36600, 36640, 43752, 51701-51703, 62320-62327, 64400-64410, 64413-64435, 64445-64450, 64461-64463, 64479-64530, 69990, 71010, 71020, 76000-76001, 76942, 76970, 76998, 77002, 92012-92014, 93000-93010, 93040-93042, 93318, 93355, 94002, 94200, 94250, 94680-94690, 94770, 95812-95816, 95819, 95822, 95829, 95955, 96360-96368, 96372, 96374-96377, 97597-97598, 97602, 99155-99157, 99211-99223, 99231-99255, 99291-99292, 99304-99310, 99315-99316, 99334-99337, 99347-99350, 99374-99375, 99377-99378, 99446-99449, 99495-99496, G0463, G0471, J0670, J1642-J1644, J2001

36580 0213T, 0216T, 0228T, 0230T, 11000-11006, 11042-11047, 12001-12007, 12011-12057, 13100-13133, 13151-13153, 35201-35206, 35226-35236, 35256-35266, 35286, 35800-35860, 36000, 36005-36013, 36400-36410, 36420-36430, 36440, 36555-36576, 36591-36592, 36597, 36600, 36640, 43752, 51701-51703, 62320-62327, 64400-64410, 64413-64435, 64445-64450, 64461-64463, 64479-64530, 69990, 71010, 71020, 76000-76001, 76942, 76970, 76998, 77002, 92012-92014, 93000-93010, 93040-93042, 93318, 93355, 94002, 94200, 94250, 94680-94690, 94770, 95812-95816, 95819, 95822, 95829, 95955, 96360-96368, 96372, 96374-96377, 97597-97598, 97602, 99155-99157, 99211-99223, 99231-99255, 99291-99292, 99304-99310, 99315-99316, 99334-99337, 99347-99350, 99374-99375, 99377-99378, 99446-99449, 99495-99496, G0463, G0471, J0670, J1642-J1644, J2001

36581 0213T, 0216T, 0228T, 0230T, 11000-11006, 11042-11047, 12001-12007, 12011-12057, 13100-13133, 13151-13153, 35201-35206, 35226-35236, 35256-35266, 35286, 35800-35860, 36000, 36005-36013, 36400-36410, 36420-36430, 36440, 36555-36576, 36591-36592, 36597, 36600, 36640, 43752, 51701-51703, 62320-62327, 64400-64410, 64413-64435, 64445-64450, 64461-64463, 64479-64530, 69990, 71010, 71020, 76000-76001, 76942, 76970, 76998, 77002, 92012-92014, 93000-93010, 93040-93042, 93318, 93355, 94002, 94200, 94250, 94680-94690, 94770, 95812-95816, 95819, 95822, 95829, 95955, 96360-96368, 96372, 96374-96377, 97597-97598, 97602, 99155-99157, 99211-99223, 99231-99255, 99291-99292, 99304-99310, 99315-99316, 99334-99337, 99347-99350, 99374-99375, 99377-99378, 99446-99449, 99495-99496, G0463, G0471, J0670, J1642-J1644, J2001

36582 0213T, 0216T, 0228T, 0230T, 11000-11006, 11042-11047, 12001-12007, 12011-12057, 13100-13133, 13151-13153, 35201-35206, 35226-35236, 35256-35266, 35286, 35800-35860, 36000, 36005-36013, 36400-36410, 36420-36430, 36440, 36555-36578, 36591-36592, 36597, 36600, 36640, 43752, 51701-51703, 62320-62327, 64400-64410, 64413-64435, 64445-64450, 64461-64463, 64479-64530, 69990, 71010, 71020, 76000-76001, 76942, 76970, 76998, 77002, 92012-92014, 93000-93010, 93040-93042, 93318, 93355, 94002, 94200, 94250, 94680-94690, 94770, 95812-95816, 95819, 95822, 95829, 95955, 96360-96368, 96372, 96374-96377, 97597-97598, 97602, 99155-99157, 99211-99223, 99231-99255, 99291-99292, 99304-99310, 99315-99316, 99334-99337, 99347-99350, 99374-99375, 99377-99378, 99446-99449, 99495-99496, G0463, G0471, J0670, J1642-J1644, J2001

36583 0213T, 0216T, 0228T, 0230T, 11000-11006, 11042-11047, 12001-12007, 12011-12057, 13100-13133, 13151-13153, 35201-35206, 35226-35236, 35256-35266, 35286, 35800-35860, 36000, 36005-36013, 36400-36410, 36420-36430, 36440, 36555-36578, 36591-36592, 36597, 36600, 36640, 43752, 51701-51703, 62320-62327, 64400-64410, 64413-64435, 64445-64450, 64461-64463, 64479-64530, 69990, 71010, 71020, 76000-76001, 76942, 76970, 76998, 77002, 92012-92014, 93000-93010, 93040-93042, 93318, 93355, 94002, 94200, 94250, 94680-94690, 94770, 95812-95816, 95819, 95822, 95829, 95955, 96360-96368, 96372, 96374-96377, 97597-97598, 97602, 99155-99157, 99211-99223, 99231-99255, 99291-99292, 99304-99310, 99315-99316, 99334-99337, 99347-99350, 99374-99375, 99377-99378, 99446-99449, 99495-99496, G0463, G0471, J0670, J1642-J1644, J2001

36584 0213T, 0216T, 0228T, 0230T, 11000-11006, 11042-11047, 12001-12007, 12011-12057, 13100-13133, 13151-13153, 35201-35206, 35226-35236, 35256-35266, 35286, 35800-35860, 36000, 36005-36013, 36400-36410, 36420-36430, 36440, 36555-36576, 36591-36592, 36597, 36600, 36640, 43752, 51701-51703, 62320-62327, 64400-64410, 64413-64435, 64445-64450, 64461-64463, 64479-64530, 69990, 71010, 71020, 76000-76001, 76942, 76970, 76998, 77002, 92012-92014, 93000-93010, 93040-93042, 93318, 93355, 94002, 94200, 94250, 94680-94690, 94770, 95812-95816, 95819, 95822, 95829, 95955, 96360-96368, 96372, 96374-96377, 97597-97598, 97602, 99155-99157, 99211-99223, 99231-99255, 99291-99292, 99304-99310, 99315-99316, 99334-99337, 99347-99350, 99374-99375, 99377-99378, 99446-99449, 99495-99496, G0463, G0471, J0670, J1642-J1644, J2001

36585 0213T, 0216T, 0228T, 0230T, 11000-11006, 11042-11047, 12001-12007, 12011-12057, 13100-13133, 13151-13153, 35201-35206, 35226-35236, 35256-35266, 35286, 35800-35860, 36000, 36005-36013, 36400-36410, 36420-36430, 36440, 36555-36578, 36591-36592, 36597, 36600, 36640, 43752, 51701-51703, 62320-62327, 64400-64410, 64413-64435, 64445-64450, 64461-64463, 64479-64530, 69990, 71010, 71020, 76000-76001, 76942, 76970, 76998, 77002, 92012-92014, 93000-93010, 93040-93042, 93318, 93355, 94002, 94200, 94250, 94680-94690, 94770, 95812-95816, 95819, 95822, 95829, 95955, 96360-96368, 96372, 96374-96377, 97597-97598, 97602, 99155-99157, 99211-99223, 99231-99255, 99291-99292, 99304-99310, 99315-99316, 99334-99337, 99347-99350, 99374-99375, 99377-99378, 99446-99449, 99495-99496, G0463, G0471, J0670, J1642-J1644, J2001

36589 0213T, 0216T, 0228T, 0230T, 11000-11006, 11042-11047, 12001-12007, 12011-12057, 13100-13133, 13151-13153, 35201-35206, 35226-35236, 35256-35266, 35286, 36000, 36005, 36400-36410, 36420-36430, 36440, 36575-36578, 36591-36592, 36597, 36600, 36640, 43752, 51701-51703, 62320-62327, 64400-64410, 64413-64435, 64445-64450, 64461-64463, 64479-64530, 69990, 76000-76001, 76942, 76970, 76998, 77002, 92012-92014, 93000-93010, 93040-93042, 93318, 93355, 94002, 94200, 94250, 94680-94690, 94770, 95812-95816, 95819, 95822, 95829, 95955, 96360-96368, 96372, 96374-96377, 97597-97598, 97602, 99155-99157, 99211-99223, 99231-99255, 99291-99292, 99304-99310, 99315-99316, 99334-99337, 99347-99350, 99374-99375, 99377-99378, 99446-99449, 99495-99496, G0463, G0471

36590 0213T, 0216T, 0228T, 0230T, 11000-11006, 11042-11047, 12001-12007, 12011-12057, 13100-13133, 13151-13153, 35201-35206, 35226-35236, 35256-35266, 35286, 36000, 36005, 36400-36410, 36420-36430, 36440, 36575-36578, 36589, 36591-36592, 36597, 36600, 36640, 43752, 51701-51703, 62320-62327, 64400-64410, 64413-64435, 64445-64450, 64461-64463, 64479-64530, 69990, 76000-76001, 76942, 76970, 76998, 77002, 92012-92014, 93000-93010, 93040-93042, 93318, 93355, 94002, 94200, 94250, 94680-94690, 94770, 95812-95816, 95819, 95822, 95829, 95955, 96360-96368, 96372, 96374-96377, 97597-97598, 97602, 99155-99157, 99211-99223, 99231-99255, 99291-99292, 99304-99310, 99315-99316, 99334-99337, 99347-99350, 99374-99375, 99377-99378, 99446-99449, 99495-99496, G0463, G0471, J0670, J2001

36597 0213T, 0216T, 0228T, 0230T, 12001-12007, 12011-12057, 13100-13133, 13151-13153, 35201-35206, 35226-35236, 35256-35266, 35286, 36000, 36002-36005, 36400-36410, 36420-36430, 36440, 36591-36592, 36600, 36640, 43752, 51701-51703, 62320-62327, 64400-64410, 64413-64435, 64445-64450, 64461-64463, 64479-64530, 69990, 71010, 71020, 76001, 76942, 76970, 76998, 77001-77002, 92012-92014, 93000-93010, 93040-93042, 93318, 93355, 94002, 94200, 94250, 94680-94690, 94770, 95812-95816, 95819, 95822, 95829, 95955, 96360-96368, 96372, 96374-96377, 99155-99157, 99211-99223, 99231-99255, 99291-99292, 99304-99310, 99315-99316, 99334-99337, 99347-99350, 99374-99375, 99377-99378, 99446-99449, 99495-99496, G0463, G0471, J0670, J1642-J1644, J2001

36598 0213T, 0216T, 0228T, 0230T, 12001-12007, 12011-12057, 13100-13133, 13151-13153, 35201-35206, 35226-35236, 35256-35266, 35286, 36000, 36005, 36400-36410, 36420-36430, 36440, 36591-36592, 36600, 36640, 43752, 51701-51703, 62320-62327, 64400-64410, 64413-64435, 64445-64450, 64461-64463, 64479-64530, 76000-76001, 77002, 92012-92014, 93000-93010, 93040-93042, 93318, 93355, 94002, 94200, 94250, 94680-94690, 94770, 95812-95816, 95819, 95822, 95829, 95955, 96360-96368, 96372, 96374-96377, 99155-99157, 99211-99223, 99231-99255, 99291-99292, 99304-99310, 99315-99316, 99334-99337, 99347-99350, 99374-99375, 99377-99378, 99446-99449, 99495-99496, G0463, G0471, J1642-J1644

Case Example #1

Indication:
The patient was a 61-year-old female with end-stage renal disease and a **poorly functioning dialysis catheter**.

Procedure:
Dialysis Catheter Removal: The patient's bilateral neck and chest areas were prepped and draped in sterile fashion. The **indwelling catheter was removed from the left neck** area using blunt and sharp dissection with 1 percent Xylocaine as local anesthesia.

Dialysis Catheter Insertion: Using ultrasound guidance, a 21-gauge needle was used to **access the right internal jugular vein** using a low posterior approach. A 4-French exchange dilator was placed over a .018 wire. A .035 Amplatz stiff wire was advanced into the inferior vena cava. Using blunt and sharp dissection, a **subcutaneous tunnel** was **created** extending from the venotomy site to just below the right clavicle. The 14-French **Hemo-Split catheter** was pulled through the tunnel. A 15-French peel-away sheath was placed over the Amplatz wire. The catheter was then **advanced under fluoroscopic guidance with the tips placed in the right atrium**. The venotomy site was closed with interrupted 4-0 Vicryl suture and the catheter was secured to the skin at the dematotomy site with 2-0 nylon suture. The catheters were primed with 5,000 units of heparinized saline. Follow-up radiography was obtained. The patient tolerated the procedure well and left the department in stable condition.

CPT/HCPCS Codes Reported:
36589, 36558, 77001

Note: There is no documentation provided of permanent ultrasound images recorded. Code 76937 should not be reported in this example.

Other HCPCS Codes Reported:
C1769x2, C1750, C1894

Case Example #2

Indication:
The patient was an 89-year-old female with end-stage renal disease with an **exposed catheter cuff**.

Procedure:
The patient's chest was prepped and draped in sterile fashion. The **indwelling catheter was exchanged** over a stiff guidewire. **A new** 14-French, 28.0 cm long Ash-Split permanent hemodialysis catheter was **advanced using fluoroscopic guidance** to place the tips in the right atrium. The catheter was primed with 5000 units of Heparinized saline via each lumen. The catheter was secured to the skin with 2-0 nylon sutures. A separate 2-0 interrupted suture was placed across a draining small sinus tract communicating with the skin near the dermatotomy site. The patient tolerated the procedure well and left the department in stable condition.

CPT/HCPCS Codes Reported:
36581, 77001

Other HCPCS Codes Reported:
C1769, C1750

Maintenance of Vascular Access Device

36593 **Declotting by thrombolytic agent of implanted vascular access device or catheter**
To remove a clot from an intravenous catheter, the physician injects a thrombolytic agent (e.g., Streptokinase) into the catheter that dissolves the clot. The patient is observed for any abnormal signs of bleeding.

36595 **Mechanical removal of pericatheter obstructive material (eg, fibrin sheath) from central venous device via separate venous access**
Pericatheter obstructive material such as a fibrin sheath is removed from around a central venous device via separate venous access. Central venous catheters often fail because of the accumulation of an obstructing thrombus or fibrin sheath around the tip of the catheter. The catheter is first checked that it can aspirate and flush forward. The pericatheter material is identified by contrast material injection. Generally, a right femoral vein access is used. A guidewire followed by an angiographic catheter are advanced into the superior vena cava and exchanged for a loop snare with its catheter, which are advanced cephalad along the length of the central venous catheter beyond the ports. The loop snare is then tightly closed about the central venous catheter to encircle it and slowly pulled down and off the tip of the catheter, stripping off the pericatheter obstructive material. This is repeated a few times and the catheter is rechecked for infusion and injection ability of the ports. A contrast study is done again to identify any fibrin and the process may be repeated until the fibrin sheath is completely removed.

36596 **Mechanical removal of intraluminal (intracatheter) obstructive material from central venous device through device lumen**
Intraluminal obstructive material, such as a thrombus or fibrin sheath, is removed from inside a central venous device through the lumen of the device. This does not require a separate access incision. The central venous catheter is first checked that it can aspirate and flush forward. The obstructing material is disrupted and removed mechanically by using an angioplasty balloon or other catheter introduced into the central venous catheter through its entry site on the skin. The catheter is checked for unimpeded, restored flow and the process may be repeated until the central venous catheter is cleared.

75901 **Mechanical removal of pericatheter obstructive material (eg, fibrin sheath) from central venous device via separate venous access, radiologic supervision and interpretation**
Pericatheter obstructive material, such as a fibrin sheath, is removed from around a central venous device via separate venous access. Central venous catheters often fail because of the accumulation of an obstructing thrombus or fibrin sheath around the tip of the catheter. The catheter is first checked that it can aspirate and flush forward. The pericatheter material is identified by contrast material injection. Generally, a right femoral vein access is used. A guidewire followed by an angiographic catheter are advanced into the superior vena cava and exchanged for a loop snare with its catheter, which are advanced cephalad along the length of the central venous catheter beyond the ports. The loop snare is then tightly closed about the CV catheter to encircle it and slowly pulled down and off the tip of the catheter, stripping off the pericatheter obstructive material. This is repeated a few times and the catheter is rechecked for infusion and injection ability of the ports. A contrast study is done again to identify any fibrin and the process may be repeated until the fibrin sheath is completely removed. This code reports only the radiological supervision and interpretation required for this procedure.

75902 **Mechanical removal of intraluminal (intracatheter) obstructive material from central venous device through device lumen, radiologic supervision and interpretation**
Intraluminal obstructive material, such as a thrombus or fibrin sheath, is removed from inside a central venous device through the lumen of the device. This does not require a separate access incision. The central venous catheter is first checked that it can aspirate and flush forward. The obstructing material is disrupted and removed mechanically by using an angioplasty balloon or other catheter introduced into the central venous catheter through its entry site on the skin. The catheter is checked for unimpeded, restored flow and the process may be repeated until the CV catheter is cleared. This code reports the radiological supervision and interpretation only required for this procedure.

VAD Access

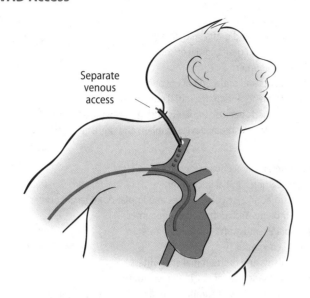

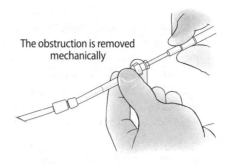

The obstruction is removed mechanically

A CVC that has become obstructed is addressed mechanically via a second venous access site. The obstructive matter is on the exterior of the catheter lumen

CPT Coding for CVAD Maintenance

Service Performed	Surgical Component	Radiology S&I Component
Mechanical removal of pericatheter obstructive material (fibrin sheath) from a central venous device via separate venous access	36595	75901
Mechanical removal of intraluminal (intracatheter) obstructive material from a central venous device through a device lumen	36596	75902
Thrombolysis of a vascular access device	36593	none

Coding Tips

1. Report both components of the procedure - the surgical component or catheter placement codes and the technical radiology S&I codes.

2. Declotting a venous access device (CPT code 36593) should not be confused with transcatheter infusion for thrombolysis (37211–37213). Also, do not confuse thrombolytic agents (e.g., tissue plasminogen activator (tPA), alteplase, streptokinase, reteplase, abbokinase, anistreplase) with anti-coagulants (e.g., heparin, coumadin). Thrombolysis requires a thrombolytic agent. Anti-coagulants (e.g., "heparin flushes") do not meet this requirement.

3. If an actual underlying venous stenosis is present and documented, then CPT code 37248 can be reported for venous balloon angioplasty.

4. Separately report thrombolysis with CPT code 36593 for declotting a central venous catheter. For prolonged infusion of thrombolytic agent, use codes 37211–37214.

5. Report all applicable pass-through HCPCS codes. Refer to the HCPCS section for possible codes.

6. Hospitals are requested to continue reporting LOCM separately with HCPCS codes Q9965–Q9967. Report contrast media by milliliter.

7. Physician Reporting: These radiology S&I codes have both a technical and professional component. To report only the professional component, append modifier 26. To report only the technical component, append modifier TC. To report the complete procedure (i.e., both the professional and technical components), submit without a modifier.

Facility HCPCS Coding

Some applicable codes may include but are not limited to:

C1769   Guidewire

Q9965   LOCM, 100-199 mg/ml iodine concentration, per ml

Q9966   LOCM, 200-299 mg/ml iodine concentration, per ml

Q9967   LOCM, 300-399 mg/ml iodine concentration, per ml

Note: See appendix B for a complete listing of reportable HCPCS Level II codes.

ICD-10-CM Coding

36593

T82.818A	Embolism of vascular prosthetic devices, implants and grafts, initial encounter
T82.848A	Pain from vascular prosthetic devices, implants and grafts, initial encounter
T82.856A	Stenosis of peripheral vascular stent, initial encounter
T82.858A	Stenosis of vascular prosthetic devices, implants and grafts, initial encounter
T82.868A	Thrombosis of vascular prosthetic devices, implants and grafts, initial encounter
T82.898A	Other specified complication of vascular prosthetic devices, implants and grafts, initial encounter
T82.9XXA	Unspecified complication of cardiac and vascular prosthetic device, implant and graft, initial encounter

36595, 36596

T82.49XA	Other complication of vascular dialysis catheter, initial encounter
T82.594A	Other mechanical complication of infusion catheter, initial encounter
T82.598A	Other mechanical complication of other cardiac and vascular devices and implants, initial encounter
T82.818A	Embolism of vascular prosthetic devices, implants and grafts, initial encounter
T82.828A	Fibrosis of vascular prosthetic devices, implants and grafts, initial encounter
T82.856A	Stenosis of peripheral vascular stent, initial encounter
T82.858A	Stenosis of vascular prosthetic devices, implants and grafts, initial encounter
T82.868A	Thrombosis of vascular prosthetic devices, implants and grafts, initial encounter
T82.898A	Other specified complication of vascular prosthetic devices, implants and grafts, initial encounter
T82.9XXA	Unspecified complication of cardiac and vascular prosthetic device, implant and graft, initial encounter
Z45.2	Encounter for adjustment and management of vascular access device

75901, 75902

T80.211A	Bloodstream infection due to central venous catheter, initial encounter
T80.212A	Local infection due to central venous catheter, initial encounter
T82.49XA	Other complication of vascular dialysis catheter, initial encounter
T82.594A	Other mechanical complication of infusion catheter, initial encounter
T82.598A	Other mechanical complication of other cardiac and vascular devices and implants, initial encounter
T82.818A	Embolism of vascular prosthetic devices, implants and grafts, initial encounter
T82.828A	Fibrosis of vascular prosthetic devices, implants and grafts, initial encounter
T82.856A	Stenosis of peripheral vascular stent, initial encounter
T82.858A	Stenosis of vascular prosthetic devices, implants and grafts, initial encounter
T82.868A	Thrombosis of vascular prosthetic devices, implants and grafts, initial encounter
T82.898A	Other specified complication of vascular prosthetic devices, implants and grafts, initial encounter
T82.9XXA	Unspecified complication of cardiac and vascular prosthetic device, implant and graft, initial encounter
Z45.2	Encounter for adjustment and management of vascular access device

CCI Edits

36593   35201-35206, 35226-35236, 35256-35266, 35286, 36005, 36591-36592, 69990, J1642-J1644

36595   0213T, 0216T, 0228T, 0230T, 11000-11006, 11042-11047, 12001-12007, 12011-12057, 13100-13133, 13151-13153, 35201-35206, 35226-35236, 35256-35266, 35286, 36000, 36005, 36400-36410, 36420-36430, 36440, 36591-36593, 36596-36600, 36640, 37211-37214, 43752, 51701-51703, 61645, 62320-62327, 64400-64410, 64413-64435, 64445-64450, 64461-64463, 64479-64530, 69990, 71010, 71020, 76000-76001, 76380, 76937, 76942, 76970, 76998, 77001-77002, 77012, 77021, 92012-92014, 93000-93010, 93040-93042, 93318, 93355, 94002, 94200, 94250, 94680-94690, 94770, 95812-95816, 95819, 95822, 95829, 95955, 96360-96368, 96372, 96374-96377, 97597-97598, 97602, 99155-99157, 99211-99223, 99231-99255, 99291-99292, 99304-99310, 99315-99316, 99334-99337, 99347-99350, 99374-99375, 99377-99378, 99446-99449, 99495-99496, G0463, G0471

36596   0213T, 0216T, 0228T, 0230T, 11000-11006, 11042-11047, 12001-12007, 12011-12057, 13100-13133, 13151-13153, 35201-35206, 35226-35236, 35256-35266, 35286, 36000, 36005, 36400-36410, 36420-36430, 36440, 36591-36593, 36597-36600, 36640, 37211-37214, 43752, 51701-51703, 61645, 62320-62327, 64400-64410, 64413-64435, 64445-64450, 64461-64463, 64479-64530, 69990, 71010, 71020, 76000-76001, 76380, 76937, 76942, 76970, 76998, 77001-77002, 77012, 77021, 92012-92014, 93000-93010, 93040-93042, 93318, 93355, 94002, 94200, 94250, 94680-94690, 94770, 95812-95816, 95819, 95822, 95829, 95955, 96360-96368, 96372, 96374-96377, 97597-97598, 97602, 99155-99157, 99211-99223, 99231-99255, 99291-99292, 99304-99310, 99315-99316, 99334-99337, 99347-99350, 99374-99375, 99377-99378, 99446-99449, 99495-99496, G0463, G0471, J0670, J1642-J1644, J2001

75901   01930, 01932, 36000, 36005, 36410, 36500, 36591-36592, 36598, 75741, 75743, 75746, 75825, 75827, 75893, 76000-76001, 76942, 76970, 76998, 77001-77002, 96360, 96365, 96372, 96375-96377, 99446-99449

75902   01930, 01932, 36000, 36005, 36410, 36500, 36591-36592, 36598, 75741, 75743, 75746, 75827, 75891, 75893, 76000-76001, 76942, 76970, 76998, 77001-77002, 96360, 96365, 96372, 96375-96377, 99446-99449

Case Example

Indication:
The patient has a malfunctioning hemodialysis catheter.

Procedure:
After informed consent was obtained, the patient was placed supine on the angiography table. The skin around the entry site of an **existing right internal jugular hemodialysis catheter was prepped** and draped in sterile fashion. Local anesthesia was achieved. Two .035 Glidewires were advanced through the existing catheter, which was removed and replaced with a long vascular sheath. The wires were advanced into the inferior vena cava. Over one wire **a Fogarty** balloon catheter was advanced within the SVC and then pulled back. The maneuver was repeated 3 or 4 times **to dislodge the fibrin sheath within the SVC. Repeat venogram** demonstrated significant improvement in the caliber of the SVC with small residual filling defects. The venogram was compared against the previous venogram obtained before fibrin stripping. The venogram at that time showed significant narrowing of the SVC. Small residual stenosis persisted at the junction of the SVC and right atrium. **No intervention was performed** at this level due to the presence of pacemaker wires. The Fogarty catheter and sheath were removed. A **new 28 cm catheter was positioned with its distal tip in the right atrium** and the proximal tip at the junction of the right atrium and the SVC. The patient tolerated the procedure well.

Impression:
Presence of fibrin sheath within the SVC hampering the function of the internal jugular hemodialysis catheter.

Successful stripping of the fibrin sheath was performed using Fogarty balloon catheter. Removal of an existing hemodialysis catheter with placement of a new permanent catheter under fluoroscopy.

CPT/HCPCS Codes Reported:
36595-52, 75901, 36581, 77001

Other HCPCS Codes Reported:
C1769 x2, C1757, C1750, C1894

Chapter 8: Minor Interventional Procedures

Arthrography

Arthrography involves injecting contrast media into a joint space and then obtaining images of the joint. The codes are unilateral and may be reported twice with modifiers RT and LT. The entire procedure may be performed using fluoroscopic guidance or a combination of fluoroscopy and CT or MRI for imaging.

70332 **Temporomandibular joint arthrography, radiological supervision and interpretation**
A radiographic contrast study is performed on the temporomandibular joint. A contrast material is injected into the joint spaces, followed by x-ray examination of the joint. This allows the physician to see the position of the structures not normally seen on conventional x-rays.

73040 **Radiologic examination, shoulder, arthrography, radiological supervision and interpretation**
The synovial joint of the shoulder is visualized internally through arthrography, the direct injection of air and/or contrast material into the joint for radiological examination. Local anesthesia is injected into the joint followed by the contrast material and/or air. A series of images are taken and interpreted. Fluoroscopic films and guidance for needle localization is included. Arthrography helps diagnose conditions of cartilage abnormalities, arthritis and bursitis, rotator cuff tear, and frozen joint. AP (front to back) views are taken with the affected arm rotated externally and internally and with the arm in a neutral, flexed position lying over the abdomen.

73085 **Radiologic examination, elbow, arthrography, radiological supervision and interpretation**
The synovial joint of the elbow is visualized internally through arthrography, the direct injection of air and/or contrast material into the joint for radiological examination. Local anesthesia is injected into the joint followed by the contrast material and/or air. A series of images are taken by the radiologist and interpreted. Fluoroscopic films and guidance for needle localization is included. Arthrography helps diagnose conditions of cartilage abnormalities, arthritis and bursitis, and frozen joint.

73115 **Radiologic examination, wrist, arthrography, radiological supervision and interpretation**
The wrist is visualized internally through arthrography, the direct injection of air and/or contrast material into the joint for radiological examination. Local anesthesia is injected into the joint followed by the contrast material and/or air. A series of images are taken and interpreted. Fluoroscopic films and guidance for needle local-ization is included. Arthrography helps diagnose conditions of cartilage abnormalities, arthritis and bursitis, and frozen joint. The hand and wrist are placed in the posteroanterior (PA) position with the hand rotated outward and the x-ray beam aimed vertically at the wrist or with the hand and wrist in PA position with the beam aimed at the wrist from a few degrees below the elbow.

73525 **Radiologic examination, hip, arthrography, radiological supervision and interpretation**
This code reports the radiological supervision and interpretation for hip arthrography. Using a fluoroscope, the physician marks the point of the femoral neck on the skin with ink. The femoral artery is palpated and marked as well to avoid inadvertent puncture. Skin traction may be applied to increase the space between the femoral head and acetabulum. The physician inserts a needle into the capsule (located by fluoroscope) and aspirates the synovial fluid for a culture check. After aspiration, a contrast agent is injected into the hip joint and the needle is removed. X-rays are then taken with the hip in neutral, external, and internal rotation. A second set of x-rays may be taken following the hip movements.

73580 **Radiologic examination, knee, arthrography, radiological supervision and interpretation**
The patient is placed supine (lying on the back) on an x-ray table with the knee flexed over a small pillow. The knee is cleansed with Betadine and covered with a sterile drape. A skin anesthetic may be applied. The physician then passes a 20-gauge needle into the femoropatellar space. Air and a contrast agent are then injected. After the injection, the patient is asked to move the knee to produce an even coating of the joint structures. Multiple x-rays are then taken of the knee. This code reports the radiological supervision and interpretation only. Use a separately reportable code for the arthrography.

73615 **Radiologic examination, ankle, arthrography, radiological supervision and interpretation**
The physician injects radiopaque fluid into the ankle for arthrography. The physician inserts a needle into the joint and aspirates if necessary. Opaque contrast solution is injected into the ankle and the needle is removed. Films are then taken of the ankle. This code reports the radiological supervision and interpretation only. Use a separately reportable code for the injection.

CPT Coding for Arthrography

Service Performed	Surgical Component	Radiology S&I Component
TMJ arthrography	21116	70332
Shoulder arthrography	23350	73040
Elbow arthrography	24220	73085
Wrist arthrography	25246	73115
Hip arthrography	27093	73525
Knee arthrography	27370	73580
Ankle arthrography	27648	73615
Sacroiliac joint arthrography	G0259 - Medicare, 27096 - non-Medicare (See Facility Coding Tip #6 below.)	76000 – Medicare, N/A – non-Medicare

Coding Tips

1. Report both components of the procedure: the surgical component and the radiology S&I codes.

2. Do not report fluoroscopy guidance codes. Fluoroscopy is included in the radiology S&I codes for all arthrogram procedures.

3. Report the appropriate computerized tomography (CT) or magnetic resonance imaging (MRI) code when imaging is performed in these modalities. For MRI imaging, report CPT® code 73222 or 73722. For CT imaging, report CPT code 73201 or 73701.

4. The surgical component codes include all injections necessary to complete the study. If more than one injection is needed to obtain a full study, report the code only once.

5. If 3D reconstruction of CT or MRI images is performed and appropriately documented, it is acceptable to report CPT code 76376 or 76377 as appropriate.

6. If the sacroiliac joint is injected to provide a therapeutic agent with or without performing arthrography, HCPCS Level II code G0260 is reported for Medicare. This code carries separate reimbursement. If no arthrography is performed, then fluoroscopy guidance is reported (CPT code 77002).

7. Both the surgical and radiology codes are unilateral. Append modifier 50 for bilateral joint studies.

8. Hospitals are requested to continue reporting LOCM separately with HCPCS codes Q9965–Q9967. Report contrast media by milliliter.

9. Physician Reporting: These radiology S&I codes have both a technical and professional component. To report only the professional component, append modifier 26. To report only the technical component, append modifier TC. To report the complete procedure (i.e., both the professional and technical components), submit without a modifier.

Facility HCPCS Coding

Some applicable codes may include but are not limited to:

Q9965   LOCM, 100-199 mg/ml iodine concentration, per ml

Q9966   LOCM, 200-299 mg/ml iodine concentration, per ml

Q9967   LOCM, 300-399 mg/ml iodine concentration, per ml

ICD-10-CM Coding

The application of these codes is too broad to adequately present ICD-10-CM diagnosis code links here. Refer to the current ICD-10-CM book.

CCI Edits

70332   36591-36592, 76000-76001, 77001-77002, 99446-99449

72240   00600, 01935-01936, 20551-20553, 36591-36592, 62284, 72255, 72265, 76000-76001, 77001-77003, 99446-99449

73085   01922, 36591-36592, 73070-73080, 76000-76001, 77001-77002, 99446-99449

73115   01922, 36591-36592, 73100-73110, 76000-76001, 77001-77002, 99446-99449

73525   36591-36592, 73501-73503, 73521-73523, 76000-76001, 77001-77002, 99446-99449

73580   01380, 01922, 36591-36592, 73560, 76000-76001, 77001-77002, 99446-99449

73615   01922, 36591-36592, 73600-73610, 76000-76001, 77001-77002, 99446-99449

Case Example

Right Shoulder Arthrogram

Indication:
Patient fell on the right shoulder while skiing. Patient had decreased range of motion and pain in the shoulder, and was unable to lift arm.

Procedure:
Under sterile conditions and following localizing procedure, 1 percent lidocaine was introduced into the skin. Thereafter, a 22-gauge **needle was introduced into the shoulder joint**. 12 cc of **Isovue-300 were instilled into the joint space** along with 3 cc of 1 percent lidocaine. The patient tolerated the procedure well.

The arm was then exercised and **films were obtained in** the internal and external rotation positions.

Findings:
The plain films showed no abnormalities of the shoulder joint. Following injection of contrast, there was normal visualization of the shoulder joint. Contrast did not extravasate into the subacromial bursa. On this examination, there was no evidence of a tear involving the supraspinatus tendon. Extravasation of contrast was seen in the subacromial bursa. There was normal outline and contour of the right shoulder joint on this study.

Impression:
The **right shoulder arthrogram was normal**. There was no evidence of a rotator cuff tear.

CPT/HCPCS Codes Reported:
73040, 23350

Other HCPCS Codes Reported:
Q9967 x 12

Image-Guided Interventional Procedures—Breast Biopsy

Image-guided breast biopsy interventions are considered minimally invasive procedures. These procedures involve placing a needle into the area of interest and removing tissue or cells for microscopic evaluation. Image guidance may be performed using special mammography stereotactic equipment, ultrasound equipment or magnetic resonance (MRI) equipment.

19081   **Biopsy, breast, with placement of breast localization device(s) (eg, clip, metallic pellet), when performed, and imaging of the biopsy specimen, when performed, percutaneous; first lesion, including stereotactic guidance**

19082   **each additional lesion, including stereotactic guidance (List separately in addition to code for primary procedure)**

A lesion in the breast is localized for biopsy. In the localization process, a movable arm holding the needle works together with the mammography unit that images the lesion from different angles at different fixed points. The mammogram information tells a computer where the coordinates are to correctly align the biopsy needle. The needle position is confirmed with more views taken. A stab incision is made in the skin. The needle is advanced to the lesion, and additional stereotactic views confirm needle placement. The tissue sample is then extracted from the lesion. If necessary, a metallic clip is inserted into the needle and pushed out into the tissue to mark the location of the biopsy. The needle is removed from the breast with the tissue sample. The tissue sample is then sent to pathology to analyze.

19083   **Biopsy, breast, with placement of breast localization device(s) (eg, clip, metallic pellet), when performed, and imaging of the biopsy specimen, when performed, percutaneous; first lesion, including ultrasound guidance**

19084   **each additional lesion, including ultrasound guidance (List separately in addition to code for primary procedure)**

Ultrasonic guidance is used for guiding needle placement into the breast tissue for the purpose of biopsy. Ultrasound is the process of bouncing sound waves far above the level of human perception through interior body structures by moving a probe over the area to be viewed. The sound waves pass through different densities of tissue and reflect back to the probe at varying speeds. The computer in the ultrasound unit then converts the waves to electrical pulses that are displayed in picture form on a screen. Once the exact needle entry site is determined along with the depth of the lesion, the optimal route from the skin to the lesion is decided. The needle is then inserted and advanced to the lesion under ultrasonic guidance. A stab incision is made in the skin. The needle is advanced to the lesion while watching in real time on the ultrasound monitor. The tissue sample is then extracted from the lesion. If necessary, a metallic clip is inserted into the needle and pushed out into the tissue to mark the location of the biopsy. The needle is removed from the breast with the tissue sample. The tissue sample is then sent to pathology to analyze.

19085   **Biopsy, breast, with placement of breast localization device(s) (eg, clip, metallic pellet), when performed, and imaging of the biopsy specimen, when performed, percutaneous; first lesion, including magnetic resonance guidance**

19086   **each additional lesion, including magnetic resonance guidance (List separately in addition to code for primary procedure)**

Magnetic resonance is used for guiding needle placement into the breast tissue for the purpose of biopsy. Magnetic resonance imaging (MRI) is a radiation-free, noninvasive technique that produces high-quality images. MRI uses the natural magnetic properties of the hydrogen atoms in our bodies that emit radiofrequency signals when exposed to radio waves within a strong electromagnetic field. These signals are processed and converted by the computer into high-resolution, three-dimensional, tomographic (cross-section) images. Some methods for magnetic resonance needle placement include coating the needle with contrast material, placing special metallic ringlets along the needle, or using a tiny receiving coil in the tip of the needle. Once the exact needle entry site is determined along with the depth of the lesion, the optimal route from the skin to the lesion is decided. The needle is then inserted and advanced to the lesion under MRI guidance. A stab incision is made in the skin. The needle is advanced to the lesion while watching in real time on the MRI monitor. The tissue sample is then extracted from the lesion. If necessary, a metallic clip is inserted into the needle and pushed out into the tissue to mark the location of the biopsy. The needle is removed from the breast with the tissue sample, which is then sent to pathology to analyze.

19281   **Placement of breast localization device(s) (eg, clip, metallic pellet, wire/needle, radioactive seeds), percutaneous; first lesion, including mammographic guidance**

19282   **each additional lesion, including mammographic guidance (List separately in addition to code for primary procedure)**

The physician places a breast localization device prior to a breast biopsy. Using image guidance, the physician places a metallic clip, pellet, wire, needle, or radioactive seed adjacent to a breast lesion to mark the site for an open breast procedure or a percutaneous breast biopsy to be performed during the same or a different encounter.

19283	**Placement of breast localization device(s) (eg, clip, metallic pellet, wire/needle, radioactive seeds), percutaneous; first lesion, including stereotactic guidance**
19284	**each additional lesion, including stereotactic guidance (List separately in addition to code for primary procedure)**

The physician places a breast localization device prior to a breast biopsy. Using image guidance, the physician places a metallic clip, pellet, wire, needle, or radioactive seed adjacent to a breast lesion to mark the site for an open breast procedure or a percutaneous breast biopsy to be performed during the same or a different encounter.

19285	**Placement of breast localization device(s) (eg, clip, metallic pellet, wire/needle, radioactive seeds), percutaneous; first lesion, including ultrasound guidance**
19286	**each additional lesion, including ultrasound guidance (List separately in addition to code for primary procedure)**

The physician places a breast localization device prior to a breast biopsy. Using image guidance, the physician places a metallic clip, pellet, wire, needle, or radioactive seed adjacent to a breast lesion to mark the site for an open breast procedure or a percutaneous breast biopsy to be performed during the same or a different encounter.

19287	**Placement of breast localization device(s) (eg, clip, metallic pellet, wire/needle, radioactive seeds), percutaneous; first lesion, including magnetic resonance guidance**
19288	**each additional lesion, including magnetic resonance guidance (List separately in addition to code for primary procedure)**

The physician places a breast localization device prior to a breast biopsy. Using image guidance, the physician places a metallic clip, pellet, wire, needle, or radioactive seed adjacent to a breast lesion to mark the site for an open breast procedure or a percutaneous breast biopsy to be performed during the same or a different encounter.

CPT Coding for Breast Biopsy

Service Performed	Code(s) Reported, Initial Lesion	Code(s) Reported, Additional Lesions
Percutaneous breast biopsy with stereotactic guidance	19081	19082
Percutaneous breast biopsy with ultrasound guidance	19083	19084
Percutaneous breast biopsy with MRI guidance	19085	19086
Percutaneous breast biopsy without image guidance	19100	19100
Open, incisional breast biopsy without image guidance	19101	

Coding Tips

1. These are comprehensive codes. Component coding does not apply.
2. Use codes 19081–19086 for percutaneous breast biopsy procedures performed with image guidance. Use the applicable code based on the type of image guidance used, i.e., stereotactic, ultrasound, or MRI.
3. Codes 19081–19086 include the placement of a localization device, e.g., metallic clip. Do not separately report 19281–19288 for the same lesion.
4. Codes 19081–19086 include specimen radiography. Do not separately report 76098.
5. For multiple lesions, report the applicable add-on code in addition to the initial procedure code when using the same imaging modality.
6. For additional biopsies performed with a different imaging modality, report another primary code for that imaging modality.
7. For percutaneous breast biopsy performed without image guidance, see codes 19100 or 19101.
8. Codes 19281–19298 are reported when a localization device is placed using imaging guidance but the subsequent biopsy procedure is performed without imaging guidance; for example, for an open incisional biopsy.
9. Specimen radiography (76098) may be additionally reported with codes 19281–19288.
10. Do not separately report mammography performed after mammographically guided procedures. It is acceptable to report mammography following ultrasound-guided procedures.
11. Report all applicable HCPCS Level II codes. Refer to the HCPCS section for possible codes.
12. Physician Reporting: These codes have both a technical and professional component. To report only the professional component, append modifier 26. To report only the technical component, append modifier TC. To report the complete procedure (i.e., both the professional and technical components), submit without a modifier.

CPT Coding for Breast Localization Procedures

Service Performed	Code(s) Reported, Initial Lesion	Code(s) Reported, Additional Lesions
Percutaneous placement of localization device with mammographic guidance	19281	19282
Percutaneous placement of localization device with stereotactic guidance	19283	19284
Percutaneous placement of localization device with ultrasound guidance	19285	19286
Percutaneous placement of localization device with MRI guidance	19287	19288
Surgical specimen radiography	76098	76098

Facility HCPCS Coding

Report any applicable supplies and HCPCS codes. Refer to appendix B for a complete list.

ICD-10-CM Coding

The application of these codes is too broad to adequately present ICD-10-CM diagnosis code links here. Refer to the current ICD-10-CM book.

CCI Edits

19081   00400, 0213T, 0216T, 0228T, 0230T, 10021-10022, 10035-10036, 12001-12007, 12011-12057, 13100-13133, 13151-13153, 19100-19101, 19281-19288, 36000, 36400-36410, 36420-36430, 36440, 36591-36592, 36600, 36640, 43752, 51701-51703, 62320-62327, 64400-64410, 64413-64435, 64445-64450, 64461-64463, 64479-64530, 69990, 76000-76001, 76098, 76380, 76942, 76970, 76998, 77002, 77011-77012, 77021, 88172, 92012-92014, 93000-93010, 93040-93042, 93318, 93355, 94002, 94200, 94250, 94680-94690, 94770, 95812-95816, 95819, 95822, 95829, 95955, 96360-96368, 96372, 96374-96377, 99155-99157, 99211-99223, 99231-99255, 99291-99292, 99304-99310, 99315-99316, 99334-99337, 99347-99350, 99374-99375, 99377-99378, 99446-99449, G0463, G0471, J0670, J2001

19082   00400, 0213T, 0216T, 0228T, 0230T, 10021-10022, 10035-10036, 12001-12007, 12011-12057, 13100-13133, 13151-13153, 19100-19101, 19281, 19282, 19283, 19284, 19285, 19286, 19287, 19288, 36000, 36400-36410, 36420-36430, 36440, 36591-36592, 36600, 36640, 43752, 51701-51703, 61650, 62320-62327, 64400-64410, 64413-64435, 64445-64450, 64461, 64463, 64479, 64483, 64486-64490, 64493, 64505-64530, 69990, 76000-76001, 76098, 76380, 76942, 76970, 76998, 77002, 77011-77012, 77021, 88172, 93000-93010, 93040-93042, 93318, 93355, 94002, 94200, 94250, 94680-94690, 94770, 95812-95816, 95819, 95822, 95829, 95955, 96360, 96365, 96372, 96374-96377, 99155-99157, 99211-99223, 99231-99255, 99291-99292, 99304-99310, 99315-99316, 99334-99337, 99347-99350, 99374-99375, 99377-99378, 99446-99449, G0463, G0471, J0670, J2001

19083   00400, 0213T, 0216T, 0228T, 0230T, 10021-10022, 10035-10036, 12001-12007, 12011-12057, 13100-13133, 13151-13153, 19100-19101, 19281-19288, 36000, 36400-36410, 36420-36430, 36440, 36591-36592, 36600, 36640, 43752, 51701-51703, 62320-62327, 64400-64410, 64413-64435, 64445-64450, 64461-64463, 64479-64530, 69990, 76000-76001, 76098, 76380, 76942, 76970, 76998, 77002, 77011-77012, 77021, 88172, 92012-92014, 93000-93010, 93040-93042, 93318, 93355, 94002, 94200, 94250, 94680-94690, 94770, 95812-95816, 95819, 95822, 95829, 95955, 96360-96368, 96372, 96374-96377, 99155-99157, 99211-99223, 99231-99255, 99291-99292, 99304-99310, 99315-99316, 99334-99337, 99347-99350, 99374-99375, 99377-99378, 99446-99449, G0463, G0471, J0670, J2001

19084   00400, 0213T, 0216T, 0228T, 0230T, 10021-10022, 10035-10036, 12001-12007, 12011-12057, 13100-13133, 13151-13153, 19100-19101, 19281, 19282, 19283, 19284, 19285, 19286, 19287, 19288, 36000, 36400-36410, 36420-36430, 36440, 36591-36592, 36600, 36640, 43752, 51701-51703, 61650, 62320-62327, 64400-64410, 64413-64435, 64445-64450, 64461, 64463, 64479, 64483, 64486-64490, 64493, 64505-64530, 69990, 76000-76001, 76098, 76380, 76942, 76970, 76998, 77002, 77011-77012, 77021, 88172, 93000-93010, 93040-93042, 93318, 93355, 94002, 94200, 94250, 94680-94690, 94770, 95812-95816, 95819, 95822, 95829, 95955, 96360, 96365, 96372, 96374-96377, 99155-99157, 99211-99223, 99231-99255, 99291-99292, 99304-99310, 99315-99316, 99334-99337, 99347-99350, 99374-99375, 99377-99378, 99446-99449, G0463, G0471, J0670, J2001

19085   00400, 0213T, 0216T, 0228T, 0230T, 10021-10022, 10035-10036, 12001-12007, 12011-12057, 13100-13133, 13151-13153, 19100-19101, 19281-19288, 36000, 36400-36410, 36420-36430, 36440, 36591-36592, 36600, 36640, 43752, 51701-51703, 62320-62327, 64400-64410, 64413-64435, 64445-64450, 64461-64463, 64479-64530, 69990, 76000-76001, 76098, 76380, 76942, 76970, 76998, 77002, 77011-77012, 77021, 88172, 92012-92014, 93000-93010, 93040-93042, 93318, 93355, 94002, 94200, 94250, 94680-94690, 94770, 95812-95816, 95819, 95822, 95829, 95955, 96360-96368, 96372, 96374-96377, 99155-99157, 99211-99223, 99231-99255, 99291-99292, 99304-99310, 99315-99316, 99334-99337, 99347-99350, 99374-99375, 99377-99378, 99446-99449, G0463, G0471, J0670, J2001

19086   00400, 0213T, 0216T, 0228T, 0230T, 10021-10022, 10035-10036, 12001-12007, 12011-12057, 13100-13133, 13151-13153, 19100-19101, 19281, 19282, 19283, 19284, 19285, 19286, 19287, 19288, 36000, 36400-36410, 36420-36430, 36440, 36591-36592, 36600, 36640, 43752, 51701-51703, 61650, 62320-62327, 64400-64410, 64413-64435, 64445-64450, 64461, 64463, 64479, 64483, 64486-64490, 64493, 64505-64530, 69990, 76000-76001, 76098, 76380, 76942, 76970, 76998, 77002, 77011-77012, 77021, 88172, 93000-93010, 93040-93042, 93318, 93355, 94002, 94200, 94250, 94680-94690, 94770, 95812-95816, 95819, 95822, 95829, 95955, 96360, 96365, 96372, 96374-96377, 99155-99157, 99211-99223, 99231-99255, 99291-99292, 99304-99310, 99315-99316, 99334-99337, 99347-99350, 99374-99375, 99377-99378, 99446-99449, G0463, G0471, J0670, J2001

19281   00400, 0213T, 0216T, 0228T, 0230T, 12001-12007, 12011-12057, 13100-13133, 13151-13153, 36000, 36400-36410, 36420-36430, 36440, 36591-36592, 36600, 36640, 43752, 51701-51703, 62320-62327, 64400-64410, 64413-64435, 64445-64450, 64461-64463, 64479-64530, 69990, 76000-76001, 76380, 76942, 76970, 76998, 77002, 77011-77012, 77021, 77061-77062, 77065-77067, 92012-92014, 93000-93010, 93040-93042, 93318, 93355, 94002, 94200, 94250, 94680-94690, 94770, 95812-95816, 95819, 95822, 95829, 95955, 96360-96368, 96372, 96374-96377, 99155-99157, 99211-99223, 99231-99255, 99291-99292, 99304-99310, 99315-99316, 99334-99337, 99347-99350, 99374-99375, 99377-99378, 99446-99449, G0202, G0204, G0206, G0463, G0471, J0670, J2001

19282   00400, 0213T, 0216T, 0228T, 0230T, 12001-12007, 12011-12057, 13100-13133, 13151-13153, 19283, 19285, 19287, 36000, 36400-36410, 36420-36430, 36440, 36591-36592, 36600, 36640, 43752, 51701-51703, 61650, 62320-62327, 64400-64410, 64413-64435, 64445-64450, 64461, 64463, 64479, 64483, 64486-64490, 64493, 64505-64530, 69990, 76000-76001, 76380, 76942, 76970, 76998, 77002, 77011-77012, 77021, 77061-77062, 77065-77067, 93000-93010, 93040-93042, 93318, 93355, 94002, 94200, 94250, 94680-94690, 94770, 95812-95816, 95819, 95822, 95829, 95955, 96360, 96365, 96372, 96374-96377, 99155-99157, 99211-99223, 99231-99255, 99291-99292, 99304-99310, 99315-99316, 99334-99337, 99347-99350, 99374-99375, 99377-99378, 99446-99449, G0202, G0204, G0206, G0463, G0471, J0670, J2001

19283   00400, 0213T, 0216T, 0228T, 0230T, 12001-12007, 12011-12057, 13100-13133, 13151-13153, 19281, 36000, 36400-36410, 36420-36430, 36440, 36591-36592, 36600, 36640, 43752, 51701-51703, 62320-62327, 64400-64410, 64413-64435, 64445-64450, 64461-64463, 64479-64530, 69990, 76000-76001, 76380, 76942, 76970, 76998, 77002, 77011-77012, 77021, 92012-92014, 93000-93010, 93040-93042, 93318, 93355, 94002, 94200, 94250, 94680-94690, 94770, 95812-95816, 95819, 95822, 95829, 95955, 96360-96368, 96372, 96374-96377, 99155-99157, 99211-99223, 99231-99255, 99291-99292, 99304-99310, 99315-99316, 99334-99337, 99347-99350, 99374-99375, 99377-99378, 99446-99449, G0463, G0471, J0670, J2001

19284   00400, 0213T, 0216T, 0228T, 0230T, 12001-12007, 12011-12057, 13100-13133, 13151-13153, 19281, 19285, 19287, 36000, 36400-36410, 36420-36430, 36440, 36591-36592, 36600, 36640, 43752, 51701-51703, 61650, 62320-62327, 64400-64410, 64413-64435, 64445-64450, 64461, 64463, 64479, 64483, 64486-64490, 64493, 64505-64530, 69990, 76000-76001, 76380, 76942, 76970, 76998, 77002, 77011-77012, 77021, 93000-93010, 93040-93042, 93318, 93355, 94002, 94200, 94250, 94680-94690, 94770, 95812-95816, 95819, 95822, 95829, 95955, 96360, 96365, 96372, 96374-96377, 99155-99157, 99211-99223, 99231-99255, 99291-99292, 99304-99310, 99315-99316, 99334-99337, 99347-99350, 99374-99375, 99377-99378, 99446-99449, G0463, G0471, J0670, J2001

19285   00400, 0213T, 0216T, 0228T, 0230T, 10036, 12001-12007, 12011-12057, 13100-13133, 13151-13153, 19281, 19283, 36000, 36400-36410, 36420-36430, 36440, 36591-36592, 36600, 36640, 43752, 51701-51703, 62320-62327, 64400-64410, 64413-64435, 64445-64450, 64461-64463, 64479-64530, 69990, 76000-76001, 76380, 76942, 76970, 76998, 77002, 77011-77012, 77021, 92012-92014, 93000-93010, 93040-93042, 93318, 93355, 94002, 94200, 94250, 94680-94690, 94770, 95812-95816, 95819, 95822, 95829, 95955, 96360-96368, 96372, 96374-96377, 99155-99157, 99211-99223, 99231-99255, 99291-99292, 99304-99310, 99315-99316, 99334-99337, 99347-99350, 99374-99375, 99377-99378, 99446-99449, G0463, G0471, J0670, J2001

19286   00400, 0213T, 0216T, 0228T, 0230T, 12001-12007, 12011-12057, 13100-13133, 13151-13153, 19281, 19283, 19287, 36000, 36400-36410, 36420-36430, 36440, 36591-36592, 36600, 36640, 43752, 51701-51703, 61650, 62320-62327, 64400-64410, 64413-64435, 64445-64450, 64461, 64463, 64479, 64483, 64486-64490, 64493, 64505-64530, 69990, 76000-76001, 76380, 76942, 76970, 76998, 77002, 77011-77012, 77021, 93000-93010, 93040-93042, 93318, 93355, 94002, 94200, 94250, 94680-94690, 94770, 95812-95816, 95819, 95822, 95829, 95955, 96360, 96365, 96372, 96374-96377, 99155-99157, 99211-99223, 99231-99255, 99291-99292, 99304-99310, 99315-99316, 99334-99337, 99347-99350, 99374-99375, 99377-99378, 99446-99449, G0463, G0471, J0670, J2001

19287   00400, 0213T, 0216T, 0228T, 0230T, 10035-10036, 12001-12007, 12011-12057, 13100-13133, 13151-13153, 19281, 19283, 19285, 36000, 36400-36410, 36420-36430, 36440, 36591-36592, 36600, 36640, 43752, 51701-51703, 62320-62327, 64400-64410, 64413-64435, 64445-64450, 64461-64463, 64479-64530, 69990, 76000-76001, 76380, 76942, 76970, 76998, 77002, 77011-77012, 77021, 92012-92014, 93000-93010, 93040-93042, 93318, 93355, 94002, 94200, 94250, 94680-94690, 94770, 95812-95816, 95819, 95822, 95829, 95955, 96360-96368, 96372, 96374-96377, 99155-99157, 99211-99223, 99231-99255, 99291-99292, 99304-99310, 99315-99316, 99334-99337, 99347-99350, 99374-99375, 99377-99378, 99446-99449, G0463, G0471, J0670, J2001

19288   00400, 0213T, 0216T, 0228T, 0230T, 10035-10036, 12001-12007, 12011-12057, 13100-13133, 13151-13153, 19281, 19283, 19285, 36000, 36400-36410, 36420-36430, 36440, 36591-36592, 36600, 36640, 43752, 51701-51703, 61650, 62320-62327, 64400-64410, 64413-64435, 64445-64450, 64461, 64463, 64479, 64483, 64486-64490, 64493, 64505-64530, 69990, 76000-76001, 76380, 76942, 76970, 76998, 77002, 77011-77012, 77021, 93000-93010, 93040-93042, 93318, 93355, 94002, 94200, 94250, 94680-94690, 94770, 95812-95816, 95819, 95822, 95829, 95955, 96360, 96365, 96372, 96374-96377, 99155-99157, 99211-99223, 99231-99255, 99291-99292, 99304-99310, 99315-99316, 99334-99337, 99347-99350, 99374-99375, 99377-99378, 99446-99449, G0463, G0471, J0670, J2001

Case Example #1

Right Breast Ultrasound Guided Core Biopsy

Clinical History:
The patient is a 54-year-old woman who on previous mammograms and ultrasound was shown to have a highly suspicious, palpable, solid, lateral, 9 o'clock right breast mass. Ultrasound guided core biopsy was recommended.

Procedure and Findings:
The right **breast** was prepped in a sterile fashion. Local anesthesia was obtained with a combination of Lidocaine and sodium bicarbonate. Under **sonographic surveillance** and using a 14-gauge Tru-Cut spring-loaded biopsy needle, I obtained two **core samples** from the mass. Appropriate pre- and post-fire positioning of the needle was verified under real time sonographic surveillance. The core samples were placed in formalin and hand-carried to Pathology.

CPT/HCPCS Codes Reported:
19083

Case Example #2

Left Breast Needle Localization #1, Anterior Upper Outer Quadrant Mass:
The left breast was prepped in a sterile fashion. Local anesthesia was obtained with a combination of Lidocaine and sodium bicarbonate. Under **sonographic surveillance**, using a 5.0 cm Kopans needle, I **localized** the irregular anterior upper outer quadrant mass from an inferolateral approach. Once the needle was shown to be in appropriate position, it was withdrawn, and the **hookwire was deployed**. The patient was taken to surgery for excision and the excised specimen was sent back to radiology for review.

Specimen Radiograph #1:
Subsequent specimen radiograph revealed that the anterior upper outer quadrant mass was included in the biopsied material.

CPT/HCPCS Codes Reported:
19285

Image-Guided Interventional Procedures—Breast, Other Than Biopsy

Image-guided breast interventions are considered minimally invasive procedures. These procedures involve placing a needle into the area of interest and removing fluid, tissue, or cells for microscopic evaluation. Image guidance may be performed using fluoroscopy, mammography, ultrasound, CT, or magnetic resonance (MRI) equipment.

19000	**Puncture aspiration of cyst of breast;**
19001	**each additional cyst (List separately in addition to code for primary procedure)**
	A needle is placed through the skin into the area of interest, and fluid is extracted for microscopic evaluation.
19030	**Injection procedure only for mammary ductogram or galactogram**
	The physician performs an injection procedure for mammary ductogram or galactogram. A cannula or needle is inserted into the duct of the breast. Contrast media is introduced into the breast duct for the purpose of radiographic study. A dissecting microscope may be used to aid in placing the cannula. The needle or cannula is removed once the study has been completed.
77053	**Mammary ductogram or galactogram, single duct, radiological supervision and interpretation**
77054	**Mammary ductogram or galactogram, multiple ducts, radiological supervision and interpretation**
	The physician applies manual pressure to the breast to elicit fluid discharge from the duct. The physician then puts a tiny catheter into the duct and injects a small amount of contrast media. Pictures of the breast are then taken with mammography equipment. The catheter is then removed.

Coding Tips

1. Report both components of the procedure—the surgical component and the radiology S&I technical component.
2. Use image guidance codes when applicable.
3. For cyst aspiration without image guidance, report only 19000 and 19001 as appropriate.
4. For cyst aspiration with image guidance, report 19000 and 19001, if applicable, and the code representing the type of image guidance used.
5. Radiologic guidance CPT codes are reported only once per patient encounter regardless of the number of needle placements performed.
6. For ductogram or galactogram of a single duct, report codes 77053 and 19030. When imaging and injecting more than one duct, report 77054 once and 19030 for each duct injected.
7. A post-procedure mammogram should not be reported separately. It is included in the imaging procedure code.
8. Report all applicable HCPCS Level II codes. Refer to the HCPCS section for possible codes.
9. Physician Reporting: These codes have both a technical and professional component. To report only the professional component, append modifier 26. To report only the technical component, append modifier TC. To report the complete procedure, submit without a modifier.

Facility HCPCS Coding

Report any applicable supplies and HCPCS codes. Refer to appendix B for a complete list.

ICD-10-CM Coding

19000–19001

N60.01	Solitary cyst of right breast
N60.02	Solitary cyst of left breast
N60.09	Solitary cyst of unspecified breast
N60.11	Diffuse cystic mastopathy of right breast
N60.12	Diffuse cystic mastopathy of left breast
N60.19	Diffuse cystic mastopathy of unspecified breast
N60.81	Other benign mammary dysplasias of right breast
N60.82	Other benign mammary dysplasias of left breast
N60.89	Other benign mammary dysplasias of unspecified breast
N63.0	Unspecified lump in unspecified breast
N63.10	Unspecified lump in the right breast, unspecified quadrant
N63.11	Unspecified lump in the right breast, upper outer quadrant
N63.12	Unspecified lump in the right breast, upper inner quadrant
N63.13	Unspecified lump in the right breast, lower outer quadrant
N63.14	Unspecified lump in the right breast, lower inner quadrant
N63.20	Unspecified lump in the left breast, unspecified quadrant

N63.21 Unspecified lump in the left breast, upper outer quadrant
N63.22 Unspecified lump in the left breast, upper inner quadrant
N63.23 Unspecified lump in the left breast, lower outer quadrant
N63.24 Unspecified lump in the left breast, lower inner quadrant
N63.31 Unspecified lump in axillary tail of the right breast
N63.32 Unspecified lump in axillary tail of the left breast
N63.41 Unspecified lump in right breast, subareolar
N63.42 Unspecified lump in left breast, subareolar

19030, 77053 & 77054
C50.011 Malignant neoplasm of nipple and areola, right female breast
C50.012 Malignant neoplasm of nipple and areola, left female breast
C50.019 Malignant neoplasm of nipple and areola, unspecified female breast
C50.021 Malignant neoplasm of nipple and areola, right male breast
C50.022 Malignant neoplasm of nipple and areola, left male breast
C50.029 Malignant neoplasm of nipple and areola, unspecified male breast
D05.10 Intraductal carcinoma in situ of unspecified breast
D05.11 Intraductal carcinoma in situ of right breast
D05.12 Intraductal carcinoma in situ of left breast
D05.80 Other specified type of carcinoma in situ of unspecified breast
D05.81 Other specified type of carcinoma in situ of right breast
D05.82 Other specified type of carcinoma in situ of left breast
D05.90 Unspecified type of carcinoma in situ of unspecified breast
D05.91 Unspecified type of carcinoma in situ of right breast
D05.92 Unspecified type of carcinoma in situ of left breast
D24.1 Benign neoplasm of right breast
D24.2 Benign neoplasm of left breast
D24.9 Benign neoplasm of unspecified breast
D48.60 Neoplasm of uncertain behavior of unspecified breast
D48.61 Neoplasm of uncertain behavior of right breast
D48.62 Neoplasm of uncertain behavior of left breast
D49.3 Neoplasm of unspecified behavior of breast
N60.01 Solitary cyst of right breast
N60.02 Solitary cyst of left breast
N60.09 Solitary cyst of unspecified breast
N60.11 Diffuse cystic mastopathy of right breast
N60.12 Diffuse cystic mastopathy of left breast
N60.19 Diffuse cystic mastopathy of unspecified breast
N60.41 Mammary duct ectasia of right breast
N60.42 Mammary duct ectasia of left breast
N60.49 Mammary duct ectasia of unspecified breast
N60.81 Other benign mammary dysplasias of right breast
N60.82 Other benign mammary dysplasias of left breast
N60.89 Other benign mammary dysplasias of unspecified breast
N60.91 Unspecified benign mammary dysplasia of right breast
N60.92 Unspecified benign mammary dysplasia of left breast
N60.99 Unspecified benign mammary dysplasia of unspecified breast
N61.0 Mastitis without abscess
N61.1 Abscess of the breast and nipple
N63.0 Unspecified lump in unspecified breast
N63.10 Unspecified lump in the right breast, unspecified quadrant
N63.11 Unspecified lump in the right breast, upper outer quadrant
N63.12 Unspecified lump in the right breast, upper inner quadrant
N63.13 Unspecified lump in the right breast, lower outer quadrant
N63.14 Unspecified lump in the right breast, lower inner quadrant
N63.20 Unspecified lump in the left breast, unspecified quadrant

N63.21	Unspecified lump in the left breast, upper outer quadrant
N63.22	Unspecified lump in the left breast, upper inner quadrant
N63.23	Unspecified lump in the left breast, lower outer quadrant
N63.24	Unspecified lump in the left breast, lower inner quadrant
N63.31	Unspecified lump in axillary tail of the right breast
N63.32	Unspecified lump in axillary tail of the left breast
N63.41	Unspecified lump in right breast, subareolar
N63.42	Unspecified lump in left breast, subareolar
N64.1	Fat necrosis of breast
N64.3	Galactorrhea not associated with childbirth
N64.4	Mastodynia
N64.51	Induration of breast
N64.52	Nipple discharge
N64.53	Retraction of nipple
N64.59	Other signs and symptoms in breast
N64.89	Other specified disorders of breast

CCI Edits

19000 00400, 0213T, 0216T, 0228T, 0230T, 12001-12007, 12011-12057, 13100-13133, 13151-13153, 36000, 36400-36410, 36420-36430, 36440, 36591-36592, 36600, 36640, 43752, 51701-51703, 62320-62327, 64400-64410, 64413-64435, 64445-64450, 64461-64463, 64479-64530, 69990, 92012-92014, 93000-93010, 93040-93042, 93318, 93355, 94002, 94200, 94250, 94680-94690, 94770, 95812-95816, 95819, 95822, 95829, 95955, 96360-96368, 96372, 96374-96377, 99155-99157, 99211-99223, 99231-99255, 99291-99292, 99304-99310, 99315-99316, 99334-99337, 99347-99350, 99374-99375, 99377-99378, 99446-99449, 99495-99496, G0463, G0471, J0670, J2001

19001 36591-36592, J2001

19030 00400, 0213T, 0216T, 0228T, 0230T, 12001-12007, 12011-12057, 13100-13133, 13151-13153, 36000, 36400-36410, 36420-36430, 36440, 36591-36592, 36600, 36640, 43752, 51701-51703, 62320-62327, 64400-64410, 64413-64435, 64445-64450, 64461-64463, 64479-64530, 69990, 76000-76001, 77001-77002, 92012-92014, 93000-93010, 93040-93042, 93318, 93355, 94002, 94200, 94250, 94680-94690, 94770, 95812-95816, 95819, 95822, 95829, 95955, 96360-96368, 96372, 96374-96377, 99155-99157, 99211-99223, 99231-99255, 99291-99292, 99304-99310, 99315-99316, 99334-99337, 99347-99350, 99374-99375, 99377-99378, 99446-99449, 99495-99496, G0463, G0471

77053 36591-36592, 99446-99449

77054 36591-36592, 77053, 99446-99449

Case Example

Patient presents with bloody nipple discharge from the left breast. The patient was brought to the mammography suite. The **left breast** was prepped in sterile fashion. Manual compression was applied, and fluid was expressed from a medial duct. The 30-gauge straight **cannula was inserted into the duct**, and a small amount of **contrast media was injected. Images were taken**. A filling defect is seen in the inferior duct, most likely representing intraductal papilloma.

CPT/HCPCS Codes Reported:
19030, 77053

Other Biopsy Procedures

CPT Coding for Image Guided Biopsy Procedures

Service Performed	Surgical Component
Percutaneous needle biopsy of muscle	20206
Superficial needle biopsy of bone	20220
Deep needle biopsy of bone	20225
Percutaneous needle biopsy of the pleura	32400
Percutaneous needle biopsy of the lung or mediastinum	32405
Needle biopsy of the salivary gland	42400
Percutaneous needle biopsy of the liver	47000
Percutaneous needle biopsy of the pancreas	48102
Percutaneous needle biopsy of an abdominal or retroperitoneal mass	49180
Percutaneous needle renal biopsy	50200
Needle biopsy of the prostate	55700
Percutaneous core needle biopsy of the thyroid	60100
Percutaneous needle biopsy of the spinal cord	62269

Coding Tips

1. Report both components of the procedure: the surgical component and the radiology S&I codes.
2. Report the appropriate image guidance code listed in the table below:

Guidance Modality Used	Radiology S&I Code
Fluoroscopy	77002
CT	77012
Ultrasound	76942
MRI	77021

3. Report the surgical component code once for each surgical site where a biopsy is performed. For example, if a biopsy is taken of two different lesions in the liver, CPT code 47000 is reported once. However, if one biopsy is performed of a lesion in the liver and a second biopsy is performed of a lesion in the right kidney, then report 47000 once and 50200 once.
4. Guidance codes include only the work provided for the imaging guidance procedure. If an evaluation is performed of the organ, then a diagnostic study code is also reported. In order to report the ultrasound guidance codes, permanently recorded images of the site are required, as well as documentation in the medical record of the process. See CPT manual instructions.
5. Report guidance codes 76942, 77002, 77003, 77012, and 77021 only once per patient encounter regardless of the number of needle placements performed.
6. Report all applicable HCPCS Level II codes. Refer to appendix B for possible codes.
   Special Note: Biopsy versus aspiration is often a point of confusion. Biopsies may be obtained using a fine needle aspiration technique. The size of the needle used to obtain the biopsy is not important. The key concept is: Was a core of tissue obtained or was a cellular aspirate obtained? When an anatomically correct surgical needle biopsy code is available, that code should be reported in lieu of the fine needle aspiration code, 10021 or 10022. Only when an anatomically correct code is not available should 10021 or 10022 be reported for a percutaneous biopsy. The physician dictating the procedure determines whether biopsy or aspiration was performed. This physician should clearly state aspiration or biopsy in the medical record. If both are stated, physician clarification should be obtained.
7. These radiology S&I codes have both a technical and professional component. To report only the professional component, append modifier 26. To report only the technical component, append modifier TC. To report the complete procedure (i.e., both the professional and technical components), submit without a modifier.

Facility HCPCS Coding

Report any applicable supplies and HCPCS codes. Refer to appendix B for a complete list.

ICD-10-CM Coding

The application of these codes is too broad to adequately present ICD-10-CM diagnosis code links here. Refer to the current ICD-10-CM book.

CCI Edits

20206 0213T, 0216T, 0228T, 0230T, 10021-10022, 12001-12007, 12011-12057, 13100-13133, 13151-13153, 24300, 25259, 26340, 36000, 36400-36410, 36420-36430, 36440, 36591-36592, 36600, 36640, 43752, 51701-51703, 62320-62327, 64400-64410, 64413-64435, 64445-64450, 64461-64463, 64479-64530, 69990, 76000-76001, 77001, 92012-92014, 93000-93010, 93040-93042, 93318, 93355, 94002, 94200, 94250, 94680-94690, 94770, 95812-95816, 95819, 95822, 95829, 95907-95913, 95955, 96360-96368, 96372, 96374-96377, 99155-99157, 99211-99223, 99231-99255, 99291-99292, 99304-99310, 99315-99316, 99334-99337, 99347-99350, 99374-99375, 99377-99378, 99446-99449, 99495-99496, G0463, G0471, J0670, J2001

20220 0213T, 0216T, 0228T, 0230T, 12001-12007, 12011-12057, 13100-13133, 13151-13153, 21750, 24300, 25259, 26340, 36000, 36400-36410, 36420-36430, 36440, 36591-36592, 36600, 36640, 38220, 43752, 51701-51703, 62320-62327, 64400-64410, 64413-64435, 64445-64450, 64461-64463, 64479-64530, 69990, 76000-76001, 77001, 92012-92014, 93000-93010, 93040-93042, 93318, 93355, 94002, 94200, 94250, 94680-94690, 94770, 95812-95816, 95819, 95822, 95829, 95955, 96360-96368, 96372, 96374-96377, 99155-99157, 99211-99223, 99231-99255, 99291-99292, 99304-99310, 99315-99316, 99334-99337, 99347-99350, 99374-99375, 99377-99378, 99446-99449, 99495-99496, G0364, G0463, G0471, J0670, J2001

20225 0213T, 0216T, 0228T, 0230T, 12001-12007, 12011-12057, 13100-13133, 13151-13153, 20220, 24300, 25259, 26340, 36000, 36400-36410, 36420-36430, 36440, 36591-36592, 36600, 36640, 38220-38221, 43752, 49010, 51701-51703, 62320-62327, 64400-64410, 64413-64435, 64445-64450, 64461-64463, 64479-64530, 69990, 92012-92014, 93000-93010, 93040-93042, 93318, 93355, 94002, 94200, 94250, 94680-94690, 94770, 95812-95816, 95819, 95822, 95829, 95955, 96360-96368, 96372, 96374-96377, 99155-99157, 99211-99223, 99231-99255, 99291-99292, 99304-99310, 99315-99316, 99334-99337, 99347-99350, 99374-99375, 99377-99378, 99446-99449, 99495-99496, G0364, G0463, G0471, J0670, J2001

32400 0213T, 0216T, 0228T, 0230T, 10021-10022, 12001-12007, 12011-12057, 13100-13133, 13151-13153, 20101, 32551, 32556-32557, 32601, 32607-32609, 36000, 36400-36410, 36420-36430, 36440, 36591-36592, 36600, 36640, 43752, 51701-51703, 62320-62327, 64400-64410, 64413-64435, 64445-64450, 64461-64463, 64479-64530, 69990, 88172, 92012-92014, 93000-93010, 93040-93042, 93318, 93355, 94002, 94200, 94250, 94680-94690, 94770, 95812-95816, 95819, 95822, 95829, 95955, 96360-96368, 96372, 96374-96377, 99155-99157, 99211-99223, 99231-99255, 99291-99292, 99304-99310, 99315-99316, 99334-99337, 99347-99350, 99374-99375, 99377-99378, 99446-99449, 99495-99496, G0463, G0471, J0670, J2001

32405 0213T, 0216T, 0228T, 0230T, 10021-10022, 12001-12007, 12011-12057, 13100-13133, 13151-13153, 20101, 32551, 32601, 32607-32609, 36000, 36400-36410, 36420-36430, 36440, 36591-36592, 36600, 36640, 43752, 51701-51703, 62320-62321, 62324-62327, 64400-64410, 64413-64435, 64445-64450, 64461-64463, 64479-64530, 69990, 88172, 92012-92014, 93000-93010, 93040-93042, 93318, 93355, 94002, 94200, 94250, 94680-94690, 94770, 95812-95816, 95819, 95822, 95829, 95955, 96360-96368, 96372, 96374-96377, 99155-99157, 99211-99223, 99231-99255, 99291-99292, 99304-99310, 99315-99316, 99334-99337, 99347-99350, 99374-99375, 99377-99378, 99446-99449, 99495-99496, G0463, G0471, J0670, J1642-J1644, J2001

42400 0213T, 0216T, 0228T, 0230T, 10021-10022, 12001-12007, 12011-12057, 13100-13133, 13151-13153, 36000, 36400-36410, 36420-36430, 36440, 36591-36592, 36600, 36640, 43752, 51701-51703, 62320-62327, 64400-64410, 64413-64435, 64445-64450, 64461-64463, 64479-64530, 69990, 92012-92014, 92502, 93000-93010, 93040-93042, 93318, 93355, 94002, 94200, 94250, 94680-94690, 94770, 95812-95816, 95819, 95822, 95829, 95955, 96360-96368, 96372, 96374-96377, 99155-99157, 99211-99223, 99231-99255, 99291-99292, 99304-99310, 99315-99316, 99334-99337, 99347-99350, 99374-99375, 99377-99378, 99446-99449, 99495-99496, G0463, G0471, J2001

47000 0213T, 0216T, 0228T, 0230T, 10021-10022, 12001-12007, 12011-12057, 13100-13133, 13151-13153, 36000, 36400-36410, 36420-36430, 36440, 36591-36592, 36600, 36640, 43752, 51701-51703, 62320-62327, 64400-64410, 64413-64435, 64445-64450, 64461-64463, 64479-64530, 69990, 92012-92014, 93000-93010, 93040-93042, 93318, 93355, 94002, 94200, 94250, 94680-94690, 94770, 95812-95816, 95819, 95822, 95829, 95955, 96360-96368, 96372, 96374-96377, 99155-99157, 99211-99223, 99231-99255, 99291-99292, 99304-99310, 99315-99316, 99334-99337, 99347-99350, 99374-99375, 99377-99378, 99446-99449, 99495-99496, G0463, G0471, J0670, J1642-J1644, J2001

48102 0213T, 0216T, 0228T, 0230T, 10021-10022, 12001-12007, 12011-12057, 13100-13133, 13151-13153, 36000, 36400-36410, 36420-36430, 36440, 36591-36592, 36600, 36640, 43752, 44950, 44970, 51701-51703, 62320-62327, 64400-64410, 64413-64435, 64445-64450, 64461-64463, 64479-64530, 69990, 92012-92014, 93000-93010, 93040-93042, 93318, 93355, 94002, 94200, 94250, 94680-94690, 94770, 95812-95816, 95819, 95822, 95829, 95955, 96360-96368, 96372, 96374-96377, 99155-99157, 99211-99223, 99231-99255, 99291-99292, 99304-99310, 99315-99316, 99334-99337, 99347-99350, 99374-99375, 99377-99378, 99446-99449, 99495-99496, G0463, G0471, J0670, J1642-J1644, J2001

49180 0213T, 0216T, 0228T, 0230T, 10021-10022, 12001-12007, 12011-12057, 13100-13133, 13151-13153, 36000, 36400-36410, 36420-36430, 36440, 36591-36592, 36600, 36640, 43752, 44950, 44970, 51701-51703, 62320-62327, 64400-64410, 64413-64435, 64445-64450, 64461-64463, 64479-64530, 69990, 92012-92014, 93000-93010, 93040-93042, 93318, 93355, 94002, 94200, 94250, 94680-94690, 94770, 95812-95816, 95819, 95822, 95829, 95955, 96360-96368, 96372, 96374-96377, 99155-99157, 99211-99223, 99231-99255, 99291-99292, 99304-99310, 99315-99316, 99334-99337, 99347-99350, 99374-99375, 99377-99378, 99446-99449, 99495-99496, G0463, G0471, J0670, J1642-J1644, J2001

50200   0213T, 0216T, 0228T, 0230T, 10021-10022, 12001-12007, 12011-12057, 13100-13133, 13151-13153, 36000, 36400-36410, 36420-36430, 36440, 36591-36592, 36600, 36640, 43752, 44950, 44970, 50205*, 51701-51703, 62320-62327, 64400-64410, 64413-64435, 64445-64450, 64461-64463, 64479-64530, 69990, 76000-76001, 76970, 76998, 92012-92014, 93000-93010, 93040-93042, 93318, 93355, 94002, 94200, 94250, 94680-94690, 94770, 95812-95816, 95819, 95822, 95829, 95955, 96360-96368, 96372, 96374-96377, 99155-99157, 99211-99223, 99231-99255, 99291-99292, 99304-99310, 99315-99316, 99334-99337, 99347-99350, 99374-99375, 99377-99378, 99446-99449, 99495-99496, G0463, G0471, J0670, J1642-J1644, J2001

55700   0213T, 0216T, 0228T, 0230T, 10021-10022, 12001-12007, 12011-12057, 13100-13133, 13151-13153, 36000, 36400-36410, 36420-36430, 36440, 36591-36592, 36600, 36640, 43752, 44950, 44970, 51701, 51703, 55873*, 62320-62327, 64400-64410, 64413-64435, 64445-64450, 64461-64463, 64479-64530, 69990, 76000-76001, 77001, 92012-92014, 93000-93010, 93040-93042, 93318, 93355, 94002, 94200, 94250, 94680-94690, 94770, 95812-95816, 95819, 95822, 95829, 95955, 96360-96368, 96372, 96374-96377, 99155-99157, 99211-99223, 99231-99255, 99291-99292, 99304-99310, 99315-99316, 99334-99337, 99347-99350, 99374-99375, 99377-99378, 99446-99449, 99495-99496, G0463, J0670, J2001

60100   0213T, 0216T, 0228T, 0230T, 10021-10022, 12001-12007, 12011-12057, 13100-13133, 13151-13153, 36000, 36400-36410, 36420-36430, 36440, 36591-36592, 36600, 36640, 43752, 51701-51703, 62320-62327, 64400-64410, 64413-64435, 64445-64450, 64461-64463, 64479-64530, 69990, 88172, 92012-92014, 93000-93010, 93040-93042, 93318, 93355, 94002, 94200, 94250, 94680-94690, 94770, 95812-95816, 95819, 95822, 95829, 95955, 96360-96368, 96372, 96374-96377, 99155-99157, 99211-99223, 99231-99255, 99291-99292, 99304-99310, 99315-99316, 99334-99337, 99347-99350, 99374-99375, 99377-99378, 99446-99449, 99495-99496, G0463, G0471, J2001

62269   01935-01936, 0213T, 0216T, 0228T, 0230T, 0333T, 0464T, 10021-10022, 12001-12007, 12011-12057, 13100-13133, 13151-13153, 36000, 36400-36410, 36420-36430, 36440, 36591-36592, 36600, 36640, 43752, 51701-51703, 62268, 62270-62272, 62320-62327, 64400-64410, 64413-64435, 64445-64450, 64461-64463, 64479-64530, 69990, 76000-76001, 77001, 77003, 92012-92014, 92585, 93000-93010, 93040-93042, 93318, 93355, 94002, 94200, 94250, 94680-94690, 94770, 95812-95816, 95819, 95822, 95829, 95860-95870, 95907-95913, 95925-95933, 95937-95940, 95955, 96360-96368, 96372, 96374-96377, 99155-99157, 99211-99223, 99231-99255, 99291-99292, 99304-99310, 99315-99316, 99334-99337, 99347-99350, 99374-99375, 99377-99378, 99446-99449, 99495-99496, G0453, G0463, G0471

Case Example #1

Sonography Monitored, Clinician Performed Percutaneous Diagnostic Native Hepatic Biopsy

Clinical History:
The patient is a 51-year-old diabetic man with end stage renal disease and elevated hepatic enzymes (suspect steatohepatitis).

Procedure:
The patient was placed in supine position. The head of the stretcher was lowered to horizontal. The patient's hands were positioned beneath the head. The **left hepatic lobe** was localized from an anterior (subcostal) approach. Depth, direction, respiratory phase and angulation of needle were calculated (using sonography). Using local anesthesia, aseptic technique and in a standard fashion, a solitary puncture 17-gauge ASAP mechanized **needle biopsy was performed** with continuous real time **monitoring** of biopsy and anesthesia needles **using sonography**. Imaging of the needle tip within the **hepatic parenchyma** was obtained with real time and hard copy imaging.

CPT/HCPCS Codes Reported:
47000, 76942

Note: Ultrasound guidance procedures require the acquisition of permanently recorded images.

Case Example #2

CT Guided Left Renal Mass Biopsy

Indications:
The patient was a 60-year-old male who had a large left renal mass, a left lung mass, as well as a right femur lesion suspicious for renal cell carcinoma with metastases.

Technique:
Under **CT guidance**, using a 19-gauge trocar, the trocar was advanced into a solid, **inferior aspect of a large left renal mass** so as to avoid biopsy of the necrotic portion. A 20-gauge cutting needle was advanced through the trocar and two 20-gauge **core biopsy specimens were obtained**. The trocar position was slightly altered and in a slightly different location; two more 20-gauge core biopsy specimens were obtained. A good solid core specimen was obtained with each pass. A small amount of Gelfoam was injected through the trocar, and the trocar was then removed. Post procedure CT demonstrated no significant perinephric hematoma.

Impression:
20-gauge **core biopsy of a large left renal mass**. Four separate specimens were obtained from a solid component in the inferior aspect of the mass.

CPT/HCPCS Codes Reported:
50200-LT, 77012

Aspiration Procedures

CPT Coding for Aspiration Procedures

Procedure	Surgery Code	Guidance Code
Breast aspiration, 1st cyst	19000	
Breast aspiration, each additional cyst	19001	
Breast aspiration with ultrasound guidance	19000	76942
Small joint aspiration with fluoro guidance	20600	77002
Small joint aspiration with CT guidance	20600	77012
Small joint aspiration with MRI guidance	20600	77021
Small joint aspiration with ultrasound guidance	20604	None
Intermediate joint aspiration with fluoro guidance	20605	77002
Intermediate joint aspiration with CT guidance	20605	77012
Intermediate joint aspiration with MRI guidance	20605	77021
Intermediate Joint Aspiration with ultrasound guidance	20606	None
Major joint aspiration with fluoro guidance	20610	77002
Major joint aspiration with CT guidance	20610	77012
Major joint aspiration with MRI guidance	20610	77021
Major joint aspiration with ultrasound guidance	20611	None
Renal cyst/pelvis aspiration with fluoro guidance	50390	77002
Renal cyst/pelvis aspiration with CT guidance	50390	77012
Renal cyst/pelvis aspiration with MRI guidance	50390	77021
Renal cyst/pelvis aspiration with ultrasound guidance	50390	76942
Thyroid cyst aspiration with CT guidance	60300	77012
Thyroid cyst aspiration with ultrasound guidance	60300	76942
Shunt tubing/reservoir aspiration	61070	75809
Spinal cord cyst or syrinx aspiration with fluoro guidance	62268	77002
Spinal cord cyst or syrinx aspiration with CT guidance	62268	77012
Spinal cord cyst or syrinx aspiration with ultrasound guidance	62268	76942
Lumbar disc aspiration	62267	77003

Coding Tips

1. Report both components of the procedure where appropriate. Refer to the table above.
2. Report the surgical component code once for each surgical site.
3. Guidance codes include only the work provided for the imaging guidance portion of the procedure. If an evaluation of the organ or surgical site is performed, a diagnostic study code is also reported. Ultrasound guidance requires permanently recorded images as well as documentation in the medical record of the process. Refer to the CPT manual for further instructions.
4. Report guidance codes only once per patient encounter regardless of the number of needle placements performed. Refer to the table above for procedures where guidance is separately reported.
5. These radiology S&I codes have both a technical and professional component. To report only the professional component, append modifier 26. To report only the technical component, append modifier TC. To report the complete procedure (both professional and technical components) submit without a modifier.

Special Note: The physician performing the procedure determines whether biopsy or aspiration was performed. This physician should clearly document aspiration or biopsy in the medical record.

Facility HCPCS Coding

Report any applicable supplies and HCPCS codes. Refer to appendix B for a complete list.

ICD-10-CM Coding

The application of these codes is too broad to adequately present ICD-10-CM diagnosis code links here. Refer to the current ICD-10-CM book.

CCI Edits

19000 00400, 0213T, 0216T, 0228T, 0230T, 12001-12007, 12011-12057, 13100-13133, 13151-13153, 36000, 36400-36410, 36420-36430, 36440, 36591-36592, 36600, 36640, 43752, 51701-51703, 62320-62327, 64400-64410, 64413-64435, 64445-64450, 64461-64463, 64479-64530, 69990, 92012-92014, 93000-93010, 93040-93042, 93318, 93355, 94002, 94200, 94250, 94680-94690, 94770, 95812-95816, 95819, 95822, 95829, 95955, 96360-96368, 96372, 96374-96377, 99155-99157, 99211-99223, 99231-99255, 99291-99292, 99304-99310, 99315-99316, 99334-99337, 99347-99350, 99374-99375, 99377-99378, 99446-99449, 99495-99496, G0463, G0471, J0670, J2001

20600 00400, 01380, 0228T, 0230T, 0232T, 10030, 10060-10061, 10140, 10160, 11010*, 11719, 20500, 20526-20553, 25259, 26340, 29065-29085, 29105-29125, 29130, 29260-29280, 29365-29425, 29505-29515, 29540-29584, 36000, 36400-36410, 36420-36430, 36440, 36591-36592, 36600, 36640, 43752, 51701-51703, 62320-62327, 64400-64410, 64413-64435, 64445-64450, 64461-64463, 64479-64489, 64494-64530, 64704-64708, 69990, 72240, 72265, 76000-76001, 76882, 76942, 76970, 76998, 77001, 92012-92014, 93000-93010, 93040-93042, 93318, 93355, 94002, 94200, 94250, 94680-94690, 94770, 95812-95816, 95819, 95822, 95829, 95907-95913, 95955, 96360-96368, 96372, 96374-96377, 99155-99157, 99211-99223, 99231-99255, 99291-99292, 99304-99310, 99315-99316, 99334-99337, 99347-99350, 99374-99375, 99377-99378, 99446-99449, 99495-99496, G0127, G0463, G0471, J0670, J2001

20605 00400, 01380, 0232T, 10030, 10060-10061, 10140, 10160, 11010*, 11900, 12011, 15852, 20526-20553, 24300, 25259, 26340, 29065-29085, 29105-29126, 29240-29260, 29405-29425, 29445, 29505-29515, 29540, 29580-29584, 29705, 36000, 36400-36410, 36420-36430, 36440, 36591-36592, 36600, 36640, 43752, 51701-51703, 64400-64410, 64413-64435, 64445-64450, 64461-64463, 64480, 64484-64489, 64494-64530, 64704, 69990, 76000-76001, 76882, 76942, 76970, 76998, 77001, 92012-92014, 93000-93010, 93040-93042, 93318, 93355, 94002, 94200, 94250, 94680-94690, 94770, 95812-95816, 95819, 95822, 95829, 95907-95913, 95955, 96360-96368, 96372, 96374-96377, 99155-99157, 99211-99223, 99231-99255, 99291-99292, 99304-99310, 99315-99316, 99334-99337, 99347-99350, 99374-99375, 99377-99378, 99446-99449, 99495-99496, G0463, G0471, J0670, J2001

20610 00400, 01380, 0232T, 10030, 10060-10061, 10140, 10160, 11010*, 11900, 12001-12002, 12020, 12031, 12044, 15851, 20500-20501, 20527-20553, 24300, 25259, 26340, 27370, 29065-29085, 29105-29125, 29130, 29240-29260, 29345-29355, 29365-29425, 29505-29515, 29530-29540, 29580-29584, 36000, 36400-36410, 36420-36430, 36440, 36591-36592, 36600, 36640, 43752, 51701-51703, 64400-64410, 64413-64435, 64445-64450, 64461-64463, 64480, 64484-64489, 64494-64530, 69990, 72255, 72265, 72295, 76000-76001, 76080, 76882, 76942, 76970, 76998, 77001, 92012-92014, 93000-93010, 93040-93042, 93318, 93355, 94002, 94200, 94250, 94680-94690, 94770, 95812-95816, 95819, 95822, 95829, 95907-95913, 95955, 96360-96368, 96372, 96374-96377, 99155-99157, 99211-99223, 99231-99255, 99291-99292, 99304-99310, 99315-99316, 99334-99337, 99347-99350, 99374-99375, 99377-99378, 99446-99449, 99495-99496, G0168, G0463, G0471, J0670, J2001

60300 0213T, 0216T, 0228T, 0230T, 10021-10022, 12001-12007, 12011-12057, 13100-13133, 13151-13153, 36000, 36400-36410, 36420-36430, 36440, 36591-36592, 36600, 36640, 43752, 62320-62327, 64400-64410, 64413-64435, 64445-64450, 64461-64463, 64479-64530, 69990, 76000-76001, 77001-77002, 92012-92014, 93000-93010, 93040-93042, 93318, 93355, 94002, 94200, 94250, 94680-94690, 94770, 95812-95816, 95819, 95822, 95829, 95955, 96360-96368, 96372, 96374-96377, 99155-99157, 99211-99223, 99231-99255, 99291-99292, 99304-99310, 99315-99316, 99334-99337, 99347-99350, 99374-99375, 99377-99378, 99446-99449, 99495-99496, G0463, J0670, J2001

61070 0213T, 0216T, 0228T, 0230T, 0333T, 0464T, 12001-12007, 12011-12057, 13100-13133, 13151-13153, 36000, 36400-36410, 36420-36430, 36440, 36591-36592, 36600, 36640, 43752, 51701-51703, 62320-62327, 64400-64410, 64413-64435, 64445-64450, 64461-64463, 64479-64530, 69990, 76000-76001, 76942, 76970, 76998, 77001-77002, 92012-92014, 92585, 93000-93010, 93040-93042, 93318, 93355, 94002, 94200, 94250, 94680-94690, 94770, 95812-95816, 95819, 95822, 95829, 95860-95870, 95907-95913, 95925-95933, 95937-95940, 95955, 96360-96368, 96372, 96374-96377, 99155-99157, 99211-99223, 99231-99255, 99291-99292, 99304-99310, 99315-99316, 99334-99337, 99347-99350, 99374-99375, 99377-99378, 99446-99449, 99495-99496, G0453, G0463, G0471, J2001

62267 01935-01936, 0213T, 0216T, 0228T, 0230T, 0333T, 0464T, 10021-10022, 12001-12007, 12011-12057, 13100-13133, 13151-13153, 20220-20225, 20240-20245, 20250-20251, 36000, 36400-36410, 36420-36430, 36440, 36591-36592, 36600, 36640, 43752, 51701-51703, 62291, 62322-62327, 62380*, 64415-64417, 64450, 64461-64463, 64479-64495, 69990, 76000-76001, 77001-77002, 92012-92014, 92585, 93000-93010, 93040-93042, 93318, 93355, 94002, 94200, 94250, 94680-94690, 94770, 95812-95816, 95819, 95822, 95829, 95860-95870, 95907-95913, 95925-95933, 95937-95940, 95955, 96360-96368, 96372, 96374-96377, 99155-99157, 99211-99223, 99231-99255, 99291-99292, 99304-99310, 99315-99316, 99334-99337, 99347-99350, 99374-99375, 99377-99378, 99446-99449, 99495-99496, G0453, G0463, G0471

62268   01935-01936, 0213T, 0216T, 0228T, 0230T, 0333T, 0464T, 10021-10022, 12001-12007, 12011-12057, 13100-13133, 13151-13153, 36000, 36400-36410, 36420-36430, 36440, 36591-36592, 36600, 36640, 43752, 51701-51703, 62270-62272, 62320-62327, 64400-64410, 64413-64435, 64445-64450, 64461-64463, 64479-64530, 69990, 76000-76001, 76800, 77001, 77003, 92012-92014, 92585, 93000-93010, 93040-93042, 93318, 93355, 94002, 94200, 94250, 94680-94690, 94770, 95812-95816, 95819, 95822, 95829, 95860-95870, 95907-95913, 95925-95933, 95937-95940, 95955, 96360-96368, 96372, 96374-96377, 99155-99157, 99211-99223, 99231-99255, 99291-99292, 99304-99310, 99315-99316, 99334-99337, 99347-99350, 99374-99375, 99377-99378, 99446-99449, 99495-99496, G0453, G0463, G0471

92287   36000, 36410, 36591-36592, 96360, 96365, 96372, 96374-96377, 99211

Case Example #1

Ultrasound Guided Cyst Aspiration Left Breast

Prior Study Comparison:
An ultrasound of the left breast was performed, which demonstrated multiple cysts of the left upper outer breast. The patient was here for cyst aspiration. The two largest cysts measured 2.5 and 2.0 cm in the greatest dimension and likely accounted for the mammographic abnormality.

Procedure:
The patient was draped and prepped in the usual sterile fashion. Under **ultrasound guidance**, using a 22-gauge needle, the two largest cysts of the outer **left breast** were aspirated and the cyst fluid was discarded. The more complex cyst of the outer left breast containing prominent internal echoes was also aspirated under ultrasound guidance using an 18-gauge needle and the cyst material was discarded. A **total of three cysts were aspirated**. The smaller cysts were not aspirated.

CPT/HCPCS Codes Reported:
19000, 19001 x 2, 76942

Note: Ultrasound guidance procedures require the acquisition of permanently recorded images.

Case Example #2

CT Guided Right Hip Injection for Pain

Technique:
The patient was placed on the CT table in a supine position. 1 percent lidocaine was used for local anesthetic in the right groin after sterile prepping and draping of this patient. **Under CT guidance**, a 22-gauge spinal needle was advanced into the **right hip joint**, confirmed with return of 2 cc of clear, colorless joint fluid. From this station, a total of 10 cc of **a solution containing 8 cc Sensorcaine, 1 cc preservative-free saline and 1 cc Kenalog was administered**. The needle was removed. There were no immediate complications. The patient reported that the hip pain felt improved after the procedure.

Impression:
CT-guided right hip injection with Sensorcaine and steroid.

CPT/HCPCS Codes Reported:
20610, 77012

Image Guided Drainage Procedures

These procedures involve placing a catheter into a collection of fluid to drain the fluid.

10030   **Image-guided fluid collection drainage by catheter (eg, abscess, hematoma, seroma, lymphocele, cyst), soft tissue (eg, extremity, abdominal wall, neck), percutaneous**

A fluid collection in the soft tissue, such as a hematoma, seroma, abscess, lymphocele, or cyst, is drained using a catheter. The area over the abnormal tissue is cleansed, and local anesthesia is administered. Imaging is performed to assist in the insertion of a needle or guidewire into the fluid collection. Small tissue samples may be collected from the site for pathological examination. A catheter is inserted to drain and collect the fluid for analysis, and then the catheter is removed. More imaging may be performed to ensure hemostasis. A bandage is then applied. In some cases, the catheter may be attached to a bag to allow for further drainage over the course of days

32550   **Insertion of indwelling tunneled pleural catheter with cuff**

The physician inserts a tunneled, indwelling pleural catheter to aid quality of life and long-term management of malignant effusion. The catheter allows drainage on an outpatient or home basis and consists of flexible rubber tubing with a safety drainage valve to provide access to the pleural cavity and prevent air and fluid entering. A polyester cuff secures the catheter in place and helps prevent infection. Using separately reportable imaging guidance, the physician inserts the catheter percutaneously through a small incision in the anterior axillary area. The pleural catheter is threaded over a guidewire to access the pleural cavity, tunneled under the skin along the chest wall, and brought out that side in the lower chest. After the catheter is placed, the patient may drain pleural fluid at home periodically into vacuum bottles by connecting the matching drainage line access tip to the valve.

32551   **Tube thoracostomy, includes connection to drainage system (eg, water seal), when performed, open (separate procedure)**

The physician removes fluid and/or air from the chest cavity by puncturing through the space between the ribs. To enter the chest cavity, the physician passes a trocar over the top of a rib, punctures through the chest tissues between the ribs, and enters the pleural cavity. Separately reportable imaging guidance may be used. With the end of the trocar in the chest cavity, the physician advances the plastic tube into the chest cavity. The sharp trocar is removed, leaving one end of the plastic catheter in place within the chest cavity. A large syringe is attached to the outside end of the catheter, and the fluid (blood or pus) is removed from the chest cavity by pulling back on the plunger of the syringe. The outside end of the tube may be connected to a drainage system, such as a water seal, to prevent air from being sucked into the chest cavity and to allow continuous or intermittent removal of air or fluid.

32552   **Removal of indwelling tunneled pleural catheter with cuff**

The physician removes a previously placed, indwelling tunneled pleural catheter with cuff. Following administration of local anesthesia along the subcutaneous catheter tunnel, blunt dissection is used to release the cuff, and the catheter is meticulously withdrawn. Conscious sedation may be required.

32555   **Thoracentesis, needle or catheter, aspiration of the pleural space with imaging guidance**

The physician removes fluid and/or air from the chest cavity by puncturing through the space between the ribs with a hollow needle (cannula) and entering the chest cavity. The fluid (blood or pus) is removed from the chest cavity by pulling back on the plunger of the syringe attached to the cannula.

32557   **Pleural drainage, percutaneous, with insertion of indwelling catheter with image guidance**

The physician removes fluid and/or air from the chest cavity. The position of the patient depends on the location of the fluid (blood or pus) on preprocedural imaging. The chest cavity is accessed by puncturing through the space between the ribs with a needle. Once the fluid is accessed via the needle(s), a guidewire is inserted to the most distal point of the fluid in the pleural cavity. A catheter (pigtail catheter) is inserted the length of the guidewire, and the chest cavity is drained. In some instances, the catheter is connected to a water seal system.

49083   **Abdominal paracentesis (diagnostic or therapeutic) with imaging guidance**

The physician inserts a needle or catheter into the abdominal cavity and withdraws and drains fluid for diagnostic or therapeutic purposes. The needle or catheter is removed at the completion of the procedure.

49084   **Peritoneal lavage, including imaging guidance, when performed**

Peritoneal lavage is usually performed to determine the presence and/or extent of internal bleeding within the peritoneum. The physician makes a small incision to insert a catheter into the abdominal cavity. Fluids are infused into the cavity and subsequently aspirated for diagnostic testing. The catheter is removed at the completion of the procedure, and the incision is closed.

49405   **Image-guided fluid collection drainage by catheter (eg, abscess, hematoma, seroma, lymphocele, cyst); visceral (eg, kidney, liver, spleen, lung/mediastinum), percutaneous**

49406   **peritoneal or retroperitoneal, percutaneous**

49407   **peritoneal or retroperitoneal, transvaginal or transrectal**

A fluid collection in the visceral organs (kidney, liver, spleen, lung, mediastinum, etc.), such as a hematoma, seroma, abscess, lymphocele, or cyst, is drained using a catheter. The area over the affected organ is cleansed, and local anesthesia is administered. Imaging is performed to assist in the insertion of a needle or guidewire into the fluid collection. Small tissue samples may be collected from the site for pathological examination. A catheter is inserted to drain and collect the fluid for analysis, and then the catheter is removed. More imaging may be performed to ensure hemostasis. A bandage is then applied. In some cases, the catheter may be attached to a bag to allow for further drainage over the course of days. In 49407, a vaginal or rectal approach is used. An intracavitary probe is used to create access through the rectal or vaginal wall, and then imaging is performed to assist in the insertion of a needle or guidewire into the fluid collection.

59074   **Fetal fluid drainage (eg, vesicocentesis, thoracocentesis, paracentesis), including ultrasound guidance**

Fetal fluid is drained in cases of pleural effusions or pulmonary cysts, and especially in fetal megavesica, a rare syndrome caused by functional obstruction of the fetal urethra. The fetus's bladder is enlarged due to the megavesica. Oligohydramnios, dilation of the lower and upper urinary tract, and hydronephrosis may also be present. Pulmonary hypoplasia can result and lead to hypoplastic abdominal musculature, urinary tract anomalies, and cryptorchidism. The fetal urinary bladder is emptied by transabdominal intrauterine vesicocentesis. Under continual ultrasound guidance, a 20-22 gauge needle is inserted through the mother's abdomen and advanced into the fetus's bladder. Fetal urine is aspirated and sent to the lab for analysis of urinary electrolytes and to determine renal function. The needle is removed, and the patient kept for monitoring for up to another hour to check for refilling in the bladder. Similar fluid drainage is done by transabdominal intrauterine thoracocentesis for fetal pleural effusion.

CPT Coding for Drainage Procedures

Procedure Description	Code(s) Reported
Pneumonostomy with Perc Drainage of Abscess or Cyst	49405
Drainage Appendiceal Abscess	49406
Drainage of Liver Abscess or Cyst	49405
Drainage of Pancreas Pseudocyst	49405
Drainage of Peritoneal Abscess	49406
Drainage of Subdiaphragmatic or Subphrenic Abscess	49406
Drainage of Retroperitoneal Abscess	49406
Drainage of Perirenal or Renal Abscess	49405
Drainage of Pelvic Abscess	49407
Drainage of perivesicular or prevesicular abscess	49406
Fetal Fluid Drainage (Includes Ultrasound Guidance)	59074
Thoracentesis by Needle with image guidance	32555
Thoracentesis by Catheter	32557
Tunneled Indwelling Catheter	32550, 75989*
Non-tunneled Insertion of Chest Tube (open)	32551, 75989*
Removal of Tunneled Indwelling Catheter	32552
Abdominal paracentesis with image guidance	49083
Peritoneal lavage including image guidance	49084

* if used

Coding Tips

1. Image guidance is included in these codes except where noted in the table. Do not separately report code 75989, 76942, 77002, 77003, 77012, or 77021.

2. Do not report these codes for open incision drainage procedures.

3. Insertion of a tunneled pleural catheter (32550) is included in the thoracentesis codes (32554–32557) and is not separately reported when performed on the same side. If performed on the opposite side of the chest, it may be reported separately when it is the only procedure performed on that side.

4. Codes 10030 and 49405–49407 may be reported for each separate fluid collection when drained with a separate catheter.

5. CPT code 59074 for drainage of fetal fluid includes ultrasound image guidance. Do not separately report CPT code 75989.

6. Report 32552 for the removal of tunneled indwelling catheters.

7. Do not report guidance code 75989 in conjunction with 32555 and 32557 for thoracentesis procedures. Imaging guidance is included. If imaging is not used, see 32554 and 32556.

8. Report all applicable HCPCS Level II codes. Refer to appendix B for possible codes.

Facility HCPCS Coding

Some applicable codes may include, but are not limited to:

C1769   Guidewire

C1729   Catheter, drainage

C1894   Introducer/sheath, other than guiding, intracardiac electrophysiological, non-laser

ICD-10-CM Coding

The application of these codes is too broad to adequately present ICD-10-CM diagnosis code links here. Refer to the current ICD-10-CM book.

CCI Edits

10030 0213T, 0216T, 0228T, 0230T, 10060-10061, 10080-10081, 10140, 10160, 11055-11057, 11401-11406, 11421-11426, 11441-11471, 11600-11606, 11620-11646, 11719-11721, 11765, 12001-12007, 12011-12057, 13100-13133, 13151-13153, 20005, 20500, 29580-29582, 36000, 36400-36410, 36420-36430, 36440, 36591-36592, 36600, 36640, 43752, 51701-51703, 61650, 62320-62327, 64400-64410, 64413-64435, 64445-64450, 64461-64463, 64479-64530, 69990, 75989, 76000-76001, 76380, 76942, 76970, 76998, 77002-77003, 77012, 77021, 92012-92014, 93000-93010, 93040-93042, 93318, 93355, 94002, 94200, 94250, 94680-94690, 94770, 95812-95816, 95819, 95822, 95829, 95955, 96360-96368, 96372, 96374-96377, 97597-97598, 97602-97608, 99155-99157, 99211-99223, 99231-99255, 99291-99292, 99304-99310, 99315-99316, 99334-99337, 99347-99350, 99374-99375, 99377-99378, 99446-99449, G0127, G0463, G0471, J0670, J2001

32550 0213T, 0216T, 0228T, 0230T, 11000-11006, 11042-11047, 12001-12007, 12011-12057, 13100-13133, 13151-13153, 32551, 32555-32556, 32560-32562, 36000, 36400-36410, 36420-36430, 36440, 36591-36592, 36600, 36640, 43752, 62320-62327, 64400-64410, 64413-64435, 64445-64450, 64461-64463, 64479-64530, 69990, 71010, 71020, 76000-76001, 76380, 76942, 76970, 76998, 77001-77002, 77012, 92012-92014, 93000-93010, 93040-93042, 93318, 93355, 94002, 94200, 94250, 94680-94690, 94770, 95812-95816, 95819, 95822, 95829, 95955, 96360-96368, 96372, 96374-96377, 97597-97598, 97602, 99155-99157, 99211-99223, 99231-99255, 99291-99292, 99304-99310, 99315-99316, 99334-99337, 99347-99350, 99374-99375, 99377-99378, 99446-99449, 99495-99496, G0463

32551 0213T, 0216T, 0228T, 0230T, 12001-12007, 12011-12057, 13100-13133, 13151-13153, 36000, 36400-36410, 36420-36430, 36440, 36591-36592, 36600, 36640, 43752, 49185, 49423-49424, 62320-62327, 64400-64410, 64413-64435, 64445-64450, 64461-64463, 64479-64530, 69990, 71010, 71020, 75989, 92012-92014, 93000-93010, 93040-93042, 93318, 93355, 94002, 94200, 94250, 94680-94690, 94770, 95812-95816, 95819, 95822, 95829, 95955, 96360-96368, 96372, 96374-96377, 99155-99157, 99211-99223, 99231-99255, 99291-99292, 99304-99310, 99315-99316, 99334-99337, 99347-99350, 99374-99375, 99377-99378, 99446-99449, 99495-99496, G0463

32552 0213T, 0216T, 0228T, 0230T, 11000-11006, 11042-11047, 12001-12007, 12011-12057, 13100-13133, 13151-13153, 36000, 36400-36410, 36420-36430, 36440, 36591-36592, 36600, 36640, 43752, 51701-51703, 62320-62327, 64400-64410, 64413-64435, 64445-64450, 64461-64463, 64479-64530, 69990, 92012-92014, 93000-93010, 93040-93042, 93318, 93355, 94002, 94200, 94250, 94680-94690, 94770, 95812-95816, 95819, 95822, 95829, 95955, 96360-96368, 96372, 96374-96377, 97597-97598, 97602, 99155-99157, 99211-99223, 99231-99255, 99291-99292, 99304-99310, 99315-99316, 99334-99337, 99347-99350, 99374-99375, 99377-99378, 99446-99449, 99495-99496, G0463, G0471, J0670, J2001

32555 0213T, 0216T, 0228T, 0230T, 12001-12007, 12011-12057, 13100-13133, 13151-13153, 20101, 32400, 32551, 32554, 36000, 36400-36410, 36420-36430, 36440, 36591-36592, 36600, 36640, 43752, 49185, 49423-49424, 51701-51703, 62320-62327, 64400-64410, 64413-64435, 64445-64450, 64461-64463, 64479-64530, 69990, 71010, 71020, 75989, 76000-76001, 76380, 76942, 76970, 76998, 77002, 77012, 77021, 92012-92014, 93000-93010, 93040-93042, 93318, 93355, 94002, 94200, 94250, 94680-94690, 94770, 95812-95816, 95819, 95822, 95829, 95955, 96360-96368, 96372, 96374-96377, 99155-99157, 99211-99223, 99231-99255, 99291-99292, 99304-99310, 99315-99316, 99334-99337, 99347-99350, 99374-99375, 99377-99378, 99446-99449, 99495-99496, G0463, G0471

32557 0213T, 0216T, 0228T, 0230T, 11000-11006, 11042-11047, 12001-12007, 12011-12057, 13100-13133, 13151-13153, 20101, 32550-32551, 32556, 36000, 36400-36410, 36420-36430, 36440, 36591-36592, 36600, 36640, 43752, 49185, 49424, 51701-51703, 62320-62327, 64400-64410, 64413-64435, 64445-64450, 64461-64463, 64479-64530, 69990, 71010, 71020, 75989, 76000-76001, 76380, 76942, 76970, 76998, 77002, 77012, 77021, 92012-92014, 93000-93010, 93040-93042, 93318, 93355, 94002, 94200, 94250, 94680-94690, 94770, 95812-95816, 95819, 95822, 95829, 95955, 96360-96368, 96372, 96374-96377, 97597-97598, 97602, 99155-99157, 99211-99223, 99231-99255, 99291-99292, 99304-99310, 99315-99316, 99334-99337, 99347-99350, 99374-99375, 99377-99378, 99446-99449, 99495-99496, G0463, G0471

49083 0213T, 0216T, 0228T, 0230T, 12001-12007, 12011-12057, 13100-13133, 13151-13153, 20102, 36000, 36400-36410, 36420-36430, 36440, 36591-36592, 36600, 36640, 43752, 49082, 51701-51703, 62320-62327, 64400-64410, 64413-64435, 64445-64450, 64461-64463, 64479-64530, 69990, 76000-76001, 76380, 76942, 76970, 76998, 77001-77002, 77012, 77021, 92012-92014, 93000-93010, 93040-93042, 93318, 93355, 94002, 94200, 94250, 94680-94690, 94770, 95812-95816, 95819, 95822, 95829, 95955, 96360-96368, 96372, 96374-96377, 99155-99157, 99211-99223, 99231-99255, 99291-99292, 99304-99310, 99315-99316, 99334-99337, 99347-99350, 99374-99375, 99377-99378, 99446-99449, 99495-99496, G0463, G0471

49084 0213T, 0216T, 0228T, 0230T, 12001-12007, 12011-12057, 13100-13133, 13151-13153, 20102, 36000, 36400-36410, 36420-36430, 36440, 36591-36592, 36600, 36640, 43752, 49082-49083, 51701-51703, 62320-62327, 64400-64410, 64413-64435, 64445-64450, 64461-64463, 64479-64530, 69990, 76000-76001, 76380, 76942, 76970, 76998, 77001-77002, 77012, 77021, 92012-92014, 93000-93010, 93040-93042, 93318, 93355, 94002, 94200, 94250, 94680-94690, 94770, 95812-95816, 95819, 95822, 95829, 95955, 96360-96368, 96372, 96374-96377, 99155-99157, 99211-99223, 99231-99255, 99291-99292, 99304-99310, 99315-99316, 99334-99337, 99347-99350, 99374-99375, 99377-99378, 99446-99449, 99495-99496, G0463, G0471

49185 0213T, 0216T, 0228T, 0230T, 12001-12007, 12011-12057, 13100-13133, 13151-13153, 32560, 36000, 36400-36410, 36420-36430, 36440, 36468, 36470-36471, 36591-36592, 36600, 36640, 43752, 44602-44605, 49320, 49424, 51701-51703, 62320-62327, 64400-64410, 64413-64435, 64445-64450, 64461-64463, 64479-64530, 69990, 76000-76001, 76080, 76380, 76942, 76970, 76998, 77001-77002, 77012, 77021, 92012-92014, 93000-93010, 93040-93042, 93318, 93355, 94002, 94200, 94250, 94680-94690, 94770, 95812-95816, 95819, 95822, 95829, 95955, 96360-96368, 96372, 96374-96377, 99155-99157, 99211-99223, 99231-99255, 99291-99292, 99304-99310, 99315-99316, 99334-99337, 99347-99350, 99374-99375, 99377-99378, 99446-99449, 99495-99496, G0463, G0471, J0670, J2001

49405 0213T, 0216T, 0228T, 0230T, 12001-12007, 12011-12057, 13100-13133, 13151-13153, 32551, 32554-32557, 32601, 32607-32609, 36000, 36400-36410, 36420-36430, 36440, 36591-36592, 36600, 36640, 43752, 44602-44605, 44950, 44970, 47000-47001, 48102, 49000-49002, 49185, 49320, 49406, 49423-49424, 51701-51703, 62320-62327, 64400-64410, 64413-64435, 64445-64450, 64461-64463, 64479-64530, 69990, 75989, 76000-76001, 76380, 76942, 76970, 76998, 77001-77003, 77012, 77021, 92012-92014, 93000-93010, 93040-93042, 93318, 93355, 94002, 94200, 94250, 94680-94690, 94770, 95812-95816, 95819, 95822, 95829, 95955, 96360-96368, 96372, 96374-96377, 99155-99157, 99211-99223, 99231-99255, 99291-99292, 99304-99310, 99315-99316, 99334-99337, 99347-99350, 99374-99375, 99377-99378, 99446-99449, G0463, G0471, J0670, J2001

49406 00910, 0213T, 0216T, 0228T, 0230T, 12001-12007, 12011-12057, 13100-13133, 13151-13153, 36000, 36400-36410, 36420-36430, 36440, 36591-36592, 36600, 36640, 43752, 44005, 44180, 44602-44605, 44701, 44820-44850, 44950, 44970, 49000-49010, 49082-49084, 49180-49185, 49255, 49320, 49322, 49400, 49402, 49423-49424, 49570, 50010, 50205, 50715, 51045, 51570, 51701-51703, 57410, 58660, 58700, 58800, 58900, 62320-62327, 64400-64410, 64413-64435, 64445-64450, 64461-64463, 64479-64530, 69990, 75989, 76000-76001, 76380, 76942, 76970, 76998, 77001-77003, 77012, 77021, 92012-92014, 93000-93010, 93040-93042, 93318, 93355, 94002, 94200, 94250, 94680-94690, 94770, 95812-95816, 95819, 95822, 95829, 95955, 96360-96368, 96372, 96374-96377, 99155-99157, 99211-99223, 99231-99255, 99291-99292, 99304-99310, 99315-99316, 99334-99337, 99347-99350, 99374-99375, 99377-99378, 99446-99449, G0463, G0471, J0670, J2001

49407 0213T, 0216T, 0228T, 0230T, 12001-12007, 12011-12057, 13100-13133, 13151-13153, 36000, 36400-36410, 36420-36430, 36440, 36591-36592, 36600, 36640, 43752, 44701, 45005, 45900-45990, 46040, 46080, 46220, 46600-46601, 46940-46942, 49082-49084, 49185, 49322, 49406, 49423-49424, 50715, 51701-51703, 57410, 58660, 58805, 58900, 62320-62327, 64400-64410, 64413-64435, 64445-64450, 64461-64463, 64479-64530, 69990, 75989, 76000-76001, 76380, 76942, 76970, 76998, 77001-77003, 77012, 77021, 92012-92014, 93000-93010, 93040-93042, 93318, 93355, 94002, 94200, 94250, 94680-94690, 94770, 95812-95816, 95819, 95822, 95829, 95955, 96360-96368, 96372, 96374-96377, 99155-99157, 99211-99223, 99231-99255, 99291-99292, 99304-99310, 99315-99316, 99334-99337, 99347-99350, 99374-99375, 99377-99378, 99446-99449, G0463, G0471, J0670, J2001

59074   0213T, 0216T, 0228T, 0230T, 12001-12007, 12011-12057, 13100-13133, 13151-13153, 36000, 36400-36410, 36420-36430, 36440, 36591-36592, 36600, 36640, 43752, 51701-51703, 57410, 62320-62327, 64400-64410, 64413-64435, 64445-64450, 64461-64463, 64479-64530, 69990, 76941-76942, 76945-76946, 76970, 76998, 92012-92014, 93000-93010, 93040-93042, 93318, 93355, 94002, 94200, 94250, 94680-94690, 94770, 95812-95816, 95819, 95822, 95829, 95955, 96360-96368, 96372, 96374-96377, 99155-99157, 99211-99223, 99231-99255, 99291-99292, 99304-99310, 99315-99316, 99334-99337, 99347-99350, 99374-99375, 99377-99378, 99446-99449, 99495-99496, G0463, G0471, J0670, J2001

Case Example #1

Ultrasound Guided Thoracentesis

Clinical Data:
Pleural effusion, lung cancer

Comparison Studies:
Multiple prior thoracentesis studies

Procedure and Findings:
After obtaining informed written consent, **ultrasound-guided thoracentesis was performed.** A site for catheter placement was localized with ultrasound. Local anesthesia was administered with 1 percent buffered lidocaine. A 6-French Arrow **catheter** was **placed** into the pleural cavity. 1.5 liters of serosanguinous **fluid was drained.** No immediate complications were noted.

Impression:
Successful ultrasound guided thoracentesis

CPT/HCPCS Codes Reported:
32557

Note: Ultrasound guidance procedures require the acquisition of permanently recorded images.

Case Example #2

Ultrasound Guided Paracentesis

Clinical Data:
Patient with ascites and history of cirrhosis

Findings:
Using sterile technique, local anesthesia with 1 percent buffered lidocaine, and **under ultrasound guidance, paracentesis was performed with arrow catheter. 5** liters of straw-colored fluid were removed. The sample was sent to the laboratory as requested.

Impression:
It was a successful **ultrasound guided paracentesis**; 5 liters of fluid were removed without immediate complication.

CPT/HCPCS Codes Reported:
49083

Note: Ultrasound guidance procedures require the acquisition of permanently recorded images.

Sclerotherapy of a Fluid Collection

49185   **Sclerotherapy of a fluid collection (eg, lymphocele, cyst or seroma), percutaneous, including contrast injection(s), sclerosant injection(s), diagnostic study, imaging guidance (eg, ultrasound, fluoroscopy) and radiological supervision and interpretation when performed**
Using image guidance the physician places a needle through the skin into the fluid collection. Contrast media may be injected to determine the location of needle placement. A guidewire is placed through the needle, and the needle is then exchanged for a catheter. The guidewire is removed. A sclerosing drug is injected and may be left in for an extended period of time, after which the drug is withdrawn. More contrast may be injected to verify the success of therapy. The catheter is withdrawn, and a dressing is placed over the access location. Additional treatments are possible to achieve desired results.

Coding Tips

1. Report 49185 once per day for each lesion treated with a separate catheter.
2. Code 49185 is reported once per access site. If multiple collections are treated through the same access, report only one unit. Usually these multiple collections are joined together.
3. For multiple collections treated through multiple accesses, report 49185 for each access and append modifier 59 or applicable X modifier to each additional code.
4. Additionally report codes for access and drainage of the fluid collection performed prior to sclerotherapy. Choose the code based on the location of the fluid collection. See the previous section for applicable codes.
5. For exchange of existing catheter, use 49423 and 75984.
6. For sclerotherapy of a lymphatic/vascular malformation, report 37241.
7. For sclerosis of veins, refer to codes 36468–36479.
8. Do not report 49185 with 49424 and 76080.

Facility HCPCS Coding

Some applicable codes may include but are not limited to:

C1729	Catheter, drainage
Q9965	LOCM, 100-199 mg/ml iodine concentration, per ml
Q9966	LOCM, 200-299 mg/ml iodine concentration, per ml
Q9967	LOCM, 300-399 mg/ml iodine concentration, per ml

ICD-10-CM Coding

B67.0	Echinococcus granulosus infection of liver
B67.5	Echinococcus multilocularis infection of liver
B67.8	Echinococcosis, unspecified, of liver
B67.90	Echinococcosis, unspecified
B67.99	Other echinococcosis
E04.1	Nontoxic single thyroid nodule
I89.8	Other specified noninfective disorders of lymphatic vessels and lymph nodes
I89.9	Noninfective disorder of lymphatic vessels and lymph nodes, unspecified
J98.4	Other disorders of lung
K76.89	Other specified diseases of liver
K86.2	Cyst of pancreas
L05.01	Pilonidal cyst with abscess
L05.91	Pilonidal cyst without abscess
L72.0	Epidermal cyst
L72.2	Steatocystoma multiplex
L72.3	Sebaceous cyst
L72.8	Other follicular cysts of the skin and subcutaneous tissue
L72.9	Follicular cyst of the skin and subcutaneous tissue, unspecified
M27.49	Other cysts of jaw
M67.40	Ganglion, unspecified site
M67.411	Ganglion, right shoulder
M67.412	Ganglion, left shoulder
M67.419	Ganglion, unspecified shoulder
M67.421	Ganglion, right elbow

M67.422	Ganglion, left elbow
M67.429	Ganglion, unspecified elbow
M67.431	Ganglion, right wrist
M67.432	Ganglion, left wrist
M67.439	Ganglion, unspecified wrist
M67.441	Ganglion, right hand
M67.442	Ganglion, left hand
M67.449	Ganglion, unspecified hand
M67.451	Ganglion, right hip
M67.452	Ganglion, left hip
M67.459	Ganglion, unspecified hip
M67.461	Ganglion, right knee
M67.462	Ganglion, left knee
M67.469	Ganglion, unspecified knee
M67.471	Ganglion, right ankle and foot
M67.472	Ganglion, left ankle and foot
M67.479	Ganglion, unspecified ankle and foot
M67.48	Ganglion, other site
M67.49	Ganglion, multiple sites
M71.20	Synovial cyst of popliteal space [Baker], unspecified knee
M71.21	Synovial cyst of popliteal space [Baker], right knee
M71.22	Synovial cyst of popliteal space [Baker], left knee
M79.81	Nontraumatic hematoma of soft tissue
M85.50	Aneurysmal bone cyst, unspecified site
M85.511	Aneurysmal bone cyst, right shoulder
M85.512	Aneurysmal bone cyst, left shoulder
M85.519	Aneurysmal bone cyst, unspecified shoulder
M85.521	Aneurysmal bone cyst, right upper arm
M85.522	Aneurysmal bone cyst, left upper arm
M85.529	Aneurysmal bone cyst, unspecified upper arm
M85.531	Aneurysmal bone cyst, right forearm
M85.532	Aneurysmal bone cyst, left forearm
M85.539	Aneurysmal bone cyst, unspecified forearm
M85.541	Aneurysmal bone cyst, right hand
M85.542	Aneurysmal bone cyst, left hand
M85.549	Aneurysmal bone cyst, unspecified hand
M85.551	Aneurysmal bone cyst, right thigh
M85.552	Aneurysmal bone cyst, left thigh
M85.559	Aneurysmal bone cyst, unspecified thigh
M85.561	Aneurysmal bone cyst, right lower leg
M85.562	Aneurysmal bone cyst, left lower leg
M85.569	Aneurysmal bone cyst, unspecified lower leg
M85.571	Aneurysmal bone cyst, right ankle and foot
M85.572	Aneurysmal bone cyst, left ankle and foot
M85.579	Aneurysmal bone cyst, unspecified ankle and foot
M85.58	Aneurysmal bone cyst, other site
M85.59	Aneurysmal bone cyst, multiple sites
N28.1	Cyst of kidney, acquired
N64.89	Other specified disorders of breast
N75.0	Cyst of Bartholin's gland
N75.1	Abscess of Bartholin's gland
N83.00	Follicular cyst of ovary, unspecified side
N83.01	Follicular cyst of right ovary
N83.02	Follicular cyst of left ovary
N83.10	Corpus luteum cyst of ovary, unspecified side
N83.11	Corpus luteum cyst of right ovary

N83.12	Corpus luteum cyst of left ovary
N83.201	Unspecified ovarian cyst, right side
N83.202	Unspecified ovarian cyst, left side
N83.209	Unspecified ovarian cyst, unspecified side
N83.291	Other ovarian cyst, right side
N83.292	Other ovarian cyst, left side
N83.299	Other ovarian cyst, unspecified side
Q33.0	Congenital cystic lung
Q44.6	Cystic disease of liver
Q45.2	Congenital pancreatic cyst
Q61.00	Congenital renal cyst, unspecified
Q61.01	Congenital single renal cyst
Q61.02	Congenital multiple renal cysts
Q61.11	Cystic dilatation of collecting ducts
Q61.19	Other polycystic kidney, infantile type
Q61.2	Polycystic kidney, adult type
Q61.3	Polycystic kidney, unspecified
Q61.8	Other cystic kidney diseases
Q61.9	Cystic kidney disease, unspecified
Q89.2	Congenital malformations of other endocrine glands
T79.2XXA	Traumatic secondary and recurrent hemorrhage and seroma, initial encounter
T88.8XXA	Other specified complications of surgical and medical care, not elsewhere classified, initial encounter

CCI Edits

49185 0213T, 0216T, 0228T, 0230T, 12001-12007, 12011-12057, 13100-13133, 13151-13153, 32560, 36000, 36400-36410, 36420-36430, 36440, 36468, 36470-36471, 36591-36592, 36600, 36640, 43752, 44602-44605, 49320, 49424, 51701-51703, 62320-62327, 64400-64410, 64413-64435, 64445-64450, 64461-64463, 64479-64530, 69990, 76000-76001, 76080, 76380, 76942, 76970, 76998, 77001-77002, 77012, 77021, 92012-92014, 93000-93010, 93040-93042, 93318, 93355, 94002, 94200, 94250, 94680-94690, 94770, 95812-95816, 95819, 95822, 95829, 95955, 96360-96368, 96372, 96374-96377, 99155-99157, 99211-99223, 99231-99255, 99291-99292, 99304-99310, 99315-99316, 99334-99337, 99347-99350, 99374-99375, 99377-99378, 99446-99449, 99495-99496, G0463, G0471, J0670, J2001

Case Example

History:
Patient with history of left parapelvic cyst.

Procedure:
Informed consent was obtained. Left posterior abdomen was sterilely prepped and draped. After giving local anesthesia, a 22-guage Chiba needle was used to **puncture the cyst** under **ultrasound guidance**. Approximately 5 ml of slightly yellowish fluid was obtained. Subsequently, contrast injected showed bi-lobed cyst. The cyst measures approximately 2 x 1.8 cm. Subsequently, the contrast was aspirated. No fistulous connection to any surrounding structures. Therefore, 5 ml of alcohol was injected under fluoroscopic guidance, displacing the contrast. This was instilled for 15 minutes. Subsequently the alcohol was removed. Repeat ultrasound shows minimal residual. The needle was removed and sterile dressing applied.

Impression:
Approximately 2 x 1.8 cm parapelvic cyst in the left kidney. This was **aspirated and contrast injected** confirmed no fistulous connection to surrounding tissue. **Sclerotherapy was performed** with 5ml of alcohol.

CPT/HCPCS Codes Reported:
49185, 49405

Endovenous Ablation Therapy

These procedures are used to treat varicose veins typically found in the lower extremity. The greater saphenous vein is most commonly treated. Radiofrequency or laser techniques are used.

36473   **Endovenous ablation therapy of incompetent vein, extremity, inclusive of all imaging guidance and monitoring, percutaneous, mechanochemical; first vein treated**

36474   **subsequent vein(s) treated in a single extremity, each through separate access sites (List separately in addition to code for primary procedure)**

The physician uses endovenous ablation therapy to treat venous incompetence in an extremity vein. Mechanochemical endovenous ablation (MOCA) uses a rotating wire in conjunction with an infused sclerosing agent to damage the wall of the vein. The most common site of treatment is the greater saphenous vein. The procedure includes any imaging guidance and monitoring. The leg is prepared and draped, and a local anesthetic is applied to the puncture site. A needle is inserted into the access site. A guidewire is placed into the vessel using ultrasound guidance. An introducer sheath is placed over the guidewire, and the guidewire is removed. A wire catheter system is introduced, and the tip is advanced to the site of the venous incompetence under ultrasound guidance. The wire catheter system is connected to a handle with a motor that provides the rotation to the wire. The system is started for about 10 seconds to create vasospasm and slowly withdrawn with continuous infusion of sclerosing agent. The ablation catheter and introducer sheath are removed, and pressure is applied to the puncture site. A compression stocking is applied for the immediate 24 hours and replaced daily for the following two weeks.

36475   **Endovenous ablation therapy of incompetent vein, extremity, inclusive of all imaging guidance and monitoring, percutaneous, radiofrequency; first vein treated**

36476   **subsequent vein(s) treated in a single extremity, each through separate access sites (List separately in addition to code for primary procedure)**

The physician uses percutaneous, radiofrequency, endovenous ablation therapy to treat venous incompetence in an extremity vein. Radiofrequency energy is used to heat and seal the vein closed. The most common site of treatment is the greater saphenous vein. The procedure includes any imaging guidance and monitoring. The leg is prepared and draped, and a local anesthetic is applied to the puncture site. A needle is inserted into the access site. A guidewire is placed into the vessel using ultrasound guidance. An introducer sheath is placed over the guidewire, and the guidewire is removed. The radiofrequency ablation catheter system is introduced, and the tip is advanced to the site of the venous incompetence under ultrasound guidance. A local anesthetic agent is injected into the tissues surrounding the vein within its fascial sheath along the course of the vein. Ultrasonography is used to position the catheter tip at the level of the terminal valve, and the catheter electrodes are deployed. The electrodes should be just distal to the valve cusps of the terminal valve. Radiofrequency energy is applied until the thermocouple temperature rises to 80° to 85°C and remains at this temperature for 10 to 15 seconds. Once this temperature is reached, the catheter tip is slowly withdrawn until it reaches the introducer sheath in the distal vein. The ablation catheter and introducer sheath are removed and pressure is applied to the puncture site.

36478   **Endovenous ablation therapy of incompetent vein, extremity, inclusive of all imaging guidance and monitoring, percutaneous, laser; first vein treated**

36479   **subsequent vein(s) treated in a single extremity, each through separate access sites (List separately in addition to code for primary procedure)**

The physician uses percutaneous, laser, endovenous ablation therapy to treat venous incompetence in an extremity vein. Laser energy is used to heat the vein and seal it closed. The most common site of treatment is the greater saphenous vein. The procedure includes any imaging guidance and monitoring. The leg is prepared and draped, and a local anesthetic is applied to the puncture site. A needle is inserted into the access site. A guidewire is placed into the vessel using ultrasound guidance. An introducer sheath is placed over the guidewire, and the guidewire is removed. The laser ablation catheter system is introduced, and the tip is advanced to the site of the venous incompetence under ultrasound guidance. A local anesthetic agent is injected into the tissues surrounding the vein within its fascial sheath. The anesthetic is injected along the course of the vein. Ultrasonography is used to position the catheter tip at the level of the terminal valve, and laser energy is applied via a laser fiber along the length of the vein as the catheter is slowly withdrawn. When the laser catheter tip reaches the introducer sheath in the distal vein, the laser energy is terminated. The ablation catheter and introducer sheath are removed, and pressure is applied at the puncture site.

36482   **Endovenous ablation of incompetent vein, extremity, by transcatheter delivery of a chemical adhesive (eg, cyanoacrylate) remote from the access site, inclusive of all imaging guidance and monitoring, percutaneous; first vein treated**

36483   **subsequent vein(s) treated in a single extremity, each through separate access sites (List separately in addition to code for primary procedure)**

The physician creates a detailed outline or mapping of the veins in the lower legs to identify all vein abnormalities, along with additional nearby structures to include deep veins and arteries, via duplex ultrasound examination. The patient is placed in the supine position, and the leg being treated is exposed. A local anesthetic is administered. Through a small incision, the physician uses a needle to position an intravenous catheter the length of the incompetent vein. A chemical adhesive, such as cyanoacrylate, is injected through the catheter via a special type of applicator and into the vein under imaging guidance. A small amount of the chemical adhesive is injected approximately every 3 cm along the vein causing sclerosis or a hardening of the vein. To minimize dispersing of the chemical adhesive, ultrasound compression of the outflow vein is often included in these procedures. Imaging guidance and monitoring are included in these procedures.

Coding Tips

1. Report 36475 and 36478 for the first or initial vein treated during the patient encounter. Report 36476 and 36479 for each additional vein treated.

2. These codes include all imaging guidance. Do not separately report fluoroscopy or ultrasound guidance (CPT codes 75894, 76000, 76001, 76937, 76942, 76998, 77022).

3. These codes include venous access. Do not separately report 36000, 36002, 36005, 36410, or 36425.

4. Report any applicable HCPCS Level II code for devices used.

5. Do not report 36478/9 with 29581-2, 36000, 36002, 36005, 36410, 36425, 36475, 36476, 37241, 75894, 76000, 76001, 76937, 76942, 76998, 77022, 93970, 93971 in the same surgical field.

6. Add-on codes 36474, 36476, and 36479 are reported only once per extremity regardless of the number of additional veins treated during the session.

7. Physician reporting: In an office setting, all devices and supplies are included in these codes and should not be separately billed.

8. Physician reporting: the application of compression bandages and/or stockings is included in codes 36473–36483 and should not be separately billed.

Facility HCPCS Coding

Some applicable codes may include, but are not limited to:

C1769   Guidewire

C1888   Catheter, ablation, non-cardiac endovascular (implantable)

C1894   Introducer/sheath, other than guiding, intracardiac electrophysiological, non-laser

C2629   Introducer/sheath, other than guiding, intracardiac

ICD-10-CM Coding

I83.001	Varicose veins of unspecified lower extremity with ulcer of thigh
I83.002	Varicose veins of unspecified lower extremity with ulcer of calf
I83.003	Varicose veins of unspecified lower extremity with ulcer of ankle
I83.004	Varicose veins of unspecified lower extremity with ulcer of heel and midfoot
I83.005	Varicose veins of unspecified lower extremity with ulcer other part of foot
I83.008	Varicose veins of unspecified lower extremity with ulcer other part of lower leg
I83.009	Varicose veins of unspecified lower extremity with ulcer of unspecified site
I83.011	Varicose veins of right lower extremity with ulcer of thigh
I83.012	Varicose veins of right lower extremity with ulcer of calf
I83.013	Varicose veins of right lower extremity with ulcer of ankle
I83.014	Varicose veins of right lower extremity with ulcer of heel and midfoot
I83.015	Varicose veins of right lower extremity with ulcer other part of foot
I83.018	Varicose veins of right lower extremity with ulcer other part of lower leg
I83.019	Varicose veins of right lower extremity with ulcer of unspecified site
I83.021	Varicose veins of left lower extremity with ulcer of thigh
I83.022	Varicose veins of left lower extremity with ulcer of calf
I83.023	Varicose veins of left lower extremity with ulcer of ankle
I83.024	Varicose veins of left lower extremity with ulcer of heel and midfoot
I83.025	Varicose veins of left lower extremity with ulcer other part of foot
I83.028	Varicose veins of left lower extremity with ulcer other part of lower leg
I83.029	Varicose veins of left lower extremity with ulcer of unspecified site
I83.10	Varicose veins of unspecified lower extremity with inflammation
I83.11	Varicose veins of right lower extremity with inflammation
I83.12	Varicose veins of left lower extremity with inflammation
I83.201	Varicose veins of unspecified lower extremity with both ulcer of thigh and inflammation

I83.202	Varicose veins of unspecified lower extremity with both ulcer of calf and inflammation
I83.203	Varicose veins of unspecified lower extremity with both ulcer of ankle and inflammation
I83.204	Varicose veins of unspecified lower extremity with both ulcer of heel and midfoot and inflammation
I83.205	Varicose veins of unspecified lower extremity with both ulcer other part of foot and inflammation
I83.208	Varicose veins of unspecified lower extremity with both ulcer of other part of lower extremity and inflammation
I83.209	Varicose veins of unspecified lower extremity with both ulcer of unspecified site and inflammation
I83.211	Varicose veins of right lower extremity with both ulcer of thigh and inflammation
I83.212	Varicose veins of right lower extremity with both ulcer of calf and inflammation
I83.213	Varicose veins of right lower extremity with both ulcer of ankle and inflammation
I83.214	Varicose veins of right lower extremity with both ulcer of heel and midfoot and inflammation
I83.215	Varicose veins of right lower extremity with both ulcer other part of foot and inflammation
I83.218	Varicose veins of right lower extremity with both ulcer of other part of lower extremity and inflammation
I83.219	Varicose veins of right lower extremity with both ulcer of unspecified site and inflammation
I83.221	Varicose veins of left lower extremity with both ulcer of thigh and inflammation
I83.222	Varicose veins of left lower extremity with both ulcer of calf and inflammation
I83.223	Varicose veins of left lower extremity with both ulcer of ankle and inflammation
I83.224	Varicose veins of left lower extremity with both ulcer of heel and midfoot and inflammation
I83.225	Varicose veins of left lower extremity with both ulcer other part of foot and inflammation
I83.228	Varicose veins of left lower extremity with both ulcer of other part of lower extremity and inflammation
I83.229	Varicose veins of left lower extremity with both ulcer of unspecified site and inflammation
I83.811	Varicose veins of right lower extremities with pain
I83.812	Varicose veins of left lower extremities with pain
I83.813	Varicose veins of bilateral lower extremities with pain
I83.819	Varicose veins of unspecified lower extremity with pain
I83.891	Varicose veins of right lower extremities with other complications
I83.892	Varicose veins of left lower extremities with other complications
I83.893	Varicose veins of bilateral lower extremities with other complications
I83.899	Varicose veins of unspecified lower extremity with other complications
I83.90	Asymptomatic varicose veins of unspecified lower extremity
I83.91	Asymptomatic varicose veins of right lower extremity
I83.92	Asymptomatic varicose veins of left lower extremity
I83.93	Asymptomatic varicose veins of bilateral lower extremities
I86.8	Varicose veins of other specified sites

CCI Edits

36473 0213T, 0216T, 0228T, 0230T, 12001-12007, 12011-12057, 13100-13133, 13151-13153, 29581-29582, 35201-35207, 35211-35286, 36000, 36002-36012, 36400-36410, 36420-36430, 36440, 36476, 36479, 36591-36592, 36600, 36640, 43752, 49185, 51701-51703, 62320-62327, 64400-64410, 64413-64435, 64445-64450, 64461-64463, 64479-64530, 69990, 75894, 76000-76001, 76380, 76937, 76940, 76942, 76970, 76998, 77002, 77012-77013, 77021-77022, 92012-92014, 93000-93010, 93040-93042, 93318, 93355, 93970-93971, 94002, 94200, 94250, 94680-94690, 94770, 95812-95816, 95819, 95822, 95829, 95955, 96360-96368, 96372, 96374-96377, 96523, 99155-99157, 99211-99223, 99231-99255, 99291-99292, 99304-99310, 99315-99316, 99334-99337, 99347-99350, 99374-99375, 99377-99378, 99446-99449, 99495-99496, G0463, G0471, J0670, J2001

36474 0213T, 0216T, 0228T, 0230T, 12001-12007, 12011-12057, 13100-13133, 13151-13153, 29581-29582, 35201-35207, 35211-35286, 36000, 36002-36005, 36400-36410, 36420-36430, 36440, 36476, 36479, 36591-36592, 36600, 36640, 43752, 51701-51703, 62320-62327, 64400-64410, 64413-64435, 64445-64450, 64461-64463, 64479-64530, 69990, 75894, 76000-76001, 76380, 76937, 76940, 76942, 76998, 77002, 77012-77013, 77021-77022, 92012-92014, 93000-93010, 93040-93042, 93318, 93970-93971, 94002, 94200, 94250, 94680-94690, 94770, 95812-95816, 95819, 95822, 95829, 95955, 96360-96368, 96372, 96374-96377, 96523, 99155-99157, 99211-99223, 99231-99255, 99291-99292, 99304-99310, 99315-99316, 99334-99337, 99347-99350, 99374-99375, 99377-99378, J0670, J2001

36475 0213T, 0216T, 0228T, 0230T, 12001-12007, 12011-12057, 13100-13133, 13151-13153, 29581-29582, 35201-35206, 35226-35236, 35256-35266, 35286, 36000, 36002-36012, 36400-36410, 36420-36430, 36440, 36473-36474, 36478, 36479, 36591-36592, 36600, 36640, 43752, 49185, 51701-51703, 62320-62327, 64400-64410, 64413-64435, 64445-64450, 64461-64463, 64479-64530, 69990, 75894, 76000-76001, 76380, 76937, 76940, 76942, 76970, 76998, 77002, 77012-77013, 77021-77022, 92012-92014, 93000-93010, 93040-93042, 93318, 93355, 93970-93971, 94002, 94200, 94250, 94680-94690, 94770, 95812-95816, 95819, 95822, 95829, 95955, 96360-96368, 96372, 96374-96377, 99155-99157, 99211-99223, 99231-99255, 99291-99292, 99304-99310, 99315-99316, 99334-99337, 99347-99350, 99374-99375, 99377-99378, 99446-99449, 99495-99496, G0463, G0471, J0670, J2001

36476	29581-29582, 36000, 36002-36005, 36410, 36425, 36591-36592, 49185, 75894, 76000-76001, 76380, 76937, 76940, 76942, 76970, 76998, 77002, 77012-77013, 77021-77022, 93970-93971
36478	0213T, 0216T, 0228T, 0230T, 12001-12007, 12011-12057, 13100-13133, 13151-13153, 29581-29582, 35201-35206, 35226-35236, 35256-35266, 35286, 36000, 36002-36012, 36400-36410, 36420-36430, 36440, 36473, 36474, 36476, 36591-36592, 36600, 36640, 43752, 49185, 51701-51703, 62320-62327, 64400-64410, 64413-64435, 64445-64450, 64461-64463, 64479-64530, 69990, 75894, 76000-76001, 76380, 76937, 76940, 76942, 76970, 76998, 77002, 77012-77013, 77021-77022, 92012-92014, 93000-93010, 93040-93042, 93318, 93355, 93970-93971, 94002, 94200, 94250, 94680-94690, 94770, 95812-95816, 95819, 95822, 95829, 95955, 96360-96368, 96372, 96374-96377, 99155-99157, 99211-99223, 99231-99255, 99291-99292, 99304-99310, 99315-99316, 99334-99337, 99347-99350, 99374-99375, 99377-99378, 99446-99449, 99495-99496, G0463, G0471, J0670, J2001
36479	29581-29582, 36000, 36002-36005, 36410, 36425, 36476, 36591-36592, 49185, 75894, 76000-76001, 76380, 76937, 76940, 76942, 76970, 76998, 77002, 77012-77013, 77021-77022, 93970-93971
36482	CCI edits for this code were not available at publication. Please check the CMS website for release.
36483	CCI edits for this code were not available at publication. Please check the CMS website for release.

Case Example #1

The patient's left leg was prepped and draped in typical aseptic fashion. One-half inch of nitroglycerin paste was placed on the calf. Using real-time **ultrasound guidance** and **micropuncture technique**, the left **lesser saphenous vein** was **entered** just above the knee. 150 micrograms of **nitroglycerin was instilled** into the vein. Using ultrasound guidance, a guidewire, sheath, and **laser were placed**. Tumescent anesthesia was placed along the course of the laser. The **laser was retracted and 679.597 Joules was given** over 54.88 seconds. The sheath was removed and hemostasis was achieved at the puncture site. The patient tolerated the procedure well with no apparent complications.

CPT/HCPCS Codes Reported:
36478

Case Example #2

Procedure:
The left lower extremity was prepped and draped to allow knee flexion in the sterile field. A 12 Mhz duplex ultrasound probe, draped in a sterile sleeve, was introduced. The entire great saphenous vein was mapped with a surgical marking pen, and notations were made of varicosity clusters and tortuous segments. Measurements of the length of the great saphenous vein, along with minimum and maximum diameters, were noted. The total length was 46cm from the entry point to 2cm below the saphenofemoral junction. The diameter of the vein ranged from 11.5mm near the saphenofemoral function to 6.7mm at the entry point. Using a 30 gauge needle, the entry site was anesthetized with 1% buffered lidocaine. The **great saphenous vein** was entered percutaneously under ultrasound guidance with a 21-gauge needle micropuncture set. A 0.018 micro wire was inserted, and the 21-gauge needle was removed. A ClosureFast catheter was introduced and placed into position so that it extended 2cm inferior to the saphenofemoral juncture. The final position of the catheter was determined by ultrasound guidance and duplex imaging. Tumescent anesthetic was delivered under ultrasound guidance. A solution of 0.1% lidocaine in 250 cc's of saline was delivered along the course of the saphenous vein. A final positioning check was made. The **RF generator** was turned on, and the catheter was withdrawn at a rate of 7cm after every 20 second RF cycle. The total time of energy delivery was 160 seconds with 8 RF cycles delivered. Repeat duplex imaging showed no flow over the entire length of the treated vein.

After ensuring hemostasis, the sheath insertion site over the saphenous vein was closed with a bandage. A compression stocking was placed on the treated vein. Post-op instructions were given.

CPT/HCPCS Codes Reported:
36475

Stab Phlebectomy

This procedure is used to treat varicose veins and is sometimes performed in hospital interventional radiology or vascular labs. Image guidance is not generally required.

37765   **Stab phlebectomy of varicose veins, one extremity; 10–20 stab incisions**

37766   **more than 20 incisions**

Stab phlebectomy for varicose veins is an ambulatory procedure that permits removal of nearly any incompetent vein below the saphenofemoral and saphenopopliteal junction. The varicose veins are identified with an indelible marking pen while the patient is standing. The patient is placed supine for further marking. Diluted lidocaine is injected into the tissues in large volumes until the perivenous tissues are engorged and distended with the anesthetic. Regional nerve blocks may be used for extensive areas. Tiny stab incisions are made with a scalpel or 18-gauge needle. The varicose vein is dissected with the phlebectomy hook. The vein is undermined along its course, all fibroadipose attachments to the vein are freed, and the vein is grasped with the hook and removed with mosquito forceps. Hemostasis is achieved by applying local compression to the veins already removed. The varicose vein is progressively extracted from one stab incision to the next. No skin closure is needed. Bandages are applied. Large pads are placed along the site of vein removal and covered with an inelastic bandage, followed by a second bandage of highly elastic material.

Coding Tips

1.   Report 37765 when 10-20 stab incisions are made.
2.   Report 37766 when more than 20 stab incisions are made.
3.   Report 37799 when less than 10 stab incisions are made.
4.   Report any applicable HCPCS Level II code for devices used.

Facility HCPCS Coding

Some applicable codes may include, but are not limited to:

C1769   Guidewire

C1894   Introducer/sheath, other than guiding, intracardiac electrophysiological, non-laser

C2629   Introducer/sheath, other than guiding, intracardiac

Lower Extremity Venous Anatomy

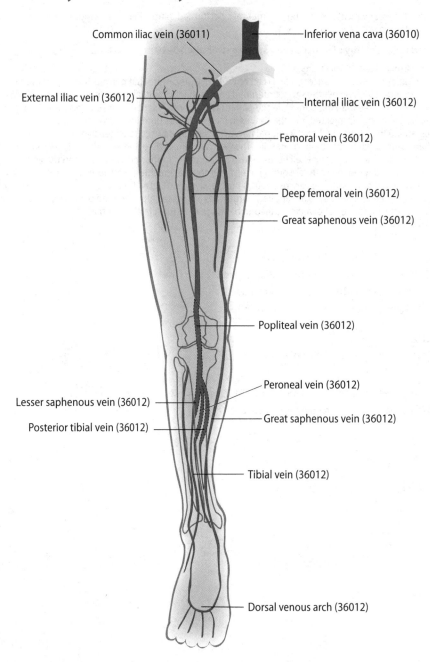

Common iliac vein (36011)

Inferior vena cava (36010)

External iliac vein (36012)

Internal iliac vein (36012)

Femoral vein (36012)

Deep femoral vein (36012)

Great saphenous vein (36012)

Popliteal vein (36012)

Peroneal vein (36012)

Lesser saphenous vein (36012)

Great saphenous vein (36012)

Posterior tibial vein (36012)

Tibial vein (36012)

Dorsal venous arch (36012)

ICD-10-CM Coding

I83.001	Varicose veins of unspecified lower extremity with ulcer of thigh
I83.002	Varicose veins of unspecified lower extremity with ulcer of calf
I83.003	Varicose veins of unspecified lower extremity with ulcer of ankle
I83.004	Varicose veins of unspecified lower extremity with ulcer of heel and midfoot
I83.005	Varicose veins of unspecified lower extremity with ulcer other part of foot
I83.008	Varicose veins of unspecified lower extremity with ulcer other part of lower leg
I83.009	Varicose veins of unspecified lower extremity with ulcer of unspecified site
I83.011	Varicose veins of right lower extremity with ulcer of thigh
I83.012	Varicose veins of right lower extremity with ulcer of calf
I83.013	Varicose veins of right lower extremity with ulcer of ankle
I83.014	Varicose veins of right lower extremity with ulcer of heel and midfoot

I83.Ø15	Varicose veins of right lower extremity with ulcer other part of foot
I83.Ø18	Varicose veins of right lower extremity with ulcer other part of lower leg
I83.Ø19	Varicose veins of right lower extremity with ulcer of unspecified site
I83.Ø21	Varicose veins of left lower extremity with ulcer of thigh
I83.Ø22	Varicose veins of left lower extremity with ulcer of calf
I83.Ø23	Varicose veins of left lower extremity with ulcer of ankle
I83.Ø24	Varicose veins of left lower extremity with ulcer of heel and midfoot
I83.Ø25	Varicose veins of left lower extremity with ulcer other part of foot
I83.Ø28	Varicose veins of left lower extremity with ulcer other part of lower leg
I83.Ø29	Varicose veins of left lower extremity with ulcer of unspecified site
I83.1Ø	Varicose veins of unspecified lower extremity with inflammation
I83.11	Varicose veins of right lower extremity with inflammation
I83.12	Varicose veins of left lower extremity with inflammation
I83.2Ø1	Varicose veins of unspecified lower extremity with both ulcer of thigh and inflammation
I83.2Ø2	Varicose veins of unspecified lower extremity with both ulcer of calf and inflammation
I83.2Ø3	Varicose veins of unspecified lower extremity with both ulcer of ankle and inflammation
I83.2Ø4	Varicose veins of unspecified lower extremity with both ulcer of heel and midfoot and inflammation
I83.2Ø5	Varicose veins of unspecified lower extremity with both ulcer other part of foot and inflammation
I83.2Ø8	Varicose veins of unspecified lower extremity with both ulcer of other part of lower extremity and inflammation
I83.2Ø9	Varicose veins of unspecified lower extremity with both ulcer of unspecified site and inflammation
I83.211	Varicose veins of right lower extremity with both ulcer of thigh and inflammation
I83.212	Varicose veins of right lower extremity with both ulcer of calf and inflammation
I83.213	Varicose veins of right lower extremity with both ulcer of ankle and inflammation
I83.214	Varicose veins of right lower extremity with both ulcer of heel and midfoot and inflammation
I83.215	Varicose veins of right lower extremity with both ulcer other part of foot and inflammation
I83.218	Varicose veins of right lower extremity with both ulcer of other part of lower extremity and inflammation
I83.219	Varicose veins of right lower extremity with both ulcer of unspecified site and inflammation
I83.221	Varicose veins of left lower extremity with both ulcer of thigh and inflammation
I83.222	Varicose veins of left lower extremity with both ulcer of calf and inflammation
I83.223	Varicose veins of left lower extremity with both ulcer of ankle and inflammation
I83.224	Varicose veins of left lower extremity with both ulcer of heel and midfoot and inflammation
I83.225	Varicose veins of left lower extremity with both ulcer other part of foot and inflammation
I83.228	Varicose veins of left lower extremity with both ulcer of other part of lower extremity and inflammation
I83.229	Varicose veins of left lower extremity with both ulcer of unspecified site and inflammation
I83.811	Varicose veins of right lower extremities with pain
I83.812	Varicose veins of left lower extremities with pain
I83.813	Varicose veins of bilateral lower extremities with pain
I83.819	Varicose veins of unspecified lower extremity with pain
I83.891	Varicose veins of right lower extremities with other complications
I83.892	Varicose veins of left lower extremities with other complications
I83.893	Varicose veins of bilateral lower extremities with other complications
I83.899	Varicose veins of unspecified lower extremity with other complications
I83.9Ø	Asymptomatic varicose veins of unspecified lower extremity
I83.91	Asymptomatic varicose veins of right lower extremity
I83.92	Asymptomatic varicose veins of left lower extremity
I83.93	Asymptomatic varicose veins of bilateral lower extremities

CCI Edits

37765   0213T, 0216T, 0228T, 0230T, 11000-11006, 11042-11047, 12001-12007, 12011-12057, 13100-13133, 13151-13153, 29581-29582, 36000, 36400-36410, 36420-36430, 36440, 36591-36592, 36600, 36640, 37785, 43752, 51701-51703, 62320-62327, 64400-64410, 64413-64435, 64445-64450, 64461-64463, 64479-64530, 69990, 92012-92014, 93000-93010, 93040-93042, 93318, 93355, 94002, 94200, 94250, 94680-94690, 94770, 95812-95816, 95819, 95822, 95829, 95955, 96360-96368, 96372, 96374-96377, 97597-97598, 97602, 99155-99157, 99211-99223, 99231-99255, 99291-99292, 99304-99310, 99315-99316, 99334-99337, 99347-99350, 99374-99375, 99377-99378, 99446-99449, 99495-99496, G0463, G0471, J0670, J2001

37766   0213T, 0216T, 0228T, 0230T, 11000-11006, 11042-11047, 12001-12007, 12011-12057, 13100-13133, 13151-13153, 29581-29582, 36000, 36400-36410, 36420-36430, 36440, 36591-36592, 36600, 36640, 37765, 37785, 43752, 51701-51703, 62320-62327, 64400-64410, 64413-64435, 64445-64450, 64461-64463, 64479-64530, 69990, 92012-92014, 93000-93010, 93040-93042, 93318, 93355, 94002, 94200, 94250, 94680-94690, 94770, 95812-95816, 95819, 95822, 95829, 95955, 96360-96368, 96372, 96374-96377, 97597-97598, 97602, 99155-99157, 99211-99223, 99231-99255, 99291-99292, 99304-99310, 99315-99316, 99334-99337, 99347-99350, 99374-99375, 99377-99378, 99446-99449, 99495-99496, G0463, G0471, J0670, J2001

Case Example

Indication:
Painful, swollen varicose veins

Procedure:
The patient's right lower leg was prepped and draped in normal sterile fashion. Local anesthesia was utilized. Using blunt and sharp dissection with an 11 blade and Mueller type 1 and 2 hooks, **25 stab incisions were made** and the **veins ligated and removed**. The incisions were closed with Indermil adhesive. Bandages were applied and the patient tolerated the procedure well.

CPT/HCPCS Codes Reported:
37766

Venous Sclerotherapy

36465	**Injection of non-compounded foam sclerosant with ultrasound compression maneuvers to guide dispersion of the injectate, inclusive of all imaging guidance and monitoring; single incompetent extremity truncal vein (eg, great saphenous vein, accessory saphenous vein)**
36466	**multiple incompetent truncal veins (eg, great saphenous vein, accessory saphenous vein), same leg**

The physician performs ultrasound-guided foam sclerotherapy (UGFS) of varicose veins. UGFS is a minimally invasive and relatively safe treatment of restricted amounts of small varicose veins. In UGFS, a noncompounded foam sclerosant is injected into an extremity truncal vein (e.g., great saphenous vein, accessory saphenous vein) using ultrasound-guided compression of the junction of the central vein (saphenofemoral junction or saphenopopliteal junction) to limit the dispersion of the injectate. The physician creates a detailed outline or mapping of the veins in the lower legs to identify all vein abnormalities along with additional nearby structures to include deep veins and arteries via duplex ultrasound examination. Once this is completed, the patient is placed in the supine position and the leg being treated is exposed. The physician guides the needle into the vein using ultrasonic guidance and injects a noncompounded foam. Foam volumes vary from 1 mL to 16 mL per treatment. The injected vein collapses and is eventually absorbed by the body. The physician may need to repeat the injection process a number of times along the vein to completely target the incompetent truncal vein.

36470	**Injection of sclerosant; single incompetent vein (other than telangiectasia)**
36471	**multiple incompetent veins (other than telangiectasia), same leg**

The physician injects a sclerosing solution into the veins of the leg. The physician inserts a tiny needle through the skin and into the vein to be treated. A solution containing a sclerosing drug is injected into a single vein for 36470 and into multiple veins for 36471. The solution causes the veins to become inflamed, collapse, and stick together so the veins close.

Coding Tips

1. Do not separately report vascular embolization when performed in the same surgical field.
2. Report ultrasound guidance, when used, with 76942.
3. Documentation should clearly state which veins were treated. This ensures the billed code matches the documentation.
4. Physician reporting: In the office setting, all devices and supplies are included in these codes and should not be separately billed.
5. Physician reporting: The application of compression bandages and/or stockings is included in codes 36470, 36471, 36465, and 36466. Do not separately bill.

Facility HCPCS Coding

There are no applicable HCPCS codes for this procedure.

ICD-10-CM Coding

I83.001	Varicose veins of unspecified lower extremity with ulcer of thigh
I83.002	Varicose veins of unspecified lower extremity with ulcer of calf
I83.003	Varicose veins of unspecified lower extremity with ulcer of ankle
I83.004	Varicose veins of unspecified lower extremity with ulcer of heel and midfoot
I83.005	Varicose veins of unspecified lower extremity with ulcer other part of foot
I83.008	Varicose veins of unspecified lower extremity with ulcer other part of lower leg
I83.009	Varicose veins of unspecified lower extremity with ulcer of unspecified site
I83.011	Varicose veins of right lower extremity with ulcer of thigh
I83.012	Varicose veins of right lower extremity with ulcer of calf
I83.013	Varicose veins of right lower extremity with ulcer of ankle
I83.014	Varicose veins of right lower extremity with ulcer of heel and midfoot
I83.015	Varicose veins of right lower extremity with ulcer other part of foot
I83.018	Varicose veins of right lower extremity with ulcer other part of lower leg
I83.019	Varicose veins of right lower extremity with ulcer of unspecified site
I83.021	Varicose veins of left lower extremity with ulcer of thigh
I83.022	Varicose veins of left lower extremity with ulcer of calf
I83.023	Varicose veins of left lower extremity with ulcer of ankle
I83.024	Varicose veins of left lower extremity with ulcer of heel and midfoot
I83.025	Varicose veins of left lower extremity with ulcer other part of foot
I83.028	Varicose veins of left lower extremity with ulcer other part of lower leg

I83.Ø29	Varicose veins of left lower extremity with ulcer of unspecified site
I83.1Ø	Varicose veins of unspecified lower extremity with inflammation
I83.11	Varicose veins of right lower extremity with inflammation
I83.12	Varicose veins of left lower extremity with inflammation
I83.2Ø1	Varicose veins of unspecified lower extremity with both ulcer of thigh and inflammation
I83.2Ø2	Varicose veins of unspecified lower extremity with both ulcer of calf and inflammation
I83.2Ø3	Varicose veins of unspecified lower extremity with both ulcer of ankle and inflammation
I83.2Ø4	Varicose veins of unspecified lower extremity with both ulcer of heel and midfoot and inflammation
I83.2Ø5	Varicose veins of unspecified lower extremity with both ulcer other part of foot and inflammation
I83.2Ø8	Varicose veins of unspecified lower extremity with both ulcer of other part of lower extremity and inflammation
I83.2Ø9	Varicose veins of unspecified lower extremity with both ulcer of unspecified site and inflammation
I83.211	Varicose veins of right lower extremity with both ulcer of thigh and inflammation
I83.212	Varicose veins of right lower extremity with both ulcer of calf and inflammation
I83.213	Varicose veins of right lower extremity with both ulcer of ankle and inflammation
I83.214	Varicose veins of right lower extremity with both ulcer of heel and midfoot and inflammation
I83.215	Varicose veins of right lower extremity with both ulcer other part of foot and inflammation
I83.218	Varicose veins of right lower extremity with both ulcer of other part of lower extremity and inflammation
I83.219	Varicose veins of right lower extremity with both ulcer of unspecified site and inflammation
I83.221	Varicose veins of left lower extremity with both ulcer of thigh and inflammation
I83.222	Varicose veins of left lower extremity with both ulcer of calf and inflammation
I83.223	Varicose veins of left lower extremity with both ulcer of ankle and inflammation
I83.224	Varicose veins of left lower extremity with both ulcer of heel and midfoot and inflammation
I83.225	Varicose veins of left lower extremity with both ulcer other part of foot and inflammation
I83.228	Varicose veins of left lower extremity with both ulcer of other part of lower extremity and inflammation
I83.229	Varicose veins of left lower extremity with both ulcer of unspecified site and inflammation
I83.811	Varicose veins of right lower extremities with pain
I83.812	Varicose veins of left lower extremities with pain
I83.813	Varicose veins of bilateral lower extremities with pain
I83.819	Varicose veins of unspecified lower extremity with pain
I83.891	Varicose veins of right lower extremities with other complications
I83.892	Varicose veins of left lower extremities with other complications
I83.893	Varicose veins of bilateral lower extremities with other complications
I83.899	Varicose veins of unspecified lower extremity with other complications
I83.9Ø	Asymptomatic varicose veins of unspecified lower extremity
I83.91	Asymptomatic varicose veins of right lower extremity
I83.92	Asymptomatic varicose veins of left lower extremity
I83.93	Asymptomatic varicose veins of bilateral lower extremities

CCI Edits

36465 CCI edits for this code were not available at publication. Please check the CMS website for release.

36466 CCI edits for this code were not available at publication. Please check the CMS website for release.

36470 0213T, 0216T, 0228T, 0230T, 12001-12007, 12011-12057, 13100-13133, 13151-13153, 36000, 36400-36410, 36420-36430, 36440, 36591-36592, 36600, 36640, 43752, 51701-51703, 62320-62327, 64400-64410, 64413-64435, 64445-64450, 64461-64463, 64479-64530, 69990, 92012-92014, 93000-93010, 93040-93042, 93318, 93355, 94002, 94200, 94250, 94680-94690, 94770, 95812-95816, 95819, 95822, 95829, 95955, 96360-96368, 96372, 96374-96377, 99155-99157, 99211-99223, 99231-99255, 99291-99292, 99304-99310, 99315-99316, 99334-99337, 99347-99350, 99374-99375, 99377-99378, 99446-99449, 99495-99496, G0463, G0471, J0670, J2001

36471 0213T, 0216T, 0228T, 0230T, 12001-12007, 12011-12057, 13100-13133, 13151-13153, 36000, 36400-36410, 36420-36430, 36440, 36470, 36591-36592, 36600, 36640, 43752, 51701-51703, 62320-62327, 64400-64410, 64413-64435, 64445-64450, 64461-64463, 64479-64530, 69990, 92012-92014, 93000-93010, 93040-93042, 93318, 93355, 94002, 94200, 94250, 94680-94690, 94770, 95812-95816, 95819, 95822, 95829, 95955, 96360-96368, 96372, 96374-96377, 99155-99157, 99211-99223, 99231-99255, 99291-99292, 99304-99310, 99315-99316, 99334-99337, 99347-99350, 99374-99375, 99377-99378, 99446-99449, 99495-99496, G0463, G0471, J0670, J2001

Case Example

Diagnosis:
Varicose veins with pain, edema and swelling

Procedure:
The patient was positioned in such a manner as to facilitate injections. The skin is anesthetized with buffered lidocaine and a 25-gauge needle is inserted through the skin and into the greater and lesser saphenous veins. Proper alignment of the needle is monitored and maintained by means of constant ultrasound imaging and guidance. Appropriate blood return from the veins was observed. After securing venous access, the **sclerosing agent**, Sotradecol, is **carefully injected into the veins**. Travel of the sclerosing drug within the veins is observed by ultrasound. A total dose of 1.5 ml of 1% Sotradecol was injected. The dose was foamed 1:4 by the Tessari method to 3.0 ml and was delivered in intraluminal injections. Each site was identified and confirmed. The patient was discharged in good condition, and no complications were encountered.

Impression:
Successful ultrasound guided sclerotherapy of the left greater and lesser saphenous veins for symptomatic varicose veins.

CPT/HCPCS Codes Reported:
36470, 76942

Sacroplasty

Sacroplasty is performed to treat patients with conditions such as osteoporosis and malignancy that are causing instability in the sacrum.

0200T   **Percutaneous sacral augmentation (sacroplasty), unilateral injection(s), including the use of a balloon or mechanical device when used, 1 or more needles, includes imaging guidance and bone biopsy, when performed**

0201T   **Percutaneous sacral augmentation (sacroplasty), bilateral injections, including the use of a balloon or mechanical device when used, 2 or more needles, includes imaging guidance and bone biopsy, when performed**

Under imaging guidance, the physician directs trocars into the sacrum. Special bone cement is mixed and then injected through the trocars into the bone. The spread of the cement is monitored with image guidance. The patient is maintained in the prone position for 30 to 45 minutes before being allowed to sit or stand.

Coding Tips

1. Codes 0200T and 0201T are comprehensive codes that include the surgical and imaging components. Do not separately report image guidance codes.
2. Bone biopsy is included in these codes. Do not separately report 20225 when biopsy is performed at the same level as sacroplasty. Bone biopsy may be additionally reported when performed at a separate level.
3. These codes are reported only once per encounter.
4. Conscious sedation is not included in these codes. Separately report 99151–99157 per payer policy and coding guidelines. Hospitals may choose to include the costs associated with the service as part of the procedure rather than reporting them separately.
5. Physician Reporting: These radiology S&I codes have both a technical and professional component. To report only the professional component, append modifier 26. To report only the technical component, append modifier TC. To report the complete procedure (i.e., both the professional and technical components), submit without a modifier.

Facility HCPCS Coding

There are no applicable HCPCS codes for these codes. Hospitals are encouraged to separately report the supplies used.

ICD-10-CM Coding

M48.48XA	Fatigue fracture of vertebra, sacral and sacrococcygeal region, initial encounter for fracture
M48.48XG	Fatigue fracture of vertebra, sacral and sacrococcygeal region, subsequent encounter for fracture with delayed healing
M48.58XA	Collapsed vertebra, not elsewhere classified, sacral and sacrococcygeal region, initial encounter for fracture
M48.58XG	Collapsed vertebra, not elsewhere classified, sacral and sacrococcygeal region, subsequent encounter for fracture with delayed healing
M80.08XA	Age-related osteoporosis with current pathological fracture, vertebra(e), initial encounter for fracture
M80.08XG	Age-related osteoporosis with current pathological fracture, vertebra(e), subsequent encounter for fracture with delayed healing
M80.08XK	Age-related osteoporosis with current pathological fracture, vertebra(e), subsequent encounter for fracture with nonunion
M80.08XP	Age-related osteoporosis with current pathological fracture, vertebra(e), subsequent encounter for fracture with malunion
M84.48XA	Pathological fracture, other site, initial encounter for fracture
M84.48XG	Pathological fracture, other site, subsequent encounter for fracture with delayed healing
M84.48XK	Pathological fracture, other site, subsequent encounter for fracture with nonunion
M84.48XP	Pathological fracture, other site, subsequent encounter for fracture with malunion
M84.58XA	Pathological fracture in neoplastic disease, other specified site, initial encounter for fracture
M84.58XG	Pathological fracture in neoplastic disease, other specified site, subsequent encounter for fracture with delayed healing
M84.58XK	Pathological fracture in neoplastic disease, other specified site, subsequent encounter for fracture with nonunion
M84.58XP	Pathological fracture in neoplastic disease, other specified site, subsequent encounter for fracture with malunion
M84.68XA	Pathological fracture in other disease, other site, initial encounter for fracture
M84.68XG	Pathological fracture in other disease, other site, subsequent encounter for fracture with delayed healing
M84.68XK	Pathological fracture in other disease, other site, subsequent encounter for fracture with nonunion
M84.68XP	Pathological fracture in other disease, other site, subsequent encounter for fracture with malunion

CCI Edits

0200T   01935-01936, 0213T, 0216T, 0228T, 0230T, 0333T, 0464T, 11000-11006, 11042-11047, 20220-20225, 20240, 22310-22315, 22505, 36000, 36400-36410, 36420-36430, 36440, 36591-36592, 36600, 36640, 38220, 38230, 38232, 43752, 51701-51703, 61650, 62322-62323, 62326-62327, 63707, 63709, 64400-64410, 64413-64435, 64445-64450, 64461, 64463, 64479, 64483, 64486-64490, 64493, 64505-64530, 69990, 75872, 76000-76001, 77002-77003, 92585, 93000-93010, 93040-93042, 93318, 93355, 94002, 94200, 94250, 94680-94690, 94770, 95812-95816, 95819, 95822, 95829, 95860-95870, 95907-95913, 95925-95933, 95937-95940, 95955, 96360, 96365, 96372, 96374-96377, 97597-97598, 97602, 99155-99157, 99446-99449, G0453, G0471

0201T   01935-01936, 0200T, 0213T, 0216T, 0228T, 0230T, 0333T, 0464T, 11000-11006, 11042-11047, 20220-20225, 20240, 22310-22315, 22505, 36000, 36400-36410, 36420-36430, 36440, 36591-36592, 36600, 36640, 38220, 38230, 38232, 43752, 51701-51703, 61650, 62322-62323, 62326-62327, 63707, 63709, 64400-64410, 64413-64435, 64445-64450, 64461, 64463, 64479, 64483, 64486-64490, 64493, 64505-64530, 69990, 75872, 76000-76001, 77002-77003, 92585, 93000-93010, 93040-93042, 93318, 93355, 94002, 94200, 94250, 94680-94690, 94770, 95812-95816, 95819, 95822, 95829, 95860-95870, 95907-95913, 95925-95933, 95937-95940, 95955, 96360, 96365, 96372, 96374-96377, 97597-97598, 97602, 99155-99157, 99446-99449, G0453, G0471

Case Example

The patient was brought to the imaging suite and placed prone on the table. Conscious sedation was administered with nursing supervision. The skin overlying the area was numbed with 1% Xylocaine. The trocar was **fluoroscopically guided into the sacrum** on the left side. Polymethylmethacrylate cement and barium powder mixture was **injected** using fluoro guidance. The procedure was repeated into the right side of the sacrum. Fluoro confirmed the cement was contained within the sacrum with no extravasation noted. The patient was moved to a stretcher and instructed to remain lying down for four hours. There were no apparent complications.

CPT/HCPCS Codes Reported:
0201T

Vertebroplasty

Vertebroplasty is performed to treat patients with conditions such as osteoporosis resulting in fractures of the vertebral bodies.

22510	**Percutaneous vertebroplasty (bone biopsy included when performed), 1 vertebral body, unilateral or bilateral injection, inclusive of all imaging guidance; cervicothoracic**
22511	**lumbosacral**
22512	**each additional cervicothoracic or lumbosacral vertebral body (list separately in addition to code for primary procedure**

Percutaneous vertebroplasty is performed by a one- or two-sided injection of a vertebral body. A local anesthetic is administered. In a separately reportable procedure, the radiologist uses imaging techniques, such as CT scanning or fluoroscopy, to guide percutaneous placement of the needle during the procedure and to monitor the injection procedure. Sterile biomaterial such as methyl methacrylate is injected from one side or both sides into the damaged vertebral body and acts as a bone cement to reinforce the fractured or collapsed vertebra. Following the procedure, the patient may experience significant, almost immediate, pain relief.

Coding Tips

1. These codes are comprehensive codes that include the surgical and imaging components. Do not separately report image guidance codes.
2. Bone biopsy is included in these codes. Do not separately report 20225 when biopsy is performed at the same level as vertebroplasty. Bone biopsy may be additionally reported when performed at a separate level.
3. These codes include conscious sedation.
4. Use only one primary code; use the add-on code for procedures performed at another level.
5. Conscious sedation is not included in these codes. Separately report 99151–99157 per payer policy and coding guidelines. Hospitals may choose to include the costs associated with the service as part of the procedure rather than reporting them separately.
6. Physician Reporting: These radiology S&I codes have both a technical and professional component. To report only the professional component, append modifier 26. To report only the technical component, append modifier TC. To report the complete procedure (i.e., both the professional and technical components), submit without a modifier.

Facility HCPCS Coding

There are no applicable HCPCS codes for these codes. Hospitals are encouraged to separately report the supplies used.

ICD-10-CM Coding

The application of these codes is too broad to adequately present ICD-10-CM diagnosis code links here. Refer to the current ICD-10-CM book.

CCI Edits

22510 01935-01936, 0213T, 0216T, 0228T, 0230T, 0333T, 0464T, 11000-11006, 11042-11047, 12001-12007, 12011-12057, 13100-13133, 13151-13153, 20220-20225, 20240, 20250, 22310, 22505, 22511, 22853-22854, 22859, 36000, 36005, 36400-36410, 36420-36430, 36440, 36591-36592, 36600, 36640, 43752, 51701-51703, 61781-61783, 62292, 62320-62327, 63707, 63709, 64400-64410, 64413-64435, 64445-64450, 64461-64463, 64479-64530, 69990, 72128-72130, 75872, 76000-76001, 76380, 76942, 76970, 76998, 77001-77003, 77012, 77021, 92012-92014, 92585, 93000-93010, 93040-93042, 93318, 93355, 94002, 94200, 94250, 94680-94690, 94770, 95812-95816, 95819, 95822, 95829, 95860-95870, 95907-95913, 95925-95933, 95937-95941, 95955, 96360-96368, 96372, 96374-96377, 97597-97598, 97602, 99155-99157, 99211-99223, 99231-99255, 99291-99292, 99304-99310, 99315-99316, 99334-99337, 99347-99350, 99374-99375, 99377-99378, 99446-99449, 99495-99496, G0453, G0463, G0471, J0670, J2001

22511 01935-01936, 0213T, 0216T, 0228T, 0230T, 0333T, 0464T, 11000-11006, 11042-11047, 12001-12007, 12011-12057, 13100-13133, 13151-13153, 20220-20225, 20240, 20251, 22310, 22505, 22853-22854, 22859, 22869-22870, 36000, 36005, 36400-36410, 36420-36430, 36440, 36591-36592, 36600, 36640, 43752, 51701-51703, 61781-61783, 62292, 62320-62327, 63707, 63709, 64400-64410, 64413-64435, 64445-64450, 64461-64463, 64479-64530, 69990, 72131-72133, 75872, 76000-76001, 76380, 76942, 76970, 76998, 77001-77003, 77012, 77021, 92012-92014, 92585, 93000-93010, 93040-93042, 93318, 93355, 94002, 94200, 94250, 94680-94690, 94770, 95812-95816, 95819, 95822, 95829, 95860-95870, 95907-95913, 95925-95933, 95937-95941, 95955, 96360-96368, 96372, 96374-96377, 97597-97598, 97602, 99155-99157, 99211-99223, 99231-99255, 99291-99292, 99304-99310, 99315-99316, 99334-99337, 99347-99350, 99374-99375, 99377-99378, 99446-99449, 99495-99496, G0453, G0463, G0471, J0670, J2001

22512   0333T, 0464T, 11000-11006, 11042-11047, 20220-20225, 22310, 36591-36592, 63707, 63709, 76000-76001, 76380, 76942, 76970, 76998, 77001-77003, 77012, 77021, 92585, 95822, 95860-95869, 95907-95913, 95925-95927, 95930-95933, 95937-95940, 97597-97598, 97602, 99155-99157, G0453

Case Example

The patient was prepped and draped and local anesthesia was administered. The **trocar** was **directed** into the **vertebral body at L-4** under fluoroscopic guidance. A total of 8 cm of **PMMA cement** was slowly **injected**. The trocar was retracted and pressure held over the site for a few minutes.

CPT/HCPCS Codes Reported:
22511

Kyphoplasty

Kyphoplasty is performed to treat patients with conditions such as osteoporosis resulting in fractures of the vertebral bodies.

22513	**Percutaneous vertebral augmentation, including cavity creation (fracture reduction and bone biopsy when performed) using mechanical device (eg, kyphoplasty), 1 vertebral body, unilateral or bilateral cannulation, inclusive of all imaging guidance; thoracic**
22514	**lumbar**
22515	**each additional thoracic or lumbar vertebral body (list separately in addition to code for primary procedure)**

The physician performs a percutaneous kyphoplasty, a modification of the percutaneous vertebroplasty, to reduce the pain associated with osteoporotic vertebral compression fractures. This procedure has the added advantage of restoring vertebral body height. The procedure is performed under separately reported radiologic guidance. The patient is placed in a prone, slightly flexed position. A small incision is made and small cannulas are inserted into the vertebral body from both sides. Balloon catheters called "tamps" are inserted into the vertebra and inflated. The tamps create a void in the soft trabecular bone and restore vertebral alignment. The balloon is removed and bone cement is injected into the cavity.

Coding Tips

1. These are comprehensive codes that include the surgical and imaging components. Do not report image guidance codes separately.

2. Bone biopsy is included in these codes. Do not report 20225 separately when biopsy is performed at the same level as vertebroplasty. Bone biopsy may be additionally reported when performed at a separate level.

3. Do not separately report fracture reduction.

4. Conscious sedation is not included in these codes. Separately report 99151–99157 per payer policy and coding guidelines. Hospitals may choose to include the costs associated with the service as part of the procedure rather than reporting them separately.

5. Use only one primary code; use the add-on code for procedures performed at another level.

6. Physician Reporting: These radiology S&I codes have both a technical and professional component. To report only the professional component, append modifier 26. To report only the technical component, append modifier TC. To report the complete procedure (i.e., both the professional and technical components), submit without a modifier.

Facility HCPCS Coding

There are no applicable HCPCS codes for these codes. Hospitals are encouraged to separately report the supplies used.

ICD-10-CM Coding

The application of these codes is too broad to adequately present ICD-10-CM diagnosis code links here. Refer to the current ICD-10-CM book.

CCI Edits

22513 01935-01936, 0213T, 0216T, 0228T, 0230T, 0333T, 0464T, 11000-11006, 11042-11047, 12001-12007, 12011-12057, 13100-13133, 13151-13153, 20220-20225, 20240, 20250, 20650, 22310, 22505, 22510, 22514, 22853-22854, 22859, 36000, 36400-36410, 36420-36430, 36440, 36591-36592, 36600, 36640, 43752, 51701-51703, 62292, 62320-62327, 63707, 63709, 64400-64410, 64413-64435, 64445-64450, 64461-64463, 64479-64530, 69990, 72128-72130, 75872, 76000-76001, 76380, 76942, 76970, 76998, 77001-77003, 77012, 77021, 92012-92014, 92585, 93000-93010, 93040-93042, 93318, 93355, 94002, 94200, 94250, 94680-94690, 94770, 95812-95816, 95819, 95822, 95829, 95860-95870, 95907-95913, 95925-95933, 95937-95941, 95955, 96360-96368, 96372, 96374-96377, 97597-97598, 97602, 99155-99157, 99211-99223, 99231-99255, 99291-99292, 99304-99310, 99315-99316, 99334-99337, 99347-99350, 99374-99375, 99377-99378, 99446-99449, 99495-99496, G0453, G0463, G0471, J0670, J2001

22514 01935-01936, 0213T, 0216T, 0228T, 0230T, 0333T, 0464T, 11000-11006, 11042-11047, 12001-12007, 12011-12057, 13100-13133, 13151-13153, 20220-20225, 20240, 20250, 20650, 22310, 22505, 22511, 22853-22854, 22859, 36000, 36400-36410, 36420-36430, 36440, 36591-36592, 36600, 36640, 43752, 51701-51703, 62292, 62320-62327, 63707, 63709, 64400-64410, 64413-64435, 64445-64450, 64461-64463, 64479-64530, 69990, 72131-72133, 75872, 76000-76001, 76380, 76942, 76970, 76998, 77001-77003, 77012, 77021, 92012-92014, 92585, 93000-93010, 93040-93042, 93318, 93355, 94002, 94200, 94250, 94680-94690, 94770, 95812-95816, 95819, 95822, 95829, 95860-95870, 95907-95913, 95925-95933, 95937-95941, 95955, 96360-96368, 96372, 96374-96377, 97597-97598, 97602, 99155-99157, 99211-99223, 99231-99255, 99291-99292, 99304-99310, 99315-99316, 99334-99337, 99347-99350, 99374-99375, 99377-99378, 99446-99449, 99495-99496, G0453, G0463, G0471, J0670, J2001

22515 11000-11006, 11042-11047, 20220-20225, 20240, 20650, 22310, 36591-36592, 63707, 63709, 76000-76001, 76380, 76942, 76970, 76998, 77001-77003, 77012, 77021, 95863-95866, 95869, 97597-97598, 97602

Case Example

Indication:
Osteoporotic fractures at L3 and L4 with loss of vertebral height.

The patient was brought to the imaging suite and placed prone on the table. Under usual sterile technique, the needle was first directed into the **L3 vertebral body** under fluoro guidance. The **balloon tamp** was inserted and carefully inflated. The PMMA cement was then prepared and slowly injected. The procedure was **repeated at the L4** level. There were no complications and the patient was released to the recovery area.

CPT/HCPCS Codes Reported:
22514, 22515

Myelography

Myelography is a diagnostic study performed to identify abnormalities in the subarachnoid space (the space between the spinal cord and the spine vertebrae). It is usually performed to identify narrowing of the space resulting in pain in the back, neck, arms, or legs. Herniated disc is one common cause of spinal canal narrowing. Other conditions such as infection, tumor, inflammation, or blood supply issues are other reasons myelography might be performed. Image guidance is commonly used to perform these procedures.

In myelography, a radiographic study using fluoroscopy is performed on the spinal cord and nerve root branches when a lesion is suspected. The procedure is performed by placing a thin needle into the spinal canal into the space that contains the spinal nerves and spinal cord. The injection site is determined and marked on the sterilized surface, and local anesthesia is injected. After the anesthetic is injected, the spinal needle is placed into the skin and using the fluoroscope for guidance, the needle is directed into the spinal canal. A nonionic, water-soluble, radiopaque contrast material is used to enhance visibility and is instilled through a lumbar area puncture into the subarachnoid space. The radiologist takes a series of pictures by sending an x-ray beam through the body, using fluoroscopy to view the enhanced structure on a television camera. The patient is angled from an erect position through a recumbent position with the body tilted so as to maintain feet higher than the head to help the flow of contrast into the study area.

62302	**Myelography via lumbar injection, including radiological supervision and interpretation; cervical**
62303	**thoracic**
62304	**lumbosacral**
62305	**2 or more regions (eg, lumbar/thoracic, cervical/thoracic, lumbar/cervical, lumbar/thoracic/cervical)**
72240	**Myelography, cervical, radiological supervision and interpretation**
72255	**Myelography, thoracic, radiological supervision and interpretation**
72265	**Myelography, lumbosacral, radiological supervision and interpretation**
72270	**Myelography, 2 or more regions (eg, lumbar/thoracic, cervical/thoracic, lumbar/cervical, lumbar/thoracic/cervical), radiological supervision and interpretation**

Coding Tips

1. Codes 62302–62305 are comprehensive procedure codes. They include the surgical and radiologic portions. These codes are used when the same physician performs both components of the procedure.
2. Do not also report 72240–72270 with 62302–62305.
3. Do not also report 62284 with 62302–62305. The injection procedure is included in these codes.
4. Conscious sedation, if used, is not included and may be reported separately.
5. Codes 72240–72270 are radiology component codes. These codes are used to report only the radiology portion when two different physician specialties are involved in performing the procedure. For example, if a neurosurgeon performs the injection component and a radiologist operates the imaging equipment and interprets the images, the neurosurgeon reports the applicable injection code, and the radiologist reports a code from 72240–72270. If the radiologist performs the injection and the imaging supervision, the applicable code from 62302–62305 is reported.
6. Hospitals should report the comprehensive procedure code, 62302–62305.
7. Hospitals should report contrast media and supplies separately.
8. If CT is used for myelography imaging, report the applicable code from 62301–62305 and the applicable CT procedure code.

Procedure	Injection Only (Physician)	Imaging Only (Physician)	Complete Procedure by Same Physician	Complete Procedure (Facility)
Cervical myelogram by C1-C2 or posterior fossa injection	61055	72240	62302	62302
Thoracic myelogram by C1-C2 or posterior fossa injection	61055	72255	62303	62303
Lumbar myelogram by C1-C2 or posterior fossa injection	61055	72265	62304	62304
Myelogram of 2 or more regions by C1-C2 or posterior fossa injection	61055	72270	62305	62305
Cervical myelogram by lumbar injection	62284	72240	62302	62302
Thoracic myelogram by lumbar injection	62284	72255	62303	62303
Lumbar myelogram by lumbar injection	62284	72265	62304	62304
Myelogram of 2 or more regions by lumbar injection	62284	72270	62305	62305

Facility HCPCS Coding

Some applicable codes may include, but are not limited to:

Q9965   LOCM, 100-199mg/ml iodine concentration, per ml

Q9966   LOCM, 200-299mg/ml iodine concentration, per ml

Q9967   LOCM, 300-399mg/ml iodine concentration, per ml

Q9958   HOCM, up to 149mg/ml iodine concentration, per ml

Q9959   HOCM, 150-199mg/ml iodine concentration, per ml

Q9960   HOCM, 200-249mg/ml iodine concentration, per ml

Q9961   HOCM, 250-299mg/ml iodine concentration, per ml

Q9962   HOCM, 300-349mg/ml iodine concentration, per ml

Q9963   HOCM, 350-399mg/ml iodine concentration, per ml

Q9964   HOCM 400 or greater mg/ml iodine concentration, per ml

ICD-10-CM Coding

The application of these codes is too broad to adequately present ICD-10-CM diagnosis code links here. Refer to the current ICD-10-CM book.

CCI Edits

62302   00600, 01935-01936, 0213T, 0216T, 0228T, 0230T, 12001-12007, 12011-12057, 13100-13133, 13151-13153, 36000, 36400-36410, 36420-36430, 36440, 36591-36592, 36600, 36640, 43752, 51701-51703, 61055, 62270-62273, 62282-62284, 62304, 62320-62327, 64400-64410, 64413-64435, 64445-64450, 64461-64463, 64479-64530, 69990, 72240, 72255, 72265, 72270, 76000-76001, 77002-77003, 92012-92014, 92585, 93000-93010, 93040-93042, 93318, 93355, 94002, 94200, 94250, 94680-94690, 94770, 95812-95816, 95819, 95822, 95829, 95860-95870, 95907-95913, 95925-95933, 95937-95941, 95955, 96360-96368, 96372, 96374-96377, 99155-99157, 99211-99223, 99231-99255, 99291-99292, 99304-99310, 99315-99316, 99334-99337, 99347-99350, 99374-99375, 99377-99378, G0453, G0471

62303   00620, 01935-01936, 0213T, 0216T, 0228T, 0230T, 12001-12007, 12011-12057, 13100-13133, 13151-13153, 36000, 36400-36410, 36420-36430, 36440, 36591-36592, 36600, 36640, 43752, 51701-51703, 61055, 62270-62273, 62282-62284, 62302, 62304, 62320-62327, 64400-64410, 64413-64435, 64445-64450, 64461-64463, 64479-64530, 69990, 72240, 72255, 72265, 72270, 76000-76001, 77002-77003, 92012-92014, 92585, 93000-93010, 93040-93042, 93318, 93355, 94002, 94200, 94250, 94680-94690, 94770, 95812-95816, 95819, 95822, 95829, 95860-95870, 95907-95913, 95925-95933, 95937-95941, 95955, 96360-96368, 96372, 96374-96377, 99155-99157, 99211-99223, 99231-99255, 99291-99292, 99304-99310, 99315-99316, 99334-99337, 99347-99350, 99374-99375, 99377-99378, G0453, G0471

62304   00630, 01935-01936, 0213T, 0216T, 0228T, 0230T, 12001-12007, 12011-12057, 13100-13133, 13151-13153, 36000, 36400-36410, 36420-36430, 36440, 36591-36592, 36600, 36640, 43752, 51701-51703, 61055, 62270-62273, 62282-62284, 62320-62327, 64400-64410, 64413-64435, 64445-64450, 64461-64463, 64479-64530, 69990, 72240, 72255, 72265, 72270, 76000-76001, 77002-77003, 92012-92014, 92585, 93000-93010, 93040-93042, 93318, 93355, 94002, 94200, 94250, 94680-94690, 94770, 95812-95816, 95819, 95822, 95829, 95860-95870, 95907-95913, 95925-95933, 95937-95941, 95955, 96360-96368, 96372, 96374-96377, 99155-99157, 99211-99223, 99231-99255, 99291-99292, 99304-99310, 99315-99316, 99334-99337, 99347-99350, 99374-99375, 99377-99378, G0453, G0471

62305   00600, 00620, 00630, 01935-01936, 0213T, 0216T, 0228T, 0230T, 12001-12007, 12011-12057, 13100-13133, 13151-13153, 36000, 36400-36410, 36420-36430, 36440, 36591-36592, 36600, 36640, 43752, 51701-51703, 61055, 62270-62273, 62282-62284, 62302-62304, 62320-62327, 64400-64410, 64413-64435, 64445-64450, 64461-64463, 64479-64530, 69990, 72240, 72255, 72265, 72270, 76000-76001, 77002-77003, 92012-92014, 92585, 93000-93010, 93040-93042, 93318, 93355, 94002, 94200, 94250, 94680-94690, 94770, 95812-95816, 95819, 95822, 95829, 95860-95870, 95907-95913, 95925-95933, 95937-95941, 95955, 96360-96368, 96372, 96374-96377, 99155-99157, 99211-99223, 99231-99255, 99291-99292, 99304-99310, 99315-99316, 99334-99337, 99347-99350, 99374-99375, 99377-99378, G0453, G0471

72240   00600, 01935-01936, 20551-20553, 36591-36592, 62284, 72255, 72265, 76000-76001, 77001-77003, 99446-99449

72255   00620, 00625-00626, 01935-01936, 36591-36592, 62284, 72265, 76000-76001, 77001-77003, 99446-99449

72265   00630, 01935-01936, 20551-20553, 36591-36592, 62284, 76000-76001, 77001-77003, 99446-99449

72270   00600, 00620, 00625-00626, 00630, 01935-01936, 36591-36592, 62284, 72240, 72255, 72265, 76000-76001, 77001-77003, 99446-99449

Case Example

The patient was placed prone on the imaging table and appropriately prepped and draped. The area **over L3–L4 interspace** was locally anesthetized. The 18-gauge **spinal needle was advanced** to the **subarachnoid space**. Spinal fluid was extracted and sent to the laboratory for evaluation. We then **injected 12cc of Omnipaque** 300. The needle was removed. The table was angled to steep Trendelenburg level, and **images were taken of the cervical region** of the spine. The patient was then slowly tilted back to horizontal and then to reverse Trendelenburg position to obtain **images of the lumbar spine region**. The radiologist performed the entire procedure.

CPT/HCPCS Codes Reported:
62305

Chapter 9: Gastrointestinal Tract Interventions

Percutaneous Cholecystostomy

47490   **Cholecystostomy, percutaneous, complete procedure, including imaging guidance, catheter placement, cholecystogram when performed, and radiological supervision and interpretation**
The physician inserts a tube into the gallbladder to allow drainage through the skin. The physician uses ultrasound guidance to place a subcostal drainage tube into the gallbladder and places a needle between the ribs into the gallbladder. The needle position is checked by aspiration. A guidewire is passed through the needle. A catheter is passed over the wire into the biliary tree. The wire is removed and the tube is left in place. This code reports the complete procedure and includes placement of the catheter under image guidance, a cholecystogram if performed, and radiological supervision and interpretation.

Coding Tips

1. This code reports a comprehensive procedure. Do not separately report radiological supervision and interpretation .
2. Image guidance is included. Do not separately report 75989, 76942, 77002, 77012, or 77021.
3. Diagnostic cholangiography is included.
4. See 47480 when the procedure is performed via an open incision.
5. Report applicable HCPCS Level II codes for devices and contrast media used. Refer to the HCPCS section for possible codes.
6. Hospitals are requested to continue reporting LOCM separately with HCPCS codes Q9965–Q9967. Report contrast media by milliliter

Percutaneous Cholecystostomy

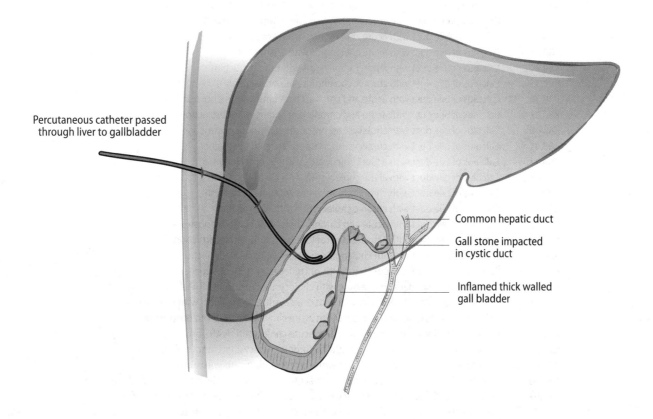

Percutaneous catheter passed through liver to gallbladder

Common hepatic duct

Gall stone impacted in cystic duct

Inflamed thick walled gall bladder

Facility HCPCS Coding

Some applicable codes may include, but are not limited to:

C1729	Catheter, drainage
C1769	Guidewire
Q9965	LOCM, 100-199 mg/ml iodine concentration, per ml
Q9966	LOCM, 200-299 mg/ml iodine concentration, per ml
Q9967	LOCM, 300-399 mg/ml iodine concentration, per ml

ICD-10-CM Coding

C23	Malignant neoplasm of gallbladder
C24.Ø	Malignant neoplasm of extrahepatic bile duct
C24.1	Malignant neoplasm of ampulla of Vater
C24.8	Malignant neoplasm of overlapping sites of biliary tract
C24.9	Malignant neoplasm of biliary tract, unspecified
K8Ø.ØØ	Calculus of gallbladder with acute cholecystitis without obstruction
K8Ø.Ø1	Calculus of gallbladder with acute cholecystitis with obstruction
K8Ø.1Ø	Calculus of gallbladder with chronic cholecystitis without obstruction
K8Ø.11	Calculus of gallbladder with chronic cholecystitis with obstruction
K8Ø.12	Calculus of gallbladder with acute and chronic cholecystitis without obstruction
K8Ø.13	Calculus of gallbladder with acute and chronic cholecystitis with obstruction
K8Ø.18	Calculus of gallbladder with other cholecystitis without obstruction
K8Ø.19	Calculus of gallbladder with other cholecystitis with obstruction
K8Ø.2Ø	Calculus of gallbladder without cholecystitis without obstruction
K8Ø.21	Calculus of gallbladder without cholecystitis with obstruction
K8Ø.3Ø	Calculus of bile duct with cholangitis, unspecified, without obstruction
K8Ø.31	Calculus of bile duct with cholangitis, unspecified, with obstruction
K8Ø.32	Calculus of bile duct with acute cholangitis without obstruction
K8Ø.33	Calculus of bile duct with acute cholangitis with obstruction
K8Ø.34	Calculus of bile duct with chronic cholangitis without obstruction
K8Ø.35	Calculus of bile duct with chronic cholangitis with obstruction
K8Ø.36	Calculus of bile duct with acute and chronic cholangitis without obstruction
K8Ø.37	Calculus of bile duct with acute and chronic cholangitis with obstruction
K8Ø.4Ø	Calculus of bile duct with cholecystitis, unspecified, without obstruction
K8Ø.41	Calculus of bile duct with cholecystitis, unspecified, with obstruction
K8Ø.42	Calculus of bile duct with acute cholecystitis without obstruction
K8Ø.43	Calculus of bile duct with acute cholecystitis with obstruction
K8Ø.44	Calculus of bile duct with chronic cholecystitis without obstruction
K8Ø.45	Calculus of bile duct with chronic cholecystitis with obstruction
K8Ø.46	Calculus of bile duct with acute and chronic cholecystitis without obstruction
K8Ø.47	Calculus of bile duct with acute and chronic cholecystitis with obstruction
K8Ø.5Ø	Calculus of bile duct without cholangitis or cholecystitis without obstruction
K8Ø.51	Calculus of bile duct without cholangitis or cholecystitis with obstruction
K8Ø.6Ø	Calculus of gallbladder and bile duct with cholecystitis, unspecified, without obstruction
K8Ø.61	Calculus of gallbladder and bile duct with cholecystitis, unspecified, with obstruction
K8Ø.62	Calculus of gallbladder and bile duct with acute cholecystitis without obstruction
K8Ø.63	Calculus of gallbladder and bile duct with acute cholecystitis with obstruction
K8Ø.64	Calculus of gallbladder and bile duct with chronic cholecystitis without obstruction
K8Ø.65	Calculus of gallbladder and bile duct with chronic cholecystitis with obstruction
K8Ø.66	Calculus of gallbladder and bile duct with acute and chronic cholecystitis without obstruction
K8Ø.67	Calculus of gallbladder and bile duct with acute and chronic cholecystitis with obstruction
K8Ø.7Ø	Calculus of gallbladder and bile duct without cholecystitis without obstruction
K8Ø.71	Calculus of gallbladder and bile duct without cholecystitis with obstruction
K8Ø.8Ø	Other cholelithiasis without obstruction
K8Ø.81	Other cholelithiasis with obstruction

K81.0	Acute cholecystitis
K81.1	Chronic cholecystitis
K81.2	Acute cholecystitis with chronic cholecystitis
K81.9	Cholecystitis, unspecified
K82.0	Obstruction of gallbladder
K82.1	Hydrops of gallbladder
K82.2	Perforation of gallbladder
K82.3	Fistula of gallbladder
K82.4	Cholesterolosis of gallbladder
K82.8	Other specified diseases of gallbladder
K82.9	Disease of gallbladder, unspecified
K83.0	Cholangitis
K83.1	Obstruction of bile duct
K83.2	Perforation of bile duct
K83.3	Fistula of bile duct
K83.4	Spasm of sphincter of Oddi
K83.5	Biliary cyst
K83.8	Other specified diseases of biliary tract
K83.9	Disease of biliary tract, unspecified
K87	Disorders of gallbladder, biliary tract and pancreas in diseases classified elsewhere

CCI Edits

47490 0213T, 0216T, 0228T, 0230T, 12001-12007, 12011-12057, 13100-13133, 13151-13153, 36000, 36400-36410, 36420-36430, 36440, 36591-36592, 36600, 36640, 43752, 47531-47534, 49405, 51701-51703, 62320-62327, 64400-64410, 64413-64435, 64445-64450, 64461-64463, 64479-64530, 69990, 74300-74301, 75989, 76000-76001, 76380, 76942, 76970, 76998, 77001-77002, 77012, 77021, 92012-92014, 93000-93010, 93040-93042, 93318, 93355, 94002, 94200, 94250, 94680-94690, 94770, 95812-95816, 95819, 95822, 95829, 95955, 96360-96368, 96372, 96374-96377, 99155-99157, 99211-99223, 99231-99255, 99291-99292, 99304-99310, 99315-99316, 99334-99337, 99347-99350, 99374-99375, 99377-99378, 99446-99449, 99495-99496, G0463, G0471

Case Example

Indication:
Acute cholecystitis

Procedure:
The patient was placed on the imaging table and sterilely prepped and draped. Using ultrasound guidance, a 19-gauge needle was **percutaneously** inserted and directed toward the gallbladder. The **gallbladder was punctured**. Position was confirmed when bile was aspirated. A 0.035 guidewire was inserted and placed in the gallbladder. The needle was exchanged for an 8-French dilator. The dilator was directed over the wire and exchanged for a 9-French **drainage catheter**. The **catheter was inserted** over the wire and placed within the gallbladder. The wire was retracted forming the pigtail within the gallbladder. Contrast injection **confirmed placement within the gallbladder**. The catheter was **connected to a drainage bag** and the patient returned to her room.

CPT/HCPCS Codes Reported:
47490

Other HCPCS Codes Reported:
C1729, C1769

Percutaneous Cholangiography

47531   **Injection procedure for cholangiography, percutaneous, complete diagnostic procedure including image guidance (eg, ultrasound and/or fluoroscopy) and all associated radiological supervision and interpretation; initial access**
Using imaging guidance, the physician injects contrast media into an existing catheter within the biliary system. Images are taken.

47532   **new access (eg, percutaneous transhepatic cholangiogram)**
Using imaging guidance, the physician inserts a needle between the ribs into the lumen of the common bile duct and checks positioning by aspiration. Contrast media is injected and images are taken. The needle is removed or a catheter is inserted and left to drain.

Coding Tips

1. Report 47531 when an existing catheter is present and only contrast injection is performed.
2. Report 47532 when a new access is created into the biliary system as in percutaneous transhepatic cholangiogram.
3. Radiologic supervision and interpretation is included—these are comprehensive codes.
4. Do not additionally report 47490 or 47533–47541 unless these procedures are performed through a separate access.
5. Code 47532 includes placing a needle and/or catheter into the biliary system.
6. Conscious sedation is not included in these codes. Separately report 99151–99157 per payer policy and coding guidelines. Hospitals may choose to include the costs associated with the service as part of the procedure rather than reporting them separately.

Facility HCPCS Coding

Some applicable codes may include but are not limited to:

Q9965   LOCM, 100-199 mg/ml iodine concentration, per ml

Q9966   LOCM, 200-299 mg/ml iodine concentration, per ml

Q9967   LOCM, 300-399 mg/ml iodine concentration, per ml

C1729   Catheter, drainage

C1769   Guidewire

Percutaneous Cholangiography

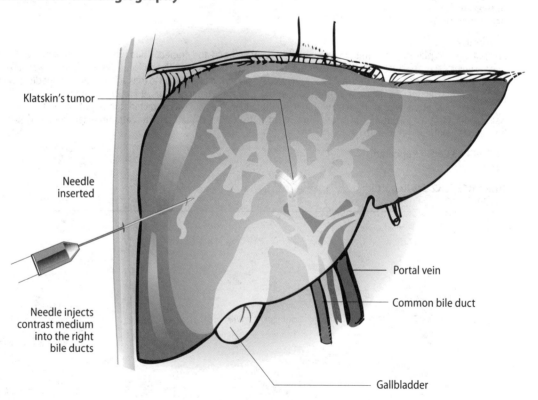

Klatskin's tumor

Needle inserted

Needle injects contrast medium into the right bile ducts

Portal vein

Common bile duct

Gallbladder

ICD-10-CM Coding

C22.0	Liver cell carcinoma
C22.1	Intrahepatic bile duct carcinoma
C22.2	Hepatoblastoma
C22.3	Angiosarcoma of liver
C22.4	Other sarcomas of liver
C22.7	Other specified carcinomas of liver
C22.8	Malignant neoplasm of liver, primary, unspecified as to type
C22.9	Malignant neoplasm of liver, not specified as primary or secondary
C23	Malignant neoplasm of gallbladder
C24.0	Malignant neoplasm of extrahepatic bile duct
C24.1	Malignant neoplasm of ampulla of Vater
C24.8	Malignant neoplasm of overlapping sites of biliary tract
C24.9	Malignant neoplasm of biliary tract, unspecified
C25.3	Malignant neoplasm of pancreatic duct
C25.9	Malignant neoplasm of pancreas, unspecified
D01.5	Carcinoma in situ of liver, gallbladder and bile ducts
D01.7	Carcinoma in situ of other specified digestive organs
D01.9	Carcinoma in situ of digestive organ, unspecified
D13.4	Benign neoplasm of liver
D13.5	Benign neoplasm of extrahepatic bile ducts
D13.6	Benign neoplasm of pancreas
D13.9	Benign neoplasm of ill-defined sites within the digestive system
D37.6	Neoplasm of uncertain behavior of liver, gallbladder and bile ducts
K74.3	Primary biliary cirrhosis
K74.4	Secondary biliary cirrhosis
K74.5	Biliary cirrhosis, unspecified
K80.00	Calculus of gallbladder with acute cholecystitis without obstruction
K80.01	Calculus of gallbladder with acute cholecystitis with obstruction
K80.10	Calculus of gallbladder with chronic cholecystitis without obstruction
K80.11	Calculus of gallbladder with chronic cholecystitis with obstruction
K80.12	Calculus of gallbladder with acute and chronic cholecystitis without obstruction
K80.13	Calculus of gallbladder with acute and chronic cholecystitis with obstruction
K80.18	Calculus of gallbladder with other cholecystitis without obstruction
K80.19	Calculus of gallbladder with other cholecystitis with obstruction
K80.20	Calculus of gallbladder without cholecystitis without obstruction
K80.21	Calculus of gallbladder without cholecystitis with obstruction
K80.30	Calculus of bile duct with cholangitis, unspecified, without obstruction
K80.31	Calculus of bile duct with cholangitis, unspecified, with obstruction
K80.32	Calculus of bile duct with acute cholangitis without obstruction
K80.33	Calculus of bile duct with acute cholangitis with obstruction
K80.34	Calculus of bile duct with chronic cholangitis without obstruction
K80.35	Calculus of bile duct with chronic cholangitis with obstruction
K80.36	Calculus of bile duct with acute and chronic cholangitis without obstruction
K80.37	Calculus of bile duct with acute and chronic cholangitis with obstruction
K80.40	Calculus of bile duct with cholecystitis, unspecified, without obstruction
K80.41	Calculus of bile duct with cholecystitis, unspecified, with obstruction
K80.42	Calculus of bile duct with acute cholecystitis without obstruction
K80.43	Calculus of bile duct with acute cholecystitis with obstruction
K80.44	Calculus of bile duct with chronic cholecystitis without obstruction
K80.45	Calculus of bile duct with chronic cholecystitis with obstruction
K80.46	Calculus of bile duct with acute and chronic cholecystitis without obstruction
K80.47	Calculus of bile duct with acute and chronic cholecystitis with obstruction
K80.50	Calculus of bile duct without cholangitis or cholecystitis without obstruction
K80.51	Calculus of bile duct without cholangitis or cholecystitis with obstruction

K80.60	Calculus of gallbladder and bile duct with cholecystitis, unspecified, without obstruction
K80.61	Calculus of gallbladder and bile duct with cholecystitis, unspecified, with obstruction
K80.62	Calculus of gallbladder and bile duct with acute cholecystitis without obstruction
K80.63	Calculus of gallbladder and bile duct with acute cholecystitis with obstruction
K80.64	Calculus of gallbladder and bile duct with chronic cholecystitis without obstruction
K80.65	Calculus of gallbladder and bile duct with chronic cholecystitis with obstruction
K80.66	Calculus of gallbladder and bile duct with acute and chronic cholecystitis without obstruction
K80.67	Calculus of gallbladder and bile duct with acute and chronic cholecystitis with obstruction
K80.70	Calculus of gallbladder and bile duct without cholecystitis without obstruction
K80.71	Calculus of gallbladder and bile duct without cholecystitis with obstruction
K80.80	Other cholelithiasis without obstruction
K80.81	Other cholelithiasis with obstruction
K81.0	Acute cholecystitis
K81.1	Chronic cholecystitis
K81.2	Acute cholecystitis with chronic cholecystitis
K81.9	Cholecystitis, unspecified
K82.0	Obstruction of gallbladder
K82.1	Hydrops of gallbladder
K82.2	Perforation of gallbladder
K82.3	Fistula of gallbladder
K82.4	Cholesterolosis of gallbladder
K82.8	Other specified diseases of gallbladder
K82.9	Disease of gallbladder, unspecified
K83.0	Cholangitis
K83.1	Obstruction of bile duct
K83.2	Perforation of bile duct
K83.3	Fistula of bile duct
K83.4	Spasm of sphincter of Oddi
K83.5	Biliary cyst
K83.8	Other specified diseases of biliary tract
K83.9	Disease of biliary tract, unspecified
K85.1	Biliary acute pancreatitis
K86.0	Alcohol-induced chronic pancreatitis
K86.1	Other chronic pancreatitis
K86.2	Cyst of pancreas
K86.3	Pseudocyst of pancreas
K86.81	Exocrine pancreatic insufficiency
K86.89	Other specified diseases of pancreas
K86.9	Disease of pancreas, unspecified
K87	Disorders of gallbladder, biliary tract and pancreas in diseases classified elsewhere
K91.5	Postcholecystectomy syndrome
Q44.0	Agenesis, aplasia and hypoplasia of gallbladder
Q44.1	Other congenital malformations of gallbladder
Q44.2	Atresia of bile ducts
Q44.3	Congenital stenosis and stricture of bile ducts
Q44.4	Choledochal cyst
Q44.5	Other congenital malformations of bile ducts
R17	Unspecified jaundice
R74.8	Abnormal levels of other serum enzymes
R94.5	Abnormal results of liver function studies

CCI Edits

47531   0213T, 0216T, 0228T, 0230T, 12001-12007, 12011-12057, 13100-13133, 13151-13153, 36000, 36400-36410, 36420-36430, 36440, 36591-36592, 36600, 36640, 43752, 47544, 51701-51703, 62320-62327, 64400-64410, 64413-64435, 64445-64450, 64461-64463, 64479-64530, 69990, 76000-76001, 76380, 76942, 76970, 76998, 77001-77002, 77012, 77021, 92012-92014, 93000-93010, 93040-93042, 93318, 93355, 94002, 94200, 94250, 94680-94690, 94770, 95812-95816, 95819, 95822, 95829, 95955, 96360-96368, 96372, 96374-96377, 99155-99157, 99211-99223, 99231-99255, 99291-99292, 99304-99310, 99315-99316, 99334-99337, 99347-99350, 99374-99375, 99377-99378, 99446-99449, 99495-99496, G0463, G0471, J0670, J2001

47532   0213T, 0216T, 0228T, 0230T, 12001-12007, 12011-12057, 13100-13133, 13151-13153, 36000, 36400-36410, 36420-36430, 36440, 36591-36592, 36600, 36640, 43752, 47544, 51701-51703, 62320-62327, 64400-64410, 64413-64435, 64445-64450, 64461-64463, 64479-64530, 69990, 76000-76001, 76380, 76942, 76970, 76998, 77001-77002, 77012, 77021, 92012-92014, 93000-93010, 93040-93042, 93318, 93355, 94002, 94200, 94250, 94680-94690, 94770, 95812-95816, 95819, 95822, 95829, 95955, 96360-96368, 96372, 96374-96377, 99155-99157, 99211-99223, 99231-99255, 99291-99292, 99304-99310, 99315-99316, 99334-99337, 99347-99350, 99374-99375, 99377-99378, 99446-99449, 99495-99496, G0463, G0471, J0670, J2001

Case Example

Procedure:

After the right flank was prepped and draped, local anesthetic was applied. Under fluoroscopy guidance a 21-gauge Chiba **needle is inserted** and **guided to the common bile duct**. Placement was confirmed with aspiration of bile. **Contrast was injected and images were obtained of the biliary ducts**. The cystic duct was also visualized. The **needle was withdrawn** and pressure held over the site for a few minutes. The patient left the department in satisfactory condition.

CPT/HCPCS Codes Reported:

47532

Biliary/Drainage Catheter Placement

47533   **Placement of biliary drainage catheter, percutaneous, including diagnostic cholangiography when performed, imaging guidance (eg, ultrasound and/or fluoroscopy), and all associated radiologic supervision and interpretation; external**

The physician introduces a catheter into the liver to drain fluid using ultrasound and/or fluoroscopy to guide the process. The puncture site on the right side of the body is incised, the needle inserted between the ribs, advanced into the liver, and into the bile duct. Contrast medium is injected to visualize the intrahepatic bile ducts. A guidewire is inserted and advanced to the point of obstruction through an optimal duct permitting access and drainage. A catheter is threaded over the guidewire and dilators may be used to enlarge the opening and the tract from the skin to the bile duct. The drainage catheter is inserted and positioned above the point of the obstruction and secured to the skin. All of the bile drains out of the body through the catheter and into a collection bag. Occasionally, the use of two separate catheters is necessary to drain the right and left biliary duct systems.

47534   **internal-external**

The physician introduces a catheter into the liver to drain fluid internally and externally, usually on patients with inoperable bile duct obstruction. The procedure is the same as in the external procedure except that a drainage catheter is inserted and positioned so that openings for drainage are above and below the obstruction and secured in place. This allows bile to flow to an external drainage system as well as into the duodenum (internal).

Coding Tips

1. Diagnostic cholangiography, imaging guidance, and radiologic supervision and interpretation are included.
2. Catheter or stent placement is included.
3. Catheter exchange is included.
4. Catheter removal is included.
5. Access and drainage catheter manipulations are included.
6. Report 47533 or 47534 once for each catheter or stent placed (multi-lobes or multi-segments).
7. Do not report 47540 with these codes for the same ductal system.
8. Codes 47542, 47543, and 47544 may be separately reported when applicable.
9. Conscious sedation is not included in these codes. Separately report 99151–99157 per payer policy and coding guidelines. Hospitals may choose to include the costs associated with the service as part of the procedure rather than reporting them separately.
10. Report applicable HCPCS Level II codes for devices and contrast media used. Refer to the HCPCS section for possible codes.
11. Hospitals should separately report contrast media with HCPCS codes Q9965–Q9967. Report contrast media by milliliter.

Facility HCPCS Coding

Some applicable codes may include but are not limited to:

C1729	Catheter, drainage
C1769	Guidewire
C2617	Stent, non-coronary, temporary, without delivery system
Q9965	LOCM, 100-199 mg/ml iodine concentration, per ml
Q9966	LOCM, 200-299 mg/ml iodine concentration, per ml
Q9967	LOCM, 300-399 mg/ml iodine concentration, per ml

Biliary Drainage Catheter

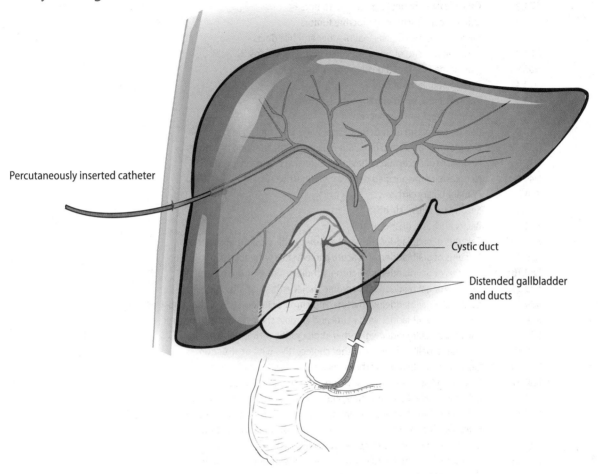

Percutaneously inserted catheter

Cystic duct

Distended gallbladder and ducts

ICD-10-CM Coding

C22.Ø	Liver cell carcinoma
C22.1	Intrahepatic bile duct carcinoma
C22.2	Hepatoblastoma
C22.3	Angiosarcoma of liver
C22.4	Other sarcomas of liver
C22.7	Other specified carcinomas of liver
C22.8	Malignant neoplasm of liver, primary, unspecified as to type
C22.9	Malignant neoplasm of liver, not specified as primary or secondary
C23	Malignant neoplasm of gallbladder
C24.Ø	Malignant neoplasm of extrahepatic bile duct
C24.1	Malignant neoplasm of ampulla of Vater
C24.8	Malignant neoplasm of overlapping sites of biliary tract
C24.9	Malignant neoplasm of biliary tract, unspecified
C25.Ø	Malignant neoplasm of head of pancreas
C25.1	Malignant neoplasm of body of pancreas
C25.2	Malignant neoplasm of tail of pancreas
C25.3	Malignant neoplasm of pancreatic duct
C25.4	Malignant neoplasm of endocrine pancreas
C25.7	Malignant neoplasm of other parts of pancreas
C25.8	Malignant neoplasm of overlapping sites of pancreas
C25.9	Malignant neoplasm of pancreas, unspecified
C78.7	Secondary malignant neoplasm of liver and intrahepatic bile duct
C78.89	Secondary malignant neoplasm of other digestive organs

C7A.1	Malignant poorly differentiated neuroendocrine tumors
C7A.8	Other malignant neuroendocrine tumors
C7B.8	Other secondary neuroendocrine tumors
D01.5	Carcinoma in situ of liver, gallbladder and bile ducts
D01.7	Carcinoma in situ of other specified digestive organs
D01.9	Carcinoma in situ of digestive organ, unspecified
D13.4	Benign neoplasm of liver
D13.5	Benign neoplasm of extrahepatic bile ducts
D13.6	Benign neoplasm of pancreas
D13.9	Benign neoplasm of ill-defined sites within the digestive system
D37.6	Neoplasm of uncertain behavior of liver, gallbladder and bile ducts
D37.9	Neoplasm of uncertain behavior of digestive organ, unspecified
D49.0	Neoplasm of unspecified behavior of digestive system
K74.3	Primary biliary cirrhosis
K74.4	Secondary biliary cirrhosis
K74.5	Biliary cirrhosis, unspecified
K80.00	Calculus of gallbladder with acute cholecystitis without obstruction
K80.01	Calculus of gallbladder with acute cholecystitis with obstruction
K80.10	Calculus of gallbladder with chronic cholecystitis without obstruction
K80.11	Calculus of gallbladder with chronic cholecystitis with obstruction
K80.12	Calculus of gallbladder with acute and chronic cholecystitis without obstruction
K80.13	Calculus of gallbladder with acute and chronic cholecystitis with obstruction
K80.18	Calculus of gallbladder with other cholecystitis without obstruction
K80.19	Calculus of gallbladder with other cholecystitis with obstruction
K80.20	Calculus of gallbladder without cholecystitis without obstruction
K80.21	Calculus of gallbladder without cholecystitis with obstruction
K80.30	Calculus of bile duct with cholangitis, unspecified, without obstruction
K80.31	Calculus of bile duct with cholangitis, unspecified, with obstruction
K80.32	Calculus of bile duct with acute cholangitis without obstruction
K80.33	Calculus of bile duct with acute cholangitis with obstruction
K80.34	Calculus of bile duct with chronic cholangitis without obstruction
K80.35	Calculus of bile duct with chronic cholangitis with obstruction
K80.36	Calculus of bile duct with acute and chronic cholangitis without obstruction
K80.37	Calculus of bile duct with acute and chronic cholangitis with obstruction
K80.40	Calculus of bile duct with cholecystitis, unspecified, without obstruction
K80.41	Calculus of bile duct with cholecystitis, unspecified, with obstruction
K80.42	Calculus of bile duct with acute cholecystitis without obstruction
K80.43	Calculus of bile duct with acute cholecystitis with obstruction
K80.44	Calculus of bile duct with chronic cholecystitis without obstruction
K80.45	Calculus of bile duct with chronic cholecystitis with obstruction
K80.46	Calculus of bile duct with acute and chronic cholecystitis without obstruction
K80.47	Calculus of bile duct with acute and chronic cholecystitis with obstruction
K80.50	Calculus of bile duct without cholangitis or cholecystitis without obstruction
K80.51	Calculus of bile duct without cholangitis or cholecystitis with obstruction
K80.60	Calculus of gallbladder and bile duct with cholecystitis, unspecified, without obstruction
K80.61	Calculus of gallbladder and bile duct with cholecystitis, unspecified, with obstruction
K80.62	Calculus of gallbladder and bile duct with acute cholecystitis without obstruction
K80.63	Calculus of gallbladder and bile duct with acute cholecystitis with obstruction
K80.64	Calculus of gallbladder and bile duct with chronic cholecystitis without obstruction
K80.65	Calculus of gallbladder and bile duct with chronic cholecystitis with obstruction
K80.66	Calculus of gallbladder and bile duct with acute and chronic cholecystitis without obstruction
K80.67	Calculus of gallbladder and bile duct with acute and chronic cholecystitis with obstruction
K80.70	Calculus of gallbladder and bile duct without cholecystitis without obstruction
K80.71	Calculus of gallbladder and bile duct without cholecystitis with obstruction
K80.80	Other cholelithiasis without obstruction
K80.81	Other cholelithiasis with obstruction

K81.0	Acute cholecystitis
K81.1	Chronic cholecystitis
K81.2	Acute cholecystitis with chronic cholecystitis
K81.9	Cholecystitis, unspecified
K82.0	Obstruction of gallbladder
K82.1	Hydrops of gallbladder
K82.2	Perforation of gallbladder
K82.3	Fistula of gallbladder
K82.4	Cholesterolosis of gallbladder
K82.8	Other specified diseases of gallbladder
K82.9	Disease of gallbladder, unspecified
K83.0	Cholangitis
K83.1	Obstruction of bile duct
K83.2	Perforation of bile duct
K83.3	Fistula of bile duct
K83.4	Spasm of sphincter of Oddi
K83.5	Biliary cyst
K83.8	Other specified diseases of biliary tract
K83.9	`Disease of biliary tract, unspecified
K85.1	Biliary acute pancreatitis
K86.0	Alcohol-induced chronic pancreatitis
K86.1	Other chronic pancreatitis
K91.5	Postcholecystectomy syndrome
K91.89	Other postprocedural complications and disorders of digestive system
Q44.0	Agenesis, aplasia and hypoplasia of gallbladder
Q44.1	Other congenital malformations of gallbladder
Q44.2	Atresia of bile ducts
Q44.3	Congenital stenosis and stricture of bile ducts
Q44.4	Choledochal cyst
Q44.5	Other congenital malformations of bile ducts
R17	Unspecified jaundice
R74.8	Abnormal levels of other serum enzymes
R94.5	Abnormal results of liver function studies
T86.40	Unspecified complication of liver transplant
T86.41	Liver transplant rejection
T86.42	Liver transplant failure
T86.43	Liver transplant infection
T86.49	Other complications of liver transplant

CCI Edits

47533
0213T, 0216T, 0228T, 0230T, 12001-12007, 12011-12057, 13100-13133, 13151-13153, 36000, 36400-36410, 36420-36430, 36440, 36591-36592, 36600, 36640, 43752, 47531-47532, 47544, 51701-51703, 62320-62327, 64400-64410, 64413-64435, 64445-64450, 64461-64463, 64479-64530, 69990, 74300-74301, 76000-76001, 76380, 76942, 76970, 76998, 77001-77002, 77012, 77021, 92012-92014, 93000-93010, 93040-93042, 93318, 93355, 94002, 94200, 94250, 94680-94690, 94770, 95812-95816, 95819, 95822, 95829, 95955, 96360-96368, 96372, 96374-96377, 99155-99157, 99211-99223, 99231-99255, 99291-99292, 99304-99310, 99315-99316, 99334-99337, 99347-99350, 99374-99375, 99377-99378, 99446-99449, 99495-99496, G0463, G0471, J0670, J2001

47534
0213T, 0216T, 0228T, 0230T, 12001-12007, 12011-12057, 13100-13133, 13151-13153, 36000, 36400-36410, 36420-36430, 36440, 36591-36592, 36600, 36640, 43752, 47531-47532, 47544, 51701-51703, 62320-62327, 64400-64410, 64413-64435, 64445-64450, 64461-64463, 64479-64530, 69990, 74300-74301, 76000-76001, 76380, 76942, 76970, 76998, 77001-77002, 77012, 77021, 92012-92014, 93000-93010, 93040-93042, 93318, 93355, 94002, 94200, 94250, 94680-94690, 94770, 95812-95816, 95819, 95822, 95829, 95955, 96360-96368, 96372, 96374-96377, 99155-99157, 99211-99223, 99231-99255, 99291-99292, 99304-99310, 99315-99316, 99334-99337, 99347-99350, 99374-99375, 99377-99378, 99446-99449, 99495-99496, G0463, G0471, J0670, J2001

Case Example

History:
A 32-year-old male with tumor involvement of the common bile duct and cholangitis.

Procedure:
The left upper quadrant was sterilely prepped and draped. Local anesthesia was applied. Under ultrasound guidance a 22-gauge Chiba needle was used to **puncture the left hepatic duct**. Purulent bile was obtained. A small amount of contrast was injected, opacifying a dilated left intrahepatic duct with distal occlusion. A 0.018" wire was advanced and the needle was exchanged for a dilator. The 0.018" wire was withdrawn and a 0.035 stiff wire introduced. The dilator was exchanged for a 5-French Kumpe catheter. Together, we were able to advance the wire into the duodenum. We injected contrast to confirm placement. The Kumpe catheter was removed and replaced with the 8-French **drainage catheter**. The drainage **catheter was advanced into the duodenum**. Contrast was injected to confirm the patency of the common hepatic duct and the common bile duct. Both were patent. The **drainage catheter was secured** to the skin at the exit site using 2-0 silk sutures. A sterile dressing was applied to the site. The catheter to an external drainage bag was left.

CPT/HCPCS Codes Reported:
47533

Other HCPCS Codes Reported:
C1769, C1729

Conversion/Exchange and Removal of Biliary Stent/Drainage Catheter

47535 **Conversion of external biliary drainage catheter to internal-external biliary drainage catheter, percutaneous, including diagnostic cholangiography when performed, imaging guidance (eg, fluoroscopy) and all associated radiologic supervision and interpretation**

The physician inserts a guidewire into an existing biliary drainage catheter and removes it. He inserts a new drainage catheter over the guidewire and advances it using fluoroscopy through the bile duct into the common bile duct and into the duodenum. The catheter is left to external drainage, and a collection bag is attached. The catheter drains bile internally into the duodenum as well as externally to the collection bag.

47536 **Exchange of biliary drainage catheter (eg, external, internal-external, or conversion of internal-external to external only), percutaneous, including diagnostic cholangiography when performed, imaging guidance (eg, fluoroscopy) and all associated radiologic supervision and interpretation**

The physician inserts a guidewire into an existing biliary drainage catheter. He removes the existing catheter and replaces it over the guidewire with a new drainage catheter. The new catheter is reconnected to the external drainage bag.

47537 **Removal of biliary drainage catheter requiring fluoroscopic guidance (eg, with concurrent indwelling biliary stents), including diagnostic cholangiography when performed, imaging guidance (eg, fluoroscopy) and all associated radiologic supervision and interpretation**

The physician inserts a guidewire into an existing external biliary drainage catheter and using fluoroscopic guidance, removes the catheter and then the guidewire.

Coding Tips

1. Diagnostic cholangiography, imaging guidance, and radiologic supervision and interpretation are included.
2. Catheter or stent placement is included.
3. Catheter exchange is included.
4. Catheter removal is included.
5. Access and drainage catheter manipulations are included.
6. Report 47533 or 47534 once for each catheter conversion, exchange or removal (multi-lobes or multi-segments).
7. Codes 47542, 47543 and 47544 may be separately reported when applicable.
8. Conscious sedation is not included in these codes. Separately report 99151–99157 per payer policy and coding guidelines. Hospitals may choose to include the costs associated with the service as part of the procedure rather than reporting them separately.
9. Report applicable HCPCS Level II codes for devices and contrast media used. Refer to the HCPCS section for possible codes.
10. Hospitals should separately report contrast media with HCPCS codes Q9965–Q9967. Report contrast media by milliliter.

Facility HCPCS Coding

Some applicable codes may include but are not limited to:

C1729 Catheter, drainage
C1769 Guidewire
C2617 Stent, non-coronary, temporary, without delivery system
Q9965 LOCM, 100-199 mg/ml iodine concentration, per ml
Q9966 LOCM, 200-299 mg/ml iodine concentration, per ml
Q9967 LOCM, 300-399 mg/ml iodine concentration, per ml

ICD-10-CM Coding

C22.0 Liver cell carcinoma
C22.1 Intrahepatic bile duct carcinoma
C22.2 Hepatoblastoma
C22.3 Angiosarcoma of liver
C22.4 Other sarcomas of liver
C22.7 Other specified carcinomas of liver
C22.8 Malignant neoplasm of liver, primary, unspecified as to type
C22.9 Malignant neoplasm of liver, not specified as primary or secondary
C23 Malignant neoplasm of gallbladder
C24.0 Malignant neoplasm of extrahepatic bile duct

C24.1	Malignant neoplasm of ampulla of Vater
C24.8	Malignant neoplasm of overlapping sites of biliary tract
C24.9	Malignant neoplasm of biliary tract, unspecified
C25.0	Malignant neoplasm of head of pancreas
C25.1	Malignant neoplasm of body of pancreas
C25.2	Malignant neoplasm of tail of pancreas
C25.3	Malignant neoplasm of pancreatic duct
C25.4	Malignant neoplasm of endocrine pancreas
C25.7	Malignant neoplasm of other parts of pancreas
C25.8	Malignant neoplasm of overlapping sites of pancreas
C25.9	Malignant neoplasm of pancreas, unspecified
C78.7	Secondary malignant neoplasm of liver and intrahepatic bile duct
C78.89	Secondary malignant neoplasm of other digestive organs
C7A.1	Malignant poorly differentiated neuroendocrine tumors
C7A.8	Other malignant neuroendocrine tumors
C7B.8	Other secondary neuroendocrine tumors
D01.5	Carcinoma in situ of liver, gallbladder and bile ducts
D01.7	Carcinoma in situ of other specified digestive organs
D01.9	Carcinoma in situ of digestive organ, unspecified
D13.4	Benign neoplasm of liver
D13.5	Benign neoplasm of extrahepatic bile ducts
D13.6	Benign neoplasm of pancreas
D37.6	Neoplasm of uncertain behavior of liver, gallbladder and bile ducts
D37.9	Neoplasm of uncertain behavior of digestive organ, unspecified
D49.0	Neoplasm of unspecified behavior of digestive system
K74.3	Primary biliary cirrhosis
K74.4	Secondary biliary cirrhosis
K74.5	Biliary cirrhosis, unspecified
K80.00	Calculus of gallbladder with acute cholecystitis without obstruction
K80.01	Calculus of gallbladder with acute cholecystitis with obstruction
K80.10	Calculus of gallbladder with chronic cholecystitis without obstruction
K80.11	Calculus of gallbladder with chronic cholecystitis with obstruction
K80.12	Calculus of gallbladder with acute and chronic cholecystitis without obstruction
K80.13	Calculus of gallbladder with acute and chronic cholecystitis with obstruction
K80.18	Calculus of gallbladder with other cholecystitis without obstruction
K80.19	Calculus of gallbladder with other cholecystitis with obstruction
K80.20	Calculus of gallbladder without cholecystitis without obstruction
K80.21	Calculus of gallbladder without cholecystitis with obstruction
K80.30	Calculus of bile duct with cholangitis, unspecified, without obstruction
K80.31	Calculus of bile duct with cholangitis, unspecified, with obstruction
K80.32	Calculus of bile duct with acute cholangitis without obstruction
K80.33	Calculus of bile duct with acute cholangitis with obstruction
K80.34	Calculus of bile duct with chronic cholangitis without obstruction
K80.35	Calculus of bile duct with chronic cholangitis with obstruction
K80.36	Calculus of bile duct with acute and chronic cholangitis without obstruction
K80.37	Calculus of bile duct with acute and chronic cholangitis with obstruction
K80.40	Calculus of bile duct with cholecystitis, unspecified, without obstruction
K80.41	Calculus of bile duct with cholecystitis, unspecified, with obstruction
K80.42	Calculus of bile duct with acute cholecystitis without obstruction
K80.43	Calculus of bile duct with acute cholecystitis with obstruction
K80.44	Calculus of bile duct with chronic cholecystitis without obstruction
K80.45	Calculus of bile duct with chronic cholecystitis with obstruction
K80.46	Calculus of bile duct with acute and chronic cholecystitis without obstruction
K80.47	Calculus of bile duct with acute and chronic cholecystitis with obstruction
K80.50	Calculus of bile duct without cholangitis or cholecystitis without obstruction
K80.51	Calculus of bile duct without cholangitis or cholecystitis with obstruction

K80.60	Calculus of gallbladder and bile duct with cholecystitis, unspecified, without obstruction
K80.61	Calculus of gallbladder and bile duct with cholecystitis, unspecified, with obstruction
K80.62	Calculus of gallbladder and bile duct with acute cholecystitis without obstruction
K80.63	Calculus of gallbladder and bile duct with acute cholecystitis with obstruction
K80.64	Calculus of gallbladder and bile duct with chronic cholecystitis without obstruction
K80.65	Calculus of gallbladder and bile duct with chronic cholecystitis with obstruction
K80.66	Calculus of gallbladder and bile duct with acute and chronic cholecystitis without obstruction
K80.67	Calculus of gallbladder and bile duct with acute and chronic cholecystitis with obstruction
K80.70	Calculus of gallbladder and bile duct without cholecystitis without obstruction
K80.71	Calculus of gallbladder and bile duct without cholecystitis with obstruction
K80.80	Other cholelithiasis without obstruction
K80.81	Other cholelithiasis with obstruction
K81.0	Acute cholecystitis
K81.1	Chronic cholecystitis
K81.2	Acute cholecystitis with chronic cholecystitis
K81.9	Cholecystitis, unspecified
K82.0	Obstruction of gallbladder
K82.1	Hydrops of gallbladder
K82.2	Perforation of gallbladder
K82.3	Fistula of gallbladder
K82.4	Cholesterolosis of gallbladder
K82.8	Other specified diseases of gallbladder
K82.9	Disease of gallbladder, unspecified
K83.0	Cholangitis
K83.1	Obstruction of bile duct
K83.2	Perforation of bile duct
K83.3	Fistula of bile duct
K83.4	Spasm of sphincter of Oddi
K83.5	Biliary cyst
K83.8	Other specified diseases of biliary tract
K83.9	Disease of biliary tract, unspecified
K85.1	Biliary acute pancreatitis
K86.0	Alcohol-induced chronic pancreatitis
K86.1	Other chronic pancreatitis
K91.5	Postcholecystectomy syndrome
K91.89	Other postprocedural complications and disorders of digestive system
Q44.0	Agenesis, aplasia and hypoplasia of gallbladder
Q44.1	Other congenital malformations of gallbladder
Q44.2	Atresia of bile ducts
Q44.3	Congenital stenosis and stricture of bile ducts
Q44.4	Choledochal cyst
Q44.5	Other congenital malformations of bile ducts
R17	Unspecified jaundice
R74.8	Abnormal levels of other serum enzymes
R94.5	Abnormal results of liver function studies
T85.510A	Breakdown (mechanical) of bile duct prosthesis, initial encounter
T85.520A	Displacement of bile duct prosthesis, initial encounter
T85.590A	Other mechanical complication of bile duct prosthesis, initial encounter
T85.79XA	Infection and inflammatory reaction due to other internal prosthetic devices, implants and grafts, initial encounter
T85.818A	Embolism due to other internal prosthetic devices, implants and grafts, initial encounter
T85.828A	Fibrosis due to other internal prosthetic devices, implants and grafts, initial encounter
T85.838A	Hemorrhage due to other internal prosthetic devices, implants and grafts, initial encounter
T85.848A	Pain due to other internal prosthetic devices, implants and grafts, initial encounter
T85.858A	Stenosis due to other internal prosthetic devices, implants and grafts, initial encounter
T85.868A	Thrombosis due to other internal prosthetic devices, implants and grafts, initial encounter

T85.898A	Other specified complication of other internal prosthetic devices, implants and grafts, initial encounter
T86.40	Unspecified complication of liver transplant
T86.41	Liver transplant rejection
T86.42	Liver transplant failure
T86.43	Liver transplant infection
T86.49	Other complications of liver transplant
Z48.03	Encounter for change or removal of drains

CCI Edits

47535 0213T, 0216T, 0228T, 0230T, 12001-12007, 12011-12057, 13100-13133, 13151-13153, 36000, 36400-36410, 36420-36430, 36440, 36591-36592, 36600, 36640, 43752, 47531-47534, 47537, 47544, 49185, 49423-49424, 51701-51703, 62320-62327, 64400-64410, 64413-64435, 64445-64450, 64461-64463, 64479-64530, 69990, 74300-74301, 76000-76001, 76380, 76942, 76970, 76998, 77001-77002, 77012, 77021, 92012-92014, 93000-93010, 93040-93042, 93318, 93355, 94002, 94200, 94250, 94680-94690, 94770, 95812-95816, 95819, 95822, 95829, 95955, 96360-96368, 96372, 96374-96377, 99155-99157, 99211-99223, 99231-99255, 99291-99292, 99304-99310, 99315-99316, 99334-99337, 99347-99350, 99374-99375, 99377-99378, 99446-99449, 99495-99496, G0463, G0471, J0670, J2001

47536 0213T, 0216T, 0228T, 0230T, 12001-12007, 12011-12057, 13100-13133, 13151-13153, 36000, 36400-36410, 36420-36430, 36440, 36591-36592, 36600, 36640, 43752, 47531-47534, 47537, 47544, 49185, 49423-49424, 51701-51703, 62320-62327, 64400-64410, 64413-64435, 64445-64450, 64461-64463, 64479-64530, 69990, 74300-74301, 76000-76001, 76380, 76942, 76970, 76998, 77001-77002, 77012, 77021, 92012-92014, 93000-93010, 93040-93042, 93318, 93355, 94002, 94200, 94250, 94680-94690, 94770, 95812-95816, 95819, 95822, 95829, 95955, 96360-96368, 96372, 96374-96377, 99155-99157, 99211-99223, 99231-99255, 99291-99292, 99304-99310, 99315-99316, 99334-99337, 99347-99350, 99374-99375, 99377-99378, 99446-99449, 99495-99496, G0463, G0471, J0670, J2001

47537 0213T, 0216T, 0228T, 0230T, 11000-11006, 11042-11047, 12001-12007, 12011-12057, 13100-13133, 13151-13153, 36000, 36400-36410, 36420-36430, 36440, 36600, 36640, 43752, 47531-47532, 47544, 51701-51703, 62320-62327, 64400-64410, 64413-64435, 64445-64450, 64461-64463, 64479-64530, 69990, 74300-74301, 76000-76001, 76380, 76942, 76970, 76998, 77002, 77012, 77021, 92012-92014, 93000-93010, 93040-93042, 93318, 94002, 94200, 94250, 94680-94690, 94770, 95812-95816, 95819, 95822, 95829, 95955, 96360-96368, 96372, 96374-96377, 97597-97598, 97602, 99155-99157, 99211-99223, 99231-99255, 99291-99292, 99304-99310, 99315-99316, 99334-99337, 99347-99350, 99374-99375, 99377-99378, J0670, J2001

Case Example

Indication:
Patient presents for **exchange of his existing biliary drainage catheter**.

Procedure:
The area around the catheter was sterilely prepped and draped. A stiff guidewire was introduced under fluoroscopic guidance. The **drainage catheter was removed**. The **new catheter** was prepped and introduced over the guidewire and **placed in the common bile duct**. Contrast was injected to confirm proper placement. The **catheter was secured to the skin** with silk sutures and **connected to a drainage bag**.

CPT/HCPCS Codes Reported:
47536

Other HCPCS Codes Reported:
C1769, C1729

Biliary Stent Placement/Drainage

47538	**Placement of stent(s) into a bile duct, percutaneous, including diagnostic cholangiography, imaging guidance (eg, fluoroscopy and/or ultrasound), balloon dilation, catheter exchange(s) and catheter removal(s) when performed, and all associated radiological supervision and interpretation, each stent; existing access**
47539	**new access, without placement of separate biliary drainage catheter**
47540	**new access, with placement of separate biliary drainage catheter**

The physician inserts a thin needle through the skin and into the liver and injects contrast media in order to diagnose and treat obstructions affecting the flow of bile from the liver to the gastrointestinal (GI) tract. Once the stricture or obstruction is identified, the physician places an introducer sheath into the biliary system. Under ultrasound or fluoroscopic guidance, a stent delivery system is placed within a narrow section of the bile duct in order to keep the duct patent. Stents may be comprised of metallic mesh or plastic tubing. A balloon-tipped catheter may be required to achieve adequate expansion of the narrow duct. The stent may be a self-expandable stent (the stent opens by itself once deployed) or balloon expandable (a balloon catheter is used to expand the stent). Once the delivery device is removed, the stent stays in place and functions to keep the duct open to allow the free flow of bile.

Coding Tips

1. Diagnostic cholangiography, imaging guidance and radiologic supervision and interpretation are included.
2. Catheter or stent placement is included.
3. Catheter exchange is included.
4. Catheter removal is included.
5. Access and drainage catheter manipulations are included.
6. Report once for each catheter or stent placed.
7. Codes 47543 and 47544 may be separately reported when applicable.
8. Do not report 47542 with these codes. Balloon dilation is included.
9. Conscious sedation is not included in these codes. Separately report 99151–99157 per payer policy and coding guidelines. Hospitals may choose to include the costs associated with the service as part of the procedure rather than reporting them separately.
10. Report applicable HCPCS Level II codes for devices and contrast media used. Refer to the HCPCS section for possible codes.
11. Hospitals should separately report contrast media with HCPCS codes Q9965–Q9967. Report contrast media by milliliter.

Facility HCPCS Coding

Some applicable codes may include but are not limited to:

C1729	Catheter, drainage
C1769	Guidewire
C2617	Stent, non-coronary, temporary, without delivery system
Q9965	LOCM, 100-199 mg/ml iodine concentration, per ml
Q9966	LOCM, 200-299 mg/ml iodine concentration, per ml
Q9967	LOCM, 300-399 mg/ml iodine concentration, per ml

Biliary Stent Placement

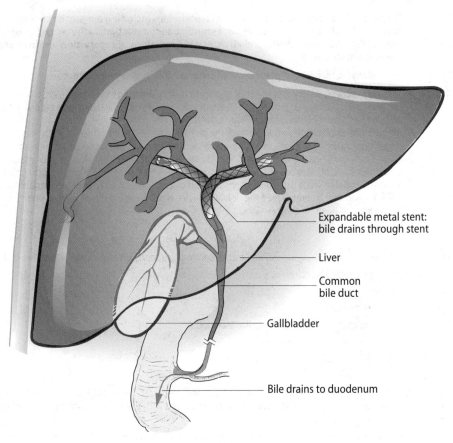

Expandable metal stent: bile drains through stent

Liver

Common bile duct

Gallbladder

Bile drains to duodenum

ICD-10-CM Coding

C22.0	Liver cell carcinoma
C22.1	Intrahepatic bile duct carcinoma
C22.2	Hepatoblastoma
C22.3	Angiosarcoma of liver
C22.4	Other sarcomas of liver
C22.7	Other specified carcinomas of liver
C22.8	Malignant neoplasm of liver, primary, unspecified as to type
C22.9	Malignant neoplasm of liver, not specified as primary or secondary
C23	Malignant neoplasm of gallbladder
C24.0	Malignant neoplasm of extrahepatic bile duct
C24.1	Malignant neoplasm of ampulla of Vater
C24.8	Malignant neoplasm of overlapping sites of biliary tract
C24.9	Malignant neoplasm of biliary tract, unspecified
C25.0	Malignant neoplasm of head of pancreas
C25.1	Malignant neoplasm of body of pancreas
C25.2	Malignant neoplasm of tail of pancreas
C25.3	Malignant neoplasm of pancreatic duct
C25.4	Malignant neoplasm of endocrine pancreas
C25.7	Malignant neoplasm of other parts of pancreas
C25.8	Malignant neoplasm of overlapping sites of pancreas
C25.9	Malignant neoplasm of pancreas, unspecified
C78.7	Secondary malignant neoplasm of liver and intrahepatic bile duct
C78.89	Secondary malignant neoplasm of other digestive organs
C7A.1	Malignant poorly differentiated neuroendocrine tumors
C7A.8	Other malignant neuroendocrine tumors

C7B.8	Other secondary neuroendocrine tumors
D01.5	Carcinoma in situ of liver, gallbladder and bile ducts
D01.7	Carcinoma in situ of other specified digestive organs
D01.9	Carcinoma in situ of digestive organ, unspecified
D13.4	Benign neoplasm of liver
D13.5	Benign neoplasm of extrahepatic bile ducts
D13.6	Benign neoplasm of pancreas
D13.9	Benign neoplasm of ill-defined sites within the digestive system
D37.6	Neoplasm of uncertain behavior of liver, gallbladder and bile ducts
D37.9	Neoplasm of uncertain behavior of digestive organ, unspecified
D49.0	Neoplasm of unspecified behavior of digestive system
K65.3	Choleperitonitis
K80.00	Calculus of gallbladder with acute cholecystitis without obstruction
K80.01	Calculus of gallbladder with acute cholecystitis with obstruction
K80.10	Calculus of gallbladder with chronic cholecystitis without obstruction
K80.11	Calculus of gallbladder with chronic cholecystitis with obstruction
K80.12	Calculus of gallbladder with acute and chronic cholecystitis without obstruction
K80.13	Calculus of gallbladder with acute and chronic cholecystitis with obstruction
K80.18	Calculus of gallbladder with other cholecystitis without obstruction
K80.19	Calculus of gallbladder with other cholecystitis with obstruction
K80.20	Calculus of gallbladder without cholecystitis without obstruction
K80.21	Calculus of gallbladder without cholecystitis with obstruction
K80.30	Calculus of bile duct with cholangitis, unspecified, without obstruction
K80.31	Calculus of bile duct with cholangitis, unspecified, with obstruction
K80.32	Calculus of bile duct with acute cholangitis without obstruction
K80.33	Calculus of bile duct with acute cholangitis with obstruction
K80.34	Calculus of bile duct with chronic cholangitis without obstruction
K80.35	Calculus of bile duct with chronic cholangitis with obstruction
K80.36	Calculus of bile duct with acute and chronic cholangitis without obstruction
K80.37	Calculus of bile duct with acute and chronic cholangitis with obstruction
K80.40	Calculus of bile duct with cholecystitis, unspecified, without obstruction
K80.41	Calculus of bile duct with cholecystitis, unspecified, with obstruction
K80.42	Calculus of bile duct with acute cholecystitis without obstruction
K80.43	Calculus of bile duct with acute cholecystitis with obstruction
K80.44	Calculus of bile duct with chronic cholecystitis without obstruction
K80.45	Calculus of bile duct with chronic cholecystitis with obstruction
K80.46	Calculus of bile duct with acute and chronic cholecystitis without obstruction
K80.47	Calculus of bile duct with acute and chronic cholecystitis with obstruction
K80.50	Calculus of bile duct without cholangitis or cholecystitis without obstruction
K80.51	Calculus of bile duct without cholangitis or cholecystitis with obstruction
K80.60	Calculus of gallbladder and bile duct with cholecystitis, unspecified, without obstruction
K80.61	Calculus of gallbladder and bile duct with cholecystitis, unspecified, with obstruction
K80.62	Calculus of gallbladder and bile duct with acute cholecystitis without obstruction
K80.63	Calculus of gallbladder and bile duct with acute cholecystitis with obstruction
K80.64	Calculus of gallbladder and bile duct with chronic cholecystitis without obstruction
K80.65	Calculus of gallbladder and bile duct with chronic cholecystitis with obstruction
K80.66	Calculus of gallbladder and bile duct with acute and chronic cholecystitis without obstruction
K80.67	Calculus of gallbladder and bile duct with acute and chronic cholecystitis with obstruction
K80.70	Calculus of gallbladder and bile duct without cholecystitis without obstruction
K80.71	Calculus of gallbladder and bile duct without cholecystitis with obstruction
K80.80	Other cholelithiasis without obstruction
K80.81	Other cholelithiasis with obstruction
K81.0	Acute cholecystitis
K81.1	Chronic cholecystitis
K81.2	Acute cholecystitis with chronic cholecystitis
K81.9	Cholecystitis, unspecified

K82.0	Obstruction of gallbladder
K82.8	Other specified diseases of gallbladder
K82.9	Disease of gallbladder, unspecified
K83.0	Cholangitis
K83.1	Obstruction of bile duct
K83.5	Biliary cyst
K83.8	Other specified diseases of biliary tract
K83.9	Disease of biliary tract, unspecified
K85.10	Biliary acute pancreatitis without necrosis or infection
K85.11	Biliary acute pancreatitis with uninfected necrosis
K85.12	Biliary acute pancreatitis with infected necrosis
K86.0	Alcohol-induced chronic pancreatitis
K86.1	Other chronic pancreatitis
K91.5	Postcholecystectomy syndrome
K91.89	Other postprocedural complications and disorders of digestive system
Q44.0	Agenesis, aplasia and hypoplasia of gallbladder
Q44.1	Other congenital malformations of gallbladder
Q44.2	Atresia of bile ducts
Q44.3	Congenital stenosis and stricture of bile ducts
Q44.4	Choledochal cyst
Q44.5	Other congenital malformations of bile ducts
T86.40	Unspecified complication of liver transplant
T86.41	Liver transplant rejection
T86.42	Liver transplant failure
T86.43	Liver transplant infection
T86.49	Other complications of liver transplant

CCI Edits

47538 0213T, 0216T, 0228T, 0230T, 11000-11006, 11042-11047, 12001-12007, 12011-12057, 13100-13133, 13151-13153, 36000, 36400-36410, 36420-36430, 36440, 36600, 36640, 43277, 43752, 47531-47534, 47536-47537, 47542, 47544, 47555-47556, 51701-51703, 62320-62327, 64400-64410, 64413-64435, 64445-64450, 64461-64463, 64479-64530, 69990, 74300-74301, 76000-76001, 76380, 76942, 76970, 76998, 77002, 77012, 77021, 92012-92014, 93000-93010, 93040-93042, 93318, 94002, 94200, 94250, 94680-94690, 94770, 95812-95816, 95819, 95822, 95829, 95955, 96360-96368, 96372, 96374-96377, 97597-97598, 97602, 99155-99157, 99211-99223, 99231-99255, 99291-99292, 99304-99310, 99315-99316, 99334-99337, 99347-99350, 99374-99375, 99377-99378, J0670, J2001

47539 0213T, 0216T, 0228T, 0230T, 11000-11006, 11042-11047, 12001-12007, 12011-12057, 13100-13133, 13151-13153, 36000, 36400-36410, 36420-36430, 36440, 36600, 36640, 43274, 43277, 43752, 47531-47534, 47536-47537, 47542, 47544, 47555-47556, 51701-51703, 62320-62327, 64400-64410, 64413-64435, 64445-64450, 64461-64463, 64479-64530, 69990, 74300-74301, 76000-76001, 76380, 76942, 76970, 76998, 77002, 77012, 77021, 92012-92014, 93000-93010, 93040-93042, 93318, 94002, 94200, 94250, 94680-94690, 94770, 95812-95816, 95819, 95822, 95829, 95955, 96360-96368, 96372, 96374-96377, 97597-97598, 97602, 99155-99157, 99211-99223, 99231-99255, 99291-99292, 99304-99310, 99315-99316, 99334-99337, 99347-99350, 99374-99375, 99377-99378, J0670, J2001

47540 0213T, 0216T, 0228T, 0230T, 11000-11006, 11042-11047, 12001-12007, 12011-12057, 13100-13133, 13151-13153, 36000, 36400-36410, 36420-36430, 36440, 36600, 36640, 43274, 43277, 43752, 47531-47534, 47536-47537, 47542, 47544, 47555-47556, 51701-51703, 62320-62327, 64400-64410, 64413-64435, 64445-64450, 64461-64463, 64479-64530, 69990, 74300-74301, 76000-76001, 76380, 76942, 76970, 76998, 77002, 77012, 77021, 92012-92014, 93000-93010, 93040-93042, 93318, 94002, 94200, 94250, 94680-94690, 94770, 95812-95816, 95819, 95822, 95829, 95955, 96360-96368, 96372, 96374-96377, 97597-97598, 97602, 99155-99157, 99211-99223, 99231-99255, 99291-99292, 99304-99310, 99315-99316, 99334-99337, 99347-99350, 99374-99375, 99377-99378, J0670, J2001

Case Example

Indication:
Biliary obstruction

History:
Cholangiocarcinoma in the bile duct. History of plastic stent placement in both hepatic ducts. These stents have been dislodged. Cholangiogram and stent placement are requested.

Procedure:
The abdomen was sterilely prepped and draped. Ultrasound shows a dilated right peripheral hepatic duct. After local anesthesia, a 22-guage Chiba needle was advanced under ultrasound guidance. Contrast was injected revealing a dilated right hepatic duct. Complete occlusion of the central portion of the right hepatic duct. A 0.018" wire was advanced and the needle was exchanged for a Neff dilator. The 0.035" Glidewire was advanced and used to select the common bile duct. A 6-French, 25 cm sheath was placed. A combination of a 0.035" Glidewire and Kumpe catheter was used to select the common bile duct and was advanced into the proximal jejunum. A Rosen wire was placed.

After local anesthesia was applied, a second 22-guage Chiba needle was used to puncture the **left peripheral hepatic duct**. Contrast injection again demonstrated a dilated hepatic duct with complete occlusion centrally. A 0.018" wire was advanced and the needle exchanged for the Neff dilator. The 0.035" J-wire was advanced and the dilator exchanged for a 6-French sheath. Next, a combination of Glidewire and Kumpe catheter was utilized in order to select the common bile duct and was advanced into the jejunum. Contrast was injected and cholangiogram was obtained in oblique projections. Subsequently, a 6 x 60 mm self-expanding noncovered **stent was advanced to the right hepatic duct and deployed from the proximal left hepatic duct to the mid common bile duct**. Contrast injection shows residual stenosis near the confluence. A 5 x 40 mm balloon dilation catheter was advanced and dilation was performed. A 5 x 37 mm **balloon expandable stent was advanced and deployed from the left hepatic duct into the common hepatic duct through the right-sided stent**. Contrast injection reveals a patent stent.

Next, an 8-French **internal/external biliary drainage catheter was placed through the right side**. The distal loop formed in the duodenum. Next, an 8-French multipurpose **catheter was advanced through the left side**. The distal loop was placed in the duodenum and confirmed with contrast injection. Both catheters were secured to the skin with 2-0 silk sutures. Sterile dressings were applied and the catheters connected to external gravity drainage bags.

Impression:
Completely occluded bilateral hepatic ducts and the confluence. **Y-shaped bilateral hepatic duct stents are placed in addition to bilateral internal/external biliary drainage catheters**. Patient will return in 3 weeks for biliary drainage check and drain catheter removal pending open stents.

CPT/HCPCS Codes Reported:
47540, 47540-XS

Other HCPCS Codes Reported:
C1769, C1729, C1725, C1874, C1887, C1893, C1894, C2625

Other Biliary Procedures

47541   **Placement of access through the biliary tree and into small bowel to assist with an endoscopic biliary procedure (eg, rendezvous procedure), percutaneous, including diagnostic cholangiography when performed, imaging guidance (eg, ultrasound and/or fluoroscopy) and all associated radiological supervision and interpretation, new access**

Placement of access through the biliary tree and into the small bowel is performed to assist in an endoscopic biliary procedure, such as rendezvous. The physician inserts a needle through the skin and liver and into a bile duct for a biliary drainage procedure. For stent placement, a drainage tube is typically placed prior to stent insertion. If this fails to resolve the obstruction, the physician inserts a guidewire and the tube is removed. A sheath is placed over the guidewire, and a stent delivery system is placed within the narrow section. Tissue samples and stone removal may be performed via this access.

47542   **Balloon dilation of biliary duct(s) or of ampulla (sphincteroplasty), percutaneous, including imaging guidance (eg, fluoroscopy), and all associated radiological supervision and interpretation, each duct (List separately in addition to code for primary procedure)**

Percutaneous balloon dilation of a biliary duct or repair of the ampulla is most often required to widen a stricture or remove stones. The repair is done due to damage caused by the stricture, stone, or dilation itself. The provider inserts a needle through the skin and into the biliary duct, and the needle is advanced through the stricture, allowing for insertion of a balloon catheter. A guidewire is inserted over the needle into the biliary duct, and the needle is removed. The balloon is placed over the guidewire. Under imaging guidance, the balloon is filled with saline in order to stretch the vessel. The size of inflation and continuity depend on the patient's diagnosis and dispensation. Once the procedure is complete, the instruments are removed and simple closure of the access site is performed.

47543   **Endoluminal biopsy(ies) of biliary tree, percutaneous, any method(s) (eg, brush, forceps, and/or needle), including imaging guidance (eg, fluoroscopy), and all associated radiological supervision and interpretation, single or multiple (List separately in addition to code for primary procedure)**

Endoluminal surgery, such as a biopsy, is performed in a hollow structure or organ (biliary tree, stomach, etc.) using common surgical techniques. Because of their nature, these procedures must be performed under endoscopic control and, ideally, via natural orifices. The physician performs a percutaneous, endoluminal biopsy of the biliary tree by brush or forceps catheters or needle using real-time imaging (ultrasound, fluoroscopy), and the specimen is deposited on a glass slide. Smears are made from the biopsy specimen, which may be used for immediate analysis (e.g., Diff-Quik) or fixed in ethanol for immunohistochemical stains. If possible, the use of an on-site cytopathologist or cytotechnologist ensures an immediate interpretation of the sample. The use of ultrasound is particularly helpful in identifying small lesions that may move during respiration. Fluoroscopy is often used in conjunction with percutaneous transhepatic biliary drainage (PTBD) as a means to access the biliary tract to conduct endoluminal biopsy.

47544   **Removal of calculi/debris from biliary duct(s) and/or gallbladder, percutaneous, including destruction of calculi by any method (eg, mechanical electrohydraulic, lithotripsy) when performed, imaging guidance (eg, fluoroscopy), and all associated radiological supervision and interpretation (List separately in addition to code for primary procedure)**

The physician removes a stone from the biliary duct after previous surgery. The common bile duct is approached by placing a scope into the tract through a previously placed drinage tube (T-tube). Manipulating basket or snare tools through the scope, the physician removes the stone(s).

Balloon Dilation of Biliary Duct

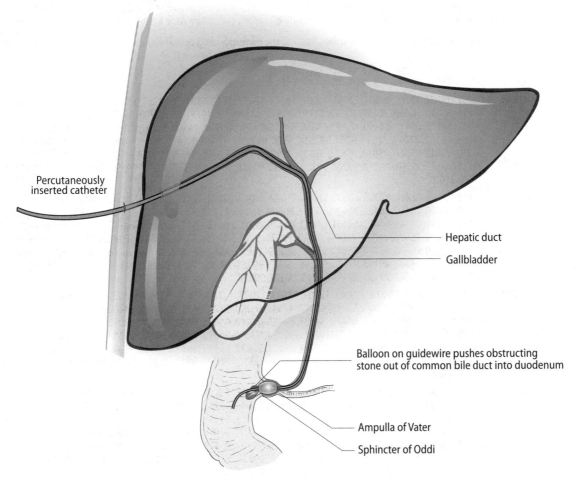

Percutaneously
inserted catheter

Hepatic duct

Gallbladder

Balloon on guidewire pushes obstructing
stone out of common bile duct into duodenum

Ampulla of Vater

Sphincter of Oddi

Coding Tips

1. Do not use 47541 when there is a biliary catheter already present.

2. If an access is present, use codes 47545–47537 as applicable.

3. Do not use 47541 with 47531–47540.

4. Codes 47542, 47543, and 47544 are add-on codes.

5. Code 47544 should not be used with codes 47531–47543 for removal of incidental sludge or debris.

6. Conscious sedation is not included in these codes. Separately report 99151–99157 per payer policy and coding guidelines. Hospitals may choose to include the costs associated with the service as part of the procedure rather than reporting them separately.

7. Report applicable HCPCS Level II codes for devices and contrast media used. Refer to the HCPCS section for possible codes.

8. Hospitals should separately report contrast media with HCPCS codes Q9965–Q9967. Report contrast media by milliliter.

Facility HCPCS Coding

Some applicable codes may include but are not limited to:

C1729	Catheter, drainage
C1769	Guidewire
C2617	Stent, non-coronary, temporary, without delivery system
Q9965	LOCM, 100-199 mg/ml iodine concentration, per ml
Q9966	LOCM, 200-299 mg/ml iodine concentration, per ml
Q9967	LOCM, 300-399 mg/ml iodine concentration, per ml

ICD-10-CM Coding

47541—This code is not identified as an add-on code by the CPT® book but describes a procedure performed at the same time as another primary procedure. Refer to the corresponding primary procedure code for ICD-10-CM diagnosis code links.

47542–47544—These codes are add-on codes. Refer to the corresponding primary procedure code for ICD-10-CM diagnosis code links.

CCI Edits

47541   0213T, 0216T, 0228T, 0230T, 12001-12007, 12011-12057, 13100-13133, 13151-13153, 36000, 36400-36410, 36420-36430, 36440, 36600, 36640, 43752, 47531-47540, 47544, 51701-51703, 62320-62327, 64400-64410, 64413-64435, 64445-64450, 64461-64463, 64479-64530, 69990, 74300-74301, 76000-76001, 76380, 76942, 76970, 76998, 77002, 77012, 77021, 92012-92014, 93000-93010, 93040-93042, 93318, 94002, 94200, 94250, 94680-94690, 94770, 95812-95816, 95819, 95822, 95829, 95955, 96360-96368, 96372, 96374-96377, 99155-99157, 99211-99223, 99231-99255, 99291-99292, 99304-99310, 99315-99316, 99334-99337, 99347-99350, 99374-99375, 99377-99378, J0670, J2001

47542   0213T, 0216T, 0228T, 0230T, 11000-11006, 11042-11047, 12001-12007, 12011-12057, 13100-13133, 13151-13153, 36000, 36400-36410, 36420-36430, 36440, 36600, 36640, 43752, 47544, 51701-51703, 62320-62327, 64400-64410, 64413-64435, 64445-64450, 64461, 64463, 64479, 64483, 64486-64490, 64493, 64505-64530, 69990, 76000-76001, 76380, 76942, 76970, 76998, 77002, 77012, 77021, 92012-92014, 93000-93010, 93040-93042, 93318, 94002, 94200, 94250, 94680-94690, 94770, 95812-95816, 95819, 95822, 95829, 95955, 96360, 96365, 96372, 96374-96377, 97597-97598, 97602, 99155-99157, 99211-99223, 99231-99255, 99291-99292, 99304-99310, 99315-99316, 99334-99337, 99347-99350, 99374-99375, 99377-99378

47543   0213T, 0216T, 0228T, 0230T, 12001-12007, 12011-12057, 13100-13133, 13151-13153, 36000, 36400-36410, 36420-36430, 36440, 36600, 36640, 43752, 47544, 51701-51703, 62320-62327, 64400-64410, 64413-64435, 64445-64450, 64461, 64463, 64479, 64483, 64486-64490, 64493, 64505-64530, 69990, 76000-76001, 76380, 76942, 76970, 76998, 77002, 77012, 77021, 92012-92014, 93000-93010, 93040-93042, 93318, 94002, 94200, 94250, 94680-94690, 94770, 95812-95816, 95819, 95822, 95829, 95955, 96360, 96365, 96372, 96374-96377, 99155-99157, 99211-99223, 99231-99255, 99291-99292, 99304-99310, 99315-99316, 99334-99337, 99347-99350, 99374-99375, 99377-99378

47544   0213T, 0216T, 0228T, 0230T, 11000-11006, 11042-11047, 12001-12007, 12011-12057, 13100-13133, 13151-13153, 36000, 36400-36410, 36420-36430, 36440, 36600, 36640, 43752, 51701-51703, 62320-62327, 64400-64410, 64413-64435, 64445-64450, 64461, 64463, 64479, 64483, 64486-64490, 64493, 64505-64530, 69990, 76000-76001, 76380, 76942, 76970, 76998, 77002, 77012, 77021, 92012-92014, 93000-93010, 93040-93042, 93318, 94002, 94200, 94250, 94680-94690, 94770, 95812-95816, 95819, 95822, 95829, 95955, 96360, 96365, 96372, 96374-96377, 97597-97598, 97602, 99155-99157, 99211-99223, 99231-99255, 99291-99292, 99304-99310, 99315-99316, 99334-99337, 99347-99350, 99374-99375, 99377-99378

Case Example

History:
Common bile duct occlusion with painless jaundice. **Patient here for endobiliary biopsy.**

Procedure:
Left upper quadrant along with the catheter were sterilely prepped and draped. After local anesthesia, an 0.035" Amplatz wire was advanced through the **existing left internal/external biliary drainage catheter**. The **catheter was removed**. An 8-French introducer sheath was advanced. Contrast was injected to confirm its position in the occluded portion of the common bile duct.

Next, 5-French biopsy forceps were advanced and **biopsy performed**. The pathologist was present for the procedure. Several samples were obtained and placed in formalin. The sheath and forceps were removed. A **new 8-French internal/external biliary drainage catheter was advanced** and distal loop formed in the small bowel loop. Contrast was injected to confirm position. Sterile dressing was applied and catheter was secured to the skin with 2-0 silk sutures.

CPT/HCPCS Codes Reported:
47536, 47543

Other HCPCS Codes Reported:
C1769, C1729

Esophageal Dilation

43450   **Dilation of esophagus, by unguided sound or bougie, single or multiple passes**
The physician dilates the esophagus using an unguided dilator into the patient's throat down into the esophagus until the end of the dilator passes the stricture. The dilator is withdrawn. This is repeated until the desired results are achieved.

43453   **Dilation of esophagus, over guide wire**
The physician dilates the esophagus by passing dilators over a guidewire. The physician uses a fluoroscope to place a guidewire into the patient's throat, down the esophagus, and into the stomach. A series of dilators are passed over the guidewire and withdrawn. The process is repeated until the esophagus is dilated to an acceptable size.

74360   **Intraluminal dilation of strictures and/or obstructions (eg, esophagus), radiological supervision and interpretation**

Coding Tips

1. For esophageal dilation using dilators over a guide wire, report code 43453 and 74360.
2. For esophageal dilation using a balloon dilator, report code 43213, 43214 or 43233.
3. For endoscopically performed dilation, see 43220 or 43226.
4. Separately report 74360 with 43450 and 43453 only.
5. Conscious sedation is not included in these codes. Separately report 99151–99157 per payer policy and coding guidelines. Hospitals may choose to include the costs associated with the service as part of the procedure rather than reporting them separately.
6. Fluoroscopy is included in CPT code 74360 and is not separately reported.
7. Report any applicable HCPCS Level II codes for devices and contrast media used. Refer to the HCPCS section for possible codes.
8. Physician Reporting: These radiology S&I codes have both a technical and professional component. To report only the professional component, append modifier 26. To report only the technical component, append modifier TC. To report the complete procedure (i.e., both the professional and technical components), submit without a modifier.

Facility HCPCS Coding

Some applicable codes may include, but are not limited to:

C1726   Catheter, balloon dilatation, non-vascular

C1727   Catheter, balloon tissue dissector, non-vascular (insertable)

C1769   Guide wire

ICD-10-CM Coding

C15.3   Malignant neoplasm of upper third of esophagus
C15.4   Malignant neoplasm of middle third of esophagus
C15.5   Malignant neoplasm of lower third of esophagus
C15.8   Malignant neoplasm of overlapping sites of esophagus
C15.9   Malignant neoplasm of esophagus, unspecified
D00.1   Carcinoma in situ of esophagus
D13.0   Benign neoplasm of esophagus
I85.00   Esophageal varices without bleeding
K20.0   Eosinophilic esophagitis
K20.8   Other esophagitis
K20.9   Esophagitis, unspecified
K21.0   Gastro-esophageal reflux disease with esophagitis
K21.9   Gastro-esophageal reflux disease without esophagitis
K22.0   Achalasia of cardia
K22.10   Ulcer of esophagus without bleeding
K22.11   Ulcer of esophagus with bleeding
K22.2   Esophageal obstruction
K22.70   Barrett's esophagus without dysplasia
K22.710   Barrett's esophagus with low grade dysplasia
K22.711   Barrett's esophagus with high grade dysplasia
K22.719   Barrett's esophagus with dysplasia, unspecified

K22.8	Other specified diseases of esophagus
K23	Disorders of esophagus in diseases classified elsewhere
Q39.3	Congenital stenosis and stricture of esophagus
Q39.4	Esophageal web
Q39.8	Other congenital malformations of esophagus
Q39.9	Congenital malformation of esophagus, unspecified
Q40.1	Congenital hiatus hernia
R13.10	Dysphagia, unspecified
R13.11	Dysphagia, oral phase
R13.12	Dysphagia, oropharyngeal phase
R13.13	Dysphagia, pharyngeal phase
R13.14	Dysphagia, pharyngoesophageal phase
R13.19	Other dysphagia
T18.100A	Unspecified foreign body in esophagus causing compression of trachea, initial encounter
T18.108A	Unspecified foreign body in esophagus causing other injury, initial encounter
T18.190A	Other foreign object in esophagus causing compression of trachea, initial encounter
T18.198A	Other foreign object in esophagus causing other injury, initial encounter

CCI Edits

43450 0213T, 0216T, 0228T, 0230T, 12001-12007, 12011-12057, 13100-13133, 13151-13153, 36000, 36400-36410, 36420-36430, 36440, 36591-36592, 36600, 36640, 43752, 51701-51703, 62320-62327, 64400-64410, 64413-64435, 64445-64450, 64461-64463, 64479-64530, 69990, 91040, 92012-92014, 93000-93010, 93040-93042, 93318, 93355, 94002, 94200, 94250, 94680-94690, 94770, 95812-95816, 95819, 95822, 95829, 95955, 96360-96368, 96372, 96374-96377, 99152, 99155-99157, 99211-99223, 99231-99255, 99291-99292, 99304-99310, 99315-99316, 99334-99337, 99347-99350, 99374-99375, 99377-99378, 99446-99449, 99495-99496, G0463, G0471

43453 0213T, 0216T, 0228T, 0230T, 12001-12007, 12011-12057, 13100-13133, 13151-13153, 36000, 36400-36410, 36420-36430, 36440, 36591-36592, 36600, 36640, 43450, 43752, 51701-51703, 62320-62327, 64400-64410, 64413-64435, 64445-64450, 64461-64463, 64479-64530, 69990, 91040, 92012-92014, 93000-93010, 93040-93042, 93318, 93355, 94002, 94200, 94250, 94680-94690, 94770, 95812-95816, 95819, 95822, 95829, 95955, 96360-96368, 96372, 96374-96377, 99152, 99155-99157, 99211-99223, 99231-99255, 99291-99292, 99304-99310, 99315-99316, 99334-99337, 99347-99350, 99374-99375, 99377-99378, 99446-99449, 99495-99496, G0463, G0471

74360 36591-36592, 74000, 76000-76001, 77001-77002, 99446-99449

Case Example

This patient is referred to us with a high-grade esophageal stricture. After administration of conscious sedation, a **guide wire** is passed through the stricture and into the stomach. An **esophageal balloon catheter** is passed over the wire and inflated under fluoroscopic guidance until satisfactory results are achieved. The patient left the department with no apparent complications.

CPT/HCPCS Codes Reported:
74360, 43453

Other HCPCS Codes Reported:
C1726, C1769

Percutaneous Transhepatic Biliary Duct Dilation and Stent Placement

47555   **Biliary endoscopy, percutaneous via T-tube or other tract; with dilation of biliary duct stricture(s) without stent**

The physician makes a small incision in the abdomen. The physician advances an endoscope through an opening in the abdominal wall or through a T-tube inserted through the abdominal wall into the common bile duct. With the endoscope, the physician is able to directly visualize portions of the biliary tract, which may be filled with contrast medium for identifying the common bile duct, biliary tree, and gallbladder (including areas of abnormality, stricture, or obstruction) under fluoroscopy. The physician advances a balloon-tipped catheter through the tract or T-tube so that it is above the site of the duct stricture, inflates the balloon and draws it back through the site of stricture to achieve dilation. This procedure may be repeated until optimal dilation is obtained. The endoscope is removed and the tract, peritoneum, and abdominal wall are approximated. The endoscope is removed. The T-tube is withdrawn and the common bile duct is sutured closed. The abdomen is sutured closed.

47556   **with dilation of biliary duct stricture(s) with stent**

The physician makes a small incision in the abdomen. The physician advances an endoscope through an opening in the abdominal wall or through a T-tube inserted through the abdominal wall into the common bile duct. With the endoscope, the physician is able to directly visualize portions of the biliary tract, which may be filled with contrast medium for identifying the common bile duct, biliary tree, and gallbladder (including areas of abnormality, stricture, or obstruction) under separately reportable fluoroscopy. The physician advances a balloon-tipped catheter through the tract or T-tube so that it is above the site of duct stricture, inflates the balloon and draws it back through the site of stricture to achieve dilation. This procedure may be repeated until optimal dilation is obtained. The physician places a stent to prevent future stricture. The endoscope is removed. The T-tube is withdrawn and the defect in the common bile duct is sutured closed. The abdomen is sutured closed.

74363   **Percutaneous transhepatic dilation of biliary duct stricture with or without placement of stent, radiological supervision and interpretation**

The physician advances an endoscope through an incision in the abdominal wall or an existing T-tube into the common bile duct. The biliary tract may be filled with contrast medium for identifying areas of abnormality, stricture, or obstruction in the common bile duct, biliary tree, and gallbladder. The physician advances a balloon-tipped catheter through the tract or T-tube so that it is above the site of the duct stricture, inflates the balloon, and draws it back through the stricture to achieve dilation. This may be repeated until optimum dilation is achieved. The physician may place a stent to prevent future stricture. This code reports only the radiological supervision and interpretation required in performing this procedure.

CPT Coding for Biliary Interventions

Service Performed	Surgical Component	Radiology S&I Component
A biliary duct stricture is dilated by percutaneous approach using imaging guidance	47555	74363
A biliary duct stricture is dilated and a stent placed by percutaneous approach using imaging guidance	47556	74363

Coding Tips

1. Biliary interventions can be complex, and several separately reportable procedures could be performed. See preceding sections for additional information.

2. It is appropriate to use 47555 and 47556 to report percutaneous biliary interventions. Specific instructions have been provided by both CMS and the CPT editorial board.

3. Separately report access and cholangiography.

4. Balloon dilation of the duct preceding biliary stent placement is not separately reported. It is included in code 47556.

5. Fluoroscopy is included in code 74363 and is not separately reported.

6. Report any applicable HCPCS Level II codes for devices and contrast media used. Refer to the HCPCS section for possible codes.

7. Physician Reporting: These radiology S&I codes have both a technical and professional component. To report only the professional component, append modifier 26. To report only the technical component, append modifier TC. To report the complete procedure (i.e., both the professional and technical components), submit without a modifier.

Facility HCPCS Coding

Some applicable codes may include, but are not limited to:

C1726	Catheter, balloon dilatation, non-vascular
C1727	Catheter, balloon tissue dissector, non-vascular (insertable)
C1729	Catheter, drainage
C1769	Guide wire
C2617	Stent, non-coronary, temporary, without delivery system
Q9958	HOCM, up to 149 mg/ml iodine concentration, per ml
Q9959	HOCM, 150-199 mg/ml iodine concentration, per ml
Q9960	HOCM, 200-249 mg/ml iodine concentration, per ml
Q9961	HOCM, 250-299 mg/ml iodine concentration, per ml
Q9962	HOCM, 300-349 mg/ml iodine concentration, per ml
Q9963	HOCM, 350-399 mg/ml iodine concentration, per ml
Q9964	HOCM, 400 or greater mg/ml iodine concentration, per ml
Q9965	LOCM, 100-199 mg/ml iodine concentration, per ml
Q9966	LOCM, 200-299 mg/ml iodine concentration, per ml
Q9967	LOCM, 300-399 mg/ml iodine concentration, per ml

ICD-10-CM Coding

C22.0	Liver cell carcinoma
C22.1	Intrahepatic bile duct carcinoma
C22.2	Hepatoblastoma
C22.3	Angiosarcoma of liver
C22.4	Other sarcomas of liver
C22.7	Other specified carcinomas of liver
C22.8	Malignant neoplasm of liver, primary, unspecified as to type
C22.9	Malignant neoplasm of liver, not specified as primary or secondary
C23	Malignant neoplasm of gallbladder
C24.0	Malignant neoplasm of extrahepatic bile duct
C24.1	Malignant neoplasm of ampulla of Vater
C24.8	Malignant neoplasm of overlapping sites of biliary tract
C24.9	Malignant neoplasm of biliary tract, unspecified
C25.0	Malignant neoplasm of head of pancreas
C25.1	Malignant neoplasm of body of pancreas
C25.2	Malignant neoplasm of tail of pancreas
C25.3	Malignant neoplasm of pancreatic duct
C25.4	Malignant neoplasm of endocrine pancreas
C25.7	Malignant neoplasm of other parts of pancreas
C25.8	Malignant neoplasm of overlapping sites of pancreas
C25.9	Malignant neoplasm of pancreas, unspecified
C78.7	Secondary malignant neoplasm of liver and intrahepatic bile duct
C78.80	Secondary malignant neoplasm of unspecified digestive organ
C78.89	Secondary malignant neoplasm of other digestive organs
C7A.1	Malignant poorly differentiated neuroendocrine tumors
C7A.8	Other malignant neuroendocrine tumors
C7B.8	Other secondary neuroendocrine tumors
D01.5	Carcinoma in situ of liver, gallbladder and bile ducts
D01.7	Carcinoma in situ of other specified digestive organs
D01.9	Carcinoma in situ of digestive organ, unspecified
D13.5	Benign neoplasm of extrahepatic bile ducts
D13.6	Benign neoplasm of pancreas
D13.9	Benign neoplasm of ill-defined sites within the digestive system
D37.6	Neoplasm of uncertain behavior of liver, gallbladder and bile ducts
D37.8	Neoplasm of uncertain behavior of other specified digestive organs

D49.Ø	Neoplasm of unspecified behavior of digestive system
K74.3	Primary biliary cirrhosis
K74.4	Secondary biliary cirrhosis
K74.5	Biliary cirrhosis, unspecified
K8Ø.Ø1	Calculus of gallbladder with acute cholecystitis with obstruction
K8Ø.11	Calculus of gallbladder with chronic cholecystitis with obstruction
K8Ø.13	Calculus of gallbladder with acute and chronic cholecystitis with obstruction
K8Ø.19	Calculus of gallbladder with other cholecystitis with obstruction
K8Ø.21	Calculus of gallbladder without cholecystitis with obstruction
K8Ø.3Ø	Calculus of bile duct with cholangitis, unspecified, without obstruction
K8Ø.31	Calculus of bile duct with cholangitis, unspecified, with obstruction
K8Ø.32	Calculus of bile duct with acute cholangitis without obstruction
K8Ø.33	Calculus of bile duct with acute cholangitis with obstruction
K8Ø.34	Calculus of bile duct with chronic cholangitis without obstruction
K8Ø.35	Calculus of bile duct with chronic cholangitis with obstruction
K8Ø.36	Calculus of bile duct with acute and chronic cholangitis without obstruction
K8Ø.37	Calculus of bile duct with acute and chronic cholangitis with obstruction
K8Ø.41	Calculus of bile duct with cholecystitis, unspecified, with obstruction
K8Ø.43	Calculus of bile duct with acute cholecystitis with obstruction
K8Ø.45	Calculus of bile duct with chronic cholecystitis with obstruction
K8Ø.47	Calculus of bile duct with acute and chronic cholecystitis with obstruction
K8Ø.5Ø	Calculus of bile duct without cholangitis or cholecystitis without obstruction
K8Ø.51	Calculus of bile duct without cholangitis or cholecystitis with obstruction
K8Ø.61	Calculus of gallbladder and bile duct with cholecystitis, unspecified, with obstruction
K8Ø.63	Calculus of gallbladder and bile duct with acute cholecystitis with obstruction
K8Ø.65	Calculus of gallbladder and bile duct with chronic cholecystitis with obstruction
K8Ø.67	Calculus of gallbladder and bile duct with acute and chronic cholecystitis with obstruction
K8Ø.71	Calculus of gallbladder and bile duct without cholecystitis with obstruction
K8Ø.81	Other cholelithiasis with obstruction
K83.Ø	Cholangitis
K83.1	Obstruction of bile duct
K83.2	Perforation of bile duct
K83.3	Fistula of bile duct
K83.4	Spasm of sphincter of Oddi
K83.5	Biliary cyst
K83.8	Other specified diseases of biliary tract
K83.9	Disease of biliary tract, unspecified
K85.1	Biliary acute pancreatitis
K86.Ø	Alcohol-induced chronic pancreatitis
K86.1	Other chronic pancreatitis
K86.81	Exocrine pancreatic insufficiency
K86.89	Other specified diseases of pancreas
K86.9	Disease of pancreas, unspecified
K87	Disorders of gallbladder, biliary tract and pancreas in diseases classified elsewhere
K91.5	Postcholecystectomy syndrome
K91.86	Retained cholelithiasis following cholecystectomy
K91.89	Other postprocedural complications and disorders of digestive system
Q44.2	Atresia of bile ducts
Q44.3	Congenital stenosis and stricture of bile ducts
Q44.4	Choledochal cyst
Q44.5	Other congenital malformations of bile ducts
R17	Unspecified jaundice
S36.13XA	Injury of bile duct, initial encounter
T86.4Ø	Unspecified complication of liver transplant
T86.41	Liver transplant rejection
T86.42	Liver transplant failure

| T86.43 | Liver transplant infection |
| T86.49 | Other complications of liver transplant |

CCI Edits

47555   0213T, 0216T, 0228T, 0230T, 12001-12007, 12011-12057, 13100-13133, 13151-13153, 36000, 36400-36410, 36420-36430, 36440, 36591-36592, 36600, 36640, 43752, 47542, 47552, 51701-51703, 62320-62327, 64400-64410, 64413-64435, 64445-64450, 64461-64463, 64479-64530, 69990, 76000-76001, 77001-77002, 92012-92014, 93000-93010, 93040-93042, 93318, 93355, 94002, 94200, 94250, 94680-94690, 94770, 95812-95816, 95819, 95822, 95829, 95955, 96360-96368, 96372, 96374-96377, 99155-99157, 99211-99223, 99231-99255, 99291-99292, 99304-99310, 99315-99316, 99334-99337, 99347-99350, 99374-99375, 99377-99378, 99446-99449, 99495-99496, G0463, G0471

47556   0213T, 0216T, 0228T, 0230T, 12001-12007, 12011-12057, 13100-13133, 13151-13153, 36000, 36400-36410, 36420-36430, 36440, 36591-36592, 36600, 36640, 43752, 47542, 47552, 47555, 51701-51703, 62320-62327, 64400-64410, 64413-64435, 64445-64450, 64461-64463, 64479-64530, 69990, 76000-76001, 77001-77002, 92012-92014, 93000-93010, 93040-93042, 93318, 93355, 94002, 94200, 94250, 94680-94690, 94770, 95812-95816, 95819, 95822, 95829, 95955, 96360-96368, 96372, 96374-96377, 99155-99157, 99211-99223, 99231-99255, 99291-99292, 99304-99310, 99315-99316, 99334-99337, 99347-99350, 99374-99375, 99377-99378, 99446-99449, 99495-99496, G0463, G0471

74363   36591-36592, 74000, 76000-76001, 77001-77002, 99446-99449

Case Example

T-Tube Cholangiogram, Common Bile Duct Brushing, Balloon Dilation of the Common Bile Duct, and Placement of a Biliary Drainage Catheter

Procedure:
The patient was placed supine on the angiography table. A small amount of contrast was injected through the **existing drainage catheter**. This demonstrated dilatation of the common bile duct with mild intra-hepatic biliary ductal dilatation. There appeared to be a high-grade **stricture** involving the distal common bile duct. A 0.035 guidewire was advanced through the existing catheter which was then removed and replaced with a 6-French vascular sheath. The **sheath was placed within the common bile duct. Contrast was injected**. This demonstrated severe dilatation of common bile duct to the level of distal common bile duct. There was opacification of a fluid collection communicating with the common bile duct. Findings were consistent with high-grade stenosis. A Bernstein catheter was advanced through the sheath along with a Glidewire. The Glidewire was used to negotiate the common bile duct stricture.

Please make note that during initial cholangiogram, there was collection of contrast adjacent to the common bile duct. The fluid collection is in congruity with the common bile duct. Findings were **consistent with a choledochocyst or common bile duct of reticulum**. A 7 mm x 4cm and an 8 mm x 4 cm **angioplasty balloon** were used to **dilate the common bile duct**. No waist was seen to suggest high-grade stenosis. After bile duct dilatation, a 10-French **biliary drainage catheter** was advanced over the wire. The catheter was **positioned with its loop within the small bowel**. The catheter **was left in place** and secured to the skin with the help of sutures. The patient tolerated the procedure well.

Impression:
Placement of a 10-French **biliary internal/external drainage catheter**.

Balloon dilatation of the common bile duct.

Choledochocyst or common bile duct of reticulum arising from the common bile duct.

CPT/HCPCS Codes Reported:
45334, 47542

Other HCPCS Codes Reported:
C1725, C1729, C1769, C1894

Percutaneous Gastrostomy Tube Placement

Percutaneous gastrostomy tubes are typically placed to allow feedings directly into the stomach.

49440	**Percutaneous placement of gastrostomy tube**

The physician places a gastrostomy tube into the stomach. A small incision is made through the skin and fascia. A large bore needle with a suture attached is passed through the incision into the lumen of the stomach. The needle is snared and the needle and suture are removed via the mouth. The gastrostomy tube is connected to the suture and passed through the mouth into the stomach and out the abdominal wall. The gastrostomy tube is sutured to the skin.

Coding Tips

1. CPT code 49440 is a comprehensive code. Radiologic supervision and interpretation is included.
2. Percutaneous jejunostomy or duodenostomy is not covered in this code. See CPT code 49441 in the next section.
3. CPT code 49440 is reported when the insertion is done nonendoscopically.
4. Fluoroscopy and radiology supervision and interpretation are included and are not separately reported.
5. Report any applicable HCPCS Level II codes for devices and contrast media used. Refer to appendix B for a list of device HCPCS codes.
6. Conscious sedation is not included in these codes. Separately report 99151–99157 per payer policy and coding guidelines. Hospitals may choose to include the costs associated with the service as part of the procedure rather than reporting them separately.

Facility HCPCS Coding

Some applicable HCPCS codes may include, but are not limited to:

C1729 Catheter, drainage

C1769 Guidewire

C1894 Introducer/sheath, other than guiding, intracardiac electrophysiological, non-laser

C2629 Introducer/sheath, other than guiding, intracardiac

ICD-10-CM Coding

The application of this code is too broad to adequately present ICD-10-CM diagnosis code links here. Refer to the current ICD-10-CM book.

CCI Edits

49440 0213T, 0216T, 11000-11006, 11042-11047, 12001-12007, 12011-12057, 13100-13133, 13151-13153, 36000, 36400-36410, 36420-36430, 36440, 36591-36592, 36600, 36640, 43191, 43197, 43200, 43210, 43235, 43246, 43752, 43760-43761, 49450, 49452-49465, 62320-62327, 64400-64410, 64413-64435, 64445-64450, 64461-64463, 64479-64530, 69990, 75984, 76000-76001, 77001-77002, 92012-92014, 93000-93010, 93040-93042, 93318, 93355, 94002, 94200, 94250, 94680-94690, 94770, 95812-95816, 95819, 95822, 95829, 95955, 96360-96368, 96372, 96374-96377, 97597-97598, 97602, 99155-99157, 99211-99223, 99231-99255, 99291-99292, 99304-99310, 99315-99316, 99334-99337, 99347-99350, 99374-99375, 99377-99378, 99446-99449, 99495-99496, G0463, J0670, J2001

Case Example

Gastrostomy Tube Placement

The patient was placed supine on the interventional radiology table. Using **ultrasound**, the inferior margin of the left hepatic lobe was **localized and marked** on the skin. **Images were taken** and **permanently stored**. A nasogastric tube was placed. The skin of the abdomen was prepped and draped in standard sterile fashion.

The stomach was insufflated with air via the nasogastric tube. After localizing an area overlying the lower gastric body cephalad to the barium-filled colon, the skin and subcutaneous soft tissues of the anterior abdominal wall were infiltrated with 1% lidocaine. Using 4 T-tacks, the anterior stomach wall was pexied to the anterior abdominal wall. In the center of the T-tacks, an 18-gauge introducer needle was placed through which a .035 Amplatz wire was advanced. The **gastrostomy tract was serially dilated** with 12- and 14-French dilators after which a 17-French peel away sheath was placed.

Finally, a 14-French **Cope gastrostomy tube was advanced through** the peel away sheath. The sheath and wire were removed. The gastrostomy tube retention balloon was inflated with 5 cc of sterile water. **Tube placement was confirmed** with injection of a small amount of contrast. The G-tube was covered with a sterile bandage. The patient tolerated the procedure well.

CPT/HCPCS Codes Reported:
49440, 76942

Percutaneous Jejunostomy or Duodenostomy Tube Placement

Percutaneous jejunostomy/duodenostomy is essentially the same procedure as percutaneous gastrostomy, only the tube is placed into the small intestine.

49441	**Insertion of duodenostomy or jejunostomy tube, percutaneous, under fluoroscopic guidance including contrast injection(s), image documentation and report**

The physician inserts a duodenostomy or jejunostomy tube via percutaneous (under the skin) approach using fluoroscopic guidance. Percutaneous image-guided gastrostomy or enterostomy procedures may be indicated for patients who have an impaired swallowing mechanism, mechanical obstruction of the upper GI tract due to malignancy, or those with aberrant upper GI anatomy. Particularly in patients who have undergone gastrectomy or gastric pull-up, the jejunum or duodenum is often a viable site for percutaneous feeding tube placement. Following administration of any necessary sedation and contrast materials, the physician identifies a suitable site for puncture of the duodenum or jejunum and a needle is inserted percutaneously. When the contrast material can be aspirated from the needle, a guidewire is inserted under fluoroscopic guidance. The tract is dilated and an appropriate catheter is inserted and secured to the skin with a stoma device. Nasogastric or orogastric tubes are removed. Antiseptic ointment and sterile dressings are applied. This code includes image documentation and report.

Coding Tips

1. CPT code 49441 separates the reporting for percutaneous insertion of a jejunostomy or duodenostomy tube from gastrostomy insertion.
2. The code is all-inclusive of imaging service. There is no radiology supervision and interpretation code to report.
3. Fluoroscopy is included and is not separately reported.
4. Report any applicable HCPCS Level II codes for devices and contrast media used. Refer to appendix B for a list of device HCPCS codes.
5. Conscious sedation is not included in these codes. Separately report 99151–99157 per payer policy and coding guidelines. Hospitals may choose to include the costs associated with the service as part of the procedure rather than reporting them separately.

Facility HCPCS Coding

Some applicable HCPCS codes may include, but are not limited to:

C1729	Catheter, drainage
C1769	Guidewire
C1894	Introducer/sheath, other than guiding, intracardiac electrophysiological, non-laser
C2629	Introducer/sheath, other than guiding, intracardiac

ICD-10-CM Coding

The application of this code is too broad to adequately present ICD-10-CM diagnosis code links here. Refer to the current ICD-10-CM book.

CCI Edits

49441	0213T, 0216T, 11000-11006, 11042-11047, 12001-12007, 12011-12057, 13100-13133, 13151-13153, 36000, 36400-36410, 36420-36430, 36440, 36591-36592, 36600, 36640, 43191, 43197, 43200, 43210, 43235, 43752, 43760-43761, 44015, 49451, 49460-49465, 62320-62327, 64400-64410, 64413-64435, 64445-64450, 64461-64463, 64479-64530, 69990, 75984, 76000-76001, 77001-77002, 92012-92014, 93000-93010, 93040-93042, 93318, 93355, 94002, 94200, 94250, 94680-94690, 94770, 95812-95816, 95819, 95822, 95829, 95955, 96360-96368, 96372, 96374-96377, 97597-97598, 97602, 99155-99157, 99211-99223, 99231-99255, 99291-99292, 99304-99310, 99315-99316, 99334-99337, 99347-99350, 99374-99375, 99377-99378, 99446-99449, 99495-99496, G0463, J0670, J2001

Case Example

The patient is placed on the interventional radiology table. Using ultrasound guidance, an anatomic window is found to allow passage of the 18-gauge needle. The **needle is passed into the duodenum**. A Rosen guidewire is passed through the needle and the needle is exchanged for a dilator. The **percutaneous tract is dilated** to allow the 10-French feeding tube to pass. The feeding tube is placed over the guidewire. Contrast media is injected to **confirm placement in the duodenum**. The retention balloon is inflated with 5 cc of sterile water. The tube insertion site is covered with a sterile bandage. The patient tolerated the procedure well.

CPT/HCPCS Codes Reported:
49441

Other HCPCS Codes Reported:
C1729, C1769, and applicable code for contrast media

Percutaneous Cecostomy Tube Placement

| 49442 | Insertion of cecostomy or other colonic tube, percutaneous, under fluoroscopic guidance including contrast injection(s), image documentation and report |

The physician inserts a cecostomy or other colonic tube via percutaneous (under the skin) approach using fluoroscopic guidance. Following identification of the gallbladder, liver, and urinary bladder by ultrasound, the physician inserts a silicone catheter into the rectum and a retention balloon is filled with air. The abdomen is prepared and draped in sterile fashion and appropriate anesthesia is administered. The colon is inflated with air via the rectal catheter and the physician assesses the position of the cecum to determine the appropriate tract site. The physician makes a small incision in the skin and inserts a puncture needle through the skin and soft tissues. Under fluoroscopic guidance, the needle is advanced into the cecum and contrast is injected to confirm the needle's position. Still using fluoroscopic guidance, a guidewire is advanced through the needle and positions the retention sutures. The physician removes the needle and clamps the sutures. A dilator is introduced over the wire, followed by an appropriately sized catheter. The catheter is locked and the physician confirms placement with contrast. The locked portion of the catheter is pulled against the cecum's anterior wall, where the retention sutures are anchored. Antiseptic ointment and sterile dressings are applied. This code includes image documentation and report.

Coding Tips

1. CPT code 49442 reports the percutaneous insertion of a cecostomy or colonic tube.

2. The code is all inclusive of imaging service. There is no radiology supervision and interpretation code to report.

3. Fluoroscopy is included and is not separately reported.

4. Report any applicable HCPCS Level II codes for devices and contrast media used. Refer to the HCPCS section for possible codes.

5. Conscious sedation is not included in these codes. Separately report 99151–99157 per payer policy and coding guidelines. Hospitals may choose to include the costs associated with the service as part of the procedure rather than reporting them separately.

Facility HCPCS Coding

Some applicable HCPCS codes may include, but are not limited to:

C1729	Catheter, drainage
C1769	Guidewire
C1894	Introducer/sheath, other than guiding, intracardiac electrophysiological, non-laser
C2629	Introducer/sheath, other than guiding, intracardiac

ICD-10-CM Coding

The application of this code is too broad to adequately present ICD-10-CM diagnosis code links here. Refer to the current ICD-10-CM book.

CCI Edits

| 49442 | 0213T, 0216T, 11000-11006, 11042-11047, 12001-12007, 12011-12057, 13100-13133, 13151-13153, 36000, 36400-36410, 36420-36430, 36440, 36591-36592, 36600, 36640, 43752, 44388, 45300, 45330, 45378, 45900-45990, 46600-46601, 49450, 49460-49465, 62320-62327, 64400-64410, 64413-64435, 64445-64450, 64461-64463, 64479-64530, 69990, 75984, 76000-76001, 77001-77002, 92012-92014, 93000-93010, 93040-93042, 93318, 93355, 94002, 94200, 94250, 94680-94690, 94770, 95812-95816, 95819, 95822, 95829, 95955, 96360-96368, 96372, 96374-96377, 97597-97598, 97602, 99155-99157, 99211-99223, 99231-99255, 99291-99292, 99304-99310, 99315-99316, 99334-99337, 99347-99350, 99374-99375, 99377-99378, 99446-99449, 99495-99496, G0463, J0670, J2001 |

Case Example

Indications:
Fecal incontinence with severe constipation, 6-year-old patient with spina bifida.

The patient is taken to the interventional radiology suite and placed in supine position on the imaging table. A Foley catheter is inserted into the rectum and the colon is inflated with air. Using fluoroscopic guidance, the **needle is inserted through the skin and into the cecum**. Contrast is injected to confirm position within the cecum. The suture anchor set is deployed into the cecum using an Amplatz guidewire. The needle is removed and the retention suture threads are clamped using the mosquito forceps. The **tract is dilated and the Cope loop catheter is placed into the cecum**. Contrast is again injected to confirm position. The catheter is connected to a drainage bag. The tube insertion site is covered with a sterile bandage. The patient tolerated the procedure well.

CPT/HCPCS Codes Reported:
49442

Other HCPCS Codes Reported:
C1729, C1769, and applicable code for contrast media

Conversion of Gastrostomy (G tube) to Jejunostomy (G-J tube)

49446   **Conversion of gastrostomy tube to gastro-jejunostomy tube, percutaneous, under fluoroscopic guidance including contrast injection(s), image documentation and report**
The physician converts a gastrostomy tube to a gastrojejunostomy tube via percutaneous (under the skin) approach using fluoroscopic guidance. Following administration of any necessary sedation and contrast materials, the physician advances a jejunostomy tube through the previously placed gastrostomy tube into the proximal jejunum. This code includes contrast injections, image documentation, and report.

Coding Tips

1.   CPT code 49446 reports the conversion of a G tube to G-J tube.

2.   The code is all inclusive of imaging service. There is no radiology supervision and interpretation code to report.

3.   Fluoroscopy is included and is not separately reported.

4.   Report any applicable HCPCS Level II codes for devices and contrast media used. Refer to Appendix B for available device HCPCS codes.

5.   Conscious sedation is not included in these codes. Separately report 99151–99157 per payer policy and coding guidelines. Hospitals may choose to include the costs associated with the service as part of the procedure rather than reporting them separately.

Facility HCPCS Coding

Some applicable HCPCS codes may include, but are not limited to:

C1729   Catheter, drainage

C1769   Guidewire

C1894   Introducer/sheath, other than guiding, intracardiac electrophysiological, non-laser

C2629   Introducer/sheath, other than guiding, intracardiac

ICD-10-CM Coding

The application of this code is too broad to adequately present ICD-10-CM diagnosis code links here. Refer to the current ICD-10-CM book.

CCI Edits

49446   0213T, 0216T, 12001-12007, 12011-12057, 13100-13133, 13151-13153, 36000, 36400-36410, 36420-36430, 36440, 36591-36592, 36600, 36640, 43752, 49452-49460, 62320-62327, 64400-64410, 64413-64435, 64445-64450, 64461-64463, 64479-64530, 69990, 75984, 76000-76001, 77001-77002, 92012-92014, 93000-93010, 93040-93042, 93318, 93355, 94002, 94200, 94250, 94680-94690, 94770, 95812-95816, 95819, 95822, 95829, 95955, 96360-96368, 96372, 96374-96377, 99155-99157, 99211-99223, 99231-99255, 99291-99292, 99304-99310, 99315-99316, 99334-99337, 99347-99350, 99374-99375, 99377-99378, 99446-99449, 99495-99496, G0463, J0670, J2001

Case Example

The patient is taken to the interventional radiology suite and placed on the imaging table. The area over the gastrostomy site is prepped and draped. A guidewire is advanced through the existing gastrostomy tube using fluoroscopic guidance. The **gastrostomy tube** is **withdrawn**. A **new tube is inserted** over the guidewire with its distal tip placed **into the proximal jejunum**. Contrast is injected and correct placement is verified. The catheter is connected to a drainage bag. The insertion site is dressed. The patient tolerated the procedure well.

CPT/HCPCS Codes Reported:
49446

Replacement and Maintenance of Gastrointestinal System Tubes

49450   **Replacement of gastrostomy or cecostomy (or other colonic) tube, percutaneous, under fluoroscopic guidance including contrast injection(s), image documentation and report**

The physician replaces an existing gastrostomy, cecostomy, or other colonic tube via percutaneous (under the skin) approach using fluoroscopic guidance and contrast monitoring. The existing tube is removed and the replacement is placed percutaneously via the existing tract. Contrast injection allows for correct positioning to be visualized with fluoroscopic images displayed on a screen. In order for this code to be reported, the new tube must be placed via the existing percutaneous access site. This procedure includes contrast injection, image documentation, and report.

49451   **Replacement of duodenostomy or jejunostomy tube, percutaneous, under fluoroscopic guidance including contrast injection(s), image documentation and report**

The physician replaces an existing duodenostomy or jejunostomy tube via percutaneous (under the skin) approach using fluoroscopic guidance and contrast monitoring. The existing tube is removed and the replacement is placed percutaneously through the abdominal wall via the existing tract. Contrast injection allows for correct positioning to be visualized with fluoroscopic images displayed on a screen. In order for this code to be reported, the new tube must be placed via the existing percutaneous access site. This procedure includes contrast injection, image documentation, and report.

49452   **Replacement of gastro-jejunostomy tube, percutaneous, under fluoroscopic guidance including contrast injection(s), image documentation and report**

The physician replaces an existing gastrojejunostomy tube via percutaneous (under the skin) approach using fluoroscopic guidance and contrast monitoring. The existing tube is removed and the replacement is placed percutaneously through the abdominal wall via the existing tract. Contrast injection allows for correct positioning to be visualized with fluoroscopic images displayed on a screen. In order for this code to be reported, the new tube must be placed via the existing percutaneous access site. This procedure includes contrast injection, image documentation, and report.

49460   **Mechanical removal of obstructive material from gastrostomy, duodenostomy, jejunostomy, gastro-jejunostomy, or cecostomy (or other colonic) tube, any method, under fluoroscopic guidance including contrast injection(s), if performed, image documentation and report**

The physician mechanically removes obstructive material from an existing tube (gastrostomy, duodenostomy, jejunostomy, gastrojejunostomy, or cecostomy) by any method. Fluoroscopic guidance and contrast imaging may be utilized. This procedure includes image documentation and report.

49465   **Contrast injection(s) for radiological evaluation of existing gastrostomy, duodenostomy, jejunostomy, gastro-jejunostomy, or cecostomy (or other colonic) tube, from a percutaneous approach including image documentationand report**

The physician injects contrast via a percutaneous approach for the radiological evaluation of existing tubes (gastrostomy, duodenostomy, jejunostomy, gastrojejunostomy, or cecostomy). Image documentation and report are included in this procedure.

Coding Tips

1. These codes report the replacement of the applicable tube using imaging guidance.
2. If imaging guidance is not used, see code 43760.
3. The codes include imaging service. There is no radiology supervision and interpretation code to report.
4. Fluoroscopy is included and is not separately reported.
5. Report any applicable HCPCS Level II codes for devices and contrast media used. Refer to appendix B for available device HCPCS codes.

Facility HCPCS Coding

Some applicable HCPCS codes may include, but are not limited to:

C1729   Catheter, drainage

C1769   Guidewire

C1894   Introducer/sheath, other than guiding, intracardiac electrophysiological, non-laser

C2629   Introducer/sheath, other than guiding, intracardiac

ICD-10-CM Coding

49450–49452

K94.00	Colostomy complication, unspecified
K94.01	Colostomy hemorrhage
K94.02	Colostomy infection
K94.03	Colostomy malfunction
K94.09	Other complications of colostomy
K94.10	Enterostomy complication, unspecified
K94.11	Enterostomy hemorrhage
K94.12	Enterostomy infection
K94.13	Enterostomy malfunction
K94.19	Other complications of enterostomy
K94.20	Gastrostomy complication, unspecified
K94.21	Gastrostomy hemorrhage
K94.22	Gastrostomy infection
K94.23	Gastrostomy malfunction
K94.29	Other complications of gastrostomy
L02.211	Cutaneous abscess of abdominal wall
L02.213	Cutaneous abscess of chest wall
L02.214	Cutaneous abscess of groin
L02.215	Cutaneous abscess of perineum
L02.216	Cutaneous abscess of umbilicus
L02.219	Cutaneous abscess of trunk, unspecified
L03.311	Cellulitis of abdominal wall
L03.313	Cellulitis of chest wall
L03.314	Cellulitis of groin
L03.315	Cellulitis of perineum
L03.316	Cellulitis of umbilicus
L03.319	Cellulitis of trunk, unspecified
L03.321	Acute lymphangitis of abdominal wall
L03.323	Acute lymphangitis of chest wall
L03.324	Acute lymphangitis of groin
L03.325	Acute lymphangitis of perineum
L03.326	Acute lymphangitis of umbilicus
L03.329	Acute lymphangitis of trunk, unspecified
Z43.1	Encounter for attention to gastrostomy
Z43.2	Encounter for attention to ileostomy
Z43.3	Encounter for attention to colostomy
Z43.4	Encounter for attention to other artificial openings of digestive tract
Z46.59	Encounter for fitting and adjustment of other gastrointestinal appliance and device

49460

K31.89	Other diseases of stomach and duodenum
K94.00	Colostomy complication, unspecified
K94.01	Colostomy hemorrhage
K94.09	Other complications of colostomy
K94.10	Enterostomy complication, unspecified
K94.11	Enterostomy hemorrhage
K94.19	Other complications of enterostomy
K94.20	Gastrostomy complication, unspecified
K94.21	Gastrostomy hemorrhage
K94.22	Gastrostomy infection
K94.23	Gastrostomy malfunction
K94.29	Other complications of gastrostomy
L02.211	Cutaneous abscess of abdominal wall
L02.212	Cutaneous abscess of back [any part, except buttock]

L02.213	Cutaneous abscess of chest wall
L02.215	Cutaneous abscess of perineum
L02.216	Cutaneous abscess of umbilicus
L02.219	Cutaneous abscess of trunk, unspecified
L03.311	Cellulitis of abdominal wall
L03.313	Cellulitis of chest wall
L03.315	Cellulitis of perineum
L03.316	Cellulitis of umbilicus
L03.319	Cellulitis of trunk, unspecified
L03.321	Acute lymphangitis of abdominal wall
L03.322	Acute lymphangitis of back [any part except buttock]
L03.323	Acute lymphangitis of chest wall
L03.324	Acute lymphangitis of groin
L03.325	Acute lymphangitis of perineum
L03.326	Acute lymphangitis of umbilicus
L03.329	Acute lymphangitis of trunk, unspecified
T85.510A	Breakdown (mechanical) of bile duct prosthesis, initial encounter
T85.511A	Breakdown (mechanical) of esophageal anti-reflux device, initial encounter
T85.518A	Breakdown (mechanical) of other gastrointestinal prosthetic devices, implants and grafts, initial encounter
T85.520A	Displacement of bile duct prosthesis, initial encounter
T85.521A	Displacement of esophageal anti-reflux device, initial encounter
T85.528A	Displacement of other gastrointestinal prosthetic devices, implants and grafts, initial encounter
T85.590A	Other mechanical complication of bile duct prosthesis, initial encounter
T85.591A	Other mechanical complication of esophageal anti-reflux device, initial encounter
T85.598A	Other mechanical complication of other gastrointestinal prosthetic devices, implants and grafts, initial encounter
T85.618A	Breakdown (mechanical) of other specified internal prosthetic devices, implants and grafts, initial encounter
T85.692A	Other mechanical complication of permanent sutures, initial encounter
T85.698A	Other mechanical complication of other specified internal prosthetic devices, implants and grafts, initial encounter
Z43.1	Encounter for attention to gastrostomy
Z43.2	Encounter for attention to ileostomy

49465

K31.89	Other diseases of stomach and duodenum
K94.00	Colostomy complication, unspecified
K94.01	Colostomy hemorrhage
K94.09	Other complications of colostomy
K94.10	Enterostomy complication, unspecified
K94.11	Enterostomy hemorrhage
K94.19	Other complications of enterostomy
K94.20	Gastrostomy complication, unspecified
K94.21	Gastrostomy hemorrhage
K94.22	Gastrostomy infection
K94.23	Gastrostomy malfunction
K94.29	Other complications of gastrostomy
L02.211	Cutaneous abscess of abdominal wall
L02.212	Cutaneous abscess of back [any part, except buttock]
L02.213	Cutaneous abscess of chest wall
L02.214	Cutaneous abscess of groin
L02.215	Cutaneous abscess of perineum
L02.216	Cutaneous abscess of umbilicus
L02.219	Cutaneous abscess of trunk, unspecified
L03.311	Cellulitis of abdominal wall
L03.312	Cellulitis of back [any part except buttock]
L03.313	Cellulitis of chest wall
L03.314	Cellulitis of groin

L03.315	Cellulitis of perineum
L03.316	Cellulitis of umbilicus
L03.319	Cellulitis of trunk, unspecified
L03.321	Acute lymphangitis of abdominal wall
L03.322	Acute lymphangitis of back [any part except buttock]
L03.323	Acute lymphangitis of chest wall
L03.324	Acute lymphangitis of groin
L03.325	Acute lymphangitis of perineum
L03.326	Acute lymphangitis of umbilicus
L03.329	Acute lymphangitis of trunk, unspecified
T85.318A	Breakdown (mechanical) of other ocular prosthetic devices, implants and grafts, initial encounter
T85.510A	Breakdown (mechanical) of bile duct prosthesis, initial encounter
T85.511A	Breakdown (mechanical) of esophageal anti-reflux device, initial encounter
T85.518A	Breakdown (mechanical) of other gastrointestinal prosthetic devices, implants and grafts, initial encounter
T85.520A	Displacement of bile duct prosthesis, initial encounter
T85.521A	Displacement of esophageal anti-reflux device, initial encounter
T85.528A	Displacement of other gastrointestinal prosthetic devices, implants and grafts, initial encounter
T85.590A	Other mechanical complication of bile duct prosthesis, initial encounter
T85.591A	Other mechanical complication of esophageal anti-reflux device, initial encounter
T85.598A	Other mechanical complication of other gastrointestinal prosthetic devices, implants and grafts, initial encounter
T85.618A	Breakdown (mechanical) of other specified internal prosthetic devices, implants and grafts, initial encounter
T85.692A	Other mechanical complication of permanent sutures, initial encounter
T85.698A	Other mechanical complication of other specified internal prosthetic devices, implants and grafts, initial encounter
Z43.1	Encounter for attention to gastrostomy
Z43.2	Encounter for attention to ileostomy

CCI Edits

49450 0213T, 0216T, 11000-11006, 11042-11047, 12001-12007, 12011-12057, 13100-13133, 13151-13153, 36000, 36400-36410, 36420-36430, 36440, 36591-36592, 36600, 36640, 43752, 43760, 49460-49465, 62320-62327, 64400-64410, 64413-64435, 64445-64450, 64461-64463, 64479-64530, 69990, 75984, 76000-76001, 77001-77002, 92012-92014, 93000-93010, 93040-93042, 93318, 93355, 94002, 94200, 94250, 94680-94690, 94770, 95812-95816, 95819, 95822, 95829, 95955, 96360-96368, 96372, 96374-96377, 97597-97598, 97602, 99155-99157, 99211-99223, 99231-99255, 99291-99292, 99304-99310, 99315-99316, 99334-99337, 99347-99350, 99374-99375, 99377-99378, 99446-99449, 99495-99496, G0463, J0670, J2001

49451 0213T, 0216T, 11000-11006, 11042-11047, 12001-12007, 12011-12057, 13100-13133, 13151-13153, 36000, 36400-36410, 36420-36430, 36440, 36591-36592, 36600, 36640, 43752, 43760, 49460-49465, 62320-62327, 64400-64410, 64413-64435, 64445-64450, 64461-64463, 64479-64530, 69990, 75984, 76000-76001, 77001-77002, 92012-92014, 93000-93010, 93040-93042, 93318, 93355, 94002, 94200, 94250, 94680-94690, 94770, 95812-95816, 95819, 95822, 95829, 95955, 96360-96368, 96372, 96374-96377, 97597-97598, 97602, 99155-99157, 99211-99223, 99231-99255, 99291-99292, 99304-99310, 99315-99316, 99334-99337, 99347-99350, 99374-99375, 99377-99378, 99446-99449, 99495-99496, G0463, J0670, J2001

49452 0213T, 0216T, 11000-11006, 11042-11047, 12001-12007, 12011-12057, 13100-13133, 13151-13153, 36000, 36400-36410, 36420-36430, 36440, 36591-36592, 36600, 36640, 43752, 43760, 49460-49465, 62320-62327, 64400-64410, 64413-64435, 64445-64450, 64461-64463, 64479-64530, 69990, 75984, 76000-76001, 77001-77002, 92012-92014, 93000-93010, 93040-93042, 93318, 93355, 94002, 94200, 94250, 94680-94690, 94770, 95812-95816, 95819, 95822, 95829, 95955, 96360-96368, 96372, 96374-96377, 97597-97598, 97602, 99155-99157, 99211-99223, 99231-99255, 99291-99292, 99304-99310, 99315-99316, 99334-99337, 99347-99350, 99374-99375, 99377-99378, 99446-99449, 99495-99496, G0463, J0670, J2001

49460 0213T, 0216T, 11000-11006, 11042-11047, 12001-12007, 12011-12057, 13100-13133, 13151-13153, 36000, 36400-36410, 36420-36430, 36440, 36591-36592, 36600, 36640, 43752, 49465, 62320-62327, 64400-64410, 64413-64435, 64445-64450, 64461-64463, 64479-64530, 69990, 75984, 76000-76001, 77001-77002, 92012-92014, 93000-93010, 93040-93042, 93318, 93355, 94002, 94200, 94250, 94680-94690, 94770, 95812-95816, 95819, 95822, 95829, 95955, 96360-96368, 96372, 96374-96377, 97597-97598, 97602, 99155-99157, 99211-99223, 99231-99255, 99291-99292, 99304-99310, 99315-99316, 99334-99337, 99347-99350, 99374-99375, 99377-99378, 99446-99449, 99495-99496, G0463, J0670, J2001

49465 0213T, 0216T, 12001-12007, 12011-12057, 13100-13133, 13151-13153, 36000, 36400-36410, 36420-36430, 36440, 36591-36592, 36600, 36640, 43752, 62320-62327, 64400-64410, 64413-64435, 64445-64450, 64461-64463, 64479-64530, 69990, 75984, 76000-76001, 92012-92014, 93000-93010, 93040-93042, 93318, 93355, 94002, 94200, 94250, 94680-94690, 94770, 95812-95816, 95819, 95822, 95829, 95955, 96360-96368, 96372, 96374-96377, 99155-99157, 99211-99223, 99231-99255, 99291-99292, 99304-99310, 99315-99316, 99334-99337, 99347-99350, 99374-99375, 99377-99378, 99446-99449, 99495-99496, G0463

Case Example #1

The patient is taken to the interventional radiology suite and placed on the imaging table. The area over the **gastrostomy site is prepped** and draped. A guidewire is advanced through the **existing gastrostomy tube** using **fluoroscopic guidance**. The **gastrostomy tube is withdrawn**. A **new tube is inserted** over the guidewire with its distal **tip placed into stomach**. Contrast is injected and correct placement is verified. The catheter is connected to a drainage bag. The insertion site is dressed. The patient tolerated the procedure well.

CPT/HCPCS Codes Reported:
49450

Case Example #2

Tube check is requested.

The patient is placed on the fluoroscopy table and prepped and draped in typical sterile fashion. The **existing catheter** is disconnected from the drainage bag. **Contrast media is slowly injected** under fluoroscopic guidance and images taken.

Findings:
The gastrostomy tube is in good position and contrast flows freely. There is no appearance of obstruction or other occlusion.

CPT/HCPCS Codes Reported:
49465

Chapter 10: Urinary Tract Diagnostics and Interventions

Nephrostogram

Nephrostograms are performed through an existing catheter previously placed into the kidney for urine drainage usually due to some sort of blockage in the collecting system or the ureter. Contrast is injected into the catheter, and images are taken.

50430   **Injection procedure for antegrade nephrostogram and/or ureterogram, complete diagnostic procedure including imaging guidance (eg, ultrasound and fluoroscopy) and all associated radiological supervision and interpretation; new access**

50431   **existing access**

The physician injects a contrast agent through a tube or indwelling catheter into the renal pelvis to study the kidney and renal collecting system. The physician determines immediate allergic response to the contrast agent by injecting a small initial dose of contrast material through an existing nephrostomy tube or indwelling ureteral catheter. If no allergic response occurs, a large quantity of contrast material is injected into the renal pelvis. The contrast is visualized as it passes from the kidneys into the ureters and the urinary bladder. Imaging guidance via fluoroscopy or ultrasound is used to observe the contrast path. When an obstruction is present, it can be readily identified on imaging because the contrast is unable to progress properly through the urinary tract. The radiologist produces a representation of the kidney, renal pelvis, and/or ureter with an x-ray. Report 50431 when this test is performed through an existing access.

74425   **Urography, antegrade, (pyelostogram, nephrostogram, loopogram), radiological supervision and interpretation**

A radiographic exam of the urinary tract is performed with injection or instillation of a contrast medium. This test is done to follow the normal flow of urine through the tract (antegrade) and may identify obstructions, abnormalities in the urinary tract, or assess function following surgery. Contrast medium is introduced percutaneously with a needle or though an existing tube, catheter, or stoma. For percutaneous needle injection, the skin is anesthetized and the needle inserted under fluoroscopic guidance into a calyx of the kidney. Contrast medium is injected and radiographs are taken.

Coding Tips

1. Codes 50430 and 50431 report a complete procedure. Do not report these codes with 50432–50435, 50693–50695 or 74425 for the same access.
2. Use 50430 for a new access into the renal collecting system.
3. Use 50431 when accessing an existing renal catheter.
4. All imaging including guidance is included and not separately reported.
5. Exchange of an existing nephrostomy is included in 50430 and 50431. Do not separately report 50435.
6. Report these codes once for each renal pelvis and associated ureter. Access into a separate renal collecting system during the same encounter is reported with an additional code.
7. Exchange of an existing catheter is separately reported.
8. Hospitals are requested to continue reporting LOCM separately with HCPCS codes Q9965–Q9967. Report contrast media by milliliter
9. Report any applicable HCPCS Level II codes for devices and contrast media used. Refer to the HCPCS section for possible codes.
10. For procedures performed by two separate physicians (eg, nephrologist and radiologist), the radiologist reports 74425 and the nephrologist reports 50430 or 50431.
11. Conscious sedation is not included in these codes. Separately report 99151–99157 per payer policy and coding guidelines. Hospitals may choose to include the costs associated with the service as part of the procedure rather than reporting them separately.

Nephrostogram

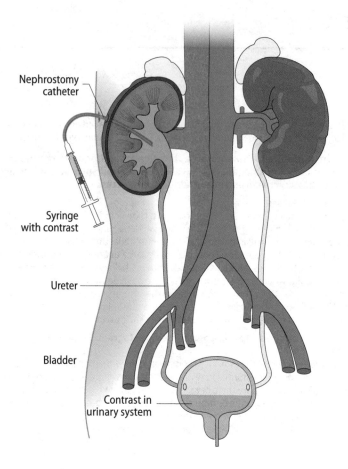

Nephrostomy catheter

Syringe with contrast

Ureter

Bladder

Contrast in urinary system

Facility HCPCS Coding

Some applicable codes may include, but are not limited to:

C1729	Catheter, drainage
C1769	Guide wire
Q9958	HOCM, up to 149 mg/ml iodine concentration, per ml
Q9959	HOCM, 150-199 mg/ml iodine concentration, per ml
Q9960	HOCM, 200-249 mg/ml iodine concentration, per ml
Q9961	HOCM, 250-299 mg/ml iodine concentration, per ml
Q9962	HOCM, 300-349 mg/ml iodine concentration, per ml
Q9963	HOCM, 350-399 mg/ml iodine concentration, per ml
Q9964	HOCM, 400 or greater mg/ml iodine concentration, per ml
Q9965	LOCM, 100-199 mg/ml iodine concentration, per ml
Q9966	LOCM, 200-299 mg/ml iodine concentration, per ml
Q9967	LOCM, 300-399 mg/ml iodine concentration, per ml

ICD-10-CM Coding

C64.1	Malignant neoplasm of right kidney, except renal pelvis
C64.2	Malignant neoplasm of left kidney, except renal pelvis
C64.9	Malignant neoplasm of unspecified kidney, except renal pelvis
C65.1	Malignant neoplasm of right renal pelvis
C65.2	Malignant neoplasm of left renal pelvis
C65.9	Malignant neoplasm of unspecified renal pelvis

C66.1	Malignant neoplasm of right ureter
C66.2	Malignant neoplasm of left ureter
C66.9	Malignant neoplasm of unspecified ureter
C67.0	Malignant neoplasm of trigone of bladder
C67.1	Malignant neoplasm of dome of bladder
C67.2	Malignant neoplasm of lateral wall of bladder
C67.3	Malignant neoplasm of anterior wall of bladder
C67.4	Malignant neoplasm of posterior wall of bladder
C67.5	Malignant neoplasm of bladder neck
C67.6	Malignant neoplasm of ureteric orifice
C67.7	Malignant neoplasm of urachus
C67.8	Malignant neoplasm of overlapping sites of bladder
C67.9	Malignant neoplasm of bladder, unspecified
C68.8	Malignant neoplasm of overlapping sites of urinary organs
C68.9	Malignant neoplasm of urinary organ, unspecified
C79.00	Secondary malignant neoplasm of unspecified kidney and renal pelvis
C79.01	Secondary malignant neoplasm of right kidney and renal pelvis
C79.02	Secondary malignant neoplasm of left kidney and renal pelvis
C79.10	Secondary malignant neoplasm of unspecified urinary organs
C79.19	Secondary malignant neoplasm of other urinary organs
C7A.093	Malignant carcinoid tumor of the kidney
D09.10	Carcinoma in situ of unspecified urinary organ
D09.19	Carcinoma in situ of other urinary organs
D30.00	Benign neoplasm of unspecified kidney
D30.01	Benign neoplasm of right kidney
D30.02	Benign neoplasm of left kidney
D30.10	Benign neoplasm of unspecified renal pelvis
D30.11	Benign neoplasm of right renal pelvis
D30.12	Benign neoplasm of left renal pelvis
D30.20	Benign neoplasm of unspecified ureter
D30.21	Benign neoplasm of right ureter
D30.22	Benign neoplasm of left ureter
D30.3	Benign neoplasm of bladder
D30.9	Benign neoplasm of urinary organ, unspecified
D3A.093	Benign carcinoid tumor of the kidney
D41.00	Neoplasm of uncertain behavior of unspecified kidney
D41.01	Neoplasm of uncertain behavior of right kidney
D41.02	Neoplasm of uncertain behavior of left kidney
D41.10	Neoplasm of uncertain behavior of unspecified renal pelvis
D41.11	Neoplasm of uncertain behavior of right renal pelvis
D41.12	Neoplasm of uncertain behavior of left renal pelvis
D41.20	Neoplasm of uncertain behavior of unspecified ureter
D41.21	Neoplasm of uncertain behavior of right ureter
D41.22	Neoplasm of uncertain behavior of left ureter
D47.Z1	Post-transplant lymphoproliferative disorder (PTLD)
D47.Z2	Castleman disease
D49.4	Neoplasm of unspecified behavior of bladder
D49.511	Neoplasm of unspecified behavior of right kidney
D49.512	Neoplasm of unspecified behavior of left kidney
D49.519	Neoplasm of unspecified behavior of unspecified kidney
D49.59	Neoplasm of unspecified behavior of other genitourinary organ
N10	Acute pyelonephritis
N11.0	Nonobstructive reflux-associated chronic pyelonephritis
N11.1	Chronic obstructive pyelonephritis
N11.8	Other chronic tubulo-interstitial nephritis
N11.9	Chronic tubulo-interstitial nephritis, unspecified

N12	Tubulo-interstitial nephritis, not specified as acute or chronic
N13.0	Hydronephrosis with ureteropelvic junction obstruction
N13.1	Hydronephrosis with ureteral stricture, not elsewhere classified
N13.2	Hydronephrosis with renal and ureteral calculous obstruction
N13.30	Unspecified hydronephrosis
N13.39	Other hydronephrosis
N13.4	Hydroureter
N13.5	Crossing vessel and stricture of ureter without hydronephrosis
N13.6	Pyonephrosis
N13.70	Vesicoureteral-reflux, unspecified
N13.71	Vesicoureteral-reflux without reflux nephropathy
N13.721	Vesicoureteral-reflux with reflux nephropathy without hydroureter, unilateral
N13.722	Vesicoureteral-reflux with reflux nephropathy without hydroureter, bilateral
N13.729	Vesicoureteral-reflux with reflux nephropathy without hydroureter, unspecified
N13.731	Vesicoureteral-reflux with reflux nephropathy with hydroureter, unilateral
N13.732	Vesicoureteral-reflux with reflux nephropathy with hydroureter, bilateral
N13.739	Vesicoureteral-reflux with reflux nephropathy with hydroureter, unspecified
N13.8	Other obstructive and reflux uropathy
N13.9	Obstructive and reflux uropathy, unspecified
N20.0	Calculus of kidney
N20.1	Calculus of ureter
N20.2	Calculus of kidney with calculus of ureter
N20.9	Urinary calculus, unspecified
N22	Calculus of urinary tract in diseases classified elsewhere
N23	Unspecified renal colic
N25.81	Secondary hyperparathyroidism of renal origin
N25.89	Other disorders resulting from impaired renal tubular function
N26.1	Atrophy of kidney (terminal)
N26.9	Renal sclerosis, unspecified
N28.1	Cyst of kidney, acquired
N28.81	Hypertrophy of kidney
N28.82	Megaloureter
N28.83	Nephroptosis
N28.84	Pyelitis cystica
N28.85	Pyeloureteritis cystica
N28.86	Ureteritis cystica
N28.89	Other specified disorders of kidney and ureter
N28.9	Disorder of kidney and ureter, unspecified
N29	Other disorders of kidney and ureter in diseases classified elsewhere
N30.10	Interstitial cystitis (chronic) without hematuria
N30.11	Interstitial cystitis (chronic) with hematuria
N30.20	Other chronic cystitis without hematuria
N30.21	Other chronic cystitis with hematuria
N41.1	Chronic prostatitis
N99.0	Postprocedural (acute) (chronic) kidney failure
N99.81	Other intraoperative complications of genitourinary system
N99.89	Other postprocedural complications and disorders of genitourinary system
Q60.3	Renal hypoplasia, unilateral
Q60.4	Renal hypoplasia, bilateral
Q60.5	Renal hypoplasia, unspecified
Q60.6	Potter's syndrome
Q61.00	Congenital renal cyst, unspecified
Q61.01	Congenital single renal cyst
Q61.02	Congenital multiple renal cysts
Q61.11	Cystic dilatation of collecting ducts
Q61.19	Other polycystic kidney, infantile type

Q61.2	Polycystic kidney, adult type
Q61.3	Polycystic kidney, unspecified
Q61.4	Renal dysplasia
Q61.5	Medullary cystic kidney
Q61.8	Other cystic kidney diseases
Q61.9	Cystic kidney disease, unspecified
Q62.0	Congenital hydronephrosis
Q62.10	Congenital occlusion of ureter, unspecified
Q62.11	Congenital occlusion of ureteropelvic junction
Q62.12	Congenital occlusion of ureterovesical orifice
Q62.2	Congenital megaureter
Q62.31	Congenital ureterocele, orthotopic
Q62.32	Cecoureterocele
Q62.39	Other obstructive defects of renal pelvis and ureter
Q64.8	Other specified congenital malformations of urinary system
Q64.9	Congenital malformation of urinary system, unspecified
T86.10	Unspecified complication of kidney transplant
T86.19	Other complication of kidney transplant

CCI Edits

50430 0213T, 0216T, 0228T, 0230T, 12001-12007, 12011-12057, 13100-13133, 13151-13153, 36000, 36011, 36400-36410, 36420-36430, 36440, 36591-36592, 36600, 36640, 43752, 50395, 50431, 51701-51703, 62320-62327, 64400-64410, 64413-64435, 64445-64450, 64461-64463, 64479-64530, 69990, 74425, 76000-76001, 76942, 76970, 76998, 77001-77002, 92012-92014, 93000-93010, 93040-93042, 93318, 93355, 94002, 94200, 94250, 94680-94690, 94770, 95812-95816, 95819, 95822, 95829, 95955, 96360-96368, 96372, 96374-96377, 99155-99157, 99211-99223, 99231-99255, 99291-99292, 99304-99310, 99315-99316, 99334-99337, 99347-99350, 99374-99375, 99377-99378, 99446-99449, 99495-99496, G0463, G0471, J0670, J2001

50431 0213T, 0216T, 0228T, 0230T, 12001-12007, 12011-12057, 13100-13133, 13151-13153, 36000, 36011, 36400-36410, 36420-36430, 36440, 36591-36592, 36600, 36640, 43752, 51701-51703, 62320-62327, 64400-64410, 64413-64435, 64445-64450, 64461-64463, 64479-64530, 69990, 74425, 76000-76001, 76942, 76970, 76998, 77001-77002, 92012-92014, 93000-93010, 93040-93042, 93318, 93355, 94002, 94200, 94250, 94680-94690, 94770, 95812-95816, 95819, 95822, 95829, 95955, 96360-96368, 96372, 96374-96377, 99155-99157, 99211-99223, 99231-99255, 99291-99292, 99304-99310, 99315-99316, 99334-99337, 99347-99350, 99374-99375, 99377-99378, 99446-99449, 99495-99496, G0463, G0471

74425 36000, 36011, 36410, 36425, 36591-36592, 74000-74010, 74020, 74400, 76000-76001, 76101-76102, 77001-77002, 96360, 96365, 96372, 96374-96377, 99446-99449

Case Example

The patient presents for a **nephrostogram** to check the status of his ureteral blockage. The area is prepped and draped in the usual sterile fashion. Under fluoroscopic guidance, the **catheter is injected** and images are taken. Images reveal the blockage is still occluding drainage through the ureter. The **catheter** is in good position **within the renal pelvis**. The catheter is then secured and reconnected to the drain bag, and a dressing is applied over the area.

CPT/HCPCS Codes Reported:
50431

Ureterogram Through Existing Access

50684 **Injection procedure for ureterography or ureteropyelography through ureterostomy or indwelling ureteral catheter**
The physician injects a contrast agent through an opening between the skin and the ureter (ureterostomy) or via an indwelling catheter into the ureter and renal pelvis to study the renal collecting system. To determine immediate allergic response to the contrast agent, the physician injects a dose of contrast material through the ureterostomy or indwelling catheter into the ureter and renal pelvis and takes an x-ray.

50690 **Injection procedure for visualization of ileal conduit and/or ureteropyelography, exclusive of radiologic service**
The physician injects a contrast agent through an existing ileal stoma into the renal pelvis or ureters to study the ileal conduit (where the ureters have been diverted into the ilium) or percutaneously or intravenously via a catheter to study the renal collecting system. To determine immediate allergic response to the contrast agent, the physician injects a small, initial dose of contrast material. If an allergic response is not evident, a larger amount of radiopaque dye is injected into the ureter and renal pelvis and radiographic pictures are obtained for a ureteropyelogram or study of the ileal conduit diversion.

74425 **Urography, antegrade (pyelostogram, nephrostogram, loopogram), radiological supervision and interpretation**
The physician uses an existing access to inject contrast media to determine if the ostomy or conduit is open and flowing freely. Various catheters, guidewires, or other devices may be used during the procedure.

Coding Tips
1. These are component codes. Report the code for the injection and 74425 for the radiologic supervision and interpretation.
2. Do not use these codes with 50433–50695.
3. Conscious sedation is not included in these codes. Separately report 99151–99157 per payer policy and coding guidelines. Hospitals may choose to include the costs associated with the service as part of the procedure rather than reporting them separately.
4. Report applicable HCPCS Level II codes for devices and contrast media used. Refer to the HCPCS section for possible codes.
5. Hospitals should separately report contrast media with HCPCS codes Q9965–Q9967. Report contrast media by milliliter.

Facility HCPCS Coding
Some applicable codes may include but are not limited to:

C1729 Catheter, drainage
C1769 Guidewire
Q9965 LOCM, 100-199 mg/ml iodine concentration, per ml
Q9966 LOCM, 200-299 mg/ml iodine concentration, per ml
Q9967 LOCM, 300-399 mg/ml iodine concentration, per ml

ICD-10-CM Coding
The application of these codes is too broad to adequately present ICD-10-CM diagnosis code links here. Refer to the current ICD-10-CM book.

CCI Edits
50684 00910, 0213T, 0216T, 0228T, 0230T, 12001-12007, 12011-12057, 13100-13133, 13151-13153, 36000, 36400-36410, 36420-36430, 36440, 36591-36592, 36600, 36640, 43752, 50715, 51701-51703, 62320-62327, 64400-64410, 64413-64435, 64445-64450, 64461-64463, 64479-64530, 69990, 76000-76001, 77001, 92012-92014, 93000-93010, 93040-93042, 93318, 93355, 94002, 94200, 94250, 94680-94690, 94770, 95812-95816, 95819, 95822, 95829, 95955, 96360-96368, 96372, 96374-96377, 99155-99157, 99211-99223, 99231-99255, 99291-99292, 99304-99310, 99315-99316, 99334-99337, 99347-99350, 99374-99375, 99377-99378, 99446-99449, 99495-99496, G0463, G0471, J1644, J2001

50690 00910, 0213T, 0216T, 0228T, 0230T, 12001-12007, 12011-12057, 13100-13133, 13151-13153, 36000, 36400-36410, 36420-36430, 36440, 36591-36592, 36600, 36640, 43752, 50715, 51701-51703, 62320-62327, 64400-64410, 64413-64435, 64445-64450, 64461-64463, 64479-64530, 69990, 92012-92014, 93000-93010, 93040-93042, 93318, 93355, 94002, 94200, 94250, 94680-94690, 94770, 95812-95816, 95819, 95822, 95829, 95955, 96360-96368, 96372, 96374-96377, 99155-99157, 99211-99223, 99231-99255, 99291-99292, 99304-99310, 99315-99316, 99334-99337, 99347-99350, 99374-99375, 99377-99378, 99446-99449, 99495-99496, G0463, G0471, J1644, J2001

74425 36000, 36011, 36410, 36425, 36591-36592, 74000-74010, 74020, 74400, 76000-76001, 76101-76102, 77001-77002, 96360, 96365, 96372, 96374-96377, 99446-99449

Case Example

Using standard sterile technique and local anesthesia, a guidewire was placed through the **indwelling external nephrostomy tube** on the right. Over the guidewire, a 5-French catheter was inserted and advanced to the proximal ureter. The guidewire was removed, and **contrast media was injected** as images were obtained over the abdomen and pelvis. This **antegrade ureterogram** demonstrates an obstruction in the distal ureter with only a thread of flow showing into the bladder.

CPT/HCPCS Codes Reported:
50684, 74425

Other HCPCS Codes Reported:
C1769

Percutaneous Placement of Nephrostomy Tube

50432   **Placement of nephrostomy catheter, percutaneous, including diagnostic nephrostogram and/or ureterogram when performed, imaging guidance (eg, ultrasound and/or fluoroscopy) and all associated radiological supervision and interpretation**

The physician inserts a catheter or intracatheter percutaneously into the renal pelvis for drainage and/or contrast injection for radiographic studies. With the patient face down and the puncture site having been identified by separately reportable means, a local anesthetic is injected. A needle with a guidewire is slowly advanced into the kidney under fluoroscopic guidance. The needle is removed and the tract may be dilated to accommodate the catheter or nephrostomy tube which is fixed in place and secured also under fluoroscopic control.

Percutaneous Nephrostomy Tube Placement

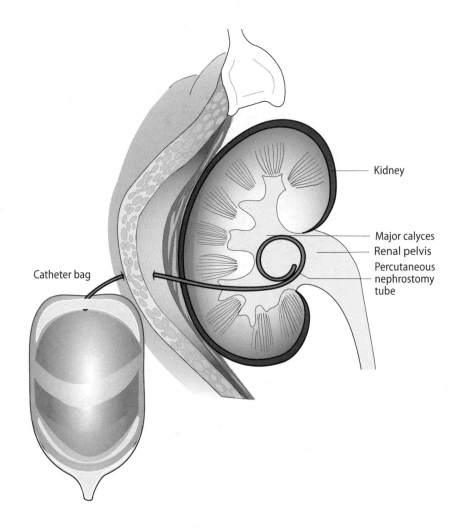

Kidney

Major calyces

Renal pelvis

Percutaneous nephrostomy tube

Catheter bag

Coding Tips

1. Code 50432 is a comprehensive code. Do not separately report imaging supervision and interpretation (74425).

2. Fluoroscopy and/or ultrasound guidance is included and is not separately reported.

3. Dilation of the tube tract is included. Do not also report 50395.

4. Nephrostomy catheter exchange is included in the code and should not be separately reported.

5. All of the elements of access into the renal pelvis are included.

6. All manipulations of the drainage catheter are included.

7. All imaging guidance is included.

8. Do not also report 50430, 50431, 50433, 50694, or 50695 for the same renal collecting system.

9. If another nephrostomy tube is placed in a separate renal collecting system, report a second unit for 50432.

10. Report any applicable HCPCS Level II codes for devices and contrast media used. Refer to the HCPCS section for possible codes.

11. Conscious sedation is not included in these codes. Separately report 99151–99157 per payer policy and coding guidelines. Hospitals may choose to include the costs associated with the service as part of the procedure rather than reporting them separately.

Facility HCPCS Coding

Some applicable codes may include, but are not limited to:

C1729	Catheter, drainage
C1769	Guide wire
Q9958	HOCM, up to 149 mg/ml iodine concentration, per ml
Q9959	HOCM, 150-199 mg/ml iodine concentration, per ml
Q9960	HOCM, 200-249 mg/ml iodine concentration, per ml
Q9961	HOCM, 250-299 mg/ml iodine concentration, per ml
Q9962	HOCM, 300-349 mg/ml iodine concentration, per ml
Q9963	HOCM, 350-399 mg/ml iodine concentration, per ml
Q9964	HOCM, 400 or greater mg/ml iodine concentration, per ml
Q9965	LOCM, 100-199 mg/ml iodine concentration, per ml
Q9966	LOCM, 200-299 mg/ml iodine concentration, per ml
Q9967	LOCM, 300-399 mg/ml iodine concentration, per ml

ICD-10-CM Coding

C64.1	Malignant neoplasm of right kidney, except renal pelvis
C64.2	Malignant neoplasm of left kidney, except renal pelvis
C64.9	Malignant neoplasm of unspecified kidney, except renal pelvis
C65.1	Malignant neoplasm of right renal pelvis
C65.2	Malignant neoplasm of left renal pelvis
C65.9	Malignant neoplasm of unspecified renal pelvis
C66.1	Malignant neoplasm of right ureter
C66.2	Malignant neoplasm of left ureter
C66.9	Malignant neoplasm of unspecified ureter
C79.00	Secondary malignant neoplasm of unspecified kidney and renal pelvis
C79.01	Secondary malignant neoplasm of right kidney and renal pelvis
C79.02	Secondary malignant neoplasm of left kidney and renal pelvis
C79.10	Secondary malignant neoplasm of unspecified urinary organs
C79.19	Secondary malignant neoplasm of other urinary organs
C7A.093	Malignant carcinoid tumor of the kidney
C80.2	Malignant neoplasm associated with transplanted organ
D09.19	Carcinoma in situ of other urinary organs
D30.10	Benign neoplasm of unspecified renal pelvis
D30.11	Benign neoplasm of right renal pelvis
D30.12	Benign neoplasm of left renal pelvis
D30.20	Benign neoplasm of unspecified ureter

D30.21	Benign neoplasm of right ureter
D30.22	Benign neoplasm of left ureter
D3A.093	Benign carcinoid tumor of the kidney
D41.00	Neoplasm of uncertain behavior of unspecified kidney
D41.02	Neoplasm of uncertain behavior of left kidney
D41.10	Neoplasm of uncertain behavior of unspecified renal pelvis
D41.11	Neoplasm of uncertain behavior of right renal pelvis
D41.12	Neoplasm of uncertain behavior of left renal pelvis
D41.20	Neoplasm of uncertain behavior of unspecified ureter
D41.21	Neoplasm of uncertain behavior of right ureter
D41.22	Neoplasm of uncertain behavior of left ureter
D47.Z1	Post-transplant lymphoproliferative disorder (PTLD)
D47.Z2	Castleman disease
D49.511	Neoplasm of unspecified behavior of right kidney
D49.512	Neoplasm of unspecified behavior of left kidney
D49.519	Neoplasm of unspecified behavior of unspecified kidney
D49.59	Neoplasm of unspecified behavior of other genitourinary organ
N10	Acute tubulo-interstitial nephritis
N11.0	Nonobstructive reflux-associated chronic pyelonephritis
N11.1	Chronic obstructive pyelonephritis
N11.8	Other chronic tubulo-interstitial nephritis
N11.9	Chronic tubulo-interstitial nephritis, unspecified
N12	Tubulo-interstitial nephritis, not specified as acute or chronic
N13.0	Hydronephrosis with ureteropelvic junction obstruction
N13.1	Hydronephrosis with ureteral stricture, not elsewhere classified
N13.2	Hydronephrosis with renal and ureteral calculous obstruction
N13.30	Unspecified hydronephrosis
N13.39	Other hydronephrosis
N13.4	Hydroureter
N13.5	Crossing vessel and stricture of ureter without hydronephrosis
N13.6	Pyonephrosis
N13.721	Vesicoureteral-reflux with reflux nephropathy without hydroureter, unilateral
N13.722	Vesicoureteral-reflux with reflux nephropathy without hydroureter, bilateral
N13.731	Vesicoureteral-reflux with reflux nephropathy with hydroureter, unilateral
N13.732	Vesicoureteral-reflux with reflux nephropathy with hydroureter, bilateral
N13.8	Other obstructive and reflux uropathy
N13.9	Obstructive and reflux uropathy, unspecified
N15.1	Renal and perinephric abscess
N15.9	Renal tubulo-interstitial disease, unspecified
N19	Unspecified kidney failure
N20.0	Calculus of kidney
N20.1	Calculus of ureter
N20.2	Calculus of kidney with calculus of ureter
N20.9	Urinary calculus, unspecified
N23	Unspecified renal colic
N25.81	Secondary hyperparathyroidism of renal origin
N25.89	Other disorders resulting from impaired renal tubular function
N25.9	Disorder resulting from impaired renal tubular function, unspecified
N28.82	Megaloureter
N28.84	Pyelitis cystica
N28.85	Pyeloureteritis cystica
N28.86	Ureteritis cystica
N28.89	Other specified disorders of kidney and ureter
N39.0	Urinary tract infection, site not specified
N39.3	Stress incontinence (female) (male)
N39.41	Urge incontinence

N39.42	Incontinence without sensory awareness
N39.43	Post-void dribbling
N39.44	Nocturnal enuresis
N39.45	Continuous leakage
N39.46	Mixed incontinence
N39.490	Overflow incontinence
N39.491	Coital incontinence
N39.492	Postural (urinary) incontinence
N39.498	Other specified urinary incontinence
N39.8	Other specified disorders of urinary system
N39.9	Disorder of urinary system, unspecified
N82.1	Other female urinary-genital tract fistulae
Q62.0	Congenital hydronephrosis
Q62.10	Congenital occlusion of ureter, unspecified
Q62.11	Congenital occlusion of ureteropelvic junction
Q62.12	Congenital occlusion of ureterovesical orifice
Q62.2	Congenital megaureter
Q62.31	Congenital ureterocele, orthotopic
Q62.32	Cecoureterocele
Q62.39	Other obstructive defects of renal pelvis and ureter
Q62.5	Duplication of ureter
Q62.60	Malposition of ureter, unspecified
Q62.61	Deviation of ureter
Q62.62	Displacement of ureter
Q62.63	Anomalous implantation of ureter
Q62.69	Other malposition of ureter
Q62.8	Other congenital malformations of ureter
R82.71	Bacteriuria
R82.79	Other abnormal findings on microbiological examination of urine
T86.10	Unspecified complication of kidney transplant
T86.11	Kidney transplant rejection
T86.12	Kidney transplant failure
T86.13	Kidney transplant infection
T86.19	Other complication of kidney transplant

CCI Edits

50432 0213T, 0216T, 0228T, 0230T, 12001-12007, 12011-12057, 13100-13133, 13151-13153, 36000, 36011, 36400-36410, 36420-36430, 36440, 36591-36592, 36600, 36640, 43752, 50390, 50395, 50430-50431, 50434-50435, 51701-51703, 62320-62327, 64400-64410, 64413-64435, 64445-64450, 64461-64463, 64479-64530, 69990, 74425, 76000-76001, 76380, 76942, 76970, 76998, 77001-77002, 77012, 77021, 92012-92014, 93000-93010, 93040-93042, 93318, 93355, 94002, 94200, 94250, 94680-94690, 94770, 95812-95816, 95819, 95822, 95829, 95955, 96360-96368, 96372, 96374-96377, 99155-99157, 99211-99223, 99231-99255, 99291-99292, 99304-99310, 99315-99316, 99334-99337, 99347-99350, 99374-99375, 99377-99378, 99446-99449, 99495-99496, G0463, G0471, J0670, J2001

Case Example

Patient presents with an obstructing ureteral stone. The patient is placed prone on the table and prepped and draped in the usual sterile fashion. The skin is anesthetized with lidocaine and under fluoroscopic guidance a **needle is placed via the left posterior flank into the renal collecting system**. Urine return confirms placement in the left renal collecting system. A guide wire is placed through the needle, the needle removed and the **tract dilated** to allow for the nephrostomy tube. An 8-French **nephrostomy tube is placed** with the **loop in the renal pelvis**. The catheter is **secured to external drainage** and the patient left the department in satisfactory condition.

CPT/HCPCS Codes Reported:
50432

Other HCPCS Codes Reported:
C1729, C1769

Percutaneous Placement Nephroureteral Catheter

50433   **Placement of nephroureteral catheter, percutaneous, including diagnostic nephrostogram and/or ureterogram when performed, imaging guidance (eg, ultrasound and/or fluoroscopy) and all associated radiological supervision and interpretation, new access**

The physician inserts a catheter through the skin and into the kidney and then through the ureter to drain urine. With the patient lying face down and the puncture site identified, a local anesthetic is injected. A needle with a guidewire is advanced into the kidney under fluoroscopic guidance. The needle is removed when urine flows back through it and, if necessary, the tract is dilated to accommodate the catheter or nephrostomy tube. The tube is advanced over the guidewire and with fluoroscopic guidance is advanced through the kidney and through the ureter into the bladder. The guidewire is removed, leaving one end of the catheter in the bladder and the other end in the renal pelvis. This catheter allows drainage of urine from the kidney through an obstruction in the ureter to the bladder.

50434   **Convert nephrostomy catheter to nephroureteral catheter, percutaneous, including diagnostic nephrostogram and/or ureterogram when performed, imaging guidance (eg, ultrasound and/or fluoroscopy) and all associated radiological supervision and interpretation, via pre-existing nephrostomy tract**

A previously placed nephrostomy catheter is converted to a nephroureteral catheter via percutaneous approach along the current nephrostomy tract. The patient is placed face down, and the conversion is performed over a stiff guidewire. Contrast is injected through the catheter to better visualize the kidney and ureter. The wire is advanced, the catheter is placed over the wire, and the wire is then removed. Imaging guidance ensures proper placement, and the new catheter is secured to the skin with sutures.

Coding Tips

1. Codes 50433 and 50434 are comprehensive codes. Do not separately report imaging supervision and interpretation (74425).
2. Dilation of the tube tract is included. Do not also report 50395.
3. Do not also report 50430, 50431, 50432, 50693, 50694, or 50695 in addition to 50433 for the same renal collecting system.
4. Do not also report 50430, 50431, 50435, 50684, or 50693 in addition to 50434 for the same renal collecting system.
5. Nephrostomy catheter exchange is included in the code and should not be separately reported.
6. All of the elements of access into the renal pelvis are included.
7. All manipulations of the drainage catheter are included.
8. All imaging guidance is included.
9. If nephroureteral catheter is removed and replaced, report 50387.
10. Report any applicable HCPCS Level II codes for devices and contrast media used. Refer to the HCPCS section for possible codes.
11. Conscious sedation is not included in these codes. Separately report 99151–99157 per payer policy and coding guidelines. Hospitals may choose to include the costs associated with the service as part of the procedure rather than reporting them separately.

Facility HCPCS Coding

Some applicable codes may include, but are not limited to:

C1729	Catheter, drainage
C1758	Catheter, ureteral
C1769	Guidewire
Q9965	LOCM, 100-199 mg/ml iodine concentration, per ml
Q9966	LOCM, 200-299 mg/ml iodine concentration, per ml
Q9967	LOCM, 300-399 mg/ml iodine concentration, per ml

ICD-10-CM Coding

C64.1	Malignant neoplasm of right kidney, except renal pelvis
C64.2	Malignant neoplasm of left kidney, except renal pelvis
C64.9	Malignant neoplasm of unspecified kidney, except renal pelvis
C65.1	Malignant neoplasm of right renal pelvis
C65.2	Malignant neoplasm of left renal pelvis
C65.9	Malignant neoplasm of unspecified renal pelvis
C66.1	Malignant neoplasm of right ureter
C66.2	Malignant neoplasm of left ureter

C66.9	Malignant neoplasm of unspecified ureter
C79.00	Secondary malignant neoplasm of unspecified kidney and renal pelvis
C79.01	Secondary malignant neoplasm of right kidney and renal pelvis
C79.02	Secondary malignant neoplasm of left kidney and renal pelvis
C79.10	Secondary malignant neoplasm of unspecified urinary organs
C79.19	Secondary malignant neoplasm of other urinary organs
C7A.093	Malignant carcinoid tumor of the kidney
C80.2	Malignant neoplasm associated with transplanted organ
D09.19	Carcinoma in situ of other urinary organs
D30.10	Benign neoplasm of unspecified renal pelvis
D30.11	Benign neoplasm of right renal pelvis
D30.12	Benign neoplasm of left renal pelvis
D30.20	Benign neoplasm of unspecified ureter
D30.21	Benign neoplasm of right ureter
D30.22	Benign neoplasm of left ureter
D3A.093	Benign carcinoid tumor of the kidney
D41.00	Neoplasm of uncertain behavior of unspecified kidney
D41.01	Neoplasm of uncertain behavior of right kidney
D41.02	Neoplasm of uncertain behavior of left kidney
D41.10	Neoplasm of uncertain behavior of unspecified renal pelvis
D41.11	Neoplasm of uncertain behavior of right renal pelvis
D41.12	Neoplasm of uncertain behavior of left renal pelvis
D41.20	Neoplasm of uncertain behavior of unspecified ureter
D41.21	Neoplasm of uncertain behavior of right ureter
D41.22	Neoplasm of uncertain behavior of left ureter
D47.Z1	Post-transplant lymphoproliferative disorder (PTLD)
D47.Z2	Castleman disease
D49.511	Neoplasm of unspecified behavior of right kidney
D49.512	Neoplasm of unspecified behavior of left kidney
D49.519	Neoplasm of unspecified behavior of unspecified kidney
D49.59	Neoplasm of unspecified behavior of other genitourinary organ
N10	Acute tubulo-interstitial nephritis
N11.0	Nonobstructive reflux-associated chronic pyelonephritis
N11.1	Chronic obstructive pyelonephritis
N11.8	Other chronic tubulo-interstitial nephritis
N11.9	Chronic tubulo-interstitial nephritis, unspecified
N12	Tubulo-interstitial nephritis, not specified as acute or chronic
N13.0	Hydronephrosis with ureteropelvic junction obstruction
N13.1	Hydronephrosis with ureteral stricture, not elsewhere classified
N13.2	Hydronephrosis with renal and ureteral calculous obstruction
N13.30	Unspecified hydronephrosis
N13.39	Other hydronephrosis
N13.4	Hydroureter
N13.5	Crossing vessel and stricture of ureter without hydronephrosis
N13.6	Pyonephrosis
N13.721	Vesicoureteral-reflux with reflux nephropathy without hydroureter, unilateral
N13.722	Vesicoureteral-reflux with reflux nephropathy without hydroureter, bilateral
N13.731	Vesicoureteral-reflux with reflux nephropathy with hydroureter, unilateral
N13.732	Vesicoureteral-reflux with reflux nephropathy with hydroureter, bilateral
N13.8	Other obstructive and reflux uropathy
N13.9	Obstructive and reflux uropathy, unspecified
N15.1	Renal and perinephric abscess
N15.9	Renal tubulo-interstitial disease, unspecified
N19	Unspecified kidney failure
N20.0	Calculus of kidney
N20.1	Calculus of ureter

N20.2	Calculus of kidney with calculus of ureter
N20.9	Urinary calculus, unspecified
N23	Unspecified renal colic
N25.81	Secondary hyperparathyroidism of renal origin
N25.89	Other disorders resulting from impaired renal tubular function
N25.9	Disorder resulting from impaired renal tubular function, unspecified
N28.82	Megaloureter
N28.84	Pyelitis cystica
N28.85	Pyeloureteritis cystica
N28.86	Ureteritis cystica
N28.89	Other specified disorders of kidney and ureter
N39.0	Urinary tract infection, site not specified
N39.3	Stress incontinence (female) (male)
N39.41	Urge incontinence
N39.42	Incontinence without sensory awareness
N39.43	Post-void dribbling
N39.44	Nocturnal enuresis
N39.45	Continuous leakage
N39.46	Mixed incontinence
N39.490	Overflow incontinence
N39.491	Coital incontinence
N39.492	Postural (urinary) incontinence
N39.498	Other specified urinary incontinence
N39.8	Other specified disorders of urinary system
N39.9	Disorder of urinary system, unspecified
N82.1	Other female urinary-genital tract fistulae
Q62.0	Congenital hydronephrosis
Q62.10	Congenital occlusion of ureter, unspecified
Q62.11	Congenital occlusion of ureteropelvic junction
Q62.12	Congenital occlusion of ureterovesical orifice
Q62.2	Congenital megaureter
Q62.31	Congenital ureterocele, orthotopic
Q62.32	Cecoureterocele
Q62.39	Other obstructive defects of renal pelvis and ureter
Q62.5	Duplication of ureter
Q62.60	Malposition of ureter, unspecified
Q62.61	Deviation of ureter
Q62.62	Displacement of ureter
Q62.63	Anomalous implantation of ureter
Q62.69	Other malposition of ureter
Q62.8	Other congenital malformations of ureter
R82.71	Bacteriuria
R82.79	Other abnormal findings on microbiological examination of urine
T83.118A	Breakdown (mechanical) of other urinary devices and implants, initial encounter
T83.128A	Displacement of other urinary devices and implants, initial encounter
T83.198A	Other mechanical complication of other urinary devices and implants, initial encounter
T83.511A	Infection and inflammatory reaction due to indwelling urethral catheter, initial encounter
T83.512A	Infection and inflammatory reaction due to nephrostomy catheter, initial encounter
T83.518A	Infection and inflammatory reaction due to other urinary catheter, initial encounter
T83.81XA	Embolism due to genitourinary prosthetic devices, implants and grafts, initial encounter
T83.82XA	Fibrosis due to genitourinary prosthetic devices, implants and grafts, initial encounter
T83.83XA	Hemorrhage due to genitourinary prosthetic devices, implants and grafts, initial encounter
T83.84XA	Pain due to genitourinary prosthetic devices, implants and grafts, initial encounter
T83.85XA	Stenosis due to genitourinary prosthetic devices, implants and grafts, initial encounter
T83.86XA	Thrombosis due to genitourinary prosthetic devices, implants and grafts, initial encounter
T83.89XA	Other specified complication of genitourinary prosthetic devices, implants and grafts, initial encounter

T83.9XXA	Unspecified complication of genitourinary prosthetic device, implant and graft, initial encounter
Z46.6	Encounter for fitting and adjustment of urinary device

CCI Edits

50433 0213T, 0216T, 0228T, 0230T, 12001-12007, 12011-12057, 13100-13133, 13151-13153, 36000, 36011, 36400-36410, 36420-36430, 36440, 36591-36592, 36600, 36640, 43752, 50395, 50430-50432, 50684, 51701-51703, 62320-62327, 64400-64410, 64413-64435, 64445-64450, 64461-64463, 64479-64530, 69990, 74425, 76000-76001, 76380, 76942, 76970, 76998, 77001-77002, 77012, 77021, 92012-92014, 93000-93010, 93040-93042, 93318, 94002, 94200, 94250, 94680-94690, 94770, 95812-95816, 95819, 95822, 95829, 95955, 96360-96368, 96372, 96374-96377, 99155-99157, 99211-99223, 99231-99255, 99291-99292, 99304-99310, 99315-99316, 99334-99337, 99347-99350, 99374-99375, 99377-99378, 99446-99449, J0670, J2001

50434 0213T, 0216T, 0228T, 0230T, 12001-12007, 12011-12057, 13100-13133, 13151-13153, 36000, 36011, 36400-36410, 36420-36430, 36440, 36591-36592, 36600, 36640, 43752, 49185, 49424, 50387, 50430-50431, 50435, 50684, 51701-51703, 62320-62327, 64400-64410, 64413-64435, 64445-64450, 64461-64463, 64479-64530, 69990, 74425, 76000-76001, 76380, 76942, 76970, 76998, 77001-77002, 77012, 77021, 92012-92014, 93000-93010, 93040-93042, 93318, 93355, 94002, 94200, 94250, 94680-94690, 94770, 95812-95816, 95819, 95822, 95829, 95955, 96360-96368, 96372, 96374-96377, 99155-99157, 99211-99223, 99231-99255, 99291-99292, 99304-99310, 99315-99316, 99334-99337, 99347-99350, 99374-99375, 99377-99378, 99446-99449, 99495-99496, G0463, G0471, J0670, J2001

Case Example

Patient presents with an obstructed left ureter. Urologist requests a nephroureteral stent placement to facilitate urinary drainage.

The patient was placed prone on the table and prepped and draped in the usual sterile fashion. The skin was anesthetized with lidocaine and under fluoroscopic guidance a **needle placed via the left posterior flank into the renal collecting system**. A guidewire was placed through the needle, and the needle was removed and exchanged for an introducer. Contrast was injected and images of the renal pelvis and ureter were obtained. The obstruction was located in distal third of the ureter. The guidewire was removed and a glidewire was inserted. Under fluoro guidance, the glidewire was used to successfully transverse the **ureteral obstruction**. The introducer was removed and an 8-French, 26 cm **nephroureteral stent was introduced**. Using fluoro, using the pushing device, **the stent was placed with the distal tip in the bladder**. The proximal tip was located in the renal pelvis. Under fluoro, the wire was then retracted slowly. The pigtail formed just distal to the ureterovesical junction. We retracted the guidewire and then slowly removed the positioner. The proximal pigtail formed in the renal pelvis. The wire was advanced back into the ureter and a **nephrostomy catheter was inserted with the loop in the renal pelvis**. The wire was removed, and the nephrostomy catheter was secured to external drainage.

CPT/HCPCS Codes Reported:
50433

Other HCPCS Codes Reported:
C1769, C1729, C1758

Ureteral Stent Placement

50693   **Placement of ureteral stent, percutaneous, including diagnostic nephrostogram and/or ureterogram when performed, imaging guidance (eg, ultrasound and/or fluoroscopy), and all associated radiological supervision and interpretation; pre-existing nephrostomy tract**

50694   **new access, without separate nephrostomy catheter**

50695   **new access, with separate nephrostomy catheter**

The physician inserts a ureteral catheter or stent percutaneously into the ureter through the renal pelvis for drainage and/or contrast injection for radiographic studies. With the patient face down and the puncture site having been identified by separately reportable means, a local anesthetic is injected. A needle with a guidewire is slowly advanced into the kidney under fluoroscopic guidance. The needle is removed and the tract may be dilated to accommodate the ureteral catheter, which is inserted into the kidney pelvis and manipulated into and down the ureter until it reaches the bladder also under fluoroscopic monitoring. An internal stent will reside in the ureter and an external stent will have one end that remains outside the body.

Ureteral Stent Placement

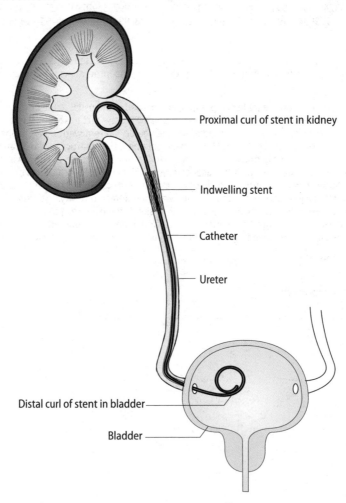

Proximal curl of stent in kidney

Indwelling stent

Catheter

Ureter

Distal curl of stent in bladder

Bladder

Coding Tips

1. These codes are comprehensive codes. Do not separately report radiologic supervision and interpretation.
2. Access into the kidney is included.
3. Drainage of fluid is included.
4. Catheter manipulations are included.
5. Diagnostic nephrostogram and/or ureterogram are included.
6. Report any applicable HCPCS Level II codes for devices and contrast media used. Refer to the HCPCS section for possible codes.
7. Conscious sedation is not included in these codes. Separately report 99151–99157 per payer policy and coding guidelines. Hospitals may choose to include the costs associated with the service as part of the procedure rather than reporting them separately.

Facility HCPCS Coding

Some applicable codes may include, but are not limited to:

C1729	Catheter, drainage
C1758	Catheter, ureteral
C1769	Guide wire
Q9958	HOCM, up to 149 mg/ml iodine concentration, per ml
Q9959	HOCM, 150-199 mg/ml iodine concentration, per ml
Q9960	HOCM, 200-249 mg/ml iodine concentration, per ml
Q9961	HOCM, 250-299 mg/ml iodine concentration, per ml
Q9962	HOCM, 300-349 mg/ml iodine concentration, per ml
Q9963	HOCM, 350-399 mg/ml iodine concentration, per ml
Q9964	HOCM, 400 or greater mg/ml iodine concentration, per ml
Q9965	LOCM, 100-199 mg/ml iodine concentration, per ml
Q9966	LOCM, 200-299 mg/ml iodine concentration, per ml
Q9967	LOCM, 300-399 mg/ml iodine concentration, per ml

ICD-10-CM Coding

C64.1	Malignant neoplasm of right kidney, except renal pelvis
C64.2	Malignant neoplasm of left kidney, except renal pelvis
C64.9	Malignant neoplasm of unspecified kidney, except renal pelvis
C65.1	Malignant neoplasm of right renal pelvis
C65.2	Malignant neoplasm of left renal pelvis
C65.9	Malignant neoplasm of unspecified renal pelvis
C66.1	Malignant neoplasm of right ureter
C66.2	Malignant neoplasm of left ureter
C66.9	Malignant neoplasm of unspecified ureter
C79.00	Secondary malignant neoplasm of unspecified kidney and renal pelvis
C79.01	Secondary malignant neoplasm of right kidney and renal pelvis
C79.02	Secondary malignant neoplasm of left kidney and renal pelvis
C79.10	Secondary malignant neoplasm of unspecified urinary organs
C79.19	Secondary malignant neoplasm of other urinary organs
C7A.093	Malignant carcinoid tumor of the kidney
D09.19	Carcinoma in situ of other urinary organs
D30.10	Benign neoplasm of unspecified renal pelvis
D30.11	Benign neoplasm of right renal pelvis
D30.12	Benign neoplasm of left renal pelvis
D30.20	Benign neoplasm of unspecified ureter
D30.21	Benign neoplasm of right ureter
D30.22	Benign neoplasm of left ureter
D41.00	Neoplasm of uncertain behavior of unspecified kidney
D41.01	Neoplasm of uncertain behavior of right kidney
D41.02	Neoplasm of uncertain behavior of left kidney

D41.1Ø	Neoplasm of uncertain behavior of unspecified renal pelvis
D41.11	Neoplasm of uncertain behavior of right renal pelvis
D41.12	Neoplasm of uncertain behavior of left renal pelvis
D41.2Ø	Neoplasm of uncertain behavior of unspecified ureter
D41.21	Neoplasm of uncertain behavior of right ureter
D41.22	Neoplasm of uncertain behavior of left ureter
D49.511	Neoplasm of unspecified behavior of right kidney
D49.512	Neoplasm of unspecified behavior of left kidney
D49.519	Neoplasm of unspecified behavior of unspecified kidney
D49.59	Neoplasm of unspecified behavior of other genitourinary organ
N1Ø	Acute tubulo-interstitial nephritis
N11.Ø	Nonobstructive reflux-associated chronic pyelonephritis
N11.1	Chronic obstructive pyelonephritis
N11.8	Other chronic tubulo-interstitial nephritis
N11.9	Chronic tubulo-interstitial nephritis, unspecified
N12	Tubulo-interstitial nephritis, not specified as acute or chronic
N13.Ø	Hydronephrosis with ureteropelvic junction obstruction
N13.1	Hydronephrosis with ureteral stricture, not elsewhere classified
N13.2	Hydronephrosis with renal and ureteral calculous obstruction
N13.3Ø	Unspecified hydronephrosis
N13.39	Other hydronephrosis
N13.4	Hydroureter
N13.5	Crossing vessel and stricture of ureter without hydronephrosis
N13.721	Vesicoureteral-reflux with reflux nephropathy without hydroureter, unilateral
N13.722	Vesicoureteral-reflux with reflux nephropathy without hydroureter, bilateral
N13.731	Vesicoureteral-reflux with reflux nephropathy with hydroureter, unilateral
N13.732	Vesicoureteral-reflux with reflux nephropathy with hydroureter, bilateral
N13.8	Other obstructive and reflux uropathy
N13.9	Obstructive and reflux uropathy, unspecified
N15.9	Renal tubulo-interstitial disease, unspecified
N2Ø.Ø	Calculus of kidney
N2Ø.1	Calculus of ureter
N2Ø.2	Calculus of kidney with calculus of ureter
N2Ø.9	Urinary calculus, unspecified
N23	Unspecified renal colic
N25.81	Secondary hyperparathyroidism of renal origin
N25.89	Other disorders resulting from impaired renal tubular function
N25.9	Disorder resulting from impaired renal tubular function, unspecified
N28.82	Megaloureter
N28.84	Pyelitis cystica
N28.85	Pyeloureteritis cystica
N28.86	Ureteritis cystica
N28.89	Other specified disorders of kidney and ureter
N39.Ø	Urinary tract infection, site not specified
N39.3	Stress incontinence (female) (male)
N39.41	Urge incontinence
N39.42	Incontinence without sensory awareness
N39.43	Post-void dribbling
N39.44	Nocturnal enuresis
N39.45	Continuous leakage
N39.46	Mixed incontinence
N39.49Ø	Overflow incontinence
N39.491	Coital incontinence
N39.492	Postural (urinary) incontinence
N39.498	Other specified urinary incontinence
N39.8	Other specified disorders of urinary system

N39.9	Disorder of urinary system, unspecified
N82.1	Other female urinary-genital tract fistulae
Q62.Ø	Congenital hydronephrosis
Q62.1Ø	Congenital occlusion of ureter, unspecified
Q62.11	Congenital occlusion of ureteropelvic junction
Q62.12	Congenital occlusion of ureterovesical orifice
Q62.2	Congenital megaureter
Q62.31	Congenital ureterocele, orthotopic
Q62.32	Cecoureterocele
Q62.39	Other obstructive defects of renal pelvis and ureter
Q62.5	Duplication of ureter
Q62.6Ø	Malposition of ureter, unspecified
Q62.61	Deviation of ureter
Q62.62	Displacement of ureter
Q62.63	Anomalous implantation of ureter
Q62.69	Other malposition of ureter
Q62.8	Other congenital malformations of ureter
R82.71	Bacteriuria
R82.79	Other abnormal findings on microbiological examination of urine

CCI Edits

50693   0213T, 0216T, 0228T, 0230T, 12001-12007, 12011-12057, 13100-13133, 13151-13153, 36000, 36011, 36400-36410, 36420-36430, 36440, 36591-36592, 36600, 36640, 43752, 49185, 49424, 50390, 50395, 50430-50435, 50684, 51701-51703, 62320-62327, 64400-64410, 64413-64435, 64445-64450, 64461-64463, 64479-64530, 69990, 74425, 76000-76001, 76380, 76942, 76970, 76998, 77001-77002, 77012, 77021, 92012-92014, 93000-93010, 93040-93042, 93318, 93355, 94002, 94200, 94250, 94680-94690, 94770, 95812-95816, 95819, 95822, 95829, 95955, 96360-96368, 96372, 96374-96377, 99155-99157, 99211-99223, 99231-99255, 99291-99292, 99304-99310, 99315-99316, 99334-99337, 99347-99350, 99374-99375, 99377-99378, 99446-99449, 99495-99496, G0463, G0471, J0670, J2001

50694   0213T, 0216T, 0228T, 0230T, 12001-12007, 12011-12057, 13100-13133, 13151-13153, 36000, 36011, 36400-36410, 36420-36430, 36440, 36591-36592, 36600, 36640, 43752, 49185, 49424, 50390, 50395, 50430-50435, 50684, 50693, 51701-51703, 62320-62327, 64400-64410, 64413-64435, 64445-64450, 64461-64463, 64479-64530, 69990, 74425, 76000-76001, 76380, 76942, 76970, 76998, 77001-77002, 77012, 77021, 92012-92014, 93000-93010, 93040-93042, 93318, 93355, 94002, 94200, 94250, 94680-94690, 94770, 95812-95816, 95819, 95822, 95829, 95955, 96360-96368, 96372, 96374-96377, 99155-99157, 99211-99223, 99231-99255, 99291-99292, 99304-99310, 99315-99316, 99334-99337, 99347-99350, 99374-99375, 99377-99378, 99446-99449, 99495-99496, G0463, G0471, J0670, J2001

50695   0213T, 0216T, 0228T, 0230T, 12001-12007, 12011-12057, 13100-13133, 13151-13153, 36000, 36011, 36400-36410, 36420-36430, 36440, 36591-36592, 36600, 36640, 43752, 49185, 49424, 50390, 50395, 50430-50435, 50684, 50693-50694, 51701-51703, 62320-62327, 64400-64410, 64413-64435, 64445-64450, 64461-64463, 64479-64530, 69990, 74425, 76000-76001, 76380, 76942, 76970, 76998, 77001-77002, 77012, 77021, 92012-92014, 93000-93010, 93040-93042, 93318, 93355, 94002, 94200, 94250, 94680-94690, 94770, 95812-95816, 95819, 95822, 95829, 95955, 96360-96368, 96372, 96374-96377, 99155-99157, 99211-99223, 99231-99255, 99291-99292, 99304-99310, 99315-99316, 99334-99337, 99347-99350, 99374-99375, 99377-99378, 99446-99449, 99495-99496, G0463, G0471, J0670, J2001

Case Example

The patient presents with a previously identified stricture of the distal left ureter. The patient is placed prone on the imaging table and the area over the left flank is prepped and draped in typical sterile fashion. Using ultrasound guidance, the **needle is advanced into the** distal portion of the **collecting system of the left kidney**. A guidewire is advanced through the needle and under fluoroscopic guidance is directed down the ureter. The **tract is then serially dilated** and an 8-French sheath is placed into the collecting system. Contrast is injected demonstrating a dilated renal pelvis and the area of stricture in the distal ureter. The guidewire is then inserted and guided through the stricture into the bladder. **A double J 8-French ureteral catheter is then guided through the area of stricture and advanced into the bladder**. Contrast is injected through the sheath and demonstrates satisfactory placement of the stent with good flow through the catheter. The guidewire is withdrawn looping the proximal end of the ureteral stent in the renal pelvis. A **separate nephrostomy drainage catheter is then placed in the renal pelvis and left to external drainage**. The catheter is secured to the skin and a sterile bandage applied over the site. There were no complications and the patient left the department in satisfactory condition.

CPT/HCPCS Codes Reported:
50695

Other HCPCS Codes Reported:
C1769, C1758, C1729

Ureteral Dilation

50706   **Balloon dilation, ureteral stricture, including imaging guidance (eg, ultrasound and/or fluoroscopy), and all associated radiological supervision and interpretation (List separately in addition to code for primary procedure)**

The physician treats a ureteral stricture by balloon dilation percutaneously by making an incision into the skin overlying the target area. The patient is anesthetized, and the incision is made. The target area is visualized by imaging guidance. A guidewire is inserted through the stricture. A catheter containing the balloon is threaded over the wire to the stricture, and the wire is removed. Balloon catheter sizes are determined based on normal ureter diameter as measured by radiological images. The balloon is inflated until the structure is minimized. The process may be repeated until the desired result is achieved. Contrast may be injected to determine adequate flow through the ureter. The catheters are removed, and the incision site is sutured closed. This procedure may be performed via transrenal access, existing renal/ureteral access, transurethral access, an ileal conduit, or ureterostomy.

Coding Tips

1. Code 50706 is an add-on code. Report in addition to the primary procedure performed. Use with 50382–50389, 50430–50435, 50684, and 50688–50695. (See previous sections.)
2. Report once per ureter with a limit of one per day.
3. Access into the ureter is not included and may be separately reported.
4. Diagnostic pyelogram/ureterogram is not included and may be separately reported.
5. Other interventions may be additionally reported.
6. Fluoroscopy and/or ultrasound guidance is included and is not separately reported.
7. Report any applicable HCPCS Level II codes for devices and contrast media used. Refer to the HCPCS section for possible codes.
8. Conscious sedation is not included in these codes. Separately report 99151–99157 per payer policy and coding guidelines. Hospitals may choose to include the costs associated with the service as part of the procedure rather than reporting them separately.

Facility HCPCS Coding

Some applicable codes may include, but are not limited to:

C1726   Catheter, balloon dilatation, non-vascular
C1729   Catheter, drainage
C1758   Catheter, ureteral
C1769   Guide wire

ICD-10-CM Coding

This is an add-on code. Refer to the corresponding primary procedure code for ICD-10-CM diagnosis code links.

CCI Edits

50706   0213T, 0216T, 0228T, 0230T, 12001-12007, 12011-12057, 13100-13133, 13151-13153, 36000, 36400-36410, 36420-36430, 36440, 36600, 36640, 43752, 51701-51703, 62320-62327, 64400-64410, 64413-64435, 64445-64450, 64461, 64463, 64479, 64483, 64486-64490, 64493, 64505-64530, 69990, 74425, 74485, 76000-76001, 76380, 76942, 76970, 76998, 77002, 77012, 77021, 92012-92014, 93000-93010, 93040-93042, 93318, 94002, 94200, 94250, 94680-94690, 94770, 95812-95816, 95819, 95822, 95829, 95955, 96360, 96365, 96372, 96374-96377, 99155-99157, 99211-99223, 99231-99255, 99291-99292, 99304-99310, 99315-99316, 99334-99337, 99347-99350, 99374-99375, 99377-99378

Case Example

Using the standard sterile technique and local anesthesia, a guidewire was placed through **the indwelling external nephrostomy tube on the left, and this tube was removed**. Over the guidewire, a 5-French Teg catheter was inserted and advanced to the level of the distal left ureter where an injection of contrast material was made as digital radiographs were obtained over the lower abdomen and pelvis in the AP projection. This **antegrade ureterogram** shows **complete obstruction of the distal ureter** with no antegrade flow demonstrated into the neobladder. With the use of a terumo glidewire, the distal left ureteral obstruction was successfully transversed, and the catheter was then advanced into the neobladder. A stiff guidewire was then inserted, and an exchange was made for a 4 mm in diameter Gruentzig balloon, which was used to **perform dilatation on the distal left ureter**. The exchange was then made for a larger 5 mm in diameter Gruentzig balloon, which was also used to perform dilatation on the distal left ureteral stenosis. Despite prolonged inflations of this balloon, there was persistent "waisting" of the balloon at the obstruction site. The balloon was subsequently deflated and withdrawn into the more proximal ureter where repeat injection of contrast material was made as digital radiographs were obtained over the pelvis in the AP and both oblique projections. Antegrade flow was demonstrated through the distal ureter into the neobladder following the balloon dilatation.

Following this balloon dilatation, the guidewire was reinserted and the balloon catheter was removed. A new 12-French Cope **nephrostomy loop was inserted and coiled within the left renal pelvis**. The proper nephrostomy tube placement was documented with digital radiographs obtained over the left side of the abdomen before and following the injection of contrast. The catheter was subsequently secured adjacent to the skin entry site with an adhesive fixation device. The catheter was then **placed to an external drainage** bag.

CPT/HCPCS Codes Reported:
50389, 50432, 50706

Other HCPCS Codes Reported:
C1769, C1726, C1729

Ureteral Embolization or Occlusion

50705   **Ureteral embolization or occlusion, including imaging guidance (eg, ultrasound and/or fluoroscopy), and all associated radiological supervision and interpretation (List separately in addition to code for primary procedure)**

Typically a nephrostomy tube is introduced into both kidneys before embolization and is replaced with a sheath during the procedure. A nephrostogram may be performed. A catheter is positioned into the distal ureter., and coils are introduced through the catheter and pushed into the desired location(s). These coils are used for the occlusion; it may take 4 to 12 coils to accomplish the end result. Gelatin sponges may also be placed within the coil groups to speed up the lumen occlusion. A nephrostogram may be performed again to verify success of the procedure at the coil positions. The sheath is replaced with a catheter, allowing for drainage, and may be replaced every eight weeks. This procedure may be performed via transrenal access, existing renal/ureteral access, transurethral access, an ileal conduit, or ureterostomy.

Coding Tips

1. Code 50705 is an add-on code. Report in addition to the primary procedure performed. Use with 50382–50389, 50430–50435, 50684, and 50688–50695. (See previous sections.)
2. Report once per ureter with a limit of one per day.
3. Access into the ureter is not included and may be separately reported.
4. Diagnostic pyelogram/ureterogram is not included and may be separately reported.
5. Other interventions may be additionally reported.
6. Report any applicable HCPCS Level II codes for devices and contrast media used. Refer to the HCPCS section for possible codes.

Facility HCPCS Coding

Some applicable codes may include, but are not limited to:

C1729	Catheter, drainage
C1758	Catheter, ureteral
C1769	Guidewire
Q9965	LOCM, 100-199 mg/ml iodine concentration, per ml
Q9966	LOCM, 200-299 mg/ml iodine concentration, per ml
Q9967	LOCM, 300-399 mg/ml iodine concentration, per ml

ICD-10-CM Coding

This is an add-on code. Refer to the corresponding primary procedure codes for ICD-10-CM diagnosis code links.

CCI Edits

50705   0213T, 0216T, 0228T, 0230T, 12001-12007, 12011-12057, 13100-13133, 13151-13153, 36000, 36400-36410, 36420-36430, 36440, 36600, 36640, 43752, 51701-51703, 62320-62327, 64400-64410, 64413-64435, 64445-64450, 64461, 64463, 64479, 64483, 64486-64490, 64493, 64505-64530, 69990, 74425, 76000-76001, 76380, 76942, 76970, 76998, 77002, 77012, 77021, 92012-92014, 93000-93010, 93040-93042, 93318, 94002, 94200, 94250, 94680-94690, 94770, 95812-95816, 95819, 95822, 95829, 95955, 96360, 96365, 96372, 96374-96377, 99155-99157, 99211-99223, 99231-99255, 99291-99292, 99304-99310, 99315-99316, 99334-99337, 99347-99350, 99374-99375, 99377-99378

Case Example

Patient presents with extravasation of urine from the right ureter. A soft catheter was placed into the ureterostomy in the left lower abdomen. Contrast was injected, and **a retrograde ileal loop study was performed**. The study demonstrated a patent left ureter. The area of extravasation from the right ureter was identified. A 7-French sheath was advanced into the ileal loop and positioned near the right ureteral connection. The catheter was advanced over a guidewire into the proximal ureter. We **placed multiple embolization coils**. We then injected gelfoam within the mesh of the coils. We then did a follow-up contrast study. This study demonstrated **complete occlusion of the right ureter**. The catheters were removed.

CPT/HCPCS Codes Reported:
50690, 74425, 50705

Other HCPCS Codes Reported:
C1769, C1894

Renal or Ureteral Catheter Removal

50382   **Removal (via snare/capture) and replacement of internally dwelling ureteral stent via percutaneous approach, including radiological supervision and interpretation**

The physician replaces the indwelling ureteral stent after removal of the old stent. A catheter or sheath is introduced into the kidney and then advanced into ureter. A snare is then directed through the sheath and is used to capture the old stent. The snare and the old stent are then removed through the sheath. A guidewire is placed, and the replacement stent is advanced into the ureter until the distal end is in the bladder and the distal loop is deployed. Stent position is confirmed with the proximal loop in the renal pelvis. The instruments are removed.

50384   **Removal (via snare/capture) of internally dwelling ureteral stent via percutaneous approach, including radiological supervision and interpretation**

The physician percutaneously removes an internally dwelling ureteral stent through the renal pelvis in 50384. With the patient under conscious sedation, a long, thin needle is advanced into the renal calyx under imaging guidance and the position is confirmed with contrast and fluoroscopy. A guidewire is threaded over the needle into the renal pelvis, the needle is removed, and a sheath placed over the guidewire. A snare device is threaded through the sheath into position, the indwelling stent is grasped, and pulled out partially through the sheath until the proximal end is outside the ureter. A guidewire is threaded through the stent, which is guided completely out. In 50382, the physician replaces the indwelling ureteral stent after removal of the old stent. The guidewire is left in place, the length of the old stent is noted, and the replacement stent is advanced into the ureter until the distal end is in the bladder and the distal loop is deployed. Stent position is confirmed with the proximal loop in the renal pelvis. The instruments are removed.

50387   **Removal and replacement of externally accessible nephro-ureteral stent (eg, external/internal stent) requiring fluoroscopic guidance, including radiological supervision and interpretation**

The physician removes and replaces an externally accessible transnephric ureteral stent under fluoroscopic guidance. A transnephric ureteral stent is one that is placed through the wall of the flank into the renal pelvis and down into the ureter to keep the ureter open. Contrast may be injected at the entry site to assess anatomy and positioning. The suture holding the pigtail in place is cut and a guidewire is threaded through the stent lumen until it exits the distal end. The original stent is removed over the guidewire. Diameter and length are noted for a new stent, which is threaded over the guidewire until the distal end forms within the bladder. Fluoroscopy is used to assess the proximal position of formation within the renal pelvis. After position is verified, the guidewire is removed and the suture is put in position to hold the pigtail in place. Contrast may be injected to check position and function. Final adjustments are made for patient comfort, and the catheter may be sutured to the skin, capped, or a drainage bag may be attached.

50389   **Removal of nephrostomy tube, requiring fluoroscopic guidance (eg, with concurrent indwelling ureteral stent)**

The physician removes an indwelling nephrostomy tube under fluoroscopic guidance that was previously placed concurrently with an indwelling ureteral stent. Nephrostomy tube removal may be done to avoid displacement of the stent. Contrast may first be injected through the indwelling catheter tube to verify placement and functioning of the stent. The suture holding the pigtail in place is cut and a guidewire is threaded through the nephrostomy tube under fluoroscopy, making certain that the pigtail or suture do not hook the stent and that the stent remains in proper position. The nephrostomy tube is pulled out over the guidewire, stent position is checked again, and the access site is dressed.

Coding Tips

1. These codes include all radiologic supervision and interpretation.

2. These codes report unilateral procedures. Append modifier 50 for bilateral procedures.

3. Code 50382 reports percutaneous approach for removal and replacement of an internal ureteral stent.

4. Code 50384 reports only the removal of an internal ureteral stent.

5. Code 50387 reports the transnephric approach for removal and replacement of a ureteral stent that is externally accessible.

6. To report code 50389, fluoroscopic guidance is required. Documentation of fluoroscopy use should be present in the medical record. For removal of a nephrostomy tube without the use of fluoroscopy, report the appropriate level of evaluation and management service according to your facility policy.

7. Report any applicable HCPCS Level II codes for devices and contrast media used. Refer to the HCPCS section for possible codes.

8. Conscious sedation is not included in these codes. Separately report 99151–99157 per payer policy and coding guidelines. Hospitals may choose to include the costs associated with the service as part of the procedure rather than reporting them separately.

Facility HCPCS Coding

Some applicable codes may include, but are not limited to:

C1729	Catheter, drainage
C1758	Catheter, ureteral
C1769	Guide wire
C1773	Retrieval device, insertable

ICD-10-CM Coding

C64.1	Malignant neoplasm of right kidney, except renal pelvis
C64.2	Malignant neoplasm of left kidney, except renal pelvis
C64.9	Malignant neoplasm of unspecified kidney, except renal pelvis
C65.1	Malignant neoplasm of right renal pelvis
C65.2	Malignant neoplasm of left renal pelvis
C65.9	Malignant neoplasm of unspecified renal pelvis
C66.1	Malignant neoplasm of right ureter
C66.2	Malignant neoplasm of left ureter
C66.9	Malignant neoplasm of unspecified ureter
C79.00	Secondary malignant neoplasm of unspecified kidney and renal pelvis
C79.01	Secondary malignant neoplasm of right kidney and renal pelvis
C79.02	Secondary malignant neoplasm of left kidney and renal pelvis
C79.10	Secondary malignant neoplasm of unspecified urinary organs
C7A.093	Malignant carcinoid tumor of the kidney
D09.19	Carcinoma in situ of other urinary organs
D30.10	Benign neoplasm of unspecified renal pelvis
D30.11	Benign neoplasm of right renal pelvis
D30.12	Benign neoplasm of left renal pelvis
D30.20	Benign neoplasm of unspecified ureter
D30.21	Benign neoplasm of right ureter
D30.22	Benign neoplasm of left ureter
D41.00	Neoplasm of uncertain behavior of unspecified kidney
D41.01	Neoplasm of uncertain behavior of right kidney
D41.02	Neoplasm of uncertain behavior of left kidney
D41.10	Neoplasm of uncertain behavior of unspecified renal pelvis
D41.11	Neoplasm of uncertain behavior of right renal pelvis
D41.12	Neoplasm of uncertain behavior of left renal pelvis
D41.20	Neoplasm of uncertain behavior of unspecified ureter
D41.21	Neoplasm of uncertain behavior of right ureter
D41.22	Neoplasm of uncertain behavior of left ureter
D49.511	Neoplasm of unspecified behavior of right kidney
D49.512	Neoplasm of unspecified behavior of left kidney
D49.519	Neoplasm of unspecified behavior of unspecified kidney
D49.59	Neoplasm of unspecified behavior of other genitourinary organ
N11.0	Nonobstructive reflux-associated chronic pyelonephritis
N11.1	Chronic obstructive pyelonephritis
N11.8	Other chronic tubulo-interstitial nephritis
N13.0	Hydronephrosis with ureteropelvic junction obstruction
N13.1	Hydronephrosis with ureteral stricture, not elsewhere classified
N13.2	Hydronephrosis with renal and ureteral calculous obstruction
N13.30	Unspecified hydronephrosis
N13.39	Other hydronephrosis
N13.4	Hydroureter
N13.5	Crossing vessel and stricture of ureter without hydronephrosis
N13.721	Vesicoureteral-reflux with reflux nephropathy without hydroureter, unilateral
N13.722	Vesicoureteral-reflux with reflux nephropathy without hydroureter, bilateral
N13.731	Vesicoureteral-reflux with reflux nephropathy with hydroureter, unilateral

N13.732	Vesicoureteral-reflux with reflux nephropathy with hydroureter, bilateral
N13.8	Other obstructive and reflux uropathy
N13.9	Obstructive and reflux uropathy, unspecified
N15.9	Renal tubulo-interstitial disease, unspecified
N20.0	Calculus of kidney
N20.1	Calculus of ureter
N20.2	Calculus of kidney with calculus of ureter
N20.9	Urinary calculus, unspecified
N23	Unspecified renal colic
N25.81	Secondary hyperparathyroidism of renal origin
N25.89	Other disorders resulting from impaired renal tubular function
N25.9	Disorder resulting from impaired renal tubular function, unspecified
N28.82	Megaloureter
N28.84	Pyelitis cystica
N28.85	Pyeloureteritis cystica
N28.86	Ureteritis cystica
N28.89	Other specified disorders of kidney and ureter
N39.0	Urinary tract infection, site not specified
N39.3	Stress incontinence (female) (male)
N39.41	Urge incontinence
N39.42	Incontinence without sensory awareness
N39.43	Post-void dribbling
N39.44	Nocturnal enuresis
N39.45	Continuous leakage
N39.46	Mixed incontinence
N39.490	Overflow incontinence
N39.491	Coital incontinence
N39.492	Postural (urinary) incontinence
N39.498	Other specified urinary incontinence
N39.8	Other specified disorders of urinary system
N39.9	Disorder of urinary system, unspecified
N82.1	Other female urinary-genital tract fistulae
Q62.0	Congenital hydronephrosis
Q62.10	Congenital occlusion of ureter, unspecified
Q62.11	Congenital occlusion of ureteropelvic junction
Q62.12	Congenital occlusion of ureterovesical orifice
Q62.2	Congenital megaureter
Q62.31	Congenital ureterocele, orthotopic
Q62.32	Cecoureterocele
Q62.39	Other obstructive defects of renal pelvis and ureter
Q62.5	Duplication of ureter
Q62.60	Malposition of ureter, unspecified
Q62.61	Deviation of ureter
Q62.62	Displacement of ureter
Q62.63	Anomalous implantation of ureter
Q62.69	Other malposition of ureter
Q62.8	Other congenital malformations of ureter
R82.71	Bacteriuria
R82.79	Other abnormal findings on microbiological examination of urine
T83.112A	Breakdown (mechanical) of indwelling ureteral stent, initial encounter
T83.113A	Breakdown (mechanical) of other urinary stents, initial encounter
T83.118A	Breakdown (mechanical) of other urinary devices and implants, initial encounter
T83.122A	Displacement of indwelling ureteral stent, initial encounter
T83.123A	Displacement of other urinary stents, initial encounter
T83.128A	Displacement of other urinary devices and implants, initial encounter
T83.192A	Other mechanical complication of indwelling ureteral stent, initial encounter

T83.193A	Other mechanical complication of other urinary stent, initial encounter
T83.198A	Other mechanical complication of other urinary devices and implants, initial encounter
T83.510A	Infection and inflammatory reaction due to cystostomy catheter, initial encounter
T83.511A	Infection and inflammatory reaction due to indwelling urethral catheter, initial encounter
T83.512A	Infection and inflammatory reaction due to nephrostomy catheter, initial encounter
T83.518A	Infection and inflammatory reaction due to other urinary catheter, initial encounter
T83.592A	Infection and inflammatory reaction due to indwelling ureteral stent, initial encounter
T83.593A	Infection and inflammatory reaction due to other urinary stents, initial encounter
T83.81XA	Embolism due to genitourinary prosthetic devices, implants and grafts, initial encounter
T83.82XA	Fibrosis due to genitourinary prosthetic devices, implants and grafts, initial encounter
T83.83XA	Hemorrhage due to genitourinary prosthetic devices, implants and grafts, initial encounter
T83.84XA	Pain due to genitourinary prosthetic devices, implants and grafts, initial encounter
T83.85XA	Stenosis due to genitourinary prosthetic devices, implants and grafts, initial encounter
T83.86XA	Thrombosis due to genitourinary prosthetic devices, implants and grafts, initial encounter
T83.89XA	Other specified complication of genitourinary prosthetic devices, implants and grafts, initial encounter
T83.9XXA	Unspecified complication of genitourinary prosthetic device, implant and graft, initial encounter
T86.10	Unspecified complication of kidney transplant
T86.19	Other complication of kidney transplant

CCI Edits

50382   0213T, 0216T, 0228T, 0230T, 11000-11006, 11042-11047, 12001-12007, 12011-12057, 13100-13133, 13151-13153, 36000, 36400-36410, 36420-36430, 36440, 36591-36592, 36600, 36640, 43752, 50384, 50385-50387, 50390, 50395, 50430-50432, 50688, 50693-50695, 51701-51703, 52332, 52356, 62320-62327, 64400-64410, 64413-64435, 64445-64450, 64461-64463, 64479-64530, 69990, 76000-76001, 76380, 76942, 76970, 76998, 77001-77002, 77012, 77021, 92012-92014, 93000-93010, 93040-93042, 93318, 93355, 94002, 94200, 94250, 94680-94690, 94770, 95812-95816, 95819, 95822, 95829, 95955, 96360-96368, 96372, 96374-96377, 97597-97598, 97602, 99155-99157, 99211-99223, 99231-99255, 99291-99292, 99304-99310, 99315-99316, 99334-99337, 99347-99350, 99374-99375, 99377-99378, 99446-99449, 99495-99496, G0463, G0471, J0670, J2001

50384   0213T, 0216T, 0228T, 0230T, 11000-11006, 11042-11047, 12001-12007, 12011-12057, 13100-13133, 13151-13153, 36000, 36400-36410, 36420-36430, 36440, 36591-36592, 36600, 36640, 43752, 50385-50387, 50390, 50395, 50430-50432, 50688, 50693-50695, 51701-51703, 52332, 52356, 62320-62327, 64400-64410, 64413-64435, 64445-64450, 64461-64463, 64479-64530, 69990, 76000-76001, 76380, 76942, 76970, 76998, 77001-77002, 77012, 77021, 92012-92014, 93000-93010, 93040-93042, 93318, 93355, 94002, 94200, 94250, 94680-94690, 94770, 95812-95816, 95819, 95822, 95829, 95955, 96360-96368, 96372, 96374-96377, 97597-97598, 97602, 99155-99157, 99211-99223, 99231-99255, 99291-99292, 99304-99310, 99315-99316, 99334-99337, 99347-99350, 99374-99375, 99377-99378, 99446-99449, 99495-99496, G0463, G0471, J0670, J2001

50387   0213T, 0216T, 0228T, 0230T, 11000-11006, 11042-11047, 12001-12007, 12011-12057, 13100-13133, 13151-13153, 36000, 36400-36410, 36420-36430, 36440, 36591-36592, 36600, 36640, 43752, 50395, 50430-50433, 50435, 50688, 50693-50695, 51701-51703, 62320-62327, 64400-64410, 64413-64435, 64445-64450, 64461-64463, 64479-64530, 69990, 74485, 76000-76001, 77001-77002, 92012-92014, 93000-93010, 93040-93042, 93318, 93355, 94002, 94200, 94250, 94680-94690, 94770, 95812-95816, 95819, 95822, 95829, 95955, 96360-96368, 96372, 96374-96377, 97597-97598, 97602, 99155-99157, 99211-99223, 99231-99255, 99291-99292, 99304-99310, 99315-99316, 99334-99337, 99347-99350, 99374-99375, 99377-99378, 99446-99449, 99495-99496, G0463, G0471, J0670, J2001

50389   0213T, 0216T, 0228T, 0230T, 11000-11006, 11042-11047, 12001-12007, 12011-12057, 13100-13133, 13151-13153, 36000, 36400-36410, 36420-36430, 36440, 36591-36592, 36600, 36640, 43752, 50430-50431, 50693-50695, 51701-51703, 62320-62327, 64400-64410, 64413-64435, 64445-64450, 64461-64463, 64479-64530, 69990, 76000-76001, 77001-77002, 92012-92014, 93000-93010, 93040-93042, 93318, 93355, 94002, 94200, 94250, 94680-94690, 94770, 95812-95816, 95819, 95822, 95829, 95955, 96360-96368, 96372, 96374-96377, 97597-97598, 97602, 99155-99157, 99211-99223, 99231-99255, 99291-99292, 99304-99310, 99315-99316, 99334-99337, 99347-99350, 99374-99375, 99377-99378, 99446-99449, 99495-99496, G0463, G0471, J0670, J2001

Case Example

Patient **presents with an externally draining nephrostomy catheter and an indwelling double J stent** with ends in the left renal pelvis and the bladder. We are **removing the nephrostomy tube** as the stent is functioning properly. The patient is placed prone on the imaging table. The area is prepped and draped in the usual sterile fashion. A stiff guide wire is inserted through the tube under fluoroscopic guidance until the pigtail tip is straightened and clears the J tip of the ureteral stent. The **catheter is removed over the wire under fluoroscopy** to ensure a clear pathway is maintained. The guide wire is then removed and a final check is made of the ureteral stent to ensure acceptable placement was maintained. A sterile dressing is applied to the nephrostomy site and the patient leaves in satisfactory condition.

CPT/HCPCS Codes Reported:
50389

Chapter 11: Diagnostic Cardiac Catheterization

CPT® coding for cardiac catheterization procedures was restructured in 2011. While some component coding still exists, comprehensive codes describe the most commonly performed heart catheterization procedures. There are two families of codes to report cardiac catheterization procedures. CPT codes 93451 through 93464 report catheterization procedures for all heart conditions other than congenital heart disease. CPT codes 93530 through 93533 report catheterization procedures specifically for congenital heart disease.

Right Heart Catheterization

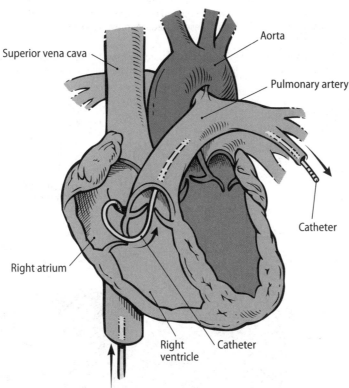

General Coding Guidelines for Cardiac Catheterization

1. The following services are inherent to the cardiac catheterization procedure and are not reported separately:
   - Fluoroscopy
   - Pulse oximetry
   - ECG monitoring
   - Administration of drugs during the procedure
   - Conscious sedation
   - Dilution and cardiac output measurements; do not report separately CPT code 93561 or 93562

2. Placement of a flow directed catheter (CPT code 93503) (e.g., Swan-Ganz) performed for hemodynamic monitoring purposes during cardiac catheterization is included and not reported separately.

3. Imaging supervision and interpretation are included in the various codes now reported for these procedures and is no longer reported separately.

4. Most contrast injection services are included in the procedure codes. Please refer to the tables below for those injections which may be reported separately as additional codes.

5. Roadmapping, any injections and imaging supervision, interpretation, and report are all included in CPT codes 93451–93461.

6. Contrast injection of the access site to assess placing a closure device is inherent to cardiac catheterization and is not reported separately. Do not report HCPCS code G0278.

7. Physicians may not report separately the procedure to place a vascular closure device. It is considered inherent in the physician work of performing the procedure.

8. Hospitals are requested to continue reporting the procedure to place a vascular closure device with HCPCS code G0269. Report separately the closure device with HCPCS code C1760; however, other third-party payers may not accept this code. Hospitals should verify with each payer regarding how to report this service. Medicare does not provide separate payment, but the costs and charges should be reported separately.

9. For physician reporting, CPT codes 93451, 93456, and 93503 should not be appended with modifier 51.

10. Hospitals should continue to report separately low osmolar contrast media (LOCM) with HCPCS codes Q9965–Q9967. Report contrast media by milliliter. Current HCPCS codes available to report contrast media used for cardiac catheterization procedures are:

    – Q9965—LOCM, 100–199 mg/ml iodine concentration, per ml
    – Q9966—LOCM, 200–299 mg/ml iodine concentration, per ml
    – Q9967—LOCM, 300–399 mg/ml iodine concentration, per ml

11. To report angiography of noncoronary vessels refer to the appropriate codes from the radiology CPT section and the vascular injection procedures CPT section. These procedures must be a distinct separate service from the cardiac catheterization procedure.

12. Conscious sedation is not included in these codes. Separately report 99151–99157 per payer policy and coding guidelines. Hospitals may choose to include the costs associated with the service as part of the procedure rather than reporting them separately.

Coronary Arteries Anterior View

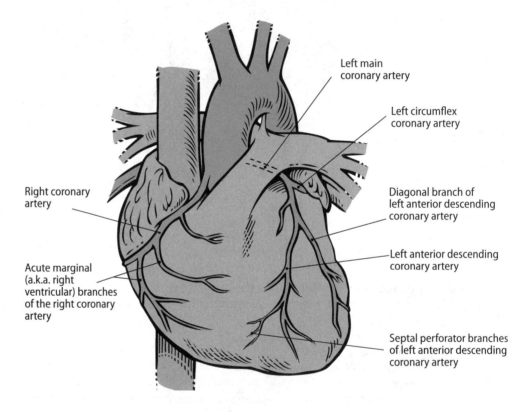

CPT Coding for Cardiac Catheterization Procedures

CPT Code	Procedure Description
93451	Right Heart Cath
93452	Left Heart Cath with or without left ventriculogram
93453	Right and Left Heart Cath with or without left ventriculogram
93454	Coronary Angiograms only
93455	Coronary artery and bypass graft angiograms
93456	Coronary artery angiograms and Right Heart Cath
93457	Coronary artery and bypass graft angiograms and Right Heart Cath
93458	Coronary artery angiograms and Left Heart Cath with or without left ventriculogram
93459	Coronary artery and bypass graft angiograms and Left Heart Cath
93460	Coronary artery angiograms and Right & Left Heart Cath
93461	Coronary artery and bypass angiograms and Right & Left Heart Cath
Add-On Codes:	
93462	Left Heart Cath by transseptal or transapical puncture
93463	Pharmacologic agent administration
93464	Physiologic exercise study
93566	Injection for right ventricular or right atrial angiography
93567	Injection for supravalvular aortography (aortic root)
93568	Injection for pulmonary angiograms
93571	Coronary flow reserve measurement, initial vessel
93572	Coronary flow reserve measurement, each additional vessel

Noncongenital Cardiac Catheterization

93451   **Right heart catheterization including measurements of oxygen saturation and cardiac output, when performed**

Catheter introduction is achieved via the femoral, subclavian, internal jugular, or antecubital vein. The catheter is directed into the right atrium, through the tricuspid valve into the right ventricle and across the pulmonary valve into the pulmonary arteries. This code applies to catheterization of the heart's right side only.

93452   **Left heart catheterization including intraprocedural injection(s) for left ventriculography, imaging supervision and interpretation, when performed**

The physician threads a catheter to the heart most commonly through an introducing sheath placed percutaneously into the femoral, brachial, or axillary artery using retrograde technique. The catheter passes through the aortic valve into the left ventricle. Blood samples, pressure and electrical recordings, and/or other tests are performed. Injection and imaging of the left ventricle is included.

93453   **Combined right and left heart catheterization including intraprocedural injection(s) for left ventriculography, imaging supervision and interpretation, when performed**

This procedure is performed to evaluate both right and left heart function. To accomplish right heart catheterization, the physician threads a catheter through an introducing sheath placed percutaneously into the femoral, subclavian, internal jugular or antecubital vein. The catheter is then threaded into the right atrium, through the tricuspid valve into the right ventricle and across the pulmonary valve into the pulmonary arteries. Left heart catheterization is also performed in this case using retrograde technique. The catheter is inserted through an introducing sheath placed percutaneously into the femoral, brachial, or axillary artery. The catheter is passed through the aortic valve into the left ventricle.

93454   **Catheter placement in coronary artery(s) for coronary angiography, including intraprocedural injection(s) for coronary angiography, imaging supervision and interpretation;**

93455   **with catheter placement(s) in bypass graft(s) (internal mammary, free arterial venous grafts) including intraprocedural injection(s) for bypass graft angiography**

93456   **with right heart catheterization**

93457   **with catheter placement(s) in bypass graft(s) (internal mammary, free arterial, venous grafts) including intraprocedural injection(s) for bypass graft angiography and right heart cath**

93458   **with left heart catheterization including intraprocedural injection(s) for left ventriculography, when performed**

93459   **with left heart catheterization including intraprocedural injection(s) for left ventriculography, when performed, catheter placement(s) in bypass graft(s) (internal mammary, free arterial, venous grafts) with bypass graft angiography**

93460   **with right and left heart catheterization including intraprocedural injection(s) for left ventriculography, when performed**

93461   **with right and left heart catheterization including intraprocedural injection(s) for left ventriculography, when performed, catheter placement(s) in bypass graft(s) (internal mammary, free arterial, venous grafts) with bypass graft angiography**

These procedures describe coronary artery diagnostic procedures with several variations depending on other services performed at the same time. Coronary angiography is completed by moving the catheter from the access point into the arterial system into the coronary arteries located just outside the heart. Injections of contrast media are performed using various angles with the imaging equipment.

93462   **Left heart catheterization by transseptal puncture through intact septum or by transapical puncture (List separately in addition to code for primary procedure**

Transseptal catheterization involves passing a catheter from the right femoral vein into the right atrium. The interatrial wall or septum is punctured and the catheter is passed into the left atrium through the mitral valve and into the left ventricle. The transapical or direct left ventricular puncture involves using a large bore needle to puncture the chest wall directly into the left ventricular cavity. These methods are used when the patient has had valve replacement and the left heart cannot be accessed any other way.

93463   **Pharmacologic agent administration (eg, inhaled nitric oxide, intravenous infusion of nitroprusside, dobutamine, milrinone, or other agent), including assessing hemodynamic measurements before, during, after, and repeat pharmacologic agent administration, when performed (List separately in addition to code from primary procedure)**

The physician administers a pharmacologic agent to invoke stress on coronary vessels in order to measure blood flow through and around the heart. This produces the same result as physical exercise. Arteries become enlarged as the body increases physical activity that requires more oxygen. When plaque is present within a vessel, it does not allow for this enlargement. This slows the ability of the oxygenated blood to reach the necessary organs, which can lead to ischemia.

| 93464 | **Physiologic exercise study (eg, bicycle or arm ergometry) including assessing hemodynamic measurements before and after (List separately in addition to code for primary procedure)** |
| | These procedures involve testing the significance of a coronary artery narrowing discovered during the cardiac catheterization procedure. Hemodynamic functions are assessed either by pharmacologic injection or by exercise. |

| 93566 | **Injection procedure during cardiac catheterization including imaging supervision, interpretation, and report; for selective right ventricular or right atrial angiography (List separately in addition to code for primary procedure)** |

| 93567 | **for supravalvular aortography (List separately in addition to code for primary procedure)** |

| 93568 | **for pulmonary angiography (List separately in addition to code for primary procedure)** |
| | Codes 93566–93568 report the injection services and imaging supervision and interpretation for right ventricle/atrium angiography, aortic root angiography, and pulmonary angiography. These codes are reported with other procedures discussed in this section. |

| 93571 | **Intravascular Doppler velocity and/or pressure derived coronary flow reserve measurement (coronary vessel or graft) during coronary angiography including pharmacologically induced stress; initial vessel (List separately in addition to code for primary procedure)** |

| 93572 | **each additional vessel (List separately in addition to code for primary procedure)** |
| | These codes report coronary flow reserve measurement procedures. They are reported with other codes discussed in this section. |

Left Heart Catheterization

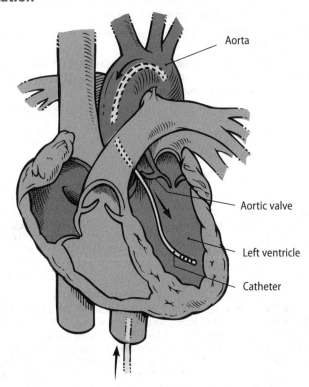

Aorta

Aortic valve

Left ventricle

Catheter

Coding Guidelines for Non-congenital Cardiac Catheterization

1. Right heart catheterization includes catheter placement in the right atrium, right ventricle, pulmonary arteries and pulmonary wedge.

2. Right heart catheterization includes obtaining blood samples for blood gases and cardiac output measurements.

3. Right heart catheterization does not include right ventricular or right atrial angiography. See 93566.

4. Refer to CPT codes 93530–93533 when congenital anomalies exist.

5. Left heart catheterization includes left ventricular (left ventriculogram) or left atrial injection. This injection code is no longer reported separately.

6. CPT codes 93454–93461 include contrast injection and imaging supervision and interpretation. These services are not reported separately.

7. CPT codes 93563–93565 are reported with congenital heart cath codes 93530–93533 only. Do not report these codes with CPT codes 93452–93461.

Facility HCPCS Coding

HCPCS Level II codes are used to report devices provided during the procedure. Hospitals should report separately supplies used during cardiac catheterization procedures. Refer to chapter 1 for more information regarding appropriate billing of supplies. Refer to the list of current device codes in appendix B.

Procedure HCPCS Codes

C9741 **Right heart catheterization with implantation of wireless pressure sensor in the pulmonary artery, including any type of measurement, angiography, imaging supervision, interpretation, and report, includes provision of patient home electronics unit**

G0269 **Placement of occlusive device into either a venous or arterial access site, post surgical or interventional procedure**

G0278 **Iliac artery angiography performed at the same time of cardiac catheterization, includes catheter placement, injection of dye, radiologic supervision and interpretation and production of images (List separately in addition to primary procedure)**

ICD-10-CM Coding

The application of these codes is too broad to adequately present ICD-10-CM diagnosis code links here. Refer to the current ICD-10-CM book.

CCI Edits

93451 01920, 0213T, 0216T, 12001-12007, 12011-12057, 13100-13133, 13151-13153, 33210, 34812, 35201-35206, 35226-35236, 35256-35266, 35286, 36000, 36005-36010, 36013-36015, 36400-36410, 36420-36430, 36440, 36555-36556, 36568-36569, 36591-36592, 36600, 36640, 43752, 51701-51703, 62320-62327, 64400-64410, 64413-64435, 64445-64450, 64461-64463, 64479-64530, 69990, 71034, 75600, 75605, 75741, 75743, 75746, 75756, 76000-76001, 78635, 92012-92014, 92961, 93000-93010, 93040-93042, 93318, 93355, 93462, 93503, 93561-93565, 94002, 94200, 94250, 94680-94690, 94770, 95812-95816, 95819, 95822, 95829, 95955, 96360-96368, 96372-96377, 99155-99157, 99211-99223, 99231-99255, 99291-99292, 99304-99310, 99315-99316, 99334-99337, 99347-99350, 99374-99375, 99377-99378, 99446-99449, 99495-99496, G0269, G0463, G0471, J0670, J1642-J1644, J2001

93452 01920, 01924-01926, 0213T, 0216T, 12001-12007, 12011-12057, 13100-13133, 13151-13153, 33210, 34812, 35201-35206, 35226-35236, 35256-35266, 35286, 36000, 36005, 36120-36140, 36200, 36245, 36400-36410, 36420-36430, 36440, 36500, 36591-36592, 36600-36640, 43752, 51701-51703, 62320-62327, 64400-64410, 64413-64435, 64445-64450, 64461-64463, 64479-64530, 69990, 71034, 75600, 75605, 75625, 75630, 75710, 75716, 75741, 75743, 75746, 75756, 75774, 75893, 76000-76001, 78635, 92012-92014, 92961, 93000-93010, 93040-93042, 93050, 93318, 93355-93451, 93503, 93561-93565, 94002, 94200, 94250, 94680-94690, 94770, 95812-95816, 95819, 95822, 95829, 95955, 96360-96368, 96372-96377, 99155-99157, 99211-99223, 99231-99255, 99291-99292, 99304-99310, 99315-99316, 99334-99337, 99347-99350, 99374-99375, 99377-99378, 99446-99449, 99495-99496, G0269, G0463, G0471, J0670, J1642-J1644, J2001

93453 01920, 01924-01926, 0213T, 0216T, 12001-12007, 12011-12057, 13100-13133, 13151-13153, 33210, 34812, 35201-35206, 35226-35236, 35256-35266, 35286, 36000, 36005-36010, 36013-36015, 36120-36140, 36200, 36245, 36400-36410, 36420-36430, 36440, 36500, 36555-36556, 36568-36569, 36591-36592, 36600-36640, 43752, 51701-51703, 62320-62327, 64400-64410, 64413-64435, 64445-64450, 64461-64463, 64479-64530, 69990, 71034, 75600, 75605, 75625, 75630, 75710, 75716, 75741, 75743, 75746, 75756, 75774, 75893, 76000-76001, 78635, 92012-92014, 92961, 93000-93010, 93040-93042, 93050, 93318, 93355-93452, 93454-93456, 93458, 93503, 93561-93565, 94002, 94200, 94250, 94680-94690, 94770, 95812-95816, 95819, 95822, 95829, 95955, 96360-96368, 96372-96377, 99155-99157, 99211-99223, 99231-99255, 99291-99292, 99304-99310, 99315-99316, 99334-99337, 99347-99350, 99374-99375, 99377-99378, 99446-99449, 99495-99496, G0269, G0463, G0471, J0670, J1642-J1644, J2001

93454   01920, 01924-01926, 0213T, 0216T, 12001-12007, 12011-12057, 13100-13133, 13151-13153, 33210-33211, 34812, 35201-35206, 35226-35236, 35256-35266, 35286, 36000, 36005, 36120-36140, 36200, 36245, 36400-36410, 36420-36430, 36440, 36500, 36591-36592, 36600-36640, 43752, 51701-51703, 62320-62327, 64400-64410, 64413-64435, 64445-64450, 64461-64463, 64479-64530, 69990, 71034, 75600, 75605, 75625, 75630, 75710, 75716, 75741, 75743, 75746, 75756, 75774, 75893, 76000-76001, 92012-92014, 92961, 93000-93010, 93040-93042, 93050, 93318, 93355-93452, 93462-93464, 93503, 93561-93565, 94002, 94200, 94250, 94680-94690, 94770, 95812-95816, 95819, 95822, 95829, 95955, 96360-96368, 96372-96377, 99155-99157, 99211-99223, 99231-99255, 99291-99292, 99304-99310, 99315-99316, 99334-99337, 99347-99350, 99374-99375, 99377-99378, 99446-99449, 99495-99496, G0269, G0463, G0471, J0670, J1642-J1644, J2001

93455   01920, 01924-01926, 0213T, 0216T, 12001-12007, 12011-12057, 13100-13133, 13151-13153, 33210-33211, 34812, 35201-35206, 35226-35236, 35256-35266, 35286, 36000, 36005, 36120-36140, 36200, 36245, 36400-36410, 36420-36430, 36440, 36500, 36591-36592, 36600-36640, 43752, 51701-51703, 62320-62327, 64400-64410, 64413-64435, 64445-64450, 64461-64463, 64479-64530, 69990, 71034, 75600, 75605, 75625, 75630, 75710, 75716, 75741, 75743, 75746, 75756, 75774, 75893, 76000-76001, 92012-92014, 92961, 93000-93010, 93040-93042, 93050, 93318, 93355-93452, 93454, 93462-93464, 93503, 93561-93565, 94002, 94200, 94250, 94680-94690, 94770, 95812-95816, 95819, 95822, 95829, 95955, 96360-96368, 96372-96377, 99155-99157, 99211-99223, 99231-99255, 99291-99292, 99304-99310, 99315-99316, 99334-99337, 99347-99350, 99374-99375, 99377-99378, 99446-99449, 99495-99496, G0269, G0463, G0471, J0670, J1642-J1644, J2001

93456   01920, 01924-01926, 0213T, 0216T, 12001-12007, 12011-12057, 13100-13133, 13151-13153, 33210, 34812, 35201-35206, 35226-35236, 35256-35266, 35286, 36000, 36005-36010, 36013-36015, 36120-36140, 36200, 36245, 36400-36410, 36420-36430, 36440, 36500, 36555-36556, 36568-36569, 36591-36592, 36600-36640, 43752, 51701-51703, 62320-62327, 64400-64410, 64413-64435, 64445-64450, 64461-64463, 64479-64530, 69990, 71034, 75600, 75605, 75625, 75630, 75710, 75716, 75741, 75743, 75746, 75756, 75774, 75893, 76000-76001, 78635, 92012-92014, 92961, 93000-93010, 93040-93042, 93050, 93318, 93355-93452, 93454-93455, 93458, 93462, 93503-93505, 93561-93565, 94002, 94200, 94250, 94680-94690, 94770, 95812-95816, 95819, 95822, 95829, 95955, 96360-96368, 96372-96377, 99155-99157, 99211-99223, 99231-99255, 99291-99292, 99304-99310, 99315-99316, 99334-99337, 99347-99350, 99374-99375, 99377-99378, 99446-99449, 99495-99496, G0269, G0463, G0471, J0670, J1642-J1644, J2001

93457   01920, 01924-01926, 0213T, 0216T, 12001-12007, 12011-12057, 13100-13133, 13151-13153, 33210, 34812, 35201-35206, 35226-35236, 35256-35266, 35286, 36000, 36005-36010, 36013-36015, 36120-36140, 36200, 36245, 36400-36410, 36420-36430, 36440, 36500, 36555-36556, 36568-36569, 36591-36592, 36600-36640, 43752, 51701-51703, 62320-62327, 64400-64410, 64413-64435, 64445-64450, 64461-64463, 64479-64530, 69990, 71034, 75600, 75605, 75625, 75630, 75710, 75716, 75741, 75743, 75746, 75756, 75774, 75893, 76000-76001, 78635, 92012-92014, 92961, 93000-93010, 93040-93042, 93050, 93318, 93355-93456, 93458-93459, 93462, 93503, 93561-93565, 94002, 94200, 94250, 94680-94690, 94770, 95812-95816, 95819, 95822, 95829, 95955, 96360-96368, 96372-96377, 99155-99157, 99211-99223, 99231-99255, 99291-99292, 99304-99310, 99315-99316, 99334-99337, 99347-99350, 99374-99375, 99377-99378, 99446-99449, 99495-99496, G0269, G0463, G0471, J0670, J1642-J1644, J2001

93458   01920, 01924-01926, 0213T, 0216T, 12001-12007, 12011-12057, 13100-13133, 13151-13153, 33210, 34812, 35201-35206, 35226-35236, 35256-35266, 35286, 36000, 36005, 36120-36140, 36200, 36245, 36400-36410, 36420-36430, 36440, 36500, 36591-36592, 36600-36640, 43752, 51701-51703, 62320-62327, 64400-64410, 64413-64435, 64445-64450, 64461-64463, 64479-64530, 69990, 71034, 75600, 75605, 75625, 75630, 75710, 75716, 75741, 75743, 75746, 75756, 75774, 75893, 76000-76001, 78635, 92012-92014, 92961, 93000-93010, 93040-93042, 93050, 93318, 93355-93452, 93454-93455, 93503, 93561-93565, 94002, 94200, 94250, 94680-94690, 94770, 95812-95816, 95819, 95822, 95829, 95955, 96360-96368, 96372-96377, 99155-99157, 99211-99223, 99231-99255, 99291-99292, 99304-99310, 99315-99316, 99334-99337, 99347-99350, 99374-99375, 99377-99378, 99446-99449, 99495-99496, G0269, G0463, G0471, J0670, J1642-J1644, J2001

93459   01920, 01924-01926, 0213T, 0216T, 12001-12007, 12011-12057, 13100-13133, 13151-13153, 33210, 34812, 35201-35206, 35226-35236, 35256-35266, 35286, 36000, 36005, 36120-36140, 36200, 36245, 36400-36410, 36420-36430, 36440, 36500, 36591-36592, 36600-36640, 43752, 51701-51703, 62320-62327, 64400-64410, 64413-64435, 64445-64450, 64461-64463, 64479-64530, 69990, 71034, 75600, 75605, 75625, 75630, 75710, 75716, 75741, 75743, 75746, 75756, 75774, 75893, 76000-76001, 78635, 92012-92014, 92961, 93000-93010, 93040-93042, 93050, 93318, 93355-93456, 93458, 93503, 93561-93565, 94002, 94200, 94250, 94680-94690, 94770, 95812-95816, 95819, 95822, 95829, 95955, 96360-96368, 96372-96377, 99155-99157, 99211-99223, 99231-99255, 99291-99292, 99304-99310, 99315-99316, 99334-99337, 99347-99350, 99374-99375, 99377-99378, 99446-99449, 99495-99496, G0269, G0463, G0471, J0670, J1642-J1644, J2001

93460   01920, 01924-01926, 0213T, 0216T, 12001-12007, 12011-12057, 13100-13133, 13151-13153, 33210, 34812, 35201-35206, 35226-35236, 35256-35266, 35286, 36000, 36005-36010, 36013-36015, 36120-36140, 36200, 36245, 36400-36410, 36420-36430, 36440, 36500, 36555-36556, 36568-36569, 36591-36592, 36600-36640, 43752, 51701-51703, 62320-62327, 64400-64410, 64413-64435, 64445-64450, 64461-64463, 64479-64530, 69990, 71034, 75600, 75605, 75625, 75630, 75710, 75716, 75741, 75743, 75746, 75756, 75774, 75893, 76000-76001, 78635, 92012-92014, 92961, 93000-93010, 93040-93042, 93050, 93318, 93355-93459, 93503, 93561-93565, 94002, 94200, 94250, 94680-94690, 94770, 95812-95816, 95819, 95822, 95829, 95955, 96360-96368, 96372-96377, 99155-99157,

99211-99223, 99231-99255, 99291-99292, 99304-99310, 99315-99316, 99334-99337, 99347-99350, 99374-99375, 99377-99378, 99446-99449, 99495-99496, G0269, G0463, G0471, J0670, J1642-J1644, J2001

93461 01920, 01924-01926, 0213T, 0216T, 12001-12007, 12011-12057, 13100-13133, 13151-13153, 33210, 34812, 35201-35206, 35226-35236, 35256-35266, 35286, 36000, 36005-36010, 36013-36015, 36120-36140, 36200, 36245, 36400-36410, 36420-36430, 36440, 36500, 36555-36556, 36568-36569, 36591-36592, 36600-36640, 43752, 51701-51703, 62320-62327, 64400-64410, 64413-64435, 64445-64450, 64461-64463, 64479-64530, 69990, 71034, 75600, 75605, 75625, 75630, 75710, 75716, 75741, 75743, 75746, 75756, 75774, 75893, 76000-76001, 78635, 92012-92014, 92961, 93000-93010, 93040-93042, 93050, 93318, 93355-93460, 93503, 93561-93565, 94002, 94200, 94250, 94680-94690, 94770, 95812-95816, 95819, 95822, 95829, 95955, 96360-96368, 96372-96377, 99155-99157, 99211-99223, 99231-99255, 99291-99292, 99304-99310, 99315-99316, 99334-99337, 99347-99350, 99374-99375, 99377-99378, 99446-99449, 99495-99496, G0269, G0463, G0471, J0670, J1642-J1644, J2001

93462 33210-33211, 36005-36010, 36013-36015, 36555-36556, 36568-36569, 36591-36592, 93050, 93561-93562, 99155-99157, G0269

93463 36591-36592, 93050, 99155-99157

93464 36591-36592, 93050, 99155-99157, 99446-99449

93566 01920, 01924-01926, 0213T, 0216T, 0228T, 0230T, 35201-35206, 35226-35236, 35256-35266, 35286, 36000, 36005, 36400-36410, 36420-36430, 36440, 36500, 36591-36592, 36600, 36640, 43752, 51701-51703, 61650, 62320-62327, 64400-64410, 64413-64435, 64445-64450, 64461, 64463, 64479, 64483, 64486-64490, 64493, 64505-64530, 71034, 75605, 75625, 75741, 75743, 75893, 76000-76001, 78635, 93000-93010, 93040-93042, 93318, 93355, 93561-93562, 94002, 94200, 94250, 94680-94690, 94770, 95812-95816, 95819, 95822, 95829, 95955, 96360, 96365, 96372, 96374-96377, 99155-99157, G0471

93567 01920, 01924-01926, 0213T, 0216T, 0228T, 0230T, 35201-35206, 35226-35236, 35256-35266, 35286, 36000, 36005, 36400-36410, 36420-36430, 36440, 36500, 36591-36592, 36600, 36640, 43752, 51701-51703, 61650, 62320-62327, 64400-64410, 64413-64435, 64445-64450, 64461, 64463, 64479, 64483, 64486-64490, 64493, 64505-64530, 71034, 75741, 75743, 75893, 76000-76001, 78635, 93000-93010, 93040-93042, 93318, 93355, 93561-93562, 94002, 94200, 94250, 94680-94690, 94770, 95812-95816, 95819, 95822, 95829, 95955, 96360, 96365, 96372, 96374-96377, 99155-99157, G0471

93568 01920, 01924-01926, 0213T, 0216T, 0228T, 0230T, 35201-35206, 35226-35236, 35256-35266, 35286, 36000, 36005, 36400-36410, 36420-36430, 36440, 36500, 36591-36592, 36600, 36640, 43752, 51701-51703, 61650, 62320-62327, 64400-64410, 64413-64435, 64445-64450, 64461, 64463, 64479, 64483, 64486-64490, 64493, 64505-64530, 71034, 75605, 75625, 75893, 76000-76001, 78635, 93000-93010, 93040-93042, 93318, 93355, 93561-93562, 93564, 94002, 94200, 94250, 94680-94690, 94770, 95812-95816, 95819, 95822, 95829, 95955, 96360, 96365, 96372, 96374-96377, 99155-99157, G0471

93571 0213T, 0216T, 0228T, 0230T, 33210-33211, 36000, 36400-36410, 36420-36430, 36440, 36591-36592, 36600, 36640, 43752, 62320-62327, 64400-64410, 64413-64435, 64445-64450, 64461, 64463, 64479, 64483, 64486-64490, 64493, 64505-64530, 93000-93010, 93040-93042, 93318, 93355, 94002, 94200, 94250, 94680-94690, 94770, 95812-95816, 95819, 95822, 95829, 95955, 96360, 96365, 96372, 96374-96377, 99155-99157, 99446-99449

93572 0213T, 0216T, 0228T, 0230T, 33210-33211, 36000, 36400-36410, 36420-36430, 36440, 36591-36592, 36600, 36640, 43752, 62320-62327, 64400-64410, 64413-64435, 64445-64450, 64461, 64463, 64479, 64483, 64486-64490, 64493, 64505-64530, 93000-93010, 93040-93042, 93318, 93355, 94002, 94200, 94250, 94680-94690, 94770, 95812-95816, 95819, 95822, 95829, 95955, 96360, 96365, 96372, 96374-96377, 99155-99157, 99446-99449

Case Example

History:
The patient is a 68-year-old white male with multiple cardiac risk factors and a history of coronary artery bypass grafting 15 years ago. Patient currently complains of dyspnea on exertion and an abnormal nuclear stress test suggestive of anterior ischemia.

Procedure:
After informed consent, the patient was brought to the cardiac catheterization lab and prepped and draped in sterile fashion. **Routine left heart catheterization with selective coronary arteriograms, left ventriculography and aortography was performed** using the modified Seldinger technique via the right femoral artery. 6-French #4 right and left Judkins catheters and a pigtail catheter were used. At the conclusion of the procedure, hemostasis was obtained by use of the VasoSeal device.

Results:
The aortic pressure measured 148/66 mmHg. The left ventricular end-diastolic pressure was 19 mmHg. There was no significant gradient on pullback across the aortic valve.

Selective left coronary angiogram:
Revealed non critical disease in the left main coronary artery. The left anterior descending was totally occluded and at the proximal segment after the takeoff of a small first diagonal branch revealed a 90% stenosis. The circumflex artery was totally occluded in its proximal segment.

Selective right coronary angiogram:
Revealed a totally occluded vessel in its mid segment.

Left ventriculography:
Revealed grossly normal left ventricular size and function without any focal wall motion abnormalities. Ejection fraction is approximately 60%. There was no significant mitral regurgitation. Aortography showed grossly normal aortic size without evidence of aneurysm or dissection. There did not appear to be any missing bypass grafts.

Selective graft angiography:
Revealed a **saphenous vein graft to the right coronary artery** which had mild diffuse disease but no significant obstructions. There was a **saphenous vein jump graft to the first diagonal branch** and onto an obtuse marginal branch, which was patent. However, there was a 50-60% stenosis at the ostium and an 80-90% stenosis at the anastomosis to the small first diagonal branch. The **left internal mammary artery graft to the LAD** was widely patent without any significant distal disease. There was a 40% stenosis in the LAD at the apex.

CPT/HCPCS Codes Reported:
93459, 93567

Other HCPCS Codes Reported:
G0269 (per payer guidelines)

Heart Catheterization Procedures for Congenital Anomalies

93530   **Right heart catheterization, for congenital cardiac anomalies**
The physician performs a right heart catheterization for congenital cardiac anomalies. The physician investigates congenital cardiac anomalies by measuring pressures, taking blood samples for oximetry, and/or injecting contrast to assess chamber size and function. The physician places an introducer sheath in a vein (typically the femoral vein) using percutaneous puncture. The physician places a lumen catheter through the introducer sheath into the femoral vein and advances it under fluoroscopic guidance to the heart chamber receiving venous circulation. The physician may use the fluid filled catheter to record intracardiac pressures, withdraw blood samples, or inject radiopaque contrast material. The physician removes the catheter and sheath from the femoral vein.

93531   **Combined right heart catheterization and retrograde left heart catheterization, for congenital anomalies**
The purpose of this procedure is to investigate congenital cardiac anomalies by measuring pressures, taking blood samples for oximetry, and/or injecting contrast to assess chamber size and function. The physician places an introducer sheath in a vein (typically the femoral) using percutaneous puncture. The physician places a lumen catheter through the introducer sheath into the femoral vein and advances it under fluoroscopic guidance to the heart chamber receiving venous circulation. The physician places an introducer sheath in an artery (typically the femoral) using percutaneous puncture. The physician places a lumen catheter through the introducer sheath into the femoral artery and advances it under fluoroscopic guidance through the aorta to the heart chamber providing arterial circulation. The physician may use the fluid filled catheters to record intracardiac pressures, withdraw blood samples, or inject radiopaque contrast material. The physician removes the catheters and sheaths from the femoral vessels. Pressure is placed on the wound for 20 to 30 minutes to stem bleeding.

93532   **Combined right heart catheterization and transseptal left heart catheterization through intact septum with or without retrograde left heart catheterization, for congenital cardiac anomalies**
The purpose of this procedure is to investigate congenital cardiac anomalies by measuring pressures, taking blood samples for oximetry, and/or injecting contrast to assess chamber size and function. The physician places an introducer sheath in a vein (typically the femoral) using percutaneous puncture. The physician places a lumen catheter through the introducer sheath into the femoral vein and advances it under fluoroscopic guidance to the heart chamber receiving venous circulation. The physician exchanges this catheter over a wire for a transseptal puncture needle, dilator, and sheath. The physician advances the transseptal puncture apparatus to the right atrium and punctures the intraatrial septum with the needle. The physician advances the needle, dilator, and transseptal sheath into the left atrium. The physician may also perform retrograde left heart catheterization as follows: The physician places an introducer sheath and lumen catheter in an artery (typically the femoral) using percutaneous puncture. The physician advances the lumen catheter under fluoroscopic guidance through the aorta to the heart chamber providing arterial circulation. The physician may use the fluid filled catheters to record intracardiac pressures, withdraw blood samples, or inject radiopaque contrast material. The physician removes the catheters and sheaths from the femoral vessels. Pressure is placed on the wound for 20 to 30 minutes to stem bleeding.

93533   **Combined right heart catheterization and transseptal left heart catheterization through existing septal opening, with or without retrograde left heart catheterization, for congenital cardiac anomalies**

The purpose of this procedure is to investigate congenital cardiac anomalies by measuring pressures, taking blood samples for oximetry, and/or injecting contrast to assess chamber size and function. The physician places an introducer sheath in a vein (typically the femoral) using percutaneous puncture. The physician places a lumen catheter through the introducer sheath into the femoral vein and advances it under fluoroscopic guidance to the heart chamber receiving venous circulation. The physician directs this catheter through an existing septal opening into the left atrium. The physician may also perform retrograde left heart catheterization as follows: The physician places an introducer sheath and lumen catheter in an artery (typically the femoral) using percutaneous puncture. The physician advances the lumen catheter under fluoroscopic guidance through the aorta to the heart chamber providing arterial circulation. The physician may use the fluid filled catheters to record intracardiac pressures, withdraw blood samples, or inject radiopaque contrast material. The physician removes the catheters and sheaths from the femoral vessels. Pressure is placed on the wound for 20 to 30 minutes to stem bleeding.

93563   Injection procedure during cardiac catheterization including imaging supervision, interpretation, and report; for selective coronary angiography during congenital heart catheterization (List separately in addition to code for primary procedure)

93564   for selective opacification of aortocoronary venous or arterial bypass graft(s) (eg, aortocoronary saphenous vein, free radial artery, or free mammary artery graft) to one or more coronary arteries and in situ arterial conduits (eg, internal mammary), whether native or used for bypass to one or more coronary arteries during congenital heart catheterization, when performed (List separately in addition to code for primary procedure)

93565   for selective left ventricular or left atrial angiography (List separately in addition to code for primary procedure)

93566   for selective right ventricular or right atrial angiography (List separately in addition to code for primary procedure)

93567   for supravalvular aortography (List separately in addition to code for primary procedure)

93568   for pulmonary angiography (List separately in addition to code for primary procedure)

These codes report the various injection procedures possible during cardiac catheterization procedures. The injection procedure codes include imaging supervision and interpretation. These codes are reported in addition to the cardiac catheterization procedure performed.

Coding Tips

1. These codes report procedures typically performed on pediatric patients; however, they are also intended to report cardiac catheterization procedures performed on adult patients with congenital cardiac anomalies.
2. Report separately contrast injection and imaging for selective coronary angiography. See CPT code 93563.
3. Report separately contrast injection and imaging for selective coronary bypass angiograms with CPT code 93564.
4. Injection and imaging for left ventriculogram or left atrium is reported separately with CPT code 93565.
5. Report contrast injection and imaging of the right ventricle or right atrium with CPT code 93566.
6. Use CPT code 93567 to report contrast injection and imaging of the aortic root.
7. Injection and imaging for pulmonary angiography is reported separately with CPT code 93568.
8. Refer to the General Coding Guidelines for Cardiac Catheterization section for additional guidelines applicable to congenital procedures.

Facility HCPCS Coding

HCPCS Level II codes are used to report the supplies provided during the procedure. Hospitals should separately report supplies used during cardiac catheterization procedures. Refer to chapter 1 for more information regarding appropriate billing of supplies. Refer to the list of current codes in appendix B.

CPT Coding for Congenital Cardiac Catheterization Procedures

CPT Code	Procedure Description
93530	Right heart cath for congenital cardiac anomalies
93531	Right heart cath & retrograde LHC for congenital cardiac anomalies
93532	RHC and transseptal LHC through intact septum with or without retrograde LHC
93533	RHC and transseptal LHC through existing septal opening with or without retrograde LHC
Add-on Codes	
93563	Injection selective coronary angiograms
93564	Injection selective coronary bypass angiograms
93565	Injection for left ventriculogram or left atrial
93566	Injection for right ventriculogram or right atrial
93567	Injection for supravalvular aorta (aortic root)
93568	Injection for pulmonary angiograms
93571	Coronary flow reserve measurement, initial vessel
93572	Coronary flow reserve measurement, each additional vessel

ICD-10-CM Coding

The application of these codes is too broad to adequately present ICD-10-CM diagnosis code links here. Refer to the current ICD-10-CM book.

CCI Edits

93530 01920, 01924-01926, 0213T, 0216T, 0228T, 0230T, 12001-12007, 12011-12057, 13100-13133, 13151-13153, 34812-34813, 35201-35206, 35226-35236, 35256-35266, 35286, 36000, 36005-36010, 36013-36015, 36400-36410, 36420-36430, 36440, 36500, 36555-36556, 36568-36569, 36591-36592, 36600, 36640, 43752, 51701-51703, 62320-62327, 64400-64410, 64413-64435, 64445-64450, 64461-64463, 64479-64530, 71034, 75600, 75605, 75741, 75743, 75746, 75756, 75893, 76000-76001, 77001-77002, 78635, 92012-92014, 92961, 93000-93010, 93040-93042, 93318, 93355, 93452, 93458-93459, 93503, 93561-93562, 94002, 94200, 94250, 94680-94690, 94770, 95812-95816, 95819, 95822, 95829, 95955, 96360-96368, 96372-96377, 99155-99157, 99211-99223, 99231-99255, 99291-99292, 99304-99310, 99315-99316, 99334-99337, 99347-99350, 99374-99375, 99377-99378, 99446-99449, 99495-99496, G0269, G0463, G0471

93531 01920, 01924-01926, 0213T, 0216T, 0228T, 0230T, 12001-12007, 12011-12057, 13100-13133, 13151-13153, 33210-33211, 34812-34813, 35201-35206, 35226-35236, 35256-35266, 35286, 36000, 36005-36010, 36013-36015, 36140, 36200, 36245, 36400-36410, 36420-36430, 36440, 36500, 36555-36556, 36568-36569, 36591-36592, 36600, 36640, 43752, 51701-51703, 62320-62327, 64400-64410, 64413-64435, 64445-64450, 64461-64463, 64479-64530, 71034, 75600, 75605, 75625, 75630, 75710, 75716, 75741, 75743, 75746, 75756, 75774, 75893, 76000-76001, 77001-77002, 78635, 92012-92014, 92961, 93000-93010, 93040-93042, 93050, 93318, 93355, 93452, 93458-93459, 93503, 93530, 93561-93562, 94002, 94200, 94250, 94680-94690, 94770, 95812-95816, 95819, 95822, 95829, 95955, 96360-96368, 96372-96377, 99155-99157, 99211-99223, 99231-99255, 99291-99292, 99304-99310, 99315-99316, 99334-99337, 99347-99350, 99374-99375, 99377-99378, 99446-99449, 99495-99496, G0269, G0463, G0471

93532 01920, 01924-01926, 0213T, 0216T, 0228T, 0230T, 12001-12007, 12011-12057, 13100-13133, 13151-13153, 33210-33211, 34812-34813, 35201-35206, 35226-35236, 35256-35266, 35286, 36000, 36005-36010, 36013-36015, 36140, 36200, 36245, 36400-36410, 36420-36430, 36440, 36500, 36555-36556, 36568-36569, 36591-36592, 36600, 36640, 43752, 51701-51703, 62320-62327, 64400-64410, 64413-64435, 64445-64450, 64461-64463, 64479-64530, 71034, 75600, 75605, 75625, 75630, 75710, 75716, 75741, 75743, 75746, 75756, 75774, 75893, 76000-76001, 77001-77002, 78635, 92012-92014, 92961, 93000-93010, 93040-93042, 93050, 93318, 93355, 93452, 93458-93459, 93503, 93530, 93561-93562, 94002, 94200, 94250, 94680-94690, 94770, 95812-95816, 95819, 95822, 95829, 95955, 96360-96368, 96372-96377, 99155-99157, 99211-99223, 99231-99255, 99291-99292, 99304-99308, 99310, 99315-99316, 99334-99337, 99347-99350, 99374-99375, 99377-99378, 99446-99449, 99495-99496, G0269, G0463, G0471

93533 01920, 01924-01926, 0213T, 0216T, 0228T, 0230T, 12001-12007, 12011-12057, 13100-13133, 13151-13153, 33210-33211, 34812-34813, 35201-35206, 35226-35236, 35256-35266, 35286, 36000, 36005-36010, 36013-36015, 36140, 36200, 36245, 36400-36410, 36420-36430, 36440, 36500, 36555-36556, 36568-36569, 36591-36592, 36600, 36640, 43752, 51701-51703, 62320-62327, 64400-64410, 64413-64435, 64445-64450, 64461-64463, 64479-64530, 71034, 75600, 75605, 75625, 75630, 75710, 75716, 75741, 75743, 75746, 75756, 75774, 75893, 76000-76001, 77001-77002, 78635, 92012-92014, 92961, 93000-93010, 93040-93042, 93050, 93318, 93355, 93452, 93458-93459, 93503, 93530, 93561-93562, 94002, 94200, 94250, 94680-94690, 94770, 95812-95816, 95819, 95822, 95829, 95955, 96360-96368, 96372-96377, 99155-99157, 99211-99223, 99231-99255, 99291-99292, 99304-99310, 99315-99316, 99334-99337, 99347-99350, 99374-99375, 99377-99378, 99446-99449, 99495-99496, G0269, G0463, G0471

93563 01920, 01924-01926, 0213T, 0216T, 35201-35206, 35226-35236, 35256-35266, 35286, 36000, 36005, 36400-36410, 36420-36430, 36440, 36500, 36591-36592, 36600, 36640, 43752, 51701-51703, 61650, 62320-62327, 64400-64410, 64413-64435, 64445-64450, 64461, 64463, 64479, 64483, 64486-64490, 64493, 64505-64530, 71034, 75605, 75625, 75741, 75743, 75893, 76000-76001, 78635, 93000-93010, 93040-93042, 93050, 93318, 93355, 93561-93562, 94002, 94200, 94250, 94680-94690, 94770, 95812-95816, 95819, 95822, 95829, 95955, 96360, 96365, 96372, 96374-96377, 99155-99157, G0471

93564 01920, 01924-01926, 0213T, 0216T, 35201-35206, 35226-35236, 35256-35266, 35286, 36000, 36005, 36400-36410, 36420-36430, 36440, 36500, 36591-36592, 36600, 36640, 43752, 51701-51703, 61650, 62320-62327, 64400-64410, 64413-64435, 64445-64450, 64461, 64463, 64479, 64483, 64486-64490, 64493, 64505-64530, 71034, 75605, 75625, 75741, 75743, 75756, 75893, 76000-76001, 78635, 93000-93010, 93040-93042, 93050, 93318, 93355, 93561-93562, 94002, 94200, 94250, 94680-94690, 94770, 95812-95816, 95819, 95822, 95829, 95955, 96360, 96365, 96372, 96374-96377, 99155-99157, G0471

93565 01920, 01924-01926, 0213T, 0216T, 35201-35206, 35226-35236, 35256-35266, 35286, 36000, 36005, 36400-36410, 36420-36430, 36440, 36500, 36591-36592, 36600, 36640, 43752, 51701-51703, 61650, 62320-62327, 64400-64410, 64413-64435, 64445-64450, 64461, 64463, 64479, 64483, 64486-64490, 64493, 64505-64530, 71034, 75605, 75625, 75741, 75743, 75893, 76000-76001, 78635, 93000-93010, 93040-93042, 93318, 93355, 93561-93562, 94002, 94200, 94250, 94680-94690, 94770, 95812-95816, 95819, 95822, 95829, 95955, 96360, 96365, 96372, 96374-96377, 99155-99157, G0471

93566   01920, 01924-01926, 0213T, 0216T, 0228T, 0230T, 35201-35206, 35226-35236, 35256-35266, 35286, 36000, 36005, 36400-36410, 36420-36430, 36440, 36500, 36591-36592, 36600, 36640, 43752, 51701-51703, 61650, 62320-62327, 64400-64410, 64413-64435, 64445-64450, 64461, 64463, 64479, 64483, 64486-64490, 64493, 64505-64530, 71034, 75605, 75625, 75741, 75743, 75893, 76000-76001, 78635, 93000-93010, 93040-93042, 93318, 93355, 93561-93562, 94002, 94200, 94250, 94680-94690, 94770, 95812-95816, 95819, 95822, 95829, 95955, 96360, 96365, 96372, 96374-96377, 99155-99157, G0471

93567   01920, 01924-01926, 0213T, 0216T, 0228T, 0230T, 35201-35206, 35226-35236, 35256-35266, 35286, 36000, 36005, 36400-36410, 36420-36430, 36440, 36500, 36591-36592, 36600, 36640, 43752, 51701-51703, 61650, 62320-62327, 64400-64410, 64413-64435, 64445-64450, 64461, 64463, 64479, 64483, 64486-64490, 64493, 64505-64530, 71034, 75741, 75743, 75893, 76000-76001, 78635, 93000-93010, 93040-93042, 93318, 93355, 93561-93562, 94002, 94200, 94250, 94680-94690, 94770, 95812-95816, 95819, 95822, 95829, 95955, 96360, 96365, 96372, 96374-96377, 99155-99157, G0471

93568   01920, 01924-01926, 0213T, 0216T, 0228T, 0230T, 35201-35206, 35226-35236, 35256-35266, 35286, 36000, 36005, 36400-36410, 36420-36430, 36440, 36500, 36591-36592, 36600, 36640, 43752, 51701-51703, 61650, 62320-62327, 64400-64410, 64413-64435, 64445-64450, 64461, 64463, 64479, 64483, 64486-64490, 64493, 64505-64530, 71034, 75605, 75625, 75893, 76000-76001, 78635, 93000-93010, 93040-93042, 93318, 93355, 93561-93562, 93564, 94002, 94200, 94250, 94680-94690, 94770, 95812-95816, 95819, 95822, 95829, 95955, 96360, 96365, 96372, 96374-96377, 99155-99157, G0471

Case Example #1

This is a 26-year-old woman with **tricuspid atresia/VSD and subpulmonary stenosis** whose palliation has consisted of a left BT shunt, classic Glenn, modified classic Fontan, and extracardiac conduit Fontan revision. She has atrial tachycardia and ascites. She is ventricularly paced.

Procedure:
Informed consent was obtained, and the patient was brought to the cardiac catheterization lab. Both groins were prepped and draped in the usual sterile fashion. **Percutaneous access** was achieved with a 7F left femoral venous sheath and a 6F left femoral arterial sheath. Baseline **right and left heart hemodynamics**, and multiple **angiograms** were obtained. There was a normal innominate vein by catheter pass. All catheters and sheaths were removed and hemostasis achieved with direct hand pressure.

Hemodynamics:
Baseline hemodynamics were obtained on room air, atrial pacing with ventricular sensing. Saturation in the superior vena cava was 60%, Fontan baffle 61%, and IVC was 64%. Left pulmonary artery saturation was 68% and right pulmonary artery 67%. Saturation in the left ventricle was 91% and the descending aorta 90%. Mean pressure in the Fontan circuit was 24mm Hg. There was no gradient to the superior or inferior vena cava or to either branch pulmonary artery. Bilateral pulmonary wedge pressure had a mean of 18mm Hg with an a-wave of 16 and a v-wave of 20. Left ventricular pressure was 100/16, ascending aorta 100/75, and descending aorta 100/75 with a mean of 86mm Hg.

Angiography/Intervention:
SVC/innominate vein: Hand contrast injection was performed in the innominate vein. There is a small collateral vessel to the pericardium from the distal innominate vein. There is unobstructed flow to the SVC.

95827 SVC/Fontan: 7F Berman **catheter in the SVC through the extracardiac conduit** demonstrates preferential flow to the right pulmonary artery. There is one collateral at the superior portion of the SVC and one junction of the SVC and RPA which fill late. The termination of these vessels is not clearly seen. There is no stenosis in the superior portion of the Fontan.

Fontan baffle/pulmonary arteries: Berman repositioned in the mid-portion of the conduit. There is mild tortuosity of the conduit although there is no gradient. There is preferential filling of the left pulmonary artery. The mid left pulmonary artery is smaller than the right pulmonary artery, but there was no pressure gradient in this region. Pulmonary venous return is unobstructed to the left atrium. There is a large atrial communication.

75825 IVC/Fontan: 7F Berman **catheter in the inferior vena cava**. The IVC and hepatic veins are dilated; there is no obstruction to the venous return and no Fontan baffle stenosis. There are no fenestrations or leaks. There is preferential flow of contrast to the left pulmonary artery.

Left ventricle: 6F pigtail catheter retrograde in the apex of the **left ventricle** demonstrates mildly depressed left ventricular systolic function and no significant mitral regurgitation. There is a hypoplastic anterior right ventricle which fills through a ventricular septal defect. The only exit of contrast from this chamber is through the VSD. There is no left ventricular outflow tract obstruction. The left ventricle appears stiff consistent with diastolic dysfunction.

Aortic root: There is no aortic insufficiency.

Descending aorta: **Pigtail withdrawn to the descending aorta** demonstrates no significant collateral flow to the pulmonary arteries. There is no coarctation. There is no ductus arteriosus.

CPT/HCPCS Codes Reported:
93531, 93568, 93565, 93567, 75825, 75827, 36010

Case Example #2

History:
A 39-year-old patient with Down syndrome and known endocardial cushion defect. She has a **primum ASD and cleft mitral valve with possible VSD**.

Approach:
Right femoral artery, right femoral vein

Procedures:
Left heart catheterization, selective coronary angiography, left ventriculogram via transseptal approach, right heart catheterization, right upper pulmonary vein angiography, right ventriculogram, pulmonary angiography

Thoracic aortogram performed in LAO position. *93567*

93563 → The left main coronary artery is angiographically normal. The left anterior descending artery is angiographically normal. The circumflex artery is angiographically normal. The right coronary artery is dominant and is angiographically normal. Left ventriculography is mildly enlarged with an ejection fraction of 55%. Mitral valve regurgitation is 1+.

93565 →
93568 → Right upper pulmonary vein angiography shows the high atrial septum is intact. **Large primum ASD is noted.** A Berman catheter was **inserted transseptally** across the mitral valve into the left ventricle. LV gram showed restrictive membranous VSD. The Berman catheter was then inserted into the main pulmonary artery. Pulmonary arteriogram showed dilated pulmonary arteries. A total of 170cc of Visipaque 270 was used during the procedure. Femoral angiography revealed patent arteries with the arteriotomy in good position suitable for closure device. A Perclose device was successfully deployed for vascular closure.

Findings:
Angiographically normal coronary arteries

Normal pulmonary artery pressures

Large primum ASD with large left to right shunt at the atrial level

Small restrictive membranous VSD

Normal LV function

Normal RV function

Enlarged pulmonary arteries

CPT/HCPCS Codes Reported:
93533, 93568, 93565, 93567, 93563

Chapter 12: Cardiac Interventional Procedures

Intra Aortic Balloon Pump Procedures—Percutaneous

Intra-aortic balloon pumps (IABPs) are used to provide patients with advanced heart failure with temporary mechanical support in pumping blood to the vital organs. These devices are placed using a percutaneous approach.

33967   **Insertion of intra-aortic balloon assist device, percutaneous**

An intra-aortic balloon catheter, usually with a 40 cc volume capacity, is inserted into the femoral artery and advanced under fluoroscopy to the distal portion of the aortic arch. After correct placement of the intra-aortic balloon assist device (IAB) in the descending aorta with its tip at the distal aortic arch, the balloon is connected to a drive console. The console consists of a pressurized gas reservoir, a monitor for ECG and pressure wave recording, adjustments for inflation/deflation timing, triggering selection switches, and battery back-up power sources. Either helium or carbon dioxide is used for inflation. Inflation and deflation are synchronized to the patient's cardiac cycle. Inflation at the onset of diastole results in proximal and distal displacement of blood volume in the aorta. Deflation occurs just prior to the onset of systole. Once the patient's cardiac performance improves, weaning from the intra-aortic balloon catheter pump (IABP) begins by gradually decreasing the balloon augmentation ratio under control of hemodynamic stability.

33968   **Removal of intra-aortic balloon assist device, percutaneous**

The physician removes an intra-aortic balloon assist device (IABP). In a previous separately reportable procedure an IABP was inserted. When the patient is stabilized they are weaned off of the IAPB. The pump is turned off and the IABP catheter with the attached balloon is withdrawn from the femoral artery. Pressure is placed over the wound in the groin for a specified period of time. A light dressing is then applied. The patient may be placed on bed rest and observed for several hours to avoid problems that could arise from bleeding or a hematoma at the puncture site.

Coding Tips

1. Fluoroscopy is included in CPT® codes 33967 and 33968 and is not reported separately.

2. Conscious sedation is not included in these codes. Separately report 99151–99157 per payer policy and coding guidelines. Hospitals may choose to include the costs associated with the service as part of the procedure rather than reporting them separately.

3. Both codes are assigned inpatient only status under OPPS. There will be no payment if reported as an outpatient.

4. For open approach insertion of an intra-aortic balloon pump, see CPT code 33970.

Facility HCPCS Coding

HCPCS Level II codes are used to report the supplies provided during the procedure. Hospitals should separately report supplies used during cardiac catheterization procedures. Refer to chapter 1 for more information regarding appropriate billing of supplies. Refer to the list of current codes in appendix B.

ICD-10-CM Coding

33967

I11.Ø	Hypertensive heart disease with heart failure
I16.Ø	Hypertensive urgency
I16.1	Hypertensive emergency
I16.9	Hypertensive crisis, unspecified
I2Ø.Ø	Unstable angina
I2Ø.1	Angina pectoris with documented spasm
I2Ø.8	Other forms of angina pectoris
I2Ø.9	Angina pectoris, unspecified
I21.Ø1	ST elevation (STEMI) myocardial infarction involving left main coronary artery
I21.Ø2	ST elevation (STEMI) myocardial infarction involving left anterior descending coronary artery
I21.Ø9	ST elevation (STEMI) myocardial infarction involving other coronary artery of anterior wall
I21.11	ST elevation (STEMI) myocardial infarction involving right coronary artery
I21.19	ST elevation (STEMI) myocardial infarction involving other coronary artery of inferior wall
I21.21	ST elevation (STEMI) myocardial infarction involving left circumflex coronary artery
I21.29	ST elevation (STEMI) myocardial infarction involving other sites
I21.3	ST elevation (STEMI) myocardial infarction of unspecified site

I21.4	Non-ST elevation (NSTEMI) myocardial infarction
I21.9	Acute myocardial infarction, unspecified
I21.A1	Myocardial infarction type 2
I21.A9	Other myocardial infarction type
I22.0	Subsequent ST elevation (STEMI) myocardial infarction of anterior wall
I22.1	Subsequent ST elevation (STEMI) myocardial infarction of inferior wall
I22.2	Subsequent non-ST elevation (NSTEMI) myocardial infarction
I22.8	Subsequent ST elevation (STEMI) myocardial infarction of other sites
I22.9	Subsequent ST elevation (STEMI) myocardial infarction of unspecified site
I24.8	Other forms of acute ischemic heart disease
I24.9	Acute ischemic heart disease, unspecified
I25.10	Atherosclerotic heart disease of native coronary artery without angina pectoris
I25.2	Old myocardial infarction
I25.3	Aneurysm of heart
I25.41	Coronary artery aneurysm
I25.42	Coronary artery dissection
I25.5	Ischemic cardiomyopathy
I25.6	Silent myocardial ischemia
I25.9	Chronic ischemic heart disease, unspecified
I34.0	Nonrheumatic mitral (valve) insufficiency
I34.1	Nonrheumatic mitral (valve) prolapse
I34.2	Nonrheumatic mitral (valve) stenosis
I34.8	Other nonrheumatic mitral valve disorders
I34.9	Nonrheumatic mitral valve disorder, unspecified
I35.0	Nonrheumatic aortic (valve) stenosis
I35.1	Nonrheumatic aortic (valve) insufficiency
I35.2	Nonrheumatic aortic (valve) stenosis with insufficiency
I35.8	Other nonrheumatic aortic valve disorders
I35.9	Nonrheumatic aortic valve disorder, unspecified
I42.0	Dilated cardiomyopathy
I42.5	Other restrictive cardiomyopathy
I42.8	Other cardiomyopathies
I42.9	Cardiomyopathy, unspecified
I46.2	Cardiac arrest due to underlying cardiac condition
I46.8	Cardiac arrest due to other underlying condition
I46.9	Cardiac arrest, cause unspecified
I47.0	Re-entry ventricular arrhythmia
I47.1	Supraventricular tachycardia
I47.2	Ventricular tachycardia
I47.9	Paroxysmal tachycardia, unspecified
I50.1	Left ventricular failure
I50.20	Unspecified systolic (congestive) heart failure
I50.21	Acute systolic (congestive) heart failure
I50.22	Chronic systolic (congestive) heart failure
I50.23	Acute on chronic systolic (congestive) heart failure
I50.30	Unspecified diastolic (congestive) heart failure
I50.31	Acute diastolic (congestive) heart failure
I50.32	Chronic diastolic (congestive) heart failure
I50.33	Acute on chronic diastolic (congestive) heart failure
I50.40	Unspecified combined systolic (congestive) and diastolic (congestive) heart failure
I50.41	Acute combined systolic (congestive) and diastolic (congestive) heart failure
I50.42	Chronic combined systolic (congestive) and diastolic (congestive) heart failure
I50.43	Acute on chronic combined systolic (congestive) and diastolic (congestive) heart failure
I50.810	Right heart failure, unspecified
I50.811	Acute right heart failure
I50.812	Chronic right heart failure

I50.813	Acute on chronic right heart failure
I50.814	Right heart failure due to left heart failure
I50.82	Biventricular heart failure
I50.83	High output heart failure
I50.84	End stage heart failure
I50.89	Other heart failure
I50.9	Heart failure, unspecified
I51.5	Myocardial degeneration
I51.9	Heart disease, unspecified
I97.0	Postcardiotomy syndrome
I97.110	Postprocedural cardiac insufficiency following cardiac surgery
I97.111	Postprocedural cardiac insufficiency following other surgery
I97.120	Postprocedural cardiac arrest following cardiac surgery
I97.121	Postprocedural cardiac arrest following other surgery
I97.130	Postprocedural heart failure following cardiac surgery
I97.131	Postprocedural heart failure following other surgery
I97.190	Other postprocedural cardiac functional disturbances following cardiac surgery
I97.191	Other postprocedural cardiac functional disturbances following other surgery
I97.710	Intraoperative cardiac arrest during cardiac surgery
I97.711	Intraoperative cardiac arrest during other surgery
I97.790	Other intraoperative cardiac functional disturbances during cardiac surgery
I97.791	Other intraoperative cardiac functional disturbances during other surgery
I97.88	Other intraoperative complications of the circulatory system, not elsewhere classified
I97.89	Other postprocedural complications and disorders of the circulatory system, not elsewhere classified
Q21.0	Ventricular septal defect
Q21.1	Atrial septal defect
Q21.2	Atrioventricular septal defect
Q21.3	Tetralogy of Fallot
Q21.4	Aortopulmonary septal defect
Q21.8	Other congenital malformations of cardiac septa
Q21.9	Congenital malformation of cardiac septum, unspecified
Q23.0	Congenital stenosis of aortic valve
Q23.1	Congenital insufficiency of aortic valve
Q23.2	Congenital mitral stenosis
Q23.3	Congenital mitral insufficiency
Q23.8	Other congenital malformations of aortic and mitral valves
Q23.9	Congenital malformation of aortic and mitral valves, unspecified
Q24.4	Congenital subaortic stenosis
Q24.5	Malformation of coronary vessels
Q24.6	Congenital heart block
Q24.8	Other specified congenital malformations of heart
Q24.9	Congenital malformation of heart, unspecified
R09.2	Respiratory arrest
R09.89	Other specified symptoms and signs involving the circulatory and respiratory systems
R57.0	Cardiogenic shock

33968

T79.A0XA	Compartment syndrome, unspecified, initial encounter
T82.513A	Breakdown (mechanical) of balloon (counterpulsation) device, initial encounter
T82.518A	Breakdown (mechanical) of other cardiac and vascular devices and implants, initial encounter
T82.523A	Displacement of balloon (counterpulsation) device, initial encounter
T82.528A	Displacement of other cardiac and vascular devices and implants, initial encounter
T82.533A	Leakage of balloon (counterpulsation) device, initial encounter
T82.538A	Leakage of other cardiac and vascular devices and implants, initial encounter
T82.593A	Other mechanical complication of balloon (counterpulsation) device, initial encounter
T82.598A	Other mechanical complication of other cardiac and vascular devices and implants, initial encounter

T82.7XXA	Infection and inflammatory reaction due to other cardiac and vascular devices, implants and grafts, initial encounter
T82.817A	Embolism of cardiac prosthetic devices, implants and grafts, initial encounter
T82.827A	Fibrosis of cardiac prosthetic devices, implants and grafts, initial encounter
T82.837A	Hemorrhage of cardiac prosthetic devices, implants and grafts, initial encounter
T82.847A	Pain from cardiac prosthetic devices, implants and grafts, initial encounter
T82.855A	Stenosis of coronary artery stent, initial encounter
T82.857A	Stenosis of cardiac prosthetic devices, implants and grafts, initial encounter
T82.867A	Thrombosis of cardiac prosthetic devices, implants and grafts, initial encounter
T82.897A	Other specified complication of cardiac prosthetic devices, implants and grafts, initial encounter
T82.898A	Other specified complication of vascular prosthetic devices, implants and grafts, initial encounter
T82.9XXA	Unspecified complication of cardiac and vascular prosthetic device, implant and graft, initial encounter
Z45.Ø9	Encounter for adjustment and management of other cardiac device

CCI Edits

33967 0213T, 0216T, 0228T, 0230T, 0454T, 11000-11006, 11042-11047, 12001-12007, 12011-12057, 13100-13133, 13151-13153, 33210-33211, 33310-33315, 34812-34813, 35201-35206, 35226, 35261-35266, 35286, 36000, 36140, 36200, 36215-36218, 36400-36410, 36420-36430, 36440, 36591-36592, 36600-36640, 43752, 51701-51703, 62320-62327, 64400-64410, 64413-64435, 64445-64450, 64461-64463, 64479-64530, 71034, 76000-76001, 77001-77002, 92012-92014, 93000-93010, 93040-93042, 93318, 93355, 93562, 94002, 94200, 94250, 94680-94690, 94770, 95812-95816, 95819, 95822, 95829, 95955, 96360-96368, 96372, 96374-96377, 97597-97598, 97602, 99155-99157, 99211-99223, 99231-99255, 99291-99292, 99304-99310, 99315-99316, 99334-99337, 99347-99350, 99374-99375, 99377-99378, 99446-99449, 99495-99496, G0463, G0471

33968 0213T, 0216T, 0228T, 0230T, 0451T-0458T, 11000-11006, 11042-11047, 12001-12007, 12011-12057, 13100-13133, 13151-13153, 33210-33211, 33310-33315, 33967, 33970, 33973, 35226, 35256, 35286, 36000, 36400-36410, 36420-36430, 36440, 36591-36592, 36600, 36640, 43752, 51701-51703, 62320-62327, 64400-64410, 64413-64435, 64445-64450, 64461-64463, 64479-64530, 92012-92014, 93000-93010, 93040-93042, 93318, 93355, 94002, 94200, 94250, 94680-94690, 94770, 95812-95816, 95819, 95822, 95829, 95955, 96360-96368, 96372, 96374-96377, 97597-97598, 97602, 99155-99157, 99211-99223, 99231-99255, 99291-99292, 99304-99310, 99315-99316, 99334-99337, 99347-99350, 99374-99375, 99377-99378, 99446-99449, 99495-99496, G0463, G0471

Case Example #1

The patient was prepped and draped in typical sterile fashion. After local anesthesia, arterial access was obtained via the left brachial artery. A 4-French Avanti sheath was placed and a guidewire inserted to provide a roadmap to identify the left axillary artery. **Direct access into the axillary artery was then made via percutaneous puncture.** A 4-French sheath was placed. The IABP kit was then introduced into the sterile field. The provided guidewire was then inserted via the sheath and directed to the descending aorta. We then exchanged the 4-French sheath with the IABP sheath. **The IABP catheter was then placed** through this sheath, over the wire and directed to the descending aorta, and placed a few centimeters below the arch. The wire was removed and the **pump device was then prepared and connected to the IABP catheter**.

CPT/HCPCS Codes Reported:
33967

Other HCPCS Codes Reported:
C1769, C1894

Case Example #2

Patient with previously placed IABP pump via right femoral artery.

Patient was prepped and draped in typical sterile fashion. **A guidewire was directed through the IABP catheter and sheath. The IABP catheter was then removed** using fluoroscopic guidance. A femoral angiogram was performed to assess for arterial injury. An 8-French closure device was then inserted.

CPT/HCPCS Codes Reported:
33968

Other HCPCS Codes Reported:
C1769, C1760

Coronary Thrombectomy

92973   **Percutaneous transluminal coronary thrombectomy mechanical (List separately in addition to code for primary procedure)**
The physician percutaneously removes a blood clot from a native or grafted coronary artery. A double lumen catheter is passed to the area of the clot. The mechanical thrombectomy device is introduced and directed to the area of the clot. The clot is broken into smaller fragments by the mechanical device and removed from the vessel by means other than aspiration. The procedure is useful to clear fatty and degenerated arteries and to modify plaques in preparation for more definitive treatment with adjunctive balloon angioplasty or stenting.

Coding Tips

1. CPT code 92973 is an "add-on" code. It is reported in addition to coronary stent placement or coronary angioplasty.
2. This code has been defined for reporting only when *mechanical* thrombectomy is performed.
3. Nonmechanical thrombectomy is a component of the base coronary intervention code and is not reported with 92973.
4. For interventional coronary coding guidelines, refer to page 17.

Facility HCPCS Coding

HCPCS Level II codes are used to report the supplies provided during the procedure. Hospitals should separately report supplies used during cardiac catheterization procedures. Refer to the introduction for more information regarding appropriate billing of supplies. Possible HCPCS codes reportable for this procedure include but may not be limited to:

C1757   Catheter, thrombectomy; embolectomy

Refer to the list of current codes in appendix B.

ICD-10-CM Coding

This is an add-on code. Refer to the corresponding primary procedure code for ICD-10-CM diagnosis code links.

CCI Edits

92973   01924-01926, 11000-11006, 11042-11047, 36591-36592, 93000-93010, 93040-93042, 93050, 94770, 97597-97598, 97602, 99155-99157

Coronary Thrombectomy

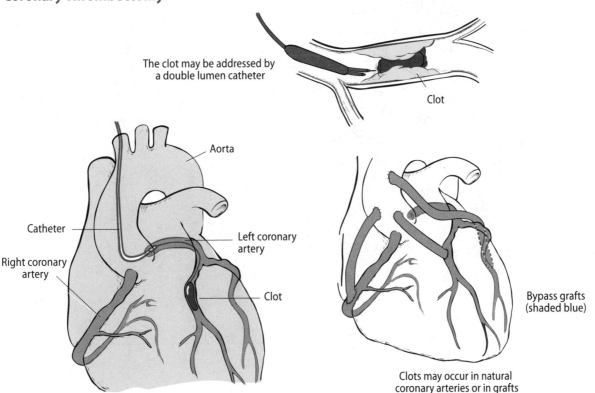

The clot may be addressed by a double lumen catheter

Clot

Aorta

Catheter

Left coronary artery

Right coronary artery

Clot

Bypass grafts (shaded blue)

Clots may occur in natural coronary arteries or in grafts

Intravascular Brachytherapy

92974   **Transcatheter placement of radiation delivery device for subsequent coronary intravascular brachytherapy (List separately in addition to code for primary procedure)**
Using fluoroscopy in a cardiac catheterization laboratory, the delivery catheter is placed in the coronary artery at the site of the in-stent restenosis (re-blockage in the artery). The transfer delivery device is connected to the delivery catheter; the transfer delivery device is used to deliver the radioactive seeds to the location. There are various methods for transcatheter placement, but commonly the methods involve the use of a guiding catheter. The radioactive seeds are positioned at the location for an appropriate length of time to administer radiation to the artery. At the completion of the radiation treatment, the radioactive seeds are returned to the transfer device. With the advent of drug-eluting stents, coronary brachytherapy is becoming an obsolete procedure.

Coding Tips

1. CPT code 92974 is an "add-on" code. It is reported in addition to the appropriate codes for coronary angiography, stent placement, angioplasty, and atherectomy.

2. For intravascular radioelement application, see 77785–77787.

Facility HCPCS Coding

HCPCS Level II codes are used to report the supplies provided during the procedure. Hospitals should separately report supplies used during cardiac catheterization procedures. Refer to chapter 1 for more information regarding appropriate billing of supplies. Refer to the list of current codes in appendix B.

ICD-10-CM Coding

This is an add-on code. Refer to the corresponding primary procedure code for ICD-10-CM diagnosis code links.

CCI Edits

92974   01924-01926, 36591-36592, 93000-93010, 93040-93042, 93050, 94770, 99155-99157

Intravascular Brachytherapy

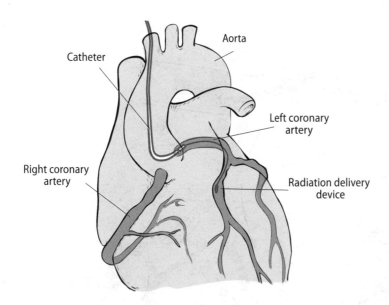

A radiation delivery device is introduced transcatheterally into a coronary artery. The procedure is in anticipation of a subsequent intravascular therapeutic procedure

Coronary Thrombolysis

92975	**Thrombolysis, coronary; by intracoronary infusion, including selective coronary angiography**
92977	**by intravenous infusion**

The physician places a hollow catheter in the aorta from the arm or leg. A small incision is made. Using fluoroscopic guidance, the physician advances the catheter tip to the coronary artery to be treated and confirms the presence of thrombus (blood clot) in the artery by injecting contrast material through the catheter into the artery. The physician infuses a thrombolytic agent (urokinase, for example) into the affected artery in order to dissolve the thrombus. The physician may perform contrast injections to assess the size and extent of the thrombus after infusion of the thrombolytic agent. The catheter is removed from the patient's body. Pressure is placed over the incision for 20 to 30 minutes to stem bleeding. The patient is observed for a period afterward. Report 92977 if intravenous infusion is used.

Coding Tips

1. The use of intracoronary thrombolysis (92975) has faded with the availability of thrombolytic drugs successfully given intravenously (92977).
2. These codes are specifically used for coronary thrombolysis.
3. CPT code 92975 includes selective coronary angiography.
4. For interventional coronary coding guidelines, refer to chapter 1.

Facility HCPCS Coding

HCPCS Level II codes are used to report the supplies provided during the procedure. Hospitals should separately report supplies used during cardiac catheterization procedures. Refer to chapter 1 for more information regarding appropriate billing of supplies. Refer to the list of current codes in appendix B.

ICD-10-CM Coding

I21.Ø1	ST elevation (STEMI) myocardial infarction involving left main coronary artery
I21.Ø2	ST elevation (STEMI) myocardial infarction involving left anterior descending coronary artery
I21.Ø9	ST elevation (STEMI) myocardial infarction involving other coronary artery of anterior wall
I21.11	ST elevation (STEMI) myocardial infarction involving right coronary artery
I21.19	ST elevation (STEMI) myocardial infarction involving other coronary artery of inferior wall
I21.21	ST elevation (STEMI) myocardial infarction involving left circumflex coronary artery
I21.29	ST elevation (STEMI) myocardial infarction involving other sites
I21.3	ST elevation (STEMI) myocardial infarction of unspecified site
I21.4	Non-ST elevation (NSTEMI) myocardial infarction
I21.9	Acute myocardial infarction, unspecified
I21.A1	Myocardial infarction type 2
I21.A9	Other myocardial infarction type
I22.Ø	Subsequent ST elevation (STEMI) myocardial infarction of anterior wall
I22.1	Subsequent ST elevation (STEMI) myocardial infarction of inferior wall
I22.2	Subsequent non-ST elevation (NSTEMI) myocardial infarction
I22.8	Subsequent ST elevation (STEMI) myocardial infarction of other sites
I22.9	Subsequent ST elevation (STEMI) myocardial infarction of unspecified site
I24.Ø	Acute coronary thrombosis not resulting in myocardial infarction
I25.11Ø	Atherosclerotic heart disease of native coronary artery with unstable angina pectoris
I25.111	Atherosclerotic heart disease of native coronary artery with angina pectoris with documented spasm
I25.118	Atherosclerotic heart disease of native coronary artery with other forms of angina pectoris
I25.119	Atherosclerotic heart disease of native coronary artery with unspecified angina pectoris
I25.7ØØ	Atherosclerosis of coronary artery bypass graft(s), unspecified, with unstable angina pectoris
I25.7Ø1	Atherosclerosis of coronary artery bypass graft(s), unspecified, with angina pectoris with documented spasm
I25.7Ø8	Atherosclerosis of coronary artery bypass graft(s), unspecified, with other forms of angina pectoris
I25.7Ø9	Atherosclerosis of coronary artery bypass graft(s), unspecified, with unspecified angina pectoris
I25.71Ø	Atherosclerosis of autologous vein coronary artery bypass graft(s) with unstable angina pectoris
I25.711	Atherosclerosis of autologous vein coronary artery bypass graft(s) with angina pectoris with documented spasm
I25.718	Atherosclerosis of autologous vein coronary artery bypass graft(s) with other forms of angina pectoris
I25.719	Atherosclerosis of autologous vein coronary artery bypass graft(s) with unspecified angina pectoris
I25.72Ø	Atherosclerosis of autologous artery coronary artery bypass graft(s) with unstable angina pectoris

I25.721	Atherosclerosis of autologous artery coronary artery bypass graft(s) with angina pectoris with documented spasm
I25.728	Atherosclerosis of autologous artery coronary artery bypass graft(s) with other forms of angina pectoris
I25.729	Atherosclerosis of autologous artery coronary artery bypass graft(s) with unspecified angina pectoris
I25.730	Atherosclerosis of nonautologous biological coronary artery bypass graft(s) with unstable angina pectoris
I25.731	Atherosclerosis of nonautologous biological coronary artery bypass graft(s) with angina pectoris with documented spasm
I25.738	Atherosclerosis of nonautologous biological coronary artery bypass graft(s) with other forms of angina pectoris
I25.739	Atherosclerosis of nonautologous biological coronary artery bypass graft(s) with unspecified angina pectoris
I25.760	Atherosclerosis of bypass graft of coronary artery of transplanted heart with unstable angina
I25.761	Atherosclerosis of bypass graft of coronary artery of transplanted heart with angina pectoris with documented spasm
I25.768	Atherosclerosis of bypass graft of coronary artery of transplanted heart with other forms of angina pectoris
I25.769	Atherosclerosis of bypass graft of coronary artery of transplanted heart with unspecified angina pectoris
I25.790	Atherosclerosis of other coronary artery bypass graft(s) with unstable angina pectoris
I25.791	Atherosclerosis of other coronary artery bypass graft(s) with angina pectoris with documented spasm
I25.798	Atherosclerosis of other coronary artery bypass graft(s) with other forms of angina pectoris
I25.799	Atherosclerosis of other coronary artery bypass graft(s) with unspecified angina pectoris
I25.82	Chronic total occlusion of coronary artery

CCI Edits

92975 01925, 0213T, 0216T, 0228T, 0230T, 12001-12007, 12011-12057, 13100-13133, 13151-13153, 35201-35206, 35226-35236, 35256-35266, 35286, 36000, 36400-36410, 36420-36430, 36440, 36500, 36591-36592, 36600, 36640, 43752, 51701-51703, 62320-62327, 64400-64410, 64413-64435, 64445-64450, 64461-64463, 64479-64530, 75893, 92012-92014, 92961, 93000-93010, 93040-93042, 93050, 93318, 93355, 93454-93461, 93463, 93563-93564, 94002, 94200, 94250, 94680-94690, 94770, 95812-95816, 95819, 95822, 95829, 95955, 96360-96368, 96372-96377, 99155-99157, 99211-99223, 99231-99255, 99291-99292, 99304-99310, 99315-99316, 99334-99337, 99347-99350, 99374-99375, 99377-99378, 99446-99449, 99495-99496, G0463, G0471

92977 35201-35206, 35226, 35261-35266, 35286, 36000, 36410, 36500, 36591-36592, 61650, 75893, 93040-93042, 93463, 96360, 96365, 96372, 96374-96377

Intravascular Coronary Ultrasound (IVUS)

92978	**Endoluminal imaging of coronary vessel or graft using intravascular ultrasound (IVUS) or optical coherence tomography (OCT) during diagnostic evaluation and/or therapeutic intervention including imaging supervision, interpretation and report; initial vessel (List separately in addition to code for primary procedure)**
92979	**each additional vessel (List separately in addition to code for primary procedure)**

Intravascular ultrasound may be used during diagnostic evaluation of a coronary vessel or graft. It may also be used both before and after a therapeutic intervention upon a coronary vessel or graft to assess patency and integrity of the vessel or graft. A needle is inserted through the skin and into a blood vessel. A guide wire is threaded through the needle into a coronary blood vessel or graft. The needle is removed. An intravascular ultrasound catheter is placed over the guide wire. The ultrasound probe is used to obtain images from inside the vessel to assess area and extent of disease prior to interventional therapy as well as adequacy of therapy after interventional therapy. The ultrasound probe provides a two-dimensional, cross-sectional view of the vessel or graft as the probe is advanced and withdrawn along the area of interest. When the ultrasound examination is complete, the catheter is removed. Report 92978 for the initial vessel or graft. In 92979, the physician advances the ultrasound catheter into additional vessels or grafts to assess patency and structure. The catheter and guide wire are removed and pressure is applied over the puncture site to stop bleeding.

Coding Tips

1. Intravascular coronary ultrasound is always performed during another interventional therapeutic procedure and is coded in addition to the primary procedure.
2. Report 92978 for the initial vessel and 92979 for each additional vessel studied.
3. Refer to Chapter 1 for guidelines on coding separate vessel interventions.
4. Report HCPCS Level II code C1753 for the ultrasound catheter. Refer to the list of current codes in appendix B.
5. IVUS catheter manipulation and repositioning within the specific vessel being examined both before and after therapeutic intervention is considered integral to the intravascular ultrasound service and is not reported separately.

Facility HCPCS Coding

HCPCS Level II codes are used to report the supplies provided during the procedure. Hospitals should separately report supplies used during cardiac catheterization procedures. Refer to chapter 1 for more information regarding appropriate billing.

C1753   Catheter, intravascular ultrasound

ICD-10-CM Coding

I20.Ø	Unstable angina
I21.Ø1	ST elevation (STEMI) myocardial infarction involving left main coronary artery
I21.Ø2	ST elevation (STEMI) myocardial infarction involving left anterior descending coronary artery
I21.Ø9	ST elevation (STEMI) myocardial infarction involving other coronary artery of anterior wall
I21.11	ST elevation (STEMI) myocardial infarction involving right coronary artery
I21.19	ST elevation (STEMI) myocardial infarction involving other coronary artery of inferior wall
I21.21	ST elevation (STEMI) myocardial infarction involving left circumflex coronary artery
I21.29	ST elevation (STEMI) myocardial infarction involving other sites
I21.3	ST elevation (STEMI) myocardial infarction of unspecified site
I21.4	Non-ST elevation (NSTEMI) myocardial infarction
I21.9	Acute myocardial infarction, unspecified
I21.A1	Myocardial infarction type 2
I21.A9	Other myocardial infarction type
I22.Ø	Subsequent ST elevation (STEMI) myocardial infarction of anterior wall
I22.1	Subsequent ST elevation (STEMI) myocardial infarction of inferior wall
I22.2	Subsequent non-ST elevation (NSTEMI) myocardial infarction
I22.8	Subsequent ST elevation (STEMI) myocardial infarction of other sites
I22.9	Subsequent ST elevation (STEMI) myocardial infarction of unspecified site
I24.Ø	Acute coronary thrombosis not resulting in myocardial infarction
I24.1	Dressler's syndrome
I24.8	Other forms of acute ischemic heart disease
I24.9	Acute ischemic heart disease, unspecified
I25.1Ø	Atherosclerotic heart disease of native coronary artery without angina pectoris
I25.11Ø	Atherosclerotic heart disease of native coronary artery with unstable angina pectoris

I25.111	Atherosclerotic heart disease of native coronary artery with angina pectoris with documented spasm
I25.118	Atherosclerotic heart disease of native coronary artery with other forms of angina pectoris
I25.119	Atherosclerotic heart disease of native coronary artery with unspecified angina pectoris
I25.2	Old myocardial infarction
I25.3	Aneurysm of heart
I25.41	Coronary artery aneurysm
I25.42	Coronary artery dissection
I25.5	Ischemic cardiomyopathy
I25.6	Silent myocardial ischemia
I25.700	Atherosclerosis of coronary artery bypass graft(s), unspecified, with unstable angina pectoris
I25.701	Atherosclerosis of coronary artery bypass graft(s), unspecified, with angina pectoris with documented spasm
I25.708	Atherosclerosis of coronary artery bypass graft(s), unspecified, with other forms of angina pectoris
I25.709	Atherosclerosis of coronary artery bypass graft(s), unspecified, with unspecified angina pectoris
I25.710	Atherosclerosis of autologous vein coronary artery bypass graft(s) with unstable angina pectoris
I25.711	Atherosclerosis of autologous vein coronary artery bypass graft(s) with angina pectoris with documented spasm
I25.718	Atherosclerosis of autologous vein coronary artery bypass graft(s) with other forms of angina pectoris
I25.719	Atherosclerosis of autologous vein coronary artery bypass graft(s) with unspecified angina pectoris
I25.720	Atherosclerosis of autologous artery coronary artery bypass graft(s) with unstable angina pectoris
I25.721	Atherosclerosis of autologous artery coronary artery bypass graft(s) with angina pectoris with documented spasm
I25.728	Atherosclerosis of autologous artery coronary artery bypass graft(s) with other forms of angina pectoris
I25.729	Atherosclerosis of autologous artery coronary artery bypass graft(s) with unspecified angina pectoris
I25.730	Atherosclerosis of nonautologous biological coronary artery bypass graft(s) with unstable angina pectoris
I25.731	Atherosclerosis of nonautologous biological coronary artery bypass graft(s) with angina pectoris with documented spasm
I25.738	Atherosclerosis of nonautologous biological coronary artery bypass graft(s) with other forms of angina pectoris
I25.739	Atherosclerosis of nonautologous biological coronary artery bypass graft(s) with unspecified angina pectoris
I25.750	Atherosclerosis of native coronary artery of transplanted heart with unstable angina
I25.760	Atherosclerosis of bypass graft of coronary artery of transplanted heart with unstable angina
I25.761	Atherosclerosis of bypass graft of coronary artery of transplanted heart with angina pectoris with documented spasm
I25.768	Atherosclerosis of bypass graft of coronary artery of transplanted heart with other forms of angina pectoris
I25.769	Atherosclerosis of bypass graft of coronary artery of transplanted heart with unspecified angina pectoris
I25.790	Atherosclerosis of other coronary artery bypass graft(s) with unstable angina pectoris
I25.791	Atherosclerosis of other coronary artery bypass graft(s) with angina pectoris with documented spasm
I25.798	Atherosclerosis of other coronary artery bypass graft(s) with other forms of angina pectoris
I25.799	Atherosclerosis of other coronary artery bypass graft(s) with unspecified angina pectoris
I25.810	Atherosclerosis of coronary artery bypass graft(s) without angina pectoris
I25.812	Atherosclerosis of bypass graft of coronary artery of transplanted heart without angina pectoris
I25.82	Chronic total occlusion of coronary artery
I25.84	Coronary atherosclerosis due to calcified coronary lesion
I25.89	Other forms of chronic ischemic heart disease
I25.9	Chronic ischemic heart disease, unspecified
R57.0	Cardiogenic shock
R94.31	Abnormal electrocardiogram [ECG] [EKG]
T82.211A	Breakdown (mechanical) of coronary artery bypass graft, initial encounter
T82.212A	Displacement of coronary artery bypass graft, initial encounter
T82.213A	Leakage of coronary artery bypass graft, initial encounter
T82.218A	Other mechanical complication of coronary artery bypass graft, initial encounter
T82.519A	Breakdown (mechanical) of unspecified cardiac and vascular devices and implants, initial encounter
T82.529A	Displacement of unspecified cardiac and vascular devices and implants, initial encounter
T82.539A	Leakage of unspecified cardiac and vascular devices and implants, initial encounter
T82.599A	Other mechanical complication of unspecified cardiac and vascular devices and implants, initial encounter
T82.818A	Embolism due to vascular prosthetic devices, implants and grafts, initial encounter
T82.828A	Fibrosis due to vascular prosthetic devices, implants and grafts, initial encounter
T82.838A	Hemorrhage due to vascular prosthetic devices, implants and grafts, initial encounter

T82.848A	Pain due to vascular prosthetic devices, implants and grafts, initial encounter
T82.858A	Stenosis of other vascular prosthetic devices, implants and grafts, initial encounter
T82.868A	Thrombosis due to vascular prosthetic devices, implants and grafts, initial encounter
T82.898A	Other specified complication of vascular prosthetic devices, implants and grafts, initial encounter
T82.9XXA	Unspecified complication of cardiac and vascular prosthetic device, implant and graft, initial encounter

CCI Edits

92978   0205T, 35201-35206, 35226, 35261-35266, 35286, 36500, 36591-36592, 75893, 93000-93010, 93040-93042, 93050, 94770, 99155-99157, 99446-99449

92979   0205T, 36500, 36591-36592, 75893, 93000-93010, 93040-93042, 93050, 94770, 99155-99157, 99446-99449

Intravascular Catheter Based Spectroscopy

0205T   **Intravascular catheter-based coronary vessel or graft spectroscopy (eg, infrared) during diagnostic evaluation and/or therapeutic intervention including imaging supervision, interpretation and report, each vessel (List separately in addition to code for primary procedure)**

During cardiac catheterization or intra-coronary intervention, a special infrared probe is placed into the vessel of concern and connected to the equipment console. The light reflected back from the coronary plaque is analyzed and further treatment decisions are made. This procedure is also known as "NIR."

Coding Tips

1. Intravascular spectroscopy is always performed during another interventional procedure.
2. CPT code 0205T is an add-on code and is reported in addition to the primary procedure.
3. Report this code in conjunction with 92920, 92924, 92928, 92933, 92937, 92941, 92943, 92975, 93454-93461, 93563, and 93564.
4. Report 0205T per vessel studied as per coronary artery coding guidelines.

Facility HCPCS Coding

HCPCS Level II codes are used to report the supplies provided during the procedure. Hospitals should separately report the supplies used for intravascular spectroscopy. Refer to chapter 1 for more information regarding appropriate billing.

ICD-10-CM Coding

This is an add-on code. Refer to the corresponding primary procedure code for ICD-10-CM diagnosis code links.

CCI Edits

0205T   35201-35206, 35226-35236, 35256-35266, 35286, 36500, 36591-36592, 75893, 93050, 99446-99449

Implantation of Wireless Pulmonary Artery Pressure Sensor

C9741   **Right heart catheterization with implantation of wireless pressure sensor in the pulmonary artery, including any type of measurement, angiography, imaging supervision, interpretation, and report**
The physician uses pulmonary artery pressure data to make treatment decisions for the patient with heart failure with the goal of reducing hospital admissions for treatment. A sensor is implanted in the pulmonary artery by right heart catheterization. A monitoring system is sent home with the patient; the wireless sensor measures the pulmonary artery pressures and records the data for physician review.

Coding Tips

1. Hospitals report C9741 for the procedure.
2. Right heart catheterization is included in C9741. Facilities do not report 93451 or 93568 separately.
3. Report device code C2624 for the wireless pressure sensor, delivery device, and monitoring system.
4. Separately report other devices used.
5. Separately report contrast media.
6. Physicians report 93451 for the right heart catheterization, 93568 for the pulmonary artery injection, and 93799 for the sensor implantation. Refer to individual payer policy for specific coding.

Facility HCPCS Coding

HCPCS Level II codes are used to report the supplies provided during the procedure. Hospitals should report supplies used during these procedures separately. A complete listing of device codes can be found in appendix B of this publication. Applicable codes for this section may include but are not limited to:

C1760	Closure device, vascular
C1766	Introducer sheath, steerable, non-peel away
C1769	Guide wire
C1887	Catheter, guiding
C1892	Introducer sheath, fixed, peel-away
C1893	Introducer sheath, fixed, non-peel-away
C1894	Introducer sheath, non-laser
C2624	Wireless pressure sensor
C2629	Introducer sheath, laser

ICD-10-CM Coding

The application of these codes is too broad to adequately present ICD-10-CM diagnosis code links here. Refer to the current ICD-10-CM book.

CCI Edits

C9741   36591-36592

Case Example

The patient was prepped and draped in the usual fashion. Access was made via the right femoral vein. A 12 French sheath was placed. A Swan-Ganz catheter was advanced through the sheath to the right atrium, right ventricle, pulmonary artery in wedge position where pressures were obtained.

A limited pulmonary angiogram was performed for the purposes of identifying an artery and position to deploy the CardioMEMS. An 0.018 wire was advanced through the Swan-Ganz catheter into the distal branch of the left pulmonary artery. The Swan-Ganz catheter was removed, and the **CardioMEMS device on a delivery system was advanced over the wire and deployed in a branch of the left pulmonary artery** supplying the inferior-posterior region. The delivery system was then removed and a Swan-Ganz catheter was reintroduced. The CardioMEMS device was calibrated. The Swan-Ganz catheter was removed, the 12 French sheath was removed, and a figure of eight stitch was placed. The patient was returned to her room in stable condition.

CPT/HCPCS Codes Reported:
C9741

Other HCPCS Codes Reported:
C2624, C1769, C1894, C1751

Percutaneous Coronary Interventions

Percutaneous coronary interventions include angioplasty, atherectomy, and stent placement within the coronary arteries or coronary bypass grafts. Lay descriptions for each of the interventional techniques are as follows:

Angioplasty: The physician makes a small incision over the site chosen for arterial system access, either the arm or the groin. The artery is cannulated with a needle and a guidewire, and then an indwelling sheath is placed. A guiding catheter is inserted through the sheath and, utilizing fluoroscopy, guided to the coronary arteries. It is positioned into the opening of the affected coronary artery and a baseline angiogram is obtained by injecting contrast media through the catheter into the coronary artery. This angiogram demonstrates the exact location and severity of the vessel occlusion. The appropriate sized balloon catheter is selected and inserted through the guiding catheter to the lesion to be treated. The physician inflates the balloon to flatten plaque obstructing the artery against the walls of the artery. See the illustration following the procedure code listing. If sufficient results are not obtained after the first inflation, the physician may reinflate the balloon for a longer period of time or at greater pressure. When desired results have been achieved, the catheters are removed.

Atherectomy: Atherectomy is performed to remove atherosclerotic plaque from the blocked coronary artery. The physician makes a small incision over the site chosen for arterial system access, either the arm or the groin. The artery is cannulated with a needle and a guidewire, and then an indwelling sheath is placed. A guiding catheter is inserted through the sheath and, utilizing fluoroscopy, guided to the coronary arteries. It is positioned into the opening of the affected coronary artery and a baseline angiogram is obtained by injecting contrast media through the catheter into the coronary artery. This angiogram demonstrates the exact location and severity of the vessel occlusion. The atherectomy device catheter is inserted through the guiding catheter and directed to the affected coronary artery. The device is positioned near the lesion or blockage. The blockage is removed using a rotary cutter device (atherectomy device). The blockage may also require angioplasty with a balloon catheter to flatten any remaining plaque. A stent is also sometimes placed if the walls of the artery are deemed to need additional support after the atherectomy. Once the desired results are obtained, the catheters are removed.

Stent placement: A stent is used to hold open a blocked or collapsed blood vessel in the heart. A peripheral artery is cannulated with a needle and a guidewire, and then an indwelling sheath is placed. A guiding catheter is inserted through the sheath and, utilizing fluoroscopy, guided to the coronary arteries. It is positioned into the opening of the affected coronary artery and a baseline angiogram is obtained by injecting contrast media through the catheter into the coronary artery. This angiogram demonstrates the exact location and severity of the vessel occlusion. Usually the lesion is predilated with an angioplasty balloon. The stent delivery system is loaded on the guidewire and both are inserted into the guiding catheter and advanced into the coronary artery. The stent is positioned in the correct location and the balloon is inflated to expand and secure the stent. The carrying balloon catheter is deflated and removed. A second, high pressure balloon catheter may be inserted and inflated to more fully expand the stent. The catheters are removed once desired results are obtained.

92920	**Percutaneous transluminal coronary angioplasty; single major coronary artery or branch**
92921	**each additional branch of a major coronary artery (List separately in addition to code for primary procedure)**
92924	**Percutaneous transluminal coronary atherectomy, with coronary angioplasty when performed; single major coronary artery or branch**
92925	**each additional branch of a major coronary artery (List separately in addition to code for primary procedure)**
92928	**Percutaneous transcatheter placement of intracoronary stent(s), with coronary angioplasty when performed; single major coronary artery or branch**
92929	**each additional branch of a major coronary artery (List separately in addition to code for primary procedure)**
92933	**Percutaneous transluminal coronary atherectomy, with intracoronary stent, with coronary angioplasty; when performed; single major coronary artery or branch**
92934	**each additional branch of a major coronary artery (List separately in addition to code for primary procedure)**
92937	**Percutaneous transluminal revascularization of or through coronary artery bypass graft (internal mammary, free arterial, venous), any combination of intracoronary stent, atherectomy and angioplasty, including distal protection when performed; single vessel**
92938	**each additional branch subtended by the bypass graft (List separately in addition to code for primary procedure)**
92941	**Percutaneous transluminal revascularization of acute total/subtotal occlusion during acute myocardial infarction, coronary artery or coronary artery bypass graft, any combination of intracoronary stent, atherectomy and angioplasty, including aspiration thrombectomy when performed, single vessel**
92943	**Percutaneous transluminal revascularization of chronic total occlusion, coronary artery, coronary artery branch, or coronary artery bypass graft, any combination of intracoronary stent, atherectomy and angioplasty, single vessel**
92944	**each additional coronary artery, coronary artery branch, or bypass graft (List separately in addition to code for primary procedure)**

Coronary Angioplasty

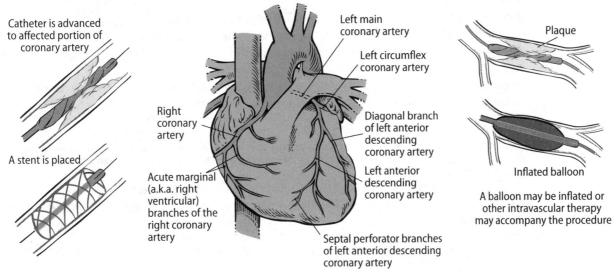

Catheter is advanced to affected portion of coronary artery

A stent is placed

Left main coronary artery

Left circumflex coronary artery

Right coronary artery

Diagonal branch of left anterior descending coronary artery

Acute marginal (a.k.a. right ventricular) branches of the right coronary artery

Left anterior descending coronary artery

Septal perforator branches of left anterior descending coronary artery

Plaque

Inflated balloon

A balloon may be inflated or other intravascular therapy may accompany the procedure

Coding Guidelines for Coronary Interventions

1. For interventional coding purposes, there are five major coronary vessels:
   - Left anterior descending coronary artery
   - Left circumflex coronary artery
   - Left main coronary artery
   - Ramus intermedius coronary arteries
   - Right coronary artery

2. A maximum of two branches are recognized as separate vessels for the left main, left anterior descending, left circumflex arteries, and right coronary arteries. The left main and ramus arteries have no recognized branches for interventional reporting purposes. This guideline applies to 92921, 92925, 92929, 92934, and 92938.

3. All interventions performed within a defined branch are reported as a single intervention. If two lesions are treated in the circumflex, only one code is reported.

4. These codes include accessing, catheterizing the vessel(s), radiologic supervision and interpretation related to the intervention, all imaging performed, and closure of the arterial access vessel. Facilities are requested to verify with individual payers for separate reporting of this service. CPT applies this rule only to physicians.

5. Do not report CPT codes from the 70000 series for test angiograms done prior to placement of a vascular closure device. This is considered part of the catheterization procedure.

6. Diagnostic coronary angiography may be reported in addition to an intervention when:
   - A full diagnostic study is performed and the decision to proceed to intervention is based upon the results of the diagnostic study
   - No prior catheter based study is available unless one of the following conditions is documented:
     - the patient's condition has changed since a prior study was performed
     - the pathology or anatomy was not adequately visualized to make a decision to proceed to intervention
     - a clinical change occurred during the procedure requiring re-evaluation of another area
   - The diagnostic study is performed at a separate session from the intervention

7. Angioplasty includes interventions performed with any type of angioplasty device, including cutting balloon and cryoplasty.

8. Atherectomy includes interventions performed with directional, rotational, or laser devices.

9. Stent placement includes all types of stents. For Medicare reporting of drug eluting stents, refer to the HCPCS code section.

10. Coronary intervention codes are built on the following hierarchy of intensiveness of the service:
    - Angioplasty—least intensive service
    - Stent
    - Atherectomy—more intensive service
    - Graft revascularization—most intensive service

11. Report the highest level of service intensity as defined by the codes.

12. Bypass grafts of any type are considered separate vessels for interventional coding purposes. Each graft is a separate vessel.

13. Grafts with more than one distal anastomosis are considered a single graft vessel.

14. For branching grafts, each branch is a separate vessel for interventional coding purposes.

15. Interventions of a native coronary vessel performed through a graft access are reported with the graft intervention codes.

16. Bypass graft codes 92937-92944 include embolic protection when used.

17. Report only one base code (92920, 92924, 92928, 92933, 92937, 92941, and 92943) per major coronary vessel treated.

18. For lesions extending from one major vessel into another major vessel treated with a single intervention, report only a single interventional code. If the lesion is a bifurcation lesion, the intervention is reported as two separate vessel interventions.

19. Code 92941, revascularization of acute occlusion, includes all interventions necessary to treat, including aspiration thrombectomy, distal protection, and intracoronary rheolytic agent injections. Mechanical thrombectomy may be separately reported.

20. The physician should clearly define the occlusion as acute or chronic to facilitate correct code assignment.

21. Refer to the following table for information on separately reportable services. Some exceptions do apply. Refer to guidelines above.

22. Hospitals should separately report supplies used during coronary interventional procedures. Refer to chapter 1 for more information regarding appropriate billing of supplies. Refer to the HCPCS Supply Codes section for applicable device codes.

Separately Reported Services—Coronary Interventions

Service Description	CPT Code(s) Reported
Mechanical thrombectomy	92973
Intravascular ultrasound	92978, 92979
Brachytherapy, intracoronary	92974
Flow reserve measurement or Doppler velocity	93971, 93972
Intravascular spectroscopy	0205T

Facility HCPCS Coding

HCPCS Level II codes are used to report the supplies provided during the procedure. Hospitals should separately report supplies used during cardiac catheterization procedures. Refer to the introduction for more information regarding appropriate billing of supplies. Refer to the list of current codes in appendix B.

Procedure HCPCS Codes

For drug-eluting stent insertion procedures, CMS requires that the following HCPCS codes be reported instead of the CPT codes.

C9600   Percutaneous transcatheter placement of drug eluting intracoronary stent(s), with coronary angioplasty when performed; single major coronary artery or branch

C9601   Percutaneous transcatheter placement of drug eluting intracoronary stent(s), with coronary angioplasty when performed; each additional branch of a major coronary artery (list separately in addition to code for primary procedure)

C9602   Percutaneous transluminal coronary atherectomy, with drug eluting intracoronary stent, with coronary angioplasty when performed; single major coronary artery or branch

C9603   Percutaneous transluminal coronary atherectomy, with drug-eluting intracoronary stent, with coronary angioplasty when performed; each additional branch of a major coronary artery (list separately in addition to code for primary procedure)

C9604   Percutaneous transluminal revascularization of or through coronary artery bypass graft (internal mammary, free arterial, venous), any combination of drug-eluting intracoronary stent, atherectomy and angioplasty, including distal protection when performed; single vessel

C9605   Percutaneous transluminal revascularization of or through coronary artery bypass graft (internal mammary, free arterial, venous), any combination of drug-eluting intracoronary stent, atherectomy and angioplasty, including distal protection when performed; each additional branch subtended by the bypass graft (List separately in addition to code for primary procedure)

C9606   Percutaneous transluminal revascularization of acute total/subtotal occlusion during acute myocardial infarction, coronary artery or coronary artery bypass graft, any combination of drug-eluting intracoronary stent, atherectomy and angioplasty, including aspiration thrombectomy when performed, single vessel

C9607	Percutaneous transluminal revascularization of chronic total occlusion, coronary artery, coronary artery branch, or coronary artery bypass graft, any combination of drug-eluting intracoronary stent, atherectomy and angioplasty; single vessel
C9608	Percutaneous transluminal revascularization of chronic total occlusion, coronary artery, coronary artery branch, or coronary artery bypass graft, any combination of drug-eluting intracoronary stent, atherectomy and angioplasty; each additional coronary artery, coronary artery branch, or bypass graft (list separately in addition to code for primary procedure)
G0269	Placement of occlusive device into either a venous or arterial access site, post surgical or interventional procedure
G0278	Iliac and/or femoral artery angiography, non-selective, performed at the same time as cardiac cath

HCPCS Supply Codes

C1714	Catheter, transluminal atherectomy, directional
C1724	Catheter, transluminal atherectomy, rotational
C1725	Catheter, transluminal angioplasty, non-laser (may include guidance, infusion/perfusion capability)
C1753	Catheter, intravascular ultrasound
C1757	Catheter, thrombectomy; embolectomy
C1760	Closure device, vascular (implantable/insertable)
C1769	Guidewire
C1874	Stent, coated/covered, with delivery system
C1875	Stent, coated/covered, without delivery system
C1876	Stent, non-coated/non-covered, with delivery system
C1877	Stent, non-coated/non-covered, without delivery system
C1884	Embolization protective system
C1885	Catheter, transluminal angioplasty, laser
C1887	Catheter, guiding (may include infusion/perfusion capability)
C1894	Introducer/sheath, other than guiding, intracardiac electrophysiological, non-laser
C2629	Introducer/sheath, other than guiding, intracardiac

ICD-10-CM Coding

The application of these codes is too broad to adequately present ICD-10-CM diagnosis code links here. Refer to the current ICD-10-CM book.

CCI Edits

92920	01924-01926, 0213T, 0216T, 0228T, 0230T, 11000-11006, 11042-11047, 12001-12007, 12011-12057, 13100-13133, 13151-13153, 33210, 34812-34813, 35201-35206, 35226-35236, 35256-35266, 35286, 36000, 36120-36140, 36160-36200, 36215-36217, 36245-36247, 36400-36410, 36420-36430, 36440, 36500, 36591-36592, 36600, 36640, 37246-37247, 43752, 51701-51703, 62320-62327, 64400-64410, 64413-64435, 64445-64450, 64461-64463, 64479-64530, 69990, 71034, 75893, 76000-76001, 77001-77002, 92012-92014, 92961, 92975, 93000-93010, 93040-93042, 93050, 93224-93227, 93318, 93355, 93454-93461, 93463, 93563-93564, 94002, 94200, 94250, 94680-94690, 94770, 95812-95816, 95819, 95822, 95829, 95955, 96360-96368, 96372-96377, 97597-97598, 97602, 99155-99157, 99211-99223, 99231-99255, 99291-99292, 99304-99310, 99315-99316, 99334-99337, 99347-99350, 99374-99375, 99377-99378, 99446-99449, 99495-99496, G0269, G0463, G0471
92921	01924-01926, 0213T, 0216T, 0228T, 0230T, 11000-11006, 11042-11047, 12001-12007, 12011-12057, 13100-13133, 13151-13153, 33210, 34812-34813, 35201-35206, 35226-35236, 35256-35266, 35286, 36000, 36120-36140, 36160-36200, 36215-36217, 36245-36247, 36400-36410, 36420-36430, 36440, 36500, 36591-36592, 36600, 36640, 37246-37247, 43752, 51701-51703, 61650, 62320-62327, 64400-64410, 64413-64435, 64445-64450, 64461, 64463, 64479, 64483, 64486-64490, 64493, 64505-64530, 69990, 71034, 75893, 76000-76001, 77001-77002, 92961, 92975, 93000-93010, 93040-93042, 93050, 93224-93227, 93318, 93355, 93454-93461, 93463, 93563-93564, 94002, 94200, 94250, 94680-94690, 94770, 95812-95816, 95819, 95822, 95829, 95955, 96360, 96365, 96372-96377, 97597-97598, 97602, 99155-99157, G0269, G0471

92924   01924-01926, 0213T, 0216T, 0228T, 0230T, 11000-11006, 11042-11047, 12001-12007, 12011-12057, 13100-13133, 13151-13153, 33210, 34812-34813, 35201-35206, 35226-35236, 35256-35266, 35286, 36000, 36120-36140, 36160-36200, 36215-36217, 36245-36247, 36400-36410, 36420-36430, 36440, 36500, 36591-36592, 36600, 36640, 37246-37247, 43752, 51701-51703, 62320-62327, 64400-64410, 64413-64435, 64445-64450, 64461-64463, 64479-64530, 69990, 71034, 75893, 76000-76001, 77001-77002, 92012-92014, 92920, 92961, 92975, 93000-93010, 93040-93042, 93050, 93224-93227, 93318, 93355, 93454-93461, 93463, 93563-93564, 94002, 94200, 94250, 94680-94690, 94770, 95812-95816, 95819, 95822, 95829, 95955, 96360-96368, 96372-96377, 97597-97598, 97602, 99155-99157, 99211-99223, 99231-99255, 99291-99292, 99304-99310, 99315-99316, 99334-99337, 99347-99350, 99374-99375, 99377-99378, 99446-99449, 99495-99496, G0269, G0463, G0471

92925   01924-01926, 0213T, 0216T, 0228T, 0230T, 11000-11006, 11042-11047, 12001-12007, 12011-12057, 13100-13133, 13151-13153, 33210, 34812-34813, 35201-35206, 35226-35236, 35256-35266, 35286, 36000, 36120-36140, 36160-36200, 36215-36217, 36245-36247, 36400-36410, 36420-36430, 36440, 36500, 36591-36592, 36600, 36640, 37246-37247, 43752, 51701-51703, 61650, 62320-62327, 64400-64410, 64413-64435, 64445-64450, 64461, 64463, 64479, 64483, 64486-64490, 64493, 64505-64530, 69990, 71034, 75893, 76000-76001, 77001-77002, 92961, 92975, 93000-93010, 93040-93042, 93050, 93224-93227, 93318, 93355, 93454-93461, 93463, 93563-93564, 94002, 94200, 94250, 94680-94690, 94770, 95812-95816, 95819, 95822, 95829, 95955, 96360, 96365, 96372-96377, 97597-97598, 97602, 99155-99157, G0269, G0471

92928   01924-01926, 0213T, 0216T, 0228T, 0230T, 11000-11006, 11042-11047, 12001-12007, 12011-12057, 13100-13133, 13151-13153, 33210, 34812-34813, 35201-35206, 35226-35236, 35256-35266, 35286, 36000, 36120-36140, 36160-36200, 36215-36217, 36245-36247, 36400-36410, 36420-36430, 36440, 36500, 36591-36592, 36600-36640, 37236, 37246-37247, 43752, 51701-51703, 62320-62327, 64400-64410, 64413-64435, 64445-64450, 64461-64463, 64479-64530, 69990, 71034, 75893, 76000-76001, 77001-77002, 92012-92014, 92920, 92924, 92961, 92975, 93000-93010, 93040-93042, 93050, 93224-93227, 93318, 93355, 93454-93461, 93463, 93563-93564, 94002, 94200, 94250, 94680-94690, 94770, 95812-95816, 95819, 95822, 95829, 95955, 96360-96368, 96372-96377, 97597-97598, 97602, 99155-99157, 99211-99223, 99231-99255, 99291-99292, 99304-99310, 99315-99316, 99334-99337, 99347-99350, 99374-99375, 99377-99378, 99446-99449, 99495-99496, C9600, G0269, G0463, G0471

92929   01924-01926, 0213T, 0216T, 0228T, 0230T, 11000-11006, 11042-11047, 12001-12007, 12011-12057, 13100-13133, 13151-13153, 33210, 34812-34813, 35201-35206, 35226-35236, 35256-35266, 35286, 36000, 36120-36140, 36160-36200, 36215-36217, 36245-36247, 36400-36410, 36420-36430, 36440, 36500, 36591-36592, 36600-36640, 37236, 37246-37247, 43752, 51701-51703, 61650, 62320-62327, 64400-64410, 64413-64435, 64445-64450, 64461, 64463, 64479, 64483, 64486-64490, 64493, 64505-64530, 69990, 71034, 75893, 76000-76001, 77001-77002, 92961, 92975, 93000-93010, 93040-93042, 93050, 93224-93227, 93318, 93355, 93454-93461, 93463, 93563-93564, 94002, 94200, 94250, 94680-94690, 94770, 95812-95816, 95819, 95822, 95829, 95955, 96360, 96365, 96372-96377, 97597-97598, 97602, 99155-99157, C9601, G0269, G0471

92933   01924-01926, 0213T, 0216T, 0228T, 0230T, 11000-11006, 11042-11047, 12001-12007, 12011-12057, 13100-13133, 13151-13153, 33210, 34812-34813, 35201-35206, 35226-35236, 35256-35266, 35286, 36000, 36120-36140, 36160-36200, 36215-36217, 36245-36247, 36400-36410, 36420-36430, 36440, 36500, 36591-36592, 36600-36640, 37236, 37246-37247, 43752, 51701-51703, 62320-62327, 64400-64410, 64413-64435, 64445-64450, 64461-64463, 64479-64530, 69990, 71034, 75893, 76000-76001, 77001-77002, 92012-92014, 92920, 92924, 92928, 92961, 92975, 93000-93010, 93040-93042, 93050, 93224-93227, 93318, 93355, 93454-93461, 93463, 93563-93564, 94002, 94200, 94250, 94680-94690, 94770, 95812-95816, 95819, 95822, 95829, 95955, 96360-96368, 96372-96377, 97597-97598, 97602, 99155-99157, 99211-99223, 99231-99255, 99291-99292, 99304-99310, 99315-99316, 99334-99337, 99347-99350, 99374-99375, 99377-99378, 99446-99449, 99495-99496, C9600, C9602, G0269, G0463, G0471

92934   01924-01926, 0213T, 0216T, 0228T, 0230T, 11000-11006, 11042-11047, 12001-12007, 12011-12057, 13100-13133, 13151-13153, 33210, 34812-34813, 35201-35206, 35226-35236, 35256-35266, 35286, 36000, 36120-36140, 36160-36200, 36215-36217, 36245-36247, 36400-36410, 36420-36430, 36440, 36500, 36591-36592, 36600-36640, 37236, 37246-37247, 43752, 51701-51703, 61650, 62320-62327, 64400-64410, 64413-64435, 64445-64450, 64461, 64463, 64479, 64483, 64486-64490, 64493, 64505-64530, 69990, 71034, 75893, 76000-76001, 77001-77002, 92961, 92975, 93000-93010, 93040-93042, 93050, 93224-93227, 93318, 93355, 93454-93461, 93463, 93563-93564, 94002, 94200, 94250, 94680-94690, 94770, 95812-95816, 95819, 95822, 95829, 95955, 96360, 96365, 96372-96377, 97597-97598, 97602, 99155-99157, C9603, G0269, G0471

92937   01924-01926, 0213T, 0216T, 0228T, 0230T, 11000-11006, 11042-11047, 12001-12007, 12011-12057, 13100-13133, 13151-13153, 33210, 34812-34813, 35201-35206, 35226-35236, 35256-35266, 35286, 36000, 36120-36140, 36160-36200, 36215-36217, 36245-36247, 36400-36410, 36420-36430, 36440, 36500, 36591-36592, 36600-36640, 37236, 37246-37247, 43752, 51701-51703, 62320-62327, 64400-64410, 64413-64435, 64445-64450, 64461-64463, 64479-64530, 69990, 71034, 75893, 76000-76001, 77001-77002, 92012-92014, 92961, 92975, 93000-93010, 93040-93042, 93050, 93224-93227, 93318, 93355, 93454-93461, 93463, 93563-93564, 94002, 94200, 94250, 94680-94690, 94770, 95812-95816, 95819, 95822, 95829, 95955, 96360-96368, 96372-96377, 97597-97598, 97602, 99155-99157, 99211-99223, 99231-99255, 99291-99292, 99304-99310, 99315-99316, 99334-99337, 99347-99350, 99374-99375, 99377-99378, 99446-99449, 99495-99496, C9604, G0269, G0463, G0471

92938   01924-01926, 0213T, 0216T, 0228T, 0230T, 11000-11006, 11042-11047, 12001-12007, 12011-12057, 13100-13133, 13151-13153, 33210, 34812-34813, 35201-35206, 35226-35236, 35256-35266, 35286, 36000, 36120-36140, 36160-36200, 36215-36217, 36245-36247, 36400-36410, 36420-36430, 36440, 36500, 36591-36592, 36600-36640, 37236, 37246-37247, 43752, 51701-51703, 61650, 62320-62327, 64400-64410, 64413-64435, 64445-64450, 64461, 64463, 64479, 64483, 64486-64490, 64493, 64505-64530, 71034, 75893, 76000-76001, 77001-77002, 92961, 92975, 93000-93010, 93040-93042, 93050, 93318, 93355, 93454-93461, 93463, 93563-93564, 94002, 94200, 94250, 94680-94690, 94770, 95812-95816, 95819, 95822, 95829, 95955, 96360, 96365, 96372-96377, 97597-97598, 97602, 99155-99157, C9605, G0269, G0471

92941   01924-01926, 0213T, 0216T, 0228T, 0230T, 11000-11006, 11042-11047, 12001-12007, 12011-12057, 13100-13133, 13151-13153, 33210, 34812-34813, 35201-35206, 35226-35236, 35256-35266, 35286, 36000, 36120-36140, 36160-36200, 36215-36217, 36245-36247, 36400-36410, 36420-36430, 36440, 36500, 36591-36592, 36600-36640, 37236, 37246-37247, 43752, 51701-51703, 62320-62327, 64400-64410, 64413-64435, 64445-64450, 64461-64463, 64479-64530, 69990, 71034, 75893, 76000-76001, 77001-77002, 92012-92014, 92920, 92924, 92928, 92933, 92937, 92961, 92975, 93000-93010, 93040-93042, 93050, 93224-93227, 93318, 93355, 93454-93461, 93463, 93563-93564, 94002, 94200, 94250, 94680-94690, 94770, 95812-95816, 95819, 95822, 95829, 95955, 96360-96368, 96372-96377, 97597-97598, 97602, 99155-99157, 99211-99223, 99231-99255, 99291-99292, 99304-99310, 99315-99316, 99334-99337, 99347-99350, 99374-99375, 99377-99378, 99446-99449, 99495-99496, C9600, C9602, C9604, C9606, G0269, G0463, G0471

92943   01924-01926, 0213T, 0216T, 0228T, 0230T, 11000-11006, 11042-11047, 12001-12007, 12011-12057, 13100-13133, 13151-13153, 33210, 34812-34813, 35201-35206, 35226-35236, 35256-35266, 35286, 36000, 36120-36140, 36160-36200, 36215-36217, 36245-36247, 36400-36410, 36420-36430, 36440, 36500, 36591-36592, 36600-36640, 37236, 37246-37247, 43752, 51701-51703, 62320-62327, 64400-64410, 64413-64435, 64445-64450, 64461-64463, 64479-64530, 69990, 71034, 75893, 76000-76001, 77001-77002, 92012-92014, 92920, 92924, 92928, 92933, 92937, 92941, 92961, 92975, 93000-93010, 93040-93042, 93050, 93224-93227, 93318, 93355, 93454-93461, 93463, 93563-93564, 94002, 94200, 94250, 94680-94690, 94770, 95812-95816, 95819, 95822, 95829, 95955, 96360-96368, 96372-96377, 97597-97598, 97602, 99155-99157, 99211-99223, 99231-99255, 99291-99292, 99304-99310, 99315-99316, 99334-99337, 99347-99350, 99374-99375, 99377-99378, 99446-99449, 99495-99496, C9600, C9602, C9604, C9606-C9607, G0269, G0463, G0471

92944   01924-01926, 0213T, 0216T, 0228T, 0230T, 11000-11006, 11042-11047, 12001-12007, 12011-12057, 13100-13133, 13151-13153, 33210, 34812-34813, 35201-35206, 35226-35236, 35256-35266, 35286, 36000, 36120-36140, 36160-36200, 36215-36217, 36245-36247, 36400-36410, 36420-36430, 36440, 36500, 36591-36592, 36600-36640, 37236, 37246-37247, 43752, 51701-51703, 61650, 62320-62327, 64400-64410, 64413-64435, 64445-64450, 64461, 64463, 64479, 64483, 64486-64490, 64493, 64505-64530, 71034, 75893, 76000-76001, 77001-77002, 92961, 92975, 93000-93010, 93040-93042, 93050, 93318, 93355, 93454-93461, 93463, 93563-93564, 94002, 94200, 94250, 94680-94690, 94770, 95812-95816, 95819, 95822, 95829, 95955, 96360, 96365, 96372-96377, 97597-97598, 97602, 99155-99157, C9608, G0269, G0471

Interventional Cardiology Case Examples

Case Example #1

Procedure:
Coronary **angioplasty and stenting** of proximal left anterior descending (**LAD**), coronary **angioplasty and stenting** of proximal and mid right coronary artery (RCA), Perclose left femoral artery (LFA), conscious sedation

Indications:
This was a 67-year-old male who presented with unstable angina. An angiography revealed presumed recent occlusion of the proximal LAD and severe stenosis of the proximal RCA. The RCA vessels were ectatic and tortuous.

Procedure Description:
The procedure was performed via a 6-French sheath placed in the LFA. A 6-French XB 3.5 catheter provided good cannulation of the left main. I advanced a Choice floppy through a 2.5 mm Maverick balloon and was able to advance this through the occlusion with the aid of the **balloon**. It was initially **advanced into a diagonal branch**, and the lesion was dilated to 12 atmospheres, establishing reperfusion. The wire was then positioned in the true lumen of the LAD distally. There was a **more distal lesion beyond the diagonal branch that was also dilated to** 10 and then 16 atmospheres. This **balloon** was then **removed** and **replaced with a 3.0 x 33 mm Velocity stent**. It was deployed at 16 atmospheres. An **additional 3.0 x 8 mm Velocity** was **deployed just distal to this at 14 atmospheres**. A 3.5 NC Ranger **balloon catheter was then used to dilate** the proximal two-thirds of the stent, with a good angiographic result. The diagonal branch remained patent both proximally and in the mid segment.

Following this, the dilating system and guiding catheter were removed and replaced with a hockey-stick guide. I then advanced the Choice floppy wire down the RCA, with some difficulty negotiating the tortuosity of the vessel. The 2.5 Maverick **balloon** was then used to **dilate the proximal and mid RCA stenosis**, with some difficulty advancing the balloon through these lesions. I then attempted to advance a 4.5 x 18 mm Velocity, but this would not pass around the initial bend because of severe tortuosity in the vessel. The stent was then removed and replaced with a 3.5 x 20 mm Maverick, which was used to dilate the proximal and mid stenosis. I again was unable to advance the 4.5 mm Velocity stent, and this was removed and replaced with a 4.0 x 13 mm Penta stent. I was able to advance the **Penta stent** across the proximal occlusion, and this was **then deployed** at 15 atmospheres. The stent balloon was then removed, and I again advanced the 4.5 x 18 mm Velocity stent. The stent hung up within the previous stent, but finally, after replacing the wire with an Ironman wire after failing to use an extra-support and body wire to advance the stent, I was able to place the hockey-stick guide down the **RCA** to just **beyond the stented segment**, and then I was finally able to advance the **stent** into the **mid stenosis**, where it was deployed at 15 atmospheres. The stent **balloon** was then **retracted proximally** and **used to dilate the proximal stent to 4.5 mm**. There was a good result. The dilating system and guiding catheter were removed. Angiography of the LFA revealed a normal-appearing vessel and Perclose was performed with good hemostasis.

Coronary Angiography:
1. LAD: The LAD appeared to be a moderate-sized vessel that was 100 percent occluded immediately beyond the first diagonal branch.

2. RCA: The RCA was a very large, ectatic-appearing vessel. After the first bend, there was an 80 percent stenosis with two 90-degree segments of angulation within the lesion. Then in the mid segment of the RCA, there was an additional 70 percent stenosis. Distally there was an area of extensive ectasia and mild disease.

Coronary Intervention:
1. **Proximal LAD:** Pre-intervention 100 percent, **post-intervention** 0 percent (3.0 x 33 mm, 3.0 x 8 mm BX dilated to 3.5 proximally)

2. **Proximal RCA:** Pre-intervention 80 percent, **post-intervention** 0 percent (4.0 x 13 mm Penta dilated to 4.5)

3. **Mid RCA:** Pre-intervention 70 percent, **post-intervention** 0 percent (4.5 x 18 mm Velocity)

Conclusion:
Successful multivessel and multilesion coronary **intervention** of the **LAD and RCA**. The recently occluded LAD was successfully recanalized, with a long lesion evident treated successfully with coronary stenting. The severely ectatic and tortuous RCA was treated successfully with sequential 4.5 mm stents in the proximal and mid vessel.

Plan:
The patient was treated with Integrilin, followed by aspirin and Plavix.

CPT/HCPCS Codes Reported:
92928-LD, 92928-RC

Note: For Medicare, report HCPCS Level II code C9600.

Other HCPCS Codes Reported:
G0269 (per payer policy)

Case Example #2

Coronary Intervention Report

1. Rotational **atherectomy**

2. **Stenting** of proximal **LAD**, coronary **stenting** distal **RCA**

3. Conscious sedation

Indications:
The patient was an 83-year-old woman who presented with severe angina and two-vessel coronary disease.

Procedure Description:
The procedure was performed via an 8-French sheath placed in the left femoral artery and a 6-French sheath in the vein. An 8-French XB 3.5 and 3.0 catheter would not fit into the left main, and finally an L3.5 provided good cannulation. A Rota floppy wire was advanced out the **LAD**, and then a 1.25 mm **bur was utilized** to cross the sequential lesions in the **proximal and mid LAD**. Seven runs with the 1.25 mm bur were required before crossing the lesion, especially in the distal end of the lesion. A 1.5 mm bur crossed easily. **This lesion** was then **dilated** with a 2.5 NC Ranger, and then a 3.0 x 13 BX **Velocity stent was deployed** in the distal part of the lesion at 10 atmospheres. A 3.0 x 8 mm BX Velocity stent was deployed then proximal, just slightly overlapping this stent. The lesions were then post dilated with a 3.0 x 9 mm NC Ranger at 15 and 16 atmospheres. This dilating system was then removed.

Attention was then given to the **RCA**, and a hockey-stick guide was utilized, which provided good cannulation. A Choice floppy wire was advanced out the RCA, and the **lesion was dilated** with a 2.5 mm NC Ranger. The lesion easily dilated and therefore, a 3.0 x 13 mm BX Velocity **stent was deployed** at 15 atmospheres. There was a good result, and the dilating system and guiding catheter were removed. The sheaths were sutured in place. The patient received an infusion of Integrilin that was started after the rotational atherectomy procedure was completed.

Coronary Angiography:

1. Left anterior descending: The LAD was a moderate sized vessel that just wrapped slightly around the apex. In the proximal and mid segment, particularly in the segment of severe disease, there was 3+ calcification. There was an 80 percent stenosis proximally just prior to the bifurcation of the septal branch. The vessel then bent at this site and there was an additional 90 percent stenosis about 1 cm further down the LAD, and again with about a 45 degree angle at this lesion. The remainder of the LAD had mild disease, and was mildly calcified.

2. Right coronary artery: The RCA was a moderate to large circulation. The vessel was moderately calcified in its proximal and mid segment, with about a 30 percent stenosis in the mid vessel. There was then a focal 90 percent stenosis distally, just prior to the posterior descending artery bifurcation.

Coronary Intervention:

1. Proximal LAD: Pre intervention 80 percent, post intervention 0 percent (3.0 x 8 mm BX Velocity)

2. Mid LAD: Pre intervention 90 percent, post intervention 0 percent (3.0 x 13 mm BX Velocity)

3. Distal RCA: Pre intervention 90 percent, post intervention 0 percent (3.0 x 13 mm BX Velocity)

Conclusion:

1. **Successful combined rotational atherectomy and stenting of severely** calcified and tortuous sequential lesions in the proxima and mid **LAD**

2. **Successful stenting** of distal **RCA** stenosis

Plan:
The patient received an 18-hour infusion of Integrilin, followed by aspirin and Plavix.

CPT/HCPCS Codes Reported:
92933-LD, 92928-RC

Note: For Medicare, report HCPCS Level II codes C9602-LD and C9600-RC.

Percutaneous Balloon Valvuloplasty

92986	Percutaneous balloon valvuloplasty; aortic valve
92987	mitral valve
92990	pulmonary valve

Valvuloplasty is a procedure for opening a blocked valve.

The approach and methods used depend upon which valve is being repaired. A peripheral artery and vein are cannulated with an indwelling sheath. A guiding catheter is positioned near the affected valve. The balloon catheter is prepared and inserted through the guiding catheter and advanced into valve with fluoroscopic guidance. The balloon is inflated to open the blocked valve. The catheters are removed.

Report 92985 if the procedure is performed on the aortic valve; 92987 if the procedure is performed on the mitral valve; and 92990 if the procedure is performed on the pulmonary valve.

Coding Tips

1. Report diagnostic cardiac catheterization, if performed, in addition to percutaneous valvuloplasty.
2. Report other interventions performed during the same encounter (e.g., coronary artery angioplasty).
3. While physicians may not separately report the placement of a mechanical arterial sealing device after the cardiac catheterization, hospitals should separately report both the supply and the procedure. Medicare has assigned a specific HCPCS Level II code for this procedure (G0269). The corresponding supply code is C1760 (Closure device, vascular [implantable or insertable]). Other third-party payers will likely not accept this code and hospitals should verify with each payer on their policy regarding this service. Medicare does not provide separate payment, but the costs and charges should still be reported separately.
4. Do not report CPT codes from the 70000 series for test angiograms done prior to placement of a vascular closure device. This is considered to be part of the catheterization procedure.
5. Hospitals should separately report supplies and contrast used during cardiac interventional procedures.
6. Conscious sedation is not included in these codes. Separately report 99151–99157 per payer policy and coding guidelines. Hospitals may choose to include the costs associated with the service as part of the procedure rather than reporting them separately.

Facility HCPCS Coding

HCPCS Level II codes are used to report the supplies provided during the procedure. Hospitals should separately report supplies used during cardiac catheterization procedures. Refer to chapter 1 for more information regarding appropriate billing of supplies. Refer to the list of current codes in appendix B.

Procedure HCPCS Codes

G0269   Placement of occlusive device into either a venous or arterial access site, post surgical or interventional procedure, if performed

Balloon Valvuloplasty

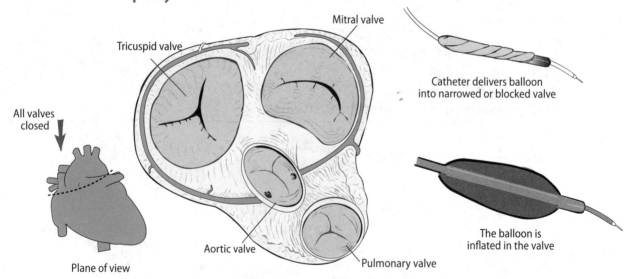

Report 92986 for the aortic valve; 92987 for the mitral valve; and report code 92987 for the pulmonary valve

Percutaneous Balloon Valvuloplasty, Mitral

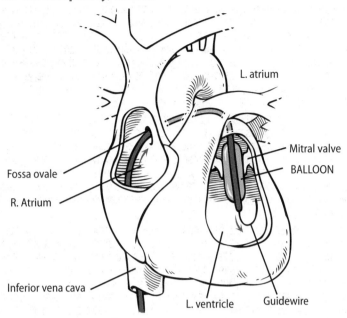

ICD-10-CM Coding

I05.0	Rheumatic mitral stenosis
I05.1	Rheumatic mitral insufficiency
I05.2	Rheumatic mitral stenosis with insufficiency
I05.8	Other rheumatic mitral valve diseases
I05.9	Rheumatic mitral valve disease, unspecified
I06.0	Rheumatic aortic stenosis
I06.1	Rheumatic aortic insufficiency
I06.2	Rheumatic aortic stenosis with insufficiency
I06.8	Other rheumatic aortic valve diseases
I06.9	Rheumatic aortic valve disease, unspecified
I08.0	Rheumatic disorders of both mitral and aortic valves
I08.8	Other rheumatic multiple valve diseases
I08.9	Rheumatic multiple valve disease, unspecified
I09.89	Other specified rheumatic heart diseases
I34.0	Nonrheumatic mitral (valve) insufficiency
I34.1	Nonrheumatic mitral (valve) prolapse
I34.2	Nonrheumatic mitral (valve) stenosis
I34.8	Other nonrheumatic mitral valve disorders
I34.9	Nonrheumatic mitral valve disorder, unspecified
I35.0	Nonrheumatic aortic (valve) stenosis
I35.1	Nonrheumatic aortic (valve) insufficiency
I35.2	Nonrheumatic aortic (valve) stenosis with insufficiency
I35.8	Other nonrheumatic aortic valve disorders
I35.9	Nonrheumatic aortic valve disorder, unspecified
I37.0	Nonrheumatic pulmonary valve stenosis
I37.1	Nonrheumatic pulmonary valve insufficiency
I37.2	Nonrheumatic pulmonary valve stenosis with insufficiency
I37.8	Other nonrheumatic pulmonary valve disorders
I37.9	Nonrheumatic pulmonary valve disorder, unspecified
Q22.1	Congenital pulmonary valve stenosis
Q23.1	Congenital insufficiency of aortic valve
Q23.3	Congenital mitral insufficiency

CCI Edits

92986   01924-01926, 0213T, 0216T, 0228T, 0230T, 11000-11006, 11042-11047, 12001-12007, 12011-12057, 13100-13133, 13151-13153, 35201-35206, 35226-35236, 35256-35266, 35286, 36000, 36120-36140, 36200, 36400-36410, 36420-36430, 36440, 36500, 36591-36592, 36600, 36640, 43752, 51701-51703, 62320-62327, 64400-64410, 64413-64435, 64445-64450, 64461-64463, 64479-64530, 75893, 92012-92014, 92961, 93000-93010, 93040-93042, 93050, 93318, 93355, 94002, 94200, 94250, 94680-94690, 94770, 95812-95816, 95819, 95822, 95829, 95955, 96360-96368, 96372-96377, 97597-97598, 97602, 99155-99157, 99211-99223, 99231-99255, 99291-99292, 99304-99310, 99315-99316, 99334-99337, 99347-99350, 99374-99375, 99377-99378, 99446-99449, 99495-99496, G0463, G0471

92987   01924-01926, 0213T, 0216T, 0228T, 0230T, 0345T, 11000-11006, 11042-11047, 12001-12007, 12011-12057, 13100-13133, 13151-13153, 35201-35206, 35226-35236, 35256-35266, 35286, 36000, 36120-36140, 36200, 36400-36410, 36420-36430, 36440, 36500, 36591-36592, 36600, 36640, 43752, 51701-51703, 62320-62327, 64400-64410, 64413-64435, 64445-64450, 64461-64463, 64479-64530, 75893, 92012-92014, 92961, 93000-93010, 93040-93042, 93050, 93318, 93355, 94002, 94200, 94250, 94680-94690, 94770, 95812-95816, 95819, 95822, 95829, 95955, 96360-96368, 96372-96377, 97597-97598, 97602, 99155-99157, 99211-99223, 99231-99255, 99291-99292, 99304-99310, 99315-99316, 99334-99337, 99347-99350, 99374-99375, 99377-99378, 99446-99449, 99495-99496, G0463, G0471

92990   01926, 0213T, 0216T, 0228T, 0230T, 11000-11006, 11042-11047, 12001-12007, 12011-12057, 13100-13133, 13151-13153, 35201-35206, 35226-35236, 35256-35266, 35286, 36000, 36400-36410, 36420-36430, 36440, 36500, 36591-36592, 36600, 36640, 43752, 51701-51703, 62320-62327, 64400-64410, 64413-64435, 64445-64450, 64461-64463, 64479-64530, 75893, 92012-92014, 92961, 93000-93010, 93040-93042, 93050, 93318, 93355-93451, 93453, 93456, 93460-93461, 94002, 94200, 94250, 94680-94690, 94770, 95812-95816, 95819, 95822, 95829, 95955, 96360-96368, 96372-96377, 97597-97598, 97602, 99155-99157, 99211-99223, 99231-99255, 99291-99292, 99304-99310, 99315-99316, 99334-99337, 99347-99350, 99374-99375, 99377-99378, 99446-99449, 99495-99496, G0463, G0471

Case Example

Indication:
Severe aortic stenosis, dyspnea on exertion, in addition to LAD lesion in the mid-LAD in the range of 80%, chronic lung disease secondary to asthma, diabetes, dyslipidemia

Procedure:
The patient was brought to the cardiac catheterization suite and scrubbed in the usual sterile fashion. The right common femoral artery and vein were accessed with micropuncture technique under ultrasound guidance. A 6-French arterial and a 7-French venous sheath were inserted respectively in the artery and vein. The right common femoral artery angiogram showed there was adequate entry of the right common femoral artery above the bifurcation and below the inguinal ligament. The right common femoral artery was pre-closed with 2 ProGlide sutures in anticipation of a large-bore 12-French sheath for the valvuloplasty. The 12-French sheath was advanced over a Supra Core wire in the right common femoral artery and a 7-French sheath over a J-wire into the right common femoral vein. **Right heart catheterization was performed.** Then, the Swan-Ganz catheter was pulled and a transvenous pacemaker was advanced in the right common femoral vein, and pacing thresholds were adequate. Following that, we proceeded with **crossing the aortic valve** with an AL1 catheter and a straight wire and a dual-lumen pigtail catheter was used for measurement of the gradient across the aortic valve. Following that, the **valve was dilated** with a 20 x 40 mm True **balloon that was inflated on 2 occasions using the rapid** pacing. The gradient across the aortic valve was re-measured with a dual lumen pigtail catheter. Hemodynamics were taken and recorded. Post-valvuloplasty the aortic pressure was 164/59 (98 mmHg). Peak to peak aortic valve gradient was 19.0 mmHg. The aortic valve area improved from 0.9 to 1.15 sq cm.

Selective angiography was performed of the left coronary artery. Angiography demonstrated mild proximal disease of the left anterior descending artery. This area was followed by an area of 30% disease in the mid portion and then by 80–90% in the distal portion of the artery. The circumflex demonstrated mild proximal disease and gives off a large obtuse marginal branch with a 50% proximal stenosis. We then **proceeded with intervention of the left anterior descending artery.** The LAD was wired with a Prowater wire. We then advanced a 2.5 x 18 mm **Resolute drug-eluting stent** across the distal artery lesion and deployed it at a maximum of 16 atm. There was still a 30% mid stent residual stenosis that was post-dilated with a 2.75 x 12 mm NC Quantum balloon inflated on 2 occasions at a max pressure of 22 atm. Repeat angiogram revealed a 10% residual stenosis in the stented segment of the LAD with TIMI-3 flow distally.

The patient received a double bolus of Integrilin and was given 600 mg of Plavix after the procedure. The 12-French sheath was removed and the 2 ProGlide sutures were deployed in the femoral artery achieving excellent hemostasis. The remaining sheath was removed and manual pressure applied. No immediate complications.

Impression and Plan:
1. Severe aortic stenosis with severe LAD artery disease in addition to moderate circumflex disease.

2. **Status post successful valvuloplasty of the aortic valve** from severe stenosis to moderate stenosis with a mean gradient improvement from 41 to 29 mmHg.

3. **Status post stenting with a drug-eluting stent of the LAD** from 80–90% down to 10% residual stenosis and TIMI-3 flow.

CPT/HCPCS Codes Reported:
92986, C9600-LD

Other HCPCS Codes Reported:
C1725, C1751, C1769, C1887, C1894, C1874, Q9967

Transvenous Atrial Septectomy/Septostomy

92992   **Atrial septectomy or septostomy; transvenous method, balloon (eg, Rashkind type) (includes cardiac catheterization)**

A Balloon is placed to enlarge the atrial septum

Certain congenital heart defects, particularly those involving transposition of the great vessels, require surgical creation or enlargement of an opening in the interatrial septum (wall) that separates the upper right and left chambers of the heart. The physician makes a small incision in the arm or leg. Two catheters are placed--a central venous catheter and a second catheter threaded up to the heart. When the foramen ovale has not closed, a deflated balloon (Rashkind-type) is passed through the foramen ovale, inflated, and pulled through the atrial septum, enlarging the opening and improving oxygenation of the blood. When the septum is intact, the deflated balloon (Rashkind-type) is passed from the right atrium through the septum to the left atrium, inflated, and then withdrawn, creating an interatrial septal defect and improving oxygenation of the blood. The catheters are removed. Pressure is placed over the incision for 20 to 30 minutes to stem bleeding. A cardiac catheterization may be included. The patient is observed for a period of time afterward.

Coding Tips

1. CPT code 92992 includes diagnostic cardiac catheterization and is not reported separately.
2. For atrial septectomy or septostomy by blade method (Park septostomy), see 92993.
3. Hospitals should separately report supplies and contrast used during cardiac interventional procedures.
4. This procedure has been designated as an inpatient only procedure. It is not covered if reported on an outpatient designated claim.
5. Conscious sedation is not included in these codes. Separately report 99151–99157 per payer policy and coding guidelines. Hospitals may choose to include the costs associated with the service as part of the procedure rather than reporting them separately.

Facility HCPCS Coding

HCPCS Level II codes are used to report the supplies provided during the procedure. Hospitals should separately report supplies used during cardiac catheterization procedures. Refer to chapter 1 for more information regarding appropriate billing of supplies. Refer to the list of current codes in appendix B.

Procedure HCPCS Codes

G0269   Placement of occlusive device into either a venous or arterial access site, post surgical or interventional procedure

Atrial Septostomy

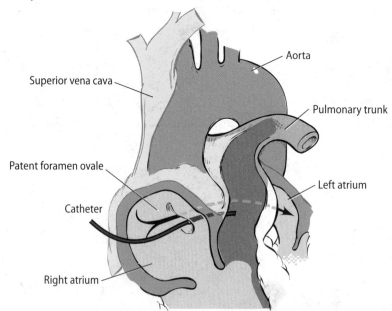

Depiction of patent foramen ovale. The procedure involves placing a catheter through the foramen ovale and enlarging the opening to allow mixing of blood between the atria. A balloon catheter may be used, or a cutting device may be required to create an opening (septostomy)

ICD-10-CM Coding

Q20.0	Common arterial trunk
Q20.1	Double outlet right ventricle
Q20.3	Discordant ventriculoarterial connection
Q21.3	Tetralogy of Fallot
Q21.8	Other congenital malformations of cardiac septa
Q22.0	Pulmonary valve atresia
Q22.4	Congenital tricuspid stenosis
Q22.6	Hypoplastic right heart syndrome
Q22.8	Other congenital malformations of tricuspid valve
Q22.9	Congenital malformation of tricuspid valve, unspecified
Q23.8	Other congenital malformations of aortic and mitral valves
Q23.9	Congenital malformation of aortic and mitral valves, unspecified
Q24.8	Other specified congenital malformations of heart
Q25.0	Patent ductus arteriosus
Q25.21	Interruption of aortic arch
Q25.29	Other atresia of aorta
Q25.5	Atresia of pulmonary artery
Q26.2	Total anomalous pulmonary venous connection

CCI Edits

92992   01926, 0213T, 0216T, 0228T, 0230T, 11000-11006, 11042-11047, 12001-12007, 12011-12057, 13100-13133, 13151-13153, 33210-33211, 35201-35206, 35226, 35261-35266, 35286, 35761, 36000, 36400-36410, 36420-36430, 36440, 36500, 36591-36592, 36600, 36640, 43752, 51701-51703, 62320-62327, 64400-64410, 64413-64435, 64445-64450, 64461-64463, 64479-64530, 75893, 92012-92014, 92961, 92993, 93000-93010, 93040-93042, 93050, 93318, 93355-93462, 93530-93533, 94002, 94200, 94250, 94680-94690, 94770, 95812-95816, 95819, 95822, 95829, 95955, 96360-96368, 96372-96377, 97597-97598, 97602, 99155-99157, 99211-99223, 99231-99255, 99291-99292, 99304-99310, 99315-99316, 99334-99337, 99347-99350, 99374-99375, 99377-99378, 99446-99449, 99495-99496, G0463, G0471

Park Septostomy

92993   **Atrial septectomy or septostomy; blade method (Park septostomy) (includes cardiac catheterization)**
The purpose of this procedure is to increase blood flow across the atrial septum in children with certain forms of cyanotic congenital heart disease. This procedure is used as an alternative to the Rashkind procedure (balloon method of atrial septostomy), typically in infants older than 1 month of age. The physician makes a small incision in the femoral vein. The physician places a transseptal sheath in the right femoral vein using standard methods, advancing the sheath to the superior vena cava under fluoroscopic or echocardiographic guidance. The physician uses a transseptal needle to cross the atrial septum, entering the left atrium. The physician introduces a guidewire into the left atrium and removes the transseptal catheter while leaving the wire in place. The physician advances a special septostomy catheter over the wire into the left atrium. This catheter has a retracted blade, which the physician extends. The physician pulls the blade slowly across the atrial septum from the left into the right atrium, under fluoroscopic or echocardiographic guidance. The physician may make several passes with the blade catheter in this fashion. The physician removes the septostomy catheter and venous sheath. Pressure is placed over the incision for 20 to 30 minutes to stem bleeding. The patient is observed for a period of time afterward.

Coding Tips

1.   CPT code 92993 includes diagnostic cardiac catheterization and is not reported separately.
2.   For atrial septectomy or septostomy by balloon method (Rashkind type), see 92992.
3.   Hospitals should separately report supplies and contrast used during cardiac interventional procedures.
4.   This procedure has been designated as an inpatient only procedure. It is not covered if reported on an outpatient designated claim.
5.   Conscious sedation is not included in these codes. Separately report 99151–99157 per payer policy and coding guidelines. Hospitals may choose to include the costs associated with the service as part of the procedure rather than reporting them separately.

Facility HCPCS Coding

HCPCS Level II codes are used to report the supplies provided during the procedure. Hospitals should separately report supplies used during cardiac catheterization procedures. Refer to chapter 1 for more information regarding appropriate billing of supplies. Refer to the list of current codes in appendix B.

Procedure HCPCS Coding

G0269   Placement of occlusive device into either a venous or arterial access site, post surgical or interventional procedure, if performed

Park Septostomy

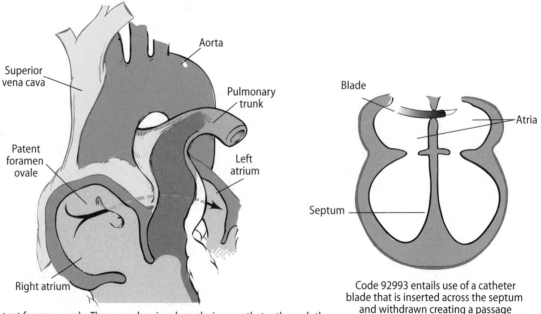

Depiction of patent foramen ovale. The procedure involves placing a catheter through the foramen ovale and enlargingthe opening to allow mixing of blood between the atria

Code 92993 entails use of a catheter blade that is inserted across the septum and withdrawn creating a passage

ICD-10-CM Coding

Q20.0	Common arterial trunk
Q20.1	Double outlet right ventricle
Q20.3	Discordant ventriculoarterial connection
Q21.3	Tetralogy of Fallot
Q21.8	Other congenital malformations of cardiac septa
Q22.0	Pulmonary valve atresia
Q22.4	Congenital tricuspid stenosis
Q22.6	Hypoplastic right heart syndrome
Q22.8	Other congenital malformations of tricuspid valve
Q22.9	Congenital malformation of tricuspid valve, unspecified
Q23.8	Other congenital malformations of aortic and mitral valves
Q23.9	Congenital malformation of aortic and mitral valves, unspecified
Q24.8	Other specified congenital malformations of heart
Q25.0	Patent ductus arteriosus
Q25.21	Interruption of aortic arch
Q25.29	Other atresia of aorta
Q25.5	Atresia of pulmonary artery
Q26.2	Total anomalous pulmonary venous connection

CCI Edits

92993   01926, 0213T, 0216T, 0228T, 0230T, 11000-11006, 11042-11047, 12001-12007, 12011-12057, 13100-13133, 13151-13153, 33210-33211, 35201-35206, 35226, 35261-35266, 35286, 35761, 36000, 36400-36410, 36420-36430, 36440, 36500, 36591-36592, 36600, 36640, 43752, 51701-51703, 62320-62327, 64400-64410, 64413-64435, 64445-64450, 64461-64463, 64479-64530, 75893, 92012-92014, 92961, 93000-93010, 93040-93042, 93050, 93318, 93355-93462, 93530-93533, 94002, 94200, 94250, 94680-94690, 94770, 95812-95816, 95819, 95822, 95829, 95955, 96360-96368, 96372-96377, 97597-97598, 97602, 99155-99157, 99211-99223, 99231-99255, 99291-99292, 99304-99310, 99315-99316, 99334-99337, 99347-99350, 99374-99375, 99377-99378, 99446-99449, 99495-99496, G0463, G0471

Percutaneous Transluminal Pulmonary Artery Angioplasty

92997   **Percutaneous transluminal pulmonary artery balloon angioplasty; single vessel**

92998   **each additional vessel (List separately in addition to code for primary procedure)**

The purpose of this procedure is to use a balloon to expand a narrowed pulmonary artery. The physician places an introducer sheath in the femoral vein, using percutaneous puncture. The physician places a special angioplasty catheter through the introducer sheath into the femoral vein and advances it under fluoroscopic guidance to the right ventricle and out into the main pulmonary artery. The physician advances the angioplasty balloon into the narrowed pulmonary artery, using injections of x-ray contrast material to guide the way. In 92998, following single vessel percutaneous transluminal pulmonary artery balloon angioplasty, the physician redirects the balloon angioplasty catheter to an additional pulmonary artery. The physician may change to a different sized balloon catheter if the additional pulmonary artery is of different size. For both procedures, the physician inflates the balloon to expand the pulmonary artery, sometimes using several balloon inflations. The physician removes the catheter and sheath from the femoral vein. Pressure is placed on the wound for 20 to 30 minutes to stem bleeding.

Coding Tips

1. Report CPT code 75741 or 75743 for the radiologic S&I, when appropriate.

2. If intravascular ultrasound is used, report 37250 in addition to 92997 or 37251 in addition to 92998.

3. Device edits apply to the codes in this section.

4. Conscious sedation is not included in these codes. Separately report 99151–99157 per payer policy and coding guidelines. Hospitals may choose to include the costs associated with the service as part of the procedure rather than reporting them separately.

Facility HCPCS Coding

Some applicable codes may include, but are not limited to:

C1725   Catheter, transluminal angioplasty, non-laser

C1885   Catheter, transluminal angioplasty, laser

C1887   Catheter, guiding

HCPCS Level II codes are used to report the supplies provided during the procedure. Hospitals should separately report supplies used during cardiac catheterization procedures. Refer to chapter 1 for more information regarding appropriate billing of supplies. Refer to the list of current codes in appendix B.

Pulmonary Artery Angioplasty

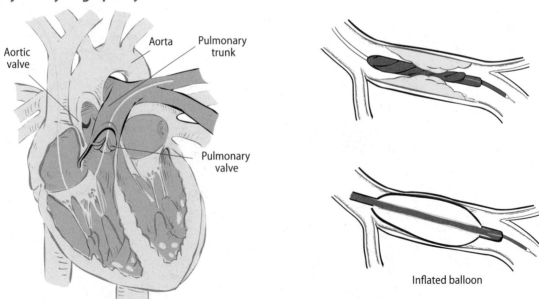

A pulmonary artery is approached transluminally by percutaneous entry. Balloon angioplasty is performed. Report 92997 for a single vessel and 92998 for each additional vessel

ICD-10-CM Coding

I26.01	Septic pulmonary embolism with acute cor pulmonale
I26.02	Saddle embolus of pulmonary artery with acute cor pulmonale
I26.09	Other pulmonary embolism with acute cor pulmonale
I26.90	Septic pulmonary embolism without acute cor pulmonale
I26.92	Saddle embolus of pulmonary artery without acute cor pulmonale
I26.99	Other pulmonary embolism without acute cor pulmonale
I28.8	Other diseases of pulmonary vessels
Q21.3	Tetralogy of Fallot
Q24.3	Pulmonary infundibular stenosis
Q25.5	Atresia of pulmonary artery
Q25.6	Stenosis of pulmonary artery
Q25.71	Coarctation of pulmonary artery
Q25.72	Congenital pulmonary arteriovenous malformation
Q25.79	Other congenital malformations of pulmonary artery

CCI Edits

92997 01924-01926, 0213T, 0216T, 0228T, 0230T, 11000-11006, 11042-11047, 12001-12007, 12011-12057, 13100-13133, 13151-13153, 33210-33211, 35201-35206, 35226-35236, 35256-35266, 35286, 36000, 36400-36410, 36420-36430, 36440, 36500, 36591-36592, 36600, 36640, 37246-37247, 43752, 51701-51703, 62320-62327, 64400-64410, 64413-64435, 64445-64450, 64461-64463, 64479-64530, 71023, 75893, 92012-92014, 92961, 93000-93010, 93040-93042, 93050, 93318, 93355, 94002, 94200, 94250, 94680-94690, 94770, 95812-95816, 95819, 95822, 95829, 95955, 96360-96368, 96372, 96374-96377, 97597-97598, 97602, 99155-99157, 99211-99223, 99231-99255, 99291-99292, 99304-99310, 99315-99316, 99334-99337, 99347-99350, 99374-99375, 99377-99378, 99446-99449, 99495-99496, G0463, G0471

92998 01924-01926, 11000-11006, 11042-11047, 33210-33211, 36591-36592, 37246-37247, 93050, 97597-97598, 97602

Endomyocardial Biopsy

93505   **Endomyocardial biopsy**
The physician threads a catheter to the heart through a central intravenous line often inserted up the femoral vein to take tissue samples of the heart's septum.

Coding Tips

1. Report CPT code 76932 when ultrasound guidance is used to obtain the biopsy. Permanently recorded images are required when reporting all ultrasound and ultrasound guidance codes.

2. Fluoroscopy is considered to be part of cardiac catheterization and is not reported separately.

3. Pulse oximetry is not reported separately.

4. Right heart catheterization (93451) should be reported only in conjunction with endomyocardial biopsy if a separate and complete diagnostic heart catheterization is indicated and performed.

Facility HCPCS Coding

HCPCS Level II codes are used to report the supplies provided during the procedure. Refer to the list of current codes in appendix B.

Endomyocardial Biopsy

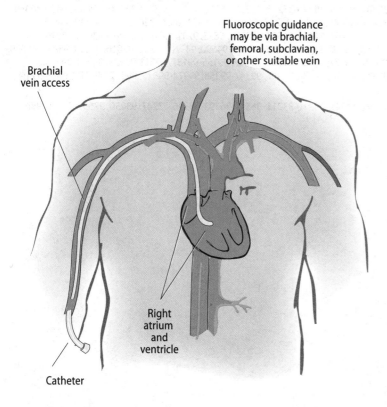

Fluoroscopic guidance may be via brachial, femoral, subclavian, or other suitable vein

Brachial vein access

Right atrium and ventricle

Catheter

A biopsy tome is inserted through the catheter and several tiny tissue samples are collected from the walls of the heart

ICD-10-CM Coding

A18.84	Tuberculosis of heart
A52.03	Syphilitic endocarditis
B37.6	Candidal endocarditis
C38.0	Malignant neoplasm of heart
C79.89	Secondary malignant neoplasm of other specified sites
D15.1	Benign neoplasm of heart
D48.7	Neoplasm of uncertain behavior of other specified sites
D49.89	Neoplasm of unspecified behavior of other specified sites
I01.1	Acute rheumatic endocarditis
I25.2	Old myocardial infarction
I25.3	Aneurysm of heart
I33.0	Acute and subacute infective endocarditis
I33.9	Acute and subacute endocarditis, unspecified
I38	Endocarditis, valve unspecified
I40.0	Infective myocarditis
I40.1	Isolated myocarditis
I40.8	Other acute myocarditis
I40.9	Acute myocarditis, unspecified
I41	Myocarditis in diseases classified elsewhere
I42.0	Dilated cardiomyopathy
I42.1	Obstructive hypertrophic cardiomyopathy
I42.2	Other hypertrophic cardiomyopathy
I42.3	Endomyocardial (eosinophilic) disease
I42.7	Cardiomyopathy due to drug and external agent
I42.8	Other cardiomyopathies
I42.9	Cardiomyopathy, unspecified
M32.11	Endocarditis in systemic lupus erythematosus
T86.21	Heart transplant rejection
T86.22	Heart transplant failure
T86.31	Heart-lung transplant rejection
T86.32	Heart-lung transplant failure

CCI Edits

93505   01920, 0213T, 0216T, 0228T, 0230T, 12001-12007, 12011-12057, 13100-13133, 13151-13153, 33210-33211, 34812-34813, 35201-35206, 35226-35236, 35256-35266, 35286, 36000, 36005-36015, 36400-36410, 36420-36430, 36440, 36500, 36591-36592, 36600, 36640, 43752, 51701-51703, 62320-62327, 64400-64410, 64413-64435, 64445-64450, 64461-64463, 64479-64530, 71034, 75600, 75605, 75741, 75743, 75746, 75756, 75893, 76000-76001, 77001-77002, 92012-92014, 92961, 93000-93010, 93040-93042, 93318, 93355-93451, 93457, 93503, 93561-93562, 94002, 94200, 94250, 94680-94690, 94770, 95812-95816, 95819, 95822, 95829, 95955, 96360-96368, 96372-96377, 99155-99157, 99211-99223, 99231-99255, 99291-99292, 99304-99310, 99315-99316, 99334-99337, 99347-99350, 99374-99375, 99377-99378, 99446-99449, 99495-99496, G0269, G0463, G0471, J0670, J2001

Case Example

Procedure:
The patient's left upper chest is prepped and draped. After local anesthesia, a needle is inserted into the left subclavian vein. Under fluoroscopic guidance, a guidewire is inserted. The needle is retracted, and an introducer sheath is placed. Through the sheath, a guiding catheter is placed and directed into the right ventricle. The **biopsy catheter** is inserted through the guiding sheath and directed to the **right ventricle**. Four biopsy samples are taken and sent to pathology. The guidewires and catheters are removed, and pressure is held over the insertion area.

CPT/HCPCS Codes Reported:
93505

Other HCPCS Codes Reported:
C1769, C1893

Catheter Closure of Atrial Septal Defect/Ventricular Septal Defect

CPT code 93580 reports percutaneous catheter closure of congenital interatrial communication (ASD). Code 93581 reports the closure of congenital interventricular communication (VSD).

93580   **Percutaneous transcatheter closure of congenital interatrial communication (ie, Fontan fenestration, atrial septal defect) with implant**

93581   **Percutaneous transcatheter closure of a congenital ventricular septal defect with implant**

A congenital ventricular septal defect is closed percutaneously by catheter. The patient is given local anesthesia and the femoral artery and vein are cannulated. A guidewire and catheter are inserted and advanced through the ventricular septum, into the right ventricle, and across the tricuspid valve into the right atrium. A separate venous sheath is placed in the jugular vein to allow passage of a snare catheter. The snare is advanced into the atrium and grasps the free wire or catheter that was threaded through the ventricular septal defect. This provides a through-and-through from the femoral vein to the ventricular septal defect and out the jugular. The jugular end is then used to pass a dilator and sheath over the defect for the positioning of the occlusive device into the left ventricle. The sheath must be in the exact position with its tip in the left ventricle for delivery of the occlusive device. If necessary, traction is used at the opposite end to secure the sheath as the dilator is carefully removed. If the sheath is displaced during removal of the dilator, the dilator is reinserted for correct positioning. Once the sheath is in place and the dilator removed, the delivery catheter loaded with an occlusive device is advanced to the center of the right atrium. The device is advanced out of the delivery catheter and into the tip of the sheath. It is then gently advanced so that the distal legs are in the left ventricle and the center of the device is in the defect. A slight withdrawing of the sheath causes the distal legs to open within the left ventricle. Further withdrawal of the sheath allows the proximal legs to open in the right ventricle. The occlusion is confirmed with angiography and the delivery system and catheters are removed.

Coding Tips

1. This procedure includes right heart catheterization and injection of contrast for atrial and ventricular angiograms. Do not report 93451–93453, 93455–93461, 93530–93533, 93564, or 93565 in addition to 93581.

2. For echocardiographic services performed in addition to 93581, see 93303-93317 and 93662 as appropriate.

3. Hospitals should report supplies and contrast used during cardiac catheterization procedures separately.

4. Conscious sedation is not included in these codes. Separately report 99151–99157 per payer policy and coding guidelines. Hospitals may choose to include the costs associated with the service as part of the procedure rather than reporting them separately.

Facility HCPCS Coding

HCPCS Level II codes are used to report the supplies provided during the procedure. Hospitals should separately report supplies used during cardiac catheterization procedures. Refer chapter 1 for more information regarding appropriate billing of supplies. Refer to the list of current codes in appendix B.

C1817   Septal defect implant system, intracardiac

ICD-10-CM Coding

Q21.0   Ventricular septal defect
Q21.1   Atrial septal defect
Q21.2   Atrioventricular septal defect

CCI Edits

93580   01926, 0213T, 0216T, 0228T, 0230T, 11000-11006, 11042-11047, 12001-12007, 12011-12057, 13100-13133, 13151-13153, 33210, 34812, 35201-35206, 35226-35236, 35256-35266, 35286, 36000, 36010, 36013-36015, 36400-36410, 36420-36430, 36440, 36555-36556, 36568-36569, 36591-36592, 36600, 36640, 43752, 51701-51703, 62320-62327, 64400-64410, 64413-64435, 64445-64450, 64461-64463, 64479-64530, 76000-76001, 77001-77002, 92012-92014, 93000-93010, 93040-93042, 93318, 93355-93461, 93503-93505, 93530-93533, 93561-93562, 93565-93566, 94002, 94200, 94250, 94680-94690, 94770, 95812-95816, 95819, 95822, 95829, 95955, 96360-96368, 96372-96377, 97597-97598, 97602, 99155-99157, 99211-99223, 99231-99255, 99291-99292, 99304-99310, 99315-99316, 99334-99337, 99347-99350, 99374-99375, 99377-99378, 99446-99449, 99495-99496, G0463, G0471

93581   01926, 0213T, 0216T, 0228T, 0230T, 11000-11006, 11042-11047, 12001-12007, 12011-12057, 13100-13133, 13151-13153, 33210, 34812, 35201-35206, 35226-35236, 35256-35266, 35286, 36000, 36010, 36013-36015, 36400-36410, 36420-36430, 36440, 36555-36556, 36568-36569, 36591-36592, 36600, 36640, 43752, 51701-51703, 62320-62327, 64400-64410, 64413-64435, 64445-64450, 64461-64463, 64479-64530, 76000-76001, 77001-77002, 92012-92014, 93000-93010, 93040-93042, 93318, 93355-93461, 93503-93505, 93530-93533, 93561-93562, 93565-93566, 94002, 94200, 94250, 94680-94690, 94770, 95812-95816, 95819, 95822, 95829, 95955, 96360-96368, 96372-96377, 97597-97598, 97602, 99155-99157, 99211-99223, 99231-99255, 99291-99292, 99304-99310, 99315-99316, 99334-99337, 99347-99350, 99374-99375, 99377-99378, 99446-99449, 99495-99496, G0463, G0471

Case Example

Procedure:
Prior left ventriculography demonstrated VSD with significant shunting. **Percutaneous VSD closure is recommended.**

Patient is prepped and draped in typical sterile fashion. Under conscious sedation, a JR4 catheter was introduced via right femoral arterial access. Under fluoro guidance, the catheter was advanced into the left ventricle. A glidewire was then inserted and used to cross the VSD into the right ventricle and then into the pulmonary artery. An ICE catheter was then introduced and used to measure the VSD.

A gooseneck snare was then introduced from the right femoral vein and advanced to the pulmonary artery to create an A-V loop across the VSD. An 8-French delivery sheath was then advanced from the venous access, directed across the VSD and into the left ventricle. Using ICE guidance, the **occluder device** was advanced, and the left-sided disk was deployed and brought back **against the left ventricular septum**. The right-sided disk was then deployed. ICE imaging was then used to evaluate clearance of the valves. No significant regurgitation was identified. The occlude device was removed and final ventriculography was done. There was **no residual shunting**. All devices were removed.

CPT/HCPCS Codes Reported:
93581, 93662

Other HCPCS Codes Reported:
C1769, C1817, C1773, C1759

Catheter Closure of Patent Ductus Arteriosus

Patent ductus arteriosus (PDA) is a persistent opening between two major blood vessels leading from the heart. The opening, called the ductus arteriosus, is a normal part of a baby's circulation before birth. This opening usually closes shortly after birth. If it fails to close, it is called a patent ductus arteriosus. A small PDA may never require treatment. A larger opening will need treatment to avoid future weakening of the heart muscle, which would cause heart failure among other complications. This opening can be closed by surgery or by the percutaneous method described here.

93582 **Percutaneous transcatheter closure of patent ductus arteriosus**

A patent ductus arteriosus is closed using a transcatheter technique. A small incision is made in an extremity artery, and a catheter is threaded through the arteries to the heart and then to the PDA. A coil or other occlusion device is deployed into the PDA via the catheter. Angiography or other imaging may be performed to check for patency of the closure device. The catheter is then removed and the incision is closed.

Coding Tips

1. Code 93582 includes congenital heart catheterization, catheter placement, and aortic arch imaging. Do not also report 36013, 36014, 36200, 75600, 75605, 93451–93461, 93530–93533, or 93567.

2. Coronary and bypass graft angiography is not included and may be separately reported using 93563 and 93564 as appropriate.

3. Pulmonary angiography is not included and may be separately reported using 93568.

4. Left ventricular and left atrial angiography are not included and may be separately reported using 93565.

5. Right ventricular and right atrial angiography are not included and may be separately reported using 93566.

6. Left heart catheterization performed by transseptal or transapical puncture is separately reported using 93462.

7. For intracardiac echo (ICE) performed during PDA closure, use 93662.

8. Device codes are required for the codes in this section. Hospitals should report all applicable device codes used. Refer to the HCPCS section for possible codes.

9. Conscious sedation is not included in these codes. Separately report 99151–99157 per payer policy and coding guidelines. Hospitals may choose to include the costs associated with the service as part of the procedure rather than reporting them separately.

Facility HCPCS Coding

Some applicable codes may include but are not limited to:

C1759   Catheter, intracardiac echocardiography

C1769   Guidewire

C1725   Catheter, angioplasty

C1817   Septal defect implant system, intracardiac

Q9965   LOCM, 100-199 mg/ml iodine concentration, per ml

Q9966   LOCM, 200-299 mg/ml iodine concentration, per ml

Q9967   LOCM, 300-399 mg/ml iodine concentration, per ml

Note: See appendix B for a complete listing of reportable HCPCS Level II codes.

ICD-10-CM Coding

Q25.Ø   Patent ductus arteriosus

CCI Edits

93582   01926, 0213T, 0216T, 0228T, 0230T, 11000-11006, 11042-11047, 12001-12007, 12011-12057, 13100-13133, 13151-13153, 33210-33211, 34812, 35201-35206, 35226-35236, 35256-35266, 35286, 36000, 36010, 36013-36015, 36200, 36400-36410, 36420-36430, 36440, 36555-36556, 36568-36569, 36591-36592, 36600, 36640, 43752, 51701-51703, 62320-62327, 64400-64410, 64413-64435, 64445-64450, 64461-64463, 64479-64530, 69990, 75600, 75605, 76000-76001, 77001-77002, 92012-92014, 93000-93010, 93040-93042, 93312-93318, 93355-93461, 93503-93505, 93530-93533, 93561-93562, 93565-93567, 94002, 94200, 94250, 94680-94690, 94770, 95812-95816, 95819, 95822, 95829, 95955, 96360-96368, 96372-96377, 97597-97598, 97602, 99155-99157, 99211-99223, 99231-99255, 99291-99292, 99304-99310, 99315-99316, 99334-99337, 99347-99350, 99374-99375, 99377-99378, 99446-99449, G0463, G0471

Case Example

Procedure:
Patient is prepped and draped in typical sterile fashion. Under conscious sedation, a JR4 catheter was introduced via right femoral arterial access. Under fluoro guidance, the catheter was advanced to the aortic arch. A glidewire was then inserted and used to cross the PDA into the pulmonary artery. An ICE catheter was then introduced and used to measure the PDA.

A gooseneck snare was then introduced from the right femoral vein and advanced to the pulmonary artery to create an A-V loop across the PDA. An 8-French delivery sheath was advanced from the venous access, directed into the **right ventricle** and then into the **pulmonary artery**. Using ICE guidance, the **occluder device** was advanced and the left-sided disk was **deployed and brought back against the aorta**. The right-sided disk was then **deployed on the pulmonary artery side**. ICE imaging was used to evaluate patency of the closure. No significant regurgitation was identified. The occluder device was removed and final pulmonary angiography and arch aortography were done. There was no residual leaking. All devices were removed.

CPT/HCPCS Codes Reported:
93582, 93662

Other HCPCS Codes Reported:
C1769, C1817, C1773, C1759

Percutaneous Transcatheter Septal Reduction Therapy

This procedure is used as an alternative for drug-refractory hypertrophic obstructive cardiomyopathy.

93583   **Percutaneous transcatheter septal reduction therapy (eg, alcohol septal ablation) including temporary pacemaker insertion when performed**

Septal reduction therapy, also known as alcohol septal ablation (ASA), is performed to decrease the size of the cardiac septal muscle in patients with hypertrophic cardiomyopathy. A small incision is made in an extremity artery (usually the femoral artery). A catheter is threaded through the arteries to the heart, and a coronary angiography is performed to locate the first septal perforator branch of the left anterior descending (LAD) artery. A balloon is inflated within the perforator, and contrast is injected to ensure no flow-back into the LAD. A slow injection of absolute alcohol is performed until a partial initial response is rendered. The balloon is deflated, and an additional coronary angiogram is performed to ensure patency of the LAD. The catheters are removed, and the incision is closed.

Coding Tips

1. Code 93583 includes the insertion of a temporary pacemaker. Do not separately report 33210 or 33211.
2. Left heart catheterization is also included in 93583. Do not separately report unless the service meets the definition of a separate diagnostic test or the prior test is inadequate.
3. Code 93583 includes angiography of the LAD for roadmapping purposes guiding this intervention.
4. Do not report 93463 for the injection of the alcohol.
5. Intracardiac transesophageal echocardiography may be separately reported with code 93662.
6. Transthoracic echo performed by a separate physician may be reported using codes 93312–93317.
7. For intracardiac echo (ICE) performed during PDA closure, use 93662.
8. Device codes are required for the codes in this section. Hospitals should report all applicable device codes used. Refer to the HCPCS section for possible codes.
9. Conscious sedation is not included in these codes. Separately report 99151–99157 per payer policy and coding guidelines. Hospitals may choose to include the costs associated with the service as part of the procedure rather than reporting them separately.

Facility HCPCS Coding

Some applicable codes may include but are not limited to:

C1759   Catheter, intracardiac echocardiography

C1769   Guidewire

Q9965   LOCM, 100-199 mg/ml iodine concentration, per ml

Q9966   LOCM, 200-299 mg/ml iodine concentration, per ml

Q9967   LOCM, 300-399 mg/ml iodine concentration, per ml

Note: See appendix B for a complete listing of reportable HCPCS Level II codes.

ICD-10-CM Coding

I42.1   Obstructive hypertrophic cardiomyopathy

I42.2   Other hypertrophic cardiomyopathy

Q24.8   Other specified congenital malformations of heart

CCI Edits

93583   01926, 0213T, 0216T, 0228T, 0230T, 11000-11006, 11042-11047, 12001-12007, 12011-12057, 13100-13133, 13151-13153, 33210-33211, 34812, 35201-35206, 35226-35236, 35256-35266, 35286, 36000, 36010, 36013-36015, 36400-36410, 36420-36430, 36440, 36555-36556, 36568-36569, 36591-36592, 36600, 36640, 43752, 51701-51703, 62320-62327, 64400-64410, 64413-64435, 64445-64450, 64461-64463, 64479-64530, 69990, 76000-76001, 77001-77002, 92012-92014, 93000-93010, 93040-93042, 93312-93318, 93355-93461, 93463, 93503-93505, 93530-93533, 93561-93563, 93565-93566, 94002, 94200, 94250, 94680-94690, 94770, 95812-95816, 95819, 95822, 95829, 95955, 96360-96368, 96372-96377, 97597-97598, 97602, 99155-99157, 99211-99223, 99231-99255, 99291-99292, 99304-99310, 99315-99316, 99334-99337, 99347-99350, 99374-99375, 99377-99378, 99446-99449, G0463, G0471

Case Example

Procedure:
The patient was prepped and draped in typical sterile fashion. Vascular access was achieved via the right femoral vein and the right femoral artery. A temporary right ventricular balloon-tipped pacing catheter was placed within the right ventricular apex. Via the arterial access, a 6-French guide catheter was directed using fluoroscopy to the left main coronary artery. A PT-2 hydrophilic coronary wire was advanced into the **second, large septal perforator**. A small over-the-wire balloon was advanced into the proximal portion of the **S2 branch** and inflated. Contrast media was injected to confirm balloon position. The wire was then removed and **2cc of 98% desiccated ethanol were delivered slowly through the balloon**. This was repeated for the **S1 branch**. Final angiography confirmed brisk flow into the LAD with **complete obliteration of the S1 and S2 branches**. A dual lumen pigtail catheter was then advanced across the aortic valve, and pressure gradients were measured with satisfactory results. All catheters were removed and hemostasis was achieved.

CPT/HCPCS Codes Reported:
93583

Other HCPCS Codes Reported:
C1769, C1887, C1725

Catheter Delivered Implantation of Aortic Valve Prostheses (TAVR)

33361	Transcatheter aortic valve replacement (TAVR/TAVI) with prosthetic valve; percutaneous femoral artery approach
33362	open femoral artery approach
33363	open axillary artery approach
33364	open iliac artery approach
33366	transapical exposure (eg, left thoracotomy)

These procedures report the insertion of an aortic valve prosthesis in patients not able to undergo traditional open surgical methods of valve replacement. The endovascular approach involves using a percutaneous approach such as femoral artery and guiding the catheter-loaded valve prosthesis through the aorta to the location of the aortic valve. The transapical approach involves making a mini-thoracotomy to expose the left ventricle. A puncture is made and a catheter inserted and then directed across the aortic valve.

Coding Tips

1. These codes do not include cardiac catheterization when performed for diagnostic purposes prior to aortic valve placement. See codes 93451–93472. Modifier XS will need to be appended to cardiac catheterization procedures performed during these aortic valve procedures.

2. All other catheterization is included and not reported separately.

3. Temporary pacing (33210) is not reported separately.

4. Fluoroscopy is included and not reported separately.

5. All contrast injections and imaging guidance related to the implantation procedure are included and not reported separately.

6. For open thoracic approach, see 33365. For a transapical approach (mini-thoracotomy), use 33366.

7. These codes have been granted inpatient-only status by CMS and are not payable if performed as outpatient.

8. Conscious sedation is not included in these codes. Separately report 99151–99157 per payer policy and coding guidelines. Hospitals may choose to include the costs associated with the service as part of the procedure rather than reporting them separately.

Facility HCPCS Coding

HCPCS Level II codes are used to report some supplies provided during the procedure. Hospitals should report separately supplies used during endovascular heart valve implantation. Refer to chapter 1 for more information regarding appropriate billing of supplies. Refer to the list of current codes in appendix B.

Transcatheter Aortic Valve Replacement (TAVR)

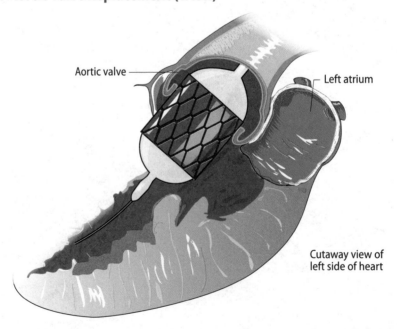

Aortic valve

Left atrium

Cutaway view of left side of heart

Procedure HCPCS Codes

There are no procedure HCPCS codes applicable to these procedures.

ICD-10-CM Coding

I06.0	Rheumatic aortic stenosis
I06.2	Rheumatic aortic stenosis with insufficiency
I08.0	Rheumatic disorders of both mitral and aortic valves
I08.8	Other rheumatic multiple valve diseases
I35.0	Nonrheumatic aortic (valve) stenosis
I35.1	Nonrheumatic aortic (valve) insufficiency
I35.2	Nonrheumatic aortic (valve) stenosis with insufficiency
I35.8	Other nonrheumatic aortic valve disorders
I35.9	Nonrheumatic aortic valve disorder, unspecified
Q23.0	Congenital stenosis of aortic valve

CCI Edits

33361 01920, 01924-01926, 0213T, 0216T, 11000-11006, 11042-11047, 12001-12007, 12011-12057, 13100-13133, 13151-13153, 20680, 21750, 32100, 32551, 32554-32557, 33140, 33210-33211, 33310-33315, 34812, 35201-35206, 35226-35236, 35256-35266, 35286, 36000, 36005, 36120-36140, 36160-36200, 36245-36247, 36400-36410, 36420-36430, 36440, 36500, 36591-36592, 36600-36640, 39000-39010, 43752, 51701-51703, 62320-62327, 64400-64410, 64413-64435, 64445-64450, 64461-64463, 64479-64530, 69990, 71034, 75600, 75605, 75625, 75630, 75710, 75716, 75741, 75743, 75746, 75756, 75774, 75893, 76000-76001, 76496, 76937, 76942, 76970, 76998, 77002, 78635, 92012-92014, 92961, 92986, 93000-93010, 93040-93042, 93306-93308, 93312-93314, 93318-93325, 93355-93461, 93503, 93530-93533, 93561-93565, 93567, 93591-93592, 94002, 94200, 94250, 94680-94690, 94770, 95812-95816, 95819, 95822, 95829, 95955, 96360-96368, 96372-96377, 97597-97598, 97602, 99155-99157, 99211-99223, 99231-99255, 99291-99292, 99304-99310, 99315-99316, 99334-99337, 99347-99350, 99374-99375, 99377-99378, 99446-99449, 99495-99496, G0269, G0463, G0471, G9157, J0670, J1644, J2001

33362 01920, 01924-01926, 0213T, 0216T, 11000-11006, 11042-11047, 12001-12007, 12011-12057, 13100-13133, 13151-13153, 20680, 21750, 32100, 32551, 32554-32557, 33140, 33210-33211, 33310-33315, 33361, 34812, 35201-35206, 35226-35236, 35256-35266, 35286, 36000, 36005, 36120-36140, 36160-36200, 36245-36247, 36400-36410, 36420-36430, 36440, 36500, 36591-36592, 36600-36640, 39000-39010, 43752, 51701-51703, 62320-62327, 64400-64410, 64413-64435, 64445-64450, 64461-64463, 64479-64530, 69990, 71034, 75600, 75605, 75625, 75630, 75710, 75716, 75741, 75743, 75746, 75756, 75774, 75893, 76000-76001, 76496, 76937, 76942, 76970, 76998, 77002, 78635, 92012-92014, 92961, 92986, 93000-93010, 93040-93042, 93306-93308, 93312-93314, 93318-93325, 93355-93461, 93503, 93530-93533, 93561-93565, 93567, 93591-93592, 94002, 94200, 94250, 94680-94690, 94770, 95812-95816, 95819, 95822, 95829, 95955, 96360-96368, 96372-96377, 97597-97598, 97602, 99155-99157, 99211-99223, 99231-99255, 99291-99292, 99304-99310, 99315-99316, 99334-99337, 99347-99350, 99374-99375, 99377-99378, 99446-99449, 99495-99496, G0269, G0463, G0471, G9157, J0670, J1644, J2001

33363 01920, 01924-01926, 0213T, 0216T, 11000-11006, 11042-11047, 12001-12007, 12011-12057, 13100-13133, 13151-13153, 20680, 21750, 32100, 32551, 32554-32557, 33140, 33210-33211, 33310-33315, 33361-33362, 34812, 34834, 35201-35206, 35226-35236, 35256-35266, 35286, 36000, 36005, 36120-36140, 36160-36200, 36215-36217, 36400-36410, 36420-36430, 36440, 36500, 36591-36592, 36600-36640, 39000-39010, 43752, 51701-51703, 62320-62327, 64400-64410, 64413-64435, 64445-64450, 64461-64463, 64479-64530, 69990, 71034, 75600, 75605, 75625, 75630, 75710, 75716, 75741, 75743, 75746, 75756, 75774, 75893, 76000-76001, 76496, 76937, 76942, 76970, 76998, 77002, 78635, 92012-92014, 92961, 92986, 93000-93010, 93040-93042, 93306-93308, 93312-93314, 93318-93325, 93355-93461, 93503, 93530-93533, 93561-93565, 93567, 93591-93592, 94002, 94200, 94250, 94680-94690, 94770, 95812-95816, 95819, 95822, 95829, 95955, 96360-96368, 96372-96377, 97597-97598, 97602, 99155-99157, 99211-99223, 99231-99255, 99291-99292, 99304-99310, 99315-99316, 99334-99337, 99347-99350, 99374-99375, 99377-99378, 99446-99449, 99495-99496, G0269, G0463, G0471, G9157, J0670, J1644, J2001

33364 01920, 01924-01926, 0213T, 0216T, 11000-11006, 11042-11047, 12001-12007, 12011-12057, 13100-13133, 13151-13153, 20680, 21750, 32100, 32551, 32554-32557, 33140, 33210-33211, 33310-33315, 33361-33363, 33417, 34812, 34820, 34833, 35201-35206, 35221-35236, 35251-35266, 35281-35286, 36000, 36005, 36120-36140, 36160-36200, 36245-36247, 36400-36410, 36420-36430, 36440, 36500, 36591-36592, 36600-36640, 39000-39010, 43752, 51701-51703, 62320-62327, 64400-64410, 64413-64435, 64445-64450, 64461-64463, 64479-64530, 69990, 71034, 75600, 75605, 75625, 75630, 75710, 75716, 75741, 75743, 75746, 75756, 75774, 75893, 76000-76001, 76496, 76937, 76942, 76970, 76998, 77002, 78635, 92012-92014, 92961, 92986, 93000-93010, 93040-93042, 93306-93308, 93312-93314, 93318-93325, 93355-93461, 93503, 93530-93533, 93561-93565, 93567, 93591-93592, 94002, 94200, 94250, 94680-94690, 94770, 95812-95816, 95819, 95822, 95829, 95955, 96360-96368, 96372-96377, 97597-97598, 97602, 99155-99157, 99211-99223, 99231-99255, 99291-99292, 99304-99310, 99315-99316, 99334-99337, 99347-99350, 99374-99375, 99377-99378, 99446-99449, 99495-99496, G0269, G0463, G0471, G9157, J0670, J1644, J2001

33366   01920, 01925, 0213T, 0216T, 0228T, 0230T, 11000-11006, 11042-11047, 12001-12007, 12011-12057, 13100-13133, 13151-13153, 20680, 21750, 32100, 32551, 32554-32557, 33140, 33254-33256, 33310-33315, 33361-33365, 33390, 33404-33406, 33410-33413, 33417, 34812, 35211-35216, 35241-35246, 35271-35276, 36000, 36010-36014, 36120-36140, 36160-36200, 36215-36217, 36245-36247, 36400-36410, 36420-36430, 36440, 36500, 36591-36592, 36600-36640, 39000-39010, 43752, 51701-51703, 62320-62327, 64400-64410, 64413-64435, 64445-64450, 64461-64463, 64479-64530, 69990, 71034, 75600, 75605, 75625, 75630, 75710, 75716, 75741, 75743, 75746, 75756, 75774, 76000-76001, 76496, 76937, 76942, 76970, 76998, 77002, 78635, 92012-92014, 92961, 92986, 93000-93010, 93040-93042, 93306-93308, 93312-93314, 93318-93325, 93355, 93452-93453, 93458-93461, 93531-93533, 93561-93565, 93567, 93591-93592, 94002, 94200, 94250, 94680-94690, 94770, 95812-95816, 95819, 95822, 95829, 95955, 96360-96368, 96372-96377, 97597-97598, 97602, 99155-99157, 99211-99223, 99231-99255, 99291-99292, 99304-99310, 99315-99316, 99334-99337, 99347-99350, 99374-99375, 99377-99378, 99446-99449, G0269, G0463, G0471, G9157, J0670, J1644, J2001

Case Example #1

Procedure:
The patient was brought to the operating suite and administered general anesthesia. The patient was prepped and draped in typical sterile fashion. Vascular access was obtained via percutaneous access into the right femoral artery and vein; **via open cutdown approach into the left femoral artery**. A temporary ventricular pacemaker was inserted using fluoroscopic guidance. A catheter was advanced to the aortic arch, and a bolus injection of contrast media was performed using 3-D CT to obtain deployment angles for the valve placement. **Using the left femoral access**, a guidewire was inserted and advanced to the proximal descending thoracic aorta. Dilation of the femoral and iliac vessels was performed step-wise to 22-French. A 22-French introducer sheath was placed over the wire and into the abdominal aorta. **We then performed balloon valvuloplasty of the aortic valve** using temporary rapid ventricular pacing. The balloon was removed, and the **transcatheter valve was advanced** through the sheath and **positioned in the aortic root**. Valve positioning was confirmed by angiography. Using temporary ventricular pacing, the valve was deployed. Intraoperative transesophageal echocardiography was then performed, confirming good seating of the valve. The catheters were removed and hemostasis achieved by arteriotomy.

CPT/HCPCS Codes Reported:
33362

Other HCPCS Codes Reported:
This code has inpatient-only status. Hospitals are encouraged to separately report all applicable devices used for the procedure, however, no HCPCS codes are necessary.

Case Example #2

Procedure:
The patient was brought to the operating suite and administered general anesthesia. The patient was prepped and draped in typical sterile fashion. We cannulated both groins, placed a pacing wire and pigtail catheter into the aorta. After orientation was obtained, we then made a **skin incision in the chest just below the right breast**. We opened up the chest and fixed the lung, which was densely adhered to the pericardium. We placed pursestrings in the apex of the heart after we had marked it, checking it for location with the echocardiogram. We then placed a **large bore needle in the heart and placed a wire across** the valve. A 7-French catheter was then placed. We then advanced a JL4 catheter into the aorta and advanced the wire down to the ascending aorta; this was changed out over superstiff wire. The large dilator of the valve was placed into the apex of the heart. When this was placed we then placed a **valvuloplasty balloon across the valve**. We began pacing and blew the balloon up. We had some mild AI at this time. A **20 Sapien valve was selected**. We placed it across the valve and began rapid pacing. We insufflated under standard protocols very slowly and got excellent position. We pulled the balloon back at this time as we stopped pacing and checked for leaks. We then pulled the wires back and removed the sheath. We began pacing as we tightened up both sutures. Excellent hemostasis was obtained. A #24 chest tube was placed and secured in place with 2-0 silk suture. The muscle and deep layers were closed followed by the subcutaneous layers. The patient tolerated the procedure well.

CPT/HCPCS Codes Reported:
33366

Other HCPCS Codes Reported:
This code has inpatient-only status. Hospitals are encouraged to separately report all applicable devices used for the procedure; however, no HCPCS codes are necessary.

Catheter Delivered Implantation of Pulmonary Valve Prostheses (TPVI)

33477   **Transcatheter pulmonary valve implantation, percutaneous approach, including pre-stenting of the valve delivery site, when performed**

Percutaneous placement of a prosthetic pulmonary valve is used primarily to treat patients with stenosis or regurgitation of a previously repaired right ventricular outflow tract (RVOT). The patient is prepped with general anesthesia in addition to endotracheal intubation. The provider inserts a needle through the skin and into an underlying vein, usually a lower extremity vein, although jugular access is also utilized. Angiography and hemodynamic studies are performed, and a guidewire is threaded through the needle and advanced into the pulmonary artery. A balloon is inflated in the RVOT conduit to evaluate for coronary compression, and an aortogram is performed to visualize the coronary arteries. Pre-stenting is commonly performed with a covered bare metal stent to decrease the risk of fractured stents, and more than one stent may be required. The needle is removed, and a catheter carrying the prosthetic valve is inserted. The prosthesis is positioned over the diseased pulmonary valve, and a balloon is inflated, deploying the prosthetic valve in place. Angiography and hemodynamic evaluations are repeated. The catheter is removed, and pressure is applied to stop bleeding at the access site. A single suture may provide hemostasis at the venous access.

Coding Tips

1.   Report only once per session.

2.   Cardiac catheterization necessary to complete the pulmonary valve procedure is included. However, diagnostic cardiac catheterization done for purposes other than placing the pulmonary valve may be separately reported. Modifier XS will be needed in these situations.

3.   Percutaneous access, sheath insertion, positioning, repositioning, and deployment of the device are all included in the code.

4.   Balloon angioplasty, valvuloplasty, and stent deployment within the treatment zone are all included.

5.   Pulmonary angiography, 92997 or 92998, is reported when performed at a site separate from the prosthetic valve insertion site.

6.   Stenting may be reported with 37236 or 37237 when performed at a site separate from the prosthetic valve insertion site.

7.   Diagnostic right and left heart catheterization may be additionally reported *provided* it meets the criteria for a separate diagnostic service discussed in chapter 1. Modifier XS will be required.

8.   Transcatheter ventricular support may be necessary during the procedure. This support is separately reportable using the correct codes (e.g., 33900–33993 among others).

9.   Report any applicable HCPCS Level II codes for devices and contrast media used. Refer to the HCPCS section for possible codes.

10. Conscious sedation is not included in these codes. Separately report 99151–99157 per payer policy and coding guidelines. Hospitals may choose to include the costs associated with the service as part of the procedure rather than reporting them separately.

Facility HCPCS Coding

HCPCS Level II codes are used to report some supplies provided during the procedure. Hospitals should report separately any supplies used during endovascular heart valve implantation. Refer to chapter 1 for more information regarding appropriate supply billing. Refer to the list of current codes in appendix B.

Transcatheter Pulmonary Valve Implantation (TPVI)

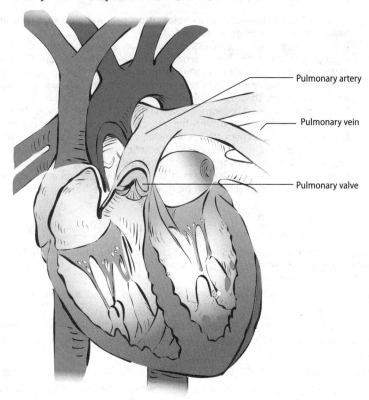

ICD-10-CM Coding

A52.Ø3	Syphilitic endocarditis
I33.9	Acute and subacute endocarditis, unspecified
I37.Ø	Nonrheumatic pulmonary valve stenosis
I37.1	Nonrheumatic pulmonary valve insufficiency
I37.2	Nonrheumatic pulmonary valve stenosis with insufficiency
I37.8	Other nonrheumatic pulmonary valve disorders
I37.9	Nonrheumatic pulmonary valve disorder, unspecified
I97.Ø	Postcardiotomy syndrome
I97.11Ø	Postprocedural cardiac insufficiency following cardiac surgery
I97.13Ø	Postprocedural heart failure following cardiac surgery
I97.19Ø	Other postprocedural cardiac functional disturbances following cardiac surgery
Q2Ø.Ø	Common arterial trunk
Q2Ø.1	Double outlet right ventricle
Q2Ø.5	Discordant atrioventricular connection
Q21.3	Tetralogy of Fallot
Q22.Ø	Pulmonary valve atresia
Q22.1	Congenital pulmonary valve stenosis
Q22.2	Congenital pulmonary valve insufficiency
Q22.3	Other congenital malformations of pulmonary valve
Q24.3	Pulmonary infundibular stenosis

CCI Edits

33477   01920, 01924, 01926, 0213T, 0216T, 0228T, 0230T, 12001-12007, 12011-12057, 13100-13133, 13151-13153, 32554-32557, 33210-33211, 33254-33256, 33310-33315, 33470-33471, 35201-35207, 35211-35286, 36000, 36010, 36013-36015, 36400-36410, 36420-36430, 36440, 36500, 36555-36556, 36568-36569, 36600, 36640, 37236, 37238-37239, 43752, 51701-51703, 62320-62327, 64400-64410, 64413-64435, 64445-64450, 64461-64463, 64479-64530, 69990, 71034, 75741, 75743, 75746, 75825, 75827, 75893, 76000-76001, 76496, 76942, 76970, 76998, 77002, 92012-92014, 92961, 92990, 92997-93010, 93040-93042, 93306-93308, 93312-93325, 93355-93461, 93503, 93530-93533, 93561-93564, 93566-93568, 94002, 94200, 94250, 94680-94690, 94770, 95812-95816, 95819, 95822, 95829, 95955, 96360-96368, 96372-96377, 99155-99157, 99211-99223, 99231-99255, 99291-99292, 99304-99310, 99315-99316, 99334-99337, 99347-99350, 99374-99375, 99377-99378, 99446-99449, G0269, G9157, J1644

Case Example

The patient was brought to the operating suite and administered general anesthesia. The patient was prepped and draped in typical sterile fashion. **Percutaneous access was made in the right femoral vein** and right femoral artery. Sheaths were placed in each vessel. An occlusion balloon was advanced via the venous access and directed to the right ventricular outflow tract. A JL4 coronary catheter was advanced via the arterial access. Using biplane fluoro, the balloon catheter was inflated, and coronary angiography was performed simultaneously to measure the distance between. This measured 12 mm and was deemed to have adequate clearance. The **porcine valve** delivery set was prepped. A stiff guidewire was directed through the inferior vena cava. The pulmonary valve delivery set was directed over the stiff guidewire. Intracardiac echo and fluoroscopy were used to **direct the valve into the RVOT** and deployed. Intracardiac echo and coronary angiography were performed to evaluate the valve patency. There was no regurgitation or perivalvular leak detected. All catheters were removed and hemostasis was achieved using a closure device.

CPT/HCPCS Codes Reported:
33477

Other HCPCS Codes Reported:
This code has inpatient-only status. Hospitals are encouraged to separately report all applicable devices used for the procedure; however, no HCPCS codes are necessary.

Percutaneous Transcatheter Closure of Left Atrial Appendage

33340   **Percutaneous transcatheter closure of the left atrial appendage with endocardial implant, including fluoroscopy, transseptal puncture, catheter placement(s), left atrial angiography, left atrial appendage angiography, radiological supervision and interpretation**

The purpose of this procedure is to prevent strokes in patients with atrial fibrillation.

A small incision is made over the right femoral vein and a catheter is passed into the right atrium. The septum is punctured and the catheter is passed into the left atrium. The LAA device loaded with the implant is then guided into the left atrium and placed into the left atrial appendage. The device is deployed and the catheters are removed.

Coding Tips

1. Do not also report CPT code 93462. Left heart catheterization by transseptal puncture is part of this procedure.
2. Separately report cardiac catheterization procedures for indications distinct from the LAA closure procedure.
3. If catheterization is performed by methods other than transseptal approach, these procedures may be separately reported for indications distinct from the LAA closure procedure.
4. Right heart catheterization may be separately reported only for indications distinct from the LAA closure procedure.
5. Catheter placement is included and is not separately reported.
6. Left atrial angiography is included and is not separately reported.
7. Conscious sedation is not included in these codes. Separately report 99151–99157 per payer policy and coding guidelines. Hospitals may choose to include the costs associated with the service as part of the procedure rather than reporting them separately.
8. This code has been granted in-patient only status and is not payable if performed as an outpatient.

Facility HCPCS Coding

Hospitals should separately report supplies and implanted devices used for this procedure. Refer to chapter 1 for more information regarding appropriate billing of supplies.

ICD-10-CM Coding

I48.Ø	Paroxysmal atrial fibrillation
I48.1	Persistent atrial fibrillation
I48.2	Chronic atrial fibrillation
I48.3	Typical atrial flutter
I48.4	Atypical atrial flutter
I48.91	Unspecified atrial fibrillation
I48.92	Unspecified atrial flutter

CCI Edits

33340   0213T, 0216T, 0228T, 0230T, 12001-12007, 12011-12057, 13100-13133, 13151-13153, 32551, 32556-32557, 33020, 33140-33141, 33210-33211, 33310-33315, 35201-35207, 35211-35286, 36000, 36400-36410, 36420-36430, 36440, 36591-36592, 36600, 36640, 43752, 51701-51703, 62320-62327, 64400-64410, 64413-64435, 64445-64450, 64461-64463, 64479-64530, 69990, 92012-92014, 92960-92961, 93000-93010, 93040-93042, 93318, 93355-93453, 93456, 93458-93462, 93530-93533, 94002, 94200, 94250, 94680-94690, 94770, 95812-95816, 95819, 95822, 95829, 95955, 96360-96368, 96372, 96374-96377, 96523, 99155-99157, 99211-99223, 99231-99255, 99291-99292, 99304-99310, 99315-99316, 99334-99337, 99347-99350, 99374-99375, 99377-99378

Case Example

Procedure:
Patient was prepped and draped in typical sterile fashion. Under general anesthesia, the TEE probe was inserted and directed to image and measure the LAA. **Vascular access was obtained in the right femoral vein and the left radial artery.** Sheaths were placed in each access. Under TEE guidance, **transseptal puncture was performed** using the Brocken-brough needle and an 8-French transseptal sheath. Left atrial pressures were taken. A stiff J-tipped guidewire was introduced and positioned in the left pulmonary vein. A pigtail catheter was advanced into the LAA. The access sheath was advanced over the pigtail. **Angiograms were obtained** for structural measurements. The appropriate sized device was selected and prepped. **The access sheath was advanced into the dominant lobe of the LAA.** Once in proper position, the pigtail catheter was removed. The **device was delivered using the preloaded catheter**. Following confirmation of correct position, the device was deployed. Final angiography and TEE imaging showed the absence of residual shunt in the LAA. All catheters were removed, and hemostasis was achieved in both access sites.

CPT/HCPCS Codes Reported:
33340

Other HCPCS Codes Reported:
This code has inpatient-only status. Hospitals are encouraged to separately report all applicable devices used for the procedure; however, no HCPCS codes are necessary.

Transcatheter Closure of Paravalvular Leak

Paravalvular regurgitation is a complication of valve replacement surgery. Percutaneous repair of this leak is an alternative therapy to avoid the high risk of open surgical repair.

93590   **Percutaneous transcatheter closure of paravalvular leak; initial occlusion device, mitral valve**

93591   **initial occlusion device, aortic valve**

93592   **each additional occlusion device (List separately in addition to code for primary procedure)**

Percutaneous transcatheter closure of a paravalvular leak (PVL) in the mitral or aortic valve can be achieved by antegrade or retrograde approach. A transesophageal echocardiogram (TEE) for a mitral valve leak or a transthoracic echocardiogram (TTE) for an aortic leak was performed within the previous six months, earlier if the patient was symptomatic. A retrograde transfemoral approach is performed utilizing a catheter and guidewire. Upon crossing the leak, the wire is removed and a stiff wire is inserted along with the device delivery system consisting of a guide catheter or sheath. The wire is removed, allowing for advancement and deployment of an occlusion device. When support becomes an issue, a transseptal access and snare may be employed to establish a rail. This entails the snaring of the initial wire within the left atrium or the formation of an apical ventricular rail by left ventricular puncture with the wire crossing the apex. In mitral PVL, if this approach does not achieve the desired results, an antegrade transseptal approach may be used. Upon completion of the procedure for 93590, TEE should indicate fluent leaflets, clear pulmonary veins, and if anterior leak, clear mitral valve. In 93591, the physician must evaluate that the coronary ostia is not covered and leaflets are fluent. For both procedures, the device deployed depends upon the defect size. Many closure devices are currently used in these procedures, such as embolization coils, double-umbrella devices, occluders, and plugs approved for other specific defects, and may be suitable in most cases. However for PVLs they are limited by size, shape, specific characteristics, and features of delivery system.

Coding Tips

1. These codes include percutaneous access.

2. These codes include fluoroscopy when used to perform the closure procedure.

3. Code 93590 includes transseptal puncture.

4. Code 93590 includes left heart catheterization when performed. Do not also report code 93452, 93453, 93458, 93459, 93460, 93461, 93531–93533, or 93565.

5. Code 93591 includes supravalvular aortography. Do not also report 93567.

6. Code 93591 includes left heart catheterization. Do not also report 93452, 93453, 93458–93461, 93531–93533, or 93565.

7. If performed, transapical left heart catheterization may be separately reported using code 93452 in addition to 93591.

8. Transesophageal echocardiography may be separately reported using code 93662.

9. Right heart catheterization and diagnostic coronary angiography may be additionally reported only when performed for diagnostic reasons unrelated to the paravalvular leak. Modifier 59 will be required.

10. Code 93592 is an add-on code and is reported in addition to 93590 and 93591 when more than one device is required to complete the closure.

11. Conscious sedation is not included in these codes. Separately report 99151–99157 per payer policy and coding guidelines. Hospitals may choose to include the costs associated with the service as part of the procedure rather than reporting them separately.

Facility HCPCS Coding

Hospitals should separately report supplies and implanted devices used for this procedure. Refer to chapter 1 for more information regarding appropriate billing of supplies. Possible HCPCS codes for this procedure could include but are not limited to:

C1769   Guidewire

C1887   Catheter, guiding

C1893   Introducer/sheath, guiding, intracardiac electrophysiological, fixed-curve, other than peel-away

ICD-10-CM Coding

T82.03XA   Leakage of heart valve prosthesis, initial encounter

T82.09XA   Other mechanical complication of heart valve prosthesis, initial encounter

T82.223A   Leakage of biological heart valve graft, initial encounter

T82.228A   Other mechanical complication of biological heart valve graft, initial encounter

CCI Edits

93590   01920, 01924-01926, 0213T, 0216T, 0228T, 0230T, 11000-11006, 11042-11047, 12001-12007, 12011-12057, 13100-13133, 13151-13153, 20680, 21750, 32100, 32551, 32554-32557, 33140, 33210-33211, 33310-33315, 34812, 35201-35206, 35226-35236, 35256-35266, 35286, 36000, 36005, 36120-36140, 36160-36200, 36215-36217, 36245-36247, 36400-36410, 36420-36430, 36440, 36500, 36591-36592, 36600-36640, 39000-39010, 43752, 51701-51703, 62320-62327, 64400-64410, 64413-64435, 64445-64450, 64461-64463, 64479-64530, 69990, 71034, 75600, 75605, 75625, 75630, 75710, 75716, 75741, 75743, 75746, 75756, 75774, 75893, 76000-76001, 76496, 76937, 76942, 76970, 76998, 77002, 78635, 92012-92014, 92961, 92986, 93000-93010, 93040-93042, 93306-93308, 93312-93314, 93318-93325, 93355-93462, 93503, 93530-93533, 93561-93565, 93567, 93591, 94002, 94200, 94250, 94680-94690, 94770, 95812-95816, 95819, 95822, 95829, 95955, 96360-96368, 96372-96377, 96523, 97597-97598, 97602, 99155-99157, 99211-99223, 99231-99255, 99291-99292, 99304-99310, 99315-99316, 99334-99337, 99347-99350, 99374-99375, 99377-99378, 99446-99449, 99495-99496, G0269, G0463, G0471, G9157, J0670, J1644, J2001

93591   01920, 01924-01926, 0213T, 0216T, 0228T, 0230T, 11000-11006, 11042-11047, 12001-12007, 12011-12057, 13100-13133, 13151-13153, 20680, 21750, 32100, 32551, 32554-32557, 33140, 33210-33211, 33310-33315, 33367-33368, 34812, 35201-35206, 35226-35236, 35256-35266, 35286, 36000, 36005, 36120-36140, 36160-36200, 36215-36217, 36245-36247, 36400-36410, 36420-36430, 36440, 36500, 36591-36592, 36600-36640, 39000-39010, 43752, 51701-51703, 62320-62327, 64400-64410, 64413-64435, 64445-64450, 64461-64463, 64479-64530, 69990, 71034, 75600, 75605, 75625, 75630, 75710, 75716, 75741, 75743, 75746, 75756, 75774, 75893, 76000-76001, 76496, 76937, 76942, 76970, 76998, 77002, 78635, 92012-92014, 92961, 92986, 93000-93010, 93040-93042, 93306-93308, 93312-93314, 93318-93325, 93355-93461, 93503, 93530-93533, 93561-93565, 93567, 94002, 94200, 94250, 94680-94690, 94770, 95812-95816, 95819, 95822, 95829, 95955, 96360-96368, 96372-96377, 96523, 97597-97598, 97602, 99155-99157, 99211-99223, 99231-99255, 99291-99292, 99304-99310, 99315-99316, 99334-99337, 99347-99350, 99374-99375, 99377-99378, 99446-99449, 99495-99496, G0269, G0463, G0471, G9157, J0670, J1644, J2001

93592   01920, 01924-01926, 0213T, 0216T, 0228T, 0230T, 11000-11006, 11042-11047, 12001-12007, 12011-12057, 13100-13133, 13151-13153, 20680, 21750, 32100, 32551, 32554-32557, 33140, 33210-33211, 33310-33315, 33367-33368, 34812, 35201-35206, 35226-35236, 35256-35266, 35286, 36000, 36005, 36120-36140, 36160-36200, 36215-36217, 36245-36247, 36400-36410, 36420-36430, 36440, 36500, 36591-36592, 36600-36640, 39000-39010, 43752, 51701-51703, 62320-62327, 64400-64410, 64413-64435, 64445-64450, 64461-64463, 64479-64530, 69990, 71034, 75600, 75605, 75625, 75630, 75710, 75716, 75741, 75743, 75746, 75756, 75774, 75893, 76000-76001, 76496, 76937, 76942, 76970, 76998, 77002, 78635, 92012-92014, 92961, 92986, 93000-93010, 93040-93042, 93306-93308, 93312-93314, 93318-93325, 93355-93461, 93503, 93530-93533, 93561-93565, 93567, 94002, 94200, 94250, 94680-94690, 94770, 95812-95816, 95819, 95822, 95829, 95955, 96360-96368, 96372-96377, 96523, 97597-97598, 97602, 99155-99157, 99211-99223, 99231-99255, 99291-99292, 99304-99310, 99315-99316, 99334-99337, 99347-99350, 99374-99375, 99377-99378, 99446-99449, 99495-99496, G0269, G0463, G0471, G9157, J0670, J1644, J2001

Case Example

Procedure:
The procedure was performed using deep sedation. TEE was used to assist in the procedure and **confirmed** moderate to severe aortic **paravalvular regurgitation**. Right femoral and right radial accesses were obtained using 6-French sheaths. Aortography was obtained via the radial access. This also demonstrated the PVL. A glidewire was inserted and advanced across the PVL. The JR4 guide catheter was advanced through the valve. A 90cm Destination sheath was telescoped over the guide catheter and across the valve. Using TEE and fluoro, an 8 mm **vascular plug was deployed across the PVL**. A tug test was performed. Final TEE imaging showed a well deployed plug into the paravalvular aortic defect with significant decreased regurgitation. The catheters were removed and hemostasis achieved.

CPT/HCPCS Codes Reported:
93591

Chapter 13: Pacemaker Insertion and Pacing Cardioverter-Defibrillator Procedures

General Guidelines

Pacemaker and implantable cardioverter-defibrillator (ICD) systems consist of the following components:

- The generator, also commonly referred to as the battery
- One or more electrodes, also commonly referred to as leads

The generator is surgically placed under the skin where the surgeon creates a "pocket" for it to reside. Generators can be single-chamber, dual-chamber, or multiple-chamber devices based upon the patient's condition. Single-chamber systems include the generator and one electrode, while dual-chamber systems involve two electrodes. New bi-ventricular devices (bi-V) typically involve three electrodes.

ICD devices also include a generator and electrodes. Coding is based upon the type of device inserted and, therefore, it is important for the documentation to include the specific type of device used, including the model number.

Coding is also based on the procedure performed. Pacemaker CPT® codes consist of insertion, replacement, upgrade, reposition, repair, or removal procedures. They can involve the generator only, the leads only, or both the generator and the leads. Code changes implemented in 2012 now report generator replacement with one code rather than two separate codes as previously reported. Codes are reported based on whether or not leads are replaced. Please refer to the sections below for details regarding appropriate reporting of these procedures.

Procedures performed in hospital cardiac catheterization labs today are typically limited to the transvenous approach. Epicardial leads involve a thoracotomy and are usually done in the operative suite. However, with the advent of recent endoscopic devices, it is possible for these to also be done in the cardiac cath lab setting. Lead removal is also primarily done by transvenous approach in the cath lab. If, however, the leads cannot be removed by transvenous approach, a thoracotomy may be necessary. Codes are available to report the type of approach used.

Fluoroscopy guidance is included in the pacemaker/ICD codes and is not separately reported.

For hospitals, it is important to have information about the device(s) implanted and/or removed. Device edits exist for nearly all of the procedures discussed in this chapter. Claim edits will result when the appropriate device/procedure combination is not present and will cause claim submission delays and subsequently payment delays.

Additionally, facilities must know if a replacement procedure is performed due to a recalled device. Hospitals are required to report the device credit amount on the claim with value code "FD." Affected devices are listed in the following table:

Devices Applicable for No Cost/Full Credit/Partial Credit Payment Adjustment

Device HCPCS Code	Short Descriptor
C1721	AICD, dual chamber
C1722	AICD, single chamber
C1777	Lead, AICD, endo single coil
C1779	Lead, pacemaker, transvenous VDD
C1785	Pacemaker, dual, rate-responsive
C1786	Pacemaker, single, rate-responsive
C1882	AICD, other than single/dual
C1895	Lead, AICD, endo dual coil
C1896	Lead, AICD, non single/dual
C1898	Lead, pacemaker, other than trans
C1899	Lead, pacemaker, AICD combination
C1900	Lead, coronary sinus
C2619	Pacemaker, dual, non rate-responsive
C2620	Pacemaker, single, non rate-responsive
C2621	Pacemaker, other than single/dual

Epicardial Electrode Insertion—Permanent Pacemaker or ICD (Cardioverter-Defibrillator)

33202   **Insertion of epicardial electrode(s); open incision (eg, thoracotomy, median sternotomy, subxiphoid approach)**

The physician places one or more electrical leads on the outside of the heart (epicardial electrodes) by open chest incision. The incision can be in the middle of the chest (midline sternotomy), a vertical incision just below the ribcage (subxiphoid), or between the ribs on the left side of the body (thoracotomy). The chest cavity is opened. After the heart is exposed, electrodes are affixed to the appropriate areas of the heart muscle. The electrodes are tested and then tunneled under the coastal margin to the upper abdomen to a pulse generator or to the infraclavicular area if the generator is in that area. The physician closes the incision in layered sutures.

33203   **endoscopic approach (eg, thoracoscopy, pericardioscopy)**

The physician places electrical leads on the outside of the heart (epicardial electrodes) using an endoscopic approach. Three trocars are placed in the left anterior chest wall and the left lung is collapsed. A small incision is made in the chest (thoracostomy) and a 12 mm trocar is placed. The thoracoscope (endoscope) is inserted. Two additional trocars are placed under thoracoscopic visualization in the inframammary anterolateral region. Under thoracoscopic guidance, the pericardium is grasped and incised. The lateral trocar is removed and the incision enlarged to allow passage of the epicardial electrode placement device and the electrodes through the intercostal space. The electrodes are placed intrapericardially. The pericardium is approximated with a single stitch to hold the electrodes in place. The electrodes are tested and then tunneled under the costal margin to the upper abdomen to a pulse generator or over the ribs to the infraclavicular area if the generator is in that area. The thoracoscope is removed and a thoracostomy tube is placed at this site. The lung is expanded and the incisions closed in layered suture.

Coding Tips

1. CPT code 33202 (Insertion of epicardial electrode[s] by open incision) may be reported in addition to other surgery requiring thoracotomy if performed. The code includes ICD electrode insertion.

2. CPT code 33203 (Insertion of epicardial electrode[s] by endoscopy) is reported when the epicardial electrode is inserted by endoscopy.

3. Report pacemaker or ICD generator insertion separately, see codes 33212, 33213, 33221, 33230, 33231, and 33240.

4. These procedures have been designated as inpatient only procedures. They are not covered if reported on an outpatient designated claim.

Facility HCPCS Coding

HCPCS Level II codes are used to report the supplies provided during the procedure. Hospitals should separately report supplies used during cardiac invasive procedures. Refer to chapter 1 for more information regarding appropriate billing of supplies. Refer to the list of current codes in appendix B.

C1777   Lead, cardioverter-defibrillator, endocardial single coil (implantable)

C1898   Lead, pacemaker, other than transvenous VDD single pass

C1899   Lead, pacemaker/cardioverter-defibrillator combination (implantable)

C1900   Lead, left ventricular coronary venous system

ICD-10-CM Coding

G90.01   Carotid sinus syncope

G90.09   Other idiopathic peripheral autonomic neuropathy

I44.0   Atrioventricular block, first degree

I44.1   Atrioventricular block, second degree

I44.2   Atrioventricular block, complete

I44.30   Unspecified atrioventricular block

I45.5   Other specified heart block

I45.6   Pre-excitation syndrome

I45.81   Long QT syndrome

I45.9   Conduction disorder, unspecified

I47.1   Supraventricular tachycardia

I48.0   Paroxysmal atrial fibrillation

I48.2   Chronic atrial fibrillation

I48.91   Unspecified atrial fibrillation

I49.2   Junctional premature depolarization

I49.5	Sick sinus syndrome
I49.8	Other specified cardiac arrhythmias
Q24.6	Congenital heart block
R00.1	Bradycardia, unspecified
T82.110A	Breakdown (mechanical) of cardiac electrode, initial encounter
T82.110D	Breakdown (mechanical) of cardiac electrode, subsequent encounter
T82.110S	Breakdown (mechanical) of cardiac electrode, sequela
T82.120A	Displacement of cardiac electrode, initial encounter
T82.120D	Displacement of cardiac electrode, subsequent encounter
T82.120S	Displacement of cardiac electrode, sequela
T82.190A	Other mechanical complication of cardiac electrode, initial encounter
T82.190D	Other mechanical complication of cardiac electrode, subsequent encounter
T82.190S	Other mechanical complication of cardiac electrode, sequela
T82.7XXA	Infection and inflammatory reaction due to other cardiac and vascular devices, implants and grafts, initial encounter
T82.7XXD	Infection and inflammatory reaction due to other cardiac and vascular devices, implants and grafts, subsequent encounter
T82.7XXS	Infection and inflammatory reaction due to other cardiac and vascular devices, implants and grafts, sequela
Z45.018	Encounter for adjustment and management of other part of cardiac pacemaker

CCI Edits

33202   00530, 00534, 00560, 0213T, 0216T, 0228T, 0230T, 0293T-0294T, 0302T-0306T, 0387T, 0389T-0391T, 0462T-0463T, 11000-11006, 11042-11047, 12001-12007, 12011-12057, 13100-13133, 13151-13153, 32551, 32556-32557, 33140-33141, 33210-33211, 33215, 36000, 36005, 36400-36410, 36420-36430, 36440, 36591-36592, 36600, 36640, 39000-39010, 43752, 51701-51703, 62320-62327, 64400-64410, 64413-64435, 64445-64450, 64461-64463, 64479-64530, 69990, 76000-76001, 76942, 76970, 76998, 77001-77002, 92012-92014, 92960-92961, 93000-93010, 93040-93042, 93260-93261, 93279-93299, 93318, 93355, 93600-93603, 93610-93612, 94002, 94200, 94250, 94680-94690, 94770, 95812-95816, 95819, 95822, 95829, 95955, 96360-96368, 96372, 96374-96377, 97597-97598, 97602, 99155-99157, 99211-99223, 99231-99255, 99291-99292, 99304-99310, 99315-99316, 99334-99337, 99347-99350, 99374-99375, 99377-99378, 99446-99449, 99495-99496, G0463, G0471

33203   00528-00529, 00540-00541, 0213T, 0216T, 0228T, 0230T, 0293T-0294T, 0302T-0306T, 0387T, 0389T-0391T, 0462T-0463T, 11000-11006, 11042-11047, 12001-12007, 12011-12057, 13100-13133, 13151-13153, 20101, 32551, 32556-32557, 32601, 32604, 32606-32609, 32659, 33140-33141, 33210-33211, 36000, 36005, 36400-36410, 36420-36430, 36440, 36591-36592, 36600, 36640, 43752, 51701-51703, 62320-62327, 64400-64410, 64413-64435, 64445-64450, 64461-64463, 64479-64530, 69990, 76000-76001, 76942, 76970, 76998, 77001-77002, 92012-92014, 92960-92961, 93000-93010, 93040-93042, 93260-93261, 93279-93299, 93318, 93355, 93600-93603, 93610-93612, 94002, 94200, 94250, 94680-94690, 94770, 95812-95816, 95819, 95822, 95829, 95955, 96360-96368, 96372, 96374-96377, 97597-97598, 97602, 99155-99157, 99211-99223, 99231-99255, 99291-99292, 99304-99310, 99315-99316, 99334-99337, 99347-99350, 99374-99375, 99377-99378, 99446-99449, 99495-99496, G0463, G0471

Insertion of New or Replacement of Permanent Pacemaker Plus Electrode Insertion

33206	**Insertion of new or replacement of permanent pacemaker with transvenous electrode(s); atrial**
33207	**ventricular**
33208	**atrial and ventricular**

Access to the central caval veins is obtained through the subclavian vein or jugular vein. The vein is penetrated with a large needle and a wire is passed through the needle into the vein. An introducer sheath is placed over the wire and it is exchanged for the pacemaker lead. Fluoroscopy is used to guide the lead to its position in the heart. A pocket for the pacemaker generator or battery is created. For a replacement procedure, an incision over the existing generator is made and the device is extracted. The lead is then tested and connected to the generator. The pocket is closed with suture.

Coding Tips

1.   Report 33206 for a single lead placed in the atrium.
2.   Report 33207 for a single lead placed in the ventricle.
3.   Report 33208 for dual leads placed: one in the atrium and one in the ventricle.
4.   These codes include the insertion of the pacemaker pulse generator (battery) and the transvenous placement of a lead(s).
5.   These codes include any repositioning.
6.   Do not report these codes in conjunction with 33227-33229.
7.   Fluoroscopy is included and is no longer separately reported.
8.   Conscious sedation is not included in these codes. Separately report 99151–99157 per payer policy and coding guidelines. Hospitals may choose to include the costs associated with the service as part of the procedure rather than reporting them separately.

Dual Chamber Pacemaker (implanted transvenously)

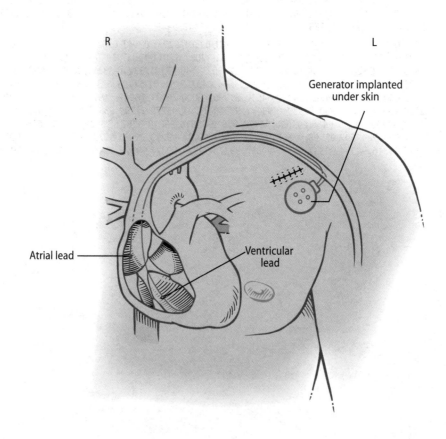

Facility HCPCS Coding

HCPCS Level II codes are used to report the devices used in these procedures. Hospitals should separately report supplies and devices used during pacemaker procedures. Refer to chapter 1 for more information regarding appropriate billing of supplies. Appendix B of this publication contains a list of current device codes applicable to this section.

C1785	Pacemaker, dual chamber, rate-responsive (implantable)
C1786	Pacemaker, single chamber, rate-responsive (implantable)
C1898	Lead, pacemaker, other than transvenous VDD single pass
C1899	Lead, pacemaker/cardioverter-defibrillator combination (implantable)
C1900	Lead, left ventricular coronary venous system
C2620	Pacemaker, single chamber, non rate-responsive (implantable)
C2621	Pacemaker, other than single or dual chamber (implantable)

ICD-10-CM Coding

I44.0	Atrioventricular block, first degree
I44.1	Atrioventricular block, second degree
I44.2	Atrioventricular block, complete
I44.30	Unspecified atrioventricular block
I44.39	Other atrioventricular block
I44.4	Left anterior fascicular block
I44.5	Left posterior fascicular block
I44.60	Unspecified fascicular block
I44.69	Other fascicular block
I44.7	Left bundle-branch block, unspecified
I45.0	Right fascicular block
I45.10	Unspecified right bundle-branch block
I45.19	Other right bundle-branch block
I45.2	Bifascicular block
I45.3	Trifascicular block
I45.4	Nonspecific intraventricular block
I45.5	Other specified heart block
I45.6	Pre-excitation syndrome
I45.81	Long QT syndrome
I45.9	Conduction disorder, unspecified
I47.1	Supraventricular tachycardia
I48.0	Paroxysmal atrial fibrillation
I48.2	Chronic atrial fibrillation
I48.91	Unspecified atrial fibrillation
I49.2	Junctional premature depolarization
I49.5	Sick sinus syndrome
I49.8	Other specified cardiac arrhythmias
I49.9	Cardiac arrhythmia, unspecified
I50.1	Left ventricular failure
I50.20	Unspecified systolic (congestive) heart failure
I50.21	Acute systolic (congestive) heart failure
I50.22	Chronic systolic (congestive) heart failure
I50.23	Acute on chronic systolic (congestive) heart failure
I50.30	Unspecified diastolic (congestive) heart failure
I50.31	Acute diastolic (congestive) heart failure
I50.32	Chronic diastolic (congestive) heart failure
I50.33	Acute on chronic diastolic (congestive) heart failure
I50.40	Unspecified combined systolic (congestive) and diastolic (congestive) heart failure
I50.41	Acute combined systolic (congestive) and diastolic (congestive) heart failure
I50.42	Chronic combined systolic (congestive) and diastolic (congestive) heart failure
I50.43	Acute on chronic combined systolic (congestive) and diastolic (congestive) heart failure
I50.810	Right heart failure, unspecified

I5Ø.811	Acute right heart failure
I5Ø.812	Chronic right heart failure
I5Ø.813	Acute on chronic right heart failure
I5Ø.814	Right heart failure due to left heart failure
I5Ø.82	Biventricular heart failure
I5Ø.83	High output heart failure
I5Ø.84	End stage heart failure
I5Ø.89	Other heart failure
I5Ø.9	Heart failure, unspecified
I51.7	Cardiomegaly
I51.9	Heart disease, unspecified
I97.11Ø	Postprocedural cardiac insufficiency following cardiac surgery
I97.111	Postprocedural cardiac insufficiency following other surgery
I97.12Ø	Postprocedural cardiac arrest following cardiac surgery
I97.121	Postprocedural cardiac arrest following other surgery
I97.13Ø	Postprocedural heart failure following cardiac surgery
I97.131	Postprocedural heart failure following other surgery
I97.19Ø	Other postprocedural cardiac functional disturbances following cardiac surgery
I97.191	Other postprocedural cardiac functional disturbances following other surgery
I97.71Ø	Intraoperative cardiac arrest during cardiac surgery
I97.711	Intraoperative cardiac arrest during other surgery
I97.79Ø	Other intraoperative cardiac functional disturbances during cardiac surgery
I97.791	Other intraoperative cardiac functional disturbances during other surgery
I97.88	Other intraoperative complications of the circulatory system, not elsewhere classified
I97.89	Other postprocedural complications and disorders of the circulatory system, not elsewhere classified
Q24.6	Congenital heart block
RØØ.1	Bradycardia, unspecified
T82.11ØA	Breakdown (mechanical) of cardiac electrode, initial encounter
T82.11ØD	Breakdown (mechanical) of cardiac electrode, subsequent encounter
T82.11ØS	Breakdown (mechanical) of cardiac electrode, sequela
T82.111A	Breakdown (mechanical) of cardiac pulse generator (battery), initial encounter
T82.111D	Breakdown (mechanical) of cardiac pulse generator (battery), subsequent encounter
T82.111S	Breakdown (mechanical) of cardiac pulse generator (battery), sequela
T82.118A	Breakdown (mechanical) of other cardiac electronic device, initial encounter
T82.118D	Breakdown (mechanical) of other cardiac electronic device, subsequent encounter
T82.118S	Breakdown (mechanical) of other cardiac electronic device, sequela
T82.119A	Breakdown (mechanical) of unspecified cardiac electronic device, initial encounter
T82.119D	Breakdown (mechanical) of unspecified cardiac electronic device, subsequent encounter
T82.119S	Breakdown (mechanical) of unspecified cardiac electronic device, sequela
T82.12ØA	Displacement of cardiac electrode, initial encounter
T82.12ØD	Displacement of cardiac electrode, subsequent encounter
T82.12ØS	Displacement of cardiac electrode, sequela
T82.121A	Displacement of cardiac pulse generator (battery), initial encounter
T82.121D	Displacement of cardiac pulse generator (battery), subsequent encounter
T82.121S	Displacement of cardiac pulse generator (battery), sequela
T82.128A	Displacement of other cardiac electronic device, initial encounter
T82.128D	Displacement of other cardiac electronic device, subsequent encounter
T82.128S	Displacement of other cardiac electronic device, sequela
T82.129A	Displacement of unspecified cardiac electronic device, initial encounter
T82.129D	Displacement of unspecified cardiac electronic device, subsequent encounter
T82.129S	Displacement of unspecified cardiac electronic device, sequela
T82.19ØA	Other mechanical complication of cardiac electrode, initial encounter
T82.19ØD	Other mechanical complication of cardiac electrode, subsequent encounter
T82.19ØS	Other mechanical complication of cardiac electrode, sequela
T82.191A	Other mechanical complication of cardiac pulse generator (battery), initial encounter
T82.191D	Other mechanical complication of cardiac pulse generator (battery), subsequent encounter

T82.191S	Other mechanical complication of cardiac pulse generator (battery), sequela
T82.198A	Other mechanical complication of other cardiac electronic device, initial encounter
T82.198D	Other mechanical complication of other cardiac electronic device, subsequent encounter
T82.198S	Other mechanical complication of other cardiac electronic device, sequela
T82.199A	Other mechanical complication of unspecified cardiac device, initial encounter
T82.199D	Other mechanical complication of unspecified cardiac device, subsequent encounter
T82.199S	Other mechanical complication of unspecified cardiac device, sequela
T82.817A	Embolism due to cardiac prosthetic devices, implants and grafts, initial encounter
T82.817D	Embolism due to cardiac prosthetic devices, implants and grafts, subsequent encounter
T82.817S	Embolism due to cardiac prosthetic devices, implants and grafts, sequela
T82.827A	Fibrosis due to cardiac prosthetic devices, implants and grafts, initial encounter
T82.827D	Fibrosis due to cardiac prosthetic devices, implants and grafts, subsequent encounter
T82.827S	Fibrosis due to cardiac prosthetic devices, implants and grafts, sequela
T82.837A	Hemorrhage due to cardiac prosthetic devices, implants and grafts, initial encounter
T82.837D	Hemorrhage due to cardiac prosthetic devices, implants and grafts, subsequent encounter
T82.837S	Hemorrhage due to cardiac prosthetic devices, implants and grafts, sequela
T82.847A	Pain due to cardiac prosthetic devices, implants and grafts, initial encounter
T82.847D	Pain due to cardiac prosthetic devices, implants and grafts, subsequent encounter
T82.847S	Pain due to cardiac prosthetic devices, implants and grafts, sequela
T82.855A	Stenosis of coronary artery stent, initial encounter
T82.857A	Stenosis of other cardiac prosthetic devices, implants and grafts, initial encounter
T82.857D	Stenosis of other cardiac prosthetic devices, implants and grafts, subsequent encounter
T82.857S	Stenosis of other cardiac prosthetic devices, implants and grafts, sequela
T82.867A	Thrombosis due to cardiac prosthetic devices, implants and grafts, initial encounter
T82.867D	Thrombosis due to cardiac prosthetic devices, implants and grafts, subsequent encounter
T82.867S	Thrombosis due to cardiac prosthetic devices, implants and grafts, sequela
T82.897A	Other specified complication of cardiac prosthetic devices, implants and grafts, initial encounter
T82.897D	Other specified complication of cardiac prosthetic devices, implants and grafts, subsequent encounter
T82.897S	Other specified complication of cardiac prosthetic devices, implants and grafts, sequela
T82.9XXA	Unspecified complication of cardiac and vascular prosthetic device, implant and graft, initial encounter
T82.9XXD	Unspecified complication of cardiac and vascular prosthetic device, implant and graft, subsequent encounter
T82.9XXS	Unspecified complication of cardiac and vascular prosthetic device, implant and graft, sequela
Z45.010	Encounter for checking and testing of cardiac pacemaker pulse generator [battery]
Z45.018	Encounter for adjustment and management of other part of cardiac pacemaker
Z95.818	Presence of other cardiac implants and grafts

CCI Edits

33206 00530, 00534, 0213T, 0216T, 0228T, 0230T, 0293T-0294T, 0302T-0306T, 0387T, 0389T-0391T, 0462T-0463T, 11000-11006, 11042-11047, 12001-12007, 12011-12057, 13100-13133, 13151-13153, 33207, 33210-33213, 33214, 33215, 33221-33222, 33227-33229, 35201-35206, 35226-35236, 35256-35266, 35286, 36000, 36005-36013, 36120-36140, 36400-36410, 36420-36430, 36440, 36555-36556, 36568-36569, 36591-36592, 36600, 36640, 43752, 51701-51703, 62320-62327, 64400-64410, 64413-64435, 64445-64450, 64461-64463, 64479-64530, 69990, 76000-76001, 76942, 76970, 76998, 77001-77002, 92012-92014, 92960-92961, 93000-93010, 93040-93042, 93260-93261, 93279-93299, 93318, 93355, 93600-93603, 93610-93612, 94002, 94200, 94250, 94680-94690, 94770, 95812-95816, 95819, 95822, 95829, 95955, 96360-96368, 96372, 96374-96377, 97597-97598, 97602, 99155-99157, 99211-99223, 99231-99255, 99291-99292, 99304-99310, 99315-99316, 99334-99337, 99347-99350, 99374-99375, 99377-99378, 99446-99449, 99495-99496, G0463, G0471

33207 00530, 00534, 0213T, 0216T, 0228T, 0230T, 0293T-0294T, 0302T-0306T, 0387T, 0389T-0391T, 0462T-0463T, 11000-11006, 11042-11047, 12001-12007, 12011-12057, 13100-13133, 13151-13153, 33210-33211, 33214, 33215, 33218, 33221, 33222, 33227-33229, 35201-35206, 35226-35236, 35256-35266, 35286, 36000, 36005-36013, 36120-36140, 36400-36410, 36420-36430, 36440, 36555-36556, 36568-36569, 36591-36592, 36600, 36640, 43752, 51701-51703, 62320-62327, 64400-64410, 64413-64435, 64445-64450, 64461-64463, 64479-64530, 69990, 76000-76001, 76942, 76970, 76998, 77001-77002, 92012-92014, 92960-92961, 93000-93010, 93040-93042, 93260-93261, 93279-93299, 93318, 93355, 93600-93603, 93610-93612, 94002, 94200, 94250, 94680-94690, 94770, 95812-95816, 95819, 95822, 95829, 95955, 96360-96368, 96372, 96374-96377, 97597-97598, 97602, 99155-99157, 99211-99223, 99231-99255, 99291-99292, 99304-99310, 99315-99316, 99334-99337, 99347-99350, 99374-99375, 99377-99378, 99446-99449, 99495-99496, G0463, G0471

33208 00530, 00534, 0213T, 0216T, 0228T, 0230T, 0293T-0294T, 0302T-0306T, 0387T, 0389T-0391T, 0462T-0463T, 11000-11006, 11042-11047, 12001-12007, 12011-12057, 13100-13133, 13151-13153, 33206-33207, 33210-33211, 33214, 33215-33217, 33221, 33222, 33227-33229, 35201-35206, 35226-35236, 35256-35266, 35286, 36000, 36005-36013, 36120-36140, 36400-36410, 36420-36430, 36440, 36555-36556, 36568-36569, 36591-36592, 36600, 36640, 43752, 51701-51703, 62320-62327, 64400-64410, 64413-64435, 64445-64450, 64461-64463, 64479-64530, 69990, 76000-76001, 76942, 76970, 76998, 77001-77002, 92012-92014, 92960-92961, 93000-93010, 93040-93042, 93260-93261, 93279-93299, 93318, 93355, 93600-93603, 93610-93612, 94002, 94200, 94250, 94680-94690, 94770, 95812-95816, 95819, 95822, 95829, 95955, 96360-96368, 96372, 96374-96377, 97597-97598, 97602, 99155-99157, 99211-99223, 99231-99255, 99291-99292, 99304-99310, 99315-99316, 99334-99337, 99347-99350, 99374-99375, 99377-99378, 99446-99449, 99495-99496, G0463, G0471

Case Examples

See case examples #2 and #3 at the end of this chapter.

Insertion or Replacement of Temporary Pacemaker

33210	**Insertion or replacement of temporary transvenous single chamber cardiac electrode or pacemaker catheter (separate procedure)**
33211	**Insertion or replacement of temporary transvenous dual chamber pacing electrodes (separate procedure)**

Access to the central caval veins is obtained through the subclavian vein or jugular vein. The vein is penetrated with a large needle and a wire is passed through it. A fluoroscope is used to guide the wire into the right atrium. A pocket for the pacemaker generator is created and the wire is tested. The wire is connected to the generator and the generator is closed in its pocket. Report 33210 or 33211 if the pacemaker generator is not implanted but temporarily placed outside the body and a transvenous single chamber cardiac electrode or pacemaker catheter (33210) or transvenous dual chamber (33211) electrode(s) are placed are inserted or replaced.

Coding Tips

1. These separate procedures by definition are usually a component of a more complex service and are not identified separately. When performed alone or with other unrelated procedures/services, they may be reported.

2. Conscious sedation is not included in these codes. Separately report 99151–99157 per payer policy and coding guidelines. Hospitals may choose to include the costs associated with the service as part of the procedure rather than reporting them separately.

Facility HCPCS Coding

HCPCS Level II codes are used to report the supplies provided during the procedure. Hospitals should separately report supplies used during cardiac invasive procedures. Refer to chapter 1 for more information regarding appropriate billing of supplies. Refer to the list of current codes in appendix B.

C1779	Lead, pacemaker, transvenous VDD single pass
C1785	Pacemaker, dual chamber, rate-responsive (implantable)
C1786	Pacemaker, single chamber, rate-responsive (implantable)
C1898	Lead, pacemaker, other than transvenous VDD single pass
C1899	Lead, pacemaker/cardioverter-defibrillator combination (implantable)
C1900	Lead, left ventricular coronary venous system
C2620	Pacemaker, single chamber, non rate-responsive (implantable)
C2621	Pacemaker, other than single or dual chamber (implantable)

ICD-10-CM Coding

G90.01	Carotid sinus syncope
G90.09	Other idiopathic peripheral autonomic neuropathy
I21.01	ST elevation (STEMI) myocardial infarction involving left main coronary artery
I21.02	ST elevation (STEMI) myocardial infarction involving left anterior descending coronary artery
I21.09	ST elevation (STEMI) myocardial infarction involving other coronary artery of anterior wall
I21.11	ST elevation (STEMI) myocardial infarction involving right coronary artery
I21.19	ST elevation (STEMI) myocardial infarction involving other coronary artery of inferior wall
I21.3	ST elevation (STEMI) myocardial infarction of unspecified site
I21.9	Acute myocardial infarction, unspecified
I21.A1	Myocardial infarction type 2
I21.A9	Other myocardial infarction type
I22.0	Subsequent ST elevation (STEMI) myocardial infarction of anterior wall
I22.1	Subsequent ST elevation (STEMI) myocardial infarction of inferior wall
I44.0	Atrioventricular block, first degree
I44.1	Atrioventricular block, second degree
I44.2	Atrioventricular block, complete
I44.30	Unspecified atrioventricular block
I45.2	Bifascicular block
I45.3	Trifascicular block
I45.5	Other specified heart block
I45.6	Pre-excitation syndrome
I45.81	Long QT syndrome

I45.9	Conduction disorder, unspecified
I46.2	Cardiac arrest due to underlying cardiac condition
I46.8	Cardiac arrest due to other underlying condition
I46.9	Cardiac arrest, cause unspecified
I47.1	Supraventricular tachycardia
I48.0	Paroxysmal atrial fibrillation
I48.1	Persistent atrial fibrillation
I48.2	Chronic atrial fibrillation
I48.3	Typical atrial flutter
I48.4	Atypical atrial flutter
I48.91	Unspecified atrial fibrillation
I48.92	Unspecified atrial flutter
I49.2	Junctional premature depolarization
I49.5	Sick sinus syndrome
I49.8	Other specified cardiac arrhythmias
I51.9	Heart disease, unspecified
I97.110	Postprocedural cardiac insufficiency following cardiac surgery
I97.111	Postprocedural cardiac insufficiency following other surgery
I97.120	Postprocedural cardiac arrest following cardiac surgery
I97.121	Postprocedural cardiac arrest following other surgery
I97.130	Postprocedural heart failure following cardiac surgery
I97.131	Postprocedural heart failure following other surgery
I97.190	Other postprocedural cardiac functional disturbances following cardiac surgery
I97.191	Other postprocedural cardiac functional disturbances following other surgery
I97.710	Intraoperative cardiac arrest during cardiac surgery
I97.711	Intraoperative cardiac arrest during other surgery
I97.790	Other intraoperative cardiac functional disturbances during cardiac surgery
I97.791	Other intraoperative cardiac functional disturbances during other surgery
I97.88	Other intraoperative complications of the circulatory system, not elsewhere classified
I97.89	Other postprocedural complications and disorders of the circulatory system, not elsewhere classified
Q24.6	Congenital heart block
R00.1	Bradycardia, unspecified
R00.2	Palpitations
R09.89	Other specified symptoms and signs involving the circulatory and respiratory systems
R55	Syncope and collapse
R57.0	Cardiogenic shock
T46.0X1A	Poisoning by cardiac-stimulant glycosides and drugs of similar action, accidental (unintentional), initial encounter
T46.0X1D	Poisoning by cardiac-stimulant glycosides and drugs of similar action, accidental (unintentional), subsequent encounter
T46.0X1S	Poisoning by cardiac-stimulant glycosides and drugs of similar action, accidental (unintentional), sequela
T46.0X2A	Poisoning by cardiac-stimulant glycosides and drugs of similar action, intentional self-harm, initial encounter
T46.0X2D	Poisoning by cardiac-stimulant glycosides and drugs of similar action, intentional self-harm, subsequent encounter
T46.0X2S	Poisoning by cardiac-stimulant glycosides and drugs of similar action, intentional self-harm, sequela
T46.0X3A	Poisoning by cardiac-stimulant glycosides and drugs of similar action, assault, initial encounter
T46.0X3D	Poisoning by cardiac-stimulant glycosides and drugs of similar action, assault, subsequent encounter
T46.0X3S	Poisoning by cardiac-stimulant glycosides and drugs of similar action, assault, sequela
T46.0X4A	Poisoning by cardiac-stimulant glycosides and drugs of similar action, undetermined, initial encounter
T46.0X4D	Poisoning by cardiac-stimulant glycosides and drugs of similar action, undetermined, subsequent encounter
T46.0X4S	Poisoning by cardiac-stimulant glycosides and drugs of similar action, undetermined, sequela
T82.110A	Breakdown (mechanical) of cardiac electrode, initial encounter
T82.110D	Breakdown (mechanical) of cardiac electrode, subsequent encounter
T82.110S	Breakdown (mechanical) of cardiac electrode, sequela
T82.120A	Displacement of cardiac electrode, initial encounter
T82.120D	Displacement of cardiac electrode, subsequent encounter

T82.120S	Displacement of cardiac electrode, sequela
T82.190A	Other mechanical complication of cardiac electrode, initial encounter
T82.190D	Other mechanical complication of cardiac electrode, subsequent encounter
T82.190S	Other mechanical complication of cardiac electrode, sequela
T82.817A	Embolism of cardiac prosthetic devices, implants and grafts, initial encounter
T82.817D	Embolism of cardiac prosthetic devices, implants and grafts, subsequent encounter
T82.817S	Embolism of cardiac prosthetic devices, implants and grafts, sequela
T82.827A	Fibrosis of cardiac prosthetic devices, implants and grafts, initial encounter
T82.827D	Fibrosis of cardiac prosthetic devices, implants and grafts, subsequent encounter
T82.827S	Fibrosis of cardiac prosthetic devices, implants and grafts, sequela
T82.837A	Hemorrhage of cardiac prosthetic devices, implants and grafts, initial encounter
T82.837D	Hemorrhage of cardiac prosthetic devices, implants and grafts, subsequent encounter
T82.837S	Hemorrhage of cardiac prosthetic devices, implants and grafts, sequela
T82.847A	Pain from cardiac prosthetic devices, implants and grafts, initial encounter
T82.847D	Pain from cardiac prosthetic devices, implants and grafts, subsequent encounter
T82.847S	Pain from cardiac prosthetic devices, implants and grafts, sequela
T82.855A	Stenosis of coronary artery stent, initial encounter
T82.857A	Stenosis of cardiac prosthetic devices, implants and grafts, initial encounter
T82.857D	Stenosis of cardiac prosthetic devices, implants and grafts, subsequent encounter
T82.857S	Stenosis of cardiac prosthetic devices, implants and grafts, sequela
T82.867A	Thrombosis of cardiac prosthetic devices, implants and grafts, initial encounter
T82.867D	Thrombosis of cardiac prosthetic devices, implants and grafts, subsequent encounter
T82.867S	Thrombosis of cardiac prosthetic devices, implants and grafts, sequela
T82.897A	Other specified complication of cardiac prosthetic devices, implants and grafts, initial encounter
T82.897D	Other specified complication of cardiac prosthetic devices, implants and grafts, subsequent encounter
T82.897S	Other specified complication of cardiac prosthetic devices, implants and grafts, sequela
T82.9XXA	Unspecified complication of cardiac and vascular prosthetic device, implant and graft, initial encounter
T82.9XXD	Unspecified complication of cardiac and vascular prosthetic device, implant and graft, subsequent encounter
T82.9XXS	Unspecified complication of cardiac and vascular prosthetic device, implant and graft, sequela
Z45.018	Encounter for adjustment and management of other part of cardiac pacemaker
Z95.818	Presence of other cardiac implants and grafts

CCI Edits

33210   00530, 00534, 0213T, 0216T, 0228T, 0230T, 0302T-0306T, 0387T, 0389T-0391T, 0462T-0463T, 11000-11006, 11042-11047, 12001-12007, 12011-12057, 13100-13133, 13151-13153, 35201-35206, 35226-35236, 35256-35266, 35286, 36000, 36005-36013, 36120-36140, 36400-36410, 36420-36430, 36440, 36555-36556, 36568-36569, 36591-36592, 36600, 36640, 43752, 51701-51703, 62320-62327, 64400-64410, 64413-64435, 64445-64450, 64461-64463, 64479-64530, 69990, 76000-76001, 76942, 76970, 76998, 77001-77002, 92012-92014, 92960, 93000-93010, 93040-93042, 93260-93261, 93279-93299, 93318, 93355, 93600-93603, 94002, 94200, 94250, 94680-94690, 94770, 95812-95816, 95819, 95822, 95829, 95955, 96360-96368, 96372, 96374-96377, 97597-97598, 97602, 99155-99157, 99211-99223, 99231-99255, 99291-99292, 99304-99310, 99315-99316, 99334-99337, 99347-99350, 99374-99375, 99377-99378, 99446-99449, 99495-99496, G0463, G0471

33211   00530, 00534, 0213T, 0216T, 0228T, 0230T, 0302T-0306T, 0387T, 0389T-0391T, 0462T-0463T, 11000-11006, 11042-11047, 12001-12007, 12011-12057, 13100-13133, 13151-13153, 33210, 35201-35206, 35226-35236, 35256-35266, 35286, 36000, 36005-36013, 36120-36140, 36400-36410, 36420-36430, 36440, 36555-36556, 36568-36569, 36591-36592, 36600, 36640, 43752, 51701-51703, 62320-62327, 64400-64410, 64413-64435, 64445-64450, 64461-64463, 64479-64530, 69990, 76000-76001, 76942, 76970, 76998, 77001-77002, 92012-92014, 92960, 93000-93010, 93040-93042, 93260-93261, 93279-93299, 93318, 93355, 93600-93603, 94002, 94200, 94250, 94680-94690, 94770, 95812-95816, 95819, 95822, 95829, 95955, 96360-96368, 96372, 96374-96377, 97597-97598, 97602, 99155-99157, 99211-99223, 99231-99255, 99291-99292, 99304-99310, 99315-99316, 99334-99337, 99347-99350, 99374-99375, 99377-99378, 99446-99449, 99495-99496, G0463, G0471

Insertion of Pulse Generator Only

33212	**Insertion of pacemaker pulse generator only; with existing single lead**
33213	**with existing dual leads**
33221	**with existing multiple leads**

An incision is made and a pocket is created for the pacemaker generator. The existing wires are tested and connected to the generator. The generator is placed into the pocket and the pocket is closed. Report 33213 if a dual chamber (atrial and ventricular) pacemaker pulse generator is inserted or 33221 for the insertion of a generator with multiple existing leads.

Coding Tips

1.   Report 33212 for a generator connected to an existing single lead.

2.   Report 33213 for a generator connected to existing dual leads.

3.   Report 33221 for a generator connected to multiple existing leads.

4.   Do not report these codes with 33233.

5.   Fluoroscopy is included and is no longer separately reported.

6.   Conscious sedation is not included in these codes. Separately report 99151–99157 per payer policy and coding guidelines. Hospitals may choose to include the costs associated with the service as part of the procedure rather than reporting them separately.

Facility HCPCS Coding

HCPCS Level II codes are used to report the devices used in these procedures. Hospitals should separately report supplies and devices used during pacemaker procedures. Refer to chapter 1 for more information regarding appropriate billing of supplies. Appendix B of this publication contains a list of current device codes applicable to this section.

C1785	Pacemaker, dual chamber, rate-responsive (implantable)
C1786	Pacemaker, single chamber, rate-responsive (implantable)
C1779	Lead, pacemaker, transvenous VDD single pass
C1898	Lead, pacemaker, other than transvenous VDD single pass
C2619	Pacemaker, dual chamber, non rate-responsive (implantable)
C2620	Pacemaker, single chamber, non rate-responsive (implantable)
C2621	Pacemaker, other than single or dual chamber (implantable)

Dual Chamber Pacemaker (implanted transvenously)

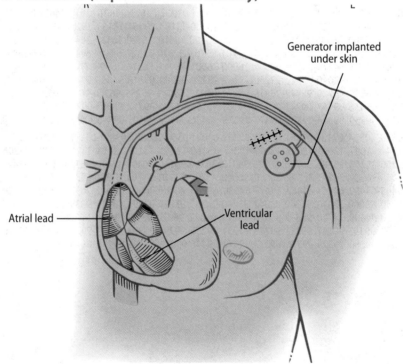

Generator implanted under skin

Atrial lead

Ventricular lead

ICD-10-CM Coding

I44.Ø	Atrioventricular block, first degree
I44.1	Atrioventricular block, second degree
I44.2	Atrioventricular block, complete
I44.3Ø	Unspecified atrioventricular block
I45.5	Other specified heart block
I45.6	Pre-excitation syndrome
I45.81	Long QT syndrome
I45.9	Conduction disorder, unspecified
I47.1	Supraventricular tachycardia
I48.Ø	Paroxysmal atrial fibrillation
I48.2	Chronic atrial fibrillation
I48.91	Unspecified atrial fibrillation
I49.2	Junctional premature depolarization
I49.8	Other specified cardiac arrhythmias
I49.9	Cardiac arrhythmia, unspecified
Q24.6	Congenital heart block
RØØ.1	Bradycardia, unspecified
T82.111A	Breakdown (mechanical) of cardiac pulse generator (battery), initial encounter
T82.121A	Displacement of cardiac pulse generator (battery), initial encounter
T82.121D	Displacement of cardiac pulse generator (battery), subsequent encounter
T82.191A	Other mechanical complication of cardiac pulse generator (battery), initial encounter
Z45.Ø18	Encounter for adjustment and management of other part of cardiac pacemaker
Z95.Ø	Presence of cardiac pacemaker

CCI Edits

33212   00530, 00534, 0213T, 0216T, 0228T, 0230T, 0293T-0294T, 0302T-0307T, 0387T, 0388T-0391T, 0462T-0463T, 11000-11006, 11042-11047, 12001-12007, 12011-12057, 13100-13133, 13151-13153, 33207-33208, 33210-33211, 33213-33214, 33217, 33222, 33224, 33233, 36000, 36005, 36400-36410, 36420-36430, 36440, 36591-36592, 36600, 36640, 43752, 51701-51703, 62320-62327, 64400-64410, 64413-64435, 64445-64450, 64461-64463, 64479-64530, 69990, 76000-76001, 76942, 76970, 76998, 77002, 92012-92014, 92960-92961, 93000-93010, 93040-93042, 93260-93261, 93279-93299, 93318, 93355, 93600-93603, 93610-93612, 94002, 94200, 94250, 94680-94690, 94770, 95812-95816, 95819, 95822, 95829, 95955, 96360-96368, 96372, 96374-96377, 97597-97598, 97602, 99155-99157, 99211-99223, 99231-99255, 99291-99292, 99304-99310, 99315-99316, 99334-99337, 99347-99350, 99374-99375, 99377-99378, 99446-99449, 99495-99496, G0463, G0471

33213   00530, 00534, 0213T, 0216T, 0228T, 0230T, 0293T-0294T, 0302T-0307T, 0387T, 0388T-0391T, 0462T-0463T, 11000-11006, 11042-11047, 12001-12007, 12011-12057, 13100-13133, 13151-13153, 33207-33208, 33210-33211, 33214, 33222, 33224, 33233, 36000, 36005, 36400-36410, 36420-36430, 36440, 36591-36592, 36600, 36640, 43752, 51701-51703, 62320-62327, 64400-64410, 64413-64435, 64445-64450, 64461-64463, 64479-64530, 69990, 76000-76001, 76942, 76970, 76998, 77002, 92012-92014, 92960-92961, 93000-93010, 93040-93042, 93260-93261, 93279-93299, 93318, 93355, 93600-93603, 93610-93612, 94002, 94200, 94250, 94680-94690, 94770, 95812-95816, 95819, 95822, 95829, 95955, 96360-96368, 96372, 96374-96377, 97597-97598, 97602, 99155-99157, 99211-99223, 99231-99255, 99291-99292, 99304-99310, 99315-99316, 99334-99337, 99347-99350, 99374-99375, 99377-99378, 99446-99449, 99495-99496, G0463, G0471

33221   00530, 00534, 0213T, 0216T, 0228T, 0230T, 0293T-0294T, 0302T-0307T, 0387T, 0388T-0391T, 0462T-0463T, 11000-11006, 11042-11047, 12001-12007, 12011-12057, 13100-13133, 13151-13153, 33210-33213, 33222, 33224, 33233, 36000, 36005, 36400-36410, 36420-36430, 36440, 36591-36592, 36600, 36640, 43752, 51701-51703, 62320-62327, 64400-64410, 64413-64435, 64445-64450, 64461-64463, 64479-64530, 69990, 76000-76001, 76942, 76970, 76998, 77002, 92012-92014, 93000-93010, 93040-93042, 93260-93261, 93279-93299, 93318, 93355, 93600-93603, 93610-93612, 94002, 94200, 94250, 94680-94690, 94770, 95812-95816, 95819, 95822, 95829, 95955, 96360-96368, 96372, 96374-96377, 97597-97598, 97602, 99155-99157, 99211-99223, 99231-99255, 99291-99292, 99304-99310, 99315-99316, 99334-99337, 99347-99350, 99374-99375, 99377-99378, 99446-99449, 99495-99496, G0463, G0471

Upgrade of Single Chamber Pacemaker System

33214   **Upgrade of implanted pacemaker system, conversion of single chamber system to dual chamber system (includes removal of previously placed pulse generator, testing of existing lead, insertion of new lead, insertion of new pulse generator)**

A single chamber system is converted or upgraded to a dual chamber system. The existing pacemaker generator pocket is opened and the single chamber generator removed. The dual chamber generator is placed into the existing pocket. The existing pacer wire is tested and connected to the generator. A second lead is placed and tested. The pocket is closed.

Coding Tips

1. A system upgrade includes removal of the previously placed pulse generator, testing of the existing lead, insertion of the new lead, and insertion of the new pulse generator. Do not separately report these services.

2. For pocket relocation, see 33222.

3. Fluoroscopic guidance is included and not separately reported.

4. Conscious sedation is not included in these codes. Separately report 99151–99157 per payer policy and coding guidelines. Hospitals may choose to include the costs associated with the service as part of the procedure rather than reporting them separately.

Facility HCPCS Coding

HCPCS Level II codes are used to report the devices used in these procedures. Hospitals should separately report supplies and devices used during pacemaker procedures. Refer to chapter 1 for more information regarding appropriate billing of supplies. Appendix B of this publication contains a list of current device codes applicable to this section.

C1779   Lead, pacemaker, transvenous VDD single pass

C1785   Pacemaker, dual chamber, rate-responsive (implantable)

C1898   Lead, pacemaker, other than transvenous VDD single pass

C2619   Pacemaker, dual chamber, non rate-responsive (implantable)

C2621   Pacemaker, other than single or dual chamber (implantable)

ICD-10-CM Coding

I44.0	Atrioventricular block, first degree
I44.1	Atrioventricular block, second degree
I44.2	Atrioventricular block, complete
I44.30	Unspecified atrioventricular block
I44.39	Other atrioventricular block
I44.4	Left anterior fascicular block
I44.5	Left posterior fascicular block
I44.60	Unspecified fascicular block
I44.69	Other fascicular block
I44.7	Left bundle-branch block, unspecified
I45.0	Right fascicular block
I45.10	Unspecified right bundle-branch block
I45.19	Other right bundle-branch block
I45.2	Bifascicular block
I45.4	Nonspecific intraventricular block
I45.5	Other specified heart block
I45.6	Pre-excitation syndrome
I45.81	Long QT syndrome
I45.9	Conduction disorder, unspecified
I47.1	Supraventricular tachycardia
I48.0	Paroxysmal atrial fibrillation
I48.2	Chronic atrial fibrillation
I48.91	Unspecified atrial fibrillation
I49.2	Junctional premature depolarization
I49.5	Sick sinus syndrome
I49.8	Other specified cardiac arrhythmias
I49.9	Cardiac arrhythmia, unspecified
I50.1	Left ventricular failure

I50.20	Unspecified systolic (congestive) heart failure
I50.21	Acute systolic (congestive) heart failure
I50.22	Chronic systolic (congestive) heart failure
I50.23	Acute on chronic systolic (congestive) heart failure
I50.30	Unspecified diastolic (congestive) heart failure
I50.31	Acute diastolic (congestive) heart failure
I50.32	Chronic diastolic (congestive) heart failure
I50.33	Acute on chronic diastolic (congestive) heart failure
I50.40	Unspecified combined systolic (congestive) and diastolic (congestive) heart failure
I50.41	Acute combined systolic (congestive) and diastolic (congestive) heart failure
I50.42	Chronic combined systolic (congestive) and diastolic (congestive) heart failure
I50.43	Acute on chronic combined systolic (congestive) and diastolic (congestive) heart failure
I50.810	Right heart failure, unspecified
I50.811	Acute right heart failure
I50.812	Chronic right heart failure
I50.813	Acute on chronic right heart failure
I50.814	Right heart failure due to left heart failure
I50.82	Biventricular heart failure
I50.83	High output heart failure
I50.84	End stage heart failure
I50.89	Other heart failure
I50.9	Heart failure, unspecified
Q24.6	Congenital heart block
R00.1	Bradycardia, unspecified
T82.110A	Breakdown (mechanical) of cardiac electrode, initial encounter
T82.111A	Breakdown (mechanical) of cardiac pulse generator (battery), initial encounter
T82.120A	Displacement of cardiac electrode, initial encounter
T82.121A	Displacement of cardiac pulse generator (battery), initial encounter
T82.190A	Other mechanical complication of cardiac electrode, initial encounter
T82.191A	Other mechanical complication of cardiac pulse generator (battery), initial encounter
T82.598A	Other mechanical complication of other cardiac and vascular devices and implants, initial encounter
Z95.0	Presence of cardiac pacemaker

CCI Edits

33214 00530, 00534, 0213T, 0216T, 0228T, 0230T, 0293T-0294T, 0302T-0306T, 0307T, 0387T-0388T, 0389T-0391T, 0462T-0463T, 11000-11006, 11042-11047, 12001-12007, 12011-12057, 13100-13133, 13151-13153, 33210-33211, 33215, 33221, 33222, 33227-33229, 33233, 35201-35206, 35226-35236, 35256-35266, 35286, 36000, 36005-36013, 36120-36140, 36400-36410, 36420-36430, 36440, 36555-36556, 36568-36569, 36591-36592, 36600, 36640, 43752, 51701-51703, 62320-62327, 64400-64410, 64413-64435, 64445-64450, 64461-64463, 64479-64530, 69990, 76000-76001, 76942, 76970, 76998, 77001-77002, 92012-92014, 92960-92961, 93000-93010, 93040-93042, 93260-93261, 93279-93299, 93318, 93355, 93600-93603, 93610-93612, 94002, 94200, 94250, 94680-94690, 94770, 95812-95816, 95819, 95822, 95829, 95955, 96360-96368, 96372, 96374-96377, 97597-97598, 97602, 99155-99157, 99211-99223, 99231-99255, 99291-99292, 99304-99310, 99315-99316, 99334-99337, 99347-99350, 99374-99375, 99377-99378, 99446-99449, 99495-99496, G0463, G0471

Electrode Repositioning

| 33215 | **Repositioning of previously implanted transvenous pacemaker or implantable (right atrial or right ventricular) electrode** |

A previously placed transvenous right atrial or right ventricular electrode is repositioned. This is done when the system does not function due to improper placement of the electrode wire itself. The generator is removed and the wire is tested to ensure the wire is not defective, merely in the wrong place. It is reattached to the generator in its new position and tested again.

Coding Tips

1. Fluoroscopic guidance is included and not separately reported.

2. Generally, no new devices are inserted. Therefore, device edits do not apply to this code.

3. Conscious sedation is not included in these codes. Separately report 99151–99157 per payer policy and coding guidelines. Hospitals may choose to include the costs associated with the service as part of the procedure rather than reporting them separately.

Facility HCPCS Coding

HCPCS Level II codes are used to report the devices used in these procedures. Hospitals should separately report supplies and devices used during pacemaker procedures. Refer to chapter 1 for more information regarding appropriate billing of supplies. Appendix B of this publication contains a list of current device codes applicable to this section.

ICD-10-CM Coding

I44.0	Atrioventricular block, first degree
I44.1	Atrioventricular block, second degree
I44.2	Atrioventricular block, complete
I44.30	Unspecified atrioventricular block
I44.39	Other atrioventricular block
I44.4	Left anterior fascicular block
I44.5	Left posterior fascicular block
I44.60	Unspecified fascicular block
I44.69	Other fascicular block
I44.7	Left bundle-branch block, unspecified
I45.0	Right fascicular block
I45.10	Unspecified right bundle-branch block
I45.19	Other right bundle-branch block
I45.2	Bifascicular block
I45.4	Nonspecific intraventricular block
I45.5	Other specified heart block
I45.6	Pre-excitation syndrome
I45.81	Long QT syndrome
I45.89	Other specified conduction disorders
I45.9	Conduction disorder, unspecified
I46.8	Cardiac arrest due to other underlying condition
I46.9	Cardiac arrest, cause unspecified
I47.0	Re-entry ventricular arrhythmia
I47.1	Supraventricular tachycardia
I47.2	Ventricular tachycardia
I47.9	Paroxysmal tachycardia, unspecified
I48.0	Paroxysmal atrial fibrillation
I48.91	Unspecified atrial fibrillation
I49.01	Ventricular fibrillation
I49.02	Ventricular flutter
I49.2	Junctional premature depolarization
I49.8	Other specified cardiac arrhythmias
I49.9	Cardiac arrhythmia, unspecified
I50.1	Left ventricular failure
I50.20	Unspecified systolic (congestive) heart failure

I5Ø.21	Acute systolic (congestive) heart failure
I5Ø.22	Chronic systolic (congestive) heart failure
I5Ø.23	Acute on chronic systolic (congestive) heart failure
I5Ø.3Ø	Unspecified diastolic (congestive) heart failure
I5Ø.31	Acute diastolic (congestive) heart failure
I5Ø.32	Chronic diastolic (congestive) heart failure
I5Ø.33	Acute on chronic diastolic (congestive) heart failure
I5Ø.4Ø	Unspecified combined systolic (congestive) and diastolic (congestive) heart failure
I5Ø.41	Acute combined systolic (congestive) and diastolic (congestive) heart failure
I5Ø.42	Chronic combined systolic (congestive) and diastolic (congestive) heart failure
I5Ø.43	Acute on chronic combined systolic (congestive) and diastolic (congestive) heart failure
I5Ø.81Ø	Right heart failure, unspecified
I5Ø.811	Acute right heart failure
I5Ø.812	Chronic right heart failure
I5Ø.813	Acute on chronic right heart failure
I5Ø.814	Right heart failure due to left heart failure
I5Ø.82	Biventricular heart failure
I5Ø.83	High output heart failure
I5Ø.84	End stage heart failure
I5Ø.89	Other heart failure
I5Ø.9	Heart failure, unspecified
RØØ.1	Bradycardia, unspecified
T82.11ØA	Breakdown (mechanical) of cardiac electrode, initial encounter
T82.12ØA	Displacement of cardiac electrode, initial encounter
T82.19ØA	Other mechanical complication of cardiac electrode, initial encounter
T82.598A	Other mechanical complication of other cardiac and vascular devices and implants, initial encounter
T82.7XXA	Infection and inflammatory reaction due to other cardiac and vascular devices, implants and grafts, initial encounter
T82.817A	Embolism due to cardiac prosthetic devices, implants and grafts, initial encounter
T82.827A	Fibrosis due to cardiac prosthetic devices, implants and grafts, initial encounter
T82.837A	Hemorrhage due to cardiac prosthetic devices, implants and grafts, initial encounter
T82.847A	Pain due to cardiac prosthetic devices, implants and grafts, initial encounter
T82.855A	Stenosis of coronary artery stent, initial encounter
T82.857A	Stenosis of other cardiac prosthetic devices, implants and grafts, initial encounter
T82.867A	Thrombosis due to cardiac prosthetic devices, implants and grafts, initial encounter
T82.897A	Other specified complication of cardiac prosthetic devices, implants and grafts, initial encounter
T82.9XXA	Unspecified complication of cardiac and vascular prosthetic device, implant and graft, initial encounter
Z45.Ø18	Encounter for adjustment and management of other part of cardiac pacemaker
Z45.Ø2	Encounter for adjustment and management of automatic implantable cardiac defibrillator
Z95.Ø	Presence of cardiac pacemaker
Z95.81Ø	Presence of automatic (implantable) cardiac defibrillator

CCI Edits

33215   00530, 00540, 0213T, 0216T, 0228T, 0230T, 0293T-0294T, 0302T-0306T, 0387T, 0389T-0391T, 0462T-0463T, 12001-12007, 12011-12057, 13100-13133, 13151-13153, 33210-33211, 33222-33223, 35201-35206, 35226-35236, 35256-35266, 35286, 36000, 36005-36013, 36120-36140, 36400-36410, 36420-36430, 36440, 36555-36556, 36568-36569, 36591-36592, 36600, 36640, 43752, 51701-51703, 62320-62327, 64400-64410, 64413-64435, 64445-64450, 64461-64463, 64479-64530, 69990, 76000-76001, 76942, 76970, 76998, 77001-77002, 92012-92014, 92960-92961, 93000-93010, 93040-93042, 93260-93261, 93279-93299, 93318, 93355, 93600-93603, 93610-93612, 94002, 94200, 94250, 94680-94690, 94770, 95812-95816, 95819, 95822, 95829, 95955, 96360-96368, 96372, 96374-96377, 99155-99157, 99211-99223, 99231-99255, 99291-99292, 99304-99310, 99315-99316, 99334-99337, 99347-99350, 99374-99375, 99377-99378, 99446-99449, 99495-99496, G0463, G0471

Insertion of Transvenous Electrode(s)

33216	**Insertion of a single transvenous electrode, permanent pacemaker or implantable defibrillator**
33217	**Insertion of 2 transvenous electrodes, permanent pacemaker or implantable defibrillator**

The insertion of a transvenous electrode is done when there is a problem with the electrode wire of the single chamber permanent pacemaker or single chamber pacing cardioverter-defibrillator. The generator is removed and the wire is first tested. When the wire is found defective, another transvenous electrode is inserted. Access to the central caval veins is obtained through the subclavian vein or jugular vein. The vein is penetrated with a large needle and a wire is passed through it. Fluoroscopy (included) is used to guide the wire into position. The wire is connected to the generator and testing is done again. Report 33217 if both electrodes on a dual chamber permanent pacemaker or dual chamber pacing cardioverter-defibrillator are inserted.

Coding Tips

1. These codes report insertion of electrodes on permanent pacemakers or cardioverter-defibrillators.
2. Do not report 33216-33217 in conjunction with 33214.
3. Fluoroscopic guidance is included and not separately reported.
4. Conscious sedation is not included in these codes. Separately report 99151–99157 per payer policy and coding guidelines. Hospitals may choose to include the costs associated with the service as part of the procedure rather than reporting them separately.

Facility HCPCS Coding

HCPCS Level II codes are used to report the supplies provided during the procedure. Hospitals should separately report supplies used during cardiac invasive procedures. Refer to chapter 1 for more information regarding appropriate billing of supplies. Refer to the list of current codes in appendix B.

C1777	Lead, cardioverter-defibrillator, endocardial single coil (implantable)
C1779	Lead, pacemaker, transvenous VDD single pass
C1895	Lead, cardioverter-defibrillator, endocardial dual coil (implantable)
C1896	Lead, cardioverter-defibrillator, other than endocardial, single or dual coil (implantable)
C1898	Lead, pacemaker, other than transvenous VDD single pass
C1899	Lead, pacemaker/cardioverter-defibrillator combination (implantable)
C1900	Lead, left ventricular coronary venous system

Transvenous Electrode Insertion

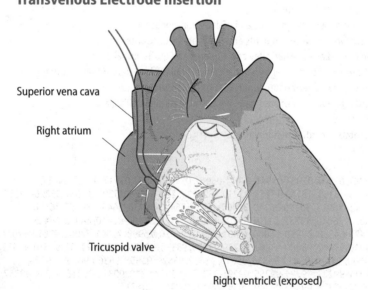

Superior vena cava

Right atrium

Tricuspid valve

Right ventricle (exposed)

A single-chamber electrode is inserted or repositioned, either ventricular or atrial in 33216

Schematic showing leads and electrodes to both right chambers

A dual-chamber electrode system is inserted or repositioned in 33217

Electrode leads are (re)positioned in a single chamber in 33216, or both in 33217. Report for repositioning when 15 days or more have passed after initial insertion

ICD-10-CM Coding

I11.0	Hypertensive heart disease with heart failure
I13.0	Hypertensive heart and chronic kidney disease with heart failure and stage 1 through stage 4 chronic kidney disease, or unspecified chronic kidney disease
I13.2	Hypertensive heart and chronic kidney disease with heart failure and with stage 5 chronic kidney disease, or end stage renal disease
I16.0	Hypertensive urgency
I16.1	Hypertensive emergency
I16.9	Hypertensive crisis, unspecified
I21.01	ST elevation (STEMI) myocardial infarction involving left main coronary artery
I21.02	ST elevation (STEMI) myocardial infarction involving left anterior descending coronary artery
I21.09	ST elevation (STEMI) myocardial infarction involving other coronary artery of anterior wall
I21.11	ST elevation (STEMI) myocardial infarction involving right coronary artery
I21.19	ST elevation (STEMI) myocardial infarction involving other coronary artery of inferior wall
I21.21	ST elevation (STEMI) myocardial infarction involving left circumflex coronary artery
I21.29	ST elevation (STEMI) myocardial infarction involving other sites
I21.3	ST elevation (STEMI) myocardial infarction of unspecified site
I21.4	Non-ST elevation (NSTEMI) myocardial infarction
I21.9	Acute myocardial infarction, unspecified
I21.A1	Myocardial infarction type 2
I21.A9	Other myocardial infarction type
I22.0	Subsequent ST elevation (STEMI) myocardial infarction of anterior wall
I22.1	Subsequent ST elevation (STEMI) myocardial infarction of inferior wall
I22.2	Subsequent non-ST elevation (NSTEMI) myocardial infarction
I22.8	Subsequent ST elevation (STEMI) myocardial infarction of other sites
I22.9	Subsequent ST elevation (STEMI) myocardial infarction of unspecified site
I25.2	Old myocardial infarction
I25.5	Ischemic cardiomyopathy
I25.6	Silent myocardial ischemia
I25.89	Other forms of chronic ischemic heart disease
I25.9	Chronic ischemic heart disease, unspecified
I42.0	Dilated cardiomyopathy
I42.5	Other restrictive cardiomyopathy
I42.8	Other cardiomyopathies
I42.9	Cardiomyopathy, unspecified
I44.0	Atrioventricular block, first degree
I44.1	Atrioventricular block, second degree
I44.2	Atrioventricular block, complete
I44.30	Unspecified atrioventricular block
I44.39	Other atrioventricular block
I44.4	Left anterior fascicular block
I44.5	Left posterior fascicular block
I44.60	Unspecified fascicular block
I44.69	Other fascicular block
I44.7	Left bundle-branch block, unspecified
I45.0	Right fascicular block
I45.10	Unspecified right bundle-branch block
I45.19	Other right bundle-branch block
I45.2	Bifascicular block
I45.4	Nonspecific intraventricular block
I45.5	Other specified heart block
I45.6	Pre-excitation syndrome
I45.81	Long QT syndrome
I45.89	Other specified conduction disorders
I45.9	Conduction disorder, unspecified
I46.2	Cardiac arrest due to underlying cardiac condition

I46.8	Cardiac arrest due to other underlying condition
I46.9	Cardiac arrest, cause unspecified
I47.0	Re-entry ventricular arrhythmia
I47.1	Supraventricular tachycardia
I47.2	Ventricular tachycardia
I48.0	Paroxysmal atrial fibrillation
I48.1	Persistent atrial fibrillation
I48.2	Chronic atrial fibrillation
I48.3	Typical atrial flutter
I48.4	Atypical atrial flutter
I48.91	Unspecified atrial fibrillation
I49.01	Ventricular fibrillation
I49.02	Ventricular flutter
I49.2	Junctional premature depolarization
I49.5	Sick sinus syndrome
I49.8	Other specified cardiac arrhythmias
I49.9	Cardiac arrhythmia, unspecified
I50.1	Left ventricular failure
I50.20	Unspecified systolic (congestive) heart failure
I50.21	Acute systolic (congestive) heart failure
I50.22	Chronic systolic (congestive) heart failure
I50.23	Acute on chronic systolic (congestive) heart failure
I50.30	Unspecified diastolic (congestive) heart failure
I50.31	Acute diastolic (congestive) heart failure
I50.32	Chronic diastolic (congestive) heart failure
I50.33	Acute on chronic diastolic (congestive) heart failure
I50.40	Unspecified combined systolic (congestive) and diastolic (congestive) heart failure
I50.41	Acute combined systolic (congestive) and diastolic (congestive) heart failure
I50.42	Chronic combined systolic (congestive) and diastolic (congestive) heart failure
I50.43	Acute on chronic combined systolic (congestive) and diastolic (congestive) heart failure
I50.810	Right heart failure, unspecified
I50.811	Acute right heart failure
I50.812	Chronic right heart failure
I50.813	Acute on chronic right heart failure
I50.814	Right heart failure due to left heart failure
I50.82	Biventricular heart failure
I50.83	High output heart failure
I50.84	End stage heart failure
I50.89	Other heart failure
I50.9	Heart failure, unspecified
Q23.8	Other congenital malformations of aortic and mitral valves
Q23.9	Congenital malformation of aortic and mitral valves, unspecified
Q24.6	Congenital heart block
Q24.8	Other specified congenital malformations of heart
R00.1	Bradycardia, unspecified
T82.110A	Breakdown (mechanical) of cardiac electrode, initial encounter
T82.120A	Displacement of cardiac electrode, initial encounter
T82.190A	Other mechanical complication of cardiac electrode, initial encounter
T82.598A	Other mechanical complication of other cardiac and vascular devices and implants, initial encounter
T82.7XXA	Infection and inflammatory reaction due to other cardiac and vascular devices, implants and grafts, initial encounter
T82.817A	Embolism due to cardiac prosthetic devices, implants and grafts, initial encounter
T82.827A	Fibrosis due to cardiac prosthetic devices, implants and grafts, initial encounter
T82.837A	Hemorrhage due to cardiac prosthetic devices, implants and grafts, initial encounter
T82.847A	Pain due to cardiac prosthetic devices, implants and grafts, initial encounter
T82.855A	Stenosis of coronary artery stent, initial encounter

T82.857A	Stenosis of other cardiac prosthetic devices, implants and grafts, initial encounter
T82.867A	Thrombosis due to cardiac prosthetic devices, implants and grafts, initial encounter
T82.897A	Other specified complication of cardiac prosthetic devices, implants and grafts, initial encounter
T82.9XXA	Unspecified complication of cardiac and vascular prosthetic device, implant and graft, initial encounter
Z45.Ø18	Encounter for adjustment and management of other part of cardiac pacemaker
Z45.Ø2	Encounter for adjustment and management of automatic implantable cardiac defibrillator
Z95.Ø	Presence of cardiac pacemaker
Z95.81Ø	Presence of automatic (implantable) cardiac defibrillator

CCI Edits

33216   00530, 00534, 0213T, 0216T, 0228T, 0230T, 0293T-0294T, 0302T-0306T, 0387T, 0389T-0391T, 0462T-0463T, 11000-11006, 11042-11047, 12001-12007, 12011-12057, 13100-13133, 13151-13153, 33206-33207, 33210-33215, 33217, 33220, 33221-33223, 33227-33228, 35201-35206, 35226-35236, 35256-35266, 35286, 36000, 36005-36013, 36120-36140, 36400-36410, 36420-36430, 36440, 36555-36556, 36568-36569, 36591-36592, 36600, 36640, 43752, 51701-51703, 62320-62327, 64400-64410, 64413-64435, 64445-64450, 64461-64463, 64479-64530, 69990, 76000-76001, 76942, 76970, 76998, 77001-77002, 92012-92014, 92960-92961, 93000-93010, 93040-93042, 93260-93261, 93279-93299, 93318, 93355, 93600-93603, 93610-93612, 94002, 94200, 94250, 94680-94690, 94770, 95812-95816, 95819, 95822, 95829, 95955, 96360-96368, 96372, 96374-96377, 97597-97598, 97602, 99155-99157, 99211-99223, 99231-99255, 99291-99292, 99304-99310, 99315-99316, 99334-99337, 99347-99350, 99374-99375, 99377-99378, 99446-99449, 99495-99496, G0463, G0471

33217   00530, 00534, 0213T, 0216T, 0228T, 0230T, 0293T-0294T, 0302T-0306T, 0387T, 0389T-0391T, 0462T-0463T, 11000-11006, 11042-11047, 12001-12007, 12011-12057, 13100-13133, 13151-13153, 33206-33207, 33210-33211, 33213-33215, 33220, 33221-33223, 33227-33228, 35201-35206, 35226-35236, 35256-35266, 35286, 36000, 36005-36013, 36120-36140, 36400-36410, 36420-36430, 36440, 36555-36556, 36568-36569, 36591-36592, 36600, 36640, 43752, 51701-51703, 62320-62327, 64400-64410, 64413-64435, 64445-64450, 64461-64463, 64479-64530, 76000-76001, 76942, 76970, 76998, 77001-77002, 92012-92014, 92960-92961, 93000-93010, 93040-93042, 93260-93261, 93279-93299, 93318, 93355, 93600-93603, 93610-93612, 94002, 94200, 94250, 94680-94690, 94770, 95812-95816, 95819, 95822, 95829, 95955, 96360-96368, 96372, 96374-96377, 97597-97598, 97602, 99155-99157, 99211-99223, 99231-99255, 99291-99292, 99304-99310, 99315-99316, 99334-99337, 99347-99350, 99374-99375, 99377-99378, 99446-99449, 99495-99496, G0463, G0471

Repair of Transvenous Electrode(s)

33218   **Repair of single transvenous electrode, permanent pacemaker or implantable defibrillator**

33220   **Repair of 2 transvenous electrodes for permanent pacemaker or pacing implantable defibrillator**
In 33218, the pacemaker or cardioverter/ defibrillator pocket is opened and the generator is removed. The electrode wire is tested. Repairs are performed. The wire is retested and then reconnected to the generator. The generator is placed back in its pocket and the pocket is closed. Report repair code 33220 if the pacemaker or cardioverter-defibrillator is a dual chamber model with two electrodes.

Coding Tips

1. These codes report only a repair procedure of electrodes.

2. For repair of one electrode with replacement of the pulse generator, see 33227-33229 or 33262-33264 and 33218.

3. For repair of two electrodes with replacement of the pulse generator, use 33220 in conjunction with 33228, 33229, 33263, and 33264 as appropriate.

4. Conscious sedation is not included in these codes. Separately report 99151–99157 per payer policy and coding guidelines. Hospitals may choose to include the costs associated with the service as part of the procedure rather than reporting them separately.

Facility HCPCS Coding

HCPCS Level II codes are used to report the supplies provided during the procedure. Hospitals should separately report supplies used during cardiac invasive procedures. Refer to chapter 1 for more information regarding appropriate billing of supplies. Refer to the list of current codes in appendix B.

ICD-10-CM Coding

The application of these codes is too broad to adequately present ICD-10-CM diagnosis code links here. Refer to the current ICD-10-CM book.

Transvenous Electrodes

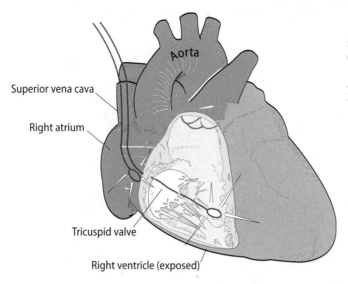

Schematic showing leads and electrodes to both right chambers

A dual-chamber electrode system is repaired in 33220

CCI Edits

33218 00530, 00534, 0213T, 0216T, 0228T, 0230T, 0293T-0294T, 0302T-0306T, 0307T, 0387T, 0388T-0391T, 0462T-0463T, 12001-12007, 12011-12057, 13100-13133, 13151-13153, 33206, 33208, 33210-33215, 33216-33217, 33221-33223, 33225, 33227-33229, 33230-33231, 33233, 33234-33235, 33240-33241, 33249, 33262-33264, 35201-35206, 35226-35236, 35256-35266, 35286, 36000, 36005-36013, 36120-36140, 36400-36410, 36420-36430, 36440, 36555-36556, 36568-36569, 36591-36592, 36600, 36640, 43752, 51701-51703, 62320-62327, 64400-64410, 64413-64435, 64445-64450, 64461-64463, 64479-64530, 69990, 76000-76001, 76942, 76970, 76998, 77001-77002, 92012-92014, 92960-92961, 93000-93010, 93040-93042, 93260-93261, 93279-93299, 93318, 93355, 94002, 94200, 94250, 94680-94690, 94770, 95812-95816, 95819, 95822, 95829, 95955, 96360-96368, 96372, 96374-96377, 99155-99157, 99211-99223, 99231-99255, 99291-99292, 99304-99310, 99315-99316, 99334-99337, 99347-99350, 99374-99375, 99377-99378, 99446-99449, 99495-99496, G0448, G0463, G0471

33220 00530, 00534, 0213T, 0216T, 0228T, 0230T, 0293T-0294T, 0302T-0306T, 0307T, 0387T, 0388T-0391T, 0462T-0463T, 12001-12007, 12011-12057, 13100-13133, 13151-13153, 33210-33215, 33218, 33221-33223, 33225, 33227-33229, 33230-33231, 33233, 33234-33235, 33240-33241, 33249, 33262-33264, 35201-35206, 35226-35236, 35256-35266, 35286, 36000, 36005-36013, 36120-36140, 36400-36410, 36420-36430, 36440, 36555-36556, 36568-36569, 36591-36592, 36600, 36640, 43752, 51701-51703, 62320-62327, 64400-64410, 64413-64435, 64445-64450, 64461-64463, 64479-64530, 69990, 76000-76001, 76942, 76970, 76998, 77001-77002, 92012-92014, 92960-92961, 93000-93010, 93040-93042, 93260-93261, 93279-93299, 93318, 93355, 94002, 94200, 94250, 94680-94690, 94770, 95812-95816, 95819, 95822, 95829, 95955, 96360-96368, 96372, 96374-96377, 99155-99157, 99211-99223, 99231-99255, 99291-99292, 99304-99310, 99315-99316, 99334-99337, 99347-99350, 99374-99375, 99377-99378, 99446-99449, 99495-99496, G0448, G0463, G0471

Pocket Relocation

The pocket created during pacemaker or ICD implantation sometimes requires relocation and can be performed as a stand-alone procedure or during a generator change procedure. The procedure involves relocating a pacemaker pocket or a cardioverter-defibrillator pocket due to infection, erosion, or complications from the original generator placement. The pocket is opened, and the generator is removed. A new pocket is formed in the subcutaneous tissue within the reach of the already present electrodes. The electrodes are brought through a new subcutaneous tunnel into the new pocket. The old pocket is closed. The existing or new generator is placed in the new pocket, and the electrodes are connected. The pocket is closed.

33222   **Relocation of skin pocket for pacemaker**

33223   **Relocation of skin pocket for implantable defibrillator**

Coding Tips

1. Report CPT code 33222 when the pocket relocation is for a pacemaker device. Report CPT code 33223 when the procedure is for a cardioverter-defibrillator device.

2. The physician should clearly describe the relocation procedure.

3. Conscious sedation is not included in these codes. Separately report 99151–99157 per payer policy and coding guidelines. Hospitals may choose to include the costs associated with the service as part of the procedure rather than reporting them separately.

Facility HCPCS Coding

There are no HCPCS codes applicable to these procedures.

ICD-10-CM Coding

L76.81	Other intraoperative complications of skin and subcutaneous tissue
M70.90	Unspecified soft tissue disorder related to use, overuse and pressure of unspecified site
M70.911	Unspecified soft tissue disorder related to use, overuse and pressure, right shoulder
M70.912	Unspecified soft tissue disorder related to use, overuse and pressure, left shoulder
M70.919	Unspecified soft tissue disorder related to use, overuse and pressure, unspecified shoulder
M70.98	Unspecified soft tissue disorder related to use, overuse and pressure other
M79.81	Nontraumatic hematoma of soft tissue
T81.4XXA	Infection following a procedure, initial encounter
T81.83XA	Persistent postprocedural fistula, initial encounter
T81.89XA	Other complications of procedures, not elsewhere classified, initial encounter
T82.121A	Displacement of cardiac pulse generator (battery), initial encounter
T82.7XXA	Infection and inflammatory reaction due to other cardiac and vascular devices, implants and grafts, initial encounter
T82.817A	Embolism of cardiac prosthetic devices, implants and grafts, initial encounter
T82.827A	Fibrosis of cardiac prosthetic devices, implants and grafts, initial encounter
T82.837A	Hemorrhage of cardiac prosthetic devices, implants and grafts, initial encounter
T82.847A	Pain from cardiac prosthetic devices, implants and grafts, initial encounter
T82.855A	Stenosis of coronary artery stent, initial encounter
T82.857A	Stenosis of cardiac prosthetic devices, implants and grafts, initial encounter
T82.867A	Thrombosis of cardiac prosthetic devices, implants and grafts, initial encounter
T82.897A	Other specified complication of cardiac prosthetic devices, implants and grafts, initial encounter
T82.9XXA	Unspecified complication of cardiac and vascular prosthetic device, implant and graft, initial encounter

CCI Edits

33222 00530, 00534, 0213T, 0216T, 0228T, 0230T, 0293T-0294T, 0302T-0306T, 0387T, 0389T-0391T, 0462T-0463T, 10060-10061, 10140, 10180, 11000-11006, 11042-11047, 12001-12007, 12011-12057, 13100-13133, 13151-13153, 33210-33211, 36000, 36005, 36400-36410, 36420-36430, 36440, 36591-36592, 36600, 36640, 43752, 51701-51703, 62320-62327, 64400-64410, 64413-64435, 64445-64450, 64461-64463, 64479-64530, 69990, 76000-76001, 76942, 76970, 76998, 77002, 92012-92014, 92960-92961, 93000-93010, 93040-93042, 93260-93261, 93279-93299, 93318, 93355, 94002, 94200, 94250, 94680-94690, 94770, 95812-95816, 95819, 95822, 95829, 95955, 96360-96368, 96372, 96374-96377, 97597-97598, 97602, 99155-99157, 99211-99223, 99231-99255, 99291-99292, 99304-99310, 99315-99316, 99334-99337, 99347-99350, 99374-99375, 99377-99378, 99446-99449, 99495-99496, G0463, G0471

33223 00530, 00534, 0213T, 0216T, 0228T, 0230T, 0293T-0294T, 0302T-0306T, 0389T-0391T, 0462T-0463T, 10060-10061, 10140, 10180, 11000-11006, 11042-11047, 12001-12007, 12011-12057, 13100-13133, 13151-13153, 33210-33211, 36000, 36005, 36400-36410, 36420-36430, 36440, 36591-36592, 36600, 36640, 43752, 51701-51703, 62320-62327, 64400-64410, 64413-64435, 64445-64450, 64461-64463, 64479-64530, 69990, 76000-76001, 76942, 76970, 76998, 77002, 92012-92014, 92960-92961, 93000-93010, 93040-93042, 93260-93261, 93279-93299, 93318, 93355, 94002, 94200, 94250, 94680-94690, 94770, 95812-95816, 95819, 95822, 95829, 95955, 96360-96368, 96372, 96374-96377, 97597-97598, 97602, 99155-99157, 99211-99223, 99231-99255, 99291-99292, 99304-99310, 99315-99316, 99334-99337, 99347-99350, 99374-99375, 99377-99378, 99446-99449, 99495-99496, G0463, G0471

Insertion of Electrode for Left Ventricular Pacing (Previously placed pacemaker or ICD)

33224   **Insertion of pacing electrode, cardiac venous system, for left ventricular pacing, with attachment to previously placed pacemaker or implantable defibrillator pulse generator (including revision of pocket, removal, insertion and/or replacement of existing generator)**

If biventricular pacing is required, an additional electrode is placed in the left ventricle. With the pacemaker or pacing cardioverter-defibrillator already in place, the physician gains access transvenously through the subclavian or jugular vein. A fluoroscope may be used for guidance and a pacing electrode is inserted in the ventricular chamber of the heart, usually in the coronary sinus tributary. The generator pocket may be revised and/or the generator removed, inserted, or replaced. The electrode is connected to the generator and the pocket is closed.

Coding Tips

1. This code reports the insertion of an electrode on a previously placed permanent pacemaker or cardioverter-defibrillator for left ventricular pacing.

2. This code is listed separately in addition to the primary procedure.

3. Pocket revision, if done, is not reported separately. Pocket revision is included in this code.

4. For insertion of a pacing electrode for left ventricular pacing placed at the time of insertion of a pacing cardioverter-defibrillator or pacemaker pulse generator, see 33225.

5. For repositioning of an electrode for left ventricular pacing, see 33226.

6. For insertion of a single chamber electrode, see 33216.

7. For insertion of a dual chamber electrode, see 33217.

8. HCPCS Level II code C1900 Lead, left ventricular coronary venous system, is reported for the electrode associated with this procedure.

Facility HCPCS Coding

HCPCS Level II codes are used to report the supplies provided during the procedure. Hospitals should separately report supplies used during cardiac invasive procedures. Refer to chapter 1 for more information regarding appropriate billing of supplies. Refer to the list of current codes in appendix B.

C1900   Lead, left ventricular coronary venous system

Pacing System

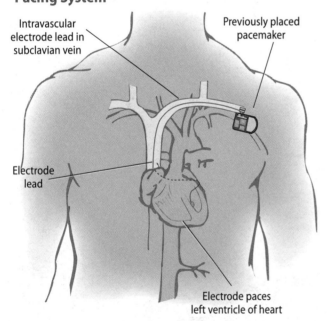

A pacing electrode is placed in the venous system and attached to a previously placed pacemaker or defibrillator generator. Revision of the pocket and/or replacement of the generator is included

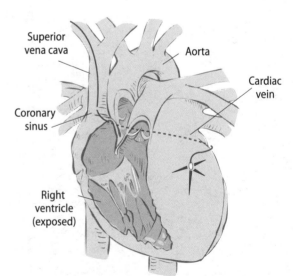

Lead is advanced through cardiac vein where it stimulates the left ventricle

ICD-10-CM Coding

I11.Ø	Hypertensive heart disease with heart failure
I13.Ø	Hypertensive heart and chronic kidney disease with heart failure and stage 1 through stage 4 chronic kidney disease, or unspecified chronic kidney disease
I13.2	Hypertensive heart and chronic kidney disease with heart failure and with stage 5 chronic kidney disease, or end stage renal disease
I16.Ø	Hypertensive urgency
I16.1	Hypertensive emergency
I16.9	Hypertensive crisis, unspecified
I21.Ø1	ST elevation (STEMI) myocardial infarction involving left main coronary artery
I21.Ø2	ST elevation (STEMI) myocardial infarction involving left anterior descending coronary artery
I21.Ø9	ST elevation (STEMI) myocardial infarction involving other coronary artery of anterior wall
I21.11	ST elevation (STEMI) myocardial infarction involving right coronary artery
I21.19	ST elevation (STEMI) myocardial infarction involving other coronary artery of inferior wall
I21.21	ST elevation (STEMI) myocardial infarction involving left circumflex coronary artery
I21.29	ST elevation (STEMI) myocardial infarction involving other sites
I21.3	ST elevation (STEMI) myocardial infarction of unspecified site
I21.4	Non-ST elevation (NSTEMI) myocardial infarction
I21.9	Acute myocardial infarction, unspecified
I21.A1	Myocardial infarction type 2
I21.A9	Other myocardial infarction type
I22.Ø	Subsequent ST elevation (STEMI) myocardial infarction of anterior wall
I22.1	Subsequent ST elevation (STEMI) myocardial infarction of inferior wall
I22.2	Subsequent non-ST elevation (NSTEMI) myocardial infarction
I22.8	Subsequent ST elevation (STEMI) myocardial infarction of other sites
I22.9	Subsequent ST elevation (STEMI) myocardial infarction of unspecified site
I25.2	Old myocardial infarction
I25.5	Ischemic cardiomyopathy
I25.6	Silent myocardial ischemia
I25.89	Other forms of chronic ischemic heart disease
I25.9	Chronic ischemic heart disease, unspecified
I42.Ø	Dilated cardiomyopathy
I42.1	Obstructive hypertrophic cardiomyopathy
I42.2	Other hypertrophic cardiomyopathy
I42.3	Endomyocardial (eosinophilic) disease
I42.4	Endocardial fibroelastosis
I42.5	Other restrictive cardiomyopathy
I42.6	Alcoholic cardiomyopathy
I42.7	Cardiomyopathy due to drug and external agent
I42.8	Other cardiomyopathies
I42.9	Cardiomyopathy, unspecified
I43	Cardiomyopathy in diseases classified elsewhere
I44.Ø	Atrioventricular block, first degree
I44.1	Atrioventricular block, second degree
I44.2	Atrioventricular block, complete
I44.3Ø	Unspecified atrioventricular block
I44.39	Other atrioventricular block
I44.4	Left anterior fascicular block
I44.5	Left posterior fascicular block
I44.6Ø	Unspecified fascicular block
I44.69	Other fascicular block
I44.7	Left bundle-branch block, unspecified
I45.Ø	Right fascicular block
I45.1Ø	Unspecified right bundle-branch block
I45.19	Other right bundle-branch block
I45.2	Bifascicular block

I45.3	Trifascicular block
I45.4	Nonspecific intraventricular block
I45.5	Other specified heart block
I45.6	Pre-excitation syndrome
I45.81	Long QT syndrome
I45.9	Conduction disorder, unspecified
I46.2	Cardiac arrest due to underlying cardiac condition
I46.8	Cardiac arrest due to other underlying condition
I46.9	Cardiac arrest, cause unspecified
I47.0	Re-entry ventricular arrhythmia
I47.1	Supraventricular tachycardia
I47.2	Ventricular tachycardia
I47.9	Paroxysmal tachycardia, unspecified
I48.0	Paroxysmal atrial fibrillation
I48.2	Chronic atrial fibrillation
I48.91	Unspecified atrial fibrillation
I49.01	Ventricular fibrillation
I49.02	Ventricular flutter
I49.2	Junctional premature depolarization
I49.5	Sick sinus syndrome
I49.8	Other specified cardiac arrhythmias
I49.9	Cardiac arrhythmia, unspecified
I50.1	Left ventricular failure
I50.20	Unspecified systolic (congestive) heart failure
I50.21	Acute systolic (congestive) heart failure
I50.22	Chronic systolic (congestive) heart failure
I50.23	Acute on chronic systolic (congestive) heart failure
I50.30	Unspecified diastolic (congestive) heart failure
I50.31	Acute diastolic (congestive) heart failure
I50.32	Chronic diastolic (congestive) heart failure
I50.33	Acute on chronic diastolic (congestive) heart failure
I50.40	Unspecified combined systolic (congestive) and diastolic (congestive) heart failure
I50.41	Acute combined systolic (congestive) and diastolic (congestive) heart failure
I50.42	Chronic combined systolic (congestive) and diastolic (congestive) heart failure
I50.43	Acute on chronic combined systolic (congestive) and diastolic (congestive) heart failure
I50.810	Right heart failure, unspecified
I50.811	Acute right heart failure
I50.812	Chronic right heart failure
I50.813	Acute on chronic right heart failure
I50.814	Right heart failure due to left heart failure
I50.82	Biventricular heart failure
I50.83	High output heart failure
I50.84	End stage heart failure
I50.89	Other heart failure
I50.9	Heart failure, unspecified
I51.7	Cardiomegaly
L76.81	Other intraoperative complications of skin and subcutaneous tissue
L76.82	Other postprocedural complications of skin and subcutaneous tissue
Q23.8	Other congenital malformations of aortic and mitral valves
Q23.9	Congenital malformation of aortic and mitral valves, unspecified
Q24.6	Congenital heart block
Q24.8	Other specified congenital malformations of heart
R00.1	Bradycardia, unspecified
T82.110A	Breakdown (mechanical) of cardiac electrode, initial encounter
T82.111A	Breakdown (mechanical) of cardiac pulse generator (battery), initial encounter
T82.120A	Displacement of cardiac electrode, initial encounter

T82.121A	Displacement of cardiac pulse generator (battery), initial encounter
T82.190A	Other mechanical complication of cardiac electrode, initial encounter
T82.191A	Other mechanical complication of cardiac pulse generator (battery), initial encounter
T82.598A	Other mechanical complication of other cardiac and vascular devices and implants, initial encounter
T82.7XXA	Infection and inflammatory reaction due to other cardiac and vascular devices, implants and grafts, initial encounter
T82.817A	Embolism of cardiac prosthetic devices, implants and grafts, initial encounter
T82.827A	Fibrosis of cardiac prosthetic devices, implants and grafts, initial encounter
T82.837A	Hemorrhage of cardiac prosthetic devices, implants and grafts, initial encounter
T82.847A	Pain from cardiac prosthetic devices, implants and grafts, initial encounter
T82.855A	Stenosis of coronary artery stent, initial encounter
T82.857A	Stenosis of cardiac prosthetic devices, implants and grafts, initial encounter
T82.867A	Thrombosis of cardiac prosthetic devices, implants and grafts, initial encounter
T82.897A	Other specified complication of cardiac prosthetic devices, implants and grafts, initial encounter
T82.9XXA	Unspecified complication of cardiac and vascular prosthetic device, implant and graft, initial encounter
Z45.018	Encounter for adjustment and management of other part of cardiac pacemaker
Z45.02	Encounter for adjustment and management of automatic implantable cardiac defibrillator
Z95.0	Presence of cardiac pacemaker
Z95.810	Presence of automatic (implantable) cardiac defibrillator

CCI Edits

33224   00530, 00540, 0213T, 0216T, 0228T, 0230T, 0293T-0294T, 0302T-0307T, 0387T, 0388T-0391T, 0462T-0463T, 11000-11006, 11042-11047, 12001-12007, 12011-12057, 13100-13133, 13151-13153, 33210-33211, 33215, 33222-33223, 33227-33229, 33230-33231, 33233, 33240-33241, 33262-33264, 35201-35206, 35226-35236, 35256-35266, 35286, 36000, 36005-36013, 36120-36140, 36400-36410, 36420-36430, 36440, 36591-36592, 36600, 36640, 43752, 51701-51703, 62320-62327, 64400-64410, 64413-64435, 64445-64450, 64461-64463, 64479-64530, 69990, 75860, 76000-76001, 76942, 76970, 76998, 77001-77002, 92012-92014, 92960-92961, 93000-93010, 93040-93042, 93260-93261, 93279-93299, 93318, 93355, 93600-93603, 93610-93612, 94002, 94200, 94250, 94680-94690, 94770, 95812-95816, 95819, 95822, 95829, 95955, 96360-96368, 96372, 96374-96377, 97597-97598, 97602, 99155-99157, 99211-99223, 99231-99255, 99291-99292, 99304-99310, 99315-99316, 99334-99337, 99347-99350, 99374-99375, 99377-99378, 99446-99449, 99495-99496, G0463, G0471

Insertion of Electrode for Left Ventricular Pacing at the Same Time as Primary Procedure

33225   **Insertion of pacing electrode, cardiac venous system, for left ventricular pacing, at time of insertion of implantable defibrillator or pacemaker pulse generator (eg, for upgrade to dual chamber system) (List separately in addition to code for primary procedure)**

If biventricular pacing is required, an additional electrode is placed in the left ventricle. During insertion of a pacing cardioverter-defibrillator or pacemaker pulse generator, the physician gains access transvenously through the subclavian or jugular vein. A fluoroscope may be used for guidance and a pacing electrode is inserted in the ventricular chamber of the heart, usually in the coronary sinus tributary. The electrode is connected to the generator and the generator pocket is closed.

Coding Tips

1. This code reports the insertion of an electrode at the time of insertion of a pacing cardioverter-defibrillator or pacemaker pulse generator for left ventricular pacing.
2. This code is listed in addition to the primary pacemaker or ICD procedure.
3. For insertion of an electrode for a previously placed pacing cardioverter-defibrillator or pacemaker pulse generator, see 33224.
4. For repositioning of an electrode for left ventricular pacing, see 33226.
5. Pocket revision is included and not separately reported.
6. HCPCS Level II code C1900 Lead, left ventricular coronary venous system, is reported for the electrode associated with this procedure. Device edits apply.

Facility HCPCS Coding

HCPCS Level II codes are used to report the supplies provided during the procedure. Hospitals should separately report supplies used during cardiac invasive procedures. Refer to chapter 1 for more information regarding appropriate billing of supplies. Refer to the list of current codes in appendix B.

C1900   Lead, left ventricular coronary venous system

Pacing System

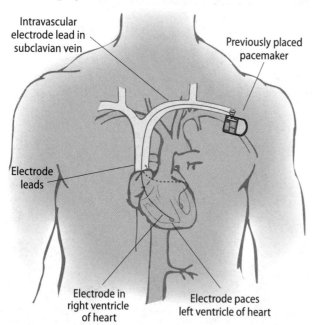

A pacing electrode is placed in the venous system at the time a pacemaker or defibrillator generators inserted. Upgrage from a single chamber to dual chamber system is included in this code.

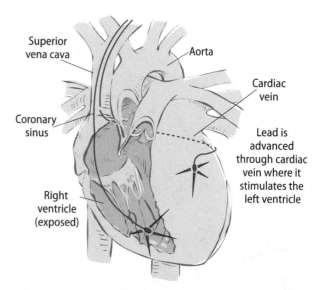

Dual chamber system

ICD-10-CM Coding

This is an add-on code. Refer to the corresponding primary procedure code for ICD-10-CM diagnosis code links.

CCI Edits

33225   0213T, 0216T, 0293T-0294T, 0302T-0306T, 0387T, 0389T-0391T, 0462T-0463T, 11000-11006, 11042-11047, 33210-33211, 33215, 36000, 36010-36013, 36120-36140, 36410, 36591-36592, 61650, 62324-62327, 64415, 64417, 64450, 64486-64490, 64493, 75860, 76000-76001, 77001-77002, 92960-92961, 93260-93261, 93279-93299, 93600-93603, 93610-93612, 96360, 96365, 97597-97598, 97602

Reposition Previously Placed Left Ventricular Electrode

33226   **Repositioning of previously implanted cardiac venous system (left ventricular) electrode (including removal, insertion and/or replacement of existing generator)**
The physician gains access transvenously through the subclavian or jugular vein. A fluoroscope may be used for guidance and the pacing electrode that is already in place in the ventricular chamber of the heart, usually in the coronary sinus tributary, is repositioned. The generator pocket may be revised and/or the generator removed, inserted, or replaced. The electrode is connected to the generator and the pocket is closed.

Coding Tips

1. This code reports the reposition of an electrode in a previously placed pacing cardioverter-defibrillator or pacemaker pulse generator for left ventricular pacing.
2. This code is listed separately in addition to the primary procedure.
3. For insertion of an electrode for a previously placed pacing cardioverter-defibrillator or pacemaker pulse generator, see 33224.
4. For insertion of an electrode at the time of insertion of a pacing cardioverter-defibrillator or pacemaker pulse generator for left ventricular pacing, see 33225.
5. For insertion of a single chamber electrode, see 33216.
6. For insertion of a dual chamber electrode, see 33217.
7. Fluoroscopy is included and not separately reported.

Facility HCPCS Coding

HCPCS Level II codes are used to report the supplies provided during the procedure. Hospitals should separately report supplies used during cardiac invasive procedures. Refer to chapter 1 for more information regarding appropriate billing of supplies. Refer to the list of current codes in appendix B.

Pacing System—Left

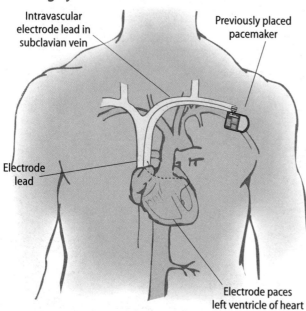

A pacing electrode in the venous system is repositioned. If the previously placed generator is revised or replaced, this code reports that service as well

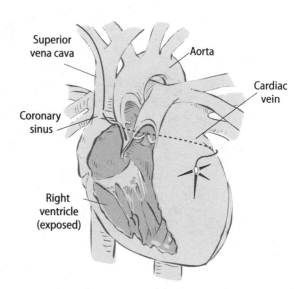

Lead is repositioned along the cardiac vein where it stimulates the left ventricle

ICD-10-CM Coding

T82.110A	Breakdown (mechanical) of cardiac electrode, initial encounter
T82.120A	Displacement of cardiac electrode, initial encounter
T82.190A	Other mechanical complication of cardiac electrode, initial encounter
T82.7XXA	Infection and inflammatory reaction due to other cardiac and vascular devices, implants and grafts, initial encounter
T82.817A	Embolism of cardiac prosthetic devices, implants and grafts, initial encounter
T82.827A	Fibrosis of cardiac prosthetic devices, implants and grafts, initial encounter
T82.837A	Hemorrhage of cardiac prosthetic devices, implants and grafts, initial encounter
T82.847A	Pain from cardiac prosthetic devices, implants and grafts, initial encounter
T82.855A	Stenosis of coronary artery stent, initial encounter
T82.857A	Stenosis of cardiac prosthetic devices, implants and grafts, initial encounter
T82.867A	Thrombosis of cardiac prosthetic devices, implants and grafts, initial encounter
T82.897A	Other specified complication of cardiac prosthetic devices, implants and grafts, initial encounter
T82.9XXA	Unspecified complication of cardiac and vascular prosthetic device, implant and graft, initial encounter
Z45.02	Encounter for adjustment and management of automatic implantable cardiac defibrillator
Z95.0	Presence of cardiac pacemaker

CCI Edits

33226 00530, 00540, 0213T, 0216T, 0228T, 0230T, 0293T-0294T, 0302T-0307T, 0387T, 0388T-0391T, 0462T-0463T, 11000-11006, 11042-11047, 12001-12007, 12011-12057, 13100-13133, 13151-13153, 33206-33208, 33210-33211, 33212-33215, 33221, 33222-33223, 33227, 33228-33229, 33230-33231, 33233, 33240-33241, 33249, 33262-33264, 35201-35206, 35226-35236, 35256-35266, 35286, 36000, 36005-36013, 36120-36140, 36400-36410, 36420-36430, 36440, 36591-36592, 36600, 36640, 43752, 51701-51703, 62320-62327, 64400-64410, 64413-64435, 64445-64450, 64461-64463, 64479-64530, 69990, 75860, 76000-76001, 76942, 76970, 76998, 77001-77002, 92012-92014, 92960-92961, 93000-93010, 93040-93042, 93260-93261, 93279-93299, 93318, 93355, 93600-93603, 93610-93612, 94002, 94200, 94250, 94680-94690, 94770, 95812-95816, 95819, 95822, 95829, 95955, 96360-96368, 96372, 96374-96377, 97597-97598, 97602, 99155-99157, 99211-99223, 99231-99255, 99291-99292, 99304-99310, 99315-99316, 99334-99337, 99347-99350, 99374-99375, 99377-99378, 99446-99449, 99495-99496, G0448, G0463, G0471

Removal and Replacement of Pacemaker Generator

33227	**Removal of permanent pacemaker pulse generator with replacement of pacemaker pulse generator; single lead system**
33228	**dual lead system**
33229	**multiple lead system**

An incision is made over the existing pacemaker generator and the pocket is opened. The old generator is removed. The existing leads are tested and the new generator is inserted. The leads are connected to the new generator and testing is done to complete parameter settings. The pocket is closed.

Coding Tips

1. Report code 33227 when the existing system is a single lead system.
2. Report 33228 when the system is a dual lead system.
3. Report 33229 when the existing system has multiple or more than two leads.
4. Do not report 33233 in conjunction with these codes as they include generator removal.
5. When electrodes are also replaced, refer to other sections in this chapter.
6. Report the appropriate device code for the procedure performed.
7. Conscious sedation is not included in these codes. Separately report 99151–99157 per payer policy and coding guidelines. Hospitals may choose to include the costs associated with the service as part of the procedure rather than reporting them separately.

Facility HCPCS Coding

HCPCS Level II codes are used to report supplies provided during the procedure. Hospitals should separately report supplies used during invasive cardiac procedures. Refer to Chapter 1 for more information regarding appropriate billing of supplies. Refer to the list of current device codes in appendix B of this publication.

C1785	Pacemaker, dual chamber, rate-responsive (implantable)
C1786	Pacemaker, single chamber, rate-responsive (implantable)
C2620	Pacemaker, single chamber, non rate-responsive (implantable)
C2621	Pacemaker, other than single or dual chamber (implantable)

Dual Chamber Pacemaker (implanted transvenously)

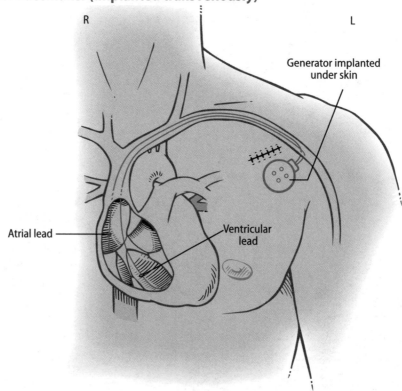

R   L

Generator implanted
under skin

Atrial lead

Ventricular
lead

ICD-10-CM Coding

T82.111A	Breakdown (mechanical) of cardiac pulse generator (battery), initial encounter
T82.121A	Displacement of cardiac pulse generator (battery), initial encounter
T82.191A	Other mechanical complication of cardiac pulse generator (battery), initial encounter
T82.7XXA	Infection and inflammatory reaction due to other cardiac and vascular devices, implants and grafts, initial encounter
T82.817A	Embolism of cardiac prosthetic devices, implants and grafts, initial encounter
T82.827A	Fibrosis of cardiac prosthetic devices, implants and grafts, initial encounter
T82.837A	Hemorrhage of cardiac prosthetic devices, implants and grafts, initial encounter
T82.847A	Pain from cardiac prosthetic devices, implants and grafts, initial encounter
T82.855A	Stenosis of coronary artery stent, initial encounter
T82.857A	Stenosis of cardiac prosthetic devices, implants and grafts, initial encounter
T82.867A	Thrombosis of cardiac prosthetic devices, implants and grafts, initial encounter
T82.897A	Other specified complication of cardiac prosthetic devices, implants and grafts, initial encounter
T82.9XXA	Unspecified complication of cardiac and vascular prosthetic device, implant and graft, initial encounter
Z45.018	Encounter for adjustment and management of other part of cardiac pacemaker

CCI Edits

33227 00530, 00534, 0213T, 0216T, 0228T, 0230T, 0293T-0294T, 0302T-0307T, 0388T, 0389T-0391T, 0462T-0463T, 11000-11006, 11042-11047, 12001-12007, 12011-12057, 13100-13133, 13151-13153, 33210-33213, 33215, 33221, 33233, 36000, 36005, 36400-36410, 36420-36430, 36440, 36591-36592, 36600, 36640, 43752, 51701-51703, 62320-62327, 64400-64410, 64413-64435, 64445-64450, 64461-64463, 64479-64530, 69990, 76000-76001, 76942, 76970, 76998, 77002, 92012-92014, 93000-93010, 93040-93042, 93260-93261, 93279-93299, 93318, 93355, 93600-93603, 93610-93612, 94002, 94200, 94250, 94680-94690, 94770, 95812-95816, 95819, 95822, 95829, 95955, 96360-96368, 96372, 96374-96377, 97597-97598, 97602, 99155-99157, 99211-99223, 99231-99255, 99291-99292, 99304-99310, 99315-99316, 99334-99337, 99347-99350, 99374-99375, 99377-99378, 99446-99449, 99495-99496, G0463, G0471

33228 00530, 00534, 0213T, 0216T, 0228T, 0230T, 0293T-0294T, 0302T-0307T, 0388T, 0389T-0391T, 0462T-0463T, 11000-11006, 11042-11047, 12001-12007, 12011-12057, 13100-13133, 13151-13153, 33210-33213, 33215, 33221, 33227, 33233, 36000, 36005, 36400-36410, 36420-36430, 36440, 36591-36592, 36600, 36640, 43752, 51701-51703, 62320-62327, 64400-64410, 64413-64435, 64445-64450, 64461-64463, 64479-64530, 69990, 76000-76001, 76942, 76970, 76998, 77002, 92012-92014, 93000-93010, 93040-93042, 93260-93261, 93279-93299, 93318, 93355, 93600-93603, 93610-93612, 94002, 94200, 94250, 94680-94690, 94770, 95812-95816, 95819, 95822, 95829, 95955, 96360-96368, 96372, 96374-96377, 97597-97598, 97602, 99155-99157, 99211-99223, 99231-99255, 99291-99292, 99304-99310, 99315-99316, 99334-99337, 99347-99350, 99374-99375, 99377-99378, 99446-99449, 99495-99496, G0463, G0471

33229 00530, 00534, 0213T, 0216T, 0228T, 0230T, 0293T-0294T, 0302T-0307T, 0388T, 0389T-0391T, 0462T-0463T, 11000-11006, 11042-11047, 12001-12007, 12011-12057, 13100-13133, 13151-13153, 33210-33213, 33215-33217, 33221, 33227-33228, 33233, 36000, 36005, 36400-36410, 36420-36430, 36440, 36591-36592, 36600, 36640, 43752, 51701-51703, 62320-62327, 64400-64410, 64413-64435, 64445-64450, 64461-64463, 64479-64530, 69990, 76000-76001, 76942, 76970, 76998, 77002, 92012-92014, 93000-93010, 93040-93042, 93260-93261, 93279-93299, 93318, 93355, 93600-93603, 93610-93612, 94002, 94200, 94250, 94680-94690, 94770, 95812-95816, 95819, 95822, 95829, 95955, 96360-96368, 96372, 96374-96377, 97597-97598, 97602, 99155-99157, 99211-99223, 99231-99255, 99291-99292, 99304-99310, 99315-99316, 99334-99337, 99347-99350, 99374-99375, 99377-99378, 99446-99449, 99495-99496, G0463, G0471

Case Example

See case example #1 at the end of this chapter.

Removal of Permanent Pacemaker Generator

33233   **Removal of permanent pacemaker pulse generator only**

In 33233, only the pulse generator is removed. The pacemaker generator pocket is opened. The generator is disconnected from the wire(s) and removed. The wire(s) are left in place in the pocket and the pocket is closed or a new pacemaker generator is inserted. If a new pacemaker is inserted, it is reported separately.

Coding Tips

1. An inactive pacemaker does not always require removal.
2. Procedure 33233 reports removal of the pacemaker generator only. For removal with replacement during the same surgical session, see 33227, 33228, or 33229.
3. For removal of transvenous pacemaker electrodes, see 33234-33235.
4. For removal of pacemaker system and/or electrodes by thoracotomy, see 33236-33238.
5. Conscious sedation is not included in these codes. Separately report 99151–99157 per payer policy and coding guidelines. Hospitals may choose to include the costs associated with the service as part of the procedure rather than reporting them separately.

Facility HCPCS Coding

HCPCS Level II codes are used to report the supplies provided during the procedure. Hospitals should separately report supplies used during cardiac invasive procedures. Refer to chapter 1 for more information regarding appropriate billing of supplies. Refer to the list of current codes in appendix B.

ICD-10-CM Coding

T82.111A	Breakdown (mechanical) of cardiac pulse generator (battery), initial encounter
T82.121A	Displacement of cardiac pulse generator (battery), initial encounter
T82.191A	Other mechanical complication of cardiac pulse generator (battery), initial encounter
T82.7XXA	Infection and inflammatory reaction due to other cardiac and vascular devices, implants and grafts, initial encounter

CCI Edits

33233   00530, 00534, 0213T, 0216T, 0228T, 0230T, 0293T-0294T, 0302T-0306T, 0388T, 0389T-0391T, 0462T-0463T, 11000-11006, 11042-11047, 12001-12007, 12011-12057, 13100-13133, 13151-13153, 33210-33211, 33215, 33222, 33236-33237, 36000, 36005, 36400-36410, 36420-36430, 36440, 36591-36592, 36600, 36640, 43752, 51701-51703, 62320-62327, 64400-64410, 64413-64435, 64445-64450, 64461-64463, 64479-64530, 69990, 76000-76001, 76942, 76970, 76998, 77002, 92012-92014, 92960-92961, 93000-93010, 93040-93042, 93260-93261, 93279-93299, 93318, 93355, 94002, 94200, 94250, 94680-94690, 94770, 95812-95816, 95819, 95822, 95829, 95955, 96360-96368, 96372, 96374-96377, 97597-97598, 97602, 99155-99157, 99211-99223, 99231-99255, 99291-99292, 99304-99310, 99315-99316, 99334-99337, 99347-99350, 99374-99375, 99377-99378, 99446-99449, 99495-99496, G0463, G0471

Pacemaker Removal

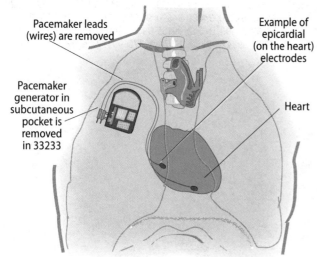

An implanted permanent pacemaker is removed in 33233

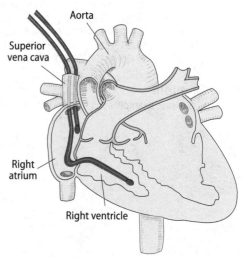

Schematic of transvenous, dual lead system

Removal of Pacemaker Electrode(s)

33234	**Removal of transvenous pacemaker electrode(s); single lead system, atrial or ventricular**
33235	**dual lead system**

In 33234 and 33235, only the transvenous electrode(s) are removed. For 33234, the generator pocket is opened and the wire is disconnected from the generator. The wire is dissected from the scar tissue which has formed around it. Once the wire is completely freed, it is twisted in a direction opposite to that used for insertion (counter clockwise). The wire is then withdrawn. Bleeding from the tracts leading to the vein is controlled with sutures. A new wire may be placed, but is reported separately. Report 33235 for a dual lead system (removal of two wires).

Coding Tips

1. Procedures 33234 and 33235 report removal of pacemaker leads without concurrent replacement. For removal with replacement of generator and leads during the same surgical session, see 33206-33208. For transvenous leads inserted when a pulse generator is in place, see 33216 and 33217.

2. For removal of a permanent pacemaker pulse generator, see 33233.

3. For removal of a pacemaker system and/or electrodes by thoracotomy, see 33236-33238.

4. Conscious sedation is not included in these codes. Separately report 99151–99157 per payer policy and coding guidelines. Hospitals may choose to include the costs associated with the service as part of the procedure rather than reporting them separately.

Facility HCPCS Coding

HCPCS Level II codes are used to report the supplies provided during the procedure. Hospitals should separately report supplies used during cardiac invasive procedures. Refer to chapter 1 for more information regarding appropriate billing of supplies. Refer to the list of current codes in appendix B.

ICD-10-CM Coding

T82.11ØA	Breakdown (mechanical) of cardiac electrode, initial encounter
T82.12ØA	Displacement of cardiac electrode, initial encounter
T82.19ØA	Other mechanical complication of cardiac electrode, initial encounter
T82.7XXA	Infection and inflammatory reaction due to other cardiac and vascular devices, implants and grafts, initial encounter

Electrode Removal

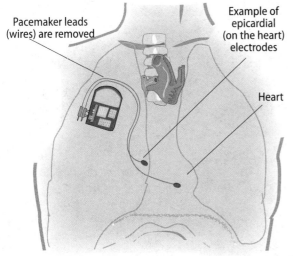

Report 33234 for removal of a transvenous single lead system (one wire

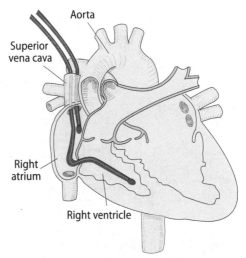

Schematic of transvenous, dual lead system

CCI Edits

33234   00530, 00534, 0213T, 0216T, 0228T, 0230T, 0293T-0294T, 0302T-0306T, 0388T, 0389T-0391T, 0462T-0463T, 11000-11006, 11042-11047, 12001-12007, 12011-12057, 13100-13133, 13151-13153, 33210-33211, 33215, 33222-33223, 35201-35206, 35226-35236, 35256-35266, 35286, 36000, 36005-36013, 36120-36140, 36400-36410, 36420-36430, 36440, 36555-36556, 36568-36569, 36591-36592, 36600, 36640, 43752, 51701-51703, 62320-62327, 64400-64410, 64413-64435, 64445-64450, 64461-64463, 64479-64530, 69990, 76000-76001, 76942, 76970, 76998, 77001-77002, 92012-92014, 92960-92961, 93000-93010, 93040-93042, 93260-93261, 93279-93299, 93318, 93355, 94002, 94200, 94250, 94680-94690, 94770, 95812-95816, 95819, 95822, 95829, 95955, 96360-96368, 96372, 96374-96377, 97597-97598, 97602, 99155-99157, 99211-99223, 99231-99255, 99291-99292, 99304-99310, 99315-99316, 99334-99337, 99347-99350, 99374-99375, 99377-99378, 99446-99449, 99495-99496, G0463, G0471

33235   00530, 00534, 0213T, 0216T, 0228T, 0230T, 0293T-0294T, 0302T-0306T, 0388T, 0389T-0391T, 0462T-0463T, 11000-11006, 11042-11047, 12001-12007, 12011-12057, 13100-13133, 13151-13153, 33210-33211, 33215, 33222-33223, 35201-35206, 35226-35236, 35256-35266, 35286, 36000, 36005-36013, 36120-36140, 36400-36410, 36420-36430, 36440, 36555-36556, 36568-36569, 36591-36592, 36600, 36640, 43752, 51701-51703, 62320-62327, 64400-64410, 64413-64435, 64445-64450, 64461-64463, 64479-64530, 69990, 76000-76001, 76942, 76970, 76998, 77001-77002, 92012-92014, 92960-92961, 93000-93010, 93040-93042, 93260-93261, 93279-93299, 93318, 93355, 94002, 94200, 94250, 94680-94690, 94770, 95812-95816, 95819, 95822, 95829, 95955, 96360-96368, 96372, 96374-96377, 97597-97598, 97602, 99155-99157, 99211-99223, 99231-99255, 99291-99292, 99304-99310, 99315-99316, 99334-99337, 99347-99350, 99374-99375, 99377-99378, 99446-99449, 99495-99496, G0463, G0471

Removal of Epicardial Pacemaker System by Thoracotomy

33236	**Removal of permanent epicardial pacemaker and electrodes by thoracotomy; single lead system, atrial or ventricular**
33237	**dual lead system**

Code 33236 reports the removal of a single lead epicardial pacemaker system and electrodes. The old pacemaker pocket is opened and the generator is removed. The old wires are cut and the incision is closed. The old chest incision is opened. The wires are pulled into the chest and they are followed onto the heart surface. The electrodes are then detached from the heart. The chest incision is closed. Report 33237 if a dual lead epicardial system is being removed.

Coding Tips

1. Procedures 33236 and 33237 report removal of the pacemaker system only. For removal with replacement of generator and leads during the same surgical session, see 33206-33208. For transvenous leads inserted when a pulse generator is in place, see 33216 and 33217.
2. For removal of a permanent pacemaker pulse generator, see 33233.
3. For removal of transvenous electrodes not requiring thoracotomy, see 33234-33235.
4. For removal of transvenous electrodes by thoracotomy, see 33238.
5. These procedures are typically performed in the surgical suite and not the cardiac cath lab or electrophysiology lab.
6. These procedures have been designated as inpatient only procedures. They are not covered if reported on an outpatient designated claim.

Facility HCPCS Coding

HCPCS Level II codes are used to report the supplies provided during the procedure. Hospitals should separately report supplies used during cardiac invasive procedures. Refer to chapter 1 for more information regarding appropriate billing of supplies. Refer to the list of current codes in appendix B.

Removal by Thoracotomy

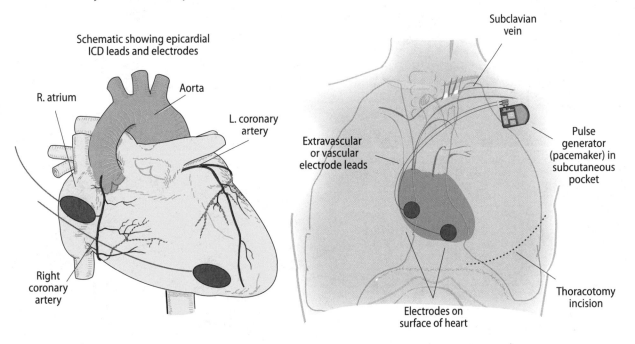

Report 33240 for insertion of pacing cardioverter defibrillator
generator and 33241 for removal of same

ICD-10-CM Coding

T82.110A	Breakdown (mechanical) of cardiac electrode, initial encounter
T82.111A	Breakdown (mechanical) of cardiac pulse generator (battery), initial encounter
T82.120A	Displacement of cardiac electrode, initial encounter
T82.121A	Displacement of cardiac pulse generator (battery), initial encounter
T82.190A	Other mechanical complication of cardiac electrode, initial encounter
T82.191A	Other mechanical complication of cardiac pulse generator (battery), initial encounter
T82.7XXA	Infection and inflammatory reaction due to other cardiac and vascular devices, implants and grafts, initial encounter

CCI Edits

33236   00530, 00534, 0213T, 0216T, 0228T, 0230T, 0293T-0294T, 0302T-0306T, 0388T, 0389T-0391T, 0462T-0463T, 11000-11006, 11042-11047, 12001-12007, 12011-12057, 13100-13133, 13151-13153, 32100, 32551, 32556-32557, 33140-33141, 33210-33211, 33215, 33222, 33227-33229, 33237-33238, 36000, 36005, 36400-36410, 36420-36430, 36440, 36591-36592, 36600, 36640, 39000-39010, 43752, 51701-51703, 62320-62327, 64400-64410, 64413-64435, 64445-64450, 64461-64463, 64479-64530, 69990, 76000-76001, 76942, 76970, 76998, 77002, 92012-92014, 92960-92961, 93000-93010, 93040-93042, 93260-93261, 93279-93299, 93318, 93355, 94002, 94200, 94250, 94680-94690, 94770, 95812-95816, 95819, 95822, 95829, 95955, 96360-96368, 96372, 96374-96377, 97597-97598, 97602, 99155-99157, 99211-99223, 99231-99255, 99291-99292, 99304-99310, 99315-99316, 99334-99337, 99347-99350, 99374-99375, 99377-99378, 99446-99449, 99495-99496, G0463, G0471

33237   00530, 00534, 0213T, 0216T, 0228T, 0230T, 0293T-0294T, 0302T-0306T, 0388T, 0389T-0391T, 0462T-0463T, 11000-11006, 11042-11047, 12001-12007, 12011-12057, 13100-13133, 13151-13153, 32100, 32551, 32556-32557, 33140-33141, 33210-33211, 33215, 33222, 33227-33229, 33238, 36000, 36005, 36400-36410, 36420-36430, 36440, 36591-36592, 36600, 36640, 39000-39010, 43752, 51701-51703, 62320-62327, 64400-64410, 64413-64435, 64445-64450, 64461-64463, 64479-64530, 69990, 76000-76001, 76942, 76970, 76998, 77002, 92012-92014, 92960-92961, 93000-93010, 93040-93042, 93260-93261, 93279-93299, 93318, 93355, 94002, 94200, 94250, 94680-94690, 94770, 95812-95816, 95819, 95822, 95829, 95955, 96360-96368, 96372, 96374-96377, 97597-97598, 97602, 99155-99157, 99211-99223, 99231-99255, 99291-99292, 99304-99310, 99315-99316, 99334-99337, 99347-99350, 99374-99375, 99377-99378, 99446-99449, 99495-99496, G0463, G0471

Removal of Permanent Electrode(s) by Thoracotomy

33238   **Removal of permanent transvenous electrode(s) by thoracotomy**

Code 33238 reports thoracotomy with removal of transvenous electrode(s) only. The right chest is opened and the superior caval vein is dissected out. Tourniquets are placed around the vein above and below the planned site of opening into the vein. The tourniquets are tightened and a hole is made in the prior to opening the chest, the pacemaker pocket was opened, the generator removed and the wires were cut. The cut ends of the wires are pulled out through the hole in the caval vein. The ends of the wires which are still in the heart are twisted counter clockwise until they are free and then are withdrawn through the caval vein. The hole in the caval veins are closed and the tourniquets are released. The chest is then closed.

Coding Tips

1.   Procedure 33238 reports removal of pacemaker components only. For removal with replacement of generator and leads during the same surgical session, see 33206-33208. For transvenous leads inserted when a pulse generator is in place, see 33216 and 33217.

2.   Note that 33238 may require vein or heart repair with graft; report this separately.

3.   For removal of transvenous electrodes not requiring thoracotomy, see 33234-33235.

4.   For removal of an epicardial pacemaker system or electrodes by thoracotomy, see 33236-33237.

5.   This procedure is typically performed in the surgical suite and not the cardiac cath lab or electrophysiology lab.

6.   This procedure has been designated as an inpatient only procedure. It is not covered if reported on an outpatient designated claim.

Facility HCPCS Coding

HCPCS Level II codes are used to report the supplies provided during the procedure. Hospitals should separately report supplies used during cardiac invasive procedures. Refer to chapter 1 for more information regarding appropriate billing of supplies. Refer to the list of current codes in appendix B.

ICD-10-CM Coding

T82.110A   Breakdown (mechanical) of cardiac electrode, initial encounter

T82.120A   Displacement of cardiac electrode, initial encounter

T82.190A   Other mechanical complication of cardiac electrode, initial encounter

T82.7XXA   Infection and inflammatory reaction due to other cardiac and vascular devices, implants and grafts, initial encounter

Electrode Removal

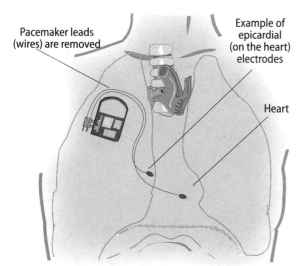

Report 33234 for removal of a transvenous single lead system (one wire per chamber), 33235 for dual lead system (two wires per chamber)

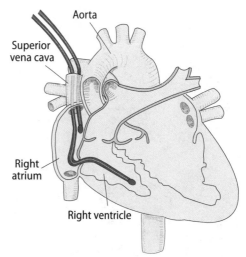

Schematic of transvenous, dual lead system

CCI Edits

33238   00530, 00534, 0213T, 0216T, 0228T, 0230T, 0293T-0294T, 0302T-0306T, 0388T, 0389T-0391T, 0462T-0463T, 11000-11006, 11042-11047, 12001-12007, 12011-12057, 13100-13133, 13151-13153, 32100, 32551, 32556-32557, 33140-33141, 33210-33211, 33215, 33222-33223, 35211-35216, 35241-35246, 35271-35276, 36000, 36005-36013, 36120-36140, 36400-36410, 36420-36430, 36440, 36591-36592, 36600, 36640, 39000-39010, 43752, 51701-51703, 62320-62327, 64400-64410, 64413-64435, 64445-64450, 64461-64463, 64479-64530, 69990, 76000-76001, 76942, 76970, 76998, 77002, 92012-92014, 92960-92961, 93000-93010, 93040-93042, 93260-93261, 93279-93299, 93318, 93355, 94002, 94200, 94250, 94680-94690, 94770, 95812-95816, 95819, 95822, 95829, 95955, 96360-96368, 96372, 96374-96377, 97597-97598, 97602, 99155-99157, 99211-99223, 99231-99255, 99291-99292, 99304-99310, 99315-99316, 99334-99337, 99347-99350, 99374-99375, 99377-99378, 99446-99449, 99495-99496, G0463, G0471

Insertion of Implantable Defibrillator Generator

33240	**Insertion of pacing implantable defibrillator pulse generator only; with existing single lead**
33230	**with existing dual leads**
33231	**with existing multiple leads**

These procedures are performed when defibrillator electrodes are already in place. The previous pocket is opened or a new pocket is created for the generator. The leads are tested and attached to the device. The generator is placed in the pocket. The pocket is closed.

Coding Tips

1. These codes are appropriate for reporting "battery" change.
2. For pocket relocation, see 33223.
3. For repositioning a previously implanted electrode, see 33215.
4. For electrode repair, see 33218-33220.
5. Fluoroscopy is included and not reported separately.
6. Do not report these codes in conjunction with 33241.
7. Conscious sedation is not included in these codes. Separately report 99151–99157 per payer policy and coding guidelines. Hospitals may choose to include the costs associated with the service as part of the procedure rather than reporting them separately.

Facility HCPCS Coding

HCPCS Level II codes are used to report the supplies provided during the procedure. Hospitals should separately report supplies used during cardiac invasive procedures. Refer to chapter 1 for more information regarding appropriate billing of supplies. Refer to the list of current codes in appendix B.

C1721	Cardioverter-defibrillator, dual chamber (implantable)
C1722	Cardioverter-defibrillator, single chamber (implantable)

Insertion of Implantable Defibrillator (ICD) (Pulse, Generator, and Lead)

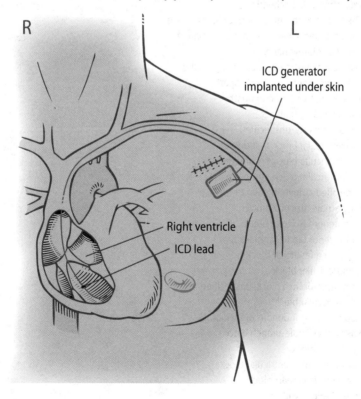

ICD-10-CM Coding

I11.0	Hypertensive heart disease with heart failure
I13.0	Hypertensive heart and chronic kidney disease with heart failure and stage 1 through stage 4 chronic kidney disease, or unspecified chronic kidney disease
I13.2	Hypertensive heart and chronic kidney disease with heart failure and with stage 5 chronic kidney disease, or end stage renal disease
I16.0	Hypertensive urgency
I16.1	Hypertensive emergency
I16.9	Hypertensive crisis, unspecified
I21.01	ST elevation (STEMI) myocardial infarction involving left main coronary artery
I21.02	ST elevation (STEMI) myocardial infarction involving left anterior descending coronary artery
I21.09	ST elevation (STEMI) myocardial infarction involving other coronary artery of anterior wall
I21.11	ST elevation (STEMI) myocardial infarction involving right coronary artery
I21.19	ST elevation (STEMI) myocardial infarction involving other coronary artery of inferior wall
I21.21	ST elevation (STEMI) myocardial infarction involving left circumflex coronary artery
I21.29	ST elevation (STEMI) myocardial infarction involving other sites
I21.3	ST elevation (STEMI) myocardial infarction of unspecified site
I21.4	Non-ST elevation (NSTEMI) myocardial infarction
I21.9	Acute myocardial infarction, unspecified
I21.A1	Myocardial infarction type 2
I21.A9	Other myocardial infarction type
I22.0	Subsequent ST elevation (STEMI) myocardial infarction of anterior wall
I22.1	Subsequent ST elevation (STEMI) myocardial infarction of inferior wall
I22.2	Subsequent non-ST elevation (NSTEMI) myocardial infarction
I22.8	Subsequent ST elevation (STEMI) myocardial infarction of other sites
I22.9	Subsequent ST elevation (STEMI) myocardial infarction of unspecified site
I25.2	Old myocardial infarction
I25.5	Ischemic cardiomyopathy
I25.6	Silent myocardial ischemia
I25.89	Other forms of chronic ischemic heart disease
I25.9	Chronic ischemic heart disease, unspecified
I42.0	Dilated cardiomyopathy
I42.1	Obstructive hypertrophic cardiomyopathy
I42.2	Other hypertrophic cardiomyopathy
I42.5	Other restrictive cardiomyopathy
I42.8	Other cardiomyopathies
I42.9	Cardiomyopathy, unspecified
I44.0	Atrioventricular block, first degree
I44.1	Atrioventricular block, second degree
I44.2	Atrioventricular block, complete
I44.30	Unspecified atrioventricular block
I44.39	Other atrioventricular block
I44.4	Left anterior fascicular block
I44.5	Left posterior fascicular block
I44.60	Unspecified fascicular block
I44.69	Other fascicular block
I44.7	Left bundle-branch block, unspecified
I45.0	Right fascicular block
I45.10	Unspecified right bundle-branch block
I45.19	Other right bundle-branch block
I45.2	Bifascicular block
I45.4	Nonspecific intraventricular block
I45.5	Other specified heart block
I45.6	Pre-excitation syndrome
I45.81	Long QT syndrome
I45.9	Conduction disorder, unspecified

I46.2	Cardiac arrest due to underlying cardiac condition
I46.8	Cardiac arrest due to other underlying condition
I46.9	Cardiac arrest, cause unspecified
I47.0	Re-entry ventricular arrhythmia
I47.1	Supraventricular tachycardia
I47.2	Ventricular tachycardia
I48.0	Paroxysmal atrial fibrillation
I48.2	Chronic atrial fibrillation
I48.91	Unspecified atrial fibrillation
I49.01	Ventricular fibrillation
I49.02	Ventricular flutter
I49.2	Junctional premature depolarization
I49.5	Sick sinus syndrome
I49.8	Other specified cardiac arrhythmias
I49.9	Cardiac arrhythmia, unspecified
I50.1	Left ventricular failure
I50.20	Unspecified systolic (congestive) heart failure
I50.21	Acute systolic (congestive) heart failure
I50.22	Chronic systolic (congestive) heart failure
I50.23	Acute on chronic systolic (congestive) heart failure
I50.30	Unspecified diastolic (congestive) heart failure
I50.31	Acute diastolic (congestive) heart failure
I50.32	Chronic diastolic (congestive) heart failure
I50.33	Acute on chronic diastolic (congestive) heart failure
I50.40	Unspecified combined systolic (congestive) and diastolic (congestive) heart failure
I50.41	Acute combined systolic (congestive) and diastolic (congestive) heart failure
I50.42	Chronic combined systolic (congestive) and diastolic (congestive) heart failure
I50.43	Acute on chronic combined systolic (congestive) and diastolic (congestive) heart failure
I50.810	Right heart failure, unspecified
I50.811	Acute right heart failure
I50.812	Chronic right heart failure
I50.813	Acute on chronic right heart failure
I50.814	Right heart failure due to left heart failure
I50.82	Biventricular heart failure
I50.83	High output heart failure
I50.84	End stage heart failure
I50.89	Other heart failure
I50.9	Heart failure, unspecified
Q23.8	Other congenital malformations of aortic and mitral valves
Q23.9	Congenital malformation of aortic and mitral valves, unspecified
Q24.6	Congenital heart block
Q24.8	Other specified congenital malformations of heart
R00.1	Bradycardia, unspecified
T82.110A	Breakdown (mechanical) of cardiac electrode, initial encounter
T82.111A	Breakdown (mechanical) of cardiac pulse generator (battery), initial encounter
T82.120A	Displacement of cardiac electrode, initial encounter
T82.121A	Displacement of cardiac pulse generator (battery), initial encounter
T82.190A	Other mechanical complication of cardiac electrode, initial encounter
T82.191A	Other mechanical complication of cardiac pulse generator (battery), initial encounter
T82.598A	Other mechanical complication of other cardiac and vascular devices and implants, initial encounter
T82.7XXA	Infection and inflammatory reaction due to other cardiac and vascular devices, implants and grafts, initial encounter
T82.817A	Embolism due to cardiac prosthetic devices, implants and grafts, initial encounter
T82.827A	Fibrosis due to cardiac prosthetic devices, implants and grafts, initial encounter
T82.837A	Hemorrhage due to cardiac prosthetic devices, implants and grafts, initial encounter
T82.847A	Pain due to cardiac prosthetic devices, implants and grafts, initial encounter
T82.855A	Stenosis of coronary artery stent, initial encounter

T82.857A	Stenosis of other cardiac prosthetic devices, implants and grafts, initial encounter
T82.867A	Thrombosis due to cardiac prosthetic devices, implants and grafts, initial encounter
T82.897A	Other specified complication of cardiac prosthetic devices, implants and grafts, initial encounter
T82.9XXA	Unspecified complication of cardiac and vascular prosthetic device, implant and graft, initial encounter
Z45.02	Encounter for adjustment and management of automatic implantable cardiac defibrillator
Z95.810	Presence of automatic (implantable) cardiac defibrillator

CCI Edits

33230 00530, 00534, 0213T, 0216T, 0228T, 0230T, 0293T-0294T, 0302T-0306T, 0389T-0391T, 0462T-0463T, 11000-11006, 11042-11047, 12001-12007, 12011-12057, 13100-13133, 13151-13153, 33210-33211, 33215-33217, 33223, 33240-33241, 36000, 36005, 36400-36410, 36420-36430, 36440, 36591-36592, 36600, 36640, 43752, 51701-51703, 62320-62327, 64400-64410, 64413-64435, 64445-64450, 64461-64463, 64479-64530, 69990, 76000-76001, 76942, 76970, 76998, 77002, 92012-92014, 93000-93010, 93040-93042, 93260-93261, 93279-93299, 93318, 93355, 93600-93603, 93610-93612, 94002, 94200, 94250, 94680-94690, 94770, 95812-95816, 95819, 95822, 95829, 95955, 96360-96368, 96372, 96374-96377, 97597-97598, 97602, 99155-99157, 99211-99223, 99231-99255, 99291-99292, 99304-99310, 99315-99316, 99334-99337, 99347-99350, 99374-99375, 99377-99378, 99446-99449, 99495-99496, G0463, G0471

33231 00530, 00534, 0213T, 0216T, 0228T, 0230T, 0293T-0294T, 0302T-0306T, 0389T-0391T, 0462T-0463T, 11000-11006, 11042-11047, 12001-12007, 12011-12057, 13100-13133, 13151-13153, 33210-33211, 33215-33217, 33223, 33230, 33240-33241, 36000, 36005, 36400-36410, 36420-36430, 36440, 36591-36592, 36600, 36640, 43752, 51701-51703, 62320-62327, 64400-64410, 64413-64435, 64445-64450, 64461-64463, 64479-64530, 69990, 76000-76001, 76942, 76970, 76998, 77002, 92012-92014, 93000-93010, 93040-93042, 93260-93261, 93279-93299, 93318, 93355, 93600-93603, 93610-93612, 94002, 94200, 94250, 94680-94690, 94770, 95812-95816, 95819, 95822, 95829, 95955, 96360-96368, 96372, 96374-96377, 97597-97598, 97602, 99155-99157, 99211-99223, 99231-99255, 99291-99292, 99304-99310, 99315-99316, 99334-99337, 99347-99350, 99374-99375, 99377-99378, 99446-99449, 99495-99496, G0463, G0471

33240 00530, 00534, 0213T, 0216T, 0228T, 0230T, 0293T-0294T, 0302T-0306T, 0389T-0391T, 0462T-0463T, 11000-11006, 11042-11047, 12001-12007, 12011-12057, 13100-13133, 13151-13153, 33210-33211, 33215-33217, 33223, 33241, 36000, 36005, 36400-36410, 36420-36430, 36440, 36591-36592, 36600, 36640, 43752, 51701-51703, 62320-62327, 64400-64410, 64413-64435, 64445-64450, 64461-64463, 64479-64530, 69990, 76000-76001, 76942, 76970, 76998, 77002, 92012-92014, 92960-92961, 93000-93010, 93040-93042, 93260-93261, 93279-93299, 93318, 93355, 93600-93603, 93610-93612, 94002, 94200, 94250, 94680-94690, 94770, 95812-95816, 95819, 95822, 95829, 95955, 96360-96368, 96372, 96374-96377, 97597-97598, 97602, 99155-99157, 99211-99223, 99231-99255, 99291-99292, 99304-99310, 99315-99316, 99334-99337, 99347-99350, 99374-99375, 99377-99378, 99446-99449, 99495-99496, G0463, G0471

Removal of Implantable Defibrillator Generator

33241   **Removal of implantable defibrillator pulse generator only**

Only the AICD pulse generator is removed. The subcutaneous generator pocket is opened and the generator is removed. The electrodes are detached from the generator and placed in the pocket. The pocket is closed.

Coding Tips

1. Fluoroscopic guidance is included and not separately reported.

2. For removal and replacement of the ICD pulse generator and electrode(s), report 33241 in conjunction with 33242 or 33244 and 33249.

3. Conscious sedation is not included in these codes. Separately report 99151–99157 per payer policy and coding guidelines. Hospitals may choose to include the costs associated with the service as part of the procedure rather than reporting them separately.

Facility HCPCS Coding

HCPCS Level II codes are used to report the devices used in these procedures. Hospitals should separately report supplies and devices used during pacemaker procedures. Refer to chapter 1 for more information regarding appropriate billing of supplies. Appendix B of this publication contains a list of current device codes applicable to this section.

ICD-10-CM Coding

T82.111A	Breakdown (mechanical) of cardiac pulse generator (battery), initial encounter
T82.121A	Displacement of cardiac pulse generator (battery), initial encounter
T82.191A	Other mechanical complication of cardiac pulse generator (battery), initial encounter
T82.598A	Other mechanical complication of other cardiac and vascular devices and implants, initial encounter
T82.7XXA	Infection and inflammatory reaction due to other cardiac and vascular devices, implants and grafts, initial encounter
T82.817A	Embolism of cardiac prosthetic devices, implants and grafts, initial encounter
T82.827A	Fibrosis of cardiac prosthetic devices, implants and grafts, initial encounter
T82.837A	Hemorrhage of cardiac prosthetic devices, implants and grafts, initial encounter
T82.847A	Pain from cardiac prosthetic devices, implants and grafts, initial encounter
T82.855A	Stenosis of coronary artery stent, initial encounter
T82.857A	Stenosis of cardiac prosthetic devices, implants and grafts, initial encounter
T82.867A	Thrombosis of cardiac prosthetic devices, implants and grafts, initial encounter
T82.897A	Other specified complication of cardiac prosthetic devices, implants and grafts, initial encounter
T82.9XXA	Unspecified complication of cardiac and vascular prosthetic device, implant and graft, initial encounter
Z45.02	Encounter for adjustment and management of automatic implantable cardiac defibrillator
Z95.810	Presence of automatic (implantable) cardiac defibrillator

CCI Edits

33241   00530, 00534, 0213T, 0216T, 0228T, 0230T, 0293T-0294T, 0302T-0306T, 0389T-0391T, 0462T-0463T, 11000-11006, 11042-11047, 12001-12007, 12011-12057, 13100-13133, 13151-13153, 33210-33211, 33215, 33223, 36000, 36005, 36400-36410, 36420-36430, 36440, 36591-36592, 36600, 36640, 43752, 51701-51703, 62320-62327, 64400-64410, 64413-64435, 64445-64450, 64461-64463, 64479-64530, 76000-76001, 76942, 76970, 76998, 77002, 92012-92014, 92960-92961, 93000-93010, 93040-93042, 93260-93261, 93279-93299, 93318, 93355, 94002, 94200, 94250, 94680-94690, 94770, 95812-95816, 95819, 95822, 95829, 95955, 96360-96368, 96372, 96374-96377, 97597-97598, 97602, 99155-99157, 99211-99223, 99231-99255, 99291-99292, 99304-99310, 99315-99316, 99334-99337, 99347-99350, 99374-99375, 99377-99378, 99446-99449, 99495-99496, G0463, G0471

Removal and Replacement of Implantable Defibrillator Generator

33262	Removal of implantable defibrillator pulse generator with replacement of pacing cardioverter-defibrillator pulse generator, single lead system
33263	dual lead system
33264	multiple lead system

The subcutaneous generator pocket is opened and the generator is removed. The electrodes are detached from the generator and connected to the new pulse generator. The system is tested. The generator is placed in the pocket and the pocket is closed. Report 33262 for a single lead system, 33263 for a dual lead system, and 33264 for a multiple lead system.

Coding Tips

1. Fluoroscopic guidance is included and not separately reported.
2. Do not report 33262-33264 in conjunction with 33241.
3. Conscious sedation is not included in these codes. Separately report 99151–99157 per payer policy and coding guidelines. Hospitals may choose to include the costs associated with the service as part of the procedure rather than reporting them separately.

Facility HCPCS Coding

HCPCS Level II codes are used to report the devices used in these procedures. Hospitals should separately report supplies and devices used during pacemaker procedures. Refer to chapter 1 for more information regarding appropriate billing of supplies. Appendix B of this publication contains a list of current device codes applicable to this section.

C1721   Cardioverter-defibrillator, dual chamber (implantable)

C1722   Cardioverter-defibrillator, single chamber (implantable)

C1882   Cardioverter-defibrillator, other than single or dual chamber (implantable)

Insertion of Implantable Cardioverter Defibrillator (ICD) (Pulse, Generator, and Lead)

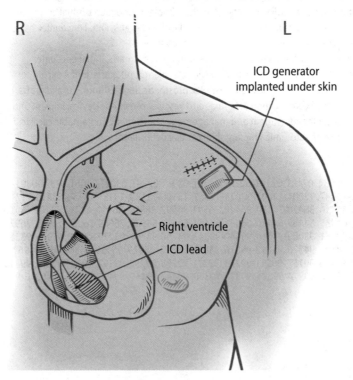

R   L

ICD generator implanted under skin

Right ventricle

ICD lead

ICD-10-CM Coding

I11.0	Hypertensive heart disease with heart failure
I13.0	Hypertensive heart and chronic kidney disease with heart failure and stage 1 through stage 4 chronic kidney disease, or unspecified chronic kidney disease
I13.2	Hypertensive heart and chronic kidney disease with heart failure and with stage 5 chronic kidney disease, or end stage renal disease
I16.0	Hypertensive urgency
I16.1	Hypertensive emergency
I16.9	Hypertensive crisis, unspecified
I21.01	ST elevation (STEMI) myocardial infarction involving left main coronary artery
I21.02	ST elevation (STEMI) myocardial infarction involving left anterior descending coronary artery
I21.09	ST elevation (STEMI) myocardial infarction involving other coronary artery of anterior wall
I21.11	ST elevation (STEMI) myocardial infarction involving right coronary artery
I21.19	ST elevation (STEMI) myocardial infarction involving other coronary artery of inferior wall
I21.21	ST elevation (STEMI) myocardial infarction involving left circumflex coronary artery
I21.29	ST elevation (STEMI) myocardial infarction involving other sites
I21.3	ST elevation (STEMI) myocardial infarction of unspecified site
I21.4	Non-ST elevation (NSTEMI) myocardial infarction
I21.9	Acute myocardial infarction, unspecified
I21.A1	Myocardial infarction type 2
I21.A9	Other myocardial infarction type
I22.0	Subsequent ST elevation (STEMI) myocardial infarction of anterior wall
I22.1	Subsequent ST elevation (STEMI) myocardial infarction of inferior wall
I22.2	Subsequent non-ST elevation (NSTEMI) myocardial infarction
I22.8	Subsequent ST elevation (STEMI) myocardial infarction of other sites
I22.9	Subsequent ST elevation (STEMI) myocardial infarction of unspecified site
I25.2	Old myocardial infarction
I25.5	Ischemic cardiomyopathy
I25.6	Silent myocardial ischemia
I25.89	Other forms of chronic ischemic heart disease
I25.9	Chronic ischemic heart disease, unspecified
I42.0	Dilated cardiomyopathy
I42.5	Other restrictive cardiomyopathy
I42.8	Other cardiomyopathies
I42.9	Cardiomyopathy, unspecified
I44.0	Atrioventricular block, first degree
I44.1	Atrioventricular block, second degree
I44.2	Atrioventricular block, complete
I44.30	Unspecified atrioventricular block
I44.39	Other atrioventricular block
I44.4	Left anterior fascicular block
I44.5	Left posterior fascicular block
I44.60	Unspecified fascicular block
I44.69	Other fascicular block
I44.7	Left bundle-branch block, unspecified
I45.0	Right fascicular block
I45.10	Unspecified right bundle-branch block
I45.19	Other right bundle-branch block
I45.2	Bifascicular block
I45.4	Nonspecific intraventricular block
I45.5	Other specified heart block
I45.6	Pre-excitation syndrome
I45.81	Long QT syndrome
I45.9	Conduction disorder, unspecified
I46.2	Cardiac arrest due to underlying cardiac condition

I46.8	Cardiac arrest due to other underlying condition
I46.9	Cardiac arrest, cause unspecified
I47.0	Re-entry ventricular arrhythmia
I47.1	Supraventricular tachycardia
I47.2	Ventricular tachycardia
I48.0	Paroxysmal atrial fibrillation
I48.2	Chronic atrial fibrillation
I48.91	Unspecified atrial fibrillation
I49.01	Ventricular fibrillation
I49.02	Ventricular flutter
I49.2	Junctional premature depolarization
I49.5	Sick sinus syndrome
I49.8	Other specified cardiac arrhythmias
I49.9	Cardiac arrhythmia, unspecified
I50.1	Left ventricular failure
I50.20	Unspecified systolic (congestive) heart failure
I50.21	Acute systolic (congestive) heart failure
I50.22	Chronic systolic (congestive) heart failure
I50.23	Acute on chronic systolic (congestive) heart failure
I50.30	Unspecified diastolic (congestive) heart failure
I50.31	Acute diastolic (congestive) heart failure
I50.32	Chronic diastolic (congestive) heart failure
I50.33	Acute on chronic diastolic (congestive) heart failure
I50.40	Unspecified combined systolic (congestive) and diastolic (congestive) heart failure
I50.41	Acute combined systolic (congestive) and diastolic (congestive) heart failure
I50.42	Chronic combined systolic (congestive) and diastolic (congestive) heart failure
I50.43	Acute on chronic combined systolic (congestive) and diastolic (congestive) heart failure
I50.810	Right heart failure, unspecified
I50.811	Acute right heart failure
I50.812	Chronic right heart failure
I50.813	Acute on chronic right heart failure
I50.814	Right heart failure due to left heart failure
I50.82	Biventricular heart failure
I50.83	High output heart failure
I50.84	End stage heart failure
I50.89	Other heart failure
I50.9	Heart failure, unspecified
Q23.8	Other congenital malformations of aortic and mitral valves
Q23.9	Congenital malformation of aortic and mitral valves, unspecified
Q24.6	Congenital heart block
Q24.8	Other specified congenital malformations of heart
R00.1	Bradycardia, unspecified
T82.111A	Breakdown (mechanical) of cardiac pulse generator (battery), initial encounter
T82.121A	Displacement of cardiac pulse generator (battery), initial encounter
T82.191A	Other mechanical complication of cardiac pulse generator (battery), initial encounter
T82.598A	Other mechanical complication of other cardiac and vascular devices and implants, initial encounter
T82.7XXA	Infection and inflammatory reaction due to other cardiac and vascular devices, implants and grafts, initial encounter
T82.817A	Embolism due to cardiac prosthetic devices, implants and grafts, initial encounter
T82.827A	Fibrosis due to cardiac prosthetic devices, implants and grafts, initial encounter
T82.837A	Hemorrhage due to cardiac prosthetic devices, implants and grafts, initial encounter
T82.847A	Pain due to cardiac prosthetic devices, implants and grafts, initial encounter
T82.855A	Stenosis of coronary artery stent, initial encounter
T82.857A	Stenosis of other cardiac prosthetic devices, implants and grafts, initial encounter

T82.867A	Thrombosis due to cardiac prosthetic devices, implants and grafts, initial encounter
T82.897A	Other specified complication of cardiac prosthetic devices, implants and grafts, initial encounter
T82.9XXA	Unspecified complication of cardiac and vascular prosthetic device, implant and graft, initial encounter
Z45.02	Encounter for adjustment and management of automatic implantable cardiac defibrillator
Z95.810	Presence of automatic (implantable) cardiac defibrillator

CCI Edits

G0463, G0471

33262 00530, 00534, 0213T, 0216T, 0228T, 0230T, 0293T, 0302T-0306T, 0389T-0391T, 0462T-0463T, 11000-11006, 11042-11047, 12001-12007, 12011-12057, 13100-13133, 13151-13153, 33210-33211, 33215-33217, 33230-33231, 33240-33241, 36000, 36005, 36400-36410, 36420-36430, 36440, 36591-36592, 36600, 36640, 43752, 51701-51703, 62320-62327, 64400-64410, 64413-64435, 64445-64450, 64461-64463, 64479-64530, 69990, 76000-76001, 76942, 76970, 76998, 92012-92014, 93000-93010, 93040-93042, 93260-93261, 93279-93299, 93318, 93355, 93600-93603, 93610-93612, 94002, 94200, 94250, 94680-94690, 94770, 95812-95816, 95819, 95822, 95829, 95955, 96360-96368, 96372, 96374-96377, 97597-97598, 97602, 99155-99157, 99211-99223, 99231-99255, 99291-99292, 99304-99310, 99315-99316, 99334-99337, 99347-99350, 99374-99375, 99377-99378, 99446-99449, 99495-99496, G0463, G0471

33263 00530, 00534, 0213T, 0216T, 0228T, 0230T, 0293T, 0302T-0306T, 0389T-0391T, 0462T-0463T, 11000-11006, 11042-11047, 12001-12007, 12011-12057, 13100-13133, 13151-13153, 33210-33211, 33215-33217, 33230-33231, 33240-33241, 36000, 36005, 36400-36410, 36420-36430, 36440, 36591-36592, 36600, 36640, 43752, 51701-51703, 62320-62327, 64400-64410, 64413-64435, 64445-64450, 64461-64463, 64479-64530, 69990, 76000-76001, 76942, 76970, 76998, 92012-92014, 93000-93010, 93040-93042, 93260-93261, 93279-93299, 93318, 93355, 93600-93603, 93610-93612, 94002, 94200, 94250, 94680-94690, 94770, 95812-95816, 95819, 95822, 95829, 95955, 96360-96368, 96372, 96374-96377, 97597-97598, 97602, 99155-99157, 99211-99223, 99231-99255, 99291-99292, 99304-99310, 99315-99316, 99334-99337, 99347-99350, 99374-99375, 99377-99378, 99446-99449, 99495-99496, G0463, G0471

33264 00530, 00534, 0213T, 0216T, 0228T, 0230T, 0293T, 0302T-0306T, 0389T-0391T, 0462T-0463T, 11000-11006, 11042-11047, 12001-12007, 12011-12057, 13100-13133, 13151-13153, 33210-33211, 33215-33217, 33230-33231, 33240-33241, 36000, 36005, 36400-36410, 36420-36430, 36440, 36591-36592, 36600, 36640, 43752, 51701-51703, 62320-62327, 64400-64410, 64413-64435, 64445-64450, 64461-64463, 64479-64530, 69990, 76000-76001, 76942, 76970, 76998, 92012-92014, 93000-93010, 93040-93042, 93260-93261, 93279-93299, 93318, 93355, 93600-93603, 93610-93612, 94002, 94200, 94250, 94680-94690, 94770, 95812-95816, 95819, 95822, 95829, 95955, 96360-96368, 96372, 96374-96377, 97597-97598, 97602, 99155-99157, 99211-99223, 99231-99255, 99291-99292, 99304-99310, 99315-99316, 99334-99337, 99347-99350, 99374-99375, 99377-99378, 99446-99449, 99495-99496, G0463, G0471

Case Example

See case example #4 at the end of this chapter.

Removal of Implantable Defibrillator Electrode(s)

33243   **Removal of single or dual chamber implantable defibrillator electrode(s); by thoracotomy**

In 33243, only the electrodes are removed. The generator pocket is opened and the electrode wires are disconnected. The old chest incision is opened and the electrodes are dissected out and removed. The chest incision is closed.

33244   **by transvenous extraction**

Code 33244 reports removal of electrodes only by transvenous extraction which is currently the most common technique for removing AICD electrodes since most cardioverter-defibrillator electrodes are now placed transvenously. The generator pocket is opened and the wire is disconnected from the generator. The wire is dissected from the scar tissue which has formed around it. Once the wire is completely freed, it is twisted in a direction opposite to that use for insertion (counter clockwise). The wire is then withdrawn. Bleeding from the tracts leading to the vein is controlled with sutures. A new wire may be placed, but is reported separately.

Coding Tips

1. Removal of both the pulse generator and electrodes requires reporting of multiple codes. For removal of an electrode by thoracotomy in conjunction with removal of the pulse generator, use 33243 with 33241.

2. For removal of an electrode by transvenous extraction in conjunction with removal of the pulse generator, use 33244 with 33241. A transvenous extraction is normally attempted initially, but if unsuccessful, a thoracotomy approach is performed.

3. For insertion or repositioning of cardioverter-defibrillator electrodes without concurrent insertion of a pulse generator, see 33215–33217.

4. For repair of cardioverter-defibrillator electrodes, see 33218 or 33220.

5. These codes are appropriate for reporting "battery" change.

6. Fluoroscopy is included and is not separately reported.

7. CPT code 33243 is designated as inpatient only. It will not be covered if reported on an outpatient designated claim.

8. Conscious sedation may be reported in addition to code 33244. Separately report 99151–99157 per payer policy and coding guidelines. Hospitals may choose to include the costs associated with the service as part of the procedure rather than reporting them separately.

Facility HCPCS Coding

HCPCS Level II codes are used to report the supplies provided during the procedure. Hospitals should separately report supplies used during cardiac invasive procedures. Refer to chapter 1 for more information regarding appropriate billing of supplies. Refer to the list of current codes in appendix B.

Dual Lead System

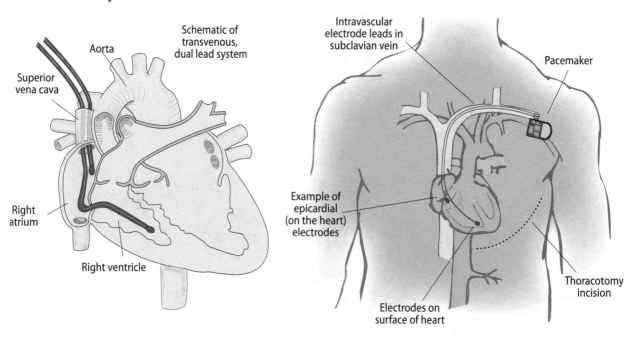

Schematic of transvenous, dual lead system

Aorta

Superior vena cava

Right atrium

Right ventricle

Intravascular electrode leads in subclavian vein

Pacemaker

Example of epicardial (on the heart) electrodes

Electrodes on surface of heart

Thoracotomy incision

ICD-10-CM Coding

T82.110A	Breakdown (mechanical) of cardiac electrode, initial encounter
T82.120A	Displacement of cardiac electrode, initial encounter
T82.190A	Other mechanical complication of cardiac electrode, initial encounter
T82.598A	Other mechanical complication of other cardiac and vascular devices and implants, initial encounter
T82.7XXA	Infection and inflammatory reaction due to other cardiac and vascular devices, implants and grafts, initial encounter
T82.817A	Embolism of cardiac prosthetic devices, implants and grafts, initial encounter
T82.827A	Fibrosis of cardiac prosthetic devices, implants and grafts, initial encounter
T82.837A	Hemorrhage of cardiac prosthetic devices, implants and grafts, initial encounter
T82.847A	Pain from cardiac prosthetic devices, implants and grafts, initial encounter
T82.855A	Stenosis of coronary artery stent, initial encounter
T82.857A	Stenosis of cardiac prosthetic devices, implants and grafts, initial encounter
T82.867A	Thrombosis of cardiac prosthetic devices, implants and grafts, initial encounter
T82.897A	Other specified complication of cardiac prosthetic devices, implants and grafts, initial encounter
T82.9XXA	Unspecified complication of cardiac and vascular prosthetic device, implant and graft, initial encounter
Z45.02	Encounter for adjustment and management of automatic implantable cardiac defibrillator
Z95.810	Presence of automatic (implantable) cardiac defibrillator

CCI Edits

33243 00530, 00534, 0213T, 0216T, 0228T, 0230T, 0293T-0294T, 0302T-0306T, 0389T-0391T, 0462T-0463T, 11000-11006, 11042-11047, 12001-12007, 12011-12057, 13100-13133, 13151-13153, 32100, 32551, 32556-32557, 33140-33141, 33210-33211, 33215, 33222-33223, 35211-35216, 35241-35246, 35271-35276, 36000, 36005-36013, 36120-36140, 36400-36410, 36420-36430, 36440, 36591-36592, 36600, 36640, 39000-39010, 43752, 51701-51703, 62320-62327, 64400-64410, 64413-64435, 64445-64450, 64461-64463, 64479-64530, 69990, 76000-76001, 76942, 76970, 76998, 77001-77002, 92012-92014, 92960-92961, 93000-93010, 93040-93042, 93260-93261, 93279-93299, 93318, 93355, 94002, 94200, 94250, 94680-94690, 94770, 95812-95816, 95819, 95822, 95829, 95955, 96360-96368, 96372, 96374-96377, 97597-97598, 97602, 99155-99157, 99211-99223, 99231-99255, 99291-99292, 99304-99310, 99315-99316, 99334-99337, 99347-99350, 99374-99375, 99377-99378, 99446-99449, 99495-99496, G0463, G0471

33244 00530, 00534, 0213T, 0216T, 0228T, 0230T, 0293T-0294T, 0302T-0306T, 0389T-0391T, 0462T-0463T, 11000-11006, 11042-11047, 12001-12007, 12011-12057, 13100-13133, 13151-13153, 33210-33211, 33215, 33222-33223, 33243, 35201-35206, 35226-35236, 35256-35266, 35286, 36000, 36005-36013, 36120-36140, 36400-36410, 36420-36430, 36440, 36591-36592, 36600, 36640, 43752, 51701-51703, 62320-62327, 64400-64410, 64413-64435, 64445-64450, 64461-64463, 64479-64530, 69990, 76000-76001, 76942, 76970, 76998, 77001-77002, 92012-92014, 92960-92961, 93000-93010, 93040-93042, 93260-93261, 93279-93299, 93318, 93355, 94002, 94200, 94250, 94680-94690, 94770, 95812-95816, 95819, 95822, 95829, 95955, 96360-96368, 96372, 96374-96377, 97597-97598, 97602, 99155-99157, 99211-99223, 99231-99255, 99291-99292, 99304-99310, 99315-99316, 99334-99337, 99347-99350, 99374-99375, 99377-99378, 99446-99449, 99495-99496, G0463, G0471

Insertion or Replacement of ICD Lead(s) and Generator

33249   **Insertion or replacement of permanent implantable defibrillator system with transvenous lead(s), single or dual chamber**

This code is used to report the insertion of a pulse generator and the transvenous electrode placement. Local anesthesia is administered. An incision is made in the infraclavicular area. The subcutaneous tissue is opened and a pocket is created for the pulse generator. Transvenous electrode placement is performed using fluoroscopic guidance. The electrode catheter is advanced through the superior vena cava into the heart and placed in the appropriate site in the right ventricle (single chamber) or in the right ventricle and atrium (dual chamber system). Multiple leads may be required for both single and dual chamber systems. Once all leads are placed, they are tested and connected to the pulse generator. The generator is placed in the prepared pocket and the incision is closed.

Coding Tips

1.   For transvenous insertion of electrodes only, see 33216 and 33217.

2.   For repair of AICD transvenous electrodes, see 33218 or 33220.

3.   Removal with reinsertion of a pacing cardioverter-defibrillator system requires reporting of multiple codes. Report 33241 and 33243 or 33244 for the removal portion of the procedure and 33249 for the reinsertion.

4.   For insertion of epicardial electrodes without concurrent pulse generator insertion, see 33202 or 33203.

5.   Fluoroscopy is included and not separately reported.

6.   Conscious sedation is not included in these codes. Separately report 99151–99157 per payer policy and coding guidelines. Hospitals may choose to include the costs associated with the service as part of the procedure rather than reporting them separately.

Facility HCPCS Coding

HCPCS Level II codes are used to report the supplies provided during the procedure. Hospitals should separately report supplies used during cardiac invasive procedures. Refer to chapter 1 for more information regarding appropriate billing of supplies. Refer to the list of current codes in appendix B.

C1721   Cardioverter-defibrillator, dual chamber (implantable)

C1722   Cardioverter-defibrillator, single chamber (implantable)

C1777   Lead, cardioverter-defibrillator, endocardial single coil (implantable)

C1882   Cardioverter-defibrillator, other than single or dual chamber (implantable)

C1895   Lead, cardioverter-defibrillator, endocardial dual coil (implantable)

C1896   Lead, cardioverter-defibrillator, other than endocardial, single or dual coil (implantable)

Insertion of Implantable Defibrillator (ICD) (Pulse, Generator, and Lead)

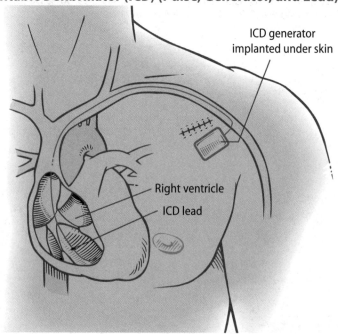

ICD generator implanted under skin

Right ventricle

ICD lead

ICD-10-CM Coding

I11.Ø	Hypertensive heart disease with heart failure
I13.Ø	Hypertensive heart and chronic kidney disease with heart failure and stage 1 through stage 4 chronic kidney disease, or unspecified chronic kidney disease
I13.2	Hypertensive heart and chronic kidney disease with heart failure and with stage 5 chronic kidney disease, or end stage renal disease
I16.Ø	Hypertensive urgency
I16.1	Hypertensive emergency
I16.9	Hypertensive crisis, unspecified
I21.Ø1	ST elevation (STEMI) myocardial infarction involving left main coronary artery
I21.Ø2	ST elevation (STEMI) myocardial infarction involving left anterior descending coronary artery
I21.Ø9	ST elevation (STEMI) myocardial infarction involving other coronary artery of anterior wall
I21.11	ST elevation (STEMI) myocardial infarction involving right coronary artery
I21.19	ST elevation (STEMI) myocardial infarction involving other coronary artery of inferior wall
I21.21	ST elevation (STEMI) myocardial infarction involving left circumflex coronary artery
I21.29	ST elevation (STEMI) myocardial infarction involving other sites
I21.3	ST elevation (STEMI) myocardial infarction of unspecified site
I21.4	Non-ST elevation (NSTEMI) myocardial infarction
I21.9	Acute myocardial infarction, unspecified
I21.A1	Myocardial infarction type 2
I21.A9	Other myocardial infarction type
I22.Ø	Subsequent ST elevation (STEMI) myocardial infarction of anterior wall
I22.1	Subsequent ST elevation (STEMI) myocardial infarction of inferior wall
I22.2	Subsequent non-ST elevation (NSTEMI) myocardial infarction
I22.8	Subsequent ST elevation (STEMI) myocardial infarction of other sites
I22.9	Subsequent ST elevation (STEMI) myocardial infarction of unspecified site
I25.2	Old myocardial infarction
I25.5	Ischemic cardiomyopathy
I25.6	Silent myocardial ischemia
I25.89	Other forms of chronic ischemic heart disease
I25.9	Chronic ischemic heart disease, unspecified
I42.Ø	Dilated cardiomyopathy
I42.1	Obstructive hypertrophic cardiomyopathy
I42.2	Other hypertrophic cardiomyopathy
I42.5	Other restrictive cardiomyopathy
I42.8	Other cardiomyopathies
I42.9	Cardiomyopathy, unspecified
I44.Ø	Atrioventricular block, first degree
I44.1	Atrioventricular block, second degree
I44.2	Atrioventricular block, complete
I44.3Ø	Unspecified atrioventricular block
I44.39	Other atrioventricular block
I44.4	Left anterior fascicular block
I44.5	Left posterior fascicular block
I44.6Ø	Unspecified fascicular block
I44.69	Other fascicular block
I44.7	Left bundle-branch block, unspecified
I45.Ø	Right fascicular block
I45.1Ø	Unspecified right bundle-branch block
I45.19	Other right bundle-branch block
I45.2	Bifascicular block
I45.4	Nonspecific intraventricular block
I45.5	Other specified heart block
I45.6	Pre-excitation syndrome
I45.81	Long QT syndrome
I45.9	Conduction disorder, unspecified

I46.2	Cardiac arrest due to underlying cardiac condition
I46.8	Cardiac arrest due to other underlying condition
I46.9	Cardiac arrest, cause unspecified
I47.0	Re-entry ventricular arrhythmia
I47.1	Supraventricular tachycardia
I47.2	Ventricular tachycardia
I48.0	Paroxysmal atrial fibrillation
I48.2	Chronic atrial fibrillation
I48.91	Unspecified atrial fibrillation
I49.01	Ventricular fibrillation
I49.02	Ventricular flutter
I49.2	Junctional premature depolarization
I49.5	Sick sinus syndrome
I49.8	Other specified cardiac arrhythmias
I49.9	Cardiac arrhythmia, unspecified
I50.1	Left ventricular failure
I50.20	Unspecified systolic (congestive) heart failure
I50.21	Acute systolic (congestive) heart failure
I50.22	Chronic systolic (congestive) heart failure
I50.23	Acute on chronic systolic (congestive) heart failure
I50.30	Unspecified diastolic (congestive) heart failure
I50.31	Acute diastolic (congestive) heart failure
I50.32	Chronic diastolic (congestive) heart failure
I50.33	Acute on chronic diastolic (congestive) heart failure
I50.40	Unspecified combined systolic (congestive) and diastolic (congestive) heart failure
I50.41	Acute combined systolic (congestive) and diastolic (congestive) heart failure
I50.42	Chronic combined systolic (congestive) and diastolic (congestive) heart failure
I50.43	Acute on chronic combined systolic (congestive) and diastolic (congestive) heart failure
I50.810	Right heart failure, unspecified
I50.811	Acute right heart failure
I50.812	Chronic right heart failure
I50.813	Acute on chronic right heart failure
I50.814	Right heart failure due to left heart failure
I50.82	Biventricular heart failure
I50.83	High output heart failure
I50.84	End stage heart failure
I50.89	Other heart failure
I50.9	Heart failure, unspecified
Q23.8	Other congenital malformations of aortic and mitral valves
Q23.9	Congenital malformation of aortic and mitral valves, unspecified
Q24.6	Congenital heart block
Q24.8	Other specified congenital malformations of heart
R00.1	Bradycardia, unspecified
T82.110A	Breakdown (mechanical) of cardiac electrode, initial encounter
T82.111A	Breakdown (mechanical) of cardiac pulse generator (battery), initial encounter
T82.120A	Displacement of cardiac electrode, initial encounter
T82.121A	Displacement of cardiac pulse generator (battery), initial encounter
T82.190A	Other mechanical complication of cardiac electrode, initial encounter
T82.191A	Other mechanical complication of cardiac pulse generator (battery), initial encounter
T82.598A	Other mechanical complication of other cardiac and vascular devices and implants, initial encounter
T82.7XXA	Infection and inflammatory reaction due to other cardiac and vascular devices, implants and grafts, initial encounter
T82.817A	Embolism due to cardiac prosthetic devices, implants and grafts, initial encounter
T82.827A	Fibrosis due to cardiac prosthetic devices, implants and grafts, initial encounter
T82.837A	Hemorrhage due to cardiac prosthetic devices, implants and grafts, initial encounter
T82.847A	Pain due to cardiac prosthetic devices, implants and grafts, initial encounter

T82.855A	Stenosis of coronary artery stent, initial encounter
T82.857A	Stenosis of other cardiac prosthetic devices, implants and grafts, initial encounter
T82.867A	Thrombosis due to cardiac prosthetic devices, implants and grafts, initial encounter
T82.897A	Other specified complication of cardiac prosthetic devices, implants and grafts, initial encounter
T82.9XXA	Unspecified complication of cardiac and vascular prosthetic device, implant and graft, initial encounter
Z45.02	Encounter for adjustment and management of automatic implantable cardiac defibrillator
Z95.810	Presence of automatic (implantable) cardiac defibrillator

CCI Edits

33249 00530, 00534, 0213T, 0216T, 0228T, 0230T, 0293T-0294T, 0302T-0306T, 0389T-0391T, 0462T-0463T, 11000-11006, 11042-11047, 12001-12007, 12011-12057, 13100-13133, 13151-13153, 32100, 33210-33211, 33215-33217, 33223, 33230-33231, 33240, 33262-33264, 35201-35206, 35226-35236, 35256-35266, 35286, 36000, 36005-36013, 36120-36140, 36400-36410, 36420-36430, 36440, 36555-36556, 36568-36569, 36591-36592, 36600, 36640, 39010, 43752, 51701-51703, 62320-62327, 64400-64410, 64413-64435, 64445-64450, 64461-64463, 64479-64530, 69990, 76000-76001, 76942, 76970, 76998, 77001-77002, 92012-92014, 92960-92961, 93000-93010, 93040-93042, 93260-93261, 93279-93299, 93318, 93355, 93600-93603, 93610-93612, 94002, 94200, 94250, 94680-94690, 94770, 95812-95816, 95819, 95822, 95829, 95955, 96360-96368, 96372, 96374-96377, 97597-97598, 97602, 99155-99157, 99211-99223, 99231-99255, 99291-99292, 99304-99310, 99315-99316, 99334-99337, 99347-99350, 99374-99375, 99377-99378, 99446-99449, 99495-99496, G0463, G0471

Leadless Pacemaker System

0387T	**Transcatheter insertion or replacement of permanent leadless pacemaker, ventricular**
0388T	**Transcatheter removal of permanent leadless pacemaker, ventricular**

The physician performs transcatheter insertion, replacement, or removal of a ventricular permanent leadless pacemaker. This pacemaker has no leads and is a single-chamber unit that is placed in the right ventricle. The size varies based on manufacturer but the pacemaker is about 7 mm x 26 mm and weighs 2 grams. The less invasive and shorter implant procedure of a leadless pacemaker reduces recovery time and eliminates complications related to the transvenous leads and the subcutaneous pulse generator used in traditional pacemaker implantation, specifically infections. The battery typically lasts from seven to 15 years, and the pacing, amplitude, and impedance are all relative to the traditional pacemaker. The femoral vein is entered, and the device is fed into the right ventricle using a special catheter. Once the device is attached, a continued connection allows for measurements to be taken and to determine positioning.

Coding Tips

1. These codes are comprehensive codes. They include fluoroscopy, right ventriculography and femoral venography when related directly to the leadless pacemaker procedure.
2. Conscious sedation is not included and may be separately reported.
3. Report any applicable HCPCS Level II codes for devices and contrast media used. Refer to the HCPCS section for possible codes.

Facility HCPCS Coding

Some applicable codes may include, but are not limited to:

C1766	Introducer/sheath, steerable, non-peel away
C1769	Guidewire
C1786	Pacemaker, single, rate-responsive
C1892	Introducer/sheath, fixed, peel-away
C1893	Introducer/sheath, fixed, non peel-away
C1894	Introducer/sheath, non-laser
C2620	Pacemaker, single, non rate-responsive
C2621	Pacemaker, other than single/dual

ICD-10-CM Coding

I44.0	Atrioventricular block, first degree
I44.1	Atrioventricular block, second degree
I44.2	Atrioventricular block, complete
I44.30	Unspecified atrioventricular block
I44.39	Other atrioventricular block
I44.4	Left anterior fascicular block
I44.5	Left posterior fascicular block
I44.60	Unspecified fascicular block
I44.69	Other fascicular block
I44.7	Left bundle-branch block, unspecified
I45.0	Right fascicular block
I45.10	Unspecified right bundle-branch block
I45.19	Other right bundle-branch block
I45.2	Bifascicular block
I45.3	Trifascicular block
I45.4	Nonspecific intraventricular block
I45.5	Other specified heart block
I45.6	Pre-excitation syndrome
I45.81	Long QT syndrome
I45.9	Conduction disorder, unspecified
I47.1	Supraventricular tachycardia
I48.0	Paroxysmal atrial fibrillation
I48.2	Chronic atrial fibrillation

I48.91	Unspecified atrial fibrillation
I49.2	Junctional premature depolarization
I49.5	Sick sinus syndrome
I49.8	Other specified cardiac arrhythmias
I49.9	Cardiac arrhythmia, unspecified
I50.1	Left ventricular failure
I50.20	Unspecified systolic (congestive) heart failure
I50.21	Acute systolic (congestive) heart failure
I50.22	Chronic systolic (congestive) heart failure
I50.23	Acute on chronic systolic (congestive) heart failure
I50.30	Unspecified diastolic (congestive) heart failure
I50.31	Acute diastolic (congestive) heart failure
I50.32	Chronic diastolic (congestive) heart failure
I50.33	Acute on chronic diastolic (congestive) heart failure
I50.40	Unspecified combined systolic (congestive) and diastolic (congestive) heart failure
I50.41	Acute combined systolic (congestive) and diastolic (congestive) heart failure
I50.42	Chronic combined systolic (congestive) and diastolic (congestive) heart failure
I50.43	Acute on chronic combined systolic (congestive) and diastolic (congestive) heart failure
I50.810	Right heart failure, unspecified
I50.811	Acute right heart failure
I50.812	Chronic right heart failure
I50.813	Acute on chronic right heart failure
I50.814	Right heart failure due to left heart failure
I50.82	Biventricular heart failure
I50.83	High output heart failure
I50.84	End stage heart failure
I50.89	Other heart failure
I50.9	Heart failure, unspecified
I51.7	Cardiomegaly
I51.9	Heart disease, unspecified
Q24.6	Congenital heart block
R00.1	Bradycardia, unspecified
T82.110A	Breakdown (mechanical) of cardiac electrode, initial encounter
T82.110D	Breakdown (mechanical) of cardiac electrode, subsequent encounter
T82.111A	Breakdown (mechanical) of cardiac pulse generator (battery), initial encounter
T82.111D	Breakdown (mechanical) of cardiac pulse generator (battery), subsequent encounter
T82.118A	Breakdown (mechanical) of other cardiac electronic device, initial encounter
T82.118D	Breakdown (mechanical) of other cardiac electronic device, subsequent encounter
T82.119A	Breakdown (mechanical) of unspecified cardiac electronic device, initial encounter
T82.119D	Breakdown (mechanical) of unspecified cardiac electronic device, subsequent encounter
T82.120A	Displacement of cardiac electrode, initial encounter
T82.120D	Displacement of cardiac electrode, subsequent encounter
T82.121A	Displacement of cardiac pulse generator (battery), initial encounter
T82.121D	Displacement of cardiac pulse generator (battery), subsequent encounter
T82.128A	Displacement of other cardiac electronic device, initial encounter
T82.128D	Displacement of other cardiac electronic device, subsequent encounter
T82.129A	Displacement of unspecified cardiac electronic device, initial encounter
T82.129D	Displacement of unspecified cardiac electronic device, subsequent encounter
T82.190A	Other mechanical complication of cardiac electrode, initial encounter
T82.190D	Other mechanical complication of cardiac electrode, subsequent encounter
T82.191A	Other mechanical complication of cardiac pulse generator (battery), initial encounter
T82.191D	Other mechanical complication of cardiac pulse generator (battery), subsequent encounter
T82.198A	Other mechanical complication of other cardiac electronic device, initial encounter
T82.198D	Other mechanical complication of other cardiac electronic device, subsequent encounter
T82.199A	Other mechanical complication of unspecified cardiac device, initial encounter
T82.199D	Other mechanical complication of unspecified cardiac device, subsequent encounter

T82.7XXA	Infection and inflammatory reaction due to other cardiac and vascular devices, implants and grafts, initial encounter
T82.7XXD	Infection and inflammatory reaction due to other cardiac and vascular devices, implants and grafts, subsequent encounter
T82.817A	Embolism due to cardiac prosthetic devices, implants and grafts, initial encounter
T82.817D	Embolism due to cardiac prosthetic devices, implants and grafts, subsequent encounter
T82.827A	Fibrosis due to cardiac prosthetic devices, implants and grafts, initial encounter
T82.827D	Fibrosis due to cardiac prosthetic devices, implants and grafts, subsequent encounter
T82.837A	Hemorrhage due to cardiac prosthetic devices, implants and grafts, initial encounter
T82.837D	Hemorrhage due to cardiac prosthetic devices, implants and grafts, subsequent encounter
T82.847A	Pain due to cardiac prosthetic devices, implants and grafts, initial encounter
T82.847D	Pain due to cardiac prosthetic devices, implants and grafts, subsequent encounter
T82.855A	Stenosis of coronary artery stent, initial encounter
T82.857A	Stenosis of other cardiac prosthetic devices, implants and grafts, initial encounter
T82.857D	Stenosis of other cardiac prosthetic devices, implants and grafts, subsequent encounter
T82.867A	Thrombosis due to cardiac prosthetic devices, implants and grafts, initial encounter
T82.867D	Thrombosis due to cardiac prosthetic devices, implants and grafts, subsequent encounter
T82.897A	Other specified complication of cardiac prosthetic devices, implants and grafts, initial encounter
T82.897D	Other specified complication of cardiac prosthetic devices, implants and grafts, subsequent encounter
T82.897S	Other specified complication of cardiac prosthetic devices, implants and grafts, sequela
T82.9XXA	Unspecified complication of cardiac and vascular prosthetic device, implant and graft, initial encounter
T82.9XXD	Unspecified complication of cardiac and vascular prosthetic device, implant and graft, subsequent encounter
T82.9XXS	Unspecified complication of cardiac and vascular prosthetic device, implant and graft, sequela
Z45.018	Encounter for adjustment and management of other part of cardiac pacemaker
Z95.0	Presence of cardiac pacemaker

CCI Edits

0387T   00530, 00534, 0213T, 0216T, 0228T, 0230T, 0293T-0294T, 0302T-0306T, 0388T-0391T, 0408T-0411T, 0414T, 0415T-0416T, 0417T-0418T, 0462T-0463T, 11000-11006, 11042-11047, 12001-12007, 12011-12057, 13100-13133, 13151-13153, 33227-33229, 35201-35206, 35226-35236, 35256-35266, 35286, 36000, 36005-36013, 36120-36140, 36400-36410, 36420-36430, 36440, 36555-36556, 36568-36569, 36591-36592, 36600, 36640, 43752, 51701-51703, 61650, 62320-62327, 64400-64410, 64413-64435, 64445-64450, 64461, 64463, 64479, 64483, 64490, 64493, 64505-64530, 69990, 75820, 76000-76001, 76942, 76970, 76998, 77001-77002, 92012-92014, 92960-92961, 93000-93010, 93040-93042, 93279-93299, 93318, 93355, 93566, 94002, 94200, 94250, 94680-94690, 94770, 95812-95816, 95819, 95822, 95829, 95955, 96360, 96365, 96372, 96374-96377, 97597-97598, 97602, 99155-99157, 99211-99223, 99231-99255, 99291-99292, 99304-99310, 99315-99316, 99334-99337, 99347-99350, 99374-99375, 99377-99378, 99446-99449, 99495-99496, G0463

0388T   00530, 00534, 0213T, 0216T, 0228T, 0230T, 0293T-0294T, 0302T-0306T, 0389T-0391T, 0412T-0414T, 0415T, 0416T, 0417T-0418T, 0462T-0463T, 11000-11006, 11042-11047, 12001-12007, 12011-12057, 13100-13133, 13151-13153, 33210-33211, 33215, 33222, 33223, 35201-35206, 35226-35236, 35256-35266, 35286, 36000, 36005-36013, 36120-36140, 36400-36410, 36420-36430, 36440, 36555-36556, 36568-36569, 36591-36592, 36600, 36640, 43752, 51701-51703, 61650, 62320-62327, 64400-64410, 64413-64435, 64445-64450, 64461, 64463, 64479, 64483, 64490, 64493, 64505-64530, 69990, 75820, 76000-76001, 76942, 76970, 76998, 77001-77002, 92012-92014, 92960-92961, 93000-93010, 93040-93042, 93279-93299, 93318, 93355, 93566, 94002, 94200, 94250, 94680-94690, 94770, 95812-95816, 95819, 95822, 95829, 95955, 96360, 96365, 96372, 96374-96377, 97597-97598, 97602, 99155-99157, 99211-99223, 99231-99255, 99291-99292, 99304-99310, 99315-99316, 99334-99337, 99347-99350, 99374-99375, 99377-99378, 99446-99449, 99495-99496, G0463

Subcutaneous ICD System Procedures (S-ICD)

Subcutaneous defibrillator systems use a single electrode placed subcutaneously to treat ventricular tachyarrhythmias. These systems do not perform pacing functions. The lead is tunneled under the skin to the left parasternal margin.

33270   **Insertion or replacement of permanent subcutaneous implantable defibrillator system, with subcutaneous electrode, inducing defibrillation threshold evaluation, induction of arrhythmia, evaluation of sensing for arrhythmia termination, and programming or reprogramming of sensing or therapeutic parameters, when performed**

33271   **Insertion of subcutaneous implantable defibrillator electrode**
The physician performs initial insertion or replacement of a permanent subcutaneous implantable defibrillator (S-ICD) system, including the pulse generator and lead. The pulse generator is placed in a subcutaneous pocket on the left side of the chest next to the ribs. Two small incisions are made above the sternum, and the lead wire is threaded through and sutured into place. The lead is connected to the pulse generator. The physician records cardiac electrical signals from the leads and paces the heart through the leads to determine pacing threshold. The physician uses the S-ICD pulse generator to pace the heart into an arrhythmia, such as ventricular tachycardia or fibrillation. The S-ICD detects and terminates the arrhythmia using pacing or by shocking the heart through the lead. The physician may reprogram the treatment parameters to optimize the device function to best treat the patient's arrhythmia.

33272   **Removal of subcutaneous implantable defibrillator electrode**
The physician performs a procedure to remove the subcutaneous implantable defibrillator lead only. The lead may be removed due to a complication or malfunction. An incision is made in the area above the sternum where the lead is located. The lead is disconnected from the pulse generator, pulled through, and removed.

33273   **Repositioning of previously implanted subcutaneous implantable defibrillator electrode**
A previously placed implanted subcutaneous defibrillator lead (electrode) is repositioned. This procedure is performed when the system does not function due to improper placement of the lead. An incision is made over the previous subcutaneous pocket on the left side of the chest next to the ribs, and the lead is disconnected from the pulse generator. The generator is removed, and the lead is tested for proper function. It is then reattached to the generator in the new position and retested.

93644   **Electrophysiologic evaluation of subcutaneous implantable defibrillator (includes defibrillation threshold evaluation, induction of arrhythmia, evaluation of sensing for arrhythmia termination, and programming or reprogramming of sensing or therapeutic parameters)**
The purpose of this study is to test the placement of the leads and whether they are working as intended. To test the leads, the physician records cardiac electrical signals from the leads and paces the heart through the leads. The physician may test the leads using the actual ICD or by hooking the lead to an external device. The physician uses the lead to pace the heart into an arrhythmia, such as ventricular tachycardia. The ICD or external device detects the arrhythmia and shocks the heart through the ICD lead. The physician may perform this test with several different levels of shock to ensure the ICD can reliably terminate the arrhythmia.

Coding Tips

1.   Insertion of subcutaneous defibrillator systems includes EP evaluation. Do not report 93644 separately.
2.   Report electrode placement with 33270 or 33271.
3.   When a second electrode is placed to allow biventricular pacing, report 33224 or 33225 in addition.
4.   Report electrode removal with 33272 separately.
5.   When generator insertion involves insertion of one or more leads, report 33270.
6.   Do not report skin pocket revision separately.
7.   Use 33273 to report repositioning of a subcutaneous lead.
8.   DFT testing during implantation is included and not reported separately. Do not use 93644 with 33270–33273.
9.   DFT testing in follow-up or at the time of replacement may be reported separately.
10.   Fluoroscopy is included in these codes.
11.   Fluoroscopy for diagnostic lead evaluation not done during implantation, revision, or replacement may be reported with 76000.

Facility HCPCS Coding

HCPCS Level II codes are used to report the supplies provided during the procedure. Hospitals should report supplies used during these procedures separately. A complete listing of device codes can be found in appendix B of this publication. Applicable codes for this section may include but are not limited to:

C1721   AICD, dual chamber

C1722   AICD, single chamber

C1882   AICD, other than single/dual

C1892	Introducer sheath, fixed, peel-away
C1893	Introducer sheath, fixed, non peel-away
C1894	Introducer sheath, non-laser
C1895	Lead, AICD, endocardial dual coil
C1896	Lead, AICD, non single/dual
C1900	Lead, coronary venous
C2629	Introducer sheath, laser

ICD-10-CM Coding

I11.0	Hypertensive heart disease with heart failure
I13.0	Hypertensive heart and chronic kidney disease with heart failure and stage 1 through stage 4 chronic kidney disease, or unspecified chronic kidney disease
I13.2	Hypertensive heart and chronic kidney disease with heart failure and with stage 5 chronic kidney disease, or end stage renal disease
I16.0	Hypertensive urgency
I16.1	Hypertensive emergency
I16.9	Hypertensive crisis, unspecified
I21.01	ST elevation (STEMI) myocardial infarction involving left main coronary artery
I21.02	ST elevation (STEMI) myocardial infarction involving left anterior descending coronary artery
I21.09	ST elevation (STEMI) myocardial infarction involving other coronary artery of anterior wall
I21.11	ST elevation (STEMI) myocardial infarction involving right coronary artery
I21.19	ST elevation (STEMI) myocardial infarction involving other coronary artery of inferior wall
I21.21	ST elevation (STEMI) myocardial infarction involving left circumflex coronary artery
I21.29	ST elevation (STEMI) myocardial infarction involving other sites
I21.3	ST elevation (STEMI) myocardial infarction of unspecified site
I21.4	Non-ST elevation (NSTEMI) myocardial infarction
I21.9	Acute myocardial infarction, unspecified
I21.A1	Myocardial infarction type 2
I21.A9	Other myocardial infarction type
I22.0	Subsequent ST elevation (STEMI) myocardial infarction of anterior wall
I22.1	Subsequent ST elevation (STEMI) myocardial infarction of inferior wall
I22.2	Subsequent non-ST elevation (NSTEMI) myocardial infarction
I22.8	Subsequent ST elevation (STEMI) myocardial infarction of other sites
I22.9	Subsequent ST elevation (STEMI) myocardial infarction of unspecified site
I25.2	Old myocardial infarction
I25.5	Ischemic cardiomyopathy
I25.6	Silent myocardial ischemia
I25.89	Other forms of chronic ischemic heart disease
I25.9	Chronic ischemic heart disease, unspecified
I42.0	Dilated cardiomyopathy
I42.1	Obstructive hypertrophic cardiomyopathy
I42.2	Other hypertrophic cardiomyopathy
I42.5	Other restrictive cardiomyopathy
I42.8	Other cardiomyopathies
I42.9	Cardiomyopathy, unspecified
I43	Cardiomyopathy in diseases classified elsewhere
I44.0	Atrioventricular block, first degree
I44.1	Atrioventricular block, second degree
I44.2	Atrioventricular block, complete
I44.30	Unspecified atrioventricular block
I44.39	Other atrioventricular block
I44.4	Left anterior fascicular block
I44.5	Left posterior fascicular block
I44.60	Unspecified fascicular block
I44.69	Other fascicular block

I44.7	Left bundle-branch block, unspecified
I45.0	Right fascicular block
I45.10	Unspecified right bundle-branch block
I45.19	Other right bundle-branch block
I45.2	Bifascicular block
I45.4	Nonspecific intraventricular block
I45.5	Other specified heart block
I45.6	Pre-excitation syndrome
I45.81	Long QT syndrome
I45.89	Other specified conduction disorders
I45.9	Conduction disorder, unspecified
I46.2	Cardiac arrest due to underlying cardiac condition
I46.8	Cardiac arrest due to other underlying condition
I46.9	Cardiac arrest, cause unspecified
I47.0	Re-entry ventricular arrhythmia
I47.1	Supraventricular tachycardia
I47.2	Ventricular tachycardia
I47.9	Paroxysmal tachycardia, unspecified
I48.0	Paroxysmal atrial fibrillation
I48.1	Persistent atrial fibrillation
I48.2	Chronic atrial fibrillation
I48.3	Typical atrial flutter
I48.4	Atypical atrial flutter
I48.91	Unspecified atrial fibrillation
I48.92	Unspecified atrial flutter
I49.01	Ventricular fibrillation
I49.02	Ventricular flutter
I49.1	Atrial premature depolarization
I49.2	Junctional premature depolarization
I49.3	Ventricular premature depolarization
I49.40	Unspecified premature depolarization
I49.49	Other premature depolarization
I49.5	Sick sinus syndrome
I49.8	Other specified cardiac arrhythmias
I49.9	Cardiac arrhythmia, unspecified
I50.1	Left ventricular failure
I50.20	Unspecified systolic (congestive) heart failure
I50.21	Acute systolic (congestive) heart failure
I50.22	Chronic systolic (congestive) heart failure
I50.23	Acute on chronic systolic (congestive) heart failure
I50.30	Unspecified diastolic (congestive) heart failure
I50.31	Acute diastolic (congestive) heart failure
I50.32	Chronic diastolic (congestive) heart failure
I50.33	Acute on chronic diastolic (congestive) heart failure
I50.40	Unspecified combined systolic (congestive) and diastolic (congestive) heart failure
I50.41	Acute combined systolic (congestive) and diastolic (congestive) heart failure
I50.42	Chronic combined systolic (congestive) and diastolic (congestive) heart failure
I50.43	Acute on chronic combined systolic (congestive) and diastolic (congestive) heart failure
I50.810	Right heart failure, unspecified
I50.811	Acute right heart failure
I50.812	Chronic right heart failure
I50.813	Acute on chronic right heart failure
I50.814	Right heart failure due to left heart failure
I50.82	Biventricular heart failure
I50.83	High output heart failure
I50.84	End stage heart failure

I50.89	Other heart failure
I50.9	Heart failure, unspecified
Q23.8	Other congenital malformations of aortic and mitral valves
Q23.9	Congenital malformation of aortic and mitral valves, unspecified
Q24.6	Congenital heart block
Q24.8	Other specified congenital malformations of heart
T82.110A	Breakdown (mechanical) of cardiac electrode, initial encounter
T82.111A	Breakdown (mechanical) of cardiac pulse generator (battery), initial encounter
T82.120A	Displacement of cardiac electrode, initial encounter
T82.121A	Displacement of cardiac pulse generator (battery), initial encounter
T82.190A	Other mechanical complication of cardiac electrode, initial encounter
T82.191A	Other mechanical complication of cardiac pulse generator (battery), initial encounter
T82.598A	Other mechanical complication of other cardiac and vascular devices and implants, initial encounter
T82.7XXA	Infection and inflammatory reaction due to other cardiac and vascular devices, implants and grafts, initial encounter
T82.817A	Embolism of cardiac prosthetic devices, implants and grafts, initial encounter
T82.827A	Fibrosis of cardiac prosthetic devices, implants and grafts, initial encounter
T82.837A	Hemorrhage of cardiac prosthetic devices, implants and grafts, initial encounter
T82.847A	Pain from cardiac prosthetic devices, implants and grafts, initial encounter
T82.855A	Stenosis of coronary artery stent, initial encounter
T82.857A	Stenosis of cardiac prosthetic devices, implants and grafts, initial encounter
T82.867A	Thrombosis of cardiac prosthetic devices, implants and grafts, initial encounter
T82.897A	Other specified complication of cardiac prosthetic devices, implants and grafts, initial encounter
T82.9XXA	Unspecified complication of cardiac and vascular prosthetic device, implant and graft, initial encounter
Z45.018	Encounter for adjustment and management of other part of cardiac pacemaker
Z45.02	Encounter for adjustment and management of automatic implantable cardiac defibrillator
Z95.0	Presence of cardiac pacemaker
Z95.810	Presence of automatic (implantable) cardiac defibrillator

CCI Edits

33270 00530, 00540, 0213T, 0216T, 0228T, 0230T, 11000-11006, 11042-11047, 12001-12007, 12011-12057, 13100-13133, 13151-13153, 33210-33211, 33271, 33273, 36000, 36400-36410, 36420-36430, 36440, 36591-36592, 36600, 36640, 43752, 51701-51703, 62310-62319, 64400-64410, 64413-64435, 64445-64450, 64461, 64463, 64479, 64483, 64486-64490, 64493, 64505-64530, 69990, 76000-76001, 76942, 76998, 92012-92014, 92960-92961, 93000-93010, 93040-93042, 93260-93261, 93279-93299, 93318, 93355, 93600-93603, 93610-93612, 93640-93644, 94002, 94200, 94250, 94680-94690, 94770, 95812-95816, 95819, 95822, 95829, 95955, 96360-96368, 96372, 96374-96376, 97597-97598, 97602, 99148-99150, 99211-99223, 99231-99255, 99291-99292, 99304-99310, 99315-99316, 99334-99337, 99347-99350, 99374-99375, 99377-99378, 99446-99449, G0471

33271 00530, 00540, 0213T, 0216T, 0228T, 0230T, 11000-11006, 11042-11047, 12001-12007, 12011-12057, 13100-13133, 13151-13153, 33210-33211, 33240, 33262, 33263-33264, 33273, 36000, 36400-36410, 36420-36430, 36440, 36591-36592, 36600, 36640, 43752, 51701-51703, 62310-62319, 64400-64410, 64413-64435, 64445-64450, 64461, 64463, 64479, 64483, 64486-64490, 64493, 64505-64530, 69990, 76000-76001, 76942, 76998, 92012-92014, 92960-92961, 93000-93010, 93040-93042, 93260-93261, 93279-93299, 93318, 93355, 93600-93603, 93610-93612, 94002, 94200, 94250, 94680-94690, 94770, 95812-95816, 95819, 95822, 95829, 95955, 96360-96368, 96372, 96374-96376, 97597-97598, 97602, 99148-99150, 99211-99223, 99231-99255, 99291-99292, 99304-99310, 99315-99316, 99334-99337, 99347-99350, 99374-99375, 99377-99378, 99446-99449, G0471

33272 00530, 00540, 0213T, 0216T, 0228T, 0230T, 11000-11006, 11042-11047, 12001-12007, 12011-12057, 13100-13133, 13151-13153, 33210-33211, 33273, 36000, 36400-36410, 36420-36430, 36440, 36591-36592, 36600, 36640, 43752, 51701-51703, 62310-62319, 64400-64410, 64413-64435, 64445-64450, 64461, 64463, 64479, 64483, 64486-64490, 64493, 64505-64530, 69990, 76000-76001, 76942, 76998, 92012-92014, 92960-92961, 93000-93010, 93040-93042, 93260-93261, 93279-93299, 93318, 93355, 94002, 94200, 94250, 94680-94690, 94770, 95812-95816, 95819, 95822, 95829, 95955, 96360-96368, 96372, 96374-96376, 97597-97598, 97602, 99148-99150, 99211-99223, 99231-99255, 99291-99292, 99304-99310, 99315-99316, 99334-99337, 99347-99350, 99374-99375, 99377-99378, 99446-99449, G0471

33273   00530, 00540, 0213T, 0216T, 0228T, 0230T, 12001-12007, 12011-12057, 13100-13133, 13151-13153, 33210-33211, 36000, 36400-36410, 36420-36430, 36440, 36591-36592, 36600, 36640, 43752, 51701-51703, 62310-62319, 64400-64410, 64413-64435, 64445-64450, 64461, 64463, 64479, 64483, 64486-64490, 64493, 64505-64530, 69990, 76000-76001, 76942, 76998, 92012-92014, 92960-92961, 93000-93010, 93040-93042, 93260-93261, 93279-93299, 93318, 93355, 93600-93603, 93610-93612, 94002, 94200, 94250, 94680-94690, 94770, 95812-95816, 95819, 95822, 95829, 95955, 96360-96368, 96372, 96374-96376, 99148-99150, 99211-99223, 99231-99255, 99291-99292, 99304-99310, 99315-99316, 99334-99337, 99347-99350, 99374-99375, 99377-99378, 99446-99449, G0471

93644   00410, 00534-00537, 0178T-0179T, 0180T, 0213T, 0216T, 0228T, 0230T, 12001-12007, 12011-12057, 13100-13133, 13151-13153, 33210-33211, 36000, 36005-36013, 36120-36140, 36400-36410, 36420-36430, 36440, 36555-36556, 36568-36569, 36591-36592, 36600, 36640, 43752, 51701-51703, 62320-62327, 64400-64410, 64413-64435, 64445-64450, 64461-64463, 64479-64530, 76942, 76970, 76998, 92012-92014, 92950, 92960-92961, 93000-93010, 93040-93042, 93050, 93260, 93282-93284, 93287, 93289, 93318, 93355-93461, 93530-93533, 93563, 93565-93568, 93618, 93640, 94002, 94200, 94250, 94680-94690, 94770, 95812-95816, 95819, 95822, 95829, 95955, 96360-96368, 96372, 96374-96377, 99155-99157, 99211-99223, 99231-99255, 99291-99292, 99304-99310, 99315-99316, 99334-99337, 99347-99350, 99374-99375, 99377-99378, 99446-99449, 99495-99496, G0463, G0471

Pacemaker Case Examples
Case Example #1

Procedure:
Permanent dual generator pacemaker replacement, with chronic lead threshold measurement

Indications:
Cordis **pacemaker at ERI**

Summary:
The patient was brought to the cardiac catheterization laboratory in the fasting state and with informed consent on the chart. He was prepped and draped in sterile fashion and premedicated with 2 mg Versed and 2 mg morphine intravenously.

The skin overlying the pulse generator was infiltrated locally with 15 cc of a 50 percent mixture of 1 percent Xylocaine and 0.25 percent Marcaine. An incision was made through the old wound and carried down to the generator pocket. After freeing up the ends of the leads as they entered the header, the generator was mobilized to the skin. Care was taken because the patient was in a unipolar pacing mode and completely pacer dependent.

The atrial lead was removed from the header of the generator, and tested. The P-wave was 10.6 mv, but impedance and threshold could not be measured. The ventricular lead was then removed from the header and immediately connected to the pacing lead in a unipolar fashion. R-waves were not evident. The ventricular lead was then attached to the ventricular port of a CPI Discovery DR Model 1275, serial 502xxx generator. The generator was programmed in unipolar fashion and appropriate capture was noted when the **generator was placed in the pocket**. Care was taken to make sure the end of the lead was beyond the set screw and the header and this was tightened to manufacturer specification. The atrial lead was then inserted and tightened in similar fashion. Both leads appeared secure to light traction. The pacemaker was then inserted into the pocket with the embossed face upward. Appropriate atrial sensing and ventricular pacing was noted at a rate of 125 (the patient had atrial fibrillation/flutter noted when not pacing). The pocket was irrigated with 10 cc of a cephalosporin antibiotic solution. The fascial layer was closed in running fashion using 3-0 chromic gut and the skin was closed in a running subcuticular manner using 4-0 Vicryl. Steri-Strips and a sterile dressing were then applied. At the time of implantation, the pacemaker was initially programmed in the DDDR mode: lower rate 75, upper rate 130 ppm, with a trial pacing at 0.5 ms, 4.0 v, with a sensitivity of 0.5 mv. Similar pacing output was present in the ventricle, with a sensitivity of 2.5 mv. The PVARP was 250 ms. Dynamic AV delay was programmed on between 80 and 180 ms. The accelerometer was programmed on with a medium activity threshold, reaction of 30 seconds, response factor of 8 and a recovery time of 5 minutes.

Atrial tachy response was programmed on initially at 170 bpm, with a fall-back mode of VDIR and a duration of 8 cycles. Once the patient was found to be in atrial fibrillation, this pacemaker was programmed again to a WIR mode at a rate of 75.

Complications:
None

Estimated Blood Loss:
15 cc

CPT/HCPCS Codes Reported:
33228

Other HCPCS Codes Reported:
C1785

Case Example #2

Procedure:
The patient was taken to the catheterization lab and prepped and draped in the usual sterile fashion. After administration of intravenous antibiotics, an incision was then made in a pocket fashion in the pre-pectoral fascia on the left side using blunt dissection. A small artery in the pocket was incised but was tied off to keep from bleeding. Good hemostasis was obtained and an antibiotic soaked sponge was placed in the pocket. **After some difficulty with access, a venogram was performed to view the subclavian.** The location was inferior to traditional landmarks. The left subclavian vein was punctured under fluoroscopy and a floppy J-wire was inserted using the standard Seldinger technique. A 9 French Safe Sheath introducer was inserted in the subclavian vein after which a **new active fixation, bipolar, steroid eluting ventricular lead was inserted and positioned in the right ventricular apex**. The patient's right ventricle was small. Electrical measurements were obtained revealing excellent function and at maximum output of 10.0 V there was no evidence of diaphragmatic stimulation. Sufficient slack was placed in the lead and the lead was sutured to the base of the pocket using 2.0 Silk. Using the retained guide wire technique, a second 7.0 French Safe Sheath introducer was inserted in the subclavian vein after which a **new active fixation, bipolar, steroid eluting atrial lead was inserted and positioned in the right atrial appendage**.

At maximum output of 10.0 V there was no evidence of phrenic nerve stimulation. Sufficient slack was placed in the lead and the lead was sutured to the base of the pocket using 2.0 Silk. The antibiotic soaked sponge was removed from the pocket. The pocket was then vigorously irrigated with Bacitracins solution and good hemostasis was confirmed. The implanted **leads were attached to a new dual chamber, rate responsive pacemaker** using the set screws and wrench provided. The pulse

Case Example #2 (Continued)

generator and the leads were coiled and placed in the pocket. The pocket was closed with a layering technique using 3-0 and 4-0 absorbable Vicryl. Upon looking one last time under fluoroscopy the generator was riding up toward the clavicle due to gravity. The pocket was revised and again irrigated with Bacitracins solution. The pocket was again closed with a layering technique using 3-0 and 4-0 Vicryl. Steri-strips and pressure dressing were applied. Post operative testing was performed revealing excellent measurements.

CPT/HCPCS Codes Reported:
33208 and 75820

Other HCPCS Codes Reported:
C1785, C1898x2, C1769, C1894

Case Example #3

Indication:
Atrial fibrillation with period of very slow ventricular response.

Procedure:
After informed consent was obtained, the patient was brought to the catheterization lab. The subclavian area was prepped and draped in a sterile manner. Xylocaine was infiltrated into the subcutaneous tissue; 25mg of fentanyl and 1mg of Versed were given IV for sedation. The subclavian vein was approached percutaneously. Guidewire was advanced to the superior vena cava. An **incision was made** along the deltopectoral groove, and a **pocket was made** under the skin. The introducer was introduced over the wire to the superior vena cava and the **right ventricular lead was advanced into position** in the **right ventricular** apex. The lead was sutured to subcutaneous tissue with a silk tie. In was connected to the pacemaker generator. The pocket was rinsed with Neosporin solution. The subcutaneous tissue was sutured with chromic and skin sutured with nylon. The position was again verified after completion under fluoroscopy and appeared to be in satisfactory position. The patient tolerated the procedure well and returned to the floor in stable condition.

CPT/HCPCS Codes Reported:
33207

Other HCPCS Codes Reported:
C1786, C1898

Case Example #4

Procedure:
ICD generator change

History:
65-year-old with an ischemic cardiomyopathy and class I/II congestive failure. He has a history of ventricular tachycardia and previous ICD implantation. He has received recent therapies for VT with painless anti-tachycardia pacing therapy. He is non pacemaker dependent. His device is under current advisory and he is **brought in for defibrillator generator change**.

Procedure Description:
The patient was brought to the EP lab in the fasting, non-sedated state. Sedation was administered with Versed 3mg and Fentanyl 75 micrograms. Thiopental was given for DFT testing. The left chest wall was prepped and draped in the normal sterile fashion. 1% lidocaine was used to infiltrate the tissues over the previously placed defibrillator and a 4.5 cm incision made. The **pocket was opened and the leads disconnected**. The atrial threshold was chronically elevated that had been stable, so this lead was utilized. The ventricular pacing thresholds were excellent. A Betadine solution was used to irrigate the pocket. The **pocket was expanded** slightly to accommodate the extended life defibrillator. The **new defibrillator** was **connected** to the leads Interrogation showed appropriate pacing and sensing and impedances. Defibrillation threshold testing was then performed. Shock on T induced ventricular fibrillation which was successfully converted with 14 joules biphasic. There were no drop outs on lead sensitivity. The lower portion of the pocket was closed with a running 2-0 Vicryl suture. A running 3-0 Vicryl suture was used to close the subcuticular tissues, and 4-0 Vicryl was used to close the skin. Final fluoroscopy demonstrated stable lead positions.

Conclusion:
Successful dual chamber ICD generator change with successful defibrillation threshold testing, 14 joules biphasic.

CPT/HCPCS Codes Reported:
33263

Other HCPCS Codes Reported:
C1721

Chapter 14: Electrophysiology and Ablation

Electrophysiology, or EP, studies are minimally invasive diagnostic studies of the electrical pathways of the heart conduction system. They are commonly performed in the cardiac cath lab or a dedicated EP lab. EP testing assesses patients for cardiac arrhythmias to correlate with clinical symptoms. Special electrode catheters are used to record the electrical pathways. In most EP studies, arrhythmias are induced in order to identify the problem.

EP mapping of arrhythmias is considered to be a distinct procedure and is reported in addition to the diagnostic EP codes using CPT® code 93609 or 93613 for three-dimensional mapping. Special computer equipment is necessary for 3-D mapping.

Catheter ablation procedures are performed to "ablate" the arrhythmia identified in an EP study. Specially designed ablation catheters and special energy creating generators are used to interrupt the pathway identified as causing the arrhythmia.

It is common for a patient to be diagnosed and treated during the same encounter. The EP study is performed and arrhythmias are identified and then ablated during the same visit. Each study should be separately reported whether performed during the same encounter or on different dates.

Heart Conduction System

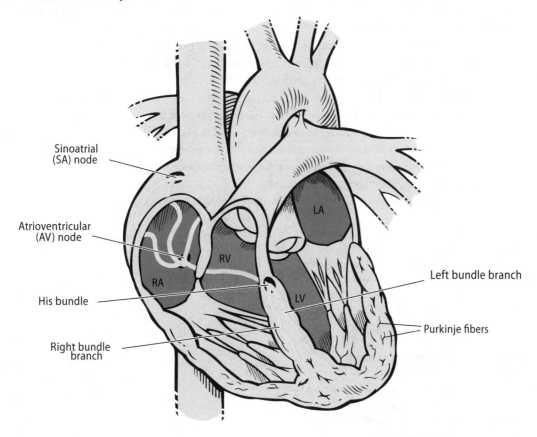

Bundle of His Recording

93600   **Bundle of His Recording**
The physician places a venous sheath, usually in a femoral vein, using standard techniques. The physician advances an electrical catheter through the venous sheath and into the right heart under fluoroscopic guidance. The physician attaches the catheter to an electrical recording device to allow depiction of the intracardiac electrograms obtained from electrodes on the catheter tip. The physician moves the catheter tip to the bundle of His, on the anteroseptal tricuspid annulus, and obtains recordings. Alternatively, the physician may obtain similar recordings by placing a catheter into the left ventricular outflow tract via the aorta

Coding Tips

1. CPT code 93600 reports bundle of His recording only. For comprehensive electrophysiologic evaluation bundle of His recording, see 93619–93622.

2. Fluoroscopy is included in 93600 and is not reported separately.

3. Physician Reporting: This code has both a technical and professional component. To report only the professional component, append modifier 26. To report only the technical component, append modifier TC. To report the complete procedure (i.e., both the professional and technical components), submit without a modifier.

Facility HCPCS Coding

HCPCS Level II codes are used to report the supplies provided during the procedure. Hospitals should separately report supplies used during cardiac invasive procedures. Refer to chapter 1 for more information regarding appropriate billing of supplies. Refer to the list of current codes in appendix B.

C1730   Catheter, electrophysiology, diagnostic, other than 3D mapping (19 or fewer electrodes)

C1731   Catheter, electrophysiology, diagnostic, other than 3D mapping (20 or more electrodes)

C1732   Catheter, electrophysiology, diagnostic/ablation, 3D or vector mapping

C1733   Catheter, electrophysiology, diagnostic/ablation, other than 3D or vector mapping, other than cool-tip

C1766   Introducer sheath, guiding, intracardiac electrophysiological, steerable, other than peel-away

C1892   Introducer/sheath, guiding, intracardiac electrophysiological, fixed-curve, peel-away

C1893   Introducer/sheath, guiding, intracardiac electrophysiological, fixed-curve, other than peel-away

C1894   Introducer/sheath, other than guiding, intracardiac, electrophysiological, non-laser

C2629   Introducer/sheath, other than guiding, intracardiac

C2630   Catheter, electrophysiology, diagnostic/ablation, other than 3D or vector mapping, cool tip

ICD-10-CM Coding

I44.Ø	Atrioventricular block, first degree
I44.1	Atrioventricular block, second degree
I44.2	Atrioventricular block, complete
I44.3Ø	Unspecified atrioventricular block
I44.39	Other atrioventricular block
I44.4	Left anterior fascicular block
I44.5	Left posterior fascicular block
I44.6Ø	Unspecified fascicular block
I44.69	Other fascicular block
I44.7	Left bundle-branch block, unspecified
I45.Ø	Right fascicular block
I45.1Ø	Unspecified right bundle-branch block
I45.19	Other right bundle-branch block
I45.2	Bifascicular block
I45.3	Trifascicular block
I45.4	Nonspecific intraventricular block
I45.5	Other specified heart block
I45.6	Pre-excitation syndrome
I45.89	Other specified conduction disorders
I45.9	Conduction disorder, unspecified
I46.2	Cardiac arrest due to underlying cardiac condition
I46.8	Cardiac arrest due to other underlying condition

I46.9	Cardiac arrest, cause unspecified
I47.0	Re-entry ventricular arrhythmia
I47.1	Supraventricular tachycardia
I47.2	Ventricular tachycardia
I47.9	Paroxysmal tachycardia, unspecified
I48.0	Paroxysmal atrial fibrillation
I48.1	Persistent atrial fibrillation
I48.2	Chronic atrial fibrillation
I48.3	Typical atrial flutter
I48.4	Atypical atrial flutter
I48.91	Unspecified atrial fibrillation
I48.92	Unspecified atrial flutter
I49.01	Ventricular fibrillation
I49.02	Ventricular flutter
I49.1	Atrial premature depolarization
I49.2	Junctional premature depolarization
I49.3	Ventricular premature depolarization
I49.40	Unspecified premature depolarization
I49.49	Other premature depolarization
I49.5	Sick sinus syndrome
I49.8	Other specified cardiac arrhythmias
I49.9	Cardiac arrhythmia, unspecified

CCI Edits

93600 00410, 00537, 0178T-0179T, 0180T, 0213T, 0216T, 0228T, 0230T, 12001-12007, 12011-12057, 13100-13133, 13151-13153, 35201-35206, 35226-35236, 35256-35266, 35286, 36000, 36005-36013, 36120-36140, 36400-36410, 36420-36430, 36440, 36555-36556, 36568-36569, 36591-36592, 36600, 36640, 43752, 51701-51703, 62320-62327, 64400-64410, 64413-64435, 64445-64450, 64461-64463, 64479-64530, 76000-76001, 76942, 76970, 76998, 77001-77002, 92012-92014, 92960-92961, 93000-93010, 93040-93042, 93050, 93318, 93355-93461, 93530-93533, 93563, 93565-93568, 93613, 94002, 94200, 94250, 94680-94690, 94770, 95812-95816, 95819, 95822, 95829, 95955, 96360-96368, 96372, 96374-96377, 99155-99157, 99211-99223, 99231-99255, 99291-99292, 99304-99310, 99315-99316, 99334-99337, 99347-99350, 99374-99375, 99377-99378, 99446-99449, 99495-99496, G0463, G0471

Intra-atrial Recording

93602   **Intra-atrial recording**
The physician places a venous sheath, usually in a femoral vein, using standard techniques. The physician advances an electrical catheter through the venous sheath and into the right heart under fluoroscopic guidance. The physician attaches the catheter to an electrical recording device to allow depiction of the intracardiac electrograms obtained from electrodes on the catheter tip. The physician moves the catheter tip to the right atrium and obtains recordings. The physician may obtain left atrial recordings by crossing the interatrial septum. Alternatively, the physician may obtain left atrial recordings by placing an arterial catheter into the aorta and crossing both the aortic and mitral valves in a retrograde fashion.

Coding Tips

1. CPT code 93602 reports intra-atrial recording only. For comprehensive electrophysiologic evaluation including intra-atrial recording, see 93619–93622.
2. Fluoroscopy is included in 93602 and is not reported separately.
3. Physician Reporting: This code has both a technical and professional component. To report only the professional component, append modifier 26. To report only the technical component, append modifier TC. To report the complete procedure (i.e., both the professional and technical components), submit without a modifier.

Facility HCPCS Coding

HCPCS Level II codes are used to report the supplies provided during the procedure. Hospitals should separately report supplies used during cardiac invasive procedures. Refer to chapter 1 for more information regarding appropriate billing of supplies. Refer to the list of current codes in appendix B.

C1730   Catheter, electrophysiology, diagnostic, other than 3D mapping (19 or fewer electrodes)

C1731   Catheter, electrophysiology, diagnostic, other than 3D mapping (20 or more electrodes)

C1732   Catheter, electrophysiology, diagnostic/ablation, 3D or vector mapping

C1733   Catheter, electrophysiology, diagnostic/ablation, other than 3D or vector mapping, other than cool-tip

C1766   Introducer sheath, guiding, intracardiac electro-physiological, steerable, other than peel-away

C1892   Introducer/sheath, guiding, intracardiac electrophysiological, fixed-curve, peel-away

C1893   Introducer/sheath, guiding, intracardiac electro-physiological, fixed-curve, other than peel-away

C1894   Introducer/sheath, other than guiding, intracardiac, electrophysiological, non-laser

C2629   Introducer/sheath, other than guiding, intracardiac

C2630   Catheter, electrophysiology, diagnostic/ablation, other than 3D or vector mapping, cool tip

ICD-10-CM Coding

I44.0   Atrioventricular block, first degree
I44.1   Atrioventricular block, second degree
I44.2   Atrioventricular block, complete
I44.30   Unspecified atrioventricular block
I44.39   Other atrioventricular block
I45.5   Other specified heart block
I45.6   Pre-excitation syndrome
I45.89   Other specified conduction disorders
I45.9   Conduction disorder, unspecified
I48.0   Paroxysmal atrial fibrillation
I48.1   Persistent atrial fibrillation
I48.2   Chronic atrial fibrillation
I48.3   Typical atrial flutter
I48.4   Atypical atrial flutter
I48.91   Unspecified atrial fibrillation
I48.92   Unspecified atrial flutter
I49.1   Atrial premature depolarization
I49.5   Sick sinus syndrome
I49.8   Other specified cardiac arrhythmias

Intra-atrial Catheter Placement

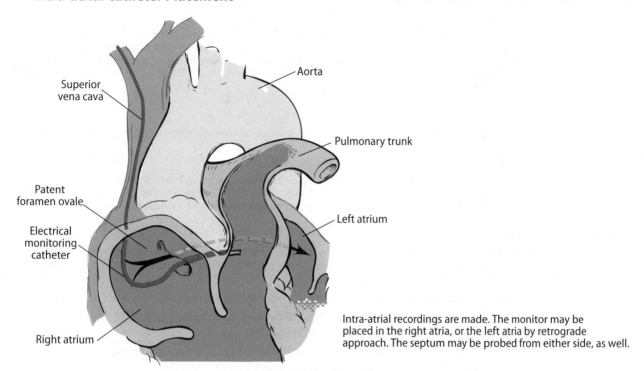

Superior vena cava

Aorta

Pulmonary trunk

Patent foramen ovale

Electrical monitoring catheter

Left atrium

Right atrium

Intra-atrial recordings are made. The monitor may be placed in the right atria, or the left atria by retrograde approach. The septum may be probed from either side, as well.

CCI Edits

93602 00410, 00537, 0178T-0179T, 0180T, 0213T, 0216T, 0228T, 0230T, 12001-12007, 12011-12057, 13100-13133, 13151-13153, 35201-35206, 35226-35236, 35256-35266, 35286, 36000, 36005-36013, 36120-36140, 36400-36410, 36420-36430, 36440, 36555-36556, 36568-36569, 36591-36592, 36600, 36640, 43752, 51701-51703, 62320-62327, 64400-64410, 64413-64435, 64445-64450, 64461-64463, 64479-64530, 76000-76001, 76942, 76970, 76998, 77001-77002, 92012-92014, 92960-92961, 93000-93010, 93040-93042, 93050, 93318, 93355-93461, 93530-93533, 93563, 93565-93568, 93613, 93624, 94002, 94200, 94250, 94680-94690, 94770, 95812-95816, 95819, 95822, 95829, 95955, 96360-96368, 96372, 96374-96377, 99155-99157, 99211-99223, 99231-99255, 99291-99292, 99304-99310, 99315-99316, 99334-99337, 99347-99350, 99374-99375, 99377-99378, 99446-99449, 99495-99496, G0463, G0471

Right Ventricular Recording

93603   **Right ventricular recording**

The physician places a venous sheath, usually in a femoral vein, using standard techniques. The physician advances an electrical catheter through the venous sheath and into the right heart under fluoroscopic guidance. The physician attaches the catheter to an electrical recording device to allow depiction of the intracardiac electrograms obtained from electrodes on the catheter tip. The physician moves the catheter tip to the right ventricle and obtains recordings.

Coding Tips

1. CPT code 93603 reports right ventricular recording only. For comprehensive electrophysiologic evaluation including right ventricular recording, see 93619-93622.

2. Fluoroscopy is included in 93603 and is not reported separately.

3. Physician Reporting: This code has both a technical and professional component. To report only the professional component, append modifier 26. To report only the technical component, append modifier TC. To report the complete procedure (i.e., both the professional and technical components), submit without a modifier.

Facility HCPCS Coding

HCPCS Level II codes are used to report the supplies provided during the procedure. Hospitals should separately report supplies used during cardiac invasive procedures. Refer to chapter 1 for more information regarding appropriate billing of supplies. Refer to the list of current codes in appendix B.

C1730   Catheter, electrophysiology, diagnostic, other than 3D mapping (19 or fewer electrodes)

C1731   Catheter, electrophysiology, diagnostic, other than 3D mapping (20 or more electrodes)

C1732   Catheter, electrophysiology, diagnostic/ablation, 3D or vector mapping

C1733   Catheter, electrophysiology, diagnostic/ablation, other than 3D or vector mapping, other than cool-tip

C1766   Introducer sheath, guiding, intracardiac electrophysiological, steerable, other than peel-away

C1892   Introducer/sheath, guiding, intracardiac electrophysiological, fixed-curve, peel-away

C1893   Introducer/sheath, guiding, intracardiac electrophysiological, fixed-curve, other than peel-away

C1894   Introducer/sheath, other than guiding, intracardiac, electrophysiological, non-laser

C2629   Introducer/sheath, other than guiding, intracardiac

C2630   Catheter, electrophysiology, diagnostic/ablation, other than 3D or vector mapping, cool tip

Right Ventricle Catheter Placement

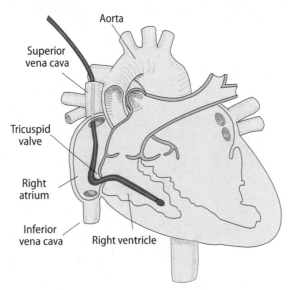

Recordings are collected from the right ventricle

ICD-10-CM Coding

I42.8	Other cardiomyopathies
I44.0	Atrioventricular block, first degree
I44.1	Atrioventricular block, second degree
I44.2	Atrioventricular block, complete
I44.30	Unspecified atrioventricular block
I44.39	Other atrioventricular block
I45.4	Nonspecific intraventricular block
I45.5	Other specified heart block
I45.6	Pre-excitation syndrome
I45.89	Other specified conduction disorders
I45.9	Conduction disorder, unspecified
I47.0	Re-entry ventricular arrhythmia
I47.1	Supraventricular tachycardia
I47.2	Ventricular tachycardia
I49.01	Ventricular fibrillation
I49.02	Ventricular flutter
I49.1	Atrial premature depolarization
I49.3	Ventricular premature depolarization
I49.9	Cardiac arrhythmia, unspecified

CCI Edits

93603   00410, 00537, 0178T-0179T, 0180T, 0213T, 0216T, 0228T, 0230T, 12001-12007, 12011-12057, 13100-13133, 13151-13153, 35201-35206, 35226-35236, 35256-35266, 35286, 36000, 36005-36013, 36120-36140, 36400-36410, 36420-36430, 36440, 36555-36556, 36568-36569, 36591-36592, 36600, 36640, 43752, 51701-51703, 62320-62327, 64400-64410, 64413-64435, 64445-64450, 64461-64463, 64479-64530, 76000-76001, 76942, 76970, 76998, 77001-77002, 92012-92014, 92960-92961, 93000-93010, 93040-93042, 93050, 93318, 93355-93461, 93530-93533, 93563, 93565-93568, 93613, 93624, 94002, 94200, 94250, 94680-94690, 94770, 95812-95816, 95819, 95822, 95829, 95955, 96360-96368, 96372, 96374-96377, 99155-99157, 99211-99223, 99231-99255, 99291-99292, 99304-99310, 99315-99316, 99334-99337, 99347-99350, 99374-99375, 99377-99378, 99446-99449, 99495-99496, G0463, G0471

EP for Mapping of Tachycardia

93609 **Intraventricular and/or intra-atrial mapping of tachycardia site(s) with catheter manipulation to record from multiple sites to identify origin of tachycardia (List separately in addition to code for primary procedure)**

The physician places an appropriate arterial or venous sheath, usually femoral, to allow access to the chamber to be mapped. The physician advances an electrical catheter through the sheath and into the appropriate chamber under fluoroscopic guidance. The physician attaches the catheter to an electrical recording device to allow depiction of the intracardiac electrograms obtained from electrodes on the catheter tip. The physician moves the catheter tip throughout the chamber to be mapped and obtains recordings. The physician compares activation times from different sites in order to identify the origin of the tachycardia.

Coding Tips

1. Intraventricular and/or intra-atrial mapping is not included in comprehensive electrophysiologic evaluation, see 93620-93622.

2. Mapping is an "add-on" code and some facilities, due to its high-frequency use, erroneously assume it is inherent in the comprehensive evaluations.

3. Fluoroscopy is not included in 93609 and is reported separately reported with 76000 or 76001.

4. For three-dimensional mapping, see 93613.

5. Conscious sedation is not included in these codes. Separately report 99151–99157 per payer policy and coding guidelines. Hospitals may choose to include the costs associated with the service as part of the procedure rather than reporting them separately.

6. Physician Reporting: This code has both a technical and professional component. To report only the professional component, append modifier 26. To report only the technical component, append modifier TC. To report the complete procedure (i.e., both the professional and technical components), submit without a modifier.

Heart Conduction System

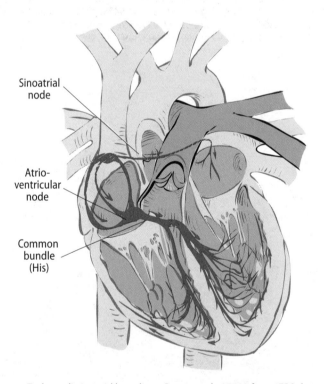

Sinoatrial node

Atrio-ventricular node

Common bundle (His)

Tachycardia is rapid heartbeat. Report code 93609 for an EPS that maps multiple sites to determine the origin of the tachycardia

Facility HCPCS Coding

HCPCS Level II codes are used to report the supplies provided during the procedure. Hospitals should separately report supplies used during cardiac invasive procedures. Refer to chapter 1 for more information regarding appropriate billing of supplies. Refer to the list of current codes in appendix B.

C1730   Catheter, electrophysiology, diagnostic, other than 3D mapping (19 or fewer electrodes)

C1731   Catheter, electrophysiology, diagnostic, other than 3D mapping (20 or more electrodes)

C1733   Catheter, electrophysiology, diagnostic/ablation, other than 3D or vector mapping, other than cool-tip

C2629   Introducer/sheath, other than guiding, intracardiac

C2630   Catheter, electrophysiology, diagnostic/ablation, other than 3D or vector mapping, cool tip

ICD-10-CM Coding

This is an add-on code. Refer to the corresponding primary procedure code for ICD-10-CM diagnosis code links.

CCI Edits

93609   00410, 00537, 33210-33211, 36000, 36005-36013, 36120-36140, 36410, 36591-36592, 92960-92961, 93000-93010, 93040-93042, 93050, 93600-93603, 93624, 94770, 99155-99157, 99446-99449

Intra-atrial Pacing

93610   **Intra-atrial pacing**

The physician places a venous sheath, usually in a femoral vein, using standard techniques. The physician advances an electrical catheter through the venous sheath and into the right heart under fluoroscopic guidance. The physician attaches the catheter to an electrical pacing device to allow transmission of pacing impulses through the catheter to the right atrium. The physician may pace the left atrium by placing the catheter in the coronary sinus or by crossing the interatrial septum. Alternatively, the physician may pace the left atrium by placing an arterial catheter into the aorta and crossing both the aortic and mitral valves in a retrograde fashion.

Coding Tips

1. CPT code 93610 reports intra-atrial pacing only. For comprehensive electrophysiologic evaluation including right ventricular recording, see 93619-93622.

2. Fluoroscopy is included in 93610 and is not reported separately.

3. Physician Reporting: This code has both a technical and professional component. To report only the professional component, append modifier 26. To report only the technical component, append modifier TC. To report the complete procedure (i.e., both the professional and technical components), submit without a modifier.

4. Code 93610 is modifier 51 exempt

Facility HCPCS Coding

HCPCS Level II codes are used to report the supplies provided during the procedure. Hospitals should separately report supplies used during cardiac invasive procedures. Refer to chapter 1 for more information regarding appropriate billing of supplies. Refer to the list of current codes in appendix B.

C1730   Catheter, electrophysiology, diagnostic, other than 3D mapping (19 or fewer electrodes)

C1731   Catheter, electrophysiology, diagnostic, other than 3D mapping (20 or more electrodes)

C1732   Catheter, electrophysiology, diagnostic/ablation, 3D or vector mapping

C1733   Catheter, electrophysiology, diagnostic/ablation, other than 3D or vector mapping, other than cool-tip

C1766   Introducer sheath, guiding, intracardiac electrophysiological, steerable, other than peel-away

C1892   Introducer/sheath, guiding, intracardiac electrophysiological, fixed-curve, peel-away

C1893   Introducer/sheath, guiding, intracardiac electrophysiological, fixed-curve, other than peel-away

C1894   Introducer/sheath, other than guiding, intracardiac, electrophysiological, non-laser

C2629   Introducer/sheath, other than guiding, intracardiac

C2630   Catheter, electrophysiology, diagnostic/ablation, other than 3D or vector mapping, cool tip

Atrial Pacing

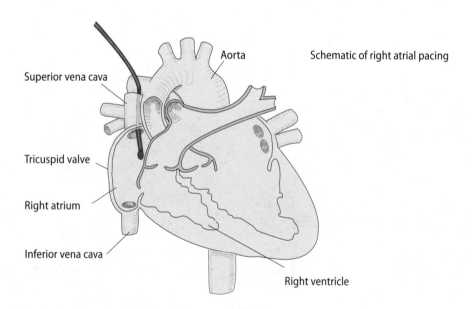

Schematic of right atrial pacing

Aorta

Superior vena cava

Tricuspid valve

Right atrium

Inferior vena cava

Right ventricle

ICD-10-CM Coding

I44.Ø	Atrioventricular block, first degree
I44.1	Atrioventricular block, second degree
I44.2	Atrioventricular block, complete
I44.3Ø	Unspecified atrioventricular block
I44.39	Other atrioventricular block
I47.2	Ventricular tachycardia
I48.Ø	Paroxysmal atrial fibrillation
I48.1	Persistent atrial fibrillation
I48.2	Chronic atrial fibrillation
I48.3	Typical atrial flutter
I48.4	Atypical atrial flutter
I48.91	Unspecified atrial fibrillation
I48.92	Unspecified atrial flutter
I49.1	Atrial premature depolarization
I49.5	Sick sinus syndrome

CCI Edits

93610 00410, 00537, 0178T-0179T, 0180T, 0213T, 0216T, 0228T, 0230T, 12001-12007, 12011-12057, 13100-13133, 13151-13153, 33210-33211, 35201-35206, 35226-35236, 35256-35266, 35286, 36000, 36005-36013, 36120-36140, 36400-36410, 36420-36430, 36440, 36555-36556, 36568-36569, 36591-36592, 36600, 36640, 43752, 51701-51703, 62320-62327, 64400-64410, 64413-64435, 64445-64450, 64461-64463, 64479-64530, 76000-76001, 76942, 76970, 76998, 77001-77002, 92012-92014, 92960-92961, 93000-93010, 93040-93042, 93050, 93318, 93355-93461, 93530-93533, 93563, 93565-93568, 93609, 93613, 93624, 94002, 94200, 94250, 94680-94690, 94770, 95812-95816, 95819, 95822, 95829, 95955, 96360-96368, 96372, 96374-96377, 99155-99157, 99211-99223, 99231-99255, 99291-99292, 99304-99310, 99315-99316, 99334-99337, 99347-99350, 99374-99375, 99377-99378, 99446-99449, 99495-99496, G0463, G0471

Intraventricular Pacing

93612 **Intraventricular pacing**
The physician places a venous sheath using standard techniques. The physician advances an electrical catheter through the venous sheath and into the right ventricle under fluoroscopic guidance. The physician attaches the catheter to an electrical pacing device to allow transmission of pacing impulses through the catheter to the right ventricle. Alternatively, the physician may pace the left ventricle by placing the catheter in the right atrium, crossing the intra-atrial septum and mitral valve. Finally, the physician may pace the left ventricle by advancing a catheter through an arterial sheath, via the aorta, across the aortic valve into the left ventricle.

Coding Tips

1. CPT code 93612 reports intraventricular pacing only. For comprehensive electrophysiologic evaluation including right ventricular recording, see 93619-93622.

2. Fluoroscopy is included in 93612 and is not reported separately.

3. Conscious sedation is included in CPT code 93612 and is not reported separately.

4. Physician Reporting: This code has both a technical and professional component. To report only the professional component, append modifier 26. To report only the technical component, append modifier TC. To report the complete procedure (i.e., both the professional and technical components), submit without a modifier.

5. Code 93612 is modifier 51 exempt.

Facility HCPCS Coding

HCPCS Level II codes are used to report the supplies provided during the procedure. Hospitals should separately report supplies used during cardiac invasive procedures. Refer to chapter 1 for more information regarding appropriate billing of supplies. Refer to the list of current codes in appendix B.

C1730 Catheter, electrophysiology, diagnostic, other than 3D mapping (19 or fewer electrodes)

C1731 Catheter, electrophysiology, diagnostic, other than 3D mapping (20 or more electrodes)

C1732 Catheter, electrophysiology, diagnostic/ablation, 3D or vector mapping

C1733 Catheter, electrophysiology, diagnostic/ablation, other than 3D or vector mapping, other than cool-tip

C1766 Introducer sheath, guiding, intracardiac electrophysiological, steerable, other than peel-away

C1892 Introducer/sheath, guiding, intracardiac electrophysiological, fixed-curve, peel-away

C1893 Introducer/sheath, guiding, intracardiac electrophysiological, fixed-curve, other than peel-away

C1894 Introducer/sheath, other than guiding, intracardiac, electrophysiological, non-laser

C2629 Introducer/sheath, other than guiding, intracardiac

C2630 Catheter, electrophysiology, diagnostic/ablation, other than 3D or vector mapping, cool tip

Ventricular Pacing

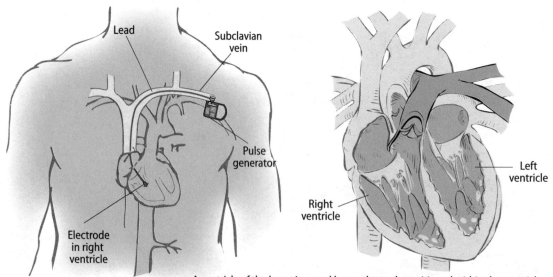

A ventricle of the heart is paced by an electrode positioned within the ventricle.
Either left or right ventricle may be addressed according to the description

ICD-10-CM Coding

I44.Ø	Atrioventricular block, first degree
I44.1	Atrioventricular block, second degree
I44.2	Atrioventricular block, complete
I44.3Ø	Unspecified atrioventricular block
I44.39	Other atrioventricular block
I44.4	Left anterior fascicular block
I44.5	Left posterior fascicular block
I44.6Ø	Unspecified fascicular block
I44.69	Other fascicular block
I44.7	Left bundle-branch block, unspecified
I45.Ø	Right fascicular block
I45.1Ø	Unspecified right bundle-branch block
I45.19	Other right bundle-branch block
I45.2	Bifascicular block
I45.3	Trifascicular block
I45.4	Nonspecific intraventricular block
I47.Ø	Re-entry ventricular arrhythmia
I47.1	Supraventricular tachycardia
I47.2	Ventricular tachycardia
I47.9	Paroxysmal tachycardia, unspecified
I48.4	Atypical atrial flutter
I49.Ø1	Ventricular fibrillation
I49.Ø2	Ventricular flutter
I49.3	Ventricular premature depolarization

CCI Edits

93612   00410, 00537, 0178T-0179T, 0180T, 0213T, 0216T, 0228T, 0230T, 12001-12007, 12011-12057, 13100-13133, 13151-13153, 33210-33211, 35201-35206, 35226-35236, 35256-35266, 35286, 36000, 36005-36013, 36120-36140, 36400-36410, 36420-36430, 36440, 36555-36556, 36568-36569, 36591-36592, 36600, 36640, 43752, 51701-51703, 62320-62327, 64400-64410, 64413-64435, 64445-64450, 64461-64463, 64479-64530, 76000-76001, 76942, 76970, 76998, 77001-77002, 92012-92014, 92960-92961, 93000-93010, 93040-93042, 93050, 93318, 93355-93461, 93530-93533, 93563, 93565-93568, 93609, 93613, 93624, 94002, 94200, 94250, 94680-94690, 94770, 95812-95816, 95819, 95822, 95829, 95955, 96360-96368, 96372, 96374-96377, 99155-99157, 99211-99223, 99231-99255, 99291-99292, 99304-99310, 99315-99316, 99334-99337, 99347-99350, 99374-99375, 99377-99378, 99446-99449, 99495-99496, G0463, G0471

Electrophysiology 3-D Mapping

93613   **Intracardiac electrophysiologic 3-dimensional mapping (List separately in addition to code for primary procedure)**

Electrophysiologic studies use electric stimulation and monitoring in the diagnosis of conduction abnormalities that predispose patients to bradyarrhythmias and to determine a patient's chance of developing ventricular and supraventricular tachyarrhythmias. The physician inserts an electrode catheter percutaneously into the right subclavian vein and, under fluoroscopic guidance, positions the electrode catheter at the right ventricular apex, both for recording and stimulating the right atrium and the right ventricle. A second electrode catheter is inserted percutaneously into the right femoral vein and positioned across the tricuspid valve for recording the His bundle electrogram. For mapping, a third electrode catheter is inserted percutaneously from the right femoral artery and advanced into the left ventricle. Ventricular tachycardia is induced by programmed ventricular stimulation from both the right and left ventricular apexes. The earliest activation site is determined and the diastolic pressure is recorded on the endocardial activation map during the ventricular tachycardia. Intracardiac electrograms with surface electrocardiograms are simultaneously displayed and recorded on a multichannel oscilloscopic photographic recorder.

Coding Tips

1. CPT code 93613 is an "add-on" code and is reported separately in addition to the primary procedure. Use 93613 in conjunction with 93620 or 93653.

2. CPT code 93613 differs from 93609 in that it is reported for three-dimensional mapping.

3. Conscious sedation is not included in these codes. Separately report 99151–99157 per payer policy and coding guidelines. Hospitals may choose to include the costs associated with the service as part of the procedure rather than reporting them separately.

4. Documentation must clearly state three-dimensional mapping was used to support reporting this code.

Facility HCPCS Coding

HCPCS Level II codes are used to report the supplies provided during the procedure. Hospitals should separately report supplies used during cardiac invasive procedures. Refer to chapter 1 for more information regarding appropriate billing of supplies. Refer to the list of current codes in appendix B.

C1730   Catheter, electrophysiology, diagnostic, other than 3D mapping (19 or fewer electrodes)

C1731   Catheter, electrophysiology, diagnostic, other than 3D mapping (20 or more electrodes)

C1732   Catheter, electrophysiology, diagnostic/ablation, 3D or vector mapping

C1733   Catheter, electrophysiology, diagnostic/ablation, other than 3D or vector mapping, other than cool-tip

C2630   Catheter, electrophysiology, diagnostic/ablation, other than 3D or vector mapping, cool tip

Mapping Catheter

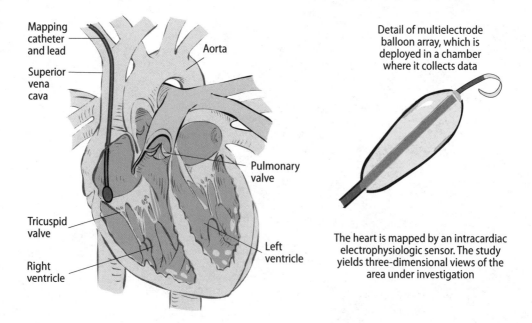

Mapping catheter and lead

Superior vena cava

Aorta

Tricuspid valve

Right ventricle

Pulmonary valve

Left ventricle

Detail of multielectrode balloon array, which is deployed in a chamber where it collects data

The heart is mapped by an intracardiac electrophysiologic sensor. The study yields three-dimensional views of the area under investigation

ICD-10-CM Coding

This is an add-on code. Refer to the corresponding primary procedure code for ICD-10-CM diagnosis code links.

CCI Edits

93613 00410, 33210-33211, 36000, 36005-36013, 36120-36140, 36410, 36591-36592, 93000-93010, 93040-93042, 93050, 93609, 94770, 99155-99157

Induction of Arrhythmia

93618   **Induction of arrhythmia by electrical pacing**

The physician places an appropriate arterial or venous sheath, usually femoral, to allow access to the chamber to be studied. The physician advances an electrical catheter through the sheath and into the appropriate chamber under fluoroscopic guidance. The physician attaches the catheter to an electrical pacing device to allow transmission of pacing impulses through the catheter to the heart chamber of interest. The physician stimulates the heart with rapid pacing or programmed electrical stimulation until the arrhythmia is induced.

Coding Tips

1. CPT code 93618 reports induction of arrhythmia only. For comprehensive electrophysiologic evaluation including arrhythmia induction, see 93620-93622.

2. Fluoroscopy is included in 93618 and is not reported separately.

3. Conscious sedation is not included in these codes. Separately report 99151–99157 per payer policy and coding guidelines. Hospitals may choose to include the costs associated with the service as part of the procedure rather than reporting them separately.

4. Physician Reporting: This code has both a technical and professional component. To report only the professional component, append modifier 26. To report only the technical component, append modifier TC. To report the complete procedure (i.e., both the professional and technical components), submit without a modifier.

Facility HCPCS Coding

HCPCS Level II codes are used to report the supplies provided during the procedure. Hospitals should separately report supplies used during cardiac invasive procedures. Refer to chapter 1 for more information regarding appropriate billing of supplies. Refer to the list of current codes in appendix B.

C1730	Catheter, electrophysiology, diagnostic, other than 3D mapping (19 or fewer electrodes)
C1731	Catheter, electrophysiology, diagnostic, other than 3D mapping (20 or more electrodes)
C1732	Catheter, electrophysiology, diagnostic/ablation, 3D or vector mapping
C1733	Catheter, electrophysiology, diagnostic/ablation, other than 3D or vector mapping, other than cool-tip
C1766	Introducer sheath, guiding, intracardiac electrophysiological, steerable, other than peel-away
C1892	Introducer/sheath, guiding, intracardiac electrophysiological, fixed-curve, peel-away
C1893	Introducer/sheath, guiding, intracardiac electrophysiological, fixed-curve, other than peel-away
C1894	Introducer/sheath, other than guiding, intracardiac, electrophysiological, non-laser
C2629	Introducer/sheath, other than guiding, intracardiac
C2630	Catheter, electrophysiology, diagnostic/ablation, other than 3D or vector mapping, cool tip

ICD-10-CM Coding

I45.89	Other specified conduction disorders
I45.9	Conduction disorder, unspecified
I47.0	Re-entry ventricular arrhythmia
I47.1	Supraventricular tachycardia
I47.2	Ventricular tachycardia
I47.9	Paroxysmal tachycardia, unspecified
I48.0	Paroxysmal atrial fibrillation
I48.1	Persistent atrial fibrillation
I48.2	Chronic atrial fibrillation
I48.3	Typical atrial flutter
I48.4	Atypical atrial flutter
I48.91	Unspecified atrial fibrillation
I48.92	Unspecified atrial flutter
I49.01	Ventricular fibrillation
I49.02	Ventricular flutter
I49.1	Atrial premature depolarization
I49.2	Junctional premature depolarization
I49.3	Ventricular premature depolarization
I49.40	Unspecified premature depolarization
I49.49	Other premature depolarization

I49.5	Sick sinus syndrome
I49.8	Other specified cardiac arrhythmias
I49.9	Cardiac arrhythmia, unspecified
R00.1	Bradycardia, unspecified
R55	Syncope and collapse

Pacing Catheter

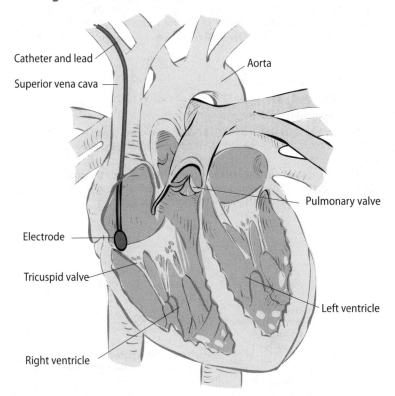

Catheter and lead

Superior vena cava

Aorta

Arrhythmia is induced through electrical pacing. Usually the procedure is performed in conjunction with mapping of an area of the heart

Pulmonary valve

Electrode

Tricuspid valve

Left ventricle

Right ventricle

CCI Edits

93618   00410, 00537, 0178T-0179T, 0180T, 0213T, 0216T, 0228T, 0230T, 12001-12007, 12011-12057, 13100-13133, 13151-13153, 33210-33211, 35201-35206, 35226-35236, 35256-35266, 35286, 36000, 36005-36013, 36120-36140, 36400-36410, 36420-36430, 36440, 36555-36556, 36568-36569, 36591-36592, 36600-36640, 43752, 51701-51703, 62320-62327, 64400-64410, 64413-64435, 64445-64450, 64461-64463, 64479-64530, 76000-76001, 76942, 76970, 76998, 77001-77002, 92012-92014, 92950, 92960-92961, 93000-93010, 93040-93042, 93050, 93318, 93355-93461, 93530-93533, 93562-93563, 93565-93568, 93603, 93609-93613, 94002, 94200, 94250, 94680-94690, 94770, 95812-95816, 95819, 95822, 95829, 95955, 96360-96368, 96372, 96374-96377, 99155-99157, 99211-99223, 99231-99255, 99291-99292, 99304-99310, 99315-99316, 99334-99337, 99347-99350, 99374-99375, 99377-99378, 99446-99449, 99495-99496, G0463, G0471

Comprehensive EP Evaluation Without Induction of Arrhythmia

93619   **Comprehensive electrophysiologic evaluation with right atrial pacing and recording, right ventricular pacing and recording, His bundle recording, including insertion and repositioning of multiple electrode catheters, without induction or attempted induction of arrhythmia**

The physician places three venous sheaths, usually in one or both femoral veins, using standard techniques. The physician advances three electrical catheters through the venous sheaths and into the right heart under fluoroscopic guidance. The physician attaches the three catheters to an electrical recording device to allow depiction of the intracardiac electrograms obtained from electrodes on the catheter tips. The physician moves the tips of the three catheters to the right atrium, the bundle of His, and the right ventricle and obtains recordings. This code should be used when 93600 is combined with 93602, 93603, 93610, and 93612.

Coding Tips

1. Code 93619 is reported when there is no attempt to induce arrhythmia.
2. Do not report 93619 in conjunction with 93600, 93602, 93610, 93612, 93618, or 93620-93622.
3. Fluoroscopy is included in 93619 and is not reported separately.
4. Conscious sedation is not included in these codes. Separately report 99151–99157 per payer policy and coding guidelines. Hospitals may choose to include the costs associated with the service as part of the procedure rather than reporting them separately.
5. Physician Reporting: This code has both a technical and professional component. To report only the professional component, append modifier 26. To report only the technical component, append modifier TC. To report the complete procedure (i.e., both the professional and technical components), submit without a modifier.

Electrophysiology Study

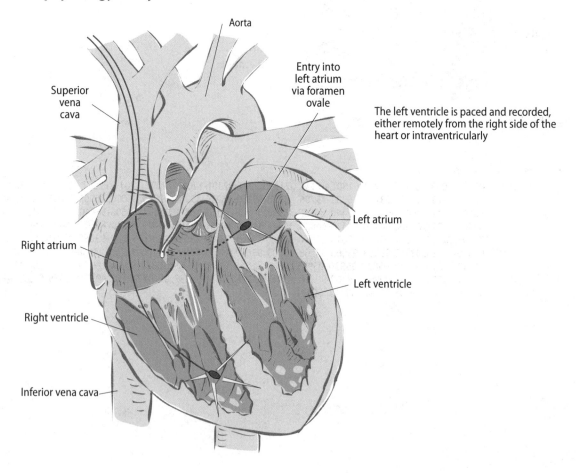

Mapping Catheter

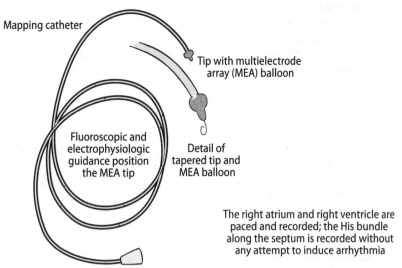

Facility HCPCS Coding

HCPCS Level II codes are used to report the supplies provided during the procedure. Hospitals should separately report supplies used during cardiac invasive procedures. Refer to chapter 1 for more information regarding appropriate billing of supplies. Refer to the list of current codes in appendix B.

C1730	Catheter, electrophysiology, diagnostic, other than 3D mapping (19 or fewer electrodes)
C1731	Catheter, electrophysiology, diagnostic, other than 3D mapping (20 or more electrodes)
C1732	Catheter, electrophysiology, diagnostic/ablation, 3D or vector mapping
C1733	Catheter, electrophysiology, diagnostic/ablation, other than 3D or vector mapping, other than cool-tip
C1766	Introducer sheath, guiding, intracardiac electrophysiological, steerable, other than peel-away
C2629	Introducer/sheath, other than guiding, intracardiac
C2630	Catheter, electrophysiology, diagnostic/ablation, other than 3D or vector mapping, cool tip
C1892	Introducer/sheath, guiding, intracardiac electrophysiological, fixed-curve, peel-away
C1893	Introducer/sheath, guiding, intracardiac electrophysiological, fixed-curve, other than peel-away
C1894	Introducer/sheath, other than guiding, intracardiac, electrophysiological, non-laser

ICD-10-CM Coding

I44.1	Atrioventricular block, second degree
I44.2	Atrioventricular block, complete
I44.3Ø	Unspecified atrioventricular block
I44.39	Other atrioventricular block
I44.4	Left anterior fascicular block
I44.5	Left posterior fascicular block
I44.6Ø	Unspecified fascicular block
I44.69	Other fascicular block
I44.7	Left bundle-branch block, unspecified
I45.Ø	Right fascicular block
I45.1Ø	Unspecified right bundle-branch block
I45.19	Other right bundle-branch block
I45.2	Bifascicular block
I45.3	Trifascicular block
I45.4	Nonspecific intraventricular block
I45.5	Other specified heart block
I45.6	Pre-excitation syndrome
I45.89	Other specified conduction disorders
I45.9	Conduction disorder, unspecified

I47.0	Re-entry ventricular arrhythmia
I47.1	Supraventricular tachycardia
I47.2	Ventricular tachycardia
I47.9	Paroxysmal tachycardia, unspecified
I48.0	Paroxysmal atrial fibrillation
I48.1	Persistent atrial fibrillation
I48.2	Chronic atrial fibrillation
I48.3	Typical atrial flutter
I48.4	Atypical atrial flutter
I48.91	Unspecified atrial fibrillation
I48.92	Unspecified atrial flutter
I49.01	Ventricular fibrillation
I49.02	Ventricular flutter
I49.1	Atrial premature depolarization
I49.2	Junctional premature depolarization
I49.3	Ventricular premature depolarization
I49.40	Unspecified premature depolarization
I49.49	Other premature depolarization
I49.5	Sick sinus syndrome
I49.8	Other specified cardiac arrhythmias
I49.9	Cardiac arrhythmia, unspecified
P29.81	Cardiac arrest of newborn
R00.1	Bradycardia, unspecified
R55	Syncope and collapse

CCI Edits

93619 00410, 00537, 0178T-0179T, 0180T, 0213T, 0216T, 0228T, 0230T, 11000-11006, 11042-11047, 12001-12007, 12011-12057, 13100-13133, 13151-13153, 33210-33211, 35201-35206, 35226-35236, 35256-35266, 35286, 36000, 36005-36013, 36120-36140, 36400-36410, 36420-36430, 36440, 36555-36556, 36568-36569, 36591-36592, 36600-36620, 36640, 43752, 51701-51703, 62320-62327, 64400-64410, 64413-64435, 64445-64450, 64461-64463, 64479-64530, 76000-76001, 76942, 76970, 76998, 77001-77002, 92012-92014, 92950, 92960-92961, 93000-93010, 93040-93042, 93050, 93318, 93355-93461, 93530-93533, 93563, 93565-93568, 93600-93603, 93610-93612, 93618, 93620-93622, 93644, 94002, 94200, 94250, 94680-94690, 94770, 95812-95816, 95819, 95822, 95829, 95955, 96360-96368, 96372, 96374-96377, 97597-97598, 97602, 99155-99157, 99211-99223, 99231-99255, 99291-99292, 99304-99310, 99315-99316, 99334-99337, 99347-99350, 99374-99375, 99377-99378, 99446-99449, 99495-99496, G0463, G0471

Comprehensive EP with Arrhythmia Induction

93620   **Comprehensive electrophysiologic evaluation including insertion and repositioning of multiple electrode catheters with induction or attempted induction of arrhythmia; with right atrial pacing and recording, right ventricular pacing and recording, His bundle recording**

The physician places three venous sheaths, usually in one or both femoral veins, using standard techniques. The physician advances three electrical catheters through the venous sheaths and into the right heart under fluoroscopic guidance. The physician attaches the three catheters to an electrical recording device to allow depiction of the intracardiac electrograms obtained from electrodes on the catheter tips. The physician moves the tips of the three catheters to the right atrium, the bundle of His, and the right ventricle and obtains recordings. The physician attaches the catheters to an electrical pacing device to allow transmission of pacing impulses through the catheters to the different heart chambers. The physician stimulates the heart with rapid pacing or programmed electrical stimulation in an attempt to induce an arrhythmia. This code is to be used when 93618 is combined with 93619.

Coding Tips

1. Report CPT code 93620 when induction of arrhythmia is attempted or is successful as part of the electrophysiology study.

2. Do not report 93620 in conjunction with 93600, 93602, 93610, 93612, 93618, or 93619.

3. Fluoroscopy is included in 93620 and is not reported separately reported.

4. Medicare has changed the way payment is made for outpatient EP procedures. When comprehensive EP evaluation is performed during the same encounter as an ablation procedure (CPT codes 93650–93652) payment is bundled into the payment for the ablation procedure. Continue to separately report the diagnostic EP evaluation procedure code(s) in addition to the ablation procedure code following current coding guidelines.

5. Conscious sedation is not included in these codes. Separately report 99151–99157 per payer policy and coding guidelines. Hospitals may choose to include the costs associated with the service as part of the procedure rather than reporting them separately.

6. Physician Reporting: This code has both a technical and professional component. To report only the professional component, append modifier 26. To report only the technical component, append modifier TC. To report the complete procedure (i.e., both the professional and technical components), submit without a modifier.

Nerve Conduction of Heart

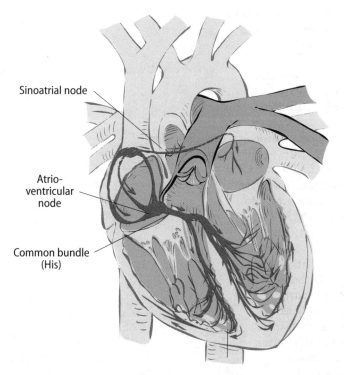

Code 93620 reports a comprehensive EPS, including multiple repositioning of the electrode catheter and induction of arrhythmias in an attempt to isolate the origin of a cardial arrhythmia

Facility HCPCS Coding

HCPCS Level II codes are used to report the supplies provided during the procedure. Hospitals should separately report supplies used during cardiac invasive procedures. Refer to chapter 1 for more information regarding appropriate billing of supplies. Refer to the list of current codes in appendix B.

C1730   Catheter, electrophysiology, diagnostic, other than 3D mapping (19 or fewer electrodes)

C1731   Catheter, electrophysiology, diagnostic, other than 3D mapping (20 or more electrodes)

C1732   Catheter, electrophysiology, diagnostic/ablation, 3D or vector mapping

C1733   Catheter, electrophysiology, diagnostic/ablation, other than 3D or vector mapping, other than cool-tip

C1766   Introducer sheath, guiding, intracardiac electrophysiological, steerable, other than peel-away

C1892   Introducer/sheath, guiding, intracardiac electrophysiological, fixed-curve, peel-away

C1893   Introducer/sheath, guiding, intracardiac electrophysiological, fixed-curve, other than peel-away

C1894   Introducer/sheath, other than guiding, intracardiac, electrophysiological, non-laser

C2629   Introducer/sheath, other than guiding, intracardiac

C2630   Catheter, electrophysiology, diagnostic/ablation, other than 3D or vector mapping, cool tip

ICD-10-CM Coding

I44.0   Atrioventricular block, first degree
I44.1   Atrioventricular block, second degree
I44.2   Atrioventricular block, complete
I44.30   Unspecified atrioventricular block
I44.39   Other atrioventricular block
I44.4   Left anterior fascicular block
I44.5   Left posterior fascicular block
I44.60   Unspecified fascicular block
I44.69   Other fascicular block
I44.7   Left bundle-branch block, unspecified
I45.0   Right fascicular block
I45.10   Unspecified right bundle-branch block
I45.19   Other right bundle-branch block
I45.2   Bifascicular block
I45.3   Trifascicular block
I45.4   Nonspecific intraventricular block
I45.5   Other specified heart block
I45.6   Pre-excitation syndrome
I45.89   Other specified conduction disorders
I45.9   Conduction disorder, unspecified
I46.2   Cardiac arrest due to underlying cardiac condition
I46.8   Cardiac arrest due to other underlying condition
I46.9   Cardiac arrest, cause unspecified
I47.0   Re-entry ventricular arrhythmia
I47.1   Supraventricular tachycardia
I47.2   Ventricular tachycardia
I47.9   Paroxysmal tachycardia, unspecified
I48.0   Paroxysmal atrial fibrillation
I48.1   Persistent atrial fibrillation
I48.2   Chronic atrial fibrillation
I48.3   Typical atrial flutter
I48.4   Atypical atrial flutter
I48.91   Unspecified atrial fibrillation
I48.92   Unspecified atrial flutter
I49.01   Ventricular fibrillation
I49.02   Ventricular flutter
I49.1   Atrial premature depolarization
I49.2   Junctional premature depolarization
I49.3   Ventricular premature depolarization

I49.40	Unspecified premature depolarization
I49.49	Other premature depolarization
I49.5	Sick sinus syndrome
I49.8	Other specified cardiac arrhythmias
I49.9	Cardiac arrhythmia, unspecified
P29.81	Cardiac arrest of newborn
R00.1	Bradycardia, unspecified
R55	Syncope and collapse

CCI Edits

93620   00410, 00537, 0178T-0179T, 0180T, 0213T, 0216T, 0228T, 0230T, 11000-11006, 11042-11047, 12001-12007, 12011-12057, 13100-13133, 13151-13153, 33210-33211, 35201-35206, 35226-35236, 35256-35266, 35286, 36000, 36005-36013, 36120-36140, 36400-36410, 36420-36430, 36440, 36555-36556, 36568-36569, 36591-36592, 36600-36620, 36640, 43752, 51701-51703, 62320-62327, 64400-64410, 64413-64435, 64445-64450, 64461-64463, 64479-64530, 76000-76001, 76942, 76970, 76998, 77001-77002, 92012-92014, 92950, 92960-92961, 93000-93010, 93040-93042, 93050, 93318, 93355-93461, 93530-93533, 93563, 93565-93568, 93600-93603, 93610-93612, 93618, 93624, 93640, 94002, 94200, 94250, 94680-94690, 94770, 95812-95816, 95819, 95822, 95829, 95955, 96360-96368, 96372, 96374-96377, 97597-97598, 97602, 99155-99157, 99211-99223, 99231-99255, 99291-99292, 99304-99310, 99315-99316, 99334-99337, 99347-99350, 99374-99375, 99377-99378, 99446-99449, 99495-99496, G0463, G0471

Comprehensive EP with Arrhythmia Induction and Left Atrial Pacing and Recording (Add-On Code)

93621   **Comprehensive electrophysiologic evaluation including insertion and repositioning of multiple electrode catheters with induction or attempted induction of arrhythmia; with left atrial pacing and recording from coronary sinus or left atrium (List separately in addition to code for primary procedure)**

The physician places four central venous sheaths using standard techniques. The physician advances four electrical catheters through the venous sheaths and into the right heart under fluoroscopic guidance. The physician attaches the four catheters to an electrical recording device to allow depiction of the intracardiac electrograms obtained from electrodes on the catheter tips. The physician moves the tips of the four catheters to the right atrium, the bundle of His, the coronary sinus, and the right ventricle and obtains recordings. The physician may attach the catheters to an electrical pacing device to allow transmission of pacing impulses through the catheters to the different heart chambers. The physician may stimulate the heart with rapid pacing or programmed electrical stimulation in an attempt to induce an arrhythmia.

Coding Tips

1. CPT code 93621 is an add-on code. Report in addition to 93620.

2. Report 93621 when coronary sinus or left atrial recording is also performed as part of an electrophysiology study.

3. Do not report 93621 in conjunction with 93656.

4. Conscious sedation is not included in these codes. Separately report 99151–99157 per payer policy and coding guidelines. Hospitals may choose to include the costs associated with the service as part of the procedure rather than reporting them separately.

5. Physician Reporting: This code has both a technical and professional component. To report only the professional component, append modifier 26. To report only the technical component, append modifier TC. To report the complete procedure (i.e., both the professional and technical components), submit without a modifier.

Electrophysiology Catheter

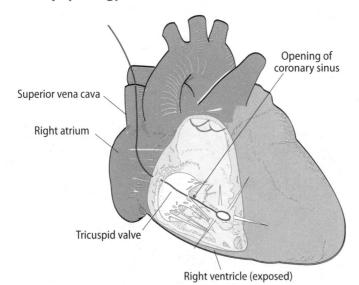

Superior vena cava

Right atrium

Tricuspid valve

Opening of coronary sinus

Right ventricle (exposed)

The catheters may be advanced through the venous system and the right side of the heart, or through to the left ventricle via the foramen ovale. The coronary sinus is the outlet of the great coronary vein and releases into the right atrium. The physician may attempt to stimulate rapid pacing or trigger an arrhythmia

Facility HCPCS Coding

HCPCS Level II codes are used to report the supplies provided during the procedure. Hospitals should separately report supplies used during cardiac invasive procedures. Refer to chapter 1 for more information regarding appropriate billing of supplies. Refer to the list of current codes in appendix B.

C1730   Catheter, electrophysiology, diagnostic, other than 3D mapping (19 or fewer electrodes)

C1731   Catheter, electrophysiology, diagnostic, other than 3D mapping (20 or more electrodes)

C1732   Catheter, electrophysiology, diagnostic/ablation, 3D or vector mapping

C1733   Catheter, electrophysiology, diagnostic/ablation, other than 3D or vector mapping, other than cool-tip

C1766   Introducer/sheath, guiding, intracardiac electrophysiological, steerable, other than peel-away

C1892   Introducer/sheath, guiding, intracardiac electrophysiological, fixed-curve, peel-away

C1893   Introducer/sheath, guiding, intracardiac electrophysiological, fixed-curve, other than peel-away

C1894   Introducer/sheath, other than guiding, intracardiac electrophysiological, non-laser

C2629   Introducer/sheath, other than guiding, intracardiac

C2630   Catheter, electrophysiology, diagnostic/ablation, other than 3D or vector mapping, cool tip

ICD-10-CM Coding

This is an add-on code. Refer to the corresponding primary procedure code for ICD-10-CM diagnosis code links.

CCI Edits

93621   00410, 00537, 11000-11006, 11042-11047, 33210-33211, 36000, 36005-36013, 36120-36140, 36410, 36555-36556, 36568-36569, 36591-36592, 92950, 92960-92961, 93000-93010, 93040-93042, 93050, 93600-93603, 93610-93612, 93618, 94770, 97597-97598, 97602, 99155-99157, 99446-99449

Comprehensive EP with Arrhythmia Induction and Left Ventricular Pacing and Recording (Add-On Code)

93622　**Comprehensive electrophysiologic evaluation including insertion and repositioning of multiple electrode catheters with induction or attempted induction of arrhythmia; with left ventricular pacing and recording (List separately in addition to code for primary procedure)**

The physician places three central venous sheaths and an arterial sheath using standard techniques. The physician advances four electrical catheters through these sheaths and into the heart under fluoroscopic guidance. The physician attaches the four catheters to an electrical recording device to allow depiction of the intracardiac electrograms obtained from electrodes on the catheter tips. The physician moves the tips of the four catheters to the right atrium, the bundle of His, the right ventricle, and the left ventricle and obtains recordings. The physician may attach the catheters to an electrical pacing device to allow transmission of pacing impulses through the catheters to the different heart chambers. The physician may stimulate the heart with rapid pacing or programmed electrical stimulation in an attempt to induce an arrhythmia.

Coding Tips

1.　CPT code 93622 is an add-on code. Report in addition to 93620.

2.　Report 93622 when left ventricular recording and pacing are also performed as part of an electrophysiology study.

3.　Conscious sedation is not included in these codes. Separately report 99151–99157 per payer policy and coding guidelines. Hospitals may choose to include the costs associated with the service as part of the procedure rather than reporting them separately.

4.　Physician Reporting: This code has both a technical and professional component. To report only the professional component, append modifier 26. To report only the technical component, append modifier TC. To report the complete procedure (i.e., both the professional and technical components), submit without a modifier.

Electrophysiology Study

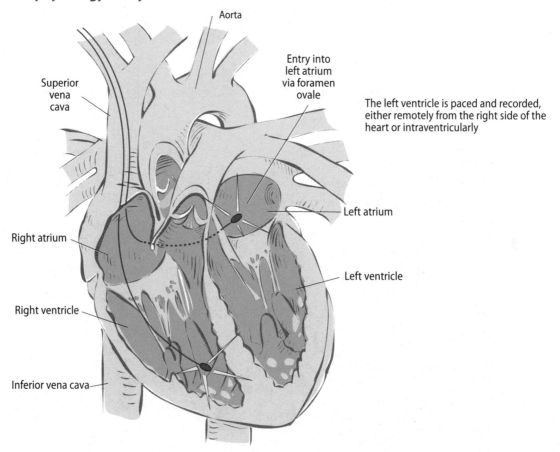

Aorta

Superior vena cava

Entry into left atrium via foramen ovale

The left ventricle is paced and recorded, either remotely from the right side of the heart or intraventricularly

Left atrium

Right atrium

Left ventricle

Right ventricle

Inferior vena cava

Facility HCPCS Coding

HCPCS Level II codes are used to report the supplies provided during the procedure. Hospitals should separately report supplies used during cardiac invasive procedures. Refer to chapter 1 for more information regarding appropriate billing of supplies. Refer to the list of current codes in appendix B.

C1730	Catheter, electrophysiology, diagnostic, other than 3D mapping (19 or fewer electrodes)
C1731	Catheter, electrophysiology, diagnostic, other than 3D mapping (20 or more electrodes)
C1732	Catheter, electrophysiology, diagnostic/ablation, 3D or vector mapping
C1733	Catheter, electrophysiology, diagnostic/ablation, other than 3D or vector mapping, other than cool-tip
C1766	Introducer/sheath, guiding, intracardiac electrophysiological, steerable, other than peel-away
C1892	Introducer/sheath, guiding, intracardiac electrophysiological, fixed-curve, peel-away
C1893	Introducer/sheath, guiding, intracardiac electrophysiological, fixed-curve, other than peel-away
C1894	Introducer/sheath, other than guiding, intracardiac electrophysiological, non-laser
C2629	Introducer/sheath, other than guiding, intracardiac
C2630	Catheter, electrophysiology, diagnostic/ablation, other than 3D or vector mapping, cool tip

ICD-10-CM Coding

This is an add-on code. Refer to the corresponding primary procedure code for ICD-10-CM diagnosis code links.

CCI Edits

93622 00410, 00537, 11000-11006, 11042-11047, 33210-33211, 36000, 36005-36013, 36120-36140, 36410, 36555-36556, 36568-36569, 36591-36592, 92950, 92960-92961, 93000-93010, 93040-93042, 93050, 93600-93603, 93610-93612, 93618, 94770, 97597-97598, 97602, 99155-99157, 99446-99449

Programmed Stimulation and Pacing—Drug Induced

93623	**Programmed stimulation and pacing after intravenous drug infusion (List separately in addition to code for primary procedure)**

The physician places an appropriate arterial or venous sheath, usually femoral, to allow access to the chamber to be studied. The physician advances an electrical catheter through the sheath and into the appropriate chamber under fluoroscopic guidance. An intravenous drug, such as isoproterenol, is infused. The physician attaches the catheter to an electrical pacing device to allow transmission of pacing impulses through the catheter to the heart chamber of interest. The physician stimulates the heart with rapid pacing or programmed electrical stimulation in an attempt to induce an arrhythmia.

Coding Tips

1. CPT code 93623 is an add-on code and should always be used in combination with the appropriate comprehensive code. Report 93623 in addition to 93619 or 93620.

2. Physician Reporting: This code has both a technical and professional component. To report only the professional component, append modifier 26. To report only the technical component, append modifier TC. To report the complete procedure (i.e., both the professional and technical components), submit without a modifier.

Facility HCPCS Coding

HCPCS Level II codes are used to report the supplies provided during the procedure. Hospitals should separately report supplies used during cardiac invasive procedures. Refer to chapter 1 for more information regarding appropriate billing of supplies. Refer to the list of current codes in appendix B.

C1730	Catheter, electrophysiology, diagnostic, other than 3D mapping (19 or fewer electrodes)
C1731	Catheter, electrophysiology, diagnostic, other than 3D mapping (20 or more electrodes)
C1732	Catheter, electrophysiology, diagnostic/ablation, 3D or vector mapping
C1733	Catheter, electrophysiology, diagnostic/ablation, other than 3D or vector mapping, other than cool-tip
C1766	Introducer/sheath, guiding, intracardiac electrophysiological, steerable, other than peel-away
C1892	Introducer/sheath, guiding, intracardiac electrophysiological, fixed-curve, peel-away
C1893	Introducer/sheath, guiding, intracardiac electrophysiological, fixed-curve, other than peel-away
C1894	Introducer/sheath, other than guiding, intracardiac electrophysiological, non-laser
C2629	Introducer/sheath, other than guiding, intracardiac
C2630	Catheter, electrophysiology, diagnostic/ablation, other than 3D or vector mapping, cool tip

ICD-10-CM Coding

This is an add-on code. Refer to the corresponding primary procedure code for ICD-10-CM diagnosis code links.

CCI Edits

93623	33210-33211, 36000, 36005-36013, 36120-36140, 36410, 36555-36556, 36568-36569, 36591-36592, 92960-92961, 93000-93010, 93040-93042, 93050, 99446-99449

EP Follow-up Study

93624   **Electrophysiologic follow-up study with pacing and recording to test effectiveness of therapy, including induction or attempted induction of arrhythmia**

Following administration of therapy (antiarrhythmic drugs, surgery, ablation, etc.), the physician places an appropriate arterial or venous sheath, usually femoral, to allow access to the chamber to be studied. The physician advances an electrical catheter through the sheath and into the appropriate chamber under fluoroscopic guidance. An intravenous drug, such as isoproterenol, is infused. The physician attaches the catheter to an electrical pacing device to allow transmission of pacing impulses through the catheter to the heart chamber of interest. The physician stimulates the heart with rapid pacing or programmed electrical stimulation in an attempt to induce an arrhythmia.

Coding Tips

1. CPT code 93624 describes follow-up EP study to determine the efficacy of pharmacological, ablation, or device therapy. It is performed after the baseline EP study.

2. Do not use CPT code 93624 to report intravenous drug testing performed at the same time as the EP study, report 93623.

3. In general, CPT Code 93624 is reported when a repeat EP study is performed to evaluate the efficacy of chronic therapy.

4. Do not report 93624 for generator evaluation of a cardioverter-defibrillator when an EP study is not performed; see 9329x.

5. Conscious sedation is not included in these codes. Separately report 99151–99157 per payer policy and coding guidelines. Hospitals may choose to include the costs associated with the service as part of the procedure rather than reporting them separately.

6. Physician Reporting: This code has both a technical and professional component. To report only the professional component, append modifier 26. To report only the technical component, append modifier TC. To report the complete procedure (i.e., both the professional and technical components), submit without a modifier.

Facility HCPCS Coding

HCPCS Level II codes are used to report the supplies provided during the procedure. Hospitals should separately report supplies used during cardiac invasive procedures. Refer to chapter 1 for more information regarding appropriate billing of supplies. Refer to the list of current codes in appendix B.

C1730	Catheter, electrophysiology, diagnostic, other than 3D mapping (19 or fewer electrodes)
C1731	Catheter, electrophysiology, diagnostic, other than 3D mapping (20 or more electrodes)
C1732	Catheter, electrophysiology, diagnostic/ablation, 3D or vector mapping
C1733	Catheter, electrophysiology, diagnostic/ablation, other than 3D or vector mapping, other than cool-tip
C1766	Introducer/sheath, guiding, intracardiac electrophysiological, steerable, other than peel-away
C1892	Introducer/sheath, guiding, intracardiac electrophysiological, fixed-curve, peel-away
C1893	Introducer/sheath, guiding, intracardiac electrophysiological, fixed-curve, other than peel-away
C1894	Introducer/sheath, other than guiding, intracardiac electrophysiological, non-laser

ICD-10-CM Coding

I44.0	Atrioventricular block, first degree
I44.1	Atrioventricular block, second degree
I44.2	Atrioventricular block, complete
I44.30	Unspecified atrioventricular block
I44.39	Other atrioventricular block
I44.4	Left anterior fascicular block
I44.5	Left posterior fascicular block
I44.60	Unspecified fascicular block
I44.69	Other fascicular block
I44.7	Left bundle-branch block, unspecified
I45.0	Right fascicular block
I45.10	Unspecified right bundle-branch block
I45.19	Other right bundle-branch block
I45.2	Bifascicular block
I45.3	Trifascicular block
I45.4	Nonspecific intraventricular block
I45.5	Other specified heart block

I45.6	Pre-excitation syndrome
I45.89	Other specified conduction disorders
I45.9	Conduction disorder, unspecified
I46.2	Cardiac arrest due to underlying cardiac condition
I46.8	Cardiac arrest due to other underlying condition
I46.9	Cardiac arrest, cause unspecified
I47.0	Re-entry ventricular arrhythmia
I47.1	Supraventricular tachycardia
I47.2	Ventricular tachycardia
I47.9	Paroxysmal tachycardia, unspecified
I48.0	Paroxysmal atrial fibrillation
I48.1	Persistent atrial fibrillation
I48.2	Chronic atrial fibrillation
I48.3	Typical atrial flutter
I48.4	Atypical atrial flutter
I48.91	Unspecified atrial fibrillation
I48.92	Unspecified atrial flutter
I49.01	Ventricular fibrillation
I49.02	Ventricular flutter
I49.1	Atrial premature depolarization
I49.2	Junctional premature depolarization
I49.3	Ventricular premature depolarization
I49.40	Unspecified premature depolarization
I49.49	Other premature depolarization
I49.5	Sick sinus syndrome
I49.8	Other specified cardiac arrhythmias
I49.9	Cardiac arrhythmia, unspecified

CCI Edits

93624   00410, 00537, 0178T-0179T, 0180T, 0213T, 0216T, 0228T, 0230T, 12001-12007, 12011-12057, 13100-13133, 13151-13153, 33210-33211, 35201-35206, 35226-35236, 35256-35266, 35286, 36000, 36005-36013, 36120-36140, 36400-36410, 36420-36430, 36440, 36555-36556, 36568-36569, 36591-36592, 36600, 36640, 43752, 51701-51703, 62320-62327, 64400-64410, 64413-64435, 64445-64450, 64461-64463, 64479-64530, 76000-76001, 76942, 76970, 76998, 77001-77002, 92012-92014, 92950, 92960-92961, 93000-93010, 93040-93042, 93050, 93318, 93355-93461, 93530-93533, 93563, 93565-93568, 93600, 93618, 93619, 93622, 93644, 94002, 94200, 94250, 94680-94690, 94770, 95812-95816, 95819, 95822, 95829, 95955, 96360-96368, 96372, 96374-96377, 99155-99157, 99211-99223, 99231-99255, 99291-99292, 99304-99310, 99315-99316, 99334-99337, 99347-99350, 99374-99375, 99377-99378, 99446-99449, 99495-99496, G0463, G0471

EP Evaluation of ICD System

93640   **Electrophysiologic evaluation of single or dual chamber pacing cardioverter-defibrillator leads including defibrillation threshold evaluation (induction of arrhythmia, evaluation of sensing and pacing for arrhythmia termination) at time of initial implantation or replacement;**
The purpose of this study is to ensure the cardioverter-defibrillator (ICD) leads are positioned well and working properly, to guarantee proper function of this device in the future. Leads are typically placed in the heart via the subclavian vein, but occasionally defibrillation patches are placed on the epicardium or under the skin. To test the leads, the physician records cardiac electrical signals from the leads and paces the heart through the leads. The physician may test the leads using the actual ICD or by hooking the lead to an external device. The physician uses the lead to pace the heart into an arrhythmia, such as ventricular tachycardia or fibrillation. The ICD or external device detects the arrhythmia and shocks the heart through the ICD lead. The physician may perform this test with several different levels of shock to ensure the ICD can reliably terminate the arrhythmia.

93641   **with testing of single or dual chamber pacing cardioverter-defibrillator pulse generator**
The purpose of this study is to ensure the cardioverter-defibrillator (ICD) and ICD leads are positioned well and working properly, to guarantee proper function of this device in the future. Leads are typically placed in the heart via the subclavian vein, but occasionally defibrillation patches are placed on the epicardium or under the skin. To test the leads, the physician records cardiac electrical signals from the leads and paces the heart through the leads. The physician attaches the leads to the ICD generator. The physician uses the ICD pulse generator to pace the heart into an arrhythmia, such as ventricular tachycardia or fibrillation. The ICD detects the arrhythmia and shocks the heart through the ICD lead. The physician may perform this test with several different levels of shock to ensure the ICD can reliably terminate the arrhythmia.

93642   **Electrophysiologic evaluation of single or dual chamber transvenous pacing cardioverter-defibrillator (includes defibrillation threshold evaluation, induction of arrhythmia, evaluation of sensing and pacing for arrhythmia termination, and programming or reprogramming of sensing or therapeutic parameters)**
The purpose of this study is to ensure the cardioverter-defibrillator (ICD) and ICD leads are positioned well and working properly, to guarantee proper function of this device in the future. The physician records cardiac electrical signals from the leads and paces the heart through the leads to determine pacing threshold. The physician uses the ICD pulse generator to pace the heart into an arrhythmia, such as ventricular tachycardia or fibrillation. The ICD detects and terminates the arrhythmia using pacing or shocking the heart through the ICD lead. The physician may reprogram the ICD's treatment parameters to optimize the device function to best treat the patient's arrhythmia.

Coding Tips

1. These codes refer to the procedures undertaken during implantation of new or replacement of cardioverter-defibrillators where arrhythmias are induced and defibrillation thresholds and sensing thresholds are determined.

2. CPT code 93640 is used for EP evaluation of ICD leads only. This code is reported for evaluation at the time of initial implant or generator replacement or system EP evaluation, including arrhythmia induction, sensing function, and defibrillation threshold testing of lead configurations.

3. CPT code 93641 is used for EP evaluation of the ICD pulse generator where the lead configuration is tested and the connected generator is tested in-vivo.

4. CPT code 93642 is used if the purpose of the procedure is to evaluate a previously implanted device, induce arrhythmia, and evaluate thresholds including reprogramming.

5. Physician Reporting: This code has both a technical and professional component. To report only the professional component, append modifier 26. To report only the technical component, append modifier TC. To report the complete procedure (i.e., both the professional and technical components), submit without a modifier.

Facility HCPCS Coding

HCPCS Level II codes are used to report the supplies provided during the procedure. Hospitals should separately report supplies used during cardiac invasive procedures. Refer to chapter 1 for more information regarding appropriate billing of supplies. Refer to the list of current codes in appendix B.

ICD-10-CM Coding

I45.89	Other specified conduction disorders
I45.9	Conduction disorder, unspecified
I47.0	Re-entry ventricular arrhythmia
I47.1	Supraventricular tachycardia
I47.2	Ventricular tachycardia
I47.9	Paroxysmal tachycardia, unspecified
I48.0	Paroxysmal atrial fibrillation
I48.1	Persistent atrial fibrillation

I48.2	Chronic atrial fibrillation
I48.3	Typical atrial flutter
I48.4	Atypical atrial flutter
I48.91	Unspecified atrial fibrillation
I48.92	Unspecified atrial flutter
I49.Ø1	Ventricular fibrillation
I49.Ø2	Ventricular flutter
I49.1	Atrial premature depolarization
I49.2	Junctional premature depolarization
I49.3	Ventricular premature depolarization
I49.4Ø	Unspecified premature depolarization
I49.49	Other premature depolarization
I49.5	Sick sinus syndrome
I49.8	Other specified cardiac arrhythmias
I49.9	Cardiac arrhythmia, unspecified
T82.817A	Embolism of cardiac prosthetic devices, implants and grafts, initial encounter
T82.827A	Fibrosis of cardiac prosthetic devices, implants and grafts, initial encounter
T82.837A	Hemorrhage of cardiac prosthetic devices, implants and grafts, initial encounter
T82.847A	Pain from cardiac prosthetic devices, implants and grafts, initial encounter
T82.855A	Stenosis of coronary artery stent, initial encounter
T82.857A	Stenosis of cardiac prosthetic devices, implants and grafts, initial encounter
T82.867A	Thrombosis of cardiac prosthetic devices, implants and grafts, initial encounter
T82.897A	Other specified complication of cardiac prosthetic devices, implants and grafts, initial encounter
T82.9XXA	Unspecified complication of cardiac and vascular prosthetic device, implant and graft, initial encounter
Z45.Ø2	Encounter for adjustment and management of automatic implantable cardiac defibrillator
Z95.81Ø	Presence of automatic (implantable) cardiac defibrillator

CCI Edits

93640   00410, 00534-00537, 0178T-0179T, 0180T, 0213T, 0216T, 0228T, 0230T, 11000-11006, 11042-11047, 12001-12007, 12011-12057, 13100-13133, 13151-13153, 33210-33211, 36000, 36005-36013, 36120-36140, 36400-36410, 36420-36430, 36440, 36555-36556, 36568-36569, 36591-36592, 36600, 36640, 43752, 51701-51703, 62320-62327, 64400-64410, 64413-64435, 64445-64450, 64461-64463, 64479-64530, 76942, 76970, 76998, 92012-92014, 92950, 92960-92961, 93000-93010, 93040-93042, 93050, 93260-93261, 93282-93284, 93287, 93289, 93318, 93355-93461, 93530-93533, 93563, 93565-93568, 93618, 93619, 93621-93622, 93624, 94002, 94200, 94250, 94680-94690, 94770, 95812-95816, 95819, 95822, 95829, 95955, 96360-96368, 96372, 96374-96377, 97597-97598, 97602, 99155-99157, 99211-99223, 99231-99255, 99291-99292, 99304-99310, 99315-99316, 99334-99337, 99347-99350, 99374-99375, 99377-99378, 99446-99449, 99495-99496, G0463, G0471

93641   00410, 00534-00537, 0178T-0179T, 0180T, 0213T, 0216T, 0228T, 0230T, 11000-11006, 11042-11047, 12001-12007, 12011-12057, 13100-13133, 13151-13153, 33210-33211, 36000, 36005-36013, 36120-36140, 36400-36410, 36420-36430, 36440, 36555-36556, 36568-36569, 36591-36592, 36600, 36640, 43752, 51701-51703, 62320-62327, 64400-64410, 64413-64435, 64445-64450, 64461-64463, 64479-64530, 76942, 76970, 76998, 92012-92014, 92950, 92960-92961, 93000-93010, 93040-93042, 93050, 93260-93261, 93282-93284, 93287, 93289, 93318, 93355-93461, 93530-93533, 93563, 93565-93568, 93618, 93619, 93621-93622, 93624, 93640, 93642-93644, 94002, 94200, 94250, 94680-94690, 94770, 95812-95816, 95819, 95822, 95829, 95955, 96360-96368, 96372, 96374-96377, 97597-97598, 97602, 99155-99157, 99211-99223, 99231-99255, 99291-99292, 99304-99310, 99315-99316, 99334-99337, 99347-99350, 99374-99375, 99377-99378, 99446-99449, 99495-99496, G0463, G0471

93642   00410, 00534-00537, 0178T-0179T, 0180T, 0213T, 0216T, 0228T, 0230T, 12001-12007, 12011-12057, 13100-13133, 13151-13153, 33210-33211, 36000, 36005-36013, 36120-36140, 36400-36410, 36420-36430, 36440, 36555-36556, 36568-36569, 36591-36592, 36600, 36640, 43752, 51701-51703, 62320-62327, 64400-64410, 64413-64435, 64445-64450, 64461-64463, 64479-64530, 76942, 76970, 76998, 92012-92014, 92950, 92960-92961, 93000-93010, 93040-93042, 93050, 93260-93261, 93282-93284, 93287, 93289, 93318, 93355-93461, 93530-93533, 93563, 93565-93568, 93618, 93619, 93624, 93640, 93644, 94002, 94200, 94250, 94680-94690, 94770, 95812-95816, 95819, 95822, 95829, 95955, 96360-96368, 96372, 96374-96377, 99155-99157, 99211-99223, 99231-99255, 99291-99292, 99304-99310, 99315-99316, 99334-99337, 99347-99350, 99374-99375, 99377-99378, 99446-99449, 99495-99496, G0463, G0471

Catheter Ablation of AV Node for Creation of Complete Heart Block

93650   **Intracardiac catheter ablation of atrioventricular node function, atrioventricular conduction for creation of complete heart block, with or without temporary pacemaker placement**

The purpose of this procedure is to create complete heart block, usually for control of the ventricular rate during atrial arrhythmias. The physician places a venous sheath, usually in a femoral vein, using standard techniques. The physician advances an electrical catheter through the venous sheath and into the right heart under fluoroscopic guidance. The physician attaches the catheter to an electrical recording device to allow depiction of the intracardiac electrograms obtained from electrodes on the catheter tip. The physician moves the catheter tip to the bundle of His, on the anteroseptal tricuspid annulus, and obtains recordings. Alternatively, the physician may obtain similar recordings by placing a catheter into the left ventricular outflow tract via the aorta. The physician maps the His bundle area and ablates the His bundle by sending cautery (radiofrequency) current through the catheter. The physician may also place a temporary pacing catheter in the right ventricle for this procedure.

Coding Tips

1. Intracardiac catheter ablation procedures are specific to the type of arrhythmia being treated. CPT code 93650 reports ablation of atrioventricular node function usually performed to control ventricular rate during atrial arrhythmias. The intent is to create complete heart block. Typically this requires concomitant pacer therapy. If a temporary back-up pacer is placed, this procedure is not coded separately. If a permanent pacemaker is inserted at the same time or subsequently, the pacemaker insertion is reported separately. Please refer to the Pacemaker chapter for further information.

2. Ablation is typically performed following diagnostic EP study. Separately report the diagnostic EP study. Please refer to the previous sections in this chapter for appropriate coding of the diagnostic EP study.

3. Fluoroscopy is included in this procedure and is not reported separately.

4. Device edits apply to this code.

5. Conscious sedation is not included in these codes. Separately report 99151–99157 per payer policy and coding guidelines. Hospitals may choose to include the costs associated with the service as part of the procedure rather than reporting them separately.

6. Physician Reporting: This code has both a technical and professional component. To report only the professional component, append modifier 26. To report only the technical component, append modifier TC. To report the complete procedure (i.e., both the professional and technical components), submit without a modifier.

Catheter Ablation

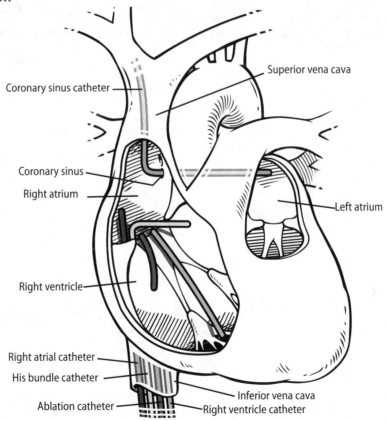

- Coronary sinus catheter
- Superior vena cava
- Coronary sinus
- Right atrium
- Left atrium
- Right ventricle
- Right atrial catheter
- His bundle catheter
- Inferior vena cava
- Ablation catheter
- Right ventricle catheter

Facility HCPCS Coding

HCPCS Level II codes are used to report the supplies provided during the procedure. Hospitals should separately report supplies used during cardiac invasive procedures. Refer to chapter 1 for more information regarding appropriate billing of supplies. Refer to the list of current codes in appendix B.

C1732	Catheter, electrophysiology, diagnostic/ablation, 3D or vector mapping
C1733	Catheter, electrophysiology, diagnostic/ablation, other than 3D or vector mapping, other than cool-tip
C1766	Introducer sheath, guiding, intracardiac electrophysiological, steerable, other than peel-away
C1892	Introducer/sheath, guiding, intracardiac electrophysiological, fixed-curve, peel-away
C1893	Introducer/sheath, guiding, intracardiac electrophysiological, fixed-curve, other than peel-away
C1894	Introducer/sheath, other than guiding, intracardiac, electrophysiological, non-laser
C2629	Introducer/sheath, other than guiding, intracardiac
C2630	Catheter, electrophysiology, diagnostic/ablation, other than 3D or vector mapping, cool tip

ICD-10-CM Coding

I48.0	Paroxysmal atrial fibrillation
I48.1	Persistent atrial fibrillation
I48.2	Chronic atrial fibrillation
I48.3	Typical atrial flutter
I48.4	Atypical atrial flutter
I48.91	Unspecified atrial fibrillation
I48.92	Unspecified atrial flutter
I49.1	Atrial premature depolarization

CCI Edits

93650   00410, 00537, 0178T-0179T, 0180T, 0213T, 0216T, 0228T, 0230T, 12001-12007, 12011-12057, 13100-13133, 13151-13153, 33210-33211, 35201-35206, 35226-35236, 35256-35266, 35286, 36000, 36005-36013, 36120-36140, 36400-36410, 36420-36430, 36440, 36555-36556, 36568-36569, 36591-36592, 36600, 36640, 43752, 51701-51703, 62320-62327, 64400-64410, 64413-64435, 64445-64450, 64461-64463, 64479-64530, 76000-76001, 76942, 76970, 76998, 77001-77002, 92012-92014, 92950, 92960-92961, 93000-93010, 93040-93042, 93050, 93318, 93355-93461, 93530-93533, 93563, 93565-93568, 93623-93624, 94002, 94200, 94250, 94680-94690, 94770, 95812-95816, 95819, 95822, 95829, 95955, 96360-96368, 96372, 96374-96377, 99155-99157, 99211-99223, 99231-99255, 99291-99292, 99304-99310, 99315-99316, 99334-99337, 99347-99350, 99374-99375, 99377-99378, 99446-99449, 99495-99496, G0463, G0471

Catheter Ablation for Treatment of Arrhythmia

93653 **Comprehensive electrophysiologic evaluation including insertion and repositioning of multiple electrode catheters with induction or attempted induction of an arrhythmia with right atrial pacing and recording, right ventricular pacing and recording (when necessary) and His bundle recording (when necessary) with intracardiac catheter ablation of arrhythmogenic focus; with treatment of supraventricular tachycardia by ablation of fast or slow atrioventricular pathway, accessory atrioventricular connection, cavo-tricuspid isthmus or other single atrial focus or source of atrial re-entry**

Catheter ablation is performed on dual atrioventricular nodal pathways, accessory atrioventricular connections, or other atrial foci causing supraventricular tachycardia (SVT). The physician places three venous sheaths, usually in one or both femoral veins, using standard techniques. The physician advances three electrical catheters through the venous sheaths and into the right heart under fluoroscopic guidance. The three catheters are attached to an electrical recording device to allow depiction of the intracardiac electrograms obtained from electrodes on the catheter tips. The tips of the three catheters are moved to the right atrium, the bundle of His, and the right ventricle, and recordings are obtained when necessary. Selective destruction (ablation) of cardiac tissue to correct the SVT is based on the recordings.

93654 **with treatment of ventricular tachycardia or focus of ventricular ectopy including intracardiac Electrophysiologic 3D mapping, when performed, and left ventricular pacing and recording, when performed**

Catheter ablation is performed on the cardiac tissue causing ventricular tachycardia or ectopy. The physician places three venous sheaths, usually in one or both femoral veins, using standard techniques. The physician advances three electrical catheters through the venous sheaths and into the right heart using fluoroscopic guidance. The three catheters are attached to an electrical recording device to allow depiction of the intracardiac electrograms obtained from electrodes on the catheter tips. The tips of the three catheters are moved to the right atrium, the bundle of His, and the right ventricle, and recordings are obtained. Left ventricle pacing and recording may also be performed. Selective destruction (ablation) of cardiac tissue to correct the tachycardia or ectopy is based on the recordings.

93655 **Intracardiac catheter ablation of a discrete mechanism of arrhythmia which is distinct from the primary ablated mechanism, including repeat diagnostic maneuvers, to treat a spontaneous or induced arrhythmia (List separately in addition to code for primary procedure)**

After the intial treatment (ablation) for supraventricular or ventricular tachycardia, a postablation evaluation is performed. If this evaluation reveals a new (not previously diagnosed) or different mechanism causing the arrhythmia, this is recorded and additional cardiac tissue is destroyed via the catheter to correct the newly discovered spontaneous or induced arrhythmia.

93656 **Comprehensive electrophysiologic evaluation including transseptal catheterizations, insertion and repositioning of multiple electrode catheters with induction or attempted induction of an arrhythmia including left or right atrial pacing/recording when necessary, right ventricular pacing/recording when necessary and His bundle recording when necessary with intracardiac catheter ablation of atrial fibrillation by pulmonary vein isolation**

During ablation by pulmonary vein isolation, also called pulmonary vein antrum isolation (PVAI), cardiac tissue responsible for the electrical irritability that causes atrial fibrillation is found at the opening of each of the four pulmonary veins that terminate in the left atrium. The physician places three venous sheaths, usually in one or both femoral veins, using standard techniques. Three electrical catheters are advanced through the venous sheaths into the right heart under fluoroscopic guidance, and the septum is punctured for access to the left atrium. The physician attaches the three catheters to an electrical recording device to allow depiction of the intracardiac electrograms obtained from electrodes on the catheter tips. The tips of the three catheters are moved to the left atrium, and selective destruction (ablation) of the cardiac tissue at the opening of the pulmonary veins is performed to correct the atrial fibrillation. The three catheters may also be maneuvered to the bundle of His and the right ventricle for pacing and to obtain recordings.

93657 **Additional linear or focal intracardiac catheter ablation of the left or right atrium for treatment of atrial fibrillation remaining after completion of pulmonary vein isolation (List separately in addition to code for primary procedure)**

The purpose of this procedure is to ablate an arrhythmogenic focus or pathway to cure supraventricular arrhythmias. The ablation is typically done following a more complex electrophysiologic study, coded elsewhere. The physician places an introducer sheath, typically in a femoral vein, using standard techniques. The physician advances an electrical catheter through the sheath and into the heart under fluoroscopic guidance. The physician attaches the catheter to an electrical recording device to allow depiction of the intracardiac electrograms obtained from electrodes on the catheter tip. The physician moves the catheter tip to the arrhythmogenic focus or pathway while guided by electrical recordings and fluoroscopic views. The physician ablates the focus or pathway by sending cautery (radiofrequency) current through the catheter.

Catheter Ablation

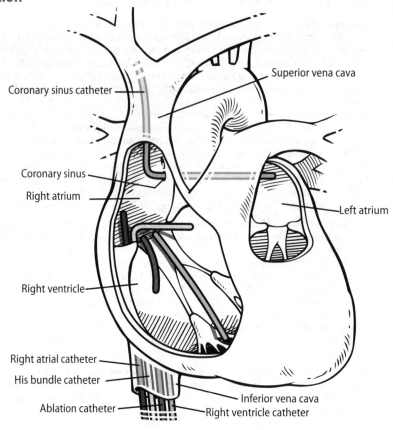

Superior vena cava

Coronary sinus catheter

Coronary sinus

Right atrium

Left atrium

Right ventricle

Right atrial catheter

His bundle catheter

Inferior vena cava

Ablation catheter

Right ventricle catheter

Coding Tips

1. Catheter ablation procedure codes include diagnostic electrophysiology. There are some exceptions. Pay close attention to the instructional notes and the CCI edits.

2. Intracardiac catheter ablation procedure codes are specific to the type of arrhythmia being treated. Use 93653 for treatment of supraventricular tachycardia caused by atrial foci. Use 93654 for treatment of ventricular tachycardia. Use 93656 for treatment of atrial fibrillation.

3. Codes 93654, 93655, and 93656 may not be reported together.

4. Additional ablation site treatments are reported with add-on codes 93655 or 93657.

5. When transseptal puncture is performed to treat tachycardia, it may be separately reported with 93462. Transseptal puncture may not be reported in addition to 93656 for treatment of atrial fibrillation. It is considered to be a component of atrial fibrillation ablation.

6. If ablation is performed without a diagnostic EP study during the same encounter, append modifier 52 to the procedure code.

7. Fluoroscopy is included in these procedures and is not reported separately.

8. Conscious sedation is not included in these codes. Separately report 99151–99157 per payer policy and coding guidelines. Hospitals may choose to include the costs associated with the service as part of the procedure rather than reporting them separately.

Facility HCPCS Coding

HCPCS Level II codes are used to report the supplies provided during the procedure. Hospitals should separately report supplies used during cardiac invasive procedures. Refer to chapter 1 for more information regarding appropriate billing of supplies. Refer to the list of current codes in appendix B.

C1730   Catheter, electrophysiology, diagnostic, other than 3D mapping (19 or fewer electrodes)

C1731   Catheter, electrophysiology, diagnostic, other than 3D mapping (20 or more electrodes0

C1732   Catheter, electrophysiology, diagnostic/ablation, 3D or vector mapping

C1733   Catheter, electrophysiology, diagnostic/ablation, other than 3D or vector mapping, other than cool-tip

C1766   Introducer/sheath, guiding, intracardiac electrophysiological, steerable, other than peel-away

C1886	Catheter, ablation
C1892	Introducer/sheath, guiding, intracardiac electrophysiological, fixed-curve, peel-away
C1893	Introducer/sheath, guiding, intracardiac electrophysiological, fixed-curve, other than peel-away
C2629	Introducer/sheath, other than guiding, intracardiac
C2630	Catheter, electrophysiology, diagnostic/ablation, other than 3D or vector mapping, cool tip

ICD-10-CM Coding

I44.3Ø	Unspecified atrioventricular block
I44.39	Other atrioventricular block
I44.4	Left anterior fascicular block
I44.5	Left posterior fascicular block
I44.6Ø	Unspecified fascicular block
I44.69	Other fascicular block
I44.7	Left bundle-branch block, unspecified
I45.Ø	Right fascicular block
I45.1Ø	Unspecified right bundle-branch block
I45.19	Other right bundle-branch block
I45.2	Bifascicular block
I45.3	Trifascicular block
I45.4	Nonspecific intraventricular block
I45.6	Pre-excitation syndrome
I45.89	Other specified conduction disorders
I46.2	Cardiac arrest due to underlying cardiac condition
I46.8	Cardiac arrest due to other underlying condition
I46.9	Cardiac arrest, cause unspecified
I47.Ø	Re-entry ventricular arrhythmia
I47.1	Supraventricular tachycardia
I47.2	Ventricular tachycardia
I47.9	Paroxysmal tachycardia, unspecified
I48.Ø	Paroxysmal atrial fibrillation
I48.1	Persistent atrial fibrillation
I48.2	Chronic atrial fibrillation
I48.3	Typical atrial flutter
I48.4	Atypical atrial flutter
I48.91	Unspecified atrial fibrillation
I48.92	Unspecified atrial flutter
I49.Ø1	Ventricular fibrillation
I49.Ø2	Ventricular flutter
I49.2	Junctional premature depolarization
I49.8	Other specified cardiac arrhythmias
I49.9	Cardiac arrhythmia, unspecified
RØØ.1	Bradycardia, unspecified

CCI Edits

93653   00410, 00537, 0178T-0179T, 0180T, 0213T, 0216T, 0228T, 0230T, 11000-11006, 11042-11047, 12001-12007, 12011-12057, 13100-13133, 13151-13153, 33210-33211, 35201-35206, 35226-35236, 35256-35266, 35286, 36000, 36005-36013, 36120-36140, 36400-36410, 36420-36430, 36440, 36555-36556, 36568-36569, 36591-36592, 36600-36620, 36640, 43752, 51701-51703, 62320-62327, 64400-64410, 64413-64435, 64445-64450, 64461-64463, 64479-64530, 69990, 76000-76001, 76942, 76970, 76998, 77001-77002, 92012-92014, 92950, 92960-92961, 93000-93010, 93040-93042, 93050, 93318, 93355-93461, 93530-93533, 93563, 93565-93568, 93600-93603, 93610-93612, 93618-93620, 93624, 93640, 93642-93644, 94002, 94200, 94250, 94680-94690, 94770, 95812-95816, 95819, 95822, 95829, 95955, 96360-96368, 96372, 96374-96377, 97597-97598, 97602, 99155-99157, 99211-99223, 99231-99255, 99291-99292, 99304-99310, 99315-99316, 99334-99337, 99347-99350, 99374-99375, 99377-99378, 99446-99449, 99495-99496, G0463, G0471

93654 00410, 00537, 0178T-0179T, 0180T, 0213T, 0216T, 0228T, 0230T, 0389T-0391T, 0417T-0418T, 0462T-0463T, 11000-11006, 11042-11047, 12001-12007, 12011-12057, 13100-13133, 13151-13153, 33210-33211, 35201-35206, 35226-35236, 35256-35266, 35286, 36000, 36005-36013, 36120-36140, 36400-36410, 36420-36430, 36440, 36555-36556, 36568-36569, 36591-36592, 36600-36620, 36640, 43752, 51701-51703, 62320-62327, 64400-64410, 64413-64435, 64445-64450, 64461-64463, 64479-64530, 69990, 76000-76001, 76942, 76970, 76998, 77001-77002, 92012-92014, 92950, 92960-92961, 93000-93010, 93040-93042, 93050, 93260-93261, 93279-93284, 93286-93289, 93318, 93355-93461, 93530-93533, 93563, 93565-93568, 93600-93603, 93609-93613, 93618-93620, 93622, 93624, 93640, 93642-93644, 93653, 93657, 94002, 94200, 94250, 94680-94690, 94770, 95812-95816, 95819, 95822, 95829, 95955, 96360-96368, 96372, 96374-96377, 97597-97598, 97602, 99155-99157, 99211-99223, 99231-99255, 99291-99292, 99304-99310, 99315-99316, 99334-99337, 99347-99350, 99374-99375, 99377-99378, 99446-99449, 99495-99496, G0463, G0471

93655 00410, 00537, 0178T-0179T, 0180T, 0213T, 0216T, 0228T, 0230T, 12001-12007, 12011-12057, 13100-13133, 13151-13153, 33210-33211, 35201-35206, 35226-35236, 35256-35266, 35286, 36000, 36005-36013, 36120-36140, 36400-36410, 36420-36430, 36440, 36555-36556, 36568-36569, 36591-36592, 36600, 36640, 43752, 51701-51703, 61650, 62320-62327, 64400-64410, 64413-64435, 64445-64450, 64461, 64463, 64479, 64483, 64486-64490, 64493, 64505-64530, 76000-76001, 76942, 76970, 76998, 77001-77002, 92950, 92960-92961, 93000-93010, 93040-93042, 93050, 93318, 93355-93461, 93530-93533, 93563, 93565-93568, 93600-93603, 93610-93612, 93618-93620, 93624, 94002, 94200, 94250, 94680-94690, 94770, 95812-95816, 95819, 95822, 95829, 95955, 96360, 96365, 96372, 96374-96377, 99155-99157, G0471

93656 00410, 00537, 0178T-0179T, 0180T, 0213T, 0216T, 0228T, 0230T, 0389T-0391T, 0417T-0418T, 0462T-0463T, 11000-11006, 11042-11047, 12001-12007, 12011-12057, 13100-13133, 13151-13153, 33210-33211, 35201-35206, 35226-35236, 35256-35266, 35286, 36000, 36005-36013, 36120-36140, 36400-36410, 36420-36430, 36440, 36555-36556, 36568-36569, 36591-36592, 36600-36620, 36640, 43752, 51701-51703, 62320-62327, 64400-64410, 64413-64435, 64445-64450, 64461-64463, 64479-64530, 69990, 76000-76001, 76942, 76970, 76998, 77001-77002, 92012-92014, 92950, 92960-92961, 93000-93010, 93040-93042, 93050, 93260-93261, 93279-93284, 93286-93289, 93318, 93355-93462, 93530-93533, 93563, 93565-93568, 93600-93603, 93610-93612, 93618-93621, 93624, 93640-93641, 93642-93644, 93653-93654, 94002, 94200, 94250, 94680-94690, 94770, 95812-95816, 95819, 95822, 95829, 95955, 96360-96368, 96372, 96374-96377, 97597-97598, 97602, 99155-99157, 99211-99223, 99231-99255, 99291-99292, 99304-99310, 99315-99316, 99334-99337, 99347-99350, 99374-99375, 99377-99378, 99446-99449, 99495-99496, G0463, G0471

93657 00410, 00537, 0178T-0179T, 0180T, 0213T, 0216T, 0228T, 0230T, 12001-12007, 12011-12057, 13100-13133, 13151-13153, 33210-33211, 35201-35206, 35226-35236, 35256-35266, 35286, 36000, 36005-36013, 36120-36140, 36400-36410, 36420-36430, 36440, 36555-36556, 36568-36569, 36591-36592, 36600, 36640, 43752, 51701-51703, 61650, 62320-62327, 64400-64410, 64413-64435, 64445-64450, 64461, 64463, 64479, 64483, 64486-64490, 64493, 64505-64530, 76000-76001, 76942, 76970, 76998, 77001-77002, 92950, 92960-92961, 93000-93010, 93040-93042, 93050, 93318, 93355-93461, 93530-93533, 93563, 93565-93568, 93600-93603, 93610-93612, 93618-93620, 93624, 94002, 94200, 94250, 94680-94690, 94770, 95812-95816, 95819, 95822, 95829, 95955, 96360, 96365, 96372, 96374-96377, 99155-99157, G0471

Intracardiac Echocardiography

93662   **Intracardiac echocardiography during therapeutic/diagnostic intervention, including imaging supervision and interpretation (List separately in addition to code for primary procedure)**
During separately reportable electrophysiologic evaluation or intracardiac catheter ablation of arrhythmogenic focus, intracardiac echocardiography (ICE) is performed. ICE uses intravascular ultrasound imaging systems in the cardiac chambers providing direct endocardial visualization. A single rotating transducer that provides a 360-degree field of view in a plane transverse to the long axis of the catheter is introduced through a long vascular sheath. Access is typically via the femoral vein. The transducer is then directed to various sites within the heart. During electrophysiologic evaluation, ICE is used to guide placement of mapping and stimulating catheters. During intracardiac ablation procedures, ICE allows for precise anatomic localization of the ablation catheter tip in relation to endocardial structures. Since the focus of some arrhythmias can be anatomically determined, it also allows the ablative procedure to be performed using anatomic landmarks.

Coding Tips

1. Report 93662 in addition to 92987, 93453, 93532, 93460-93462, 93580, 93581, 93621, 93622, 93653, 93654, or 93656.
2. Do not report internal cardioversion (92961) with 93662.
3. Electrophysiologic evaluation or intracardiac catheter ablation procedures are reported separately.

Facility HCPCS Coding

HCPCS Level II codes are used to report the devices used in these procedures. Hospitals should separately report supplies and devices used during pacemaker procedures. Refer to chapter 1 for more information regarding appropriate billing of supplies. Appendix B of this publication contains a list of current device codes applicable to this section.

C1759   Catheter, intracardiac echocardiography

ICD-10-CM Coding

This is an add-on code. Refer to the corresponding primary procedure code for ICD-10-CM diagnosis code links.

CCI Edits

93662   00537, 36591-36592, 93050, 99446-99449

EP and Ablation Case Examples

Case Example #1

Electrophysiologic Testing

Indications:
Recurrent supraventricular tachycardia, known ventricular tachycardia with ventricular fibrillation arrest, status post defibrillator placement, ischemic disease

Procedure:
After standard prepping and draping, the right groin was infiltrated with local lidocaine anesthesia. Seldinger technique was used to cannulate the right femoral vein and a guidewire and sheath were inserted. A second cannulation was made inferior to the first and a guidewire and sheath were inserted. A similar process was followed on the left with two sheaths inserted.

Initially, a 6-French **decapolar catheter** was advanced from the right femoral venous access **to the coronary sinus**. A 6-French **quadripolar catheter** was advanced from the left femoral venous access **to the right ventricular septum**. A 5-French quadripolar **catheter** was advanced from the left femoral venous access **to the AV junction for His bundle recording**, and a 6-French quadripolar **catheter** was advanced from the right femoral venous access **to the high right atrium**. The catheters were manipulated around the pre-existing defibrillator lead in the right ventricle and atrial pacing lead in the right atrium.

Basic CL was 1000 Msec in a paced atrial rhythm. AH interval was 150 Msec with HA of 50 Msec. Initial pacing was performed from the right ventricle. There was 1:1 retrograde conduction at 600, 500 and 450 Msec. VA block occurred at 400 Msec. Retrograde activation sequence was normal.

Atrial pacing was then **performed**. Antegrade conduction was present at 600 Msec. Wenckebach was present at 500 Msec. Single extrastimuli were introduced at the high right atrium at a CL of 600 Msec. AV nodal effective refractory period was 480 Msec.

Case Example #1 (Continued)

The patient was heavily sedated at this time. **Isuprel was then begun** at 0.5 mcg. During the Isuprel an AH jump could be documented with a marked increase in AV, AH intervals from approximately 200 to 300 Msec on 20 Msec decrements in S2. No echo beats were seen and no supraventricular tachycardia was induced. Isuprel was increased to 1 mcg/min. With ventricular pacing at a CL of 500 Msec, **sustained supraventricular tachycardia was induced**. There was 1:1 retrograde conduction at 500 and this yielded prolonged antegrade conduction via the slow pathway and retrograde conduction using the fast pathway. The tachycardia was terminated by burst pacing from the right ventricle at a CL of 450 Msec. The pattern is one of AV nodal reentry tachycardia. The CL was 534 Msec with an AH of 380 Msec and HV of 52 Msec. **Single extrastimuli was delivered from the right ventricular septum with His bundle refractory** and there was no retrograde pre-excitation. Atrial **pacing** at a CL of 600 Msec yielded an AV nodal effective refractory period of 380 Msec. Interestingly, there was no induction of supraventricular tachycardia with atrial pacing. **Multiple inductions were performed using right ventricular pacing** at 500 Msec. This was highly reproducible.

Following this the right atrial catheter was removed and a white Webster **ablation catheter advanced** from the right femoral venous access. This was positioned on the **tricuspid annulus**. The first **application of RF energy** did yield junctional tachycardia. However, there was evidence of retrograde block during the junctional tachycardial and therefore energy was terminated. **Multiple other applications of RF energy were delivered**. This would typically be accompanied by retrograde block and on **repeat testing** it was found that in the absence of any antegrade abnormality, there was an absence of ventricular atrial conduction following ablation, pacing at a CL of 600 Msec. This accounts for the retrograde block during junctional rhythm with ablation. Nonetheless, this did limit the application of RF energy and this was done in a very slow fashion so that RF would be delivered for 20 or 30 seconds and then conduction reassessed to make sure there was no change in antegrade conduction. No antegrade abnormalities were ever noted. There were several inductions of junctional tachycardia.

Due to difficulties manipulating the catheter around the preexisting defibrillator wires, it was decided to place an SRO sheath. This was advanced over a long J-tip guidewire to the right atrium. It was flushed and the ablation catheter re-advanced through the SRO sheath. This gave a little better control of the catheter at the ablation site. The **ablation site** was **radiographically at the site of the proximal poles of the coronary sinus catheter**. It was in the mid to superior aspect of the coronary sinus, although it was well separated from the His bundle catheter. Following multiple applications of radiofrequency energy, supraventricular tachycardia was never seen again. Multiple applications of ventricular pacing were performed. Even on 1 mcg of Isuprel for a prolonged period of time, there was no conduction from the ventricle to the atrium at CL of 600 Msec or lower. 1-1 conduction was noted at a CL of 700 Msec. Single extrastimuli from the high right atrium demonstrated an AV nodal ERP of 290 Msec. There was a prolonged AH just prior to AV nodal refractoriness. No echo beats were seen and no supraventricular tachycardia could be induced. Wenckebach CL was 300 Msec.

Impression:

1. **Easily inducible sustained supraventricular tachycardia** using AV nodal reentrant mechanism. Tachycardia was reproducibly **induced on Isuprel** from the right ventricle. We did not induce tachycardia from the atrium.

2. Slow pathway **ablation** with absence of ventriculo-atrial conduction at the conclusion of the procedure with no change in antegrade conduction.

3. Residual AH jump, consistent with slow pathway but no echo beats of SVT.

4. The patient's defibrillator had been programmed to detect but not treat arrhythmias during the procedure. Following the procedure it was reactivated to provide for treatment for ventricular tachyarrhythmias in the high range. We will maintain a monitoring zone only to evaluate the patient for any recurrence of supraventricular tachycardia.

Procedure Codes Reported:
93623, 93653

Other Codes Reported:
Report the applicable catheter device codes.

Case Example # 2

Atrial Flutter RF Ablation Report

History:
This 75-year-old patient has a history of **medically refractory type I atrial flutter** and has had an unsuccessful attempt at radiofrequency ablation. He continues to have persistent arrhythmia despite medications.

Procedure:
After providing informed consent, the patient was taken to the EP lab in a post absorptive state and placed in the supine position. Noninvasive blood pressure, arterial oxygen saturation and ECG monitoring were started. Anterior and posterior defibrillation pads were applied to the chest. The right and left femoral areas were then prepared and draped in the usual sterile fashion. Sedation medication was given. Appropriate local anesthesia was applied to the puncture sited using 1% lidocaine. Venous access was accomplished using standard Seldinger technique. Two 6.5 French sheaths and one 7 French sheath was placed within the left femoral vein. The sheaths were aspirated and then flushed with heparinized saline. Under fluoroscopic guidance, two 6 French quadripolar **catheters** were then **advanced into the high right atrium** (appendage), **and into the coronary sinus.** A 7 French quadripolar orange tip **steerable mapping catheter** was then advanced to the **lateral tricuspid annulus region**. An 8 French sheath and a 6 French sheath were placed in the right femoral vein. From the right femoral approach, a 6 French quadripolar **catheter was placed** across the tricuspid valve in the region of the His-bundle. After initial catheter placement, the catheters were connected to the **EP digital recording system**. Bipolar intracardiac signals were then recorded utilizing filter settings of 30 Hz to 500 Hz. Baseline recordings and measurements were obtained. The patient received intravenous heparin throughout the procedure. **Comprehensive mapping** of the tricuspid annulus was performed. This was followed by **RF ablation**. Following, RFA, a **comprehensive EP study was performed. Programmed stimulation** was performed. Induction of arrhythmias was then **performed from the high right atrium**. A total of 4 extrastimuli were utilized. No arrhythmias were induced. At the completion of the procedure, all catheters were withdrawn and pressure applied at the puncture sites to assure hemostasis. The patient was returned to his room with no apparent complications.

Arrhythmias Observed:
In the baseline state, atrial flutter with variable block was present. The atrial flutter cycle length was 342 msec. The flutter wave morphology indicated negative waves in II, III and avF, with positive waves in V1. The patient remained hemodynamically stable during atrial flutter. During atrial flutter, the observed ventricular cycle length varied between 628 and 1321 msec. The QRS duration was 122 msec. The corrected QT interval was 325 msec and the resting HV interval was 58 msec.

Intracardiac Mapping Procedure:
Comprehensive **3-dimensional intracardiac mapping was performed** utilizing steerable quadripolar ablation catheters. Mapping was performed during atrial flutter. Comprehensive mapping of the tricuspid annulus was completed. Mid-diastolic potentials and split potentials were recorded within the mid portion of the tricuspid isthmus between the tricuspid annulus and the inferior vena cava. Analysis of the atrial activation pattern was performed. Entrainment pacing was performed. The electrophysiologic characteristics of the arrhythmia were compatible with orthodromic atrial flutter.

Radiofrequency Ablation Procedure:
Following comprehensive mapping, a total of 9 **applications of radiofrequency energy** were delivered to the medial tricuspid isthmus region. Energy was applied in a unipolar fashion between the tip of the ablation catheter and a dispersive pad placed on the patient's right posterior chest region. The anterior rim of the annulus was targeted first and a continuous drag was performed back to the inferior vena cava. During the second application, sinus rhythm resumed. There was a prolonged episode of sinus bradycardia. Prior to the onset of the radiofrequency ablation procedure, the patient's defibrillator was interrogated and found to be functioning appropriately. The device was programmed to the DDI configuration with lower rate of 40 prior to the RF ablation. After the RF ablation procedure, the device was reprogrammed to the DDIR configuration with the lower rate of 70. No significant impedance rise occurred during the procedure. Following successful RF ablation, a comprehensive electrophysiologic study was performed. During RFA, the maximum observed impedance was 92 ohms, maximum voltage 77 volts, maximum generator output 70 watts, maximum current 950 mA, maximum temperature achieved 64 degrees, and the longest duration of application was 3 minutes.

Conclusions:
1. Orthodromic atrial flutter with variable AV block (type I).
2. **Successful radiofrequency ablation** (type I atrial flutter).
3. Bidirectional block in the tricuspid isthmus at the completion of the procedure
4. Normal ICD function.

Procedure Codes Reported:
93613, 93620, 93650, and 93642

Other Codes Reported:
Report the applicable catheter device codes.

Case Example #3

Radiofrequency Ablation Report

History:
This 82-year-old patient has a **history of medically refractory paroxysmal supraventricular tachycardia**.

Procedure:
After obtaining informed consent, the patient was taken to the EP lab in a post absorptive state and placed in the supine position. Noninvasive blood pressure, arterial oxygen saturation and ECG monitoring were started. Anterior and posterior defibrillation pads were applied to the chest. The right and left femoral areas were then prepared and draped in the usual sterile fashion. Sedation medication was given. Appropriate local anesthesia was applied to the puncture sited using 1% lidocaine. Venous access was accomplished using standard Seldinger technique. Three 6.5F sheaths were placed within the left femoral vein. The sheaths were aspirated and then flushed with heparinized saline. Under fluoroscopic guidance, three 6F quadripolar **catheters** were then **advanced into the right ventricular apex, high right atrium (appendage), and into the coronary sinus**. An 8F sheath and a 6F sheath were placed in the right femoral vein. The sheaths were aspirated and flushed with heparinized saline. From the right femoral approach, a 6F quadripolar **catheter** was **placed** across the tricuspid valve in the **region of the His-bundle**. After initial catheter placement, the catheters were connected to the EP digital recording system. Bipolar intracardiac signals were then recorded utilizing filter settings of 30Hz to 500Hz. Baseline recordings and measurements were obtained. **Programmed stimulation was performed**. A **supraventricular study** was performed using standard atrial extra stimulus techniques. This was followed by incremental **atrial pacing**. A **ventricular study** was performed from the right ventricular apex using standard ventricular extra stimulus techniques. **Incremental ventricular pacing** was then performed. Sinus node function was assessed. **Induction of arrhythmias** was then **performed** from the **high right atrium**.

✓ Comprehensive **mapping of the tachycardia** was then **performed**. This was followed by **RF ablation**. A **comprehensive EP study** was repeated before and after the administration of **intravenous isoproterenol**. At the completion of the procedure, all catheters were withdrawn and pressure was applied to the puncture sites to assure hemostasis. The patient was returned to his room in stable condition and without apparent complications.

Conduction Abnormalities:
Antegrade conduction was normal. Dual AV nodal physiology was observed. There was no evidence of aberrant ventricular conduction or infra-His block. There was no evidence of an accessory pathway demonstrated during this study. Retrograde conduction was concentric and decremental.

Arrhythmias Observed:
The patient had evidence of dual AV nodal physiology and a history of supraventricular tachycardia. Although we gave him graded **doses of intravenous isoproterenol** and used aggressive atrial and ventricular **pacing protocols**, no supraventricular tachycardia could be induced. Additionally, we never saw any consistent AV nodal echo beats.

Intracardiac Mapping Procedure:
Comprehensive intracardiac mapping was performed utilizing steerable quadripolar ablation catheters. **Three-dimensional mapping was not utilized** during this procedure. Mapping was performed during tachycardia and sinus rhythm. Slow pathway potentials were recorded. Comprehensive mapping of the right atrial septum was followed by mapping of the lower mitral annulus inside the coronary sinus.

RF Ablation Procedure:
Because of his history of documented narrow QRS complex tachycardia and the finding of dual AV nodal pathways, we decided to proceed with **empiric slow pathway ablation. Following comprehensive mapping**, a total of six applications of **radiofrequency energy** were **delivered** to the low septal **atrium** in the P1 position. Energy was applied in a unipolar fashion between the tip of the ablation catheter and a dispersive pad placed on the patient's right posterior chest region. Accelerated junctional rhythm was observed during the delivery of energy. During RFA, the maximum observed impedance was 108 ohms, maximum voltage was 51 volts, maximum generator output 27 watts, maximum current 542 mA, maximum temperature achieved 52 degrees and the longest duration of application was 60 seconds. No AV block occurred during the procedure. No significant impedance rise occurred during the procedure.

Case Example #3 (Continued)

Post Ablation EP Study:

Following empiric radiofrequency ablation, there was a significant prolongation of the AV nodal refractory periods as well as the AV nodal Wenckebach cycle length. Residual dual AV nodal physiology was present. No echo beats could be induced.

Conclusions:

1. Normal SA nodal function.

2. Normal AV nodal function.

   a. Dual AV nodal pathways.

3. Normal His-Purkinje responses.

   a. No evidence of infra-His block.

4. Intact retrograde VA conduction with decremental concentric properties.

5. No evidence of accessory pathway.

6. History of sustained narrow QRS complex tachycardia.

   a. No inducible sustained supraventricular tachycardia following the administration of IV isoproterenol.

7. Apparently successful empiric RF modification of the slow antegrade Av nodal pathway.

Procedure Codes Reported:
93609, 93623, and 93653

Other Codes Reported:
Report the applicable catheter device codes.

93609 - Tachycardia

Case Example #4

Electrophysiology Study Report

History:

A 47-year-old woman with palpitations since age 16, documented AVNRT and AT. She has a normal ejection fraction and stress testing was normal. She has been maintained on lopressor and flecanide with minimal effect and has continued to have daily tachycardia.

Procedure:

The patient was brought to the EP lab, and the right groin was prepped and draped in the usual sterile fashion. The sheaths were inserted using modified Seldinger approach. The catheters were advanced to their respective positions under fluoroscopic guidance. **Coronary sinus, RA and RV apex pacing and recording were performed. HIS recording performed. Isuprel was given to assist tachycardia induction. Three-dimensional mapping using ESI was performed. Ablation was performed in the anterior lateral right atrium distant from the HIS bundle, SA node, and phrenic nerve locations.** At the conclusion of the procedure the sheaths were removed and hemostasis achieved without difficulty.

Procedure Codes Reported:
93613, 93623, and 93653

Other Codes Reported:
Report the applicable catheter device codes.

Appendix A: APCs and Payment Rates

Following is information for the addendum B table from the 2018 OPPS final rule, crosswalking CPT®/HCPCS codes to their associated APCs and payment rates.

CPT/HCPCS Code	Descriptor	CI	SI	APC	Relative Weight	Payment Rate	National Unadjusted Copayment	Minimum Unadjusted Copayment
0075T	Perq stent/chest vert art		C					
0076T	S&i stent/chest vert art		C					
0200T	Perq sacral augmt unilat inj		J1	5114	71.2909	$5,606.03		$1,121.21
0201T	Perq sacral augmt bilat inj		J1	5114	71.2909	$5,606.03		$1,121.21
0202T	Post vert arthrplst 1 lumbar		C					
0205T	Inirs each vessel add-on		N					
0206T	Cptr dbs alys car elec dta		Q1	5733	0.7116	$55.96		$11.20
0228T	Njx tfrml eprl w/us cer/thor		T	5443	8.5474	$672.13		$134.43
0229T	Njx tfrml eprl w/us cer/thor		N					
0230T	Njx tfrml eprl w/us lumb/sac		T	5443	8.5474	$672.13		$134.43
0231T	Njx tfrml eprl w/us lumb/sac		N					
0234T	Trluml perip athrc renal art		J1	5193	133.6503	$10,509.72		$2,101.95
0235T	Trluml perip athrc visceral		C					
0236T	Trluml perip athrc abd aorta		J1	5193	133.6503	$10,509.72		$2,101.95
0237T	Trluml perip athrc brchiocph		J1	5193	133.6503	$10,509.72		$2,101.95
0238T	Trluml perip athrc iliac art		J1	5194	203.7145	$16,019.29		$3,203.86
0254T	Evasc rpr iliac art bifur		C					
0255T	Evasc rpr iliac art bifr s&i	CH	D					
0290T	Laser inc for pkp/lkp recip		N					
0293T	Ins lt atrl press monitor	CH	D					
0294T	Ins lt atrl mont pres lead	CH	D					
0312T	Laps impltj nstim vagus		J1	5464	354.6704	$27,889.86		$5,577.98
0313T	Laps rmvl nstim array vagus		T	5461	36.6139	$2,879.17		$575.84
0314T	Laps rmvl vgl arry&pls gen		Q2	5461	36.6139	$2,879.17		$575.84
0315T	Rmvl vagus nerve pls gen		Q2	5461	36.6139	$2,879.17		$575.84
0316T	Replc vagus nerve pls gen		J1	5463	233.5777	$18,367.62		$3,673.53
0317T	Elec alys vagus nrv pls gen		Q1	5741	0.4798	$37.73		$7.55
0329T	Mntr io press 24hrs/> uni/bi		E1					
0330T	Tear film img uni/bi w/i&r		Q1	5732	0.4044	$31.80		$6.36
0331T	Heart symp image plnr		S	5593	15.2932	$1,202.60		$240.52
0332T	Heart symp image plnr spect		S	5593	15.2932	$1,202.60		$240.52
0333T	Visual ep acuity screen auto		E1					
0335T	Extraosseous joint stblztion		J1	5114	71.2909	$5,606.03		$1,121.21
0337T	Endothel fxnassmnt non-invas		Q1	5733	0.7116	$55.96		$11.20
0338T	Trnscth renal symp denrv unl		J1	5192	64.6607	$5,084.66		$1,016.94
0339T	Trnscth renal symp denrv bil		J1	5192	64.6607	$5,084.66		$1,016.94
0345T	Transcath mtral vlve repair		C					
0387T	Leadless c pm ins/rpl ventr		J1	5194	203.7145	$16,019.29		$3,203.86

CPT/HCPCS Code	Descriptor	CI	SI	APC	Relative Weight	Payment Rate	National Unadjusted Copayment	Minimum Unadjusted Copayment
0388T	Leadless c pm remove ventr	CH	T	5183	31.6976	$2,492.57		$498.52
0389T	Prog eval inper leadls pm		Q1	5741	0.4798	$37.73		$7.55
0390T	Periproc eval inper ledls pm		N					
0391T	Intergt eval inper leadls pm		Q1	5741	0.4798	$37.73		$7.55
0394T	Hdr elctrnc skn surf brchytx		S	5622	2.7954	$219.82		$43.97
0395T	Hdr elctr ntrst/ntrcv brchtx		S	5624	9.0806	$714.06		$142.82
0396T	Intraop kinetic balnce sensr		N					
0397T	Ercp w/optical endomicroscpy		N					
0398T	Mrgfus strtctc les abltj	CH	S	1576		$17,500.50		$3,500.10
0399T	Myocardial strain imaging		N					
0400T	Mltispectrl digital les alys		N					
0401T	Mltispectrl digital les alys		N					
0402T	Collagen crosslinking cornea	CH	J1	5503	23.0330	$1,811.22		$362.25
0403T	Diabetes prev standard curr		E1					
0404T	Trnscrv uterin fibroid abltj		J1	5416	79.9497	$6,286.92	$1,405.70	$1,257.39
0405T	Ovrsght xtrcorp liv asst pat		B					
0406T	Sin ndsc plmt drg elut mplnt		Q2	5153	16.8321	$1,323.61		$264.73
0407T	Sin ndsc plmt drg elut mplnt		Q2	5153	16.8321	$1,323.61		$264.73
0408T	Insj/rplc cardiac modulj sys		J1	5231	281.1561	$22,108.99		$4,421.80
0409T	Insj/rplc car modulj pls gn		J1	5231	281.1561	$22,108.99		$4,421.80
0410T	Insj/rplc car modulj atr elt		J1	5222	93.7291	$7,370.48		$1,474.10
0411T	Insj/rplc car modulj vnt elt		J1	5222	93.7291	$7,370.48		$1,474.10
0412T	Rmvl cardiac modulj pls gen		Q2	5221	36.4686	$2,867.74		$573.55
0413T	Rmvl car modulj tranvns elt		Q2	5221	36.4686	$2,867.74		$573.55
0414T	Rmvl & rpl car modulj pls gn		J1	5231	281.1561	$22,108.99		$4,421.80
0415T	Repos car modulj tranvns elt		T	5181	7.7894	$612.53		$122.51
0416T	Reloc skin pocket pls gen		T	5054	19.9440	$1,568.32		$313.67
0417T	Prgrmg eval cardiac modulj		Q1	5741	0.4798	$37.73		$7.55
0418T	Interro eval cardiac modulj		Q1	5741	0.4798	$37.73		$7.55
0419T	Dstrj neurofibroma xtnsv		T	5053	6.2080	$488.17		$97.64
0420T	Dstrj neurofibroma xtnsv		T	5053	6.2080	$488.17		$97.64
0421T	Waterjet prostate abltj cmpl	CH	J1	5375	47.1256	$3,705.77		$741.16
0422T	Tactile breast img uni/bi		Q1	5521	0.7899	$62.11		$12.43
0423T	Assay secretory type ii pla2		A					
0424T	Insj/rplc nstim apnea compl		J1	5464	354.6704	$27,889.86		$5,577.98
0425T	Insj/rplc nstim apnea sen ld		J1	5462	77.0028	$6,055.19		$1,211.04
0426T	Insj/rplc nstim apnea stm ld		J1	5463	233.5777	$18,367.62		$3,673.53
0427T	Insj/rplc nstim apnea pls gn		J1	5463	233.5777	$18,367.62		$3,673.53
0428T	Rmvl nstim apnea pls gen		Q2	5461	36.6139	$2,879.17		$575.84
0429T	Rmvl nstim apnea sen ld		Q2	5461	36.6139	$2,879.17		$575.84
0430T	Rmvl nstim apnea stimj ld		Q2	5461	36.6139	$2,879.17		$575.84
0431T	Rmvl/rplc nstim apnea pls gn		J1	5463	233.5777	$18,367.62		$3,673.53
0432T	Repos nstim apnea stimj ld		T	5461	36.6139	$2,879.17		$575.84

CPT/HCPCS Code	Descriptor	CI	SI	APC	Relative Weight	Payment Rate	National Unadjusted Copayment	Minimum Unadjusted Copayment
0433T	Repos nstim apnea sensing ld		T	5461	36.6139	$2,879.17		$575.84
0434T	Interro eval npgs apnea		S	5742	1.4646	$115.17		$23.04
0435T	Prgrmg eval npgs apnea 1 ses		S	5742	1.4646	$115.17		$23.04
0436T	Prgrmg eval npgs apnea study		S	5724	11.4822	$902.91		$180.59
0437T	Impltj synth rnfcmt abdl wal		N					
0438T	Tprnl plmt biodegrdabl matrl	CH	D					
0439T	Myocrd contrast prfuj echo		N					
0440T	Abltj perc uxtr/perph nrv		J1	5432	58.8442	$4,627.27		$925.46
0441T	Abltj perc lxtr/perph nrv		J1	5432	58.8442	$4,627.27		$925.46
0442T	Abltj perc plex/trncl nrv		J1	5432	58.8442	$4,627.27		$925.46
0443T	R-t spctrl alys prst8 tiss		N					
0444T	1st plmt drug elut oc ins		N					
0445T	Sbsqt plmt drug elut oc ins		N					
0446T	Insj impltbl glucose sensor		T	5053	6.2080	$488.17		$97.64
0447T	Rmvl impltbl glucose sensor		Q2	5051	2.1483	$168.93		$33.79
0448T	Remvl insj impltbl gluc sens		T	5053	6.2080	$488.17		$97.64
0449T	Insj aqueous drain dev 1st		J1	5492	45.9141	$3,610.50		$722.10
0450T	Insj aqueous drain dev each		N					
0451T	Insj/rplcmt aortic ventr sys		C					
0452T	Insj/rplcmt dev vasc seal		C					
0453T	Insj/rplcmt mech-elec ntrfce		J1	5222	93.7291	$7,370.48		$1,474.10
0454T	Insj/rplcmt subq electrode		J1	5222	93.7291	$7,370.48		$1,474.10
0455T	Remvl aortic ventr cmpl sys		C					
0456T	Remvl aortic dev vasc seal		C					
0457T	Remvl mech-elec skin ntrfce		Q2	5221	36.4686	$2,867.74		$573.55
0458T	Remvl subq electrode		Q2	5221	36.4686	$2,867.74		$573.55
0459T	Relocaj rplcmt aortic ventr		C					
0460T	Repos aortic ventr dev eltrd		T	5221	36.4686	$2,867.74		$573.55
0461T	Repos aortic contrpulsj dev		C					
0462T	Prgrmg eval aortic ventr sys		S	5743	3.3302	$261.87		$52.38
0463T	Interrog aortic ventr sys		S	5743	3.3302	$261.87		$52.38
0464T	Visual ep test for glaucoma		S	5721	1.7334	$136.31		$27.27
0465T	Supchrdl njx rx w/o supply		T	5694	3.7838	$297.54		$59.51
0466T	Insj ch wal respir eltrd/ra		N					
0467T	Revj/rplmnt ch respir eltrd		Q2	5461	36.6139	$2,879.17		$575.84
0468T	Rmvl ch wal respir eltrd/ra		Q2	5461	36.6139	$2,879.17		$575.84
0469T	Rta polarize scan oc scr bi	NC	E1					
0470T	Oct skn img acquisj i&r 1st	NC	M					
0471T	Oct skn img acquisj i&r addl	NC	N					
0472T	Prgrmg io rta eltrd ra	NC	Q1	5743	3.3302	$261.87		$52.38
0473T	Reprgrmg io rta eltrd ra	NC	Q1	5742	1.4646	$115.17		$23.04
0474T	Insj aqueous drg dev io rsvr	NC	J1	5492	45.9141	$3,610.50		$722.10
0475T	Rec ftl car sgl 3 ch i&r	NC	M					

CPT/HCPCS Code	Descriptor	CI	SI	APC	Relative Weight	Payment Rate	National Unadjusted Copayment	Minimum Unadjusted Copayment
0476T	Rec ftl car sgl elec tr data	NC	Q1	5734	1.3357	$105.03		$21.01
0477T	Rec ftl car sgl xrtj alys	NC	Q1	5734	1.3357	$105.03		$21.01
0478T	Rec ftl car 3 ch rev i&r	NC	M					
0479T	Fxjl abl lsr 1st 100 sq cm	NC	T	5052	3.9521	$310.78		$62.16
0480T	Fxjl abl lsr ea addl 100sqcm	NC	N					
0481T	Njx autol wbc concentrate	NC	Q1	5735	4.1964	$329.99		$66.00
0482T	Absl quan myocrd bld flo pet	NC	N					
0483T	Tmvi percutaneous approach	NC	C					
0484T	Tmvi transthoracic exposure	NC	C					
0485T	Oct mid ear i&r unilateral	NC	Q1	5732	0.4044	$31.80		$6.36
0486T	Oct mid ear i&r bilateral	NC	Q1	5732	0.4044	$31.80		$6.36
0487T	Trvg biomchn mapg w/reprt	NC	Q1	5734	1.3357	$105.03		$21.01
0488T	Diabetes prev online/elec	NC	E1					
0489T	Regn cell tx scldr hands	NC	E1					
0490T	Regn cell tx scldr h mlt inj	NC	E1					
0491T	Abl lsr opn wnd 1st 20 sqcm	NC	T	5052	3.9521	$310.78		$62.16
0492T	Abl lsr opn wnd addl 20 sqcm	NC	N					
0493T	Near ifr spectrsc of wounds	NC	N					
0494T	Prep & cannulj cdvr don lung	NC	C					
0495T	Mntr cdvr don lng 1st 2 hrs	NC	C					
0496T	Mntr cdvr don lng ea addl hr	NC	C					
0497T	Xtrnl pt act ecg in-off conn	NC	Q1	5741	0.4798	$37.73		$7.55
0498T	Xtrnl pt act ecg r&i pr 30 d	NC	M					
0499T	Cysto f/urtl strix/stenosis	NC	E1					
0500T	Hpv 5+ hi risk hpv types	NC	A					
0501T	Cor ffr derived cor cta data	NC	M					
0502T	Cor ffr data prep & transmis	NC	N					
0503T	Cor ffr alys gnrj ffr mdl	NC	S	1516		$1,450.50		$290.10
0504T	Cor ffr data review i&r	NC	M					
10021	Fna w/o image		T	5052	3.9521	$310.78		$62.16
10022	Fna w/image		T	5071	7.2843	$572.81		$114.57
10030	Guide cathet fluid drainage		T	5071	7.2843	$572.81		$114.57
10035	Perq dev soft tiss 1st imag		T	5071	7.2843	$572.81		$114.57
10036	Perq dev soft tiss add imag		N					
10040	Acne surgery		Q1	5051	2.1483	$168.93		$33.79
10060	Drainage of skin abscess		T	5051	2.1483	$168.93		$33.79
10061	Drainage of skin abscess		T	5052	3.9521	$310.78		$62.16
10080	Drainage of pilonidal cyst		T	5071	7.2843	$572.81		$114.57
10081	Drainage of pilonidal cyst		T	5071	7.2843	$572.81		$114.57
10120	Remove foreign body		T	5052	3.9521	$310.78		$62.16
10121	Remove foreign body		J1	5072	17.1415	$1,347.94		$269.59
10140	Drainage of hematoma/fluid		J1	5072	17.1415	$1,347.94		$269.59
10160	Puncture drainage of lesion		T	5052	3.9521	$310.78		$62.16

CPT/HCPCS Code	Descriptor	CI	SI	APC	Relative Weight	Payment Rate	National Unadjusted Copayment	Minimum Unadjusted Copayment
10180	Complex drainage wound		J1	5073	29.5628	$2,324.70		$464.94
11981	Insert drug implant device		Q1	5734	1.3357	$105.03		$21.01
11982	Remove drug implant device		Q1	5735	4.1964	$329.99		$66.00
11983	Remove/insert drug implant		Q1	5735	4.1964	$329.99		$66.00
19000	Drainage of breast lesion		T	5071	7.2843	$572.81		$114.57
19001	Drain breast lesion add-on		N					
19020	Incision of breast lesion		J1	5072	17.1415	$1,347.94		$269.59
19030	Injection for breast x-ray		N					
19081	Bx breast 1st lesion strtctc		J1	5072	17.1415	$1,347.94		$269.59
19082	Bx breast add lesion strtctc		N					
19083	Bx breast 1st lesion us imag		J1	5072	17.1415	$1,347.94		$269.59
19084	Bx breast add lesion us imag		N					
19085	Bx breast 1st lesion mr imag		J1	5072	17.1415	$1,347.94		$269.59
19086	Bx breast add lesion mr imag		N					
19100	Bx breast percut w/o image		J1	5072	17.1415	$1,347.94		$269.59
19101	Biopsy of breast open		J1	5091	34.6871	$2,727.65		$545.53
19105	Cryosurg ablate fa each		J1	5091	34.6871	$2,727.65		$545.53
19281	Perq device breast 1st imag		Q1	5071	7.2843	$572.81		$114.57
19282	Perq device breast ea imag		N					
19283	Perq dev breast 1st strtctc		Q1	5071	7.2843	$572.81		$114.57
19284	Perq dev breast add strtctc		N					
19285	Perq dev breast 1st us imag		Q1	5071	7.2843	$572.81		$114.57
19286	Perq dev breast add us imag		N					
19287	Perq dev breast 1st mr guide		Q1	5071	7.2843	$572.81		$114.57
19288	Perq dev breast add mr guide		N					
19294	Prep tum cav iort prtl mast	NC	N					
19296	Place po breast cath for rad		J1	5093	93.9419	$7,387.22		$1,477.45
19297	Place breast cath for rad		N					
19298	Place breast rad tube/caths		J1	5092	61.1875	$4,811.54		$962.31
19300	Removal of breast tissue		J1	5091	34.6871	$2,727.65		$545.53
20206	Needle biopsy muscle		J1	5072	17.1415	$1,347.94		$269.59
20220	Bone biopsy trocar/needle		J1	5072	17.1415	$1,347.94		$269.59
20225	Bone biopsy trocar/needle		J1	5072	17.1415	$1,347.94		$269.59
20500	Injection of sinus tract		T	5163	14.4730	$1,138.10		$227.62
20501	Inject sinus tract for x-ray		N					
20520	Removal of foreign body		J1	5072	17.1415	$1,347.94		$269.59
20525	Removal of foreign body		J1	5073	29.5628	$2,324.70		$464.94
20600	Drain/inj joint/bursa w/o us		T	5441	3.1116	$244.68		$48.94
20604	Drain/inj joint/bursa w/us		T	5441	3.1116	$244.68		$48.94
20605	Drain/inj joint/bursa w/o us		T	5441	3.1116	$244.68		$48.94
20606	Drain/inj joint/bursa w/us		T	5442	6.9096	$543.34		$108.67
20610	Drain/inj joint/bursa w/o us		T	5441	3.1116	$244.68		$48.94
20611	Drain/inj joint/bursa w/us		T	5441	3.1116	$244.68		$48.94

CPT/HCPCS Code	Descriptor	CI	SI	APC	Relative Weight	Payment Rate	National Unadjusted Copayment	Minimum Unadjusted Copayment
21116	Injection jaw joint x-ray		N					
22510	Perq cervicothoracic inject		J1	5113	33.6365	$2,645.04		$529.01
22511	Perq lumbosacral injection		J1	5113	33.6365	$2,645.04		$529.01
22512	Vertebroplasty addl inject		N					
22513	Perq vertebral augmentation		J1	5114	71.2909	$5,606.03		$1,121.21
22514	Perq vertebral augmentation		J1	5114	71.2909	$5,606.03		$1,121.21
22515	Perq vertebral augmentation		N					
23350	Injection for shoulder x-ray		N					
24220	Injection for elbow x-ray		N					
25246	Injection for wrist x-ray		N					
27093	Injection for hip x-ray		N					
27095	Injection for hip x-ray		N					
27096	Inject sacroiliac joint		B					
27370	Injection for knee x-ray		N					
27648	Injection for ankle x-ray		N					
32400	Needle biopsy chest lining		J1	5072	17.1415	$1,347.94		$269.59
32405	Percut bx lung/mediastinum		J1	5072	17.1415	$1,347.94		$269.59
32550	Insert pleural cath		J1	5341	37.0182	$2,910.96		$582.20
32551	Insertion of chest tube	CH	T	5182	12.4994	$982.90		$196.58
32552	Remove lung catheter		Q2	5181	7.7894	$612.53		$122.51
32553	Ins mark thor for rt perq		S	5613	15.0898	$1,186.60		$237.32
32554	Aspirate pleura w/o imaging		T	5181	7.7894	$612.53		$122.51
32555	Aspirate pleura w/ imaging		T	5181	7.7894	$612.53		$122.51
32556	Insert cath pleura w/o image		J1	5302	18.1506	$1,427.29		$285.46
32557	Insert cath pleura w/ image	CH	T	5182	12.4994	$982.90		$196.58
32560	Treat pleurodesis w/agent		T	5181	7.7894	$612.53		$122.51
32561	Lyse chest fibrin init day		T	5181	7.7894	$612.53		$122.51
32562	Lyse chest fibrin subq day		T	5181	7.7894	$612.53		$122.51
32960	Therapeutic pneumothorax		T	5181	7.7894	$612.53		$122.51
32994	Ablate pulm tumor perq crybl	NC	J1	5361	57.0778	$4,488.37		$897.68
32998	Ablate pulm tumor perq rf		J1	5361	57.0778	$4,488.37		$897.68
32999	Chest surgery procedure		T	5181	7.7894	$612.53		$122.51
33010	Drainage of heart sac	CH	T	5182	12.4994	$982.90		$196.58
33011	Repeat drainage of heart sac	CH	T	5182	12.4994	$982.90		$196.58
33202	Insert epicard eltrd open		C					
33203	Insert epicard eltrd endo		C					
33206	Insert heart pm atrial		J1	5223	123.9549	$9,747.32		$1,949.47
33207	Insert heart pm ventricular		J1	5223	123.9549	$9,747.32		$1,949.47
33208	Insrt heart pm atrial & vent		J1	5223	123.9549	$9,747.32		$1,949.47
33210	Insert electrd/pm cath sngl		J1	5222	93.7291	$7,370.48		$1,474.10
33211	Insert card electrodes dual		J1	5222	93.7291	$7,370.48		$1,474.10
33212	Insert pulse gen sngl lead		J1	5222	93.7291	$7,370.48		$1,474.10
33213	Insert pulse gen dual leads		J1	5223	123.9549	$9,747.32		$1,949.47

CPT/HCPCS Code	Descriptor	CI	SI	APC	Relative Weight	Payment Rate	National Unadjusted Copayment	Minimum Unadjusted Copayment
33214	Upgrade of pacemaker system		J1	5223	123.9549	$9,747.32		$1,949.47
33215	Reposition pacing-defib lead	CH	T	5183	31.6976	$2,492.57		$498.52
33216	Insert 1 electrode pm-defib		J1	5222	93.7291	$7,370.48		$1,474.10
33217	Insert 2 electrode pm-defib		J1	5222	93.7291	$7,370.48		$1,474.10
33218	Repair lead pace-defib one		T	5221	36.4686	$2,867.74		$573.55
33220	Repair lead pace-defib dual		T	5221	36.4686	$2,867.74		$573.55
33221	Insert pulse gen mult leads		J1	5224	223.6167	$17,584.32		$3,516.87
33222	Relocation pocket pacemaker		T	5054	19.9440	$1,568.32		$313.67
33223	Relocate pocket for defib		T	5054	19.9440	$1,568.32		$313.67
33224	Insert pacing lead & connect		J1	5223	123.9549	$9,747.32		$1,949.47
33225	L ventric pacing lead add-on		N					
33226	Reposition l ventric lead	CH	T	5183	31.6976	$2,492.57		$498.52
33227	Remove&replace pm gen singl		J1	5222	93.7291	$7,370.48		$1,474.10
33228	Remv&replc pm gen dual lead		J1	5223	123.9549	$9,747.32		$1,949.47
33229	Remv&replc pm gen mult leads		J1	5224	223.6167	$17,584.32		$3,516.87
33230	Insrt pulse gen w/dual leads		J1	5231	281.1561	$22,108.99		$4,421.80
33231	Insrt pulse gen w/mult leads		J1	5232	393.7127	$30,959.99		$6,192.00
33233	Removal of pm generator		Q2	5222	93.7291	$7,370.48		$1,474.10
33234	Removal of pacemaker system		Q2	5221	36.4686	$2,867.74		$573.55
33235	Removal pacemaker electrode		Q2	5221	36.4686	$2,867.74		$573.55
33236	Remove electrode/thoracotomy		C					
33237	Remove electrode/thoracotomy		C					
33238	Remove electrode/thoracotomy		C					
33240	Insrt pulse gen w/singl lead		J1	5231	281.1561	$22,108.99		$4,421.80
33241	Remove pulse generator		Q2	5221	36.4686	$2,867.74		$573.55
33243	Remove eltrd/thoracotomy		C					
33244	Remove elctrd transvenously		Q2	5221	36.4686	$2,867.74		$573.55
33249	Insj/rplcmt defib w/lead(s)		J1	5232	393.7127	$30,959.99		$6,192.00
33250	Ablate heart dysrhythm focus		C					
33251	Ablate heart dysrhythm focus		C					
33254	Ablate atria lmtd		C					
33255	Ablate atria w/o bypass ext		C					
33256	Ablate atria w/bypass exten		C					
33257	Ablate atria lmtd add-on		C					
33258	Ablate atria x10sv add-on		C					
33259	Ablate atria w/bypass add-on		C					
33261	Ablate heart dysrhythm focus		C					
33262	Rmvl& replc pulse gen 1 lead		J1	5231	281.1561	$22,108.99		$4,421.80
33263	Rmvl & rplcmt dfb gen 2 lead		J1	5231	281.1561	$22,108.99		$4,421.80
33264	Rmvl & rplcmt dfb gen mlt ld		J1	5232	393.7127	$30,959.99		$6,192.00
33265	Ablate atria lmtd endo		C					
33266	Ablate atria x10sv endo		C					
33270	Ins/rep subq defibrillator		J1	5232	393.7127	$30,959.99		$6,192.00

CPT/HCPCS Code	Descriptor	CI	SI	APC	Relative Weight	Payment Rate	National Unadjusted Copayment	Minimum Unadjusted Copayment
33271	Insj subq impltbl dfb elctrd		J1	5222	93.7291	$7,370.48		$1,474.10
33272	Rmvl of subq defibrillator		Q2	5221	36.4686	$2,867.74		$573.55
33273	Repos prev impltbl subq dfb		T	5221	36.4686	$2,867.74		$573.55
33282	Implant pat-active ht record		J1	5222	93.7291	$7,370.48		$1,474.10
33284	Remove pat-active ht record		Q2	5071	7.2843	$572.81		$114.57
33340	Perq clsr tcat l atr apndge		C					
33361	Replace aortic valve perq		C					
33362	Replace aortic valve open		C					
33363	Replace aortic valve open		C					
33364	Replace aortic valve open		C					
33365	Replace aortic valve open		C					
33366	Trcath replace aortic valve		C					
33418	Repair tcat mitral valve		C					
33419	Repair tcat mitral valve		N					
33420	Revision of mitral valve		C					
33477	Implant tcat pulm vlv perq		C					
33967	Insert i-aort percut device		C					
33968	Remove aortic assist device		C					
33981	Replace vad pump ext		C					
33982	Replace vad intra w/o bp		C					
33983	Replace vad intra w/bp		C					
33987	Artery expos/graft artery		C					
33988	Insertion of left heart vent		C					
33989	Removal of left heart vent		C					
33990	Insert vad artery access		C					
33991	Insert vad art&vein access		C					
33999	Cardiac surgery procedure		T	5181	7.7894	$612.53		$122.51
36000	Place needle in vein		N					
36002	Pseudoaneurysm injection trt		T	5181	7.7894	$612.53		$122.51
36005	Injection ext venography		N					
36010	Place catheter in vein		N					
36011	Place catheter in vein		N					
36012	Place catheter in vein		N					
36013	Place catheter in artery		N					
36014	Place catheter in artery		N					
36015	Place catheter in artery		N					
36100	Establish access to artery		N					
36120	Establish access to artery	CH	D					
36140	Intro ndl icath upr/lxtr art		N					
36160	Establish access to aorta		N					
36200	Place catheter in aorta		N					
36215	Place catheter in artery		N					
36216	Place catheter in artery		N					

CPT/HCPCS Code	Descriptor	CI	SI	APC	Relative Weight	Payment Rate	National Unadjusted Copayment	Minimum Unadjusted Copayment
36217	Place catheter in artery		N					
36218	Place catheter in artery		N					
36221	Place cath thoracic aorta	CH	Q2	5183	31.6976	$2,492.57		$498.52
36222	Place cath carotid/inom art	CH	Q2	5183	31.6976	$2,492.57		$498.52
36223	Place cath carotid/inom art	CH	Q2	5184	54.2330	$4,264.67		$852.94
36224	Place cath carotd art	CH	Q2	5184	54.2330	$4,264.67		$852.94
36225	Place cath subclavian art	CH	Q2	5183	31.6976	$2,492.57		$498.52
36226	Place cath vertebral art	CH	Q2	5184	54.2330	$4,264.67		$852.94
36227	Place cath xtrnl carotid		N					
36228	Place cath intracranial art		N					
36245	Ins cath abd/l-ext art 1st		N					
36246	Ins cath abd/l-ext art 2nd		N					
36247	Ins cath abd/l-ext art 3rd		N					
36248	Ins cath abd/l-ext art addl		N					
36251	Ins cath ren art 1st unilat	CH	Q2	5183	31.6976	$2,492.57		$498.52
36252	Ins cath ren art 1st bilat	CH	Q2	5183	31.6976	$2,492.57		$498.52
36253	Ins cath ren art 2nd+ unilat	CH	Q2	5184	54.2330	$4,264.67		$852.94
36254	Ins cath ren art 2nd+ bilat	CH	Q2	5183	31.6976	$2,492.57		$498.52
36260	Insertion of infusion pump	CH	T	5184	54.2330	$4,264.67		$852.94
36261	Revision of infusion pump		T	5221	36.4686	$2,867.74		$573.55
36262	Removal of infusion pump		Q2	5221	36.4686	$2,867.74		$573.55
36299	Vessel injection procedure		N					
36465	Njx noncmpnd sclrsnt 1 vein	NC	T	5054	19.9440	$1,568.32		$313.67
36466	Njx noncmpnd sclrsnt mlt vn	NC	T	5054	19.9440	$1,568.32		$313.67
36468	Njx sclrsnt spider veins		Q1	5051	2.1483	$168.93		$33.79
36470	Njx sclrsnt 1 incmptnt vein		T	5052	3.9521	$310.78		$62.16
36471	Njx sclrsnt mlt incmptnt vn		T	5052	3.9521	$310.78		$62.16
36473	Endovenous mchnchem 1st vein	CH	T	5183	31.6976	$2,492.57		$498.52
36474	Endovenous mchnchem add-on		N					
36475	Endovenous rf 1st vein	CH	T	5183	31.6976	$2,492.57		$498.52
36476	Endovenous rf vein add-on		N					
36478	Endovenous laser 1st vein	CH	T	5183	31.6976	$2,492.57		$498.52
36479	Endovenous laser vein addon		N					
36481	Insertion of catheter vein		N					
36482	Endoven ther chem adhes 1st	NC	T	5184	54.2330	$4,264.67		$852.94
36483	Endoven ther chem adhes sbsq	NC	N					
36500	Insertion of catheter vein		N					
36510	Insertion of catheter vein		N					
36555	Insert non-tunnel cv cath	CH	T	5182	12.4994	$982.90		$196.58
36556	Insert non-tunnel cv cath	CH	T	5182	12.4994	$982.90		$196.58
36557	Insert tunneled cv cath	CH	T	5184	54.2330	$4,264.67		$852.94
36558	Insert tunneled cv cath	CH	T	5183	31.6976	$2,492.57		$498.52
36560	Insert tunneled cv cath	CH	T	5183	31.6976	$2,492.57		$498.52

CPT/HCPCS Code	Descriptor	CI	SI	APC	Relative Weight	Payment Rate	National Unadjusted Copayment	Minimum Unadjusted Copayment
36561	Insert tunneled cv cath	CH	T	5183	31.6976	$2,492.57		$498.52
36563	Insert tunneled cv cath	CH	T	5184	54.2330	$4,264.67		$852.94
36565	Insert tunneled cv cath	CH	T	5183	31.6976	$2,492.57		$498.52
36566	Insert tunneled cv cath	CH	T	5184	54.2330	$4,264.67		$852.94
36568	Insert picc cath		T	5181	7.7894	$612.53		$122.51
36569	Insert picc cath	CH	T	5182	12.4994	$982.90		$196.58
36570	Insert picvad cath	CH	T	5183	31.6976	$2,492.57		$498.52
36571	Insert picvad cath	CH	T	5183	31.6976	$2,492.57		$498.52
36575	Repair tunneled cv cath		T	5181	7.7894	$612.53		$122.51
36576	Repair tunneled cv cath	CH	T	5182	12.4994	$982.90		$196.58
36578	Replace tunneled cv cath	CH	T	5183	31.6976	$2,492.57		$498.52
36580	Replace cvad cath	CH	T	5182	12.4994	$982.90		$196.58
36581	Replace tunneled cv cath	CH	T	5183	31.6976	$2,492.57		$498.52
36582	Replace tunneled cv cath	CH	T	5183	31.6976	$2,492.57		$498.52
36583	Replace tunneled cv cath	CH	T	5184	54.2330	$4,264.67		$852.94
36584	Replace picc cath	CH	T	5182	12.4994	$982.90		$196.58
36585	Replace picvad cath	CH	T	5183	31.6976	$2,492.57		$498.52
36589	Removal tunneled cv cath		Q2	5181	7.7894	$612.53		$122.51
36590	Removal tunneled cv cath		Q2	5181	7.7894	$612.53		$122.51
36591	Draw blood off venous device		Q1	5734	1.3357	$105.03		$21.01
36592	Collect blood from picc		Q1	5734	1.3357	$105.03		$21.01
36593	Declot vascular device		T	5694	3.7838	$297.54		$59.51
36595	Mech remov tunneled cv cath	CH	T	5183	31.6976	$2,492.57		$498.52
36596	Mech remov tunneled cv cath	CH	T	5182	12.4994	$982.90		$196.58
36597	Reposition venous catheter	CH	T	5182	12.4994	$982.90		$196.58
36598	Inj w/fluor eval cv device		T	5693	2.4299	$191.08		$38.22
36901	Intro cath dialysis circuit		T	5181	7.7894	$612.53		$122.51
36902	Intro cath dialysis circuit		J1	5192	64.6607	$5,084.66		$1,016.94
36903	Intro cath dialysis circuit		J1	5193	133.6503	$10,509.72		$2,101.95
36904	Thrmbc/nfs dialysis circuit		J1	5192	64.6607	$5,084.66		$1,016.94
36905	Thrmbc/nfs dialysis circuit		J1	5193	133.6503	$10,509.72		$2,101.95
36906	Thrmbc/nfs dialysis circuit		J1	5194	203.7145	$16,019.29		$3,203.86
36907	Balo angiop ctr dialysis seg		N					
36908	Stent plmt ctr dialysis seg		N					
36909	Dialysis circuit embolj		N					
37182	Insert hepatic shunt (tips)		C					
37183	Remove hepatic shunt (tips)		J1	5192	64.6607	$5,084.66		$1,016.94
37184	Prim art m-thrmbc 1st vsl	CH	J1	5192	64.6607	$5,084.66		$1,016.94
37185	Prim art m-thrmbc sbsq vsl		N					
37186	Sec art thrombectomy add-on		N					
37187	Venous mech thrombectomy	CH	J1	5192	64.6607	$5,084.66		$1,016.94
37188	Venous m-thrombectomy add-on	CH	T	5183	31.6976	$2,492.57		$498.52
37191	Ins endovas vena cava filtr	CH	T	5184	54.2330	$4,264.67		$852.94

CPT/HCPCS Code	Descriptor	CI	SI	APC	Relative Weight	Payment Rate	National Unadjusted Copayment	Minimum Unadjusted Copayment
37192	Redo endovas vena cava filtr	CH	T	5183	31.6976	$2,492.57		$498.52
37193	Rem endovas vena cava filter	CH	T	5183	31.6976	$2,492.57		$498.52
37195	Thrombolytic therapy stroke		T	5694	3.7838	$297.54		$59.51
37197	Remove intrvas foreign body	CH	T	5183	31.6976	$2,492.57		$498.52
37200	Transcatheter biopsy	CH	T	5184	54.2330	$4,264.67		$852.94
37211	Thrombolytic art therapy	CH	T	5184	54.2330	$4,264.67		$852.94
37212	Thrombolytic venous therapy	CH	T	5183	31.6976	$2,492.57		$498.52
37213	Thromblytic art/ven therapy	CH	T	5182	12.4994	$982.90		$196.58
37214	Cessj therapy cath removal	CH	T	5182	12.4994	$982.90		$196.58
37215	Transcath stent cca w/eps		C						
37216	Transcath stent cca w/o eps		E1						
37217	Stent placemt retro carotid		C						
37218	Stent placemt ante carotid		C						
37220	Iliac revasc		J1	5192	64.6607	$5,084.66		$1,016.94
37221	Iliac revasc w/stent		J1	5193	133.6503	$10,509.72		$2,101.95
37222	Iliac revasc add-on		N						
37223	Iliac revasc w/stent add-on		N						
37224	Fem/popl revas w/tla		J1	5192	64.6607	$5,084.66		$1,016.94
37225	Fem/popl revas w/ather		J1	5193	133.6503	$10,509.72		$2,101.95
37226	Fem/popl revasc w/stent		J1	5193	133.6503	$10,509.72		$2,101.95
37227	Fem/popl revasc stnt & ather		J1	5194	203.7145	$16,019.29		$3,203.86
37228	Tib/per revasc w/tla		J1	5193	133.6503	$10,509.72		$2,101.95
37229	Tib/per revasc w/ather		J1	5194	203.7145	$16,019.29		$3,203.86
37230	Tib/per revasc w/stent		J1	5194	203.7145	$16,019.29		$3,203.86
37231	Tib/per revasc stent & ather		J1	5194	203.7145	$16,019.29		$3,203.86
37232	Tib/per revasc add-on		N						
37233	Tibper revasc w/ather add-on		N						
37234	Revsc opn/prq tib/pero stent		N						
37235	Tib/per revasc stnt & ather		N						
37236	Open/perq place stent 1st		J1	5193	133.6503	$10,509.72		$2,101.95
37237	Open/perq place stent ea add		N						
37238	Open/perq place stent same		J1	5193	133.6503	$10,509.72		$2,101.95
37239	Open/perq place stent ea add		N						
37241	Vasc embolize/occlude venous		J1	5193	133.6503	$10,509.72		$2,101.95
37242	Vasc embolize/occlude artery		J1	5193	133.6503	$10,509.72		$2,101.95
37243	Vasc embolize/occlude organ		J1	5193	133.6503	$10,509.72		$2,101.95
37244	Vasc embolize/occlude bleed		J1	5193	133.6503	$10,509.72		$2,101.95
37246	Trluml balo angiop 1st art		J1	5192	64.6607	$5,084.66		$1,016.94
37247	Trluml balo angiop addl art		N						
37248	Trluml balo angiop 1st vein		J1	5192	64.6607	$5,084.66		$1,016.94
37249	Trluml balo angiop addl vein		N						
37252	Intrvasc us noncoronary 1st		N						
37253	Intrvasc us noncoronary addl		N						

CPT/HCPCS Code	Descriptor	CI	SI	APC	Relative Weight	Payment Rate	National Unadjusted Copayment	Minimum Unadjusted Copayment
37765	Stab phleb veins xtr 10-20	CH	T	5183	31.6976	$2,492.57		$498.52
37766	Phleb veins - extrem 20+	CH	T	5183	31.6976	$2,492.57		$498.52
38200	Injection for spleen x-ray		N					
38790	Inject for lymphatic x-ray		N					
38792	Ra tracer id of sentinl node		Q1	5591	4.4435	$349.42		$69.89
38794	Access thoracic lymph duct		N					
42400	Biopsy of salivary gland		T	5071	7.2843	$572.81		$114.57
42405	Biopsy of salivary gland		J1	5164	27.9630	$2,198.90		$439.78
43752	Nasal/orogastric w/tube plmt		Q1	5735	4.1964	$329.99		$66.00
43753	Tx gastro intub w/asp		Q1	5722	3.1641	$248.81		$49.77
43754	Dx gastr intub w/asp spec		Q1	5722	3.1641	$248.81		$49.77
43755	Dx gastr intub w/asp specs		S	5721	1.7334	$136.31		$27.27
43756	Dx duod intub w/asp spec		Q1	5301	9.4542	$743.44		$148.69
43757	Dx duod intub w/asp specs		T	5301	9.4542	$743.44		$148.69
43760	Change gastrostomy tube		T	5371	2.9187	$229.51		$45.91
43761	Reposition gastrostomy tube		T	5371	2.9187	$229.51		$45.91
43830	Place gastrostomy tube		J1	5302	18.1506	$1,427.29		$285.46
43831	Place gastrostomy tube		T	5301	9.4542	$743.44		$148.69
43832	Place gastrostomy tube		C					
44500	Intro gastrointestinal tube		T	5301	9.4542	$743.44		$148.69
47000	Needle biopsy of liver		J1	5072	17.1415	$1,347.94		$269.59
47001	Needle biopsy liver add-on		N					
47010	Open drainage liver lesion		C					
47015	Inject/aspirate liver cyst		C					
47100	Wedge biopsy of liver		C					
47380	Open ablate liver tumor rf		C					
47381	Open ablate liver tumor cryo		C					
47382	Percut ablate liver rf		J1	5361	57.0778	$4,488.37		$897.68
47383	Perq abltj lvr cryoablation		J1	5361	57.0778	$4,488.37		$897.68
47400	Incision of liver duct		C					
47531	Injection for cholangiogram		Q2	5341	37.0182	$2,910.96		$582.20
47532	Injection for cholangiogram		Q2	5341	37.0182	$2,910.96		$582.20
47533	Plmt biliary drainage cath		J1	5341	37.0182	$2,910.96		$582.20
47534	Plmt biliary drainage cath		J1	5341	37.0182	$2,910.96		$582.20
47535	Conversion ext bil drg cath		J1	5341	37.0182	$2,910.96		$582.20
47536	Exchange biliary drg cath		J1	5341	37.0182	$2,910.96		$582.20
47537	Removal biliary drg cath		Q2	5301	9.4542	$743.44		$148.69
47538	Perq plmt bile duct stent		J1	5361	57.0778	$4,488.37		$897.68
47539	Perq plmt bile duct stent		J1	5361	57.0778	$4,488.37		$897.68
47540	Perq plmt bile duct stent		J1	5361	57.0778	$4,488.37		$897.68
47541	Plmt access bil tree sm bwl		J1	5341	37.0182	$2,910.96		$582.20
47542	Dilate biliary duct/ampulla		N					
47543	Endoluminal bx biliary tree		N					

CPT/HCPCS Code	Descriptor	CI	SI	APC	Relative Weight	Payment Rate	National Unadjusted Copayment	Minimum Unadjusted Copayment
47544	Removal duct glbldr calculi		N					
47550	Bile duct endoscopy add-on		C					
47552	Biliary endo perq dx w/speci		J1	5341	37.0182	$2,910.96		$582.20
47553	Biliary endoscopy thru skin		J1	5341	37.0182	$2,910.96		$582.20
47554	Biliary endoscopy thru skin		J1	5361	57.0778	$4,488.37		$897.68
47555	Biliary endoscopy thru skin		J1	5341	37.0182	$2,910.96		$582.20
47556	Biliary endoscopy thru skin		J1	5361	57.0778	$4,488.37		$897.68
47801	Placement bile duct support		C					
48102	Needle biopsy pancreas		J1	5072	17.1415	$1,347.94		$269.59
48510	Drain pancreatic pseudocyst		C					
49082	Abd paracentesis		T	5301	9.4542	$743.44		$148.69
49083	Abd paracentesis w/imaging		T	5301	9.4542	$743.44		$148.69
49084	Peritoneal lavage		T	5301	9.4542	$743.44		$148.69
49180	Biopsy abdominal mass		J1	5072	17.1415	$1,347.94		$269.59
49185	Sclerotx fluid collection		T	5071	7.2843	$572.81		$114.57
49400	Air injection into abdomen		N					
49402	Remove foreign body adbomen		J1	5341	37.0182	$2,910.96		$582.20
49405	Image cath fluid colxn visc		J1	5072	17.1415	$1,347.94		$269.59
49406	Image cath fluid peri/retro		J1	5072	17.1415	$1,347.94		$269.59
49407	Image cath fluid trns/vgnl		J1	5072	17.1415	$1,347.94		$269.59
49411	Ins mark abd/pel for rt perq		S	5613	15.0898	$1,186.60		$237.32
49412	Ins device for rt guide open		C					
49418	Insert tun ip cath perc		J1	5341	37.0182	$2,910.96		$582.20
49419	Insert tun ip cath w/port	CH	T	5184	54.2330	$4,264.67		$852.94
49421	Ins tun ip cath for dial opn		J1	5341	37.0182	$2,910.96		$582.20
49422	Remove tunneled ip cath	CH	Q2	5183	31.6976	$2,492.57		$498.52
49423	Exchange drainage catheter		J1	5302	18.1506	$1,427.29		$285.46
49424	Assess cyst contrast inject		N					
49425	Insert abdomen-venous drain		C					
49426	Revise abdomen-venous shunt		J1	5341	37.0182	$2,910.96		$582.20
49427	Injection abdominal shunt		N					
49429	Removal of shunt	CH	Q2	5183	31.6976	$2,492.57		$498.52
49435	Insert subq exten to ip cath		N					
49436	Embedded ip cath exit-site		J1	5302	18.1506	$1,427.29		$285.46
49440	Place gastrostomy tube perc		J1	5302	18.1506	$1,427.29		$285.46
49441	Place duod/jej tube perc		J1	5302	18.1506	$1,427.29		$285.46
49442	Place cecostomy tube perc		T	5312	11.9071	$936.33		$187.27
49446	Change g-tube to g-j perc		J1	5302	18.1506	$1,427.29		$285.46
49450	Replace g/c tube perc		T	5301	9.4542	$743.44		$148.69
49451	Replace duod/jej tube perc		T	5301	9.4542	$743.44		$148.69
49452	Replace g-j tube perc		T	5301	9.4542	$743.44		$148.69
49460	Fix g/colon tube w/device		T	5301	9.4542	$743.44		$148.69
49465	Fluoro exam of g/colon tube	CH	Q1	5522	1.5100	$118.74		$23.75

CPT/HCPCS Code	Descriptor	CI	SI	APC	Relative Weight	Payment Rate	National Unadjusted Copayment	Minimum Unadjusted Copayment
49999	Abdomen surgery procedure		T	5301	9.4542	$743.44		$148.69
50080	Removal of kidney stone		J1	5376	96.5936	$7,595.73		$1,519.15
50081	Removal of kidney stone		J1	5376	96.5936	$7,595.73		$1,519.15
50200	Renal biopsy perq		J1	5072	17.1415	$1,347.94		$269.59
50382	Change ureter stent percut		J1	5373	21.5622	$1,695.57		$339.12
50384	Remove ureter stent percut		Q2	5373	21.5622	$1,695.57		$339.12
50385	Change stent via transureth		J1	5373	21.5622	$1,695.57		$339.12
50386	Remove stent via transureth		Q2	5373	21.5622	$1,695.57		$339.12
50387	Change nephroureteral cath		J1	5373	21.5622	$1,695.57		$339.12
50389	Remove renal tube w/fluoro		Q2	5372	7.1921	$565.56		$113.12
50390	Drainage of kidney lesion		T	5071	7.2843	$572.81		$114.57
50391	Instll rx agnt into rnal tub		T	5371	2.9187	$229.51		$45.91
50395	Create passage to kidney		J1	5374	34.2919	$2,696.58		$539.32
50396	Measure kidney pressure	CH	J1	5373	21.5622	$1,695.57		$339.12
50430	Njx px nfrosgrm &/urtrgrm		Q2	5372	7.1921	$565.56		$113.12
50431	Njx px nfrosgrm &/urtrgrm		Q2	5372	7.1921	$565.56		$113.12
50432	Plmt nephrostomy catheter		J1	5373	21.5622	$1,695.57		$339.12
50433	Plmt nephroureteral catheter		J1	5373	21.5622	$1,695.57		$339.12
50434	Convert nephrostomy catheter	CH	J1	5373	21.5622	$1,695.57		$339.12
50435	Exchange nephrostomy cath	CH	J1	5373	21.5622	$1,695.57		$339.12
50592	Perc rf ablate renal tumor		J1	5361	57.0778	$4,488.37		$897.68
50593	Perc cryo ablate renal tum		J1	5362	96.5829	$7,594.89		$1,518.98
50600	Exploration of ureter		C					
50684	Injection for ureter x-ray		N					
50686	Measure ureter pressure		S	5721	1.7334	$136.31		$27.27
50688	Change of ureter tube/stent		J1	5373	21.5622	$1,695.57		$339.12
50690	Injection for ureter x-ray		N					
50693	Plmt ureteral stent prq		J1	5374	34.2919	$2,696.58		$539.32
50694	Plmt ureteral stent prq		J1	5374	34.2919	$2,696.58		$539.32
50695	Plmt ureteral stent prq		J1	5374	34.2919	$2,696.58		$539.32
50705	Ureteral embolization/occl		N					
50706	Balloon dilate urtrl strix		N					
51600	Injection for bladder x-ray		N					
51605	Preparation for bladder xray		N					
51610	Injection for bladder x-ray		N					
51700	Irrigation of bladder		T	5371	2.9187	$229.51		$45.91
51701	Insert bladder catheter		Q1	5734	1.3357	$105.03		$21.01
51702	Insert temp bladder cath		Q1	5734	1.3357	$105.03		$21.01
51703	Insert bladder cath complex		S	5721	1.7334	$136.31		$27.27
51705	Change of bladder tube		T	5371	2.9187	$229.51		$45.91
51710	Change of bladder tube		T	5372	7.1921	$565.56		$113.12
51715	Endoscopic injection/implant		J1	5374	34.2919	$2,696.58		$539.32
51720	Treatment of bladder lesion		T	5371	2.9187	$229.51		$45.91

CPT/HCPCS Code	Descriptor	CI	SI	APC	Relative Weight	Payment Rate	National Unadjusted Copayment	Minimum Unadjusted Copayment
53899	Urology surgery procedure		T	5371	2.9187	$229.51		$45.91
54230	Prepare penis study		N					
54231	Dynamic cavernosometry		J1	5373	21.5622	$1,695.57		$339.12
54235	Penile injection		T	5371	2.9187	$229.51		$45.91
54240	Penis study		S	5721	1.7334	$136.31		$27.27
54250	Penis study		T	5371	2.9187	$229.51		$45.91
55700	Biopsy of prostate		J1	5373	21.5622	$1,695.57		$339.12
55705	Biopsy of prostate		J1	5373	21.5622	$1,695.57		$339.12
55706	Prostate saturation sampling		J1	5374	34.2919	$2,696.58		$539.32
55720	Drainage of prostate abscess		J1	5373	21.5622	$1,695.57		$339.12
55725	Drainage of prostate abscess		J1	5373	21.5622	$1,695.57		$339.12
55874	Tprnl plmt biodegrdabl matrl	NC	T	5375	47.1256	$3,705.77		$741.16
55875	Transperi needle place pros	CH	J1	5375	47.1256	$3,705.77		$741.16
55876	Place rt device/marker pros		S	5613	15.0898	$1,186.60		$237.32
58340	Catheter for hysterography		N					
60100	Biopsy of thyroid		T	5071	7.2843	$572.81		$114.57
60300	Aspir/inj thyroid cyst		T	5071	7.2843	$572.81		$114.57
61623	Endovasc tempory vessel occl		J1	5193	133.6503	$10,509.72		$2,101.95
61624	Transcath occlusion cns		C					
61626	Transcath occlusion non-cns		J1	5193	133.6503	$10,509.72		$2,101.95
61630	Intracranial angioplasty		C					
61635	Intracran angioplsty w/stent		C					
61640	Dilate ic vasospasm init		E1					
61641	Dilate ic vasospasm add-on		E1					
61642	Dilate ic vasospasm add-on		E1					
61645	Perq art m-thrombect &/nfs		C					
61650	Evasc prlng admn rx agnt 1st		C					
61651	Evasc prlng admn rx agnt add		C					
62267	Interdiscal perq aspir dx		T	5071	7.2843	$572.81		$114.57
62268	Drain spinal cord cyst		T	5443	8.5474	$672.13		$134.43
62269	Needle biopsy spinal cord		J1	5072	17.1415	$1,347.94		$269.59
62270	Spinal fluid tap diagnostic		T	5442	6.9096	$543.34		$108.67
62272	Drain cerebro spinal fluid		T	5442	6.9096	$543.34		$108.67
62273	Inject epidural patch		T	5442	6.9096	$543.34		$108.67
62280	Treat spinal cord lesion		T	5443	8.5474	$672.13		$134.43
62281	Treat spinal cord lesion		T	5443	8.5474	$672.13		$134.43
62282	Treat spinal canal lesion		T	5443	8.5474	$672.13		$134.43
62284	Injection for myelogram		N					
62287	Percutaneous diskectomy		J1	5432	58.8442	$4,627.27		$925.46
62290	Njx px discography lumbar		N					
62291	Njx px discography crv/thrc		N					
62292	Njx chemonucleolysis lmbr		J1	5431	20.4791	$1,610.39		$322.08
62294	Injection into spinal artery		T	5443	8.5474	$672.13		$134.43

CPT/HCPCS Code	Descriptor	CI	SI	APC	Relative Weight	Payment Rate	National Unadjusted Copayment	Minimum Unadjusted Copayment
62302	Myelography lumbar injection	CH	Q2	5573	8.6707	$681.83		$136.37
62303	Myelography lumbar injection	CH	Q2	5573	8.6707	$681.83		$136.37
62304	Myelography lumbar injection	CH	Q2	5573	8.6707	$681.83		$136.37
62305	Myelography lumbar injection	CH	Q2	5573	8.6707	$681.83		$136.37
62320	Njx interlaminar crv/thrc		T	5442	6.9096	$543.34		$108.67
62321	Njx interlaminar crv/thrc		T	5442	6.9096	$543.34		$108.67
62322	Njx interlaminar lmbr/sac		T	5442	6.9096	$543.34		$108.67
62323	Njx interlaminar lmbr/sac		T	5442	6.9096	$543.34		$108.67
62324	Njx interlaminar crv/thrc		T	5443	8.5474	$672.13		$134.43
62325	Njx interlaminar crv/thrc		T	5443	8.5474	$672.13		$134.43
62326	Njx interlaminar lmbr/sac		T	5443	8.5474	$672.13		$134.43
62327	Njx interlaminar lmbr/sac		T	5443	8.5474	$672.13		$134.43
62350	Implant spinal canal cath		J1	5432	58.8442	$4,627.27		$925.46
62351	Implant spinal canal cath		J1	5114	71.2909	$5,606.03		$1,121.21
62355	Remove spinal canal catheter		Q2	5431	20.4791	$1,610.39		$322.08
62360	Insert spine infusion device		J1	5471	209.0602	$16,439.66		$3,287.94
62361	Implant spine infusion pump		J1	5471	209.0602	$16,439.66		$3,287.94
62362	Implant spine infusion pump		J1	5471	209.0602	$16,439.66		$3,287.94
62365	Remove spine infusion device		Q2	5432	58.8442	$4,627.27		$925.46
62367	Analyze spine infus pump		S	5743	3.3302	$261.87		$52.38
62368	Analyze sp inf pump w/reprog		S	5743	3.3302	$261.87		$52.38
62369	Anal sp inf pmp w/reprg&fill		S	5743	3.3302	$261.87		$52.38
62370	Anl sp inf pmp w/mdreprg&fil		S	5743	3.3302	$261.87		$52.38
62380	Ndsc dcmprn 1 ntrspc lumbar		J1	5114	71.2909	$5,606.03		$1,121.21
68850	Injection for tear sac x-ray		N					
70010	Contrast x-ray of brain	CH	Q2	5572	5.8032	$456.34	$111.70	$91.27
70015	Contrast x-ray of brain	CH	Q2	5573	8.6707	$681.83		$136.37
70328	X-ray exam of jaw joint		Q1	5521	0.7899	$62.11		$12.43
70330	X-ray exam of jaw joints		Q1	5521	0.7899	$62.11		$12.43
70332	X-ray exam of jaw joint		Q2	5523	3.1184	$245.22		$49.05
70390	X-ray exam of salivary duct		Q2	5523	3.1184	$245.22		$49.05
72240	Myelography neck spine	CH	Q2	5573	8.6707	$681.83		$136.37
72255	Myelography thoracic spine	CH	Q2	5573	8.6707	$681.83		$136.37
72265	Myelography l-s spine	CH	Q2	5573	8.6707	$681.83		$136.37
72270	Myelogphy 2/> spine regions	CH	Q2	5573	8.6707	$681.83		$136.37
72275	Epidurography		N					
72285	Discography cerv/thor spine		Q2	5431	20.4791	$1,610.39		$322.08
74190	X-ray exam of peritoneum		Q2	5524	6.1888	$486.66		$97.34
74328	X-ray bile duct endoscopy		N					
74329	X-ray for pancreas endoscopy		N					
74330	X-ray bile/panc endoscopy		N					
74340	X-ray guide for gi tube		N					
74355	X-ray guide intestinal tube		N					

CPT/HCPCS Code	Descriptor	CI	SI	APC	Relative Weight	Payment Rate	National Unadjusted Copayment	Minimum Unadjusted Copayment
74360	X-ray guide gi dilation		N					
74363	X-ray bile duct dilation		N					
74425	Contrst x-ray urinary tract	CH	Q2	5571	3.2138	$252.72		$50.55
74470	X-ray exam of kidney lesion		Q2	5523	3.1184	$245.22		$49.05
74485	X-ray guide gu dilation		Q2	5373	21.5622	$1,695.57		$339.12
74740	X-ray female genital tract		Q2	5523	3.1184	$245.22		$49.05
74742	X-ray fallopian tube		N					
74775	X-ray exam of perineum	CH	S	5522	1.5100	$118.74		$23.75
75600	Contrast exam thoracic aorta	CH	Q2	5183	31.6976	$2,492.57		$498.52
75605	Contrast exam thoracic aorta	CH	Q2	5184	54.2330	$4,264.67		$852.94
75625	Contrast exam abdominl aorta	CH	Q2	5183	31.6976	$2,492.57		$498.52
75630	X-ray aorta leg arteries	CH	Q2	5183	31.6976	$2,492.57		$498.52
75635	Ct angio abdominal arteries		Q2	5571	3.2138	$252.72		$50.55
75658	Artery x-rays arm	CH	D					
75705	Artery x-rays spine	CH	Q2	5184	54.2330	$4,264.67		$852.94
75710	Artery x-rays arm/leg	CH	Q2	5183	31.6976	$2,492.57		$498.52
75716	Artery x-rays arms/legs	CH	Q2	5183	31.6976	$2,492.57		$498.52
75726	Artery x-rays abdomen	CH	Q2	5184	54.2330	$4,264.67		$852.94
75731	Artery x-rays adrenal gland		Q2	5181	7.7894	$612.53		$122.51
75733	Artery x-rays adrenals	CH	Q2	5183	31.6976	$2,492.57		$498.52
75736	Artery x-rays pelvis	CH	Q2	5184	54.2330	$4,264.67		$852.94
75741	Artery x-rays lung	CH	Q2	5183	31.6976	$2,492.57		$498.52
75743	Artery x-rays lungs	CH	Q2	5183	31.6976	$2,492.57		$498.52
75746	Artery x-rays lung	CH	Q2	5182	12.4994	$982.90		$196.58
75756	Artery x-rays chest	CH	Q2	5183	31.6976	$2,492.57		$498.52
75774	Artery x-ray each vessel		N					
75801	Lymph vessel x-ray arm/leg		Q2	5181	7.7894	$612.53		$122.51
75803	Lymph vessel x-ray arms/legs		Q2	5181	7.7894	$612.53		$122.51
75805	Lymph vessel x-ray trunk	CH	Q2	5182	12.4994	$982.90		$196.58
75807	Lymph vessel x-ray trunk	CH	Q2	5183	31.6976	$2,492.57		$498.52
75809	Nonvascular shunt x-ray		Q2	5522	1.5100	$118.74		$23.75
75810	Vein x-ray spleen/liver	CH	Q2	5182	12.4994	$982.90		$196.58
75820	Vein x-ray arm/leg		Q2	5181	7.7894	$612.53		$122.51
75822	Vein x-ray arms/legs	CH	Q2	5182	12.4994	$982.90		$196.58
75825	Vein x-ray trunk	CH	Q2	5183	31.6976	$2,492.57		$498.52
75827	Vein x-ray chest		Q2	5181	7.7894	$612.53		$122.51
75831	Vein x-ray kidney	CH	Q2	5183	31.6976	$2,492.57		$498.52
75833	Vein x-ray kidneys	CH	Q2	5183	31.6976	$2,492.57		$498.52
75840	Vein x-ray adrenal gland	CH	Q2	5183	31.6976	$2,492.57		$498.52
75842	Vein x-ray adrenal glands	CH	Q2	5184	54.2330	$4,264.67		$852.94
75860	Vein x-ray neck	CH	Q2	5183	31.6976	$2,492.57		$498.52
75870	Vein x-ray skull		Q2	5181	7.7894	$612.53		$122.51
75872	Vein x-ray skull epidural		Q2	5181	7.7894	$612.53		$122.51

CPT/HCPCS Code	Descriptor	CI	SI	APC	Relative Weight	Payment Rate	National Unadjusted Copayment	Minimum Unadjusted Copayment
75880	Vein x-ray eye socket		Q2	5181	7.7894	$612.53		$122.51
75885	Vein x-ray liver w/hemodynam	CH	Q2	5183	31.6976	$2,492.57		$498.52
75887	Vein x-ray liver w/o hemodyn	CH	Q2	5182	12.4994	$982.90		$196.58
75889	Vein x-ray liver w/hemodynam	CH	Q2	5183	31.6976	$2,492.57		$498.52
75891	Vein x-ray liver	CH	Q2	5183	31.6976	$2,492.57		$498.52
75893	Venous sampling by catheter	CH	Q2	5184	54.2330	$4,264.67		$852.94
75894	X-rays transcath therapy		N					
75898	Follow-up angiography	CH	Q2	5182	12.4994	$982.90		$196.58
75901	Remove cva device obstruct		N					
75902	Remove cva lumen obstruct		N					
75952	Endovasc repair abdom aorta	CH	D					
75953	Abdom aneurysm endovas rpr	CH	D					
75954	Iliac aneurysm endovas rpr	CH	D					
75956	Xray endovasc thor ao repr		C					
75957	Xray endovasc thor ao repr		C					
75958	Xray place prox ext thor ao		C					
75959	Xray place dist ext thor ao		C					
75970	Vascular biopsy		N					
75984	Xray control catheter change		N					
75989	Abscess drainage under x-ray		N					
76000	Fluoroscopy <1 hr phys/qhp	CH	S	5522	1.5100	$118.74		$23.75
76001	Fluoroscope exam extensive		N					
76376	3d render w/intrp postproces		N					
76377	3d render w/intrp postproces		N					
76496	Fluoroscopic procedure		Q1	5521	0.7899	$62.11		$12.43
76497	Ct procedure		Q1	5521	0.7899	$62.11		$12.43
76498	Mri procedure		S	5521	0.7899	$62.11		$12.43
76499	Radiographic procedure		Q1	5521	0.7899	$62.11		$12.43
76930	Echo guide cardiocentesis		N					
76932	Echo guide for heart biopsy		N					
76936	Echo guide for artery repair		S	5722	3.1641	$248.81		$49.77
76937	Us guide vascular access		N					
76940	Us guide tissue ablation		N					
76941	Echo guide for transfusion		N					
76942	Echo guide for biopsy		N					
76945	Echo guide villus sampling		N					
76946	Echo guide for amniocentesis		N					
76948	Echo guide ova aspiration		N					
76965	Echo guidance radiotherapy		N					
77001	Fluoroguide for vein device		N					
77002	Needle localization by xray		N					
77003	Fluoroguide for spine inject		N					
77011	Ct scan for localization		N					

CPT/HCPCS Code	Descriptor	CI	SI	APC	Relative Weight	Payment Rate	National Unadjusted Copayment	Minimum Unadjusted Copayment
77012	Ct scan for needle biopsy		N					
77021	Mr guidance for needle place		N					
77022	Mri for tissue ablation		N					
77053	X-ray of mammary duct		Q2	5523	3.1184	$245.22		$49.05
77054	X-ray of mammary ducts		Q2	5523	3.1184	$245.22		$49.05
92920	Prq cardiac angioplast 1 art		J1	5192	64.6607	$5,084.66		$1,016.94
92921	Prq cardiac angio addl art		N					
92924	Prq card angio/athrect 1 art		J1	5193	133.6503	$10,509.72		$2,101.95
92925	Prq card angio/athrect addl		N					
92928	Prq card stent w/angio 1 vsl		J1	5193	133.6503	$10,509.72		$2,101.95
92929	Prq card stent w/angio addl		N					
92933	Prq card stent/ath/angio		J1	5194	203.7145	$16,019.29		$3,203.86
92934	Prq card stent/ath/angio		N					
92937	Prq revasc byp graft 1 vsl		J1	5193	133.6503	$10,509.72		$2,101.95
92938	Prq revasc byp graft addl		N					
92941	Prq card revasc mi 1 vsl	CH	C					
92943	Prq card revasc chronic 1vsl		J1	5193	133.6503	$10,509.72		$2,101.95
92944	Prq card revasc chronic addl		N					
92950	Heart/lung resuscitation cpr		S	5722	3.1641	$248.81		$49.77
92953	Temporary external pacing		Q3	5781	6.5190	$512.63		$102.53
92960	Cardioversion electric ext		S	5781	6.5190	$512.63		$102.53
92961	Cardioversion electric int		S	5781	6.5190	$512.63		$102.53
92973	Prq coronary mech thrombect		N					
92974	Cath place cardio brachytx		N					
92975	Dissolve clot heart vessel		C					
92977	Dissolve clot heart vessel		T	5694	3.7838	$297.54		$59.51
92978	Endoluminl ivus oct c 1st		N					
92979	Endoluminl ivus oct c ea		N					
92986	Revision of aortic valve		J1	5192	64.6607	$5,084.66		$1,016.94
92987	Revision of mitral valve		J1	5193	133.6503	$10,509.72		$2,101.95
92990	Revision of pulmonary valve		J1	5193	133.6503	$10,509.72		$2,101.95
92992	Revision of heart chamber		C					
92993	Revision of heart chamber		C					
92997	Pul art balloon repr percut		J1	5193	133.6503	$10,509.72		$2,101.95
92998	Pul art balloon repr percut		N					
93451	Right heart cath		J1	5191	35.7776	$2,813.41	$865.56	$562.69
93452	Left hrt cath w/ventrclgrphy		J1	5191	35.7776	$2,813.41	$865.56	$562.69
93453	R&l hrt cath w/ventriclgrphy		J1	5191	35.7776	$2,813.41	$865.56	$562.69
93454	Coronary artery angio s&i		J1	5191	35.7776	$2,813.41	$865.56	$562.69
93455	Coronary art/grft angio s&i		J1	5191	35.7776	$2,813.41	$865.56	$562.69
93456	R hrt coronary artery angio		J1	5191	35.7776	$2,813.41	$865.56	$562.69
93457	R hrt art/grft angio		J1	5191	35.7776	$2,813.41	$865.56	$562.69
93458	L hrt artery/ventricle angio		J1	5191	35.7776	$2,813.41	$865.56	$562.69

CPT/HCPCS Code	Descriptor	CI	SI	APC	Relative Weight	Payment Rate	National Unadjusted Copayment	Minimum Unadjusted Copayment
93459	L hrt art/grft angio		J1	5191	35.7776	$2,813.41	$865.56	$562.69
93460	R&l hrt art/ventricle angio		J1	5191	35.7776	$2,813.41	$865.56	$562.69
93461	R&l hrt art/ventricle angio		J1	5191	35.7776	$2,813.41	$865.56	$562.69
93462	L hrt cath trnsptl puncture		N					
93463	Drug admin & hemodynmic meas		N					
93464	Exercise w/hemodynamic meas		N					
93503	Insert/place heart catheter	CH	T	5182	12.4994	$982.90	.	$196.58
93505	Biopsy of heart lining	CH	T	5183	31.6976	$2,492.57	.	$498.52
93530	Rt heart cath congenital		J1	5191	35.7776	$2,813.41	$865.56	$562.69
93531	R & l heart cath congenital		J1	5191	35.7776	$2,813.41	$865.56	$562.69
93532	R & l heart cath congenital		J1	5191	35.7776	$2,813.41	$865.56	$562.69
93533	R & l heart cath congenital		J1	5191	35.7776	$2,813.41	$865.56	$562.69
93561	Cardiac output measurement		N					
93562	Card output measure subsq		N					
93563	Inject congenital card cath		N					
93564	Inject hrt congntl art/grft		N					
93565	Inject l ventr/atrial angio		N					
93566	Inject r ventr/atrial angio		N					
93567	Inject suprvlv aortography		N					
93568	Inject pulm art hrt cath		N					
93571	Heart flow reserve measure		N					
93572	Heart flow reserve measure		N					
93580	Transcath closure of asd		J1	5194	203.7145	$16,019.29		$3,203.86
93581	Transcath closure of vsd		J1	5194	203.7145	$16,019.29		$3,203.86
93582	Perq transcath closure pda		J1	5194	203.7145	$16,019.29		$3,203.86
93583	Perq transcath septal reduxn		C					
93590	Perq transcath cls mitral		J1	5194	203.7145	$16,019.29		$3,203.86
93591	Perq transcath cls aortic		J1	5194	203.7145	$16,019.29		$3,203.86
93592	Perq transcath closure each		N					
93600	Bundle of his recording		J1	5212	67.5765	$5,313.95		$1,062.79
93602	Intra-atrial recording		J1	5212	67.5765	$5,313.95		$1,062.79
93603	Right ventricular recording		J1	5211	11.5621	$909.20		$181.84
93609	Map tachycardia add-on		N					
93610	Intra-atrial pacing		J1	5212	67.5765	$5,313.95		$1,062.79
93612	Intraventricular pacing		J1	5212	67.5765	$5,313.95		$1,062.79
93613	Electrophys map 3d add-on		N					
93615	Esophageal recording		J1	5211	11.5621	$909.20		$181.84
93616	Esophageal recording		J1	5211	11.5621	$909.20		$181.84
93618	Heart rhythm pacing		J1	5211	11.5621	$909.20		$181.84
93619	Electrophysiology evaluation		J1	5212	67.5765	$5,313.95		$1,062.79
93620	Electrophysiology evaluation		J1	5212	67.5765	$5,313.95		$1,062.79
93621	Electrophysiology evaluation		N					
93622	Electrophysiology evaluation		N					

CPT/HCPCS Code	Descriptor	CI	SI	APC	Relative Weight	Payment Rate	National Unadjusted Copayment	Minimum Unadjusted Copayment
93623	Stimulation pacing heart		N					
93624	Electrophysiologic study		J1	5212	67.5765	$5,313.95		$1,062.79
93631	Heart pacing mapping		N					
93640	Evaluation heart device		N					
93641	Electrophysiology evaluation		N					
93642	Electrophysiology evaluation		J1	5211	11.5621	$909.20		$181.84
93644	Electrophysiology evaluation		N					
93650	Ablate heart dysrhythm focus		J1	5212	67.5765	$5,313.95		$1,062.79
93653	Ep & ablate supravent arrhyt		J1	5213	235.4500	$18,514.85		$3,702.97
93654	Ep & ablate ventric tachy		J1	5213	235.4500	$18,514.85		$3,702.97
93655	Ablate arrhythmia add on		N					
93656	Tx atrial fib pulm vein isol		J1	5213	235.4500	$18,514.85		$3,702.97
93657	Tx l/r atrial fib addl		N					
93660	Tilt table evaluation		S	5723	5.6508	$444.36		$88.88
93662	Intracardiac ecg (ice)		N					
96373	Ther/proph/diag inj ia		S	5693	2.4299	$191.08		$38.22
96416	Chemo prolong infuse w/pump		S	5694	3.7838	$297.54		$59.51
96420	Chemo ia push tecnique		S	5694	3.7838	$297.54		$59.51
96422	Chemo ia infusion up to 1 hr		S	5693	2.4299	$191.08		$38.22
96423	Chemo ia infuse each addl hr		S	5691	0.4709	$37.03		$7.41
99151	Mod sed same phys/qhp <5 yrs		N					
99152	Mod sed same phys/qhp 5/>yrs		N					
99153	Mod sed same phys/qhp ea		N					
99155	Mod sed oth phys/qhp <5 yrs		N					
99156	Mod sed oth phys/qhp 5/>yrs		N					
99157	Mod sed other phys/qhp ea		N					
C1714	Cath, trans atherectomy, dir		N					
C1721	Aicd, dual chamber		N					
C1722	Aicd, single chamber		N					
C1724	Cath, trans atherec,rotation		N					
C1725	Cath, translumin non-laser		N					
C1726	Cath, bal dil, non-vascular		N					
C1727	Cath, bal tis dis, non-vas		N					
C1729	Cath, drainage		N					
C1730	Cath, ep, 19 or few elect		N					
C1731	Cath, ep, 20 or more elec		N					
C1732	Cath, ep, diag/abl, 3d/vect		N					
C1733	Cath, ep, othr than cool-tip		N					
C1750	Cath, hemodialysis,long-term		N					
C1751	Cath, inf, per/cent/midline		N					
C1752	Cath,hemodialysis,short-term		N					
C1753	Cath, intravas ultrasound		N					
C1757	Cath, thrombectomy/embolect		N					

CPT/HCPCS Code	Descriptor	CI	SI	APC	Relative Weight	Payment Rate	National Unadjusted Copayment	Minimum Unadjusted Copayment
C1758	Catheter, ureteral		N					
C1759	Cath, intra echocardiography		N					
C1760	Closure dev, vasc		N					
C1766	Intro/sheath,strble,non-peel		N					
C1767	Generator, neuro non-recharg		N					
C1768	Graft, vascular		N					
C1769	Guide wire		N					
C1772	Infusion pump, programmable		N					
C1773	Ret dev, insertable		N					
C1777	Lead, aicd, endo single coil		N					
C1778	Lead, neurostimulator		N					
C1779	Lead, pmkr, transvenous vdd		N					
C1785	Pmkr, dual, rate-resp		N					
C1786	Pmkr, single, rate-resp		N					
C1787	Patient progr, neurostim		N					
C1788	Port, indwelling, imp		N					
C1874	Stent, coated/cov w/del sys		N					
C1875	Stent, coated/cov w/o del sy		N					
C1876	Stent, non-coa/non-cov w/del		N					
C1877	Stent, non-coat/cov w/o del		N					
C1880	Vena cava filter		N					
C1882	Aicd, other than sing/dual		N					
C1883	Adapt/ext, pacing/neuro lead		N					
C1884	Embolization protect syst		N					
C1885	Cath, translumin angio laser		N					
C1886	Catheter, ablation		N					
C1887	Catheter, guiding		N					
C1888	Endovas non-cardiac abl cath		N					
C1889	Implant/insert device, noc		N					
C1892	Intro/sheath,fixed,peel-away		N					
C1893	Intro/sheath, fixed,non-peel		N					
C1894	Intro/sheath, non-laser		N					
C1895	Lead, aicd, endo dual coil		N					
C1896	Lead, aicd, non sing/dual		N					
C1897	Lead, neurostim test kit		N					
C1898	Lead, pmkr, other than trans		N					
C1899	Lead, pmkr/aicd combination		N					
C1900	Lead, coronary venous		N					
C2617	Stent, non-cor, tem w/o del		N					
C2618	Probe/needle, cryo		N					
C2619	Pmkr, dual, non rate-resp		N					
C2620	Pmkr, single, non rate-resp		N					
C2621	Pmkr, other than sing/dual		N					

CPT/HCPCS Code	Descriptor	CI	SI	APC	Relative Weight	Payment Rate	National Unadjusted Copayment	Minimum Unadjusted Copayment
C2623	Cath, translumin, drug-coat	CH	N					
C2624	Wireless pressure sensor		N					
C2625	Stent, non-cor, tem w/del sy		N					
C2626	Infusion pump, non-prog,temp		N					
C2627	Cath, suprapubic/cystoscopic		N					
C2628	Catheter, occlusion		N					
C2629	Intro/sheath, laser		N					
C2630	Cath, ep, cool-tip		N					
C9600	Perc drug-el cor stent sing		J1	5193	133.6503	$10,509.72		$2,101.95
C9601	Perc drug-el cor stent bran		N					
C9602	Perc d-e cor stent ather s		J1	5194	203.7145	$16,019.29		$3,203.86
C9603	Perc d-e cor stent ather br		N					
C9604	Perc d-e cor revasc t cabg s		J1	5193	133.6503	$10,509.72		$2,101.95
C9605	Perc d-e cor revasc t cabg b		N					
C9606	Perc d-e cor revasc w ami s		J1	5194	203.7145	$16,019.29		$3,203.86
C9607	Perc d-e cor revasc chro sin		J1	5194	203.7145	$16,019.29		$3,203.86
C9608	Perc d-e cor revasc chro add		N					
C9728	Place device/marker, non pro		S	5613	15.0898	$1,186.60		$237.32
C9733	Non-ophthalmic fva		Q2	5523	3.1184	$245.22		$49.05
C9734	U/s trtmt, not leiomyomata		J1	5114	71.2909	$5,606.03	.	$1,121.21
C9741	Impl pressure sensor w/angio		J1	5200	414.9030	$32,626.31	$9,081.23	$6,525.27
C9744	Abd us w/contrast		S	5571	3.2138	$252.72		$50.55
C9745	Nasal endo eustachian tube	NC	J1	5165	55.1718	$4,338.49		$867.70
C9746	Trans imp balloon cont	NC	J1	5377	199.6126	$15,696.74		$3,139.35
G0259	Inject for sacroiliac joint		N					
G0260	Inj for sacroiliac jt anesth		T	5442	6.9096	$543.34		$108.67
G0269	Occlusive device in vein art		N					
G0278	Iliac art angio,cardiac cath		N					
G0293	Non-cov surg proc,clin trial		Q1	5732	0.4044	$31.80		$6.36
G0294	Non-cov proc, clinical trial		Q1	5732	0.4044	$31.80		$6.36
G0364	Bone marrow aspirate &biopsy	CH	D					
G0365	Vessel mapping hemo access		S	5522	1.5100	$118.74		$23.75
Q9950	Inj sulf hexa lipid microsph	CH	N					
Q9951	Locm >= 400 mg/ml iodine,1ml		N					
Q9953	Inj fe-based mr contrast,1ml		N					
Q9954	Oral mr contrast, 100 ml		N					
Q9955	Inj perflexane lip micros,ml		N					
Q9956	Inj octafluoropropane mic,ml		N					
Q9957	Inj perflutren lip micros,ml		N					
Q9958	Hocm <=149 mg/ml iodine, 1ml		N					
Q9959	Hocm 150-199mg/ml iodine,1ml		N					
Q9960	Hocm 200-249mg/ml iodine,1ml		N					
Q9961	Hocm 250-299mg/ml iodine,1ml		N					

CPT/HCPCS Code	Descriptor	CI	SI	APC	Relative Weight	Payment Rate	National Unadjusted Copayment	Minimum Unadjusted Copayment
Q9962	Hocm 300-349mg/ml iodine,1ml		N					
Q9963	Hocm 350-399mg/ml iodine,1ml		N					
Q9964	Hocm>= 400mg/ml iodine, 1ml		N					
Q9965	Locm 100-199mg/ml iodine,1ml		N					
Q9966	Locm 200-299mg/ml iodine,1ml		N					
Q9967	Locm 300-399mg/ml iodine,1ml		N					

Appendix B: HCPCS Level II Codes

The following is a list of HCPCS Level II device codes current as of November 2017 for interventional radiology and cardiology. These codes are appropriate for hospital providers to report with the associated procedures.

Device Code	Description
C1714	Catheter, transluminal atherectomy, directional
C1721	Cardioverter-defibrillator, dual chamber (implantable)
C1722	Cardioverter-defibrillator, single chamber (implantable)
C1724	Catheter, transluminal atherectomy, rotational
C1725	Catheter, transluminal angioplasty, non-laser (may include guidance, infusion/perfusion capability)
C1726	Catheter, balloon dilatation, non-vascular
C1727	Catheter, balloon tissue dissector, non-vascular (insertable)
C1729	Catheter, drainage
C1730	Catheter, electrophysiology, diagnostic, other than 3d mapping (19 or fewer electrodes)
C1731	Catheter, electrophysiology, diagnostic, other than 3d mapping (20 or more electrodes)
C1732	Catheter, electrophysiology, diagnostic/ablation, 3d or vector mapping
C1733	Catheter, electrophysiology, diagnostic/ablation, other than 3d or vector mapping, other than cool-tip
C1750	Catheter, hemodialysis/peritoneal, long-term
C1751	Catheter, infusion, inserted peripherally, centrally or midline (other than hemodialysis)
C1752	Catheter, hemodialysis/peritoneal, short-term
C1753	Catheter, intravascular ultrasound
C1754	Catheter, intradiscal
C1755	Catheter, intraspinal
C1756	Catheter, pacing, transesophageal
C1757	Catheter, thrombectomy/embolectomy
C1758	Catheter, ureteral
C1759	Catheter, intracardiac echocardiography
C1760	Closure device, vascular (implantable/insertable)
C1766	Introducer/sheath, guiding, intracardiac electrophysiological, steerable, other than peel-away
C1768	Graft, vascular
C1769	Guide wire
C1773	Retrieval device, insertable (used to retrieve fractured medical devices)

Device Code	Description
C1777	Lead, cardioverter-defibrillator, endocardial single coil (implantable)
C1779	Lead, pacemaker, transvenous vdd single pass
C1785	Pacemaker, dual chamber, rate-responsive (implantable)
C1786	Pacemaker, single chamber, rate-responsive (implantable)
C1788	Port, indwelling (implantable)
C1817	Septal defect implant system, intracardiac
C1874	Stent, coated/covered, with delivery system
C1875	Stent, coated/covered, without delivery system
C1876	Stent, non-coated/non-covered, with delivery system
C1877	Stent, non-coated/non-covered, without delivery system
C1880	Vena cava filter
C1882	Cardioverter-defibrillator, other than single or dual chamber (implantable)
C1883	Adaptor or extension, pacing/neurostimulator lead
C1884	Embolization protective system
C1885	Catheter, transluminal angioplasty, laser
C1886	Catheter, extravascular tissue ablation, any modality (insertable)
C1887	Catheter, guiding (may include infusion/perfusion capability)
C1888	Catheter, ablation, non-cardiac, endovascular (implantable)
C1889	Implant, insertable device, not otherwise classified
C1892	Introducer/sheath, guiding, intracardiac electrophysiological, fixed-curve, peel-away
C1893	Introducer/sheath, guiding, intracardiac electrophysiological, fixed-curve, other than peel-away
C1894	Introducer/sheath, other than guiding, other than intracardiac electrophysiological, non-laser
C1895	Lead, cardioverter-defibrillator, endocardial dual coil (implantable)
C1896	Lead, cardioverter-defibrillator, other than endocardial single or dual coil (implantable)
C1898	Lead, pacemaker, other than transvenous vdd single pass
C1899	Lead, pacemaker/cardioverter-defibrillator combination (implantable)
C1900	Lead, left ventricular coronary venous system

Device Code	Description
C2617	Stent, non-coronary, temporary, without delivery system
C2618	Probe/needle, cryoablation
C2619	Pacemaker, dual chamber, non rate-responsive (implantable)
C2620	Pacemaker, single chamber, non rate-responsive (implantable)
C2621	Pacemaker, other than single or dual chamber (implantable)
C2623	Catheter, transluminal angioplasty, drug-coated, non-laser
C2624	Implantable wireless pulmonary artery pressure sensor with delivery catheter, including all system components
C2625	Stent, non-coronary, temporary, with delivery system
C2626	Infusion pump, non-programmable, temporary (implantable)
C2627	Catheter, suprapubic/cystoscopic
C2628	Catheter, occlusion
C2629	Introducer/sheath, other than guiding, other than intracardiac electrophysiological, laser
C2630	Catheter, electrophysiology, diagnostic/ablation, other than 3d or vector mapping, cool-tip

Code Definitions

3D mapping catheter (C1732)—Refers to a catheter used for mapping the electrophysiologic properties of the heart. Signals are identified by a specialized catheter and changed into a 3-dimensional map of a specific region of the heart.

Adaptor for a pacing lead (C1883)—Interposed between an existing pacemaker lead and a new generator. The end of the adaptor lead has the appropriate connector pin that will enable utilization of the existing pacemaker lead with a new generator that has a different receptacle. These are required when a generator is replaced or when two leads are connected to the same port in the connector block.

Balloon dilatation catheter, non-vascular (C1726)—Catheter used to dilate strictures or stenoses through the insertion of an uninflated balloon affixed to the end of a flexible catheter, followed by the inflation of the balloon at the specified site (e.g., common bile duct, ureter, small or large intestine). [For the reporting of vascular balloon dilatation catheters, see category "Transluminal angioplasty catheter" (C1725 and C1885).]

Balloon tissue dissector catheter (C1727)—Balloon tipped catheter used to separate tissue planes, used in procedures such as hernia repairs.

Catheter, ablation, non-cardiac, endovascular (implantable) (C1888)—Used to obliterate or necrose tissues in an effort to restore normal anatomic and physiologic function.

Cardioverter-defibrillator, other than single or dual chamber (C1882)—Includes cardiac resynchronization devices.

Coated stent (C1874, C1875)—Refers to a stent bonded with drugs (e.g., heparin) or layered with biocompatible substances (e.g., phosphorylcholine).

Cool-tip electrophysiology catheter (C2630)—Ablation catheter that contains a cooling mechanism and has temperature sensing capability.

Covered stent (C1874, C1875)—Refers to a stent layered with silicone or a silicone derivative (e.g., PTFE, polyurethane).

Drainage catheter (C1729)—Intended to be used for percutaneous drainage of fluids. (Note: This category does NOT include Foley catheters or suprapubic catheters. Refer to category C2627 to report suprapubic catheters.)

Electrophysiology catheter (C1730, C1731, C1732, C1733, C2630)—Assists in providing anatomic and physiologic information about the cardiac electrical conduction system. Electrophysiology catheters are categorized into two main groups: (1) diagnostic catheters that are used for mapping, pacing, and/or recording only, and (2) ablation (therapeutic) catheters that also have diagnostic capability. The electrophysiology ablation catheters are distinct from non-cardiac ablation catheters. Electrophysiology catheters designated as "cool-tip" refer to catheters with tips cooled by infused and/or circulating saline. Catheters designated as "other than cool-tip" refer to the termister tip catheter with temperature probe that measures temperature at the tissue catheter interface.

Embolization protective system (C1884)—A system designed and marketed for use to trap, pulverize, and remove atheromatous or thrombotic debris from the vascular system during an angioplasty, atherectomy, or stenting procedure.

Extension for a pacing lead (C1883)—Provides additional length to an existing pacing lead but does not have the capability of an adaptor.

Guiding catheter (C1887)—Intended for the introduction of interventional/diagnostic devices into the coronary or peripheral vascular systems. It can be used to inject contrast material, function as a conduit through which other devices pass, and/or provide a mechanism for measuring arterial pressure, and maintain a pathway created by the guide wire during the performance of a procedure.

Left ventricular coronary venous system lead (C1900)—Designed for left heart placement in a cardiac vein via the coronary sinus and is intended to treat the symptoms associated with heart failure.

Pacemaker, other than single or dual chamber (C2621)—Includes cardiac resynchronization devices as well as other pacemakers that are neither single nor dual chamber.

Peel-away introducer/sheath (C1892)—A non-absorbable sheath or introducer that separates into two pieces. This device is used primarily when removal of the sheath is required after a catheter or lead is in the desired position.

Retrieval device, insertable (C1773)—A device designed to retrieve other devices or portions thereof (e.g., fractured catheters, leads) lodged within the vascular system. This can also be used to retrieve fractured medical devices or to exchange introducers/sheaths.

Septal defect implant system (C1817)—An intracardiac metallic implant used for closure of various septal defects within the heart. The septal defect implant system includes a delivery catheter. The category code for the septal defect implant system (C1817) includes the delivery catheter; therefore, the delivery catheter should not be reported separately.

Stents with delivery system (C1874, C1876, C2625)—Stents packaged with delivery systems generally include the following components: stent mounted or unmounted on a balloon angioplasty catheter, introducer, and sheath. These components should not be reported separately.

Temporary non-coronary stent (C2617, C2625)—Usually composed of a substance, such as plastic or other non-absorbable material, designed to permit removal. Typically, this type of stent is placed for a period of less than one year.

Transluminal angioplasty catheter (C1725, C1885)—Designed to dilate stenotic blood vessels (arteries and veins). For vascular use, the terms "balloon dilatation catheter" and "transluminal angioplasty catheter" are frequently used interchangeably. [For the reporting of non-vascular balloon dilatation catheters, see the category "Balloon dilatation catheter" (C1726).]

Transvenous VDD single pass pacemaker lead (C1779)—A transvenous pacemaker lead that paces and senses in the ventricle and senses in the atrium.

Vascular closure device (implantable/insertable) (C1760)—Used to achieve hemostasis at arterial puncture sites following invasive or interventional procedures using biologic substances (e.g., collagen) or suture through the tissue tract.

Vector mapping catheter (C1732)—Refers to an electrophysiology catheter with an "in-plane" orthogonal array of electrodes. This catheter is used to locate the source of a focal arrhythmia.

Wireless pressure sensor (C2624)—Used to measure pressure within the pulmonary artery to assist physicians in treatment decisions for patients with heart failure. The sensor is implanted via right heart catheterization and includes monitoring system that records data.

Appendix C: Claim Forms

UB-04 Form

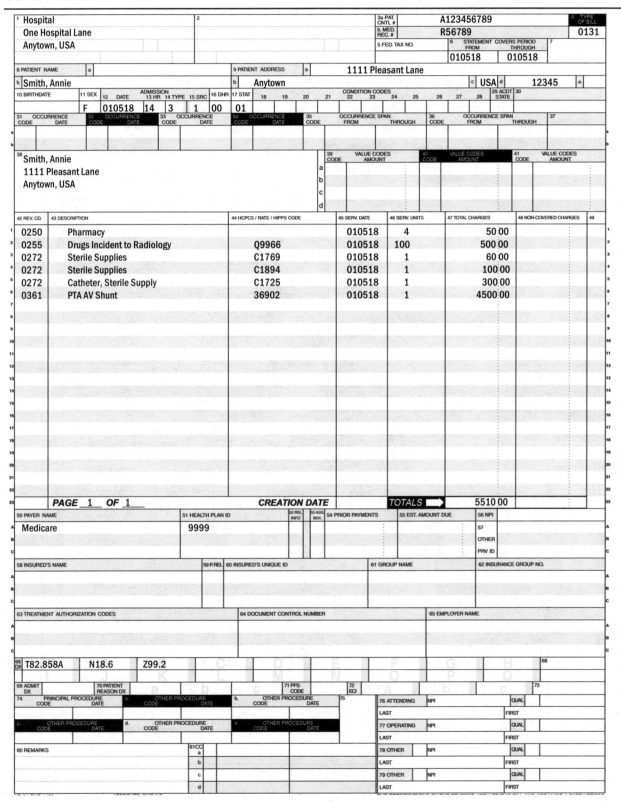

CMS-1500 Form

```
┌─────────────────────────────────────────────────────────────────────────┐
│ 1500                                                                      │
│ HEALTH INSURANCE CLAIM FORM                                               │
│ APPROVED BY NATIONAL UNIFORM CLAIM COMMITTEE 08/05                        │
│ PICA                                                              PICA     │
│ 1. MEDICARE [X]  ...  1a. INSURED'S I.D. NUMBER  A123456789                │
│ 2. PATIENT'S NAME  Smith, Annie      3. BIRTH DATE MM DD CCYY  SEX F[X]    │
│    4. INSURED'S NAME                                                       │
│ 5. ADDRESS  1111 Pleaseant Lane   6. RELATIONSHIP Self[X]                  │
│ 7. INSURED'S ADDRESS                                                       │
│ CITY Anytown  STATE XX                                                     │
│ 8. STATUS Single[X]  Employed[X]                                          │
│ ZIP 12345  TEL (111)111-1111                                              │
│ 9. OTHER INSURED'S NAME      10. CONDITION RELATED TO:                     │
│ 11. POLICY GROUP None                                                     │
│   a. EMPLOYMENT? NO[X]                                                     │
│   b. AUTO ACCIDENT? NO[X]   b. EMPLOYER BBB Inc                           │
│   c. OTHER ACCIDENT? NO[X]                                                 │
│   d. ANOTHER HEALTH BENEFIT PLAN? NO[X]                                    │
│ 12. SIGNED Signature on file   13. SIGNED SOF                             │
│ 14. DATE OF CURRENT 01 05 18                                              │
│ 17. REFERRING PROVIDER   17b NPI                                          │
│ 18. HOSPITALIZATION FROM 01 05 18                                         │
│ 20. OUTSIDE LAB? NO[X]                                                     │
│ 21. DIAGNOSIS  1. T82.858A  2. N18.6  3. Z99.2                            │
│ 24. SERVICE  01 05 18  01 05 18  21  36902  DX 1  $4000.00  1  1C 1111111111│
│ 25. FEDERAL TAX ID XXX-XX-XXXX [X]SSN  26. ACCT R56789  27. ACCEPT[X]YES   │
│ 28. TOTAL $4000.00  29. PAID $0.00  30. BALANCE $4000.00                   │
│ 31. SIGNED 80F   32. Hospital One Hospital Lane Anytown, USA               │
│ 33. Hospital Physicians Center One Hospital Lane Anytown, USA  1111111111  │
│ NUCC Instruction Manual www.nucc.org  APPROVED OMB-0938-0999 FORM CMS-1500 (08-05)│
└─────────────────────────────────────────────────────────────────────────┘
```

Appendix D: 2018 Inpatient Only CPT Codes

The following is a listing of interventional radiology and cardiology procedures classified with status indicator C for payment on an inpatient only basis.

CPT/HCPCS	Descriptor	CI	SI
0075T	Perq stent/chest vert art		C
0076T	S&i stent/chest vert art		C
0235T	Trluml perip athrc visceral		C
0254T	Evasc rpr iliac art bifur		C
0345T	Transcath mtral vlve repair		C
0451T	Insj/rplcmt aortic ventr sys		C
0452T	Insj/rplcmt dev vasc seal		C
0455T	Remvl aortic ventr cmpl sys		C
0456T	Remvl aortic dev vasc seal		C
0459T	Relocaj rplcmt aortic ventr		C
0461T	Repos aortic contrpulsj dev		C
0483T	Tmvi percutaneous approach	NC	C
0484T	Tmvi transthoracic exposure	NC	C
33202	Insert epicard eltrd open		C
33203	Insert epicard eltrd endo		C
33236	Remove electrode/thoracotomy		C
33237	Remove electrode/thoracotomy		C
33238	Remove electrode/thoracotomy		C
33243	Remove eltrd/thoracotomy		C
33250	Ablate heart dysrhythm focus		C
33251	Ablate heart dysrhythm focus		C
33254	Ablate atria lmtd		C
33255	Ablate atria w/o bypass ext		C
33256	Ablate atria w/bypass exten		C
33257	Ablate atria lmtd add-on		C
33258	Ablate atria x10sv add-on		C
33259	Ablate atria w/bypass add-on		C
33261	Ablate heart dysrhythm focus		C
33265	Ablate atria lmtd endo		C
33266	Ablate atria x10sv endo		C
33340	Perq clsr tcat l atr apndge		C
33361	Replace aortic valve perq		C
33362	Replace aortic valve open		C
33363	Replace aortic valve open		C
33364	Replace aortic valve open		C
33365	Replace aortic valve open		C
33366	Trcath replace aortic valve		C

CPT/HCPCS	Descriptor	CI	SI
33367	Replace aortic valve w/byp		C
33368	Replace aortic valve w/byp		C
33369	Replace aortic valve w/byp		C
33390	Valvuloplasty aortic valve		C
33391	Valvuloplasty aortic valve		C
33405	Replacement aortic valve opn		C
33406	Replacement aortic valve opn		C
33410	Replacement aortic valve opn		C
33411	Replacement of aortic valve		C
33412	Replacement of aortic valve		C
33413	Replacement of aortic valve		C
33414	Repair of aortic valve		C
33417	Repair of aortic valve		C
33418	Repair tcat mitral valve		C
33420	Revision of mitral valve		C
33422	Revision of mitral valve		C
33425	Repair of mitral valve		C
33426	Repair of mitral valve		C
33427	Repair of mitral valve		C
33460	Revision of tricuspid valve		C
33463	Valvuloplasty tricuspid		C
33464	Valvuloplasty tricuspid		C
33465	Replace tricuspid valve		C
33468	Revision of tricuspid valve		C
33477	Implant tcat pulm vlv perq		C
33880	Endovasc taa repr incl subcl		C
33881	Endovasc taa repr w/o subcl		C
33883	Insert endovasc prosth taa		C
33884	Endovasc prosth taa add-on		C
33886	Endovasc prosth delayed		C
33889	Artery transpose/endovas taa		C
33891	Car-car bp grft/endovas taa		C
33967	Insert i-aort percut device		C
33968	Remove aortic assist device		C
34701	Evasc rpr a-ao ndgft	NC	C
34702	Evasc rpr a-ao ndgft rpt	NC	C
34703	Evasc rpr a-unilac ndgft	NC	C
34704	Evasc rpr a-unilac ndgft rpt	NC	C
34705	Evac rpr a-biiliac ndgft	NC	C
34706	Evasc rpr a-biiliac rpt	NC	C

CPT/HCPCS	Descriptor	CI	SI
34707	Evasc rpr ilio-iliac ndgft	NC	C
34708	Evasc rpr ilio-iliac rpt	NC	C
34709	Plmt xtn prosth evasc rpr	NC	C
34710	Dlyd plmt xtn prosth 1st vsl	NC	C
34711	Dlyd plmt xtn prosth ea addl	NC	C
34712	Tcat dlvr enhncd fixj dev	NC	C
34808	Endovas iliac a device addon		C
34812	Opn fem art expos		C
34813	Femoral endovas graft add-on		C
34820	Opn iliac art expos		C
34830	Open aortic tube prosth repr		C
34831	Open aortoiliac prosth repr		C
34832	Open aortofemor prosth repr		C
34833	Opn ilac art expos cndt crtj		C
34834	Opn brach art expos		C
37182	Insert hepatic shunt (tips)		C
37215	Transcath stent cca w/eps		C
37217	Stent placemt retro carotid		C
37218	Stent placemt ante carotid		C
37616	Ligation of chest artery		C
37617	Ligation of abdomen artery		C

CPT/HCPCS	Descriptor	CI	SI
37618	Ligation of extremity artery		C
61624	Transcath occlusion cns		C
61630	Intracranial angioplasty		C
61635	Intracran angioplsty w/stent		C
61645	Perq art m-thrombect &/nfs		C
61650	Evasc prlng admn rx agnt 1st		C
61651	Evasc prlng admn rx agnt add		C
75956	Xray endovasc thor ao repr		C
75957	Xray endovasc thor ao repr		C
75958	Xray place prox ext thor ao		C
75959	Xray place dist ext thor ao		C
92941	Prq card revasc mi 1 vsl	CH	C
92975	Dissolve clot heart vessel		C
92992	Revision of heart chamber		C
92993	Revision of heart chamber		C
93583	Perq transcath septal reduxn		C

Appendix E: 2018 Status Indicators for OPPS Payment

Indicator	Item/Code/Service	OPPS Payment Status
A	Services furnished to a hospital outpatient that are paid under a fee schedule or payment system other than OPPS, for example: • Ambulance Services • Separately payable clinical diagnostic laboratory services • Separately payable non-implantable prosthetics and orthotics • Physical, Occupational, and Speech Therapy • Diagnostic Mammography • Screening Mammography	Not paid under OPPS. Paid by MACs under a fee schedule or payment system other than OPPS. Services are subject to deductible or coinsurance unless indicated otherwise. Not subject to deductible or coinsurance. Not subject to deductible.
B	Codes that are not recognized by OPPS when submitted on an outpatient hospital Part B bill type (12x and 13x).	Not paid under OPPS. • May be paid by MACs when submitted on a different bill type, for example, 75x (CORF), but not paid under OPPS. • An alternate code that is recognized by OPPS when submitted on an outpatient hospital Part B bill type (12x and 13x) may be available.
C	Inpatient Procedures	Not paid under OPPS. Admit patient. Bill as inpatient.
D	Discontinued Codes	Not paid under OPPS or any other Medicare payment system.
E1	Items and Services: • Not covered by any Medicare outpatient benefit category • Statutorily excluded by Medicare • Not reasonable and necessary	Not paid by Medicare when submitted on outpatient claims (any outpatient bill type).
E2	Items and Services: For which pricing information and claims data are not available	Not paid by Medicare when submitted on outpatient claims (any outpatient bill type).
F	Corneal Tissue Acquisition; Certain CRNA Services and Hepatitis B Vaccines	Not paid under OPPS. Paid at reasonable cost.
G	Pass-Through Drugs and Biologicals	Paid under OPPS; separate APC payment.
H	Pass-Through Device Categories	Separate cost-based pass-through payment; not subject to copayment.
J1	Hospital Part B services paid through a comprehensive APC	Paid under OPPS; all covered Part B services on the claim are packaged with the primary "J1" service for the claim, except services with OPPS SI=F,G, H, L and U; ambulance services; diagnostic and screening mammography; all preventive services; and certain Part B inpatient services.

Indicator	Item/Code/Service	OPPS Payment Status
J2	Hospital Part B Services That May Be Paid Through a Comprehensive APC	Paid under OPPS; Addendum B displays APC assignments when services are separately payable. (1) Comprehensive APC payment based on OPPS comprehensive-specific payment criteria. Payment for all covered Part B services on the claim is packaged into a single payment for specific combinations of services, except services with OPPS SI=F,G, H, L and U; ambulance services; diagnostic and screening mammography; all preventive services; and certain Part B inpatient services. (2) Packaged APC payment if billed on the same claim as a HCPCS code assigned status indicator "J1." (3) In other circumstances, payment is made through a separate APC payment or packaged into payment for other services.
K	Nonpass-Through Drugs and Nonimplantable Biologicals, Including Therapeutic Radiopharmaceuticals	Paid under OPPS; separate APC payment.
L	Influenza Vaccine; Pneumococcal Pneumonia Vaccine	Not paid under OPPS. Paid at reasonable cost; not subject to deductible or coinsurance.
M	Items and Services Not Billable to the MAC	Not paid under OPPS.
N	Items and Services Packaged into APC Rates	Paid under OPPS; payment is packaged into payment for other services. Therefore, there is no separate APC payment.
P	Partial Hospitalization	Paid under OPPS; per diem APC payment.
Q1	STV-Packaged Codes	Paid under OPPS; Addendum B displays APC assignments when services are separately payable. (1) Packaged APC payment if billed on the same date of service as a HCPCS code assigned status indicator "S," "T," or "V." (2) Composite APC payment if billed with specific combinations of services based on OPPS composite-specific payment criteria. Payment is packaged into a single payment for specific combinations of services. (3) In other circumstances, payment is made through a separate APC payment.
Q2	T-Packaged Codes	Paid under OPPS; Addendum B displays APC assignments when services are separately payable. (1) Packaged APC payment if billed on the same date of service as a HCPCS code assigned status indicator "T." (2) In other circumstances, payment is made through a separate APC payment.

Indicator	Item/Code/Service	OPPS Payment Status
Q3	Codes That May Be Paid Through a Composite APC	Paid under OPPS; Addendum B displays APC assignments when services are separately payable. Addendum M displays composite APC assignments when codes are paid through a composite APC. (1) Composite APC payment based on OPPS composite-specific payment criteria. Payment is packaged into a single payment for specific combinations of services. (2) In other circumstances, payment is made through a separate APC payment or packaged into payment for other services.
Q4	Conditionally packaged laboratory tests	Paid under OPPS or CLFS. (1) Packaged APC payment if billed on the same claim as a HCPCS code assigned published status indicator "J1," "J2," "S," "T," "V," "Q1," "Q2," or "Q3." (2) In other circumstances, laboratory tests should have an SI=A and payment is made under the CLFS.
R	Blood and Blood Products	Paid under OPPS; separate APC payment.
S	Procedure or Service, Not Discounted When Multiple	Paid under OPPS; separate APC payment.
T	Procedure or Service, Multiple Procedure Reduction Applies	Paid under OPPS; separate APC payment.
U	Brachytherapy Sources	Paid under OPPS; separate APC payment.
V	Clinic or Emergency Department Visit	Paid under OPPS; separate APC payment.
Y	Non-Implantable Durable Medical Equipment	Not paid under OPPS. All institutional providers other than home health agencies bill to DMERC.

Glossary

ablation. Removal or destruction of a body part or tissue or its function. Ablation may be performed by surgical means, hormones, drugs, radiofrequency, heat, chemical application, or other methods.

abuse. Medical reimbursement term that describes an incident that is inconsistent with accepted medical, business, or fiscal practices and directly or indirectly results in unnecessary costs to the Medicare program, improper reimbursement, or reimbursement for services that do not meet professionally recognized standards of care or which are medically unnecessary. Examples of abuse include excessive charges, improper billing practices, billing Medicare as primary instead of other third-party payers that are primary, and increasing charges for Medicare beneficiaries but not to other patients.

accredited record technician. Former AHIMA certification describing medical records practitioners; now known as a registered health information technician (RHIT).

actual charge. Charge a physician or supplier bills for a service rendered or a supply item.

acute care facility. Health care institution primarily engaged in providing treatment to inpatients and diagnostic and therapeutic services for medical diagnosis, treatment, and care of injured, disabled, or sick persons who are in an acute phase of illness.

add-on code. CPT code representing a procedure performed in addition to the primary procedure and designated with a + symbol in the CPT book. Add-on codes are never reported for stand-alone services but are reported secondarily in addition to the primary procedure.

adjudication. Processing and review of a submitted claim resulting in payment, partial payment, or denial. In relationship to judicial hearings, it is the process of hearing and settling a case through an objective, judicial procedure.

advanced cardiac life support. Certification for health care professionals who have achieved proficiency in providing emergent care of cardiac and respiratory systems and medication management.

adventitia. Outermost layer of connective tissue covering an organ or other tissue.

AHIMA. American Health Information Management Association. Association of health information management professionals that offers professional and educational services, providing these certifications: RHIA, RHIT, CCA, CCS, CCS-P, CDIP, CHDA, CHPS, and CHTS.

all-inclusive rate. In health care contracting, a flat fee charged by a facility on a daily basis (per diem) or for a total stay. The all-inclusive reimbursement rate usually pertains to state psychiatric hospitals. The UB-04 is used for billing all-inclusive rate accommodations and/or ancillary services. The only billable revenue codes under this rate are 0100 (all-inclusive room and board plus ancillary) and 0101 (all-inclusive room and board).

allowable charge. Fee schedule amount for a medical service as determined by the physician fee schedule methodology published annually by CMS.

ambulatory surgery center. Any distinct entity that operates exclusively for the purpose of providing surgical services to patients not requiring hospitalization. To receive reimbursement for treatment of Medicare patients, an ASC must have an agreement with the Centers for Medicare and Medicaid Services (CMS) and meet certain required conditions.

American Academy of Professional Coders. National organization for coders and billers offering certification examinations based on physician-, facility-, or payer-specific guidelines. Upon successful completion of the selected examination, the credential for that examination is obtained. The following list represents the credentials currently being offered through the AAPC: CIC, COC, CPB, CPC, CPC-P, and CRC certifications, as well as a variety of specialty-specific certifications.

American Medical Association. Professional organization for physicians. The AMA is the secretariat of the National Uniform Claim Committee (NUCC), which has a formal consultative role under HIPAA. The AMA also maintains the Physicians' Current Procedural Terminology (CPT) coding system.

amniocentesis. Surgical puncture through the abdominal wall, with a specialized needle and under ultrasonic guidance, into the interior of the pregnant uterus and directly into the amniotic sac to collect fluid for diagnostic analysis or therapeutic reduction of fluid levels.

ancillary services. Services, other than routine room and board charges, that are incidental to the hospital stay. These services include operating room; anesthesia; blood administration; pharmacy; radiology; laboratory; medical, surgical, and central supplies; physical, occupational, speech pathology, and inhalation therapies; and other diagnostic services.

angioscopy. Visualization of capillary blood vessels with a microscope, or the inside of a blood vessel with a fiberoptic-equipped catheter.

anterior. Situated in the front area or toward the belly surface of the body; an anatomical reference point used to show the position and relationship of one body structure to another.

anterolateral. Situated in the front and off to one side.

anteromedial. Situated in the front and to the side of the central point or midline.

anteroposterior. Front to back.

anteroposterior x-ray. X-ray view taken from the front of the body to the back.

anticoagulant. Substance that reduces or eradicates the blood's ability to clot.

appeal. Specific request made to a payer for reconsideration of a denial or adverse coverage or payment decision and potential restriction of benefit reimbursement.

arc beam. Radiation beam that is not stationary but moves around an axis in a curved path.

arteriogram. Radiograph of arteries.

artery. Vessel through which oxygenated blood passes away from the heart to any part of the body.

arthrocentesis. Puncture and aspiration of fluid from a joint for diagnostic or therapeutic purposes or injection of anesthetics or corticosteroids.

arthrogram. X-ray of a joint after the injection of contrast material.

arthrography. Radiographic study of a joint and its internal structures. Air or contrast medium is injected into the joint just before the images are taken.

ASC payment indicators. Ambulatory surgical center payment indicators. Beginning January 1, 2008, the ASC payment group rate was deleted and replaced with 16 payment indicators. To review the full list of payment indicators, go to CMS website http://www.cms.hhs.gov/ASCPayment/04_CMS-1517-F.asp#TopOfPage.

ASC surgical procedure. One of the allowable surgical procedures performed on an outpatient basis in an ambulatory surgical center.

aspirate. To withdraw fluid or air from a body cavity by suction.

assignment. In medical reimbursement, the arrangement in which the provider submits the claim on behalf of the patient and is reimbursed directly by the patient's plan. By doing so, the provider agrees to accept what the plan pays.

atrial septal defect. Cardiac anomaly consisting of a patent opening in the atrial septum due to a fusion failure, classified as ostium secundum type, ostium primum defect, or endocardial cushion defect.

audit. Examination or review that establishes the extent to which performance or a process conforms to predetermined standards or criteria. An audit may target utilization, quality of care, coding, or reimbursement.

authorization. Verbal or written agreement indicating that a third-party payer will pay for services rendered by the provider as set forth in the authorization.

average payment rate. Amount of money CMS could pay an HMO for services provided to Medicare recipients under a risk contract.

axillary. Area under the arm.

balance billing. Arrangement prohibited in Medicare regulations and some payer contracts whereby a provider bills the patient for charges in excess of the contracted allowable rate or medical necessity denials not reimbursed by the payer. Insurance plan exclusions may still be billable.

beneficiary. Person entitled to receive Medicare or other payer benefits who maintains a health insurance policy claim number.

bilateral. Consisting of or affecting two sides.

brachytherapy. Form of radiation therapy in which radioactive pellets or seeds are implanted directly into the tissue being treated to deliver their dose of radiation in a more directed fashion. Brachytherapy provides radiation to the prescribed body area while minimizing exposure to normal tissue.

C-arm. Portable x-ray fluoroscopy machine often used in surgery.

catheter. Flexible tube inserted into an area of the body for introducing or withdrawing fluid.

Centers for Medicare and Medicaid Services. Federal agency that oversees the administration of the public health programs such as Medicare, Medicaid, and State Children's Insurance Program.

centesis. Puncture.

central axis. Midline of any given body section around which the specified body parts are organized or rotate; the midpoint of directly opposing beams in radiation treatment.

cerebral angiography. Injection of contrast medium (dye) into an artery, x-raying the blood vessel system of the brain.

cine. Movement usually related to motion pictures.

cineradiography. High-speed x-ray images taken in exposure ranges of nanoseconds to milliseconds to capture a series of images of an organ or organ system in motion, such as the vocal cords or heart.

claim manual. Administrative guidelines used by claims processors to adjudicate claims according to company policy and procedure.

claims review. Examination of a submitted demand for payment by a Medicare contractor, insurer, or other group to determine payment liability, eligibility, reasonableness, or necessity of care provided.

clean claim. Submitted bill for services rendered that does not need to be investigated by the payer, passes all internal billing edits and payer specific edits, and is paid without the need for further information.

CMS manuals. Official government manuals prepared by CMS that detail procedures for processing and paying Medicare claims, preparing reimbursement forms, and billing procedures. These manuals were converted to web-based manuals (referred to as IOM, or Internet-only manuals) on October 1, 2003. At the time of the conversion, the manuals were streamlined, updated, and consolidated. Manuals may be accessed at http://www.cms.gov/manuals.

CMS-1500. Universal claim form used to file professional claims. Recently updated from version (08/05) to (02/12) in order to ensure appropriate reporting of ICD-10-CM codes and to ensure additional diagnosis codes could be reported, as needed.

Cobalt-60. Radioactive isotope.

coder. Professional who translates documented, written diagnoses and procedures into numeric and alphanumeric codes.

coding guidelines. Criteria that specifies how procedure, diagnosis, or supply codes are to be translated and used in various situations. Coding guidelines are issued by the AHA, AMA, CMS, NCHVS, and various other groups. Guidelines may vary by payer, type of coding system, and intended use.

coinsurance. Percentage of the allowed charges paid by a beneficiary toward the cost of care.

commercial carriers. For-profit insurance companies issuing health coverage.

common working file. System of local databases containing total beneficiary histories developed by CMS to improve Medicare claims processing. Medicare fiscal intermediaries, and/or carriers, interact with these databases to obtain data on eligibility, utilization, Medicare secondary payer (MSP), and other detailed claims information.

complete procedure. According to the AMA's CPT coding guidelines, a procedure performed by one physician who is responsible for all pre- and postinjection services, including administration of local anesthesia, placement of needle, injection of contrast materials, supervision of the study and interpretation of the study results. Hospitals should use the CPT codes for the complete procedure to bill for the technician's work and for the equipment, film, room, and clerical support.

compliance. Satisfying official coding and/or billing requirements.

compliance plan. Established methods to eliminate errors in coding, billing, and other issues through auditing and monitoring, training, or other corrective actions. Such a plan also provides an avenue for employees and others to report problems.

contrast material. Radiopaque substance placed into the body to enable a system or body structure to be visualized, such as nonionic and low osmolar contrast media (LOCM), ionic and high osmolar contrast media (HOCM), barium, and gadolinium.

coordination of benefits. Agreement that prevents double payment for services when the member is covered by two or more sources. The agreement dictates which organization is primarily and secondarily responsible for payment.

coronary care unit. Facility or service area dedicated to patients suffering from heart attack, stroke, or other serious cardiopulmonary problems.

Correct Coding Initiative. Official list of codes from the Centers for Medicare and Medicaid Services' (CMS) National Correct Coding Policy Manual for Medicare Services that identifies services considered an integral part of a comprehensive code or mutually exclusive of it.

Coverage Issues Manual. Revised and renamed the National Coverage Determination Manual in the CMS manual system, it contained national coverage decisions and specific medical items, services, treatment procedures, or technologies paid for under the Medicare program. This manual has been converted to the Medicare National Coverage Determinations Manual (NCD manual), Pub. 100-03.

CPT modifier. Two-character code used to indicate that a service was altered in some way from the stated CPT or HCPCS Level II description, but not enough to change the basic definition of the service.

CRNA. Certified registered nurse anesthetist. Nurse trained and specializing in the administration of anesthesia. Anesthesia services rendered by a CRNA must be reported with HCPCS Level II modifier QX, QY, or QZ.

crosswalk. Cross-referencing of CPT codes with ICD-10-CM, anesthesia, dental, or HCPCS Level II codes.

Current Procedural Terminology. Definitive procedural coding system developed by the American Medical Association that lists descriptive terms and identifying codes to provide a uniform language that describes medical, surgical, and diagnostic services for nationwide communication among physicians, patients, and third parties.

cutaneous. Relating to the skin.

cutdown. Small, incised opening in the skin to expose a blood vessel, especially over a vein (venous cutdown) to allow venipuncture and permit a needle or cannula to be inserted for the withdrawal of blood or administration of fluids.

date of service. Day the encounter or procedure is performed or the day a supply is issued.

debridement. Removal of dead or contaminated tissue and foreign matter from a wound.

denial. Refusal by an insurance plan to pay for services, procedures, or supplies. A denial may be made due to coverage limitations, medical necessity issues, or failure to follow appropriate prior authorization or claim submission guidelines.

diagnosis code. Numeric or alphanumeric code that describes the patient's medical condition, symptoms, or reason for the encounter.

diagnostic services. Examination or procedure performed on a patient to obtain information to assess the medical condition of the patient or to identify the nature and cause of a sign or symptom.

digital subtraction angiography. Diagnostic imaging technique that applies computer technology to fluoroscopy for the purpose of visualizing the same vascular structures observable with conventional angiography.

direct claim payment. Method where members deal directly with the payer rather than submitting claims through the employer.

discharge date. For medical facilities, the date the patient is formally released, expires, or is transferred. In other situations, the date that medical care or treatment ended.

dorsal. Pertaining to the back or posterior aspect.

dosimetry. Component in the administration of radiation oncology therapy in which a radiation dose is calculated to a specific site, including implant or beam orientation and exposure, isodose strengths, tissue inhomogeneities, and volume.

downcoding. Reporting a lower-level code for a service so that an additional code may be used rather than using one higher-level and more comprehensive code.

echography. Radiographic imaging that uses sound waves reflected off the different densities of anatomic structures to create images.

electrocardiogram. Recording of the electrical activity of the heart on a moving strip of paper that detects and records the electrical potential of the heart during contraction.

electronic data interchange. Transference of claims, certifications, quality assurance reviews, and utilization data via computer in X12 format. May refer to any electronic exchange of formatted data.

electronic media claim. Automated claims processing method that uses a data storage tool to transfer claims data to the payer. EMC has been replaced by electronic data interchange (EDI).

embolectomy. Surgical excision of a blood clot or other foreign material that broke away from its original source and traveled in the blood stream, becoming lodged in a blood vessel and blocking circulation.

embolization. Placement of a clotting agent, such as a coil, plastic particles, gel, foam, etc., into an area of hemorrhage to stop the bleeding or to block blood flow to a problem area, such as an aneurysm or a tumor.

endarterectomy. Removal of the thickened, endothelial lining of a diseased or damaged artery. Occlusion is often found in heavy or long-term tobacco users. Endarterectomy is performed on many different vessels, such as the carotids, the pulmonary artery, the common femoral, vertebral, and aortoiliac arteries and is coded accordingly.

endocarditis. Inflammatory disease of the interior lining of the heart chamber and heart valves, most commonly caused by bacteria.

established patient. *1)* Patient who has received professional services in a face-to-face setting within the last three years from the same physician/qualified health care professional or another physician/qualified health care professional of the exact same specialty and subspecialty who belongs to the same group practice. *2)* For OPPS hospitals, patient who has been registered as an inpatient or outpatient in a hospital's provider-based clinic or emergency department within the past three years.

explanation of benefits. Statement mailed to the member and provider explaining claim adjudication and payment.

explanation of Medicare benefits. Medicare statement mailed to the member and provider explaining claim adjudication and payment.

facet. Smooth surface area where the transverse and articular processes of certain vertebrae articulate with another vertebra.

fine needle aspiration. 22- or 25-gauge needle attached to a syringe is inserted into a lesion/tissue and a few cells are aspirated for biopsy and diagnostic study. Aspiration is also used to remove fluid from a benign cyst.

first order selective. Catheter placement into the first vessel that branches off the aorta; catheter placement into the first vessel that branches off the vessel into which percutaneous insertion was made.

flank. Part of the body found between the posterior ribs and the uppermost crest of the ilium, or the lateral side of the hip, thigh, and buttock.

fluoroscopy. Radiology technique that allows visual examination of part of the body or a function of an organ using a device that projects an x-ray image on a fluorescent screen.

focused medical review. Process of targeting and directing medical review efforts on Medicare claims where the greatest risk of inappropriate program payment exists. The goal is to reduce the number of noncovered claims or unnecessary services. CMS analyzes national data such as internal billing, utilization, and payment data and provides its findings to the FI. Local medical review policies are developed identifying aberrances, abuse, and overutilized services. Providers are responsible for knowing national Medicare coverage and billing guidelines and local medical review policies, and for determining whether the services provided to Medicare beneficiaries are covered by Medicare.

fraud and abuse. Method of obtaining unauthorized benefits. Fraud is an intentional deception, misrepresentation, or statement that is known to be false. Abuse is a practice that is inconsistent with accepted medical, business, or fiscal practices.

galactogram. Following injection of a radiopaque dye into the ducts of the breast, radiographic pictures are taken of the milk-producing mammary ducts.

general anesthesia. State of unconsciousness produced by an anesthetic agent or agents, inducing amnesia by blocking the awareness center in the brain, and rendering the patient unable to control protective reflexes, such as breathing.

government mandates. Services mandated by state or federal law.

HCPCS. Healthcare Common Procedure Coding System.

HCPCS Level I. Healthcare Common Procedure Coding System Level I. Numeric coding system used by physicians, facility outpatient departments, and ambulatory surgery centers (ASC) to code ambulatory, laboratory, radiology, and other diagnostic services for Medicare billing. This coding system contains only the American Medical Association's Physicians' Current Procedural Terminology (CPT) codes. The AMA updates codes annually.

HCPCS Level II. Healthcare Common Procedure Coding System Level II. National coding system, developed by CMS, that contains alphanumeric codes for physician and nonphysician services not included in the CPT coding system. HCPCS Level II covers such things as ambulance services, durable medical equipment, and orthotic and prosthetic devices.

HCPCS modifiers. Two-character code (AA-ZZ) that identifies circumstances that alter or enhance the description of a service or supply. They are recognized by carriers nationally and are updated annually by CMS.

health care provider. Entity that administers diagnostic and therapeutic services.

health information. Information, whether oral or recorded in any form or medium, that is created or received by a covered entity; relates to the past, present, or future physical or mental health or condition of an individual; the provision of health care to an individual; or for the past, present, or future payment for the provision of health care to an individual.

health insurance claim number. Number issued by the Social Security Administration to individuals or beneficiaries entitled to Medicare benefits. The HICN card provides the beneficiary information necessary for processing Medicare claims.

Healthcare Common Procedure Coding System. Two levels of codes used by Medicare and other payers to describe procedures and supplies. Level I includes all of the codes listed in CPT, and Level II are alphanumeric supply and procedure codes.

Healthcare Common Procedure Coding System modifiers. Alphanumeric code used to identify circumstances that alter or enhance the description of a service or supply reported to Medicare or other payers.

hysterosalpingography. Radiographic pictures taken of the uterus and the fallopian tubes after the injection of a radiopaque dye.

ICD-10-CM. International Classification of Diseases, 10th Revision, Clinical Modification. Clinical modification of the alphanumeric classification of diseases used by the World Health Organization, already in use in much of the world, and used for mortality reporting in the United States. The implementation date for ICD-10-CM diagnostic coding system to replace ICD-9-CM in the United States was October 1, 2015.

ICD-10-PCS. International Classification of Diseases, 10th Revision, Procedure Coding System. Beginning October 1, 2015, inpatient hospital services and surgical procedures must be coded using ICD-10-PCS codes, replacing ICD-9-CM, Volume 3 for procedures.

imaging. Radiologic means of producing pictures for clinical study of the internal structures and functions of the body, such as x-ray, ultrasound, magnetic resonance, or positron emission tomography.

International Classification of Diseases, 10th Revision, Clinical Modification. Clinical modification of ICD-10 developed for use in the United States. Replaced ICD-9-CM as of October 1, 2015.

International Classification of Diseases, 9th Revision, Clinical Modification. Clinical modification of the international statistical coding system used to report, compile, and compare health care data, using numeric and alphanumeric codes to help plan, deliver, reimburse, and quantify medical care in the United States. Replaced by ICD-10-CM as of October 1, 2015.

interpretation. Professional health care provider's review of data with a written or verbal opinion.

interventional radiology. Performance of invasive procedures using imaging guidance.

interventional radiology component coding. Coding allowing a physician, regardless of specialty, to specifically identify and report those aspects of the service provided, whether the procedural component, the radiological component, or both.

invalid ICD-9-CM code. Diagnosis code that is not specific because a digit is missing. Medicare and private payers will reject claims containing invalid ICD-9-CM codes. Effective October 1, 2015, the ICD-9-CM coding system was replaced by ICD-10-CM.

Joint Commission on Accreditation of Healthcare Organizations. Organization that accredits health care organizations. In the future, the JCAHO may play a role in certifying these organizations' compliance with the HIPAA A/S requirements. Previously known as the Joint Commission for the Accreditation of Hospitals.

lateral x-ray. X-ray taken from the side.

ligation. Tying off a blood vessel or duct with a suture or a soft, thin wire.

limitation of liability. Signed waiver a provider must obtain from the patient before performing a service that appears on a list of services Medicare classifies as medically unnecessary. The waiver notifies the patient in advance that the service may be denied coverage and that the patient is responsible for payment.

linking codes. To establish medical necessity, CPT and HCPCS Level II codes must be supported by the ICD-10-CM diagnosis and injury codes submitted on the claim form and supported by the documentation.

local anesthesia. Induced loss of feeling or sensation restricted to a certain area of the body, including topical, local tissue infiltration, field block, or nerve block methods.

local medical review policy. Carrier-specific policy applied in the absence of a national coverage policy to make local Medicare coverage decisions, including the development of a draft policy based on a review of medical literature, an understanding of local practice, and the solicitation of comments from the medical community and Carrier Advisory Committee.

magnetic resonance imaging. Radiation-free, noninvasive technique that produces high quality, multiple plane images of the inside of the body by using the natural magnetic properties of the hydrogen atoms within the body that emit radiofrequency signals when exposed to radio waves in a strong magnetic field.

mandated providers. Providers of medical care, such as psychologists, optometrists, podiatrists, and chiropractors, whose licensed services must, under state or federal law, be included in coverage offered by a health plan.

maximum out-of-pocket costs. Limit on total patient payments including copayments, deductibles, and coinsurance under a benefit contract in a specified time period.

mediastinum. Collection of organs and tissues that separate the pleural sacs. Located between the sternum and spine above the diaphragm, it contains the heart and great vessels, trachea and bronchi, esophagus, thymus, lymph nodes, and nerves.

medical documentation. Patient care records, including operative notes; physical, occupational, and speech-language pathology notes; progress notes; physician certification and recertifications; and emergency room records; or the patient's medical record in its entirety. When Medicare coverage cannot be determined based on the information submitted on the claim, medical documentation may be requested. The Medicare Administrative Contractor (MAC) will deny a claim for lack of medical necessity if medical documentation is not received within the stated time frame defined by the MAC (usually within 35-45 days after the date of request).

medical necessity. Medically appropriate and necessary to meet basic health needs; consistent with the diagnosis or condition and national medical practice guidelines regarding type, frequency, and duration of treatment; rendered in a cost-effective manner.

medical review. Review by a Medicare administrative contractor, carrier, and/or quality improvement organization (QIO) of services and items provided by physicians, other health care practitioners, and providers of health care services under Medicare. The review determines if the items and services are reasonable and necessary and meet Medicare coverage requirements, whether the quality meets professionally recognized standards of health care, and whether the services are medically appropriate in an inpatient, outpatient, or other setting as supported by documentation.

Medicare carrier. Organization that contracts with CMS to adjudicate professional claims under Part B, the supplemental medical insurance program. Medicare carriers are responsible for daily claims processing, utilization review, record maintenance, dissemination of information based on CMS regulations, and determining whether services are covered and payments are appropriate. This organization has been replaced by Medicare administrative contractors.

Medicare Carriers Manual. Manual the Centers for Medicare and Medicaid Services provides to Medicare carriers containing instructions for processing and paying Medicare claims, preparing reimbursement forms, billing procedures, and adhering to Medicare regulations. This has been replaced by the Medicare manual system.

Medicare fee schedule. Fee schedule based upon physician work, expense, and malpractice designed to slow the rise in cost for services and standardize payment to physicians regardless of specialty or location of service with geographic adjustments.

Medicare Part A. Hospital insurance coverage that includes hospital, nursing home, hospice, home health, and other inpatient care. Claims are submitted to intermediaries for reimbursement.

Medicare Part B. Supplemental medical insurance that includes outpatient hospital care and physician and other qualified professional care. Claims from providers or suppliers other than a hospital are submitted to carriers for reimbursement. Hospital outpatient claims are submitted to their FI/MAC.

Medicare secondary payer. Specified circumstance when other third-party payers have the primary responsibility for payment of services and Medicare is the secondary payer. Medicare is secondary to workers' compensation, automobile, medical no-fault and liability insurance, EGHPs, LGHPs, and certain employer health plans covering aged and disabled beneficiaries. The MSP program prohibits Medicare payment for items or services if payment has been made or can reasonably be expected to be made by another payer, as described above.

modifier. Two characters that can be appended to a HCPCS code as a means of identifying circumstances that alter or enhance the description of a service or supply.

myelogram. Radiological images of the spinal cord after injection of contrast medium.

myelography. Introduction of radiographic contrast medium into the sac surrounding the spinal cord and nerves.

noncovered procedure. Health care treatment not reimbursable according to provisions of a given insurance policy, or in the case of Medicare, in accordance with Medicare laws and regulations.

noncovered services. Health care services that are not reimbursable according to provisions of a given insurance policy.

nonspecific code. Catch-all code that identifies the diagnosis as ill-defined, other, or unspecified. A nonspecific code may be a valid choice if no other code closely describes the diagnosis.

oblique x-ray view. Slanted view of the object being x-rayed.

Office of Inspector General. Agency within the Department of Health and Human Services that is ultimately responsible for investigating instances of fraud and abuse in the Medicare and Medicaid and other government health care programs.

outpatient code editor. Centers for Medicare and Medicaid Services' outpatient software program that analyzes hospital outpatient claims to detect incorrect billing and coding data, assign an ambulatory payment classification for covered services, and determine the appropriate payment. Medicare contractors use the OCE to test the validity of ICD-10-CM and HCPCS coding and to conduct compatibility edits. The OCE performs editing functions related to HCPCS codes, HCPCS modifiers, and ICD-10-CM diagnosis codes. It identifies individual errors and indicates the action to take with the claim (e.g., return to provider [RTP], suspend, deny). Effective October 1, 2015, ICD-9-CM codes were replaced by ICD-10-CM.

pacemaker. Implantable cardiac device that controls the heart's rhythm and maintains regular beats by artificial electric discharges. This device consists of the pulse generator with a battery and the electrodes, or leads, which are placed in single or dual chambers of the heart, usually transvenously.

paper claim. Claim that is submitted on paper, including optical character recognition (OCR) claims and claims that are converted to electronic format by Medicare. Medicare will not pay clean paper claims until the 26th day after the claim is received.

participating provider. Provider who has contracted with the health plan to deliver medical services to covered persons.

percutaneous transluminal coronary angioplasty. Procedure used to treat coronary artery obstruction. A balloon catheter is placed in the affected artery and the balloon is inflated to flatten the plaque against the wall of the artery and open the obstruction.

pericardium. Thin and slippery case in which the heart lies that is lined with fluid so that the heart is free to pulse and move as it beats.

posterior. Located in the back part or caudal end of the body.

posteroanterior x-ray. X-ray view taken from back to front.

posterolateral. Located in the back and off to the side.

professional component. Portion of a charge for health care services that represents the physician's (or other practitioner's) work in providing the service, including interpretation and report of the procedure. This component of the service usually is charged for and billed separately from the inpatient hospital charges.

radioactive substances. Materials used in the diagnosis and treatment of disease that emit high-speed particles and energy-containing rays.

radiograph. Image made by an x-ray.

radiological examination. Plain films of specific sites.

radiopaque dye. Medium injected into the body that is impenetrable by x-rays.

retrograde. Moving against the usual direction of flow.

revascularization. Restoration of blood flow and oxygen supply to a body part. This may apply to an extremity, the heart, or penis.

revenue code. Identifies a specific accommodation or ancillary charge on the bill. The revenue code field was expanded to allow four-digit codes for use in the future.

roentgenogram. Film produced by x-ray.

separate procedures. Services commonly carried out as a fundamental part of a total service and, as such, do not usually warrant separate identification. These services are identified in CPT with the parenthetical phrase (separate procedure) at the end of the description and are payable only when performed alone.

sequencing codes. Codes reported according to ranking guidelines defining severity, time, and skill required to treat the diagnosed condition and cost of the service for procedures.

stent. Tube to provide support in a body cavity or lumen.

stereoradiography. Preparation of radiographs with appropriate shift of the x-ray tube or film so that the images can be viewed stereoscopically to give a three-dimensional appearance.

stereotaxis. Three-dimensional method for precisely locating structures.

supervision and interpretation. Radiology services that usually contain an invasive component and are reported by the radiologist for supervision of the procedure and the personnel involved with performing the examination, reading the film, and preparing the written report.

supination. Lying on the back; turning the palm toward the front or upward; raising the medial margin of the foot by an inverting and adducting movement.

surgical package. Normal, uncomplicated performance of specific surgical services, with the assumption that, on average, all surgical procedures of a given type are similar with respect to skill level, duration, and length of normal follow-up care.

suture. Numerous stitching techniques employed in wound closure: *1)* Buried suture: Continuous or interrupted suture placed under the skin for a layered closure. *2)* Continuous suture: Running stitch with tension evenly distributed across a single strand to provide a leakproof closure line. *3)* Interrupted suture: Series of single stitches with tension isolated at each stitch, in which all stitches are not affected if one becomes loose, and the isolated sutures cannot act as a wick to transport an infection. *4)* Purse-string suture: Continuous suture placed around a tubular structure and tightened, to reduce or close the lumen. *5)* Retention suture: Secondary stitching that bridges the primary suture, providing support for the primary repair; a plastic or rubber bolster may be placed over the primary repair and under the retention sutures.

tangential port. Radiation beam that glides across the body surface.

technical component. Portion of a health care service that identifies the provision of the equipment, supplies, technical personnel, and costs attendant to the performance of the procedure other than the professional services.

thoracentesis. Surgical puncture of the chest cavity with a specialized needle or hollow tubing to aspirate fluid from within the pleural space for diagnostic or therapeutic reasons.

thrombolysis. Chemical process of dissolving or breaking down a blood clot by inducing a complex chain of events involving the action of plasminogen to solubilize fibrin clots and degrade fibrinogen.

thrombolytic agent. Drugs or other substances used to dissolve blood clots in blood vessels or in tubes that have been placed into the body.

tomogram. X-ray or radiograph of one select layer or slice of the body made by tomography.

tomograph. Method of precise x-ray.

transcatheter. Procedure or treatment performed via a catheter.

transverse. Crosswise at right angles to the long axis of a structure or part.

trocar. Cannula or a sharp pointed instrument used to puncture and aspirate fluid from cavities.

ultrasound. Imaging using ultra-high sound frequency bounced off body structures.

unbundling. Separately packaging costs or services that might otherwise be billed together including billing separately for health care services that should be combined according to the industry standards or commonly accepted coding practices.

undocumented services. Billed service for which the supporting documentation has not been recorded or is unavailable to substantiate the service.

ureteropyelogram. Radiologic study of the renal pelvis and the ureter.

venography. Radiographic study of the veins.

ventricular septal defect. Congenital cardiac anomaly resulting in a continual opening in the septum between the ventricles that, in severe cases, causes oxygenated blood to flow back into the lungs, resulting in pulmonary hypertension.

waiver of liability. Provision established by Medicare to protect beneficiaries and physicians from liability when services are denied as inappropriate or medically unnecessary. Under the provision, if the Medicare beneficiary knew or should have known that the services billed for were not covered, the beneficiary is liable for paying for the services. If neither the beneficiary nor the hospital knew or reasonably could have been expected to know that the services were not covered, Medicare is liable for paying the claim. If the provider should have known and the beneficiary is protected from liability, then liability falls with the provider, and the hospital cannot bill the beneficiary for services other than deductibles and coinsurance amounts, even though no Medicare payment has been made. Beneficiaries who do not know that services were noncovered are protected from liability when the services are not reasonable and/or necessary (including adverse level of care determinations) and when custodial care is involved.